DICTIONARY OF
SCOTTISH
QUOTATIONS

Dictionary of

SCOTTISH
QUOTATIONS

Edited by
Angela Cran
James Robertson

Gaelic consultant
John MacInnes

MAINSTREAM
PUBLISHING

EDINBURGH AND LONDON

Introduction, selection and arrangement copyright © Angela Cran and
James Robertson 1996

Quotations by Hugh MacDiarmid appear by permission of Carcanet
Press Ltd; quotations by Edwin Muir appear by permission of Faber and
Faber Ltd

Lyrics by The Proclaimers appear courtesy of Charlie and Craig Reid
and Warner Chappell Music Ltd; lyrics by Runrig appear courtesy of
Runrig and Chrysalis Music Ltd

Thug Comhairle nan Leabhraichean seachad barantas
airson trusadh nan cuibhreannan Gàidhlig san leabhar seo.

MAINSTREAM PUBLISHING COMPANY (EDINBURGH) LTD
7 Albany Street
Edinburgh EH1 3UG

First published in 1996

ISBN 1 85158 812 4

A CIP catalogue record for this book is available from the British Library

Subsidised by THE SCOTTISH ARTS COUNCIL

Typeset in Ehrhardt by Bibliocraft, Dundee, in conjunction with
Æsthetex, Edinburgh

Printed and bound in Great Britain by Butler & Tanner Ltd, Frome

for John, Margaret, John and Betty

Who, if he were wisely considerate of
things at large, would ever embark upon
any work much more considerable than
a halfpenny post-card? . . .

ROBERT LOUIS STEVENSON

Contents

Acknowledgements

In the course of compiling this book, we have been helped in many ways by a large number of people. In particular, we would like to thank:

John MacInnes of the School of Scottish Studies, University of Edinburgh, for his scholarship and advice in compiling the Gaelic quotations; Ian MacDonald and the Gaelic Books Council for their financial assistance and general support for the project; Alan Lawson of Æsthetex Ltd for his programming expertise and dedication; and Neil Graham, Production Manager at Mainstream.

For help in gathering quotations, we are indebted to many individuals but especially to Valentina Bold, Andrew Burnet, Kevin Dunion, Rosemary Goring, Linda Gray, Moira Jeffrey, Alan Lawson, Frederic Lindsay, Murdo Macdonald, Seonaid McDonald, Annie Matheson, Hazel Muir, Neil Robertson, Elizabeth Small, Peter Small, Roland Tanner, Alan Taylor.

For general help and advice, our thanks to Viv Adams of the Scottish Society of Playwrights, Carol Anderson, Iain Bayne and Marlene Ross of Runrig, Deirdre Grieve, Siri Hansen, Joy Hendry, Catherine Johnson, Billy Kay, James Lumsden, Kenny Macdonald of Braw Music, Andreas Schöter, Christopher Whyte.

For their patience and friendly professionalism, we thank the staff of Edinburgh City Libraries, especially those in the Scottish Library; the staff of the National Library of Scotland; the staff of Edinburgh University Library; Tessa Ransford and the staff of the Scottish Poetry Library.

We are especially grateful to all those who have allowed us to quote from their work. We have made every effort to clear copyright where applicable, and to trace copyright owners. In the event of an error or oversight, we would be happy to hear from any copyright owners whom we have not been able to contact.

Finally, we would like to extend our appreciation to the writers, editors and compilers of the many important books on different aspects of Scottish culture which have been published in recent years; and to the editors of *Cencrastus*, *Chapman*, *Edinburgh Review*, *Lines Review*, *Radical Scotland*, *Scottish Affairs*, *Verse* and other periodicals. These have been invaluable in our research, and without them, our task would have been much more difficult.

Introduction

This is, to the best of our knowledge, the first large-scale work of its kind ever produced. There have been several pocket-sized collections of Scottish quotations in the past, but by far the most detailed work to date has been Alan Bold's *Scottish Quotations* (Mercat Press, 1985). Although on a smaller scale than this book, it was in many respects ground-breaking, but has been out of print for some years. And as various important Scottish reference books appeared over the last decade or so – covering language, culture, literature, religion, history, art, music and other areas – the lack of a substantial quotations source seemed to become only more obvious. It was to remedy this situation that we decided to gather the material for this book.

Why do we feel such a dictionary to be necessary? First, a revitalised and self-confident Scottish culture demands it: it is one more step in the reconstruction of an articulate, progressive, self-determining society. Second, other general dictionaries of quotations by and large fail to deal adequately with the Scottish dimension. The 'usual suspects' – Burns, Scott and Stevenson – are well represented in them, but divorced from their native context. We feel it is enriching, not parochial, to set these internationally known figures alongside their lesser known influences and contemporaries, such as Robert Fergusson, Susan Ferrier and John Galt. By contrast, other figures whose reputations are or should be international, have often been poorly represented, or neglected entirely: Hugh MacDiarmid, Lord Kelvin, Mary Somerville, John Muir, R B Cunninghame Graham and Mary Slessor all, to some extent, fall into this category. This is not, however, to blame other editors – they have had different priorities and agendas to fulfil – but only to point out a need that we felt should be addressed; in any case, the Scots themselves have not always been foremost in recognising the achievements of their compatriots. But we hope this dictionary creates a new space in which some 840 individuals – most, but not all of them, Scots – can rub shoulders and opinions with each other.

We should immediately say something about the presence of women in the *Dictionary*. It was a priority of ours to represent Scottish women as fully as possible. We were faced with some major obstacles in trying to achieve this. History, until very recently, has tended to relegate the role of women to one of support and succour: Elspeth King referred, in her recent book on Glasgow's women[1], to a 'hidden history', which has all too often meant a silent history. In this, Scotland may have been no better or no worse than other countries, but the fact remains that it is extremely difficult, perhaps hundreds of years after their deaths, to open the mouths of women made dumb by history. Nevertheless,

---

[1] *The Hidden History of Glasgow's Women: The Thenew Factor* (1993)

from Lady Elphinstone to Elsie Inglis, from Mary, Queen of Scots to Margaret Oliphant, women's voices have persisted in being heard through the din of male pronouncement and argument, and we hope that, while we have not achieved a 50:50 ratio, we have built a solid foundation for making female Scotland, past and present, better heard now and in the future. As Naomi Mitchison wrote in 1941, 'Nobody can be a power in their age unless they are part of its voice.'

We were also determined, at the outset, that the *Dictionary* should reflect Scottish culture as comprehensively as possible. The bulk of the quotations here are in either English or Scots, but it was essential, we felt, that Gaelic be represented alongside these languages. Clearly this entailed entering a huge and in many respects quite different cultural arena, and we are aware that we have only scratched the surface of what might be included, but, for example, the poetry of Duncan Ban Macintyre should be recognised alongside that of Robert Burns as part of the voice of 18th-century Scotland. We are indebted to Dr John MacInnes of the School of Scottish Studies for his advice and authoritative selection of the Gaelic quotations.

As for the quotations in Scots, we have resisted the temptation to standardise or otherwise interfere with the language as it appears in historical texts (except for occasional clarification). This means, for example, that we have retained those 'apologetic' apostrophes which are now seen as redundant by most modern writers, but which were so predominant from the vernacular revival of the 18th century through to the mid-20th century. The variations in Scots orthography, then, are not editorial inconsistencies but a legacy of the sources.

There is, we hope, a democratic spirit to our selection, which extends it beyond the platitudes of the great and good. We had to restrict what we could include from areas like the ballads, bairn rhymes and traditional songs: all of these could be, and of course have been, the subject of many books in their own right. But we did not want to ignore them. (On the other hand, we did reluctantly decide, for reasons of space, to exclude the huge field of 'proverbs' altogether.) We should stress, however, that it is in the nature of ballads, rhymes and folk songs to have no single 'definitive' version. The extracts included here are either what we believe to be the best-known versions, or those best known to us: in no other sense would we claim them to be 'correct'.

We have tried to provide a context for those quotations which are not in themselves self-explanatory. We found, in discussion with various people, that a lack of context was the most common complaint against dictionaries of quotations, and so we have provided such explanations wherever we can. Sometimes too we have extended quotations to include material surrounding the best-known phrase or sentence. This is to clarify what is actually being said, although it can make the entry seem less 'quotable'. An example is Stevenson's definition of marriage as 'one long conversation, chequered by disputes': on the face of it this is a somewhat negative statement, but the sentences that follow it make it quite clear that, on this occasion at least, he was paying the institution a compliment.

The two indexes provide different ways into the text, and make this a useful and workable source for the quick reference check. But we hope that the *Dictionary* will also be good for browsing, and that in browsing readers may find themselves discovering more than they had expected. Certainly, as editors we have learned a huge amount about people we in some cases knew very little of before we began; and if this book sends readers back to the original sources, then we feel it will have achieved something as a bonus.

A number of the quotations have been cross-referenced so that readers can pursue ideas and remarks across the pages. There is a story to be told, for example, in the reactions to Dr Johnson's definition of 'Oats', which he admitted he put in *his* dictionary to vex the Scots – on the evidence of the responses of Robert Fergusson, Lord Elibank, Andrew Shirrefs and others, he clearly succeeded.

Since Dr Johnson has been mentioned, we should explain our reasons for including him and numerous other non-Scottish figures. It was not our original intention to do so, but it soon became clear that we could not leave out the sometimes irritating but always interesting jibes of 'that great Cham of Literature' (as Smollett called him). Once we had conceded to Johnson, we could not keep out Sydney Smith, Dorothy Wordsworth, T W H Crosland or Jimmy Hill. We did not want to omit John Steinbeck's challenging remark about Scotland, nor Virginia Woolf's description of Skye as a 'jelly fish'. But to have included every instance of ourselves being seen 'as ithers see us' would have required a second volume, and so we have kept these entries to what might be called 'a necessary minimum'.

This could apply to the whole dictionary. We have gathered some 4,000 quotations, but it might have been 40,000. This kind of book is, in fact, never-ending; never complete, never the last word, and never immune to the need for updating and revising. But we do think it is reasonably comprehensive. Obviously there will be omissions: all editors have to make choices. Some readers may be disappointed that their favourite writer or least favourite politician is absent; others may disagree with our selection of quotations from those who are included. We would argue, with Maurice Lindsay, against making for Scotland 'a kind of wholeness or ultimate category . . . Scotland's an attitude of mind.' Or, in the words of Lady Perth, as recorded by Dean Ramsay: 'Weel, weel, some fowk like parritch and some like puddocks.'

If, however, the *Dictionary* becomes, as we hope, an essential item on the bookshelf, then this edition will be not just a building-block, but a foundation stone. And for future expanded, revised, reorganised or otherwise altered editions, we would welcome comments, criticisms and suggestions from those who read and use this one.

Edinburgh, July 1996

How to use the Dictionary

Quotations

The quotations are arranged alphabetically by author/speaker, usually by surname, eg **Anderson, Alexander**, but in some instances (usually Gaelic), by first name, eg **Màiri Mhór nan Oran**. Entries will be found under the name by which we consider the author/speaker is best known, which may be a pseudonym, title or nickname: eg, James Leslie Mitchell will be found under **Gibbon, Lewis Grassic**, Robert MacQueen under **Braxfield, Lord**, and Henry the Minstrel under **Blind Harry**. Gaelic authors/speakers are usually given under their Gaelic names, eg Derick Thomson appears as **MacThòmais, Ruaraidh**. In most cases, there are cross-references to the main entry from alternative names. Other sources of quotations which have no specified author appear alphabetically by title, eg **Declaration of Arbroath, Gude and Godlie Ballatis, Statistical Account of Scotland**. There are generic groupings for **Anonymous, Bairn rhymes, Ballads, Metrical Psalms, Traditional Gaelic tales, Traditional songs**.

Within each author/speaker entry, quotations are ordered chronologically as far as possible (including where a date is not specified). In the case of **Ballads** and **Traditional songs**, however, the order is alphabetical by title. Where poems, essays, etc are quoted from a collection, they are generally ordered as they appear in that collection. Undated attributions are usually given at the end of the entry.

The following conventions have been used in the Dictionary:

†	indicates an English translation of a Gaelic, French or Latin original;
. . .	usually indicates that part of the quotation is omitted, except in the rare instances where the ellipsis is contained within the original quotation. An ellipsis at the start or end indicates that a quotation begins or ends mid-sentence;
In	before a source title usually indicates a work by another author (eg a collection of songs, or essays, or stories etc) in which the quotation appears; **Quoted in** before a source title specifically indicates a secondary source where the quotation is cited;
Cf.	indicates a cross-reference to another quotation in the *Dictionary*, eg Cf. Walter Scott 25 refers the reader to quotation number 25 under **Scott, Walter**;
See	at the end of an entry refers the reader to a source outwith the *Dictionary*, eg See Shakespeare, *Macbeth*, Act 1, sc.2.

Other abbreviations used in the book are as follows:

Attrib.	Attributed	ll.	lines
b.	born	n.d.	no date
Bk(s)	Book(s)	No.	Number
c.	circa	Nos	Numbers
ch.	chapter(s)	p.	page
d.	died	pp.	pages
ed.	editor	sc.	scene
eds	editors	st.	stanza(s)
eg	for example	v.	versus
fl.	flourished	Vol.	Volume
ie	that is	Vols	Volumes
l.	line		

Subject Index

This is a list of forty-seven broad subject categories, under which the majority of quotations have been sorted. References are in the form of the name of the author/speaker/work, as it appears in the main part of the book, followed by the number of the relevant quotation(s). For example, Baxter, Stanley 3, 4, 5, 7 under the heading **Comedy and Humour** indicates that quotations numbered 3, 4, 5 and 7 under the entry **Baxter, Stanley** refer in some way to comedy and/or humour.

The reader's attention is particularly drawn to the **People** and **Places** categories, which provide easy access to quotations about specific individuals or places. For example, to identify quotations about Dundee, look up the sub-heading **Dundee** under the **Places** heading; listed below it will be those people included in the *Dictionary* who pass comment on Dundee, along with the number(s) of the related quotation(s), as above. The **People** category works in the same way.

Keyword Index

This lists keywords and the phrases containing them, alphabetically by keyword. Every quotation in the *Dictionary* is represented by at least one, and often by more than one, keyword and its associated phrase. For example, the quotation 'Freedom an' whisky gang thegither' can be found by looking under either 'whisky' or 'freedom'. The index gives a shortened version of the author/speaker's name followed by the quotation number and page number, eg MACKEN 7, 226 refers to quotation number 7 under **Mackenzie** on page 226. Where more clarification is required, the author/speaker is further identified by an initial, eg H MACKEN 3, 226 refers to Henry rather than R F Mackenzie.

Please note that English, Scots and Gaelic (and occasionally French and Latin) keywords are all contained in the same index. In the case of Scots, readers should be aware that there are often variant spellings of the same keyword, which are listed alphabetically as they appear in the quotations: if you cannot find a specific Scots keyword, it may appear close by with a variant spelling. In the case of Gaelic, keywords are also listed as they appear in the quotations, not in their root form, eg for the phrase 'chaidil mi raoir air a' bhuailidh' the keywords appear as 'chaidil' and 'bhuailidh', not 'caidil' and 'buailidh'.

SUBJECT INDEX

Subject Categories

SUBJECT INDEX

Class

Comedy and Humour

Drink and Drinking

Economics, Commerce and Money

Film and Photography

Food

Football

Health and Medicine

History and Historical Moments

Land and Landscape

Journalism and Broadcasting

Language

Literature, Reading and Writing

Love and Sex

Poets and Poetry

Politics and Government

Publishing and Bookselling

Religion

Royalty and Nobility

Science and Technology

Scotland and the Scots

QUOTATIONS

A

Adam, James and Adam, Robert
1730–94 (James), 1728–92 (Robert)
Architectural partners, and brothers

1 'Movement' is meant to express the rise and
fall, the advance and recess, with other diversity
of form, in the different parts of a building,
so as to add greatly to the picturesque of
the composition. For the rising and falling,
advancing and receding, with the convexity and
concavity and other forms of the great parts,
have the same effect in architecture that hill
and dale, foreground and distance, swelling and
sinking, have in landscape.

*The Works in Architecture of Robert and James
Adam* (3 Vols, 1773–1822), Introduction

Adam, Jean 1710–65
Poet

1 What do I owe to ought below the sun,
My worth does in a different channel run.
The cause of my creation was as high
As his who does an earthly sceptre sway;
Out of the dust he sprung as well as I,
No more than I can he Atropos fly.

'The Impartial Law of God in Nature', *Miscellany
Poems* (1734)

An early protest against sexual discrimination

2 For there's nae luck about the house
There's nae luck ava;
There's little pleasure in the house
When our gudeman's awa'.

'There's Nae Luck about the House'

Also known as 'The Song of the Mariner's
Wife', it is sometimes attributed to William
Julius Mickle (1735–88)

Ailean Dall (Allan MacDougall, Blind Allan) c.1750–1829
Poet

1 Thàinig oirnn a dh'Albainn crois,
Tha daoine bochda nochdte ris,
Gun bhiadh, gun aodach, gun chluain:
Tha 'n àird a tuath air a sgrios.

† There has come on us in Scotland a cross,
poor people are naked before it;
without food, without clothing, without
pasture:
the land of the north is utterly destroyed.

On the Highland Clearances. 'Oran nan
Ciobairean Gallda' ('Song to the Lowland
Shepherds')

Sorley MacLean, whose English translation
this is, explains that the word 'sgrios' ('utterly
destroyed') is the word used 'in the Gaelic
translation of the Bible for such holocausts as
visited on Sodom and Gomorrah, and. . . the
one regularly used for eternal damnation'. See
his essay, 'Vale of Tears: a view of Highland
history to 1886' in M MacLean & C Carrell
(eds), *As an Fhearann* (*From the Land*, 1986)

Aireach Muileach, An t- (The Mull Herdsman) 18th century
Poet

1 Cha b'e an creideamh ach am brosgal
Chuir thu ghiùlan crois a' Phàpa.

† It was not religion but fawning that caused
you to carry the cross of the Pope.

Traditional. On the conversion to Catholicism
of the Jacobite poet Alasdair Mac Mhaighstir
Alasdair (Alexander MacDonald)

A variant reading gives 'sodal-cùrtach' ('court
sycophancy') for 'brosgal'

Airlie, Jimmy
Trade unionist

1 We are not going to grovel to any Tory butcher.
We are going to fight, we have no alternative,
the key and basic fight – the right to work!

Speaking as a shop steward and organiser of the
Upper Clyde Shipbuilders work-in. Quoted on
BBC television news (9 Aug 1971)

Alasdair Mac Mhaighstir Alasdair (Alexander MacDonald) c.1695–c.1770
Jacobite poet

1 Is toil liom Cailein Ghlinn Iubhair:
B' fhearr liom gum b' iubhar 's nach fearna.

† I like Colin of Glenure: I wish he were yew-
wood and not alder.

Traditional. Said of Colin Campbell of Glenure
(designated the 'Red Fox' in R L Stevenson's
Kidnapped), afterwards the victim of the Appin
murder in 1752. Yew is a 'noble' wood, alder a
'base' wood: 'I wish he were a MacDonald and
not a Campbell' is the implication. Cf. Giolla
Críost Brúilingeach 1

2 Ach 's fheudar dhòmh-sa nis bhith falbh
bhuaibh,

23

Ghàidhealaibh calma mo ghràidh. . .
Sibh a rinn fo làimh na Trianaid mise dhiòn
  o mhiorun chàich,
mo dhearg nàimhdean neartmhor lìonmhor
  chuir an lìon feadh ghleann is àrd;
mheud 's a thaisbean sibh dur dìlseachd, 's còir
  nach dìochuimhnich gu bràth,
a bhàrr gur sibh as luaith' a shìn rium toic air
  tìr 's an talamh àrd.

† But I shall now have to leave you, my beloved
  hardy Gaels. . .
  It was you who, in the providence of the
  Trinity, protected me from others' hate, my
  arch-enemies, powerful, numerous, who set
  their net over glen and hill; what you displayed
  of faithfulness should never be forgotten, and
  you were also the first to offer your support
  on shore and on upland.

> 'Dealachadh a' Phrionnsa 's na Gàidheil'
> ('Prince Charlie's Parting with the Highlanders'),
> quoted in William Matheson, 'Gaelic Bards and
> Minstrels', in *Scottish Tradition* No.16 (1993).
> See also J L Campbell (ed.), *Highland Songs of
> the Forty-Five* (1933; revised edition 1984)

3 An uair dh'éireamaid gu h-allail
  Am bàrr nan tonn sin,
  B'éiginn an t-abhsadh a bhearradh
  Gu grad-phongail.

  'S 'n uair a thuiteamaid le ion-slugaidh
  Sìos 's na gleanntaibh,
  Bheirteadh gach seòl a bhiodh aice
  Am bàrr nan crann dith.

† When the ship was poised on wave crest
  in proud fashion
  it was needful to strike sail
  with quick precision.

  When the valleys nearly swallowed us
  by suction
  we fed her cloth to take her up to
  resurrection.

> 'Birlinn Chlann Raghnaill' ('The Galley of
> Clanranald', c.1750), translated by Iain Crichton
> Smith, in R Watson, *The Poetry of Scotland* (1995)

4 An fhairge 'g a maistreadh 's 'g a sluistreadh
  Troimh a chéile,
  Gu 'n robh ròin is mialan mòra
  Am barrachd éiginn':

  Onfhadh is confhadh na mara,
  'S falbh na luinge,
  Sradadh an eanchainnean geala,
  Feadh gach tuinne. . .

† The ocean churning, mixing, stirring
  its abyss,
  seals and huge sea creatures howling
  in distress.

  Impetuous tumult of the waters,
  the ship's going,
  sparking their white brains about

an eerie snowing.

> 'Birlinn Chlann Raghnaill' ('The Galley of
> Clanranald', c.1750), translated by Iain Crichton
> Smith, in R Watson, *The Poetry of Scotland* (1995)

Alexander, Sir William (Earl of Stirling)
c.1567–1640
Courtier, poet and politician

1 What thing so good which not some harme
  may bring?
  Even to be happy is a dangerous thing.

> *Darius* (1603), Act 1, Chorus

2 The deepest rivers make least din,
  The silent soule doth most abound in care. . .

> *Aurora* (1604), Song 1

Alison, Isabel d.1681
Covenanting martyr

1 . . . I leave my testimony against all the blood
  shed on both scaffolds, and in the fields, and
  seas; and against all the cruelty used against
  the people of the Lord – I leave my testimony
  against profanity of all sorts; and likewise against
  lukewarmness and indifference in the Lord's
  matters. . .

> 'The Dying Testimony and Last Words of Isabel
> Alison' (26 Jan 1681). Quoted in D P Thomson,
> *Women of the Scottish Church* (1975), ch.6
>
>> In her late twenties, she was hanged in the
>> Grassmarket, Edinburgh, along with Marion
>> Harvie, a servant girl from Bo'ness. Her
>> crime had been to publicly criticise the
>> harsh treatment of people sympathetic to the
>> Covenanters' cause

Anderson, Alexander ('Surfaceman')
1845–1909
Railway navvy and poet

1 The bairnies cuddle doon at nicht,
  Wi' muckle faucht an' din;
  O try and sleep, ye waukrife rogues,
  Your faither's comin' in.
  They never heed a word I speak;
  I try to gie a froon,
  But aye I hap them up an' cry,
  'O, bairnies, cuddle doon.'

> 'Cuddle Doon', *Ballads and Sonnets* (1879), st.1

2 What a plague is this o' mine,
  Winna steek his e'e,
  Though I hap him ow'r the head
  As cosie as can be.
  Sleep! an' let me to my wark,
  A' thae claes to airn;

Jenny wi' the airn teeth,
Come an' tak' the bairn.

'Jenny wi' the Airn Teeth', *Ballads and Sonnets*
(1879), st.1. Cf. James Nicholson 1

Anderson, Basil Ramsay 1861–88

Shetland poet

1 At last, despite baid sheep an kael,
Maunse an his krö began ta fail,
Time booed his rigg an shöre his tap,
An laid his krö in mony a slap;
Snug-shorded by his ain hert-steyn,
He lost his senses een by een,
Till, lyin helpless laek a paet,
Nor kael nor mutton he could aet;
Sae dee'd, as what we au maun dö,
Hae we, or hae we no, a krö.

'Auld Maunsie's Krö', in *Shetland Verse: Remnants
of the Norn* (1953)

krö: a small stone enclosure

2 O, some say da fram an da fraemd ir da best –
Da fram may be fair, an da fraemd may be free;
Bit I laek da heym-folk abö au da rest,
An I laek da heym-folk at bide by da sea.

'Heym-Folk', in *Shetland Verse: Remnants of the
Norn* (1953)

Da fram an da fraemd: foreign places and
foreigners

Anderson, Ian 1947–

*Rock singer (with Jethro Tull), flautist and
fish farmer*

1 I would be quite happy if, 20 years from
now, people remembered I stood on one leg
and played the flute and had something to do
with fish.

Said in interview in 1987. Quoted in *The Scotsman*
(8 May 1996)

Anderson, John 1893–1962

Philosopher and educationist

1 The general conclusion is that all the objects of
science, including minds and goods, are things
occurring in space and time. . . And therefore
all ideals, ultimates, symbols, agencies and the
like are to be rejected, and no such distinction
as that of facts and principles, or facts and
values, can be maintained. There are only facts,
ie occurrences in space and time.

'Empiricism' (1927), in *Studies in Empirical
Philosophy* (1962)

2 It should always be remembered that culture is
opposed not to commerce but to commercialism;
the question is whether or not investigation is
to be subordinated to the making of profits.

'University Reform' (1935). Reprinted in
D Z Phillips (ed.), *Education and Enquiry: John
Anderson* (1980)

3 In connection with 'the discipline of study itself'
it is argued that I exaggerate the intellectual
element in education, that not all children are
fitted for an intellectual training. My answer
is that the only alternative to the development
of understanding is the development of
submissiveness.

'Religion in Education' (1943), footnote.
Reprinted in D Z Phillips (ed.), *Education and
Enquiry: John Anderson* (1980)

4 The field of education. . . is a battlefield
between liberality and illiberality – between
cosmopolitanism and patriotism, between the
treatment of the child as 'the heir of all the
ages' and the treatment of him as job-fodder.

'Education and Practicality' (1944). Reprinted in
D Z Phillips (ed.), *Education and Enquiry: John
Anderson* (1980)

Angus, Marion 1866–1946

Poet

1 She was skilled in music and the dance
And the old arts of love
At the court of the poisoned rose
And the perfumed glove,
And gave her beautiful hand
To the pale Dauphin
A triple crown to win –
And she loved little dogs
And parrots
And red-legged partridges
And the golden fishes of the Duc de Guise
And a pigeon with a blue ruff
She had from Monsieur d'Elboeuf.

On Mary, Queen of Scots. 'Alas! Poor Queen',
The Tinker's Road and other verses (1924), st.1

2 Bit aye, wae's me!
The hindmaist tune he made. . .
'Twas juist a dune wife
Greetin' in her plaid,
Winds o' a' the years,
Naked wa's atween,
And heather creep, creepin'
Ower the bonnie dryin' green.

'The Fiddler', *The Tinker's Road and other verses*
(1924), st.3

3 Lassie, think lang, think lang,
Ere his step comes ower the hill.
Luve gi'es wi' a lauch an' a sang,
An' whiles for nocht bit ill.

'Think Lang', *The Tinker's Road and other verses*
(1924), st.1

4 I'm coming near to Forever and Ever,
With its flower and leaf unfalling,
Where you, poor Time, are an ancient measure,
Fit for a dream's recalling.

'On a Birthday', *Lost Country* (1937), st.2. First
published in *The Glasgow Herald* (29 Sep 1932)

Annan, James Craig 1864–1946
Photographer

1 The aim of a picture is not to demonstrate any
theory or fact, but is to excite a certain sensory
pleasure.

Address at the opening of an exhibition of
his works, reported in *Amateur Photographer*
(2 Feb 1900)

Annand, J(ames) K(ing) 1908–93
Poet

1 Said the whitrick to the stoat,
'I see ye've on your winter coat.
I dinna see the sense ava!
Ye're shairly no expectin snaw?'

'Fur Coats', *Sing it Aince for Pleisure* (1965), st.1

2 It's nocht but fun and games aa day,
Nae mair wark but lots o play
Until neist year the schule-bell caas
Them back to the maister and his tawse.

'Holidays', *Sing it Aince for Pleisure* (1965)

3 Burd alane on a barren mountain tap
A man can think upon the wey o things
Wi mind as clear's the cleanness o the wind,
The blueness o the lift, the greenness
O the waters in the corrie's rockbund lochan.

Two Voices (1968)

4 Intil the pitmirk nicht we northwart sail
Facin the bleffarts and the gurly seas
That ser' out muckle skaith to mortal men.

'Arctic Convoy', *Two Voices* (1968)

5 He'll ne'er be o our kind
That canna cheynge his mynd.
Ye need a cheery hert
To play the gangrel pairt,
Never worriet
Fasht or hurriet
Back and forrit
Around the warld.

'The Gangrel Scholars', *Songs from Carmina
Burana* (1978), st.3

Anonymous

1 Ingigerth is the most beautiful of women

Runic graffiti left by Vikings (1153) on the wall
of Maes Howe chambered tomb, Orkney

Historic Scotland's booklet on Maes Howe (text
by Patrick Ashmore), points out that beside
this inscription is a drawing of a slavering dog

2 Quhen Alexander our kynge was dede,
That Scotland lede in lauche and le,
Away was sons of alle and brede,
Of wyne and wax, of gamyn and gle,
Our golde was changit into lede.
Crist, born into virgynyte,
Succoure Scotlande and ramede,
That is stade in perplexite.

'Quhen Alexander our kynge was dede' (14th
century). Quoted in Andrew of Wyntoun's
Orygynale Cronykil (written c.1420)

The earliest surviving piece of Scots verse, it
laments the fatal fall of Alexander III from
his horse at Kinghorn in 1286

3 Fier comme un Ecossais

† Touchy as a Scot

French medieval proverb (14th or 15th century)

Many Scots, especially soldiers, travelled
widely throughout Europe, and France in
particular, in the later Middle Ages. Walter
Scott used the phrase in *Quentin Durward*
(1823), ch.2, and Hugh MacDiarmid used it
in *A Drunk Man Looks at the Thistle* (1926),
ll.2304–18

4 Perfervidum ingenium Scotorum

† The ardent temper of the Scots

Phrase of uncertain origin, perhaps misquoted
from George Buchanan's *Rerum Scoticarum
Historia* (1582), Vol.16, ch.51, where the phrase
'Scotorum praefervida ingenia' ('the ardent tempers of the Scots') appears. Cf. John Stuart Blackie 4

5 Ni fallat fatum, Scoti, quocunque locutum
Invenient lapidem, regnare tenentur ibidem.

† If fate faileth not, the Scots, in whatever place
they find this stone, there shall they reign.

Inscription supposed to have been written on
the Stone of Destiny. See William F Skene, *The
Coronation Stone* (1869)

6 The Scottis sall bruke that realme as
native ground
Gif weirdis faill nocht quhairevir this chair
is found.

Old rhyme associated with the Stone of Destiny,
based on the inscription in above entry

7 Pìobaireachd Dhomhnaill Duibh
Pìobaireachd Dhomhnaill
Pìob agus bratach air faich Inbhir Lòchaidh.

Chaidh an diugh, chaidh an diugh
Chaidh an diugh oirnne
Chaidh an diugh is an dé
Is chaidh a h-uile latha oirnne.

† Pibroch of Donald Dubh, pibroch of Donald,
a pipe and a banner on the field of Inverlochy.
Today, today, today has gone against us;

today and yesterday and every day has gone against us.

> Song connected with a battle at Inverlochy (23 Jun 1429)

8 . . . eight bolls of malt to Friar John Cor wherewith to make aqua vitae.

> Entry in the *Scottish Exchequer Rolls* (1494)
>
>> This is the earliest known reference to the distilling of Scotch whisky

9 Brissit brawnis and brokin banis,
Stryf, discorde and waistie wanis,
Cruikit in eild, syn halt withall,
Thir are the bewteis of the fute-ball.

> 'The Bewteis of the Fute-ball' (15th or 16th century), *The Maitland Manuscript* (1582)

10 Than they come to the townis end
Withouttin more delay,
He before, and scho before,
To see wha was maist gay.
All that lukit them upon
Leuch fast at their array;
Some said that they were merkat folk;
Some said the Queen of May
Was comit
Of Peblis to the play.

> 'Peblis to the Play' (15th or 16th century), st.9

11 Was never in Scotland hard nor sene
Sic dansing nor deray,
Nother in Falkland on the grene,
Nor Peblis to the play,
As was of wooeris as I wene
At Chrystis Kirk on ane day.
Thair come our Kittie weschen clene
In hir new kirtill of gray,
Full gay,
At Chrystis Kirk on the grene.

> 'Christ's Kirk on the Green' (15th or 16th century), st.1
>
>> Sometimes attributed to James I

12 Thocht raging stormes movis us to schaik,
And wind makis waters us ouerflow,
We yeild thairto bot dois not brek,
And in the calme bent up we grow.

So baneist men, thocht princes raige,
And prisoners be not disparit,
Abyde the calm, quhill that it suaige;
For tyme sic caussis hes reparit.

> 'The Reid in the Loch Sayis' (15th or 16th century), *The Maitland Manuscript* (1582)

13 London, thou art of townes *A per se*.
Soveraign of cities, semeliest in sight,
Of high renoun, riches, and royaltie;
Of lordis, barons, and many goodly knyght;
Of most delectable lusty ladies bright;
Of famous prelatis in habitis clericall;
Of merchauntis full of substaunce and myght:

London, thou art the flour of Cities all.

> 'To the City of London' (1501), st.1
>
>> Written by a member of the Scots diplomatic mission visiting London to negotiate the marriage of James IV to Margaret, daughter of Henry VII. Often attributed to William Dunbar, but without firm evidence

14 In Auchtermuchty thair dwelt ane man,
Ane husband, as I hard it tawld,
Quha weill cowld tippill owt a can
And nather luvit hungir nor cawld. . .

> 'The Wife of Auchtermuchty' (15th or 16th century), st.1

15 Than up he gat on ane knowe-heid,
On her to cry, on her to shout,
Scho heard him, and she heard him not,
Bot stoutly steer'd the stottis about.
Scho draif the day unto the nicht;
Scho lowsit the pleuch, and syne come hame;
Scho fand all wrang that sould bene richt:
I trow the man thocht richt grit schame.

> 'The Wife of Auchtermuchty' (15th or 16th century), st.12

16 God and Sanct Petir was gangand be the way
heiche up in Ardgyle quhair thair gait lay.
Sanct Petir said to God in a sport word,
'Can ye nocht mak a Helandman of this hors turd?'
God turnd owre the hors turd with his pykit staff
and up start a Helandman blak as on draff.
Quod God to the Helandman, 'Quhair wilt thou now?'
'I will doun in the Lawland, Lord, and thair steill a kow.'

> 'How the first Helandman of God was maid of ane hors turd in Argylle, as is said' (16th century), *Bannatyne Manuscript* (1568)

17 'Fy!' quod Sanct Petir, 'thou will nevir do weill,
and thou bot new maid sa sone gais to steill.'
'Umff', quod the Helandman and swere be yon kirk
'Sa lang as I may geir gett to steill, will I nevir wirk.'

> 'How the first Helandman of God was maid of ane hors turd in Argylle, as is said' (16th century), *Bannatyne Manuscript* (1568)

18 My hairt is heich aboif, my body is full of blis,
For I am sett in lufe als weill as I wald wis.
I lufe my lady pure and scho luvis me agane;
I am hir serviture, scho is my soverane;
Scho is my verry harte, I am hir howp and heill;
Scho is my joy inwart, I am hir luvar leill. . .

> 'My Hairt is Heich Aboif' (16th century), *Bannatyne Manuscript* (1568)

19 Mad ailt beth follan & madh ail beth slan
cuir na h-imsnimha troma diot & creid gurob
dimhaoin duit ferg do denamh. . . coigill fion

& bhi do suìper bec & nar budh dimaoin let ceimniughadh tar eis na codach & seachain codlad in medhoin laoi. . . Na connuiph co fada ar fual & na h-eigin go laidir do timperacht.

† If you wish to be sound and healthy, banish heavy worries and believe that it is foolish to be angry. . . . Use wine sparingly and let your supper be light. Do not neglect a walk after the repast, and avoid sleeping at noon. . . Do not retain the urine, nor press forcibly your anus.

> Extract from a medical manuscript (1611–14) written largely by Angus O' Conacher. Quoted in Donald MacKinnon (ed.), *Catalogue of Gaelic Manuscripts in Scotland* (1912), Manuscript 60

20 Thug thu an ear dhiom is thug thu an iar dhiom
Thug thu ghealach is thug thu ghrian dhiom
Thug thu an cridhe a bha 'nam chliabh bhuam
'S cha mhór a ghaoil ghil nach dug 's mo
Dhia bhuam.

† You took the east from me and you took the west from me
You took the moon and you took the sun from me
You took the heart within my breast from me
And almost, white love, you took my God from me.

> This verse appears in different Scottish songs, but originates in the Irish song 'Dónal Og'

21 Neart na gile neart na gréine
Bhith eadar Dòmhnall Gorm 's a léine.
Neart an fhochainn anns a' Chéitean
Bhith eadar Dòmhnall Gorm 's a léine.
Neart nan tonna troma treubhach
Bhith eadar Dòmhnall Gorm 's a léine.
Neart a' bhradain as braise leumas
Bhith eadar Dòmhnall Gorm 's a léine.

† Strength of the moon, strength of the sun
Be between Donald Gorm and his shirt.
Strength of the growing corn in May-time
Be between Donald Gorm and his shirt.
Strength of the heavy valiant waves
Be between Donald Gorm and his shirt.
Strength of the salmon boldest in leaping
Be between Donald Gorm and his shirt.

> 'Tàladh Dhòmhnaill Ghuirm' ('The Lullaby of Donald Gorm', chief of Sleat, who died in 1617). Quoted in W J Watson (ed.), *Bardachd Ghàidhlig* (3rd edition, 1959)

22 Thig trì nithean gun iarraidh:
An t-eagal, an t-iadach, 's an gaol;
'S gur beag a chùis mhaslaidh
Ged ghlacadh leo mis air a' h-aon,
'S a liughad bean uasal
A fhuaradh sa' chiont an robh mi –
A thug an gaol fuadain
Air ro bheagan duaise ga chionn.

† Three things come without asking: fear, jealousy and love; and it is no cause of disgrace that I for one have been seized by them, seeing how many a noble lady has been found guilty as I – who gave clandestine love with very little gain in return.

> 'Thig trì nithean gun iarraidh' ('Three things come without asking'). Quoted in John Mackenzie, *Sar-Obair nam Bard Gaelach* (*Beauties of Gaelic Poetry*, 1877)
>
> > This song is usually ascribed to the daughter of Fraser of Reelig

23 Nec tamen consumebatur

† And yet it was not consumed

> This phrase and the image of the Burning Bush of Exodus 3.2 has been the unofficial symbol of the Church of Scotland since the printer George Mossman used it on the cover of the proceedings of the General Assembly of 1691

24 A choin ghlais, comfhurtail is ga bheil thu 'nad shìneadh an sin, nam bu mhise thusa, dhèanainn mo leaba anns an fhraoch a nochd.

† Grey hound, comfortable as you are lying there, if I were you, I'd make my bed in the heather tonight.

> By tradition, said by a Campbell soldier to a dog on the night of the Massacre of Glencoe (5 Feb 1692)
>
> > The MacDonalds of the household, understanding the warning thus given, left that evening and escaped with their lives

25 Why Should I be Sad on my Wedding-Day?

> Title of tune (17th century)
>
> > On the day that the Scots Parliament approved the Act of Union in 1707, this lament was played from the bells of the High Kirk of St Giles. The tune re-emerged in a livelier form in the 19th century as 'The Campbells are Coming'

26 God grant that Marshal Wade
May by thy mighty aid
Victory bring.
May he sedition hush
And like a torrent rush
Rebellious Scots to crush,
God save the King.

> One of two verses added to 'God Save the King' and sung nightly by English audiences at Covent Garden and elsewhere in late 1745, when London was threatened by the advancing Jacobite army. Cf. John Purser 2

27 I met ayont the Kairny,
Jenny Nettles, Jenny Nettles,
Singing till her Bairny,
Robin Rattles' Bastard;
To flee the Dool upo' the Stool,
And ilka ane that mocks her,
She round about seeks Robin out,
To stap it in his Oxter.

> 'Jenny Nettles' (18th century), st.2. Cf. Hugh MacDiarmid 9

'Dool upo' the Stool' refers to the kirk stool
of repentance

28 The King ower the Water!

Jacobite toast (18th century), usually drunk in
claret

29 Some hae meat and canna eat
And some wad eat that want it;
But we hae meat and we can eat,
And sae the Lord be thankit.

'The Selkirk Grace' (18th century), often
attributed to Robert Burns

30 If you had seen these roads before they
were made,
You would hold up your hands and bless
General Wade.

Rhyme celebrating George Wade's Highland
military road-building (18th century)

31 Up the Lawnmarket,
Doun the West Bow,
Up the lang ladder,
And doun the pickle tow.

Rhyme celebrating the four stages of the route
from Edinburgh's Tolbooth to the place of
execution in the Grassmarket (18th century)

32 Whaur's yer Wullie Shakespeare noo?

Patriotic cry from a member of the audience at
the first Edinburgh performance of John Home's
tragedy *Douglas* (14 Dec 1756)

The play was vastly overrated by the Scottish
literati. The earliest reference to this incident is
in David Erskine Baker, *Biographia Dramatica*
(1812 edition), where the phrase used is 'Weel,
lads; what think you of Wully Shakspeare
now?' The identity of the patriot is not known,
but Ernest Mossner in his *Life of David Hume*
(1954), ch.27, describes him as an Aberdeen
man at the first *London* performance at Covent
Garden in 1757, who shouted, 'Ou fie, lads!
fat think ye o yir Willy Shakespeare noo?'

33 Nine Inch will Please a Lady

Title of song, *The Merry Muses of Caledonia*
(c.1800)

Many of the songs in this volume were
gathered by Robert Burns, and cleaned up by
him for polite versions. In their 'uncensored'
versions some were possibly written, or at the
very least added to and developed, by him

34 Green grow the rashes O,
Green grow the rashes O,
The lasses they hae wimble bores,
The widows they hae gashes O.

'Green Grow the Rashes O', *The Merry Muses
of Caledonia* (c.1800), chorus. Cf. Robert Burns 2

35 O gie the lass her fairin' lad,
O gie the lass her fairin',
An' something else she'll gie to you,
That's waly worth the wearin';
Syne coup her o'er amang the creels,

When ye hae taen your brandy,
The mair she bangs the less she squeels,
An' hey for houghmagandie.

'Gie the Lass her Fairin'', *The Merry Muses of
Caledonia* (c.1800), st.1

36 John Anderson, my jo, John,
When first that ye began,
Ye had as good a tail-tree
As ony ither man;
But now it's waxen wan, John,
And wrinkles to and fro;
I've twa gae-ups for ae gae-down,
John Anderson, my jo.

'John Anderson, my Jo', *The Merry Muses of
Caledonia* (c.1800), st.2. Cf. Robert Burns 86

37 Roseberry to his lady says,
'My hinnie and my succour,
O shall we do the thing ye ken,
Or shall we take our supper?'

Wi' modest face, sae fu' o' grace,
Replied the bonny lady;
'My noble lord do as you please,
But supper is na ready.'

'Supper is na Ready', *The Merry Muses of
Caledonia* (c.1800)

38 Scotland free or a desert

Political slogan coined during the 'Radical
Rising' of 1820

It was later taken up and re-used by the
leftwing 79 Group in the Scottish National
Party during the 1980s. Cf. Anne Frater 1

39 Within this circular idea
Call'd vulgarly a tomb,
The ideas and impressions lie
That constituted Hume.

'On the Circular Monument on Edinburgh's
Calton Hill to the Philosopher David Hume'.
First published in *A Scotch Haggis* (c.1820)

The author of this rhyme mocking Hume's
sceptical philosophy may have been Adam
McCheyne, father of Robert Murray
McCheyne (1813–43), the evangelical minister

40 Listen to me, as when ye heard our father
Sing long ago the song of other shores –
Listen to me, and then in chorus gather
All your deep voices as ye pull your oars:
*Fair these broad meads – these hoary woods
are grand;*
But we are exiles from our fathers' land.

'Canadian Boat Song', *Blackwood's Edinburgh
Magazine* (Sep 1829), st.1 and chorus

This first appeared in 'Noctes Ambrosianae'
no.46, supposedly translated from a Gaelic
original. The authorship is unknown, though
sometimes attributed to John Galt, D M Moir,
or, with less likelihood, Walter Scott

41 From the lone shieling of the misty island
Mountains divide us, and the waste of seas –

Yet still the blood is strong, the heart is Highland,
And we in dreams behold the Hebrides.

'Canadian Boat Song', *Blackwood's Edinburgh Magazine* (Sep 1829), st.2. Cf. Compton Mackenzie 4

42 Glencalvie people the wicked generation

Scratched on the window of Croick parish church, Easter Ross (24 May 1845)

The Rosses of Glencalvie were evicted from their homes by James Gillanders, factor to the landowner Major Charles Robertson of Kindeace, and were forced to take shelter overnight in the kirkyard at Croick

43 We have no leaders; we are all leaders; we are all acting together.

Skye crofters, speaking in unison in defence of their claims for land rights. *The Scotsman* (19 Nov 1884)

44 The Free kirk, the wee kirk,
The kirk without the steeple;
The Auld kirk, the cauld kirk,
The kirk without the people.

Rhyme on the relative demerits of the post-Disruption (1843) Free Church and Church of Scotland

45 Is treasa tuath na tighearna
† The tenant is stronger than the laird

Slogan used by agitators for land reform on Skye (1884)

46 A guid cause maks a strong arm

Proverb, adopted by suffragettes and used on their banners during the late 19th and early 20th centuries

47 Jute, Jam and Journalism

Phrase celebrating the 'three Js', traditionally the main components of Dundee's economy (19th/20th century)

48 Ye maunna tramp on the Scots thistle, Laddie!

Advertising slogan for Isdale and McCallum's Thistle soap (from late 1880s). The slogan was later adopted by suffragettes, and appeared on a banner as a 'Message to Mr Asquith' in London (Sep 1908), when Scottish suffragettes led by Flora Drummond gathered to greet one of their compatriots on her release from Holloway Prison. See Elspeth King, *The Scottish Women's Suffrage Movement* (1978)

49 The earth belongs unto the Lord
And all that it contains;
Except the Western Isles alone,
And they are all MacBrayne's.

Rhyme parodying Metrical Psalm 24, on David MacBrayne (1818–1907), whose shipping company dominated the transport economy of the West Highlands and Islands for much of the 19th and 20th centuries

Several variations exist on the theme of what exactly 'belongs' to MacBrayne

50 Not a Headache in a Gallon

Advertising slogan for Cambus Patent Still Grain Whisky (1906)

Coined by William Ross, chairman of the Distillers Company Limited (DCL), as part of a campaign to have grain and blended whisky acknowledged as whisky rather than simply plain spirit. Malt distillers disputed DCL's argument, but a Royal Commission found against them in 1908

51 This bloody town's a bloody cuss –
No bloody trains, no bloody bus,
And no one cares for bloody us –
In bloody Orkney.

'The Bloody Orkneys', st.1. First published in *The Orkney Blast*, a forces newspaper, during the Second World War, as the work of a Captain Blair

Many versions and verses exist, eg in Maurice Lindsay (ed.), *Scottish Comic Verse* (1981). The identity of Captain Blair is uncertain

52 Best bloody place is bloody bed
With bloody ice on bloody head;
You might as well be bloody dead –
In bloody Orkney.

'The Bloody Orkneys', last stanza

53 Here's tae us; wha's like us?
Damn few, and they're aa deid.

Widely used toast of obscure origin

Variations include the substitution of 'gey' for 'damn', and of 'Deil the yin!' for the entire response

54 What is a Scot but an uninspired Irishman?

Derogatory remark quoted by John Grierson in 'The Salt of the Earth' (address to the Rotary Club of Ottawa, 29 Nov 1943). Reprinted in Forsyth Hardy (ed.), *John Grierson's Scotland* (1979)

55 This is the tree that never grew
This is the bird that never flew
This is the fish that never swam
This is the bell that never rang.

Rhyme associated with Glasgow's coat of arms, based on the legends of St Mungo, the city's patron saint. The order of the lines frequently differs. Cf. Michael Marra 2

56 Wha daur meddle wi me?

Aggressive paraphrase of the royal motto 'Nemo me impune lacessit' ('No one provokes me with impunity')

57 Glasgow's Miles Better

Slogan used in campaign led by Provost Michael Kelly to improve Glasgow's image (1980s)

58 Better to break the law than break the poor

Anti-Poll Tax slogan adopted by protesters in Glasgow (from 1989)

The Poll Tax was eventually abandoned by the Conservative government in 1992. Cf. Ian Bell 1

59 Why do we always get Julians and Timothys? Let's get some Wullies in charge.

Remark by a member of the public made at a protest against Timothy Clifford's directorship of the National Galleries of Scotland, following his high-profile campaign for Canova's 'Three Graces'. Quoted in *The Scotsman* (6 Oct 1994). Cf. Timothy Clifford, Julian Spalding

60 There's nae ill intill't.

Comment by a reader (c.1994) on the enduring appeal of the D C Thomson publication, *The People's Friend*

Anthony, Jack (originally John Herbertson) 1900–62
Comedian

1 Nae bother at aw!

Catchphrase

Aonghas Mac Alasdair Ruaidh
see **MacDonald (of Glencoe), Angus**

Arbuthnot, John 1667–1735
Physician to Queen Anne, and satirist

1 Law is a Bottom-less Pit

Title of one of several satirical pamphlets against the Duke of Marlborough, published in 1712

2 Hocus was an old cunning attorney.

Law is a Bottom-Less Pit (1712), ch.5

3 Hame's hame, be it never so hamely.

The History of John Bull (1712), ch.3, 'John Bull Still in His Senses'

Argyll, 4th Duke of (John Campbell) 1693–1770
General, known as 'Handsome Jack Campbell'

1 I have received undoubted intelligence that on the 28th of last month the Pretender's son passed over from the Isle of South Uist to the Isle of Skye, disguised in women's clothes and accompanying a daughter of MacDonald of Milton . . .

From an order issued by him (9 Jul 1746). National Library of Scotland manuscript 3736. Cf. Charles Edward Stewart 6

Arniston, Lord see **Dundas, Robert**

Arnold, Matthew 1822–88
English poet and critic

1 I have been up in Ross-shire, and a more impressive country I never saw. After being used to this Lake country, over which you could throw a pocket-handkerchief, the extent of the Highlands gives a sense of vastness; and then the desolation . . . miles and miles and miles of mere heather and peat and rocks, and not a soul. And then the sea comes up into the land on the west coast, and the mountain forms are there quite magnificent.

Letter to Lady de Rothschild (25 Sep 1864)

2 . . . I have a great *penchant* for the Celtic races, with their melancholy and unprogressiveness.

Letter to Lady de Rothschild (25 Sep 1864)

3 I never much liked Carlyle. He seemed to me to be 'carrying coals to Newcastle', as our proverb says; preaching earnestness to a nation which had plenty of it by nature, but was less abundantly supplied with several other useful things.

On Thomas Carlyle. Letter to M. Fontanès (25 Mar 1881)

4 In my two days in that stormy wind on Loch Ruthven I managed to set up a flying faceache, which comes on at night, when I am warm in bed, and bothers me a great deal.

Letter to his wife (11 Sep 1882)

5 I am very glad to have seen the Caledonian Canal, but don't want to see it again. Ben Nevis I should like to see again, and to make the ascent of him.

Letter to his wife (11 Sep 1882)

Artúr Dall Mac Gurcaigh (Blind Arthur Mac Gurcaigh) 13th–14th century
Poet

1 Fir arda ag eagar na loingse,
ar loime luath leanas cuairt:
ní bhí lámh gan ghalgha gasta,
i n-ár stargha snasta suairc.

Do chotúnaibh is díobh eagrar
aghaidh na mbárc fá chruth liag,
do choradhaibh na gcrios gclárdhonn:
Lochlannaigh is ármuinn iad.

† Tall men are arraying the fleet, which swiftly holds its course on the sea's bare surface: no hand lacks a trim warspear, in battle of targes, polished and comely.

Of quilted hauberks is arrayed the barks' forefront in form of jewels, of warriors with brown-faced girdles: Norsemen and nobles are they.

Poem (probably composed in 1310). In W J

Watson (ed.), *Scottish Verse from the Book of the Dean of Lismore* (1937), st.2–3

> Written as a 'brosnachadh catha' (incitement to battle) prior to the (unsuccessful) expedition of John MacSween, a supporter of the English against Robert the Bruce, to win back his lands in Knapdale from John of Menteith. Historically, the poem is important for its detailing of Norse design in ships and weaponry

Ascherson, (Charles) Neal 1932–

Journalist and political commentator

1 Those who resist devolution on the grounds that they are 'internationalists' usually turn out to be 'British patriots', the most insular and isolationist of all creeds. Politicians who say they want Scottish self-government in order to end a separation from the outside world rather than to commence one, seem to be on harder ground.

> 'Scottish Contradictions', a paper for the Church of Scotland Colloquy on Devolution (1976), reprinted in *Games with Shadows* (1988)

2 . . . Europe is not a civilised place, a region which is polished but rather lifeless. It is a barbaric continent, heaving with a crude vigour which is now beginning to crack apart the marble slabs of imperial order laid across it by the post-war settlement 40 years ago.

> 'Tiring the Romans', *The Observer* (1985), reprinted in *Games with Shadows* (1988)

3 Rioting is at least as English as thatched cottages and honey still for tea.

> 'The English Riot', *The Observer* (1985), reprinted in *Games with Shadows* (1988)

4 The Presbyterian faith is an incomparable metaphor for the unity of creation, for the inner conflict between our sense of freedom and our scientific understanding that, in another way, we control nothing that happens.

> 'Pity, Love and the Accident of Birth', *The Observer* (1986), reprinted in *Games with Shadows* (1988)

5 'Truth Will Prevail.' 'Don't be afraid – and don't steal.' You cannot guarantee that a nation-state that applies these principles will never be crushed. But you can be certain that such a nation will rise again.

> 'Don't Be Afraid – and Don't Steal!' Lecture at Scottish National Party Conference, Dunoon (Sep 1986), reprinted in *Games with Shadows* (1988)
>
> The first quotation is adapted from 'Magna est veritas, et praevalet' ('Great is truth, and it prevails'), in 1 Esdras 4.41 (Vulgate Bible). The second comes from Thomas Masaryk, the 'father of Czechoslovak independence', in 1918

6 It is commonly and comfortably said that there is nothing basically wrong with British institutions – 'the finest in the world' – but that they are not working well at present because the economy is in such a bad state. The reverse is true. The reason that the British economy does not work is that British institutions are in terminal decay.

> 'Ancient Britons and the Republican Dream', John P Mackintosh Memorial Lecture (16 Nov 1986), reprinted in *Games with Shadows* (1988)

7 If the cult of the archaic nation is demolished, the monarchy – no longer called upon to sanctify it – will reduce to the scale of a harmless focus of attention and newspaper scuttlebutt. It is not the last king or queen who should be beheaded. It is the last Druid whose brains should be knocked out with the last volume of Walter Bagehot.

> 'Ancient Britons and the Republican Dream', John P Mackintosh Memorial Lecture (16 Nov 1986), reprinted in *Games with Shadows* (1988). Cf. Naomi Mitchison 7, Tom Nairn 2

8 Once again, English history is presented as a perfectly-landscaped garden, all the lines of sight converging from trim lawn and ornamental lake to where we stand on the 'now' of a country-house terrace.

This is history only in the sense that the Old Testament is history: the account of a divinely-ordained pilgrimage. But I don't see Canaan when I look out of the window; rather, a kindly and long-suffering nation increasingly puzzled about its identity and in sore trouble.

> On government proposals for a core school curriculum of English history. 'Tell the Children. . .', *The Observer* (1987), reprinted in *Games with Shadows* (1988)

9 What is Edinburgh for? To be a city. That isn't the tautology it sounds. Edinburgh is not meant to be a park or a suburb or a heritage resource or a conference venue or a tourist Mecca or even a 'Festival City'. Many of us could attach a policy or a name to attempts to make this town into one of each of those. The truth is that it can have something of all of them, but only as seasoning.

> 'Edinburgh, the European City'. Address to 'Civilising the City' conference, 1990, published in *Radical Scotland* No.45 (Jun/Jul 1990)

10 It seems to me that Edinburgh has never quite discovered an alternative *raison d'être* in all the 283 years since the last session of the Scottish parliament. For different reasons, Prague, too, has seemed at a loose end for most of the last 40 years, and Budapest and Bucharest and Vilnius as well. In the end, it turns out that the most European of urban destinies is to be the capital of a nation regaining the use of its limbs.

> 'Edinburgh, the European City'. Address to

'Civilising the City' conference, 1990, published in *Radical Scotland* No.45 (Jun/Jul 1990)

Atholl, Duchess of (*née* Katharine Marjory Ramsay) 1874–1960

Conservative politician, first Scottish woman MP and, as Minister of Education (1924–9), first Conservative woman minister

1 I agree unreservedly... in regarding the children of this country as our best and most valuable raw material.

Speaking at a debate on proposed education cuts in the House of Commons (17 Dec 1925)

2 I am aware that Herr Hitler has recently reminded us that *Mein Kampf* was written some years ago, before his accession to power. But if it thus represents views which he has discarded, why is the book still being published with these statements in it? Above all, why is the English translation, first published in 1933, so expurgated that none of the passages quoted, or other similar ones, are to be found in it? That edition is only about one-third of the length of the original.

Late 1935. Quoted in Sheila Hetherington, *Katharine Atholl 1874–1960: Against the Tide* (1989), ch.16

She had read the original German version of Hitler's work, and was one of a group called the 'Friends of Europe' who succeeded in having published an unexpurgated English translation of it, in an attempt to alert British politicians to Hitler's threat

3 I feel bound to say that so long as Germany is governed under a system disposed to racial discrimination, which has led to the persecution of Jews in Germany, it would be a gross betrayal of our trusteeship to hand over natives and helpless races to their rule.

Speaking at a Conservative fete at Dunira House, near Comrie (Aug 1936), opposing the idea of giving in to Hitler's demands that mandated territories in Africa be returned to Germany. Quoted in Sheila Hetherington, *Katharine Atholl 1874–1960: Against the Tide* (1989), ch.17

4 Neither in London, Paris, nor anywhere else have I addressed meetings organised by any political party other than the Conservative and Unionist Party; surely, however, no-one can object to members from different political parties speaking from the same platform on behalf of humanitarian purposes such as Spanish Relief or for a great and good cause such as the League of Nations and collective security.

Defending herself against accusations that she had participated in meetings supported by communists (Jun 1937). Although the complaint against her

was not upheld, she faced increased hostility from within her Party; she subsequently became known by some members as 'the Red Duchess'. Quoted in Sheila Hetherington, *Katharine Atholl 1874–1960: Against the Tide* (1989), ch.18

5 I am standing as an Independent so that Unionists, Liberals and Socialists may be able to support me without voting against their several parties. Real unity will be founded on a readiness to put country before party. Munich has not brought appeasement. On the contrary, Hitler's speeches and the officially controlled German press have become increasingly aggressive. And there has been a renewed persecution of Jewish people of unparalleled brutality.

Kinross and West Perthshire by-election campaign (Dec 1938). Quoted in Sheila Hetherington, *Katharine Atholl 1874–1960: Against the Tide* (1989), ch.19

As an opponent of fascism and Prime Minister Neville Chamberlain's 'peace in our time' appeasement policy, she came in for such criticism that she resigned her seat, prompting a by-election. This she lost to the National Government candidate, William McNair Snadden, by 1,313 votes. In March 1939, Germany went on to occupy the whole of Czechoslovakia and, following Hitler's invasion of Poland (Sep 1939), Britain and France declared war on Germany. Chamberlain resigned in 1940

Ayala, Don Pedro de 15th century

Spanish ambassador to the court of James IV

1 The women are courteous in the extreme. I mention this because they are really honest, though very bold. They are absolute mistresses of their houses and even of their husbands, in all things concerning the administration of their property, income as well as expenditure. They are very graceful and handsome women.

Letter to the Spanish court (25 Jul 1498). Quoted in P Hume Brown (ed.), *Early Travellers in Scotland* (1891)

Ayton, Sir Robert 1570–1638

Poet and courtier to James VI and I

1 Philo lov'd Sophia and she againe
Did pay him home with coy disdaine.
Yet when he dye'd, he left her all he had.
What doe you thinke? The man was mad.

'An Epigram'

2 I loved thee once; I'll love no more –
Thine be the grief as is the blame;
Thou art not what thou wast before,
What reason I should be the same?

'To an Inconstant Mistress', st.1

3 He that can love unloved again
Hath better store of love than brain. . .

'To an Inconstant Mistress', st.1

4 . . . To live upon Tobacco and on hope,
The ones but smoake, the other is but winde.

'Upone Tabacco'

Aytoun, W(illiam) E(dmonstoune)
1813–65

Lawyer and humorist

1 Fhairson swore a feud
Against the clan M'Tavish;
Marched into their land
To murder and to rafish;
For he did resolve
To extirpate the vipers,
With four-and-twenty men
And five-and-thirty pipers.

'The Massacre of the Macpherson' (1845), st.1

2 'He is coming! he is coming!'
Like a bridegroom from his room,
Came the hero from his prison
To the scaffold and the doom.
There was glory on his forehead,
There was lustre in his eye,
And he never walked to battle

More proudly than to die. . .

'The Execution of Montrose', *Lays of the Scottish Cavaliers* (1849). Cf. Marquis of Montrose 5

3 The grim Geneva ministers
With anxious scowl drew near,
As you have seen the ravens flock
Around the dying deer.

'The Execution of Montrose', *Lays of the Scottish Cavaliers* (1849)

4 'Strike! and when the fight is over,
If ye look in vain for me,
Where the dead are lying thickest,
Search for him that was Dundee!'

'The Burial March of Dundee', *Lays of the Scottish Cavaliers* (1849)

5 The deep, unutterable woe
Which none save exiles feel.

'The Island of the Scots', *Lays of the Scottish Cavaliers* (1849), st.12

6 Better to be born a peasant
Than to live an exiled king!

'Charles Edward at Versailles, on the anniversary of Culloden', *Lays of the Scottish Cavaliers* (1849)

7 Nowhere beats the heart so kindly
As beneath the tartan plaid.

'Charles Edward at Versailles, on the anniversary of Culloden', *Lays of the Scottish Cavaliers* (1849)

B

Bailie, The 1873–1926
Glasgow satirical magazine

1 It has been whispered that the lady who is a 'Man You Know' shows sometimes an inclination to espouse the cause of the 'shrieking sisterhood' who rave about 'Women's rights' and 'Women's wrongs' until honest men are well nigh 'deaved wi' skirlin'!'. . . It would be a misfortune that a gracious dame should, from a mistaken sense of duty, sink down to the level of agitators who sport their petticoats on platforms and contaminate themselves and outrage their sex. . .

> On women's rights activist Mrs Jane Arthur (1827–1907), after she was elected to the Paisley School Board in 1873, becoming the first woman in Scotland to sit on any school board (25 Jun 1873)
>
> > *The Bailie*, which profiled prominent men, afforded Jane Arthur the privilege of being the first woman to appear in the 'Men You Know' series of biographical sketches

Baillie, Lady Grizel (*née* Home) 1665–1746
Poet and songwriter

1 There ance was a may, and she loo'd na men;
She biggit her bonnie bower doun in yon glen;
But now she cries, Dool! and well-a-day!
Come doun the green gait and come here away!

When bonny young Johnny came o'er the sea,
He said he saw naething sae lovely as me;
He hecht me baith rings and mony braw things;
And werena my heart licht, I wad dee.

> 'Werena my Heart Licht I wad Dee', first published in Allan Ramsay, *The Tea-Table Miscellany* (1724), st.1–2

Baillie, Joanna 1762–1851
Playwright and poet

1 The theatre is a school in which much good or evil may be learned.

> *A Series of Plays* (1798), Introductory Discourse

2 GEOFFRY: Some men are born to feast, and not to fight;
Whose sluggish minds, e'en in fair honour's field,
Still on their dinner turn –

Let such pot-boiling varlets stay at home,
And wield a flesh-hook rather than a sword.

> *Count Basil: A Tragedy*, in *A Series of Plays* (1798), Act 1, sc.1

3 COUNT ROSENBERG: . . . what custom hath endear'd
We part with sadly, tho' we prize it not. . .

> *Count Basil: A Tragedy*, in *A Series of Plays* (1798), Act 1, sc.2

4 MASKS' SONG: Child, with many a childish wile,
Timid look, and blushing smile,
Downy wings to steal thy way,
Gilded bow, and quiver gay,
Who in thy simple mien would trace
The tyrant of the human race?

> On Cupid. *Count Basil: A Tragedy*, in *A Series of Plays* (1798), Act 3, sc.3

5 COL HARDY: Nay, heaven defend us from a violent woman; for that is the devil himself!

> *The Tryal: A Comedy*, in *A Series of Plays* (1798), Act 4, sc.1

6 FREEMAN: Pamper'd vanity is a better thing perhaps than starved pride.

> *The Election* (1811), Act 2, sc.2

7 ORRA: Can spirit from the tomb, or fiend from hell,
More hateful, more malignant be than man –
Than villainous man?

> *Orra* (1812), Act 3, sc.2

8 'I stood,' said Wallace, 'for the right,
When ye in holes shrunk from the light;
My plumes spread to the blazing sun
Which coweringly ye sought to shun.
Ye are the owls, who from the gloom
Of cleft and cranny boasting come. . .'

> Wallace's reproach to the Scots nobles. 'A Metrical Legend of William Wallace', *Metrical Legends of Exalted Characters* (1821), st.73

9 O! who shall lightly say that fame
Is nothing but an empty name!
When mem'ry of the mighty dead
To earth-worn pilgrim's wistful eye
The brightest rays of cheering shed,
That point to immortality?

> 'The Legend of Christopher Columbus', *Metrical Legends of Exalted Characters* (1821), st.61

10 The gowan glitters on the sward,
The lav'rock's in the sky,

And collie on my plaid keeps ward,
And time is passing by.
Oh no! sad and slow,
And lengthen'd on the ground,
The shadow of our trysting bush,
It wears so slowly round!

> 'The Gowan Glitters on the Sward', st.1
>
>> Also known as 'The Lover's Watch' and 'The Shepherd's Song'

11 I' the kirk sic commotion last Sabbath she made,
Wi' babs o' red roses and breast-knots o'erlaid!
The Dominie stickit the psalm very nearly:
O gin my wife wad dress hooly and fairly!
Hooly and fairly, hooly and fairly,
O gin my wife wad dress hooly and fairly!

> 'Hooly and Fairly', st.4

12 Kind was she, and my friends were free,
But poverty parts good company.

> 'Poverty Parts Good Company', st.1. Cf. Traditional songs 74

13 Tam o' the Lin was fu' o' pride,
And his weapon he girt to his valorous side,
A scabbard o' leather wi' de'il-haet within –
'Attack me wha daur!' quo' Tam o' the Lin.

> 'Tam o' the Lin', st.1

14 Tam o' the Lin he married a wife,
And she was the torment, the plague o' his life;
She lays sae about her, and makes sic a din –
'She frightens the bailie', quo' Tam o' the Lin.

> 'Tam o' the Lin', st.7
>
>> 'Bailie' is given as 'baby' in some editions

15 The bride she is winsome and bonny,
Her hair it is snooded sae sleek,
And faithfu' and kind is her Johnny,
Yet fast fa' the tears on her cheek.
New pearlins are cause of her sorrow,
New pearlins and plenishing too;
The bride that has a' to borrow
Has e'en right mickle ado.
Woo'd and married and a'!
Woo'd and married and a'!
Isna she very weel aff
To be woo'd and married at a'?

> 'Woo'd and Married and A'', st.1. Cf. Joanna Picken 1, Alexander Ross 1

16 Ladies of four score and upwards cannot expect to be robust, and need not be gay.

> Letter to Mary Somerville (1843), quoted in Margaret S Carhart, *The Life and Work of Joanna Baillie* (1923), p.62

Baillie, William see Polkemmet, Lord

Bain, Ewen 1925–89
Cartoonist, creator of 'Angus Og'

1 The difference between devolution and evolution is that devolution takes longer.

> Quoted in Rob Brown, 'Beyond the East-West Divide', *Scotland on Sunday* (2 Jun 1996)
>
>> Derived from a Bain cartoon in the *Scots Independent* (Jan 1978), which depicts a man reading a newspaper article on devolution while his son reads a book on evolution. The caption is: 'No, son, they're not the same thing – devolution takes longer!'

Baird, John Logie 1888–1946
Pioneer in the development of television

1 Seeing by wireless.

> His answer to the question, 'What is television?' (1923). Quoted in T McArthur & P Waddell, *The Secret Life of John Logie Baird* (1986), ch.6
>
>> He also used this phrase as the title of an article in *Chambers Journal* (Nov 1923). Even earlier, he had used the phrase 'seeing by telephone'

Bairn rhymes

1 There cam a man tae oor toun,
Tae oor toun, tae oor toun;
There cam a man tae oor toun,
An they ca'd him Aiken Drum.

He played upon a ladle,
A ladle, a ladle;
He played upon a ladle,
An his name was Aiken Drum.

> 'Aiken Drum'. Cf. Traditional songs 60

2 Wha learnt ye tae dance, Babbity-Bowster,
Babbity-Bowster?
Wha learnt ye tae dance, Babbity-Bowster,
brawly?

> 'Babbity-Bowster'

3 Bobbie Shafto's gane tae sea,
Siller buckles on his knee,
He'll come back an mairry me,
Bonny Bobbie Shafto.

> 'Bobbie Shafto'

4 The bonnie muir hen
Has feathers enou,
The bonnie muir hen
Has feathers enou.
There's some o them black,
And there's some o them blue;
The bonnie muir hen
Has feathers enou.

> 'The Bonnie Muir Hen'

5 Burke and Hare,
They were a pair,
Killed a wife,
And didna care.

Then they pit her
In a box,
And sent her aff
Tae Doctor Knox.

'Burke and Hare'

Rhyme on Burke and Hare, the murderers
who supplied bodies to anatomists, and Robert
Knox, their chief customer

6 Doun the close and up the stair,
But and ben wi Burke and Hare.
Burke's the butcher, Hare's the thief,
Knox the boy that buys the beef.

Another rhyme on Burke and Hare

7 Dance to your daddy, my bonnie laddie,
Dance to your daddy, my little lamb!
An ye'll get a fishie in a little dishie,
An ye'll get a fishie when the boat comes in!

'Dance to your Daddy'

8 Bloodthirsty Dee
Each year needs three,
But bonnie Don
She needs none.

'Dee'

9 Ae mile o' Don's worth twa o' Dee
Except for salmon, stane and tree.

'Don'

10 Hush ye, hush ye, little pet ye,
Hush ye, hush ye, do not fret ye,
The Black Douglas shall not get ye.

'Hush ye, Hush ye'

Lullaby reputedly sung by the wives of English
troops garrisoned in Scotland during the
campaigns of Bruce and his lieutenant, Lord
James Douglas. According to Walter Scott,
at Roxburgh Castle a woman was singing it
to her child one night when Douglas himself
appeared beside her saying, 'You are not so
sure of that', and proceeded to take the castle
by surprise. See *Tales of a Grandfather*, 1st
Series (1828), ch.9

11 The lion and the unicorn
Fechtin for the croun;
Up jumped the wee dog,
An knocked them baith doun.

Some gat white breid,
An some gat broun;
But the lion beat the unicorn,
Roon aboot the toun.

'The Lion and the Unicorn'

12 Nievie, nievie, nick, nack,
Whit haun will ye tak?
Tak the richt, tak the wrang,

I'll beguile ye gin I can.

'Nievie, Nievie, Nick, Nack'

13 Old Mother Riley at the pawnshop door,
Baby in her arms and a bundle on the floor.
She asked for ten bob, she only got four,
And she nearly pull't the hinges aff the
pawnshop door.

'Old Mother Riley'

14 O, Pearlin Jean!
O, Pearlin Jean!
She haunts the hoose,
She haunts the green,
An glowers on me
Wi her wul-cat een.

'Pearlin Jean'

Pearlin Jean was a ghost reputed to haunt
Allanbank House near Duns, Berwickshire

15 Pisky, Pisky, say Amen!
Doun on your knees and up again!

Presby, Presby, never bend!
Sit on your seat on Man's chief end!

On the rival forms of worship of Episcopalians
and Presbyterians

16 Rainy, rainy rattlestanes!
Dinna rain on me;
Rain on Johnny Groat's hoose,
Far ayont the sea!

'Rainie, Rainie Rattlestanes'

17 Skinny malinky lang legs, big banana feet,
Went tae the pictures an' couldnae find a
seat. . .

'Skinny Malinky Lang Legs'

There are many variants of this rhyme, eg
'umberella' for 'big banana'. Just one of the
lines that frequently follows the above is 'When
the picture started, Skinny Malinky farted'.
In Matt McGinn's version, Skinny was 'neat',
'sweet', but had 'helluva sweaty feet'

18 Says Tweed to Till:
'What gars ye rin sae still?'
Says Till to Tweed:
'Though ye rin fast
An I rin slaw,
For ae man ye droon,
I droon twa.'

'Tweed and Till'

Balfour, Arthur James (1st Earl of Balfour) 1848–1930

*Conservative politician, British Prime Minister
(1902–6) and Foreign Secretary (1916–19)*

1 Science is of no party. It seeks no object, selfish
or unselfish, good or bad. It is unmoved by any
emotion; it feels no pity, nor is it stirred by any

wrong. Its sole aim is the investigation of truth and the discovery of law, wholly indifferent to the use to which those investigations and those discoveries may afterwards be put.

'Politics and Political Economy' (1885)

2 I look forward to a time when Irish patriotism will as easily combine with British patriotism as Scottish patriotism combines now.

Speech in Glasgow (Dec 1889)

3 It is unfortunate, considering that enthusiasm moves the world, that so few enthusiasts can be trusted to speak the truth.

Letter to Mrs Drew (19 May 1891)

4 Persecution is only an attempt to do that overtly and with violence which the community is, in self-defence, perpetually doing unconsciously and in silence.

Rectorial address, Glasgow University (26 Nov 1891)

5 The energies of our system will decay, the glory of the sun will be dimmed, and the earth, tideless and inert, will no longer tolerate the race which has for a moment disturbed its solitude. Man will go down into the pit, and all his thought will perish.

The Foundations of Belief (1895), Part 1, ch.1

6 You can have no distinction between the feeling which a Scotchman has for Scotland and the feeling he has for that Empire of which Scotland is no small part. Each reacts upon the other, each moves the other, and turns it into a motive for ever more strenuous efforts for the great cause in which both Scotland and the Empire are interested.

Speech on receiving the freedom of Glasgow (14 Jan 1896)

7 Our Scottish theory. . . is that every country has need of Scotchmen, but that Scotland has no need of the citizens of any other country.

Speech at Edinburgh University (20 Jan 1904)

8 Fashion, whether in clothes or operas, whether in manners or in morals, is an influence which, though it may produce some hypocrites, most certainly produces many more true believers. And tradition, though infinitely more than mere fashion, is fashion still.

Lecture, 'Beauty, and the Criticism of Beauty', at Oxford University (24 Nov 1910)

9 His Majesty's Government view with favour the establishment in Palestine of a national home for the Jewish people, and will use their best endeavours to facilitate the achievement of this object, it being clearly understood that nothing shall be done which may prejudice the civil and religious rights of existing non-Jewish

communities in Palestine, or the rights and political status enjoyed by Jews in any other country.

Letter to Lord Rothschild (2 Nov 1917), which became known as the Balfour Declaration

Balfour, Lady Frances 1858–1931
Churchwoman, suffragist and writer

1 The farther away the Church gets from the ideal that in Christ there is neither male nor female, and that there is a glorious liberty granted to the children of God, the less alive will be its hold on the Christianity of the world. . . Which of us can afford to let the truth slip past on the stream of time?

On the need for equality of opportunity for women in the Church. Introduction to E Picton-Turnbull, *Christ and Woman's Power* (1919)

2 It has been said that Queen Victoria never saw a railway ticket. I doubt if my grandmother ever did, and I am certain, if my mother saw one, she never took it at a railway station.

Ne Obliviscaris: Dinna Forget (1930), Vol.1, ch.3, 'Ancestry'

3 Scotland has had to forge its religion on the anvil of the will of the people.

Ne Obliviscaris: Dinna Forget (1930), Vol.2, ch.19, 'The Church of Scotland'

4 There are some Scots who become so completely Anglicanised by Whitehall, that they will not fight for Scottish Rights, and when Scottish Records are brought over the Border for 'safer keeping', it sounds as if Scotland was considered still a country of untutored savages. Someday we must hope that we may again find a true blue secretary for Scotland installed in office.

Ne Obliviscaris: Dinna Forget (1930), Vol.2, ch.21, 'Changes and Chances'

5 It was very much like the position of anglers on a Scottish river, bent on having good sport and constantly maddened by swarms of midges, no equipment saved the man from their stinging importunity, they were everywhere.

On militant suffragette action. *Ne Obliviscaris: Dinna Forget* (1930), Vol.2, ch.23, 'At Last'

6 Golf has ceased to be a peculiarly national game. It is now no longer a pastime for the impecunious Scot, armed with two or three clubs and a feather ball, it has become a professional sport, pursued by devastating hordes of foreigners among whom the American tongue rises shrill and strident. Locusts are the only things in natural history that these strangers resemble, and after their departure the countryside is bare of all that made it a place fit for its own natives to live in.

Ne Obliviscaris: Dinna Forget (1930), Vol.2,

ch.27, 'Dominions Beyond the Sea'. Cf.
Andrew Lang 5

7 Motor cars were to be the great means of
propulsion in the coming age. . . And the
unending roads are now made, with their tarmac
shiny surfaces, their curb bound borders, their
loathsome motor pumps, their destruction of
every lovely turn and bend, and flowers wither
wherever they are driven.

Ne Obliviscaris: Dinna Forget (1930), Vol.2, ch.29,
'The Reign of King Edward'

Ballads

1 O Allison Gross, that lives in yon tower,
The ugliest witch in the north countrie. . .

'Allison Gross', st.1

2 'Oh, mother, mother, mak my bed,
And mak it saft and narrow;
Since my love died for me today,
I'll die for him tomorrow.'

'Barbara Allan', st.9

3 It fell about the Lammas tide,
When the muir-men win their hay,
The doughty Douglas bound him to ride
Into England, to drive a prey.

'The Battle of Otterburn', st.1

4 But I have dreamed a dreary dream,
Beyond the Isle of Skye;
I saw a dead man win a fight,
And I think that man was I.

'The Battle of Otterburn', st.19

5 There was twa sisters in a bower,
Binnorie, O Binnorie;
There came a knight to be their wooer,
By the bonnie mill-dams o' Binnorie.

'Binnorie', st.1. Cf. Ballads 44

6 Ye Highlands and ye Lawlands,
O where hae ye been?
They hae slain the Earl of Murray
And laid him on the green.

'The Bonnie Earl of Murray', st.1

In 1592, James VI commanded George Gordon,
6th Earl of Huntly to bring James Stewart, 2nd
Earl of Moray before him to answer a charge
of disloyalty to the Crown. A feud existed
between the two houses, and Huntly took the
opportunity of having his rival murdered at
Donibristle in Fife. Moray was stabbed by
one Gordon of Buckie, who compelled his
lord, Huntly, to be involved in the violence.
Huntly struck a half-hearted blow to Moray's
face, and the dying man, reputedly as vain
as he was handsome, managed to gasp, 'You
have spoiled a better face than your own.'
See Walter Scott, *Tales of a Grandfather*, 1st
Series (1828), ch.33

7 He was a braw gallant,
And he play'd at the glove;
And the bonnie Earl of Murray,
Oh he was the Queen's love!

O lang will his lady
Look owre the castle Doune,
Ere she see the Earl of Murray
Come sounding thro' the toun.

'The Bonnie Earl of Murray', st.5–6

In spite of the ballad, there is no historical
evidence of a liaison between James Stewart,
2nd Earl of Moray, and Queen Anne

8 It fell on a day, and a bonnie simmer day,
When green grew aits and barley,
That there fell out a great dispute
Between Argyll and Airlie.

Argyll has raised an hundred men,
An hundred harness'd rarely,
And he's awa by the back o' Dunkell,
To plunder the bonnie house o' Airlie.

'The Bonnie House o' Airlie', st.1–2

A Covenanting army under the Earl of Argyll
destroyed Airlie Castle, the home of the
Royalist Ogilvies, in 1640 when the Earl of
Airlie was in England supporting Charles I.
Argyll is alleged to have raped Lady Margaret
Ogilvy in front of his troops when she refused
to save the castle by surrendering herself to him

9 O may she comes, and may she goes,
Down by yon gardens green,
And there she spied a gallant squire
As squire had ever been.

'The Bonny Hyn', st.1

10 'They call me Jack when I'm abroad,
Sometimes they call me John;
But when I'm in my father's bower
Jock Randal is my name.'

'Ye lee, ye lee, ye bonny lad,
Sae loud's I hear ye lee!
For I'm Lord Randal's yae daughter,
He has nae mair nor me.'

'The Bonny Hyn', st.7–8

11 O the broom, and the bonnie, bonnie broom,
The broom of the Cowdenknowes;
And aye sae sweet as the lassie sang,
I' the bucht, milking the yowes.

'The Broom of Cowdenknowes', st.1

12 Clerk Saunders and May Margaret
Walk'd owre yon garden green;
And deep and heavy was the love
That fell this twa between.

'A bed, a bed,' Clerk Saunders said,
'A bed for you and me!'
'Fye na, fye na,' said May Margaret,
'Till anes we married be!'

'Clerk Saunders', st.1–2

13 There was a wee cooper who lived in Fife,
    Nickity, nackity, noo, noo, noo
    And he has gotten a gentle wife.
    Hey Willie Wallacky, how John Dougall,
    Alane, quo Rushety roue roue roue.

    She wadna bake, nor she wadna brew,
    For the spoiling o' her comely hue.

    She wadna card, nor she wadna spin,
    For the shaming o' her gentle kin.
        'The Cooper o' Fife', st.1–3 and refrain

14 The carline she was stark and sture,
    She aff the hinges dang the door. . .
        'Cospatrick', st.16

15 She hadna sailed a league, a league,
    A league but barely three,
    When dismal grew his countenance
    And drumlie grew his ee.

    They hadna sailed a league, a league,
    A league but barely three,
    Until she espied his cloven foot,
    And she wept right bitterlie.
        'The Demon Lover', st.10–11

16 He strack the tap-mast wi his hand,
    The fore-mast wi his knee;
    And he brake that gallant ship in twain,
    And sank her in the sea.
        'The Demon Lover', st.15

17 Late at een, drinkin' the wine,
    And ere they paid the lawin',
    They set a combat them between,
    To fight it in the dawin'.

    'O stay at hame, my noble lord,
    O stay at hame, my marrow!
    My cruel brother will you betray
    On the dowie houms o' Yarrow!'
        'The Dowie Houms o' Yarrow', st.1–2

18 'Yestreen I dream'd a dolefu' dream;
    I ken'd there wad be sorrow!
    I dream'd I pu'd the heather green,
    On the dowie banks o' Yarrow.'

    She gaed up yon high, high hill –
    I wat she gaed wi' sorrow –
    An' in a den spied nine dead men,
    On the dowie houms o' Yarrow.
        'The Dowie Houms o' Yarrow', st.11–12

19 'Why dois your brand sae drap wi bluid,
    Edward, Edward,
    Why dois your brand sae drap wi bluid,
    And why sae sad gang ye O?' –
    'O I hae killed my hawk sae guid,
    Mither, mither;
    O I hae killed my hawk sae guid,
    And I had nae mair but he, O.'
        'Edward', st.1

20 Then up and started our gudewife,
    Gied three skips on the floor:
    'Gudeman, ye've spoken the foremost word,
    Get up and bar the door.'
        'Get Up and Bar the Door', st.11

21 Glenkindie was ance a harper gude,
    He harped to the king;
    Glenkindie was ance the best harper
    That e'er harped on a string.

    He'd harpit a fish out o' saut water,
    Or water out o' a stane,
    Or milk out o' a maiden's breast
    That bairn had never nane.
        'Glenkindie', st.1–2

22 I wish I were where Helen lies,
    Night and day on me she cries;
    O that I were where Helen lies,
    On fair Kirkconnell lea!
        'Helen of Kirkconnell', st.1

23 'It's I, Jamie Telfer o' the fair Dodhead,
    And a harried man I think I be!
    There's naething left at the fair Dodhead
    But a waefu' wife and bairnies three.'
        'Jamie Telfer', st.9

24 Some speiks of lords, some speiks of lairds,
    And siclyke men of hie degrie;
    Of a gentleman I sing a sang,
    Some time called Laird of Gilnockie.
        'Johnie Armstrang', st.1

25 'Away, away, thou traitor strang!
    Out o' my sicht thou mayst sune be!
    I grantit nevir a traitors lyfe,
    And now I'll not begin with thee.'
        'Johnie Armstrang', st.8

        Armstrang was a renowned Dumfriesshire
        reiver, summoned to meet with James V in
        1529 at Carlinrigg near Hawick. He and his
        men were immediately seized and hanged, in
        spite of his protestations of loyalty. Before
        being strung up Armstrang said to the King:
        'I am but a fool to ask grace at a graceless face.'
        See Walter Scott, *Tales of a Grandfather*, 1st
        Series (1828), ch.27

26 'Come to your bed,' says Johnie Faa;
    'Come to your bed, my dearie;
    For I vow and I swear by the hilt o' my sword,
    That your lord shall nae mair come near ye.'
        'Johnie Faa', st.7

27 Dan he took oot his pipes ta play,
    Bit sair his hert wi döl and wae.

    And first he played da notes o noy,
    An dan he played da notes of joy.
        'King Orfeo', st.6–7
        Shetland ballad. Noy: sadness

28 It's Lamkin was a mason good
As ever built wi stane;
He built Lord Wearie's castle,
But payment got he nane.

'Lamkin', st.1

29 But the nourice was a fause limmer
As e'er hung on a tree;
She laid a plot wi Lamkin,
Whan her lord was o'er the sea.

'Lamkin', st.6

30 Then Lamkin's tane a sharp knife,
That hang down by his gaire,
And he has gien the bonny babe
A deep wound and a sair.

'Lamkin', st.12

31 'O wha will shoe my bonnie foot?
And wha will glove my hand?
And wha will lace my middle jimp
Wi' a lang, lang linen band?'

'The Lass of Lochroyan', st.1

32 'Will ye gang to the Hielands, Lizie Lindsey?
Will ye gang to the Hielands wi me?
And I will gie ye a cup of the curds,
Likewise a cup of green whey.'

'Lizie Lindsey' or 'Donald of the Isles', st.4

Robert Burns collected a fragment of a later
version of this ballad under the title 'Leezie
Lindsay', in which the second couplet of the
above stanza is replaced with 'Will ye go to
the Hielands, Leezie Lindsay/My pride and
my darling to be?'

33 This ae nighte, this ae nighte,
– *Every nighte and alle,*
Fire and fleet and candle-lighte,
And Christe receive thy saule.

'A Lyke-Wake Dirge', st.1

34 Marie Hamilton's to the kirk gane,
Wi' ribbons in her hair;
The king thought mair o' Marie Hamilton
Than ony that were there.

'Marie Hamilton' or 'The Queen's Marie', st.1

35 'Yestreen the queen had four Maries,
The night she'll hae but three;
There was Marie Seaton, and Marie Beaton,
And Marie Carmichael, and me.'

'Marie Hamilton' or 'The Queen's Marie', st.19

This ballad seems to conflate a reference to
the 'four Maries' who attended Mary, Queen
of Scots (whose surnames were in fact Seaton,
Beaton, Livingston and Fleming) with the
story of Mary Hamilton, who was executed in
1719 in Russia after the murder of a child she
had had illegitimately by Tsar Peter the Great

36 The muckin' o' Geordie's byre,
And shoolin the grape sae clean,

Has gard me weit my cheiks
And greit with baith my een.

'The Muckin o' Geordie's Byre', st.1

37 The king sits in Dumfermline town,
Drinking the blude-red wine;
'O whare will I get a skeely skipper,
To sail this new ship of mine?'

'Sir Patrick Spens', st.1

38 Our king has written a braid letter,
And seal'd it with his hand,
And sent it to Sir Patrick Spens,
Was walking on the strand.

'To Noroway, to Noroway,
To Noroway o'er the faem;
The king's daughter of Noroway,
'Tis thou maun bring her hame.'

'Sir Patrick Spens', st.3–4

39 'I saw the new moon late yestreen,
Wi the auld moon in her arm;
And if we gang to sea, master,
I fear we'll come to harm.'

'Sir Patrick Spens', st.13

40 And lang, lang may the ladyes sit,
Wi their fans into their hand,
Before they see Sir Patrick Spens
Come sailing to the strand.

And lang, lang may the maidens sit,
Wi their goud kaims in their hair,
A' waiting for their ain dear loves,
For them they'll see nae mair.

Half-owre, half-owre to Aberdour,
'Tis fifty fathoms deep,
And there lies gude Sir Patrick Spens,
Wi' the Scots lords at his feet.

'Sir Patrick Spens', st.24–6

41 O I forbid you, maidens a',
That wear gowd on your hair,
To come or gae by Carterhaugh,
For young Tam Lin is there.

There's nane that gaes by Carterhaugh,
But they leave him a wad,
Either their rings or green mantles,
Or else their maidenhead.

Janet has kilted her green kirtle
A little aboon her knee,
And she has braided her yellow hair
A little aboon her bree,
And she's awa to Carterhaugh
As fast as she can hie.

'Tam Lin', st.1–3

42 True Thomas lay on Huntlie bank,
A ferlie he spied wi' his ee,
And there he saw a lady bright,
Come riding down by the Eildon Tree.

'Thomas the Rhymer', st.1

43 As I was walking all alane,
I heard twa corbies making a mane;
The tane unto the t'other say,
'Where sall we gang and dine to-day?'

'In behint yon auld fail dyke,
I wot there lies a new-slain knight;
And naebody kens that he lies there,
But his hawk, his hound, and lady fair.

'His hound is to the hunting gane,
His hawk to fetch the wild-fowl hame,
His lady's taen anither mate,
So we may mak our dinner sweet.

'Ye'll sit on his white hause-bane,
And I'll pike out his bonny blue een:
Wi ae lock o his gowden hair
We'll theek our nest when it grows bare.'

'The Twa Corbies', st.1–4

44 There was twa sisters in a bower,
Edinburgh, Edinburgh
There was twa sisters in a bower
Stirling for ay
There was twa sisters in a bower,
There cam a knight to be their wooer.
Bonnie Saint Johnston stands upon Tay

'The Twa Sisters', st.1. Cf. Ballads 5

45 As I was walking all alane
Between a water and a wa',
And there I spied a wee wee man,
And he was the least that e'er I saw.

'The Wee Wee Man', st.1

46 There lived a wife at Usher's Well,
And a wealthy wife was she;
She had three stout and stalwart sons,
And sent them o'er the sea.

'The Wife of Usher's Well', st.1

47 'The cock doth craw, the day doth daw,
The channerin' worm doth chide. . .'

'The Wife of Usher's Well', st.11

Balmerino, Lord Arthur 1688–1746

Jacobite, who fought in both the 'Fifteen and 'Forty-Five Risings

1 No intrusion at all, sir; for I have done nothing to make my conscience uneasy. I shall die with a true heart and undaunted; for I think no man fit to live that is not fit to die; nor am I in any ways concerned at what I have done.

To a visitor to his prison who apologised for intruding on his last few hours on a matter of business (Aug 1746). *Scots Magazine* (Aug 1746)

George II is reputed to have said, when inundated with appeals for clemency on behalf of the Jacobite lords Kilmarnock and Cromarty, 'Heaven help me, will no one say a word in behalf of Lord Balmerino! He, though a rebel, is at least an honest one!'

2 If I had a thousand lives, I would lay them all down here in the same cause.

On the scaffold before his execution by beheading, in London (18 Aug 1746). Quoted in a letter from Horace Walpole to Horace Mann (21 Aug 1746)

Banks, Iain 1954–

Novelist

1 All our lives are symbols. Everything we do is part of a pattern we have at least some say in. The strong make their own patterns and influence other people's, the weak have their courses mapped out for them. The weak and the unlucky and the stupid. The Wasp Factory is part of the pattern because it is part of life and – even more so – part of death. . . The Wasp Factory is beautiful and deadly and perfect.

The Wasp Factory (1984), ch.7, 'Space Invaders'

2 It was the day my grandmother exploded.

The Crow Road (1992), opening sentence

Bankton, Lord see MacDouall, Andrew

Barbour, John c.1320–95

Poet, prelate and author of the epic narrative poem The Brus, *on the life of King Robert I, the Bruce*

1 Storyss to rede ar delitabill,
Suppose that thai be nocht but fabill. . .

The Brus (c.1375), Bk 1, ll.1–2

2 A! fredome is a noble thing!
Fredome mayss man to haiff liking,
Fredome all solace to man giffis:
He levys at ess that frely levys!
A noble hart may haiff nane ess,
Nay ellys nocht that may him pless,
Gyff fredome failyhe. . .

The Brus (c.1375), Bk 1, ll.225–31

3 Than with ane voce all can thai cry –
'Gud King, forouten mair delay,
To-morn, als soyn as ye se day,
Ordane yow haill for the battale,
For dout of ded we sall nocht fale;
Na nane payn sall refusit be
Till we have maid our cuntre fre.'

The Brus (c.1375), Bk 12, ll.200–6 (Bruce's soldiers responding to his call to fight at Bannockburn)

4 For we have three great avantage:
The first is, that we have the richt;

And for the richt ilk man suld ficht.

> *The Brus* (c.1375), Bk 12, ll.234–7 (Bruce exhorting his troops at Bannockburn)

5 And quhen the Ingliss King had sicht
Of thame kneland, he said on hy –
'Yon folk knelis till ask mercy.'
Schir Ingerame said, 'Ye say suth now;
Thai ask mercy but nocht at yow.
For thair trespass to God thai cry.
I tell yow a thing sekirly,
That yon men will wyn all or de,
For dout of ded thar sall nane fle.'

> *The Brus* (c.1375), Bk 12, ll.480–8 (the Scots soldiers pray before battle)

6 God grant that thai, that cummyne ar
Of his ofspring, maynteyme the land,
And hald the folk weill to warrand,
And maynteyme richt and ek laute,
As weill as in his tyme did he!

> *The Brus* (c.1375), Bk 13, ll.708–12 (The poet's hopes for Bruce's descendants)

Barclay, William 1907–78
Religious writer and broadcaster

1 Prayer is not a monologue in which we do all the talking; prayer is listening more than it is talking. The highest form of prayer is silence when we wait on God and listen to God. . .

> *The Plain Man's Book of Prayers* (1959), Introduction. Cf. James VI and I 5

2 It may well be that the future of religion lies with broadcasting. It is a strange fact that, when one broadcasts, there is no sensation of loneliness and no sensation of talking into nothing. . . A Church of the air is not an impossible dream.

> *Testament of Faith* (1975), ch.4

Bàrd Mac an t-Saoir, Am (The Bard McIntyre) 14th–15th century
Poet

1 Créad í an long-sa ar Loch Inse,
nó an bhféadtar a h-airinnse?
créad thug an long ar an loch,
's nach féad an fonn a folach?. . .

Seanlong gan iarnaí gan dair,
níor fhidir sinne a samhail;
aonlong í do leathar lán:
go tuinn ní h-eathar iomlán.

† What ship is this on Loch Inch, or can it be reported? What has brought the ship on the loch, that the land can not conceal it?. . .

An old ship without anchors, without oak timber; we have not known its like; she is all one ship of leather: she is not a ship complete for sea-going.

> Poem on a fantastical ship crewed entirely by women, st.1, 5. In W J Watson (ed.), *Scottish Verse from the Book of the Dean of Lismore* (1937)

2 Créad é an lucht ud san luing dhuibh
'gá tarraing idir tonnaibh?
an lucht gan chaidreabh gan chéill,
bantracht an aigne aimhréidh.

Buidhean bhrosgalach bhruidhneach
labhar dhuanach dhíochuimhneach
shiorrach chonasach chíocrach
ghionach dhona dhroichíotach. . .

Fágmaid ar an sruth síonach
an long dhona dhroichdhíonach,
's a lán do bhantracht na mbéad
san sál gan salm gan sáilchréad.

† What is yon crew in the black ship, pulling her among the waves? – A crew without fellowship, without sense, a woman-band of mind disordered.

A band loud-voiced and talkative, loquacious, chanting, negligent; flighty, quarrelsome, greedy, ravenous, evil, of ill desires. . .

Let us leave on the stormy stream the evil leaky ship, and its load of noxious women, in the brine, without psalm or sea-creed.

> Poem on a fantastical ship crewed entirely by women, st.7–8, 13. In W J Watson (ed.), *Scottish Verse from the Book of the Dean of Lismore* (1937)

Barnard, Lady Anne
see **Lindsay, Lady Anne**

Barrie, Sir J(ames) M(atthew) 1860–1937
Playwright and novelist

1 What she had been, what I should be, these were the two great subjects between us in my boyhood, and while we discussed the one we were deciding the other, though neither of us knew it.

> *Margaret Ogilvy* (1896), ch.2
>
> > This book was a highly sentimental portrait of his mother

2 I remember being asked by two maiden ladies about the time I left the university, what I was to be, and when I replied brazenly, 'An author,' they flung up their hands, and one exclaimed reproachfully, 'And you an MA!'

> *Margaret Ogilvy* (1896), ch.3

3 CRICHTON: His lordship may compel us to be equal upstairs, but there will never be equality in the servants' hall.

> *The Admirable Crichton* (1902), Act 1

4 CRICHTON: The divisions into classes, my lord, are not artificial. They are the natural outcome of a civilised society. There must always be a master and servants in all civilised communities, my lady, for it is natural, and whatever is natural is right.
LORD LOAM: It is very unnatural for me to stand here and allow you to talk such nonsense.
CRICHTON: Yes, my lord, it is. That is what I have been striving to point out to your lordship.

The Admirable Crichton (1902), Act 1

5 PETER: Children know such a lot now. Soon they don't believe in fairies, and every time a child says, 'I don't believe in fairies' there is a fairy somewhere that falls down dead.

Peter Pan (1904), Act 1

6 PETER: To die will be an awfully big adventure.
Peter Pan (1904), Act 3

7 PETER: Do you believe in fairies? Say quick that you believe! If you believe, clap your hands!

Peter Pan (1904), Act 4

8 HOOK: Back, you pewling spawn. I'll show you now the road to dusty death. A holocaust of children, there is something grand in the idea!

Peter Pan (1904), Act 5, sc.1. See Shakespeare, *Macbeth*, Act 4, sc.5, ll.22–3

9 ALICK: What *is* charm, exactly, Maggie?
MAGGIE: Oh, it's – it's a sort of bloom on a woman. If you have it, you don't need to have anything else; and if you don't have it, it doesn't much matter what else you have.

What Every Woman Knows (1908), Act 1

10 DAVID: A young Scotsman of your ability let loose upon the world with £300, what could he not do? It's almost appalling to think of; especially if he went among the English.

What Every Woman Knows (1908), Act 1

11 DAVID: My lady, there are few more impressive sights in the world than a Scotsman on the make.

What Every Woman Knows (1908), Act 2

12 MAGGIE: I've sometimes thought, John, that the difference between us and the English is that the Scotch are hard in all other respects but soft with women, and the English are hard with women but soft in all other respects.
JOHN: You've forgotten the grandest moral attribute of a Scotsman, Maggie, that he'll do nothing which might damage his career.

What Every Woman Knows (1908), Act 2

13 JOHN: I remember reading of some one that said it needed a surgical operation to get a joke into a Scotsman's head.

MAGGIE: Yes, that's been said.
JOHN: What beats me, Maggie, is how you could insert a joke with an operation.

What Every Woman Knows (1908), Act 2.
Cf. Sydney Smith 4

14 VENABLES: You Scots, Mrs Shand, are such a mixture of the practical and the emotional that you escape out of an Englishman's hand like a trout.

What Every Woman Knows (1908), Act 3

15 MAGGIE: Every man who is high up loves to think that he has done it all himself; and the wife smiles, and lets it go at that. It's our only joke. Every woman knows that.

What Every Woman Knows (1908), Act 4.
Cf. Lady Fairbairn 1

16 KATE: One's religion is whatever he is most interested in, and yours is Success.

The Twelve-Pound Look (1910). Cf. Thomas Carlyle 36

17 KATE: I didn't give you up willingly, Harry. I invented all sorts of theories to explain you. Your hardness – I said it was a fine want of mawkishness. Your coarseness – I said it goes with strength. Your contempt for the weak – I called it virility. Your want of ideals was clear-sightedness. Your ignoble views of women – I tried to think them funny. Oh, I clung to you to save myself. But I had to let go; you had only the one quality, Harry, success; you had it so strong that it swallowed all the others.

The Twelve-Pound Look (1910)

18 HARRY: Seems to me you're feared of being a ghost. I dare say, to a timid thing, being a ghost is worse than seeing them.

Mary Rose (1920), Act 3

19 M'Connachie. . . is the name I give to the unruly half of myself: the writing half. We are complement and supplement. I am the half that is dour and practical and canny, he is the fanciful half; my desire is to be the family solicitor, standing firm on my hearthrug among the harsh realities of the office furniture; while he prefers to fly around on one wing. I should not mind him doing that, but he drags me with him.

'Courage', Rectorial Address at St Andrews (3 May 1922), in *Plays and Stories* (1962)

20 Courage is the thing. All goes if courage goes!

'Courage', Rectorial Address at St Andrews (3 May 1922), in *Plays and Stories* (1962)

21 You all have dark secrets, all the men among you, and even I. I should like to tell you my dark secret. When I was at school in the south of Scotland – it was a mixed school – one day

the girls took a plebiscite about which boy had the sweetest smile. It came to my ears that I had won. Think of my elation. But the tragedy is that it made me self-conscious, and I have never been able to smile since.

Speech to the Worcestershire Association dinner (29 Feb 1928), in *M'Connachie and JMB: Speeches by J M Barrie* (1938)

We are undoubtedly a sentimental people, and it sometimes plays queer games with that other celebrated sense of ours, the practical. The wild dances these two have had as partners, making everybody dizzy but ourselves! I say this with feeling.

On the Scots. Speech to the Royal Scottish Corporation (30 Nov 1928), in *M'Connachie and JMB: Speeches by J M Barrie* (1938)

The characters we think we 'create'. That is surely the most comic word in an author's vocabulary. The heroine, of course, is the worst one. Very obedient until she gets into your book, but you are a lucky writer if in a week thereafter you know her by sight.

Speech to the Royal Literary Fund (9 May 1930), in *M'Connachie and JMB: Speeches by J M Barrie* (1938)

Let us treat children and fairies in a more summary manner. I never could abide them . . . Nowadays if in reading a book I come across a word beginning with 'c' or 'f' I toss it aside.

Speech to the Royal Literary Fund (9 May 1930), in *M'Connachie and JMB: Speeches by J M Barrie* (1938)

I can't abide children, never could. It was merely pretend on my part to get round their mothers and so spend an idle hour in dalliance. I know a boy of four who, when he wakes up and sees the sun, calls out 'Good morning, God.' His own idea. Horrible.

Speech for the Great Ormond Street Hospital for Children (3 Dec 1930), in *M'Connachie and JMB: Speeches by J M Barrie* (1938)

Bateman, Meg 1959–
Poet

Nist cha tig e tuilleadh
is nì e tàir orm
a chionn 's gu robh mi measail air.

Now he comes no more,
indeed he despises me,
because I was so fond of him.

'A chionn 's gu robh mi measail air' ('Because I was so fond of him'), *Orain Ghaoil* (1990)

Cailleach air bàsachadh aig baile,
ròpa t' acaire a' caitheamh;
nist tha mi a' faicinn nad shùilean

briseadh-cridhe na cùise.

† An old woman dies at home,
your anchor rope is fraying;
now I can see in your eyes
the heart-break of the matter.

'Sìoladh na Gàidhlig' ('The Loss of Gaelic'), *Orain Ghaoil* (1990)

Baxter, Jim 1939–
Rangers and Scotland footballer

1 They canna play nane.

On the England team, prior to the Scotland v. England 1967 international at Wembley. Quoted in John Rafferty, *100 Years of Scottish Football* (1973)

Scotland won 3–2, the first team to beat England since their 1966 World Cup victory

2 . . . I never said to myself 'Oh, I'm Scottish.' I never did the Bill Shankly thing. It wouldn't have bothered me to have been born a German or an Italian. If I'd been born in Berwick instead of Beath I'd have done it to Scotland if I had been picked. Aye, simple as that.

On twice being on the winning side against England at Wembley. Quoted in Roddy Forsyth, *The Only Game* (1990), ch.2

Baxter, Stanley 1926–
Comic actor and pantomime star

1 The legend that Scots are mean originated with Sir Harry Lauder when he was a low comedian before becoming 'that grand old minstrel' as Churchill had it. Because of the awful image of the Scot Lauder gave the world his memory is not exactly revered by many. The smear of meanness has become a crashing bore to millions of Scots who never saw Lauder. The painful truth is that the Scot can be stupidly generous and the most oft-used sayings in Scottish pubs are – 'It's MA round,' 'I'm on the bell' and the more aggressive, 'Ye're havin' a double!'

'There was a Scotsman, a Scotsman, and a Scotsman. . .', in Miles Kington (ed.) *Punch on Scotland* (1977)

2 I like the tradition of Principal Boy played by a woman. A Prince Charming played by a boy merely looks camp, it doesn't work. It is too effete a part to be played by a male. And Dame should be played by a man.

On pantomime. Quoted in Vivien Devlin, *Kings, Queens and People's Palaces: An Oral History of the Scottish Variety Theatre, 1920–1970* (1991), ch.7

3 If a thing is not funny after the tenth time of repeating it, it's not funny.

Quoted by comedy scriptwriter John Robertson

in Vivien Devlin, *Kings, Queens and People's Palaces: An Oral History of the Scottish Variety Theatre, 1920–1970* (1991), ch.9

4 It is interesting that the vast majority of Scots comics have come from Glasgow... Glaswegian has undoubtedly been the *lingua franca*. Glaswegians laugh with you if you speak in broad Glaswegian, and the rest of Scotland probably laughs more at it.

Quoted in Vivien Devlin, *Kings, Queens and People's Palaces: An Oral History of the Scottish Variety Theatre, 1920–1970* (1991), ch.10

5 Scottish humour has so much to do with dialect. It is all to do with the way things are said. The 'dinnaes', the 'wees', the 'doon the stairs' and so on. Gags translated directly into English can be terribly unfunny. If you take out words like 'glaikit', or 'stotious', and you have to say 'stupid' and 'drunk' instead, it is just not the same. It is essentially a thing of language, and the life of the audience.

Quoted in Vivien Devlin, *Kings, Queens and People's Palaces: An Oral History of the Scottish Variety Theatre, 1920–1970* (1991), ch.10

6 To be so randy... and so literate.

On James Boswell, whom he would like to have been. Quoted in *Scotland on Sunday* (3 Dec 1995), 'Profile'

7 If people cease to be able to laugh, they're ill. I equate sanity with the ability to laugh.

Quoted in *Scotland on Sunday* (3 Dec 1995), 'Profile'

Bean Torra-Dhamh see Clark, Mary

Beattie, James 1735–1803
Philosopher and poet

1 Some deemed him wondrous wise, and some believed him mad.

The Minstrel, Bk 1 (1771), st.16

2 In the deep windings of the grove no more
The hag obscene, and grisly phantom dwell;
Nor in the fall of mountain-stream, or roar
Of winds, is heard the angry spirit's yell.

The Minstrel, Bk 2 (1774), st.47

3 We who live in Scotland are obliged to study English from books, like a dead language... We are slaves to the language we write, and are continually afraid of committing *gross* blunders; and, when an easy, familiar, idiomatical phrase occurs, dare not adopt it, if we recollect no authority, for fear of Scotticisms. In a word, *we* handle English as a person who cannot fence handles a sword; continually afraid of hurting ourselves with it, or letting it fall, or making

some awkward motion that shall betray our ignorance.

Quoted in W Forbes (ed.), *An Account of the Life and Writings of James Beattie, LL.D.* (1806), Vol.2, p.16

Beattie, Johnny 1926–
Comedian

1 I decided a long time ago, in 1962 or so, that Dame was the thing to do; you gotta fly, you gotta do pantomime, get the high-heeled shoes on... And from that day I've never played anything other than Dame.

Quoted in Vivien Devlin, *Kings, Queens and People's Palaces: An Oral History of the Scottish Variety Theatre, 1920–1970* (1991), ch.7

2 There will always be pantomime. I'm sure there will so I won't throw my bra away yet.

Quoted in Vivien Devlin, *Kings, Queens and People's Palaces: An Oral History of the Scottish Variety Theatre, 1920–1970* (1991), ch.7

Beith, John Hay see Hay, Ian

Belhaven, Lord (John Hamilton, 2nd Lord Belhaven) 1656–1708
Opponent of the Treaty of Union

1 I think I see a Free and Independent Kingdom delivering up That which all the World hath been fighting for, since the days of Nimrod; yea, that for which most of all the Empires, Kingdoms, States, Principalities and Dukedoms of Europe, are at this very time engaged in the most Bloody and Cruel Wars that ever were, to wit, a Power to Manage their own Affairs by themselves, without the Assistance and Counsel of any other.

Speech in the Scottish Parliament (2 Nov 1706), quoted in Daniel Defoe, *History of the Union* (1785)

2 But above all, My Lord, I think I see our Ancient Mother Caledonia, like Caesar sitting in the midst of our Senate, Rufully looking round about her, Covering her self with her Royal Garment, attending the Fatal Blow, and breathing out her last with a *Et tu qoque mi fili*.

Speech in the Scottish Parliament (2 Nov 1706), quoted in Daniel Defoe, *History of the Union* (1785)

3 My Lord, patricide is a greater crime than parricide, all the world over...

Speech in the Scottish Parliament (2 Nov 1706), quoted in Daniel Defoe, *History of the Union* (1785)

None can Destroy Scotland, save Scotland's self; hold your Hands from the Pen, you are Secure.

Speech in the Scottish Parliament (2 Nov 1706) imploring the Members not to sign the Treaty of Union. Quoted in Daniel Defoe, *History of the Union* (1785)

5 Good God! What, is this an entire surrender?

Speech in the Scottish Parliament (2 Nov 1706), quoted in Daniel Defoe, *History of the Union* (1785)

At this point, exasperated, Belhaven broke off his speech and sat down

Bell, Alexander Graham 1847–1922

Inventor of the telephone

1 Mr Watson, come here, I want you.

Spoken to his assistant (10 Mar 1876)

The first intelligible message sent by telephone

Bell, Ian

Journalist and author

1 If the poll tax is dead it was killed by non-payment, a tactic which each of the three main parties insisted was pointless and wrong... It was left to a rag-tag army of ordinary people to destroy a bad law.

The Observer (24 Mar 1991). Cf. Anonymous 58

2 Perhaps it's time to stop talking about what 'Scotland' wants, and stop proclaiming what 'Scotland' thinks... [the election results] suggest that we chatterers in the Central Belt should do a little more travelling and much less talking.

The Herald (17 Apr 1992)

On misjudged press analysis of electoral feeling in the whole country in the run-up to the general election of 11 April 1992. Cf. Andrew Marr 1

3 The War of Major's Mince.

On Prime Minister John Major and his Government's tactics for getting the European Union's ban on British beef products lifted during the BSE crisis. Headline in *The Scotsman* (24 May 1996)

Bell, J(ohn) J(oy) 1871–1934

Novelist and poet

1 ... Macgregor dashed his new hat on the floor. 'I'll no' wear it! I'll no' wear it! I winna be gentry! I winna be gentry!' he moaned, and rushed from the house, sobbing as if his heart would break.

Wee Macgregor (first serialised in the *Glasgow Evening News*, 1901, published in book form, 1902; revised edition, 1933), ch.9, 'Macgregor's New Hat'

2 '... it's a daft story onywey... There's naebody gets kilt in it. I like stories aboot folk gettin' their heids cut aff, or stabbit through an' through wi' swords an' spears. An' there's nae wild beasts. I like stories aboot black men gettin' ett up, an' white men killing lions, an' teagurs, an' bears, an' – '

'Whist, whist, laddie,' cried Lizzie.

'Aw, the wean's fine,' said John, smiling. 'Dod, I doot I like thur kin' o' stories best masel'.'

Wee Macgreegor, (first serialised in the *Glasgow Evening News*, 1901, published in book form, 1902; revised edition, 1933), ch.19, '"Arms and the Boy"'

3 'Always somebody goin' away,
Somebody gettin' home.'

'On the Quay', *Clyde Songs and other Verse* (1905)

Bell, Joseph 1837–1911

Surgeon

1 Why bother yourself about the cataract of drivel for which Conan Doyle is responsible? I am sure he never imagined that such a heap of rubbish would fall on my devoted head in consequence of his stories.

Letter (1901), quoted in *Joseph Bell: an Appreciation by an Old Friend* (Anonymous, 1913), p.14

Arthur Conan Doyle modelled the character of Sherlock Holmes, at least in part, on his medical teacher, the observant Dr Bell

2 ... every good teacher, if he is to make his men good doctors, must get them to cultivate the habit of noticing the little apparent trifles. Any really good doctor ought to be able to tell before a patient has fairly sat down, a good deal of what is the matter with him or her.

Quoted in *Joseph Bell: an Appreciation by an Old Friend* (Anonymous, 1913), p.24

3 You cannot expect the ordinary 'bobby', splendid fellow as he is so far as pluck and honesty go, to stand eight hours on his legs and then develop great mental strength, he doesn't get enough blood to his brain to permit of it.

Quoted in *Joseph Bell: an Appreciation by an Old Friend* (Anonymous, 1913), p.24

Bellany, John 1942–

Painter

1 There may have been a lot of churches in Port Seton but the pubs were full too! The sacred and profane go hand-in-hand.

On growing up in Port Seton. Quoted in John McEwen, *John Bellany* (1994), ch.1

2 He wasn't a one-to-one man in the pub, like Sydney Goodsir Smith. He might let you tug the hem of his garment once in a while, but that was all. He was an élitist; a platform man.

> On Hugh MacDiarmid. Quoted in John McEwen, *John Bellany* (1994), ch.4

3 I went to the Royal Academy – the dregs of the art world.

> Recalling a visit to the RA while a student in London in the 1960s. Quoted in John McEwen, *John Bellany* (1994), ch.5

4 You can't paint from a vacuum. Whether you're in a state of serenity or absolute anguish. . . if you're being honest it comes through in the work.

> Quoted in John McEwen, *John Bellany* (1994), ch.6

5 But I want to live as long as Picasso.

> On being told (Dec 1987) by hospital consultants that there was nothing more they could do for him. He went on to have a successful liver transplant. As quoted by his wife, Helen Bellany, in John McEwen, *John Bellany* (1994), ch.8
>
> Pablo Picasso lived from 1881 to 1973

Bellenden, John d.1587

Churchman and historian, translator into Scots of Boece's Scotorum Historiae

1 Manhede but prudence is ane fury blind, And bringis man to schame and indegence.

> *History and Chronicles of Scotland* (1536), 'The Proheme of the History', st.14
>
> but: without

2 So singing, fidling, and piping not effer is For men of honour nor of hie estate, Because it spoutis swete venome in thair eris And makis thair mindis al effeminate.

> *History and Chronicles of Scotland* (1536), 'The Proheme of the History', st.21

3 Ane young madin, namit Katherine Douglas, quhilk was eftir maryit on Alexander Lovell of Bolunny, stekit the dure; and becaus the bar was away that suld have closit the dure, scho schot hir arme into the place quhare the bar suld have passit. Scho was bot young, and hir bonis not solide, and thairfore, hir arm was sone brokin in schonder, and the dure doung up, be force.

> *History and Chronicles of Scotland* (1536), Bk 17, ch.8
>
> A famous detail of the murder of James I at Perth (21 Feb 1437)

Bernstein, Marion fl.1876

Glasgow poet and music teacher, who wrote for the Glasgow Weekly Mail

1 I dreamt that the nineteenth century
Had entirely passed away
And had given place to a more advanced
And very much brighter day.

For Woman's Rights were established quite
And man could the fact discern
That he'd long been teaching his grandmamma
What she didn't require to learn.

There were female chiefs in the Cabinet,
(Much better than males I'm sure!)
And the Commons were three parts feminine,
While the Lords were seen no more!

> 'A Dream', *Mirren's Musings: A Collection of Songs and Poems* (1876), st.1–3

2 Beast-taming seems to me
Not quite a woman's mission;
The brutes might stay for me,
In bachelor condition.

But, since you choose to wed
And risk your limbs and lives,
Consider what I've said
All ye unhappy wives.

Exert your common sense
And form a combination
For mutual defence
Against assassination.

> 'Married and "Settled"', *Mirren's Musings: A Collection of Songs and Poems* (1876), st.5–7
>
> > Domestic violence against women was an issue of great public concern in the 1870s. Cf. Jessie Russell 1

3 If beating can reform a wife
It might reform a husband too,
Since such are the effects of strife –
My sisters, I advise that you

Should try it, not with fists – Oh no!
For that would seem like some weak joker;
In husband-curing let each blow
Be given with the kitchen poker!

> 'A Rule to Work Both Ways', *Mirren's Musings: A Collection of Songs and Poems* (1876), st.1–2

Berwick, Thurso see Blythman, Morris

Bird, Isabella (married name Bishop)
1831–1904

English traveller and writer

1 The appearance of the lower part of the High Street was as little pleasant as usual. Knots of men who never seem to 'move on' stared at the

passers-by on the South Bridge. . . There were dirty little children as usual rolling in the gutter or sitting stolidly on the kerb-stone; as usual, haggard, wrinkled, vicious faces were looking out of the dusty windows above, and an air of joylessness, weariness, and struggle hung over all. Truly has this street been named the *Via Dolorosa*.

Notes on Old Edinburgh (1869), ch.1

Limited water and unlimited whisky, crowded dens and unwholesome air; we need nothing more to make a city full of drunkards.

Notes on Old Edinburgh (1869), ch.1

If there be anything more mournful than the poverty and immorality of the poor, it is the vicious selfishness of the rich.

Notes on Old Edinburgh (1869), ch.4

'So this is Blackfriar's Wynd,' remarked one of our party, as we passed down the crowded alley. '*No, it's hell's mouth*,' exclaimed a forlorn woman, who was dragging a drunken man to his joyless home.

Notes on Old Edinburgh (1869), ch.4

Birnie, Pate (Patrick) fl.1660

Fiddler from Kinghorn, Fife

The auld man's mare's deid,
The poor man's mare's deid,
The auld man's mare's deid,
A mile aboon Dundee.

She was cut luggit, paich lippit,
Steel waimit, staincher fittit,
Chanler chafttit, lang neckit,
Yet the brute did die!

'The Auld Man's Mare's Deid', in James Johnson (ed.), *The Scots Musical Museum* (1787–1803)

Black, Sir Douglas 1913–

Physician, government chief health scientist (1973–7), Chairman of the Research Working Group on Inequalities in Health (1977–80)

In Britain we have homelessness and massive unemployment, potent causes of illness, and we have a health service which is being covertly denationalised, at great expense. . . After a lifetime of professional detachment, I am both sad and angry to see the attempted destruction of a system of health care which was as comprehensive as any in the world, and at a lower cost than any other comparable system.

Article in the *British Medical Journal*, quoted in *The Guardian* (17 Dec 1993)

2 Our view that poverty and its effects was the root cause of the ill-health associated with it, naturally led us to advocate a wider strategy of social measures. After all, the surest way to alleviate the effects of poverty must be to alleviate poverty itself.

On the Black Report. Article in the *British Medical Journal*, quoted in *The Guardian* (17 Dec 1993)

His Research Working Group's report (the Black Report) had called for spending on social measures to counter poor health, but was never implemented by the Conservative government, which deemed it too costly

Black Agnes or Annes of Dunbar, Countess of March 14th century

Patriotic defender of Dunbar

1 Montagu, for al the power that thou may, or lang time by pas I sal ger thi sow fery [farrow] agayn hir wil.

Quoted in *Liber Pluscardensis* (probably compiled 1461, ed. F J H Skene, 1877), Bk 9, ch.36

Besieged by an English army under Sir William Montagu in 1337, Black Agnes defended Dunbar Castle with great courage, famously mocking the damage caused by the English bombardment by dusting the ramparts with a handkerchief. Montagu had a siege-engine named the Sow brought under the walls, but the Scots destroyed it with huge boulders, forcing the soldiers inside to abandon it. When the English commander finally gave up the siege, Agnes bade him farewell with 'Adieu, adieu, Monsure Montagu'

Blackadder, Elizabeth 1931–

Painter

1 There is the danger, perhaps, of being put down only as a watercolourist – the feeling that it is not so serious a medium and that it is somehow feminine.

'Artist's comment', in Bill Hare, *Contemporary Painting in Scotland* (1992), p.32

Blackhall, Sheena (*née* Middleton) 1947–

Poet and short-story writer

1 If half they said wis Gospel,
We'd be damned for ivermore;
The curse o Scotland's villages. . .
The sklaikin at the door.

'Sklaik', *The Cyard's Kist* (1984)

2 There's a hole i' the sky,
At the back o' the day
Tae gang til't naebody daurs
For there, like a barfit bairn, stauns nicht
Wi his neive stap-fu o' stars.

'Bairn-Sang', *The Cyard's Kist* (1984), st.1

3 Fowk spik aboot Scots –
Ay, wir ain Doric leid –
As if 'twis a dodo
Wha'd drappit doon deid!. . .

I've news fur them –
Scots disna bide in a buik!
It's alive an it's kickin,
Gin they wid bit look.

'Doric's no Dodo', *The Spik o' the Lan'* (1986).
Cf. Anna Buchan 3

4 Sadie Dempster looked, and felt, like a camel
which had inadvertently swallowed its hump,
as her father handed her over to the granite
reception block of the city's maternity hospital.

'The Conveyor Belt', in *Chapman* No.49
(Summer 1987)

5 I am a Doric stereotype –
Abune ma brose I rift,
I skirl an birl at echtsome reels,
An darn ma hose fur thrift.

I am a Doric stereotype –
That thing ye'll niver meet. . .
I fyles chant Buddhist mantras
An read René Magritte.

'I am a Doric Stereotype', *Stagwyse* (1995).
Cf. David Rorie 3

Blackie, John Stuart 1809–95

Scholar, linguist and nationalist

1 Who owns these ample hills? – a lord who lives
Ten months in London, and in Scotland two;
O'er the wide moors, with gun in hand,
    he drives;
And, Scotland, this is all he knows of you!

'Absentee Proprietors', *Lays and Legends of
Ancient Greece with other poems* (1857)

2 Converse with men makes sharp the
    glittering wit,
But God to man doth speak in solitude.

'Highland Solitude', *Lays and Legends of Ancient
Greece with other poems* (1857). Cf. Lord Byron 17

3 An old grey chapel on an old grey beach,
Grey waste of rocks unpictured by a tree,
And far as hungry vision's range can reach,
The old grey mist upon the old grey sea:
These shows for sense; but the deep
    truth behind
They only know who read the mind with mind.

'The Tourists', *Lays of the Highlands and
Islands* (1872)

4 MACDONALD: The oatcakes, you remember, Dr
Johnson says, are food for men in Scotland
and horses in England; and you see the reason
here both how Scotchmen are so superior to

Englishmen, and English horses to all other
horses. If beer and beef-steaks have made
Englishmen, oatmeal cakes and oatmeal
porridge have made Scotchmen.

HILARIUS: Specially Scotch brains. There is a
notable seasoning of phosphorus in oats which
produces the *praefervidum ingenium Scotorum.*

Altavona (1882), Dialogue 3, sc.4. Cf. Anonymous 4,
Samuel Johnson 1

5 Ownership in land exists for the sake of the
people; not the people for the sake of the
ownership.

The Scottish Highlanders and the Land Laws (1885),
ch.2, 'The Land Laws'

6 It is always the factor who does the dirty
business; the landlord is always a good
gentleman; and the land laws are always and
everywhere on the side of the strong.

The Scottish Highlanders and the Land Laws (1885),
ch.2, 'The Crofters' Commission'

7 For we bought the hills with English gold
And what we bought we'll keep;
The hills 'tis clear were meant for deer,
And not for men or sheep.

Then come and scour the Bens with me, ye
    jolly stalkers all,
With lawyers to defend your right, and gillies
    at your call!
Those crofter carles may cross the sea but we
    are masters here,
And say to all, both great and small, *let none
disturb the deer.*

'A Song of Jolly Deer-Stalkers', *The Scottish
Highlanders and the Land Laws* (1885), chorus
and st.10

Blackie wrote this satire to the tune of 'The
British Grenadiers'

Blacklock, Thomas 1721–91

Blind poet and preacher

1 Life is a bumper filled by fate. . .

'On Punch, an Epigram', *Poems* (1796)

2 Say, then, Physicians of each kind,
Who cure the body, or the mind;
What harm in drinking can there be,
Since punch and life so well agree?

'On Punch, an Epigram', *Poems* (1796)

Blair, Hugh 1718–1800

*Minister and writer, Professor of Rhetoric
and Belles Lettres at Edinburgh University
(1762–83)*

1 . . . many circumstances of those times which
we call barbarous, are favourable to the poetical

spirit. That state, in which human nature shoots wild and free, though unfit for other improvements, certainly encourages the high exertion of fancy and passion.

'A Critical Dissertation on the Poems of Ossian' (1763)

> He argued enthusiastically for the authenticity of James Macpherson's 'translations' of Ossianic epic poetry, and his authority persuaded many of the Scottish literati to accept the poems as genuine

Blair, Robert 1593–1666

Covenanter, minister in St Andrews

1 A good king, evil used.

On Charles I. Quoted in Thomas M'Crie (ed.), *The Life of Mr Robert Blair* (1848), p.261

2 He is an egregious dissembler and a great liar. Away with him, he is a greeting divil!

On Oliver Cromwell, said to fellow-Covenanter David Dickson. Quoted in Thomas M'Crie (ed.), *The Life of Mr Robert Blair* (1848), p.310

Blair, Robert 1699–1746

Poet

1 Oft, in the lone church-yard at night I've seen
By glimpse of moonshine chequering through the trees,
The school-boy, with his satchel in his hand,
Whistling aloud to bear his courage up...

The Grave (1743)

2 Sure 'tis a serious thing to die! my soul!
What a strange moment must it be, when near
The journey's end, thou hast the gulf in view!

The Grave (1743)

3 Death's shafts fly thick! Here falls the village swain,
And there his pamper'd lord! The cup goes round,
And who so artful as to put it by?

The Grave (1743)

4 On this side and on that, men see their friends
Drop off, like leaves in autumn; yet launch out
Into fantastic schemes, which the long livers
In the world's hale and undegenerate days
Could scarce have leisure for; fools that we are!
Never to think of Death and of ourselves
At the same time: as if to learn to die
Were no concern of ours.

The Grave (1743)

> 'Long livers' refers to those early Biblical characters who supposedly lived for hundreds of years

5 What is this world!
What, but a spacious burial-field unwall'd,

Strew'd with Death's spoils, the spoils of animals
Savage and tame, and full of dead men's bones?
The very turf on which we tread once liv'd...

The Grave (1743)

Blair, Tony 1953–

Scottish-born politician, Labour Party leader (1994–)

1 Now we know what Margaret Thatcher meant when she said privatisation would set the people free.

On Group 4's prison escort service. Quoted in *The Independent* (1 Oct 1993)

> As Shadow Home Secretary, he was commenting on a number of prisoner escapes which received much media attention

2 I got fed up with all the sex and sleaze and backhanders of rock 'n' roll so I went into politics.

On why he left the pop group Ugly Rumours. Quoted in *The Independent* (12 Nov 1994)

3 Any parent wants the best for their children. I am not going to make a choice for my child on the basis of what is the politically correct thing to do.

On his decision to send his son to a grant-maintained school. Quoted in *The Independent* (4 Dec 1994)

4 Those who seriously believe that we cannot improve on words written for the world of 1918 when we are now in 1995 are not learning from our history but merely living in it.

On changing Clause IV of the Labour Party's constitution, which called for public ownership of the means of production. Quoted in *The Independent* (15 Jan 1995)

Blind Allan see Ailean Dall

Blind Arthur Mac Gurcaigh see Artùr Dall Mac Gurcaigh

Blind Harper, The see Clàrsair Dall, An

Blind Harry (Harry or Henry the Minstrel) c.1440–92

Poet and chronicler of the life of William Wallace

1 Now leiff thy myrth, now leiff thy haill plesance;
Now leiff thy bliss, now leiff thy childis age;

Now leiff thy youth, now folow thy hard chance;
Now leiff thy lust, now leiff thy mariage;
Now leiff thy luff, for thow sall loss a gage
Quhilk nevir in erd sall be redemyt agayne;
Folow fortoun, and all hir fers owtrage;
Go leiff in wer, go leiff in cruell payne.

> *The Wallace* (c.1477), Bk.6, ll.81–8 (The lover summoned to war)

2 'Madem,' he said, 'as God giff me gud grace,
Prynsace or queyn, in quhat stait so thai be,
In till hir tym scho was als der to me.'

> *The Wallace* (c.1477), Bk.8, ll.1382–4 (Wallace tells the Queen of England of his love for his murdered wife, Mirren Braidfute)

3 Sotheroun lordys scornyt him in termys rud,
And said; 'Behald, yon Scot ettis his awn blud.'
The king thocht ill thai maid sic derisioun,
He bad haiff watter to Bruce off Huntyntoun.
Thai bad him wesche; he said, that wald
   he nocht:
'This blud is myn, that hurtis most my thocht.'

> *The Wallace* (c.1477), Bk.10, ll.535–40 (Bruce in the English camp after the Battle of Falkirk, beset with guilt, is mocked for eating with bloody hands)
>
> 'The king' is Edward I of England

4 'In thee was wyt, fredom, and hardines;
In thee was treuth, manheid, and nobilnes;
In thee was rewll, in thee was governans;
In thee was vertu with outyn varians;
In thee lawte, in thee was gret largnas;
In thee gentrice, in thee was stedfastnas.
Thow was gret causs off wynnyng off Scotland;
Thocht I began, and tuk the wer on hand.
I vow to God, that has the warld in wauld,
Thy dede sall be to Sotheroun full der sauld.
Martyr thow art for Scotlandis rycht and me;
I sall thee venge, or ellis tharfor dee.'

> *The Wallace* (c.1477), Bk.10, ll.571–82 (Wallace's lament for his great friend Sir John the Graham, killed at Falkirk)

5 Than Wallace smyld a litill at his langage.
'I grant,' he said, 'part Inglissmen I slew
In my quarrel, me thocht nocht halff enew.
I mowyt na were bot for to win our awin;
To God and man the rycht full weill is knawin.'

> *The Wallace* (c.1477), Bk.11, ll.1384–8 (Wallace responds to the accusation of treason at his trial at Westminster)

Blythman, Morris
(pseudonym **Thurso Berwick**) 1919–81
Folk songwriter, poet and school teacher

1 O Scotland hasnae got a King
An she hasnae got a Queen,
For ye canny hae the saicint Liz

When the first yin's never been.

Nae Liz the Twa,
Nae Lillibet the Wan,
Nae Liz will ever dae:
For we'll mak oor land republican
In a Scottish breakaway. . .

> 'The Scottish Breakaway' (1952), st.1 and chorus, in *Rebel Ceilidh Song Book '67* (1966)
>
> The proclamation of Elizabeth as queen in 1952 caused controversy, as many Scots disputed her designation as Elizabeth II, given that there had never been an Elizabeth I of Scotland. Cf. Lord Cooper 3

Bogle, Eric 1944–
Folksinger and songwriter, who emigrated to Australia in 1969

1 The Band Played Waltzing Matilda

> Title of song (1972)

2 Well, the suffering, the sorrow, the glory,
   the shame,
The killing, the dying, it was all done in vain;
For Willie McBride it all happened again,
And again and again and again and again.

> 'No Man's Land', st.4
>
> Also popularly known as 'The Green Fields of France'

3 Did they beat the drum slowly,
Did they sound the fife lowly,
Did the rifles fire o'er ye
As they lowered you down?
Did the bugles sing the 'Last Post' in chorus,
Did the pipes play 'The Flowers o' the Forest'?

> 'No Man's Land', chorus

Bold, Alan 1943–
Poet and critic

1 Our job is to try
To change things.
After Hiroshima
You ask a poet to sing.

> 'Recitative', *Society Inebrious* (1965)

2 This happened near the core
Of a world's culture. This
Occurred among higher things.
This was a philosophical conclusion.
Everybody gets what he deserves.

The bare drab rubble of the place.
The dull damp stone. The rain.
The emptiness. The human lack.

> 'June 1967 at Buchenwald', *A Perpetual Motion Machine* (1969)
>
> The words 'JEDEM DAS SEINE' ('to each his own') are on the gate of Buchenwald concentration camp

3 . . . Scotland, land of the omnipotent No.

'A Memory of Death', *A Perpetual Motion Machine* (1969)

4 The typical Scot has bad teeth, a good chance of cancer, a liver under severe stress and a heart attack pending. He smokes like a chimney, drinks like a fish and regularly makes an exhibition of himself. He is a loser and he knows it. He is forever trying to cover up the pathological cracks in his character.

'An Open Letter on the Closed Mind', in *Chapman* No.35–6 (Jul 1983)

5 The voyage is in motion, how the seas
Turn over, how the earth is insecure,
How much anguish going from here to there:
This journey over endless ecstasies.

'The Voyage of John Bellany: A Triptych' (1986), final stanza

Written for John Bellany's first major retrospective exhibition in the Scottish National Gallery of Modern Art, Edinburgh. Published in *John Bellany: Paintings, Watercolours and Drawings 1964–86* (SNGMA, 1986)

Bonar, Horatius 1808–89

Free Church preacher and hymnwriter

1 Here, O my Lord, I see Thee face to face;
Here would I touch and handle things unseen,
Here grasp with firmer hand the eternal grace,
And all my weariness upon Thee lean.

Hymn, 'Here, O my Lord, I see Thee', st.1

2 Go, labour on: spend and be spent,
Thy joy to do the Father's will. . .

Hymn, 'Go, Labour On', st.1

3 Men die in darkness at thy side,
Without a hope to cheer the tomb;
Take up the torch and wave it wide,
The torch that lights time's thickest gloom.

Hymn, 'Go, Labour On', st.3

Bone, Sir (David) Muirhead 1876–1953

Etcher and war artist

1 Glasgow's tenement life, Glasgow's working life, is a superb feast for any artist. . . I bless the Academy I found in the Glasgow streets. The grand indifference of the great city taught one concentration and gave one solitude.

In 'Talks with Great Scots, No.4, Muirhead Bone', *Scotland* (Spring 1937). Quoted in Duncan MacMillan, *Scottish Art 1460–1990* (1990), ch.16

Boothby, Bob (Sir Robert Boothby, 1st Baron Boothby of Buchan and Rattray Head) 1900–86

Conservative politician, MP for East Aberdeenshire (1924–58)

1 Prior to 1707 the Scottish people were a pack of miserable savages, living in incredible poverty and squalor, and playing no part in the development of civilisation. Since 1707, they have been partners in the greatest undertaking the world has ever seen.

The Nation (9 Mar 1929)

Borthwick, Jane Laurie 1813–97

Hymnwriter and translator of German hymns

1 Still on the homeward journey
Across the desert plain,
Beside another landmark,
We pilgrims meet again.
We meet in cloud and sunshine,
Beneath a changeful sky,
With calm and storm before us,
As in the days gone by.

Hymn, 'Still on the Homeward Journey', st.1

Boswell, Sir Alexander 1775–1822

Songwriter and poet, son of James Boswell

1 At Willie's wedding on the green,
The lassies, bonnie witches,
Were busked out in aprons clean,
And snaw-white Sunday's mutches:
Auld Maysie bade the lads tak tent,
But Jock wad na believe her;
But soon the fool his folly kent,
For – Jenny dang the Weaver.

'Jenny Dang the Weaver', *Songs, Chiefly in the Scots Dialect* (1803), st.1

Boswell, James 1740–95

Writer and biographer of Samuel Johnson

1 I should have mentioned last night that I met with a monstrous big whore in the Strand, whom I had a great curiosity to lubricate, as the saying is. I went into a tavern with her, where she displayed to me all the parts of her enormous carcass; but I found that her avarice was as large as her a—, for she would by no means take what I offered her. I therefore with all coolness pulled the bell and discharged the reckoning, to her no small surprise and mortification. . . I walked off with the gravity of a Barcelonian bishop.

Journal (13 Apr 1763)

2 I was much agitated; and recollecting his prejudice against the Scotch, of which I had heard much, I said to Davies, 'Don't tell where I come from.' – 'From Scotland,' cried Davies, roguishly. 'Mr Johnson, (said I) I do indeed come from Scotland, but I cannot help it.'

> On being first introduced to Dr Johnson. *Life of Samuel Johnson* (1791), 16 May 1763

>> Boswell went on to say that he meant his admission as 'light pleasantry' rather than 'humiliating abasement at the expence of my country', but it did not save him from Johnson's sarcastic response: 'That, Sir, I find is what a very great many of your countrymen cannot help.'

3 . . . the English are better animals than the Scots; they are nearer the sun; their blood is richer, and more mellow: but when I humour any of them in an outrageous contempt of Scotland, I fairly own I treat them as children. And thus I have, at some moments, found myself obliged to treat even Dr Johnson.

> *Journal of a Tour to the Hebrides* (1786), Introduction

4 Mr Keith breakfasted with us. Dr Johnson expatiated rather too strongly upon the benefits derived to Scotland from the Union, and the bad state of our people before it. I am entertained with his copious exaggeration upon that subject: but I am uneasy when people are by, who do not know him as well as I do, and may be apt to think him narrow-minded. I therefore diverted the subject.

> Journal entry (29 Aug 1773), *Journal of a Tour to the Hebrides* (1786)

5 We passed through Glensheal, with prodigious mountains on each side. We saw where the battle was fought in the year 1719; Dr Johnson owned he was now in a scene of as wild nature as he could see; but he corrected me sometimes in my inaccurate observations. 'There,' said I, 'is a mountain like a cone.' JOHNSON. 'No, sir . . . It is indeed pointed at the top; but one side of it is larger than the other.' Another mountain I called immense. JOHNSON. 'No; it is no more than a considerable protuberance.'

> Journal entry (1 Sep 1773), *Journal of a Tour to the Hebrides* (1786)

6 In the evening the company danced as usual. We performed, with much activity, a dance which, I suppose, the emigration from Sky[e] has occasioned. They call it 'America'.

> Journal entry (2 Oct 1773), *Journal of a Tour to the Hebrides* (1786). Cf. Runrig 1

7 . . . last year when a ship sailed from Portree for America, the people on shore were almost distracted when they saw their relations go off; they lay on the ground, tumbled, and tore the grass with their teeth. This year there was not a tear shed. The people on shore seemed to think that they would soon follow. This indifference is a mortal sign for the country.

> Journal entry (2 Oct 1773), *Journal of a Tour to the Hebrides* (1786)

8 We cannot tell the precise moment when friendship is formed. As in filling a vessel drop by drop, there is at last a drop which makes it run over; so in a series of kindnesses there is at last one which makes the heart run over.

> *Life of Samuel Johnson* (1791), Sep 1777

9 For my own part I think no innocent species of wit or pleasantry should be suppressed; and that a good pun may be admitted among the smaller excellencies of lively conversation.

> *Life of Samuel Johnson* (1791), Jun 1784

Bothchanain, Dùghall (Dugald Buchanan) 1716–68
Teacher and evangelical poet

1 Cha bu ghaisgeach Alasdair Mór
No Caesar thug an Ròimh gu géill
Oir ged a thug iad buaidh air càch
Dh'fhan iad 'nan tràill' da miannaibh fhéin.

Cha ghaisg' an nì bhith liodairt dhaoin'
'S cha chliù bhith ann an caonnaig tric
Chan uaisle inntinn ardan borb
'S cha treubhantas bhith garg gun iochd.

Ach 's gaisgeach esan a bheir buaidh
Air eagal beatha 's uamhann bàis
'S a chòmhlaicheas le misnich crì
A h-uile nì ata dhan dàn.

† No hero was Alexander the Great nor Caesar who conquered Rome, for though they defeated others they remained slaves to their own desires.
It is not heroism to wound and maim, nor is it fame to be often in fight; barbarous hauteur is not nobility of mind, nor is it valour to be cruel and fierce.
A hero is he who has subdued the fears of life and dread of death, who meets with the heart's courage everything that fate has in store.

> 'An Gaisgeach' ('The Hero', 1767)

2 Air meadhon oidhch' 'n uair bhios an saogh'l
Air aomadh thairis ann an suain
Grad dhùisgear suas an cinne-daonn'
Le glaodh na trompaid 's airde fuaim.

† At midnight when the world is laid aside in slumber, mankind will suddenly be woken by the trumpet of highest sound.

> 'Là a' Bhreitheanais' ('Day of Judgment', 1767)

Le h-osaig dhoinionnach a bhéil
An saogh'l so reubaidh e gu garg
'S mar dhùn an t-seangain dol 'na ghluas'
Grad bhrùchdaidh 'n uaigh a nios a mairbh.

With a tempest blast from his mouth he [the
Archangel] shall fiercely rend this world; like
an ant-hill beginning to move, the graves will
suddenly pour out their dead.

'Là a' Bhreitheanais' ('Day of Judgment', 1767)

A' ghrian, ard-lòcharan nan speur
Do ghlòir a phearsa géillidh grad
An dealradh drillseach thig o ghnùis
A solus mùchaidh e air fad.

Cuiridh i uimpe culaidh bhròin
'S bidh ghealach mar gun dòirt oirr' fuil
Is crathar cumhachdan nan speur
A' tilgeadh nan reult' as am bun.

Bidh iad air uideal anns an speur
Mar mheas air ghéig ri h-anradh garbh
Tuiteam mar bhraona dh'uisge dlùth
'S an glòir mar shùilean duine mhairbh.

The sun, high lamp of the heavens, will
yield to the glory of His person [Christ]: the
dazzling brightness of His countenance will
utterly quench its light.

It will put on a robe of mourning and the
moon will be as if blood had been spilt on her;
the forces of the skies shall be shaken and the
stars thrown from their place.

They will be tossed about in the heavens
like fruit on a branch in a raging storm, falling
like drops of close thick rain, and their glory
like the eyes of the dead.

'Là a' Bhreitheanais' ('Day of Judgment', 1767)

Boulton, Sir Harold Edwin 1859–1935
Songwriter

Speed, bonnie boat, like a bird on the wing,
'Onward!' the sailors cry.
Carry the lad that's born to be king
Over the sea to Skye.

'Skye Boat Song', in Harold Boulton and Annie
MacLeod (eds), *Songs of the North* (1885), chorus

For my heart's a boat in tow
And I'd give the world to know
Why she means to let me go
As I sing horee, horo.

'Loch Tay Boat Song', chorus

Boyd, Eddie (Edward) 1916–89
Writer for film, television and radio

Scotland, the rock where I was hewn, is one
of the few countries in the world that not only
accepts boredom in the arts but actually justifies

it. There may perhaps be an economic reason
for this. You invest your time and money to
watch some play so putrid, it glows green in
the dark, then justify its tedium by saying. . .
if nothing else it has to be significant. One
good critic could demolish all this *dreck*, but
one good critic is precisely what we do not
have. Instead, we are lumbered with pin-money
pundits, walled up academics or old ladies
of both sexes writing parts for stockbrokers
not to read.

'Across the Airwaves' (a radio programme on
Boyd made by the BBC but never broadcast),
published in *Cencrastus* No.27 (Autumn 1987).
Cf. Helen Cruickshank 9

Boyd, Mark Alexander 1563–1601
Poet

1 Fra banc to banc, fra wod to wod, I rin
Ourhailit with my feble fantasie,
Lyc til a leif that fallis from a trie
Or til a reid ourblawin with the wind.
Twa gods gyds me: the ane of tham is blind,
Ye, and a bairn brocht up in vanitie;
The nixt a wyf ingenrit of the se,
And lichter nor a dauphin with hir fin.

Unhappie is the man for evirmaire
That teils the sand and sawis in the aire;
Bot twyse unhappier is he, I lairn,
That feidis in his hairt a mad desyre,
And follows on a woman throw the fyre,
Led be a blind and teichit be a bairn.

'Sonet'

Boyd wrote almost entirely in Latin, so it is
ironic that he is remembered now solely for
this exquisite Scots sonnet on the trials of
love, represented by the 'wyf' Venus and the
'blind bairn' Cupid

Boyd Orr, John (1st Baron Boyd Orr of Brechin Mearns) 1880–1971
*Biologist, first Director of United Nations Food
and Agriculture Organisation (1945–8), Nobel
Peace Prize winner (1949)*

1 Hungry people judge a Government by the food
it makes available. In the present conflict of
ideologies the food supply will be the deciding
factor. As someone once said, if you offered
an Asian Roosevelt's four freedoms or four
sandwiches he would take the four sandwiches.

The White Man's Dilemma: Food and the Future
(1953), ch.4

President Franklin D Roosevelt's four
freedoms, as set out in a message to Congress
in 1941, were freedom of speech, freedom
of worship, freedom from want and freedom
from fear. Cf. Peter Ritchie-Calder 1

2 The Western Powers are faced with the rising waves of revolt of Asia, Africa, and Latin America against poverty. They can try to resist it by force or buy it off by the offer of technical assistance and trifling loans with political strings attached to them, which will break on the first strain. In that case they will ultimately be destroyed or submerged. On the other hand. . . they could recognise the inevitable and use their overwhelming industrial superiority to create a new world of plenty.

> *The White Man's Dilemma: Food and the Future* (1953), ch.11

3 What people call Communism is hunger becoming articulate.

> Quoted in P Ritchie-Calder, *On Human Rights* (1967)

Boyle, Jimmy 1944–

Convicted murderer, now writer and sculptor (see also Tom McGrath)

1 Blood is pumping through my whole body. It's passing through my heart to the sole of my feet. I live. I hate; oh God, how I hate. . .
You who sit out there, what the fuck do you know? How can I expect you to understand what it means to be in the control of people who look on me as an animal? I want to destroy your system. I want to live. . .

> *The Pain of Confinement* (1984), 26 Jun 1976

2 I want to see the stars without seeing bars. I want to be caught in a busy shopping crowd. I want to see children playing nonsense games. I want to see a dog pissing against a lamp-post. I want to take my girlfriend for a walk. I want to sleep a whole night beside her. I want to see all of you suffer less. I want away from institutions.

> *The Pain of Confinement* (1984), 26 Jun 1976

3 It comes down to freedom. You can keep a person in the most luxurious hotel and give him what he wants but if you restrict his movements to a room of that hotel then it will become his hell. Ultimately, the *need* is for freedom.

> *The Pain of Confinement* (1984), 30 May 1977

4 I have caused much suffering and have suffered but the disease is larger than me. An environment has been created that has encouraged change and I'm the vehicle that the lesson is travelling in.

> On the filming of *A Sense of Freedom* (1981). Quoted in Forsyth Hardy, *Scotland in Film* (1990), ch.9

5 If you cut people off from the outside world to a degree whereby they become more resentful and more aggressive to society for putting

them in that position, then when they come out they are timebombs. . . Yes, some people need to be taken out of the community if they commit a crime but if you are going to degrade them and humiliate them in the process of this confinement then you are going beyond the bounds of civilised society.

> Interviewed in *Radical Scotland* No.9 (Jun/Jul 1984)

6 . . . the inarticulate expression of the inequalities of life.

> On crime. Interviewed in *Radical Scotland* No.9 (Jun/Jul 1984)

Brahan Seer, The (Coinneach Odhar or Pale Kenneth) 16th or 17th century

Highland wizard, famed for his powers of prophecy

1 When two false teachers shall come across the seas who will revolutionise the religion of the land, and nine bridges shall span the river Ness, the Highlands will be overrun with ministers without grace and women without shame.

> In Alexander Mackenzie, *The Prophecies of the Brahan Seer* (1977 edition), p.47
>
> For explanations of this and the other predictions, see Mackenzie's book and Elizabeth Sutherland's *Ravens and Black Rain* (1985)

2 Sheep shall eat men, men will eat sheep, the black rain will eat all things; in the end old men shall return from new lands.

> In Alexander Mackenzie, *The Prophecies of the Brahan Seer* (1977 edition), p.49
>
> Predicting the clearances and repopulation of the Highlands

3 Oh! Drummossie, thy bleak moor shall, ere many generations have passed away, be stained with the best blood of the Highlands. Glad am I that I will not see that day, for it will be a fearful period; heads will be lopped off by the score, and no mercy will be shown or quarter given on either side.

> In Alexander Mackenzie, *The Prophecies of the Brahan Seer* (1977 edition), p.64
>
> Predicting the Battle of Culloden

4 I see a chief, the last of his house, both deaf and dumb. He will be the father of four fair sons, all of whom he will follow to the tomb. He will live careworn and die mourning, knowing that the honours of his line are to be extinguished for ever, and that no future chief of the Mackenzies shall bear rule at Brahan or in Kintail. After lamenting over the last and most promising of his sons, he himself shall sink into the grave, and the remnant of his possessions shall be inherited by a white-coifed lassie from the East,

and she is to kill her sister. And as a sign by which it may be known that these things are coming to pass, there shall be four great lairds in the days of the last deaf and dumb Seaforth – Gairloch, Chisholm, Grant and Raasay – of whom one shall be buck-toothed, another hare-lipped, another half-witted, and the fourth a stammerer. . . and when Seaforth looks around him and sees them, he may know that his sons are doomed to death, that his broad lands shall pass away to the stranger, and that his race shall come to an end.

> In Alexander Mackenzie, *The Prophecies of the Brahan Seer* (1977 edition), p.109

> > Known as the Doom of the Seaforths, this was the Brahan Seer's last and most detailed prediction, which was fulfilled in the early 19th century

Braxfield, Lord (Robert MacQueen)
1722–99

Court of Session judge, known as the 'hanging judge', who inspired R L Stevenson's Lord Hermiston in Weir of Hermiston

1 Come awa, Maister Horner, come awa, and help us to hang ane o' thae daamned scoondrels.

> Spoken in 1793 to a juror handpicked by him, who was about to enter the jury-box at the trial of Thomas Muir for sedition. Quoted in Lord Cockburn, *Memorials of his Time* (1856), ch.2

2 A government in every country should be just like a corporation, and in this country it is made up of the landed interest which alone has a right to be represented. As for the rabble, who have nothing but personal property, what hold has the nation of them?

> At the trial of Thomas Muir (1793), over which he presided. Cf. Thomas Muir 1

3 The laddie has clear tint his Scotch and fund nae English.

> Said in 1794 of Francis, later Lord, Jeffrey, who was fresh at the Scottish Bar after attending Oxford University. Quoted in W Forbes Gray, *Some Old Scots Judges* (1914)

> > 'The only part of a Scotchman I mean to abandon,' Jeffrey had written to a friend from Oxford, 'is the language; and language is all I expect to learn in England.' Quoted in J A Greig, *Francis Jeffrey of the Edinburgh Review* (1948), ch.4, p.57

4 Muckle he made o' that; he was hanget.

> This was Braxfield's outrageous response, at the trial of a political reformer in 1794, to the panel's plea that all great men, even Jesus Christ, had been reformers. Quoted in Lord Cockburn, *Memorials of his Time* (1856), ch.2

5 Gentlemen, ye may just pack up your papers and gang hame; the tane o' ye's rifting punch,

and the ither's belching claret – and there'll be nae gude got out o' ye the day!

> Addressing two hungover advocates, one of whom was Charles Hay, later Lord Newton. Quoted in John Kay, *Original Portraits* (1877 edition), Vol.1, p.169

6 Lissy, I am looking out for a wife, and I thought you just the person that would suit me. Let me have your answer, aff or on, the morn, and nae mair about it.

> Proposing to his second wife. Quoted in John Kay, *Original Portraits* (1877 edition), Vol.1, p.169

7 Lord! ye've little to complain o'; ye may be thankfu' ye're no married to her.

> Said to his butler, who had given notice because of Lady Braxfield's constant scolding. Quoted in Lord Cockburn, *Memorials of his Time* (1856), ch.2

8 Let them bring me prisoners, and I'll find them law.

> Said prior to a political trial when doubts had been raised about the likelihood of a succeful prosecution. Quoted in Lord Cockburn, *Memorials of his Time* (1856), ch.2

9 Ye're a verra clever chiel', man, but ye wad be nane the waur o' a hanging.

> Said to an eloquent defendant on trial before him. Quoted in J G Lockhart, *Memoirs of the Life of Sir Walter Scott, Bart.* (1837–8), ch.48

10 What a glorious thing it is to speak nonsense!

> Free translation of Horace's 'Dulce est desipere in loco'. Quoted in John Ramsay of Ochtertyre, *Scotland and Scotsmen in the Eighteenth Century* (1888 edition), Vol.1, p.390

11 Hang a thief when he's young and he'll no steal when he's auld.

> Attrib. See Robert Ford, *Thistledown, A Book of Scotch Humour* (1914), ch.11

Breadheid, Janet d.1662
Woman tried and executed for witchcraft at Inshoch in Moray

1 He was a meikle, roch, blak man, cloven footed, verie cold; and I fand his nature within me als cold as spring-well-water.

> On sex with the Devil. Quoted in Robert Pitcairn (ed.), *Ancient Criminal Trials of Scotland* (1833), Vol.3

> > Her description is almost word for word identical to that of Issobell Gowdie, with whom she was supposed to have been involved. Cf. Issobell Gowdie 1

Brewster, Sir David 1781–1868
Scientist, inventor of the kaleidoscope

1 . . . it was impossible not to perceive that it would prove of the highest service in all the

ornamental arts, and would, at the same time, become a popular instrument for the purpose of rational amusement.

Treatise on the Kaleidoscope (1819)

> He discovered the principle of the kaleidoscope in 1814–15, but was unsuccessful in patenting it before others flooded the market with thousands of cheap imitations of his design

2 You can form no conception of the effect which the instrument excited in London. . . They are exhibited publicly on the streets for a penny. . . Infants are seen carrying them, the coachmen on their boxes are busy using them, and thousands of poor people make their bread by making and selling them.

> On the kaleidoscope. Quoted in M M Gordon, *The Home Life of Sir David Brewster* (1869), p.97

3 . . . may there not be a type of reason of which the intellect of Newton is the lowest degree? May there not be a telescope more penetrating, and a microscope more powerful than ours?

> On the possible existence of a 'plurality of worlds'. *More Worlds Than One: the Creed of the Philosopher and the Hope of the Christian* (1854)

Bridie, James (pseudonym of Osborne Henry Mavor) 1888–1951

Playwright and doctor

1 AMELIA: And what is the hall-mark of greatness? KNOX: To be assailed by the mob.

> *The Anatomist* (1930), Act 1

> The play centres on the figure of Robert Knox, the surgeon who was the chief recipient of bodies provided by Burke and Hare

2 KNOX: What do I care for your opinions? I am a man of science. I want your reasons.

> *The Anatomist* (1930), Act 1

3 KNOX: I'm not the sort of man to die in a night-shirt looking like an angel.

> *The Anatomist* (1930), Act 3

4 KNOX: London! Pompous Ignorance sits enthroned there and welcomes Pretentious Mediocrity with flattery and gifts. . . I cannot tell you. . . what there is in London to awaken in a realist any feeling but loathing and contempt. Yet she entraps great men and sucks their blood. Her streets are littered with their bones.

> *The Anatomist* (1930), Act 3

5 KNOX: Woman, have you no heart? Have you no manners? You must know that no real lady would make her lover talk about his wife. It embarrasses him beyond bearing.

> *The Anatomist* (1930), Act 3

6 His was an unfathomable sense of the incongruous that burned like the heat in the

centre of the world and could not have burst into flame without destroying. This demoniacal sense belongs, in some degree or other, to the Scottish nation alone, though never has it grown to such magnificent proportions in any individual as it did in young Auchinleck.

> On James Boswell. *One Way of Living* (1939), ch.1

7 I like Roman Catholic priests better than any other kind of priest. They are very expert in the art of living.

> *One Way of Living* (1939), ch.2

8 'Guid gi'e us a guid conceit o' oursel's', is the Scotsman's most earnest prayer. . .

> *One Way of Living* (1939), ch.3

9 . . . we do not rate highly the Scotsman who has succeeded in becoming an Englishman, unless his Rugby is exceptionally good. We are too apt to search him closely for signs of affectation; and in Scotland alien affectations are treated very harshly indeed. We are kinder to our own.

> *One Way of Living* (1939), ch.3

10 I may have been repulsive, but I was not bad. Please remember this.

> *One Way of Living* (1939), ch.4

11 I did not like being a general practitioner though the life had its compensations. . . I learned how to talk to people and improved somewhat my technique in lying.

> *One Way of Living* (1939), ch.7

12 In Scotland there is only one recent tradition of persecution, and that is the persecution of artists and the light-headed and the light-hearted by the unco-guid.

> Quoted by Alasdair Cameron in 'Bridie: The Scottish Playwright', *Chapman* No.55-6 (Spring 1989)

13 When I first went to London at a very early age I saw its mean streets with the eyes of Dickens and its squares and terraces through the eyes of Thackeray. When I went to India it was the India of Kipling that I saw. Perthshire and Stirlingshire, Edinburgh, and the Scottish border overwhelmingly mean Scott to me.

It is one of the qualities of great literature that it can do this thing – that it can cover places in the visible earth with a strange light long after the eyes of the author have been closed for ever.

> Speech as President of the Edinburgh Sir Walter Scott Club at its annual dinner (1947), quoted in *Sir Walter Scott: an Edinburgh Keepsake* (1971)

14 THE DE´IL: This is my Baikie.
A slate-grey township half as old as Peckham, Grew in Italian villas, built in the fifties,

And Scots baronial mansions
Handy by train for the City,
For shipbuilders, stockbrokers, wholesale
  grocers to die in,
Lulled by the wash of the waves of the Clyde...

  The Baikie Charivari (1953), Prologue

5 THE DE´IL: No sae genteel, these days, no sae
  genteel;
When the bungaloids burgeon and gowfers gowf
And keelies squeal on the foreshore
And screwtaps gang crash on the rocks and the
  reeking omnibuses belch...
O Baikie, my beloved, my washpot, my own.

  The Baikie Charivari (1953), Prologue

6 *Him* write a play? Ah kenn't his faither!

  His version of the standard Scots put-down.
  Quoted by Jack House, 'Leisure Interests',
  in *The Third Statistical Account of Scotland:
  Glasgow* (1958)

7 Open your window, the night is beastly derk,
The phentoms are dencing in the West
  End Perk,
Open your window, your lover brave to see,
I'm here all alone, and there's no one
  here but me!

  'The West End Perk', *The British Students' Song
  Book* (n. d.), chorus

Brodie, William (Deacon Brodie)
1741–88

*Respectable Edinburgh citizen by day,
housebreaker by night*

1 To my good friends and companions Brown
and Ainslie I bequeath my villainy and whole
other bad qualities, not doubting but their own
will secure them a rope at last...
  And lastly my neck being now about to
be embraced by a halter I recommend to all
Rogues, Sharpers, Thieves and Gamblers, as
well in high as in low stations to take care of
theirs by leaving of all wicked practices and
becoming good members of society.

  His last will and testament, written on the day
  of his execution (1 Oct 1788). Aeneas Morison,
  The Trial of William Brodie (1788), quoted in J
  S Gibbon, *Deacon Brodie: Father to Jekyll and
  Hyde* (1977)

Brooksbank, Mary (*née* Soutar)
1897–1980

Poet and mill worker

1 Dinna speak tae me o' the guid auld days,
For wha mair than me kens better;

Wha ran barefitted in ragged claes
In summer days and winter.

Guid days they were for some, nae doot,
But never for me or mine;
Puir, hard-working, aye daein' withoot,
And hungry mony's the time.

  '18 Dempster Street – The Guid Auld Bad Days',
  Sidlaw Breezes (1966), st.5–6

2 My language is crude for it's my belief,
A millionaire's just a shameless thief;
To flatter the soldier is never my fashion,
You see, I just call him a hired assassin.

  'To the Erudite', *Sidlaw Breezes* (1966), st.3

3 The slick politician, our franchise beseeching,
Flattering, cajoling, exhorting and preaching;
Voting for Labour, our social wrongs righting,
Vote what you like, you do your own fighting.

These literati, fine livings they've earned
Teaching us what we've long ago learned;
Their windy polemics like asses they bray,
Why do they speak when they've nothing to say?

  'To the Erudite', *Sidlaw Breezes* (1966), st.6–7

4 Oh, dear me, the mill's gaen fest,
The puir wee shifters canna get a rest,
Shiftin' bobbins, coorse and fine,
They fairly mak' ye work for your ten and nine.

  'Oh Dear Me', also called 'The Jute Mill Song',
  Sidlaw Breezes (1966), st.1

5 Oh, dear me, the warld's ill divided,
Them that work the hardest are aye wi' least
  provided...

  'Oh Dear Me', also called 'The Jute Mill Song',
  Sidlaw Breezes, st.3

6 Exhorted to watch out for traitors, spies
While the sirens were wailing their warning.
And you wondered just who manufactured
  the lies
When you looked at the mess in the morning.

  'War', *Sidlaw Breezes* (1966), st.4

7 Be it red or be it blue,
Whit's the odds tae me or you;
In Westminster's hall o' fame,
They cerry on the same auld game.

  'The General Election', *Sidlaw Breezes*
  (1966), st.14

8 My heart's sair wrocht wi' passion,
My heid's sae sair wi' thocht;
Noo tholin' is the fashion,
Wi' promises we're bocht.

And I'm jist ae wee woman,
The kind they used tae burn;
Time seems lang in comin',
It's daft tae seek tae turn.

  'All Over The World', *Sidlaw Breezes*
  (1966), st.1–2

Brougham, Henry Peter (1st Baron Brougham and Vaux) 1778–1869

Lawyer, statesman, campaigner for popular education and against slavery

1 The poesy of this young lord belongs to the class which neither gods nor men are said to permit... His effusions are spread over a dead flat, and can no more get above or below the level, than if they were so much stagnant water.

Review (unsigned) of Byron's *Hours of Idleness*, in *Edinburgh Review* No.22 (Jan 1808)

2 He is at best, he says, but an intruder into the groves of Parnassus; he never lived in a garret, like thorough-bred poets; and 'though he once roved a careless mountaineer in the Highlands of Scotland', he has not of late enjoyed this advantage... let us take what we get and be thankful. What right have we poor devils to be nice? We are well off to have got so much from a man of this lord's station, who does not live in a garret, but 'has the sway' of Newstead Abbey.

Review of Byron's *Hours of Idleness*, in *Edinburgh Review* No.22 (Jan 1808)

3 The schoolmaster is abroad, and I trust to him, armed with his primer, more than I do the soldier in full military array, for upholding and extending the liberties of the country.

Speech in House of Commons (29 Jan 1828), after the Duke of Wellington became Prime Minister

4 Education makes a people easy to lead, but difficult to drive; easy to govern but impossible to enslave.

Speech in House of Commons (29 Jan 1828)

Brown, George Douglas 1869–1902

Novelist

1 When the Deacon was not afraid of a man he stabbed him straight: when he was afraid of him he stabbed him on the sly.

The House with the Green Shutters (1901), ch.2

2 In every little Scotch community there is a distinct type known as 'the bodie'. 'What does he do, that man?' you may ask, and the answer will be, 'Really, I could hardly tell ye what he does – he's juist a bodie!'

The House with the Green Shutters (1901), ch.5

3 'Jock Goudie' – an envious bodie will pucker as if he had never heard the name – 'Jock Goudie? Wha's *he* for a Goudie? Oh ay, let me see now. He's a brother o' – eh,' – (tit-tit-titting on his brow) – oh, just a brother o' Drucken Will Goudie o' Auchterwheeze! Oo-ooh, I ken *him* fine. His grannie keepit a sweetie-shop in Strathbungo.'

The House with the Green Shutters (1901), ch.5

4 When Gourlay was to be approached there was always a competition for who was to be hindmost.

The House with the Green Shutters (1901), ch.5

5 ... so flushed and riotous can the Scottish mind become over a commercial prospect that it sometimes sends native caution by the board, and a man's really fine idea becomes an empty balloon, to carry him off to the limbo of vanities. There is a megalomaniac in every parish of Scotland. Well, not so much as that; they're owre canny for that to be said of them.

The House with the Green Shutters (1901), ch.11

6 Gourlay felt for the house of his pride even more than for himself – rather the house was himself; there was no division between them. He had built it bluff to represent him to the world. It was his character in stone and lime. He clung to it, as the dull, fierce mind, unable to live in thought, clings to a material source of pride.

The House with the Green Shutters (1901), ch.24

7 'Tis a brutal and a bloody work... There is too much black for the white in it. Even so it is more complimentary to Scotland, I think, than the sentimental slop of Barrie, and Crockett, and Maclaren. It was antagonism to their method that made me embitter the blackness; like Old Gourlay I was going to 'show the dogs what I thought of them'. Which was a gross blunder, of course. A novelist should never have an axe of his own to grind.

Letter to his friend Ernest Barker (24 Oct 1901) after the publication of *The House with the Green Shutters*. Quoted in James Veitch, *George Douglas Brown* (1952), Part 4, ch.2

J M Barrie, S R Crockett and Ian Maclaren were the 'kailyard' novelists criticised by J H Millar. Cf. J H Millar 1, Lady Nairne 11

8 Every clachan in Scotland *is* a hot-bed of scandal and malevolence.

Letter to Ernest Barker. Quoted in James Veitch, *George Douglas Brown* (1952), Part 4, ch.2

Brown, George Mackay 1921–96

Orkney poet and novelist

1 Go sad or sweet or riotous with beer
Past the old women gossiping by the hour,
They'll fix on you from every close and pier
An acid look to make your veins run sour.

'The Old Women', *Loaves and Fishes* (1959), st.1

2 My father passed with his penny letters
Through closes opening and shutting
   like legends
When barbarous with gulls

Hamnavoe's morning broke

On the salt and tar steps.

'Hamnavoe', *Loaves and Fishes* (1959), st.1–2

3 The boats drove furrows homeward, like
    ploughmen
  In blizzards of gulls.

  'Hamnavoe', *Loaves and Fishes* (1959), st.7

4 The kirk, in a gale of psalms, went heaving
    through
  A tumult of roofs, freighted for heaven.
    Ploughboy
  And milklass tarried under
  The buttered bannock of the moon.

  'Hamnavoe', *Loaves and Fishes* (1959), st.9

5 So fierce and sweet the song on the
    plucked string,
  Know now for truth
  Those hands have cut from the net
  The strong
  Crab-eaten corpse of Jock washed from a boat
  One old winter, and gathered the mouth of
    Thora to his mouth.

  'Old Fisherman with Guitar', *The Year of the
  Whale* (1965), st.2

6 Decay of language is always the symptom of a
  more serious sickness.

  An Orkney Tapestry (1969), 'Islands and People'

7 In Scotland when people congregate they tend
  to argue and discuss and reason; in Orkney
  they tell stories.

  An Orkney Tapestry (1969), 'Islands and People'

8 A town like Stromness, even thirty years ago,
  used to be alive with 'characters', the kind
  of delightfully surrealistic folk you read about
  in Russian novels. There are less and less of
  them now. It is as if people were ashamed to
  be different from one another.
    One senses a growing coldness – the coldness
  of people who have received the fatal blessing
  of prosperity.

  'The Broken Heraldry', in Karl Miller (ed.),
  Memoirs of a Modern Scotland (1970)

9 Perhaps. . . the quality of life grows poorer
  as progress multiplies its gifts on a simple
  community.

  Fishermen With Ploughs (1971), Introduction

10 Man goes, man voyages, into the blackest sun.

  'The Blind Helmsman', *Fishermen with
  Ploughs* (1971)

11 A silent conquering army,
  The island dead,
  Column on column, each with a stone banner
  Raised over his head.

  'Kirkyard', *Poems New and Selected* (1971), st.1

12 It is the writer's task to relate the legend. . . to
  this age of television, uranium, and planet-flight.

  'An Autobiographical Essay', in Maurice Lindsay
  (ed.), *As I Remember* (1979)

13 . . . it is a constant in history that a strong
  neighbour never shows much consideration or
  care for the impoverished neighbour on the
  other shore, but is never happy till he has
  the key, the title deeds and every last stick of
  furniture.

  On historical relations between Scotland and
  Orkney. 'The View from Orkney', *The Sunday
  Mail Story of Scotland* (1988), No.12

14 History can show few benign mergings of people
  with people. Flame and blood is always the
  cement.

  'The View from Orkney', *The Sunday Mail Story
  of Scotland* (1988), No.12

15 All a writer needs is a cheap pad and a
  10-penny biro.

  Quoted in obituary article in *Scotland on Sunday*
  (14 Apr 1996)

Brown, (James) Gordon 1951–
Labour politician and MP

1 No chancellor until this one has come to the
  House [of Commons] and said that because he
  has money available to him the rich will get the
  benefits and the poor will make the sacrifices.

  On Chancellor Nigel Lawson's 'giveaway' budget
  of 1988. Quoted in *The Observer* (1 May 1988)

2 The tiger, once the king of the jungle,
  now just the fireside rug, decorative and
  ostentatious certainly, but there essentially to
  be walked all over.

  On the President of the Board of Trade, Michael
  Heseltine. Quoted in *The Independent* (11 Jul 1992)

3 Socialism is an ideology often more successfully
  caricatured by our enemies than defined by our
  friends.

  Quoted in *The Independent* (25 Jun 1994).
  Cf. Nicholas Fairbairn 10

4 For the Tories to become believers in
  intervention for industry, skills, training and
  education will make them look like tourists in a
  foreign country with a phrase-book they don't
  understand.

  Quoted in *The Independent* (11 Jun 1995)

Brown, Hamish 1934–
Mountaineer and author

1 The critic who decries walking the Munros
  because it means climbing dozens of boring

hills is commenting not on the richness of the hills, but on his own dulled vision. No hill is dull between the sunset and the sea. By the time you have topped a hundred Munros (the incurable stage usually) you will know Scotland – and yourself – in a fuller, richer way...

'The Munros – A Personal View', in Donald Bennet (ed.), *The Munros* (1985)

Bruce, George 1909–
Poet

1 A song for Scotland this,
For the people
Of the clearances,
For the dead tenements,
For the dead herring
On the living water.
A song for Scotland this.

'A Song for Scotland', *Sea Talk* (1944)

2 O impregnable and very ancient rock,
Rejecting the violence of water,
Ignoring its accumulations and strategy,
You yield to history nothing.

'Kinnaird Head', *Sea Talk* (1944)

3 This is a known land,
A land without myth.

'A Land without Myth', *Sea Talk* (1944)

4 Old tales, old customs and old men's dreams
Obscure this town. Memories abound.
In the mild misted air, and in the sharp air
Toga and gown walk the pier.
The past sleeps in the stones.

'St Andrews, June – 1946', *Selected Poems* (1947), st.1

5 'She's jinkit again,
the bitch!'
said the man wi' the spade.

On the refusal of the Scots language to die. 'Urn Burial (R I P Scots Tongue)', *Perspectives: Poems 1970–86* (1987)

Bruce, James 1730–94
Explorer

1 It is easier to guess than to describe the situation of my mind at that moment – standing in that spot which had baffled the genius, industry, and inquiry, of both ancients and moderns, for the course of near three thousand years. Kings had attempted this discovery at the head of armies, and each expedition was distinguished from the last, only by the difference of the numbers which had perished... Though a mere Briton, I triumphed here, in my own mind, over kings and their armies...

On reaching, as he believed, the source of the Nile (in fact he was at Lake Tana, source of the Blue Nile), on 4 November 1770. *Travels to Discover the Source of the Nile* (1790), Vol.5, Bk 6, ch.12

Bruce, Michael 1746–67
Poet

1 Sweet bird! thy bow'r is ever green,
Thy sky is ever clear;
Thou hast no sorrow in thy song,
No winter in thy year!

'Ode to the Cuckoo', st.6

A variant version of this poem was published under the name of John Logan (1746–88), minister of South Leith and a friend of Bruce, and some doubt remains as to whose was the original poem

Bruce, Robert (Robert I) 1274–1329
Victor of Bannockburn, King of Scotland from 1306

1 I have broken my good battle-axe.

Attrib. Quoted in Walter Scott, *Tales of a Grandfather*, 1st Series (1828), ch.10

A knight, Sir Henry de Bohun, rode out from the assembled English army in an attempt to kill Bruce before the battle (23 Jun 1314). Bruce evaded his charge and despatched him with an axe-blow to the head, with the above result

2 Ni me Scotorum libertas prisca moveret
Tot mala non paterer orbis ob imperium.

† Had I not been moved by the old freedom of the Scots
I would not have tholed so many evils even to rule the world.

Attrib. Referring to the tribulations undergone in his struggle to liberate Scotland. Quoted in Walter Bower, *Scotichronicon* (1440–9), Vol.6, Bk 12, ch.11

Bruce Lockhart, Sir Robert Hamilton 1887–1970
Diplomat, secret agent and writer

1 ... whisky has made us what we are. It goes with our climate and with our nature. It rekindles old fires in us, our hatred of cant and privilege, our conviviality, our sense of nationhood, and, above all, our love of Scotland. It is our release from materialism, and I often think that without it we should have long been extinct as a race, for we should have been so irritatingly efficient that a worse persecution than the Hebrews ever suffered would have been our inevitable fate.

Scotch (1959 edition), ch.3

2 As an enemy, there is no Scot who does not know its dangers, and almost no Scottish family without its whisky skeletons. They rattle in my own cupboard, and I myself have been near enough to destruction to respect whisky, to fear it, and to continue to drink it.

Scotch (1959 edition), ch.3

Brunton, Mary (*née* Balfour) 1778–1818
Novelist

1 Lady Pelham viewed her niece with triumphant admiration. . . declaring, that she had never seen her look half so lovely. Yet, with skilful malice, she contrived to awaken Laura's natural bashfulness, by saying, as they were alighting at Mrs Clermont's door, 'Now my dear don't mortify me tonight by any of your Scotch *gaucheries*. Remember every eye will be turned upon you.'

Self-Control (1810/11), ch.28

Buchan, Anna (pseudonym O. Douglas) 1877–1948
Novelist, sister of John Buchan

1 Joan laughed. 'I believe, Mother, that if a marriage comes to grief, you always, in your heart, blame the woman.'
'Yes,' said Mrs Heggie firmly, 'I do. Men, even the good ones, are kittle cattle; God didn't give them much sense, and it's the woman's job to make the best of them.'

Jane's Parlour (1937), ch.16. Cf. Helena Kennedy 1

2 To be alone might or might not be one's misfortune, but to be lonely is largely one's own fault. . . The people who really are lonely are the women who have enough to live on, and who for some reason or another have not kept up a home, and simply wander about leading an aimless life. One meets them in the hydros and hotels; they know every hotel in the Riviera and, poor dears, they are very lonely because they are not old enough to enjoy a rest, and they have never worked hard enough to deserve a rest.

Speech at the opening of a Christmas sale in Glasgow, quoted in Wendy Forrester, *Anna Buchan and O. Douglas* (1995), ch.9

3 To restore the Scots vernacular is beyond the power of any Act of Parliament, because the life on which it depended is gone. Scots can only survive as a book-tongue, and as a book-tongue it must be cherished. Surely our educational authorities, who are so anxious to teach us all kinds of fancy things, will make an effort to preserve this most valuable national asset.

Speech at a Burns Night during World War II,

quoted in Wendy Forrester, *Anna Buchan and O. Douglas* (1995), ch.9. Cf. Sheena Blackhall 3

4 That any Scot would *choose* to die and be buried in England appalled me.

On learning that her great-uncle and aunt had no plans ever to return to Scotland. *Unforgettable, Unforgotten* (1945), ch.5

Buchan, Elspeth (*née* Simpson, known as 'Luckie Buchan') 1738–91
Founder of religious sect in Irvine, known as the Buchanites

1 . . . I never was fed nor cloathed, nor educate by parents according to the flesh; but he who feeds the ravens, clothes the lilies, teaches babes, has had a goodly heritage prepared for me, and has made Jesus Christ my tutor, and the angels his servants, ministering spirits. . .

Letter to an English clergyman. Quoted in Harry Graham, *A Group of Scottish Women* (2nd edition, 1908), ch.12

2 . . . if we were of the world, it would love us, but, because we are not of the world but God has chosen us out of the world, therefore doth the world hate us. . .

Letter to an Edinburgh teacher who challenged the beliefs of the Buchanites. Quoted in Harry Graham, *A Group of Scottish Women* (2nd edition, 1908), ch.13

3 I go where my words will not be rejected.

Attrib. Last words. Quoted in Harry Graham, *A Group of Scottish Women* (2nd edition, 1908), ch.12

Buchan, John (1st Baron Tweedsmuir) 1875–1940
Novelist and, from 1935 until his death, Governor-General of Canada

1 'Pardon,' he said, 'I'm a bit rattled to-night. You see, I happen at this moment to be dead.'
I sat down in an armchair and lit my pipe.
'What does it feel like?' I asked. I was pretty certain that I had to deal with a madman.

The Thirty-Nine Steps (1915), ch.1, 'The Man who Died' (Scudder and Hannay in conversation)

2 'You think that a wall as solid as the earth separates civilisation from barbarism. I tell you the division is a thread, a sheet of glass.'

The Power-House (1916), ch.3, 'Tells of a Midsummer Night' (Andrew Lumley to Edward Leithen)

3 'Civilisation is a conspiracy.'

The Power-House (1916), ch.3, 'Tells of a Midsummer Night' (Andrew Lumley to Edward Leithen)

4 Tommy in such a situation was a tower of strength, for, whatever his failings in politics, I knew no one I would rather have with me to go tiger-shooting.

> *The Power-House* (1916), ch.4, 'I Follow the Trail of the Super-Butler'

5 'Back to Glasgow to do some work for the cause,' I said lightly.
'Just so,' he said with a grin. 'It's a great life if you don't weaken.'

> *Mr Standfast* (1919), ch.5, 'Various Doings in the West'

6 'You will not find him in Russia. He is what we call the middle-class, which we who were foolish used to laugh at. But he is the stuff which above all others makes a great people. He will endure when aristocracies crack and proletariats crumble. In our own land we have never known him, but till we create him our land will not be a nation.'

> *Huntingtower* (1922), ch.16, 'In which a Princess Leaves a Dark Tower and a Provision Merchant Returns to his Family' (Alexis Nicolaevitch on the retired Glasgow grocer Dickson McCunn)

7 I believe that every Scotsman should be a Scottish Nationalist. If it could be proved that a separate Scottish Parliament were desirable, that is to say that the merits were greater than the disadvantages, Scotsmen should support it. I would go further. Even if it were not proved desirable, if it could be proved to be desired by any substantial majority of the Scottish people, then Scotland should be allowed to make the experiment.

> Speech in Parliament (24 Nov 1932)

8 ... romance... is a revolt against the despotism of facts.

> *Sir Walter Scott* (1932), ch.7, Part 3

9 We can only pay our debt to the past by putting the future in debt to ourselves.

> Address to the people of Canada, on the coronation of George VI (12 May 1937)

10 It is a miserable business to watch a great country like Germany wallowing in a viler mud than the Middle Ages.

> Letter to former British Prime Minister, Stanley Baldwin (Dec 1938). Quoted in Wendy Forrester, *Anna Buchan and O. Douglas* (1995), ch.12

11 I was especially fascinated by the notion of hurried journeys... We live our lives under the twin categories of time and space, and when the two come together we get the great moment. Whether failure or success is the result, life is sharpened, intensified, idealised. A long journey, even with the most lofty purpose, may be a dull thing to read of if it is made at leisure; but a hundred yards may be a breathless business if only a few seconds are granted to complete it.

> *Memory Hold-The-Door* (1941), ch.8

12 The essence of civilisation lies in man's defiance of an impersonal universe. It makes no difference that a mechanised universe may be his own creation if he allows his own handiwork to enslave him.

> *Memory Hold-the-Door* (1941), ch.12

13 The dominant thought of youth is the bigness of the world, of age its smallness. As we grow older we escape from the tyranny of matter and recognise that the true centre of gravity is in the mind.

> *Memory Hold-the-Door* (1941), ch.12

14 One of the misfortunes of advancing age is that you get out of touch with the sunrise. You take it for granted, and it is over and done with before you settle yourself for the daily routine. That is one reason, I think, why, as we grow older, the days seem shorter. We miss the high moments of their beginning.

> *Memory Hold-the-Door* (1941), 'Pilgrim's Rest', ch.1, Part 1

15 The cold infernal North magnified instead of dwarfing humanity. What a marvel was this clot of vivified dust!... The universe seemed to spread itself before him in immense distances lit and dominated by a divine spark which was man. An inconsiderable planet... that vegetable world on which every living thing was in the last resort a parasite! Man, precariously perched on this rotating scrap-heap, yet so much master of it that he could mould it to his transient uses and, while struggling to live, could entertain thoughts and dreams beyond the bounds of time and space! Man so weak and yet so great, the chief handiwork of the Power that had hung the stars in the firmament!

> *Sick Heart River* (1941), Part 3, section 16

Buchan, Norman 1922–90
Labour MP, folksong collector and writer

1 Not a glen but it has its but and ben. Not a granny but she is old and frail and we have to be kind to her. And what a waving of tartan around the hieland hames, ain wee hooses, stars o' Rabbie Burns. We cannot help but feel that the Glasgow street cry, 'Ye canny shove yer granny aff the bus,' has more of truth and reality than the slobbering over her in a distant and imaginary hieland hame.

> On the persistence of 'kailyairdery' in Scottish song. *101 Scottish Songs* (1962), Introduction. Cf. Alexander Petrie 4, Traditional songs 65, 73

2 . . . the normal sign of a bad song is that it calls Scotland 'Caledonia'. 'Jamie Raeburn' is the exception that proves the rule!

'Folk and Protest', in E J Cowan (ed.), *The People's Past* (1980). Cf. Traditional songs 45

Buchan, Tom 1931–95

Poet

1 Scotland the wee, crèche of the soul, of thee I sing

land of the millionaire draper, whisky vomit and the Hillman Imp

'Scotland the wee', *Dolphins at Cochin* (1969)

2 Stenhousemuir, Glenrothes, Auchterarder, Renton

– one way street to the coup of the mind.

'Scotland the wee', *Dolphins at Cochin* (1969)

Buchanan, Dugald
see Bothchanain, Dùghall

Buchanan, George 1506–82

Humanist scholar and tutor to James VI

1 They who are styled queens in other languages, are only called kings' wives in ours.

Rerum Scoticarum Historia (1582; translated by James Aikman, 1845), Vol.2, p.116

Buchanan puts these words into a speech by James Kennedy, Bishop of St Andrews, opposing the appointment of Mary of Gueldres as regent for her son James III in 1460; but they also represent his own opposition to Mary of Guise and Mary, Queen of Scots

2 Better this nor steilling sheipe, or sitting ydle, quhilk is as ill.

Responding to Andrew Melville's surprise at finding him, in his dying year, teaching a servant to read and write. Quoted in James Melville's *Diary* (1829 edition), p.86

Buchanan, George 1890–1955

Labour politician and 'Red Clydeside' MP

1 . . . [in Glasgow] you have the tragedy going on day after day, a death rate of four times the number of children than the death rate in a well-to-do division, and this is not because our people are poor, or Scottish, or Irish, or drunkards. It is not even because this Parliament is brutal towards our people. It is because this Parliament cannot devote the time to the work, and furthermore because it has no knowledge of the problems with which we are confronted.

Speech in House of Commons in support of Home Rule for Scotland (May 1924)

Buchanan, Robert William 1841–1901

Poet and journalist

1 She just wore
Enough for modesty – no more.

White Rose and Red (1871), Part 1

2 To the wedding of Shon Maclean,
Twenty Pipers together
Came in the wind and the rain
Playing across the heather;
Backward their ribbons flew,
Blast upon blast they blew,
Each clad in tartan new,
Bonnet, and blackcock feather:
And every Piper was fou,
Twenty Pipers together!

'The Wedding of Shon Maclean', chorus 1

3 At the wedding of Shon Maclean,
Twenty Pipers together,
Blowing with might and main,
Thro' wonderful lungs of leather!

'The Wedding of Shon Maclean', chorus 6

Buckle, Henry Thomas 1821–62

English historian

1 Herein lies the apparent paradox, and the real difficulty, of Scotch history. That knowledge should not have produced the effects which have elsewhere followed it; that a bold and inquisitive literature should be found in a grossly superstitious country, without diminishing its superstition; that the people should constantly withstand their kings, and as constantly succumb to their clergy; that while they are liberal in politics, they should be illiberal in religion. . . that these discrepancies should coexist, seems at first sight a strange contradiction, and is surely a phenomenon worthy of our careful study.

History of Civilisation in England (1857–62), Vol.3, ch.1, 'Condition of Scotland to the End of the 14th Century'

The second and third parts of Buckle's massive study of intellectual development in England are in fact concerned with, respectively, Spain and Scotland

2 . . . they looked for future fortune, not to Scotland, but to England. London became the centre of their intrigues and their hopes. . . It became evident that their patriotism was but a selfish passion. They ceased to love a country which could give them nothing, and, as a natural consequence, their country ceased to love them.

On the Scottish aristocracy after the Union of 1707. *History of Civilisation in England* (1857–62), Vol.3, ch.3, 'Condition of Scotland During the 17th and 18th Centuries'

3 What more need I say? What further evidence
need I bring to elucidate the real character of
one of the most detestable tyrannies ever seen
on the earth? When the Scotch Kirk was at
the height of its power, we may search history
in vain for any institution which can compete
with it, except the Spanish Inquisition. . .
One difference, however, there was, of vast
importance. In political matters, the Church,
which was servile in Spain, was rebellious in
Scotland. Hence the Scotch always had one
direction in which they could speak and act
with unrestrained liberty. In politics, they found
their vent. There, the mind was free. And this
was their salvation.

> *History of Civilisation in England* (1857–62), Vol.3,
> ch.4, 'An Examination of the Scotch Intellect
> During the 17th Century'

4 . . . that monkish rabble. . .

> On Scottish theologians of the 17th century.
> *History of Civilisation in England* (1857–62), Vol.3,
> ch.5, 'An Examination of the Scotch Intellect
> During the 18th Century'

5 Even in the capital of Scotland, in that centre
of intelligence which once boasted of being the
Modern Athens, a whisper will quickly circulate
that such an one is to be avoided, for that he is
a free-thinker; as if free-thinking were a crime,
or as if it were not better to be a free-thinker
than a slavish thinker.

> *History of Civilisation in England* (1857–62), Vol.3,
> ch.5, 'An Examination of the Scotch Intellect
> During the 18th Century'

Burnet, Gilbert 1643–1715

*Edinburgh-born churchman, made Bishop
of Salisbury by William of Orange after the
Revolution of 1689*

1 A secularist, he shook off Presbyterianism as
a viper, utilised Episcopacy as the readiest
political tool, and finally put on Popery as a
comfortable shroud to die in.

> On Charles II. Quoted in N M Cameron, D F
> Wright et al., *Dictionary of Scottish Church
> History and Theology* (1993)

Burnet, John 1863–1928

*Philosopher and classicist, Professor of Greek
at St Andrews University (1891–1926)*

1 The most important side of any department of
knowledge is the side in which it comes into
touch with every other department. To insist
on this is the true function of humanism.

> *Essays and Addresses* (1929)

Burnett, James see Monboddo, Lord

Burns, Elizabeth 1957–

Poet and short-story writer

1 . . . may the perfume of her garden
that she tells us is so famous
turn sour as burning flesh
and may her pink and white skin
be stripped from her bones
and spat to herring gulls

> 'The Laird's Wife Visits the Poorhouse', *New
> Writing Scotland 7* (1989)

2 In the afternoon I sit against the apple tree
feeling the dent of bark on my bare shoulders
I close my eyes and the murmur of their voices
blurs with the birdsong that maybe
when we listen to the finished record
will have swum inside the poems

> 'Valda's Poem/Sleevenotes', *Ophelia and other
> poems* (1991)

>> The sleevenotes on Hugh MacDiarmid's
>> record *Whaur Extremes Meet* (1978) described
>> its recording at Brownsbank Cottage, Biggar,
>> with MacDiarmid and Norman MacCaig inside
>> talking and drinking whisky while outside,
>> Valda Grieve, MacDiarmid's wife, gardened
>> in her swimsuit

3 Oh wilted church, what rags of hymns you sing
what mumbled scraps of prayers you speak
on the narrow track to your imagined heaven

Oh gaunt church, gaunt people
so silent and not dancing
not screaming

> 'Jesus Speaks to the Church at Eastertime',
> *Ophelia and other poems* (1991)

Burns, Robert 1759–96

Poet and songwriter

1 For my own part I never had the least thought
or inclination of turning Poet till I got heartily
in Love, and then Rhyme and Song were, in a
manner, the spontaneous language of my heart.

> First Commonplace Book (1783)

2 Green grow the rashes, O;
Green grow the rashes, O;
The sweetest hours that e'er I spend,
Are spent amang the lasses, O.

> 'Green Grow the Rashes' (1784), chorus.
> Cf. Anonymous 34

3 There's nought but care on ev'ry han',
In every hour that passes, O:
What signifies the life o' man,
An 'twere na for the lasses, O.

> 'Green Grow the Rashes' (1784), st.1

4 From scenes like these, old Scotia's grandeur
     springs,
   That makes her lov'd at home, rever'd abroad;
   Princes and lords are but the breath of kings,
   'An honest man's the noblest work of God'. . .
   'The Cotter's Saturday Night' (1785), st.19

   > In the Kilmarnock edition of his poems Burns
   > misquoted Alexander Pope's line as 'the noble
   > work of God'; this was corrected in subsequent
   > editions

5 Some books are lies frae end to end,
   And some great lies were never penn'd. . .
   'Death and Doctor Hornbook, A True Story'
   (1785), st.1

6 The clachan yill had made me canty,
   I was na fou, but just had plenty. . .
   'Death and Doctor Hornbook, A True Story'
   (1785), st.3

7 The heart ay's the part ay
   That makes us right or wrang.
   'Epistle to Davie, a Brother Poet' (1785), st.5

8 If honest Nature made you fools,
   What sairs your grammars?
   Ye'd better taen up spades and shools,
   Or knappin-hammers.
   'Epistle to J Lapraik, An Old Scotch Bard,
   1 April 1785' (1785), st.11

9 A set o' dull, conceited hashes
   Confuse their brains in college-classes,
   They gang in stirks, and come out asses,
   Plain truth to speak;
   An' syne they think to climb Parnassus
   By dint o' Greek!
   'Epistle to J Lapraik, An Old Scotch Bard,
   1 April 1785' (1785), st.12

10 Gie me ae spark o' Nature's fire,
   That's a' the learning I desire;
   Then, tho' I drudge thro' dub an' mire,
   At pleugh or cart,
   My Muse, tho' hamely in attire,
   May touch the heart.
   'Epistle to J Lapraik, An Old Scotch Bard,
   1 April 1785' (1785), st.13

11 O Fergusson! thy glorious parts
   Ill-suited law's dry, musty arts!
   My curse upon your whunstane hearts,
   Ye E'nbrugh Gentry!
   The tythe o' what ye waste at cartes
   Wad stow'd his pantry!
   'Epistle to William Simpson, Ochiltree'
   (1785), st.4

   > Robert Fergusson (1750–74), by whose poetry
   > Burns was greatly influenced, died a pauper
   > in the Edinburgh bedlam

12 In days when mankind were but callans
   At Grammar, Logic, an' sic talents,

They took nae pains their speech to balance,
Or rules to gie,
But spak their thoughts in plain, braid Lallans,
Like you or me.
'Epistle to William Simpson, Ochiltree' (1785),
'Postscript', st.2

13 There's some are fou o' love divine;
   There's some are fou o' brandy;
   An' monie jobs that day begin,
   May end in houghmagandie
   Some ither day.
   'The Holy Fair' (1785), st.27

14 O Thou, that in the Heavens does dwell,
   Wha, as it pleases best Thysel,
   Sends ane to Heaven, an' ten to Hell,
   A' for Thy glory,
   And no for onie guid or ill
   They've done before Thee!

   I bless and praise Thy matchless might,
   When thousands Thou hast left in night,
   That I am here before Thy sight,
   For gifts an' grace
   A burning and a shining light
   To a' this place.
   'Holy Willie's Prayer' (1785), st.1–2

15 But Lord, remember me and mine
   Wi' mercies temporal and divine,
   That I for grace an' gear may shine,
   Excell'd by nane;
   And a' the glory shall be Thine,
   Amen, Amen!
   'Holy Willie's Prayer' (1785), st.17

16 O Whisky! soul o' plays an' pranks!
   Accept a Bardie's gratefu' thanks!
   When wanting thee, what tuneless cranks
   Are my poor verses!
   Thou comes – they rattle i' their ranks,
   At ither's arses!
   'Scotch Drink' (1785), st.18

17 Wee sleekit, cow'rin, tim'rous beastie,
   O, what a panic's in thy breastie!
   Thou need na start awa sae hasty
   Wi' bickering brattle!
   I wad be laith to rin an' chase thee,
   Wi' murdering pattle!
   'To A Mouse, On Turning her up in her Nest
   with the Plough, November, 1785' (1785), st.1

18 But Mousie, thou art no thy lane,
   In proving foresight may be vain:
   The best-laid schemes o' mice an' men
   Gang aft agley,
   An' lea' us nought but grief an' pain,
   For promis'd joy!
   'To A Mouse, On Turning her up in her Nest
   with the Plough, November, 1785' (1785), st.7

19 O Thou, whatever title suit thee! –
   Auld Hornie, Satan, Nick, or Clootie –

Wha in yon cavern grim an' sootie,
Clos'd under hatches,
Spairges about the brunstane cootie,
To scaud puir wretches!

Hear me, Auld Hangie, for a wee,
An' let poor damnèd bodies be. . .

'Address to the Deil' (1786), st.1–2

20 An' now, Auld Cloots, I ken ye're thinkin,
A certain Bardie's rantin, drinkin,
Some luckless hour will send him linkin
To your black Pit;
But, faith! he'll turn a corner jinkin,
An' cheat you yet.

'Address to the Deil' (1786), st.20

21 Edina! Scotia's darling seat!

'Address to Edinburgh' (1786), st.1

22 O ye wha are sae guid yoursel,
Sae pious and sae holy,
Ye've nought to do but mark and tell
Your neebours' fauts an folly!

'Address to the Unco Guid, or the Rigidly
Righteous' (1786), st.1

23 Then gently scan your brother Man,
Still gentler sister Woman;
Tho' they may gang a kennin wrang,
To step aside is human.

'Address to the Unco Guid, or the Rigidly
Righteous' (1786), st.7

24 Freedom an' whisky gang thegither,
Tak aff your dram!

'The Author's Earnest Cry and Prayer, to the
Right Honorable and Honorable, the Scotch
Representatives in the House of Commons'
(1786), st.30

25 But facts are chiels that winna ding,
An' downa be disputed. . .

'A Dream' (1786), st.4

26 A fig for those by law protected!
Liberty's a glorious feast!
Courts for cowards were erected,
Churches built to please the priest.

'The Jolly Beggars', or 'Love and Liberty, a
Cantata' (?1786), chorus

27 Let them cant about decorum
Who have characters to lose!

'The Jolly Beggars', or 'Love and Liberty, a
Cantata' (?1786), st.5

28 Man's inhumanity to Man
Makes countless thousands mourn!

'Man was made to Mourn, A Dirge' (1786), st.7

29 If I'm design'd yon lordling's slave –
By Nature's law design'd –
Why was an independent wish

E'er planted in my mind?
If not, why am I subject to
His cruelty, or scorn?
Or why has Man the will and pow'r
To make his fellow mourn?

'Man was made to Mourn, A Dirge' (1786), st.9

30 Now westlin winds, and slaught'rin guns
Bring Autumn's pleasant weather;
The moorcock springs on whirring wings
Amang the blooming heather. . .

'Now Westlin Winds' or 'Song, composed in
August' (1786), st.1

31 It was upon a Lammas night,
When corn rigs are bonie,
Beneath the moon's unclouded light,
I held awa to Annie. . .

'The Rigs o' Barley', or 'Corn Rigs Are Bonie'
(1786), st.1

32 I hae been blythe wi' Comrades dear;
I hae been merry drinking;
I hae been joyfu' gath'rin gear;
I hae been happy thinking. . .

'The Rigs o' Barley', or 'Corn Rigs Are Bonie'
(1786), st.4

33 Corn rigs, an' barley rigs,
An' corn rigs are bonie:
I'll ne'er forget that happy night,
Amang the rigs wi' Annie.

'The Rigs o' Barley', or 'Corn Rigs Are Bonie'
(1786), chorus

34 Fair fa' your honest, sonsie face,
Great chieftain o' the puddin'-race!
Aboon them a' ye tak your place,
Painch, tripe, or thairm;
Weel are ye wordy of a grace
As lang's my arm.

The groaning trencher there ye fill,
Your hurdies like a distant hill,
Your pin wad help to mend a mill
In time o' need,
While thro' your pores the dews distil
Like amber bead.

'To a Haggis' (1786), st.1–2

35 Auld Scotland wants nae skinking ware
That jaups in luggies;
But, if ye wish her gratefu' prayer,
Gie her a Haggis!

'To a Haggis' (1786), st.8

36 Ha! whare ye gaun, ye crowlin ferlie?
Your impudence protects you sairly;
I canna say but ye strunt rarely
Owre gauze and lace,
Tho' faith! I fear ye dine but sparely
On sic a place.

'To a Louse, On Seeing one on a Lady's Bonnet
at Church' (1786), st.1

37 O wad some Power the giftie gie us
To see oursels as ithers see us!
It wad frae monie a blunder free us,
An' foolish notion:
What airs in dress an' gait wad lea' us,
An' ev'n devotion!

'To a Louse, On Seeing one on a Lady's Bonnet at Church' (1786), st.8

38 Wee, modest, crimson-tipped flow'r,
Thou's met me in an evil hour;
For I maun crush amang the stoure
Thy slender stem:
To spare thee now is past my pow'r,
Thou bonie gem.

'To A Mountain Daisy, On Turning one down with the Plough, in April 1786' (1786), st.1

39 Twa dogs, that were na thrang at hame,
Forgathered ance upon a time.

'The Twa Dogs' (1786), ll.5–6

40 His lockèd, letter'd, braw brass-collar,
Show'd him the gentleman an' scholar;
But tho' he was o' high degree,
The fient a pride, nae pride had he;
But wad hae spent an hour caressin,
Ev'n wi' a tinkler-gipsy's messin. . .

'The Twa Dogs' (1786), ll.13–18

41 The tither was a ploughman's collie,
A rhyming, ranting, raving billie. . .

'The Twa Dogs' (1786), ll.23–4

42 An' tho' fatigu'd wi' close employment,
A blink o' rest's a sweet enjoyment.

'The Twa Dogs' (1786), ll.109–10

43 The men cast out in party-matches.
Then sowther a' in deep debauches;
Ae night they're mad wi' drink and whoring,
Niest day their life is past enduring.

'The Twa Dogs' (1786), ll.215–18

44 Kind, honest-hearted Willie,
I'm sitten down here, after seven and forty miles ridin, e'en as forjesket and forniaw'd as a forfoughten cock, to gie you some notion o' my landlowper-like stravaguin sin the sorrowfu' hour that I sheuk hands and parted wi' auld Reikie. . .

Letter to William Nicol ('1st June 1787 – or I believe the 39th o' May rather')

45 I met wi' twa dink quines in particular, ane o' them a sonsie, fine, fodgel lass, baith braw and bonie; the tither was a clean-shankit, straught, tight, weel-far'd winch, as blythe's a lintwhite on a flowrie thorn, and as sweet and modest's a new blawn plumrose in a hazle shaw. . . They play'd me sik a deevil o' a shavie that I daur say if my harigals were turn'd out, ye wad see twa nicks i' the heart o' me like the mark o' a kail-whittle in a castock. –

I was gaun to write you a lang pystle, but, Gude forgie me, I gat myself sae notouriously bitchify'd the day after kail-time that I can hardly stoiter but and ben.

Letter to William Nicol ('1st June 1787 – or I believe the 39th o' May rather')

46 Farming, the only thing of which I know any thing, and Heaven above knows, but little do I understand even of that. . .

Letter to James Smith (11 Jun 1787)

47 . . . the story of Wallace poured a Scottish prejudice in my veins which will boil along there till the flood-gates of life shut in eternal rest.

Letter to Dr John Moore (2 Aug 1787)

48 The great misfortune of my life was, never to have AN AIM.

Letter to Dr John Moore (2 Aug 1787)

49 Those who think that composing a Scotch song is a trifling business – let them try.

Letter to James Hoy (6 Nov 1787)

50 There are just two creatures I would envy, a horse in his native state traversing the forests of Asia, or an oyster on some of the desert shores of Europe. The one has not a wish without enjoyment, the other has neither wish nor fear.

Letter to Margaret Chalmers (19 Dec 1787)

51 The Poetic Genius of my Country found me as the prophetic bard Elijah did Elisha – at the *plough*; and threw her inspiring mantle over me. She bade me sing the loves, the joys, the rural scenes and rural pleasures of my native Soil, in my native tongue; I tuned my wild, artless notes, as she inspired.

Address 'To the Noblemen and Gentlemen of the Caledonian Hunt', the preface to the 1787 'Edinburgh' edition of his poems

52 O thou, my elder brother in misfortune,
By far my elder brother in the Muse. . .

'Apostrophe to Fergusson' (1787)

53 No sculptured Marble here, nor pompous lay,
'No storied Urn nor animated Bust':
This simple stone directs pale Scotia's way,
To pour her sorrows o'er the Poet's dust.

Inscription (written 1787) on the headstone of Robert Fergusson in Canongate Kirkyard, Edinburgh, erected and paid for by Burns

The second line refers to Thomas Gray's 'Elegy Written in a Country Churchyard' (1751)

54 When death's dark stream I ferry o'er –
A time that surely *shall* come –
In Heaven itself I'll ask no more
Than just a Highland welcome!

'Impromptu, on being hospitably entertained in the Highlands in 1787' (1787, published 1800). Cf. Lord Byron 45

55 John Barleycorn was a hero bold,
Of noble enterprise;
For if you do but taste his blood,
'Twill make your courage rise.

'John Barleycorn, A Ballad' (1787), st.13

56 Robin was a rovin boy,
Rantin, rovin, rantin, rovin,
Robin was a rovin boy,
Rantin, rovin Robin!

There was a lad was born in Kyle,
But whatna day o' whatna style,
I doubt it's hardly worth the while
To be sae nice wi' Robin.

'There was a lad', or 'Rantin' Rovin' Robin'
(1787), chorus and st.1

57 Cauld blaws the wind frae east to west,
The drift is driving sairly;
Sae loud and shill's I hear the blast,
I'm sure it's winter fairly.

Up in the morning's no for me,
Up in the winter early;
When a' the hills are cover'd wi' snaw,
I'm sure it's winter fairly.

'Up in the Morning Early' (1787), st.1 and chorus.
Cf. John Hamilton (1761–1814) 1, Harry Lauder 8

shill: shrill

58 My creed is pretty nearly expressed in the last
clause of Jamie Dean's grace, an honest weaver
in Ayrshire: 'Lord grant that we may lead a
gude life! for a gude life maks a gude end, at
least it helps weel!'

Letter to Agnes McLehose (8 Jan 1788)

59 . . . mine is the Religion of the bosom. – I
hate the very idea of controversial divinity; as I
firmly believe, that every honest, upright man,
of whatever sect, will be accepted of the Deity.

Letter to Agnes McLehose (12 Jan 1788)

60 I like to have quotations ready for every
occasion. – They give one's ideas so pat, and
save one the trouble of finding expression
adequate to one's feelings.

Letter to Agnes McLehose (14 Jan 1788).
Cf. Robert Burns 110

61 Why will Great people not only deafen us with
the din of their equipage, and dazzle us with
their fastidious pomp, but they must also be
so very dictatorially wise?

Letter to Agnes McLehose (27 Jan 1788)

62 O, what a peacemaker is a guid weel-willy
pintle! It is the mediator, the guarantee, the
umpire, the bond of union, the solemn league
and covenant, the plenipotentiary, the Aaron's
rod, the Jacob's staff, the prophet Elisha's pot
of oil, the Ahasuerus' Sceptre, the sword of
mercy, the philosopher's stone, the Horn of
Plenty, and Tree of Life between Man and
Woman.

Letter to Robert Ainslie (3 Mar 1788)

Written after a reunion with Jean Armour, to
whom, he wrote, he gave 'such a thundering
scalade that electrified the very marrow of
her bones.'

63 I have a sore warfare in this world! The Devil,
the World and the Flesh, are three formidable
foes. The first, I generally try to fly from; the
second, Alas! generally flies from me; but the
third is my plague, worse than the ten plagues
of Egypt.

Letter to William Nicol (8 Mar 1788)

64 – Be not in a hurry; let us go on correctly; and
your name shall be immortal.

Letter to James Johnson (15 Nov 1788)

Johnson published *The Scots Musical Museum*
in six volumes (1787–1803). However, it was
Burns himself that did much of the work,
collecting songs and tunes, and editing most
of the volumes.

65 Should auld acquaintance be forgot,
And never brought to mind?
Should auld acquaintance be forgot,
And auld lang syne?

'Auld Lang Syne' (1788), st.1

66 For auld lang syne, my dear,
For auld lang syne,
We'll tak a cup o' kindness yet
For auld lang syne!

'Auld Lang Syne' (1788), chorus

67 We twa hae run about the braes,
And pou'd the gowans fine,
But we've wandered monie a weary fit,
Sin' auld lang syne.

'Auld Lang Syne' (1788), st.3

68 Hey, the dusty Miller,
And his dusty coat;
He will win a shilling,
Or he spend a groat:
Dusty was the coat,
Dusty was the colour;
Dusty was the kiss
That I got frae the Miller!

'The Dusty Miller' (1788), st.1

69 Farewell, ye dungeons dark and strong,
The wretch's destinie!
M'Pherson's time will not be long
On yonder gallows-tree.

Sae rantingly, sae wantonly,
Sae dauntingly gaed he;
He play'd a spring, and danc'd it round
Below the gallows-tree.

'M'Pherson's Farewell' (1788), st.1 and chorus

Based on an older ballad, 'MacPherson's Rant'. James MacPherson, a gypsy freebooter and fiddler, was hanged at the market cross in Banff (16 Nov 1700). The last tune he played before execution is reputed to have been his 'Rant', or 'Testament', after which he smashed his fiddle across his knee

70 Of a' the airts the wind can blaw
I dearly like the west,
For there the bonie lassie lives,
The lassie I lo'e best.

'Of A' the Airts the Wind can Blaw', or 'I Love my Jean' (1788), st.1

71 O rattlin, roarin Willie,
O, he held to the fair;
An' for to sell his fiddle
And buy some other ware;
But parting wi' his fiddle,
The saut tear blin't his e'e –
And rattlin, roarin Willie,
Ye're welcome hame to me.

'Rattlin Roarin Willie' (1788), st.1

72 Go, fetch to me a pint o' wine,
And fill it in a silver tassie,
That I may drink before I go
A service to my bonie lassie!

'The Silver Tassie' or 'My Bonie Mary' (1788), st.1

73 A Poet and a Beggar are in so many points of view alike, that one might take them for the same individual character under different designations; were it not that though, with a trifling Poetic license, most Poets may be styled Beggars, yet the converse of the proposition does not hold, that every Beggar is a Poet. – In one particular however they remarkably agree; if you help either the one or the other to a mug of ale or the picking of a bone, they will very willingly repay you with a Song.

Letter to John McMurdo (9 Jan 1789)

74 I myself can affirm, both from bachelor and wedlock experience, that Love is the Alpha and the Omega of human enjoyment. – All the pleasures, all the happiness of my humble Compeers, flow immediately and directly from this delicious source. – It is that spark of celestial fire which lights up the wintry hut of Poverty, and makes the chearless mansion, warm, comfortable and gay.

Letter to Alexander Cunningham (24 Jan 1789)

75 . . . my success has encouraged such a shoal of ill-spawned monsters to crawl into public notice, under the title of Scots Poets, that the very term, Scots Poetry, borders on the burlesque.

Letter to Frances Anna Dunlop (4 Mar 1789)

76 I do not care three farthings for Commentators & authorities. – An honest candid enquirer after truth, I revere; but illiberality & wrangling I equally detest.

Letter to Frances Anna Dunlop (17 Jul 1789)

77 Flow gently, sweet Afton, among thy
green braes!
Flow gently, I'll sing thee a song in thy praise!
My Mary's asleep by the murmuring stream –
Flow gently, sweet Afton, disturb not
her dream!

'Afton Water' (1789), st.1

78 Curs'd be the man, the poorest wretch in life,
The crouching vassal to the tyrant wife!
Who has no will but by her high permission;
Who has not sixpence but in her possession;
Who must to her his dear friend's secret tell;
Who dreads a curtain-lecture worse than hell.

'The Henpecked Husband' or 'The Tyrant Wife' (1789)

79 We are na fou, we're nae that fou,
But just a drappie in our e'e!
The cock may craw, the day may daw,
And ay we'll taste the barley bree!

'Willie Brew'd a Peck o' Maut' (1789), chorus

80 I am out of all patience with this vile world for one thing. – Mankind are by nature benevolent creatures; except in a few scoundrelly instances, I do not think that avarice of the good things we chance to have is born with us; but we are placed here amid so much Nakedness, & Hunger, & Poverty, & Want, that we are under a damning necessity of studying Selfishness in order that we may Exist!

Letter to Peter Hill (2 Mar 1790)

81 What hidden trap-doors of disaster, what unseen arrows of misfortune, waylay, & beset our path of life!

Letter to Frances Anna Dunlop (9 Jul 1790)

82 How wretched is the man that hangs on & by the favors of the Great! To shrink from every dignity of Man at the approach of a lordly piece of Self-consequence, who, amid all his tinsel glitter & stately hauteur, is but a creature formed as thou art – & perhaps not so well formed as thou art – came into the world a puling infant as thou didst, & must go out of it as all men must, a stinking corpse – & should the important piece of clay-dough deign to cast his supercilious eye over you, & make a motion as if to signify his tremendous fiat – then – in all the quaking pangs & staring terrors of self-annihilation, to stutter in crouching syllables – 'Speak! Lord!! for thy servant heareth!!!' If such is the damned state of the poor devil, from my soul I pity him!

Letter to Alexander Cunningham (8 Aug 1790)

83 My fingers are so wore to the bone in holding the noses of his Majesty's liege subjects to the grindstone of Excise that I am totally unfitted for wielding a pen in any generous subject.
Letter to Dr James Anderson (1 Nov 1790)

84 Ay waukin, O,
Waukin still and weary:
Sleep I can get nane,
For thinkin on my dearie.
'Ay Waukin, O' (1790), chorus

85 O, for him back again!
O, for him back again!
I wad gie a' Knockhaspie's land
For Highland Harry back again.
'Highland Harry Back Again' (1790), chorus

86 John Anderson my jo, John,
When we were first acquent;
Your locks were like the raven,
Your bonie brow was brent;
But now your brow is beld, John,
Your locks are like the snaw,
But blessings on your frosty pow,
John Anderson, my jo!
'John Anderson, My Jo' (1790), st.1.
Cf. Anonymous 36

87 An ye had been whare I hae been,
Ye wad na been sae canty, O!
An ye had seen what I hae seen,
On the braes o' Killiecrankie, O!
'Killiecrankie' (1790), chorus

88 My heart's in the Highlands, my heart is not here,
My heart's in the Highlands a chasing the deer,
A-chasing the wild deer and following the roe –
My heart's in the Highlands, wherever I go!
'My Heart's in the Highlands' (1790), chorus

89 My love, she's but a lassie yet,
My love she's but a lassie yet!
We'll let her stand a year or twa,
She'll no be half sae saucy yet!
'My Love, She's But a Lassie Yet' (1790), chorus

90 When chapman billies leave the street,
And drouthy neebors, neebors meet;
As market-days are wearing late,
An' folk begin to tak the gate;
While we sit bousing at the nappy,
An' getting fou and unco happy,
We think na on the lang Scots miles,
The mosses, waters, slaps, and styles,
That lie between us and our hame,
Whare sits our sulky, sullen dame,
Gathering her brows like gathering storm,
Nursing her wrath to keep it warm.
'Tam o' Shanter, A Tale' (1790), ll.1–12

91 (Auld Ayr, wham ne'er a town surpasses,
For honest men and bonny lasses.)
'Tam o' Shanter, A Tale' (1790), ll.15–16

92 Ah! gentle dames! it gars me greet,
To think how mony counsels sweet,
How mony lengthen'd sage advices,
The husband frae the wife despises!
'Tam o' Shanter, A Tale' (1790), ll.33–6

93 Tam lo'ed him like a vera brither;
They had been fou for weeks thegither.
'Tam o' Shanter, A Tale' (1790), ll.43–4

94 The storm without might rair and rustle,
Tam did na mind the storm a whistle.
'Tam o' Shanter, A Tale' (1790), ll.51–2

95 Kings may be blest but Tam was glorious,
O'er a' the ills o' life victorious!
'Tam o' Shanter, A Tale' (1790), ll.57–8

96 But pleasures are like poppies spread,
You seize the flower, its bloom is shed;
Or like the snow falls in the river,
A moment white – then melts for ever;
Or like the borealis race,
That flit ere you can point their place;
Or like the rainbow's lovely form
Evanishing amid the storm.
Nae man can tether time or tide;
The hour approaches Tam maun ride. . .
'Tam o' Shanter, A Tale' (1790), ll.59–68

97 Inspiring bold John Barleycorn!
What dangers thou canst make us scorn!
Wi' tippeny, we fear nae evil;
Wi' usquabae, we'll face the devil!
'Tam o' Shanter, A Tale' (1790), ll.105–8

98 Three lawyers' tongues, turn'd inside out,
Wi' lies seam'd like a beggar's clout;
Three priests' hearts, rotten, black as muck,
Lay stinking, vile, in every neuk.
'Tam o' Shanter, A Tale' (1790), ll.143–6

> Burns omitted these four lines from later editions of the poem, on the advice of Alexander Fraser Tytler. They have acquired a certain notoriety as a result

99 As Tammie glowr'd, amaz'd, and curious,
The mirth and fun grew fast and furious;
The piper loud and louder blew,
The dancers quick and quicker flew,
They reel'd, they set, they cross'd, they cleekit,
Till ilka carlin swat and reekit,
And coost her duddies to the wark,
And linket at it in her sark!
'Tam o' Shanter, A Tale' (1790), ll.147–54

100 Ah, Tam! Ah, Tam! thou'll get thy fairin!
In hell they'll roast thee like a herrin!
In vain thy Kate awaits thy comin!
Kate soon will be a woefu' woman!
'Tam o' Shanter, A Tale' (1790), ll.205–8.
Cf. Matthew Fitt 1

01 Whene'er to drink you are inclin'd,
Or cutty sarks run in your mind,
Think, ye may buy the joys o'er dear –
Remember Tam o' Shanter's mare.

'Tam o' Shanter, A Tale' (1790), ll.225–8

02 First when Maggy was my care,
Heaven, I thought, was in her air;
Now we're married, spier nae mair;
But whistle o'er the lave o't.

'Whistle O'er the Lave O't' (1790), st.1

Another version of this song, with indelicate overtones, appeared in 'The Jolly Beggars' (?1786)

03 Poverty! Thou half-sister of Death, thou cousin-german of Hell, where shall I find force of execration equal to thy demerits!

Letter to Peter Hill (17 Jan 1791)

04 When Political combustion ceases to be the object of Princes & Patriots, it then, you know, becomes the lawful prey of Historians & Poets.

On the Jacobite song 'There'll never be Peace till Jamie Comes Hame'. Letter to Alexander Cunningham (12 Mar 1791)

05 Ae fond kiss, and then we sever!
Ae fareweel, and then for ever!
Deep in heart-wrung tears I'll pledge thee,
Warring sighs and groans I'll wage thee.

'Ae Fond Kiss' (1791), st.1

06 Had we never lov'd sae kindly,
Had we never lov'd sae blindly!
Never met – or never parted,
We had ne'er been broken-hearted.

Fare-thee-weel, thou first and fairest!
Fare-thee-weel, thou best and dearest!
Thine be ilka joy and treasure,
Peace, Enjoyment, Love and Pleasure!

'Ae Fond Kiss' (1791), st.4–5

07 Ye banks and braes o' bonie Doon,
How can ye bloom sae fresh and fair;
How can ye chant, ye little birds,
And I sae weary fu' o' care!

'The Banks o' Doon' (1791), st.1

08 And my fause luver staw my rose –
But ah! he left the thorn wi' me.

'The Banks o' Doon' (1791), st.2

09 . . . of all Nonsense, Religious Nonsense is the most nonsensical. . .

Letter to Alexander Cunningham (10 Sep 1792)

10 Do you know, I pick up favourite quotations, & store them in my mind as ready armour, offensive, or defensive, amid the struggle of this turbulent existence.

Letter to Frances Anna Dunlop (6 Dec 1792). Cf. Robert Burns 60

111 The Deil cam fiddlin' thro' the town,
And danc'd awa wi' th' Exciseman,
And ilka wife cries, 'Auld Mahoun,
I wish you luck o' the prize, man!'

'The Deil's Awa wi' th' Exciseman' (1792), st.1

112 There's threesome reels, there's foursome reels,
There's hornpipes and strathspeys, man,
But the ae best dance e'er cam to the land
Was 'The Deil's Awa wi' th' Exciseman'.

'The Deil's Awa wi' th' Exciseman' (1792), st.3

113 Duncan Gray cam here to woo
(Ha, ha, the wooing o't!)
On blythe Yule-Night when we were fou
(Ha, ha, the wooing o't!)
Maggie coost her head fu' high,
Look'd asklent and unco skeigh,
Gart poor Duncan stand abeigh –
Ha, ha, the wooing o't!

'Duncan Gray' (1792), st.1

114 Here's freedom to him that wad read,
Here's freedom to him that wad write!
There's nane ever feared that the truth should be heard,
But they wham the truth wad indite.

'Here's a Health to Them that's Awa'' (1792), st.3

115 The golden hours on angel wings
Flew o'er me and my dearie;
For dear to me as light and life
Was my sweet Highland Mary.

'Highland Mary' (1792), st.2

116 When o'er the hill the eastern star
Tells bughtin' time is near, my jo,
And owsen frae the furrow'd field
Return sae dowf and weary, O;
Down by the burn, where scented birks
Wi' dew are hangin' clear, my jo,
I'll meet thee on the lea-rig,
My ain kind dearie, O!

'The Lea-Rig' or 'My Ain Kind Dearie' (1792), st.1. Cf. Robert Fergusson 22

117 O when she cam ben she bobbed fu' law,
O when she cam ben, she bobbed fu' law;
And when she cam ben she kiss'd Cockpen,
And syne deny'd she did it at a'.

'O When She Cam Ben She Bobbed' (1792), st.1. Cf. Lady Nairne 8

118 It was in sweet Senegal that my foes did me enthral
For the lands of Virginia-ginia, O;
Torn from that lovely shore, and must never see it more,
And alas! I am weary, weary, O!

'The Slave's Lament' (1792), st.1

119 Fareweel to a' our Scottish fame,
Fareweel our ancient glory!

Fareweel ev'n to the Scottish name,
Sae famed in martial story!
Now Sark rins over the Solway sands,
An' Tweed rins to the ocean,
To mark where England's province stands –
Such a parcel of rogues in a nation!

'Such a Parcel of Rogues in a Nation' (1792), st.1

120 But pith and power, till my last hour,
I'll mak this declaration: –
'We're bought and sold for English gold' –
Such a parcel of rogues in a nation!

'Such a Parcel of Rogues in a Nation' (1792), st.3

On the Union of 1707, which was popularly
held to have been effected only through bribery
and corruption. Cf. Christian Watt 6

121 By yon castle wa' at the close of the day,
I heard a man sing tho' his head it was grey;
And as he was singing the tears down came,
There'll never be peace till Jamie comes hame.

The Church is in ruins, the State is in jars:
Delusions, oppressions, and murderous wars;
We dare na weel say't, but we ken wha's
to blame –
There'll never be peace till Jamie comes hame.

'There'll Never be Peace till Jamie Comes Hame'
(1792), st.1–2. Cf. Walter Scott 34

122 Willie Wastle dwalt on Tweed,
The spot they ca'd it Linkumdoddie.
Willie was a wabster guid
Could stown a clue wi' onie body.
He had a wife was dour and din,
O, Tinkler Maidgie was her mither!
Sic a wife as Willie had,
I wad na gie a button for her.

'Willie Wastle' (1792), st.1

123 Ye Jacobites by name, give an ear, give an ear!
Ye Jacobites by name, give an ear,
Ye Jacobites by name,
Your fautes I will proclaim,
Your doctrines I maun blame – you shall hear!

'Ye Jacobites By Name' (1792), st.1

Frequently sung with the word 'lend'
substituted for 'give'

124 Tho' this was fair, and that was braw,
And yon the toast of a' the town,
I sigh'd, and said amang them a',
'Ye are na Mary Morison.'

'Mary Morison' (1793), st.2

Hugh MacDiarmid reckoned this last line
(in its context) the best that Burns ever
wrote. See Norman MacCaig's address at the
MacDiarmid centenary, Langholm, quoted in
Chapman No.69–70 (Autumn 1992)

125 Hear, Land o' Cakes, and brither Scots,
Frae Maidenkirk to Johnny Groats! –
If there's a hole in a' your coats,

I rede you tent it;
A chield's amang you takin' notes,
And, faith, he'll prent it.

'On the Late Captain Grose's Peregrinations
Thro' Scotland' (1793), st.1.

Naomi Mitchison called the selection of her
wartime diaries *Among You Taking Notes* (1985)

126 Scots, wha hae wi' Wallace bled,
Scots, wham Bruce has aften led,
Welcome to your gory bed
Or to victorie!
Now's the day, and now's the hour:
See the front o' battle lour;
See approach proud Edward's power –
Chains and slaverie!

'Scots Wha Hae' or 'Bruce's Address at
Bannockburn' (1793), st.1

Of this poem, Sir James Murray, instigator and
first editor of the *Oxford English Dictionary*,
commented in a letter (9 Jul 1912): 'Even
Burns thought that Scotch was defiled by
"bad grammar" and tried to conform his
Scotch to *English* Grammar! transforming eg
the Scotch "Scots 'at hae" into *Scots wha hae*
which no sober Scotch man in his senses ever
naturally said'

127 I am sensible that my taste in Music must be
inelegant & vulgar, because people of undisputed
& cultivated taste can find no merit in many
of my favourite tunes. – Still, because I am
cheaply pleased, is that any reason why I should
deny myself that pleasure?

Letter to George Thomson (Sep 1794)

128 Ca' the yowes to the knowes,
Ca' them whare the heather grows,
Ca' them whare the burnie rowes,
My bonie dearie!

'Ca' the Yowes to the Knowes' (1794), chorus.
Cf. Isobel Pagan 2

Burns added verses to an older song at least
partly written by Isobel Pagan. This is Burns's
second version, reworked for Johnson's *Scots
Musical Museum*

129 Contented wi' little and cantie wi' mair,
Whene'er I forgather wi' Sorrow and Care,
I gie them a skelp as they're creepin' alang,
Wi' a cog o' guid swats and an auld
Scottish sang.

'Contented wi' Little' (1794), st.1

130 O my luve's like a red, red rose,
That's newly sprung in June;
O my luve's like the melodie
That's sweetly play'd in tune.

As fair art thou, my bonie lass,
So deep in luve am I;
And I will luve thee still, my dear,
Till a' the seas gang dry.

Till a' the seas gang dry, my dear,
And the rocks melt wi' the sun:
O I will love thee still, my dear,
While the sands o' life shall run.

And fare thee weel, my only luve!
And fare thee weel awhile.
And I will come again, my luve,
Tho' 't were ten thousand mile!

'A Red, Red Rose' (1794)

1 Is there for honest Poverty
That hings his head, and a' that;
The coward-slave, we pass him by,
We dare be poor for a' that!
For a' that, and a' that,
Our toils obscure, and a' that,
The rank is but the guinea's stamp,
The man's the gowd for a' that.

'For a' that and a' that' (1795), st.1

2 A man's a man for a' that.

'For a' that and a' that' (1795), st.2

3 Ye see yon birkie ca'd a lord,
Wha struts, and stares, and a' that,
Though hundreds worship at his word,
He's but a coof for a' that.

'For a' that and a' that' (1795), st.3

4 For a' that, an a' that,
It's comin' yet for a' that,
That Man to Man the warld o'er,
Shall brothers be, for a' that.

'For a' that and a' that' (1795), st.5

5 An' Charlie he's my darling
My darling, my darling,
Charlie he's my darling –
The young Chevalier!

'Charlie he's my Darling' (1796), chorus.
Cf. James Hogg 6

6 Gin a body meet a body
Comin thro' the rye,
Gin a body kiss a body
Need a body cry?

'Comin thro' the Rye' (1796), st.2. Cf. James
Clerk Maxwell 6

7 There's Death in the cup – so beware!
Nay, more – there is danger in touching;
But wha can avoid the fell snare?
The man and his wine's so bewitching!

'Inscription on a Goblet' (1796)

8 It was a' for our rightfu' King
We left fair Scotland's strand;
It was a' for our rightfu' King
We e'er saw Irish land, my dear –
We e'er saw Irish land.

'It was a' for our Rightfu' King' (1796), st.1

9 Oh wert thou in the cauld blast
On yonder lea, on yonder lea;
My plaidie to the angry airt,

I'd shelter thee, I'd shelter thee.

'Oh Wert Thou in the Cauld Blast' (1796), st.1

140 Don't let the Awkward Squad fire over me!

Attrib.

Apparently spoken from his death-bed to
a fellow member of the Royal Dumfries
Volunteers. However, his wishes were ignored
and at his funeral the Volunteers fired three
volleys over his grave. Quoted in Catherine
Carswell, *The Life of Robert Burns* (1930), ch.30

Burns, Tommy 1956–

Football player and Celtic manager (1994–   )

1 In Glasgow half the fans hate you and the other
half think they own you.

On playing for Celtic (1987). Quoted in Kenny
MacDonald, *Scottish Football Quotations* (1994)

Byrne, John 1940–

Painter and playwright

1 SPANKY: Dames like her only go for a guy with
style. . . style, that's what counts.

The Slab Boys (1978), Act 1

2 PHIL: All we ever knew about dames was their
arms stuck out sideyways when they ran.

The Slab Boys (1978), Act 2

3 SPANKY: I wonder what it is like being dead?
PHIL: Listen, kid. . . you're nineteen with
a wardrobe full of clothes. . . you've got
everything to live for.

Cuttin' a Rug (1979), Act 2

Byron, Lord (George Gordon Noel Byron) 1788–1824

Poet

1 Away, ye gay landscapes! ye gardens of roses!
In you let the minions of luxury rove;
Restore me the rocks, where the snow-flake
reposes,
Though still they are sacred to freedom
and love:
Yet, Caledonia! belov'd are thy mountains,
Round their white summits though
elements war;
Though cataracts foam 'stead of smooth flowing
fountains,
I sigh, for the valley of dark Loch na Garr.

'Lachin Y Gair', *Hours of Idleness* (1806), st.1

2 England! thy beauties are tame and domestic,
To one who has rov'd on the mountains afar;
Oh! for the crags that are wild and majestic,

The steep frowning glories of dark Loch
na Garr.

'Lachin Y Gair', *Hours of Idleness* (1806), st.5

3 I would I were a careless child,
Still dwelling in my Highland cave,
Or roaming through the dusky wild,
Or bounding o'er the dark blue wave;
The cumbrous pomp of Saxon pride,
Accords not with the freeborn soul,
Which loves the mountain's craggy side,
And seeks the rocks where billows roll.

'Stanzas', *Hours of Idleness* (1806), st.1

4 Good God! I hope not. I would rather the country was sunk in the sea. *I*, the Scotch accent!

Responding to a comment that he had 'a slight
Scotch accent' (1808). Quoted in E C Mayne,
Byron (1924 edition), ch.2

The *Edinburgh Review*'s vicious review of
Hours of Idleness had just appeared, and no
doubt affected Byron's reaction. Cf. Henry
Brougham 1, 2

5 Prepare for rhyme – I'll publish, right or wrong:
Fools are my theme, let Satire be my song.

English Bards and Scotch Reviewers (1809), ll.5–6

In the Preface to this, he writes: 'As to the
Edinburgh Reviewers; it would, indeed, require
a Hercules to crush the Hydra; but if the
Author succeeds in merely "bruising one of
the heads of the serpent", though his own
hand should suffer in the encounter, he will
be amply satisfied.'

6 'Tis pleasant, sure, to see one's name in print;
A Book's a Book, altho' there's nothing in't.

English Bards and Scotch Reviewers (1809), ll.51–2

7 A man must serve his time to every trade
Save Censure; critics all are ready made.
Take hackneyed jokes from Miller, got by rote,
With just enough of learning to misquote...

English Bards and Scotch Reviewers (1809), ll.63–6

Joe Miller's Jests by John Mottley (1692–1750)
was published in 1739. A 'Joe Miller' is a dull
joke, named after Joseph Miller (1684–1738),
an English actor and, apparently, second-rate
humorist

8 I don't know what Scrope Davies meant by
telling you I liked Children, I abominate the
sight of them so much that I have always had
the greatest respect for the character of *Herod*.

Letter to Augusta Leigh (30 Aug 1811), in L A
Marchand (ed.), *Byron's Letters and Journals*,
Vol.2 (1973)

9 ... Caledonia's ours.
And well I know within that bastard land
Hath Wisdom's goddess never held command:
A barren soil where Nature's germs, confin'd
To stern sterility can stint the mind,

Whose thistle well betrays the niggard earth,
Emblem of all to whom the land gives birth;
Each genial influence nurtur'd to resist,
A land of meanness, sophistry and mist...

The Curse of Minerva (1812), ll.130–8

10 Each breeze from foggy mount and marshy plain
Dilutes with drivel every drizzly brain,
Till, burst at length, each watery head o'erflows,
Foul as their soil, and frigid as their snows.

The Curse of Minerva (1812), ll.139–42

11 I have been in some of the most oppressed
provinces of Turkey; but never under the most
despotic of infidel governments did I behold
such squalid wretchedness as I have seen since
my return in the very heart of a Christian
country. And what are your remedies? After
months of inaction, and months of action worse
than inactivity, at length comes forth the grand
specific, the never-failing nostrum of all state
physicians, from the days of Draco to the
present time... Death... Is there not blood
enough upon your penal code, that more must
be poured forth to ascend to Heaven and testify
against you?

Arguing against the death penalty for Luddites.
Maiden speech in the House of Lords (27 Feb
1812)

12 Are we aware of our obligations to a *mob*? It is
the mob that labour in your fields, and serve in
your houses – that man your navy, and recruit
your army – that have enabled you to defy all
the world – and can also defy you, when neglect
and calamity have driven them to despair. You
may call the people a mob, but do not forget
that a mob too often speaks the sentiments of
the people.

Maiden speech in the House of Lords (27 Feb
1812)

13 ... thou fatal Waterloo!
Millions of tongues record thee, and anew
Their children's lips shall echo them, and say –
'Here, where the sword united nations drew,
Our countrymen were warring on that day!'
And this is much, and all which will not
pass away.

Childe Harold's Pilgrimage (1812–18), Canto 3
(1816), st.35

Quoted in the White House by Winston
Churchill to Franklin D Roosevelt (Jan 1942)
when they decided to change the term Associated Powers to United Nations in the treaty
they wished to be signed by all free nations

14 To fly from, need not be to hate, mankind...

Childe Harold's Pilgrimage (1812–18), Canto 3, st.69

15 I live not in myself, but I become
Portion of that around me; and to me,
High mountains are a feeling, but the hum

Of human cities torture. . .

Childe Harold's Pilgrimage (1812–18), Canto 3, st.72

6 I have not loved the world, nor the world me;
I have not flattered its rank breath, nor bow'd
To its idolatries a patient knee. . .

Childe Harold's Pilgrimage (1812–18), Canto 3, st.113

7 'Tis solitude should teach us how to die;
It hath no flatterers; vanity can give
No hollow aid; alone – man with his God must strive. . .

Childe Harold's Pilgrimage (1812–18), Canto 4, st.33. Cf. John Stuart Blackie 2

8 . . . the Ariosto of the North. . .

Childe Harold's Pilgrimage (1812–18), Canto 4, st.40

On Walter Scott. In a letter to his publisher John Murray from Venice (17 Sep 1817), Byron wrote 'If you think Scott will dislike it – say so – & I expunge. – I do not call him the "*Scotch* Ariosto" which would be sad *provincial* eulogy – but the "Ariosto of the *North*" – meaning of *all countries* that are not the *South*.'

9 Alas! our young affections run to waste,
Or water but the desert.

Childe Harold's Pilgrimage (1812–18), Canto 4, st.120

10 There is a pleasure in the pathless woods,
There is a rapture on the lonely shore,
There is society, where none intrudes,
By the deep Sea, and music in its roar:
I love not Man the less, but Nature more,
From these our interviews, in which I steal
From all I may be, or have been before,
To mingle with the Universe, and feel
What I can ne'er express, yet cannot all conceal.

Childe Harold's Pilgrimage (1812–18), Canto 4, st.178

11 Roll on, thou deep and dark blue ocean – roll!
Ten thousand fleets sweep over thee in vain;
Man marks the earth with ruin – his control
Stops with the shore.

Childe Harold's Pilgrimage (1812–18), Canto 4, st.179

12 . . . I do think. . . the mighty stir made about scribbling and scribes, by themselves and others – a sign of effeminacy, degeneracy, and weakness. Who would write, who had anything better to do?

Journal (24 Nov 1813), in L A Marchand (ed.), *Byron's Letters and Journals*, Vol.3 (1974)

13 All are inclined to believe what they covet, from a lottery-ticket up to a passport to Paradise, – in which, from description, I see nothing very tempting.

Journal (27 Nov 1813), in L A Marchand (ed.), *Byron's Letters and Journals*, Vol.3 (1974)

24 I by no means rank poetry or poets high in the scale of intellect – this may look like Affectation – but it is my real opinion. . . I prefer the talents of *action* – of war – or the Senate – or even of Science – to all the speculations of those mere dreamers of another existence. . . and spectators of this.

Letter to Annabella Milbanke (29 Nov 1813), in L A Marchand (ed.), *Byron's Letters and Journals*, Vol.3 (1974)

25 What an antithetical mind! – tenderness, roughness – delicacy, coarseness – sentiment, sensuality – soaring and grovelling, dirt and deity – all mixed up in that one compound of inspired clay!

On Robert Burns. Journal (13 Dec 1813), in L A Marchand (ed.), *Byron's Letters and Journals*, Vol.3 (1974)

26 Mark! where his carnage and his conquests cease!
He makes a solitude – and calls it – peace!

The Bride of Abydos (1813), Canto 2, st.20. Cf. Galgacus 1

27 . . . but what is Hope? nothing but the paint on the face of Existence; the least touch of truth rubs it off, and then we see what a hollow-cheeked harlot we have got hold of.

Letter to Thomas Moore (28 Oct 1815), in L A Marchand (ed.), *Byron's Letters and Journals*, Vol.4 (1975)

28 She walks in beauty, like the night
Of cloudless climes and starry skies;
And all that's best of dark and bright
Meet in her aspect and her eyes:
Thus mellow'd to that tender light
Which heaven to gaudy day denies.

'She Walks in Beauty', *Hebrew Melodies* (1815), st.1

29 There's not a joy the world can give like that it takes away,
When the glow of early thought declines in feeling's dull decay.

'Stanzas for Music' (1815), st.1

30 If I should meet thee
After long years,
How should I greet thee? –
With silence and tears.

'When we two parted' (1815)

31 And so – you want to come to London – it is a damned place – to be sure – but the only one in the world – (at least in the English world) for fun – though I have seen parts of the Globe that I like better – still upon the whole it is the completest either to help one in feeling oneself alive – or forgetting that one is so.

Letter to James Hogg (1 Mar 1816), in L A

Marchand (ed.), *Byrons Letters and Journals*, Vol.5 (1976)

32 So, we'll go no more a roving
So late into the night,
Though the heart be still as loving,
And the moon be still as bright.
'So, We'll Go No More A Roving' (1817), st.1.
Cf. Traditional songs 47

33 Though the night was made for loving,
And the day returns too soon,
Yet we'll go no more a roving
By the light of the moon.
'So, We'll Go No More A Roving' (1817), st.3

34 MANFRED: Old man! 'tis not so difficult to die.
Manfred (2nd edition, 1818), Act 3, sc.4, l.151
This line was removed without Byron's consent from the first published edition

35 What men call gallantry, and gods adultery,
Is much more common where the climate's sultry.
Don Juan (1819–24), Canto 1, st.63

36 Sweet is revenge – especially to women.
Don Juan (1819–24), Canto 1, st.124

37 Pleasure's a sin, and sometimes sin's a pleasure.
Don Juan (1819–24), Canto 1, st.133

38 Man's love is of his life a thing apart,
'Tis woman's whole existence.
Don Juan (1819–24), Canto 1, st.194
In some versions of the poem, 'his' is given as 'man's'

39 There's nought, no doubt, so much the spirit calms
As rum and true religion.
Don Juan (1819–24), Canto 2, st.34

40 Let us have wine and woman, mirth and laughter,
Sermons and soda water the day after.
Don Juan (1819–24), Canto 2, st.178

41 Man, being reasonable, must get drunk;
The best of life is but intoxication:
Glory, the grape, love, gold, in these are sunk
The hopes of all men, and of every nation.
Don Juan (1819–24), Canto 2, st.179

42 Marriage from love, like vinegar from wine –
A sad, sour, sober beverage – by time
Is sharpen'd from its high celestial flavour,
Down to a very homely household savour.
Don Juan (1819–24), Canto 3, st.5

43 Think you, if Laura had been Petrarch's wife,
He would have written sonnets all his life?
Don Juan (1819–24), Canto 3, st.8

44 Even good men like to make the public stare.
Don Juan (1819–24), Canto 3, st.81

45 His Highness gazed upon Gulbeyaz' charms,
Expecting all the welcome of a lover,
(A 'Highland welcome' all the wide world over.)
Don Juan (1819–24), Canto 6, st.13.
Cf. Robert Burns 54

46 A lady of a 'certain age', which means
Certainly aged.
Don Juan (1819–24), Canto 6, st.69

47 But I am half a Scot by birth, and bred
A whole one, and my heart flies to my head, –

As 'Auld Lang Syne' brings Scotland, one and all,
Scotch plaids, Scotch snoods, the blue hills, and clear streams,
The Dee, the Don, Balgounie's Brig's *black wall*,
All my boy feelings, all my gentler dreams
Of what I *then dreamt*, clothed in their own pall,
Like Banquo's offspring.
Don Juan (1819–24), Canto 10, st.17–18

48 I '*scotched*, not killed,' the Scotchman in my blood,
And love the land of 'mountain and of flood'.
Don Juan (1819–24), Canto 10, st.19.
Cf. Walter Scott 8, 96

49 And, after all, what is a lie? 'Tis but
The truth in masquerade.
Don Juan (1819–24), Canto 11, st.37

50 The English winter – ending in July,
To recommence in August.
Don Juan (1819–24), Canto 13, st.42. Cf. Billy Connolly 10

51 'Tis strange – but true; for Truth is always strange,
Stranger than Fiction...
Don Juan (1819–24), Canto 14, st.101

52 He who first met the Highlands' swelling blue,
Will love each peak that shews a kindred hue,
Hail in each crag a friend's familiar face,
And clasp the mountain in his mind's embrace.
The Island, or Christian and his Comrades (1823), Canto 2, st.12

53 Damn it, Tom, don't be poetical.
To his friend the poet Thomas Moore, as they watched the sun set over Venice. Quoted in Walter Scott's *Journal* (13 Mar 1826)

54 I awoke one morning and found myself famous.
On the 'overnight' success of the first two cantos of *Childe Harold's Pilgrimage*, published 1812. Quoted in Thomas Moore, *Letters and Journals of Lord Byron* (1830), Vol. 1, p.346

C

Caimbeul, Maoilios M
(Myles Campbell) 1944–
Poet

1 Muile nam monaidhean farsaing
agus nam bailtean gun daoine;
an clamhan air chaithris 'na rioghachd
ag éisdeachd ri beul-aithris na gaoithe.

† Mull of the spacious moors
and the deserted townships;
the buzzard wakeful in his kingdom
listening to the oral tradition of the wind.

> 'An Clamhan' ('The Buzzard'), *Bailtean*
> (*Villages/Towns*, 1987)

2 Aile a gheallas Earrach;
ged a tha e fuar fhathast,
tha spiorad uaine san aire
aig talamh is daoin'.

† A promise of spring in the air;
although it is still cold,
people and earth
are aware of a green spirit.

> 'Latha Faoiltich' ('A January Day'), *Bailtean*
> (*Villages/Towns*, 1987), st.7

Cairncross, Sir Alexander Kirkland
1911–

Economist

1 A trend is a trend is a trend
But the question is, will it bend?
Will it alter its course
Through some unforeseen force
And come to a premature end?

> 'Stein Age Forecaster', in 'Economic Forecasting',
> *Economic Journal* (Dec 1969)

2 It is common for professional economists, when
they first come in contact with administrators,
to feel that the administrator is grossly
ignorant of elementary economics. Sometimes
this is justified; but it is equally true that the
professional economist may be grossly ignorant
of administration.

> 'Economists in Government', *Essays in Economic
> Management* (1971)

Cairns, Joyce 1947–

Painter

1 I see life as a comedy. It's about living
and experience, a burlesque with evil

undertones.

> 'Artist's comment', in Bill Hare, *Contemporary
> Painting in Scotland* (1992), p.40

Caldwell, James
Glasgow glazier and glass merchant

1 Suffragettes may break windows, but I am the
wee boy can put them in.

> Advertisement which ran for about a year in
> *Forward* (1912–13)
>
> > Window-smashing was one of the strategies
> > resorted to by militant suffragettes

Cameron, Andy
Comedian

1 We're on the road wi Ally's Army,
We're gaun tae the Argentine,
And we'll really shake them up
When we win the World Cup
'Cos Scotland is the greatest football team.

> 'Ally's Army' (1978), chorus
>
> > The boundless optimism of this song (referring
> > to Ally MacLeod, the team manager) typified
> > the worst excesses of Scotland's pre-realist
> > 1978 World Cup experience. Journalist Ian
> > Archer, in the 1985 BBC documentary *Only a
> > Game?*, summed it up when he said, 'We just
> > had to skulk around and not talk to English
> > people. Everybody in this country was reduced
> > by what happened over there.'

2 . . . the song sold so many copies and I put
all the money from the single into an LP –
financed it all myself – and the album came
out the day after Iran drew 1-1 with Scotland.
A man in Dundee did a roaring trade, selling
it for a penny and giving you a hammer to
smash it with.

> On the fate of the album made on the strength
> of the success of the song 'Ally's Army'. Quoted
> in Roddy Forsyth, *The Only Game: The Scots
> and World Football* (1990), ch.5

Cameron (of Lochiel), Donald
c.1695–1748

*Chief of Clan Cameron, known as 'Gentle
Lochiel'*

1 I will share the fate of my Prince, and so shall
every man over whom nature or fortune hath

given me any power.

To Prince Charles Edward Stewart (Aug 1745)

> Lochiel was unwilling to support Charles's attempt to regain the throne, and on being summoned to meet him after his arrival in Scotland tried to dissuade him from it. Charles insisted that he would raise his standard and remarked, 'Lochiel, who my father has often told me was our firmest friend, may stay at home, and learn from the newspapers the fate of his Prince.' Lochiel then gave the above response, and his decision was influential in bringing out many other chiefs

Cameron (of Lochiel), Sir Ewen
1629–1719
Influential Royalist and Jacobite clan chief

1 Is coma leis an Righ Eoghainn; is coma le Eoghainn co-dhiùbh.

† The King doesn't care for Ewen; Ewen doesn't care anyway.

> Attrib. Said at a time when he was in disfavour at court

Cameron, James Mark 1911–85
Journalist

1 I love short trips to New York; to me it is the finest three-day town on earth.

> *Witness* (1966)

2 . . . an assemblage of recognisably nudging clichés that was defined in our literary terms as 'couthy'. . . Everything had to be written in paragraphs one sentence long, and as far as possible in what was held to be the homely idiom of the Scottish working class, which is to say a costive coyness larded with apostrophes and Doricisms which bore as much likeness to the demotic speech of the Gorbals, say, as it did to Greek.

> On writing for the *Sunday Post* in 1930s Glasgow. *Point of Departure* (1967), ch.2

3 Considerable value was placed on what were known as 'human stories', which by definition concerned animals. To this end I would be obliged to write under the title of Percy the Poodle, or An Unloved Alley-cat. In this character I authored some work so truly horrible that it met with heartfelt acclaim.

> *Point of Departure* (1967), ch.2

4 . . . beautiful, in its monstrous way; a writhing lovely mass. Then. . . the sound of the explosion. . . not a bang, it was a rumble, not overloud, but it thudded into all the corners of the morning like a great door slammed in the deepest hollows of the sea.

On the atom bomb tests at Bikini (1946). *Point of Departure* (1967), ch.3

5 . . . objectivity in some circumstances is both meaningless and impossible. I still do not see how a reporter attempting to define a situation involving some sort of ethical conflict can do it with sufficient demonstrable neutrality to fulfil some arbitrary concept of 'objectivity'. . . I always tended to argue that objectivity was of less importance than the truth, and that the reporter whose technique was informed by no opinion lacked a very serious dimension.

> *Point of Departure* (1967), ch.4

6 The spectacle of the conscientious journalist bemoaning the idealistic shortcomings of his profession is both pitiable and platitudinous, like that of the rueful whore.

> *Point of Departure* (1967), ch.5

7 Hiroshima. . . the most spectacular, destructive, and almost certainly wickedest man-made catastrophe ever known.

> *Point of Departure* (1967), ch.16

8 Today we journalists spend our time splashing in the shallows, reaching on occasions the rare heights of the applauded mediocre. It looks, perhaps, easier than it is.

> To the individual in this machine it brings its own dilemma: the agonising narrow line between sincerity and technique, between the imperative and the glib – so fine and delicate a boundary that one frequently misses it altogether, especially with a tight deadline, a ringing phone, a thirst, and an unquiet mind.

> *Point of Departure* (1967), ch.18

9 Hope subsides, but curiosity remains. Every day is, necessarily, and even now, a point of departure.

> *Point of Departure* (1967), ch.18

Cameron, Richard c.1648–1680
Covenanting preacher and martyr

1 Lord, spare the green and take the ripe.

> Prayer before a skirmish with government forces at Ayrsmoss near Auchinleck (22 Jul 1680) in which Cameron himself was killed

Campbell, Angus Peter
Poet, journalist and broadcaster

1 From Pennsylvania to Paris they all now knew what Scotland in general, and the Highlands in particular, was like: a place where comic tartan-wearing country folk went around singing happily of their lot in a northern Shangri La.

On the merits of the 1954 film *Brigadoon*. Quoted in Malcolm MacLean and Christopher Carrell (eds), *As an Fhearann* (*From the Land*, 1986), 'The Moving Picture'

> Arthur Freed, the film's producer, defended the decision to film in the studio rather than on location by saying, 'I went to Scotland but I could find nothing that looked like Scotland.' Quoted in Forsyth Hardy, *Scotland in Film* (1990), ch.1

Campbell, Anna see Chaimbeul, Anna

Campbell, Sir Colin (Lord Clyde)
1796–1863

Soldier

1 By means of patience, common-sense and time, impossibility becomes possibility.

> Written in his memorandum book (1832) as a junior officer

2 We'll hae nane but Hielan bonnets here!

> Exhorting the troops of his Highland Brigade to capture the Russian positions at the Battle of the Alma (1854) in the Crimean War

>> This phrase became the refrain of a song celebrating this episode, written by Alexander Maclagan (1811–79)

3 Bring forward the tartan! Let my own lads at them!

> At the relief of Lucknow (Nov 1857) in India, ordering the 93rd Highlanders into attack

>> Later adopted as the motto of the Scottish Tartans Society, 'Bring Forrit the Tartan'

Campbell, Donald 1940–

Poet and playwright

1 The kind of audience I want is what Brecht called the cigar-smoking audience. They could watch a play, understand it, but respond to it in a non-reverential manner. A lot of theatre today is carried on in 'controlled conditions'. . . I want an audience that goes to a play like they'd go to a pub, or to church, or to a pop concert or a football game, or to play snooker.

> Interview in *Radical Scotland* No.21 (Jun/Jul 1986)

Campbell, John see Argyll, 4th Duke of

Campbell (of Islay), John Francis
1822–85

Folklorist

1 To wash gold, a man must be skilled in practical hydraulics; to know where to seek, he must

know the nature of burns; to find the source of the gold, he must be wise in other ways.

> *Something from 'The Diggins' in Sutherland* (pamphlet, 20 Apr 1869)

Campbell, Myles
see Caimbeul, Maoilios M

Campbell, Thomas 1777–1844

Poet and journalist, editor of The New Monthly Magazine *from 1820 to 1830*

1 On the green banks of Shannon, when Sheelah was nigh,
No blithe Irish lad was so happy as I;
No harp like my own could so cheerily play,
And wherever I went was my poor dog Tray.

> 'The Harper' (1799), st.1

2 'Tis distance lends enchantment to the view,
And robes the mountain in its azure hue.

> *Pleasures of Hope* (1799), Part 1, ll.7–8

3 What millions died – that Caesar might be great!

> *The Pleasures of Hope* (1799), Part 2, l.174

4 Cease, every joy, to glimmer on my mind,
But leave – oh! leave the light of Hope behind!
What though my winged hours of bliss
  have been,
Like angel-visits, few and far between,
Her musing mood shall every pang appease,
And charm – when pleasures lose the power
  to please!

> *The Pleasures of Hope* (1799), Part 2, ll.375–80

5 Lochiel, Lochiel! beware of the day;
For, dark and despairing, my sight I may seal,
But man cannot cover what God would reveal;
'Tis the sunset of life gives me mystical lore,
And coming events cast their shadow before.

> 'Lochiel's Warning' (1802)

>> A Highland seer is prophesying the fate of the 'Forty-Five, and Lochiel's role in it

6 And yet, amidst that joy and uproar,
Let us think of them that sleep,
Full many a fathom deep,
By thy wild and stormy steep,
Elsinore!

> 'The Battle of the Baltic' (1809), st.8

7 On Linden, when the sun was low,
All bloodless lay th' untrodden snow;
And dark as winter was the flow
Of Iser, rolling rapidly.

> 'Hohenlinden' (1809), st.1

8 A chieftain to the Highlands bound
Cries 'Boatman, do not tarry!

And I'll give thee a silver pound
To row us o'er the ferry.'

'Lord Ullin's Daughter' (1809), st.1

9 And call they this Improvement? – to have
changed,
My native Clyde, thy once romantic shore,
Where Nature's face is banished and estranged,
And Heaven reflected in thy wave no more;
Whose banks, that sweetened May-day's
breath before,
Lie sere and leafless now in summer's beam,
With sooty exhalations covered o'er;
And for the daisied green sward, down
thy stream
Unsightly brick-lanes smoke, and clanking
engines gleam.

'Lines on Revisiting a Scottish River' (1827), st.1

Campbell-Bannerman, Sir Henry
1836–1908

*Liberal MP for Stirling (1868–1908), British
Prime Minister (1905–8)*

1 A phrase often used is that 'war is war', but
when one comes to ask about it one is told
that no war is going on, or that it is not war.
When is a war not a war? When it is carried
on by methods of barbarism in South Africa.

Speech to the National Reform Union (14 Jun
1901). Quoted in John Wilson, *CB: A Life of
Sir Henry Campbell-Bannerman* (1973), ch.22

He was protesting against British brutality,
including the use of concentration camps,
against the Boers

2 I seldom venture as you have done into the
wilds of the Scotch Highlands. They are not the
working & really dominant part of the country: I
find the humdrum lowlands interesting enough:
and I keep my temper even by avoiding even
the sight of the shooting tenant and ghillie-
dom which is the curse of Celtic Caledonia.

Letter (Oct 1905), quoted in John Wilson,
CB: A Life of Sir Henry Campbell-Bannerman
(1973), ch.11

3 Good government can never be a substitute
for government by the people themselves.

Speech at Stirling (23 Nov 1905), quoted in the
Daily News (24 Nov 1905)

Cant, Bob 1945–

Writer and voluntary sector worker

1 Lesbians and gay men are, for the most
part, invisible in Scotland. The few public
references that are made to us – by teachers,
by preachers, by politicians, by pundits –
imply that we are Other, that we are 'these

people', that we do not belong. . .

Silence in the public arena has been a major
mode of control of homosexual people both
in Scotland and in the UK as a whole.

In Bob Cant (ed.), *Footsteps and Witnesses:
Lesbian and Gay Lifestories from Scotland* (1993),
Introduction

Carlyle, Alexander ('Jupiter Carlyle')
1722–1805

*'Moderate' Church of Scotland minister of
Inveresk (1748–1805) and man of letters*

1 She was gorgeously dressed: her face was
like the moon, and patched all over, not for
ornament, but for use. For these eighty years
I have been wandering in this wilderness, I
have seen nothing like her. . . she appeared to
me to be the lady with whom all well-educated
children were acquainted, the Great Scarlet
Whore of Babylon.

On meeting Lady Grange as a child. *Autobiography* (first published 1860, ed. J H Burton; 1910
edition), ch.1, p.15, footnote

The eccentric Lady Grange was afterwards
removed to St Kilda by her husband and held
in captivity there and on other islands until
her death. Cf. Lady Grange 1

2 This lady was famous, even in the Annandale
border, both at the bowl and in battle: she
could drink a Scots pint of brandy with ease;
and when the men grew obstreperous in their
cups, she could either put them out of doors,
or to bed, as she found most convenient.

On Lady Bridekirk of Dumfriesshire, c.1733.
Autobiography (1860; ed. J H Burton, 1910), ch.1,
p.28, footnote

3 . . . a mistake into which the English authors
have fallen. . . is, that the people of Scotland
have no humour. That this is a gross mistake,
could be proved by innumerable songs, ballads,
and stories that are prevalent in the south of
Scotland. . . Since we began to affect speaking
a foreign language, which the English dialect
is to us, humour, it must be confessed, is less
apparent in conversation.

Autobiography (1860; ed. J H Burton, 1910),
ch.5, p.232

4 Mr Robert Alexander, wine merchant, a very
worthy man, but a bad speaker, entertained
us all with warm suppers and excellent claret,
as a recompense for the patient hearing of his
ineffectual attempts, when I often thought he
would have beat out his brains on account of
their constipation.

On meetings of the Select Society (formed in
1754). *Autobiography* (1860; ed. J H Burton,
1910), ch.7, p.312

5 . . . that liquor, without which no Scotch gentleman in those days could be exhilarated.

> On claret. *Autobiography* (1860; ed. J H Burton, 1910), ch.9, p.367

Carlyle, Jane Welsh (*née* Jane Baillie Welsh) 1801–66

Letter writer and diarist, wife of Thomas Carlyle

1 He scratched the fenders dreadfully – I must have a pair of carpet-shoes and hand-cuffs prepared for him the next time – his tongue only should be left at liberty: his other members are most fantastically awkward. . .

> On an early visit by her future husband to her mother's house. Letter to her cousin Eliza Stodart (c.12 Feb 1822), in C R Sanders and K J Fielding (eds), *Collected Letters of Thomas and Jane Welsh Carlyle*, Vol.2 (1970), p.38

2 Really there is nothing at all amusing in one's mode of existence here. A tea-party, a quarrel or a *report* of a marriage now and then, are the only excitements this precious little Borough affords.

> On life in her mother's house in Haddington. Letter to Eliza Stodart (30 Mar 1823), in C R Sanders and K J Fielding (eds), *Collected Letters of Thomas and Jane Welsh Carlyle*, Vol.2 (1970), p.317

3 And Byron is dead! I was told it all at once in a room full of people, My God if they had said that the sun or the moon had gone out of the heavens it could not have struck me with the idea of a more awful and dreary blank in creation than the words, Byron is dead. . .

> Letter (20 May 1824) to her future husband, in C R Sanders and K J Fielding (eds), *Collected Letters of Thomas and Jane Welsh Carlyle*, Vol.3 (1970), p.69

4 If I have an antipathy for any class of people it is for *fine ladies*. . . Woe to the fine lady who should find herself set down at Craigenputtock for the first time in her life, left alone with her thoughts, no *'fancy bazaar'* in the same kingdom with her, no place of amusement within a day's journey; the very church, her last imaginable resource, seven miles off. I can fancy with what horror she would look on the ridge of mountains that seemed to enclose her from all earthly bliss! with what despair in her accents she would enquire if there was not even a 'charity sale' within reach.

> Letter to Eliza Miles (16 Jun 1832), in C R Sanders and K J Fielding (eds), *Collected Letters of Thomas and Jane Welsh Carlyle*, Vol.6 (1970), pp.171–2

5 . . . I am more and more persuaded that there is no complete misery in the world that does not emanate from the bowels.

> Letter to Eliza Stodart (c. Aug 1834), in C R Sanders and K J Fielding (eds), *Collected Letters of Thomas and Jane Welsh Carlyle*, Vol.7 (1977), p.251

6 To see how they live and waste here it is a wonder the whole City does not bankrape, and go out o' sight – flinging platefuls of what they are pleased to denominate *'crusts'* (that is, what I consider all the best of the bread) into the ash-pits – I often say with honest self-congratulation, in Scotland we have no such thing as *'crusts'*.

> Letter from Chelsea to her mother-in-law, Mrs Carlyle (1 Sep 1834), in C R Sanders and K J Fielding (eds), *Collected Letters of Thomas and Jane Welsh Carlyle*, Vol.7 (1977), p.288

7 On the whole, tho' the English Ladies seem to have their wits more at their finger-ends and have a great advantage over me in that respect, I never cease to be glad that I was born on the other side the Tweed, and that those who are nearest and Dearest to me are Scotch.

> Letter from Chelsea to her mother-in-law, Mrs Carlyle (1 Sep 1834), in C R Sanders and K J Fielding (eds), *Collected Letters of Thomas and Jane Welsh Carlyle*, Vol.7 (1977), p.288

8 Of late weeks Carlyle has. . . been getting on better with his writing, which has been uphill work since the burning of the first manuscript. . . One chapter more brings him to the end of his *second first* volume, and then we shall sing a *te deum* and get drunk. . .

> Letter to Mrs Jean Aitken (Aug 1835), in C R Sanders and K J Fielding (eds), *Collected Letters of Thomas and Jane Welsh Carlyle*, Vol.8 (1981), p.194
>
> > In March 1835, Thomas Carlyle had lent the only copy of the manuscript of Book 1 of his *History of the French Revolution* to John Stuart Mill, who accidentally set it on fire; only a few pages survived. Carlyle took five months to rewrite the book, the second version of which Jane thought was 'a little less vivacious, perhaps, but better thought and put together. . .'

9 . . . Quelle vie! let no woman who values peace of soul ever dream of marrying an Author! – that is to say if he is an honest one, who makes a conscience of *doing* the thing he pretends to do.

> Letter to John Sterling (1 Feb 1837), in C R Sanders and K J Fielding (eds), *Collected Letters of Thomas and Jane Welsh Carlyle*, Vol.9 (1981), p.134

10 . . . genuine, unsophisticated nature, I grant you, is all very amiable and harmless – but beautiful nature which Man has *exploited* as a Reviewer does a work of genius – making it a peg to hang his own conceits upon. . .

beautiful nature which you look out upon from pea-green arbours – which you dawdle about in on the backs of donkeys – and where you are haunted with an everlasting smell of roast meat – all that I do declare to be the greatest of bores, and I would rather spend my days amidst acknowledged brick houses and paved streets than [in] any such fools' paradise.

> Letter to Thomas Carlyle (29 Aug 1837), in C R Sanders and K J Fielding (eds), *Collected Letters of Thomas and Jane Welsh Carlyle*, Vol.9 (1981), p.299.

11 I am always wondering since I came here how I can ever in my angriest mood talk about leaving you for good and all – for to be sure if I *were* to leave you today *on that principle* I should need absolutely to go back tomorrow *to see how you were taking it!*

> Letter from Liverpool to Thomas Carlyle (2 Jul 1844), in C R Sanders and K J Fielding (eds), *Collected Letters of Thomas and Jane Welsh Carlyle*, Vol.18 (1990), p.99

12 If I were going. . . to take up a mission, it would be the reverse of Fanny Wright's – instead of boiling up *individuals* into the *species* I would draw a chalk circle round every individuality – and preach it to keep within *that*, and preserve and cultivate its identity at the expense of ever so much lost gilt lacker of other people's *isms*.

> Letter to Thomas Carlyle (5 Aug 1845), in C R Sanders and K J Fielding (eds), *Collected Letters of Thomas and Jane Welsh Carlyle*, Vol.19 (1993), p.131
>
> Fanny (Frances) Wright (1795–1852) was a Scottish-born radical reformer and abolitionist, who emigrated to the USA in 1818

13 . . . nobody out of Bedlam even educated in Edinburgh can contrive to doubt of Death. One may go a fair way in Scepticism – may get to disbelieve in God and Devil, in Virtue and in Vice, in Love, in one's own Soul. . . *isms* world without end, everything in short that the human mind ever believed in or 'believed that it believed in' – only *not* in *Death*!

> Letter to Thomas Carlyle (15 Jul 1846), in C R Sanders and K J Fielding (eds), *Collected Letters of Thomas and Jane Welsh Carlyle*, Vol.20 (1993), p.240

14 When one has been threatened with a great injustice, one accepts a smaller as a favour.

> Diary entry (21 Nov 1855). *Letters and Memorials of Jane Welsh Carlyle* (ed. J A Froude, 1882), Vol.2
>
> She had spent most of the day at the Kensington tax office, arguing that as her husband had not earned anything from his writing in the last year, his tax bill should be cancelled. After much wrangling, it was reduced

15 . . . not a hundredth part of the thoughts in my head have ever been or ever will be spoken or written – as long as I keep my senses, at least.

> Letter to Thomas Carlyle (16 Jul 1858). *Letters and Memorials of Jane Welsh Carlyle* (ed. J A Froude, 1882), Vol.2

16 Blessed be the inventor of photography! I set him above even the inventor of chloroform! It has given more positive pleasure to poor suffering humanity than anything that has 'cast up' in my time or is like to – this art by which even the 'poor' can possess themselves of tolerable likenesses of their absent dear ones. And mustn't it be acting favourably on the morality of the country?

> Letter to Mrs Stirling (21 Oct 1859). *Letters and Memorials of Jane Welsh Carlyle* (ed. J A Froude, 1882), Vol.3

17 My dear, if Mr Carlyle's digestion had been better there is no telling what he might have done.

> Said in response to Mrs Oliphant's remark about 'the way in which Mr Carlyle alone, of all his peers, seemed to have trodden the straight way'. Quoted by Mrs Oliphant in her article 'Thomas Carlyle', *Macmillan's Magazine* (Apr 1881)

Carlyle, Thomas 1795–1881
Historian, essayist and philosopher

1 Poets such as Byron and Rousseau are like opium eaters; they raise their minds by brooding over and embellishing their sufferings, from one degree of fervid exaltation and dreary greatness to another, till at length they run *amuck* entirely, and whoever meets them would do well to run them thro' the body.

> Letter to William Graham (28 Jan 1821), in C R Sanders and K J Fielding (eds), *Collected Letters of Thomas and Jane Welsh Carlyle*, Vol.1 (1970), p.316
>
> In *Sartor Resartus* (1833–4), Bk 2, ch.9, Carlyle confirmed his low opinion of Byron when he wrote, 'Close thy Byron; open thy Goethe'

2 . . . this accursed, stinking, reeky mass of stones and lime and dung.

> On Edinburgh. Letter to his brother John (10 Feb 1821), in C R Sanders and K J Fielding (eds), *Collected Letters of Thomas and Jane Welsh Carlyle*, Vol.1 (1970), p.325

3 *The Man should bear rule in the house and not the Woman.* This is an eternal axiom, the Law of Nature herself which no mortal departs from unpunished. I have meditated on this many long years, and every day it grows plainer to me: I must not and I cannot live in a house of which I am not head. I should be miserable myself, and make all about me miserable.

Letter to Jane Welsh, his future wife (2 Apr 1826), in C R Sanders and K J Fielding (eds), *Collected Letters of Thomas and Jane Welsh Carlyle*, Vol.4 (1970), p.69. Cf. Lord Kames 13

4 It is the nature of a woman, again, (for she is essentially *passive* not *active*) to cling to the man for support and direction, to comply with his humours and feel pleasure in doing so, simply because they are his; to reverence while she loves him, to conquer him not by her force but her weakness, and perhaps (the cunning gypsy!) after all to command him by obeying him.

Letter to Jane Welsh (2 Apr 1826), in C R Sanders and K J Fielding (eds), *Collected Letters of Thomas and Jane Welsh Carlyle*, Vol.4 (1970), p.69

5 The three great elements of modern civilisation, Gunpowder, Printing, and the Protestant religion.

'The State of German Literature' (1827), *Critical and Miscellaneous Essays*. Cf. R B Cunninghame Graham 12

6 . . . a well-written Life is almost as rare as a well-spent one. . .

'Jean Paul Friedrich Richter' (1827), *Critical and Miscellaneous Essays*

7 Were we required to characterise this age of ours by any single epithet, we should be tempted to call it, not an Heroical, Devotional, Philosophical, or Moral Age, but, above all others, the Mechanical Age. It is the Age of Machinery. . .

'Signs of the Times' (1829), *Critical and Miscellaneous Essays*

8 We remove mountains, and make seas our smooth highway; nothing can resist us. We war with rude Nature; and, by our resistless engines, come off always victorious, and loaded with spoils.

'Signs of the Times' (1829), *Critical and Miscellaneous Essays*

9 . . . the Bible Society. . . is found, on inquiry, to be altogether an earthly contrivance: supported by collection of moneys, by fomenting of vanities, by puffing, intrigue and chicane; a machine for converting the Heathen.

'Signs of the Times' (1829), *Critical and Miscellaneous Essays*

10 Men are grown mechanical in head and in heart, as well as in hand.

'Signs of the Times' (1829), *Critical and Miscellaneous Essays*

11 The truth is, men have lost their belief in the Invisible, and believe, and hope, and work only in the Visible; or, to speak it in other words: This is not a Religious age.

'Signs of the Times' (1829), *Critical and Miscellaneous Essays*

12 The time is sick and out of joint.

'Signs of the Times' (1829), *Critical and Miscellaneous Essays*. See Shakespeare, *Hamlet*, Act 1, sc.5, l.188

13 To reform a world, to reform a nation, no wise man will undertake; and all but foolish men know, that the only solid, though a far slower reformation, is what each begins and perfects on *himself*.

'Signs of the Times' (1829), *Critical and Miscellaneous Essays*, concluding sentence

14 History is the essence of innumerable Biographies.

'On History' (1830), *Critical and Miscellaneous Essays*

15 Man is a Tool-using Animal. . . Nowhere do you find him without Tools: without Tools he is nothing, with Tools he is all.

Sartor Resartus (1833–4), Bk 1, ch.5

16 Be not the slave of Words.

Sartor Resartus (1833–4), Bk 1, ch.8

17 Language is called the Garment of Thought: however, it should rather be, Language is the Flesh-Garment, the Body, of Thought.

Sartor Resartus (1833–4), Bk 1, ch.11

18 Man's Unhappiness as I construe, comes of his Greatness; it is because there is an Infinite in him, which with all his cunning he cannot quite bury under the Finite.

Sartor Resartus (1833–4), Bk 2, ch.9

19 Is not Sentimentalism twin-sister to Cant, if not one and the same with it?

History of the French Revolution (1837), Vol.1, Bk 2, ch.7

20 . . . History a distillation of Rumour. . .

History of the French Revolution (1837), Vol.1, Bk 7, ch.5

21 . . . does the reader inquire. . . what the difference between Orthodoxy or *My-doxy* and Heterodoxy or *Thy-doxy* might be?

History of the French Revolution (1837), Vol.2, Bk 4, ch.2

22 'A Republic?' said the Seagreen, with one of his dry husky *unsportful* laughs, 'What is that?' O seagreen Incorruptible, thou shalt see!

On Maximilien Robespierre. *History of the French Revolution* (1837), Vol.2, Bk 4, ch.4

23 What a man *kens* he *cans*.

History of the French Revolution (1837), Vol.3, Bk 3, ch.4

24 Aristocracy of Feudal Parchment has passed away with a mighty rushing; and now, by a natural course, we arrive at Aristocracy of the Moneybag.

History of the French Revolution (1837), Vol.3, Bk 7, ch.7

25 . . . there is no heroic poem in the world but is at bottom a biography, the life of a man: also, it may be said, there is no life of a man, faithfully recorded, but is a heroic poem of its sort, rhymed or unrhymed.

'Sir Walter Scott' (1838), *Critical and Miscellaneous Essays*

This essay appeared first as a review of J G Lockhart's *Memoirs of the Life of Sir Walter Scott, Bart.*

26 Under all speech that is good for anything there lies a silence that is better. Silence is deep as Eternity; speech is shallow as Time.

'Sir Walter Scott' (1838), *Critical and Miscellaneous Essays*

27 No man lives without jostling and being jostled; in all ways he has to *elbow* himself through the world, giving and receiving offence.

'Sir Walter Scott' (1838), *Critical and Miscellaneous Essays*

28 . . . the sickliest of recorded ages, when British Literature lay all puking and sprawling in Werterism, Byronism, and other Sentimentalism tearful or spasmodic (fruit of internal *wind*).

'Sir Walter Scott' (1838), *Critical and Miscellaneous Essays*

On the 18th century. 'Nature was kind enough', Carlyle added, to send two healthy men to counter this sickness – Scott and Cobbett

29 The Scotch national character originates in many circumstances; first of all, in the Saxon stuff there was to work on; but next, and beyond all else except that, in the Presbyterian Gospel of John Knox. It seems a good national character; and on some sides not so good. Let Scott thank John Knox, for he owed him much, little as he dreamed of debt in that quarter! No Scotchman of his time was more entirely Scotch than Walter Scott: the good and the not so good, which all Scotchmen inherit, ran through every fibre of him.

'Sir Walter Scott' (1838), *Critical and Miscellaneous Essays*

30 Alas, Scott, with all his health, was *infected*; sick of the fearfulest malady, that of Ambition!. . . Walter Scott, one of the gifted of the world, whom his admirers call the most gifted, must kill himself that he may be a country gentleman, the founder of a race of Scottish lairds.

On the building of Abbotsford. 'Sir Walter Scott' (1838), *Critical and Miscellaneous Essays*

31 . . . these Historical Novels have taught all men this truth. . . that the bygone ages of the world were actually filled by living men, not by protocols, state-papers, controversies and abstractions of men. Not abstractions were they, not diagrams and theorems; but men, in buff or other coats and breeches, with colour in their cheeks, with passions in their stomach, and the idioms, features and vitalities of very men.

On the Waverley Novels. 'Sir Walter Scott' (1838), *Critical and Miscellaneous Essays*

32 A witty statesman said, you might prove anything by figures.

Chartism (1839), ch.2

33 Tables are like cobwebs, like the sieve of Danaides; beautifully reticulated, orderly to look upon, but which will hold no conclusion.

On statistics. *Chartism* (1839), ch.2

34 A man willing to work, and unable to find work, is perhaps the saddest sight that Fortune's inequality exhibits under this sun.

Chartism (1839), ch.4. Cf. Robert Louis Stevenson 103

35 Surely of all 'rights of man', this right of the ignorant man to be guided by the wiser, to be, gently or forcibly, held in the true course by him, is the indisputablest.

Chartism (1839), ch.6

36 It is well said, in every sense, that a man's religion is the chief fact with regard to him.

On Heroes, Hero-Worship and the Heroic in History (1841), Lecture 1, 'The Hero as Divinity'. Cf. J M Barrie 16

37 That great mystery. . . the illimitable, silent, never-resting thing called Time, rolling, rushing on, swift, silent, like an all-embracing ocean-tide, on which we and all the Universe swim like exhalations, like apparitions which *are*, and then *are not*: this is forever very literally a miracle; a thing to strike us dumb, – for we have no word to speak about it.

On Heroes, Hero-Worship and the Heroic in History (1841), Lecture 1, 'The Hero as Divinity'

38 No sadder proof can be given by a man of his own littleness than disbelief in great men.

On Heroes, Hero-Worship and the Heroic in History (1841), Lecture 1, 'The Hero as Divinity'

39 The greatest of faults, I should say, is to be conscious of none.

On Heroes, Hero-Worship and the Heroic in History (1841), Lecture 2, 'The Hero as Prophet'

40 In Books lies the *soul* of the whole Past Time; the articulate audible voice of the Past, when the

body and material substance of it has altogether vanished like a dream.

On Heroes, Hero-Worship and the Heroic in History (1841), Lecture 5, 'The Hero as Man of Letters'

No magic *Rune* is stranger than a Book. All that Mankind has done, thought, gained or been: it is lying as in magic preservation in the pages of Books.

On Heroes, Hero-Worship and the Heroic in History (1841), Lecture 5, 'The Hero as Man of Letters'

The true University of these days is a Collection of Books.

On Heroes, Hero-Worship and the Heroic in History (1841), Lecture 5, 'The Hero as Man of Letters'

Burke said there were Three Estates in Parliament; but, in the Reporters' Gallery yonder, there sat a *Fourth Estate* more important far than they all.

On Heroes, Hero-Worship and the Heroic in History (1841), Lecture 5, 'The Hero as Man of Letters'

A man lives by believing something; not by debating and arguing about many things. A sad case for him when all that he can manage to believe is something he can button in his pocket, and with one or the other organ eat and digest! Lower than that he will not get. . . Genuine Acting ceases in all the world's work; dextrous Similitude of Acting begins. The world's wages are pocketed, the world's work is not done. Heroes have gone out; quacks have come in.

On Heroes, Hero-Worship and the Heroic in History (1841), Lecture 5, 'The Hero as Man of Letters'

Adversity is sometimes hard upon a man; but for one man who can stand prosperity, there are a hundred that will stand adversity.

On Heroes, Hero-Worship and the Heroic in History (1841), Lecture 5, 'The Hero as Man of Letters'

Brothers, I am sorry I have got no Morrison's Pill for curing the maladies of Society.

Past and Present (1843), Bk 1, ch.4

Fire is the best of servants; but what a master!

Past and Present (1843), Bk 2, ch.9

Carlyle had good reason to know: eight years earlier, the manuscript of the first volume of his *History of the French Revolution* was accidentally burnt while in the possession of John Stuart Mill. Cf. Jane Welsh Carlyle 8

All work, even cotton-spinning, is noble; work alone is noble. . . And in like manner too, all dignity is painful; a life of ease is not for any man, nor for any god.

Past and Present (1843), Bk 3, ch.4

49 Cash-payment is not the sole nexus of man with man. . .

Past and Present (1843), Bk 3, ch.9

50 In the long-run every Government is the exact symbol of its People, with their wisdom and unwisdom; we have to say, Like People like Government.

Past and Present (1843), Bk 4, ch.4

51 The Leaders of Industry, if Industry is ever to be led, are virtually the Captains of the World!. . . But let the Captains of Industry consider: once again, are they born of other clay than the old Captains of Slaughter. . . ?

Past and Present (1843), Bk 4, ch.4

52 The sunny plains and deep indigo transparent skies of Italy are all indifferent to the great sick heart of a Sir Walter Scott: on the back of the Apennines, in wild spring weather, the sight of bleak Scotch firs, and snow-spotted heath and desolation, brings tears into his eyes.

Past and Present (1843), Bk 4, ch.5

This passage refers to J G Lockhart's description of Scott, in his last year (1832), travelling in Italy for his health. See *Memoirs of the Life of Sir Walter Scott, Bart.*, ch.82

53 Friday last at Lord Mahon's to breakfast. . . Niagara of eloquent commonplace talk from Macaulay.

Journal (14 Mar 1848)

R M Milnes (Baron Houghton), in his *Notebook* (1838), p.157, quoted Carlyle as saying, 'Macaulay is well for a while, but one wouldn't *live* under Niagara.'

54 Respectable Professors of the Dismal Science.

On political economists. *Latter-Day Pamphlets* (1850), No.1, 'The Present Time'

55 Talk that does not end in any kind of action is better suppressed altogether.

Inaugural address as Rector of Edinburgh University (2 Apr 1866)

56 Work is the grandest cure of all the maladies and miseries that ever beset mankind.

Inaugural address as Rector of Edinburgh University (2 Apr 1866)

57 Maid-servants, I hear people complaining, are getting instructed in the 'ologies.

Inaugural address as Rector of Edinburgh University (2 Apr 1866)

58 If Jesus Christ were to come to-day, people would not even crucify him. They would ask him to dinner, and hear what he had to say, and make fun of it.

Quoted in D A Wilson, *Carlyle at his Zenith* (1927), p.238

Carmichael, Kay

Social work lecturer and political activist

1 [The women of Scotland] have been strong
women, going down in history as sometimes
being stronger than their men as they defied the
soldiers, the landlords and the factors. Their
names are not known, they are lost in history,
but we must make sure that the women of
today are given a place in the new Assembly,
and that their talents are used.

> On proposals for a Scottish Assembly or
> Parliament. Quoted in *Radical Scotland* No.26
> (Apr/May 1987)

Carmina Gadelica 1855–99

*Collection of Gaelic lore made by Alexander
Carmichael (1832–1912) and published in five
volumes (Vols 1–2, 1900; Vol.3, 1940; Vol.4,
1941; Vol.5, 1954)*

1 Gum beannaicheadh Dia do chrois
Mun téid thu thar lear;
Aon ghalar dh'am bi ad chois,
Cha tobhair e thu leis.

† May God bless thy cross
Before thou go over the sea;
Any illness that thou mayest have,
It shall not take thee hence.

> 'Soisgeul Chrìosd' ('The Gospel of Christ'),
> st.1 (Vol.3)
>
> > 'Soisgeul Chrìosd' was the name given to
> > a charm worn to safeguard a person from
> > drowning at sea and evil on land: a word,
> > phrase or verse from one of the Gospels
> > written on parchment or paper and placed in
> > a linen bag sewn into the clothing under the
> > left arm, or in the case of a child hung round
> > the neck on linen cord

2 Is gil thu na 'n eal air loch làthaich,
Is gil thu na faoileag bhàn an t-sruth,
Is gil thu na sneachd nam beann arda,
Is gil thu na gràdh ainglean nan nimh.

† Thou art whiter than the swan on miry lake,
Thou art whiter than the white gull of the
current,
Thou art whiter than the snow of the high
mountains,
Thou art whiter than the love of the angels
of heaven.

> 'Soisgeul Chrìosd' ('The Gospel of Christ'),
> st.9 (Vol.3)

3 A dhaolag, a dhaolag,
An cuimhne leat an la 'n dé
Chaidh Mac De seachad?

† Little beetle, little beetle,
Rememberest thou yesterday
The Son of God went by?

> 'Duan an Daoil' ('Poem of the Beetle') (Vol.2)

This rhyme is connected with a legend that,
when the Jews were searching for Christ to
arrest and execute him, they asked two beetles
if he had passed that way. The gravedigger
beetle readily answered that they had seen
him only yesterday, while the smaller 'sacred'
beetle said it had been a year ago yesterday.
'Because of his ready officiousness against
Christ,' wrote Carmichael, 'the gravedigger
beetle is always killed when seen; while for
his desire to shield Christ, the sacred beetle is
spared, but because he told a lie he is always
turned on his back.'

4 Mathas sùla dhuit,
Mathas ùidhe dhuit,
Mathas rùn mo chléibhe.

† The good of eye be thine,
The good of liking be thine,
The good of my heart's desire.

> 'Dùrachd' ('Good wish'), st.1 (Vol.3)

5 Guth an Dé mhóir,
Agus cha mhór ach e.

† The voice of the great God,
And none is great but He.

> 'Torann' ('Thunder') (Vol.3)

6 Fàilte dhut, a ghealach ùr,
Ailleagan iùil na bàidh!
Ta mi lùbadh dhut mo ghlùn,
Ta mi curnadh dhut mo ghràidh.

† Hail to thee, thou new moon,
Guiding jewel of gentleness!
I am bending to thee my knee,
I am offering thee my love.

> 'A' Ghealach Ur' ('The New Moon'), st.1 (Vol.3)

7 Latha sìth agus sonais
Latha solais mo bhàis;
Làmh Mhìcheil dha m'iarraidh
Latha geal grianach mo shlàint.

† Day of peace and of joy
The bright day of my death;
May Michael's hand seek me
On the white sunny day of my salvation.

> 'Latha a' Bhàis' ('The Day of Death'), st.3 (Vol.3)

8 Fàilte ort féin, a ghrian nan tràth,
'S tu siubhal ard nan speur;
Do cheumaibh treun air sgéith nan ard,
'S tu màthair àigh nan reul.

† Hail to thee, thou sun of the seasons,
As thou traversest the skies aloft;
Thy steps are strong on the wing of the
heavens,
Thou art the glorious mother of the stars.

> 'A' Ghrian' ('The Sun'), st.1 (Vol.3)

9 SMEORACH: Dhomhaill mhóir bhochd!
Dhomhaill mhóir bhochd!
Dhomhaill mhóir bhochd!
Tha 'm pathadh ort!

Tha 'm pathadh ort!
Sgob as e!
Sgob as e!
Chuile diod!
Chuile diod!

† MAVIS: Poor big Donald!
Poor big Donald!
Poor big Donald!
You are thirsty!
You are thirsty!
Drink it off!
Drink it off!
Every drop!
Every drop!

> Rhyme associated with tales of a man with a
> hangover who hears this song of the mavis or
> thrush (Vol.4)

10 AN TARBH GAIDHEALACH: 'S ann air an druim
fhraoich a rugadh mi,
'S ann air an druim fhraoich a rugadh mi,
'S ann air an druim fhraoich a rugadh mi,
'S air bainne bó gaoil a thogadh mi.

AN TARBH GALLDA: Air làr an taigh mhóir a
rugadh mi,
Air làr an taigh mhóir a rugadh mi,
Air làr an taigh mhóir a rugadh mi,
'S air mil 's air beòir 's air fìon 's air feòir a
thogadh mi.

† THE HIGHLAND BULL: 'Tis on the heather ridge
I was born...
And on the milk of a beloved cow was reared.
THE LOWLAND BULL: 'Tis on the floor of the
big house I was born...
And on honey and beer and wine and grasses
was reared.

> 'An Tarbh Gàidhealach' ('The Highland
> Bull') (Vol.4)

>> This item is followed by the note,
>> 'Thionndaidh an tarbh Gàidhealach air agus
>> mharbh e an tarbh Gallda' ('The Highland bull
>> turned on the Lowland bull and killed him')

11 Fhir a shiubhlas gu subhach,
Chan éirich dhut beud na pudhar
Ris a' ghréin na ris an dubhar
'S garbhag an t-sléibh air a shiubhal.

† Thou man who travellest blithely,
Nor hurt nor harm shall befall thee
Nor in sunshine nor in darkness
If but the club-moss be on thy pathway.

> 'Garbhag an t-Sléibhe' ('The Club-Moss') (Vol.4)

12 Sobhrach, sobhrach
'S feada-coille,
Biadh na cloinne
'S t-samhradh;
Geimileachd, geimileachd,
Fìon agus feadagan,
Biadh nam fear
Sa gheamhradh.

† Primrose, primrose
And wood-sorrel,
The children's food
In summer;
'Geimileachd, geimileachd',
Wine and plovers,
The food of men
In winter.

> 'An t-Sobhrach' ('The Primrose') (Vol.4)

13 A sheamarag nan duilleag,
A sheamarag nan dual,
A sheamarag na guidhe,
A sheamarag mo luaidh.

† Thou shamrock of foliage,
Thou shamrock of entwining,
Thou shamrock of the prayer,
Thou shamrock of love.

> 'An t-Seamarag' ('The Shamrock'), st.1 (Vol.4)

14 Thréig an cadal mi o h-Inid,
Tric mi tionntan
Feuch am faic mi do long shiubhlach
Air cuan dubhghorm.

Loma-luath do dharach liathghlas
O shlios Lochlann,
Gach bord cho mìn ri cluaimh nan eala
Air luinn locha.

† Sleep has forsaken me since Shrovetide,
Often I turn
In hope to see thy speeding ship
On blue-black ocean.

Surpassing swift thy bark grey-timbered
From the slope of Lochlann,
Each plank of her smooth as the swans'
plumage
On a loch's billows.

> 'Thréig an cadal mi' ('Sleep has forsaken me'),
> st.1–2 (Vol.4)

15 Chraobh nan ubhal, gun robh Dia leat,
Gun robh gile, gun robh grian leat,
Gun robh gaoth an ear 's an iar leat,
Gun robh gach nì a thànaig riamh leat...

† O apple tree, may God be with thee,
May the moon and the sun be with thee,
May the east and west winds be with thee,
May everything that ever existed be
with thee...

> Address to a warrior-lover, symbolised by the
> apple-tree (Vol.5)

Carnegie, Andrew 1835–1919

*Dunfermline-born American industrialist and
philanthropist*

1 A Working Boy though not bound.

> Signature to letter sent to the Pittsburgh *Dispatch*
> (9 May 1853). Quoted in B J Hendrick, *The Life*

of Andrew Carnegie (1932), Vol.1, ch.4

> He wrote to complain that the Pittsburgh Mechanics' and Apprentices' Library, established as a charity for 'working boys', had recently changed its rules so that only those learning a trade and 'bound' to an employer for a certain period could make use of its resources

2 Pioneering does not pay.

> c.1870. On the steel-making process developed, at great personal cost, by Henry Bessemer. Quoted in B J Hendrick, *The Life of Andrew Carnegie* (1932), Vol.1, ch.10

3 How beautiful is Dunfermline seen from the Ferry Hills, its grand old abbey towering over all, seeming to hallow the city and to lend a charm and dignity to the lowliest tenement. . . What Benares is to the Hindoo, Mecca to the Mohammedan, Jerusalem to the Christian, all that is Dunfermline to me.

> *Our Coaching Trip* (1882), p.185

4 . . . the employer of labour will find it much more to his interest, wherever possible, to allow his works to remain idle and await the result of a dispute than to employ a class of men that can be induced to take the place of other men who have stopped work. . . There is an unwritten law among the best workmen: 'Thou shalt not take thy neighbour's job.'

> On strikes and strike-breaking. 'Results of the Labour Struggle', *Forum* (Aug 1886)

5 While the law [of competition] may be sometimes hard for the individual, it is best for the race, because it insures the survival of the fittest in every department.

> 'Wealth', *North American Review* (Jun 1889)

6 Upon the sacredness of property civilisation itself depends – the right of the labourer to his hundred dollars in the savings bank, and equally the legal right of the millionaire to his millions.

> 'Wealth', *North American Review* (Jun 1889)

7 Surplus wealth is a sacred trust which its possessor is bound to administer in his lifetime for the good of the community.

> 'Wealth', *North American Review* (Jun 1889)

8 The day is not far distant when the man who dies leaving behind him millions of available wealth, which was free for him to administer during life, will pass away 'unwept, unhonoured, and unsung,', no matter to what uses he leave the dross which he cannot take with him. Of such as these the public verdict will then be: 'The man who dies thus rich dies disgraced.' Such, in my opinion, is the true gospel concerning wealth, obedience to which

is destined some day to solve the problem of the rich and the poor, and to bring 'Peace on earth, among men good will.'

> 'Wealth', *North American Review* (Jun 1889)

> This conclusion to Carnegie's influential essay was what made it popularly known as the 'Gospel of Wealth'. 'Unwept, unhonoured, and unsung' comes from Scott's *Lay of the Last Minstrel*. Cf. Walter Scott 7

9 Never employ one of these rioters. Let grass grow over works.

> Telegram sent to company chairman Henry Clay Frick (Jul 1892) in the wake of violent confrontation between workers and strike-breakers at Carnegie's Homestead steel works in Pennsylvania

10 I was brought up among Chartists and Republicans. . . My childhood's desire was to get to be a man and kill a king.

> To W T Stead (1897). Quoted in J F Wall, *Andrew Carnegie* (1970), p.2

11 Steel is Prince or Pauper.

> Quoted in B J Hendrick, *The Life of Andrew Carnegie* (1932), Vol.1, ch.19

> The phrase refers to Carnegie's opposition to profit-sharing schemes for employees in steel-making, on the grounds that steel's economic performance was too uneven for poorer workers to be able to sustain the lean periods

12 Golf is an indispensable adjunct to high civilisation.

> On leaving $200,000 to Yale University to build a golf course

13 Death to Privilege

> Motto used by Carnegie on the family coat of arms, which he designed himself

Carr, Walter 1925–
Comedian and actor

1 . . . the great art of all comedy, of all acting, is to make it look spontaneous. . . to make it sound as if you have just thought of it that second.

> Quoted in Vivien Devlin, *Kings, Queens and People's Palaces: An Oral History of the Scottish Variety Theatre, 1920–1970* (1991), ch.7

2 I think the key traditions of Scottish comedy lie in homeliness. . . To be successful, a good comic must know the lives and experiences of his audience. You must know what it was like to have a stairhead, and to put white clay round, when you washed the steps. You need to be a constant observer of people and remember what your mother and funny aunties said and did. . . that is the basis of our comedy.

> Quoted in Vivien Devlin, *Kings, Queens and*

People's Palaces: An Oral History of the Scottish Variety Theatre, 1920–1970 (1991), ch.10

Carstairs, George Morrison 1916–91
Psychiatrist

1 I am going to talk about teenagers and that means, almost inevitably, that I am going to talk about violence and sex. . .

This Island Now (1962 BBC Reith Lectures), Lecture 3, 'Vicissitudes of Adolescence', opening words

These lectures caused controversy because of Carstairs's liberal views on sex and sexuality

2 I suggest that the creative artist's role in the future may be to keep alive the sense of significance in local and national traditions, and so to combat the deadening effect of uniformity. . . we shall participate most fruitfully in the coming world community if we keep alive a good measure of our eccentricities, our private visions and our peculiar variations on the pattern of mankind.

This Island Now (1962 BBC Reith Lectures), Lecture 6, 'The Changing British Character'

As an example of what he meant, Carstairs quoted from the Scots poetry of Hugh MacDiarmid and Sydney Goodsir Smith

Carswell, Catherine Roxburgh (*née* Macfarlane) 1879–1946
Novelist and critic

1 . . . she stooped once more to the ground, and leaning on her two palms kissed the moist grass till the taste of the earth was on her lips. 'If I forget thee, O Duntarvie,' she whispered, 'let my right hand forget its cunning.' (She was not clear about the meaning of this phrase: but she loved working with her hands, and the words expressed her emotion better than any other words she knew.)

Open the Door (1920), ch.2, section 4 (Joanna). Cf. Robert Louis Stevenson 43

2 Of my writing he said, 'I see. It is like the camomile – the more it is trodden on the faster it grows.'

The Camomile (1922), 'The Journal', 2, 'Studies and Inventions, Feb 17th' (Ellen on Don John)

See Shakespeare, *Henry IV, Part 1*, Act 2, sc.4

3 . . . it *is*, as a rule, a disgrace for a woman never to lose her virginity. Not a disgrace because of what people say, but for her inmost self. I couldn't bear not to get married!

The Camomile (1922), 'The Journal', 2, 'Studies and Inventions, Feb 22nd' (Ellen)

4 She would say I had no right to use any such knowledge as material for fiction, all such knowledge being 'sacred'. Oh, that word! Are not the uses of art more sacred than a million domesticities?

The Camomile (1922), 'The Journal', 2, 'Studies and Inventions, May 1st' (Ellen on Laura)

5 But anyhow it wasn't a woman who betrayed Jesus with a kiss.

Said to John Middleton Murry, literary critic, editor and friend of D H Lawrence (1924). Recorded in her book on Lawrence, *The Savage Pilgrimage* (1932)

Carswell deeply admired Lawrence and was suspicious of Murry's 'effusive' feelings for him. When Murry gave Lawrence a kiss and saw her discomfort, he said, 'Women can't understand this. This is an affair between men. Women can have no part or place in it.' 'Maybe,' replied Carswell, and made the above remark

6 Any notion of Robert as a dreamy-eyed young man weaving rhymes while loitering behind the plough, is as prettified as his portraits. An unwelcome energy informed his speech and his movements. Into his Freemasonry, his friendships and loves, he poured the full violence of living.

The Life of Robert Burns (1930), ch.15

Her warts-and-all portrayal of Burns caused uproar on its publication: newspapers were inundated with letters of (mainly) complaint; the Burns Federation tried unsuccessfully to have the book withdrawn; and Carswell herself received a bullet through the post with a note signed 'Holy Willie', demanding that she use it on herself so that the world would be left 'a better and cleaner place'. (See Thomas Crawford, Introduction to 1990 edition)

7 In a life-long crucifixion Burns summed up what the common poor man feels in widely severed moments of exaltation, insight and desperation. In the recognition and acceptance of this he may have found some solace. . .

The Life of Robert Burns (1930), ch.24

8 Men and women quite suddenly realised that here lay one who was the Poet of his Country – perhaps of mankind – as none had been before, because none before had combined so many human weaknesses with so great an ardour of living and so generous a warmth of admission. Certainly none had ever possessed a racier gift of expression for his own people.

On the death of Burns. *The Life of Robert Burns* (1930), ch.30

9 Youth. . . is proffered advice, middle-age compulsion. But reports concerning old age are so vague and various that each entrant is at liberty to seek a personal procedure.

Lying Awake: An Unfinished Autobiography and Other Posthumous Papers, (ed. John Carswell, 1950), ch.1, 'The Clock'

10 What is wrong with the vegetarians is lack of aesthetic ears and eyes. Who can maintain that a raw quacking duck or cackling hen sounds better than a plucked sizzling one being taken from the oven? Or that a pig is pleasanter to look at coated with mud in its sty than with well browned crackling on the table?

Lying Awake: An Unfinished Autobiography and Other Posthumous Papers, (ed. John Carswell, 1950), ch.6, 'Town and Country'

11 Bach is for me the bread and wine of music. But Mozart takes me to the Milky Way and brings me into the Pleiades and Orion's Belt.

Lying Awake: An Unfinished Autobiography and Other Posthumous Papers, (ed. John Carswell, 1950), ch.10, 'Music: the Arts'

12 The contempt of the hard worker for the idler is as nothing compared to the contempt of the idler for the hard worker. Both are justified.

Lying Awake: An Unfinished Autobiography and Other Posthumous Papers, (ed. John Carswell, 1950), ch.11, 'Letters and Women'

13 When the wife of an artist, painter, singer or what not, goes about saying she 'doesn't understand anything about her husband's particular art', you may be sure that he is not very good in his line. Many women have no understanding of the arts, but all women know talent when they share a bed with it.

Lying Awake: An Unfinished Autobiography and Other Posthumous Papers, (ed. John Carswell, 1950), ch.11, 'Letters and Women'

14 I never can see. . . why in almost everything appreciation of quality should debar one from the appreciation of qualities. Pure gold is pure gold. But there are times when it is more interesting to look over a handful of the precious stuff mixed with dross or cunningly combined with baser metals to form a new amalgam.

Lying Awake: An Unfinished Autobiography and Other Posthumous Papers, (ed. John Carswell, 1950), ch.11, 'Letters and Women'

15 I can truly see only when alone. The most congenial companion takes the edge off my seeing.

Lying Awake: An Unfinished Autobiography and Other Posthumous Papers, (ed. John Carswell, 1950), ch.11, 'Letters and Women'

16 If to have expressive words and balanced phrases ringing in one's head is to be a writer, then I am one.

Lying Awake: An Unfinished Autobiography and Other Posthumous Papers, (ed. John Carswell, 1950), ch.11, 'Letters and Women'

17 Men can and often *do* love their wives but not the women their wives are.

Lying Awake: An Unfinished Autobiography and Other Posthumous Papers, (ed. John Carswell, 1950), ch.12, 'Men and Women'

18 I have found that men, in all other ways admirable, have insisted upon flattery, upon extreme tact, upon suppression of opinion, in short, upon the sort of extreme and conscious consideration one shows to children or to persons suffering from nervous ailments.

Lying Awake: An Unfinished Autobiography and Other Posthumous Papers, (ed. John Carswell, 1950), ch.12, 'Men and Women'. Cf. Marion Reid 1

19 Earnest youth best lays the foundations for a frivolous old age.

Lying Awake: An Unfinished Autobiography and Other Posthumous Papers, (ed. John Carswell, 1950), ch.12, 'Men and Women'

20 Each soul must cut some time or other the umbilical cord and stand up in its essential integrity, knowing that there is a birth independent of heredity, nation, accident and all else. And if there is not there is no creative soul.

Letter to F Marian McNeill (24 Apr 1928). Quoted in *Lying Awake: An Unfinished Autobiography and Other Posthumous Papers*, (ed. John Carswell, 1950)

Carswell, John c.1520–72
Native of Argyll, Bishop of the Isles from 1567

1 Agas is mór an doille agas an dorchadas peacaidh agas aineòlais agas indtleachta do lucht deachtaidh agas sgrìobhtha agas chumhdaigh na Gaoidheilge gurab mó is mian léo agas gurab mó ghnàthuidheas siad eachtradha dìmhaoineacha buaidheartha brègacha saoghalta, do cumadh ar Thuathaibh Dé Dhanond, agas ar Mhacaibh Mileadh, agas ar na curadhaibh, agas [ar] Fhind mhac Cumhaill gona Fhianaibh, agas ar mhóran eile nach àirbhim agas nach indisim andso, do chumhdach agas do choimh-leasughagh, do chiond luathuidheachta dìmhaoinigh an t-saoghail d'fhaghàil dòibh féin, iná briathra dìsle Dé agas slighe foirfe na fìrinde do sgrìobhadh agas do dheachtadh agas do chumhdach. Oir is andsa leis an t-saoghal an bhrèg go mór iná an fhìrinde.

† And great indeed is the blindness and darkness of sin and ignorance, and of the mind, among composers and writers and patrons of Gaelic, in that they prefer and are accustomed to maintain and improve vain hurtful lying worldly tales composed about the Tuatha Dé Danann and about the Sons of Milesius, and about the heroes and Fionn mac Cumhaill and his warriors, and about many others whom I do not recount or mention here, with a view to obtaining for themselves vain worldly gain, rather than to write and compose and

to preserve the very Word of God and the perfect ways of truth. For the world loves the lie much more than the truth.

Epistle addressed to the Earl of Argyll and to readers of Carswell's Gaelic translation of the Church of Scotland's *Book of Common Order* (*Foirm na n-Urrnuidheadh*, 1567)

Foirm na n-Urrnuidheadh was the first printed book in any of the Celtic languages. Cf. James Loch 2

Cartland, Dame (Mary) Barbara Hamilton 1901–

Romantic novelist born in England but claiming direct descent from Robert the Bruce

1 Really I just love Scotland. In fact, every time I've been in Scotland I write a book after it. I think the Scots are doing very well indeed, the only thing is they all vote Labour, nobody votes Conservative. It's sad you know. I wrote to the Prime Minister and said, can't we do something about it?

Quoted in *The Scotsman* (21 Nov 1995)

Casson, Sir Lewis 1875–1969

English actor-manager and producer

1 The National Theatre of Scotland is Pantomime.

Said after seeing a pantomime in the Metropole Theatre, Glasgow. Quoted in Vivien Devlin, *Kings, Queens and People's Palaces: An Oral History of the Scottish Variety Theatre, 1920–1970* (1991), ch.7

Catechism, The Shorter
see Shorter Catechism, The

Caton-Jones, Michael 1957–

Film director

1 In any small community there is always somebody with the gumption to get out. I just knew I was smarter than the rest.

On making it in Hollywood after leaving his hometown, Broxburn, in West Lothian. Quoted in *The Independent* (10 Oct 1993)

Chaimbeul, Anna (Anna Campbell)
18th century

Poet of Scalpay, Harris

1 Chuala mi gun deach do bhàthadh
Gura truagh nach mi bha làmh riut
Ge b'e sgeir no bogh' an tràigh thu
Ge b'e tiùrr am fàg an làn thu.

Dh' olainn deoch ge b'oil le m' chàirdibh
Cha b' ann a dh' fhìon dearg na Spàinne
Ach a dh' fhuil do chuim, 's i b' fhearr leam.

† I heard that you were drowned; alas, that I was not beside you on whatever skerry or reef the ebbing sea casts you, in whatever tide-wrack the falling sea leaves you.

I would drink a drink in spite of my kinsfolk, not of the red wine of Spain but the blood of your body – a better drink to me.

'Ailein Duinn, shiubhlainn leat' ('Brown-haired Alan, I'd go with you'). In Gilleasbuig Mac-na-Ceardaich (ed.), *An t-Oranaiche* (*The Gaelic Songster*, 1879)

This is the only composition known to be by Anna Campbell

Chalmers, Thomas 1780–1847

Theologian, social reformer and leading Free Church minister

1 There are two kinds of pride. . . that which lords it over inferiors and. . . that which rejoices in repressing the insolence of superiors. The first I have none of – the second I glory in.

Said, as private tutor in a wealthy Arbroath family, to his employer (1798). Quoted in W Hanna, *Memoirs of the Life and Writings of Thomas Chalmers* (1849–52), Vol.1, p.32

2 . . . it is better for the poor to be worse fed and worse clothed, than that they should be left ignorant of those Scriptures, which are able to make them wise unto salvation through the faith that is in Christ Jesus.

The Influence of Bible Societies on the Temporal Necessities of the Poor (1814)

3 I have already professed myself, and will profess myself again, an out and out and, I maintain it, the only consistent Radical. The dearest object of my earthly existence is the elevation of the common people, humanised by Christianity and raised by the strength of their moral habits to a higher platform of human nature. . .

Address to the Presbytery of Edinburgh (1834). Quoted in W G Blaikie, *Thomas Chalmers* (1896), ch.5

4 To make Ireland what he wanted it to be, O'Connell gave forth his watchword, 'Agitate, agitate, agitate'. . . Scotland. . . seeks the Christian freedom of her Church and the Christian good of her people, and to make out this, let her watchword be – 'Organise, organise, organise.'

Speech at a public meeting in Edinburgh on the church patronage issue (16 Feb 1842)

5 Though we quit the Establishment, we go out on the Establishment principle; we quit

a vitiated Establishment, but would rejoice in returning to a pure one.

> On the Disruption (18 May 1843). Quoted in Margaret Oliphant, *Thomas Chalmers* (1893), ch.6
>
>> In spite of leading those ministers who left the Church of Scotland to form the Free Church, Chalmers always believed in the idea of an established church

6 Who cares about the Free Church, compared with the Christian good of Scotland? Who cares about any church but as an instrument of Christian good? For be assured that the moral and religious well-being of the population is of infinitely higher importance than the advancement of any sect.

> Lecture (1844) to raise public interest in his 'West Port experiment' of evangelical social work among the poor of Edinburgh. Quoted in W G Blaikie, *Thomas Chalmers* (1896), ch.6

7 Eh, Tommy, if a' the gowks in the world were brought together, they would fill a great muckle house.

> Said to his grandson. Quoted in Margaret Oliphant, *Thomas Chalmers* (1893), ch.7

8 Mr — , you must cut out one half of that sermon. *It doesn't matter which half.*

> Said to a theology student at Edinburgh University. Quoted in William Knight, *Some Nineteenth-Century Scotsmen* (1903)

Charles I 1600–49

King of Scotland, England and Ireland (1625–49)

1 I see all the birds are flown.

> On entering the English House of Commons (4 Jan 1642) to arrest the 'Five Members' leading the opposition to his government

2 As for church ambition, it doth not at all terminate in seeking to be Pope. . . Papacy in a multitude may be as dangerous as in one.

> Debating church government with Alexander Henderson (1646). Quoted in Agnes Mure Mackenzie, *Scottish Pageant*, Vol.3 (1949), p.89
>
>> The King was negotiating the terms of his surrender with the Scottish Covenanting army, which was holding him captive

3 I die a Christian, according to the profession of the Church of England, as I found it left me by my father.

> Last words on the scaffold before his execution (30 Jan 1649). Quoted in J Rushworth, *Historical Collections* (1701), Part 4, Vol.2, p.1430

Charleson, Ian 1949–90

Actor

1 You know me, if there are two people out there who I can impress I'd be there if I could.

Said to Richard Eyre, director of *Hamlet* at the National Theatre, London, after having to withdraw (Nov 1989) from the title role, less than eight weeks before his death from an Aids-related illness. Quoted in *For Ian Charleson: A Tribute* (1990)

Charteris, Catherine Morice Anderson 1835–1918

Founder of the Church of Scotland Woman's Guild

1 If the sight of the woes of others calls any of you to work beyond what have been hitherto the ordinary limits of women's work. . . you need not fear surely to listen to the voice, nor think that it calls you beyond a woman's province. 'Whatsoever He saith unto you, do it.'

> *Life and Work: Woman's Guild Supplement* (1901). Quoted in N M Cameron, D F Wright et al., *Dictionary of Scottish Church History and Theology* (1993)

Christie, Campbell 1937–

General Secretary of the Scottish Trades Union Congress (1986–)

1 It is one of the contradictions of our society that two-thirds of people are stressed out due to overwork, while one-third are stressed due to under-employment and poverty.

> Quoted in *The Independent* (22 Apr 1995)

Churchill, Winston Spencer 1874–1965

British Prime Minister (1940–5, 1951–5); Liberal MP for Dundee (1908–22)

1 There is nothing which conflicts with the integrity of the United Kingdom in the setting up of a Scottish Parliament for the discharge of Scottish business. . . Certainly I am of opinion that if such a scheme can be brought into existence it will mean a great enrichment not only of the national life of Scotland, but of the politics and public life of the United Kingdom.

> Speech as Liberal candidate for Dundee (1911)

2 VOICE: You will be at the bottom of the poll.
CHURCHILL: If I am going to be at the bottom of the poll, why don't you allow me my last dying kick?

> At an extremely rowdy election meeting, Dundee (13 Nov 1922). Quoted in M Gilbert, *Winston S Churchill*, Vol.4 (1975), ch.47
>
>> Churchill lost his seat, which he had held despite much personal unpopularity. T E Lawrence, writing to a friend two days after the election, complained, 'What bloody shits

the Dundeans must be', but Churchill was
more conciliatory in defeat: 'If you saw the
kind of lives the Dundee folk have to live,'
he wrote on the same day (18 Nov) to
H A L Fisher, 'you would admit they have many
excuses.' Quoted in M Gilbert, *Winston
S Churchill*, Vol.4 (1975), ch.47

3 I would never accept the view that Scotland
should be forced into the serfdom of Socialism
as a result of a vote in the House of Commons.

> General Election speech in Edinburgh (14
> Feb 1950)

Clark, Mary (Bean Torra-Dhamh)
c.1740–c.1815

Poet and hymnwriter of Laggan, Badenoch

1 Chuir iad cas air reachd na firinn
Is ghluais iad dichiollach 'san droch-bheart
Claoidh nam bochd 's gan lot le miorun –
Banntraich 's dilleachdain gun choiseachd:
B' uamhasach an cleachdadh tire –
Croich is binn air aird gach cnocain:
Cuirt nan spleadh gun lagh gun fhirinn –
Is tric a dhit an ti bha neo-chiont'.

† They placed their foot on the rule of truth
and proceeded diligently in mischief
harassing the poor and wounding them with
  malice –
widows and orphans without the power of
  walking:
fearful was the custom of the country –
a gallows and sentence on the summit of
  every hillock:
a court of mock justice, without law,
  without truth –
often did it condemn the innocent.

> On the Gaelic world, pre-1745. 'Beachd Gràis
> air an t-saoghal' ('The world from the viewpoint
> of Grace'). In Alexander MacRae (ed.), *Bean
> Torra Dhamh* (n.d.)

Clàrsair Dall, An (The Blind Harper, Roderick Morison) c.1656–c.1714

One of the last clarsach minstrels in Scotland

1 Chaidh a' chuibhle mun cuairt,
ghrad thionndaidh gu fuachd am blàths:
gum faca mi uair
Dùn ratha nan cuach 'n seo thràigh,
far 'm biodh tathaich nan duan,
iomadh mathas gun chruas, gun chàs:
dh'fhalbh an latha sin uainn,
's tha na taighean gu fuarraidh fàs.

Tha Mac-alla fo ghruaim
anns an talla 'm biodh fuaim a' cheòil
'n ionad tathaich nan cliar,
gun aighear, gun mhiadh, gun phòit. . .

† The wheel [of fortune] has come full circle,
warmth has suddenly turned cold. But I once
saw here a bountiful castle, well-stocked with
drinking-cups that have now gone dry, a
song-haunted place abounding in good things,
given without stint or question. That day has
gone from us, and the buildings are chill and
desolate.

Echo is dejected in the hall where music
was wont to sound, in the place resorted to by
poet-bands, now without mirth, or pleasure,
or drinking. . .

> 'Oran do Mhac Leòid Dhùn Bheagain' ('A Song
> to MacLeod of Dunvegan'). In W Matheson (ed.),
> *An Clàrsair Dall* (*The Blind Harper*, 1970), st.1–2

> > This song castigates Roderick MacLeod of
> > Dunvegan (c.1674–99) for his 'spendthrift
> > habits, neglect of his estate and lack of
> > the virtues expected of a chief.' See Derick
> > Thomson (ed.), *The Companion to Gaelic
> > Scotland* (1983)

2 'Is mi Mac-alla bha uair
'g éisdeachd faram nan duan gu tiugh,
far 'm bu mhuirneach am beus
an am dubhradh do 'n ghréin 'san t-sruth;
far am b'fhoirmeil na seòid,
iad gu h-organach ceòlmhor cluth:
ge nach fhaicte mo ghnùis,
chluinnte aca 'san Dùn mo ghuth.'

† 'I am Echo, who once listened to the carolling
of songs in rich profusion, accompanied by a
ground-bass pleasing to the ear, what time the
sun was becoming dim in the ocean flood. It
was a place where gallants might be found in
high glee, enjoying the music of organs at their
ease. Though my face could not be seen, my
voice could be heard by them in the Castle.'

> 'Oran do Mhac Leòid Dhùn Bheagain' ('A Song
> to MacLeod of Dunvegan'). In W Matheson (ed.),
> *An Clàrsair Dall* (*The Blind Harper*, 1970), st.6

3 '. . . fir ag cnapraich mu 'n chlàr
is cath air a ghnàth chur leò;
dà chomhairleach ghearr
gun labhairt, ge b'ard an glòir,
's a righ, bu titheach an guin
do dhaoine gun fhuil, gun fheòil.'

† '. . . men rattled dice as they sat round the
board, engaged in battle as was their wont. Two
counsellors there were, short of stature, and
not speaking, however loud their clamour. And
O Lord, how keen was their spite, considering
that they were men without flesh or blood.'

> 'Oran do Mhac Leòid Dhùn Bheagain' ('A Song
> to MacLeod of Dunvegan'). In W Matheson (ed.),
> *An Clàrsair Dall* (*The Blind Harper*, 1970), st.10

> > The 'counsellors' are pieces on the board

4 . . . bho nach léir dhaibh an call,
miad an déidh air cùirt Ghall cha sguir,
gus an togar do 'n Fhraing,

a dhol ann an geall na chuir;
siod an niosgaid a' fàs
air an iosgaid 's a cràdh 'na bun.

† . . . since they cannot visualise their losses,
their fondness for court life among southron
strangers is unabated, until they hie them to
France, [there] to give a bond for their outlay.
Then does the boil fester on the thigh with
its pain at the root.

'Oran do Mhac Leòid Dhùn Bheagain' ('A Song
to MacLeod of Dunvegan'). In W Matheson (ed.),
An Clàrsair Dall (*The Blind Harper*, 1970), st.17

5 Masa ceòl fidileireachd, tha gu leòr siod dheth.
† If fiddling is music, that is enough of it.

Quoted in W Matheson (ed.), *An Clàrsair Dall*
(*The Blind Harper*, 1970)

His response to hearing a harp tune played
on the fiddle. He also wrote a tune called
'Contempt for Fiddlers'

Clephane, Elizabeth Cecilia 1830–69
Free Church hymnwriter

1 Beneath the Cross of Jesus
I fain would take my stand –
The shadow of a mighty rock
Within a weary land;
A home within a wilderness,
A rest upon the way,
From the burning of the noontide heat
And the burden of the day.

Hymn, 'Beneath the Cross of Jesus', st.1

Clerk, John (Lord Eldin) 1757–1832
Lawyer and judge

1 WOMAN (on passing him on the High Street
of Edinburgh): There goes Johnnie Clerk, the
lame lawyer.
CLERK: No, madam; I may be a lame man, but
not a *lame lawyer*!

Quoted in John Kay, *Original Portraits* (1877
edition), Vol.2, p.439

Clerk had a pronounced limp from a
childhood illness

2 LORD CHANCELLOR: 'Mr Clerk, do you spell
water in Scotland with two t's?'
JOHN CLERK: 'Na, my Lord, we dinna spell *water*
wi twa t's, but we spell *mainners* wi twa n's.'

On Scots pronunciation and English prejudice,
while arguing an appeal case before the House
of Lords. Quoted in various sources, with minor
variations, eg Dean Ramsay, *Reminiscences of
Scottish Life and Character* (1858), ch.5

Cleveland, John 1613–58
English satirical poet

1 Had Cain been Scot, God would have chang'd
his doom,
Not forced him wander, but confin'd him home.
Like Jews they spread, and as Infection flie,
As if the Divell had Ubiquitie.
Hence 'tis, they live as Rovers; and defie
This or that Place, Rags of Geographie.
They're Citizens o' the World; they're all in all,
Scotland's a Nation Epidemicall.

'The Rebell Scot' (1644), ll.63–70

The poem attacked the involvement of
the Scots in the English civil war campaigns of 1644

2 I wrong the Devill, should I picke the bones.
That dish is his: for when the Scots decease,
Hell like their Nation feeds on Barnacles.
A Scot, when from the Gallows-tree got loose,
Drops into Styx, and turns a Soland-Goose.

'The Rebell Scot' (1644), ll.122–6

Clifford, Timothy 1946–
*English director of the National Galleries of
Scotland (1984–)*

1 At times it's very good, at times it's bloody
awful. It's a lesser school with a few high points.

On Scottish art. Quoted in *Scotland on Sunday*
(16 Jan 1994)

2 Absolute nonsense. They didn't influence
anybody.

On claims that the influence of Scottish artists
has been greatly undervalued. Quoted in *Scotland
on Sunday* (16 Jan 1994)

Clyde, Lord (James Avon Clyde)
1863–1944
Judge

1 I cannot understand why the light which the law
of our own country sheds on a question such
as this should be deliberately hidden under a
bushel of alien authority.

Complaining against the citation of English case
law in civil cases where perfectly good Scots
authority exists. MacKintosh's Judicial Factor
v. Lord Advocate (1935)

Cockburn, Mrs Alison (*née* Rutherford)
1712–94
Poet and songwriter

1 I've seen the smiling of Fortune beguiling,
I've felt all its favours and found its decay;

Sweet was its blessing, kind its caressing,
But now it is fled, fled far, far away.

> 'The Flowers of the Forest' (1765), st.1.
> Cf. Jean Elliot 1
>
>> Believed to have been written some twenty
>> years earlier, and inspired by a commercial
>> disaster in which seven local lairds were
>> bankrupted in one year

2 I am just returned from a Highland expedition,
and was much delighted with the magnificence
of nature in her awful simplicity. These
mountains, and torrents, and rocks would
almost convince one that it was some Being
of infinite power that had created them. Plain
corn countries look as if men had made them;
but I defy all mankind put together to make
anything like the Pass of Killiecranky [sic].

> Letter to David Hume. Quoted in Sarah Tytler
> and J L Watson, *The Songstresses of Scotland*
> (1871), Vol.1

Cockburn, Lord (Henry Thomas Cockburn) 1779–1854

Judge

1 Dinner is the English meal, breakfast the
Scotch. An Englishman's certainty of getting
a good dinner, seems to make him indifferent
about his breakfast, while the substantiality of
a Scotchman's breakfast impairs, or at least
might impair, his interest in his dinner.

> *Circuit Journeys* (11 Apr 1841)

2 A band of five horrible women, – real Glasgow
faggots, – incorrigible devils, were sent to
Botany in a batch, for a ferocious robbery,
committed on a decent stranger they had
inveigled into their den. I was greatly diverted
by overhearing the account which one of them
gave, in a soliloquy, of her learned judges, as
she was leaving the bar, 'Twa d—d auld grey-
headed blackguards! They gie us plenty o' their
law, but deevilish little joostice!'

> *Circuit Journeys* (3 May 1843)

3 . . . Dundee, the palace of Scottish blackguardism, unless perhaps Paisley be entitled to
contest this honour with it.

> *Circuit Journeys* (27 Apr 1844)

4 Argyleshire stots make the stupidest jurymen.

> *Circuit Journeys* (18 Sep 1845)

5 Britain is at present an asylum of railway
lunatics, and one symptom of their malady
consists in their being possessed of the idea
that all seclusion is a grievance.

> *Circuit Journeys* (21 Sep 1845)

6 I never see a scene of Scotch beauty, without
being thankful that I have beheld it before it has
been breathed over by the angel of mechanical
destruction.

> On rural railway development. *Circuit Journeys*
> (20 Sep 1846)

7 Eskgrove was a personified compound of avarice,
indecency, official insolence and personal
cowardice, great law, and practical imbecility.

> On the judge Lord Eskgrove (?1729–1804). *Circuit
> Journeys* (24 Sep 1847)

8 Her Majesty passed through Perth station
while we were there, on her way home. She
left Balmoral by the highway this forenoon;
got on the railway at Cupar-Angus, and was in
Edinburgh, by Stirling, in two and a half hours.
All the stations were crowded with people,
panting for a sight of her; and her gracious
condescension was expressed by whisking past
them at the rate of about thirty miles per hour,
with all her windows shut. Immense folly! When
I'm a queen, I shall hold it to be my dignity
to go slow.

> *Circuit Journeys* (27 Sep 1849)

9 . . . Dundee, certainly now, and for many years
past, the most blackguard place in Scotland. . .
a sink of atrocity, which no moral flushing
seems capable of cleansing. A Dundee criminal,
especially if a lady, may be known, without
any evidence about character, by the intensity
of the crime, the audacious bar air, and the
parting curses.

> *Circuit Journeys* (1 May 1852)

10 . . . the last purely Scotch age that Scotland
was destined to see. . . Almost the whole
official state, as settled at the union, survived;
and all graced the capital, unconscious of the
economical scythe which has since mowed
it down.

> On Edinburgh at the end of the 18th century.
> *Life of Lord Jeffrey* (1852), Vol.1, p.157

11 *Scots* is the affected pronunciation and spelling
of a paltry, lisping, puppy Englishman. A *good*
Caledonian calls himself a *Skotcchman*. Even
the Suthrons don't call themselves *Englismen*.
They keep their H, but won't give us ours!

> Letter to John Marshall (25 Mar 1854). Quoted
> in K Miller, *Cockburn's Millennium* (1975), ch.14

12 Two vices especially, which have been long
banished from all respectable society, were
very prevalent, if not universal, among the
whole upper ranks – swearing and drunkenness.
Nothing was more common than for gentlemen
who had dined with ladies, and meant to
rejoin them, to get drunk. To get drunk in a
tavern seemed to be considered as a natural, if

not an intended consequence of going to one. Swearing was thought the right, and the mark, of a gentleman. And, tried by the test, nobody, who had not seen them, could now be made to believe how many gentlemen there were.

Memorials of his Time (1856), ch.1

13 I never heard of him [the philosopher Adam Ferguson] dining out, except at his relation Dr Joseph Black's, where his son Adam (the friend of Scott) used to say that it was delightful to see the two philosophers rioting over a boiled turnip.

Memorials of his Time (1856), ch.1

14 Nobody could sit down like the lady of Inverleith [Mrs Rocheid]. She would sail in like a ship from Tarshish, gorgeous in velvet or rustling silk, and done up in all the accompaniments of fan, earrings and finger-rings, falling sleeves, scent-bottle, embroidered bag, hoop, and train – all superb, yet all in purest taste; and managing all this heavy rigging with as much ease as a full-blown swan does its plumage, she would take possession of the centre of a huge sofa. . .

Memorials of his Time (1856), ch.1

15 I remember one of her grand-daughters stumbling, in the course of reading the news-papers to her, on a paragraph which stated that a lady's reputation had suffered from some indiscreet talk on the part of the Prince of Wales. Up she of fourscore sat, and said with an indignant shake of her shrivelled fist and a keen voice – 'The dawmned villain! does he kiss and tell!'

On the elderly Margaret Watson, mother of the soldier Sir David Dundas. *Memorials of his Time* (1856), ch.1

16 One lamentable error we certainly have committed, are committing, and, so far as appears, will ever commit. We massacre every town tree that comes in a mason's way; never sacrificing mortar to foliage.

Memorials of his Time (1856), ch.5

17 No apology is thought necessary for murdering a tree; many for preserving it.

Memorials of his Time (1856), ch.5

18 As quiet as the grave – or Peebles.

Remark coined, or at least used, by Lord Cockburn

Coinneach Odhar (Pale Kenneth) see Brahan Seer, The

Colkitto see MacDonald, Colla Ciotach

Colquhoun, Lady Janet (*née* Sinclair) 1781–1846
Writer, diarist and philanthropist

1 This day I am thirty years old. Let me now bid a cheerful adieu to my youth. My young days are now surely over, and why should I regret them? Were I never to grow old I might be always here, and might never bid farewell to sin and sorrow.

Diary entry (17 Apr 1811). Quoted in James Hamilton, *A Memoir of Lady Colquhoun* (1849)

2 Impressed with the shortness of my abode in this world, which is to me a reviving, as well as awful idea. Indeed, I would not live here always.

Diary entry (24 Jul 1814). Quoted in James Hamilton, *A Memoir of Lady Colquhoun* (1849)

3 Be very cautious of your friendships. Shun, as the plague, those who have not the fear of God, whatever other attractive qualities they may possess. . .

Undated letter to her daughters, to be read after her death. Quoted in James Hamilton, *A Memoir of Lady Colquhoun* (1849)

4 . . . can the disciple of Christ here seek for enjoyment? Will he not rather feel in a tainted atmosphere, where every breath may bring infection along with it, and where the most vigilant guard cannot always prevent the contagion?

On the theatre. 'Thoughts on the Religious Profession and Defective Practice of the Higher Classes of Society' (1823), ch.2. Published in *The Works of Lady Colquhoun of Luss* (1852)

5 Happiness is the universal pursuit among all classes of intelligent people with whom our world is peopled. . .

'Impressions of the Heart Relative to the Nature and Excellence of Genuine Religion' (1825), ch.1. Published in *The Works of Lady Colquhoun of Luss* (1852)

Coltart, Robert
Candy-maker, who sold his sweets round markets and fairs in the Borders

1 Ally, bally, ally bally bee,
Sittin' on yer mammy's knee,
Greetin' for anither bawbee,
Tae buy mair Coulter's candy.

'Coulter's Candy', st.1. Quoted in Norman Buchan, *101 Scottish Songs* (1962). Frequently sung with 'a wee' in place of 'anither'

Coltrane, Robbie
(originally **Robin McMillan**) 1950–
Actor

1 By and large television is wallpaper, and getting worse. It goes for viewers who sit with the

sound half-down and blether right through the programme. Just because 18 million people have their sets switched on, it doesn't mean they are watching.

Quoted in *Radio Times* (Oct 1994)

2 You know why they don't drink in California? Because they spend so much time telling lies, they can't remember them if they drink.

Quoted in *Radio Times* (Oct 1994)

Columba, St (Colum Cille, 'Colm of the Cell') 521–97

Irish-born Christian missionary to Scotland, founder of monastery in Iona

1 There are some, although only a few, on whom divine grace has bestowed the gift of contemplating, clearly and distinctly, and with a mind miraculously enlarged, even the whole world entire, with the ocean and the sky about it, at one and the same moment as if under a single ray of the sun [*quasi sub uno solis radio*].

Explaining his powers of prophecy to the monk Lugbe. Quoted in St Adamnan (c.625–704, abbot of Iona from 679), *Life of Columba*

2 Noles ultra progedi, nec hominem tangas. Retro citius revertere.

† You will go no further, nor touch the man. Turn back instantly.

His command to a monster in Loch Ness about to devour a man swimming out to a boat. Quoted in St Adamnan, *Life of Columba*

'Hearing the voice of the saint,' the story continues, 'the beast fled back terrified, as rapidly as if it were being pulled by ropes.'

3 Small and mean though this place is, great and special honour will be conferred upon it, not only by the kings of the Scots and their people, but also by the rulers of barbarous and foreign nations. And saints, too, even of other churches, shall regard it with no common reverence.

On Iona, shortly before his death. Quoted in St Adamnan, *Life of Columba*

4 A nest of singing birds.

Attrib. On Iona

5 I mo chridhe, I mo ghràidh
An àite guth manaich bidh geum bà
Ach man dig an saoghal gu crìch
Bidh I mar a bhà.

† In Iona of my heart, Iona of my love
In place of the voices of monks, there shall be the lowing of a cow
But before the world comes to an end
Iona shall be as it was.

Attrib.

Complaynt of Scotland, The 1549

1 . . . the natural love of your native cuntre suld be inseperablye rutit in your hartis, considerand that your lyvis, your bodeis, your habitatione, your frendis, your lyvyngis, and sustentan, your hail, your pace, your refuge, the rest of your eild, ande your sepulture is in it.

The Complaynt of Scotland (1549), ch.8

The *Complaynt* was a polemical work defending Scottish independence and identity, published anonymously but possibly the work of Robert Wedderburn, one of the compilers of the *Gude and Godlie Ballatis*

2 . . . we may verray weil belief that quhou beit that the kyng of ingland garris tret scottis men witht gold and silver as thai war his frendis yit doutles he wald be rytht glaid sa that everye scottis man hed ane ythyr scottis man in his bellye.

The Complaynt of Scotland (1549), ch.12

3 . . . there is nocht twa nations undir the firmament that ar mair contrar and different fra uthers, nor is inglis men and scottis men quhoubeit that thai be witht in ane ile and nythtbours, and of ane langage: for inglis men ar subtil and scottis men ar facile, inglis men ar ambitius in prosperite, and scottis men ar humain in prosperite, inglis men are humil quhen thai ar subjeckit be forse and violence, and scottis men ar furious quhen thai ar violently subjeckit, inglis men ar cruel quhene thai get victorie, and scottis men ar merciful quhen thai get victory. And to conclude it is onpossibil that scottis men and inglis men can remane in concord undir ane monarche or ane prince, be cause there naturis and conditions ar as indefferent as is the nature of scheip and wolvis.

The Complaynt of Scotland (1549), ch.13

Conn, Stewart 1936–

Poet and playwright

1 But the real Renaissance is also to be found
In the witches and wizards of mankind:
The iron wheels on which they turned
Did much to liberate the human mind.

'Renaissance Thought', *Stoats in the Sunlight* (1968)

2 I wonder, will it ever be
Springtime again, the blood flow freely;
Or has man blighted all hope of recovery?

We are on borrowed time, you and I,
And have been from the outset.
All that is left, is to live lovingly.

'Springtime', *In the Kibble Palace* (1987), st.4–5. Cf. Douglas Dunn 15

3 Muir still worshipping his open spaces, the
   supreme
   escape from that father who drove him below
   ground.
   What better than a Wilderness, to liberate
   the mind.

   On the environmentalist John Muir. 'Air and
   Water', *In the Blood* (1995), st.5

Connery, Sean Thomas 1930–
Actor

1 The problem with interviews of this sort is to
   get across the fact, without breaking your arse,
   that one is not Bond, that one was functioning
   reasonably well before Bond, and that one is
   going to function reasonably well after Bond.

   Interview in *Playboy* (Nov 1965)

2 I suppose more than anything else I'd like to
   be an old man with a good face, like Hitchcock
   or Picasso. They know life is not a popularity
   contest.

   Quoted in John Millar, 'Sean Connery', in Eddie
   Dick (ed.), *From Limelight to Satellite* (1990)

3 We have friends all over the world. They are
   waiting to see if Scotland will go for it –
   or cop out.

   Contemplating whether Scots would vote for the
   Scottish National Party and independence in the
   1992 general election. Quoted in *The Independent*
   (21 Mar 1992)

4 I'm not against feminism at all. I'm only against
   women who whine and complain too much.

   Quoted in *The Independent* (1 Aug 1992)

5 I'm what I always have been – a Scot, a bit
   introspective. I don't tell lies and I prefer
   straight dealing.

   Quoted in John Hunter, *Great Scot: The Life of
   Sean Connery* (1993), ch.7

Connolly, Billy 1942–
Comedian

1 If it wasnae for yer wellies where wud ye be?
   Ye'd be in the hospital or infirmary.
   For you would have a dose of the flu or even
   pleurisy
   If ye didnae have yer feet in yer wellies.

   'The Welly Boot Song', chorus. Cf. David Shaw 1

   The song was written by George McEwan
   and popularised by Connolly (early 1970s)

2 He says: 'Is that her?' He says, 'Aye.' He
   says, 'What did you leave her bum sticking

out for?' He says, 'I need somewhere to park
my bike.'

   Punchline to joke about a man who tells his friend
   he's killed his wife and buried her in the back
   green. Said in BBC television interview with
   Michael Parkinson, *Parkinson* (broadcast 1975)

3 I often think that life is like an ashtray – full
   of wee dowts.

   Minister's sermon. Quoted in Jonathan Margolis,
   The Big Yin: The Life & Times of Billy Connolly
   (1994), ch.5, 'Diced Carrots'

4 Land of polluted river
   Bloodshot eyes and sodden liver
   Land of my heart forever
   Scotland the Brave.

   Quoted in Jonathan Margolis, *The Big Yin: The
   Life & Times of Billy Connolly* (1994), ch.5,
   'Diced Carrots'. Cf. Cliff Hanley 1

5 It's no' the eighteen Guinnesses that does it,
   it's the diced carrots.

   On drunks' vomit. Quoted in Jonathan Margolis,
   The Big Yin: The Life & Times of Billy Connolly
   (1994), ch.5, 'Diced Carrots'

6 The one drink to avoid is Advocaat: the
   alcoholic's omelette.

   Gullible's Travels (1982), 'Hygiene and Fitness
   on the Road'

7 Still, they [the Americans] got Andrew Carnegie
   about whom it was said that he gave money
   away as silently as a waiter falling down a flight
   of stairs with a tray of glasses.

   Gullible's Travels (1982), 'America'

8 My definition of an intellectual is someone who
   can listen to the *William Tell Overture* without
   thinking of the Lone Ranger.

   Gullible's Travels (1982), 'Europe'

9 One thing I do envy the royals is their wee
   chins: shaving must be a doddle – whoosh, and
   it's all done in one stroke.

   Gullible's Travels (1982), 'England'

10 There are two seasons in Scotland: June
   and winter.

   Gullible's Travels (1982), 'Scotland'.
   Cf. Lord Byron 50

11 He's handsome, he's rich, he's funny and he's
   happy. . . my envy knows no bounds.

   On Ally McCoist. In foreword to *Ally McCoist:
   My Story* (1992)

12 *Braveheart* is pure Australian shite. Unless
   William Wallace went about with Dulux on
   his fuckin' face, in pigtails and a kilt. And
   then there's Rob Roy, poncing about the
   heather talking about honour. He was a spy,
   a thief, a blackmailer – a cunt, basically. And

people are swallowing it. . . It's part of a new Scottish racism, which I loathe – this thing that everything that's horrible is English. It's conducted by the great unread and the conceited wankers in the SNP, those dreary little pricks in Parliament who rely on bigotry for support. Ask the people in Bosnia about nationalism and what good it does. . . I would suggest that if your nationality is the strongest suit you can play then you are in deep shit.

> Interview with Bob Flynn in *The Guardian* (17 Apr 1996). Cf. Michael Forsyth 1

3 We are the most alone people in the world. It's like being on the moon out there. If you make a mistake – and it's usually a mistake of judgment – you die. But it's brilliant. You're like an outlaw, you create your own reality, your own rules.

> On comedians. Interview with Bob Flynn in *The Guardian* (17 Apr 1996)

Conti, Tom 1941–
Actor

1 The only function of theatre is as an entertainment to take you out of the day's hardships. People go to the theatre to have a good time, not to be educated. If you want to be educated go to bloody university.

> Quoted in *The Scotsman* (11 Mar 1996)

Cook, Robin (Robert Finlayson Cook) 1946–
Labour politician

1 I have not been an extravagant supporter of the Scottish dimension. But I have changed my mind. I don't give a bugger if Thatcher has a mandate or not – I will simply do whatever I can to stop her.

> Addressing a Scottish Socialist Society conference, Mitchell Library, Glasgow (2 Jul 1983), shortly after Mrs Thatcher's second General Election triumph. The occasion marked his conversion to the cause of Scottish devolution

2 We need a minimum wage because we will not build industries that are an international success on the back of wages that are an international disgrace.

> Said as Trade and Industry spokesman at the Labour Party Conference, Blackpool. Quoted in *The Independent* (4 Oct 1994)

Cooper (of Culross), Lord (Thomas Mackay Cooper) 1892–1955
Judge

1 The formidable and still rising torrent of acts, regulations and orders has been the subject of many an unavailing protest by lawyers and laymen alike, and the rule to which we still pay lip service that every citizen is presumed to know the law has long since degenerated into a pious fiction.

> *The Scottish Legal Tradition* (1949), 'The Present Position'

2 . . : law is the reflection of the spirit of a people, and so long as the Scots are conscious that they are a people, they must preserve their law.

> *The Scottish Legal Tradition* (1949), 'The Prospects for the Future'

3 The principle of the unlimited sovereignty of Parliament is a distinctively English principle which has no counterpart in Scottish constitutional law.

> Opinion given in the case of MacCormick v. Lord Advocate (1953). Quoted in *The Scottish Legal Tradition* (1991 edition), Appendix
>
> John MacCormick, leader of the Scottish Covenant movement, raised a case against the use of the style 'Elizabeth II', as determined in the Royal Titles Act 1953, to describe the new Queen. It was argued that as there had never been an Elizabeth I of Scotland there could not be an Elizabeth II either of Scotland or of the United Kingdom of Great Britain and Northern Ireland. Lord Cooper found no Parliamentary authority for the style adopted, but on the other hand dismissed MacCormick's action as incompetent, in that the Court of Session had no authority to pass judgment on the issue. The case remains a powerful example of the curious constitutional position in which Scotland, and the other constituent parts of the United Kingdom, stand. Cf. Morris Blythman 1

Corrie, Joe 1894–1968
Miner, playwright and poet

1 Crawlin' aboot like a snail in the mud,
Covered wi' clammy blae,
ME, made after the image o' God –
Jings! but it's laughable, tae.

> 'The Image o' God' (1926), st.1

2 BOB: (*at mirror*) My face is no' half broon, faither.
JOCK: They'll soon take the broon off your face: they'll soon make a mushroom o' ye. It's a hell o' a job, hunger and rags, water and bad air, and up at fower o' clock on the cauld, snawy mornin's, and under the heel o' a set o' tyrants for starvation wages. And what can we dae, just suffer it oot and say naething.
BOB: I ken what's needed. . .
LIZZIE: It's a revolution that's needed, Bob.

> *In Time o' Strife* (1927, first performed throughout the Fife coalfield 1928), Act 3

3 JEAN: That's the spirit, my he'rties! sing! sing!
tho' they ha'e ye chained to the wheels and
the darkness. Sing! tho' they ha'e ye crushed
in the mire. Keep up your he'rts, my laddies,
you'll win through yet, for there's nae power
on earth can crush the men that can sing on a
day like this.

> *In Time o' Strife* (1927), Act 3, final words
>> As the men are forced back to work, the
>> General Strike of 1926 over, they are defiantly
>> singing 'The Red Flag'

4 We have borne good sons to broken men,
Nurtured them on our hungry breast,
And given them to our masters when
Their day of life was at its best.

> 'Miners' Wives', *The Image o' God and other
> poems* (1937), st.1

5 We have stood through the naked night to watch
The silent wheels that raised the dead . . .

> 'Miners' Wives', *The Image o' God and other
> poems* (1937), st.4

6 Of hunger let us sing,
Praise the Lord for its mad pain,
Not the hunger of the belly,
But the hunger of the brain,
The hunger that makes mortals strive,
And dream, and do, and dare,
To make this Earth a Heaven
That will be good and fair.

> 'Of Hunger Let Us Sing', st.1

7 I was going from hunger away,
To a land that promised me bread,
But I could not sing with the hopes to be,
For my heart was dead.

> 'The Emigrant', st.3

8 Noo he is there, back-bencher Tam,
And listens daily to the farce
O' Tweedledum and Tweedledee,
And never rises off his arse.

> 'Rebel Tam', st.3
>> On the tendency of Labour radicals to be
>> subdued once elected as Westminster MPs.
>> Cf. David Kirkwood 1

Cousin, Annie Ross (*née* Cundell)
1824–1906
Hymnwriter

1 The sands of time are sinking;
The dawn of heaven breaks;
The summer morn I've sighed for,
The fair, sweet morn, awakes.

> Hymn, 'The Sands of Time are Sinking', st.1

2 And glory, glory dwelleth
In Immanuel's land.

> Hymn, 'The Sands of Time are Sinking', st.1

Cranston, Kate (Catherine) 1850–1934
Glasgow tea-room owner

1 Would ladies please refrain from combing out
their hair, as there have been complaints of
hair being carried away on people's skirts.

> Notice in the Ladies' Room in one of her
> tea-rooms. Recalled by Miss Jenny Logan in
> Anna Blair, *More Tea at Miss Cranston's* (1991),
> Introduction
>> Her tea-rooms were well known for their
>> artistic interiors, several of which were
>> designed by Charles Rennie Mackintosh

Crawford, Robert 1959–
*Poet and critic, Professor of Scottish Literature
at St Andrews University*

1 Ghetto-makars, tae the knackirs'
Wi aw yir schemes, yir smug dour dreams
O yir ain feet. Yi're beat
By yon new Scoatlan loupin tae yir street . . .

> 'Ghetto-Blastir', *Sterts & Stobies* (1985), st.1

2 Throw all your stagey chandeliers in wheel-
barrows and move them north
To celebrate my mother's sewing-machine
And her beneath an eighty-watt bulb, pedalling
Iambs on an antique metal footplate . . .

> 'Opera', *A Scottish Assembly* (1990)

3 Semiconductor country, land crammed with
intimate expanses,
Your cities are superlattices, heterojunctive
Graphed from the air, your cropmarked
farmlands
Are epitaxies of tweed.

> 'Scotland', *A Scottish Assembly* (1990), st.1

4 To be miniaturised is not small-minded.
To love you needs more details than the Book
of Kells –
Your harbours, your photography, your
democratic intellect
Still boundless, chip of a nation.

> 'Scotland', *A Scottish Assembly* (1990), st.4

5 . . . Listen –

Not to dour centuries of trudging,
Marching, and taking orders;

Today I have heard the feet of my country
Breaking into a run.

> 'Radio Scottish Democracy', *Talkies* (1992)

Crawfurd, Helen (*née* Jack) 1877–1954
Suffragette and Communist activist

1 I had always resented any suggestion of the
inferiority of women . . . The status of women

implied in the Old and New Testament, 'Let your women keep silent in the churches', made me rebel but I think it was my respect for women more than this which made me a feminist.

'Memoirs', unpublished 1940s typescript, p.46. Quoted in W Knox (ed.), *Scottish Labour Leaders 1918–39* (1984)

2 I never was a Pacifist. I hated and still hate war but I hate injustice and duplicity more.

'Memoirs', unpublished 1940s typescript, p.128. Quoted in W Knox (ed.), *Scottish Labour Leaders 1918–39* (1984)

Crosland, T W H

English poet and journalist

1 Your proper child of Caledonia believes in his rickety bones that he is the salt of the earth. . . This arrogation has served him passing well. It has brought him into unrivalled esteem. He is one species of human animal that is taken by all the world to be fifty per cent cleverer and pluckier and honester than the facts warrant. He is the daw with a peacock's tail of his own painting. He is the ass who has been at pains to cultivate the convincing roar of a lion. He is the fine gentleman whose father toils with a muck-fork.

The Unspeakable Scot (1902), ch.1, 'The Superstition'

2 . . . I concede that the Scotch really do love learning. I gather, too, from unbiased sources that they starve their mothers and make gin-mules of their fathers to get it. . .

The Unspeakable Scot (1902), ch.1, 'The Superstition'

3 . . . journalism suits the Scot because it is a profession into which you can crawl without inquiry as to your qualifications, and because it is a profession in which the most middling talents will take you a long way.

The Unspeakable Scot (1902), ch.4, 'The Scot in Journalism'

4 After illicit love and flaring drunkenness, nothing appeals so much to Scotch sentiment as having been born in the gutter.

The Unspeakable Scot (1902), ch.7, 'The Bard'

5 . . . while at the present moment his popularity is of the widest. . . the circumstance that he wrote in the vernacular must ultimately relegate him to a position of comparative obscurity. As Scotland gradually extricates herself from the slough of barbarism in which she wallows so joyfully, she will inevitably shed her uncouth dialect, and, as soon as that is accomplished,

Burns, excepting as a curiosity, will no longer exist.

The Unspeakable Scot (1902), ch.10, 'The Scot in Letters'

6 Under the inspiring tutelage of the National Bard, Scotland has become one of the drunkenest nations in the world.

The Unspeakable Scot (1902), ch.12, 'The Scot in his Cups'

7 Whiskey [sic], and that of the crudest and most shuddering quality, is undoubtedly the Scotchman's peculiar vanity. The amount that he can consume without turning a hair is quite appalling.

The Unspeakable Scot (1902), ch.12, 'The Scot in his Cups'

8 The garb of old Gaul is no doubt very fetching from the point of view of the weak-minded, but of its effeminacy there can be no doubt. Really it is a costume for small and pretty boys who are too young to be breeched. In view of its associations and of its innate childishness, not to say immodesty, it is a great pity that any Englishman should go out of his way to wear it.

On the kilt. *The Unspeakable Scot* (1902), ch.14, 'The Scot by Adoption'. Cf. Sir Henry Erskine 1

9 . . . the Scotch possess neither the requisite agitators, nor the requisite pluck to indulge in serious demonstrations against the Imperial Government. So that they have to content themselves with futile grumbling and petty acts of disloyalty.

The Unspeakable Scot (1902), ch.15, 'The Scot and England'

10 Try to forget that the Battle of Bannockburn was won by the Scotch in 1314. The dates of Flodden and Culloden are much better worth remembering, though most Englishmen have forgotten both of them.

No.8 in a series of rules 'for the general guidance of young Scotchmen who wish to succeed in this country [England]'. *The Unspeakable Scot* (1902), ch.16, 'The Way Out'

Cruickshank, Helen B(urness)
1886–1975

Poet, secretary of Scottish PEN (1927–34)

1 Up the Noran Water
In by Inglismaddy,
Annie's got a bairnie
That hasna got a daddy.
Some say it's Tammas's
An' some say it's Chay's;
An' naebody expec'it it,
Wi' Annie's quiet ways.

'Shy Geordie', *Up the Noran Water* (1934), st.1

2 This man set the flame
of his native genius
under the cumbering whin
of the untilled field;
Lit a fire in the Mearns
to illumine Scotland,
clearing the sullen soil
for a richer yield.

> On Lewis Grassic Gibbon, composed just after
> his death. 'Spring in the Mearns' (1935), st.6.
> Collected in *Sea Buckthorn* (1954)

3 Sae smoor yersel', my man,
Pit oot yer licht,
Grey hair that's tow
To a lassie's lowe
Is an unco sicht.

> 'An Unco Sicht', *Sea Buckthorn* (1954), st.2

4 Laughter and gibes and scorn
they brave for her:
their pounds, their silver, and their pence
they give;
their time, their talent and their youth for her
that she may live.

> 'Lines for the Scottish Watch', *Sea Buckthorn*
> (1954), st.1

>> The 'her' in the poem is Scotland. The Scottish
>> Watch was a youth movement founded by
>> Wendy Wood, which hoped to interest young
>> people in the cultural and political development
>> of Scotland. Its activities included ceilidh
>> dancing on the esplanade of Edinburgh Castle

5 They agonise in sordid
tenements,
with children stabled worse than sheep
or kye.
O, how can grace or peace or health abide
such poverty?

> 'Lines for the Scottish Watch', *Sea Buckthorn*
> (1954), st.3

6 I mind o' the Ponnage Pule
On a shinin' mornin',
The saumon fishers
Nettin' the bonny brutes –
I' the slithery dark o' the boddom
O' Charon's Coble
Ae day I'll faddom my doots.

> 'The Ponnage Pool', *The Ponnage Pool* (1968), st.4

7 But where this passionate self will go,
God knows,
Who knows whence the lightning comes, and
whither it goes.

> 'At the End', *Collected Poems* (1971)

8 While I am not teetotal, a drunk woman I find
revolting and Burns orgies detestable.

> *Octobiography* (1976), ch.9

9 Criticism in Scotland, of books as well as plays,
is often bedevilled because we all know each
other too well. The clique can cast its chill over
its rivals; the claque delude with false praise.

> *Octobiography* (1976), ch.15. Cf. Eddie Boyd 1

10 I am not asked out to drinking parties and
have never been in a Rose Street pub. I can't
be a poet.

> *Octobiography* (1976), ch.20

Cumming, Alan
Actor

1 At the start he's a pain in the arse. You can
imagine him spending all his time listening to
Morrissey and reading Sylvia Plath.

> On Shakespeare's Hamlet. Quoted in *The
> Independent* (21 Nov 1993)

Cunningham, Allan 1784–1842
*Poet and contemporary of James Hogg and
Walter Scott*

1 A wet sheet and a flowing sea,
A wind that follows fast,
And fills the white and rustling sail,
And bends the gallant mast –
And bends the gallant mast, my boys,
While, like the eagle free,
Away the good ship flies, and leaves
Old England on the lee.

> 'A Wet Sheet and a Flowing Sea' (1825), st.1

2 Wha the deil hae we got for a king,
But a wee, wee German lairdie?
An' whan we gaed to bring him hame,
He was delving in his kail-yairdie;
Sheughing kail, an' laying leeks,
But the hose and but the breeks,
Up his beggar duds he cleeks,
The wee, wee German lairdie.

> 'The Wee, Wee German Lairdie', *Poems and
> Songs* (1847), st.1

3 He's pu'd the rose o' English louns,
An' brak the harp o' Irish clowns,
But our thistle will jag his thumbs,
The wee, wee German lairdie.

> 'The Wee, Wee German Lairdie', *Poems and
> Songs* (1847), st.2

4 O gude ale comes and gude ale goes,
Gude ale gars me sell my hose,
Sell my hose and pawn my shoon,
Gude ale hauds my heart aboon:
Gude ale keeps me bare and busy,
Brandy makes me dull and dizzy,
Gars me sleep and sough i' my shoon,
Gude ale hauds my heart aboon.

> 'Gude Ale Hauds My Heart Aboon', st.1

5 Hame, hame, hame, O hame fain wad I be,
O hame, hame, hame, to my ain countrie!

'Hame, Hame, Hame', chorus

6 The sun rises bright in France,
And fair sets he;
But he has tint the blythe blink he had
In my ain countrie!

'The Sun Rises Bright in France', st.1

7 The bird comes back to summer,
And the blossom to the bee;
But I'll win back, O never,
To my ain countrie.

'The Sun Rises Bright in France', st.4

8 . . . in every quarter of the world you will find
a Scot, a rat, and a Newcastle grindstone.

Quoted by Cunningham as a remark made by
a Mr Bolton to Walter Scott in 1821. See J G
Lockhart, *Memoirs of the Life of Sir Walter Scott,
Bart.* (1837–8), ch.52

Probably derived from Thomas Fuller, *History
of the Worthies of England* (1662): 'A Scotsman
and a Newcastle grindstone travel all the
world over'

Cunningham, Roseanna 1951–

*Nationalist politician, MP for Perth and Kinross
(1995–)*

1 Until a woman is free to be as incompetent
as the average male then she will never be
completely equal.

Said in the run-up to the Perth and Kinross by-
election. Quoted in *The Independent* (14 May 1995)

2 I am sure everyone would rather listen to
the bagpipes than windbags like John Carlisle
droning on in this way. A pibroch is preferable
to the hot air we get from Westminster.

Responding (16 Feb 1996) to comments made by
John Carlisle, an English Conservative MP, in
the House of Commons. Quoted in *The Scotsman*
(17 Feb 1996)

Carlisle objected to the bagpipes thus: 'I like
to fish and shoot in Scotland, and I love the
people, but unfortunately the sound of the
bagpipes turns me completely off – they're
so squeaky.'

Cunninghame Graham, R(obert)
B(ontine) 1852–1936

*Writer, adventurer, traveller, Liberal MP and
nationalist*

1 I never withdraw. I simply said what I meant.

On being asked by the Speaker of the House
of Commons to withdraw an unparliamentary
remark (1 Dec 1888). Quoted in C Watts &

L Davies, *Cunninghame Graham: A Biography*
(1979), ch.4

He had described as 'a dishonourable trick
to avoid discussion' a Tory motion blocking
a debate on notorious conditions of labour
for chain-makers at Cradley Heath near
Birmingham. When the Speaker asked him
to withdraw from the House since he would
not withdraw the expression, Cunninghame
Graham answered, 'Certainly, sir. I will go to
Cradley Heath.' George Bernard Shaw adapted
'I never withdraw' to 'I never apologise' in
his play *Arms and the Man* (1898)

2 I never yet was able to discover why it is, when
a body of white troops, well-armed with all
the newest murderous appliances of scientific
warfare, shoot down men whose ignorance of
their proper calling clearly proves them to be
savages, the act is invariably spoken of as a
'glorious victory'. . . if the aforesaid braceless,
breechless knaves, in precisely the same manner,
shoot our 'glorious troops', their proceeding
becomes a 'bloody massacre', a 'treacherous
ambuscade' or something of a low-priced nature
of that sort.

Letter to *The Daily Graphic* (Nov 1890)

Cunninghame Graham wrote three letters
to the paper in quick succession, outlining
the plight of the Sioux on the Pine Ridge
reservation, South Dakota, and predicting that
their Ghost Dance religion would be ended by
the bullets of the US Army. Before the year
was out the 'battle' or 'massacre' of Wounded
Knee had taken place

3 I wonder if the British public realises that it
is the Sioux themselves who are the Ghosts
dancing. Ghosts of a primeval race. Ghosts of
Ghosts who for three hundred years, through
no crimes committed by themselves (except that
of being born), if it be not a crime to love better
the rustle of the grass than the shrieking of the
engine, have suffered their long purgatory.

Letter to *The Daily Graphic* (Nov 1890)

4 At least we owe the men from whom we
have taken their all, replacing the beaver and
the buffalo with whisky and smallpox, some
reparation besides a small-bore bullet. . . It
puzzles me to think, except for the horse,
what benefit the Indian race has gained from
civilisation.

Letter to *The Daily Graphic* (Dec 1890)

5 Why is it that the races of English and Scotch
have never really amalgamated? So close, so like,
so wizened by the same east wind. . . St George
for Merrie England. No one in his wildest fits
of patriotism ever talked of Merrie Scotland.
Loyal, abstemious, business-like, haggis-eating,
tender, disagreeable, true, a Scotsman may be,
but merry, never.

'De Heretico Comburendo', *Father Archangel
of Scotland and other essays* (1896)

6 What is a 'nigger'?. . . generally all those of almost any race whose skins are darker than our own, and whose ideas of faith, matrimony, banking, and therapeutics, differ from those held by the dwellers of the meridian of Primrose Hill. . .

'Bloody Niggers', *The Social-Democrat* (Apr 1897)

7 . . . to-day a Scotchman stands confessed a sentimental fool, a canting cheat, a grave, sententious man, dressed in a 'stan o' black', oppressed with the tremendous difficulties of the jargon he is bound to speak, and above all weighed down with the responsibility of being Scotch. I know he prays to Gladstone and to Jehovah turn about, finds his amusement in comparing preachers, can read and write and cypher, buys newspapers, tells stories about ministers, drinks whisky, fornicates gravely but without conviction, and generally disports himself after a fashion which would land a more imaginative and less practically constituted man within the precincts of a lunatic asylum before a week was out.

On the Scottish 'type' as presented to the world by the Kailyard School of writers. 'A Survival', *The Ipané* (1899)

8 Success, which touches nothing that it does not vulgarise, should be its own reward. In fact, rewards of any kind are but vulgarities.

We applaud successful folk, and straight forget them, as we do ballet-dancers, actors and orators. They strut their little hour, and then are relegated to peerages, to baronetcies, to books of landed gentry, and the like.

'Success', *Success* (1902). See Shakespeare, *Macbeth*, Act 5, sc.6, l.25

9 He has all the qualifications for a great Liberal Prime Minister. He wears spats and he has a beautiful set of false teeth.

On Sir Henry Campbell-Bannerman (British Prime Minister 1905–8). Quoted in James Bridie, *One Way of Living* (1939), ch.5

10 God forbid that I should go to any heaven in which there are no horses. . .

Letter to President Theodore Roosevelt (27 Mar 1917)

11 The enemies of Scottish nationalism are not the English, for they were ever a great and generous folk, quick to respond when justice calls. Our real enemies are among us, born without imagination.

Speech at Bannockburn (21 Jun 1930). Cf. Alasdair Gray 10

12 That pillar of our civilisation, the Hotchkiss gun.

Quoted in A F Tschiffley, *Don Roberto* (1937), ch.10. Cf. Thomas Carlyle 5

13 The strife of parties means nothing but the rotation of rascals in office.

Quoted in A F Tschiffley, *Don Roberto* (1937), ch.10

14 The proletarian has no country; all are equally prisons to him alike.

Quoted in A F Tschiffley, *Don Roberto* (1937), ch.10

15 There are only two classes, the genuine and the humbug.

Quoted in Alanna Knight, 'Some Notes on Robert Bontine Cunninghame Graham', in *Beattock for Moffat and the Best of R B Cunninghame Graham* (1979)

16 I believe, and it is good for man to believe in something fervently, even in Voodoo, that intense vitality is of itself a sort of genius. Genius I mean for life, for most men hardly ever are alive, passing from golf to tennis, and ending up with bridge, till they ascend to join in singing Rule Britannia in the heavenly choirs.

Quoted in Tom Hubbard, 'R B Cunninghame Graham', *Cencrastus* No.8 (Spring 1982)

Currie, Ken 1960–
Painter

1 The problems of an emerging, challenging indigenous Scottish culture are well-known as we struggle against the many forms of cultural imperialism that have stunted its growth. This is not simply cultural nationalism, but a desire to assert the hegemony of an authentic culture against the damaging and divisive dominant representations of Scotland. It will be a culture inseparable from politics and ideas – a culture of ideas – a popular and ultimately political culture. Painters must be at the heart of this struggle.

'New Glasgow Painting in Context', *Edinburgh Review* No.72 (1986)

D

Dalglish, Kenny 1951–
Football player and manager

1 When you're gaun to somebody else's hoose, you've got to try to look dacent.

> Responding to a friend's comment about the top-hat-and-tails outfit in which he went to Buckingham Palace to receive his MBE. Quoted in Hugh McIlvanney, 'Accentuating the Wonder of Liverpool', *The Observer* (14 Feb 1988). Reprinted in *McIlvanney on Football* (1994)

2 Very soon we will be down to one-a-side – one will be a priest and the other a minister.

> Said as manager of Blackburn Rovers, on the increasing tendency of referees to send off players for swearing. Quoted in *The Independent* (6 Mar 1993)

Dallán Forgaill 6th century
Monk

1 Raunais raind co figuir eter libru léig.
Legais rúna, ro-chuaid eter scolaib screptra,
sceo ellacht imm-uaim n-éscai im rith,
raith rith la gréin ngescaig,
sceo réin rith.
Rímfed rind nime, nech in-choí cech ndiruais
ro-Columb ó Chille – cúalammar.
He separated the elements according
   to figures
among the books of the Law.
He read mysteries and distributed the
   Scriptures among the schools,
and he put together the harmony concerning
   the course of the moon,
the course which it ran with the rayed sun,
and the course of the sea.
He could number the stars of heaven, the one
   who could tell all the rest
which we have heard from Colum Cille.

> Poem to Colum Cille (St Columba), supposedly begun c.575 but not completed until after the saint's death in 597

Dalrymple, Sir David see Hailes, Lord

Dalrymple, James see Stair, 1st Viscount

Dalrymple, John see Stair, 1st Earl of

Dalyell, Tam 1932–
Labour politician, MP for West Lothian (1962–83) and for Linlithgow (1983–)

1 We would have the absurd situation in which Scottish and Welsh MPs [at Westminster] could continue to legislate on subjects which had been devolved to the Assemblies in their own countries. They would not be responsible to their own constituents for such legislation, nor would they be answerable to the English voters who would be affected by it.

> *Devolution: The End of Britain?* (1977), ch.11, 'The Slide to Independence'

>> This statement defines the 'West Lothian Question', a key issue of the 1970s devolution debate, so named after Dalyell's constituency, since it was he who most persistently articulated it. He gave examples of what he would and would not be able to vote on: 'Betting, bookies and gaming in Blackburn, Lancashire, but not Blackburn, West Lothian. . . Waterways in Winchester, but not in Winchburgh.'

2 Scottish and Welsh interference in purely English affairs would be strongly resented, particularly since the participation of these MPs could well be decisive in deciding whether such legislation was introduced or not.

> *Devolution: The End of Britain?* (1977), ch.11, 'The Slide to Independence'

>> It has been pointed out that interchanging 'Scottish and Welsh' with 'English', and replacing 'could well be' with 'would always', produced a good explanation of the existing situation and why a need was felt for some form of constitutional change

3 Myths about a nation's history should be treated with considerable caution at the best of times: if they also incorporate an unjustified – and wholly unhistorical – sense of national grievance, they should be handled with especial care. Like the Irish, the Scots have a strong and pervasive sense of history, yet all too often they prefer the romantic myth to the complicated truth. . .

> *Devolution: The End of Britain?* (1977), ch.12, 'The Unrealities'

4 The truth of the matter is that we Scots have always been more divided amongst ourselves than pitted against the English. Scottish history before the union of parliaments is a gloomy,

violent tale of murders, feuds and tribal
revenge. . . Only after the Act of Union did
Highlanders and Lowlanders, Picts and Celts,
begin to recognise one another as fellow-citizens.

> *Devolution: The End of Britain?* (1977), ch.12,
> 'The Unrealities'

5 I make no apology for returning yet again to
the subject of the sinking of the *Belgrano*.

> Speech in the House of Commons (13 May 1983)

6 The Prime Minister is a sustained, brazen
deceiver now hiding cynical performances. . .
I say that she is a bounder, a liar, a deceiver,
a cheat and a crook.

> In the House of Commons (29 Oct 1988), on
> Margaret Thatcher's alleged involvement in the
> leak of the Solicitor General's letter during the
> Westlands Affair
>
> > Dalyell was suspended from the Commons
> > for refusing to withdraw these remarks

7 I believe that with Mrs Thatcher pique and
temper can be the father and mother of policy.

> *Misrule: How Mrs Thatcher Misled Parliament
> from the Sinking of the Belgrano to the Wright
> Affair* (1987), ch.5

Davidson, John c.1549–1604

Presbyterian minister

1 Busk, busk him as bonnily as you can, bring
him in as fairly as you will, we see the horns
of his mitre weel enough.

> On James VI's attempt to reintroduce bishops by
> manipulating the appointment of superintendents
> to the Kirk. Quoted in Walter Scott, *Tales of a
> Grandfather*, 2nd Series (1829), ch.36

Davidson, John 1857–1909

Poet and journalist

1 But I don't allow it's luck and all a toss;
There's no such thing as being starred and
crossed;
It's just the power of some to be a boss,
And the bally power of others to be bossed. . .

> 'Thirty Bob a Week', *Ballads and Songs*
> (1894), st.2

2 . . . the difficultest job a man can do,
is to come it brave and meek with thirty
bob a week,
and feel that that's the proper thing for you.

> 'Thirty Bob a Week', *Ballads and Songs*
> (1894), st.15

3 It's a naked child against a hungry wolf;
It's playing bowls upon a splitting wreck;

It's walking on a string across a gulf
With millstones fore-and-aft about your neck;
But the thing is daily done by many and
many a one;
And we fall, face forward, fighting, on the deck.

> 'Thirty Bob a Week', *Ballads and Songs*
> (1894), st.16

4 In anguish we uplift
A new unhallowed song:
The race is to the swift;
The battle to the strong.

> 'War Song', *The Last Ballad* (1899), st.1

5 In many a mountain-pass,
Or meadow green and fresh,
Mass shall encounter mass
Of shuddering human flesh;
Opposing ordnance roar
Across the swaths of slain,
And blood in torrents pour
In vain – always in vain,
For war breeds war again!

> 'War Song', *The Last Ballad* (1899), st.7

6 When the pods went pop on the broom,
green broom,
And apples began to be golden-skinned,
We harboured a stag in the Priory coomb,
And we feathered his trail up-wind, up-wind,
We feathered his trail up-wind –
A stag of warrant, a stag, a stag,
A runnable stag, a kingly crop,
Brow, bay and tray and three on top,
A stag, a runnable stag.

> 'A Runnable Stag', *Holiday and other poems*
> (1906), st.1

Davidson, Julie

Journalist

1 She haunts the sculleries and parlours of
Scotland's social history like an irreversible
curse. She patrols our psyche like a
bossy traffic warden, comic incarnation of
the authoritarian drudge. She is Margaret
Ogilvy writ large, speaking in balloons, the
martyred mother figure who stalks the pages
of Scottish literature. She is Black Agnes
of the but-and-ben, scolding her menfolk,
stiffening their backbone, sacrificing herself
and her daughters on the altar of their
incompetence.

> On 'Ma Broon', character in the *Sunday Post*'s
> strip cartoon 'The Broons'. *The Scotsman* (19
> Feb 1979)
>
> > Margaret Ogilvy was the mother of J M Barrie,
> > who wrote a highly sentimental biography of
> > her in 1896. Cf. Black Agnes of Dunbar 1

Davie, Elspeth (*née* **Dryer**) 1918–95
Writer and painter, wife of George Davie

1 Breaking the long silence of a shy person is a mighty undertaking. One feels that the words which break such a silence must be pretty stupendous ones for they must shatter the silence of eternity itself. Usually they are the most facetious ever uttered.

> Journal entry (3 Apr 1939). Quoted in *Chapman* No.81 (1995)

2 . . . an extraordinary interesting mind and a great talker – the Dr Johnson of Varsity as he is called.

> On her first meeting with her future husband, George Davie. Journal entry (11 Jul 1939). Quoted in *Chapman* No.81 (1995)

3 So often it is one's ordinary life which is unreal and small. In great Art one comes to grips with what is really true and it seems unnecessary to applaud or praise, and there are no words left. The silence in recognition of greatness is the silence of people looking at stars or mountains.

> Journal entry (20 Nov 1939). Quoted in *Chapman* No.81 (1995)

4 A short story. . . is seldom an easy amble along a well-marked lane. More often it's a bit of a tightrope walk, a balancing act over a sort of Niagara of sights, sounds and sensations that we'd love to look down at, but can't in case we fall off the wire. We have to get across, and what's more, do it with a certain amount of grace.

> 'Notes on the Short Story', in *Chapman* No.81 (1995)

5 . . . learning to read is the only way of learning to write. It is not a case of becoming obsessed with somebody's style and trying to copy it. Rather, it is being in the emotional company of books – being warmed, sustained, comforted, stimulated and made more courageous.

> 'Notes on the Short Story', in *Chapman* No.81 (1995)

6 The desolating and the unfamiliar is happening continually between our getting up and our going to bed. It is of this day-to-day business of living, its mysteriousness and its absurdity, that I would like to write.

> Quoted in obituary article, *The Scotsman* (15 Nov 1995)

Davie, George 1912–
Philosopher and historian of education, husband of Elspeth Davie

1 The Democratic Intellect

> Title of book (1961). Cf. Walter Elliot 2

Davie's title derives from a phrase coined by Elliot, 'democratic intellectualism'

2 This Scottish Enlightenment – was it an exotic bloom where Scotland was concerned? How far was it the mere preserve of a leisure class, which had immured itself in the New Town of Edinburgh? This point of view, though still widespread, is, I believe, seriously confused, being due to a failure to distinguish the aesthetic side. . . from the side I wish to discuss: the passion for ideas.

> 'Hume, Reid and the Passion for Ideas', *Edinburgh in the Age of Reason: a Commemoration* (1967)

3 When a writer, typical of the last generation – Professor J Y T Greig in his *Life of David Hume* – proclaimed that modern Scotland was unthinkable apart from the Union, his words betrayed a point of view which takes it for granted that modern Scotland does not bear thinking of at all.

> 'Nationalism and the Unthinkable' (1969), published in *Edinburgh Review* No.83 (1990)

4 Elsewhere the Enlightenment may have gradually faded out, leaving behind an honoured though very controversial memory. In Scotland it went out not with a whimper but a bang and was by a sort of common consent almost instantly forgotten.

> 'The Scottish Enlightenment' (Historical Association pamphlet, 1981)

5 It used to be noted that visitors to Scotland without a taste for metaphysics were liable to be nonplussed by the questions publicly debated, because of the tendency for arguments about mundane matters to develop into arguments about first principles and for ordinary problems about material things to turn into rarefied problems of the relation of matter to mind.

> *The Crisis of the Democratic Intellect* (1986), prologue

Deacon Blue see **Ross, Ricky**

Dean of Lismore, Book of the
Compiled c.1500

Manuscript of largely Gaelic verse collected by Dugald MacGregor of Fortingall and his son James, Dean of Lismore

1 'Sloinnidh, a dheaghlaocha, dhamhsa,'
adubhairt Fionn fuair gach ioth;
'cuiridh mar sin ar eól inne
cá ceól libh as binne ar bioth.'

Do ráidh Conán gurbh í an imirt
aoincheól as binne fuair féin;
maith lámh an fhir ré h-eadh bruidhne,

fear sin gan chuimhne ar chéill.

† 'Tell me, you goodly warriors,' quoth Fionn
who conquered every land; 'let me thus know,
what music do ye deem the sweetest on earth?'
   Conan declared that [the noise of] gaming
was the sweetest music himself had ever found;
good was that man's hand so long as fighting
lasted, but he was a man who forgot sense.

> Quoted in Neil Ross (ed.), *Heroic Poetry from
> the Book of the Dean of Lismore* (1939)

2 'Ceól as mó rugas do roghainn,'
do ráidh Diarmaid na ndearc mall,
'a roghrádh gion go rabh dhamhsa,
comhrádh ban ansa ann.'

† 'The music on which my choice has most
fallen,' said Diarmaid of lingering eye, 'my
favourite of all, is the converse of women,
even though all their love was not for me.'

> Quoted in Neil Ross (ed.), *Heroic Poetry from
> the Book of the Dean of Lismore* (1939)

3 Duibhe ná fiach barr a fhuilt,
deirge a ghruadh ioná fuil laoigh;
fá míne ioná cubhar sreabh,
gile ioná an sneachta cneas Fraoich.

Caise ioná an casnaidhe a fholt,
guirme a rosg ná oighreadh leac;
deirge ioná partaing a bhéal,
gile a dhéad ioná bláth feath.

† Blacker than raven his locks, redder his cheeks
than calf's blood; softer than foam of streams,
whiter than snow the skin of Fraoch.
   More curled than ringlets from the wood-
plane his hair, bluer his eyes than a sheet
of ice; his mouth redder than scarlet, his teeth
whiter than woodbine bloom.

> Description of the hero Fraoch, who in fighting
> a monster lost his life, st.29–30. Quoted in Neil
> Ross (ed.), *Heroic Poetry from the Book of the
> Dean of Lismore* (1939)

4 Is fearr sgíos cos bharr gnímh ghlain
ná fos agus sgíos meanman;
mairidh sgíos meanman go bráth:
cha mhair sgíos cos acht aontráth.

† Better is tiredness of feet after a bright deed
than inertness and tiredness of spirit: tiredness
of spirit remains for ever, tiredness of feet
remains but for a space.

> 15th or 16th century. Quoted in W J Watson
> (ed.), *Scottish Verse from the Book of the Dean of
> Lismore* (1937)

5 Is dú éirghe i n-aghaidh Gall,
nocha dóigh éirghe udmhall;
faobhair claidheamh, reanna ga,
cóir a gcaitheamh go h-aobhdha.

† Meet it is to rise against Saxons; we expect
no wavering rising: edges of swords, points
of spears, it is right to ply them blithely.

> Poem addressed to Archibald, Earl of Argyll

and Chancellor of Scotland, before the Battle of
Flodden (1513), st.2. Quoted in W J Watson (ed.),
*Scottish Verse from the Book of the Dean of
Lismore* (1937)

> This is an example of 'brosnachadh catha'
> (incitement to battle). Argyll was in fact killed
> in the battle

6 Alasdair, 'ndo thréig tú an ghruaim
nó a bhféad sibh a cur uaibh ar lár?
a nd'fhan sibh 'n bhliadhain gan ghean?
nó a mbí sibh mar sean go bráth?

Chaoidhche ní nd'fhuaras do ghean,
ó ataoi tú go sean liath:
más ar ghruaim bhitheas an rath,
's mór fhuair thú de mhath ó Dhia.

† Alasdair, have you shed the gloom or can you
throw it from you? Have you remained this
year without cheer, or will you be so for ever?
Never have I found your cheer, now that you
are old and grey; if grace goes with gloom,
great is the good you have got from God.

> 15th or 16th century. Quoted in W J Watson
> (ed.), *Scottish Verse from the Book of the Dean of
> Lismore* (1937). The author is given as Donnchadh
> Mac an Phearsúin (Duncan MacPherson)

Declaration of Arbroath, The 1320

1 But after all, if this prince [Robert Bruce]
shall leave the principles he hath so nobly
pursued, and consent that we or our kingdom be
subjected to the king or the people of England,
we will immediately endeavour to expel him,
as our enemy, and as the subverter both of
his own and our rights, and will make another
king, who will defend our liberties; for, so long
as there shall but one hundred of us remain
alive, we will never subject ourselves to the
dominion of the English. For it is not glory,
it is not riches, neither is it honour, but it is
freedom alone that we fight and contend for,
which no honest man will lose but with his life.

> The Declaration was a letter sent to Pope
> John XXII by the Scottish barons seeking
> recognition of Scotland's independence from
> England, and also clearly stating the consti-
> tutional principle that sovereignty lies with
> the people, not the crown. Cf. Lord Cooper 3

Defoe, Daniel 1660–1731
English pamphleteer, novelist and traveller

1 A rough, unhewn, uncultivated Spot,
Of old so fam'd, and so of late forgot:
NEGLECTED SCOTLAND shews her awful
  BROW,
Not always quite so near to Heaven as now.

> 'Caledonia, a Poem in Honour of Scotland' (1706)

As an observer and informant for the English government, he was in Scotland while the Union of Parliaments was being debated, and recorded the bitter divisions which the proposal caused

2 As Cromwell's Soldiers initiated them thus into the Arts and Industry of the Husbandman, so they left them the *English* accent upon their Tongues, and they preserve it also to this Day; for they speak perfect *English*, even much better than in the most southerly Provinces of *Scotland*; nay, some will say that they speak it as well as at *London*; though I do not grant that neither. It is certain they keep the Southern Accent very well, and speak very good *English*.

On Invernesians. *A Tour Through the Whole Island of Great Britain* (1724–7)

Demarco, Richard 1930–
Art promoter and gallery owner, co-founder of the Traverse Theatre

1 I thank God for the Edinburgh Festival. It gives Edinburgh a sense of its true destiny as a city worthy of comparison with all those Italian cities that first gave meaning to the word 'civilised'.

'A Renaissance Vision', *The Sunday Mail Story of Scotland* (1988), No.26

Dewar, Donald 1937–
Labour politician and MP

1 He could start a party in an empty room – and often did – filling it with good cheer, Gaelic songs, and argument.

On Labour Party leader John Smith, at his funeral service in Edinburgh (19 May 1994)

2 . . . The people have lost a friend – someone who was on their side and they know it.

On John Smith (19 May 1994)

Dickson, David c.1583–1663
Covenanting minister of Irvine

1 The work gangs bonnily on!

Attrib., in Henry Guthry, *Memoirs of Scottish Affairs, Civil and Ecclesiastical* (1702)

Dickson is supposed to have uttered these words (29 Oct 1645) at the foot of the Glasgow gallows, approving the spate of executions which followed the defeat of Montrose's royalist army at Philiphaugh. Many historians, including John Buchan in his biography of Montrose, think that Dickson, a man of great learning, was wrongly imputed by Guthry

Discipline, First Book of 1561
Document written by John Knox and others, laying down the guiding principles of Church of Scotland government and administration

1 It appertaineth to the people and to every severall Congregation to elect their Minister.

Book of Discipline (1621 edition), 4th Head

First published as part of Knox's *History of the Reformation in Scotland* (1586)

2 For altogether this is to be avoided, that any man be violently intruded or thrust in upon any congregation.

Book of Discipline (1621 edition), 4th Head

This and the clause quoted above were the fundamental Presbyterian principles on which the disputes leading to the Disruption of 1843 were centred

3 Of necessitie therefore we judge it, that every severall Kirk have one School-maister appointed, such a one at least as is able to teach Grammar and the Latine tongue, if the town be of any reputation.

Book of Discipline (1621 edition), 5th Head, Part 5

Discipline, Second Book of 1578
A more detailed and stricter version of the First Book of Discipline

1 It is ane title falslie usurpit be antichryst to call him self heid of the kirk and aucht not to be attributit to angell or to mane, of quhat estait soevir he be, saiffing to Chryst, the heid and onlie monarche in this kirk.

Second Book of Discipline (1621 edition), 1st Head, paragraph 12

Docherty, Tommy 1928–
Football player and manager

1 The ideal board of directors should be made up of three men – two dead and the other dying.

1977. Quoted in Kenny MacDonald, *Scottish Football Quotations* (1994)

2 They offered me a handshake of £10,000 to settle amicably. I told them they would have to be a lot more amicable than that.

After being sacked as manager of Preston (1981). Quoted in Kenny MacDonald, *Scottish Football Quotations* (1994)

3 To the Scots, football's a lovely incurable disease.

Only a Game?, BBC documentary (1985)

4 Jimmy Hill is to football what King Herod was to babysitting.

In interview with Clive Anderson on *Clive*

Anderson Talks Back (broadcast on Channel 4, Jun 1992)

> Jimmy Hill is considered by many Scots to be the *bête-noir* of football commentary. In the World Cup finals of 1982, for example, he infamously described David Narey's goal for Scotland against Brazil as a 'toe poke'. Cf. Jimmy Hill 1

5 Football management these days is like a nuclear war. No winners, just survivors.

> 1992. Quoted in Peter Ball and Phil Shaw (eds), *The Umbro Book of Football Quotations* (1993)

Dodd, Kenn 1931–
English comedian

1 I became a stand-up comedian. . . and played. . . the House of Terror, the Glasgow Empire. Here the audience would say to English comedians, 'Awa hame and bile yer heid'.

> Interview on *Desert Island Discs*, broadcast on BBC Radio 4 (8 June 1990). Reproduced in Vivien Devlin, *Kings, Queens and People's Palaces: An Oral History of the Scottish Variety Theatre, 1920–1970* (1991), ch.10. Cf. Jimmy Logan 3

Dods, Meg or Margaret (pseudonym of Isobel Johnstone) 1781–1857
Cookery writer, novelist and journalist

1 Carving has ever been esteemed one of the minor arts of polite life, – a test at first sight of the breeding of men, as its dexterous and graceful performance is presumed to mark a person trained in good fashion.

> *The Cook and Housewife's Manual* (1826; 10th edition, 1854), Part 1, 'Directions for Carving'
>
> > Isobel Johnstone took as her pseudonym the name of the innkeeper in Walter Scott's novel, *St Ronan's Well* (1823). Cf. Walter Scott 85

2 . . . the Cook, like the Surgeon, must first look on, observe carefully, and then put to her hand; for it would be quite as easy to teach surgery by book, as many of the manual operations of cookery.

> *The Cook and Housewife's Manual* (1826; 10th edition, 1854), Part 3, ch.1, 'Made Dishes'

3 An English traveller in Scotland. . . states in his very pleasant book that our Club have fallen into a mistake in the name of these cakes, and that *petticoat-tails* is a corruption of the French *Petites Gatelles*. It may be so: in Scottish culinary terms there are many corruptions, though we rather think the name *Petticoat-tails* has its origin in the shape of the cakes, which is exactly that of the bell-hoop petticoats of our ancient Court ladies.

On Scotch Petticoat-tails, triangular cakes of shortbread. *The Cook and Housewife's Manual* (1826; 10th edition, 1854), Part 3, ch.5, 'Creams, Jellies etc'

Dòmhnaíl Donn (Donald MacDonald of Bohuntin) d.1691
Poet and cattle thief

1 A Cheit, tog an ceann.

† Kate, take away the head.

> By tradition, these words were spoken to his sister by his tongue just after he was beheaded
>
> > He was executed by Grant of Glen Urquhart when he was caught trying to elope with the latter's daughter

Dòmhnall Ruadh Chorùna (Donald MacDonald of Coruna) 1887–1967
Poet

1 An t-sealg 's an t-iasgach bha sinne dìon dhaibh
Am measg fuil is crèadh ann an sliabh na Fraing,
Cha bhlais ar beul-ne air sgath gu sìorraidh –
Tha laghan dèante nach fhiach sinn ann –
Ach dha na h-uaislean a bh' air a' chluasaig
'S a' phlangaid shuarach 's i suas mun ceann;
Bhiomaide 'n uair sin a-muigh aig uabhas
'S am peileir luaidhe mar cluais le srann.

† The hunting and fishing which we were
   defending for them
in the blood and clay of the soil of France,
we shall never taste a morsel of that –
the laws decree that our rights are worthless.
But the gentry will – they who sleep on pillows,
with their despicable blankets over their heads,
while we faced frightful odds,
the whine of bullets constantly round our ears.

> 'Oran na Seilge' ('Hunting Song'), in *Dòmhnall Ruadh Chorùna* (1969; 1995), st.6

Donaldson, David 1916–96
Painter

1 If you keep the original inspiration – that which fascinates you at the beginning – for a year, or a month or half an hour or for however long it takes – you might arrive at a conclusion.

> 'Artist's comment', in Bill Hare, *Contemporary Painting in Scotland* (1992), p.72

2 I was a wee bastard who was bairned up a close in Coatbridge.

> Quoted in W Gordon Smith, *David Donaldson: Painter and Limner to Her Majesty the Queen in Scotland* (1996), 'The Childhood Years'

Donaldson, Margaret Caldwell 1926–

Psychologist

1 When we make laws which compel our children
to go to school we assume collectively an
awesome responsibility. For a period of ten
years, with minor variations from country to
country, the children are conscripts; and their
youth does nothing to alter the seriousness of
this fact.

Children's Minds (1978), ch.1

2 . . . if we are not willing to try and to keep
trying, in the light of knowledge attained, to
help our children meet the demands which we
impose on them, then we must not call them
stupid. We must rather call ourselves indifferent
or afraid.

Children's Minds (1978), ch.11

3 Human beings know more about life's dangers
than other animals, and have to deal with a
greater range of fears. . . We know that thieves
break in, that rapists and muggers strike, that
jobs can be lost. We know that love can be lost.
We know that, sooner or later, we must die.

Human Minds (1992), ch.2

4 . . . every one of us exists at the expense of
countless unborn sisters and brothers.

Human Minds (1992), ch.4

Donegan, Lonnie (originally Anthony Donegan) 1931–

Skiffle singer and guitarist

1 Does Your Chewing Gum Lose Its Flavour
(On The Bedpost Overnight)

Title of song (1959)

2 My Old Man's a Dustman

Title of song (1960)

Donnchadh Mac Cailéin (Duncan, son of Colin)

Medieval poet

1 Cia don phléid as ceann uidhe
ó do theasta an deaghdhuine?
tá na deoir ar éis an fhir,
an phléid gan treoir ré faicsin.

Tá 'na díleacht giodh olc linn
an phléid ar n-éag do Lachlann;
is béad sin ar lár gach lis,
an phléid ar easbhaidh eólais.

† Whom does begging make its goal, now that
the worthy man is dead? Tears follow the
man; begging is seen helpless.

After Lachlann's death begging, though sore
we deem it, is an orphan; it is a sad thing in
the midst of every court, that begging knows
not where to go.

Poem lamenting the death of Lachlann Galbraith,
st.1–2. Quoted in W J Watson (ed.), *Scottish
Verse from the Book of the Dean of Lismore* (1937)

Donnchadh Mór ó Leamhnacht (Great Duncan from Lennox) 14th–15th century

Poet, possibly Duncan, 8th Earl of Lennox

1 Mairg duine do chaill a ghuth,
agus 'gá bhfuil sruth do dhán,
agus nach fhéad gabháil leó,
agus nach eól bheith 'na thámh. . .

Is mairg nach sguir dá dhring drang,
agus do-ní a rann do rádh,
agus nach cluintear a chruit,
agus nach tuigthear a dhán.

† Woe to the man who has lost his voice, and
who has a flood of song, and who cannot sing
them, and knows not how to hold his peace. . .

Woe to him who ceases not from his ding-
dong, and still recites his verse; whose harp
is not heard nor his song understood.

'Mairg duine' ('Woe to the man'), st.1, 3. Quoted
in W J Watson (ed.), *Scottish Verse from the Book
of the Dean of Lismore* (1937)

Donnchadh Og (Young Duncan)

dates unknown

Poet

1 Seacht saighde atá ar mo thí,
tá gach saighead díobh 'gam lot,
ag teacht eadram agus Dia,
ó's é sin as mian lem chorp.

† Seven shafts there be that seek me out; each
shaft of them wounds me, coming between
me and God, for such is my body's desire.

Poem on the Seven Deadly Sins, st.1. Quoted in
W J Watson (ed.), *Scottish Verse from the Book
of the Dean of Lismore* (1937)

Donoghue v. Stevenson 1932

1 In consequence of the nauseating sight of the
snail in said circumstances, and of the noxious
condition of the said snail-tainted ginger beer
consumed by her, the pursuer sustained the
shock and illness hereinafter condescended on.

Extract from pleadings in the case of Donoghue
v. Stevenson

This was a landmark case in the law of delict,
decided on appeal to the House of Lords in
1932, in favour of the pursuer Mrs Donoghue.

On 26 Aug 1928, at the Wellmeadow Cafe in Paisley, she discovered the decomposed remains of a snail in an opaque ginger beer bottle, some of the contents of which she had already drunk, and sued the manufacturer, Stevenson, for damages, even though she had no relationship in contract with him

Donovan (full name Donovan Leitch)
1944–

Singer and songwriter

1 Catch the Wind
   Title of song (1965)

2 Mellow Yellow
   Title of song (1966)

3 Hurdy Gurdy Man
   Title of song (1968)

Douglas, Archibald (5th Earl of Angus)
c.1449–1514

Statesman and nobleman, known as 'Bell-the-Cat'

1 I am he who will bell the cat.
   Attrib. Said in 1482 at Lauder. Quoted in Walter Scott, *Tales of a Grandfather*, 1st Series (1828), ch.22

   The story is that a faction of the nobility gathered to discuss how to counter the power of Robert Cochrane, Earl of Mar and favourite of James III. Lord Gray recounted the fable of the mice who wished to hang a bell round the neck of the cat to warn them of its approach: all were agreed on the plan, but none would volunteer to put it into effect. At this point, Douglas made his famous remark. Shortly afterwards, Cochrane and his associates arrived at Lauder, were seized and hanged over the bridge there

Douglas, Bill 1934–91

Film director

1 What interests me is reaching into the soul of a person, other than the mask presented so often. There is so much to be read in a person's face. I use the camera to read the face and it will speak volumes if you listen to it.
   Quoted in Andrew Noble, 'Bill Douglas's Trilogy', in Eddie Dick (ed.), *From Limelight to Satellite* (1990)

2 For as long as I remember I always liked the pictures... That was my real home, my happiest place when I was lucky enough to be there. Outside, whether in the village or the city, whether I was seven or seventeen, it always seemed to be raining or grey and my heart would sink to despairing depths. I hated reality. Of course I had to go to school – sometimes. And I had to go home and apply myself to the things one has to do. But the next picture, how to get in, was the thing that occupied my mind.
   Quoted in Andrew Noble, 'Bill Douglas, 1934–91: A Memoir', in Eddie Dick, Andrew Noble & Duncan Petrie (eds), *Bill Douglas: A Lanternist's Account* (1993)

3 When you write, write only what you see, what you want the audience to see. Nothing more. Every shot is a sentence.
   On scriptwriting. As recalled by Colin Young, quoted in Andrew Noble, 'Bill Douglas, 1934–91: A Memoir', in Eddie Dick, Andrew Noble & Duncan Petrie (eds), *Bill Douglas: A Lanternist's Account* (1993)

Douglas, Gavin c.1474–1522

Poet, Bishop of Dunkeld and translator of Virgil's Aeneid

1 Fyrst I protest, beaw schirris, be your leif,
   Beis weill avisit my wark or ye repreif,
   Consider it warly, reid oftar than anys;
   Weill at a blenk sle poetry nocht tayn is,
   And yit forsuyth I set my bissy pane
   As that I couth to mak it braid and plane,
   Kepand na sudron bot our awyn langage,
   And spekis as I lernyt quhen I was page.
   Eneados (1513), Prologue to Bk 1, ll.105–12

2 The batalis and the man I wil discrive
   Fra Troyis boundis first that fugitive
   By fait to Ytail come and cost Lavyne,
   Our land and sey katchit with mekil pyne
   By fors of goddis abufe, from every steid,
   Of cruell Juno throu ald remembrit fede.
   Eneados (1513), Bk 1, i, ll.1–6

3 Heich as a hill the jaw of watir brak
   And in ane hepe cam on thame with a swak.
   Eneados (1513), Bk 1, iii, ll.21–2

4 In obscure lycht, quhair mune may nocht
   be kend...
   On the darkness of Hell. *Eneados*, Bk 6, iv, l.72

5 The frosty regioun ryngis of the yer,
   The tyme and sesson bittir, cald and paill,
   Tha schort days that clerkis clepe brumaill,
   Quhen brym blastis of the northyn art
   Ourquhelmyt had Neptunus in his cart,
   And all to schaik the levis of the trees,
   The rageand storm ourweltrand wally seys.
   Ryveris ran reid on spait with watir browne,
   And burnys hurlys all thar bankis downe,
   And landbrist rumland rudely with sik beir,

So lowd ne rumyst wild lyoun or ber. . .

Eneados (1513), Prologue to Bk 7, ll.12–22

6 Thik drumly skuggis dyrkynt so the hevyn,
  Dym skyis oft furth warpit feirfull levyn,
  Flaggis of fire, and mony felloun flaw,
  Scharpe soppys of sleit and of the snypand snaw.
  The dolly dichis war all donk and wait,
  The law valle flodderit all with spait,
  The plane stretis and every hie way
  Full of floschis, dubbis, myre and clay.

Eneados (1513), Prologue to Bk 7, ll.47–54

7 Hornyt Hebowd, quhilk we clepe the
    nycht owle,
  Within hir cavern hard I schowt and yowle,
  Laithly of form, with crukyt camscho beke,
  Ugsum to heir was hir wild elrich screke.
  The wild geis claking eik by nyghtis tyde
  Atour the cite fleand hard I glyde.

Eneados (1513), Prologue to Bk 7, ll.105–10

8 For to behald, it was ane gloir to se
  The stabillit wyndis and the cawmyt sea,
  The soft sessoun, the firmament serene,
  The lown illuminat air and firth amene.

On the arrival of Spring. *Eneados* (1513),
Prologue to Bk 12, ll.51–4

9 And al small fowlys syngis on the spray:
  'Welcum the lord of lycht and lamp of day,
  Welcum fostyr of tendir herbys grene,
  Welcum quyknar of floryst flowris scheyn. . .'

Eneados (1513), Prologue to Bk 12, ll.251–4

Douglas, James see Morton, 4th Earl of

Douglas, (George) Norman 1868–1952
Travel writer, essayist and novelist

1 . . . many of us would do well to *mediterraneanise*
  ourselves for a season, to quicken those ethic
  roots from which has sprung so much of what
  is best in our natures.

Siren Land (1911), 'Uplands of Sorrento'

2 'Shall I give you my recipe for happiness? I find
  everything useful and nothing indispensable.
  I find everything wonderful and nothing
  miraculous. I reverence the body. I avoid first
  causes like the plague.'

South Wind (1917), ch.15 (Mr Keith)

3 . . . I like to taste my friends but not to eat
  them; in other words, I hold the old-fashioned
  view that all interrogation, all social curiosity,
  is vulgar and therefore to be avoided. . .

A Plea for Better Manners (1924 pamphlet)

4 I pick up an ordinary novel now and then, and
  ask myself whether we shall go on reading this

flatulent balderdash much longer. I hope not.
For what is the ordinary novel but a string
of foregone conclusions; a barrel-organ wound
up to play one particular tune?. . . Life would
indeed be a bore, if constructed on the lines
of the ordinary novel.

A Plea for Better Manners (1924 pamphlet)

5 What struck me in these islands was their
  bleakness, the number of ridiculous little
  churches, the fact that bogs do not require a
  level surface for their existence but can also run
  uphill, and that ponies sometimes have a black
  stripe like the wild ass. . . Nightmarish regions,
  swathed in boreal mists. . . On returning to
  Deeside we felt as if we had entered the Tropics.

On Orkney and Shetland in 1891. *Looking Back*
(1933), p.64

Douglas, O. see Buchan, Anna

Douglas, Ronald MacDonald 1896–1987
Writer and nationalist

1 . . . do try to sound the *r*, although not with the
  exaggerated trill usually given to it by so-called
  Scotch comedians. But, and again this to my
  English readers, don't even attempt to get the
  guttural sounds of *ach*, and *loch*. You will only
  strangle yourselves. To say *ach!* correctly you
  need generations of Scots blood behind you,
  and you must have been born with the peat-
  reek in your nostrils, and the sight of the hills
  as the first thing ever you clapped your eyes on.

Advice on pronunciation, *The Scots Book* (1935)

Douglas, Sheila 1932–
Folksinger and folklorist

1 The Scottish folk tradition is a shared and
  democratic tradition, which is what makes it one
  of the best, like a great river fed by a myriad of
  different streams. . . [It is] carried on in songs
  that never get broadcast or recorded, because
  naturally they are too dangerous.

'A Window on the Folk Revival', *Cencrastus*
No.35 (Winter 1989)

Douglas (of Fingland), William fl.1700
Poet

1 Maxwelton banks are bonnie,
  Whar early fa's the dew;
  Whar me and Annie Laurie
  Made up the promise true;
  Made up the promise true,
  And never forget will I;

And for bonnie Annie Laurie
I'd lay me down and die.

'Annie Laurie' (17th century), st.1. Cf. Alicia
Anne Spottiswoode 1

The authorship is uncertain, but now generally
ascribed to Douglas

2 She's backit like the peacock;
She's breastit like the swan. . .

'Annie Laurie' (17th century), st.2

Douglas-Home, Alexander
see Home (of the Hirsel), Lord

Douglas-Home, Caroline 1937–
Daughter of Lord Home of the Hirsel

1 He is used to dealing with estate workers.
I cannot see how anyone can say he is out
of touch.

On her father, who had just become Conservative
leader and Prime Minister (20 Oct 1963).
Cf. Lord Home 2

Doyle, Sir Arthur Conan 1859–1930
Novelist, creator of Sherlock Holmes

1 London, that great cesspool into which all the
loungers of the Empire are irresistibly drained.

A Study in Scarlet (1887), ch.1, 'Mr Sherlock
Holmes'

2 'Wonderful!' I ejaculated.
'Common-place,' said Holmes.

A Study in Scarlet (1887), ch.3, 'The Lauriston
Gardens Mystery'

3 'There is a mystery about this which stimulates
the imagination; where there is no imagination,
there is no horror.'

A Study in Scarlet (1887), ch.5, 'Our Advertisement Brings a Visitor'

4 'How often have I said to you that when
you have eliminated the impossible, whatever
remains, *however improbable*, must be the truth?'

The Sign of Four (1890), ch.6, 'Sherlock Holmes
Gives a Demonstration'

Many of Holmes's 'laws' may have had
their origins in the remarks of Dr Joseph
Bell (1837–1911), under whom Conan Doyle
studied medicine in Edinburgh, and who was
fond of quoting the maxims of an earlier
eminent surgeon, James Syme (1799–1870).
Cf. Joseph Bell 1

5 'You see, but you do not observe.'

'A Scandal in Bohemia', *Adventures of Sherlock
Holmes* (1891)

6 'It is a capital mistake to theorise before one
has data. Insensibly one begins to twist facts to
suit theories, instead of theories to suit facts.'

'A Scandal in Bohemia', *Adventures of Sherlock
Holmes* (1891)

7 'As a rule,' said Holmes, 'the more bizarre a
thing is the less mysterious it proves to be. It
is your commonplace, featureless crimes which
are really puzzling.'

'The Red-Headed League', *Adventures of Sherlock
Holmes* (1891)

8 'It is quite a three-pipe problem, and I beg that
you won't speak to me for fifty minutes.'

'The Red-Headed League', *Adventures of Sherlock
Holmes* (1891)

9 'My name is Sherlock Holmes. It is my business
to know what other people don't know.'

'The Adventure of the Blue Carbuncle',
Adventures of Sherlock Holmes (1891)

10 'It is my belief, Watson, founded upon my
experience, that the lowest and vilest alleys in
London do not present a more dreadful record
of sin than does the smiling and beautiful
countryside.'

'The Adventure of the Copper Beeches',
Adventures of Sherlock Holmes (1891)

11 'Is there any point to which you would wish
to draw my attention?'
'To the curious incident of the dog in the
night-time.'
'The dog did nothing in the night-time.'
'That was the curious incident,' remarked
Sherlock Holmes.

'Silver Blaze', *The Memoirs of Sherlock
Holmes* (1894)

12 'Excellent!' I cried.
'Elementary,' said he.

'The Crooked Man', *Memoirs of Sherlock
Holmes* (1894)

This is the closest to the phrase 'Elementary,
my dear Watson' in any of Conan Doyle's
stories. In 1929 the first Holmes film with
sound, *The Return of Sherlock Holmes*, ended
with the line 'Elementary, my dear Watson,
elementary'

13 'He is the Napoleon of crime, Watson. He is
the organiser of half that is evil and of nearly
all that is undetected in this great city.'

'The Final Problem', *The Memoirs of Sherlock
Holmes* (1894) (Holmes on his arch-enemy,
Professor Moriarty)

14 It is the mute hound that bites the hardest.

Sir Nigel (1906), ch.14

15 Mediocrity knows nothing higher than itself;
but talent instantly recognises genius. . .

The Valley of Fear (1915), ch.1, 'The Warning'

Drummond, Flora 1879–1949

Telegraphist and suffragette, known as 'the General'

1 We were told by Socialists that we would be better to wait for socialism, that we would put the clock of socialism back twenty years. Oh dear! To think of the socialism that we would turn back!

> *Forward* (9 Feb 1907)

> > Drummond, a member of the Independent Labour Party, was angered by the anti-female suffrage attitudes of some men in the ILP. She described herself as 'a married woman and a socialist in a hurry'. Quoted in Elspeth King, *The Hidden History of Glasgow's Women* (1993), ch.7

2 Do you realise what I, as a wife and mother, am wanting? I want women to be looked upon as human beings in the eyes of the law. . . I have been twice to prison, and am prepared to go as many times as necessary.

> *Votes for Women* (29 Oct 1908)

> > From a report of her appearance in court, on a charge of distributing a suffragette bill

Drummond (of Hawthornden), William 1585–1649

Poet

1 Phoebus arise,
And paint the sable Skies
With azure, white, and Red. . .

> 'Phoebus Arise', *Poems 1* (1614), song 2

2 Sound hoarse sad Lute, true Witnesse of my Woe,
And strive no more to ease selfe-chosen Paine
With Soule-enchanting Sounds, your Accents straine
Unto these Teares uncessantly which flow.

> 'Sound Hoarse Sad Lute', *Poems 1* (1614), sonnet 28

3 Then sound sad Lute, and beare a mourning Part,
Thou Hell may'st moove, though not a Womans Heart.

> 'Sound Hoarse Sad Lute', *Poems 1* (1614), sonnet 28

4 On this colde World of Ours,
Flowre of the Seasons, Season of the Flowrs,
Sonne of the Sunne sweet Spring,
Such hote and burning Dayes why doest thou bring?

> 'On this Colde World of Ours', *Poems 1* (1614), madrigal 6

5 There burst hee foorth; All yee, whose Hopes relye

On God, with mee amidst these Desarts mourne,
Repent, repent, and from olde errours turne.
Who listned to his voyce, obey'd his crye?
Onlie the Ecchoes, which hee made relent,
Rung from their Marble Caves, 'repent, repent.'

> 'For the Baptiste', *Flowres of Sion* (1623), sonnet 11

6 This world a Hunting is,
The Pray poore Man, the Nimrod fierce is Death. . .

> 'The World a Game', *Flowres of Sion* (1623), madrigal 4

7 So after all the Spoile, Disgrace, and Wrake,
That Time, the World, and Death could bring combind,
Amidst that Masse of Ruines they did make,
Safe and all scarre-lesse yet remaines my Minde. . .

> 'Content and Resolute', *Flowres of Sion* (1623), sonnet 24

8 Death is the sade Estranger of acquantance, the eternall Divorcer of Mariage, the Ravisher of Children from their Parentes, the stealer of Parents from the Children, the Interrer of Fame, the sole cause of Forgetfulnesse, by which the living talke of those gone away as of so many Shadowes, or fabulous Paladines. . .

> *A Cypresse Grove* (1623)

9 The halfe of our Life is spent in Sleepe; which hath such a resemblance to Death, that often it separates the Soule from the Bodie, and teacheth it a sort of beeing above it, making it soare beyond the Spheare of sensuall Delightes, and attaine to Knowledge, unto which, while the Bodie did awake, it dared scarce aspire. And who would not rather than remaine chained in this loathsome Galley of the World, Sleep ever (that is dye). . . ?

> *A Cypresse Grove* (1623)

10 God is not in the bitter divisione and alienatione of affections, nor the raging flames of seditiones, nor in the Tempeste of the turbulent whirl-windes of contradictiones and disputationes, but in the calme and gentle breathinges of peace and concord.

> A speech on toleration, *The History of Scotland* (1655)

> > Drummond puts these words into the mouth of a privy councillor addressing James V in 1540, during the earliest stirrings of the Reformation

11 In all nations it is observed that there are some families fatal to the ruin of the Commonwealth and some persons fatal to the ruin of the house and race of which they are descended.

> Of the Douglases. Quoted in Agnes Mure Mackenzie, *Scottish Pageant*, Vol.1 (1946), p.31

Dryden, John 1631–1700
English poet, essayist and dramatist

1 Treacherous Scotland to no int'rest true.
   'Heroic Stanzas on the Death of Cromwell'
   (1659), st.17

Dubhghall mac an Ghiolla Ghlais fl.1500
Poet

1 Clann Ghriogóir an dream nach tréith,
   'n-am nach beidís réidh ré rígh;
   Goill, giodh fuileachtach na fir,
   ní chuireadh siad sin i mbrígh.

   Ní mó leó Gaoidhil ná Goill,
   na saoirfhir ó chloinn an ríogh;
   aicme Ghriogóir na gcolg gcruaidh
   ó bhorb shluagh ní ghabhadh sníomh.

† The race of Gregor is a folk not weak when a
   king and they are not at one; Saxons, though
   they be bloody men, our warriors set them at
   naught.
      Of Gael they reck no more than of Saxon,
   those free-born men of the King's race;
   Gregor's clan of hard swords, they were not
   dismayed by a fierce host.
   Poem in praise of John, chief of Clan Gregor,
   st.8–9. Quoted in W J Watson (ed.), *Scottish
   Verse from the Book of the Dean of Lismore* (1937)

2 Ag sin trí freiteacha Finn:
   breith a ghill ní facas riamh;
   lámh badh mhath iorghail i ngreis;
   dob ionmhain leis fuileach fiadh.

† Here are the three matters vowed by Fionn;
   winning of his wager was never seen; a hand
   good at quarrel in a fray; he well loved the
   stag a-bleeding.
   Poem in praise of John, chief of Clan Gregor,
   st.14. Quoted in W J Watson (ed.), *Scottish Verse
   from the Book of the Dean of Lismore* (1937)

Duffy, Carol Ann 1955–
Poet

1 The politeness of strangers worries me,
   like surgical gloves.
   'Absolutely', *Selling Manhattan* (1987), st.2

2 . . . Love makes buildings home
   and out of dreary weather, sometimes,
   rainbows come.
   'By Heart', *Selling Manhattan* (1987), st.5

3 . . . I remember my tongue
   shedding its skin like a snake, my voice
   in the classroom sounding just like the
   rest. Do I only think
   I lost a river, culture, speech, sense of first space

and the right place?
   'Originally', *The Other Country* (1990), st.3

4 I write the headlines for a Daily Paper.
   It's just a knack one's born with all-right-Squire.
   You do not have to be an educator,
   just bang the words down like they're
   screaming *Fire!*
   'Poet for Our Times', *The Other Country*
   (1990), st.1

5 The poems of the decade. . . *Stuff 'em! Gotcha!*
   The instant tits and bottom line of art.
   'Poet for Our Times', *The Other Country*
   (1990), st.5

6 Some days, although we cannot pray, a prayer
   utters itself. So, a woman will lift
   her head from the sieve of her hands and stare
   at the minims sung by a tree, a sudden gift.
   'Prayer', *Mean Time* (1993), st.1

Dunbar, William c.1460–c.1520
Poet at the court of James IV

1 He that hes gold and grit riches,
   And may be into mirrynes,
   And dois glaidnes fra him expell,
   And levis in to wrechitnes,
   He wirkis sorrow to him sell.
   'Ane His Awin Ennemy', st.1

2 Now all this tyme lat us be mirry,
   And sett nocht by this warld a chirry;
   Now, quhill thair is gude wyne to sell,
   He that dois on dry breid wirry,
   I gif him to the Devill of hell.
   'Ane His Awin Ennemy', st.5

3 Iersch brybour baird, vyle beggar with
      thy brattis,
   Cuntbittin crawdoun Kennedy, coward
      of kynd. . .
   'The Flyting of Dunbar and Kennedie', ll.49–50

4 Renunce, rebald, thy rymyng, thow bot royis,
   Thy trechour tung hes tane ane heland strynd;
   Ane lawland ers wald mak a bettir noyis.
   'The Flyting of Dunbar and Kennedie', ll.54–6

5 Wan wisage widdefow, out of thy wit gane wyld,
   Laithly and lowsy, als latherand as ane leik,
   Sen thow with wirschep wald sa fane be styld,
   Haill, soverane senyeour! Thy bawis hingis
      throw thy breik.
   'The Flyting of Dunbar and Kennedie', ll.101–4

6 Ryght as the stern of day begouth to schyne,
   Quhen gone to bed war Vesper and Lucyne,
   I raise and by a rosere did me rest. . .
   'The Goldyn Targe', st.1

For mirth of May, wyth skippis and
  wyth hoppis,
The birdis sang upon the tender croppis
With curiouse note. . .

'The Goldyn Targe', st.3

Now of wemen this I say for me,
Off erthly thingis nane may bettir be;
They suld haif wirschep and grit honoring
Off men, aboif all uthir erthly thing;
Rycht grit dishonour upoun him self he takkis
In word or deid quha evir wemen lakkis;
Sen that of wemen cumin all ar we,
Wemen ar wemen, and sa will end and de.

'In Prais of Wemen', ll.1–8

In secreit place this hyndir nycht,
I hard any berne say till ane bricht,
'My huny, my hart, my hoip, my heill,
I have bene lang your luifar leill,
And can of yow get confort nane;
How lang will ye with danger deill?
Ye brek my hart, my bony ane!'

'In Secreit Place This Hyndir Nycht', st.1

Quod he, 'My kyd, my capirculyoun,
My bony baib with the ruch brylyoun,
My tendir gyrle, my wallie gowdye,
My tyrlie myrlie, my crowdie mowdie;
Quhone that oure mouthis dois meit at ane,
My stang dois storkyn with your towdie;
Ye brek my hairt, my bony ane!'

'In Secreit Place This Hyndir Nycht', st.7

He gaiff to hir ane apill rubye;
Quod scho, 'Gramercye! my sweit cowhubye.'

'In Secreit Place This Hyndir Nycht', st.9

I that in heill wes and gladnes,
Am trublit now with great seiknes,
And feblit with infermite;
Timor mortis conturbat me.

Our plesance heir is all vane glory,
This fals warld is bot transitory,
The flesche is brukle, the Fend is sle;
Timor mortis conturbat me.

The stait of man dois change and vary,
Now sound, now seik, now blith, now sary,
Now dansand mery, now like to dee;
Timor mortis conturbat me.

'Lament for the Makaris', st.1–3

Sen for the deid remeid is none,
Best is that we for dede dispone,
Eftir our deid that lif may we;
Timor mortis conturbat me.

'Lament for the Makaris', st.25

In to thir dirk and drublie dayis,
Quhone sabill all the hevin arrayis
With mystie vapouris, cluddis, and skyis,

Nature all curage me denyis
Off sangis, ballattis, and of playis.

'Meditatioun in Wyntir', st.1

15 Be mirry, man! and tak nocht far in mynd
The wavering of this wrechit warld of sorrow;
To God be humill, and to thy freynd be kynd,
And with thy nychbouris glaidly len and
  borrow. . .

'No Tressour Availis Without Glaidnes', st.1

16 Lang heff I maed of ladyes quhytt,
Nou of ane blak I will indytt,
That landet furth of the last schippis;
Quhou fain wald I descryve perfytt,
My ladye with the mekle lippis.

'Of Ane Blak-Moir', st.1

17 Quhai for hir saek, with speir and scheld,
Preiffis maest mychttelye in the feld,
Sall kis and withe her go in grippis;
And fra thyne furth hir luff sall weld:
My ladye with the mekle lippis.

And quhai in felde receaves schaem,
And tynis thair his knychtlie naem,
Sall cum behind and kis hir hippis,
And nevir to uther confort claem:
My ladye with the mekle lippis.

'Of Ane Blak-Moir', st.4–5

18 Quho thinkis that he hes sufficence,
Off gudis hes no indigence;
Thocht he have nowder land nor rent,
Grit mycht, nor hie magnificence,
He hes anewch that is content.

'Of Content', st.1

19 Quhat is this lyfe bot ane straucht way to deid,
Quhilk has a tyme to pas, and nane to duell;
A slyding quheill us lent to seik remeid;
A fre chois gevin to Paradice or Hell;
A pray to deid, quhome vane is to repell;
A schoirt torment for infineit glaidnes,
Als schort ane joy for lestand hevynes.

'Of Life'

20 Now culit is dame Venus brand;
Trew luvis fyre is ay kindilland,
And I begyn to undirstand,
In feynit luve quhat foly bene:
Now cumis aige quhair yewth hes bene,
And trew luve rysis fro the splene.

Quhill Venus fyre be deid and cauld,
Trew luvis fyre nevir birnis bauld;
So as the ta lufe waxis auld,
The tothir dois incres moir kene:
Now cumis aige quhair yewth hes bene,
And trew lufe rysis fro the splene.

'Of Luve Erdly and Divine', st.1–2

21 I haif experience by my sell;
In luvis court anis did I dwell,

Bot quhair I of a joy cowth tell,
I culd of truble tell fyftene. . .

'Of Luve Erdly and Divine', st.5

22 This waverand warldis wretchidnes,
The failyeand and frutless bissines,
The mispent tyme, the service vane,
For to considder is ane pane.

'Of the Warldis Instabilitie', st.1

23 The sugurit mouthis with myndis thairfra,
The figurit speiche with faceis tua,
The plesand toungis with hartis unplane,
For to considder is ane pane.

'Of the Warldis Instabilitie', st.3

24 My heid did yak yester nicht,
This day to mak that I na micht,
So sair the magryme dois me menyie,
Perseing my brow as ony ganyie,
That scant I luik may on the licht.

'On His Heid-Ake', st.1

25 I will na preistis for me sing,
Dies illa, Dies ire;
Na yit na bellis for me ring,
Sicut semper solet fieri;
Bot a bag pipe to play a spryng. . .

'The Testament of Mr Andro Kennedy', ll.105–9

This is the first reference in Scots to bagpipes.
See John Purser, *Scotland's Music* (1992), ch.6

26 Blyth Aberdeane, thow beriall of all tounis,
The lamp of bewtie, bountie, and blythnes;
Unto the heaven ascendit thy renoun is
Off vertew, wisdome, and of worthines. . .

'To Aberdein', st.1

27 Be blyth and blisfull, burgh of Aberdein.

'To Aberdein', st.1

28 Apon the Midsummer evin, mirriest of nichtis,
I muvit furth allane, neir as midnicht wes past,
Besyd ane gudlie grein garth, full of gay flouris,
Hegeit, of ane huge hicht, with hawthorne treis;
Quhairon ane bird, on ane bransche, so birst
out hir notis
That never ane blythfullar bird was on the
beuche harde. . .

'The Tretis of the Tua Mariit Wemen and the
Wedo', ll.1–6

29 As birs of ane brym bair, his berd is als stif,
Bot soft and soupill as the silk is his sary lume;
He may weill to the syn assent, bot sakles is
his deidis.

'The Tretis of the Tua Mariit Wemen and the
Wedo', ll.95–7

Duncan, son of Colin
see **Donnchadh Mac Cailéin**

Duncan from Lennox, Great
see **Donnchadh Mór ó Leamhnacht**

Duncan, Young see **Donnchadh Og**

Duncanson, Major Robert fl.1692
Soldier

1 You are hereby ordered to fall upon the Rebells,
the McDonalds of Glenco, and putt all to the
sword under seventy. You are to have a special
care that the old fox and his sones doe upon no
account escape your hands you are to secure
all the avenues thatt no man escape. This you
are to putt in executione att fyve of the clock
precisely. . .

From the order (dated 12 Feb 1692) to Captain
Robert Campbell of Glenlyon, for the Massacre
of Glencoe

The 'old fox' refers to Alasdair MacIain, chief
of the Glencoe MacDonalds

Dundas, Henry (1st Viscount Melville)
1742–1811

*Statesman and lawyer, Lord Advocate and
effective 'uncrowned King of Scotland'
1775–1805*

1 When it is said that no alternative is left to the
New Englanders but to starve or rebel, this is
not the fact, for there is another way, to submit.

Speech in the House of Commons (1775)

He was one of the fiercest opponents of any
concessions to the American colonists, and one
of the strongest supporters of the subsequent
war against them. During this speech he is
credited with coining the word 'starvation'.
It was, according to Michael Fry (*The Dundas
Despotism*, 1992, ch.3), 'fastidiously omitted
from the record, but he certainly uttered it,
to be drowned by roars of laughter from a
House of Latinists.' For years after, he was
known as 'Starvation Dundas'

2 . . . my secession from all public life at this time
would be a very fatal step to the strength and
hold Government has of Scotland. . . a variety
of circumstances happen to concur in my person
to render me a cement of political strength
to the present administration, which, if once
dissolved, would produce very ruinous effects.

Letter to Lord Grenville (Feb 1789), declining
the position of Lord President of the Court of
Session (a post held previously by his father and
half-brother) which would have required him to
curtail his political career. Quoted in Michael
Fry, *The Dundas Despotism* (1992), ch.4

The unofficial title 'uncrowned King of
Scotland' would be inherited in the 20th
century by Secretary of State Tom Johnston

3 The expediency of resistance [to unpopular government] is not a point which the generality of mankind can safely consider. . . Every ignorant man would conceive he had a right to resist everything which did not accord with his opinions, and the result might be shocking to humanity. Such language tends to bring all government into disgrace or, at least, to render it precarious.

> Speech in the House of Commons opposing political reform (1790s). Quoted in Michael Fry, *The Dundas Despotism* (1992), ch.5

Dundas, Robert (Lord Arniston)
1685–1753

Judge, Lord President of the Court of Session (1748–53), father of Henry Dundas

1 My lord, I never wish to talk on law after meals. The moment a cause is determined, I desire not to argue over it again: I would as soon converse with a whore after business was over.

> Said to Patrick Grant, Lord Elchies (1690–1754), who was in the habit of talking nothing but law after dinner. Quoted in John Ramsay of Ochtertyre, *Scotland and Scotsmen in the Eighteenth Century* (1888 edition), Vol.1, p.93, footnote

Dundee, Viscount
see Graham (of Claverhouse), John

Dunn, Douglas 1942–

Poet, Professor of English at St Andrews University

1 The street's patricians, they are ignored.
Their anger proves something, their disen-
  chantments
Settle round me like a cold fog.

They are the individualists of our time.
They know no fashions, copy nothing but
  their minds.
Long ago, they gave up looking in mirrors.

> 'The Patricians', *Terry Street* (1969), st.6–7

2 I want to be touched by them, know their lives,
Dance in my own style, learn something new.
At night, I even dream of ideal communities.
Why do they live where they live, the rich and
  the poor?

Tonight, when their hair is ready, after tea,
They'll slip through laws and the legs of
  policemen.
I won't be there, I'll be reading books elsewhere.
There are many worlds, there are many laws.

> 'Young Women in Rollers', *Terry Street* (1969), st.9–10

3 The happy life is dreamt, just like the love
Before the first, and is not quite enough.
Insufficient perfections – what else is there?

> 'The Happier Life', *The Happier Life* (1972)

4 They will not leave me, the lives of other people.
I wear them near my eyes like spectacles.

> 'The Hunched', *The Happier Life* (1972)

5 My poems should be Clyde-built, crude
  and sure,
With images of those dole-deployed
To honour the indomitable Reds,
Clydesiders of slant steel and angled cranes;
A poetry of nuts and bolts, born, bred,
Embattled by the Clyde, tight and impure.

> 'Clydesiders', *Love or Nothing* (1974), st.2

6 They ruined us. They conquered continents.
We filled their uniforms. We cruised the seas.
We worked their mines and made their
  histories.
You work, we rule, they said. We worked;
  they ruled.
They fooled the tenements. All men were fooled.
It still persists. It will be so, always.
Listen. An out-of-work apprentice plays
God Save the Queen on an Edwardian flute.
He is, but does not know it, destitute.

> 'Empires', *Barbarians* (1979)

7 Share with me, then, the sad glugs in
  your bottles;
Throw a stolen spud for me on the side-
  embers.

> 'An Address on the Destitution of Scotland', *St Kilda's Parliament* (1981), st.3

8 . . . But know, I worked and tried:
And hope still for a small posterity
And, through a chink in time, to hear
  men say,
That, wasting these best talents of my life,
I fed my children and I loved my wife.

> 'John Wilson in Greenock, 1786', *St Kilda's Parliament* (1981)
>
>> John Wilson (1720–89), author of the poem 'Clyde', was appointed headmaster of Greenock Grammar School, a post he accepted having signed an agreement to give up 'the profane and unprofitable art of poem-making'. Cf. John Wilson 1

9 I'm a Francophile, I don't believe in common sense; it's an Anglo-Saxon virtue. Scotsmen, like Frenchmen, don't believe in common sense, we believe in intelligence.

> Interview in John Haffenden (ed.), *Viewpoints: Poets in Conversation* (1981)

10 'No, don't stop writing your grievous poetry.
It will do you good, this work of your grief.
Keep writing until there is nothing left.

It will take time, and the years will go by.'
   'December', *Elegies* (1985)

11 Why be discreet? A broken heart is
     what I have –
     A pin to burst the bubble of shy poetry. . .
       'The Stories', *Elegies* (1985)

12 She spoke of what I might do 'afterwards'.
     'Go, somewhere else.' I went north to
     Dundee.
     Tomorrow I won't live here any more,
     Nor leave alone. *My love, say you'll*
     come with me.
       'Leaving Dundee', *Elegies* (1985)

13 Photography exposes everyone to the worst
     of what's happened since its invention was
     perfected. A result for literature is that realism
     can never be as adequate – it seems compelled
     to become dirtier and dirtier. Decency is in
knowing about what's happened, and what can
happen, and of being aware of the possible
squalor and toxicity of life, but at the same
time. . . refusing to allow one's life to become
disablingly contaminated with the crimes
against humanity and nature which in our
century are so *visible*. On television, you can
see horrors, filmed *as they happened*. You can
turn away and carry on talking about roses
– we've become so careless, morally helpless,
ineffective.
     Interview with Robert Crawford (12 Jun 1985),
     in *Verse* No.4 (1985)

14 In a country like this
     Our ghosts outnumber us. . .
       'At Falkland Palace', *Northlight* (1988)

15 Look to the living, love them, and hold on.
       'Disenchantments', *Dante's Drum-kit* (1993).
       Cf. Stewart Conn 2

E

Elcho, Lord (David Elcho) 1721–87
Jacobite soldier

1 There you go for a damned cowardly Italian!

Called out to Charles Edward Stewart as he withdrew from the field at Culloden (16 Apr 1746). Quoted in Walter Scott's *Journal* (10 Feb 1826)

Scott's source is not known. It was not Lord Elcho's *Short Account of the Affairs of Scotland, 1744–6* (published 1907), although this clearly shows tempers fraying as the outcome of the battle became obvious

Eldin, Lord see Clerk, John

Elliot, Jean 1727–1805
Poet and songwriter

1 I've heard the lilting at our yowe-milking,
Lasses a-lilting before the dawn o' day;
But now they are moaning on ilka green loaning;
'The Flowers of the Forest are a' wede away.'

'The Flowers of the Forest' (c.1755), st.1.
Cf. Mrs Alison Cockburn 1

Based on a traditional version of which only a fragment survives, this song was written as a lament for the Battle of Flodden (9 Sep 1513), in which James IV and thousands of his men were slain by the English. First published anonymously, it is Elliot's only surviving work

2 Dule and wae for the order sent our lads to the Border;
The English, for ance, by guile wan the day;
The Flowers of the Forest, that foucht aye the foremost,
The prime o' our land, are cauld in the clay.

'The Flowers of the Forest' (c.1755), st.5

Elliot, Walter 1888–1958
Conservative politician, Secretary of State for Scotland (1936–8), and writer

1 The gateway of Scotland is the Firth of Forth. It lies almost at the balancing point of Europe between the Mediterranean and the Baltic. . . Scotland is European, with its own sea-access to the springs of European thought. . .

'Politics', in Duke of Atholl et al., *A Scotsman's Heritage* (1932)

2 The Disruption was much more than a quarrel about Church government. It was the fall of a régime. The democratic intellectualism which had lasted for so many centuries was challenged in its own house.

On the Disruption of 1843. 'Politics', in Duke of Atholl et al., *A Scotsman's Heritage* (1932). Cf. George Davie 1

3 The machine and the intellectual have not yet found any formula which will let them work together. The machine brings wealth; wealth fortifies the nobleman; wealth rots the thinker. There is only one relation in which the machine brings no flood of affluence or of discontent to its controller, and that is in the steamship; and there you will find the Scot, exiled from his house of thought, watching in the engine-room the combination of action and certainty which his soul craves and finding like M'Andrew, 'predestination in the stride of yon connecting rod'.

'Politics', in Duke of Atholl et al., *A Scotsman's Heritage* (1932)

4 Argument to the Scot is a vice more attractive than whisky. We would carry argument to the point of plunging ourselves into poverty as we have often, in the past, plunged ourselves into civil war.

Speech in the House of Commons (May 1942). Quoted in Andrew Marr, *The Battle for Scotland* (1992), ch.3

5 We have seen enough of life to be certain that there is a hostile element in affairs as well as a friendly. The believers in continual automatic progress were on the wrong track. Evil exists.

This is the real problem of government; to reconcile these two apparently irreconcilables – force and goodwill. It is an endless adventure.

'What Sort of Warriors?' Rectorial address at Glasgow University (6 Feb 1948)

Elphinstone, Lady fl.1670s
Society lady and staunch Whig

1 . . . when I entered the world there was one Knox deaving us a' with his clavers, and now that I am going out of it, there is one Clavers deaving us with his knocks.

Said to John Graham of Claverhouse (1670s). Quoted in Walter Scott, *Journal* (27 Nov 1827)

At the age of 103, she reputedly said this to 'Bluidy Clavers' when he sought an audience to ask her what remarkable things she had seen in her long life

Erskine, Sir Henry ?1720–65

Poet

1 In the garb of old Gaul, with the fire of
  old Rome,
  From the heath-cover'd mountains of Scotia
  we come,
  Where the Romans endeavour'd our country to gain,
  But our ancestors fought, and they fought
  not in vain.

> 'In the Garb of Old Gaul', st.2.

>> This militaristic poem (later set to music
>> by General John Reid, 1721–1807), directed
>> against France during the Seven Years War
>> (1756–63), makes use of a common phrase for
>> the kilt, the wearing of which was – ironically
>> – banned from 1747 to 1782 except in the
>> Highland regiments of the British Army

Erskine, Thomas (1st Baron Erskine)
1750–1823

Advocate, writer and politician

1 On Waterloo's ensanguined plain
  Lie tens of thousands of the slain;
  But none by sabre or by shot
  Fell half so flat as Walter Scott.

> On Scott's poem 'The Field of Waterloo' (1815)

Eskgrove, Lord (David Rae) ?1729–1804

Judge

1 Young woman! you will now consider yourself
  as in the presence of Almighty God, and of
  this High Court. Lift up your veil; throw off
  all modesty, and look me in the face.

> Said to a female witness of great beauty, at
> the trial of Glengarry for murder, when she
> entered the court wearing a veil. Quoted in Lord
> Cockburn, *Memorials of his Time* (1856), ch.2

2 And so, gentle-men, having shown you that
  the pannell's argument is utterly impossibill,
  I shall now proceed for to show you that it is
  extremely improbabill.

> In Lord Cockburn, *Memorials of his Time* (1856), ch.2

3 He [Lord Eskgrove] had to condemn two or
  three persons to die who had broken into
  a house at Luss, and assaulted Sir James
  Colquhoun and others, and robbed them of
  a large sum of money. He first, as was his
  almost constant practice, explained the nature
  of the various crimes, assault, robbery, and
  hamesucken – of which last he gave them the
  etymology; and he then reminded them that they
  attacked the house and the persons within it,
  and robbed them, and then came to this climax
  – 'All this you did; and God preserve us! joost
  when they were sitten doon to their denner!'

> In Lord Cockburn, *Memorials of his Time* (1856), ch.2

4 [Lord Eskgrove] rarely failed to signalise himself
  in pronouncing sentences of death. It was
  almost a matter of style with him to console
  the prisoner by assuring him that, 'whatever
  your religi-ous persua-shon may be, or even if,
  as I suppose, you be of no persua-shon at all,
  there are plenty of rever-end gentle-men who
  will be most happy for to show you the way
  to yeternal life.'

> In Lord Cockburn, *Memorials of his Time* (1856), ch.2

5 I heard him [Lord Eskgrove], in condemning
  a tailor to death for murdering a soldier by
  stabbing him, aggravate the offence thus, 'and
  not only did you murder him, whereby he was
  berea-ved of his life, but you did thrust, or push,
  or pierce, or project, or propell, the le-thall
  weapon through the belly-band of his regimen-
  tal breeches, which were his Majes-ty's!'

> In Lord Cockburn, *Memorials of his Time* (1856), ch.2

Evaristi, Marcella 1953–

Playwright

1 CESARE: Well, you try being five years old in
  a Glasgow school and introducing yourself as
  Cesare. Caesar. God Almighty I'd have been
  dead by dinner time.

> On why he re-named himself 'Harry'. *Commedia*
> (1982), Act 1, sc.1

Ewen, John 1741–1821

Hawker, jeweller and poet

1 O weel may the boatie row,
  And better may she speed;
  And leesome may the boatie row,
  That wins the bairnies' bread!

  The boatie rows, the boatie rows,
  The boatie rows indeed;
  And weel may the boatie row,
  That wins my bairnies' breid!

> 'The Boatie Rows', st.1 and chorus.
> Cf. Traditional songs 63

2 I cuist my line in Largo Bay,
  And fishes I catch'd nine:
  There was three to boil, and three to fry,
  And three to bait the line.

> 'The Boatie Rows', st.2

Ewing, Margaret (Anne) (*née* McAdam)
1945–

Nationalist politician and MP

1 Scotland is playing tartan waitress instead of
  hostess . . .

> Said on the occasion of the European Summit
> (Dec 1992), which was held in Edinburgh. Quoted
> in Maurice Smith, *Paper Lions: The Scottish Press
> and National Identity* (1994), ch.1

Ewing, Winnie (Winifred Margaret, née Woodburn) 1929–

Nationalist politician, Member of the European Parliament for the Highlands and Islands (1975–)

1 As I took my seat it was said by political pundits that 'a chill ran along the Labour back benches looking for a spine to run up'.

> On arriving at Westminster after winning the 1967 Hamilton by-election for the SNP. 'Road to the Isles', *The Sunday Mail Story of Scotland* (1988), No.16

2 Once Robert Mugabe of Zimbabwe asked me how my party was faring, and when I told him, in 1981, that it was not doing all that well, he told me that it was because 'the people of Scotland are not yet sufficiently oppressed'.

> 'Road to the Isles', *The Sunday Mail Story of Scotland* (1988), No.16

F

Fairbairn, Sir Nicholas Hardwick
1933–95

Lawyer, Conservative politician and MP

1 The great preponderance of Scottish newspapers and Scottish television emit a
chorus of unremitting complaint and envious
resentment. They are little Scotlanders,
suspicious of everything, be it beneficial or not, and yearning to return to
those far-off days when Scotland was
an independent oatmeal republic with a
squabbling parliament presiding over abject
poverty.

> Editorial in the first issue of the magazine *Scottish
> Conservative* (Winter 1989)

>> He went on to say that his Party was that of
>> 'big Scotlanders. . . [who] thanks to 10 years
>> of Thatcher government, [are] the pacemakers
>> of British industry and commerce and finance,
>> conscious that we have the unicorn's share of
>> investment, government finance and subsidy,
>> which is infinitely more than the lion's share.'

2 This means that all the Scots worldwide who
happen not to have been born in Scotland and
not to be resident have no say in the affairs
of Scotland.
But everybody who is born in Scotland, be
he Greek, Tasmanian or the bastard child of
an American serviceman, qualify to vote in
Scotland.

> On the Scottish National Party's proposal to give
> citizenship in an independent Scotland to anyone
> living or born there. Quoted in *The Scotsman*
> (4 Apr 1992)

>> His comments, a week before a General
>> Election, caused outrage, but he retained his
>> Perth and Kinross parliamentary seat with a
>> reduced majority

3 Look at the food – oatcakes, haggis, broth –
it's all peasant fare. This was a peasant country
before the Union.

> Quoted in *The Observer* (5 Apr 1992)

4 The reason they think I'm bonkers is
because I have original views and speak
my mind.

> Quoted in *The Independent* (3 Jul 1993)

5 She is short on looks, absolutely deprived of
any dress sense, has a figure like a Jurassic
monster, no tact and wants to upstage
everyone.

> On Sarah Ferguson, the Duchess of York. Quoted
> in *The Independent* (31 Jul 1993)

6 I see no reason for anonymity. Are women some
feebleness that they have to be protected? Not
at all, they are the tauntresses.

> On anonymity for rape victims in cases brought
> to trial (Oct 1993). Quoted in obituary article,
> *The Scotsman* (20 Feb 1995)

7 I don't think he's up to the task. He is vin
ordinaire and he should be château-bottled.

> On Prime Minister John Major. Quoted in *The
> Independent* (9 Apr 1994)

8 A rise in VAT would have hit stately home
owners harder than anyone else. You need more
heating as you head up the kingdom away from
Essex. Luckily, we have thick walls and our
own wood.

> Speaking from his home, Fordell Castle, in Fife,
> after the government was defeated in the House
> of Commons (6 Dec 1994) over its plans to
> further increase the VAT rate on domestic fuel
> to 17.5 per cent. Quoted in *The Independent*
> (10 Dec 1994)

9 The women in the House of Commons are
mostly hideous. They have no fragrance. I
dislike women who deny their femininity. . .
They are just cagmags, scrubheaps, old tattles.

> Quoted in obituary article, *The Scotsman*
> (20 Feb 1995)

10 . . . the ever hopeful in pursuit of the ever
hopeless.

> On socialists. Quoted in obituary article, *The
> Scotsman* (20 Feb 1995). Cf. Gordon Brown 3

Fairbairn, Lady Sam (*née* Suzanne Wheeler)

Second wife of Sir Nicholas Fairbairn

1 Behind every great man is an exhausted woman.

> Quoted in *The Independent* (16 Apr 1994).
> Cf. J M Barrie 15

Farmer, Tom 1940–

*Businessman, founder and chairman of
Kwik-Fit*

1 Women dream of falling in love with a Kwik-
Fit fitter.

> *Marketing* (9 Feb 1989)

Fell, Alison 1944–
Poet and novelist

1 There's no word for the feeling women
have of being in the wrong before
they even open their mouths,
Dale Spender says.

  'Significant Fevers', *Kisses for Mayakovsky* (1984)

  Dale Spender (1943–   ), Australian feminist writer

2 Life is as short as a shoelace,
but who knows it?

  'Significant Fevers', *Kisses for Mayakovsky* (1984)

3 Pushing forty, we vow
that when the time comes
rather than wither
ladylike and white
we will henna our hair
like Colette, we too
will be gold and red
and go out
in a last wild blaze.

  'Pushing Forty', *Kisses for Mayakovsky* (1984), st.2

Ferguson, Adam 1723–1816
Philosopher

1 We speak of art as distinguished from nature;
but art itself is natural to man. He is in some
measure the artificer of his own frame, as well
as his fortune, and is destined, from the first age
of his being, to invent and contrive. . . While
he appears equally fitted to every condition, he
is. . . unable to settle in any. At once obstinate
and fickle, he complains of innovations, and
is never sated with novelty. He is perpetually
busied in reformations, and is continually
wedded to his errors.

  An Essay on the History of Civil Society (1767),
  Part 1, section 1

2 . . . his emblem is a passing stream, not a
stagnating pool. We may desire to direct his love
of improvement to its proper object, we may
wish for stability of conduct; but we mistake
human nature, if we wish for a termination of
labour, or a scene of repose.

  On mankind's restlessness. *An Essay on the History
  of Civil Society* (1767), Part 1, section 1.
  Cf. Frances Wright 10

3 Affection operates with the greatest force, where
it meets with the greatest difficulties: In the
breast of the parent, it is most solicitous amidst
the dangers and distresses of the child: In the
breast of a man, its flame redoubles where
the wrongs or sufferings of his friend, or his
country, require his aid.

  An Essay on the History of Civil Society (1767),
  Part 1, section 3

4 It is here indeed [in a commercial society], if
ever, that man is sometimes found a detached
and a solitary being: he has found an object
which sets him in competition with his fellow-
creatures, and he deals with them as he does
with his cattle and his soil, for the sake of the
profits they bring. The mighty engine which
we suppose to have formed society, only tends
to set its members at variance, or to continue
their intercourse after the bands of affection
are broken.

  An Essay on the History of Civil Society (1767),
  Part 1, section 3

5 Oppression and cruelty are not always necessary
to despotical government; and even when
present, are but a part of its evils. It is founded
on corruption, and on the suppression of all the
civil and political virtues. . . and would erect
the peace of society itself on the ruins of that
freedom and confidence from which alone the
enjoyment, the force, and the elevation of the
human mind, are found to arise.

  An Essay on the History of Civil Society (1767),
  Part 6, section 6

Ferguson, Christina
see Nic Fhearghais, Cairistìona

Fergusson, George see Hermand, Lord

Fergusson, J(ohn) D(uncan) 1874–1961
Painter

1 To earn the name artist it seems clear that one
must *create* something, must make something,
be a '*makar*'.

  Modern Scottish Painting (1943), ch.5, 'Art and
  Philosophy'

2 . . . I think that any intelligent person will
be able to decide that black is certainly not
fundamentally characteristic of the Scottish
temperament. It is characteristic of Calvinism,
night, degeneration, despair, disease and
death. . . Everyone in Scotland should refuse
to have anything to do with *black or dirty and
dingy colours*, and insist on clean colour in
everything.

  Modern Scottish Painting (1943), ch.6, 'Scotland
  and Colour'

3 Scotland should have an independent art. No
one has a right to decide for others what *is* art
and what isn't. The public has a right to decide
for itself, and to like what is considered to be
bad art if they choose.

  Modern Scottish Painting (1943), ch.7, 'Independent Art'. Cf. Julian Spalding 3

4 . . . it is pretty clear that most people have not even thought of *quality* of paint, and that many think that quantity of paint is quality. Quality of paint like quality of line or quality of tone is not a thing that can be fixed. It is the artist's statement in paint of his reaction to form created by the play of light, and is poor or full according to the painter's sensibility and experience of life.

Modern Scottish Painting (1943), ch.8, 'The Journeyman Artist'

5 Art is, or ought to be, the purest form of free self-expression and free self-expression is the life of any free country.

Modern Scottish Painting (1943), ch.11, 'Responsibility of Art Schools and Directors'

6 The effects of Calvinism on Scotland have been as destructive as the effects of prohibition in America. . . In the case of America, a young and vigorous nation, a stupid law inevitably produced lawlessness. In the case of Scotland the submissive submitted, and the others just left for some place where life was reasonably human.

Modern Scottish Painting (1943), ch.12, 'Calvinism and Art'

Fergusson, Robert 1750–74

Poet, major influence on Robert Burns

1 Braid Claith lends fock an unco heeze,
Makes mony kail-worms butter-flies,
Gies mony a doctor his degrees
For little skaith:
In short, you may be what you please
Wi' gude Braid Claith.

For thof ye had as wise a snout on
As Shakespeare or Sir Isaac Newton,
Your judgment fouk wou'd hae a doubt on,
I'll tak my aith,
Till they cou'd see ye wi' a suit on
O' gude Braid Claith.

'Braid Claith' (1772), st.8–9

2 Come prie, frail man! for gin thou art sick,
The oyster is a rare cathartic,
As ever doctor patient gart lick
To cure his ails;
Whether you hae the head or heart-ake,
It ay prevails.

'Caller Oysters' (1772), st.5

3 A' ye wha canna stand sae sicker,
Whan twice you've toom'd the big ars'd bicker,
Mix caller oysters wi' your liquor,
And I'm your debtor,
If greedy priest or drouthy vicar
Will thole it better.

'Caller Oysters' (1772), st.13

4 Now mirk December's dowie face
Glours our the rigs wi' sour grimace,
While thro' his *minimum* of space,
The bleer-ey'd sun,
Wi' blinkin light and stealing pace,
His race doth run.

'The Daft-Days' (1772), st.1

5 *Fidlers*, your pins in temper fix,
And roset weel your fiddle-sticks,
But banish vile Italian tricks
From out your quorum:
Nor *fortes* wi' *pianos* mix,
Gie's *Tulloch Gorum*.

For nought can cheer the heart sae weil
As can a canty Highland reel;
It even vivifies the heel
To skip and dance:
Lifeless is he wha canna feel
Its influence.

'The Daft-Days' (1772), st.8–9. Cf. John Skinner 2

6 On Scotia's plains, in days of yore,
When lads and lasses tartan wore,
Saft Music rang on ilka shore,
In hamely weid;
But harmony is now no more,
And music dead.

'Elegy on the Death of Scots Music' (1772), st.1

7 Now foreign sonnets bear the gree,
And crabbit queer variety
Of sound fresh sprung frae Italy,
A bastard breed!
Unlike that saft-tongu'd melody
Which now lies dead.

'Elegy on the Death of Scots Music' (1772), st.9

8 Wanwordy, crazy, dinsome thing,
As e'er was fram'd to jow or ring,
What gar'd them sic in steeple hing
They ken themsel',
But weel wat I they coudna bring
Waur sounds frae hell.

'To the Tron-Kirk Bell' (1772), st.1

9 Auld Reikie! wale o' ilka town
That Scotland kens beneath the moon;
Whare couthy chiels at e'ening meet
Their bizzing craigs and mous to weet. . .

'Auld Reikie, A Poem' (1773), ll.1–4

10 On stair wi' tub, or pat in hand,
The barefoot housemaids looe to stand,
That antrin fock may ken how snell
Auld Reikie will at morning smell:
Then, with an inundation big as
The burn that 'neath the Nore Loch Brig is,
They kindly shower Edina's roses,
To quicken and regale our noses.

'Auld Reikie, A Poem' (1773), ll.33–40

1 Near some lamp-post, wi' dowy face,
Wi' heavy een, and sour grimace,
Stands she that beauty lang had kend,
Whoredom her trade, and vice her end.

'Auld Reikie, A Poem' (1773), ll.87–90

2 He could, by Euclid, prove lang sine
A ganging point compos'd a line;
By numbers too he cou'd divine,
Whan he did read,
That three times three just made up nine;
But now he's dead.

'Elegy, on the Death of Mr David Gregory, late professor of Mathematics in the University of St Andrews' (1773), st.3

3 Weel kens the gudewife that the pleughs require
A heartsome meltith, and refreshing synd
O' nappy liquor, o'er a bleezing fire:
Sair wark and poortith douna weel be join'd.

'The Farmer's Ingle' (1773), st.3

4 May Scotia's simmers ay look gay and green,
Her yellow har'sts frae scowry blasts decreed;
May a' her tenants sit fu' snug and bien,
Frae the hard grip of ails and poortith freed,
And a lang lasting train o' peaceful hours
succeed.

'The Farmer's Ingle' (1773), st.13

This poem gave Burns the idea for 'The Cotter's Saturday Night'

5 Black be the day that e'er to England's ground
Scotland was eikit by the Union's bond. . .

'The Ghaists: a Kirk-Yard Eclogue' (1773), ll.57–8

The lines are spoken by George Heriot's ghost, complaining at southern interference in the finances of his charitable hospital school in Edinburgh

6 Unyoke then, man, an' binna sweer
To ding a hole in ill-haind gear:
O think that eild, wi' wyly fitt,
Is wearing nearer bit by bit;
Gin yence he claws you wi' his paw,
What's siller for?

'Hame Content, A Satire' (1773), ll.53–8

7 Daft gowk, in macaroni dress,
Are ye come here to shew your face,
Bowden wi' pride o' simmer gloss,
To cast a dash at Reikie's cross;
And glowr at mony twa-legg'd creature,
Flees braw by art, tho' worms by nature?

'On Seeing a Butterfly in the Street' (1773), ll.1–6

'Macaroni' was one of Fergusson's favourite epithets for a dandy

8 And may they scad their lips fu' leal,
That dip their spoons in ither's kail.

'On Seeing a Butterfly in the Street' (1773), ll.71–2

19 Thanks to the gods, who made me poor!
No *lukewarm* friends molest my door,
Who always shew a busy care
For being legatee or heir:
Of this stamp none will ever follow
The youth that's favour'd by Apollo.

'Rob. Fergusson's Last Will' (1773), ll.13–18

20 Now gae your wa's – Tho' anes as gude
As ever happit flesh and blude,
Yet part we maun – the case sae hard is,
Amang the writers and the bardies,
That lang they'll brook the auld I trow,
Or neibours cry, 'Weel brook the new';
Still making tight wi' tither steek,
The tither hole, the tither eik,
To bang the birr o' winter's anger,
And had the hurdies out o' langer.

'To My Auld Breeks' (1773), ll.1–10

21 But hear me lads! gin I'd been there,
How I wad trimm'd the bill o' fare!
For ne'er sic surly wight as he
Had met wi' sic respect frae me.
Mind ye what Sam, the lying loun!
Has in his Dictionar laid down?
That aits in England are a feast
To cow an' horse, an' sican beast,
While in Scots ground this growth was common
To gust the gab o' man and woman.

'To the Principal and Professors of the University of St Andrews, on their Superb Treat to Dr Samuel Johnson' (1773), ll.23–32. Cf. Samuel Johnson 1

22 Will ye gang o-er the lee-rigg,
My ain kind deary O!
And cuddle there sae kindly
Wi' me, my kind deary O?

At thornie-dike and birken-tree
We'll daff, and ne'er be weary O;
They'll scug ill een frae you and me,
Mine ain kind deary O.

'The Lee Rigg' (first published 1782), st.1–2

Robert Burns acknowledged Fergusson's song, together with a still older, anonymous version, as an influence on his own 'The Lea-Rig'. Cf. Robert Burns 116

Ferrier, Susan Edmondstone 1782–1854
Novelist

1 Worldly prudence is very suitable at seventy, but at seventeen it is absolutely disgusting; in the one it is the result of experience, in the other it is the offspring of a little mind and base contracted heart.

Letter to Walter Ferrier (1809 or 1810), in John A Doyle (ed.), *Memoir and Correspondence of Susan Ferrier* (1898), ch.1

2 . . . the only good purpose of a book is to inculcate morality, and convey some lesson of instruction as well as delight. . .

> Letter to Miss Charlotte Clavering (1809 or 1810), in John A Doyle (ed.), *Memoir and Correspondence of Susan Ferrier* (1898), ch.2

3 . . . you can do nothing but write, and though I approve of it as an amusement I by no means commend it as the business of life – too much application is bad for the health and will spoil your eyes and complexion. . .

> Letter to Miss Charlotte Clavering (Feb 1810), in John A Doyle (ed.), *Memoir and Correspondence of Susan Ferrier* (1898), ch.2

4 . . . I mean to choose a nobler path, and intend to immortalise myself by giving to the world a work which shall be read when reading is no more! A work whose fame shall extend from the Taboozamanoo Islands to the last stone of the Mull of Kantyre [sic]!

> Letter to Miss Charlotte Clavering (1810), in John A Doyle (ed.), *Memoir and Correspondence of Susan Ferrier* (1898), ch.2

5 I maintain there is but one crime a woman could never forgive in her husband, and that is a *kicking*. Did you ever read anything so exquisite as the new canto of 'Childe Harold'? It is enough to make a woman fly into the arms of a tiger; nothing but a kick could ever have hardened her heart against such genius.

> Letter to Miss Charlotte Clavering (?1816), in John A Doyle (ed.), *Memoir and Correspondence of Susan Ferrier* (1898), ch.2

6 'Edication!. . . If a woman can nurse her bairns, mak their claes, and manage her hooss, what mair need she do? If she can play a tune on the spinnet, and dance a reel, and play a rubber at whist – nae doot these are accomplishments, but they're soon learnt. Edication! pooh!'

> *Marriage* (1818), Vol.1, ch.13 (Glenfern to Henry)

7 'What renders his death Particularly distressing, is, that Lady Maclaughlan is of opinion it was entirely owing to eating Raw oysters, and damp feet. This ought to be a warning to all Young people to take care of Wet feet, and Especially eating Raw oysters, which are certainly Highly dangerous, particularly where there is any Tendency to Gout.'

> *Marriage* (1818), Vol.1, ch.23 (Letter from Miss Grizzy to Lady Juliana)

8 'I'm certain – indeed, I think there's no doubt of it – that reading does young people much harm. It puts things into their heads that never would have been there, but for books. I declare, I think reading's a very dangerous thing.'

> *Marriage* (1818), Vol.2, ch.4 (Lady Grizzy)

9 ' . . . what can I do with a girl who has been educated in Scotland? She must be vulgar –

all Scotchwomen are so. They have red hands and rough voices; they yawn, and they blow their noses, and talk, and laugh loud, and do a thousand shocking things. Then, to hear the Scotch brogue – oh, heavens! I should expire every time she opened her mouth!'

> *Marriage* (1818), Vol.2, ch.6 (Lady Juliana to Lady Emily)

10 'If a person speaks sense and truth, what does it signify how it is spoken?'

> *Marriage* (1818), Vol.2, ch.6 (Lady Emily to Lady Juliana)

11 'What a selfish cold-hearted thing is grandeur!', thought Mary, as Lady Emily and she sat like two specks in the splendid saloon, surrounded by all that wealth could purchase, or luxury invent. . .

> *Marriage* (1818), Vol.2, ch.12

12 'Married ladies only celebrated for their good dinners, or their pretty equipages, or their fine jewels. How I should scorn to be talked of as the appendage to any soups or pearls!'

> *Marriage* (1818), Vol.2, ch.20 (Lady Emily to Mary)

13 'Oh! the insipidity of a mere Miss! a soft simpering thing with pink cheeks, and pretty hair, and fashionable clothes; – *sans* eyes for anything but flattery – *sans* taste for anything but balls – *sans* brains for anything at all!'

> *Marriage* (1818), Vol.2, ch.20 (Lady Emily to Mary)

14 'Civility is too much for a man one means to refuse. You'll never get rid of a stupid man by civility.'

> *Marriage* (1818), Vol.3, ch.7 (Lady Emily to Mary)

15 'Spendthrifts and ne'erdoweels on the tae side; fules and tawpies on the t'ither – a true picture o' the warld.'

> *The Inheritance* (1824), ch.18 (Mr Ramsay)

16 'A smokey house and a scolding wife have, indeed, always been looked upon as the *ne plus ultra* of human misery; but that is only amongst the rich. When you have seen more of the poor you will be satisfied there are still greater evils. . .'

> *The Inheritance* (1824), ch.64 (Mr Lyndsay to Gertrude)

17 Dinners are commonly dull things, unless there is some *bel esprit* to take the lead and act as *sauce piquante* to the company. . .

> *The Inheritance* (1824), ch.74

18 'Scotch songs!' repeated Mrs Waddell, with astonishment and contempt. 'I hope, cousin, you don't think me *quite* so vulgar as to sing Scotch

songs. I assure you they are quite exploded from the drawing-room now; they are called kitchen songs. . .'

> *The Inheritance* (1824), ch.74 (Mrs Waddell to Gertrude)

9 But who can count the beatings of the lonely heart?

> *The Inheritance* (1824), ch.102

0 . . . the Highlands may be said to open for the season as the King's Theatre shuts; and, thanks to grouse and deer, the one has become almost as fashionable a place of amusement as the other.

> *Destiny* (1831), ch.2

1 'It was the saying, sir, of one of the wisest judges who ever sat upon the Scottish bench, that a *poor* clergy made a *pure* clergy; a maxim which deserves to be engraven in letters of gold on every manse in Scotland.'

> *Destiny* (1831), ch.10 (Inch Orran to Mr M'Dow)

2 '. . . I do assure you, it is a very tiresome thing to be trained up to be a person of consequence. . . '

> *Destiny* (1831), ch.47 (Lady Waldegrave to Edith)

3 . . . Sunday – day of rest to the poor and the toil-worn, of weariness to the rich and the idle.

> *Destiny* (1831), ch.51

Findlater, Mary 1865–1963

Poet and novelist, sister of Jane Findlater (1866–1946) with whom she co-wrote several novels

1 Alas! for Youth & Beauty! Paint is hard enough on a young face but an aged, seamed, harrowed one, covered with powder and with reddened mouth is unspeakably ghastly.

> Letter to Marion Cadell (28 May 1915), quoted in Eileen Mackenzie, *The Findlater Sisters* (1964), ch.5

2 I do feel now as if the whole world, & all its present history, is being boiled down into an unctuous BBC Broth – or as if an immense-voiced, common-minded sort of gargantuan Governess had control of the news we are allowed to hear & was telling us even what we had to think about it. Yet how good some of it is! I know we should hate not to have it now.

> On the BBC in the early 1930s. Quoted in Eileen Mackenzie, *The Findlater Sisters* (1964), ch.6

Finlay, Ian 1906–

New Zealand-born art historian and critic

1 A ship, like a medieval church, is the creation of many minds and of a still larger number of

hands, and if it achieves beauty this is not to be denied simply because it was not produced in the studio of a single man of genius.

> *Art in Scotland* (1948), ch.11

Finlay, Ian Hamilton 1925–

Poet, sculptor and painter

1 When I have talked for an hour I feel lousy –
Not so when I have danced for an hour:
The dancers inherit the party
While the talkers wear themselves out and
  sit in corners alone, and glower.

> 'The Dancers Inherit the Party', *The Dancers Inherit the Party* (1960)

2 Poor. Old. Tired. Horse.

> Title of his poetry and arts magazine, which he edited from 1961 to its close in 1967. The title is taken from a line in American poet Robert Creeley's poem 'Please', in *A Form of Women* (1959)

3 A model of order, even if set in a space filled with doubt.

> On Concrete Poetry. Letter to Pierre Garnier (17 Sep 1963), reprinted on the card, 'The Guillotine' (1991)

4 When I hear the words 'Arts Council' I reach for my water-pistol.

> On his headed paper (c.1970)

5 Arts Councils are the insane asylums of bureaucracy.

> 'An Alphabet', *Studio International* Vol.195, No.991/2 (1981)

6 When the *Shepherdperson* came in, surely Pan was out.

> *More Detached Sentences on Gardening*, in *PN Review* No.42 (1984)

7 Art that stops short at art is not enough.

> Interview with Everest Potter, 'A Forgotten Art', *Arts Magazine* Vol.62, No.1 (Sep 1987). Quoted in Alec Finlay (ed.), *Wood Notes Wild: Essays on the poetry and art of Ian Hamilton Finlay* (1995), Editor's foreword

8 The French Revolution
Scorned circumlocution.
'It depends what you mean'
Meant Madame Guillotine.

> From 'Clerihews for Liberals' (1987). Quoted in Alec Finlay (ed.), *Wood Notes Wild: Essays on the poetry and art of Ian Hamilton Finlay* (1995)

9 Reverence is the Dada of the 1980s as irreverence was the Dada of 1918.

> *The Little Critic* 4 (Victoria Miro Gallery, London, 1988). Quoted in Alec Finlay (ed.), *Wood Notes Wild: Essays on the poetry and art of Ian Hamilton Finlay* (1995), Editor's foreword

10 Conflict is one of the givens of the universe. The only way it can ever be tamed or managed or civilised is within culture. You cannot pretend that it does not exist.

> Quoted in Malise Ruthven, 'Gardens, Politics of Little Sparta', *Architectural Digest* (Jul 1989), and again in Alec Finlay (ed.), *Wood Notes Wild: Essays on the poetry and art of Ian Hamilton Finlay* (1995), Editor's foreword

11 When our friends leave us they take away our shores.

> *Detached Sentences on Friendship* (1991)

12 Landscapes are *ideas* as much as things.

> Quoted in Patrick Eyres, 'A People's Arcadia', *New Arcadians' Journal* No.33–4 (1992), and again in Alec Finlay (ed.), *Wood Notes Wild: Essays on the poetry and art of Ian Hamilton Finlay* (1995), Editor's foreword

13 I became quite inspired, not so much from inside but from outside. . . . I became obsessed with the vision of a classical garden, which was absolutely absurd considering this was just a moorland and I had only a spade.

> On contemplating the landscape at his home in Dunsyre, which became his garden, Little Sparta. Interview with Paul Crowther, *Art and Design* (1994), quoted in Alec Finlay (ed.), *Wood Notes Wild: Essays on the poetry and art of Ian Hamilton Finlay* (1995), 'Notes for the Reader'

14 Gardening activity is of five kinds, namely, sowing, planting, fixing, placing, maintaining. In so far as gardening is an Art, all these may be taken under one head, composing.

> 'Detached Sentences on Gardening', in 'A Walk Around Stonypath, Little Sparta', *Chapman* No.78–9 (1994)

15 What a Possibility lies in a newly dug turf!

> *Domestic Pensées* (unpublished). Quoted in Alec Finlay (ed.), *Wood Notes Wild: Essays on the poetry and art of Ian Hamilton Finlay* (1995), Editor's foreword

16 Garden Centres must become the Jacobin Clubs of the new Revolution.

17 TO APOLLO.
HIS MUSIC. HIS MISSILES. HIS MUSES.

> Inscription on the Garden Temple, the Temple of Apollo at the heart of Little Sparta

18 Terror is the piety of the revolution.

> Inscription in the Garden Temple at Little Sparta

19 Strathclyde Region made war on Little Sparta
Strathclyde Region is no more

> Postcard issued by the 'Committee of Public Safety, Little Sparta' (1996)

Finlay the Red Bard
see **Fionnlagh Ruadh**

Finniston, Sir Monty 1912–
Industrialist and businessman, chairman of British Steel Corporation (1973–6)

1 I do not believe that people who are inexpert, inexperienced and ignorant of an industry can be expected to know more about it than an expert who has spent all his life in it. I do not think any civil servant can tell me my job. I may not be as intelligent. I certainly was not educated at Oxford or Cambridge – I was educated at a far better place, Glasgow.

> On being sacked as chairman of British Steel. Quoted in *The Daily Mail* (19 Mar 1976)

2 Give them an inch and they take a mile. They always have to make their play you see. And there are so many of them; if one is exhausted, they can roll out another. There's only one of me.

> On the 17 government ministers he had to deal with as chairman of BSC. Quoted in the London *Evening Standard* (8 Sep 1976)

3 All markets, even free ones, need planning – and planning well ahead.

> 'Necessity and Invention' in K Cargill (ed.), *Scotland 2000* (1987)

4 Ignorance is not an asset at any time – and certainly not in industry. Education and training are the cures for ignorance.

> 'Necessity and Invention' in K Cargill (ed.), *Scotland 2000* (1987)

5 The bustle of talented people doing share deals at their VDUs in the Scottish Stock Exchange is superficially impressive. . . [But] the Scottish equivalent of the City seemed to show too little understanding of the needs and risks of modern industry and the requirement for investors to match that need and risk with a more relaxed and sympathetic attitude towards investment. . . in my opinion the country has for the past twenty-five years (some would say longer) suffered and still suffers from economic AIDS – Acquired Industrial Deficiency Syndrome.

> 'Necessity and Invention' in K Cargill (ed.), *Scotland 2000* (1987)

Fionnlagh Ruadh (Finlay the Red Bard)
16th century
Poet to John, chief of Clan Gregor

1 Theast aon diabhal na nGaoidheal,
sgéal as cóir do chommaoidheamh,
bhaoi ré daorlot cheall is chros,

an maoltorc mall gan mhathas.

A h-ifreann thánaig ar dtús:
usaide an sgéal a iomthús,
mar thá a bheatha rís ar bail
i gceathaibh ghrís an diabhail.

† The prime devil of the Gael is dead, a tale fit
to be vaunted, who ignobly wounded churches
and crosses, the bald boar dull and worthless.

From hell he came at first: his origin makes
it the easier to believe the news, how that his
existence is again prosperous among the hot
ash showers of the Devil.

Poem in dispraise of Allan, chief of Clan Ranald
(died c.1509), st.1–2. Quoted in W J Watson
(ed.), *Scottish Verse from the Book of the Dean of
Lismore* (1937)

2 Ní h-iongnadh a bheith i bpéin:
fada ó b'ionchrochtha Ailéin;
ná luaidh ar láthair an fhir
chuaidh go a mháthair 's go a phiuthair.

Mithigh a nois sgur dot aoir,
a mheic Ruaidhrí, a ainmhín;
a Ailéin nach greasann greas,
caithréim t'easgaine is oircheas.

† No marvel that he is in torment; it is long
since Allan was gallows-ripe; mention not the
manly vigour of the man who went in to his
mother and to his sister.

Time now to cease from satire of thee, thou
son of Roderick, thou man of violence; thou
Allan whose wont is not to press a fight, fit
is the triumph of thy cursing.

Poem in dispraise of Allan, chief of Clan
Ranald, st.16–17. Quoted in W J Watson (ed.),
*Scottish Verse from the Book of the Dean of
Lismore* (1937)

3 Mar chaochladh gaoithe do chnocaibh
ruith na saoithe i ndeachaidh;
mór gceád lér aidhbhsech a siubhal.
théid mar thaidhbhse seachaibh;
each do-ní siorruith ré saighid,
a gníomhraidh is greanta. . .

† As the shifting of wind from hill-tops is the
running of the troop he charges; to many
hundreds his career is dreadful, he that passes
like a phantom; a steed that keeps pace ever
with an arrow, his deeds are brilliant. . .

Poem in praise of MacGregor's horse, ll.17–22.
Quoted in W J Watson (ed.), *Scottish Verse from
the Book of the Dean of Lismore* (1937)

Fitt, Matthew 1968–

Poet

1 ye wur that pischt
that yir ain voamit
goat aff the flair
an ran ben tae the cludgie

an spewed its ring

'Kate O' Shanter's Tale', *Chapman* No.65
(Summer 1991). Cf. Robert Burns 100

2 an juist whit
in the nemm o the wee man
duid ye dae tae the horse
ma best brawest cuddie, puir meg
that wis the tocher aff ma ain faithir
ye'v went an broke it
ye'r an eejit, shanter
a fukkin eejit
ah dinna ken whit ye wur playin at
bit ye better fynn that tail
pronto

'Kate O' Shanter's Tale', *Chapman* No.65
(Summer 1991)

Fleming, Sir Alexander 1881–1955

Chemist, discoverer of penicillin

1 Every research-worker should have a certain
amount of time to himself. . . Momentous
things may happen in a man's free time.

c.1946. Quoted in André Maurois, *The Life of
Sir Alexander Fleming* (1959), ch.15

2 This thirst for immediate results is by no means
uncommon, but it is extremely harmful. Really
valuable research is a long-term affair.

c.1946. Quoted in André Maurois, *The Life of
Sir Alexander Fleming* (1959), ch.15

3 It is the lone worker who makes the first advance
in a subject: the details may be worked out by a
team, but the prime idea is due to the enterprise,
thought and perception of an individual.

Rectorial address at Edinburgh University (1951)

4 When you gamble, you may eventually go broke,
but with research you may make a failure, then
another failure, then others, but you never
go broke.

Quoted in L J Ludovici, *Fleming, Discoverer of
Penicillin* (1952), ch.4

5 You catch it on Monday, you're cured on Tuesday and on Wednesday you may catch it again.

On the effectiveness of penicillin as a cure for
gonorrhoea. Quoted in L J Ludovici, *Fleming,
Discoverer of Penicillin* (1952), ch.12

6 A good gulp of whisky at bedtime – it's not
very scientific, but it helps.

Response when asked about a cure for colds.
News summary (22 Mar 1954)

Fleming, Marjory 1803–11

Child writer, popularly known as 'Pet Marjorie'

1 The most Devilish thing is 8 times 8 & 7 times
7 it is what nature itselfe cant endure

'Journal 2' (1810), in F Sidgwick (ed.), *The
Complete Marjory Fleming* (1934)

2 Many girls have not the advantage I have and I [am] very very glad that satan has not geven me boils and many other Misfortunes.

'Journal 2' (1810), in F Sidgwick (ed.), *The Complete Marjory Fleming* (1934)

3 To Day I pronunced a word which should never come out of a ladys lips it was that I caled John a Impudent Bitch.

'Journal 2' (1810), in F Sidgwick (ed.), *The Complete Marjory Fleming* (1934)

4 I would rather have a man dog then a women dog because they do not bear like women dogs, it is a hard case it is shoking.

'Journal 2' (1810), in F Sidgwick (ed.), *The Complete Marjory Fleming* (1934)

5 I hope I will be religious agoin but as for reganing my charecter I despare.

'Journal 2' (1810), in F Sidgwick (ed.), *The Complete Marjory Fleming* (1934)

6 An annibaptist is a thing I am not a member of: – I am a Pisplikan just now & a Prisbeteren at Kercaldy my native town which thugh dirty is clein in the country.

'Journal 3' (1811), in F Sidgwick (ed.), *The Complete Marjory Fleming* (1934)

7 Love is a very papithatick thing as well as troublesom & tiresome but O Isabella forbid me to speak about it.

'Journal 3' (1811), in F Sidgwick (ed.), *The Complete Marjory Fleming* (1934)

8 Fighting is what ladies is not gualyfied for they would not make a good figure in battle or in a dual.

'Journal 3' (1811), in F Sidgwick (ed.), *The Complete Marjory Fleming* (1934)

Fletcher (of Saltoun), Andrew
1655–1716

Patriot and opponent of the Treaty of Union of 1707

1 I knew a very wise man so much of Sir Chr—'s sentiment, that he believed if a man were permitted to make all the ballads, he need not care who should make the laws of a nation.

An Account of a Conversation Concerning a Right Regulation of Governments for the Common Good of Mankind (1704). Cf. Ian Hamilton 1

2 The Scots deserve no pity, if they voluntarily surrender their united and separate interests to the Mercy of an united Parliament, where the English have so vast a Majority. . . This will be the issue of that darling Plea, of being one and not two; it will be turned upon the Scots with a Vengeance; and their 45 Scots Members

may dance round to all Eternity, in this Trap of their own making.

State of the Controversy betwixt United and Separate Parliaments (1706)

A critique of the proposed Union

3 It is only fit for the slaves who sold it.

Referring to Scotland (1707), on his departure from it after the signing of the Treaty of Union. Quoted in G W T Ormond, *Fletcher of Saltoun* (1897), p.139

4 Lord have mercy on my poor country that is so barbarously oppressed.

Attrib. Dying words (Sep 1716)

Ford, Robert 1846–1905
Folklorist and collector of songs and humorous anecdotes

1 The rapid and general railway service that now obtains, not to speak of the ubiquitous bicycle, has brought the village so close to the town, the hill so near to the street recently, that the rising generations in the country are catching up the howling rhapsodies of the music halls only a day later than the people of the city.

On the decline of rural folksong. *Vagabond Songs and Ballads of Scotland* (1904 edition), Preface

2 . . . an Englishman's wit (he has little or no humour) being an acquired taste, comes out 'on parade' – it is a gay thing – while Scotch folks' humour, being the common gift of Nature to all and sundry in the land, differing only in degree, slips out most frequently when and where least expected.

Thistledown (1914), ch.2, 'Characteristics of Scotch Humour'

3 'Hoots, Janet, ye think there's naebody good enough for Heaven but yersel', and the minister.'

'Deed,' replied Janet, 'I hae sometimes very grave doots about the minister.'

Thistledown (1914), ch.4, 'The Pulpit and the Pew'

Punch in 1880 (Vol.79, p.275), captioned a cartoon on the same theme: 'Ah whiles hae ma doobts aboot the meenister.'

Forsyth, Bill 1947–
Film director

1 You are allowed one chance in Scotland, and if you blow it, that's your lot. It is just luck if it comes off. Afterwards, you are terrified, but at the time you don't realise what is happening.

After the première of *That Sinking Feeling* (29 Aug 1979). Interview with Liz Taylor in *The Scotsman*, quoted in Forsyth Hardy, *Scotland in Film* (1990), ch.9

2 It would be impossible to make films in Scotland without thermal underwear.

> *Sight and Sound* (Spring 1984). Quoted in Allan Hunter, 'Bill Forsyth: The Imperfect Anarchist', in Eddie Dick (ed.), *From Limelight to Satellite* (1990)

3 It is the humour of despair, the humour of the gallows. The humour of awful circumstances or predicaments. I think that is where humour comes from. From situations where the only way out is to laugh for survival's sake. At the bottom of every joke is a piece of despair. . . If someone falls on a banana skin you get a laugh but someone gets hurt.

> On the similarities between Glaswegian and New York humour. Quoted in Allan Hunter, 'Bill Forsyth: The Imperfect Anarchist', in Eddie Dick (ed.), *From Limelight to Satellite* (1990)

4 I think we're basically all odd. I think we all have a tension between what we think we are and what other people think we are. . . Strangeness is in everyone, it's just a matter of whether you choose to reveal it or not.

> Quoted in Allan Hunter, 'Bill Forsyth: The Imperfect Anarchist', in Eddie Dick (ed.), *From Limelight to Satellite* (1990)

5 We're not Scottish, we're northern European and highly industrialised, developed westerners. Whatever is uniquely Scottish about us would be so difficult to put across in such a crass medium as film that it's not worth the attempt.

> Quoted in Allan Hunter, 'Bill Forsyth: The Imperfect Anarchist', in Eddie Dick (ed.), *From Limelight to Satellite* (1990)

Forsyth, Janice

Broadcaster and journalist

1 These days the Sex Pistols' idea of anarchy in the UK is probably taking a full shopping trolley into the express queue at Sainsburys.

> On the announcement of the Sex Pistols' come-back tour. *The Scotsman*, 'Weekend' (23 Mar 1996)

Forsyth, Michael Bruce 1954–

Conservative politician, MP for Stirling (1983–), Secretary of State for Scotland (1995–)

1 . . . the cult of the defeated Wallace eclipses the successes of the crowned Bruce. . . [Both were] national heroes in a country which professes to have no heroes. Wallace was an heroic failure; Bruce was a spectacular success. A loser and a winner: it is Wallace who is in fashion today. That must tell us something about the contemporary Scots ethos.

> Williamson Memorial Lecture, quoted in *The Scotsman* (27 Apr 1996)

On the popularity of 'loser' William Wallace, as portrayed in the film *Braveheart*, compared with that of Robert the Bruce. Cf. Billy Connolly 12

2 If Prince Charles Edward Stuart had won at Culloden 250 years ago this month there would have been precious few songs about him. We might not have gone so far as to put the Butcher Cumberland on shortbread tins, but Bonnie Prince Charlie, in the Scottish psyche, would have been irredeemably diminished by success.

> Williamson Memorial Lecture, quoted in *The Scotsman* (27 Apr 1996)

3 Labour's tartan tax.

> Phrase coined (c.1995) to describe the Labour Party's proposal for a Scottish Assembly with tax-varying powers

Forsyth, Roddy

Football broadcaster, journalist and author

1 Walk into a pub in Scotland and, if you know anything about football, you'll never talk alone. If you know nothing you can be even better company. You can be a good listener.

> *The Only Game: Scots and World Football* (1990), ch.1

Fraser, G(eorge) S(utherland) 1915–80

Poet

1 Glitter of mica at the windy corners,
Tar in the nostrils, under blue lamps budding
Like bubbles of glass and the blue buds of a tree,
Night-shining shopfronts, or the sleek sun
  flooding
The broad abundant dying sprawl of the Dee. . .

> 'Hometown Elegy (for Aberdeen in Spring)', *Hometown Elegy* (1944)
>
> > Jessie Kesson used the phrase 'Glitter of mica' as the title for her 1963 novel

2 . . . The fat sky gurgles like a swollen bladder
With the foul rain that rains on poverty.

> 'Lean Street', *Hometown Elegy* (1944), st.5

3 He sings alone who in this province sings.
I kick a lamp-post, and in drink I rave:
With Byron and with Lermontov
Romantic Scotland's in the grave.

> 'Meditation of a Patriot', *Hometown Elegy* (1944), st.2

Fraser, James 1726–1808

Secretary of the Bank of Scotland (1802–8)

1 Let me beg the favour that you will believe, that what I am about to say and to recommend, comes from a man who has always wished yours

and your family's interest and happiness. For some time past, even for some years, there have been suggestions made, that like other men Mr Geddie grows old, and that an Agent younger and capable of more activity would be more acceptable to the Town and County and more for the success of the branch at Cupar... I would not like to receive orders to intimate to you that your Agency is to cease, but would much rather receive a Letter of Resignation from my good old friend, naming a convenient day for giving up your charge...

Letter to Robert Geddie, Agent (Manager) at Cupar (8 Mar 1802). Bank of Scotland archive, 1/146/1 Letter Book

2 I lose not a post in answering your enquiry of yesterday. A Change [in management] I find will take place. The thing is yet open for application. Tho' I could wish to serve you; yet as the choise will probably be determined, not wholey by capacity, nor even by merit, but in great measure by influence in the town and County, I cannot bid you come forward; This is my way; plain, tho' sometimes not pleasant, but candid.

Letter to George Fernie, Cupar, in answer to his application for the post of Agent at the branch there (17 Mar 1802). Bank of Scotland archive, 1/146/1 Letter Book

Fraser, Olive 1909–77
Poet and playwright

1 Come, lamefoot brain, and dance and be
A merry carnival for me.
We are alive in spite of all
Hobgoblins who our wits did call.

'Lines Written After a Nervous Breakdown II' (1964), in *The Wrong Music: The Poems of Olive Fraser* (1989, ed. Helena M Shire)

2 I was the wrong music
The wrong guest for you
When I came through the tundras
And thro' the dew.

'The Unwanted Child', *The Pure Account* (1981), st.1

Fraser, Simon see Lovat, Lord

Fraser Darling, Sir Frank 1903–79
Natural historian and ecologist

1 It is of the very nature of humanity to alter the complex of living things wherever man is found. Man must be considered as part of the natural history of the earth's surface, however unnatural he may be... The animal, lacking the power of reflection, is as much at the mercy of the environment as the environment has to endure that particular animal; but man has power quite beyond his own physical strength; he can make the desert bloom, or ultimately fill an oceanic island with the beauty of bird song, and equally he makes deserts as spectacularly as any horde of locusts.

Natural History in the Highlands and Islands (1947), ch.4

2 Even as I write, Highland fox-hunting organisations have expressed 'satisfaction' at kills not only of foxes but badgers, otters, weasels and stoats. These same men will soon be yapping their dissatisfaction at plagues of voles and rabbits and calling on that universal Aunt Sally of Scotland, the Department of Agriculture, 'to do something'.

Natural History in the Highlands and Islands (1947), ch.4

3 We are apt to view with pleasure a rugged Highland landscape and think we are here away from the works of the mind and hand of man, that here is wild nature. But more often than not we are looking at a man-made desert: the summits of the hills and the inaccessible sea cliffs alone are as time and evolution made them.

Natural History in the Highlands and Islands (1947), Conclusion

4 What is meant by a national park? There is every reason to believe that, in the minds of many who will have a large say as to whether they will or will not be, they are considered largely as lungs for urban industrial populations. So they should be, and let none of us who live in easier surroundings be one little bit scornful of this tremendous necessity...

Natural History in the Highlands and Islands (1947), Conclusion. Cf. John Muir 6

5 Wild life does not exist for man's delectation. Man may find it beautiful, edifying, amusing, useful and all the rest of it, but that is not why it is there, nor is that a good enough reason for our allowing it to remain. Let us give beast and bird and flower the place to live *in its own right*...

Natural History in the Highlands and Islands (1947), Conclusion

Frater, Anne 1967–
Poet

1 'Alba saor no na fàsach.'
Saorsa no gainmheach
canaidh iad ruinn an aon rud:

'Gheibh sibh sin . . .
ach cumaidh sinne an ola.'

† 'Scotland free or a desert.'
Freedom or sand
they'll say the same thing to us:
'You can have that . . .
but we'll keep the oil.'

> 'Smuain' ('A Thought'). In C Whyte (ed.), *An
> Aghaidh na Sìorraidheachd* (*In the Face of Eternity*,
> 1991). Cf. Anonymous 38

Frazer, Sir J(ames) G(eorge) 1854–1941
Anthropologist and folklorist

1 The awe and dread with which the untutored
savage contemplates his mother-in-law are
amongst the most familiar facts of anthropology.

> *The Golden Bough* (1922 edition), ch.18, 'The
> Perils of the Soul'

2 The abundance, the solidity, and the splendour
of the results already achieved by science
are well fitted to inspire us with a cheerful
confidence in the soundness of its method.
Here at last, after groping about in the dark
for countless ages, man has hit upon a clue to
the labyrinth, a golden key that opens many
locks in the treasury of nature. It is probably
not too much to say that the hope of progress
– moral and intellectual as well as material –
in the future is bound up with the fortunes
of science, and that every obstacle placed in
the way of scientific discovery is a wrong to
humanity.

> *The Golden Bough* (1922 edition), ch.69, 'Farewell
> to Nemi'

3 The advance of knowledge is an infinite
progression towards a goal that for ever recedes.

> *The Golden Bough* (1922 edition), ch.69, 'Farewell
> to Nemi'

4 The principle of the survival of the fittest
applies to books as well as to men. Bad books
perish, but good books survive, because the
world will not willingly let them die. Therefore,
the older a book, the stronger the testimony of
humanity to its excellence.

> 'Address to the International Association of
> Antiquarian Booksellers' (26 Jan 1927). Published
> in *Garnered Sheaves* (1931)

5 . . . we may perhaps best define an uncivilised
race as one which is ignorant of the art of
writing: the acquisition of the art of writing is
the touchstone of civilisation.

> 'The Scope and Method of Mental Anthropology',
> *Garnered Sheaves* (1931)

Fulton, Rikki 1924–
Actor, comedian and writer

1 Francie and Josie were ethnic, they were
unmistakably Glaswegian and the audiences
simply took them to their hearts . . . However,
Edinburgh audiences took to them for a very
different reason. They found them extremely
amusing because they could laugh at two
Glaswegian layabouts.

> Quoted in Vivien Devlin, *Kings, Queens and
> People's Palaces: An Oral History of the Scottish
> Variety Theatre, 1920–1970* (1991), ch.3

>> Francie and Josie were characters played as a
>> double act by Fulton and Jack Milroy from
>> 1960. The first Francie and Josie sketch,
>> however, was performed in 1958 with Stanley
>> Baxter as Francie and Fulton as Josie

2 I do believe humour is a personal thing which
is born in the main when people are under
pressure, or are suppressed . . . In Scotland,
humour may reflect the history of Scotland.
One of the hallmarks is a preoccupation with
death and funerals.

> Quoted in Vivien Devlin, *Kings, Queens and
> People's Palaces: An Oral History of the Scottish
> Variety Theatre, 1920–1970* (1991), ch.10

Fyffe, Will 1885–1947
Comedian, singer and stage and screen actor

1 I belong to Glasgow,
Dear old Glasgow town!
But what's the matter with Glasgow?
For it's going round and round.
I'm only a common old working chap,
As anyone can see,
But when I get a couple of drinks on a
  Saturday,
Glasgow belongs to me.

> 'I Belong to Glasgow' (1921), chorus

2 Twelve and a tanner a bottle,
That's what it cost me the day,
Twelve and a tanner a bottle,
Man it takes a' your pleasure away.
Afore ye can get a wee drappie
Ye have tae spend a' that ye've got,
So hoo can a fella be happy
When happiness costs such a lot?

> 'Twelve and a Tanner a Bottle' (1930), chorus

>> Fyffe sang this song in his film debut, *Elstree
>> Calling*, on the 'price of food' (ie whisky)

3 When a man takes a drink, he's a man. When
ye're teetotal – Ach! . . . When ye're teetotal
ye've got a rotten feeling that everybody's
your boss.

> Quoted in Albert Mackie, *The Scotch Comedians*
> (1973), ch.4

G

Galford, Ellen 1947–
American-born novelist

1 . . . I'm quite happy to be in Scottish
Literature. . . but if there are going to be sort of
ghetto strands I want to be in all the ghettos. . .
I don't just want to be in Lesbian or just in
Scottish or just in mainstream, I want to be
on all those shelves.

> Resisting simplistic categorisation of her work
> in bookshops and elsewhere. Interviewed in
> Caroline Gonda, 'An Other Country?: Mapping
> Scottish/Lesbian/Writing', in Christopher Whyte
> (ed.), *Gendering the Nation: Studies in Modern
> Scottish Literature* (1995)

Galgacus (or Calgacus) fl. 84 AD
Caledonian leader

1 Here at the end of the world, the last refuge
of freedom, we have lived unmolested to this
day, and that fame has kept us secure; for
everything unknown is magnified [*omne ignotum
pro magnifico est*]. But now the furthermost
parts of Britain are laid bare, there are no other
people left, nothing but waves and rocks, and
these more deadly Romans. . . raptors of the
world, who, now that they have devastated
all the earth, turn their attention even to the
sea. . . Plunder, massacre, rape, they call these
things empire: they make a desert and call it
peace [*solitudinem faciunt pacem appellant*].

> Attrib. His speech before the battle of Mons
> Graupius (AD 84). Quoted in Tacitus, *Agricola*,
> ch.30. Cf. Lord Byron 26, Samuel Johnson 5

Galloway, Janice 1956–
Novelist and short-story writer

1 Love/Emotion = embarrassment: Scots equa-
tion. Exceptions are when roaring drunk or
watching football. Men do rather better out of
this loophole.

> *The Trick is to Keep Breathing* (1990)

2 I'm gawky, not a natural swimmer. But I can
read up a little, take advice. I read somewhere
the trick is to keep breathing, make out it's
not unnatural at all. They say it comes with
practice.

> *The Trick is to Keep Breathing* (1990)

3 You don't remember just by telling yourself
you should, by sheer act of will. You don't get

to pick and choose. The same way you don't
get to forget. Memory. A bastard really. A
complete bastard.

> *Foreign Parts* (1994), ch.10

4 . . . she knew even less about what passed for
Scottish history. Macbeth. St Columba. Your
own country's medieval life restricted to an
English play and a velcro shape off the felt table
at Sunday school. Robert the Bruce. Kings
and generals, Men of letters. Of the mass of
people, less than nothing. Women didn't come
into the reckoning at all.

> *Foreign Parts* (1994), ch.11

5 I'd trade a lot for tenderness. I really would.

> *Foreign Parts* (1994), ch.16

6 The knight on a white charger is never going
to come, Rona. You know why? Because he's
down the pub with the other knights, that's
why. Or on the bloody golf course or at the
football or constructing Great Art or some such
bloody thing that has nothing to do with the
forging of sound interpersonal relationships
AT ALL.

> *Foreign Parts* (1994), ch.16

7 Any feminism that overlooks class or race or
sexuality issues is not worth the name. Shutting
feminism off from other issues in life is just
simplistic. It doesn't know its arse from its
political elbow.

> Profile in *The Big Issue* No.75 (26 Apr– 9 May
> 1996)

Galt, John 1779–1839
Novelist

1 Before this year, the drinking of tea was little
known in the parish, saving among a few of
the heritors' houses on a Sabbath evening; but
now it became very rife. Yet the commoner
sort did not like to let it be known that they
were taking to the new luxury – especially the
elder women, who, for that reason, had their
ploys in out-houses and by-places, just as the
witches lang syne had their sinful possets and
galravitchings; – and they made their tea for
common in the pint-stoup, and drank it out of
caps and luggies, for there were but few among
them that had cups and saucers.

> *Annals of the Parish* (1821), ch.2, 'Year 1761'

2 The auld carles kecklet with fainness as they saw
the young dancers, and the carlins sat on forms

as mim as May puddocks, with their shawls pinned apart to show their muslin napkins. But after supper, when they had got a glass of punch, their heels showed their mettle, and grannies danced with their oyes, holding out their hands as if they had been spinning with two rocks.

On a pay-wedding, *Annals of the Parish* (1821), ch.48, 'Year 1807'

oyes: grandchildren

. . . on the Monday, when the spinners went to the mill, they were told that the company had stopped payment. Never did a thunder-clap daunt the heart like this news, for the bread in a moment was snatched from more than a thousand mouths.

Annals of the Parish (1821), ch.49, 'Year 1808'

. . . the stupendous rock of Dumbarton Castle, that Gibraltar of antiquity. . .

The Ayrshire Legatees (1821), ch.4, 'The Town', Letter 8 (Miss Rachel Pringle)

But you will be surprised to hear that no such thing as whusky is to be had in the public-houses, where they drink only a dead sort of beer. . . As for the water, a drink of clear, wholesome good water is not within the bounds of London; and, truly, now may I say that I have learnt what the blessing of a cup of cold water is.

The Ayrshire Legatees (1821), ch.4, 'The Town', Letter 11 (Mrs Pringle)

Trully, it may be said that the croun of England is upon the downfal, and surely we are all seething in the pot of revolution, for the scum is mounting uppermost.

The Ayrshire Legatees (1821), ch.7, 'Discoveries and Rebellions', Letter 22 (Mrs Pringle)

In a word, man in London is not quite so good a creature as he is out of it.

The Ayrshire Legatees (1821), ch.7, 'Discoveries and Rebellions', Letter 23 (Andrew Pringle)

'O Sir Thomas! Sir Thomas! there's nae plaster for a wounded conscience, nor solder for a broken heart.'

Sir Andrew Wylie (1822), ch.41, 'A Remonstrance' (Andrew Wylie)

'Ye have said sae,' replied the laird; 'but everybody kens that duchesses, especially o' the English breed, are nae better than they should be.'

Sir Andrew Wylie (1822), ch.94, 'The Fireside' (the laird of Craiglands)

It is, in our opinion, a more awful thing to be born than to die. . .

Sir Andrew Wylie (1822), ch.105, 'The Conclusion'

11 Having thus reached to a seat in the council, I discerned that it behoved me to act with circumspection, in order to gain a discreet dominion over the same, and to rule without being felt, which is the great mystery of policy.

The Provost (1822), ch.3, 'A Dirgie'

12 . . . the ill-less vanity of being thought far ben with the great is among others of her harmless frailties.

On Mrs Pawkie, the Provost's wife. *The Provost* (1822), ch.35, 'Tests of Success'

13 'Mr Walkinshaw, I'm nae prophet, as ye weel ken; but I can see that the day's no far aff when ministers of the gospel in Glasgow will be seen chambering and wantoning to the sound o' the kist fu' o' whistles, wi' the seven-headed beast routing its choruses at every ouercome o' the spring.'

The Entail (1823), ch.4 (Cornelius Luke to Claud Walkinshaw)

14 'Mr Walkinshaw,' said the honest writer after a pause of about a minute, 'there's no Christianity in this.'
'But there may be law, I hope.'

The Entail (1823), ch.18 (Mr Keelevin, the lawyer, in conversation with Claud Walkinshaw, who has determined to cut his son off from his inheritance)

15 'Ye had better come hame,' said Watty, 'for there's a sheep's-head in the pat, wi' a cuff o' the neck like ony Glasgow bailie's. Ye'll no get the like o't at Kilmarkeckle, where the kail's sae thin that every pile o' barley runs roun' the dish, bobbing and bidding gude-day to its neighbour.'

The Entail (1823), ch.23

16 'So out o' my house, and daur no longer to pollute my presence, ye partan-handit, grip-and-haud smiddy-vice Mammon o' unrighteousness.'

The Entail (1823), ch.91 (Leddy Grippy ejects Milrookit and instigates a lawsuit against him)

17 'Wha ever heard o' thousands o' pounds gotten for sax weeks' bed, board, and washing like mine? But it was a righteous judgment on the Nabal, Milrookit, whom I'll never speak to again in this world, and no in the next either, I doot, unless he mends his manners.'

The Entail (1823), ch.93 (Leddy Grippy wins her case)

18 'Eh! little did I think that I was ever to hae the honour and glory of ca'ing a nail intil the timber hip o' the Virgin Mary! Ah, lucky, ye would na hae tholed the dirl o' the dints o' my hammer as she did. But she's a saint, and ye'll ne'er deny that ye're a sinner.'

Ringan Gilhaize (1823), Vol.1, ch.14 (James Coom,

a Reformer, on repairing for the local Abbot
'that aged and worthy grannie of the papistry,
our leddy the Virgin Mary')

19 'When the sword, Johnnie, is in the hand, it's an
honourable thing to deal stoutly wi' the foe; but
when forlorn and dejectit, and more houseless
than the beasts of the field, he's no longer an
adversary, but a man that we're bound by the
laws of God and nature to help.'

Ringan Gilhaize (1823), Vol.2, ch.15 (Gideon
Kemp to Johnnie Jamieson, seeking compassion
for the fugitive Covenanter Ringan)

20 From the time of the *North Briton* of the un-
principled Wilkes, a notion has been entertained
that the moral spine in Scotland is more flexible
than in England. The truth however is, that
an elementary difference exists in the public
feelings of the two nations quite as great as
in the idioms of their respective dialects. The
English are a justice-loving people, according
to charter and statute; the Scotch are a wrong-
resenting race, according to right and feeling:
and the character of liberty among them takes
its aspect from that peculiarity.

Ringan Gilhaize (1823), Postscript

Garden, Mary (originally Davidson)
1874–1967

Soprano who lived much of her life in America

1 I began my career at the top, I stayed at the
top, and I left at the top. When, many years
later, the time came to leave it all, I did so
without any hesitation.

Mary Garden's Story (1952, with Louis
Biancolli), p.40

She became an overnight success in 1900
when, on the illness of the principal singer,
she stepped into the title role midway through
a performance of Charpentier's *Louise* at the
Opéra-Comique in Paris

2 My passion was opera, and that was the only
real 'romance' of my life.

Mary Garden's Story (1952, with Louis Biancolli),
closing sentence

3 You mustn't have a big stomach and be a big
fat lady. You have to be thin to sing it.

On the ideal requirements for performing the
role of Mélisande, in Debussy's *Pelléas et
Mélisande*

Garioch, Robert (pseudonym of Robert
Garioch Sutherland) 1909–81

Poet

1 In simmer, when aa sorts forgether
in Embro to the ploy,
fowk seek out friens to hae a blether,

or faes they'd fain annoy;
smorit wi British Railways' reek
frae Glesca or Glen Roy
or Wick, they come to hae a week
of cultivatit joy,
or three,
in Embro to the ploy.

'Embro to the Ploy', st.1, *Complete Poetical Works*
(1983, ed. Robin Fulton). Cf. Anonymous 10

2 Bumpity doun in the corrie gaed whuddran
the pitiless whun stane,
Sisyphus dodderan eftir it, shair of his cheque
at the month's end.

'Sisyphus', *Complete Poetical Works* (1983, ed.
Robin Fulton)

3 Badenoch in simmer, wi nae clegs about.

'The Muir', *Complete Poetical Works* (1983, ed.
Robin Fulton)

His analogy for Heaven

4 Canongate kirkyaird in the failing year
is auld and grey, the wee roseirs are bare,
five gulls leam white agin the dirty air:
why are they here? There's naething for
them here.

'At Robert Fergusson's Grave', *Complete Poetical
Works* (1983, ed. Robin Fulton)

5 . . . Strang, present dool
ruggs at my hairt. Lichtlie this gin ye daur:
here Robert Burns knelt and kissed the mool.

'At Robert Fergusson's Grave', *Complete Poetical
Works* (1983, ed. Robin Fulton)

6 Shote! here's the poliss,
the Gayfield poliss,
an thull pi'iz in the nick fir
pleyan fi'baw in the street!
Yin o thum's a faw'y,
like a muckle foazie taw'y,
bi' the ither's lang and skinnylike,
wi umburrelly feet.

'Fi'baw in the Street', *Complete Poetical Works*
(1983, ed. Robin Fulton), st.1

7 I'm early up, this Friday morn,
and feelin maist byordnar gay;
ma heid's as caller as a herrin,
I'm faur owre weill to wark the day.

'Owre Weill', *Complete Poetical Works* (1983, ed.
Robin Fulton), st.1

8 . . . here in Edinburgh, the people have
no spontaneous art; therefore, they have
no potential consciousness. They may shout
'Scotland!' at an international match; but this
kind of nationalism is a mere habit formed by
conditioning from without. . . In like manner
they are wont to wash down haggis with whisky
in honour of Robert Burns, and by the natural
reaction of these national chemicals, proceeding

within their paunches, generate a sententious aromatic fume that dislodges from their brains their little stock of platitudes. You may find more intellectual honesty at Murrayfield than at a Burns Supper. But in neither of these places do you find any genuine Scottish feeling.

> In the *Scots Observer* (1933–4), quoted in Raymond Ross, 'Edinburgh Grooves: Robert Garioch's Edinburgh', *Cencrastus* No.29 (Spring 1988)

Gaughan, Dick 1948–
Folksinger, musician and songwriter

1 It is not possible to take politics out of folk music.

> Interview on Radio Scotland, *Travelling Folk*, quoted in Bert Wright, 'Politics and the Folksong Revival – Commitment or Complacency?', *Radical Scotland* No.24 (Dec 1986/Jan 1987). Cf. Hamish Henderson 8

2 A human without a memory is a helpless victim of incomprehensible forces. Those who have no recollection of the past cannot understand the present and are unprepared for the future. If this is true for individuals, it must also be true for collections of individuals, or nations.

> On the importance of history, refuting Henry Ford's dictum that 'History is bunk'. 'A Different Kind of Love Song', *The Sunday Mail Story of Scotland* (1988), No.35

Geddes, Jenny fl.1637
Edinburgh vegetable stallkeeper

1 Deil colic the wame o' thee, thou false thief! Dost thou say mass at my lug?

> Attrib. Shouted at St Giles Cathedral (23 Jul 1637), to Bishop David Lindsay, as he attempted to read from Archbishop Laud's Book of Liturgy. She followed up her words by flinging her folding stool at the bishop's head, and a riot ensued
>
> > In fact, there is no firm proof of the existence of Jenny Geddes, although the riot was real enough, and she became an important figure in Presbyterian lore. By the second half of the 17th century her story featured in all histories of the period, with many variations on the form of words she used

Geddes, Sir Patrick 1854–1932
Planner, biologist and sociologist

1 Vivendo discimus

By living we learn

> Motto adopted by him (c.1887) to express his educational philosophy

2 Man thinks more, woman feels more. He discovers more but remembers less; she is more receptive and less forgetful.

> *The Evolution of Sex* (1889), written with J Arthur Thomson, p.271

3 Here then are some of the ideas of the 'Evergreen'. It makes no promise of perpetual life, but sinks only to link the Autumn of our own Age with an approaching Spring, and pass, through Decadence, towards Renascence.

> Note (with Victor Branford) to *The Evergreen* ('Autumn', 1895)
>
> > *The Evergreen*, a 'Northern seasonal' review edited by Geddes and William Sharp, appeared in four issues (1895–6). This is one of the earliest references to a cultural 'renaissance' in modern Scotland

4 Education is not merely by and for the sake of thought, it is in a still higher degree by and for the sake of action. Just as the man of science must think and experiment alternately, so too must artist, author and scholar alternate creation or study with participation in the life around them. For it is only by thinking things out as one lives them, and living things out as one thinks them, that a man or a society can really be said to think or even live at all.

> Lecture (1895), quoted in Philip Boardman, *The Worlds of Patrick Geddes* (1978), ch.5

5 Civics as an art, a policy, has. . . to do, not with U-topia but with Eutopia; not with imagining an impossible no-place where all is well, but with making the most and best of each and every place, and especially of the city in which we live.

> 'City Development: A Study of Parks, Gardens, and Culture-Institutes' (1904). Quoted in Philip Boardman, *The Worlds of Patrick Geddes* (1978), ch.7

6 Look with me at this sad old city – you see her pinioned by her judges and preyed on by their wig-lice, that countless vermin of lawyerlings, swollen and small. You see her left in squalor by her shopkeepers, the bawbee-worshipping bailie-bodies, and pushioned by her doctors; you hear her dulled by the blithers of her politicians and deived by the skreigh of the newsboy-caddies who squabble at their heels, and you know how she has been paralysed by the piffle of her professors, more than half-docted or driven into alternate hidebound or hysteric nightmares by every chilly dogmatism, every flaring hell-blast imagined by three centuries and more of diabologiac Divines.

> On Edinburgh. Letter to R B Cunninghame Graham (31 Aug 1909), quoted in Philip Boardman, *The Worlds of Patrick Geddes* (1978), ch.7

7 Consider the lily; face its elemental biological-moral fact. 'Pure as a lily' is not really a phrase

of hackneyed sham morals; for it does not mean weak, bloodless, sexless. Its purity lies in that it has something to be pure; its glory in being the most frank and open manifestation of sex in all the organic world.

Sex (1914), written with J Arthur Thomson

8   Town-planning is not mere place-planning, nor even work-planning. If it is to be successful it must be folk-planning. This means that its task is not to coerce people into new places against their associations, wishes and interest – as we find bad schemes trying to do. Instead its task is to find the right places for each sort of people; places where they will really flourish. To give people in fact the same care that we give when transplanting flowers, instead of harsh evictions and arbitrary instructions to 'move on', delivered in the manner of officious amateur policemen.

'Report on the Towns in the Madras Presidency' (1917). Quoted in J Tyrwhitt (ed.), *Patrick Geddes in India* (1947)

9   How many people think twice about a leaf? Yet the leaf is the chief product and phenomenon of Life: this is a green world, with animals comparatively few and small, and all dependent upon the leaves. By leaves we live.

'Biology and its Social Bearings: How a Botanist Looks at the World' (1919). Quoted in Amelia Defries, *The Interpreter Geddes: The Man and his Gospel* (1927), p.175

This lecture was Geddes's last as Professor of Botany at Dundee University College, a post he held for thirty years in spite of considerable disapproval of his controversial views

10   Set the child observing Nature, not with labelled and codified lessons, but with its own treasures and beauty feasts – as of stones, minerals, crystals, of living fishes and butterflies, of wild flowers, fruits and seeds. Above all, the cultivated plants and the kindly domesticated animals, which have domesticated and civilised man in the past, and have now to be brought back to civilise him to peace again.

'Biology and its Social Bearings: How a Botanist Looks at the World' (1919). Quoted in Amelia Defries, *The Interpreter Geddes: The Man and his Gospel* (1927), p.186

11   Each child needs its own plot in the school-garden, and its own bench in the workshop; but it should also go on wider and wider excursions, and these increasingly of its own choice. We need to give everyone the outlook of the artist, who begins with the art of seeing – and then in time we shall follow him into the seeing of art, even the creating of it.

'Biology and its Social Bearings: How a Botanist Looks at the World' (1919). Quoted in Amelia Defries, *The Interpreter Geddes: The Man and his Gospel* (1927), p.186

12   . . . we must cease to think merely in terms of separated departments and faculties, and must correlate these in the living mind; in the social life as well – indeed, this above all. . . Beyond the attractive yet dangerous apples of the separate sciences, the Tree of Life thus comes into view.

'Biology and its Social Bearings: How a Botanist Looks at the World' (1919). Quoted in Amelia Defries, *The Interpreter Geddes: The Man and his Gospel* (1927), pp.188–90

13   When an idea is dead it is embalmed in a textbook.

Quoted in Philip Boardman, *The Worlds of Patrick Geddes* (1978), ch.9

14   Sympathy, Synthesis and Synergy

His 'three Ss', which represented 'an emotional, intellectual and co-operative engagement' with the categories of place, folk and work. See M Macdonald on Geddes in David Daiches (ed.), *The New Companion to Scottish Culture* (1993)

15   Sometimes the Beautiful is more useful than the Useful.

Attrib.

Gibbon, Lewis Grassic (pseudonym of James Leslie Mitchell) 1901–35
Novelist and journalist

1   Glasgow – that strange, deplorable city which has neither sweetness nor pride, the vomit of a cataleptic commercialism. . .

On Glasgow, *The Thirteenth Disciple* (1931), ch.3, 'The Walls of the World', section 5

2   So that was Kinraddie that bleak winter of nineteen eleven and the new minister, him they chose early next year, he was to say it was the Scots countryside itself, fathered between a kailyard and a bonny brier bush in the lee of a house with green shutters.

Sunset Song (1932), Prelude, 'The Unfurrowed Field'

The references are to literary trends: the smalltown sentimental values of the 'kailyard' school, epitomised by Ian Maclaren's stories in *Beside the Bonnie Brier Bush* (1894), were subverted in George Douglas Brown's *The House with the Green Shutters* (1901)

3   You saw their faces in firelight, father's and mother's and the neighbours', before the lamps lit up, tired and kind, faces dear and close to you, you wanted the words they'd known and used, forgotten in the far-off youngness of their lives, Scots words to tell to your heart, how they wrung it and held it, the toil of their days and unendingly their fight. And the next minute that passed from you, you were English, back

to the English words so sharp and clean and true – for a while, for a while, till they slid so smooth from your throat you knew they could never say anything that was worth the saying at all.

Sunset Song (1932), Part 1, 'Ploughing'

. . . [Chris] looked round Kinraddie in the evening light, seeing it so quiet and secure and still, thinking of the seeds that pushed up their shoots from a thousand earthy mouths. . . Scotland lived, she could never die, the land would outlast them all, their wars and their Argentines, and the winds come sailing over the Grampians still with their storms and rain and the dew that ripened the crops – long and long after all their little vexings in the evening light were dead and done.

Sunset Song (1932), Part 4, 'Harvest'

. . . you can do without the day if you've a lamp quiet-lighted and kind in your heart.

Sunset Song (1932), Epilude, 'The Unfurrowed Field', closing sentence

Oh, Segget it's a dirty hole,
A kirk without a steeple,
A midden-heap at ilka door
And damned uncivil people.

Cloud Howe (1933), Part 1, 'Cirrus'

'There is no hope for the world at all. . . except it forget the dream of the Christ. . . and turn and seek with unclouded eyes, not that sad vision that leaves hunger unfed, the wail of children in unending dark, the cry of human flesh eaten by beasts. . . But a stark, sure creed that will cut like a knife, a surgeon's knife through the doubt and disease – men with unclouded eyes may yet find it, and far off yet in the times to be, on an earth at peace, living and joyous, the Christ come back. . . '

Cloud Howe (1933), Part 4, 'Nimbus' (Robert Colquohoun's final sermon)

'My class? It was digging its living in sweat while yours lay down with a whine in the dirt.'

Grey Granite (1934), Part 1, 'Epidote' (Chris to Watson)

'There will always be you and I, I think, Mother. It's the old fight that maybe will never have a finish, whatever the names we give to it – the fight in the end between FREEDOM and GOD.'

Grey Granite (1934), Part 4, 'Zircon' (Ewan to Chris)

Edinburgh. . . a disappointed spinster, with a hare-lip and inhibitions. . . Dundee, a frowsy fisher-wife addicted to gin and infanticide. . . Aberdeen a thin-lipped

peasant woman who has borne eleven and buried nine.

'Glasgow', *Scottish Scene, or the Intelligent Man's Guide to Albyn* (1934)

Having written that Glasgow defied personification, Gibbon produced these images of the other three cities

11 Bleakness, not meanness or jollity, is the keynote to Aberdonian character, not so much lack of the graces or graciousness of existence as lack of colour in either of these. And this is almost inevitable for anyone passing their nights and days in The Silver City by the Sea. It is comparable to passing one's existence in a refrigerator.

'Aberdeen', *Scottish Scene, or the Intelligent Man's Guide to Albyn* (1934)

12 Union Street has as much warmth in its face as a dowager duchess asked to contribute to the Red International Relief.

'Aberdeen', *Scottish Scene, or the Intelligent Man's Guide to Albyn* (1934)

13 About half of the women of Aberdeen appear to rejoice in the name of Grizel – and rejoice with justness, for my saner self tells me it is a lovely and incisive name. But for some strange reason I can never hear it pronounced without thinking of a polar bear eating an Eskimo.

'Aberdeen', *Scottish Scene, or the Intelligent Man's Guide to Albyn* (1934)

14 The Episcopalian Church in Scotland gave to life and ritual mildly colourful trappings, a sober display; it avoided God with a shudder of genteel taste.

'Religion', *Scottish Scene, or the Intelligent Man's Guide to Albyn* (1934)

15 It is a strange and disgusting cult of antique fear and antique spite. It looks upon all the gracious and fine things of the human body – particularly the body of a woman – with sickened abhorrence, it detests music and light and life and mirth, the God of its passionate convictions is a kind of immortal Peeping Tom, an unsleeping celestial sneak-thief. . .

On Free Church Presbyterianism. 'Religion', *Scottish Scene, or the Intelligent Man's Guide to Albyn* (1934)

16 One sees rise ultimately. . . in place of Religion – Nothing. . . One does not seek to replace a fever by an attack of jaundice.

'Religion', *Scottish Scene, or the Intelligent Man's Guide to Albyn* (1934)

Gillies, Valerie 1948–

Poet

1 Someone has laid
four unripe pears
along the window-ledge.

They cling on to the sill
like ticks on a ewe's neck.

'Ticks', *Bed of Stone* (1984), st.1–2

2 To lift another woman's child
is like carrying a bundle of barbed wire.
And one who will let himself be held
Stirs every bereaved desire.

'Infertility Patient', *The Chanter's Tune* (1990), st.1

3 On their dung-yellow rock,
gannets rest a beak-stab apart.

'Bass Rock', *The Ringing Rock* (1995), st.2

Giolla Coluim Mac an Ollaimh (Giolla Coluim MacMhuirich) late 15th century

Poet

1 Beagán do shloinneadh na bhfaighdheach
sloinnfead duibh,
an uair thigid fir na faighdhe
d'fhaighdhe chruidh.

Bíd go mín cairdeamhail caibhneach
mar is dluigh,
's an uair chuirthear iad air chairdeas
cia nach tuig?

Gabhaid míghean roimhéin ghairbhe
agus ruid;
cromaid cnuasuighid a mailghe
muin ar muin:
'Go bráth nocha chara caingne
sinne dhuit.'

† Somewhat of the thiggers' character I will
recount to you, when those thiggers come to
make request for gear.
   They are courteous, friendly, kindly, as
is meet; and when they are bidden to stay
for friendship's sake, which of them fails to
understand?
   They take a fit of displeasure, rough ill
humour, and of peevishness; they bend and
gather their eyebrows one after another.
'Never,' say they, 'will we be friends to you
in a dispute.'

Poem on the practice of 'thigging', which some
developed into an art, st.3–5. Quoted in W J
Watson (ed.), *Scottish Verse from the Book of the
Dean of Lismore* (1937). Cf. Henry Mackenzie 5

Alexander Carmichael (1832–1912), collector
of *Carmina Gadelica*, knew an old man 'who
went round thigging with the daughter of
his chief. . . [and] returned home with a
miscellaneous herd, enough to stock a large
farm.' (*Carmina Gadelica*, Vol.2, p.275)

2 Beagán do shloinneadh na bhfaighdheach
sloinnfidh mé:
meic Uí Shúiligh, meic Uí Anmoich
iad i gcéin.

Meic Uí Mhoichéirghe, lá samhraidh
iarras gréin;
meic Uí Shirthigh, meic Uí Shanntaigh
iad go léir.

† Some little of the thiggers' styles I will set
forth; they are
Roving-eye-sons, Fly-by-night-sons while
yet afar off.
They are Early-rising-sons, who on a summer's
day demand more sun; Spyer-sons, Greedy-
sons are they all.

Poem on 'thigging', st.10–11. Quoted in W J
Watson (ed.), *Scottish Verse from the Book of the
Dean of Lismore* (1937)

3 Ní h-éibhneas gan Chlainn Domhnaill,
ní comhnairt bheith 'na n-éagmhais;
an chlann dob fhearr san gcruinne:
gur dhíobh gach duine céatach.

† It is no joy without Clan Donald; it is no
strength to be without them; the best race
in the round world; to them belongs every
goodly man.

Poem praising Clan Donald, st.1. Quoted in
W J Watson (ed.), *Scottish Verse from the Book
of the Dean of Lismore* (1937)

4 Níorbh iad na droichfhir bhodhra,
ná na fir lobhra laga;
ré dol i n-ionad bhuailte
fir nach cruaidhe na craga.

† Not they the miserly men and deaf, nor yet
men weak and feeble; to go where blows were
struck they were men than whom the rocks
were not harder.

Poem praising Clan Donald, st.9. Quoted in
W J Watson (ed.), *Scottish Verse from the Book
of the Dean of Lismore* (1937)

Giolla Críost Brúilingeach mid-15th century

Poet, probably one of a hereditary line of poet-harpers from Gigha

1 Mag Uidhir as mion meanma,
slat don mhuine mhaoithfhearna;
glac uallach na bhfonn bhfada
Mac dualach donn Diarmada.

† Maguire of paltry spirit is a rod from the
thicket of soft alder; the proud theme of
long melodious strains is the brown-tressed
MacDiarmaid.

Poem celebrating the gift of a harp from his
patron, st.24. Quoted in W J Watson (ed.), *Scottish
Verse from the Book of the Dean of Lismore* (1937)

Alder was considered a base or ignoble wood.
Cf. Alasdair Mac Mhaighstir Alasdair 1

Giolla Glas mac an Táilliúir
?15th century

Poet, probably the father of Dubhghall mac an Ghiolla Ghlais

1 Níor argain tú i gcogadh creach
féadáil fileadh ná cléireach;
b'fhear gan réim feall do chraidhe
ar spréidh cheall nó chomraighe.

* In warfare of forays, thou didst not harry the gear of poets or of churchmen; thou wert a man whose heart harboured no treacherous course against the stock of churches or of sanctuary.

Elegy on Duncan, son of Gregor, keeper of the castle of Glenorchy, who died in July 1518, st.15. Quoted in W J Watson (ed.), *Scottish Verse from the Book of the Dean of Lismore* (1937)

Glen, William 1789–1826
Poet

1 On hills that are by right his ain,
He roams a lonely stranger;
On ilka hand he's press'd by want,
On ilka side by danger.
Yestreen I met him in a glen,
My heart near burstit fairly,
For sairly changed indeed was he –
Oh! wae's me for Prince Charlie!

'Wae's me for Prince Charlie', *Poems Chiefly Lyrical* (1815), st.3

This Jacobite lyric, highly popular in its day, is put into the mouth of a wee 'bonnie, bonnie bird' that has flown past the fugitive prince

Glendale Martyr, The
see **MacPherson, John**

Glover, Jean 1758–1801
Songwriter

1 Owre the muir amang the heather,
Owre the muir amang the heather,
There I met a bonnie lassie
Keepin' a' her yowes thegither.

'Owre the Muir Amang the Heather', chorus

This song was recorded by Robert Burns in James Johnson (ed.), *The Scots Musical Museum* (1839). A note made by Burns reads, 'This song is a composition of Jean Glover, a girl who was not only a whore, but also a thief. . . I took the song down from her singing as she was strolling through the country with a sleight-of-hand blackguard'

Glover, Sue
Playwright

1 ELLEN: 'Don't be ridiculous, Ellen,' says the maister. 'We can't do away with the bondage. I can't employ a man who hasn't a woman to work with him. . . I'm all for progress,' he says, 'but I won't do away with the bondage,' he says. 'We need the women. Who else would do the work?. . . Women's work, for women's pay.'

Bondagers (1991), Act 1, sc.10

Gold, Jimmy see Naughton, Charles

Goram, Andy (Andrew Lewis) 1964–
Football goalkeeper

1 I'd be an 18-stone alcoholic bricklayer playing for Penicuik Athletic – assuming they could find a jersey to fit me.

On what he would be like without the support and influence of his wife. Quoted by Kevin McCarra in *The Times* (14 Aug 1995)

Gordon, Alexander (4th Duke of Gordon) 1743–1827
Songwriter

1 There's cauld kail in Aberdeen,
And castocks in Stra'bogie;
Gin I hae but a bonnie lass,
Ye're welcome to your cogie.
And ye may sit up a' the night,
And drink till it be braid daylight;
Gie me a lass baith clean and tight
To dance the reel o' Bogie.

'Cauld Kail in Aberdeen', st.1

There are five or more versions of this old song, this one being perhaps the best known. Cf. Lady Nairne 4

Gordon, Alexander see Rockville, Lord

Gordon, Duchess of (née Jane Maxwell, known as 'Jenny of Monreith') c.1749–1812
Society lady and supporter of Prime Minister William Pitt, 'the Younger'

1 I have been acquainted with David Hume and William Pitt, and therefore I am not afraid to converse with anybody.

Quoted in Harry Graham, *A Group of Scottish Women* (2nd edition, 1908), ch.14

2 Rax me a spaul o' that bubbly jock.

Attrib. Quoted in Harry Graham, *A Group of Scottish Women* (2nd edition, 1908), ch.14

Said at a formal dinner, to an uncomprehend-
ing Englishman who was carving a turkey
while boasting about his great understanding
of the Scottish vernacular

Gordon, Harry (originally Alexander Ross) 1893–1957

Comedian, 'The Laird of Inversnecky'

1 Laughter is the sensation of feeling good all
over and showing it principally in one spot. . .
A ripple of laughter is worth an ocean of tears.
To laugh is to be free of worry.

> *Why I am a Comedian*, a talk broadcast on BBC
> Radio, Scottish Home Service (18 Mar 1949).
> Reproduced in Vivien Devlin, *Kings, Queens and
> People's Palaces: An Oral History of the Scottish
> Variety Theatre, 1920–1970* (1991), ch.6

2 I put on my heid, this lady's wig, aroon my
neck, a feathery boa, arrange my hat at an angle
so, a handbag, brolly, and there ye are, I'm
ready for the opening of the Kirk Bazaar.

> From *The Opening of the Kirk Bazaar*, broadcast
> on BBC Radio, Scottish Home Service (27 Sep
> 1951). Reproduced in Vivien Devlin, *Kings,
> Queens and People's Palaces: An Oral History of the
> Scottish Variety Theatre, 1920–1970* (1991), ch.6

3 Ye gang oot there for sixteen miles and ye come
to a signpost. On ae side it says, 'You are just
entering Inversnecky', and on the ither, 'You
are just leaving Inversnecky'. It takes ye an oor
by train fae Aberdeen and an oor an' a half
by bus an' if ye wait for a lift it micht take a
lifetime!

> On how to get to the mythical 'Inversnecky'.
> Quoted in Iain Watson, *Harry Gordon, the Laird
> of Inversnecky* (1993)

Gow, Niel 1727–1807

Fiddler

1 Gang down to your suppers, ye daft limmers,
and dinna haud me reelin' here, as if hunger
and drouth were unkent in the land – a body
can get naething dune for you.

> Quoted in John Purser, *Scotland's Music*
> (1992), ch.15
>
> > Said to the ladies at a party, who would not
> > stop dancing to his playing although supper
> > had been called. He often had to play for
> > hours at a time without a break

2 They may praise your braid roads that gains by
'em: for my part, when I'se gat a wee droppy
at Perth, I'se just as lang again in getting hame
by the new road as by the auld one!

> Attrib. Said to the Duke of Atholl, on hearing
> someone else praising a road he had just had
> built. Quoted in Robert Southey, *Journal of a
> Tour in Scotland in 1819* (first published 1929),
> entry for 24 August

3 Gow and time are even now,
Gow beat time, now time's beat Gow.

> Anonymous epitaph, composed shortly after his
> death. Quoted in Mary Anne Alburger, *Scottish
> Fiddlers and Their Music* (1983), p.117

Gowdie, Issobell d.1662

*Woman from Auldearn, Nairnshire, tried and
executed for witchcraft*

1 I sall goe intill ane haire,
With sorrow, and sych [sigh], and meikle caire;
And I sall goe in the Divellis nam,
Ay whill I come hom againe!

> Incantation used for turning herself into a hare.
> From her second confession (3 May 1662), quoted
> in Robert Pitcairn (ed.), *Ancient Criminal Trials
> of Scotland* (1833), Vol.3
>
> > Gowdie made four confessions over a period
> > of several weeks, implicating herself and
> > numerous other women in devil-worship and
> > witchcraft. Cf. Janet Breadheid 1

2 The Devill wold giv us the brawest lyk money
that ever wes coyned; within fowr and twantie
houris it wold be horse-muke. Alace! I deserv
not to be sitting heir, for I hav done so manie
evill deidis, especiallie killing of men, &c. I
deserv to be reivin upon iron harrowes, and
worse, if it culd be devysit!

> From her third confession (15 May 1662), quoted
> in Robert Pitcairn (ed.), *Ancient Criminal Trials
> of Scotland* (1833), Vol.3

3 He is lying in his bed – and he is seik and sair,
Let him ly in till that bedd monthes two and
dayis thrie mair!

> Incantation used against Mr Harie Forbes to make
> him die. From her fourth confession (27 May
> 1662), quoted in Robert Pitcairn (ed.), *Ancient
> Criminal Trials of Scotland* (1833), Vol.3
>
> > Forbes was the minister at Auldearn and one
> > of those before whom she was on trial

Graham (of Duntrune), Clementina Stirling 1782–1877

Society lady and impersonator

1 I have a *flech* [flea] that loupit aff him upon my
aunty, the Lady Brax, when she was helping
him on wi' his short gown; my aunty rowed
it up in a sheet of white paper, and she keepit
it in the tea-canister, and she ca'd it aye the
King's Flech; and the Laird, honest man, when
he wanted a guid cup of tea, sought aye a cup
of the *Prince's mixture*. . . It is now set on the
pivot of my watch, and a' the warks gae round
the *flech* in place of turning on a diamond.

> *Mystifications* (1911), 'Soirée at Mr Russell's'

She was well known for her 'mystifications', ie adopting the persona of an eccentric elderly woman and thus fooling one or more guests at social occasions. Here, in the guise of 'Lady Pitlyal', her favourite character, she was responding to the question, whether in her youth she had secured any souvenirs of Bonnie Prince Charlie

2 It greets a' winter, and girns a' simmer.

> *Mystifications* (1911), 'A Party at Lord Gillies's'

>> In character as 'Mrs Arbuthnott of Balwylie', describing the poor soil of her land at Balwylie

Graham, James see Montrose, James Graham, Marquis of

Graham (of Claverhouse), John (Viscount Dundee) 1648–89

Anti-Covenanter and Jacobite soldier, killed at Killiecrankie

1 To man I can be answerable, and, as for God, I will take Him in my own hands.

> Traditional. Said to the widow of the Covenanter John Brown of Priesthill (1 May 1685), whom he had just had shot in front of her and her children

Graham, W(illiam) S(ydney) 1918–86

Poet

1 Thunder falls round the fieldmice and the house.
Through all the suburbs children trundle cries.

> 'I, No More Real than Evil in my Roof', *Cage Without Grievance* (1942), st.3

2 Listen. Put on morning.
Waken into falling light.
A man's imagining
Suddenly may inherit
The handclapping centuries
Of his one minute on earth.

> 'Listen. Put on Morning', *The White Threshold* (1949)

3 . . . Clydeside,
Webbed in its foundries and loud blood,
Binds up the children's cries alive.

> 'The Children of Greenock', *The White Threshold* (1949), st.5

4 The muse has felled me in this bed
That in the wall is set.
Lie over to me from the wall or else
Get up and clean the grate.

> 'Baldy Bane', *The Nightfishing* (1955), st.1

5 I sit with the gas turned
Down and time knocking

Somewhere through the wall.
Wheesht, children, and sleep
As I break the raker up,
It is only the stranger
Hissing in the grate.

> 'The Dark Dialogues', *Malcolm Mooney's Land* (1970), section 2

6 What does it matter if the words
I choose, in the order I choose them in,
Go out into a silence I know
Nothing about, there to be let
In and entertained and charmed
Out of their master's orders? And yet
I would like to see where they go
And how without me they behave.

> 'Approaches to How They Behave', *Malcolm Mooney's Land* (1970), section 1

Grahame, Kenneth 1859–1932

Writer of children's books

1 'Believe me, my young friend, there is *nothing* – absolutely nothing – half so much worth doing as simply messing about in boats. . . or *with* boats. . . . In or out of 'em, it doesn't matter.'

> *The Wind in the Willows* (1908), ch.1 (Water Rat to Mole). Cf. Robert Louis Stevenson 2

2 'Glorious, stirring sight!' murmured Toad, never offering to move. 'The poetry of motion! The *real* way to travel! The *only* way to travel! Here today – in next week tomorrow! Villages skipped, towns and cities jumped – always somebody else's horizon! O bliss! O poop-poop! O my! O my!'

> On the motor-car which had just forced his cart into the ditch. *The Wind in the Willows* (1908), ch.2

3 The Piper at the Gates of Dawn

> Chapter title, *The Wind in the Willows* (1908), ch.7

>> This was used by the rock band Pink Floyd as the title of an album in 1967

Grange, Lady (*née* Rachel Chiesly) d.1745

Wife of James Erskine, Lord Grange (1679–1754), who had her abducted and held captive for 13 years

1 . . . and then rushed in some Highland men whom I had seen frequently attending my Lord Lovat and if I remember well had his livery upon them, threw me down upon the floor in a barbarous manner and I cried out 'Murder' then they stopped my mouth and dung out several of my teeth. . .

> 'A Copy of My Lady Grange's Letter' (from

St Kilda, Jan 1738), Scottish Records Office
GD124/15/1506

> In 1732, apparently after discovering her
> husband was having an affair, Lady Grange
> threatened to make public his Jacobite
> conspiring, which led to her abduction. She
> was held captive on several remote islands,
> including St Kilda, and eventually died insane.
> Cf. Alexander Carlyle 1

Grant (of Laggan), Mrs Anne (née MacVicar) 1755–1838
Poet and essayist

1 'O where, tell me where is your Highland
laddie gone?
O where, tell me where, is your Highland
laddie gone?'
'He's gone, with streaming banners, where
noble deeds are done;
And my sad heart will tremble till he comes
safely home.'

> 'O Where, Tell Me Where', *Poems on Various
> Subjects* (1802), st.1.

> > Written on the occasion of the departure of
> > the Marquis of Huntly's regiment for Holland
> > in 1799, this is based upon an earlier, popular
> > version of the song. In his *Journal* entry for
> > 30 Nov 1825, Walter Scott referred to Mrs
> > Grant as being 'proud as a Highland-woman,
> > vain as a poetess, and absurd as a bluestocking'

2 'But I will hope to see him yet, in Scotland's
bonnie bounds;
But I will hope to see him yet, in Scotland's
bonnie bounds.
His native land of liberty shall nurse his glorious
wounds,
While wide, through all our Highland hills his
warlike name resounds.'

> 'O Where, Tell Me Where', *Poems on Various
> Subjects* (1802), st.5

3 I am all anti-Pinkerton, and delight in the Celtic.
You cannot think what a source of pleasure
my little acquaintance with that emphatic and
original language has afforded me. . . I never
desire to hear an English word out of their
[her children's] mouths till they are four or
five years old.

> On Gaelic. John Pinkerton (1758–1826) wrote
> two histories of Scotland, the first of which
> (*An Inquiry into the History of Scotland
> Preceding the Reign of Malcolm III*, 1789)
> promoted his controversial view that Celtic
> people were far inferior to Scots. Cf. John
> Pinkerton 1

4 Principle built on piety is a pedestal on which
one may safely lean.

> Letter to Miss Charlotte Grant (8 Mar 1789),
> in *Letters from the Mountains* (1803)

5 . . . whatever you learn, do not learn to despise
peace, friendship, and needlework.

> Letter to Miss Charlotte Grant (8 Mar 1789),
> in *Letters from the Mountains* (1803)

6 Enthusiasm is the wine of life; it cheers and
supports the mind; though excess, in either
case, produces intoxication and madness.

> Letter to Mrs Smith (3 Aug 1789), in *Letters
> from the Mountains* (1803)

7 Needlework, good old court needlework, is the
thing. It exercises fancy, fixes attention, and,
by perseverance and excellence in it, habituates
the mind to patient application, and to those
peaceful and still-life pleasures which form the
chief enjoyment of every amiable woman.

> Letter to Mrs Brown (13 Feb 1790), in *Letters
> from the Mountains* (1803)

8 Fashion is an epidemical frenzy, that follows
and overtakes us everywhere, though we, in
following it, can overtake it nowhere.

> Letter to Mrs Brown (13 Feb 1790), in *Letters
> from the Mountains* (1803)

9 What business women have with any science
but that which serves to improve and adorn
conversation, I cannot comprehend. . . I wish
people would begin to work tapestry again.

> Letter to Mrs Furzer (27 Apr 1797), in *Letters
> from the Mountains* (1803)

10 Retirement is certainly the only safe asylum
for delicate minds and delicate constitutions.

> On 'retirement' from society. Letter to Mrs
> Furzer (27 Apr 1797), in *Letters from the
> Mountains* (1803)

Grant (of Carron), Elizabeth 1745–1814
Songwriter

1 Roy's wife of Aldivalloch,
Roy's wife of Aldivalloch,
Wat ye how she cheated me,
As I cam o'er the braes o' Balloch.

> 'Roy's Wife of Aldivalloch', chorus

Grant (of Rothiemurchus), Elizabeth 1797–1885
Diarist

1 Neil [sic] Gow's delightful violin. . . had so
over excited me the evening before that my
father had had to take me a little walk by the
river side in the moonlight before I was rational
enough to be left to sleep.

> *Memoirs of a Highland Lady* (1898), ch.3,
> '1804–1806'

2 We were proud of having a brother at Eton then.
Now I look back with horrour on that school of

corruption, which the strongest minded could not enter without being polluted and where weaker characters made shipwreck of all worth.

Memoirs of a Highland Lady (1898), ch.5, '1807–1809'

3 In after years I did not fail in admiration of our northern Capital, but at this period I can't remember any feeling about Inverness except the pleasure of getting out of it. . .

Memoirs of a Highland Lady (1898), ch.6, '1809'

4 Too much work we hardly any of us have, but work too dry, work too absorbing, work unsuitable, is the work cut out for and screwed on to every young mind of every nature that falls under the iron rule of School or College.

Memoirs of a Highland Lady (1898), ch.8, '1810–1811'

5 . . . accomplished girls, portionless and homeless, were made into governesses, and for the less instructed there was nothing dreamed of but the dress making. . .

Memoirs of a Highland Lady (1898), ch.9, '1811–1812'

6 Nothing can exceed the dreariness of Drumochter – all heather, bog, granite, and the stony beds of winter torrents, unrelieved by one single beauty of scenery. . .

Memoirs of a Highland Lady (1898), ch.10, '1812'

7 Wines, all our set were famous for having of the best and in startling variety – it was a mania; their cellars and their books divided the attention of the husband; the wife, alas, was more easily satisfied with the cookery. Except in a real old-fashioned Scotch house, where no dish was attempted that was not national, the various abominations served up in corner dishes under French names were merely libels upon housekeeping.

On dining habits in Edinburgh. *Memoirs of a Highland Lady* (1898), ch.21, '1818–1819'

8 If old men will marry young women, young widows should be left quite independent as some return for the sacrifice, the full extent of which they are not aware of till too late.

Memoirs of a Highland Lady (1898), ch.25, '1823–1827'. Cf. Christian Watt 2

Grant, James 1822–67

Soldier, novelist and historian

1 The world is neither Scottish, English, nor Irish, neither French, Dutch, nor Chinese, but *human*, and each nation is only the partial development of a universal humanity. . . All true progress consists not in the eradication of the generic peculiarities of races, but in the wise direction of those peculiarities. England will not be better by becoming French, or German, or Scottish, but by becoming more truly and more nobly English; and Scotland will never be improved by being transformed into an inferior imitation of England, but by being made a better and truer Scotland.

First report of the National Association for the Vindication of Scottish Rights (1852)

2 Unfortunately, the old fallacy with regard to the education of women, viz, that the higher instruction was not necessary for them, is not yet exploded, but we are slowly realising that any knowledge calculated to improve the human mind should be communicated to women, no less than to men.

A History of the Burgh Schools of Scotland (1876), Vol.1, ch.16

Vol.2 was completed but never published

3 It would indeed seem as if Providence intended that the sexes should influence each other from their birth to their death, and at no time is this influence more necessary than when their characters are being formed. Possibly the character of the girls may, by being taught with the boys, suffer to some extent from the rough and boisterous manners of their companions; but, on the other hand, it is certain that the boys will suffer *more* from the absence of the girls than the girls from the presence of the boys.

On co-education. *A History of the Burgh Schools of Scotland* (1876), Vol.1, ch.16

Gray, Alasdair James 1934–

Painter, poet and novelist

1 'Man is the pie that bakes and eats himself and the recipe is separation.'

Lanark (1981), ch.11, 'Diet and Oracle'

2 'Glasgow is a magnificent city,' said McAlpin. 'Why do we hardly every notice that?' 'Because nobody imagines living here,' said Thaw.

Lanark (1981), ch.22, 'Kenneth McAlpin'

3 'What is Glasgow to most of us? A house, the place we work, a football park or golf course, some pubs and connecting streets. That's all. No, I'm wrong, there's also the cinema and library. And when our imagination needs exercise we use these to visit London, Paris, Rome under the Caesars, the American West at the turn of the century, anywhere but here and now. Imaginatively Glasgow exists as a music-hall song and a few bad novels. That's all we've given to the world outside. It's all we've given to ourselves.'

Lanark (1981), ch.22, 'Kenneth McAlpin'

Ironically Gray's novel has been largely responsible for destroying the argument of its character Duncan Thaw

4 'What I hate most is their conceit. Their institute breaks whole populations into winners and losers and calls itself *culture* . . . They believe their greed holds up the continents. They don't call it greed, of course, they call it profit, or (among themselves, where they don't need to fool anyone) *killings*. They're sure that only their profit allows people to make and eat things.'
'Maybe that's true.'
'Yes, because they make it true. But it isn't necessary.'

On the rulers of society. *Lanark* (1981), ch.36, 'Chapterhouse'

5 I started making maps when I was small showing places, resources, where the enemy and where love lay. I did not know
time adds to land. Events drift continually down,
effacing landmarks, raising the level, like snow.

I have grown up. My maps are out of date.
The land lies over me now.
I cannot move. It is time to go.

Lanark (1981), ch.44, 'End'

6 Work as if you were living in the early days of a better nation Scotland 1983

Embossed on the hardback edition of *Unlikely Stories, Mostly* (1983)

This (apart from 'Scotland 1983') is in fact a line from a poem by the Canadian author Dennis Lee (1939–), as Gray acknowledges at the end of the first part of the prologue to *1982 Janine*

7 This slip has been inserted by mistake.

Erratum slip inserted in the book *Unlikely Stories, Mostly* (1983)

8 Seen from Selkirk America is a land of endless pornographic possibility.

1982 Janine (1984), ch.1

9 The truth is that we are a nation of arselickers, though we disguise it with surfaces: a surface of generous, openhanded manliness, a surface of dour practical integrity, a surface of futile maudlin defiance like when we break goalposts and windows after football matches on foreign soil and commit suicide on Hogmanay by leaping from fountains in Trafalgar Square. Which is why, when England allowed us a referendum on the subject, I voted for Scottish self-government. Not for one minute did I think it would make us more prosperous, we are a poor little country, always have been, always will be, but it would be a luxury to blame ourselves for the mess we

are in instead of the bloody old Westminster parliament.

1982 Janine (1984), ch.4

10 'The curse of Scotland is these wee hard men. I used to blame the English for our mediocrity. I thought they had colonised us by sheer cunning. They aren't very cunning. They've got more confidence and money than we have, so they can afford to lean back and smile while our own wee hard men hammer Scotland down to the same dull level as themselves.'

1982 Janine (1984), ch.11. Cf. R B Cunninghame Graham 11

11 Everyone wanted the moon until one day a great nation became wealthy enough to woo her. So scientists and technicians went pimping to this great nation and got rich by selling a quick moonfuck. . . now nobody wants the moon. She holds nothing but shattered rockets and rundown machines that litter her crust like used contraceptives proving that Kilroy was here.

1982 Janine (1984), 'Moondream'

12 God is a bleak fact in a book of stones
a cold voice in a room of iron clocks
a frozen hoof that clatters on my bones.

'Bare Bloodhymn', *Old Negatives* (1989)

Gray, Sir Alexander 1882–1968
Poet and economist

1 This is my country,
The land that begat me.
These windy spaces
Are surely my own.
And those who here toil
In the sweat of their faces
Are flesh of my flesh
And bone of my bone.

'Scotland', *Gossip* (1928), st.4

Gray, Muriel 1959–
Writer and broadcaster

1 You remember your first mountain in much the same way you remember having your first sexual experience, except that walking doesn't make as much mess and you don't cry for a week if Ben Nevis forgets to phone next morning.

The First Fifty: Munro-Bagging Without A Beard (1991), Introduction. Cf. Norman MacCaig 20

2 I'm terrified, terrified of the celebration of mediocrity in Scotland, and that's what's changing my political colours. It's making me think what would happen if we were totally sealed off to the outside world. Of course I want political autonomy but not cultural autonomy.

You just have to watch the Scottish Baftas to want to kill yourself.

> On her new preference for Scottish devolution rather than independence. Interview with Alastair McKay, in *Scotland on Sunday* (14 Jan 1996)

Stop applauding things that are crap.

> On being asked if she had any advice for the Scottish people. Interview with Alastair McKay, in *Scotland on Sunday* (14 Jan 1996)

>> In the same interview she said of the television show *Noel Edmonds' House Party*, 'anybody who says it's a bad programme is an idiot'

Gregory, John 1724–73
Physician and Professor of Medicine

Be cautious in displaying your good sense. It will be thought you assume a superiority over the rest of the company. But if you happen to have any learning, keep it a profound secret, especially from the men, who generally look with a jealous and malignant eye on a woman of great parts and a cultivated understanding.

A man of real genius and candour is far superior to this meanness. But such a one will seldom fall in your way; and if by accident he should, do not be anxious to show the full extent of your knowledge.

> 'A Father's Legacy to his Daughters', *Scots Magazine* No.26 (1774)

Do not marry a fool; he is the most intractable of all animals; he is led by his passions and caprices, and is incapable of hearing the voice of reason. . . But the worst circumstance that attends a fool is his constant jealousy of his wife's being thought to govern him. This renders it impossible to lead him, and he is continually doing absurd and disagreeable things for no other reason but to show he dares do them.

> 'A Father's Legacy to his Daughters', *Scots Magazine* No.26 (1774)

Grierson, John 1898–1972
Film producer, sometimes known as the 'father of Documentary'

Film-making belongs like all show business to that magical world in which two and two can make five, but also three and even less. It is, by that token, not a business to which the presbyterian mind is natively and nationally attuned.

> 'A Scottish Film Industry' in *Saltire Review* (Summer 1960). Reprinted in Forsyth Hardy (ed.), *John Grierson's Scotland* (1979)

The film will come to serve Scotland when we dig into our Scottish pockets and, in the name of all things vital and beautiful, make the film

reach out to the great shapes, the dramatic and poetic shapes, which give depth to what we do.

> 'A Mind for the Future', St Andrew's Day lecture, broadcast on BBC Scottish Home Service (1962). Reprinted in Forsyth Hardy (ed.), *John Grierson's Scotland* (1979)

3 . . . I don't think we should feel that we are engaging in small or provincial affairs when we take thought of our own small country, for they are not necessarily so. It is only we ourselves who in the smallness of our observation make them small. . . The arc of the sky over us is as wide as any, the land under has seen as much of the light and as much of the light of love as any.

> 'By Our Doorstep', *Scotland on the Screen* (Aug 1968). Reprinted in Forsyth Hardy (ed.), *John Grierson's Scotland* (1979)

4 Documentary can achieve an intimacy of knowledge and effect impossible to the shimsham mechanics of the studio and the lily-fingered interpretation of the metropolitan actor.

> Quoted in Cliff Hanley, 'Notable Scots', *The Sunday Mail Story of Scotland* (1988), No.26

Grieve, Christopher Murray
see **MacDiarmid, Hugh**

Grieve, Sir Robert 1910–95
Administrator, Chief Planner at the Scottish Office (1960–4), first chairman of the Highlands and Islands Development Board (1965–70)

1 Can man plan?

> Rhetorical question often posed by him

>> When considering whether to accept the chairmanship of the HIDB, he was persuaded by his wife May's argument, 'Bob, you've got to do it, or they'll get somebody worse.' Quoted in *The Scotsman* (Diary, 12 Dec 1995)

Grieve, Valda (*née* Trevlyn) 1906–89
Cornish nationalist, wife of Christopher Murray Grieve

1 Now you're awake
And find you're not an astronaut
Just a poet
Thousands of people and switches
Put Neil Armstrong on the Moon
You gripped the curly snake Cencrastus
And made it alone. . .

> 'Haud Forrit: to Hugh MacDiarmid on his eightieth birthday' (1972), reprinted in *Chapman* No.58 (Autumn 1989)

>> In 1963, the idea that MacDiarmid should be made the first Freeman of Langholm, his

hometown, was suggested, but was greeted with much local opposition. On 10 March 1972, Neil Armstrong, the first man on the moon, received that honour, largely on the strength of his Borders surname

2 Hell! What need have you to care
You are meeting your eightieth year
Head held high, haud forrit MacDiarmid
Like Muhammad Ali – you're the greatest.

'Haud Forrit: to Hugh MacDiarmid on his eightieth birthday' (1972), reprinted in *Chapman* No.58 (Autumn 1989)

3 Last night I dreamed.
Now I'm awake
I'm cold, it's dark and lonely.
Hesitatingly I reach out
And find no hand to clasp.

'Grey Ghost', quoted in *Chapman* No.58 (Autumn 1989)

Grimond, Jo(seph) (Lord Grimond)
1913–93

Liberal MP for Orkney and Shetland (1945–83) and Liberal Party leader (1956–67, and briefly in 1976)

1 In bygone days, commanders were taught that when in doubt, they should march their troops towards the sound of gunfire. I intend to march my troops towards the sound of gunfire.

Speech at the Liberal Party conference (14 Sep 1963). Cf. David Steel 1

Gude and Godlie Ballatis, The
1567, with subsequent editions in 1578, 1600 and 1621

A collection of adaptations and paraphrases from Scripture, Lutheran in tone, which utilised popular Scots songs and other forms. It was compiled by three brothers, James (d.1553), John (d.1556) and Robert (d.1557) Wedderburn

1 All my hart, ay this is my sang,
With doubill mirth and joy amang;
Sa blyith as byrd my God to sang:
Christ hes my hart ay.

'Christ hes my hart ay', st.1

2 Go, hart, unto the Lamp of licht,
Go, hart, do service and honour;
Go, hart, and serve him day and nicht,
Go, hart, unto thy Saviour.

'Go, hart, unto the Lamp of licht', st.1

3 God send everie preist ane wyfe,
And everie Nunne ane man,
That thay micht leve that haly lyfe,
As first the Kirk began.

'God send everie preist ane wyfe', st.1

4 Johne, cum kis me now,
Johne, cum kis me now;
Johne, cum kis me by and by
And mak no moir adow.

'Johne, cum kis me now', st.1

5 O Man, ryse up, and be not swier,
Prepair aganis this gude New Yeir.
My New Yeir gift thow hes in stoir,
Sen I am he that coft thee deir:
Gif me thy hart, I ask no moir.

'O Man, ryse up', st.1

6 Be war, I am ane Jelous God,
I am na image, stock or wod;
Thairfor give nane of that my gloir,
Sen I to hevin mon be the ro[a]d:
Gif me thy hart, I ask no moir.

'O Man, ryse up', st.6

7 The Paip, that pagane full of pryde,
He hes us blindit lang;
For quhair the blind the blind dois gyde,
Na wonder baith ga wrang. . .

'The Paip, that pagane full of pryde', st.1

8 Quho is at my windo? quho?
Go from my window, go!
Cry na mair thair, lyke ane stranger,
But in at my dure thow go.

'Quho is at my windo?', st.22

9 The hunter is Christ, that huntis in haist,
The hundis ar Peter and Paull,
The Paip is the fox, Rome is the rox,
That rubbis us on the gall.

'With huntis up', st.4

Gunn, George 1956–
Poet and playwright

1 Her hat, her hat, oh like
a cake universe, so ridiculous

I loved its fabulous presence
& her coat so dead
& strung, the unlovely
metal swish of car, of power

'The Queen Mother Drives Through Dunnet 1968', *Into the Anarchic* (1985), st.3–4. Reprinted in *Sting* (1991)

2 MEG:. . . I've got a laddie from Wick til give ye a hand. He seems a fine enough loon but ye can never tell with a Gallagh. Ye canna understand what they say half the time.
SANDY: They dinna have the Gàidhlig, poor souls. Just that clackin Scots tongue. It's like the skraik o a hen.

The Gold of Kildonan (1989), Act 2, sc.2

Gallagh: the name Sutherland folk (themselves 'Caitach' or 'Cattachs') use for Caithness folk

3 there is no high place here to raise your voice
this is an anarchist landscape
where angels learn of gales & choice
is Holborn's point or Wrath's distant cape

'Dunnet Head', *Sting* (1991), st.4

Dunnet Head, Caithness: the northernmost point of the Scottish mainland

4 list after list like nineteen fourteen
roughneck & roustabout, crane-op & cook
name after name in numbing insistence
singing
'Back in Buchan the barley is turning
in Scotland now the Summer is green'

'Piper', *Sting* (1991)

Dedicated to the '167 dead of the Piper "Alpha" ', the oil rig which exploded in the North Sea on 6 July 1988

Gunn, Neil M(iller) 1891–1973
Novelist

1 Whisky is concerned about the limitations of the mind; it is masculine and penetrative. It can be coarse and aggressive. But, perfectly conceived, it is creative fire.

Whisky and Scotland (1935), 'Blending'

2 . . . you walk out upon Caithness, and at once experience an austerity in the flat clean wind-swept lands that affects the mind almost with a sense of shock. There is something more in it than contrast. It is a movement of the spirit that finds in the austerity, because strength is there also, a final serenity.

'Caithness and Sutherland', in George Scott-Moncrieff (ed.), *Scottish Country* (1935)

3 Of all forms of life, surely the most vile. The cleg was silent, the colour of old horse manure, a sort of living ghost of evil. The tenderest skin never felt him land. Not content with filling his belly with one's blood – for which he might have been forgiven in a difficult world – he must go on to leave behind him a filthy poison to swell the flesh in maddening irritation for days.

Highland River (1937), ch.19

4 If I were an unemployed man in the High-lands, a broken fisherman, a three-months gillie, I should prefer to work in a factory in the Highlands rather than in one in Lanarkshire, South Wales or the Midlands of England. . . I should demand a man's work, and I should demand it in my own land. I might hate the forces, national or local, that had so misgoverned and impoverished the Highlands as to compel me away from my fishing or crofting and into a factory. But better a factory than starvation; better a self-respecting worker in my own trade union than a half-sycophant depending on the whims of a passing tourist.

' "Gentlemen – the Tourist!": the New Highland Toast', *Scots Magazine* (Mar 1937)

Gunn was arguing in favour of the develop-ment of hydro-electric power and questioning the notion of tourism as the economic salvation of the Highlands

5 . . . not all the deserving old women attending to all the tourists of the world and prattling of the scenic beauty of empty glens can save the ancient heritage from decay and death.

' "Gentlemen – the Tourist!": the New Highland Toast', *Scots Magazine* (Mar 1937)

6 . . . when I turn to the Mod and try to see what it is doing for Gaeldom, I find it difficult to be impressed. Despite its concern with the things of the spirit, it is essentially neither a creative body nor an inspiration towards creation. At the core, it stands for the remembrance of things past, and does not envisage a future in terms of that past. . .
And that is why no real Gael, in his heart, believes in the Mod. And when he is a decent man he is troubled, because here in truth are precious things of the spirit, and he knows that the life that bred them is dying.

'The Ferry of the Dead', *Scots Magazine* (Oct 1937)

7 Iona is the island of light.

'The New Community of Iona', *Scots Magazine* (Dec 1938)

8 This mass-worship has become so insidious that it creeps between a man and his vision of a flower. The individual is no longer of value except as a unit in the mass. The shortest way to a concentration camp is by the expression of individual inspiration.

'Memories of the Months: A Balance Sheet', writing as Dane McNeil in the *Scots Magazine* (Jan 1941)

Gunn opposed what he called 'the great modern heresy', the ideal which was 'no longer the unity of the individual but the unity of the herd'

9 All the theorists who argue so nobly against nationalism and for peace miss this simple point, it seems to me. When the blood fondly says, 'This is my land,' it is at that moment profoundly in harmony and at peace.

When it cannot say that, something has gone wrong, and it is that something that is the evil thing.

'My Bit of Britain', *The Field* (2 Aug 1941)

10 Let the philosophers and political theorists build up their opposing systems, let science add to the pool of common knowledge its marvellous discoveries, but somewhere somehow the individual has to stand on his own two feet and reckon with it all.

The Serpent (1943), ch.20

11 A tireless, tough, and God-fearing people, taking their lives in their hands, on these treacherous coasts, in their small open boats – and sending their tens of thousands of barrels of herring deep into Germany, into the Baltic Sea, and far into Russia.

On the herring fishers of Caithness and Sutherland. 'The Wonder Story of the Moray Firth', first published in *Anarchy* (1968), reprinted in Alistair McCleery (ed.), *Landscape and Light: Essays by Neil M Gunn* (1987)

Guthrie, Sir James 1859–1930
Painter

1 But hang it, Newbery, this man ought to be an artist!

Said in 1891 to Francis Newbery, Director of Glasgow School of Art, on being told that the winning watercolourist in the student exhibition he was assessing there was an architectural student. The student was Charles Rennie Mackintosh. Quoted in Roger Billcliffe, *Mackintosh Watercolours* (1978)

Gutteridge, Sue
Poet and sociologist

1 Married female friendship –
An art form, bred of constrictions
Which are the stuff of it.
Fitted in the spaces between the children.
Half sentences thrown across the noise
of playing
Or fighting.

'For Eileen', *Original Prints II: New Writing from Scottish Women* (1987)

H

Haig, Douglas (1st Earl of Bemersyde)
1861–1928

Commander-in-chief of British Army (1915–18)

The work performed by a newspaper correspondent is most degrading. They can't tell
the truth even if they want to. The British
public likes to read sensational news, and the
best war correspondent is he who can tell the
most thrilling lies.

> Letter to his sister Henrietta (5 Jun 1898) during
> the Sudan campaign

A very weak-minded fellow, I'm afraid, and,
like the feather pillow, bears the marks of the
last person who has sat on him!

> On the then Secretary for War, the Earl of Derby.
> Letter to his wife (14 Jan 1918)

Every position must be held to the last man:
there must be no retirement. With our backs
to the wall, and believing in the justice of our
cause, each one of us must fight on to the end.
The safety of our Homes and the Freedom
of mankind alike depend upon the conduct of
each one of us at this critical moment.

> Order (12 Apr 1918) exhorting troops in the
> trenches to resist the German spring offensive
> of that year. Quoted in A Duff Cooper, *Haig*
> (1936), Vol.2, ch.23

Hailes, Lord (Sir David Dalrymple)
1726–92

Judge and historian

Next to the passions of man, I know not
anything which has so fatally checked the
growth and progress of truth as that prejudice
which tries every fact and custom related in
history by the standard of our own manners.
When we read of facts or customs dissimilar
from what we see every day, we generally
pronounce them to be fictitious. This is the
brief decision of ignorance.

> *Annals of Scotland* (1776)

What! my lord, do you require artificial heat
like us mere moderns?

> Said to Lord Monboddo, who had joined him
> as he warmed himself in front of the fire in
> Parliament House
>
> > Monboddo held the view that the life and
> > virtues of the ancient Greeks were far superior
> > to anything human society had achieved since.

After Hailes returned to his seat, Monboddo
retorted, 'Well said of him that leads the life of
a bug!' Quoted in John Ramsay of Ochtertyre,
Scotland and Scotsmen in the Eighteenth Century
(1888 edition), Vol.1, p.412, footnote.
Cf. Lord Kames 8

Hamilton, Elizabeth 1758–1816

Novelist and songwriter

1 It is by giving free scope to the imagination,
that one becomes thoroughly acquainted with
the real disposition of one's own heart. . . I
sincerely believe that the great disadvantage of
perpetually living in a crowd, is the check it
puts upon the free excursions of imagination.

> Letter to a young female friend (1801), quoted
> in Miss Berger, *Memoirs of the late Mrs
> Elizabeth Hamilton with a Selection from her
> Correspondence*. . . (1818)

2 'Towels!' cried Mrs MacClarty; 'na, na, we
manna pretend to towels; we just wipe up the
things wi' what comes in the gait.'

> *The Cottagers of Glenburnie* (1808), ch.7 (Mrs
> MacClarty explains the absence of dish-towels
> in her house to Mrs Mason)

3 'We cou'dna be fashed. . .'

> *The Cottagers of Glenburnie* (1808), ch.7 (Mrs
> MacClarty's catchphrase)

4 'Ay,' said Mrs MacClarty, 'I aye feared she
would be owre nice for us. She has been sae
lang amang the Englishes, that she maun hae a
hantel o' outlandish notions. But we are owre
auld to learn, and we just do weel eneugh.'

> On Mrs Mason. *The Cottagers of Glenburnie*
> (1808), ch.7

5 'Those who wait till evening for sunrise,' said
Mrs Mason, 'will find that they have lost
the day.'

> *The Cottagers of Glenburnie* (1808), ch.8

6 The village of Aberdour, which belongs to the
Earl of Morton, has little to boast beyond the
charms of situation, for it contains not one
tolerable house, except the parsonage: but the
inhabitants, though not of the higher order,
are all above poverty. . .

> Letter to Dr S— (16 Sep 1811), quoted in Miss
> Berger, *Memoirs of the late Mrs Elizabeth Hamilton
> with a Selection from her Correspondence*. . . (1818)

7 O' a' roads to happiness ever were tried,
There's nane half so sure as ane's ain
fireside.

My ain fireside, my ain fireside,
There's nought to compare wi' my ain fireside.

'My Ain Fireside', st.3 and chorus

Hamilton, Ian 1925–

*Writer, advocate and reclaimer of the Stone
of Destiny in 1950*

1 Although the English still make our laws and
for the most part neglect us, we make our own
songs, paint our own pictures and put on our
own plays. So long as a nation goes on making
and singing its own songs it will never die.

'Bringing it Home', *The Sunday Mail Story of
Scotland* (1988), No.4. Cf. Andrew Fletcher 1

2 The world would be near its end if it were all
one big family. It is going foreign and coming
home again that is the very spice of life itself.

'Bringing it Home', *The Sunday Mail Story of
Scotland* (1988), No.4

3 My prime qualification was that I did not
know my place. I never have. So many Scots,
forgetting that one of the great features of our
history is the mobility between classes, have
lapsed into the English habit of thought best
expressed in the words, 'I wouldn't presume.'
I hope I know my place.' I always presume. I
have never known my place.

On his qualification for recovering the Stone of
Destiny from Westminster Abbey (24 Dec 1950).
Quoted in Ludovic Kennedy, *In Bed with an
Elephant* (1995), ch.12. Cf. Kay Matheson 1

Hamilton, Janet (*née* Thomson) 1795–1873

Spinner, weaver and poet

1 Oh, the dreadfu' curse o' drinkin'!
Men are ill, but tae my thinkin',
Leukin' through the drucken fock,
There's a Jenny for ilk Jock.

'Oor Location', *Poems and Ballads* (1873)

2 Frae whence cums misery, want, an' wo,
The ruin, crime, disgrace an' shame,
That quenches a' the lichts o' hame?
Ye needna speer, the feck ot's drawn
Out o' the change-house an' the pawn.

'Oor Location', *Poems and Ballads* (1873)

3 Owre a' kin's o' ruination,
Drink's the king in oor location.

'Oor Location', *Poems and Ballads* (1873)

4 Selfish, unfeeling men!
Have ye not had your will?
High pay, short hours; yet your cry, like
the leech,

Is, Give us, give us still.
She who tambours – tambours
For fifteen hours a day –
Would have shoes on her feet, and dress for
church,
Had she a third of your pay.

'A Lay of the Tambour Frame', *Poems and Ballads*
(1873), st.5

tambour: a circular frame used to keep fabric
taut while embroidering it

5 Still the tambourer bends
Wearily o'er the frame.
Patterns oft vary, for fashions will change –
She is ever the same.

'A Lay of the Tambour Frame', *Poems and Ballads*
(1873), st.7

6 Auld Scotlan' gangs yirmin an chanerin' alane,
She wunners whaur a' her trig lassocks
ha'e gane;
She's trampit the kintra, an' socht thro'
the toons,
An' fan' the fule hizzies – blawn oot like
balloons!

'Crinoline', *Poems Sketches and Essays* (1885), st.1

Hamilton, John see Belhaven, Lord

Hamilton, John c.1511–71

Archbishop of St Andrews

1 The office of a Preist and Byschop is nocht to
leive in idilnes, nocht to leive in fornicatioun
and huirdome, nocht to be occupeit in halking
and hunting, bot to leive ane haly lyfe, chaist
in body and saule, to pray to God for the pepil,
to offer giftis and sacrifice to God for the pepil,
to preche the word of God to the pepil, and
lyk lanternis of lycht to gife exempil to haly
lyfe to the pepil, quhow thai suld contemne all
inordinat lufe of carnal plesour, of warldly geir,
and temporal dignitie and to leive a christin
lyfe to the plesour of God.

Catechism (1552). Quoted in T G Law (ed.), *The
Catechism of John Hamilton* (1884)

Hamilton, John 1761–1814

Music tutor and songwriter

1 Cauld blaws the wind frae north to south,
The drift is drifting sairly;
The sheep are cowerin' in the heugh;
Oh, sirs, it's winter fairly!
Now, up in the mornin's no for me,
Up in the mornin' early;
I'd rather go supperless to my bed
Than rise in the mornin' early.

'Up in the Mornin' Early', st.1. Cf. Robert Burns 57,
Harry Lauder 8

Hamilton, William 1665–1751

Poet

1 Alas, alas, quo' bonny Heck,
On former Days when I reflect!
I was a Dog much in Respect
For doughty Deed:
But now I must hing by the Neck
Without Remeed.

'The Last Dying Words of Bonny Heck, a
famous Grey-hound in the Shire of Fife', in
James Watson, (ed.), *Choice Collection of Comic
and Serious Scots Poems*, Vol.1 (1706), st.1

Hamilton, William 1704–54

Poet

1 Busk ye, busk ye, my bonny, bonny bride,
Busk ye, busk ye, my winsome marrow;
Busk ye, busk ye, my bonny, bonny bride,
And think nae mair on the braes of Yarrow.

'The Braes of Yarrow', st.1

2 Pale tho' thou art, yet best, yet best belov'd,
O could my warmth to life restore thee!
Yet lie all night between my breasts;
No youth lay ever there before thee.

'The Braes of Yarrow', st.28

Hanley, Cliff 1922–

Glasgow novelist and broadcaster

1 Land of my high endeavour,
Land of the shining river,
Land of my heart forever,
Scotland the brave.

'Scotland the Brave', chorus. Quoted in Norman
Buchan, *101 Scottish Songs* (1962). Cf. Billy
Connolly 4

2 [Golf] is an intensely Presbyterian activity. In
golf, you do not play against an opponent. You
may play alongside one, but he can't touch
your ball or interfere with your swing. You are
on your own, one man matching his effort and
his conscience against the enigma of life. You
may lie about the number of strokes you took
to kill a snake in the heather; but you know,
and so does the Big Handicapper in the Sky
from Whom nothing is hidden.

The Scots (1980), ch.23, 'Stir Crazy'

3 A real leader of men is somebody who is afraid
to go anywhere by himself.

Quoted in Alan Bold (ed.), *Scottish Quotations*
(1985)

4 Scotland is not a place, of course. It is a state of
mind. Probably every country is and we should
be cautious when we assume we are unique.
Other people may be just as crazy as we are.

'A State of Mind', *The Sunday Mail Story of
Scotland* (1988), No.10. Cf. Maurice Lindsay 2,
Brian McCabe 3

Hannah, George 1896–1947

Painter

1 Art is a common impulse. . . the urge to make
something, to design, to paint, carve, sing and
dance is latent in all human beings. . . It is
this part of our being which prevents us from
succumbing to that robot-like dullness which
dictators would like to batter us into, and it
is from this bubbling inner well that we must
derive the strength to transform our lives.
Individual experience can only possess depth
and solidity if it mirrors communal experience.
This experience [is] the spirit, the life-blood
of all real art.

In John Singer (ed.), *Million* (1943). Quoted
in Duncan Macmillan, *Scottish Art 1460–1990*
(1990), ch.20

Hardie, (James) Keir 1856–1915

*Labour politician, Party leader, and a founder
of the Independent Labour Party*

1 From his childhood onward this boy will be
surrounded by sycophants and flatterers by
the score – [*Cries of* 'Oh, oh!'] – and will
be taught to believe himself as of a superior
creation. [*Cries of* 'Oh, oh!'] A line will be
drawn between him and the people whom he
is to be called upon some day to reign over.
In due course, following the precedent which
has already been set, he will be sent on a tour
round the world, and probably rumours of a
morganatic alliance will follow – [*Loud cries of*
'Oh, oh!' *and* 'Order!'] – and the end of it all
will be that the Country will be called upon to
pay the bill.

Speech in the House of Commons (28 Jun 1894)

He was alone in opposing a motion
being passed in the House of Commons,
congratulating Queen Victoria on the birth,
to the Duke and Duchess of York, of a son
(the future Edward VIII). He objected to the
waste of parliamentary time as much as to the
sycophancy

2 Can a Man be a Christian on a Pound a Week?

Title of pamphlet (1901)

3 . . . I think it could be shown that the position
of women, as of most other things, has always
been better, nearer to equality with man,
in Celtic than in non-Celtic races. Thus in
Scotland a woman speaks of her 'man', whilst
in Staffordshire he is always spoken of as 'the
master'.

The Citizenship of Women (1906)

4 Killing No Murder

> Title of pamphlet (1911)

>> The pamphlet attacked the Liberal Government for refusing to take responsibility for the killing of two striking workers by troops at Llanelli in Wales

5 I often feel sick at heart with politics and all that pertains thereof. If I were a thirty years younger man. . . I would, methinks, abandon house and home and wife and child, if need be. . . to proclaim afresh and anew the full message of the Gospel of Jesus of Nazareth.

> Said in 1913. Quoted in H Addison, *Contrast in Philosophies* (1982), p.53

Harry or Henry the Minstrel
see Blind Harry

Harvey, Alex 1935–82
Rock singer

1 There are only two types of music: rock and roll.

> Quoted in Stewart Cruickshank, 'Scottish Rock Music, 1955–93', in P H Scott (ed.), *Scotland: A Concise Cultural History* (1993)

Havergal, Giles 1938–
Artistic director of the Citizen's Theatre, Glasgow (1969–   )

1 People say, 'what on earth are you doing, doing Ibsen and Schiller and Lermontov and Proust in the Gorbals?' And the answer is, of course, that if you really believe that these are the great works of art then you must believe that they can and should be shared.

> Interview with Andrew Burnet in *The List* No.76 (Sep 1988)

Hay, Deòrsa Caimbeul (George Campbell Hay) 1915–84
Poet

1 Leaving those men, whose hearts
are hearths that have no fire,
my greetings, westward go
to lovely long Kintyre.

> 'Kintyre', *Wind on Loch Fyne* (1948), st.1

2 Long is sgioba, long is sgioba,
gaoth is gillean, gaoth is gillean,
muir is misneach, muir is misneach,
sgòd an ruigheadh, sgòd an ruigheadh,

seòl is sitheadh, seòl is sitheadh,
creach is iomairt, creach is iomairt,
creach is iolach, creach is iolach,
fraoch is frionas, glaodh is frioghan,
gaoth is gillean, gaoth is gillean,
long is sgioba, long is sgioba.

† A ship and a crew, a ship and a crew; wind and lads, wind and lads; sea and spirit, sea and spirit; a sheet stretched hard, a sheet stretched hard; a sail and coursing, a sail and coursing; foray and turmoil, foray and turmoil; foray and outcry, foray and outcry; rage and anger, yelling and bristling; wind and lads, wind and lads; a ship and a crew, a ship and a crew.

> 'Seeker, Reaper', *Wind on Loch Fyne* (1948)

3 She's a stieve sea-strider, she's a storm-
course-keeper,
she's a tide-scour-bucker, she's a quick-
light-leaper,
she's a stem-teerer, keel-teerer, seeker,
finder, reaper.

> 'Seeker, Reaper', *Wind on Loch Fyne* (1948)

4 C' ainm an nochd a th'orra,
na sràidean bochda anns an sgeith gach uinneag
a lasraichean 's a deatach,
a sradagan is sgreadail a luchd thuinidh. . .
Có an nochd a phàidheas
sean chis àbhaisteach na fala cumant?

† What is their name tonight,
the poor streets where every window spews
its flame and smoke,
its sparks and the screaming of its
inmates. . .
Who tonight is paying
the old accustomed tax of common blood?

> 'Bisearta' ('Bizerta'), *O na Ceithir Airdean* (*From the Four Airts*, 1952), st.2

5 Bha 'm beul onorach a dhìt thu
pladach, bideach 'sa ghnùis ghlais;
bha Ceartas sreamshùileach o sgrùdadh
a leabhar cunntais 's iad sìor phailt.

Ach am beul a dhearbhadh breugach,
bha e modhail, éibhinn, binn;
fhuair mi eirmseachd is sgeòil uaith
's gun e ro eòlach air tràth bidh.

† The honourable mouth that condemned you
was blubberish and tiny in the grey face;
and Justice was blear-eyed from scrutinising
its account-books, that ever showed abundance.

But the mouth which was found lying
was mannerly, cheerful and melodious;
I got sharp repartee and tales from it,
though it was not too well acquainted
with a meal.

> 'Atman', *O na Ceithir Airdean* (*From the Four Airts*, 1952), st.2–3

Hay, Sir Gilbert c.1419–60
Diplomat, poet and scholar

1 Syndry folk thare is, that has the body rycht
lytill, and yit thai have the hert and the curage
grete, and that is a grace of God. . . Certainly
nocht force na strenth corporale makis a man
to wyn the bataill. Bot force spirituale, that is
to say, hardy curage, makis victory. . .

> *The Buke of the Law of Armys* (1456), Part 3, ch.4

> This and his other works are translations
> from French and Latin originals

2 Unworthy war he suld be a lord or a maister that
knew never quhat it is to be a servand, for he
may never wele tak na knawe the suetenes that
it is to be the lord, bot gif he had sum knaulage
of the sourness that it is, and payne to a gude
hert, to be ane underlout or a servand. . .

> *The Buke of the Order of Knychthede* (c.1456), ch.2

3 And quhasa ever drynkis wyne in our mekle
habundance, tharof cummys mony maladyes
and othir misgovernaunces. For it stoppis the
wittis of man and hynderis the knaulage, it
troublis the harnis, waykis the vertues naturale
carporale and spirituale. . . and makis man
to be unthochtfull of his honour, and prouffit
foryettand, and hurtis and woundis the fyve
wittis that governis the man, and makis him
all othir in his complexioun naturale. . .

> *The Buke of the Governaunce of Princis*
> (c.1456), ch.32

> harnis: brain

Hay, Ian (pseudonym of John Hay Beith) 1876–1952
Novelist and playwright

1 CHRIS: That's funny.
BUTTON: What do you mean, funny? Funny
peculiar or funny ha-ha?

> *Housemaster* (1938), Act 3

Haynes, Dorothy K(ate) 1918–87
Writer

1 It's amazing how angry the clergy can get
without actually swearing.

> *Haste Ye Back* (1973), ch.4, 'The Good Times'

Haynes, Jim 1933–
*American co-founder, and second artistic
director, of the Traverse Theatre, Edinburgh*

1 Friends and lovers are the most important part
of my life.

> *Thanks for Coming!* (1984), Introduction

2 The Traverse isn't in Scotland, it's in the world.

> Quoted in Joyce McMillan, *The Traverse Theatre
> Story 1963–1988* (1988), ch.2

>> Journalist Ronald 'Bingo' Mavor described
>> Haynes's time as Traverse director: 'Everybody
>> went to the Traverse, and Jim would introduce
>> you to Timothy Leary, the Lord Provost, and
>> a man who was growing blue carrots in the
>> interval between acts. . . ' Quoted in Joyce
>> McMillan, as above

Henderson, Hamish 1919–
Folklorist, poet and songwriter

1 Then fareweel ye banks o' Sicily,
Fare ye weel, ye valley an' shaw.
There's nae Jock will mourn the kyles o' ye –
Puir bluidy swaddies are weary.

> 'The Highland Division's Farewell to Sicily'
> (1943), chorus 1

2 There were our own, there were the others.
Their deaths were like their lives, human
and animal.
There were no gods and precious few heroes.

> *Elegies for the Dead in Cyrenaica* (1948), 'First
> Elegy: End of a Camapign'

3 The red will be worn, my lads, and Scotland
will march again.
Noo great John Maclean has come hame tae
the Clyde.

> 'The John Maclean March' (1948), last verse

4 In our cities the folk tradition has never
completely disappeared, in spite of all the
inroads made upon it, and it is still possible to
graft these flowering branches from the North
and West upon a living tree.

> Programme notes for the second People's Festival
> Ceilidh in Edinburgh (1952). Quoted in Adam
> T McNaughtan, 'Hamish Henderson – Folk
> Hero', in *Chapman* No.42 (Winter 1985)

5 Roch the wind in the clear day's dawin,
Blaws the cloods heelster-gowdie ow'r the bay,
But there's mair nor a roch wind blawin
Through the great glen o the warld the day.

> 'The Freedom Come-All-Ye', st.1

>> The sentiments of this song (written 'For
>> the Glasgow Peace Marchers, May 1960',
>> and published in *Ding Dong Dollar: Anti-
>> Polaris Songs*, 1961) were suggested by Harold
>> Macmillan's 'wind of change' speech in Cape
>> Town (1960)

6 O come all ye at hame wi freedom,
Never heed whit the hoodies croak for doom;
In your hoose aa the bairns o Adam
Can find breid, barley-bree an painted room.
When Maclean meets wi's freens in Springburn,
Aa the roses and geans will turn tae bloom,

And a black boy frae yont Nyanga
Dings the fell gallows o the burghers doon.

'The Freedom Come-All-Ye', st.3

7 Folk-song has no use for the conventional
hypocrisies and taboos of respectable society.
It handles the joys, miseries, and above all
the comedy of sex with medieval directness.
Needless to say, this has never endeared it to
the Holy Willies of Scottish life.

'The Underground of Song' in *The Scots
Magazine* (Feb 1963), reprinted in *Alias
MacAlias* (1992)

8 . . . by embarking on the study of folk material,
we were engaged willy-nilly in a political act.

Quoted in Bert Wright, 'Politics and the Folksong
Revival – Commitment or Complacency?', *Radical
Scotland* No.24 (Dec 1986/Jan 1987). Cf. Dick
Gaughan 1

Henderson, James 16th–17th century
Soldier of fortune and traveller

1 I am a young man, and gif I haif litill, I haif
als litill to fear. I have my swerd undishonorit,
and that is aneuch to me: yet gif evir God send
me a fortune, I hoip to use it weill.

Letter home from the Netherlands (Sep 1608),
quoted in Agnes Mure Mackenzie, *Scottish
Pageant*, Vol.2 (1948), p.296

Hendry, Joy 1953–
Editor of Chapman, *critic and poet*

1 The Predicament of Scotland, the State
of Scotland, is a pre-occupation which is
admittedly inward and introverted; some say
that it is no healthy pre-occupation. But until
there is a State of Scotland, we have no choice
but to be so obsessed. Would it were not so. But
we can stop *talking* about the State of Scotland
only when we are in a position to *do* something
about it.

Chapman No.35–6 (Jul 1983), 'The State of
Scotland – a Predicament for the Scottish
Writer?', editorial. Cf. Roderick Watson 1

2 The moment you utter a Scots word you are
making a revolutionary statement.

Speaking at Scots poetry conference, Dundee
(19 Apr 1986). Quoted in *Radical Scotland* No.21
(Jun/Jul 1986)

3 The Double Knot in the Peeny

Title of essay. In Gail Chester and Sigrid Nielsen
(eds), *In Other Words: Writing as a Feminist* (1987)

She coined this phrase to describe the double
disdvantage, for Scottish women writers,
created by being both Scottish and female

Hendry, Stephen 1969–
Professional snooker player

1 Someone would have to play unbelievable
snooker to beat me. But as for the future – I
don't care.

On winning his fifth world championship title in
1995. Quoted in *The Herald* (1 May 1995)

2 If anyone had told me I would win so many
titles when I first began my career I would
have thought they were mad.

On winning his sixth world championship title
in 1996. Quoted in *The Scotsman* (7 May 1996)

3 I've probably got another two or three titles in
me. As long as I still get the buzz from playing
the big events, I'll carry on.

Quoted in *The Scotsman* (8 May 1996)

Henryson, Robert c.1425–90
Poet

1 O lord, that is to mankind haill succure,
Preserve us fra this perrelus pestilens!

'Ane Prayer for the Pest', ll.7–8

2 Use derth, O lord, or seiknes and hungir soir,
And slak thy plaig that is so penetryfe:
The pepill ar perreist – quha may remeid
thairfoir,
Bot thow, O lord, that for thame lost thy lyfe?

'Ane Prayer for the Pest', ll.25–8

3 'My fair sister,' quod scho, 'have me excusit;
This rude dyat and I can not accord.
To tender meit my stomok is ay usit,
For quhy I fair alsweill as ony lord.
Thir wydderit peis and nuttis, or thay
be bord,
Wil brek my teith and mak my wame ful
sklender,
Quhilk usit wes before to meitis tender.'

'The Two Mice', *Fables*, ll.218–24 (the town
mouse to the upland mouse)

4 Grit aboundance and blind prosperitie
Oftymes makis ane evill conclusioun.
The sweitest lyfe, thairfoir, in this cuntrie,
Is sickernes, with small possessioun.

'The Two Mice', *Fables*, ll.377–80

5 Fy, puft up pryde, thow is full poysonabill!

'The Cock and the Fox, *Fables*, l.593

6 The hardbakkit hurcheoun, and the hirpland
hair . . .

'The Trial of the Fox', *Fables*, l.903

hurcheoun: hedgehog

7 'O lamit lyoun, liggand heir sa law,
Quhair is the mycht off thy magnyfycence,
Off quhome all brutal beist in eird stude aw,

And dred to luke upon thy excellence?
But hoip or help, but succour or defence,
In bandis strang heir man I ly, allace,
Till I be slane; I se nane uther grace.'

'The Lion and the Mouse', *Fables*, ll.1531–7 (the lion's lament, caught in the net)

8 'Grit fule is he that puttis in dangeir
His lyfe, his honour, for ane thing off nocht.
Grit fule is he that will not glaidlie heir
Counsall in tyme, quhill it availl him mocht.
Grit fule is he that hes na thing in thocht
Bot thing present, and efter quhat may fall
Nor off the end hes na memoriall.'

'The Preaching of the Swallow', *Fables*, ll.1860–6

9 For in this warld thair is na thing lestand;
Is na man wait how lang his stait will stand,
His lyfe will lest, nor how that he sall end
Efter his deith, nor quhidder he sall wend.

'The Preaching of the Swallow', *Fables*, ll.1940–3

10 Ane doolie sessoun to ane cairfull dyte
Suld correspond and be equivalent:
Richt sa it wes quhen I began to wryte
This tragedie. . .

The Testament of Cresseid, ll.1–4

11 O fair Cresseid, the flour and A per se
Of Troy and Grece, how was thow fortunait
To change in filth all thy feminitie,
And be with fleschelie lust sa maculait,
And go amang the Greikis air and lait,
Sa gigotlike takand thy foull plesance!
I have pitie thow suld fall sic mischance!

The Testament of Cresseid, ll.78–84

12 Nocht is your fairnes bot ane faiding flour,
Nocht is your famous laud and hie honour
Bot wind inflat in uther mennis eiris,
Your roising reid to rotting sall retour. . .

The Testament of Cresseid, ll.461–4

13 'Lovers be war and tak gude heid about
Quhome that ye lufe, for quhome ye suf-
fer paine.
I lat you wit, thair is richt few thairout
Quhome ye may traist to have trew lufe
agane. . .

The Testament of Cresseid, ll.561–4

Herbert, W(illiam) N 1961–
Poet

1 Beauty, resilient as girstle, reveals
itself: I see all of Scotland

rolling down and up on death's yoyo.
There is no passport to this country.

'Dingle Dell', in Daniel O'Rourke (ed.), *Dream State: The New Scottish Poets* (1994)

Herdman, John 1941–
Novelist and critic

1 . . . in Scotland to challenge the position of
drink as a consideration to which priority must
unfailingly be granted appears, if not unmanly,
at least anti–life.

'Muir, Scotland, Drink and Free-will', in *Chapman* No.35–6 (Jul 1983)

2 It is a well-known failing of the insane to
take a mere adjunct or accident as a defining
characteristic. In my childhood I learned from
my mother that our lunatic asylums are filled
with mentally disturbed persons who can be
divided into two principal categories: those
labouring under the impression that they are
Napoleon, and those, seated on pieces of toast,
who believe themselves to be poached eggs.

'The Day I Met the Queen Mother', in Hamish
Whyte and Janice Galloway (eds), *The Day I
Met The Queen Mother: New Writing Scotland 8*
(1990). Reprinted in *Imelda* (1993)

Hermand, Lord (George Fergusson) 1743–1827
Judge

1 But then we're told that there's a statute against
all this. A statute! what's a statute? Words.
Mere words! And am *I* to be tied down by
words? No, my Laards; I go by the law of
right reason.

Quoted in Lord Cockburn, *Memorials of his Time*
(1856), ch.2

2 We are told that there was no malice, and that
the prisoner must have been in liquor! Why,
he was drunk! And yet he murdered the very
man who had been drinking with him! They
had been carousing the whole night; and yet
he stabbed him; after drinking a whole bottle
of rum with him; Good God, my Laards, if
he will do this when he is drunk, what will he
not do when he's sober?

Quoted in Lord Cockburn, *Memorials of his Time*
(1856), ch.2

3 Sir! I sucked in the being and attributes of God
with my mother's milk!

At the court case concerning the appointment of
the allegedly atheistic John Leslie to the Chair
of Mathematics at Edinburgh University, 1805.
Quoted in Lord Cockburn, *Memorials of his Time*
(1856), ch.3

4 A sceptic, Sir, I hate! With my whole heart I
detest him! *But, Moderator, I love a Turk!*

Quoted in Lord Cockburn, *Memorials of his Time*
(1856), ch.3

See entry above

5 What shall we come to at last! I believe I
shall be left alone on the face of the earth –
drinking claret!

> Quoted in Lord Cockburn, *Memorials of his Time*
> (1856), ch.4

>> Like many judges of the period, Hermand
>> was a great drinker, and lamented what he
>> saw as the enfeebled appetites of the younger
>> generation, and in particular the declining
>> taste for claret

Heseltine, Michael 1933–

*English Conservative politician, Deputy British
Prime Minister (1992–)*

1 Scotland is an absolutely critical part of the
UK. It has very serious representation in the
English Cabinet – distinguished Scots playing
a whole role in running the UK. We're all in
this together and trying to break it up into
bits, after hundreds of years of one of the most
successful partnerships in history, is crazy.

> Defending the constitutional status quo against
> Labour plans for a Scottish parliament. Quoted
> in *The Scotsman* (2 Feb 1996)

2 Labour running Britain with beer and
sandwiches at No.10 Downing Street in the
1970s was one thing. But running Scotland
over pasta and chianti in Islington is quite
another thing!

> On the Labour leadership's change of policy
> over a referendum on devolution for Scotland.
> Quoted in *The Scotsman* (28 Jun 1996)

Higgins, Lizzie 1929–

*Traditional singer, the daughter of singer
Jeannie Robertson*

1 To me, the Scottish balladry, the Scottish folk
pipe singin', is the word: magic. Proper, sheer,
naked, magic. . . It's about human beings, their
loves, their liberty or their broken hearts, the
death, the grief, the sorrow, the. . . cups o'
happiness flowin' over. . . It's like evolution. . .

> Recorded in Aberdeen (9 Nov 1976), quoted in
> Ailie Munro, *The Folk Music Revival in Scotland*
> (1984), ch.6

Hill, Aaron 1685–1750

English dramatist

1 Scotland! thy weather's like a modish wife!
Thy winds and rains, forever are at strife:
So Termagant, a while her Thunder tries,
And, when she can no longer scold – she cries.

> 'Writ on a Window in the Highlands of
> Scotland' (1728)

Hill, David Octavius 1802–70

Pioneering photographer

1 The rough surface and unequal texture
throughout of the paper is the main cause of
the Calotype failing in details before the process
of Daguerrotypes – and this is the very life
of it. They look like the imperfect work of a
man – and not the much diminished perfect
work of God.

> On the artistic advantages of the calotype process.
> Letter to Henry Bicknell (17 Jan 1849), quoted
> in Sara Stevenson, 'Photography', in P H Scott (ed.),
> *Scotland: A Concise Cultural History* (1993)

Hill, Jimmy

English football commentator

1 I know there's a certain amount of aggression
against me in Scotland. I'm not sure why,
really, but perhaps that is the difference
between the two countries; the Englishman
assumes that nobody dislikes him while the
Scotsman wouldn't be happy without an
enemy. . . But I look upon Scotland as part
of the British Empire, as it were, and when
I was a kid I used to look at all the pink on
the map and say, 'Isn't that marvellous! We
own all that.'

> Quoted in Roddy Forsyth, *The Only Game: The
> Scots and World Football* (1990), ch.2. Cf. Tommy
> Docherty 4

Hirst, Sir Michael 1946–

*Conservative politician, Chairman of the
Scottish Conservative and Unionist Party
(1993–)*

1 The one and only lesson that our parliamentary
party could usefully learn from Labour is the
discipline of hunger for power.

> Quoted in *The Independent* (14 May 1995)

Hislop, Joseph John 1884–1977

Opera singer

1 We'll no hae grannie lang noo!

> Quoted in Michael Turnbull, 'Joseph Hislop',
> *Stretto* Vol.7, No.2 (1987)

>> Apparently whispered to William Anderson, a
>> Scottish bass, towards the end of a performance
>> of *La Bohème* at Covent Garden, London,
>> as the character Mimi died on stage. He
>> was referring to opera singer Nellie Melba
>> (1861–1931) who, as Mimi, was his opposite
>> number in the show. She is said to have been
>> most unfriendly to the rest of the cast. See
>> John Purser, *Scotland's Music* (1992), p.244

Hogg, James 1770–1835

Poet and novelist, known as 'The Ettrick Shepherd'

1 Having been bred amongst mountains I am always unhappy when in a flat country. Whenever the skirts of the horizon come on a level with myself I feel myself quite uneasy and have generally a headache.

> Letter to Sir Walter Scott (25 Jul 1802)

2 Will ye gang wi' me, lassie,
To the braes o' Birniebouzle?
Baith the earth an' sea, lassie,
Will I rob to fend ye...

> 'Birniebouzle', *The Forest Minstrel* (1810), st.1
>
> > A popular version of this song has the lines 'Gin ye'll mairry me, lassie/At the kirk o' Birnie Bouzle/Till the day ye dee, lassie/Ye will ne'er repent it'

3 'Lock the door, Lariston, lion of Liddesdale;
Lock the door, Lariston, Lowther comes on;
The Armstrongs are flying,
The widows are crying,
The Castletown's burning, and Oliver's gone!'

> 'Lock the Door, Lariston' (1811), st.1

4 May everilke man in the land of Fife
Read what the drinkeris dree,
And nevir curse his puir auld wife,
Rychte wicked altho scho be.

> 'The Witch of Fife' (revised version), *The Queen's Wake* (1814)

5 Bonnie Kilmeny gaed up the glen,
But it wasna to meet Duneira's men,
Nor the rosy monk of the isle to see,
For Kilmeny was pure as pure could be.

> 'Kilmeny', *The Queen's Wake* (1814)

6 Our Highland hearts are true and leal,
And glow without a stain;
Our Highland swords are metal keen,
And Charlie he's our ain.

And Charlie he's my darling,
My darling, my darling;
Charlie he's my darling,
The young Chevalier.

> 'Charlie He's My Darling', *The Jacobite Relics of Scotland*, Vol.2 (1821), st.5 and chorus. Cf. Robert Burns 135

7 What is the greatest bliss that the tongue of man can name?
'Tis to woo a bonny lassie when the kye comes hame.

> 'When the Kye Comes Hame' (1823), st.1
>
> > First published as 'The Sweetest Thing the Best Thing' in *The Three Perils of Man* (1822), and then as 'When the Kye Come Hame' in *Blackwood's Magazine* (May 1823). Hogg later

changed 'come' to 'comes' on the grounds that he would 'choose rather to violate a rule in grammar, than a Scottish phrase so common'

8 But let the tempest tout an' blaw,
Upon his loudest winter horn,
Good night, an' joy be wi' you a' –
We'll maybe meet again the morn.

> 'Good Night an' Joy be wi' you a'', in R A Smith (ed.), *Scottish Minstrel* Vol.6 (1824), st.1

9 'What a wonderful boy he is!' said my mother. 'I'm feared he turn out to be a conceited gowk,' said old Barnet, the minister's man.

> *The Private Memoirs and Confessions of a Justified Sinner* (1824)

10 'Man's thoughts are vanity, sir; they come unasked, an gang away without a dismissal, an' he canna help them.'

> *The Private Memoirs and Confessions of a Justified Sinner* (1824) (John Barnet to the minister)

11 D'ye ken the big village of Balmaquhapple,
The great muckle village of Balmaquhapple?
'Tis steeped in iniquity up to the thrapple,
And what's to become of poor Balmaquhapple?

> 'The Great Muckle Village of Balmaquhapple', in *Blackwood's Magazine* (Jun 1826), st.1

12 'Confound thae deevils incarnate, for they're the curse o' a het simmer. O' a' God's creturs, the wasp is the only ane that's eternally out o' temper. There's nae sic thing as pleasin him.'

> 'Noctes Ambrosianae' No.9 (*Blackwood's Magazine*, Oct 1826)
>
> > The character of the 'Shepherd' in these sketches (published 1822–35) was unmistakably that of Hogg, but the words put into his mouth were largely written by John Wilson ('Christopher North')

13 'Gie me the real Glenleevit... and I weel believe that I could mak drinkable toddy out o' sea-water. The human mind never tires o' Glenleevit, ony mair than o' cauler air. If a body could just find oot the exac proper proportion o' quantity that ought to be drank every day, and keep to that, I verily trow that he micht leeve for ever, without dying at a', and that doctors and kirkyards would go out of fashion.'

> On Glenlivet malt whisky. 'Noctes Ambrosianae' No.11, *Blackwood's Magazine* (Jan 1827)
>
> See entry above

14 Where the pools are bright and deep,
Where the grey trout lies asleep,
Up the river and o'er the lea,
That's the way for Billy and me.

> 'A Boy's Song', *The Poetic Mirror* (2nd edition, 1829–31), st.1

15 The best thing in life is to mak
The maist o't that we can.

> 'The Lass o' Carlisle', in *Fraser's Magazine* (Jul 1830), chorus 2

16 In my young days, we had singing matches almost every night, and, if no other chance or opportunity offered, the young men attended at the ewe-bught or the cows milking, and listened and joined the girls in their melting lays. . . And then, with the exception of *Wads*, and a little kissing and toying in consequence, song, song alone, was the sole amusement.

> 'On the Changes in the Habits, Amusements, and Conditions of the Scottish Peasantry' (1831–2). Quoted in Judy Steel (ed.), *A Shepherd's Delight* (1985)
>
>> Wads: various games played for forfeits

17 Life is a weary, weary, weary,
Life is a weary coble o' care;
The poets mislead you,
Wha ca' it a meadow,
For life is a puddle o' perfect despair.

> 'Life is a Weary Coble o' Care', st.1

18 O! love! love! laddie,
Love's like a dizziness!
It winna let a puir body
Gang about his business!

> 'Love's Like a Dizziness', chorus

Hogg, Margaret (*née* Laidlaw) 1730–1813

Mother of James Hogg, singer of traditional Border ballads

1 There war never ane o' my sangs prentit till ye prentit them yoursel', an' ye hae spoilt them awthegither. They were made for singin' an' no for readin'; but ye hae broken the charm noo, an' they'll never be sung mair. An' the worst thing of a', they're nouther richt spell'd nor richt setten doun.

> To Walter Scott (c.1803). Quoted in James Hogg, *Domestic Manners and Private Life of Sir Walter Scott* (1834)
>
>> Scott had used Mrs Hogg as a source for some of his *Minstrelsy of the Scottish Border* (1802–3), and she was not best pleased with the results

Holland, Sir Richard c.1415–82

Poet and courtier

1 Quhen ilk thing has the awne, suthly we se
Thy nakit cors bot of clay a foule carioun,
Hatit and hawless; quharof art thou hie?
We cum pure, we gang pure, baith king and commoun.

> *The Buke of the Howlat* (c.1448), ll.980–3.
> Cf. Sir David Lindsay 5
>
>> the awne: its own

Holloway, Richard 1933–

Episcopal Bishop of Edinburgh (1986–   )

1 I think faith and doubt are co-active. One of the things I find most dangerous and damaging for human beings is over-certainty. It is the cause of most human misery.

> *The Scotsman* (11 Jan 1996)

Home (of the Hirsel), Lord (Alexander Frederick Douglas-Home) 1903–95

Conservative politician, British Prime Minister (1963–4)

1 When I have to read economic documents I have to have a box of matches and start moving them into position to simplify and illustrate the points to myself.

> *The Observer* (16 Sep 1962)
>
>> Harold Wilson referred to him as 'the matchsticks premier' after this admission

2 As far as the fourteenth earl is concerned, I suppose Mr Wilson, when you come to think of it, is the fourteenth Mr Wilson.

> Television interview (21 Oct 1963)
>
>> He was responding to the Labour leader Harold Wilson's accusations that, as a hereditary peer, he was reactionary and out of touch with the times: 'After half a century of democratic advance, the whole process has ground to a halt with a 14th Earl'. Cf. Caroline Douglas-Home 1

3 Representation without the power to tax is a recipe for political irresponsibility. . . My point is that this Act should not become law until Parliament has had another look at its obvious flaws. . . A No vote need not imply any disloyalty to the principle of devolution. The important thing is to achieve the right pattern consistent with the efficiency of government and the unity of the UK.

> On the forthcoming referendum on Labour's proposed Scottish Assembly. Speech at Edinburgh University Conservative and Unionist Association (14 Feb 1979)
>
>> His suggestion was that a rejection of Labour's scheme would allow the next Conservative government to bring forward plans for a stronger, more effective assembly

4 . . . the peace-maker may have to rethink his philosophy, for the two wars have shown that good is not automatically blessed, and that security is not guaranteed by good intentions. Quite the contrary, for conciliation, negotiation, compromise, tolerance – all the civilised words of the Christian and democratic vocabulary – have too often turned out to be a trap.

> *Letters to a Grandson* (1983), Introduction

5 I am going to stick my neck out and say that the British Government was wrong about re-armament and that Chamberlain was right at Munich.

Letters to a Grandson (1983), Letter 8

> He was parliamentary private secretary to Prime Minister Neville Chamberlain in 1938, and was with him at the signing of the Munich Agreement with Hitler

Home, Henry see Kames, Lord

Home, John 1722–1808
Playwright and Church of Scotland minister

1 My name is Norval: on the Grampian hills
My father feeds his flocks; a frugal swain,
Whose constant cares were to increase his store,
And keep his only son, myself, at home.

Douglas (1757), Act 2

2 Bold and erect the Caledonian stood,
Old was his mutton and his claret good;
'Let him drink port,' the English states-
man cried –
He drank the poison, and his spirit died.

'Epigram on Enforcement of High Duty on French Wines'

> Claret was the most popular wine in Scotland in the 18th century, but was gradually overtaken by changing fashions, many of them imported from England. Cf. Lord Neaves 5

Hood, Stuart 1915–
Novelist and critic

1 We may record the past for various reasons: because we find it interesting; because by setting it down we can deal with it more easily; because we wish to escape from the prison where we face our individual problems, wrestle with our particular temptations, triumph in solitude and in solitude accept defeat and death. Autobiography is an attempted jail-break. The reader tunnels through the same dark.

Pebbles from my Skull (1963; republished in 1985 as *Carlino*), Epilogue

2 . . . that mixture of sentimentality, militarism and bogus history – the Edinburgh Tattoo.

'The Backwardness of Scottish Television', in Karl Miller (ed.), *Memoirs of a Modern Scotland* (1970)

House, Jack 1906–91
Journalist, known as 'Mr Glasgow'

1 Glasgow has known two kinds of leisure over the past 50 years – the customary leisure at the end of the day's work and at week-ends;

and the enforced leisure which accompanies unemployment. . . . Enforced leisure set men to hanging about street corners. . . to gambling on waste ground and by the side of the River Clyde and canals, and, strangely enough, to hiking and mountaineering. Some of the most intrepid of Glasgow climbers owe their skill to unemployment.

The Third Statistical Account of Scotland: Glasgow (1958), ch.19, 'Leisure Interests: Changes in the Use of Leisure'

2 A remarkable sight in Glasgow is to be seen any week day about noon in the gramophone department of Lewis's Store in Argyle Street. Large numbers of young people apparently forego their lunch in order to stand about in this department listening to gramophone records being played over loud-speakers. Most of the young people become animated only when dance music or jazz is played.

The Third Statistical Account of Scotland: Glasgow (1958), ch.19, 'Leisure Interests: Changes in the Use of Leisure'

3 'Perpendicular drinking' has been said to be the trouble with Glasgow pubs, and it has even been suggested that the Glasgow invention of square-toed shoes was to enable the Glasgow man to get closer to the bar.

The Third Statistical Account of Scotland: Glasgow (1958), ch.19, 'Leisure Interests: Pubs'

4 The 'Hampden Roar' is the name given to the amazing ululations produced from thousands of throats when the Scottish football fans are urging on the Scottish team in an international match, especially against England. It is an almost frightening sound, and English football players have been quoted as saying that the Hampden Roar is the equivalent of two goals for Scotland. Unfortunately this has not always proved true.

The Third Statistical Account of Scotland: Glasgow (1958), ch.19, 'Leisure Interests: Football'

5 There are also the 'hikers', who clothe themselves in remarkable garments – especially the females – hang themselves about with impedimenta, travel to a tram terminus and then proceed to walk backwards as they look for car-drivers who will give them a lift.

The Third Statistical Account of Scotland: Glasgow (1958), ch.19, 'Leisure Interests: Holiday Habits'

6 It was actually said that when he was appearing as Dame, certain ladies in the audience would especially come to see this scene so that they could see his latest outfit and then go and buy one like it.

> On pantomime dame, Harry Gordon. Quoted in Vivien Devlin, *Kings, Queens and People's Palaces: An Oral History of the Scottish Variety Theatre, 1920–1970* (1991), ch.7

Hume, David 1711–76

Philosopher and central figure of the Scottish Enlightenment

1   . . . as a Boy he was a fat, stupid, lumbering Clown, but full of sensibility and Justice, – one day at my home, when he was about 16 a most unpleasant odour offended the Company before dinner. . . 'O the Dog. . . the Dog,' cried out everyone 'put out the Dog; 'tis that vile Beast Pod, kick him down stairs. . . pray.' –

Hume stood abashed, his heart smote him. . . 'Oh do not hurt the Beast' he said 'it is not Pod, it is Me!'

> As told by Lady Dalrymple to her grand-daughter Lady Anne Lindsay. Quoted in E C Mossner, *The Life of David Hume* (1980), ch.5
>
> 'How very few people', the anecdote concludes, 'would take the odour of a stinking Conduct from a guiltless Pod to wear it on their own rightful Shoulders.'

2   Poets themselves, tho' liars by profession, always endeavour to give an air of truth to their fictions; and where that is totally neglected, their performances, however ingenious, will never be able to afford much pleasure.

> *A Treatise of Human Nature* (1739), Bk 1, Part 3, section 10, 'Of the Influence of Belief'

3   Generally speaking, the errors in religion are dangerous; those in philosophy only ridiculous.

> *A Treatise of Human Nature* (1739), Bk 1, Part 4, section 7

4   Human Nature is the only science of man; and yet has been hitherto the most neglected.

> *A Treatise of Human Nature* (1739), Bk 1, Part 4, section 7

5   In general we may remark, that the minds of men are mirrors to one another. . .

> *A Treatise of Human Nature* (1739), Bk 2, Part 2, section 5. Cf. Adam Smith 3

6   There is no method of reasoning more common, and yet none more blameable, than in philosophical debates to endeavour to refute any hypothesis by a pretext of its dangerous consequences to religion and morality. When any opinion leads us into absurdities, 'tis certainly false; but 'tis not certain an opinion is false, because 'tis of dangerous consequence. Such topics, therefore, ought entirely to be foreborn, as serving nothing to the discovery of truth, but only to make the person of an antagonist odious.

> *A Treatise of Human Nature* (1739), Bk 2, Part 3, section 2
>
> Hume, as a sceptic challenging the religious society of his day, knew better than anyone the relevance of this passage

7   We speak not strictly and philosophically when we talk of the combat of passion and of reason. Reason is, and ought only to be the slave of the passions, and can never pretend to any other office than to serve and obey them.

> *A Treatise of Human Nature* (1739), Bk 2, Part 3, section 3. Cf. Thomas Reid 6

8   'Tis not contrary to reason to prefer the destruction of the whole world to the scratching of my finger. . .

> *A Treatise of Human Nature* (1739), Bk 2, Part 3, section 3

9   Vice and virtue, therefore, may be compar'd to sounds, colours, heat and cold, which, according to modern philosophy, are not qualities in objects, but perceptions in the mind. . .

> *A Treatise of Human Nature* (1739), Bk 3, Part 1, section 1

10 In every system of morality, which I have hitherto met with, I have always remark'd, that the author proceeds for some time in the ordinary way of reasoning, and establishes the being of a God, or makes observations concerning human affairs; when of a sudden I am surpriz'd to find, that instead of the usual copulations of propositions, *is*, and *is not*, I meet with no proposition that is not connected with an *ought*, or an *ought not*. This change is imperceptible; but is, however, of the last consequence.

> *A Treatise of Human Nature* (1739), Bk 3, Part 1, section 1

11 Avarice, the spur of industry. . .

> 'Of Civil Liberty', *Essays Moral, Political and Literary I* (1742)

12 Money. . . is none of the wheels of trade: it is the oil which renders the motion of the wheels more smooth and easy.

> 'Of Money', *Essays Moral, Political and Literary I* (1742)

13 Nothing endears so much a friend as sorrow for his death. The pleasure of his company has not so powerful an influence.

> 'Of Tragedy', *Essays Moral, Political and Literary I* (1742)

14 The best excuse that can be made for avarice is, that it generally prevails in old men, or in men of cold tempers, where all the other affections are extinct; and the mind being incapable of remaining without some passion or pursuit, at last finds out this monstrously absurd one, which suits the coldness and inactivity of its temper.

> 'Of Avarice', unpublished essay, *Essays Moral, Political and Literary* (ed. E F Miller, 1985)

15 The great end of all human industry is the attainment of happiness. For this were arts invented, sciences cultivated, laws ordained,

and societies modelled, by the most profound wisdom of patriots and legislators. Even the lonely savage, who lies exposed to the inclemency of the elements and the fury of wild beasts, forgets not, for a moment, this grand object of his being.

'The Stoic', *Essays, Moral, Political and Literary I* (1742)

Indulge your passion for science, says she [Nature], but let your science be human, and such as may have a direct reference to action and society. . . Be a philosopher; but, amidst all your philosophy, be still a man.

An Enquiry Concerning Human Understanding (1748), section 1

Hume's mother is reputed to have said of her son, 'Oor Davie's a fine gude-natured cratur, but uncommon waik-minded'

Custom, then, is the great guide of human life. . . Without the influence of custom, we should be entirely ignorant of every matter of fact beyond what is immediately present to the memory and senses. . . There would be an end at once of all action, as well as of the chief part of speculation.

An Enquiry Concerning Human Understanding (1748), section 5, Part 1

When anyone tells me, that he saw a dead man restored to life, I immediately consider within myself, whether it be more probable, that this person should either deceive or be deceived, or that the fact, which he relates, should really have happened. I weigh the one miracle against the other; and. . . always reject the greater miracle. If the falsehood of his testimony would be more miraculous, than the event which he relates; then, and not till then, can he pretend to command my belief or opinion.

An Enquiry Concerning Human Understanding (1748), section 10, Part 1

. . . we may conclude that the *Christian Religion* not only was at first attended with miracles, but even at this day cannot be believed by any reasonable person without one. Mere reason is insufficient to convince us of its veracity: And whoever is moved by *Faith* to assent to it, is conscious of a continued miracle in his own person, which subverts all the principles of his understanding, and gives him a determination to believe what is most contrary to custom and experience.

An Enquiry Concerning Human Understanding (1748), section 10, Part 2

Morals and criticism are not so properly objects of the understanding as of taste and sentiment. Beauty, whether moral or natural, is felt, more properly than perceived.

An Enquiry Concerning Human Understanding (1748), section 12, Part 3

21 If we take in our hand any volume; of divinity or school metaphysics, for instance; let us ask, *Does it contain any abstract reasoning concerning quantity or number?* No. *Does it contain any experimental reasoning concerning matter of fact and existence?* No. Commit it then to the flames: for it can contain nothing but sophistry and illusion.

An Enquiry Concerning Human Understanding (1748), section 12, Part 3

22 Absolute, unprovoked, disinterested malice has never perhaps place in any human breast; or if it had, must there pervert all the sentiments of morals, as well as the feelings of humanity.

An Enquiry Concerning the Principles of Morals (1751), section 5, Part 2

23 Every thing in the world is purchased by labour. . .

'Of Commerce', *Essays Moral, Political and Literary II* (1752)

24 . . . where the riches are in few hands, these must enjoy all the power, and will readily conspire to lay the whole burthen on the poor, and oppress them still further, to the discouragement of all industry.

'Of Commerce', *Essays Moral, Political and Literary II* (1752). Cf. Sir James Mackintosh 2

25 About seven months ago, I got a house of my own, and completed a regular family; consisting of a head, viz myself, and two inferior members, a maid and a cat.

Letter to Dr John Clephane (5 Jan 1753), in J Y T Greig (ed.), *Letters of David Hume* (1932), Vol.1

He stayed at Riddle's Court, Lawnmarket, Edinburgh in 1752–3

26 Notwithstanding all the Pains, which I have taken in the Study of the English Language, I am still jealous of my Pen. As to my Tongue, you have seen, that I regard it as totally desperate and irreclaimable.

Letter to John Wilkes (16 Oct 1754), in J Y T Greig (ed.), *Letters of David Hume* (1932), Vol.1

Like many otherwise intelligent men of his age, he spent his life trying to rid himself of 'Scotticisms'

27 Is it not strange that, at a time when we have lost our Princes, our Parliaments, our independent Government, even the Presence of our chief Nobility, are unhappy, in our Accent & Pronunciation, speak a very corrupt Dialect of the Tongue which we make use of; is it not strange, I say, that, in these Circumstances, we shou'd really be the People most distinguish'd for Literature in Europe?

Letter to Gilbert Elliot of Minto (2 July 1757), in J Y T Greig (ed.), *Letters of David Hume* (1932), Vol.1

28 Doubt, uncertainty, suspence of judgment appear the only result of our most accurate scrutiny, concerning this subject [religion]. But such is the frailty of human reason... that even this deliberate doubt could scarcely be upheld; did we not enlarge our view, and opposing one species of superstition to another, set them a-quarrelling; while we ourselves, during their fury and contention, happily make our escape into the calm, though obscure, regions of philosophy.

> *The Natural History of Religion* (1757), Part 15, 'General Corollary'

29 I do not believe there is one Englishman in fifty, who, if he heard that I had broke my Neck to night, woud not be rejoic'd with it. Some hate me because I am not a Tory, some because I am not a Whig, some because I am not a Christian, and all because I am a Scotsman. Can you seriously talk of my continuing an Englishman? Am I, or are you, an Englishman? Will they allow us to be so? Do they not treat with Derision our Pretensions to that Name, and with Hatred our just Pretensions to surpass & to govern them? I am a Citizen of the World...

> Letter to Gilbert Elliot of Minto (22 Sep 1764), in J Y T Greig (ed.), *Letters of David Hume* (1932), Vol.1

>> He was contrasting his reception throughout Europe with his treatment in England, and finished his letter by expressing a preference to live in France, where he then was, over any other country

30 ... reading and sauntering and lownging and dozing, which I call thinking, is my supreme Happiness, I mean my full Contentment.

> Letter to Hugh Blair (1 Apr 1767), in J Y T Greig (ed.), *Letters of David Hume* (1932), Vol.2

31 I believe this is the historical age and this the historical nation.

> Letter to William Strahan (Aug 1770), in J Y T Greig (ed.), *Letters of David Hume* (1932), Vol.2

>> He was commenting on the plethora of works of history then being produced in Scotland

32 It is difficult for a man to speak long of himself without vanity; therefore I will be short.

> 'My Own Life' (written 18 Apr 1776, published 1777)

33 Never literary attempt was more unfortunate than my Treatise of Human Nature. It fell *dead-born from the press* without reaching such distinction, as even to excite a murmur among the zealots.

> 'My Own Life' (written 18 Apr 1776, published 1777)

34 ... a man of sixty-five, by dying, cuts off only a few years of infirmities; and though I see many symptoms of my literary reputation's breaking out at last with additional lustre, I know, that I had but few years to enjoy it. It is difficult to be more detached from life than I am at present.

> 'My Own Life' (written 18 Apr 1776, published 1777)

>> He was suffering from intestinal cancer, and had only a few months to live

35 He [Hume] then said flatly that the Morality of every Religion was bad, and, I really thought, was not jocular when he said that when he heard a man was religious, he concluded he was a rascal, though he had known some instances of very good men being religious.

> On his death-bed (7 Jul 1776), as reported by James Boswell in his *Journal* (3 Mar 1777)

36 'Well,' said I, 'Mr Hume, I hope to triumph over you when I meet you in a future state; and remember you are not to pretend that you was joking with all this Infidelity.' 'No, No,' said he, 'But I shall have been so long there before you come that it will be nothing new.'

> Boswell and Hume in conversation (7 Jul 1776), quoted in Boswell's *Journal* (3 Mar 1777)

Hume, Tobias c.1569–1645
Composer and mercenary soldier

1 Cease Leaden Slumber dreaming
My Genius presents the cause of sweet musickes meaning...

> 'The Queenes New Yeeres Gift', *Poeticall Music* (1607)

2 ... Love makes men scorn all coward fears,
So doth tobacco.
Love often sets men by the ears,
So doth tobacco.
Tobacco, tobacco,
Sing sweetly for tobacco!
Tobacco is like love, o love it.
For you see I have proved it.

> Quoted in John Purser, *Scotland's Music* (1992), ch.10. Cf. James VI and I 15

Hunter, Anne (*née* Home) 1742–1821
Poet and songwriter

1 My mother bids me bind my hair
With bands of rosy hue,
Tie up my sleeves with ribbons rare,
And lace my bodice blue.

'For why,' she cries, 'sit still and weep,
While others dance and play?'
Alas! I scarce can go, or creep,
While Lubin is away.

> 'My Mother Bids me Bind my Hair', st.1–2

Hunter, William 1718–83

Anatomist and obstetrician

1 Some physiologists will have it that the stomach is a mill; – others, that is a fermenting vat; – others again that it is a stew-pan; – but in my view of the matter, it is neither a mill, a fermenting vat, nor a stew-pan – but a *stomach*, gentlemen, a *stomach*.

> Epigraph in J A Paris, *A Treatise on Diet* (1824), quoted from a manuscript note made by Hunter on one of his lectures

Huston, John 1906–87

American film director

1 As long as actors are going into politics, I wish, for Christ's sake, that Sean Connery would become king of Scotland.

> Quoted in John Millar, 'Sean Connery', in Eddie Dick (ed.), *From Limelight to Satellite* (1990)
>
> > Huston directed *The Man Who Would Be King* (1975), in which Connery starred with Michael Caine

Hutcheson, Francis 1694–1746

Irish-born philosopher, Professor of Moral Philosophy at the University of Glasgow from 1729

1 Wisdom denotes the pursuing of the best ends by the best means.

> *An Inquiry into the Original of our Ideas of Beauty and Virtue* (1725), Treatise 1, section 5

2 ... that action is best, which procures the greatest happiness for the greatest numbers; and that, worst, which, in like manner, occasions misery.

> *An Inquiry Concerning Moral Good and Evil* (1725), section 3

3 Some strange love of simplicity in the structure of human nature, or attachment to some favourite hypothesis, has engaged many writers to pass over a great many simple perceptions, which we may find in ourselves. We have got the number five fixed for our external senses, though a larger number might as easily be defended. We have multitudes of perceptions which have no relation to any external sensation...

> *An Essay on the Nature and Conduct of the Passions and Affections* (1730), Preface

Hutton, James 1726–97

Scientist, often regarded as the 'father' of modern geology

1 A bag of gravel is a history to me.

> Letter to James Lind (1772), quoted in G Bruce & P H Scott, *A Scottish Postbag: Eight Centuries of Scottish Posts* (1986)

2 Lord pity the arse that's clagged to a head that will hunt stones... I begin to be tired of speaking to stones and long for a fresh bit of mortality to make sauce to them.

> After an arduous geological tour of Wales, on horseback, in 1774. Letter to George Clerk Maxwell (Scottish Record Office GD 18/5749)

3 Time, which measures every thing in our idea, and is often deficient in our schemes, is to nature endless and as nothing; it cannot limit that by which it alone has existence.

> 'Theory of the Earth', *Transactions of the Royal Society of Edinburgh* (1788), Vol.1, Part 1

4 The result... of our present enquiry is that we find no vestige of a beginning, no prospect of an end.

> On the immensity of geological time, 'Theory of the Earth', *Transactions of the Royal Society of Edinburgh* (1788), Vol.1, Part 2

I

Iain Dubh Mac Iain Mhic Ailein (Black John MacDonald) c.1650–c.1740
Poet

1 Bliadhna leumadh dhar milleadh,
  an cóig deug 's am mil' eile
  's na seachd ceud a rinn imeachd,
  chaill sinn ùrròs ar fine
  's geur a leus air ar cinne ram beò.

† The year in which our enemy sprang to destroy
  us, the fifteen and the other thousand with
  the seven hundred that have sped [1715], we
  lost the fragrant rose of our clan. The sting
  of it will be a sharp one for our clan as long
  as they live.

> Verse composed on the Jacobite rising of 1715,
> in 'Oran nam Fineachan Gàidhealach' ('Song of
> the Highland Clans')

2 'S i seo an aimsir an dearbhar an targanach
    dhuinn,
  's bras meanmnach fir Alba fon armaibh air tùs
  nuair dh'éireas gach treunfhear 'na éideadh
    glan ùr
  le rùn feirg' agus gairge gu seirbheis a' chrùin.

† This is the time when the prophecy will be
  fulfilled for us, with the men of Scotland
  mettlesome and spirited, armed in the van [of
  the battle], each valiant man will rise in brand
  new garb, with angry and fierce determination
  in the service of the crown.

> Attrib. 'Marbhrann do Mhac Mhic Ailein' ('Elegy
> for Allan, chief of Clan Ranald')

> The prophecy referred to is almost certainly
> that of Thomas the Rhymer, foretelling that
> the Gaels will be restored to their proper place
> in Scotland

Iain Lom (Bare John MacDonald) c.1625–c.1707
Poet of the MacDonalds of Keppoch

1 Ro Bhlàr Inbhir Lochaidh chunnaic Alasdair
  mac Colla Iain Lom am bard 'na shuidhe air
  cnocan an àite a bhith ag ullachadh airson
  a' bhlàir. 'Nach eil thu a dol a shabaid idir,
  Iain?' ars Alasdair.
  'Ma théid mise mharbhadh,' ars Iain Lom,
  'có nì òran-molaidh dhut?'
  B'e sin cuid a' bhaird.

† Before the Battle of Inverlochy (1645) Alasdair
  mac Colla saw Iain Lom the poet sitting on a
  hillock instead of preparing for battle. 'Aren't
  you going to fight at all, Iain?' said Alasdair.

'If I get killed,' said Iain Lom, 'who will make
a praise-song for you?'
That was the poet's part.

> Traditional

2 MAC CAILEIN MOR, IARLA ARRA GHAIDHEAL: Iain,
  Iain, cha sguir thu gu bràth de chagnadh nan
  Caimbeulach?
  IAIN LOM: Chan e bhith 'gur cagnadh bu duilich
  leam, ach nach b'urrainn domh bhur slugadh.

† EARL OF ARGYLL: Iain, Iain, will you never
  cease gnawing at the Campbells?
  IAIN LOM: It's not gnawing at you that I find
  hard, but that I cannot swallow you.

> Attrib.

> Argyll had offered a large reward for the
> poet's head because of the influence of his
> songs of invective against the Campbells.
> Iain Lom, knowing that a poet must not
> be harmed, went to Inveraray in person
> to claim the reward. Argyll was much
> amused and entertained him as a guest for
> a week. When he showed him a collection
> of dead blackcocks and asked him if he
> had ever seen so many in one place, Iain
> Lom said he had, at Inverlochy (where
> Montrose had inflicted a heavy defeat on the
> Campbells in 1645). The above exchange then
> took place

Iain Mac Mhurchaidh (John MacRae) 18th century
Poet, who emigrated to America and fought on the Royalist side in the War of Independence

1 Tha sinne 'n ar n-Innseanaich, cinnteach
    gu leòir;
  Fo dhubhar nan craobh, cha bhi h-aon
    againn beò;
  Madaidh alluidh 'us béistean ag éigheach 's
    gach fròig;
  Gu bheil sinne 'nar n-éiginn bho 'n là thréig
    sinn Righ Deòrs'.

† We've become Indians surely enough.
  Skulking under trees, not one of us will be
    left alive,
  with wolves and beasts howling in every lair.
  We've come to ruin since the day we forsook
    King George.

> 'Dean Cadalan Sàmhach, a Chuilean Mo Rùin'
> ('Sleep Softly, my Darling Beloved'). Quoted in
> Margaret MacDonell, *The Emigrant Experience:
> Songs of Highland Emigrants in North America*
> (1982), st.4

Imlach, Hamish 1940–96
Folksinger

Ah-ha, Glory Hallelujah,
The cod liver oil and the orange juice.

> 'Cod Liver Oil and Orange Juice', chorus
>
>> The song was written by Ron Clark and Carl
>> MacDougall (1962). Imlach became famous
>> for performing it, and he later used it as the
>> title for his autobiography

I would hate to die with a heart attack and
have good liver, kidneys and brain. When I die
I want everything to be knackered.

> *Cod Liver Oil and the Orange Juice: Reminiscences
> of a Fat Folksinger* (1992), ch.12

I often thought I'd have made much more
money as a professional invalid than I ever did
as a professional singer.

> *Cod Liver Oil and the Orange Juice: Reminiscences
> of a Fat Folksinger* (1992), ch.12

If you think there are too many stories in
this book about shitty underpants then you
obviously haven't drunk and eaten to excess
on a regular basis.

> *Cod Liver Oil and the Orange Juice: Reminiscences
> of a Fat Folksinger* (1992), ch.13

Inglis, Elsie Maud 1864–1917
*Surgeon, medical reformer, founder member
of the Scottish Women's Suffragette Federation, and organiser of the Scottish Women's
Hospitals*

. . . when I have the vote I shall vote that
all men who turn their wives and families out
of doors at eleven o'clock at night, especially
when the wife is ill, shall be horse-whipped.
And if they make the excuse that they were
tipsy, I should give them double. They would
very soon learn to behave themselves.

> As a medical student in Glasgow, after visiting
> the homes of the poor (c.1891). Quoted in Margot
> Lawrence, *Shadows and Swords: a Biography of
> Elsie Inglis* (1971), ch.5

2 I cannot think of anything more calculated to
bring home to men the fact that women *can
help* intelligently in any kind of work. So much
of our work is done where they can not see it.
They'll see every bit of this. . .

> On setting up the Scottish Women's Hospitals.
> Letter to Mrs Fawcett (9 Oct 1914), quoted
> in Margot Lawrence, *Shadows and Swords: a
> Biography of Elsie Inglis* (1971), ch.9
>
>> Following the Austrian declaration of war on
>> Serbia at the start of World War I (Jul 1914),
>> she had offered her services to the Royal
>> Army Medical Corps and to the Red Cross.
>> Both had turned her down, the response of

the RAMC representative in Edinburgh being
'My good lady, go home and sit still'

3 I heard those girls' voices laughing and
chattering, and I thought there might be
something in what a Russian woman said to
me *a propos* of the great cheerfulness of the
Unit. 'There is certainly something great in the
British character which the continental nations
don't possess,' and when I said 'I don't know,
we all have our strong points and our weak
ones,' she said 'There is no other nation that
goes into trouble laughing'.

> Report III, quoted in Margot Lawrence, *Shadows
> and Swords: a Biography of Elsie Inglis* (1971), ch.1

4 The traditional male disbelief in our capacity
cannot be argued away; it can only be
worked away.

> Report III, quoted in Margot Lawrence, *Shadows
> and Swords: a Biography of Elsie Inglis* (1971), ch.4

5 It was a great day in my life when I discovered
that I did not know what fear was.

> Quoted in Margot Lawrence, *Shadow of Swords:
> a Biography of Elsie Inglis* (1971), ch.14
>
>> She was referring to an incident in late 1915.
>> While working in Krushevatz in Serbia, she
>> refused to sign, despite immense pressure
>> from the German CO, a certificate confirming
>> the good behaviour of the German Army that
>> had occupied the hospital in which her unit
>> was working

6 We are in the very centre of the storm and it
just feels exactly like having the rain pouring
down, and the wind beating in gusts, and not
being able to see for the water in one's eyes
and just holding on and saying 'It cannot last,
it is so bad'. . . The hospitals are packed
with wounded. We decided we must stand by
our hospitals; it was too awful leaving badly
wounded men with no proper care. . .

> Letter from Russia to Mrs Simson (6 Nov 1916).
> Quoted in Margot Lawrence, *Shadows and Swords:
> a Biography of Elsie Inglis* (1971), ch.13

7 When a Scotsman says he'll see us out – I
know he'll see us out! When anybody else
says it I keep my eye on the means of
exit myself!

> Letter from Russia to Mrs McLaren (19 Dec
> 1916), quoted in Margot Lawrence, *Shadow of
> Swords: a Biography of Elsie Inglis* (1971), ch.19
>
>> On Commander Gregory of the Armoured
>> Cars Division, who told her he would
>> see her and her workers safely out of
>> Galatz, Russia

8 Hard-working, conscientious, good-tempered,
plucky, cheerful and the better bred they are
the better they stand roughing it.

> On the ideal characteristics of recruits to the
> Scottish Women's Hospitals. Letter to Lady

Ashmore (9 Jan 1917), quoted in Margot Lawrence, *Shadows and Swords: a Biography of Elsie Inglis* (1971), ch.1

9 The worst of being a doctor is that one's mistakes matter so much.

Quoted in Margot Lawrence, *Shadows and Swords: a Biography of Elsie Inglis* (1971), ch.6

After her death in 1917, a Serbian Orthodox priest remarked 'If she were a Serbian, we would declare her a saint. In Scotland, she is only a doctor.' (See Lawrence, ch.27)

Irvine, Jack
Businessman and journalist

1 . . . all readers can get tired with their paper. But it's like a man being tired and bored with his wife: it's a terrible effort to ditch her and find a bimbo, and besides you're comfortable, like an old pair of slippers.

Speculating on why bored Sunday newspaper readers did not switch to buying the *Sunday Scot*, of which he was editor. That paper folded (10 Mar 1991) after 14 issues. Quoted in Maurice Smith, *Paper Lions: The Scottish Press and National Identity* (1994), ch.10

Iseabail Ní Mheic Ciléin (Isabel of Argyll) 15th century
Poet, member of the household, or perhaps daughter, of the Earl of Argyll

1 Is mairg dá ngalar an grádh,
gé bé fáth fá n-abrainn é;
deacair sgarachtainn ré pháirt;
truagh an cás i bhfeilim fein.

An grádh-soin tugas gan fhios,
ó's é mo leas gan a luadh,
mara bhfaigh mé furtacht tráth,
biaidh mo bhláth go tana truagh.

† Alas for him whose sickness is love, for what cause soever I should say it; hard it is to be free of it; sad is the plight in which I am myself.
That love which I have given in secret, since it profits me to declare it not: if I find not quick relief, my bloom will be slight and meagre.

'Is mairg dá ngalar an grádh' ('Alas for him whose sickness is love'), st.1–2. Quoted in W J Watson (ed.), *Scottish Verse from the Book of the Dean of Lismore* (1937)

J

Jackson, Alan 1938–

Poet

Curse you apples on that tree,
And curse our human destiny.
An ape, a bull, I'd rather be
Than civil suffering conscious me.

> 'Curse you apples on that tree', *Underwater Wedding* (1961)

All over the world, perhaps mostly in the West, young people are finding that they'd rather go barefoot than wear Daddy's shoes.

> 'The Knitted Claymore: An Essay on Culture and Nationalism', *Lines Review* No.37 (Jun 1971)

. . . one thing that is not true is that Scotland lost its independence. Scotland, ie the Scottish people, never had any to lose. They, like the English, French, German and many other peoples, were subjects; subjects of the sacred pirates and the social order which controlled them by a combination of mystification and power.

> On the Union with England. 'The Knitted Claymore: An Essay on Culture and Nationalism', *Lines Review* No.37 (Jun 1971)

I'm all for Home Rule as long as it is understood my home is in Cathcart Place. Let's be glad that one king and one bloody frontier have gone and recognise that the world has suffered enough from men surrendering their freedoms to ideologies, nation-states, religions and football clubs.

> 'The Knitted Claymore: an Essay on Culture and Nationalism', *Lines Review* No.37 (Jun 1971)

Presumably because of nationalist successes at the polls, men I thought had slunk away to prickly sulks on couches of thistle or even to realise which decade of which century they lived in, came breengin' hurriedly back, reknitting their half unravelled claymores and pulling behind them pramfuls of young poets waving tartan rattles.

> 'The Knitted Claymore: an Essay on Culture and Nationalism', *Lines Review* No.37 (Jun 1971)

Och, I wish you hadn't come right now;
You've put me off my balance.

I was just translating my last wee poem
Into the dear auld Lallans.

> 'A Scotch Poet Speaks', *Idiots Are Freelance* (1973)

7 certainly the remedy's
inside the disease
and the meaning of being ill
's to bring the eye
to the heart.

> 'Certainly the remedy's', *Idiots are Freelance* (1973)
>
>> A slightly altered version of this appeared under the dustjacket of Alasdair Gray's novel *1982 Janine* (1984)

8 From my window I see the rectangular blocks of man's
insolent mechanical ignorance rise, with hideous exactitude,
against the sun
against the sky.
It is the University.

> 'From my window', 'The Attic Poems', in *Salutations: Collected Poems 1960–89* (1990)

9 I bring you salutations from the planets,
I bring you watch and welcome from the stars.
Be brave, all you who care for this endeavour,
We have yet to live and die through many wars.

> 'Salutations', *Salutations: Collected Poems 1960–89* (1990)

Jacob, Violet (*née* Kennedy-Erskine) 1863–1946

Poet and novelist

1 The action of a gorged vulture trying to rise off the ground is the most ungainly thing in the world. The greed, the grotesque lack of dignity, the devil-take-the-hindmost of it all made me think of the words of an old woman I knew in Scotland, who, speaking of the crowding relations of a rich man just dead, said 'Where the money is, there will the blayguards be gathered thegither!'

> Diary entry (13 Jun 1899), in Carol Anderson (ed.), *Violet Jacob: Diaries and letters from India 1895–1900* (1990)

2 ' . . . Damn me, but I hate old women! They should have their tongues cut out.'

> *Flemington* (1911), ch.25 (Duke of Cumberland)

3 O Jean, my Jean, when the bell ca's the congregation
Owre valley an' hill wi' the ding frae its iron mou',
When a'body's thochts is set on his ain salvation,

Mine's set on you.

There's a reid rose lies on the Buik o' the
    Word afore ye
That was growin' braw on its bush at the
    keek o' day,
But the lad that pu'd yon flower i' the
    mornin's glory
He canna pray.

> 'Tam i' the Kirk', *Songs of Angus* (1915), st.1–2

4 Craigo Woods, wi' the splash o' the cauld
    rain beatin'
I' the back end o' the year,
When the clouds hang laigh wi' the weicht o'
    their load o' greetin'
And the autumn wind's asteer. . .

> 'Craigo Woods', *Songs of Angus* (1915), st.1

5 There's a road to a far-aff land, an' the land
    is yonder
Whaur a' men's hopes are set;
We dinna ken foo lang we maun hae to wander,
But we'll a' win to it yet. . .

> 'Craigo Woods', *Songs of Angus* (1915), st.3

6 'Oh, tell me what was on yer road, ye roarin'
    norlan' Wind,
As ye cam' blawin' frae the land that's niver
    frae my mind?
My feet they traivel England, but I'm deein'
    for the north.'
'*My man, I heard the siller tides rin up the Firth
o' Forth.*'

> 'The Wild Geese', *Songs of Angus* (1915), st.1

7 '*And far abune the Angus straths I saw the wild
geese flee,
A lang, lang skein o' beatin' wings, wi' their heids
towards the sea,
And aye their cryin' voices trailed ahint them
on the air–*'
'O Wind, hae maircy, haud yer whisht, for I
    daurna listen mair!'

> 'The Wild Geese', *Songs of Angus* (1915), st.4

8 They gae'd frae mill and mart; frae wind-
    blawn places,
And grey toon-closes; i' the empty street
Nae mair the bairns ken their steps, their faces,
Nor stand tae listen to the trampin' feet.

> 'Glory', *More Songs of Angus and Others* (1918)
>
> On war. Poem dedicated to her son Harry,
> 'A.H.J.', who died from his injuries after the
> Battle of the Somme (1916)

9 Guid fortune's blate whaur she's weel desairv't
The sinner fu' and the godly stairv't. . .

> 'Pride', *Bonnie Joann and other poems* (1921), st.4

10 . . . the shilpit sun is thin
Like an auld man deein' slow
And a shade comes creepin' in

When the fire is fa'in low;
Then I feel the lang een set
Like a doom upon ma heid,
For the warlock's livin' yet –
But the rowan's deid!

> 'The Rowan', *The Northern Lights and Other
> Poems* (1927), st.2

James I (Stewart) 1394–1437
King of Scotland (1406–37; de facto from 1424)

1 If God grant me life, though it be but the life
of a dog, there shall be no place in my realm
where the key shall not keep the castle and the
brackenbush the cow.

> Reputedly said on his return to Scotland (1424)
> after 18 years' captivity in England. Quoted in
> Walter Bower, *Scotichronicon* (1440–9), Vol.8,
> Bk 16, ch.34

2 In this processe my wilsum wittis gye,
And with your bryght lanternis wele convoye
My pen, to write my turment and my joye.

> On writing, addressing the Muses. *The Kingis
> Quair* (c.1424), st.19

3 The bird, the best, the fisch eke in the see,
They lyve in fredome everich in his kynd;
And I a man, and lakkith libertee. . .

> *The Kingis Quair* (c.1424), st.27

4 Worschippe, ye that loveris bene, this May,
For of your blisse, the kalendis ar begonne,
And sing with us, 'away, winter, away!
Cum somer, cum, the suete sesoun and sonne!'

> *The Kingis Quair* (c.1424), st.34

5 And therewith kest I doun myn eye ageyne,
Quhare as I sawe, walking under the tour,
Full secretly, new cummyn hir to pleyne,
The fairest or the freschest yonge floure
That ever I sawe, me thoght, before that houre,
For quhich sodayn abate, anon astert
The blude of all my body to my hert.

> *The Kingis Quair* (c.1424), st.40
>
> This passage records the captive King's first
> sight of Lady Joan Beaufort, who would
> become his Queen

James II (Stewart) 1430–60
King of Scotland (1437–60)

1 It is decreyet and ordanyt that the
wapinschawings be haldin be the lordis and the
barronis spiritual and temporall foure tymis in
the yeir, and that the futball and golf be utterly
cryit downe, and not to be usit.

> Parliamentary proclamation (Mar 1457)
>
> 'Wapinschawings' were gatherings of the
> populace to make sure that each man was
> properly armed according to his rank; golf

and 'futball' were seen by the king to be annoying distractions from these

James V (Stewart) 1512–42
King of Scotland (1513–42)

Adieu, Farewell, it came with a lass, it will pass with a lass.

> Said on his death-bed (14 Dec 1542), on learning of the birth of his daughter Mary. Quoted in Robert Lindsay of Pitscottie (c.1532–80), *The Historie and Cronicles of Scotland* (1570s; 1899 edition), Bk 29, ch.31
>
> > He was referring to the Crown of Scotland, which had come to the Stewart line by marriage to Marjorie, daughter of Robert the Bruce. Other versions include the Scots, 'It cam wi a lass, it will gang wi a lass'

James VI and I (Stewart) 1566–1625
King of Scotland (from 1567), and also of England (from 1603)

Of all these straits the best is out of doubt
That courage wise, and wisedome should be stoute.

> 'A Sonnet, when the King was Surprised by the Earle Bothwell' (c.1593)
>
> > Francis Hepburn, Earl of Bothwell (c.1563–1624), continually caused trouble for James between about 1588 and 1595. James's poem, in which courage and wisdom argue the merits of self-defence and preservation, probably refers to 24 July 1593, when Bothwell burst in upon the King at Holyrood before he was dressed, and attempted to control royal policy by holding him a prisoner

2 . . . the highest benche is sliddriest to sit upon.

> On the burden of kingship. *The True Lawe of Free Monarchies* (1598)

3 God gives not Kings the stile of *Gods* in vaine,
For on his throne his Scepter doe they swey;
And as their subjects ought them to obey,
So Kings should feare and serve their
     God againe.

> Sonnet prefacing *Basilikon Doron* (1599)
>
> > This book was subtitled *His Majesties Instructions to his Dearest Sonne, Henry the Prince*, who died in 1612 at the age of 18. Quotations from *Basilikon Doron* are all from the 1603 edition

4 . . . learne to know and love that God, whome-to ye have a double obligation; first, for that he made you a man; and next, for that he made you a little God to sitte on his throne, and rule over other men.

> *Basilikon Doron* (1599), Bk 1

5 [Faith] muste be nourished by prayer, which is nothing else but a friendly talking with God.

> *Basilikon Doron* (1599), Bk 1. Cf. William Barclay 1

6 . . . the true difference betwixt a lawfull good King and a usurping Tyrant. . . . The one acknowledgeth himselfe ordained for his people, having receaved from God a burthen of government whereof he must be countable: the other thinketh his people ordayned for him, a pray to his passions and inordinate appetites, as the fruits of his magnanimitie.

> *Basilikon Doron* (1599), Bk 2

7 As for the Hie-lands, I shortly comprehend them al in two sorts of people: the one that dwelleth in our maine land, that are barbarous for the most parte, and yet mixed with some shewe of civilitie; the other, that dwelleth in the Iles, and are allutterlie barbares.

> *Basilikon Doron* (1599), Bk 2

8 And Craftes-men thinke, we should be content with their worke, howe bad and deare so ever it be: and if they in any thing be controlled, up goeth the blew-blanket.

> On strikes. *Basilikon Doron* (1599), Bk 2
>
> > The Blue Blanket was the banner of the Trades of Edinburgh

9 And as I have counselled you to be slowe in taking on a warre; so advise I you to be slowe in peace-making. Before ye aggree, look that the grounde of your warres be satisfied in your peace; and that ye see a good suretie for you and your people: otherwaies a honorable & just warre is more tolerable, than a dishonorable and dis-advantageous peace.

> *Basilikon Doron* (1599), Bk 2

10 . . . that filthy vice of Flattery, the pest of all Princes, and wracke of Republickes.

> *Basilikon Doron* (1599), Bk 2. Cf. Sir David Lindsay 14

11 Be also moderate in your rayment; neither over superfluous, like a deboshed waister; nor yet over base, like a miserable wretche; not artificiallie trimmed & decked, like a Courtizane; nor yet over sluggishly clothed, like a country-clowne; not over lightly, like a Candie-souldier, or a vaine young Courtier; nor yet over gravelie, like a Minister.

> *Basilikon Doron* (1599), Bk 3

12 And as for the chesse, I thinke. . . it is over wise and Philosophicke a follie. For where all suche light plaies are ordained to free mens heades for a time from the fashious thoughts on their affaires, it by the contrarie filleth and troubleth mens heades with as many fashious toies of the play, as before it was filled with thoughts on his affaires.

> *Basilikon Doron* (1599), Bk 3. Cf. Walter Scott 119

13 . . . what honour or policie can moove us to imitate the barbarous and beastly maners of the wilde, godlesse, and slavish *Indians*, especially

in so vile and stinking a custome?. . . Why doe we not as well imitate them in walking naked as they doe? in preferring glasses, feathers, and such toyes, to golde and precious stones, as they do? yea why do we not denie God and adore the Devill, as they doe?

A Counterblaste to Tobacco (1604)

14 . . . is it not both great vanitie and uncleanenesse, that at the table, a place of respect, of cleanlinesse, of modestie, men should not be ashamed, to sit tossing of *Tobacco pipes*, and puffing of the smoke of *Tobacco* one to another, making the filthy smoke and stinke thereof, to exhale athwart the dishes, and infect the aire, when very often, men that abhorre it are at their repast?

A Counterblaste to Tobacco (1604)

15 A custome lothsome to the eye, hatefull to the Nose, harmefull to the braine, daungerous to the Lungs, and in the black stinking fume thereof, neerest resembling the horrible Stigian smoke of the pit that is bottomelesse.

A Counterblaste to Tobacco (1604). Cf. Tobias Hume 2

16 No bishop, no king.

At Hampton Court, concluding a conference on possible church reform (14 Jan 1604)

17 Here I sit and govern Scotland with my pen. I write and it is done; and by the Clerk of the Council I govern Scotland now, which others could not do by the sword.

Speech to the English Parliament (1607)

18 That is done today with a penny, that will not be done hereafter with an hundred pounds, and that will be mended now in a day, which hereafter will not be mended in a year. . .

On the repair of roads and bridges. Speech in the Star Chamber (20 Jun 1616)

19 Jesus Christ did the same and therefore I cannot be blamed. Christ had his John and I have my George.

Attrib. (1617). To his counsellors, defending his infatuation with George Villiers, Duke of Buckingham

20 Look not to find the softness of a down pillow in a crown, but remember that it is a thorny piece of stuff and full of continual cares.

'Meditations on St Matthew' (1620)

21 The heavens that wept perpetually before,
Since we came hither show theyr smilinge cleere.
This goodly house it smiles, and all this store
Of huge provvision smiles upon us heere.
The Buckes & Stagges in fatt they seeme
to smile:

God send a smilinge boy within a while.

'Verses made by the Kinge, when hee was entertayned at Burly in Rutland-shire by my Lord Marquesse of Buckingham' (Aug 1621)

22 I will govern according to the common weal, but not according to the common will.

Address to the House of Commons (Dec 1621)

23 God's wounds, I will pull down my breeches and they shall also see my arse.

On the trials of appearing before a demanding public. Quoted in Antonia Fraser, *King James* (1974), ch.4

24 A beggar's mantle fringed with gold.

Attrib. On Fife.

25 These are rare attainments for a damsel, but pray tell me, can she spin?

Attrib.

Apparently said when introduced to a girl who had knowledge of Greek, Latin and Hebrew

26 Have I three kingdoms and thou must needs fly into my eye?

Attrib. To a fly. Quoted in John Selden, *Table Talk* (1689)

27 He was a bold man who first swallowed an oyster.

Attrib.

Jamie, Kathleen 1962–
Poet

1 Stop thinking now, and put on your shoes.

'Karakoram Highway', *The Way We Live* (1987)

2 To the way it fits, the way it is, the way it seems to be: let me bash out praises – pass the tambourine.

'The Way We Live', *The Way We Live* (1987)

3 The museums of Scotland are wrang.
They urnae arraheids
but a show o grannies' tongues,
the hard tongues o grannies
aa deid an gaun
back to thur peat and burns,
but for thur sherp
chert tongues, that lee
fur generations in the land
like wicked cherms, that lee
aa douce in the glessy cases in the gloom
o oor museums, an
they arenae lettin oan.

'Arraheids', *The Queen of Sheba* (1994)

4 our spires and doocoots
institutes and tinkies' benders,
old Scots kings and dancing fairies

give strength to my house

on whose roof we can balance,
carefully stand and see
clear to the far off mountains,
cities, rigs and gardens,

Europe, Africa, the Forth and Tay bridges,
even dare to let go, lift our hands
and wave to the waving citizens
of all those other countries.

'The Republic of Fife', *The Queen of Sheba*
(1994), st.8–10

Skeins o geese write a word
across the sky. A word
struck lik a gong
afore I wis born.
The sky moves like cattle, lowin.

'Skeins o geese', *The Queen of Sheba* (1994), st.1

Jamieson, Robert Alan 1958–

Poet and novelist

Let aa tochts be lichthooses
Aa wyrds dir baems.

'Lion', *Shoormal* (1986)

Harry listen Harry please
We canna bide nae langer.
Da aert is tired man, sae is du,
We'll sell da sheep, we'll sell da coo.
Gie up da lease.

Come man awa
For we maun ging
Across da Soond o Papa

'Sang oda Post War Exiles', *Shoormal* (1986)

Jeffrey, Francis (Lord Jeffrey)
1773–1850

Critic, lawyer and judge

There was no objection to the blue-stocking,
provided the petticoat came low enough down.

On novelist Elizabeth Hamilton, author of *The
Cottagers of Glenburnie* (1808). Quoted in Lord
Cockburn, *Memorials of His Time* (1856), ch.4

... Scotch is not to be considered as a provincial dialect – the vehicle only of rustic vulgarity
and rude local humour. It is the language of a
whole country – long an independent kingdom,
and still separate in its laws, character, and
manners... it is an ignorant, as well as an
illiberal prejudice, which would confound it with
the barbarous dialects of Yorkshire or Devon.

Review of Cromek's *Reliques of Robert Burns*, in
Edinburgh Review No.26 (Jan 1809)

Argument from authority is, in general, the
weakest and the most tedious of all arguments;
and learning, we are inclined to believe, has

more often played the part of a bully than of a
fair auxiliary; and been oftener used to frighten
people than to convince them, – to dazzle and
overawe, rather than to guide and enlighten.

Review of *Letters from a Late Eminent Prelate
to one of his Friends*, in *Edinburgh Review* No.26
(Jan 1809)

The 'eminent prelate' under review was
William Warburton (1698–1779), Bishop of
Gloucester and a controversial theologian

4 This will never do!

Opening words of review of William
Wordsworth's *The Excursion*, in *Edinburgh
Review* No.47 (Nov 1814)

5 This, we think, has the merit of being the very
worst poem we ever saw imprinted in a quarto
volume...

Opening words of review of William
Wordsworth's *The White Doe of Rylstone*, in
Edinburgh Review No.50 (Oct 1815)

6 A man must love his fellows before he loves
their liberty; and if he has not learned to interest
himself in their enjoyments, it is impossible that
he can have any genuine concern in their liberty.

Review of G Crayon, *Bracebridge Hall*, in
Edinburgh Review No.74 (Nov 1822)

7 You have no mission upon earth, whatever you
may fancy, half so important as to be innocently
happy...

Letter to Thomas Carlyle (Aug 1828), quoted in
D A Wilson, *Carlyle to 'The French Revolution'*
(1924), p.62

8 You will never persuade anybody that the
regulation of life is such a mighty laborious
business as you would make it, or that it is not
better to go lightly through it, with the first
creed that comes to hand, than to spend the
better part of it in an anxious verification of
its articles.

Letter to Thomas Carlyle (Aug 1828), quoted in
D A Wilson, *Carlyle to 'The French Revolution'*
(1924), p.63

9 I am proud of my country; there is not another
country on earth where such a deed could have
been done.

On learning of the Disruption (18 May 1843),
when hundreds of ministers left the Church
of Scotland on the principle of opposing lay
patronage. Quoted in Margaret Oliphant, *Thomas
Chalmers* (1893), ch.6

Jeffrey, John 1959–

Rugby player and farmer

1 I accept the suspension without complaint,
but I deny damaging the cup.

Quoted in Derek Douglas, *The Book of World
Rugby Quotations* (1991)

On being suspended for six months following an

incident after Scotland's victory over England in the 1988 Calcutta Cup match. The 110-year-old cup had disappeared during the post-match dinner in Edinburgh, and was allegedly drop-kicked in the street by unidentified players. Scotland official Bob Munro was later quoted as saying, 'It will now have to be called the Calcutta Shield.' English RFU Secretary Dudley Wood remarked, 'In case I was out when the trophy was brought back from Scotland, I told them they could slip it under the door.' (*Daily Telegraph*, 23 Dec 1988)

Johnson, Dr Samuel 1709–84

English lexicographer, critic and wit

1 OATS – A grain, which in England is generally given to horses, but in Scotland supports the people.

> *A Dictionary of the English Language* (1755). Cf. John Stuart Blackie 4, Robert Fergusson 21, Andrew Shirrefs 2
>
> Johnson later said to James Boswell, 'Why, I own, that by my definition of *oats* I meant to vex them [the Scots].' See Boswell, *Life of Samuel Johnson* (1791), 21 Mar 1783. Lord Elibank's riposte to Johnson is also well known: 'But where will you find such horses, and such men?'

2 Mr Ogilvie then took a new ground, where, I suppose, he thought himself perfectly safe; for he observed, that Scotland had a great many noble wild prospects. JOHNSON. 'I believe, Sir, you have a great many. Norway, too, has noble wild prospects; and Lapland is remarkable for prodigious noble wild prospects. But, Sir, let me tell you, the noblest prospect which a Scotchman ever sees is the high road that leads him to England!'

> Quoted in James Boswell, *Life of Samuel Johnson* (1791), 6 Jul 1763

3 Much may be made of a Scotchman, if he be *caught* young.

> Quoted in James Boswell, *Life of Samuel Johnson* (1791), Spring 1772
>
> Said of Lord Mansfield, who had been educated in England

4 I here began to indulge old Scottish sentiments, and to express warm regret, that by our union with England, we were no more – our independent kingdom was lost. JOHNSON. 'Sir, never talk of your independency, who could let your Queen remain twenty years in captivity, and then be put to death, without even a pretence of justice, without your ever attempting to rescue her; and such a Queen too! as every man of any gallantry of spirit woud have sacrificed his life for.' Worthy MR JAMES KERR, Keeper of the Records. 'Half our nation was bribed by English money.' JOHNSON. 'Sir,

that is no defence: that makes you worse.'

> On Mary, Queen of Scots. Quoted in James Boswell, *Journal of a Tour to the Hebrides* (1786), 16 Aug 1773

5 Your country consists of two things, stone and water. There is, indeed, a little earth above the stone in some places, but a very little; and the stone is always appearing. It is like a man in rags; the naked skin is still peeping out.

> To Sir Allan MacLean, while in Mull. Quoted in James Boswell, *Journal of a Tour to the Hebrides* (1786), 21 Oct 1773

6 We supped well; and after supper, Dr Johnson, whom I had not seen taste any fermented liquor during all our travels, called for a gill of whisky. 'Come,' said he, 'let me know what it is that makes a Scotchman happy!'

> Quoted in James Boswell, *Journal of a Tour to the Hebrides* (1786), 23 Oct 1773

7 To hinder insurrection, by driving away the people, and to govern peaceably, by having no subjects, is an expedient that argues no great profundity of politicks. To soften the obdurate, to convince the mistaken, to mollify the resentful, are worthy of a statesman; but it affords a legislator little self-applause to consider, that where there was formerly an insurrection, there is now a wilderness.

> On enforced emigration in the Highlands and Islands. *A Journey to the Western Islands of Scotland* (1775), 'Ostig in Sky'. Cf. Galgacus 1

8 A Scotchman must be a very sturdy moralist, who does not love Scotland better than truth: he will always love it better than inquiry; and if falsehood flatters his vanity, will not be very diligent to detect it.

> *A Journey to the Western Islands of Scotland* (1775), 'Ostig in Sky'
>
> Johnson was referring specifically to the general Scottish enthusiasm for James Macpherson's 'translations' (1760) of ancient Ossianic poetry. He was extremely doubtful of the existence of the original Gaelic texts, but any such scepticism in a Scot was considered by many tantamount to a betrayal of patriotism. It was after another discussion of the authenticity of Macpherson's work that Johnson made the remark, 'Patriotism is the last refuge of a scoundrel.' (Boswell, *Life of Johnson*, 1791, 7 Apr 1775)

9 That man is little to be envied, whose patriotism would not gain force upon the plain of Marathon, or whose piety would not grow warmer among the ruins of Iona.

> *A Journey to the Western Islands of Scotland* (1775), 'Inch Kenneth'

10 Seeing Scotland, Madam, is only seeing a worse England. It is seeing the flower gradually fade away to the naked stalk. Seeing the Hebrides,

indeed, is quite a different scene.

> Said to Mrs Hester Thrale, who had expressed a wish to see Scotland. Quoted in James Boswell, *Life of Samuel Johnson* (1791), 7 Apr 1778

Johnston, Ellen ?1835–73

Lanarkshire, Glasgow and Dundee weaver and poet, who published her work as the 'Factory Girl'

1 My stepfather could not bear to see me longer basking in the sunshine of freedom and therefore took me into the factory where he worked, to learn power-loom weaving, when about ten years of age, from which time I became a factory girl; but no language can paint the suffering which I afterwards endured from my tormentor. . . Like Rasselas, there was a dark history engraven on the tablet of my heart. . . a dark shadow, as a pall, enshrouded my soul, shutting out life's gay sunshine from my bosom – a shadow which has haunted me like a vampire, but at least for the present must remain the mystery of my life.

> *Autobiography, Poems and Songs of Ellen Johnston, the Factory Girl* (2nd edition, 1869)

> > Elspeth King suggests that the 'mystery' of Ellen Johnston's life was probably sexual abuse by her stepfather. See *The Hidden History of Glasgow's Women: The Thenew Factor* (1993), ch.5

2 The spring is come at last, my freens, cheer up, you sons of toil,
Let the seeds of independence be sown in labour's soil
And tho' the nipping blast of care should blight your wee bit crop,
Oh dinna let your spirits sink, cling closer aye to hope.

> 'The Working Man', *Autobiography, Poems and Songs of Ellen Johnston, the Factory Girl* (2nd edition, 1869), st.1

3 The weans sit greeting in oor face, and we ha'e nocht to gie.
What care some gentry if they're weel though a' the puir wad dee!

It is the puir man's hard-won toil that fills the rich man's purse;
I'm sure his gouden coffers they are het wi' mony a curse;
Were it no for the working men what wad the rich men be?
What care some gentry if they're weel though a' the puir wad dee?

> 'The Last Sark' (written 1859), *Autobiography, Poems and Songs of Ellen Johnston, the Factory Girl* (2nd edition, 1869) st.4–5

Johnston, Maurice ('Mo') 1963–

Footballer

1 I might even agree to become Rangers' first Catholic if they paid me £1 million *cash* and bought me Stirling Castle to live in!

> *Mo: the Maurice Johnston Story* (1988), ch.5

2 . . . I am a Celtic man through and through and so I dislike Rangers because they are a force in Scottish football and therefore a threat to the club I love. But more than that I hate the religious policy they maintain. Why won't they sign a Catholic?

> *Mo: the Maurice Johnston Story* (1988), ch.7

3 I'm coming to a really big club, possibly the biggest in Europe. I'm just delighted to be joining the club.

> On signing for Rangers Football Club (10 Jul 1989). Quoted in *The Scotsman* (11 Jul 1989)

> > He was the first Catholic to sign for Rangers in the club's 116-year history

Johnston, Tom 1881–1965

Labour politician, Secretary of State for Scotland (1941–5)

1 We can never have Socialism without complete democracy, and every privilege broken, every barrier burst, every sex and social hallucination swept aside makes clearer the road.

> *Forward* (20 Oct 1906)

> > *Forward* was a weekly socialist newspaper, launched on 13 Oct 1906 and originally edited by Johnston

2 Generation after generation, these few families of tax-gatherers have sucked the life-blood of our nation; in their prides and lusts they have sent us to war, family against family, class against class, race against race; that they might live in idleness and luxury, the labouring mass has sweated and starved; they have pruned the creeds of our Church and stolen its revenues; their mailed fists have crushed the newer thought, and their vanities the arts. . .

> *Our Scots Noble Families* (1909), 'A General Indictment', p.viii

3 . . . they have barred us by barbed wire fences from the bens and glens: the peasant has been ruthlessly swept aside to make room for the pheasant, and the mountain hare now brings forth her young on the hearthstone of the Gael!

> *Our Scots Noble Families* (1909), 'A General Indictment', p.viii

4 Show the people that our Old Nobility is not noble, that its lands are stolen lands – stolen either by force or fraud; show people that the title-deeds are rapine, murder, massacre,

cheating, or Court harlotry. . . let the people clearly understand that our present House of Lords is composed largely of descendants of successful pirates and rogues; do these things and you shatter the Romance that keeps the nation numb and spellbound while privilege picks its pockets.

Our Scots Noble Families (1909), 'A General Indictment', p.x

5 . . . yesterday she was battering at a university door, today she cries for a voice in the laws which govern her, tomorrow she will demand economic equality with man. . . She will demand payment for maternity, recognising that child-rearing is as valuable a service to the state as the carrying of sandwich boards or the hammering of nails. If unmarried, she will demand equal wages and equal advantages for work she can do as skilfully as a man. She will break down senseless conventions. She will invade Parliament via the ballot box. She will teach from the pulpits, sway the world from Downing Street, edit *The Times*, judge women's cases from the bench and plead them from the Bar, become occasionally Provostess of Glasgow, design the newest flying machine, discover the latest bacteria. . .

On the likely effects of women's suffrage. *Forward* (12 Nov 1910)

6 . . . I have become, and increasingly become, uneasy lest we should get political power without our first having, or at least simultaneously having, an adequate economy to administer. What purport would there be in our getting a Scots Parliament in Edinburgh if it has to administer an emigration system, a glorified Poor Law, and a graveyard!

Memories (1952), ch.9, 'A Nation Once Again'

7 Civilisation is the womanisation of brave men.

Quoted in Elspeth King, *The Hidden History of Glasgow's Women: The Thenew Factor* (1993), ch.7

Johnston was a staunch supporter of the women's suffrage movement

Johnstone, Isobel see Dods, Meg

Johnstone, Thomas 19th century
Music-hall entertainer

1 O, wi cheeks as red as roses and een sae bonnie blue,
Dancin and glancin, she pierced me through and through;
She fairly won my fancy and she stole awa my hairt,
Ay, drivin intae Glesca in my soor-mulk cairt.

'The Soor-Mulk Cairt' (c.1890), st.4

Johnstone, William 1897–1981
Painter, art teacher and, from his retiral in 1960, farmer

1 Paint, turpentine, indian ink, watercolours are all waiting for me. As I go to my studio I hear my father saying, sadly, 'Ah, Johnstone, think what a great farmer you might have been!'

Points in Time (1980), concluding words

Jones, John Paul (originally John Paul) 1747–92
Galloway-born American admiral, considered the founder of the US Navy

1 Don't tread on me

Motto on the Revolutionary flag flown on his ship the *Alfred* (1776)

The flag showed a rattlesnake coiled at the foot of a pine tree

2 I have not yet begun to fight.

Responding to a call to surrender during an engagement against the British (23 Sep 1779) off the Yorkshire coast, as his ship, *Le Bonhomme Richard*, began to sink. Quoted in Mrs Reginald De Koven, *Life and Letters of John Paul Jones* (1914), Vol.1, p.455

K

Kames, Lord (Henry Home) 1696–1782
Judge and philosopher

I have often amused myself with a fanciful
resemblance of law to the river Nile. When we
enter upon the municipal law of any country
in its present state, we resemble a traveller
who, crossing the Delta, loses his way among
the numberless branches of the Egyptian river.
But when we begin at the source and follow
the current of law, it is in that course not
less easy than agreeable, and all its relations
and dependencies are traced with no greater
difficulty than are the many streams into which
that magnificent river is divided before it is
lost in the sea.

Historical Law Tracts (1757), preface

Self-conceit is none of the smallest blessings
from heaven.

Introduction to the Art of Thinking (1761)

> David Hume was reported by James Boswell
> to have said, 'When one says of another man
> that he is the most arrogant man in the world,
> it is only to say that he is very arrogant; but
> when one says it of Lord Kames, it is an
> absolute truth.' Quoted in Boswell's *Private
> Papers* (ed. G Scott & F A Pottle, 1928–34),
> Vol.15, p.12

In the first passion, women have commonly
an affection for the lover; afterwards they love
for the pleasure of loving.

Introduction to the Art of Thinking (1761)

> 'A period of time spent with Lord Kames's
> works', David Daiches comments in *The
> Paradox of Scottish Culture* (1964), Lecture 2,
> 'produces a curious effect of having lived in
> a world of cotton wool.'

A fine woman seen naked once in her life is
made a desired object by novelty. But let her go
naked for a month, how much more charming
will she appear when dressed with propriety
and elegance!

Sketches of the History of Man (1774; revised
1813 edition), Vol.1, p.258

Genuine manners never were represented more
to the life by a Tacitus nor a Shakespeare. Such
painting is above the reach of pure invention:
it must be the work of knowledge and feeling.

> Defending James Macpherson's 'translations' of
> the ancient Gaelic poetry of Ossian, *Sketches of
> the History of Man* (1774; revised 1813 edition),
> Vol.1, p.361

6 The promiscuous use of women would unqualify
them in a great measure to procreate. The
carnal appetite in man resembles his appetite
for food: each of them demands gratification,
after short intervals. . . women who indulge
that appetite to excess, seldom have children;
and if all women were common, all women
would in effect be common prostitutes.

> *Sketches of the History of Man* (1774; revised
> 1813 edition), Vol.1, p.414

7 It is deplorable, that in English public schools
patriotism makes no branch of education:
young men, on the contrary, are trained up
to selfishness. *Keep what you get, and get what
you can*, is a lesson that boys learn early at
Westminster, Winchester, and Eton.

> *Sketches of the History of Man* (1774; revised
> 1813 edition), Vol.2, p.147

8 By no means, my lord, you must walk first that
I may see your tail!

> Said to his fellow judge, Lord Monboddo, who
> had stepped aside to allow Kames to precede
> him. Quoted in John Kay, *Original Portraits* (1877
> edition), Vol.1, p.15

> > Monboddo believed that humans were born
> > with tails and that there was a conspiracy
> > of midwives to remove them from new-born
> > infants. Although ridiculed at the time, his
> > views on the similarities between humans and
> > orang-outangs seem more sensible now. Cf.
> > Lord Hailes 2

9 That's checkmate to you, Matthew!

> Said in 1780 to a defendant, Matthew Hay,
> who was on trial for murder at the court in
> Ayr, when the jury returned a 'guilty' verdict.
> Quoted in Lord Cockburn, *Memorials of His
> Time* (1856), ch.2

> > The previous spring, Lord Kames had been
> > a guest of Hay's, and played a game of chess
> > with him which they had not had time to
> > conclude

10 The mind of man is a rich soil, productive
equally of lovely flowers and noisome weeds.
Good passions and impressions are flowers
which ought carefully to be cultivated: bad
passions and impressions are weeds which ought
to be discouraged at least, if they cannot be
totally rooted out. Such moral culture is no
slight art: it requires a complete knowledge of
the human heart, of all its mazes, and of all
its biasses.

> *Loose Hints upon Education, chiefly concerning the
> Culture of the Heart* (1782 edition), Introduction

11 A man says what he knows; a woman what is agreeable: knowledge is necessary to the former; taste is sufficient to the latter.

> *Loose Hints upon Education, chiefly concerning the Culture of the Heart* (1782 edition), section 6

12 Women, destined by nature to be obedient, ought to be disciplined early to bear wrongs without murmuring. This is a hard lesson; and yet it is necessary even for their own sake: sullenness or peevishness may alienate the husband; but tend not to soothe his roughness, nor to moderate his impetuosity.

> *Loose Hints upon Education, chiefly concerning the Culture of the Heart* (1782 edition), section 8

13 A man indeed bears rule over his wife's person and conduct: his will is law. Providence, however, has provided her with means to bear rule over his will. He governs by law, she by persuasion. Nor can her influence ever fail, if supported by sweetness of temper and zeal to make him happy.

> *Loose Hints upon Education, chiefly concerning the Culture of the Heart* (1782 edition), section 8. Cf. Thomas Carlyle 3

14 . . . a woman of sense prudently educated, makes a delicious companion to a man of parts and knowledge.

> *Loose Hints upon Education, chiefly concerning the Culture of the Heart* (1782 edition), section 9

15 A boy who is flogged into grammar-rules, makes a shift to apply them; but he applies them by rote, like a parrot. Boys, for a knowledge they acquire of any language, are not indebted to dry rules, but to practice and observation.

> *Loose Hints upon Education, chiefly concerning the Culture of the Heart* (1782 edition), section 9. Cf. Walter Scott 99

16 Fare ye a' weel, ye bitches!

> Said in 1782 to the other judges in the Court of Session, as he took his leave of them for the last time. He died eight days later. Quoted in John Kay, *Original Portraits* (1877 edition), Vol.1, p.15
>
> > 'Bitch' was one of Kames's favourite words used to excess in all and any circumstances. James Boswell once cited Lord Kames as an example of the Scottish advancement in literature to a sceptical Dr Johnson: ' "But, Sir, we have Lord Kames." JOHNSON. "You *have* Lord Kames. Keep him; ha, ha, ha! We don't envy you him." ' See Boswell, *Life of Samuel Johnson* (1791), Spring 1768

17 Ye bitch, would ye have me stay with my tongue in my cheek till death comes to fetch me!

> Said four days before his death on 27 December 1782, in reply to someone expressing surprise that he was dictating to an amanuensis when so unwell. Quoted in John Kay, *Original Portraits* (1877 edition), Vol.1, p.15

Kay, Billy 1951–
Writer and broadcaster

1 Dundee is the great untapped source in Scotland, it's got a unique sub-culture which hasn't been delved into. . . it's a cultural gold mine.

> Interview in *Cencrastus* No.20 (Spring 1985)

2 Educationalists often refer to the Inarticulate Scot, as if it were a hereditary disease, instead of the effect of shackling people with one language, when they are much more articulate in another.

> *Scots: The Mither Tongue* (1986), ch.1, 'The Mither Tongue?'

3 . . . one nation's language is another's corrupt dialect if a political border happens to be drawn in the wrong place.

> *Scots: The Mither Tongue* (1986), ch.9, 'Wha's Like Us?'

Kay, Jackie 1961–
Poet and playwright

1 Whit is an Afro-Scot anyway?
mibbe she can dance a reel and a salsa
remember Fannie Lou Hamer and Robert Burns. . .

> 'Kail and Callalou', in *Original Prints II: New Writing from Scottish Women* (1987)

2 . . . Scottish people will either refuse to recognise my Scottish accent, or my Scottishness, or they'll say, 'Are you American?' And Black people will just hear my accent or think it really funny and say they've never met such a person before. And so being Black and Scottish is always treated as a kind of anomaly, which I suppose it is. But I think that's changing quite rapidly and it will change more.

> Interview with Rebecca E Wilson, in Gillean Somerville-Arjat and Rebecca E Wilson (eds), *Sleeping with Monsters: Conversations with Scottish and Irish Women Poets* (1990)

3 So slow as torture he discloses bit by bit
my mother's name, my original name
the hospital I was born in, the time I came.

Outside Edinburgh is soaked in sunshine
I talk to myself walking past the castle.
So, so, so, I was a midnight baby after all.

> 'The Adoption Papers – Chapter 2: The Original Birth Certificate', *The Adoption Papers* (1991)

4 Ma ma didn't touch her turkey
Finally she said What did I do
I know what they call you, transvite.
You look a bloody mess you do.
She had a black eye, a navy dress.

> 'Dressing Up', *The Adoption Papers* (1991), st.5

... The tartan tammy
Sitting proudly on top of her pony;
the tartan scarf swinging like a tail.
The nose pressed to the window.
'England's not so beautiful, is it?'
And we haven't even crossed the border.

'Sassenachs', *Two's Company* (1992)

Every note she sang, she bent her voice to
her will.

On the blues singer, Bessie Smith. 'The Same
Note', *Other Lovers* (1993)

Keats, John 1795–1821
English poet

A Scotch Girl stands in terrible awe of the
Elders – poor little Susannas. – They will
scarcely laugh – they are greatly to be pitied
and the Kirk is greatly to be damn'd... These
Kirkmen have done Scotland harm – they have
banished puns and laughing and Kissing...
I would sooner be a wild deer than a Girl
under the dominion of the Kirk.

After making a journey to Scotland in 1818.
Quoted in Willa Muir, *Mrs Grundy in Scotland*
(1936), ch.6, 'Scotswomen'

Keith, George (5th Earl Marischal)
c.1553–1623
Founder of Marischal College, Aberdeen

Thai haif said. Quhat say thai? Lat thame say.

Response to questions about the sources of his
wealth, and whether it was right to establish
a new Protestant college (1593) in buildings
which had formerly belonged to the Franciscan
order of friars

His words became the Keith family motto.
They are still engraved in the stonework of
Marischal College

Kelman, James 1946–
Novelist

Not Not While the Giro

Title of short-story collection (1983)

Honestly, there's nothing else apart from that.
To obliterate the narrator, get rid of the artist,
so all that's left is the story.

Interview with Duncan McLean (July 1985), in
Edinburgh Review No.71 (1985)

Greyhound for Breakfast

Title of short-story collection (1987)

The lectures in philosophy were to be attended
at all costs... it was here you learned to
question at the level most likely to frighten

authority... a university which does not have
a philosophy section has lost the right to be
known as a university.

Letter in *Scotland on Sunday* (Jan 1989), opposing
Strathclyde University's proposal to close its
philosophy department

5 I think the most ordinary person's life is fairly
dramatic; all you've got to do is follow some
people around and look at their existence for
24 hours, and it will be horror. It will just
be horror... For 80% of our society life is
constantly dramatic in a way that the 20%
who control the wealth and power find totally
incomprehensible.

Interview with Kirsty McNeill (20 Feb 1989),
in *Chapman* No.57 (Summer 1989)

6 How Late it Was, How Late

Title of novel (1994)

7 I come from a country called Scotland. I don't
need to *ask* for my independence.

On his lack of respect for the SNP or any political
party 'which requires someone in Whitehall to
pat them on the head.' Quoted in *The Independent*
(8 Oct 1994)

8 When people talk about the so-called expletives
they're not talking about the real issue, you
know. The real issue is to do with suppression
– the standard English literary voice won't
allow it. I mean, the term 'fuck' can be used
in about 17 different ways, one of which is the
cause of its exclusion.

Quoted in *The Independent* (13 Oct 1994)

9 My culture and my language have the right
to exist, and no one has the authority to
dismiss that.

Speech accepting the Booker Prize (11 Oct 1994)
for his novel *How Late it Was, How Late*

One of the Booker judges, Rabbi Julia
Neuberger, opposed the decision to award the
Prize to Kelman, calling it 'a disgrace'. She
said 'Kelman is deeply inaccessible for a lot
of people. I am implacably opposed to the
book. I feel outmanoeuvred.' Quoted in *The
Independent* (13 Oct 1994)

Kelvin, Lord (William Thomson)
1824–1907
Scientist and inventor

1 There is at present in the material world
a universal tendency to the dissipation of
mechanical energy... Within a finite period of
time past the earth must have been, and within
a finite period of time to come, the earth must
again be, unfit for the habitation of man as at
present constituted...

Address to the Royal Society of Edinburgh (1852)

2 A tree contains more mystery of creative power than the sun, from which all its mechanical energy is borrowed. An earth without life, a sun, and countless stars, contain less wonder than that grain of mignonette.

Lecture, 'On the Origin and Transformation of Motive Power' (29 Feb 1856), at the Royal Institution, London

3 Every theory is merely a combination of established truths.

The Athenaeum (4 Oct 1856)

4 One object which we have constantly kept in view is the grand principle of the *Conservation of Energy*. According to modern experimental rules, especially those of Joule, Energy is as real and indestructible as *Matter*.

A Treatise on Natural Philosophy (co-written with Peter Guthrie Tait, 1867), Preface

5 The earth is filled with evidences that it has not been going on for ever in the present state, and that there is a progress of events towards a state infinitely different from the present.

Lecture, 'Geological Time' (27 Feb 1868), to the Geological Society of Glasgow

He was challenging the geological theory of 'uniformitarianism' as established by Hutton. Cf. James Hutton 4

6 Dead matter cannot become living without coming under the influence of matter previously alive... This seems to me as sure a teaching of science as the law of gravitation... I am ready to adopt, as an article of scientific faith, true through all space and through all time, that life proceeds from life, and from nothing but life.

Address as President of the British Association, Edinburgh (2 Aug 1871)

7 I often say that when you can measure what you are speaking about, and express it in numbers, you know something about it; but when you cannot express it in numbers, your knowledge is of a meagre and unsatisfactory kind: it may be the beginning of knowledge, but you have scarcely, in your thoughts, advanced to the stage of *science*.

Lecture to the Institution of Civil Engineers (3 May 1883)

8 I never satisfy myself until I can make a mechanical model of a thing. If I can make a mechanical model I can understand it.

Baltimore Lectures (Oct 1884)

9 The expenditure of chalk is often a saving of brains.

On the importance of physically writing out formulas. Baltimore Lectures (Oct 1884)

10 The object of a university is teaching, not testing... the object of examination is to promote the teaching. The examination should be, in the first place, daily. No professor should meet his class without talking to them. He should talk to them and they to him... Every lecture should be a conference of teachers and students.

Address at University College, Bangor, Wales (2 Feb 1885)

11 Paradoxes have no place in science. Their removal is the substitution of true for false statements and thoughts.

Address to the Royal Institution (1887), quoted in S P Thompson, *The Life of William Thomson, Baron Kelvin of Largs* (1910), Vol.2, ch.25

12 One word characterises the most strenuous of the efforts for the advancement of science that I have made perseveringly during fifty-five years; that word is failure. I know no more of electric and magnetic force, or of the relation between ether, electricity, and ponderable matter, or of chemical affinity, than I knew and tried to teach my students of natural philosophy fifty years ago in my first session as Professor.

Speech at the jubilee of his professorship at Glasgow University (16 Jun 1896)

John Buchan, writing in the *Scottish Review* (26 Dec 1907) commented that this was no mock humility: 'Because he knew so much, he realised how little he knew.'

13 ... to account for the commencement of life on the earth mathematics and dynamics fail us. We must pause, face to face with the mystery and miracle of the creation of living creatures.

'The Age of the Earth as an Abode Fitted for Life', address to the Victoria Institute (2 Jun 1897)

14 Do not be afraid of being free-thinkers. If you think strongly enough you will be forced by science to the belief in God, which is the foundation of all Religion. You will find science not antagonistic, but helpful to Religion.

Giving the vote of thanks for a course of lectures on 'Christian Apologetics' by Rev Professor Henslow, London (May 1903)

15 The mystery of radium, no doubt we shall solve it one day; but the freedom of the will, that is a mystery of another kind.

Said to Sir Edward Fry (1903), quoted in S P Thompson, *The Life of William Thomson, Baron Kelvin of Largs* (1910), Vol.2, ch.25

16 More ships have been lost by bad logic than by bad seamanship.

Quoted in S P Thompson, *The Life of William Thomson, Baron Kelvin of Largs* (1910), Vol.2, ch.25

17 When you call a thing mysterious, all that it means is that you don't understand it.

Quoted in S P Thompson, *The Life of*

William Thomson, Baron Kelvin of Largs (1910), Vol.2, ch.25

Mathematics is the only true metaphysics.

Quoted in S P Thompson, *The Life of William Thomson, Baron Kelvin of Largs* (1910), Vol.2, ch.25

Do not imagine that mathematics is hard and crabbed and repulsive to common sense. It is merely the etherealisation of common sense.

Quoted in S P Thompson, *The Life of William Thomson, Baron Kelvin of Largs* (1910), Vol.2, ch.25

The art of reading mathematics is judicious skipping.

Quoted in Andrew Gray, *Lord Kelvin* (1908), ch.16

The High Church. . . is high only in the sense that game is high – when it is decomposing.

Attrib.

Kennaway, James 1928–68

Novelist

'Whisky. For the gentlemen that like it and for the gentlemen that don't like it, whisky.'

Tunes of Glory (1956), ch.1

I suppose I'm what is called an outsider now. No team spirit, no society in the accepted sense. A lot of amusing acquaintances, a handful of friends who are becoming less not more close, neither English nor Scottish, nor richer nor poorer, uneasy.

But God, how much better it is than being with the 90%; than being a potato. One should count one's blessings, even if it implies one's conceit.

Letter to his mother, never sent (Sep 1961), James and Susan Kennaway, *The Kennaway Papers* (1981), p.72

We look into the dark and there's always someone there. We look into the dark and see the faces of those we have already destroyed, by our own ignorance of ourselves; our immaturity.

We look into the dark, sweet cousin, and no wonder we are afraid.

Household Ghosts (1961), Part 5, 'From the Lab'

Words are so suspect, as we know. Much as I've tried them before the horrid little Scot locked up inside has betrayed my best intentions.

Letter (1 Mar 1964), James and Susan Kennaway, *The Kennaway Papers* (1981), pp.90–1

Had one only kept a locked notebook one would never have sent all those telegrams and letters

over the years: all sincere: none the truth. No wonder we like women. They are our sisters. Writers, I mean, by us.

Diary entry (Mar 1965), James and Susan Kennaway, *The Kennaway Papers* (1981), p.99

6 The wicked games, the weapons we use to destroy others with ourselves: there is no measuring the lengths to which we go in order to avoid the loneliness of death.

The Cost of Living Like This (1969), ch.1

7 Jealousy is wild and filthy, we know; is demanding, obsessive, leading always to thoughts of violence; but Lord, it is a living emotion. We are never more totally alive than when the loved one is lying in someone else's arms.

The Cost of Living Like This (1969), ch.1

8 'Notice the blood. It is also red.'

Silence (1972)

Spoken by Larry Ewing, the white doctor, about the dying black woman, Silence, who saved his life in the midst of racial conflict in an unspecified American city

9 Doctors, like mini-cab drivers, are the other idiots to whom we trust our lives.

James and Susan Kennaway, *The Kennaway Papers* (1981), p.9

Kennedy, A L (Alison) 1965–

Novelist and short-story writer

1 Go into any place where history is stored and listen. Hold your breath. Hear how still it is. Librarians and archivists will keep their visitors quiet, but this particular silence has nothing to do with them. It runs through buzzing computer rooms and waits in busy record offices, it is always there. It is the sound of nothingness. It is the huge, invisible, silent roar of all the people who are too small to record. They disappear and leave the past inhabited only by murderers and prodigies and saints.

'The Role of Notable Silences in Scottish History', *Night Geometry and the Garscadden Trains* (1990). Cf. Nan Shepherd 2

2 We have small lives, easily lost in foreign droughts, or famines; the occasional incendiary incident, or a wall of pale faces, crushed against grillwork, one Saturday afternoon in Spring. This is not enough.

'Night geometry and the Garscadden trains', *Night Geometry and the Garscadden Trains* (1990)

3 All beds have ghosts. They play host to deaths, conceptions, births and indiscretions. They support us in our dreams and in our nightmares and they remember things. Overlooking our

armchairs and our cupboards, we fill our beds with inadvertent haunting.

'The Last', *Night Geometry and the Garscadden Trains* (1990)

4 Thank you, but this really has nothing to do with me.

Accepting the Saltire First Book of the Year award for *Night Geometry and the Garscadden Trains* (1990). Quoted by Gillian Glover in *The Scotsman* (1 Dec 1995)

5 'Being alive is important. Everything *else* is a waste of time.'

Looking for the Possible Dance (1993)

6 Scots down south either turn into Rob Roy McStrathspeyandreel or simply become Glaswegian – no one will understand you, if you don't.

'Christine', *Now That You're Back* (1994)

7 Guilt is of course not an emotion in the Celtic countries, it is simply a way of life – a kind of gleefully painful social anaesthetic.

So I am Glad (1995)

Kennedy, Charles 1959–
Liberal Democrat politician, MP for Skye, Ross and Cromarty (1983–)

1 Voting Tory is like being in trouble with the police. You'd rather the neighbours didn't know.

Speaking at the 1994 Liberal Democrat Conference, on the unreliability of opinion polls. Quoted in *The Independent* (21 Sep 1994)

Kennedy, Helena 1950–
Barrister, broadcaster and writer

1 At every point in my Catholic girlhood the Virgin Mary was presented to us as our role model. Men were simply victims of their own appetites, hardly capable of free will when it came to sex or violence, and it was up to us to act as the restraining influence. After all, woman was responsible for the original sin. It was only later I came to the conclusion that Eve had been framed.

Eve Was Framed: Women and British Justice (1992), ch.1. Cf. Anna Buchan 1

2 Transportation from Paradise is one thing, but a sentence of eternal damnation when the conviction had to be based on the uncorroborated testimony of a co-accused must surely constitute a breach of international standards on human rights. Poor old Eve. I wonder if she would have done any better with a good defence lawyer.

Eve Was Framed: Women and British Justice (1992), ch.1

Kennedy, Ludovic 1919–
Writer and broadcaster

1 Although she has the reputation of being privately charming and considerate. . . I have always found her public persona almost totally repulsive – pretentious, arrogant, raucous, patronising, humourless, vain.

On Margaret Thatcher. *In Bed with an Elephant* (1995), ch.19

In a footnote, he writes, 'To which I would add, after having seen the three television programmes on her premiership mounted by the BBC after her fall from power, histrionic, self-pitying and partly deranged.'

2 During her time in office Mrs Thatcher was always banging on about 'our heritage' and the importance of history, largely I fancy because she lacked any sense of them herself. . .

In Bed with an Elephant (1995), ch.19

This chapter is titled 'The Sermon on the Mound', referring to Prime Minister Thatcher's controversial address (May 1988) to the General Assembly of the Church of Scotland, which meets annually in its hall on the Mound, Edinburgh

Keppel, Lady Caroline 18th century
Songwriter

1 What's this dull town to me?
Robin's not near.
What was't I wished to see?
What wished to hear?
Where's all the joy and mirth
Made this town heav'n on earth?
Oh, they're all fled with thee,
Robin Adair.

'Robin Adair', st.1

The song was set to an old Irish melody, 'Eileen Aroon', which was popularised in Scotland in the early 18th century by a blind Irish harper called Hempson. Lady Keppel was in fact English, the daughter of the 2nd Earl of Albermarle: she fell in love with and married an Irish surgeon, Robin Adair; but the song is generally considered Scottish (a Scotticised version was written by Robert D Jamieson) in spite of its pedigree. See Robert Ford, *Song Histories* (1900)

Kerr, Jim see Simple Minds

Kesson, Jessie 1916–94
Novelist and playwright

1 Skene never had the colour of its sound. It lay on the threshold of Deeside, a doormat against which hurrying tourists wiped their feet, their

eyes straining ever forwards towards the greater glories of the Moor of Dinnet and Lochnagar. Skene lay sulking eternally under this slight, its grey face lined and loured with the perpetual shadow of the Cairngorm Mountains.

The White Bird Passes (1958), ch.8

'I don't want to dust and polish... And I don't want to work on a farm. I want to write poetry. Great poetry. As great as Shakespeare.'

The White Bird Passes (1958), ch.10 (Janie to one of the Trustees of the orphanage, when asked what she would like to do on leaving the place)

... it's all just a question of money again. If you're poor you're plain mad. If you're rich they've got an easier name for you. A Nervous Breakdown.

Glitter of Mica (1963). Cf. G S Fraser 1

... though you sang *Scots Wha Hae* and *Highland Laddie*, the paradox remained: the soldier, except in times of war, in moments of high sentimental fervour, in retrospect or in song, was regarded as the lowest form of life. 'Where's my Mam?'... 'She's run off with a Sodger!'

Glitter of Mica (1963)

Edinburgh. Glasgow. Aberdeen. Dundee. How small Scotland sounded, summed up by its four main cities, but what a width of world its little villages stravaiged.

Glitter of Mica (1963)

Woods are my territory.

Interview with Julie Davidson in *The Scotsman* (21 Apr 1980)

I've told so many lies about my age I've made my children illegitimate.

Interview with Julie Davidson in *The Scotsman* (21 Apr 1980)

You should get yourself acquainted with cemeteries... You have no fear of death if you see enough graves.

Interview with William Foster in *The Scotsman* (20 Aug 1983)

... my Scotland, two corners of the North-East, in Morayshire and Aberdeenshire, are small enough to be contained both spiritually and emotionally. I carry their climate intact – within myself.

On why she would never be homesick for Scotland. 'My Scotland', *Scottish Review* No.35 (Aug 1984)

... if God said to me: 'All the drink in the world is finished, Jessie,' I would say: 'A pity about that God. I enjoy a drink a bitty.' But if he said all the fags in the world were finished, I'd be under the first bus.

Interview with Andrew Young in *The Glasgow Herald* (20 Jun 1985)

King, Elspeth 1949–

Museum curator and social historian

1 This book is dedicated to the unnamed and countless Scottish women who perished in the witch-hunts of the sixteenth and seventeenth centuries (a war against women which generated no war memorials) and to those who have been witch-hunted in the centuries since.

Dedication in her book *The Hidden History of Glasgow's Women: The Thenew Factor* (1993)

2 St Thenew, one of the few Scottish-born pre-Reformation female saints, was the mother of St Mungo, patron saint of Glasgow. She is on record as Scotland's first recorded rape victim, battered woman and unmarried mother. In the course of history she has had a name, sex and nationality change; her story is virtually unknown, and she is remembered only in the place-name 'St Enoch'.

Illustrating 'male priorities in the writing of history', which she terms 'the Thenew Factor'. *The Hidden History of Glasgow's Women: The Thenew Factor* (1993), Introduction

3 ... imprisoned witches... were kept awake, day and night, so that they would have no further contact with Satan. Sleep deprivation is now widely recognised as a commonplace tool in the torture kit of oppressive regimes, and it was practised to perfection in seventeenth-century Scotland.

The Hidden History of Glasgow's Women: The Thenew Factor (1993), ch.2

Kirkpatrick, Sir Roger 13th–14th century

Knight and follower of Robert Bruce

1 I'll mak siccar.

Attrib.

When Bruce met his rival claimant to the throne, John 'the Red' Comyn, in Greyfriars Kirk in Dumfries (Feb 1306), they came to blows and Bruce stabbed Comyn. Outside he told the waiting Kirkpatrick what had happened: 'I doubt I have killed him.' 'Do you leave such a matter in doubt?' replied Kirkpatrick. 'I'll mak siccar.' And, entering the kirk, he finished Comyn off. G W S Barrow, in *Robert Bruce and the Community of the Realm of Scotland* (1965), ch.9, notes that there is no historical evidence for this 'famous but wholly fabulous tale'

Kirkwood, David 1872–1955

Labour MP, one of the group of 'Red Clydesiders'

1 John, we'll soon change all this.

To John Wheatley, on their arrival at Westminster in 1922 as members of the newly elected group of radical Labour MPs for the Glasgow area

Before leaving Glasgow, Kirkwood told the crowd that had gathered to see the new MPs off, 'We'll bring the fresh air of Scotland into the House of Commons'. Cf. Joe Corrie 8

Knapp, Jimmy (James) 1940–

Railway workers' union leader

1 The trouble with employers is that they like ballots as long as you lose them.

Quoted in *The Independent* (17 Jun 1989)

Knox, John c.1513–72

Protestant reformer

1 To promote a Woman to beare rule, superioritie, dominion, or empire above any Realme, Nation or Citie, is repugnant to Nature; contumelie to God, a thing most contrarious to his revealed will and approved ordinance; and finallie it is the subversion of good Order, of all equitie and justice. . .

The First Blast of the Trumpet Against the Monstrous Regiment of Women (1558), opening sentence. Cf. George MacLeod 7

This work was intended as the first of three attacks against female rule, specifically against Mary of Guise, Regent of Scotland, her daughter Mary Stewart, and Mary Tudor, Queen of England. Later, Knox would claim to Mary Stewart (Queen of Scots) that, although he stood by everything he wrote, his principal target was Mary Tudor, 'that wicked Jezebel of England'. See John Knox, *History of the Reformation in Scotland* (1586; ed. W C Dickinson, 1949), Vol.2, p.15

2 For who can denie but it repugneth to nature, that the blind shall be appointed to leade and conduct such as do see? That the weake, the sicke, and impotent persons shall norishe and kepe the whole and strong? And finallie, that the foolishe, madde, and phrenetike shal governe the discrete, and give counsel to such as be sober of mind? And such be al women, compared unto men in bearing of authoritie. For their sight in civile regiment is but blindnes; their strength, weaknes; their counsel, foolishnes; and judgment, phrensie, if it be rightly considered.

The First Blast of the Trumpet Against the Monstrous Regiment of Women (1558)

3 Woman in her greatest perfection was made to serve and obey man, not to rule and command him.

The First Blast of the Trumpet Against the Monstrous Regiment of Women (1558)

4 . . . she [was] maid Regent in the year of God 1554; and a croune putt upone hir head, als

seimlye a sight (yf men had eis) as to putt a saddil upon the back of ane unrewly kow.

On Mary of Guise, whom he loathed. *History of the Reformation in Scotland* (1586), Bk 1

5 One Messe. . . was more fearful. . . then gif ten thousand armed enemyes war landed in any pairte of the Realme, of purpose to suppress the hoill religioun.

Preaching (31 Aug 1561) against Mary, Queen of Scots hearing mass. *History of the Reformation in Scotland* (1586), Bk 4

6 Conscience, Madam, requyres knowlege; and I fear that ryght knowlege ye have none.

To Mary, Queen of Scots, at their first meeting (4 Sep 1561). *History of the Reformation in Scotland* (1586), Bk 4

7 If thair be not in hir. . . a proud mynd, a crafty witt, and ane indurat hearte against God and his treuth, my judgment faileth me.

On Mary, Queen of Scots, after their first meeting (4 Sep 1561). *History of the Reformation in Scotland* (1586), Bk 4

8 In presence of hir Counsall sche keapt hir self [very] grave, (for under the dule wead sche could play the hypocryte in full perfectioun); but how soon that ever hir Frenche fillockis, fydlaris, and otheris of that band, gatt the howse allone, thair mycht be sean skipping not verry cumlie for honest wemen.

On Mary's hypocrisy (in widow's weeds) and frivolity. *History of the Reformation in Scotland* (1586), Bk 4. Cf. David Lindsay 10

9 We call hir nott a hoore. . . but sche was brought up in the company of the wyldast hooremongaris (yea, of such as no more regarded incest, then honest men regard the company of their lauchfull wyeffis); in the company of such men (we say) was our Queyn brought up. What sche was and is, her self best knowis, and God (we doubt nott) will farther declair.

On Mary's upbringing in France. *History of the Reformation in Scotland* (1586), Bk 4

10 And of dansing. . . I [do] not utterlie dampne it, provyding that two vices be avoided: the formare, That the principall vocatioun of those that use that exercise be not neglected for the pleasur of dansing; Secoundly, That they daunse not, as the Philisteanis thair fatheris, for the pleasur that thai tack in the displeasur of Goddis people. For yf any of boyth thai do, as thai shall receave the reward of dansaris, and that will be drynk in hell. . .

On dancing (1562). *History of the Reformation in Scotland* (1586), Bk 4

11 . . . a sweatt morsall for the Devillis mouth.

On Annabella Murray, Lady Erskine, a lady at

the court of Mary, Queen of Scots (1563). *History of the Reformation in Scotland* (1586), Bk 4

> Previously, Knox used one of his fávourite epithets to describe Lady Erskine – a 'verray Jesabell' (Bk 3)

Without the preaching place, Madam, I think few have occasioun to be offendit at me; and thair, Madam, I am nott Maister of my self, but man obey Him who comandis me to speik plane, and to flatter no flesche upoun the face of the earth.

> To Mary, Queen of Scots (May/Jun 1563). *History of the Reformation in Scotland* (1586), Bk 4. Cf. 4th Earl of Morton 1

Madam, in Goddis presence I speak: I never delyted in the weaping of any of Goddis creatures; yea, I can skarslie weill abyde the tearis of my awin boyes whome my awin hand correctis, much less can I rejoise in your Majesties weaping. But seing that I have offered unto you no just occasioun to be offended. . . I man sustean (albeit unwillinglie) your Majesties tearis rather than I dar hurte my conscience, or betray my Commounwealth through my silence.

> To Mary, Queen of Scots (May/Jun 1563). *History of the Reformation in Scotland* (1586), Bk 4

14 I am not a man of law that has my tongue to sell for silver or favour of the world.

> Attrib.

15 What I have been to my country, albeit this unthankful age will not know, yet the ages to come will be compelled to bear witness to the truth.

> Said in old age. Quoted in P Hume Brown, *John Knox* (1895), Vol.2, Bk 5, ch.6

L

Lady's Review of Reviews
Feminist magazine, launched in April 1901

1 Scottish women are not behind any more than Scottish men in everything that pertains to forward movements, and we think the time has come for a country which has its own social customs, its own law, and even its own religion, to have its own Ladies' Magazine. We would be sorry to see the time arrive when everything is done from London.

    Editorial in first issue, quoted in Elspeth King, *The Hidden History of Glasgow's Women: The Thenew Factor* (1993), ch.10. The magazine folded in September 1901 after six issues

Laing, R(onald) D(avid) 1927–89
Psychiatrist

1 We are born into a world where alienation awaits us. We are potentially men, but are in an alienated state, and the state is not simply a natural system. Alienation as our present destiny is achieved only by outrageous violence perpetrated by human beings on human beings.

    The Politics of Experience (1967), Introduction

2 Long before a thermonuclear war can come about, we have had to lay waste our own sanity. We begin with the children. It is imperative to catch them in time. . . Children are not yet fools, but we shall turn them into imbeciles like ourselves, with high IQs if possible.

    The Politics of Experience (1967), ch.3, 'The Mystification of Experience'

3 We are effectively destroying ourselves by violence masquerading as love.

    The Politics of Experience (1967), ch.3, 'The Mystification of Experience'

4 Madness need not be all breakdown. It may also be breakthrough. It is potentially liberation and renewal as well as enslavement and existential death.

    The Politics of Experience (1967), ch.6, 'Transcendental Experience'

5 I think Calvinism has done more damage to Scotland than drugs ever did.

    Speaking in Iona Abbey (Oct 1984)

6 Aye, there's enough angst here to keep me busy.

    Said to Jim McMillan at Glasgow airport, on returning to Scotland from London (1984)

Lamb, Charles 1775–1834
English essayist and poet

1 I have been trying all my life to like Scotchmen, and am obliged to desist from the experiment in despair. They cannot like me – and in truth, I never knew one of that nation who attempted to do it. . .

    'Jews, Quakers, Scotchmen, and other Imperfect Sympathies', in *London Magazine* (Aug 1821). Reprinted as 'Imperfect Sympathies', *Essays of Elia* (1823)

2 The tediousness of these people is certainly provoking. I wonder if they ever tire one another!

    On the Scots. 'Jews, Quakers, Scotchmen, and other Imperfect Sympathies', in *London Magazine* (Aug 1821). Reprinted as 'Imperfect Sympathies', *Essays of Elia* (1823)

Lambie, John
Football manager

1 Brilliant. Tell him he's Pele.

    On being informed that one of his Partick Thistle strikers, Colin McGlashan, had suffered a head injury and could not remember who he was. Quoted in *The Independent* (20 Mar 1993)

2 I'm not going to praise them – we were a disgrace in that first half. I can tell you that won't be the team for Saturday.

    After his Partick Thistle team had defeated Albion Rovers 11-1. The score was 2-0 at half-time. Quoted in *The Independent* (14 Aug 1993)

Lamond, Mary 1860–1948
Leading churchwoman in the Church of Scotland

1 The women workers of the Church of Scotland thank the Assembly for recognition of their services. . . I would say they are quite worthy of any encouragement. Perhaps they are also worthy of a greater share in Church counsels than you have yet given them.

    Speech at the General Assembly (1929)

Lamont, Donald 1874–1958
Tiree-born minister and prolific writer of articles and essays

1 Bha na seann lighichean gaolach air a bhith leigeil fala á daoine, ach tha mi an dùil gum

b' fheàrr leam cupan fala a bhith air a leigeil asam seach cuid de na cungaidhean oillteil aca a ghabhail. Ann am baile Dhun-éideann, àrd-bhaile na dotaireachd, so na stuthannan as am biodh na lighichean a' deanamh chungaidhean aon uair: eanchainn nathrach, mionach figheadair, glothagaich is seangain, geir ghobhar is fuil mhuc, losgannan is seilcheagan, salchar each is chalman is pheucagan, daolagan is cnuimheagan, is burraghlas eile de'n t-seòrsa sin.

† The old physicians were fond of bleeding people, but I think I would rather have a cupful of blood taken from me than take some of their horrible medicines. In the city of Edinburgh, capital of medicine, these are the substances from which physicians at one time made their medicines: snake's brain, spider's entrails, frogspawn and ants, goat's suet and pig's blood, frogs and snails, the dung of horses and pigeons and peacocks, beetles and grubs, and other rubbish of that kind.

'Riaghailt na Slàinte' ('The Rule of Health'). In T M Murchison (ed.), *Prose Writings of Donald Lamont* (1960)

2 Ach rud glé neònach, bha na stuthannan sin a' leigheas dhaoine a cheart cho mhaith is a tha na stuthannan a bhios dotairean a' toirt dhuinn an diugh fo ainmean eile. Nan tugadh tu bogsa phileachan do dhuine agus innseadh dha gur e mionach seilcheig a bha annta air a mheasgadh ri blonaig cait, bhiodh cunnart ann gun gabhadh e an galair-buidhe, a thuilleadh air rud air bith a bha ceàrr air cheana, ach nan tugadh tu dha a' cheart bhogsa agus so air a sgrìobhadh air,
Quinia Sulph. . . gr.j
Tinct. Calumbae . . f.zl
Acid. Sulph. Dilut. . . m.x
Syrup Aurant . . f.ziss
Infus. Calumbae . . ad f. zj
theagamh gun deanadh e feum anabarrach dha.

† But a very strange thing, these substances healed quite as well as the substances doctors give us today under other names. If you were to give a box of pills to a person and tell him that they were snail's entrails mixed with cat's fat, he'd be in danger of taking jaundice, in addition to whatever was wrong with him already; but if you gave him the same box with this written on it [Quinia Sulph. etc.], no doubt it would do him no end of good.

'Riaghailt na Slàinte' ('The Rule of Health'). In T M Murchison (ed.), *Prose Writings of Donald Lamont* (1960)

Lamont, Norman 1942–
Conservative politician and Chancellor of the Exchequer (1990–3)

1 I have long ago learnt that the only true things in the newspapers are the advertisements.
On speculative reports that he intended to challenge John Major for the leadership of the Conservative Party. Quoted in *The Independent* (3 Dec 1994)

Lang, Andrew 1844–1912
Journalist, essayist and poet

1 *St Andrews by the Northern Sea,*
A haunted town it is to me!
A little city, worn and grey,
The grey North Ocean girds it round,
And o'er the rocks, and up the bay,
The long sea-rollers surge and sound. . .
'Almae Matres (St Andrews, 1862. Oxford, 1865)'

2 . . . The drifting surge, the wintry year,
The college of the scarlet gown.
St Andrews by the Northern Sea,
That is a haunted town to me!
'Almae Matres (St Andrews, 1862. Oxford, 1865)'

3 So gladly, from the songs of modern speech
Men turn, and see the stars, and feel the free
Shrill wind beyond the close of heavy flowers,
And through the music of the languid hours,
They hear like ocean on a western beach
The surge and thunder of the Odyssey.
'The Odyssey' (1879)

4 A book is a friend whose face is constantly changing.
The Library (1881), ch.1

5 Golf is a thoroughly national game; it is as Scotch as haggis, cockie-leekie, high cheekbones, or rowanberry jam.
'Golf', in *Lost Leaders* (1889). Cf. Frances Balfour 6

6 You can cover a great deal of country in books.
'To the Gentle Reader', st.5

Lang, Ian 1940–
Conservative politician and Secretary of State for Scotland (1990–5)

1 Scotland's greatest days have been since the Union. Our greatest economic growth, our cultural flowering, our art and our heritage come from the last three hundred years.
Speaking in a debate on Scotland's constitutional future in the Usher Hall, Edinburgh (18 Jan 1992)

2 'Karaoke Kinnock' – the man who will sing any song you want him to.
On the Labour leader, Neil Kinnock, in the run-

up to the 1992 general election. Quoted in *The Independent* (24 Mar 1992)

3 Scotland has said no to nationalism. Britain has said no to socialism. That is a double whammy.

On retaining his Galloway and Upper Nithsdale seat against the SNP, and on overall Conservative victory in the 1992 general election. Quoted in *The Scotsman* (10 Apr 92)

4 History is littered with dead opinion polls.

Quoted in *The Independent* (16 Apr 1994)

Lauder, Sir Harry (originally Harry MacLennan) 1870–1950

Comedian and entertainer

1 When I came up to London, well, I thought the men were free,
Because they stood and look'd and laugh'd and wink'd and blink'd at me –
In fact, they went as far as ask me home with them to tea.
Said I, 'No – porridge is the stuff for Mary!'

'Bonnie Hielan' Mary' (1901), st.1

2 'Will ye stop yer tickling, Jock!
Oh, stop yer tickling, Jock!
Dinna mak' me laugh so hearty, or you'll mak' me choke.
Oh! I wish you'd stop yer nonsense – just look at all the folk,
Will ye stop yer tickling – tickle-ickle-ickle-ing – Stop yer tickling, Jock!'

'Stop Yer Tickling, Jock!' (1904), chorus

3 I love a lassie, a bonnie, bonnie lassie,
She's as pure as the lily in the dell.
She's as sweet as the heather
The bonnie bloomin' heather –
Mary, ma Scotch Bluebell.

'I Love a Lassie' or 'Ma Scotch Bluebell' (1905), chorus

4 Every nicht I used to hing my troosers up
On the back o' the bedroom door.
I rue the day – I must have been a jay!
I'll never hing them up any more;
For the wife she used to ramble thro' my pooches
When I was fast asleep aneath the quilt;
In the mornin' when I woke,
I was always stony broke –
That's the reason noo I wear the kilt!

'That's the Reason Noo I Wear a Kilt' (1906), written by Harry Lauder and A B Kendall

5 Just a wee deoch-an-doris,
Just a wee yin, that's a'.
Just a wee deoch-an-doris,
Afore we gang awa'.
There's a wee wifey waitin'

In a wee but-an-ben;
If ye can say 'It's a braw bricht moonlicht nicht',
Ye're a' richt, ye ken.

'Just a Wee Deoch-an-Doris' (1911), written by R F Morrison and popularised by Lauder

6 Roamin' in the gloamin' on the bonnie banks o' Clyde.
Roamin' in the gloamin' wae my lassie by my side.
When the sun has gone to rest,
That's the time that we love best –
O, it's lovely roamin' in the gloamin'!

'Roamin' in the Gloamin'' (1911), chorus

7 Keep right on to the end of the road,
Keep right on to the end.
Tho' the way be long let your heart be strong,
Keep right on round the bend.
Tho' you're tired and weary
Still journey on, till you come to your happy abode,
Where all you love you've been dreaming of
Will be there, at the end of the road.

'The End of the Road' (1924), chorus

8 O! it's nice to get up in the mornin'
When the sun begins to shine,
At four or five or six o'clock in the good old summertime;
When the snow is snowin',
And it's murky overhead,
O! it's nice to get up in the mornin'
But it's nicer to lie in bed.

'It's Nice to Get Up in the Mornin' (but it's Nicer to Lie in Bed)', chorus. Cf. Robert Burns 57, John Hamilton (1761–1814) 1

9 He's a braw, braw Hielan laddie, Private Jock McDade.
There's not anither sodger like him in the Scotch Brigade.
Rear'd among the heather, you can see he's Scottish built
By the wig, wig, wiggle, wiggle-waggle o' the kilt.

'The Waggle o' the Kilt', chorus

10 I stand for nationality and the simple human things which are its roots.

Quoted in H V Morton, *In Search of Scotland* (1929), ch.7, Part 5

11 I don't like this slimming business. It's no natural. . . It's an absurd, nay, a tragic, business when fashion fads interfere with the shape o' the human body. . .
. . . I like a womanly woman. Nane o' your walking-sticks for Harry Lauder!

Ticklin' Talks (1934), 'Gie me the lass that's plump'

12 If folk think I'm mean, they'll no' expect too much.

> Quoted in A D Mackie, *The Scotch Comedians* (1973), ch.3

13 Aye, I'm tellin' ye. . . happiness is one of the few things in this world that doubles every time you share it with someone else.

> Quoted in John Keay and Julia Keay (eds), *Collins Encyclopaedia of Scotland* (1994), p.598

Lauderdale, Duke of (John Maitland) 1616–82

Statesman, sometimes known as 'King of Scotland'

1 It were better that the west bore nothing but windle-straws and sandy-laverocks than that it should bear rebels to the King.

> Attrib. Quoted in Walter Scott, *Tales of a Grandfather*, 2nd Series (1829), ch.51
>
> Said in January 1678, when it was pointed out to him that his policy of oppressing the Covenanting south-west would totally disrupt the agricultural cycle there

2 Let Mitchell glorify God in the Grassmarket.

> Attrib., at the trial of James Mitchell (Jan 1678) for the attempted murder of Archbishop Sharp ten years earlier. Quoted in Walter Scott, *Tales of a Grandfather*, 2nd Series (1829), ch.51
>
> Mitchell, when asked why he had tried to assassinate Sharp, said it was for 'the glory of God', hence Lauderdale's remark

Law, Denis 1940–

Footballer

1 As we came round the corner from the eighteenth green a crowd of members were at the clubhouse window cheering and waiting to tell me that England had won the World Cup. It was the blackest day of my life.

> On England's victory in the World Cup final (1966). Quoted in P Ball & P Shaw, *The Book of Football Quotations* (1984)

2 I've always been two different people on the park and off it. It's like looking at a stranger and I can hardly bear to watch.

> As told to Hugh McIlvanney. Quoted in Richard Holt, 'The King Over the Border: Denis Law and Scottish Football', in Grant Jarvie and Graham Walker (eds), *Scottish Sport in the Making of a Nation* (1994)

Lawrence, D(avid) H(erbert) 1885–1930

English novelist and poet

1 So this is your Scotland. It is rather nice, but dampish and Northern and one shrinks a trifle inside one's skin. For these countries one should be an amphibian.

> Letter to Dorothy Brett (14 Aug 1928)

Leacock, Stephen 1869–1944

Canadian humorist

1 . . . there is a real and typical Scottish humour that turns upon the Scottish natural character and outlook upon life. If one had to name it, it could be called Grim Humour.

> *Humour* (1935), ch.8

2 . . . the Scotchman. . . would as soon tell a funny story in a churchyard as in a bar-room, beside a sick-bed as beside a side-board. There is no irreverence involved.

> *Humour* (1935), ch.8

3 It is a peculiar element in Scottish humour, as appreciated by Scotchmen, that the harder it is to see, the better it is esteemed. If it is obvious, it is of less account. This rests on the intellectuality of the Scotch; having little else to cultivate, they cultivated the intellect. The export of brains came to be their chief item of commerce.

> *Humour* (1935), ch.8

Leighton, Robert 1611–84

Bishop of Dunblane and (from 1670) Archbishop of Glasgow, religious moderate

1 . . . scaling heaven with ladders fetched out of hell.

> His view of religious persecution. Quoted in N M Cameron, D F Wright et al., *Dictionary of Scottish Church History and Theology* (1993)

Lennox, Annie 1954–

Pop singer and songwriter

1 Love is a Stranger

> Title of Eurythmics song (1982), on *Sweet Dreams (Are Made of This)* (1983)

2 Sweet Dreams (Are Made of This)

> Title of Eurythmics song and album (1983)

3 Here Comes the Rain Again

> Title of Eurythmics song, on *Touch* (1983)

4 Sisters Are Doin' It For Themselves

> Title of Eurythmics song, on *Be Yourself Tonight* (1985)

5 Song writing is like psychic wrestling.

> Quoted in Lucy O'Brien, *Annie Lennox* (1991), ch.6

Leonard, Tom 1944–

Poet

1 That supposed insult 'the language of the gutter'
puts forward a revealing metaphor for society.
The working-class rubbish, with all its bad
pronunciation and the dreadful swear words,
is only really fit for draining away out of sight;
the really great artists though will recycle even
this, to provide some 'comic relief' to offset
the noble emotions up top.

'The Proof of the Mince Pie', in *Scottish
International* (1973). Reprinted in *Intimate Voices:
Selected Work 1965–83* (1984)

2 There are basically two ways of speaking in
Britain: one which lets the listener know that
one paid for one's education, the other which
lets the listener know that one didn't. Within
these two categories there are wide variations,
the line between the two is not always clear,
and there are always loads of exceptions to
any rule. But one can say that of the two
categories, the latter – the 'free' education one
– has much the wider variety. It is this very
variety of regional working-class accents which
the 'bought' education has promised to keep its
pupils free from, and to provide them instead
with a mode of pronunciation which ironically
enough is called 'Received'.

'The Locust Tree in Flower, and why it
had Difficulty Flowering in Britain', in *Poetry
Information 16* (Winter 1976–7). Reprinted in
Intimate Voices: Selected Work 1965–83 (1984)

Leslie, Bishop John 1527–96

Clergyman and historian

1 . . . ther wes ane Italiane with the King, quha
wes maid Abbot of Tungland, and wes of
curious ingyne. . . he causet mak ane pair of
wingis of fedderis, quhilks beand fessinit apoun
him, he flew off the castell wall of Striveling,
bot schortlie he fell to the ground and brak his
thee bane; bot the wyt thairof he asscryvit to
that thair wes sum hen fedderis in the wingis,
quhilk yarnit and covet the mydding and not
the skyis.

Historie of Scotland (completed 1571, published
1830), p.76

This early attempt at flight took place at
Stirling in the reign of James IV, c.1510

Leslie, John
see **Rothes, 7th Earl and 1st Duke of**

Leyden, John 1775–1811

Poet and traveller

1 As you pass through Jura's sound,
Bend your course by Scarba's shore,

Shun, O shun, the gulf profound,
Where Corrivrekin's surges roar!

'The Mermaid', st.11

Liddell, Eric Henry 1902–45

Athlete and missionary

1 I'm not running.

Said prior to the 1924 Olympic Games, Paris,
on learning that the heats for the 100 metres
event were to be held on a Sunday. Quoted
in D P Thomson, *Eric H Liddell: Athlete and
Missionary* (1971), ch.7

He would not compromise his religious
principles by running on a Sunday. Instead
he contested the 200 and 400 metres events,
winning bronze and gold medals respectively

2 The secret of my success over the 400 metres
is that I run the first 200 metres as hard as
I can. Then, for the second 200 metres, with
God's help, I run faster.

After winning the Olympic gold medal in a new
world record time. Quoted in D P Thomson,
Eric H Liddell: Athlete and Missionary (1971), ch.9

Lindsay, Lady Anne (married name
Lady Anne Barnard) 1750–1826

Songwriter

1 When the sheep are in the fauld, and the kye
a' at hame,
When a' the weary warld to sleep are gane,
The waes o' my heart fa' in showers frae my e'e,
While my gudeman lies sound by me.

'Auld Robin Gray' (c.1771), st.1

2 I gang like a ghaist, and I carena to spin;
I daurna think o' Jamie, for that wad be a sin.
But I'll do my best a gude wife to be,
For auld Robin Gray, he is kind to me!

'Auld Robin Gray' (c.1771), st.9

Lindsay or Lyndsay (of the Mount),
Sir David c.1486–1555

Poet and dramatist

1 Quhen thow wes young, I bure thee in
myne arme
Full tenderlie, tyll thow begouth to gang,
And in thy bed oft happit thee full warme,
With lute in hand, syne, sweitlie to thee sang. . .

The Dreme of Schir David Lyndsay (1528),
'Epistil', st.2

He was tutor or 'usher' to James V but
temporarily lost favour, as the young King
fell under the control of Archibald Douglas,
6th Earl of Angus, the estranged husband

of James's mother, Margaret Tudor. Here,
Lindsay addresses the King directly, invoking
the closeness of their former relationship

2 And thus, as we wer talking to and fro,
We saw a boustius berne cum ouir the bent,
But hors, on fute, als fast as he mycht go,
Quhose rayment wes all raggit, revin and rent,
With visage leyne, as he had fastit Lent:
And forwart fast his wayis he did advance,
With ane rycht malancolious countynance.

The Dreme of Schir David Lyndsay (1528),
'The Complaynt of the Commoun Weill of
Scotland', st.1

3 Auld Wille Dile, wer he on lyve,
My lyfe full weill he could discryve:
Quhow, as ane chapman beris his pak,
I bure thy Grace upon my bak,
And sumtyme, strydlingis on my nek,
Dansand with mony bend and bek.
The first sillabis that thow did mute
Was 'pa Da Lyn': upon the lute
Than playt I twenty spryngis, perqueir,
Quhilk wes gret piete for to heir.

The Complaynt of Schir David Lyndsay (1529–30),
ll.85–94

Addressing King James V, as in *The Dreme*

4 Als James the Secunde, roye of gret renoun,
Beand in his superexcelland glore,
Throuch reakles schuttyng of ane gret cannoun
The dolent deith, allace, did hym devore...

*The Testament and Complaynt of Our Soverane
Lordis Papyngo* (1538), ll.437–40

James II was killed at the siege of Roxburgh
in 1460 by an exploding cannon

5 At morne, ane king with sceptour, sweird,
and croun;
Att evin, ane dede deformit carioun.

On James III, murdered after the Battle of
Sauchieburn (1488). *The Testament and Complaynt
of Our Soverane Lordis Papyngo* (1538), ll.484–5.
Cf. Sir Richard Holland 1

6 Quho that Antique Stories reidis
Considder may the famous deidis
Of our Nobill Progenitouris,
Quhilk suld to us be richt mirrouris...

*The Historie of Ane Nobil and Wailyeand Squyer,
William Meldrum, Umquhyle Laird of Cleische
and Bynnis* (c.1550–3), ll.1–4

7 With that, this lustie young Squyar
Saw this Ladie so plesantlie
Cum to his Chalmer quyetlie,
In Kyrtill of fyne Damais broun,
Hir goldin traissis hingand doun.
Hir Pappis wer hard, round and quhyte,
Quhome to behald wes greit delyte.
Lyke the quhyte lyllie wes hir lyre;
Hir hair was like the reid gold wyre;

Hir schankis quhyte withouttin hois,
Quhairat the Squyer did rejois.
And said than, now vailye quod vailye,
Upon the Ladie thow mak ane sailye.

*The Historie of Ane Nobil and Wailyeand Squyer,
William Meldrum...* (c.1550–3), ll.940–52

8 Of warldlie Ioy it is weill kend
That sorrow bene the fatall end...

*The Historie of Ane Nobil and Wailyeand Squyer,
William Meldrum...* (c.1550–3), ll.1183–4

9 And, quhen he lay upon the ground,
They gaif him monie cruell wound,
That men on far micht heir the knokkis,
Like boucheouris hakkand on thair stokkis.

*The Historie of Ane Nobil and Wailyeand Squyer,
William Meldrum...* (c.1550–3), ll.1357–60

10 Duill weidis I think hypocrisie & scorne,
With huidis heklit doun ouirthort thair ene.
With men of armes my bodie salbe borne;
Into that band see that no blak be sene.
My luferay salbe reid, blew, and grene;
The reid for Mars, the grene for freshe Venus,
The blew for lufe of God Mercurius.

*The Historie of Ane Nobil and Wailyeand Squyer,
William Meldrum...* (c.1550–3), 'Testament',
ll.127–33. Cf. John Knox 8

11 FLATTERIE: Quhat buik is that, harlot, into
thy hand?
Out, walloway, this is the New Testament,
In Englisch toung, and prentit in England!
Herisie, herisie! Fire, fire incontinent!

VERITIE: Forsuith, my freind, ye have ane wrang
judgement,
For in this buik thair is na heresie,
Bot our Christs word, baith dulce and redolent,
Ane springing well of sinceir veritie.

Ane Satyre of the Thrie Estaitis (c.1552), Part 1,
ll.1152–9

12 DILIGENCE: Swyith, begger bogill, haist the away!
Thow art over pert to spill our play.
PAUPER: I wil not gif for al your play worth an
sowis fart,
For thair is richt litill play at my hungrie hart.

Ane Satyre of the Thrie Estaitis (c.1552), Part 1,
ll.1962–5

13 REX HUMANITAS: Quhat is the caus the Common-
weil is crukit?
JOHNE THE COMMON-WEILL: Becaus the
Common-weil hes bene overlukit.
REX: Quhat gars the luke sa with ane dreirie hart?
JOHNE: Becaus the Thrie Estaits gangs all
backwart.

Ane Satyre of the Thrie Estaitis (c.1552), Part 2,
ll.2446–9

The 'Thrie Estaitis' of Scotland – Merchand,
Spiritualitie and Temporalitie – are shown in

the play to be corrupt and badly in need of reform, hence they 'gangs all backwart'

14 JOHNE THE COMMON-WEILL: Thou feinyeit Flattrie, the Feind fart in thy face: Quhen ye was guyder of the Court we gat litill grace!

Ane Satyre of the Thrie Estaitis (c.1552), Part 2, ll.2466–7. Cf. James VI and I 10

15 JOHNE: Sic pykand peggrall theifis ar hangit, Bot he that all the warld hes wrangit, Ane cruell tyrane, ane strang transgressour, Ane common publick plain oppressour, By buds may he obteine favours. . .

Ane Satyre of the Thrie Estaitis (c.1552), Part 2, ll.2662–6

buds: bribes

16 GUDE COUNSALL: Schir, red ye never the New Testament? SPIRITUALITIE: Na, sir, be him that our Lord Jesus sauld, I red never the New Testament nor Auld, Nor ever thinks to do, sir, be the Rude: I heir freiris say that reiding dois na gude.

Ane Satyre of the Thrie Estaitis (c.1552), Part 2, ll.2932–6

17 PERSOUN: Quhair thou sayis pride is deidlie sin, I say pryde is bot honestie, And covetice of warldlie win Is bot wisdome, I say for me. Ire, hardines and gluttonie Is nathing ellis but lyfis fude; The naturall sin of lecherie Is bot trew luife: all thir ar gude.

Ane Satyre of the Thrie Estaitis (c.1552), Part 2, ll.3564–71

Lindsay uses the Parson to show the parlous state into which the Church has fallen

Lindsay, (John) Maurice 1918–

Poet, writer and editor

1 The hurlygush and hallyoch o the watter skinklan i the moveless simmer sun harles aff the scaurie mountain wi a yatter that thru ten-thoosan centuries has run.

'Hurlygush', *Hurlygush* (1948), st.1

2 Scotland's a sense of change, an endless becoming for which there was never a kind of wholeness or ultimate category. Scotland's an attitude of mind.

'Speaking of Scotland', *One Later Day* (1964), st.4. Cf. Cliff Hanley 4, Brian McCabe 3

3 Children are taught this leader or that king built castles and scored victories; his battle scars, honour and guilt inextricably mixed.

Who laid the stones, put death into his wars?

'Responsibilities', *Comings and Goings* (1971), st.4

4 The party's almost over. Though at times a trifle odd, I've thoroughly enjoyed it. Thank you for having me, God.

'To Catch the Last Post', *Collected Poems 1940–90* (1990)

Lindsay or Lindesay (of Pitscottie), Robert c.1532–80

Historian

1 . . . sa lang as the king is young greit men ringis at thair awin pleasouris and libertie oppressand all men as thay will but doubt be punischit thaireftir.

On the minority of James II (1437). *The Historie and Cronicles of Scotland* (written 1570s; 1899 edition), Bk 1, ch.1

2 . . . yit he [the Earl of Douglas] inquyreit at the said Schir Patrick gif he had dynit quha ansuerit he had nocht, than the erle said 'thair is na talk to be had betuix ane fou man and ane fastand. Thairfoir ye sall dyne, and we sall talk together at lenth.'

The Historie and Cronicles of Scotland (written 1570s; 1899 edition), Bk 1, ch.20. Cf. Walter Scott 84

This refers to an incident in 1449. The Earl of Douglas had imprisoned a servant of the King, the Tutor of Bombie, who was nephew to Sir Patrick Gray. Gray came to Douglas to demand his release, but 'quhan thay war at the denner crakand of mirrie matteris the erle gart quyetlie tak out the Tutour of Bombie out of presoun and have him to the greine and thair strak of his heid and tuik the samyn away fra him. . .'

3 . . . this scheip was of so greit statur and tuik so mekill timber that scho waistit all the wodis in Fyfe except Falkland wode, [for]by all the tymmer that was gottin out of Noraway.

On the building of James IV's flagship the *Great Michael* in 1512. *The Historie and Cronicles of Scotland* (written 1570s; 1899 edition), Bk 3, ch.13

4 This ambassadour of the paipis seand this great bancat and treumph being maid in ane wildernes, quhair thair was not toune neir be 20 myle, thocht it ane great mervell that sic ane thing sould be in Scotland considerand that it was bot the erse of the warld. . .

On the papal envoy's surprise at the huge temporary timber palace erected by the Earl of Atholl near Pitlochry for James V's hunting trip (1531). *The Historie and Cronicles of Scotland* (written 1570s; 1899 edition), Bk 4, ch.21

Lingard, Joan 1932–
Novelist and children's writer

1 Isobel smiled. . . Poor mother, she thought, she's had five children but she's as barren as Rannoch Moor. What did she know of life with her church committees and her Madeira cakes and her husband who was more Calvinistic than Calvin himself?
The Prevailing Wind (1964), ch.4

2 'She is a nice lady even though she thinks I am not nice. A nice Edinburgh lady who is never late for her husband's tea.'
An Edinburgh lady who is loyal to her husband, who loves her children. . . who works diligently sweeping the dirt from the corners of her house, whose tear-washed eyes betray a self-induced martyrdom of sadness; a wife and mother who has known what it is to be peacefully content with a fire at her feet and children sleeping in upstairs rooms but who has never known what it is to be wildly, deliriously happy and want to shout it out of every window up to the stars in the sky.
The Prevailing Wind (1964), ch.8

Linklater, Eric 1899–1974
Novelist

1 'There won't be any revolution in America,' said Isadore. Nitkin agreed. 'The people are all too clean. They spend all their time changing their shirts and washing themselves. You can't feel fierce and revolutionary in a bathroom.'
Juan in America (1931), Bk 5, Part 3

2 In red leather volumes in the Memorial on the Castle Rock were the myriad names of the Scottish dead, and here in the lively squalor of a lousy tavern were their comrades who had survived, and whose names were nowhere written – unless perhaps on the wall of a jakes. . . Kings had fallen and nations perished, armies had withered and cities been ruined for this and this alone: that poor men in stinking pubs might have great wealth of memory.
Magnus Merriman (1934), ch.5

3 Patriotism and the waving of flags was an empty pride, but love of one's own country, of the little acres of one's birth, was the navel-string of life.
Magnus Merriman (1934), ch.34

4 Light is the dominating factor in its scenery. . . Except Hoy, there are no hills high enough to intercept it. There are no trees to diminish it. There is, on the entire circumference, the sea to reflect it.
'Orkney', in George Scott-Moncrieff (ed.), *Scottish Country* (1935)

5 . . . the lovely small town of Stromness, where the people have miniature wharfs instead of gardens, and the children learn to row a boat before they can walk.
'Orkney', in George Scott-Moncrieff (ed.), *Scottish Country* (1935)

6 . . . you may regard life either as the general adventure or the general burden. That much of it is burdensome, no one can deny. . . but if from the beginning you think of life as a burden, you will immediately feel tired, and thereby suffer a disadvantage: you will lack energy that might have procured enjoyment. It is more profitable to see life as an adventure: not as something to be carried, but as something to be broken into.
'The Art of Adventure', Rectorial Address to Aberdeen University (1945)

7 'If there is any creature in the world more miserable than a refugee,' said Simon, 'it is a refugee's horse.'
'There is no liberation for horses,' said Angelo.
'None,' said Simon.
Angelo sighed. 'They have at least been spared that.'
Private Angelo (1946), ch.12

8 'Courage is a common quality in men of little sense,' said Lucrezia. 'I think you over-rate it. A good understanding is much rarer and more important.'
Private Angelo (1946), ch.21

Lithgow, William c.1585–1645
Poet and traveller

1 The pleasant banks of Clyde
Where orchards, castles, towns, and wood
Are planted by his side;
And chiefly Lanerk thou,
Thy country's laureat lamp,
In which this bruised body now
Did first receive the stamp.

In *The Rare Adventures and Painful Peregrinations* (1632)

Lithgow was born in Lanark. His travels took him to Spain where his anti-Catholic views led to his being tortured and permanently maimed by the Inquisition

Little, Janet 1759–1813
Poet and farmworker, known as 'the Scotch Milkmaid'

1 . . . But then a rustic country quean
To write – was e'er the like o't seen?
A milk maid poem-books to print;

Mair fit she wad her dairy tent;
Or labour at her spinning wheel,
An' do her wark baith swift an' weel.
Frae that she may some profit share,
But winna frae her rhyming ware.
Does she, poor silly thing, pretend
The manners of our age to mend?
Mad as we are, we're wise enough
Still to despise sic paultry stuff.

'Given to a Lady Who Asked Me To Write A
Poem', *The Poetical Works of Janet Little the
Scotch Milkmaid* (1792)

Livingstone, David 1813–73
Missionary and explorer

1 No one knows the value of water till he is
deprived of it. . . I have drunk water swarming
with insects, thick with mud and putrid with
Rhinoceros urine and buffaloes' dung, and no
stinted draughts of it either.

Private Journals 1851–3 (ed. I Schapera, 1960),
12 May 1851

2 Aye, they have a great population, viz. 21
millions of the greatest bores that the moon
ever saw.

On America. Letter to his parents (26 Sep 1852)

3 I shall open a way to the interior or perish.

To his brother Charles, prior to his 1854
expedition from West to East Africa via the
Zambesi. Quoted in T Jeal, *Livingstone* (1973),
ch.10. Cf. Mungo Park 2

4 I go back to Africa to try to make an open path
for commerce and Christianity.

Lecture at Cambridge University (4 Dec 1857),
which resulted in the forming of the Universities'
Mission to Central Africa

5 The strangest disease I have seen in this country
seems really to be broken-heartedness, and it
attacks free men who have been captured and
made slaves.

1870. *Last Journals of David Livingstone in Central
Africa* (ed. H Waller, 1874), Vol.2, p.93

6 You have brought me new life.

In response to Henry Stanley's 'Doctor
Livingstone, I presume', on Stanley's reaching
him at Ujiji on Lake Tanganyika (Nov 1871).
Quoted in H M Stanley, *How I Found Livingstone*
(1872), p.416

7 All I can say in my lonliness [sic] is, may
heaven's rich blessing come down on every one
– American, English, Turk – who will help to
heal this open sore of the world.

On the slave trade. *Last Journals of David
Livingstone in Central Africa* (ed. H Waller, 1874),
Vol.2, p.182

These words, with 'solitude' substituted
for 'lonliness', appear on his gravestone in
Westminster Abbey

Loch, James 1780–1855
*Lawyer, commissioner and 'improver' for the
Sutherland estates, and MP for Wick and the
Northern Burghs (1830–55)*

1 . . . they contracted habits and ideas, quite
incompatible with the customs of regular
society, and civilised life, adding greatly to
those defects which characterise persons living
in a loose and unformed state of society.

On the Gaels, whom he found to be the victims
of 'every species of deceit and idleness'. *An
Account of the Improvements. . . on the Estate of
Sutherland* (1820), quoted in Ian Grimble, *The
Trial of Patrick Sellar* (1962), ch.2. Cf. David
Stewart 1

2 . . . that barrier which the prevalence of the
Celtic tongue presents to the improvement
and civilisation of the district, wherever it may
prevail. . . a language in which no book was
ever written.

*An Account of the Improvements. . . on the Estate
of Sutherland* (1820). Quoted in Ian Grimble,
The Trial of Patrick Sellar (1962), ch.2

As Grimble points out, the first publication of
a Gaelic prose work in Scotland had occurred
in 1567. Cf. John Carswell 1

3 In a few years the character of the whole of
this population will be completely changed. . .
The children of those who are removed from
the hills will lose all recollection of the habits
and customs of their fathers.

On the supposed benefits of the Sutherland
clearances. *An Account of the Improvements. . .
on the Estate of Sutherland* (1820), quoted in Ian
Grimble, *The Trial of Patrick Sellar* (1962), ch.2

Lochhead, Liz 1947–
Poet and playwright

1 . . . How does she feel?
Her children grow up with foreign accents,
swearing in fluent Glaswegian. Her face
is sullen. Her coat is drab plaid, hides
but for a hint at the hem, her sari's
gold embroidered gorgeousness. She has
a jewel in her nostril.
The golden hands with the almond nails
that push the pram turn blue
in the city's cold climate.

'Something I'm Not', *Memo for Spring* (1972)

2 I think of those prizes that were ours for
the taking
and wonder when the choices got made

we don't remember making.

'The Choosing', *Memo for Spring* (1972)

3 . . . Linen
washed in public here.
We let out of the bag who we are.

'Laundrette', *Islands* (1978), st.4

4 Wasp waist and cone breast, I see them yet.
I hope, I hope
there's been a change of more than silhouette.

'The Grim Sisters', *The Grimm Sisters* (1981)

5 I will keep fit in leotards.

Go vegetarian. Accept.
Support good causes.
Be frugal, circumspect.
Keep cats. Take tidy fits.
Go to evening classes.
Keep a nest-egg in the bank.
Try Yoga. Cut your losses.
Accept. Admit you're a bit of a crank. . .

'The Furies – II: Spinster', *The Grimm
Sisters* (1981)

6 I'll be a bad lot.
I've a brass neck. There is mayhem in my smile.
No one will guess it's not my style.

'The Furies – III: Bawd', *The Grimm
Sisters* (1981)

7 God
the brickwall you are these days
it doesn't even crack when you smile.
Believe me I spent a lot of time
working with my fingernails at mortar and lime
before I started to bash and
batter my head at it, that brick wall.
Now, even when I stop,
it doesn't stop hurting at all.

'Six Disenchantments', *The Grimm Sisters* (1981)

8 . . . the people's poet
is reading to us from his most recent work.
Natty in tattersall,
boyish and fifty on the bare stage
under the blue light –
if the sidespots have rosecoloured filters, well
that won't wash with him –
listen,
his quick light voice not tripping ever
over his own peppery rhythms, the sibilants
and little silver sparkles of spittle. . .

On Edwin Morgan. 'The People's Poet', *Dreaming
Frankenstein & Collected Poems* (1984)

9 Hammered like a bolt
diagonally through Scotland (my
small dark country) this
train's a
swaying caveful of half-
seas over oil-men (fuck

this fuck that fuck
everything) bound for Aberdeen and
North Sea Crude. . .

'Inter-City', *Dreaming Frankenstein & Collected
Poems* (1984)

10 Is it for the mere satisfaction of seeing
into every room at once, even
the ones as children we were locked out of,
that we reduce
what we most deeply fear might be trivial
to what we can be sure
is perfectly cute?

'The Dollhouse Convention', *Dreaming
Frankenstein & Collected Poems* (1984)

11 She'll crumple all the
tracts and adverts, shred
all the wedding dresses, snap
all the spike-heel icicles
in the cave she will claw out of –
a woman giving birth to herself.

'Mirror's Song', *Dreaming Frankenstein &
Collected Poems* (1984)

12 Oh, we spill the beans and we swill our gin
and discover that we're Sisters Under The Skin.
Oh, I know her inside out –
thanks to the sessions
of truly hellish, unembellished
True Confessions.

'True Confessions' (rap), *True Confessions &
New Cliches* (1985)

13 Women
Rabbit rabbit rabbit women
Tattle and titter
Women prattle
Women waffle and witter

Men Talk. Men Talk.

Women into Girl Talk
About Women's Trouble
Trivia 'n' Small Talk
They yap and they babble

Men Talk. Men Talk.

'Men Talk' (rap), *True Confessions & New
Cliches* (1985)

14 Men
Think First, Speak Later
Men Talk.

'Men Talk' (rap), *True Confessions & New
Cliches* (1985)

15 TARTUFFE: . . . Ah'll thank yi
Afore ye speak tae me tae tak' this hanky
In the name o' a' that's holy and religious –
DORINE: Whit fur?
TARTUFFE: To cover up yir. . . yir. . . whidjies.
It's evil sichts lik' yon, I'm sure it is,

That swall men's thochts wi' impurities.
DORINE: You must be awfy fashed wi'
flesh tae fire
Yir appetites sae quick wi' Base Desire.
As fur masel', Ah'm no that easy steered.
If you were barescud-nakit, aye and geared
Up guid and proaper, staunin' hoat for
houghmagandie
I could lukk and lukk ett you, and no'
get randy.

> *Tartuffe* (1985), Act 3, sc.2

16 DORINE: Because
Ah'm a wummin doesny mean ma fingers urny
itchin' fur a stick,
Or Ah dinny notice hoo yir erse is the right
shape fur a kick!
LOYAL: Because yir a wummin disny mean that
yir above the law.
Git tae vote, eh? Well, ye git tae go tae
jile an a'.

> *Tartuffe* (1985), Act 5, sc.4

17 LA CORBIE: It's a peatbog, it's a daurk forest.
It's a cauldron o' lye, a saltpan or a coal mine.
If you're gey lucky it's a bricht bere meadow
or a park o' kye.
Or mibbe. . . it's a field o' stanes.
It's a tenement or a merchant's ha'.
It's a hure hoose or a humble cot. Princes Street
or Paddy's Merkit.
It's a fistfu' o' fish or a pickle o' oatmeal.
It's a queen's banquet o' roast meats and
junketts.
It depends. It depends. . .

> On Scotland. *Mary Queen of Scots Got Her Head Chopped Off* (1987) Act 1, sc.1

Lockhart, J(ohn) G(ibson) 1794–1854
Critic, novelist and biographer of Walter Scott

1 Whenever Scotland could be considered as
standing separate on any question from the
rest of the empire, he was not only apt,
but eager to embrace the opportunity of
again rehoisting, as it were, the old signal
of national independence. . . He confesses,
however, in his Diary, that he was aware how
much it became him to summon calm reason
to battle imaginative prepossessions on this
score; and I am not aware that they ever led
him into any serious practical error. . . Had
any Anti-English faction, civil or religious,
sprung up in his own time in Scotland,
he would have done more than any living
man could have hoped to do, for putting
it down.

> On Walter Scott. *Memoirs of the Life of Sir Walter Scott, Bart.* (1837–8), ch.84

Lockhart, Sir Robert Hamilton Bruce
see **Bruce Lockhart, Sir Robert Hamilton**

Logan, Jimmy (originally James Short) 1928–
Comedian and entertainer

1 Sausages is the boys.

> Catchphrase. Quoted in A D Mackie, *The Scotch Comedians* (1973), ch.11

2 Smashin', in't it?

> Catchphrase. Quoted in A D Mackie, *The Scotch Comedians* (1973), ch.11

3 The Empire Theatre in Glasgow was well
known as the 'Graveyard of English comics'.
The reason was that many of the English
comedians came up here and would begin their
act with ' 'ello, 'ello, 'ello, how are yer? alright
luv?' And they didn't attempt to make any
rapport with the audience.

> Quoted in Vivien Devlin, *Kings, Queens and People's Palaces: An Oral History of the Scottish Variety Theatre, 1920–1970* (1991), ch.10.
> Cf. Ken Dodd 1

London Evening Standard
English newspaper

1 . . . the subsidy junkies [who wail] like a
trampled bagpipe. . .

> On the Scots (1987). Quoted in Maurice Smith, *Paper Lions: The Scottish Press and National Identity* (1994)

Lorimer, W(illiam) L(aughton)
see **New Testament in Scots**

Lorne, Tommy (pseudonym of Hugh Corcoran) 1890–1935
Comedian

1 In the name o' the wee man!

> Catchphrase (often rendered simply as 'In the name!')

2 I'll get ye, and if I don't get ye, the
coos'll get ye.

> Catchphrase

Lovat, Lord (Simon Fraser) c.1667–1747
Clan chief and Jacobite

1 On his return from the House of Lords to the
Tower, an old woman not very well favoured,
had pressed through the crowd and screamed

in at the window of the coach, 'You'll get that
nasty head of yours chopped off, you ugly old
Scotch dog,' to which he answered, 'I believe
I shall, you ugly old English bitch.'

> Traditional. Quoted in John Hill Burton, *Life
> of Simon Lord Lovat* (1847), ch.9

>> Lord Lovat was found guilty of sedition after
>> the failure of the 'Forty-Five and sentenced
>> to death (by beheading) in the House of Lords
>> (19 Mar 1747)

2 The more mischief the better sport.

> Said at his execution (9 Apr 1747)

>> A huge crowd had assembled in London to
>> watch the execution. Part of a stand collapsed,
>> killing and injuring some of the spectators,
>> causing the ever cynical Lovat to make
>> his remark

3 God save us – why should there be such a
bustle about taking off an old grey head that
cannot get up three steps without two men to
support it.

> At his execution (9 Apr 1747)

4 My dear James, I am going to Heaven, but you
must continue to crawl a little longer in this
evil world.

> On the scaffold, to his clansman James Fraser
> (9 Apr 1747)

>> His final words were Horace's 'Dulce et
>> decorum est pro patria mori' ('It is sweet
>> and noble to die for one's country'), by all
>> accounts delivered with his customary sneer

Lucas, E(dward) V(errall) 1868–1938
English humorist and essayist

1 Oatmeal marks not only the child's breakfast, it
is the favourite food of the Edinburgh reviewers.
Thus do extremes meet.

> *Domesticities* (1900), ch.4

Lyell, Sir Charles 1795–1875
Geologist

1 *No causes whatsoever . . . ever acted, but
those now acting*: and they never acted with
different degrees of energy from that which
they now exert.

> On the theory of 'uniformitarianism' in geological
> process. *Principles of Geology* (1830–3)

>> Lyell's Hutton-influenced theories were hugely
>> influential throughout the 19th century

2 A scientific hypothesis is elegant and exciting
insofar as it contradicts common sense.

> Attrib.

Lyle, Thomas 1792–1859
Poet

1 Let us haste to Kelvin Grove, bonnie lassie, O,
Thro' its mazes let us rove, bonnie lassie, O,
Where the rose in all her pride
Decks the hollow dingle side,
Where the midnight fairies glide, bonnie
lassie, O.

> 'Kelvin Grove', st.1. Cf. Traditional songs 59

Lynch, Benny 1913–46
Boxer

1 I felt I was fighting for Scotland and my
true happiness lies in the fact that I did
not let Scotland down. My countrymen were
looking to me to triumph, and since the
referee raised my hand in token of victory I
have often thought what I would have done
had I failed.

> On winning the World Flyweight boxing title
> (9 Sep 1935)

Lyndsay, Sir David
see Lindsay (of the Mount), Sir David

Lyndsay, John (Johnne Lyndesay)
16th century
Associate of Archbishop James Beaton

1 My Lord, yf ye burne any mo, except ye follow
my counsall, ye will utterlye destroy your selves.
Yf ye will burne thame, lett thame be brunt
in how sellaris [hollow cellars]; for the reik of
Maister Patrik Hammyltoun hes infected as
many as it blew upoun.

> His advice to Beaton on the burning of heretics.
> Quoted in John Knox, *History of the Reformation
> in Scotland* (1586), Bk 1

>> Lyndsay's remarks followed the public
>> execution of Patrick Hamilton at St Andrews
>> (29 Feb 1528). Hamilton was the first martyr
>> of the Scottish Reformation: he was roasted
>> rather than just burned alive at the stake,
>> causing widespread popular revulsion

Lyon, Mrs Agnes (*née* L'Amy)
1762–1840
Songwriter

1 Ye've surely heard o' famous Niel,
The man that played the fiddle weel;
I wat he was a canty chiel,
An' dearly lo'ed the whisky, O!
An' aye sin he wore tartan hose,
He dearly lo'ed the Athole Brose;

An' wae was he, you may suppose,
To bid fareweel to whisky, O.

'Niel Gow's Farewell to Whisky', st.1

Words written to an air by Niel Gow

Lyte, Henry Francis 1793–1847

Hymnwriter

1 Abide with me: fast falls the eventide;
The darkness deepens; Lord, with me abide:
When other helpers fail, and comforts flee,
Help of the helpless, O abide with me.

Hymn, 'Abide with me', st.1

2 Change and decay in all around I see. . .

Hymn, 'Abide with me', st.2

Allan Massie used this phrase as the title of
his first novel (1978)

3 Pleasant are Thy courts above,
In the land of light and love;
Pleasant are Thy courts below,
In this land of sin and woe.

Hymn, 'Pleasant are Thy courts above', st.1

4 Praise, my soul, the King of heaven;
To His feet thy tribute bring;
Ransomed, healed, restored, forgiven,
Who like me His praise should sing?

Hymn, 'Praise my soul', st.1

5 Angels, help us to adore Him;
Ye behold Him face to face;
Sun and moon, bow down before Him;
Dwellers all in time and space.

Hymn, 'Praise, my soul', st.5

M

Mac a' Ghobhainn, Iain
see **Smith, Iain Crichton**

MacAmhlaigh, Domhnall (Donald MacAulay) 1930–
Poet

1 Chan iarr iad orm ach
gal aithreachais peacaidh
nach buin dhomh
's gu faigh mi saorsa
fhuadan nach tuig mi. . .

They ask of me only
to weep repentance for a sin
that does not concern me
and I shall get in return an alien
freedom I don't understand. . .

> 'Féin-fhìreantachd' ('Selfrighteousness'),
> *Seòbhrach ás a' Chlaich* (1967)

2 Choisich thu crotach
le do bhata
sìos ris a' ghàradh;
stad thu 's thog
thu cudthrom do chrom-chinn,
chuir thu do bhois
eadar do shùilean 's a' ghrian.

You walked, feeble,
with your stick,
down by the wall;
you stopped and raised
the weight of your bent head,
you put your hand
between your eyes and the sun.

> 'An t-Sean Bhean' ('Old Woman'), *Seòbhrach ás
> a' Chlaich* (1967)

3 Siud an t-eilean ás an t-sealladh
mar a shiùbhlas am bàta,
mar a chunnaic iomadh bàrd e
eadar liunn is iargan,
's fir eile a bha 'n teanga fo fiacaill,
's deòir a' dalladh –
dùbhradh neo-dhearbht is uinneagan a' fannadh.

There goes the island out of sight
as the boat sails on,
as seen by many a bard
through sorrow and beer
and by others, tongue under tooth,
and tears blinding –
an ill-defined shadow and windows fading.

> 'Comharra Stiuiridh' ('Landmark'), *Seòbhrach ás
> a' Chlaich* (1967)

Mac an t-Saoir, Donnchadh Bàn (Duncan Ban Macintyre) 1724–1812
Poet

1 'S e Deòrsa rinn an eucoir,
'S ro dhiombach tha mi féin deth,
On thug e dhinn am féileadh
'S gach eudach a bhuineadh dhuinn.

† 'Tis George has done the unfair thing,
and I am much incensed at him,
since he deprived us of the kilt
and all our native garments.

> 'Oran do'n Bhriogais' ('Song to the Breeches').
> In A MacLeod (ed.), *Orain Dhonnchaidh Bhàin*
> (*The Songs of Duncan Ban Macintyre*, 1952)

>> The song refers to the Disclothing Act of
>> 1747, which banned the wearing of Highland
>> dress and was not repealed till 1782

2 Nan tigeadh oirnne Tearlach
'S gun éireamaid 'na champa,
Gheibhte breacain charnaid
'S bhiodh aird air na gunnachan.

† If Charles were to descend on us,
and we rose to take the field with him,
red-tinted tartans could be got,
and the guns would be forthcoming.

> 'Oran do'n Bhriogais' ('Song to the Breeches').
> In A MacLeod (ed.), *Orain Dhonnchaidh Bhàin*
> (*The Songs of Duncan Ban Macintyre*, 1952)

3 'N uair bhios cion an stòrais air daoinibh ganna,
Cha leigeadh nighean Deòrsa mo phòca falamh;
Cumaidh i rium òl anns na taighibh-leanna,
'S pàighidh i gach stòpan a nì mi cheannach.

Nì i mar bu mhiann leam a h-uile car dhomh,
Chan innis i breug dhomh no sgeul am
    mearachd;
Cumaidh i mo theaghlach cho math 's bu
    mhath leam,
Ge nach dèan mi saothair no obair shalach.

† While needy men are short of means, George's
    daughter
would not allow my pocket to be empty;
she will provide me with drink in the
    ale-houses,
and pay for every flagon that I purchase.

She serves me at every turn just as I
    would have it;
she tells me no untruth nor erroneous story;
she will support my household as well as I
    could wish,
though I do not toil nor engage in dirty labour.

> 'Oran do'n Mhusg' ('Song to the Musket'). In

A MacLeod (ed.), *Orain Dhonnchaidh Bhàin* (*The Songs of Duncan Ban Macintyre*, 1952)

The poet had left the Highlands and joined the City Guard of Edinburgh. His musket ('George's daughter', after the ancient custom of naming weapons) provides him with everything, in effect becoming his wife

4 Bha mi 'n dé 'san aonach
'S bha smaointean mór air m' aire-sa,
Nach robh 'n luchd-gaoil a b' àbhaist
Bhith siubhal fàsaich mar rium ann;
'S a' bheinn as beag a shaoil mi
Gun dèanadh ise caochladh,
On tha i nis fo chaoraibh
'S ann thug an saoghal car asam.

† Yesterday I was on the moor,
and grave reflections haunted me:
that absent were the well-loved friends
who used to roam the waste with me;
since the mountain, which I little thought
would suffer transformation,
has now become a sheep-run,
the world, indeed, has cheated me.

'Cead Deireannach nam Beann' ('Final Farewell to the Hills'). In A MacLeod (ed), *Orain Dhonnchaidh Bhàin* (*The Songs of Duncan Ban Macintyre*, 1952)

5 An là sin thug iad Cùil-lodair,
Cha robh fhortan siud ach searbh dhuinn;
Choisinn Diùc Uilleam 'san drochuair,
'S gur mór an rosad e d' ar cairdean;
Chaill na cinn-feadhna am fearann
'S an tuath-cheathairn an cuid armachd,
Cha bhi oirnn ach ad is casag
An àite nam breacana dearga.

† That day they fought at Culloden,
bitter to us was the outcome;
Duke William won in the evil hour –
'twas a great misfortune to our friends:
the chieftains lost their estates
and the tenantry their weapons;
we shall wear only hat and long coat
instead of the scarlet tartans.

'Oran Eile air Blàr na h-Eaglaise Brice' ('Another Song of the Battle of Falkirk'). In A MacLeod (ed.), *Orain Dhonnchaidh Bhàin* (*The Songs of Duncan Ban Macintyre*, 1952)

6 Cha robh meas de Chlanna Ghàidheil
On dh'fhalbh Teàrlach uainn air fògradh;
Dh'fhàg e sinn mar uain gun mhàthair,
Gun adhbhar ghàire gun sòlas. . .

† The Highland clans were not respected
since Charles went from us into exile;
he left us like motherless lambs,
without cause of hilarity or comfort. . .

'Oran Eile air Blàr na h-Eaglaise Brice' ('Another Song of the Battle of Falkirk'). In A MacLeod (ed.), *Orain Dhonnchaidh Bhàin* (*The Songs of Duncan Ban Macintyre*, 1952)

7 An t-urram thar gach beinn
Aig Beinn Dòbhrain;
De na chunnaic mi fon ghrèin,
'S i bu bhòidhche leam:
Munadh fada rèidh,
Cuilidh 'm faighte fèidh,
Soilleireachd an t-slèibh
Bha mi sònrachadh. . .

† Respect beyond each ben
for Ben Doran;
of all beneath the sun
the most glorious:
long unbroken moor,
sanctuary of deer,
upland that is clearly
worth talking of. . .

'Moladh Beinn Dòbhrain' ('The Praise of Ben Doran'). In Derick S Thomson (ed.), *Gaelic Poetry in the Eighteenth Century* (1993)

8 'S e Coir' a' Cheathaich nan aighean siùbhlach
An coire rùnach as ùrar fonn;
Gu lurach miadarach min geal sùghmhor
Gach luisean flùar bu chùbhraidh leam;
Gu mollach dùbhghorm torrach lùisreagach
Corrach plùranach dlùthghlan grinn
Caoin ballach dìtheanach cannach mìsleanach
Gleann a' mhìltich as lìonmhor mang.

† The Misty Corrie of hinds aye roving,
the dearest corrie of verdant ground;
where every herb with its flower grew fragrant
on grassy leas rich and smooth all round;
yet shaggy, dark-green, with herbs abundant,
steep-sided, fine, full of lovely flowers,
soft, dappled, blooming, pretty, sweet-grassed,
glen of arrow-grass that's full of fawns.

'Oran Coire a' Cheathaich' ('Song of the Misty Corrie'). In Derick S Thomson (ed.), *Gaelic Poetry in the Eighteenth Century* (1993), st.1

McArthur, Alexander and Long, H Kingsley
Novelists

1 No Mean City
Title of novel (1935) about gang warfare in the Gorbals, Glasgow

2 And Gorbals life goes on its way – just as if nobody could help it.
No Mean City (1935), ch.20, 'Checkmate', final sentence of novel

Macaulay, Thomas Babington (1st Baron Rothley) 1800–59
English historian and essayist

1 In the Gaelic tongue, Glencoe signifies the Glen of Weeping: and in truth that pass is the

most dreary and melancholy of all the Scottish
passes, the very Valley of the Shadow of Death.

History of England from the Accession of James II
(1849–61), Vol.5, ch.18

McCabe, Brian 1951–
Novelist and poet

1 I am a man and I make my man-sense
of a cloud, the smoke, some cows and a tree.
But no landscape can make sense of my me.

'Making Senses', *One Atom to Another* (1987)

2 No doubt he'd come home by instinct, the poor
man's taxi.

The Other McCoy (1990)

3 'To Scotland as a concept,' said MacRae.
'No. A state of mind,' corrected Grogan.
'He's right, it's different,' said McCoy.
And they all toasted Scotland as a state
of mind.

The Other McCoy (1990). Cf. Cliff Hanley 4,
Maurice Lindsay 2

MacCaig, Norman Alexander 1910–96
Poet

1 Straws like tame lightnings lie about the grass
And hang zigzag on hedges.

'Summer Farm', *Riding Lights* (1955), st.1

2 A hen stares at nothing with one eye,
Then picks it up.

'Summer Farm', *Riding Lights* (1955), st.2

3 Self under self, a pile of selves I stand
Threaded on time, and with metaphysic hand
Lift the farm like a lid and see
Farm within farm, and in the centre, me.

'Summer Farm', *Riding Lights* (1955), st.4

4 I nod and nod to my own shadow and thrust
A mountain down and down.
Between my feet a loch shines in the brown,
Its silver paper crinkled and edged with rust.
My lungs say No;
But down and down this treadmill hill must go.

'Climbing Suilven', *Riding Lights* (1955), st.1

5 The wind hangs nursery rhymes on branches;
The sun leans ladders against the apple trees.

'Edinburgh spring', *Riding Lights* (1955), st.1

6 The night tinkles like ice in glasses.
Leaves are glued to the pavement with frost.
The brown air fumes at the shop windows,
Tries the doors, and sidles past.

'November night, Edinburgh', *The Sinai Sort*
(1957), st.1

7 So I stand here, a guilty primitive,
My education down about my knees,
Caught in the act of living, if to live
Is to be all one's possibilities,
A sum of generations six foot high,
Learning to live and practising to die.

'Growing down', *The Sinai Sort* (1957), st.6

8 You whose ambition is to swim the Minch
Or write a drum concerto in B flat
Or run like Bannister or box like Lynch
Or find the Ark wrecked on Mt Ararat –
No special training's needed: thin or fat,
You'll do it if you never once supplant
As basis of your commissariat
Glenfiddich, Bruichladdich and Glengrant.

'Ballade of good whisky', *A Round of Applause*
(1962), st.1

9 Who'd laugh the louder, the Devil or
God, to see
Two rosy bourgeois howling at each other?

'Street Preacher', *Measures* (1965), st.2

10 . . . With lifted head
And no shoulders at all, it periscopes round –
Steps, like an aunty, forward – gives itself
shoulders
And vanishes, a shilling in a pound,
Making no sight as other things make no sound.

'Heron', *Measures* (1965), st.2

11 He does more than he does.
When he goes hunting
he aims at a bird and
brings a landscape down.

Or he dynamites a ramshackle
idea – when
the dust settles,
what structures shine in the sun.

'Hugh MacDiarmid', *Surroundings* (1966), st.3–4

12 I love frogs that sit
like Buddha, that fall without
parachutes, that die
like Italian tenors.

'Frogs', *Surroundings* (1966), st.2

13 The dwarf with his hands on backwards
sat, slumped like a half-filled sack
on tiny twisted legs from which
sawdust might run,
outside the three tiers of churches built
in honour of St Francis, brother
of the poor, talker with birds, over whom
he had the advantage
of not being dead yet.

'Assisi', *Surroundings* (1966), st.1

14 I sit with my back to the engine, watching
the landscape pouring away out of my eyes.
I think I know where I'm going and have

some choice in the matter.

'Crossing the Border', *Rings on a Tree* (1968)

15 I sit with my back to the future, watching
time pouring away into the past. I sit, being
  helplessly
lugged backwards
through the Debatable Lands of history. . .

'Crossing the Border', *Rings on a Tree* (1968)

16 Because I see the world poisoned
by cant and brutal self-seeking,
must I be silent about
the useless waterlily, the dunnock's nest
in the hedgeback?

'Balances', *Rings on a Tree* (1968), st.1

17 Hear my words carefully.
Some are spoken
not by me, but
by a man in my position.

'A man in my position', *A Man In My
Position* (1969)

18 I never saw more frogs
than once at the back of Ben Dorain.
Joseph-coated, they ambled and jumped
in the sweet marsh grass
like coloured ideas.

'One of the many days', *A Man In My
Position* (1969)

19 Glaciers, grinding West, gouged out
these valleys, rasping the brown sandstone,
and left, on the hard rock below – the
ruffled foreland –
this frieze of mountains, filed
on the blue air – Stac Polly,
Cul Beag, Cul Mor, Suilven,
Canisp – a frieze and
a litany.

Who owns this landscape?
Has owning anything to do with love?
For it and I have a love-affair, so nearly human
we even have quarrels. . .

'A man in Assynt', *A Man In My Position* (1969)

20 . . . I love it
with special gratitude, since
it sends me no letter, is never
jealous and, expecting nothing
from me, gets nothing but
cigarette packets and footprints.

'A man in Assynt', *A Man In My Position* (1969).
Cf. Muriel Gray 1

21 Who owns this landscape? –
The millionaire who bought it or
the poacher staggering downhill in the early
  morning
with a deer on his back?

'A man in Assynt', *A Man In My Position* (1969)

22 And the mind
behind the eye, within the passion,
remembers with certainty that the tide
  will return
and thinks, with hope, that that other ebb,
that sad withdrawal of people, may, too,
reverse itself and flood
the bays and the sheltered glens
with new generations replenishing the land
with its richest of riches and coming, at last,
into their own again.

'A man in Assynt', *A Man In My Position* (1969)

23 We like the unlikely. The terrible thing is
we like it, too, when it's terrible.
When the quiet clerk poisons his family,
when the doctor says *Cancer*, when the tanks
clank on the innocent frontier,
inside the fear, the rage and the horror
a tiny approval smirks, ashamed of itself.

'The unlikely', *A Man In My Position* (1969)

24 I'm a sprinter, not a long-distance runner. . .
I'm a spontaneous hit-or-miss writer. . .

Interview in *Scottish Field* (1972)

25 The government decreed that
on the anniversary of his birth
the people should observe
two minutes pandemonium.

'After his death', *The White Bird* (1973)
On his friend Hugh MacDiarmid, who in fact
did not die until 1978

26 There's a Schiehallion anywhere you go.
The thing is, climb it.

'Landscape and I', *The World's Room* (1974), st.6

27 She flowed through fences like a piece of
black wind.

'Praise of a collie', *Tree of Strings* (1977)

28 He would walk into my mind as if it were a
town and he a torchlight procession of one,
lighting up the streets of my mind and some
of the nasty little things that were burrowing
into the corners.

On Hugh MacDiarmid, at his funeral (13
Sep 1978)

29 I have a hundred horsepower revulsion from
writing about myself. . .

Letter to Maurice Lindsay. Quoted in 'My
Way of It', in Maurice Lindsay (ed.), *As I
Remember* (1979)

30 Poetry teaches a man to do more than observe
merely factual errors and measurable truths. It
trains him to have a shrewd nose for the fake,
the inflated, the imprecise and the dishonest.

'My Way of It', in Maurice Lindsay (ed.), *As I
Remember* (1979)

To have unexamined emotional responses is as immature, as dangerous, as to have unexamined beliefs. And what proportion, I wonder, of the misunderstandings and miseries in the world are due to no more than the stock use of big words – liberty, patriotism, democracy and all their dreary clan – and the stock response to them?

'My Way of It', in Maurice Lindsay (ed.), *As I Remember* (1979)

Stop looking like a purse. How could a purse squeeze under the rickety door and sit, full of satisfaction, in a man's house?

'Toad', *The Equal Skies* (1980)

A jewel in your head? Toad, you've put one in mine, a tiny radiance in a dark place.

'Toad', *The Equal Skies* (1980)

The English are extraordinary people. Extreme Scottish Nationalists, even MacDiarmid, and he was the most extreme Scottish Nationalist ever, accused them of practising genocide. That's not the way the English destroy a people. They destroy a people by pretending they're not there. There's no purpose in it whatever.

Interview in *Cencrastus*, No.8 (Spring 1982)

. . . there's more to a mountain than the cairn on top of it: the countless experiences offered to your feet, your five senses and your muscles and – I'm trying to avoid the word, but I can't – a feeling of freedom, of dealing with the natural, physical world, obeying its natural laws – savage enough, some of them, till you compare them with the worse perversions of the blessed intelligence of men.

Foreword in Hamish Brown, *Poems of the Scottish Hills: an Anthology* (1982)

Experience teaches that it doesn't.

'Bruce and that spider – the truth', *A World of Difference* (1983)

I was born an atheist. The first thing I said when I sprang out of my mother's womb was, 'Down with Popery!' I said it in Gaelic of course!

Interview with Isobel Murray and Bob Tait (Feb 1986), in Isobel Murray (ed.), *Scottish Writers Talking* (1996)

Zen Calvinist.

His response to being asked what his religion was. Quoted in *Scottish Book Collector* (Aug 1987)

Take away the contradictions and what's left? Heaven.

Only the gods could settle as happy natives

in that place of no contradictions, that place of certainty, the place of peace.

'Thinking of contradictions', *Voice-Over* (1988)

40 What does he do at home? Sit at attention? Or does he stay in the lobby like a hatstand?

'Neighbour', *Voice-Over* (1988)

41 It was a friend who rescued my poetry from being a vomitorium of unrelated images. He read my first book and said: 'Here's your book, Norman. When are you going to publish the answers?' And I started on the rocky road to lucidity and simplicity.

Interview with David Campbell, in *The Scotsman* (14 Nov 1990)

42 Beware, I'm in my anecdotage.

Interview with David Campbell, in *The Scotsman* (14 Nov 1990)

43 Two fags. Unless it's a wee one then it's one fag.

On how long it took him to write a poem. Interview with Ian Walton, 'Still Counting my Fingers', in *Poetry Now*, Vol.1, No.4 (Autumn 1992)

44 I pat slaters on the head and call earwigs by their first name. . .

Recorded interview (BBC Scotland). Reproduced in *Speaking Likeness* exhibition, Scottish National Portrait Gallery, Edinburgh (1996)

45 Study brevity.

Advice given to students who wrote long-winded essays. Quoted in his obituary by Alasdair MacRae, *The Scotsman* (24 Jan 1996)

MacCallum, Rev Donald 1849–1929
Church of Scotland minister and anti-landlord campaigner in the Highlands

1 The land is our birthright, even as the air, the light of the sun and the water belong to us as our birthright.

Quoted in Malcolm MacLean and Christopher Carrell (eds), *As an Fhearann (From the Land*, 1986), 'Land for the People, 1873–1986'

McCance, William 1894–1970
Painter and printmaker

1 In my opinion Scotland is the great White Hope of European art. . . When the Scot can purge himself of the illusion that art is reserved for the sentimentalist and realise that he, the Scot, has a natural gift for construction, combined with a racial aptitude for metaphysical thought and a deep emotional nature, then out of this combination can arise an art which will be

pregnant with Idea and will have within it the seeds of greatness.

'The Idea in Art', *The Modern Scot*, I (No.2, 1930). Quoted in Duncan Macmillan, *Scottish Art 1460–1990* (1990), ch.19

McCaskill, Ian
Televison weatherman

1 What they really want is a red-nosed clown with a physics degree.

On the ideal requirements for his job. Quoted on BBC Radio 4's *Midweek* (July 1992)

McCheyne, Robert Murray 1813–43
Evangelical Church of Scotland minister

1 You don't know what Moderatism is. It is a plant that our Heavenly Father never planted, and I trust it is now to be rooted out.

Letter to a friend (1837) on the divisions between Evangelicals and Moderates in the Kirk preceding the Disruption of 1843. Quoted in N M Cameron, D F Wright et al., *Dictionary of Church History and Theology* (1993)

MacCodrum, Iain (John MacCodrum)
1693–1779
North Uist poet

1 Gum beannaicheadh Dia bùrn Loch Hàstain –
Ge math fhàileadh 's fhèarr a bhlas;
'S ma bha e mar so gu léir
Bu mhór am beud a leigeil as.

† May God bless the water of Loch Hasten –
Though good its smell, better its taste;
And if it was all like this
'Twas a great pity to drain it away.

Quoted in W Matheson (ed.), *The Songs of John MacCodrum* (1938)

This was his response to the local factor who was supervising the draining of Loch Hasten in Paible. The poet did not arrive until the work was over and a keg of whisky had been broached for the workers' refreshment. 'So, Iain, sin agad glaine de bhùrn Loch Hàstain,' were the factor's words ('Here, John, there you have a glass of the water of Loch Hasten.')

2 Nach gasda chùis-bhùirt
A bhith cneatraich air ùrlar,
Gun phrannadh air lùtha,
Gun siubhlaichean grinn,
A' sparradh o-draochain
An earball o-dròchain,
A' sparradh o-dròchain
An tòin o-dro-bhì;
Màl caol cam
Le thaosg rann,

Gaoth mar ghreann reòta
Throimh na tuill fhiara
Nach dionaich na meòirean,
Nach tuigear air dòigh
Ach o-theoin is o-thì.

† Is it not a fine laughing-stock to splutter away at a theme without playing of variation or lovely grace-notes, ramming *odroochan* in the tail of *odrochan*, ramming *odrochan* in the rear of *odrovi*; a narrow crooked bag, half-full of slavers, a wind like the chill of frost through the squint holes that the fingers cannot cover, only *ohon* and *ohi* can be understood aright.

'Diomoladh Pìoba Dhomhnaill Bhàin' ('The Dispraise of Donald Ban's Pipes'). In W Matheson (ed.), *The Songs of John MacCodrum* (1938), st.7

McColgan, Liz 1964–
Middle- and long-distance runner

1 If you want it you've got to go for it, so I just kept saying to myself 'work, work, work'. I proved I wanted it more than anybody else.

On winning the 10,000m at the World Championship in Tokyo (1991), about one year after giving birth. Quoted in Rodger Baillie (ed.), *100 Years of Scottish Sport* (1994), 'Strike for Gold'

BBC commentator Brendan Foster enthused about her win: 'The greatest run in the history of British distance running, men or women, any time, any place, anywhere. That's the best I've ever seen and, better than that, it's better than any I've read about.' Quoted in the *Daily Telegraph* (30 Dec 1991)

MacColl, Ewan (originally Jimmie Miller)
1915–89
English-born folksinger and left-wing playwright

1 I found my love by the gasworks crofts
Dreamed a dream by the old canal
Kissed my girl by the factory wall
Dirty old town, dirty old town

'Dirty Old Town' (1950), st.1 (Robbins Music Corporation)

On Salford, Lancashire, where he grew up

2 The first time ever I saw your face
I thought the sun rose in your eyes,
and the moon and the stars were the gifts you gave
to the dark and the empty skies.

'The First Time Ever I Saw Your Face' (written for Peggy Seeger, 1957), st.1 (Stormking Music)

3 Oh the work was hard and the hours were long
And the treatment sure it took some bearing
There was little kindness and the kicks was many
as we hunted for the shoals of herring.

'The Shoals of Herring' (from the BBC radio

ballad broadcast, *Singing the Fishing*, 1960), st.3
(Ewan MacColl Ltd)

4 If jeans were the uniform of the revival, then
hair was its banner. . . It grew longer and
longer, both on men and women, until it
became difficult to distinguish one sex from
the other. Then came the beards, proliferating
and luxuriating in an incredible way. There
were times when one had the impression of
singing into an impenetrable hedge of hair, a
veritable Birnam Wood of whiskers.

Journeyman: an autobiography (1990), ch.22,
'Into the Folk Revival'

5 If actors became bitter every time a theatre
folded, they would be one of the most
disillusioned groups of people on this earth.

Journeyman: an autobiography (1990), 'Epilogue'

6 Strange is the love you have for your children.
It creeps into your life furtively like a stray
cat unsure of its welcome, and then suddenly
it has occupied every cell of your being.

Journeyman: an autobiography (1990), 'Epilogue'

McColl, Jim 1935–
*Gardener, presenter of BBC television pro-
gramme,* The Beechgrove Garden

1 There are the enthusiasts, the mildly interested
and the sheep in any field of human endeavour.

Quoted in *Scotland on Sunday* (21 Apr 1996)

MacColla, Fionn (pseudonym of Thomas Douglas Macdonald) 1906–75
Novelist and polemicist

1 . . . the typical monument of the pre-
Reformation spirit is cathedrals, of the
Reformation spirit, industrial slums.

At the Sign of the Clenched Fist (1967), Part 3,
'The Valve'

MacColla was virulently anti-Calvinist and
blamed what he saw as the 'cultural desert'
of Scottish life on the effect of a 'nay-saying'
Presbyterian philosophy

2 It is the distinction of 'Scottish education', since
it became universal and compulsory, to have
extinguished two languages in three generations.

At the Sign of the Clenched Fist (1967), Part 3,
'The Valve'

3 . . . what the Reformation did was to snuff out
what must otherwise have developed into the
most brilliant national culture in history.

At the Sign of the Clenched Fist (1967), Part 3,
'The Valve'. Cf. William Soutar 9

4 . . . the Gas Chamber of the Scots, and
especially of the Gael.

On the British Empire. *Too Long In This
Condition* (1975)

The reference is to the use of Highlanders in
particular as expendable soldiers, as typified
by General Wolfe's judgment of them.
Cf. James Wolfe 1

McCombe, David 1932–
Resident of Hawick and Lottery winner

1 A day out of Hawick is a day wasted.

On his family's plans not to leave their home
town after winning £1.59 million in the National
Lottery. Quoted in *The Scotsman* (31 Oct 1995)

The phrase is commonplace and over the years
has been applied to many different towns and
villages throughout Scotland

MacDhubhghaill, Féidhlim (Felim MacDugall) dates unknown
Medieval poet

1 Ní math siubhal san Domhnach,
gé bé chongbhas an t-saoire;
ní math míochlú do cheannach,
ní math feamach mná baoithe. . .

Ní math easbog gan bhairrín,
ní math anaoibh ar sheanóir;
ní math sagart ar leathshúil,
ní math pearsún go dearóil.

† It is not good to travel on Sunday, for
whomsoever keeps that day free from work;
it is not good to purchase an evil name; not
good to dally with a lewd woman. . .

Not good is a bishop lacking a mitre; not
good a senior in ill-humour; not good a priest
lacking an eye; not good a parson in poverty.

'Ní math siubhal san Domhnach' ('It is not good
to travel on Sunday'), st.1, 3. Quoted in W J
Watson (ed.), *Scottish Verse from the Book of the
Dean of Lismore* (1937)

2 Ní math bean gan bheith náireach,
ní math cláirseach gan téada. . .

Ní math éadach gan úcadh,
ní math súgradh gan gháire . . .

† Not good is a woman without modesty; not
good a harp without strings. . .

Not good is cloth without waulking; sport
is not good lacking laughter. . .

'Ní math siubhal san Domhnach' ('It is not good
to travel on Sunday'), st.5, 10. Quoted in W J
Watson (ed.), *Scottish Verse from the Book of the
Dean of Lismore* (1937)

3 Fuath liom bheith anmoch ag triall,
fuath liom cliar ara mbí bean;
fuath liom dobrón i dtigh n-óil,
fuath liom baile mór gan ghean.

Fuath liom droichbhean ag fear math,
fuath liom flath ara mbí gruaim;

fuath liom deoch anbhfann 's í daor;
fuath liom duine saor gan stuaim.

† I hate to be late journeying; I hate a poet-
band that includes a woman; I hate sadness
in a drinking-house; I hate a great homestead
without cheer.

I hate to see a good husband with a bad wife;
I hate a prince weighed down with gloom; I
hate a weak drink that is yet dear; I hate a
freeman without dignity.

'Fuath liom' ('I hate'), st.1–2. Quoted in W J
Watson (ed.), *Scottish Verse from the Book of the
Dean of Lismore* (1937)

MacDiarmid, Hugh (pseudonym of Christopher Murray Grieve) 1892–1978

*Poet, nationalist and communist who
spearheaded the modern Scottish literary
Renaissance*

1 Mars is braw in crammasy,
Venus in a green silk goun...

'The Bonnie Broukit Bairn', *Sangschaw* (1925)

2 ... Nane for thee a thochtie sparin',
Earth, thou bonnie broukit bairn!
– *But greet, an' in your tears ye'll droun
The haill clanjamfrie!*

'The Bonnie Broukit Bairn', *Sangschaw* (1925).
Cf. James Tytler 3

3 Ae weet forenicht i' the yow-trummle
I saw yon antrin thing,
A watergaw wi' its chitterin' licht
Ayont the on-ding...

'The Watergaw', *Sangschaw* (1925), st.1

4 Oh to be at Crowdieknowe
When the last trumpet blaws,
An' see the deid come loupin' owre
The auld grey wa's.

'Crowdieknowe', *Sangschaw* (1925), st.1

5 – *Fegs, God's no blate gin he stirs up
The men o' Crowdieknowe!*

'Crowdieknowe', *Sangschaw* (1925), st.4

6 I' the how-dumb-deid o' the cauld hairst nicht
The warl' like an eemis stane
Wags i' the lift;
An' my eerie memories fa'
Like a yowdendrift.

'The Eemis Stane', *Sangschaw* (1925), st.1

7 I' mony an unco warl' the nicht
The lift gaes black as pitch at noon,
An' sideways on their chests the heids
O' endless Christs roll doon.

'The Innumerable Christ', *Sangschaw* (1925), st.3

8 ... – And I lo'e Love
Wi' a scunner in't.

'Scunner', *Penny Wheep* (1926), st.2

9 I met ayont the cairney
A lass wi' tousled hair
Singin' till a bairnie
That was nae langer there.

'Empty Vessel', *Penny Wheep* (1926), st.1.
Cf. Anonymous 27

10 ... the bubblyjock swallowed the bagpipes
And the blether stuck in its throat.

'The Bubblyjock', *Penny Wheep* (1926)

11 *It's soon', no' sense, that faddoms the herts o' men,
And by my sangs the rouch auld Scots I ken
E'en herts that ha'e nae Scots 'll dirl richt thro'
As nocht else could – for here's a language rings
Wi' datchie sesames, and names for nameless things.*

'Gairmscoile', *Penny Wheep* (1926), st.9

12 I amna fou' sae muckle as tired – deid dune.
It's gey and hard wark coupin' gless for gless
Wi' Cruivie and Gilsanquhar and the like,
And I'm no juist as bauld as aince I wes.

A Drunk Man Looks at the Thistle (1926), ll.1–4

13 To prove my saul is Scots I maun begin
Wi' what's still deemed Scots and the
folk expect,
And spire up syne by visible degrees
To heichts whereo' the fules ha'e never recked.

A Drunk Man Looks at the Thistle (1926), ll.21–4

14 Mair nonsense has been uttered in his name
Than in ony's barrin' liberty and Christ.

On Robert Burns. *A Drunk Man Looks at the
Thistle* (1926), ll.57–8

15 I'll ha'e nae hauf-way hoose, but aye be whaur
Extremes meet – it's the only way I ken
To dodge the curst conceit o' bein' richt
That damns the vast majority o' men.

A Drunk Man Looks at the Thistle (1926), ll.141–4

These lines are engraved on MacDiarmid's
gravestone at Langholm

16 Drums in the Walligate, pipes in the air,
Come and hear the cryin' o' the Fair.

A' as it used to be, when I was a loon
On Common-Ridin' day in the Muckle Toon.

A Drunk Man Looks at the Thistle (1926), ll.455–8

On the annual Common Riding in Langholm,
his birthplace

17 O wha's the bride that cairries the bunch
O' thistles blinterin' white?
Her cuckold bridegroom little dreids
What he sall ken this nicht.

A Drunk Man Looks at the Thistle (1926), ll.612–5

18 O wha's been here afore me, lass,
And hoo did he get in?
– *A man that deed or I was born
This evil thing has din.*

A Drunk Man Looks at the Thistle (1926), ll.620–3

And let the lesson be – to be yersel's,
Ye needna fash gin it's to be ocht else.
To be yersel's – and to mak' that worth bein'.
Nae harder job to mortals has been gi'en.

A Drunk Man Looks at the Thistle (1926), ll.743–6

'Let there be Licht,' said God, and there was
A little. . .

A Drunk Man Looks at the Thistle (1926), ll.2101–2

He canna Scotland see wha yet
Canna see the Infinite,
And Scotland in true scale to it.

A Drunk Man Looks at the Thistle (1926), ll.2527–9

Yet ha'e I Silence left, the croon o' a'.

A Drunk Man Looks at the Thistle (1926), l.2671

The number of people who can copulate
properly may be few; the number who can
write well are infinitely fewer.

Review of D H Lawrence's *Lady Chatterley's
Lover* in *The New Age* (27 Sep 1928)

Lourd on my hert as winter lies
The state that Scotland's in the day.
Spring to the North has aye come slow
But noo dour winter's like to stay
For guid,
And no' for guid!

*To Circumjack Cencrastus, or The Curly
Snake* (1930)

The problems o' the Scottish soul
Are nocht to Harry Lauder. . .

*To Circumjack Cencrastus, or The Curly
Snake* (1930)

Scots steel tempered wi' Irish fire
Is the weapon that I desire.

To Circumjack Cencrastus, or The Curly Snake
(1930), 'The Weapon'

Better a'e gowden lyric
Than a social problem solved. . .

*To Circumjack Cencrastus, or The Curly
Snake* (1930)

Man's the reality that mak's
A' things possible, even himsel'.

*To Circumjack Cencrastus, or The Curly
Snake* (1930)

A livin' man upon a deid man thinks
And ony sma'er thocht's impossible.

'At My Father's Grave', *First Hymn to Lenin
and other poems* (1931)

*Are my poems spoken in the factories and fields,
In the streets o' the toon?
Gin they're no', then I'm failin' to dae
What I ocht to ha' dune.*

Second Hymn to Lenin (1932)

31 *Oh, it's nonsense, nonsense, nonsense,
Nonsense at this time o' day
That breid-and-butter problems
S'ud be in ony man's way.*

Second Hymn to Lenin (1932)

32 Unremittin', relentless,
Organised to the last degree,
Ah, Lenin, politics is bairns' play
To what this maun be!

Second Hymn to Lenin (1932)

'This' in the last line refers to poetry

33 *This Bolshevik bog! Suits me doon to the grun'!*

'Tarras', *Scots Unbound and other poems* (1932),
Part 1, st.1

34 . . . your small black shape by the edge
of the sea,
– A bullet-hole through a great scene's beauty,
God through the wrong end of a telescope.

'Of John Davidson', *Scots Unbound and other
poems* (1932)

Davidson, whose poetry MacDiarmid greatly
admired, committed suicide in Penzance,
Cornwall, in 1909

35 Nae maitter hoo faur I've travelled sinsyne
The cast o' Dumfriesshire's aye in me like wine;
And my sangs are gleids o' the candent spirit
Its sons inherit.

Dedication to his wife Valda and son Michael,
Stony Limits and other Poems (1934), st.2

36 There are plenty of ruined buildings in the
world but no ruined stones.

'On a Raised Beach', *Stony Limits and other
poems* (1934)

37 These stones go through Man, straight to God,
if there is one.
What have they not gone through already?
Empires, civilisations, aeons. Only in them
If in anything, can His creation confront Him.
They came so far out of the water and halted
forever.

'On a Raised Beach', *Stony Limits and other poems*
(1934). Cf. Hugh Miller 10

38 What happens to us
Is irrelevant to the world's geology
But what happens to the world's geology
Is not irrelevant to us.
We must reconcile ourselves to the stones,
Not the stones to us.

'On a Raised Beach', *Stony Limits and other
poems* (1934)

39 'I see herrin'.' – I hear the glad cry
And 'gainst the moon see ilka blue jowl
In turn as the fishermen haul on the nets
And sing: 'Come, shove in your heids
and growl.'

'Shetland Lyrics: With the Herring Fishers',
Stony Limits and other poems (1934), st.1

40 The rose of all the world is not for me.
I want for my part
Only the little white rose of Scotland
That smells sharp and sweet – and breaks
the heart.

'The Little White Rose', *Stony Limits and other poems* (1934)

41 There is so much that is bad in all the poetry
that Scots people know and admire that it is
not surprising that for their pet example of a
good bad poet they should have to go outside
the range of poetry, good, bad, or indifferent,
altogether. McGonagall is in a very special
category, and has it entirely to himself.

'The Great McGonagall', *Scottish Eccentrics* (1936)

42 It is one of the favourite ideas of the bourgeoisie
– who thereby get their culture and art-products
cheap or whose mean souls are compensated by
the indigence of their superiors – that artists
are all the better for hardship, and that easy
conditions and good living are apt to spoil them.

'The Strange Case of William Berry', *Scottish Eccentrics* (1936). Cf. Robert Louis Stevenson 102

43 Scottish women of any historical importance
or interest are curiously rare, and although
these may have played dramatic parts in great
affairs and manifested no little courage and
contriving power, their psychologies present
next to nothing that is out of the ordinary.
A long list of famous Englishwomen is easy
to compile; it is impossible to draw up any
corresponding list of Scotswomen.

'Elspeth Buchan: Friend Mother in the Lord', *Scottish Eccentrics* (1936)

44 . . . my function in Scotland during the past
twenty to thirty years has been that of the cat-
fish that vitalises the other torpid denizens of
the aquarium.

Lucky Poet (1943), 'Author's Note: On Being a Hippopotamus'

45 My aim all along has been (in Ezra Pound's
term) the most drastic *desuetization* of Scottish
life and letters, and, in particular, the de-
Tibetanization of the Highlands and Islands, and
getting rid of the whole gang of high mucky-
mucks, famous fatheads, old wives of both sexes,
stuffed shirts, hollow men with headpieces
stuffed with straw, bird-wits, lookers-under-
beds, trained seals, creeping Jesuses, Scots Wha
Ha'evers, village idiots, policemen, leaders of
white-mouse factions and noted connoisseurs
of bread and butter, glorified gangsters, and
what 'Billy' Phelps calls Medlar Novelists (the
medlar being a fruit that becomes rotten before
it is ripe), Commercial Calvinists, makers of
'noises like a turnip' and all the touts and toadies
and lickspittles of the English Ascendancy, and

their infernal women-folk, and all their skunkoil
skulduggery.

Lucky Poet (1943), ch.3, 'The Kind of Poetry I Want'

46 . . . the great source of the paralysing ideology
of defeatism in Scotland, the spread of which
is responsible at once for the acceptance of
the Union and the low standard of nineteenth-
century Scots literature. . .

On Walter Scott's Waverley Novels. *Lucky Poet* (1943), ch.4, 'Robert Burns, Sir Walter Scott and Others'

47 'A disgrace to the community.' – Mr Justice
Mugge

His proposed epitaph. *Lucky Poet* (1943), ch.9, 'Valedictory'

48 We do not like the confiding, the intimate,
the ingratiating, the hail-fellow-well-met, but
prefer the unapproachable, the hard-bitten, the
recalcitrant, the sinister, the malignant, the
saturnine, the cross-grained and the cankered,
and the howling wilderness to the amenities
of civilisation, the irascible to the affable, the
prickly to the smooth. We have no damned
fellow-feeling at all. . .

'The Dour Drinkers of Glasgow', *The American Mercury* (Mar 1952)

49 I dream of poems like the bread-knife
Which cuts three slices at once. . .

The Kind of Poetry I Want (1961)

50 A poetry like an operating theatre,
Sparkling with a swift, deft energy,
Energy quiet and contained and fearfully alert,
In which the poet exists only as a nurse during
an operation. . .

The Kind of Poetry I Want (1961)

51 My job, as I see it, has never been to lay a tit's
egg, but to erupt like a volcano emitting not
only flame but a lot of rubbish.

Letter to George Bruce (1 Jul 1964)

52 He is in fact a zombie, personifying the
obsolescent traditions of an aristocratic and big
landlord order, of which Thomas Carlyle said
that no country had been oppressed by a worse
gang of hyenas than Scotland. He is not really a
Scotsman, of course, but only a sixteenth part of
one, and all his education and social affiliations
are anti-Scottish. Sir Walter warned long ago
that a Scotsman unscotched would become only
a damned mischievous Englishman, and that
is precisely what has happened in this case.

On Sir Alec Douglas-Home, the Conservative Prime Minister, against whom MacDiarmid stood as a Communist candidate in the Kinross and West Perthshire constituency, in the 1964 General Election. Quoted in *The Daily Worker* (4 Sep 1964). Cf. Walter Scott 96

If you ask: Do I have a personal antipathy to Sir Alec Home, I say yes I have. This campaign is a personal issue. After all, I have a personality, and Home doesn't.

Quoted in *The Sun* (14 Oct 1964)

There is no one really alive in Edinburgh yet.
They are all living on the tiniest fraction
Of the life they could easily have,
Like people in great houses who prefer
To live in their cellars and keep all the rest
  sealed up.

'Talking with Five Thousand People in Edinburgh', *The Hugh MacDiarmid Anthology* (1972)

For I am like Zamyatin. I must be a Bolshevik
Before the Revolution, but I'll cease to be
  one quick
When Communism comes to rule the roost,
For real literature can exist only when it's
  produced
By madmen, hermits, heretics,
Dreamers, rebels, sceptics,
– And such a door of utterance has been
  given to me
As none may close whosoever they be.

'Talking with Five Thousand People in Edinburgh', *The Hugh MacDiarmid Anthology* (1972)

Scotland small? Our multiform, our infinite
  Scotland *small*?
Only as a patch of hillside may be a cliché corner
To a fool who cries 'Nothing but heather!'. . .

Dìreadh 1 (1974)

Let what can be shaken, be shaken,
And the unshakeable remain.
The Inaccessible Pinnacle is not inaccessible.

Dìreadh 3 (1974)

The Inaccessible Pinnacle, on Sgurr Dearg in Skye, is the most notoriously difficult of all Scotland's Munros (mountains over 3000 ft)

MacDonald, Alexander
see **Alasdair Mac Mhaighstir Alasdair**

MacDonald (of Glencoe), Angus (Aonghas Mac Alasdair Ruaidh)
c.1665–1745

Poet

Chunna mi crìoch air m'fhear-cinnidh
'Ga chàramh 'n diugh an Tom Aingeal;
Iuchair nam bàrd, rìgh nam filidh,
Dia dhèanamh sìth ri t'anam.
B'fhuath leat Màiri, b'fhuath leat Uilleam,
Is b'fhuath leat Sìol Diarmaid uile,
'S a h-uile neach nach biodh rìoghail

Dh'innseadh tu dhaibh e gun iarraidh.
Tha gaol an Leóghainn 's fuath an Tuirc
Anns an uaigh 's am bheil do chorp,
Gun tugadh Dia mathanas duit,
Bha thu dìoghaltach 'san olc.

† I saw an end to my kinsman, today laid to rest in Tom Aingeal: key of bards, king of poets; may God make peace with your soul. You hated Mary, you hated William; you hated all of the seed of Diarmad [Campbell]; to all who failed to be loyal [to the Stewart line], you would let them know it without their asking. Love of the Lion, loathing of the Boar, are in the grave where your body lies. May God forgive you: you were vengeful against evil.

Spoken at the burial of the poet Iain Lom (c.1624–c.1707)

MacDonald, Bare John see **Iain Lom**

MacDonald, Black John
see **Iain Dubh Mac Iain Mhic Ailein**

MacDonald, Colla Ciotach (Colkitto)
c.1570–1647

Soldier and opponent of the Campbells

1 MAC CAILEIN MOR, IARLA ARRA GHAIDHEAL: Có 's fhearr do chrochadh no do dhicheannadh? COLLA CIOTACH: Nach b'e sin an dà dhiùghaidh gun aon roghainn!

† EARL OF ARGYLL: Which do you prefer: your being hanged or beheaded? COLKITTO: Now there's an offer of worthless alternatives [literally, two things-to-be-rejected], and not a thing to choose between them.

Attrib.

According to tradition, he was hanged on a gallows made from the oars of his own ship

MacDonald (of Bohuntin), Donald
see **Dòmhnall Donn**

MacDonald (of Coruna), Donald
see **Dòmhnall Ruadh Chorùna**

McDonald, Ellie 1937–
Poet

1 *The glaid gangs free, my bonnie lad
kens nocht o daith nor birth,
the wind but cairts aa human pain
tae ilka howe o yirth*

Whit seeks tae come inby the nicht,

nae bield has ever haen,
but haiks its gangrel body, whaur
eternities cry doun.

> 'The Gangan Fuit', *The Gangan*
> *Fuit* (1991), st.3–4

2   An whit's it worth
gin the warld's melled
intil a village, tae speak
o Scots ingine or egalitarian thocht

or waur – o language. . .

I'm threipin awa
til an auld sang the nicht.
Are ye needin ony guisers
wha sing in a minor key?

> 'Halloween', *The Gangan Fuit* (1991)

3   The road I traivel has nae end.
The sang that circled aince
abune the broch, the cloister an the keep
rings i the pends an closies o the city.
Our past is an auld-farrant bairn we cairry
for the sang o the poet is in its hert.

> 'Pathfinder', in *Chapman* No.83 (1996)

MacDonald, George 1824–1905
Poet and novelist

1   I learned that it is better, a thousand-fold, for a
proud man to fall and be humbled, than to hold
up his head in his pride and fancied innocence.
I learned that he that will be a hero, will barely
be a man; that he that will be nothing but a
doer of his work, is sure of his manhood.

> *Phantastes* (1858), ch.22

2   . . . it is by loving, and not by being loved, that
one can come nearest the soul of another. . .

> *Phantastes* (1858), ch.24

3   Here lie I, Martin Elginbrodde:
Hae mercy o' my soul, Lord God;
As I wad do, were I Lord God,
And ye were Martin Elginbrodde.

> *David Elginbrod* (1863), Bk 1, ch.13

4   Let me, if I may, be ever welcomed to my room
in winter by a glowing hearth, in summer by a
vase of flowers; if I may not, let me then think
how nice they would be, and busy myself in my
work. I do not think the road to contentment
lies in despising what we have not got. Let us
acknowledge all good, all delight that the world
holds, and be content without it.

> *Annals of a Quiet Neighbourhood* (1867), ch.11,
> 'Sermon on God and Mammon'

5   'You have tasted of death now,' said the Old
Man. 'Is it good?'
'It is good,' said Mossy. 'It is better than life.'

'No,' said the Old Man: 'it is only more life.'

> 'The Golden Key' (1867)

6   As the thoughts move in the mind of a man,
so move the worlds of men and women in the
mind of God, and make no confusion there,
for there they had their birth, the offspring of
his imagination. Man is but a thought of God.

> 'The imagination: its function and its cul-
> ture' (1867)

7   They all were looking for a king
To slay their foes and lift them high:
Thou cam'st, a little baby thing
That made a woman cry.

> 'That Holy Thing' (1883), st.1

8   There is endless room for rebellion against
ourselves.

> *Unspoken Sermons* (Second Series, 1885)

9   And no scripture is of private interpretation,
so is there no feeling in a human heart which
exists in that heart alone – which is not, in
some form or degree, in every heart.

> *Unspoken Sermons* (Second Series, 1885)

10   . . . self is but the shadow of life. When it is
taken for life itself, and set as the man's centre,
it becomes a live death in the man, a devil he
worships as his God; the worm of the death
eternal he clasps to his bosom as his one joy.

> *Unspoken Sermons* (Second Series, 1885)

11   A great good is coming to us all – too big for
this world to hold.

> On death. Letter to his wife Louisa (27 Oct
> 1891). Quoted in Greville MacDonald, *George
> MacDonald and His Wife* (1924), Bk 10, ch.2

Macdonald, Gus (Angus John) 1940–
Journalist and broadcaster, Managing Director of Scottish Television (1990–)

1   If you lose the argument of investing in Silicon
Glen, certainly you lose jobs. If you lose the
ability to create images of yourself and to
conduct arguments within your own society
through broadcasting, to keep control under
some reasonably democratic aegis, you lose far
more than a wage packet.

> Quoted in *Cencrastus* No.28 (Winter 1987–8)

MacDonald, Mary (*née* MacDougall or MacLucas) 1817–c.1890
Poet from Mull

1   Leanabh an àigh
An Leanabh aig Màiri
Rugadh san stàball

Rìgh nan dùl,
Thàinig dh'an fhàsach,
'S dh'fhuilig 'nar n-àite;
Sona dh'an àireamh
Bhitheas dha dlùth.
The Child of glory
The Child of Mary,
Born in the stable
The King of all,
Who came to the wilderness
And in our stead suffered;
Happy they are counted
Who to Him are near.

'Leanabh an Aigh' ('The Child of Glory'), st.1.
Collected in *Carmina Gadelica* (Vol.3)

This is the original of the carol 'Child in
the Manger', which appears in the Church
Hymnary as loosely translated by Lachlan
MacBean (1853–1931)

MacDonald, (James) Ramsay
1866–1937

*Labour politician, first Labour British Prime
Minister (1923–4, 1929–31) and National
Government Prime Minister (1931–5)*

The League of Nations grows in moral courage.
Its frown will soon be more dreaded than a
nation's arms, and when that happens you and
I shall have security and peace.

Speech at the Guild Hall, London (9 Nov 1929)

We hear war called murder. It is not: it is
suicide.

The Observer (4 May 1930)

Yes, tomorrow every Duchess in London will
be wanting to kiss me.

Said after forming the coalition National
Government (25 Aug 1931). Quoted in Philip
Snowden, *Autobiography* (1934), Vol.2, p.957

The National Government was predominantly
Conservative, and MacDonald, the illegitimate
son of a Morayshire farmworker, was
considered by many to have betrayed the
Labour movement in order to prop up an
ailing capitalist system

Macdonald, Sharman 1951–

Playwright and novelist

FIONA: Do you miss sex?
VARI: I've read every book in existence on the
female orgasm. I've never had one.
MORAG: Still. We'll get into heaven.

When I Was a Girl, I Used to Scream and Shout. . .
(1985), Act 2, sc.1

VARI: I have acquired a major accomplishment.
Compromise. Listen. This is what I chose. I'm

happy till you march in with no bottom and a
social conscience.

On being married. *When I Was a Girl, I Used
to Scream and Shout. . .* (1984), Act 2, sc.2

3 ELLEN: English teachers have got dicks, Rose.
ROSE: Peaceful dicks.
ELLEN: That's an oxymoron isn't it?

Borders of Paradise (1995), Act 1

4 JOHN: She's wired up wrong. Gets worse when
she's premenstrual. Doesn't get tense, my
mother, just can't park the car.

Borders of Paradise (1995), Act 1

Macdonald, Thomas Douglas
see MacColla, Fionn

MacDonnell, A(rchibald) G(ordon)
1895–1941

Novelist

1 England, their England

Title of his satirical novel (1933)

2 'But, Glennie,' went on Donald, 'where did
you learn that fine Buchan accent? You never
used to talk like that. Is it since you came south
that you've picked it up?'
 The big professional looked a little
shamefaced and drew Donald back into the
dark corner.
 'It's good for trade,' he whispered in the pure
English of Inverness. 'They like a Scot to be
real Scottish. They think it makes a man what
they call "a character". God knows why, but
there it is. So I just humour them by talking
like a Guild Street carter who's having a bit of
back-chat with an Aberdeen fishwife. It makes
the profits something extraordinary.'

England, their England (1933), ch.8

Glennie, the professional at a wealthy English
golf-club, explains the benefits of turning on
the Doric to the members

3 Scotland has suffered in the past, and is
suffering now, from too much England.

My Scotland (1937)

MacDouall, Andrew (Lord Bankton)
?1685–1760

Judge

1 Am I fou yet? How many cups have I drunk?

To his wife, while drinking tea. Quoted in John
Ramsay of Ochtertyre, *Scotland and Scotsmen
in the Eighteenth Century* (1888 edition), Vol.1,
p.131, footnote

MacDougall, Allan see Ailean Dall

MacDugall, Felim
see MacDhubhghaill, Féidhlim

McEvoy, John
see Traditional songs 80

McGahey, Mick (Michael) 1925–
Mineworkers' union leader

1 Communists don't infiltrate unions, we are
born into them.

> *Financial Times* (29 Jan 1974)

2 Pontius Pilate didn't hold a ballot vote for
Barabbas and Jesus Christ. Jesus never got a
ballot vote but he went on to found a mass
movement.

> Responding to criticism of the National Union
> of Mineworkers' refusal to ballot its members on
> strike action in 1984–5. Quoted in *The Financial
> Times* (24 Nov 1986)

3 I want a British socialist state where people
are able to develop their talents in life. I think
it's criminal for people to be unemployed, I
think it's criminal for to have deprivation, to
have slums. . . Why have slums when half the
building trade are unemployed? It's a negation
in terms of real democracy to deprive people of
decent homes, a decent job, a worthwhile life.

> Interview, quoted in *Speaking Likeness* ex-
> hibition, Scottish National Portrait Gallery,
> Edinburgh (1996)

MacGill-Eain, Somhairle
(Sorley MacLean) 1911–
Poet

1 Cha grinneas anfhann na gealaich,
no maise fhuaraidh na mara,
no baoth-sgeulachd onfhaidh a' chladaich
tha an nochd a' drùdhadh air m'aigne.

Anfhannachd an strì,
aognuidheachd am brìgh,
gealtachd anns a' chrìdh,
gun chreideamh an aon ni.

† It is not the frail beauty of the moon
nor the cold loveliness of the sea
nor the empty tale of the shore's uproar
that seeps through my spirit tonight.

Faintness in fight
death-pallor in effect,
cowardice in the heart
and belief in nothing.

> 'A' Chorra-Ghritheach' ('The Heron', 1932–40),
> *O Choille gu Bearradh* (*From Wood to Ridge:
> Collected Poems*, 1989), st.2–3

2 A nighean a' chùil bhuidhe, throm-bhuidh, òr-
bhuidh,

fonn do bheòil-sa 's gaoir na h-Eòrpa,
a nighean gheal chasurlach aighearach
bhòidheach,
cha bhiodh masladh ar latha-ne searbh 'nad
phòig-sa.

† Girl of the yellow, heavy-yellow, gold-
yellow hair,
the song of your mouth and Europe's
shivering cry,
fair, heavy-haired, spirited, beautiful girl,
the disgrace of our day would not be bitter
in your kiss.

> 'Gaoir na h-Eòrpa' ('The Cry of Europe',
> 1932–40), *O Choille gu Bearradh* (*From Wood to
> Ridge: Collected Poems*, 1989), st.1

3 Tric 's mi gabhail air Dùn-éideann
baile glas gun ghathadh gréine,
's ann a lasadh e le d' bhòidhche,
baile lòghmhor geal-reultach.

† Often when I called Edinburgh
a grey town without darting sun,
it would light up with your beauty,
a refulgent, white-starred town.

> 'Dùn-éideann' ('Edinburgh', 1932–40), *O Choille
> gu Bearradh* (*From Wood to Ridge: Collected
> Poems*, 1989)

4 Lìonmhoireachd anns na speuran,
òr-chriathar muillionan de reultan,
fuar, fad as, lòghmhor, àlainn,
tosdach, neo-fhaireachdail, neo-fhàilteach.

Lànachd an eòlais m' an cùrsa,
failmhe an aineolais gun iùl-chairt,
cruinne-cé ag gluasad sàmhach,
aigne leis fhéin anns an àruinn.

† Multitude of the skies,
golden riddle of millions of stars,
cold distant lustrous beautiful,
silent, unfeeling, unwelcoming.

Fullness of knowledge in their course
emptiness of chartless ignorance,
a universe moving in silence,
a mind alone in its bounds.

> 'Lìonmhoireachd' ('Multitude', 1932–40), *O
> Choille gu Bearradh* (*From Wood to Ridge: Collected
> Poems*, 1989), st.1–2

5 Choisich mi cuide ri mo thuigse
a muigh ri taobh a' chuain:
bha sinn còmhla ach bha ise
a' fuireach tiotan bhuam.

† I walked with my reason
out beside the sea.
We were together but it was
keeping a little distance from me.

> 'An Roghainn' ('The Choice', 1932–40), *O Choille
> gu Bearradh* (*From Wood to Ridge: Collected Poems*,
> 1989), st.1

6 An dèanar a' chochur de'n dàn,
de thruaighe 's de ghlòir na cruinne,

a' bhréine bhreòite, oillteil, thruagh,
t'àilleachd is uaisle luinneag?

Thachd an fhiabhras iomadh truagh
's dh'fhàg i iomadh athair breòite,
ach dh'fhàg ceòl cumha Phàdraig Mhóir
àmhghar a chloinne glòrmhor.

Will a synthesis be made of Fate,
of the misery and glory of the universe,
the frail bruised loathsome wretched filth,
your beauty and the nobleness of lyrics?

Fever has choked many a poor one
and has left many a father bruised, sore
    and frail,
but the music of Patrick's Lament
left the distress of his children glorious.

'Cochur' ('A Synthesis', 1932–40), *O Choille gu
Bearradh* (*From Wood to Ridge: Collected Poems*,
1989), st.9–10

Am faca Tu i, Iùdhaich mhóir,
ri'n abrar Aon Mhac Dhé?
Am fac' thu a coltas air Do thriall
ri stri an fhìon-lios chéin?

Hast Thou seen her, great Jew,
who art called the One Son of God?
Hast Thou seen on Thy way the like of her
labouring in the distant vineyard?

'Ban-Ghàidheal' ('A Highland Woman', 1932–40),
O Choille gu Bearradh (*From Wood to Ridge:
Collected Poems*, 1989), st.1

Agus labhair T' eaglais chaomh
mu staid chaillte a h-anama thruaigh;
agus leag an cosnadh dian
a corp gu sàmhchair dhuibh an uaigh.

Is thriall a tìm mar shnighe dubh
a' drùdhadh tughaidh fàrdaich bochd;
mheal ise an dubh chosnadh cruaidh;
is glas a cadal suain an nochd.

And Thy gentle church has spoken
about the lost state of her miserable soul,
and the unremitting toil has lowered
her body to a black peace in a grave.

And her time has gone like a black sludge
seeping through the thatch of a poor dwelling:
the hard Black Labour was her inheritance;
grey is her sleep tonight.

'Ban-Ghàidheal', ('A Highland Woman',
1932–40), *O Choille gu Bearradh* (*From Wood to
Ridge: Collected Poems*, 1989), st.6–7

Chan eil mo shùil air Calbharaigh
no air Betlehem an àigh
ach air cùil ghrod an Glaschu
far bheil an lobhadh fàis. . .

My eye is not on Calvary
nor on Bethlehem the Blessed,
but on a foul-smelling backland in Glasgow,
where life rots as it grows. . .

'Calbharaigh' ('Calvary', 1932–40), *O Choille*

gu Bearradh (*From Wood to Ridge: Collected
Poems*, 1989)

10 A bhàta dhuibh, a Ghreugaich choimhlionta,
cluas siùil, balg siùil làn is geal,
agus tu fhéin gu foirfeach ealanta
sàmhach uallach gun ghiamh gun ghais. . .

† Black boat, perfect Greek,
sail tack, sail belly full and white,
and you yourself complete in craft,
silent, spirited, flawless. . .

'Am Bàta Dubh ('The Black Boat', 1932–40),
O Choille gu Bearradh (*From Wood to Ridge:
Collected Poems*, 1989)

11 . . . esan bha 'n Glaschu,
ursann-chatha nam feumach,
Iain mór MacGill-Eain,
ceann is fèitheam ar sgeula.

† . . . he who was in Glasgow
the battle-post of the poor,
great John Maclean,
the top and hem of our story.

'Clann Ghill-Eain' ('The Clan MacLean',
1932–40), *O Choille gu Bearradh* (*From Wood to
Ridge: Collected Poems*, 1989)

12 Chunnaic mi Adharc an Sgùrr Dheirg
Ag éirigh ann an dùbhlan feirg
Anns an deifir bh' air na speuran,
'S 'nan cathadh a thilgeil nan reultan
Trianaid an Sgumain air éirigh.

† I saw the horn of Sgurr Dearg
rising in furious challenge
in the haste of the skies;
and throwing the stars in spindrift
the trinity of the Sguman risen.

'An Cuilithionn' ('The Cuillin', 1939), *O Choille
gu Bearradh* (*From Wood to Ridge: Collected Poems*,
1989), Part 2

13 Thar lochan fala clann nan daoine,
thar breòiteachd blàir is strì an aonaich,
thar bochdainn caithimh fiabhrais amhghair,
thar anacothrom eucoir ainneart ànraidh,
thar truaighe eu-dochas gamhlas cuilbheart,
thar ciont is truaillidheachd, gu furachair,
gu treunmhor chithear an Cuilithionn
's e 'g éirigh air taobh eile duilghe.

† Beyond the lochs of the blood of the
    children of men,
beyond the frailty of plain and the labour of
    the mountain,
beyond poverty, consumption, fever, agony,
beyond hardship, wrong, tyranny, distress,
beyond misery, despair, hatred, treachery,
beyond guilt and defilement; watchful,
heroic, the Cuillin is seen
rising on the other side of sorrow.

'An Cuilithionn' ('The Cuillin', 1939), *O Choille
gu Bearradh* (*From Wood to Ridge: Collected Poems*,
1989), Part 7

217

14 . . . coin chiùine cuthaich mo bhàrdachd,
madaidhean air tòir na h-àilleachd,
àilleachd an anama 's an aodainn,
fiadh geal thar bheann is raointean,
fiadh do bhòidhche ciùine gaolaich,
fiadhach gun sgur, gun fhaochadh.

† . . . the mild mad dogs of my poetry,
wolves in chase of beauty, beauty of soul
and face,
a white deer over hills and plains,
the deer of your gentle beloved beauty,
a hunt without halt, without respite.

'Coin is Madaidhean-Allaidh' ('Dogs and Wolves',
1939–41), *O Choille gu Bearradh* (*From Wood to
Ridge: Collected Poems*, 1989)

15 Sgatham le faobhar-roinn gach àilleachd
a chuir do bhòidhichead 'nam bhàrdachd;
's dèanam dàin cho lom aognaidh
ri bàs Liebknecht no daorsa. . .

† Let me lop off with sharp blade every grace
that your beauty put in my verse,
and make poems as bare and chill
as Liebknecht's death or slavery. . .

'Sgatham' ('Let me lop. . .', 1939–41), *O Choille
gu Bearradh* (*From Wood to Ridge: Collected
Poems*, 1989)

16 Thig am chomhair, oidhche chiùin,
gorm reultachd athair agus driùchd. . .

† Come before me, gentle night,
starred blue sky and dew. . .

'Oidhche Chiùin' ('Gentle Night', 1939–41), *O
Choille gu Bearradh* (*From Wood to Ridge: Collected
Poems*, 1989)

17 Chan fhaic mi fàth mo shaothrach
bhith cur smaointean an cainnt bhàsmhoir,
a nis is siùrsachd na Roinn-Eòrpa
'na murt stòite 's na cràdhlot;
ach thugadh dhuinn am muillion bliadhna
'na mhìr an roinn chianail fhàsmhoir,
gaisge 's foighidinn nan ciadan
agus mìorbhail aodainn àlainn.

† I do not see the sense of my toil
putting thoughts in a dying tongue
now when the whoredom of Europe
is murder erect and agony;
but we have been given the million years,
a fragment of a sad growing portion,
the heroism and patience of hundreds
and the miracle of a beautiful face.

'Chan fhaic mi' ('I do not see. . .', 1939–41),
O Choille gu Bearradh (*From Wood to Ridge:
Collected Poems*, 1989)

18 Tha aodann ga mo thathaich,
ga mo leantuinn dh'oidhche 's latha:
tha aodann buadhmhor nighne
's e sìor agairt.

† A face haunts me,
following me day and night,

the triumphant face of a girl
is pleading all the time.

'An Tathaich' ('The Haunting', 1939–41), *O
Choille gu Bearradh* (*From Wood to Ridge: Collected
Poems*, 1989), st.1

19 Chan eil eòl air an t-slighe
th' aig fiarachd cham a' chridhe
's chan eil eòl air a' mhilleadh
do'n tàrr gun fhios a cheann-uidhe.

† There is no knowledge of the course
of the crooked veering of the heart,
and there is no knowledge of the damage
to which its aim unwittingly comes.

'Coilltean Ratharsair' ('The Woods of Raasay',
1940), *O Choille gu Bearradh* (*From Wood to
Ridge: Collected Poems*, 1989), st.40

20 Cuiridh mi làmh air corran na gealaich
agus òrd ceann-chruaidh thairis
air an òr fhann is troimhe:
is canadh Dia gur h-e an toibheum.

† I will put a handle on the sickle of the moon
and a steel-headed hammer over the feeble gold
and through it: and let God call it blasphemy.

'Gealach Ur' ('A New Moon'), *Dàin do Eimhir
agus Dàin Eile* (*Poems to Eimhir and Other Poems*,
1943), st.1

21 Uair is uair agus mi briste
thig mo smuain ort is tu òg,
is lìonaidh an cuan do-thuigsinn
le làn-mara 's mìle seòl.

† Again and again when I am broken
My thought comes on you when you
were young,
And the incomprehensible ocean fills
With floodtide and a thousand sails.

'Reothairt' ('Spring Tide', 1941–4), *O Choille gu
Bearradh* (*From Wood to Ridge: Collected Poems*,
1989), st.1

22 Chunnaic mi gaisgeach mór á Sasuinn,
fearachan bochd nach laigheadh sùil air;
cha b' Alasdair á Gleanna Garadh –
is thug e gal beag air mo shùilean.

† I saw a great warrior of England,
a poor manikin on whom no eye would rest;
no Alasdair of Glen Garry;
and he took a little weeping to my eyes.

'Curaidhean' ('Heroes', 1942–3), *O Choille gu
Bearradh* (*From Wood to Ridge: Collected Poems*,
1989), st.8

23 'Na shuidhe marbh an 'Glaic a' Bhàis'
fo Dhruim Ruidhìseit,
gill' òg 's a logan sìos m' a ghruaidh
's a thuar grìsionn;

Smaoinich mi air a' chòir 's an àgh
a fhuaire e bho Fhurair,
bhith tuiteam ann an raon an àir
gun éirigh tuilleadh. . .

Sitting dead in 'Death Valley'
below the Ruweisat Ridge
a boy with his forelock down about his cheek
and his face slate-grey;

I thought of the right and the joy
that he got from his Fuehrer,
of falling in the field of slaughter
to rise no more...

'Glac a' Bhàis' ('Death Valley', 1942–3), *O Choille gu Bearradh* (*From Wood to Ridge: Collected Poems*, 1989), st.1–2

Tha tìm, am fiadh, an Coille Hallaig.

Time, the deer, is in the wood of Hallaig.

Epigraph to 'Hallaig' (1953–4), *O Choille gu Bearradh* (*From Wood to Ridge: Collected Poems*, 1989)

Ann an Screapadal mo chinnidh,
far robh Tarmad 's Eachunn Mór,
tha 'n nigheanan 's am mic 'nan coille
ag gabhail suas ri taobh an lóin.

In Screapadal of my people,
where Norman and Big Hector were,
their daughters and their sons are a wood
going up beside the stream.

'Hallaig' (1953–4), *O Choille gu Bearradh* (*From Wood to Ridge: Collected Poems*, 1989), st.3

... 's nuair theàrnas grian air cùl Dhùn Cana
thig peileir dian á gunna Ghaoil;

's buailear am fiadh a tha 'na thuaineal
a' snòtach nan làraichean feòir;
thig reothadh air a shùil 'sa choille:
chan fhaighear lorg air fhuil ri m' bheò.

... and when the sun goes down behind
  Dun Cana
a vehement bullet will come from the gun
  of Love;

and will strike the deer that goes dizzily,
sniffing at the grass-grown ruined homes;
his eye will freeze in the wood,
his blood will not be traced while I live.

'Hallaig' (1953–4), *O Choille gu Bearradh* (*From Wood to Ridge: Collected Poems*, 1989), st.13–14

Carson a dh'fhàg e Dùis MhicLeòid,
Na bruthaichean gorma 's na lochan,
Na rubhannan, na h-eileanan 's na tràighean,
An t-aran, an fheòil 's am fìon
'S an t-eathar mór ud air an fhàire,
An Cuilithionn far an robh e riamh?

Why did he leave the Land of MacLeod,
the green braes and the lochs,
the headlands, the islands and the shores,
the bread, the flesh and the wine,
and that big boat on the horizon,
the Cuillin where it always was?

'Uamha 'n Oir' ('The Cave of Gold', post-1972), *O Choille gu Bearradh* (*From Wood to Ridge: Collected Poems*, 1989), Part 1, st.7

28 Chunnaic e each mór a spéis
Air sréin 's air teadhair aig na bha...

† He saw the great horse of his aspirations
bridled and tethered by the past...

'Uamha 'n Oir' ('The Cave of Gold', post-1972), *O Choille gu Bearradh* (*From Wood to Ridge: Collected Poems*, 1989), Part 2, st.14

29 Thogadh ròn a cheann
Agus cearban a sheòl,
Ach an diugh anns an linnidh
Togaidh long-fo-thuinn a turraid
Agus a druim dhubh shlìom
A' maoidheadh an ní a dheanadh
Smùr de choille, de lianagan 's de chreagan,
A dh'fhàgadh Screapadal gun bhòidhche
Mar a dh' fhàgadh e gun daoine.

† A seal would lift its head
and a basking-shark its sail,
but today in the sea-sound
a submarine lifts its turret
and its black sleek back
threatening the thing that would make
dross of wood, of meadows and of rocks
that would leave Screapadal without beauty
just as it was left without people.

'Screapadal' (post-1972), *O Choille gu Bearradh* (*From Wood to Ridge: Collected Poems*, 1989), st.10

McGinn, Matt 1928–77
Glasgow songwriter and folksinger

1 Your daddy coories doon my darling,
Doon in a three foot seam,
So you can coorie doon my darling,
Coorie doon and dream.

'Coorie Doon' (1962), also known as 'The Miner's Lullaby', st.4. In *McGinn of the Calton: the Life and Works of Matt McGinn* (1987)

2 Did ye find a red Yo-Yo, red Yo-Yo, red Yo-Yo,
Did ye find a red Yo-Yo wi' a wee yellow string?

'The Red Yo-Yo' (1964), chorus. In *McGinn of the Calton: the Life and Works of Matt McGinn* (1987)

3 I work a' day and I work a' night,
Tae hell wi' you Jack, I'm all right.
Three nights and a Sunday double time.

'Three Nights and a Sunday' (1964), chorus. In *McGinn of the Calton: the Life and Works of Matt McGinn* (1987)

4 The leaders o' the nation made money
  hand o'er fist
By grinding down the people by the fiddle and
  the twist,
Aided and abetted by the preacher and
  the Press –
John called for revolution and he called for
  nothing less.

Dominie, Dominie,
There was nane like John Maclean,
The fighting Dominie.

'The Ballad of John Maclean' (1967), st.4 and chorus. In *McGinn of the Calton: the Life and Works of Matt McGinn* (1987)

5 He kept bees in the old town of Effen
An Effen beekeeper was he
And one day this Effen beekeeper
Was stung by a big Effen bee

Now this big Effen beekeeper's wee Effen wife
For the big Effen polis she ran
For there's nobody can sort out a big Effen bee
Like a big Effen polisman can

'The Bee from the Old Town of Effen', st.1–2. In *McGinn of the Calton: the Life and Works of Matt McGinn* (1987)

In a note to this poem the 'sleepy little town of Effen' is described as lying 'nine hundred and twenty-two and a half miles outside Ecclefechan, in fact, in France'

6 The butchers of Glasgow have all got their pride
But they'll tell you that Willie's the prince
For Willie the butcher he slaughtered his wife
And he sold her for mutton and mince.

'The Butchers of Glasgow', st.1. In *McGinn of the Calton: the Life and Works of Matt McGinn* (1987)

7 I'm looking for a job with a sky-high pay,
A four-day week and a two-hour day,
It's maybe just because I'm inclined that way
But I never did like being idle!

'I'm Looking for a Job', chorus. In *McGinn of the Calton: the Life and Works of Matt McGinn* (1987)

McGonagall, William c.1825–1902

Self-styled 'poet and tragedian', regarded by many as the worst poet ever published

1 Alas! Lord and Lady Dalhousie are dead, and buried at last,
Which causes many people to feel a little downcast...

'The Death of Lord and Lady Dalhousie', *Poetic Gems* (1890), st.1

2 'Twas in the month of December, and in the year 1883,
That a monster whale came to Dundee,
Resolved for a few days to sport and play,
And devour the small fishes in the silvery Tay.

'The Famous Tay Whale', *Poetic Gems* (1890), st.1

3 Then hurrah! for the mighty monster whale,
Which has got 17 feet 4 inches from tip to tip of a tail!
Which can be seen for a sixpence or a shilling,
That is to say, if the people all are willing.

'The Famous Tay Whale', *Poetic Gems* (1890), st.14

4 Beautiful Railway Bridge of the Silv'ry Tay!
Alas! I am very sorry to say
That ninety lives have been taken away
On the last Sabbath day of 1879,
Which will be remember'd for a very long time.

'The Tay Bridge Disaster', *Poetic Gems* (1890), st.1

5 Ye lovers of the picturesque, if ye wish to drown your grief,
Take my advice, and visit the ancient town of Crieff;
The climate is bracing, and the walks lovely to see
Besides, ye can ramble over the district, and view the beautiful scenery.

'Beautiful Crieff', *More Poetic Gems* (1962), st.1

6 The man that gets drunk is little else than a fool,
And is in the habit, no doubt, of advocating for Home Rule;
But the best Home Rule for him, as far as I can understand,
Is the abolition of strong drink from the land.

'The Demon Drink', *Last Poetic Gems* (1968), st.9

McGonagall was politically conservative, a Unionist and a teetotaller

McGrath, John Peter 1935–

English-born playwright, film producer and director, artistic director of 7:84 Scotland (1973–88)

1 BILLY: But we came, more and more of us, from all over Europe, in the interests of a trade war between two lots of shareholders, and in time, the Red Indians were reduced to the same state as our fathers after Culloden – defeated, hunted, treated like the scum of the earth, their culture polluted and torn out with slow deliberation and their land no longer their own.

The Cheviot, the Stag and the Black, Black Oil (1973)

2 JOHN:... the tragedy of the Highlands has become a saleable commodity.

The Cheviot, the Stag and the Black, Black Oil (1973)

3 ANDY MCCHUCKEMUP (a Glasgow Property-operator's man): The motel – as I see it – is the thing of the future... So – picture it, if yous will, right there at the top of the glen, beautiful vista – The Crammem Inn, High Rise Motorcroft – all finished in natural, washable, plastic granitette. Right next door, the 'Frying Scotsman' All Night Chipperama – with a wee ethnic bit, Fingal's Cafe – serving seaweed suppers in the basket and draught Drambuie. And to cater for the younger set, yous've got your Grouse-a-go-go... So – picture it, if

yous will – a drive-in clachan on every hill-top where formerly there was hee-haw but scenery.

The Cheviot, the Stag and the Black, Black Oil (1973)

`GENERAL` JOE SMITH: I've been deid and cauld in the earth two hundred year, and I've slept in my grave through mony's the disaster – aye – through Napoleon's wars and the Kaiser's wars and Hitler's wars too. But the thunderous apathy of the devolution vote has finally aroused me from the sleep of the just – Ye had yer chance to beat yer ain drum and what did you dae?... *Naethin'*...

Joe's Drum (1979)

5 Working-class audiences like laughs; middle-class audiences in the theatre tend to think laughter makes the play less serious.

A Good Night Out (1981), ch.3

... for many people [television]... goes with carpet slippers, cocoa and biscuits to nibble; it is an amenity, like soft toilet-paper.

A Good Night Out (1981), ch.6

McGrath, Tom 1940–
Dramatist and poet

MAW: When he was younger, he wantit tae be an altar boy. But he wusnae allowed because he didnae huv any sandshoes – and ah couldnae afford tae buy him any. It wus oanly the toaffs that could afford tae kneel oan God's altar.

The Hardman (with Jimmy Boyle, 1977), Act 1

2 BYRNE: Sometimes violence has a reason on the streets – it's political, or religious, or a junkie killing for drugs – either a reason or an excuse. But in the world that I come from, violence is its own reason. Violence is an art form practised in and for itself.

The Hardman (with Jimmy Boyle, 1977), Act 1

3 BYRNE: Ma road's mapped oot fur me. Ah keep a chib over the door an a blade in ma bedroom. That's when ahm no oan the run or oot causin damage. Ah'm for the Bar-L. It's inevitable.

The Hardman (with Jimmy Boyle, 1977), Act 1
Bar-L: Barlinnie Prison, Glasgow

McGregor, Archie
Editor of football fanzine The Absolute Game

People would get fairly desperate – it would be like having no sex. It's been important for Scotland culturally for the past one hundred years, particularly for the working class, and a lot of us like to claim Scotland as the cradle of football.

On whether Scotland could survive without football. Quoted in *Scotland on Sunday* (5 Apr 1992)

MacGregor, Sir Ian Kinloch 1912–
Scottish-born American business executive, Chairman of the National Coal Board (1983–6)

1 People are now discovering the price of insubordination and insurrection. And, boy, are we going to make it stick.

Said during the miners' strike. Quoted in the *Sunday Telegraph* (10 Mar 1985)

McGregor, Iona
Novelist

1 We have become visible to ourselves and each other, as well as to the general public who are now aware that we exist in large numbers. When word is out, that can bring its own problems; but the worst oppression is self-oppression.

On gay and lesbian self-confidence in spite of recent anti-homosexual legislation (Section 28/29 of the 1989 Local Government Act banned the promotion of homosexuality in schools). 'Visibility Eighties Rising', in Toni Davidson (ed.), *And Thus Will I Freely Sing: An Anthology of Gay and Lesbian Writing from Scotland* (1989)

2 'When did you first realise?' remains a question of endless interest to homosexuals. (The final seal of equality will be the freedom to ask 'When did you first realise you were heterosexual?')

Introduction to Joanne Winning (ed.), *The Crazy Jig: Gay and Lesbian Writing from Scotland 2* (1992)

Macgregor, Jimmie 1932–
Broadcaster and folksinger

1 Oh, he's fitba' crazy, he's fitba' mad,
And the fitba' it has robbed him o' the wee bit sense he had.
And it would take a dozen skivvies, his clothes to wash and scrub,
Since our Jock became a member o' that terrible fitba' club.

'Fitba' Crazy' (1959)
Adapted from Joe Gordon's version

MacGregor, Peter 1848–98
Poet

1 'S cian bhon rèitich iad air falbh sinn
Lag is treun thar sléibhtean Albainn,
'S 'gar co-éigneachadh thar fairge
Gus an do shealbhaich damh nan cròc iad...

Gun do dh'fhògair iad gu lèir sinn
As ar còirichean le eucoir,
'S ar blàth chòmhnardan fo fhéidh
Is luchd na Beurla gabhail spòrs dheth.

† It is a long time since they cleared us away,
weak and strong alike, over the hills of
Scotland, compelling us to go ourselves and
leaving the antlered stag in possession. . .

They unjustly banished us all from our
rightful possessions. Our sheltered fields
are under deer to make sport for those of
English speech.

'Teann a-nall is éisd na facail' ('Draw near and
hear the words'). Quoted in Iain Thornber, *The
Gaelic Bards of Morvern* (1985)

MacGregor, Stuart 1942–73
Poet and songwriter

1 My father's name was Harry
My mother's name was Ann,
Come sit beside me, come dry all my tears
I've been wronged by a Sandy Bell's man.

'The Sandy Bell's Man', *Poems and Songs*
(1974), chorus

Sandy Bell's: a famous pub in Edinburgh

2 The west wind blows to Coshieville, and with
the winds came we,
But where the river hugs the wood
And blackthorns flower in May there stood
A single rowan tree
So young and slender, so were you,
I loved you both as there you grew
The day I took the road that leads
By Rannoch to the sea.

'Coshieville', *Poems and Songs* (1974), st.1

McIlvanney, Hugh 1933–
Sports journalist

1 A sense of proportion is anathema to the
Glasgow drinker. When he goes at the bevvy
it is a fight to the death.

'One for the High Road', in Miles Kington (ed.),
Punch on Scotland (1977)

2 During the past six months, MacLeod's
pronouncements on his assignment have shown
all the objective restraint of the Highland Light
Infantry going over the top.

On Scotland manager Ally MacLeod's prepara-
tions for the 1978 World Cup in Argentina. 'The
Pride of our Ally', *The Observer* (28 May 1978).
Reprinted in *McIlvanney on Football* (1994)

3 Barring the kind of miracle that no one here
is prepared to believe in, the party is surely
over and the Scots are left with little but dirty
glasses and the stale smell of spent euphoria.

Following the defeat by Peru in Scotland's
opening game of the World Cup finals. 'Scotland:
The Party is Over, 3–1', *The Observer* (4 Jun
1978). Reprinted in *McIlvanney on Football* (1994)

4 If there is ever a World Cup for self-
destructiveness, few nations will have the nerve
to challenge the Scots. It seems astonishing
that the race has never produced a kamikaze
pilot, but perhaps the explanation is that all the
volunteers insisted on attacking sewage farms.

'A Case of Kamikaze in Cordoba', *The Observer*
(11 Jun 1978). Reprinted in *McIlvanney on
Football* (1994)

5 Some of us have been acknowledging through
most of our lives that the game is hopelessly
ill-equipped to carry the burden of emotional
expression the Scots seek to load upon it. What
is hurting so many now is the realisation that
something they believed to be a metaphor for
their pride has all along been a metaphor for
their desperation.

'A Case of Kamikaze in Cordoba', *The Observer*
(11 Jun 1978). Reprinted in *McIlvanney on
Football* (1994)

6 With his drill-sergeant's hairstyle, his boxer's
stance and his staccato, hard-man's delivery he
did not fit everybody's idea of a romantic. But
that's what he was, an out-and-out, 22-carat
example of the species. His secret was that
he sensed deep down that the only practical
approach to sport is the romantic one. How
else could a manager persuade grown men that
they could glory in a boy's game?

On Bill Shankly. 'A Man with More than
Education', *The Observer* (4 Oct 1981). Reprinted
in *McIlvanney on Football* (1994)

7 . . . a volcano trapped in an iceberg.

On Lester Piggott. 'The Master's Last Furlong?',
The Observer (2 Jun 1985). Reprinted in
McIlvanney on Horseracing (1995)

8 Busby emanated presence, substance, the quality
of strength without arrogance. No man in my
experience ever exemplified better the ability
to treat you as an equal while leaving you with
the sure knowledge that you were less than
he was. Such men do not have to be elected
leaders. Some democracy of the instincts and
the blood elects them to be in charge.

On Matt Busby. 'Farewell to the Ultimate
Football Man', *The Sunday Times* (23 Jan 1994).
Reprinted in *McIlvanney on Football* (1994)

9 On the matter of origins, it is one of the most remarkable facts in football that the small coalfield
which once spread across part of Lanarkshire
and southern Ayrshire produced three of the
greatest managers and most formidable individuals the game has ever known: Busby himself;
Bill Shankly. . . and Jock Stein. . . Plainly, there
were more than coal seams running through
that bleak landscape in the West of Scotland.
There were seams of rich humanity, of working-
class pride and wit and energy and character.

'Farewell to the Ultimate Football Man', *The

Sunday Times (23 Jan 1994). Reprinted in *McIlvanney on Football* (1994)

10 Race trains are like troop trains without the dread. We have camaraderie and coarse humour, an adrenaline flood that sharpens the senses and boosts the appetite for living. But running through it all is the blissful reassurance that the conflict we are approaching is make-believe, an arena in which everyday reality is suspended in favour of a theatrically heightened version.

McIlvanney on Horseracing (1995), Introduction

McIlvanney, William 1936–

Novelist, poet and essayist

1 . . . the heart of any place is the relationships you have there. Geography is people.

'Growing up in the West', in Karl Miller (ed.), *Memoirs of a Modern Scotland* (1970)

2 Outside the walls, the machinery was clanking on, and whether it needed your hand or your eyes or your legs or yourself to run on made no difference to anything. That was simply what it needed. That was all that mattered. You didn't. Personal responses were irrelevant.

Docherty (1975), Bk 2, ch.15

3 'We walk a nerra line. Ah ken hoo nerra it is. Ah've walked it a' ma days. Us an' folk like us hiv goat the nearest thing tae nothin' in this world. A' that filters doon tae us is shite. We leeve in the sewers o' ither bastards' comfort. The only thing we've goat is wan anither. That's why ye never sell yer mates.'

Docherty (1975), Bk 3, ch.5 (Tam Docherty)

4 . . . I think Scots is like English in its underwear, you know it likes to dismantle pretensions. . . You know you can't fake it, you can't be as hypocritical, I think it's very difficult to be pompous in Scots.

Quoted in Billy Kay, *Scots – The Mither Tongue* (1986), ch.11, 'The Future Oors?'

5 In the library the first time
I stood in a pool of awe.
Wonder for taking, acres of promises.
The lady with the specs
And the hair-tuft on her cheek
Asking me if I had washed my hands.

'In the Library', *In Through the Head: Selected Poems* (1988)

6 Bless this house, wherever it is,
This house and this and this and this,

Pitched shaky as small nomad tents
Within Victorian permanence,

Where no name stays long, no families meet
In Observatory Road and Clouston Street. . .

'Bless this House: a sampler for Glasgow bedsits', *In Through the Head: Selected Poems* (1988)

7 It's not that we lost, but that it meant so much. Losing a football match shouldn't be confused with loss of identity. I suspect that the kind of commitment Scots invest in football means that there's less left for more important concerns.

On Scotland's performance in the 1978 World Cup finals in Argentina. 'Before: February 1979 – Referendum', in *Surviving the Shipwreck* (1991)

8 . . . Margaret Thatcher is not just a perpetrator of bad policies. She is a cultural vandal. She takes the axe of her own simplicity to the complexities of Scottish life. She has no understanding of the hard-earned traditions she is destroying. And if we allow her to continue, she will remove from the word 'Scottish' any meaning other than the geographical.

'Stands Scotland Where It Did?' Speech at the Scottish National Party's annual conference, Dundee (Sep 1987). Published in *Surviving the Shipwreck* (1991)

9 There is a deeply ingrained tradition in Scotland that we will not finally judge one another by material standards. A country as poor as we have been for so long has at least learnt that there are more important measures of a human being than the financial – more significant assessments of a nation than the stock market. We have a humane tradition to uphold second to that of no other nation.

'Stands Scotland Where It Did?', *Surviving the Shipwreck* (1991)

10 . . . Scotland is one of the most intense talking-shops I have ever been in. Here the Ancient Mariner haunts many pubs and Socrates sometimes wears a bunnet, and women at bus-stops say serious things about the world.

'The Shallowing of Scotland', Part 6, 'A Socialist Scotland?', *Surviving the Shipwreck* (1991)

11 . . . the selling of Glasgow as some sort of yuppie freehold is a diminution of Glasgow. . . The reality is much more complex. Glasgow is a great city. Glasgow is in trouble. Glasgow is handsome. Glasgow is ugly. Glasgow is kind. Glasgow is cruel. Some people in Glasgow live full and enlightened lives. Some people in Glasgow live lives bleaker than anyone should live – and die deaths bleaker than anyone should die.

On 'Glasgow's Miles Better' and other promotional campaigns. 'Where Greta Garbo Wouldn't Have Been Alone', *Surviving the Shipwreck* (1991)

12 So much of Glasgow humour is disbelief under anaesthetic. It is anger with the fuse snuffed but still smoking.

'Where Greta Garbo Wouldn't Have Been Alone', *Surviving the Shipwreck* (1991)

13 Humane irreverence more than the big ships, Glasgow's greatest export.

'Where Greta Garbo Wouldn't Have Been Alone', *Surviving the Shipwreck* (1991)

14 When someone rejects utterly your beliefs and your identity, the only pride, the only pragmatism, is to return that rejection in total. Those who live by the anathema should perish by the anathema.

Pre-election essay, *Scotland on Sunday* (8 Mar 1992)

He was specifically advocating the removal of the remaining nine Conservative MPs in Scotland. In the general election the following month, the Conservative Party returned 11 MPs in Scotland

Macintosh, Charles 1766–1843

Chemist and manufacturer of dyes and waterproof clothing

1 I fear that the development of the railways will destroy the need for waterproof coats.
Attrib.

Macintyre, Duncan Ban
see **Mac an t-Saoir, Donnchadh Bàn**

Mack, John

Folksinger and songwriter

1 O ye canny spend a dollar when ye're deid, O ye canny spend a dollar when ye're deid: Singin' Ding. . . Dong. . . Dollar; Everybody holler
Ye canny spend a dollar when ye're deid.

'Ding Dong Dollar' (1961), chorus, in *Rebels Ceilidh Song Book No.2* (n.d.)

Sung in protest at the US nuclear submarine base in the Holy Loch, Argyll

McKail, Hugh 1640–66

Covenanting preacher and martyr

1 Friends and fellow-sufferers, be not afraid. Every step of this ladder is a degree nearer Heaven.

On mounting the gallows in Edinburgh (22 Dec 1666). Quoted in James Stirling and Sir James Stewart, *Naphtali, or The Wrestlings of the Church of Scotland For the Kingdom of Christ* (1667)

Mackay (of Clashfern), Lord (James Mackay) 1927–

Judge and Lord Chancellor (1987–)

1 The law cannot make two people continue to love each other.

On his proposed divorce law reforms in England

and Wales. Quoted in *The Independent* (12 Dec 1993)

Mackay, John Alexander 1889–1983

Church of Scotland missionary and ecumenical theologian

1 Let the Church know herself, whose she is and what she is. . . This means concretely that the Church recognise herself to be the Church of Christ, the organ of God's purpose in Him. It must be her ceaseless concern to rid herself of all subjugation to a prevailing culture, an economic system, a social type, or a political order.

Study paper ('Let the Church be the Church') presented at the Oxford Conference on Life and Work (1937), quoted in N M Cameron, D F Wright et al., *Dictionary of Scottish Church History and Theology* (1993)

Mackay was later put to the test of his own principles when, as Moderator of the Presbyterian Church in the USA (1953), he defended himself and others against McCarthyite accusations of collaborating with Communism

Mackay, John Henry 1864–1933

Scots-born poet, novelist, anarchist and campaigner for homosexual freedom

1 Yet since you think it a dirty thing Have dragged it through mud and infamy And kept in the dark under lock and key – This love will I freely sing.

'The Nameless Love', st.2. Originally published in German under the pseudonym 'Sagitta' in *Der Eigene* (1905). Translated by Hubert Kennedy and published in Toni Davidson (ed.), *And Thus Will I Freely Sing* (1989)

Mackay, Robert see **Rob Donn**

McKelvey, Willie (William) 1934–

Labour MP for Kilmarnock and Loudon

1 I would have resigned if I had anything to resign from.

On the Labour Party's U-turn on holding a referendum on Scottish devolution. Quoted in *The Scotsman* (29 Jun 1996)

Mackenzie, Sir (Edward Montague) Compton 1883–1972

English-born novelist and Scottish nationalist

1 Women do not find it difficult nowadays to behave like men, but they often find it extremely difficult to behave like gentlemen.

Literature in My Time (1923), ch.22

2 One day a novelist with that [ie homosexual] temperament will have the courage to write about himself as he is, not as he would be were he actually Jane or Gladys or Aunt Maria.

> Said in 1927. Quoted in Edwin Morgan, Introduction to Toni Davidson (ed.), *And Thus Will I Freely Sing* (1989)

3 Do you plan to be a politician? Statesmanship is now a profession. You need no longer trouble to stimulate a detached and disinterested patriotism. You will not be expected to rise above place-hunting. Your career will depend on the skill with which you can mingle impudence on the hustings with modesty on the back benches. If you should be fortunate enough to represent a Scottish constituency you will be able to give up to party what was meant for country, and you will call the sacrifice a realisation of larger issues.

> Rectorial address at Glasgow University (1932)

4 As a girl Caroline Macdonald had suffered from the Lone Shieling complex. She had seen the fairies in a peach-orchard on the shores of Lake Ontario. She had repined at not having been christened Flora, but had derived a measure of consolation from the thought that Caroline was the feminine of Charles.

> *The Monarch of the Glen* (1941), ch.1.
> Cf. Anonymous 41

5 'A nation which thinks that the news of the world in the six o'clock bulletin is a tiresome postponement of the football results is marching in blinkers along the road to ruin.'

> *The North Wind of Love* (1944), Bk 1, p.30 (John Ogilvie)

6 What comes from the sea should go to the people.

> On the wreck of the SS *Politician* off Eriskay (1941), from which the people of Barra salvaged approximately 5,000 cases of whisky. His novel *Whisky Galore* (1947) was based on this incident

7 Doubloons, ducats, and ducatoons, moidores, pieces of eight, sequins, guineas, rose and angel nobles, what are these to vaunt above the liquid gold carried by the *Cabinet Minister*? It may be doubted if such a representative collection of various whiskies has ever been assembled before... There were Highland Gold and Highland Heart, Tartan Milk and Tartan Perfection, Bluebell, Northern Light, Preston Pans, Queen of the Glens, Chief's Choice and Prince's Choice, Islay Dew, Silver Whistle, Salmon's Leap, Stag's Breath, Stalker's Joy, Bonnie Doon, Auld Stuarts, King's Own, Trusty Friend, Old Cateran, Scottish Envoy, Norval, Bard's Bounty, Fingal's Cave, Deirdre's Farewell, Lion Rampart, Road to the Isles, Pipe Major, Moorland Gold and Moorland Cream, Thistle Cream, Shinty, Blended Heather, Glen Gloming, Mountain Tarn, Cromag, All the Year Round, Clan MacTavish and Clan MacNab, Annie Laurie, Over the Border, and Caberfèidh.

> *Whisky Galore* (1947), ch.10, 'Whisky Galore'

8 Well, I think it has become a kind of folk-tale... rather like Aladdin... because it goes on and on....

> On the film of his novel, *Whisky Galore* (directed by Alexander Mackendrick, 1948). BBC Radio interview (1966), quoted in Murray Grigor, 'Whisky Galore!', in Eddie Dick (ed.), *From Limelight to Satellite* (1990)

Mackenzie, Sir George 1636–91

Jurist, writer, Lord Advocate and founder of the Advocates' Library

1 ... a statue of dust kneaded with tears, moved by the hid engines of his restless passions; a clod of earth, which the shortest fever can burn to ashes and the least shower of rheums wash away to nothing...

> On mankind. *Religio Stoici* (1663)

2 The mad-cap zealots of this bigot age, intending to mount Heaven, Elias-like, in zeal's fiery chariot, do, like foolish Phaeton, not only fall themselves from their flaming seat, but by their furious over-driving, envelop the world in unquenchable combustions: and when they have set the whole globe on a blaze, this they term a new light.

> *Religion Stoici* (1663)

3 If laws and lawgivers did not make heretics vain, by taking too much notice of their extravagancies, the world should be no more troubled with them... It fares with them as with tops, which how long they are scourged keep foot and run pleasantly, but fall how soon they are neglected and left to themselves.

> *Religio Stoici* (1663)

4 To me it appears undeniable that the Scottish idiom of the British tongue is more fitting for pleading than either the English idiom or the French tongue: for certainly a pleader must use a brisk, smart, and quick way of speaking: whereas the English, who are a grave nation, use too slow and grave a pronunciation, and the French a too soft and effeminate one. And therefore I think the English is fit for haranguing, the French for complimenting, but the Scots for pleading. Our pronunciation is like ourselves, fiery, abrupt, sprightly, and bold...

> *Pleadings in Some Remarkable Cases before the Supreme Court of Scotland* (1672), Preface

5 Albeit witchcraft be the greatest of crimes, since it includes in it the grossest heresies and

blasphemies, I do conclude that of all crimes it requires the clearest relevancy and most convincing probation. . . It is dangerous that those who are of all others the most simple should be tried for a crime which is of all others the most mysterious.

Laws and Customs of Scotland (1678)

6 . . . this Parnassus and bosom of the Muses.

Of the Advocates' Library (forerunner of the National Library of Scotland), on formally opening it (1689)

Mackenzie, Henry 1745–1831
Novelist and essayist

1 The Man of Feeling

Title of novel (1771), which began a cult of sentimentality. Mackenzie himself became known by the book's title

He was also known as *Ultimus Scotorum*, on account of his being the last relic of a great era. Walter Scott, dedicating *Waverley* to him in 1814, called him 'our Scottish Addison'

2 In Scotland we can be very bitter in our Wrath, seldom jocose in our Satire; We can lash an Adversary but want the Art of laughing at him, which is frequently the severer Revenge of the two.

Letter to his cousin Elizabeth Rose (11 Oct 1774)

3 'Tis pity that the [Scots] Language. . . will probably soon become so antiquated as not to be understood: Glossaries do but very ill supply this Defect; it is a cool Operation to stop in the midst of a Sentiment or Description to scrutinise the Sense of a Vocable.

Letter to his cousin Elizabeth Rose (17 Aug 1775)

4 . . . this Heaven-taught ploughman. . .

On Robert Burns, in *The Lounger*, No.97 (9 Dec 1786)

Burns wore out two copies of *The Man of Feeling*, a book he said he valued 'next to the Bible'. Mackenzie preferred and praised Burns's English poems over his Scots ones, and for the most part ignored the latter

5 THIGGING. A good custom: a new married couple going round their friends and relations for assistance to set up house; has softened into wedding presents.

Anecdotes and Egotisms (ed. H W Thompson, 1927), ch.1. Cf. Giolla Coluim Mac an Ollaimh 1

6 ABUSE. Silent contempt is the most mortifying reception of abuse to the abuser. One of our *poissardes*, a fishwife of Newhaven, heard with seeming indifference and in silence the violent abuse of a sister of the trade. After trying in vain to rowze her into anger or provoke her

to a reply, the violent dame put her hands to her sides; her face grew red as a coal, and she uttered with a violent scream, 'Speak, you bitch, or I'll burst!'

Anecdotes and Egotisms (ed. H W Thompson, 1927), ch.5

7 Burns, originally virtuous, was seduced by dissipated companions, and after he got into the Excise addicted himself to drunkenness, tho' the rays of his genius sometimes broke through the mist of his dissipation; but the habit had got too much power over him to be overcome, and it brought him, with a few lucid intervals, to an early grave.

Anecdotes and Egotisms (ed. H W Thompson, 1927), ch.9

Mackenzie, R(obert) F(raser) 1910–87
Teacher and liberal educationist

1 Few things are as unChristian as the Scottish educational system. The intense competitiveness, the intense seeking for individual gain, the carelessness about the under-dog, the hitting of young children with a leather belt belong to an older world. It's a dark, troubled psyche that broods over the Scottish classroom.

The Unbowed Head: Events at Summerhill Academy 1968–74 (1976), ch.2

2 It is of the nature of our decaying society that it keeps its headmasters, and the company of directors and inspectors and ministry officials, so busy on the details of administration that they have no time to foresee the future and plan for it. When the ship goes down, they'll all be at their posts, filling in forms.

The Unbowed Head: Events at Summerhill Academy 1968–74 (1976), ch.4

He was headteacher at Summerhill Academy, Aberdeen and introduced a 'permissive' regime there. He was eventually removed from his post

3 After all those years in Scottish education, it is only now that I have become aware that the schools are not on our side. They are the agencies of the rulers. They bring us up to do what we are told, and not to speak back, to learn our lessons and pass the examinations. Above all not to ask questions.

A Search for Scotland (1989), ch.17

4 The young are looking far beyond the bounds of the political parties and the kirks for something that can only be described as a rebirth. . .
They could make Scotland a clearinghouse of ideas. They haven't a hangup like us adults on whether it is the will of the elected Westminster parliament or the will of the Scottish people that is sovereign and paramount when we talk

about government. They don't try to undo that tangled knot; they just cut it.

A Search for Scotland (1989), ch.18

Mackie, Alastair 1925–95
Poet

1 Her face was thrawed.
She wisna aa come.
   'Pietà', *Clytach* (1972)

2 Aifter the boombers cleck
and the sodgers traik thro the skau
there's an auld air sterts up –
bubblin and greetin.
It's a ballant mithers sing
on their hunkers i the stour
for a bairn deid.

It's the cauldest grue i the universe
yon skelloch.
It niver waukens the deid.
   'Pietà', *Clytach* (1972)

3 Elbucks on the herbour waa
the mongol quine
collogues
wi hersel. . .

She wints for naething. Yet
she's singin till the distance.
Ayont the hert-brak her een
are set for ever on an unkent airt.
   'Mongol Quine', *Clytach* (1972), st.1, 6

MacKinnon, Donald 1839–1914
Scholar and editor, first Professor of Celtic at Edinburgh University (1882–1914)

1 Cha robh focal sgoile aig Rob Donn; ach anns a' char so cha robh e air leth air cuid de na bàird as àirde cliù 'nar measg. . . Ach mur a robh sgoil aca bha foghlum aca, agus bha ionnsachadh aca. Chaill iadsan agus gu sònraichte chaill sinne móran a chionn nach b' urrainn iad leughadh no sgrìobhadh. Ach chan fhaod sinn a smuaineachadh gu robh an duine nach b' urrainn leughadh anns an am ud 'na dhuine aineolach mar a tha an duine nach urrainn leughadh an diugh. . . Chan e a mhàin gu robh eòlas aig na daoine so air bàrdachd, air eachdraidh agus air deas-ghnàthan nan Gàidheal, ach bha fiosrachadh earbsach aca mu thimcheall cùisean agus modh-riaghlaidh na rìoghachd 'nan latha féin nach faigh thu aig móran de sgoilearan no aig cuid de mhaighistirean-sgoile ar latha-ne.

† Rob Donn had not a word of formal schooling; but in that respect he was no different from some of the most famous poets among us. . . But if they lacked schooling, they did have learning and education. They lost much and in particular we have lost, because they could not read or write. But we must not think that a person who could not read in that age was ignorant as a person who cannot read today is ignorant. . . It is not only that those men and women knew poetry and history and the customs of the Gael: they possessed reliable information about the affairs and principles of government of the kingdom in their time such as you find among few literate people, or even among the schoolmasters, of our own day.

   'Rob Donn', in L MacKinnon (ed.), *Prose Writings of Donald MacKinnon* (1956)

2 Is ann do'n bhàrd féin a bhuineas a ràdh co dhiùbh a théid no nach téid roinn shònraichte d'a shaothair a chumail air ais o'n t-sluagh. Ach ma tha thusa ag gabhail os làimh dol a chruinneachadh saothair bàird as déidh a bhàis cha tig e dhuit teachd eadar coguis a' bhàird agus còir an t-sluaigh, agus a ràdh, 'Tha an t-òran so no an t-òran ud eile salach, neo-airidh air a' bhàrd. Nam biodh e-féin beò dh'aontaicheadh e leam. Fàgaidh mi iad so a mach.' Is e do dhleasdanas-sa na gheibh thu de fhìor shaothair a' bhàird a thoirt seachad air a' cheart dòigh air am faigh thu i, no gun ghnothach a ghabhail ris an obair idir.

† It is for the poet himself to say whether a certain portion of his work is to be kept back from the public. But if you are going to undertake to collect a poet's work after his death, it is not fitting for you to come between the poet's conscience and the rights of the public and say: 'This song or that is dirty, unworthy of the poet. If he were alive himself he would agree with me. I'll leave it out.' It is your duty to deliver whatever you get of the real work of the poet in the exact form in which you find it or else have nothing to do with it at all.

   'Rob Donn', in L MacKinnon (ed.), *Prose Writings of Donald MacKinnon* (1956)

3 Tha e 'na chùis-iongnaidh dhuinne an diugh a bhith leughadh beachdan luchd-turuis mu'n Ghàidhealtachd còrr agus ceud bliadhna roimhe so. . . Tha aon. . . duine tuigseach, beachdail, a sgrìobh mu chóig bliadhna deug roimh Chùil-lodair, Mr Burt, ag coimeas mullach nam beann àrda ri 'ceann sgràbach'; ag innseadh 'cho uamhasach agus a tha an sealladh an uair a dh'amhaircear air na beanntan o'n ear gus an iar agus a chithear am meudachd ana-cuibhseach, an cumadh oillteil, agus an dorchadas eagalach a tha eatorra leis an dubhar a tha gach aon a' tilgeadh.' Ach dh'fhalbh an latha so. Thug Seumas Mac Mhuirich seachad bàrdachd Oisein anns a' Bheurla o chionn cóig deug agus cóig fichead bliadhna, agus riamh o'n am sin tha litreachas nan Gall agus nan Sasannach cho

làn de mhaise na tìre agus a bha i roimhe cho
falamh. Coma an tràths' co dhiùbh is e Mac
Mhuirich a rinn 'Oisean' no nach e, b'fhìor
Ghàidheal e a dh'aon chor. B'e a' cheud aon a
sheinn am port so do na Goill; agus tha iad gu
dìcheallach 'ga dhannsadh gus an là' an diugh.

† It is a matter of astonishment for us today
to read the views of travellers about the
Highlands more than a century ago. . .
One. . . an intelligent, observant man, who
wrote some fifteen years before Culloden, Mr
Burt, compares the high mountain summits
to 'a shaggy head'; telling 'how fearful the
sight is when one looks at the mountains from
east to west and sees their immoderate size,
their horrible shape, and the terrible darkness
between them because of the shadow that each
of them casts.' But that day has gone. James
Macpherson produced the poetry of Ossian in
English a hundred and fifteen years ago, and
ever since then the literature of the Lowlanders
and the English is as full of the beauty of the
landscape as it was previously empty. Never
mind now whether it was Macpherson who
created 'Ossian' or not; he was a true Gael
in this respect. He was the first to play this
melody for the Lowlands; and they dance it
diligently to the present day.

'Bàrdachd Nàduir' ('Nature Poetry'), in
L MacKinnon (ed.), *Prose Writings of Donald
MacKinnon* (1956)

4 Tòisichear air obair an latha le ùrnuigh
dhùrachdaich an Gàidhlig; théid earrann de'n
Bhìobull a leughadh, is na Ceistean a chur.
Tha an sin sgrìobhadh is cunntas, cunntas is
sgrìobhadh, gu feasgar. Leughar am Bìobull.
Co-dhùnar le ùrnuigh. Bheirear na camain
am follais, is bithear ag iomain gus an toir an
oidhche as ar sùilean e.

'Sgoil thruagh! teagasg bochd!' their an
Leughadair. 'Tigh-sgoil truagh,' their mise,
agus teagasg easbhaidheach; ach teagasg, an
tomhas, a dh'fhaodadh a bhith air a leantainn
le buannachd am móran de na Sgoilean
Gàidhealach air an là an diugh. . . Am measg
nan seann mhaighistirean-sgoil Gàidhealach
gheibhte air uairibh na daoine a b'fhòghluimte
anns an tìr.

† The work of the day begins with an earnest
prayer in Gaelic; a portion of the Bible is read
and questions asked from the Catechism. Then
writing and reckoning, reckoning and writing,
until evening. The Bible is read. The day is
concluded with prayer. The shinty-sticks are
brought out, we play until night takes it from
our eyes.

'Miserable school! wretched teaching!' the
Reader will say. 'A miserable schoolhouse,' I
say, and inadequate instruction; but teaching
that, to a certain degree, might be followed

with profit in many of the Highland Schools
today. . . Among the old Highland schoolmasters there were at times to be found the
most learned men in the land.

'Seann Sgoil' ('The Old School', 1874), in
L MacKinnon (ed.), *Prose Writings of Donald
MacKinnon* (1956)

Mackintosh, Charles Rennie 1868–1928
Art Nouveau architect, designer and painter

1 . . . if Architecture has national peculiarities
impressed upon it, then it must be history –
the world's history written in stone.

'Untitled Paper on Architecture' (c.1892), in
Pamela Robertson (ed.), *Charles Rennie Mackintosh: the Architectural Papers* (1990)

2 . . . I think we should be a little less cosmopolitan and rather more national in our Architecture,
as we are with language, new words and phrases
will be incorporated gradually, but the wholesale
introduction of Japanese sentences for example
would be denounced and rightly by the purist.

'Untitled Paper on Architecture' (c.1892), in
Pamela Robertson (ed.), *Charles Rennie Mackintosh: the Architectural Papers* (1990)

3 Artists (I mean of course Architects) must be
as select in those whom they desire to please as
in those whom they desire to imitate. Without
the love of fame they can never do anything
excellent: but by an excessive and unsatiable
thirst after it they will come to have vulgar
views, they will degrade their style and their
taste will be entirely corrupted.

'Untitled Paper on Architecture' (c.1892), in
Pamela Robertson (ed.), *Charles Rennie Mackintosh: the Architectural Papers* (1990)

4 . . . architecture has the biggest programme,
the widest range of sympathy and action of all
the arts – it is more practical – it demands more
technical workshop knowledge, it deals with
a greater number of materials – of subjects –
of fellow workmen than any other art, except
perhaps music. At least this is being more
generally admitted for the day is happily passing
away when architecture may be deemed a thing
of quantities of dilettanteism and drains.

'Architecture' (1893), in Pamela Robertson (ed.),
*Charles Rennie Mackintosh: the Architectural
Papers* (1990)

5 Old architecture lived because it had a purpose.
Modern architecture, to be real, must not be
a mere envelope without contents.

'Architecture' (1893), in Pamela Robertson (ed.),
*Charles Rennie Mackintosh: the Architectural
Papers* (1990)

6 You ask how are you to judge architecture.
Just as you judge painting or sculpture – form,
colour, proportion, all visible qualities – and

the one great invisible quality in all art, soul.

> 'Architecture' (1893), in Pamela Robertson (ed.), *Charles Rennie Mackintosh: the Architectural Papers* (1990)

7 Don't meddle with other people's ideas when you have all your work cut out of you in trying to express your own – Shake off all the props – the props tradition and authority offer you – and go alone. Crawl – stumble – stagger – but go alone – You cannot learn to walk without tumbles and knocks and bruises, but you will never learn to walk so long as there are props.

> 'Seemliness' (1902), in Pamela Robertson (ed.), *Charles Rennie Mackintosh: the Architectural Papers* (1990)

8 Art is the flower – Life is the green leaf. Let every artist strive to make his flower a beautiful living thing – something that will convince the world that there may be – there are things more precious – more beautiful more lasting than life.

> 'Seemliness' (1902), in Pamela Robertson (ed.), *Charles Rennie Mackintosh: the Architectural Papers* (1990). Cf. Patrick Geddes 9

9 . . . something vital, something good, the only possible art for all and the highest achievement of our time.

> On Modernism. Quoted in Duncan Macmillan, *Scottish Art in the 20th Century* (1994), ch.1

Mackintosh, Sir James 1765–1832
Philosopher, reformer and historian

1 The Commons, faithful to their system, remained in a wise and masterly inactivity . . .

> On the Third Estate's refusal to compromise its demands for voting reforms in the French States-General. *Vindiciae Gallicae* (1791), section 1
>> This book was a defence of the French Revolution, responding to Edmund Burke's condemnation of it

2 The accumulation of that power which is conferred by wealth in the hands of the few, is the perpetual source of oppression and neglect to the mass of mankind.

> *Vindiciae Gallicae* (1791), section 1. Cf. David Hume 24

3 Men will not long dwell in hovels, with the model of a palace before their eyes.

> On expectations for improvement raised by the spread of liberal ideas under the Ancien Regime. *Vindiciae Gallicae* (1791), section 1

4 Were that House [of Commons] really to become the vehicle of the popular voice, the privileges of other bodies, in opposition to the sense of the people and their representatives,

would be but as dust in the balance . . . We desire to avert revolution by reform – subversion by correction.

> On political reform in Britain. *Vindiciae Gallicae* (1791), section 5

5 Affectation, the most ridiculous of faults . . . the frivolous work of polished idleness.

> *Dissertation on the Progress of Ethical Philosophy* (1830), 'Remarks on Thomas Brown'

6 Men are never so good or so bad as their opinions.

> *Dissertation on the Progress of Ethical Philosophy* (1830), 'Jeremy Bentham'

Maclaren, Ian (pseudonym of John Watson) 1850–1907
Minister and writer

1 'Lord Jesus, remember my dear maister, for he's been a kind freend to me and mony a puir laddie in Drumtochty. Bind up his sair heart and give him licht at eventide, and may the maister and his scholars meet some mornin' where the schule never skails, in the Kingdom o' oor Father.'

> *Beside the Bonnie Brier Bush* (1894), 'Domsie', ch.3 (the dying words of George Howe, the story's 'lad o' pairts')
>> Maclaren's book, the archetypal kailyard novel, was a huge bestseller in Scotland, England and America

2 There are such things as drains, and sometimes they may have to be opened, but one would not for choice have one opened in his library.

> 'Ugliness in Fiction', in *Literature* No.1 (1897)

MacLaren, John 1667–1750
Evangelical Church of Scotland minister

1 My friends, I know well what you say in your own defence: it is not the liquor that makes you sit so long, but the company. But, I trow, when the liquor is done there is an end to the company.

> From a sermon against hard drinking. Quoted in John Ramsay of Ochtertyre, *Scotland and Scotsmen in the Eighteenth Century* (1888 edition), Vol.1, p.259, footnote

McLaren, Priscilla (née Bright) 1815–1906
English-born first president of the first Scottish women's suffrage society (the Edinburgh National Society for Women's Suffrage)

1 Scotland has witnessed many a noble gathering in the cause of liberty, but never one nobler

than the one I look upon tonight, over which I have the honour to preside.

> At a women's suffrage demonstration held in St Andrews Hall, Glasgow (3 Nov 1882), to celebrate the winning of the municipal franchise by Scottish women. Quoted in *The Glasgow Herald* (4 Nov 1882)

MacLean, Alistair 1922–87
Novelist

1 Ach, any fool can write a book.

> Giving advice to Bill Knox, himself at the start of a career as a writer, shortly after the publication of his bestselling first novel, *HMS Ulysses* (1955). Quoted in Jack Webster, *Alistair MacLean* (1991), ch.11

2 Ice Station Zebra

> Title of novel (1963)

3 When Eight Bells Toll

> Title of novel (1966)

4 Where Eagles Dare

> Title of novel (1967)

MacLean, Dougie 1954–
Singer, songwriter and instrumentalist

1 If I should become a stranger
You know that it would make me more than sad
Caledonia's been everything I've ever had

> 'Caledonia', on *Craigie Dhu* (1983)

McLean, Duncan 1964–
Writer

1 I do reckon Burns' poetry is well worth getting intimate with – no matter how many stuffed-shirt-and-sporran, secret-handshaking, hairy-balled and lily-livered, tartan-Tory half-wits agree with me.

> On the bicentenary of the death of Robert Burns. 'The Mortal Memory', *The List*, No.270 (Jan 1996)

Maclean, John 1879–1923
Revolutionary Marxist, appointed Soviet Consul in Glasgow following the Russian Revolution

1 The times we live in are so stirring and full of change that it is not impossible to believe we are in the rapids of revolution.

> Speech to the Renfrewshire Co-operative Conference (25 Nov 1911)

2 The only war that is worth waging is the Class War. . .

> *The Vanguard* (1915)

At his trial (10 Nov 1915) for making anti-recruiting statements prejudicial to the war effort at his weekly political meetings in Bath Street, Glasgow, Maclean explained his position: 'I said "I have been enlisted in the Socialist Army for fifteen years, the only army worth fighting for. God damn all other armies!" Take out of that what meaning you like.' He was fined £5

3 No human being on the face of the earth, no government is going to take from me my right to speak, my right to protest against wrong, my right to do everything that is for the benefit of mankind. I am not here, then, as the accused; I am here as the accuser of capitalism dripping with blood from head to foot.

> Speech at his trial for sedition in Edinburgh (9 May 1918)

4 We are out for life and all that life can give us.

> Speech at his trial for sedition in Edinburgh (9 May 1918)

5 Scotland must again have independence, but not to be ruled by traitor kings or chiefs, lawyers and politicians. The communism of the clans must be re-established on a modern basis. . . The country must have but one clan, as it were – a united people working in co-operation and co-operatively, using the wealth that is created. We can safely say, then: back to communism and forward to communism.

> *All Hail! The Scottish Communist Republic!* (Aug 1920)
>
>> This pamphlet was reissued in 1922 under its better known title, *All Hail! The Scottish Workers' Republic!*

6 I for one am out for a Scottish Workers' Republic.

> Speech at his trial for sedition in Glasgow (25 Oct 1921)

7 Lenin's gramophone.

> On Willie Gallacher, leading Communist politician, who persuaded Lenin to oppose Maclean's demands for a Scottish Communist Party. Quoted in Nan Milton, Biographical Introduction to John Maclean, *In the Rapids of Revolution* (1978)
>
>> 'I for one will not follow a policy dictated by Lenin until Lenin knows the situation more clearly than he possibly can know it [from Gallacher]', Maclean wrote in a pamphlet, 'The Irish Tragedy' (1920). In his election address of 1922 he said, 'I am not prepared to let Moscow dictate to Glasgow.'

MacLean, Sorley
see **MacGill-Eain, Somhairle**

McLellan, Andrew 1944–

Church of Scotland minister

1 . . . the best kind of nationalism that knows how to love our own nation more without loving other nations less.

> On the movement for a Scottish parliament, speaking at the launch of the Scottish Constitutional Convention's document on Home Rule, *Scotland's Parliament, Scotland's Right* (30 Nov 1995). Quoted by Lesley Riddoch in *The Scotsman* (1 Dec 1995)

2 Christians ought to observe the law and support the state. But ever since New Testament times, Christians have also felt that they have an obligation to God and that may occasionally come into conflict with the obligation to the state.
  When that happens, Christians have found that what, in prayer and conscience, they take to be the will of God, takes precedence over the laws of the state.

> Speaking as outgoing convenor of the Church and Nation Committee at the General Assembly (22 May 1996). Quoted in *The Scotsman* (23 May 1996)

> He was justifying the Assembly's decision to give guidelines to congregations which decided to give sanctuary to foreign asylum seekers facing deportation by the government

McLellan, Robert 1907–85

Dramatist and short-story writer

1 THE KING: God, I'm wabbit!

> *Jamie the Saxt* (1937), Act 1

2 THE KING: Mistress Edward, gie me a dram! I hae been gey near shot doun, hackit to bits, and staned to daith!

> *Jamie the Saxt* (1937), Act 4

3 MIRREN: For what we are aboot to receive may the Lord be thankit. May He prosper the cause o the true Kirk, and gar the licht o His mercie shine on aa its members. May He bring ilka singin, sweirin, tea-drinkin, horse-racin Episcopalian sinner to a true understaundin o the error o his weys, and veesit ilka Jacobite rebel wi the eternal torment o the lowin brunstane pit.

> *Torwatletie* (1946), Act 1

4 CHARLES: I am British, father. The terms 'Scotch' and 'English' became obsolete with the Union.
  LORD STANEBYRES: Did they? I'll wager ye winna fin mony Englishmen caain themselves British and stertin to talk and dress like Scotsmen. . . Ye may think ye mak no a bad shape at it,

but compared wi a real Englishman ye're like a bubbly-jock wi a chuckie in its thrapple. As for yer claes, they wad sit weill on a lassie, but they're haurdly fit weir for a man. Hae they been peyed for?

> *The Flouers o Edinburgh* (1947), Act 1

> In a famous stage direction, McLellan wrote of the character Charles: 'He speaks his formal English with a marked Scots accent, and his part must *on no account* be played by an English actor.'

5 LORD STANEBYRES: He's tryin to speak English.
  LADY ATHELSTANE: I ken. But what wey? He kens we aa speak Scots here. He spak Scots himsell afore he gaed awa. What's come ower ye, Chairlie?
  CHARLES: I simply refuse to be provincial.
  LADY ATHELSTANE: Oh. I hope ye'll pardon the rest o us for juist bidin naitural.

> *The Flouers o Edin.burgh* (1947), Act 1

> Set in 18th-century Edinburgh, the play centres on the desire of the upper classes to rid themselves of Scotticisms and learn to speak and write English

6 LORD STANEBYRES: I'm quite content wi my Scots.
  BALDERNOCK: Ye're fleein in the face o progress.
  LORD STANEBYRES: Progress is a cheynge for the better. This'll be a cheynge for the waur. Whan the haill Toun sterts to talk like Chairlie, it'll be gey ill to thole.

> *The Flouers o Edinburgh* (1947), Act 1

7 CHARLES: Father, what are you talking about? What possible connection can exist between goats in the Sahara and sheep in the Highlands?
  LORD STANEBYRES: They baith hae the same kind o teeth.

> *The Flouers o Edinburgh* (1947), Act 2

Maclennan, Robert Adam Ross 1936–

Liberal Democrat politician, MP for Caithness and Sutherland (1966–   )

1 Tony Blair has pushed moderation to extremes, he has gone over the top with restraint, he has reduced his party to a sort of smiling anaemia.

> On the new leader of the Labour Party. Quoted in *The Independent* (25 Sep 1994)

MacLeod, Donald fl.1814–57

Rossal stonemason, whose accounts of the Sutherland clearances appeared in the Edinburgh Weekly Chronicle (1840–1)

1 I was present at the pulling down and burning of the house of William Chisholm, Badinloskin, in which was lying his wife's mother, an old bed-

ridden woman of nearly 100 years of age, none of the family being present. . . On [Mr Sellar's] arrival I told him of the poor old woman being in a condition unfit for removal. He replied, 'Damn her, the old witch, she has lived too long; let her burn.' Fire was immediately set to the house, and the blankets in which she was carried were in flames before she could be got out. . . She died within five days.

> Letter 4 in the *Edinburgh Weekly Chronicle* (1840–1). Reprinted in *Gloomy Memories* (1857), his riposte to Harriet Beecher Stowe's *Sunny Memories of Foreign Lands* (1854). Cf. Harriet Beecher Stowe 1

2 Can you or any other believe that a poor sinner like Donald MacLeod would be allowed for so many years to escape with impunity, had he been circulating and publishing calumnious, absurd falsehoods against such personages as the House of Sutherland. No, I tell you, if money could secure my punishment, without establishing their own shame and guilt, that it would be considered well-spent long ere now, – they would eat me in penny pies if they could get me cooked for them.

> Addressed to Harriet Beecher Stowe, in *Gloomy Memories* (1857)
>
> > Responding to her suggestion that his published account of the Sutherland clearances was imaginative and partly fictional

3 I have read from speeches delivered by Mr Loch at public dinners among his own party, 'that he would never be satisfied until the Gaelic language and the Gaelic people would be extirpated root and branch from the Sutherland estate; yes, from the highlands of Scotland.'

> *Gloomy Memories* (1857). Cf. James Loch 1, 2

4 Sufferings have been inflicted in the Highlands as severe as those occasioned by the policy of the brutal Roman kings in England; deer have extended ranges, while men have been hunted within a narrower and still narrower circle. The strong have fainted in the race for life; the old have been left to die.

> *Gloomy Memories* (1857)

5 It is a Satanic imposture, that the stewardship of God's soil is freely convertible into a mischevious power of oppressing the poor. The proper use of property is to make property useful; where this is not done, it were better for land owners to have been born beggars, than to live in luxury while causing the wretched to want and weep.

> *Gloomy Memories* (1857)

Macleod, Fiona (pseudonym of William Sharp) 1855–1905

Poet and novelist of the 'Celtic twilight' school

1 Here in the heart of summer, sweet is life
to me still,
But my heart is a lonely hunter that hunts on
a lonely hill.

> 'The Lonely Hunter', *From the Hills of Dream* (1901), st.6
>
> > The American novelist Carson McCullers (1917–67) adapted the last line for the title of her 1940 novel *The Heart is a Lonely Hunter*

2 And as a silent leaf the white bird passes,
Winnowing the dusk by dim forgetful streams.

> 'The Valley of White Poppies', *Poems and Dramas* (1912), st.4
>
> > Jessie Kesson used the phrase 'the white bird passes' as the title for her first novel (1958)

MacLeod, George Fielden (Baron MacLeod of Fuinary) 1895–1991

Church of Scotland minister and founder of the Iona Community

1 The Churchless Million are largely the blame of the Church herself and, until we set our house in order, we dare not blame one single soul. If only she would lift up her eyes and look into the fields, she would still find them ripe unto the harvest. If the Church cares even now to take her serious part, the answer to Scotland for Christ is as certain as the dawn.

> *Are Not the Churchless Million Partly the Church's Fault?* (Church of Scotland pamphlet, 1933)

2 Success is hearing the voice of God no louder than thunder in distant hills on a summer day.

> Quoted in *Can These Stones Live?* (BBC film, 30 Sep 1964)
>
> > This remark was made, according to MacLeod, by a stranger who approached him while he sat, depressed, on a hill in Iona in 1940, at a time when the Community was suspected of being a nest of pacifists, communists and revolutionaries

3 Criticism is good for a movement. More often than not the criticism can teach you things, and also rallies invariably more friends than foes.

> Sermon, 'God Pays on Time'. Quoted in R Ferguson, *George MacLeod, Founder of the Iona Community* (1990), ch.13

4 I do not hate the Communists because of their ultimate programme, which is indistinguishable from the Christian one, but I do not like their methods.

> Speech in support of the Labour candidate for Hillhead, Glasgow. Quoted in *The Glasgow Herald* (18 Feb 1950)

5 You go down into that dark, seemingly grave-like valley that is called pacifism, a valley largely untrodden since the first three centuries of Christianity. When you first find yourself there, phantom serpents seem to be hissing at you, 'cowardice!' and 'treason!' All the centuries-old tradition of Scotland and our fathers whisper around you and half of your best friends, if only by their silent eyes, seem to be saying, 'Mad! Mad! Mad!' and yet there is no halting place of sanity higher up.

The time is past when men can speak of war as an instrument of policy. . . I for one cannot press that button. Can you?

Speaking at the General Assembly (24 May 1952) against the atomic bomb

6 I simply argue that the Cross be raised again at the centre of the market-place as well as on the steeple of the church. I am recovering the claim that Jesus was not crucified in a cathedral between two candles, but on a cross between two thieves; on the town garbage-heap; at a crossroad so cosmopolitan that they had to write his title in Hebrew and in Latin and in Greek. . . at the kind of place where cynics talk smut, and thieves curse, and soldiers gamble. Because that is where churchmen should be and what churchmanship should be about.

Only One Way Left (1956). Cf. Norman Shanks 1

7 . . . when is it God's purpose that his people should rebel against lawful authority? This for years was John Knox's great agony. . . We all know what his final answer was. . .

Unless the 'sovereignty of the monstrous regiment of the damned bomb' is annulled soon, may it be that the real celebration of the Reformers will be seen in the witness of those who, for the freedom of men and, indeed, for the continuance of civilisation, unilaterally rise up against the possibility of its use? High treason? Yes indeed. And was not Knox a traitor?

Article in *The Glasgow Herald* (1960). Quoted in R Ferguson, *George MacLeod, Founder of the Iona Community* (1990), ch.21. Cf. John Knox 1

MacLeod, Kenneth
see MacLeòid, Coinneach

MacLeod, Norman 1812–72

Church of Scotland minister of the Barony Church, Glasgow (1851–72), chaplain to Queen Victoria

1 People talk of early morning in the country with bleating sheep, singing larks and purling brooks. I prefer the roar which greets my ears

when a thousand hammers, thundering on boilers of steam vessels which are to bridge the Atlantic or Pacific, usher in a new day – the type of a new era. I feel men are awake with me, doing their work, and that the world is rushing on to fulfil its mighty destinies, and that I must do my work, and fulfil my grand and glorious end.

Quoted in R Ferguson, *George MacLeod, Founder of the Iona Community* (1990), ch.7

Norman MacLeod was the grandfather of George MacLeod

2 Courage, brother! do not stumble, Though thy path be dark as night; There's a star to guide the humble: 'Trust in God and do the right.'

Hymn, 'Courage, brother! do not stumble', st.1

The last line appears on Earl Haig's tomb at Dryburgh Abbey

MacLeòid, Coinneach (Kenneth MacLeod) 1871–1955

Folklorist, songwriter and minister in Colonsay and Gigha

1 Theirteadh gum 'bu dual do isean an ròin dol thun na mara', 's tha e ceart cho dual don Eileanach a shùil agus a chridhe 's a làmh a thionndadh ris a' Chuan Shiar. 'S gun tighinn air sin idir, ar leam gu bheil rud-eigin an litreachas na mara, doimhneachd is dian-theas is balbh-neart, nach eil idir cho tric rim faotainn an litreachas na beinne.

† It was said that 'it is in the nature of the seal's pup to go to the sea', and it is quite as natural for the Islander to turn his eye and his heart and his hand to the Western Ocean. And without mentioning that at all, it seems to me that there is something in the literature of the sea, a profundity and an intense heat and a hushed strength, that is not at all so frequently to be found in the literature of the mountain.

'Duatharachd na Mara' ('The Mystery of the Sea'), in T M Murchison (ed.), *Sgrìobhaidhean Choinnich MhicLeòid (The Gaelic Prose of Kenneth MacLeod*, 1988)

2 A rèir beachd an t-sluaigh bu bheò-chreutair an Cuan Siar, le faireachdainnean daonda, 's le cumhachd thar comas nàduir, thar comas aona chuid maith no uilc. Ach cha do shaoil neach riamh sin a thaobh na beinne; air a h-àirdead is ar a maisead bu bheinn i iochd air n-achd, 's ged thachradh na daoine, cha charaicheadh na cnuic.

† According to the belief of the people the Western Ocean was a living being, with human feelings, and with a power beyond the power

of nature, beyond either the power of good or evil. But no one ever thought that about the mountain; no matter how high or how beautiful it was, the mountain was a mountain, of necessity; and although people might come together, the hills would not stir.

> 'Duatharachd na Mara' ('The Mystery of the Sea'), in T M Murchison (ed.), *Sgrìobhaidhean Choinnich MhicLeòid* (*The Gaelic Prose of Kenneth MacLeod*, 1988)

3 Sure, by Tummel and Loch Rannoch and Lochaber I will go,
By heather tracks wi' heaven in their wiles;
If it's thinkin' in your inner heart braggart's in my step,
You've never smelt the tangle o' the Isles.
Oh, the far Coolins are puttin' love on me,
As step I wi' my cromak to the Isles.

> 'The Road to the Isles', chorus

Mac Mhaighstir Alasdair, Alasdair
see **Alasdair Mac Mhaighstir Alasdair**

Mac Mhurchaidh, Iain
see **Iain Mac Mhurchaidh**

MacMillan, Hector 1929–
Playwright

1 UNA: We're bound t'make it an addict t'somethin. Maybe whisky would be less damagin than prejudice.

> Refusing whisky because she is pregnant. *The Sash My Father Wore* (1973), Act 2

2 BRIDGET: If you hadda listened t'the church, you wouldn't be standin there with a big pregnant belly on you, an no sign of a ring on your finger!
UNA: No! I'd have a ring on me finger, and never done being pregnant!

> *The Sash My Father Wore* (1973), Act 2

3 CAMERON: We should fling the hale fukn religious thing oot the fukn windae!. . . Jesus Christ. There's too many Gods. Everybody's got wan. Everybody's got the *right* wan!

> *The Sash My Father Wore* (1973), Act 2

McMillan, Joyce 1952–
Theatre critic and journalist

1 . . . art is not the only thing on Demarco's mind, and certainly not the only thing on Haynes'; both are great socialisers, and keen and unapologetic woman-fanciers of the kind that flourished briefly in the window of opportunity between the decline of Victorian morality and the rise of feminism.

> On the early 1960s outlook of Richard Demarco and Jim Haynes, two of the founders of the Traverse Theatre, Edinburgh. Quoted in *The Traverse Theatre Story 1963–1988* (1988), ch.1

2 . . . whatever the source of the anti-English passion, it's of no use to Scotland now. At worst, it gives the nationalist movement a poisoned strength that can only lead to racism and chauvinism; at best, a burning hatred for Jimmy Hill is a poor substitute for a positive vision of Scotland reborn as a modern, inventive and enlightened social democracy in Europe.

> 'Tartan special', in *Scotland on Sunday* (15 Jul 1990)

McMillan, Margaret 1860–1931
American-born pioneer of nursery education and campaigner for social reform in Britain

1 What is the use of saying 'We must begin with children'? Too late. We must begin with the babies.

> Written c.1894, her first year as a member of the Bradford School Board. Quoted in Elizabeth Bradburn, *Margaret McMillan: Portrait of a Pioneer* (1989), ch.8

2 The State compels the children to work – it makes the demand for sustenance urgent, intolerable. But it does not compel parents to feed their children. Hence it is certain that to some of these hungry little ones free education is less of a boon than an outrage.

> Campaigning for the provision of school meals paid for by the state. *Early Childhood* (1901), pp.152–3
>
> > The Education (Provision of Meals) Bill was passed by the new Liberal government in December 1906, introducing the first state-subsidised meals for school children

3 The classroom of today is not the classroom of yesterday. It is full of new light – and of new shadows. As time goes on, some will make strange discoveries. And some, for the sake of comfort, may pull down the blinds. But the brave will not pull down the blinds. They will go on fearlessly to note conditions – to unearth the causes of defect, disease, suffering, and failure, to set these open to the sunshine of an enlightened public opinion, and to lay the foundations of a happier order of social life, and a new era of human progress.

> *Labour and Childhood* (1907), p.205

4 The entrance of women into Parliament should, and will, we believe, be the death knell of misery, slow torture, early death and neglect of children. The nation will be disgraced whose

women, having power, do not take care of its little ones.

> 'Dawn of the Women's Day in Politics', *The Labour Leader* (31 Oct 1918). Quoted in Elizabeth Bradburn, *Margaret McMillan: Portrait of a Pioneer* (1989), ch.18

Parents do not cease to be parents necessarily when they cease to be drudges. Nor does their work cease necessarily when they have washed, fed, and clothed their children. For a human being, even if he be very poor, is a soul, is he not, as well as a body?

> 'Nursery Schools and Parents', in the *Times Educational Supplement* (6 Mar 1919)

Education should make even the poorest district beautiful and create Edens in the heart of mean streets. . .

> 'Leaflet for the Visitors present at the Stone-Laying Ceremony' at the Rachel McMillan College (6 Nov 1929). Quoted in Elizabeth Bradburn, *Margaret McMillan: Portrait of a Pioneer* (1989), ch.22
>
> > The training college for nursery and infant teachers was established as a tribute to her sister, Rachel (1859–1917), with whom she had set up a Baby Camp in Deptford in 1911. In 1918, Margaret had opened the Rachel McMillan Open-air Nursery School. She dreamed that this was the first step towards gathering all 'neglected, suffering, dirty little children now playing in the gutter, and near roaring traffic and hooting cars. . . into gardens at last'

7 Reform. Reform. That's what Scotland needs. What memories of suffering and cruelty I have of my native land.

> Remembering her own schooling in Inverness. Letter to Rev J Mackenzie (7 Jul 1930). Quoted in Elizabeth Bradburn, *Margaret McMillan: Portrait of a Pioneer* (1989), ch.2

8 Progress is not a triumphant riding on; it is a painful stumbling on.

> *The Nursery School* (1930). Quoted in Elizabeth Bradburn, *Margaret McMillan: Portrait of a Pioneer* (1989), ch.19

9 Educate every child as if he were your own.

> Her motto, quoted by G Yorath in Elizabeth Bradburn, *Margaret McMillan: Portrait of a Pioneer* (1989), ch.21
>
> > She was herself a single woman who did not give birth to any children

McMillan, Roddy 1923–79
Actor and playwright

1 BOB: There's roughly three kinds o blokes get loose efter school. . . Third kind's the wans wi the itch. . . the fullas ah'm talking aboot don't seem tae need whit the rest o us need. They've a kinna instinct, an' it gets them through. Some o them turn intae bookies, some do well at the buyin an' sellin, but occasionally ye get wan an' he really makes a name. Nae real start in life, but he's got the itch.

> *The Bevellers* (1973), Act 1

2 ALEX: Get away fae it. Ye spend yur days grindin gless, an' at the finish yur life's like slurry at the bottom o the wheel. Yur back's like the bent bit o an oul' tree an' yur hauns are like jaurries aboot the knuckles. . . Get somethin' else – anythin'. Get intae the sun an' the fresh air.

> *The Bevellers* (1973), Act 1

Macmurray, John 1891–1976
Philosopher

1 If we confess, as I think we must, that we live in a world that has gone mad, we have to remember that madness is a malady of the human mind. The world outside us can't be mad: only the world inside us is capable of sanity and insanity. Plainly, there is something serious the matter with us. We have lost our hold on reality, and the world will continue to reflect the Bedlam inside us until we recover our sanity.

> *Freedom in the Modern World* (1932), 'The Modern Dilemma', section 1, 'Is there a Modern Dilemma?'

2 Freedom depends upon Reality. The sense of constraint in human life is always the result of unreality in human life. We are free only when we are real.

> *Freedom in the Modern World* (1932), 'Reality and Freedom', section 1, 'About Philosophy and its Problems'

3 The strongest condemnation of modern industrial life is not that it is cruel and materialistic and wearisome and false, but simply that it is ugly and has no sense of beauty. Moral conduct *is* beautiful conduct. If we want to make the world better, the main thing we have to do is to make it more beautiful.

> *Freedom in the Modern World* (1932), 'Reality and Freedom', section 12, 'The Final Summary: Self-Realisation'

4 We shall never be saved by science, though we may be destroyed by it. It is to art and religion that we must look; and both of these depend on freedom of feeling.

> *Freedom in the Modern World* (1932), 'Reality and Freedom', section 12, 'The Final Summary: Self-Realisation'

5 Self-realisation is the true moral ideal.

> *Freedom in the Modern World* (1932), 'Reality

and Freedom', section 12, 'The Final Summary: Self-Realisation'

6 Freedom is our nature. But our nature lies always beyond us, and has to be intended and achieved. The obstacle lies in our fear, and the craving for security which expresses it. So at every crisis we are faced with a free choice between freedom and security. If we choose security, and make that our aim, we lose freedom, and find in the end that security eludes us. . . If we choose freedom we may find the security we do not seek, though of this there can be no guarantee: yet it is the only path that offers promise of security.

Conditions of Freedom (1950), ch.3

7 All meaningful knowledge is for the sake of action, and all meaningful action for the sake of friendship.

The Self as Agent (1957), 'Introductory'

8 The business of a university is to be the cultural authority of the region that it serves. In virtue of this it can and should hold together every aspect of human culture, in its widest sense, in a unity.

'The Idea of a University', *Times Educational Supplement for Scotland* (4 Dec 1970)

McNaughtan, Adam 1939–

Glasgow songwriter and folksinger

1 Oh where is the Glasgow where I used tae stey,
The white wally closes done up wi' pipe cley;
Where ye knew every neighbour frae first floor tae third,
And tae keep your door locked was considered absurd?
Do you know the folk steying next door tae you?

'The Glasgow I Used to Know', st.1. Quoted in Norman Buchan and Peter Hall (eds), *The Scottish Folksinger* (1973)

2 Oh where is the Glasgow that I used tae know,
Big Wullie, wee Shooey, the steamie, the Co.,
The shilpet wee bauchle, the glaiket big dreep,
The ba' on the slates, an' yer gas in a peep?
If ye scrape the veneer aff, are these things still there?

'The Glasgow I Used to Know', st.6. Quoted in Norman Buchan and Peter Hall (eds), *The Scottish Folksinger* (1973)

3 Oh ye cannae fling pieces oot a twenty storey flat,
Seven hundred hungry weans'll testify to that.
If it's butter, cheese or jeely, if the breid is plain or pan,
The odds against it reaching earth are ninety-nine tae wan.

'Skyscraper Wean', chorus. Quoted in Norman

Buchan and Peter Hall (eds), *The Scottish Folksinger* (1973)

A Glasgow song, highlighting one of the potential problems of moving from a tenement to a multi-storey flat

4 The boay says, 'Right, Ah'll dae it, but Ah'll huvti play it crafty.
So that naeb'dy will suspect me, Ah'll kid oan that Ah'm a daftie.'

'Oor Hamlet'. Quoted in Gordon Jarvie (ed.), *The Scots Reciter* (1993)

5 Hamlet, Hamlet! Aw the gory!
Hamlet, Hamlet! End of story.
Hamlet, Hamlet! Ah'm away!
If you think this is boring, you should read the bloody play!

'Oor Hamlet'. Quoted in Gordon Jarvie (ed.), *The Scots Reciter* (1993)

MacNeacail, Aonghas 1942–

Poet

1 sgrìobh thu air m' anam
do nàdur, a bhidse gun chridhe, is dhùin
thu an leabhar gu grad mus d'ràinig
sinn deireadh ar sgeulachd. . .

† you etched your nature
on my spirit, heartless bitch, and
snapped shut the book before we had reached
the end of our story. . .

'dàn' ('poem/fate'), *An Seachnadh agus dàin eile* (*The Avoiding and other poems*, 1986)

2 'tha gàidhlig beò'
a dh'aindeoin gach saighead
's i streap nan sithean
fiùran daraich fo h-achlais
a sùilean dùbhlanach
a' sìneadh gu fàire fad' as. . .

† 'gaelic is alive'
despite all arrows
she climbs the hillside
sapling of oak in her arms
her defiant eyes
reaching the far-off horizon. . .

'tha gàidhlig beò' ('gaelic is alive'), *An Seachnadh agus dàin eile* (*The Avoiding and other poems*, 1986)

3 ach dèan dannsa dèan dannsa
's e obair th'ann a bhith dannsa

† but be dancing be dancing
it is work to be dancing

'tha gàidhlig beò' ('gaelic is alive'), *An Seachnadh agus dàin eile* (*The Avoiding and other poems*, 1986)

4 cha b'eachdraidh ach cuimhne
màiri mhòr, màiri mhòr
a dìtidhean ceòlar,
cha b'eachdraidh ach cuimhne

na h-òrain a sheinn i
dha muinntir an cruaidh-chàs
dha muinntir an dùbhlan. . .

it wasn't history but memory
great mary macpherson
her melodic indictments,
it wasn't history but memory
the anthems she sang
for her people distressed
for her people defiant. . .

'oideachadh ceart' ('a proper schooling'), in
C Whyte (ed.), *An Aghaidh na Siorraidheachd*
(*In the Face of Eternity*, 1991)

McNeill, F(lorence) Marian 1885–1973
Folklorist and social historian

Since the Reformation, which effected a
radical change in the national character, the
proverbial Scot has been reared on porridge
and the Shorter Catechism, a rigorous diet, but
highly beneficial to those possessed of sound
digestive organs.

The Scots Kitchen (1929), ch.2, 'The National
Larder'

. . . in the haggis we have concocted from
humble, even despised ingredients, a veritable
plat de gourmets. It contains a proportion of
oatmeal, for centuries the national staple, whilst
the savoury and wholesome blending of the
cereal with onion and suet. . . is typically
Scottish. Further, it is a thoroughly democratic
dish, equally available and equally honoured
in castle, farm and croft. Finally, the use of
the paunch of the animal as the receptacle of
the ingredients gives the touch of romantic
barbarism so dear to the Scottish heart.

The Scots Kitchen (1929), 'Dishes of Meat'

It is an age of science, they say. Maybe so, but
the province of science is bounded by the five
senses, and how much lies beyond!

The Silver Bough Vol.1 (1957), ch.1, 'Introductory'

Primitive man was an intense realist: otherwise
he could not have survived. If he worshipped the
sun and the moon and the heavenly bodies, it
was not primarily for their inherent mystery. . .
but because they mysteriously regulated the
seasons and brought him food.

The Silver Bough Vol.1 (1957), ch.1, 'Introductory'

Magic is not religion, but magic and religion
have developed by similar processes from
primitive thought and ritual; magic is not
science, but magic, alchemy and science form
a direct sequence.

The Silver Bough Vol.1 (1957), ch.6, 'Magic'

MacNeill, Hector 1746–1818
Poet and novelist

1 They're *now* nae langer wi' affection
Skreen'd by their Laird's ance warm protection,
Nor by your Ladyship's kind care;
But driven out helpless, naked, bare,
To meet cauld poortith's nipping blast,
And on the wide warld houseless cast
To beg for help, since rich new Comers
Hae changed to frost their ance warm summers!

On the Highland Clearances. *Bygane Times, and
Late Come Changes* (2nd edition, 1811)

2 Come under my plaidie, the nicht's gaun to fa';
Come in frae the cauld blast, the drift and
the snaw;
Come under my plaidie, and sit down beside me,
There's room in't, dear lassie, believe me,
for twa.

'Come Under My Plaidie', st.1

3 I lo'ed ne'er a laddie but ane,
He lo'ed ne'er a lassie but me;
He's willing to mak me his ain,
And his ain I am willing to be.
He has coft me a rokelay o' blue,
And a pair o' mittens o' green;
The price was a kiss o' the mou,
And I paid him the debt yestreen.

'I Lo'ed Ne'er a Laddie but Ane', st.1

Robert Burns ascribed this opening stanza to
John Clunie, minister of Borthwick (d.1819);
MacNeill added several more verses

4 My luve's in Germanie, send him hame, send
him hame;
My luve's in Germanie, send him hame.
My luve's in Germanie,
Fighting brave for royalty,
He may ne'er his Jeanie see –
Send him hame.

'My Luve's in Germanie', st.1

Although claimed by MacNeill, the authorship
of this song (to the tune of 'Ye Jacobites by
Name') remains doubtful

Maconochie, Allan
see **Meadowbank, 1st Lord**

Maconochie-Welwood, Alexander
see **Meadowbank, 2nd Lord**

MacPherson, Archie 1935–
Sports commentator and writer

1 MACPHERSON: Well, I don't know why the ref
ruled out that goal. He didn't look offside to me.
Possibly hand ball? What do you think, Davie?

DAVIE PROVAN: Archie, the ball hit the side-netting. It's a bye-kick.

> Football commentary on Radio Clyde. Quoted by Graham Spiers in *Scotland on Sunday* (24 Dec 1995)

Macpherson, James 1736–96
Poet, 'translator' of Ossianic Gaelic poetry

1 Dark Cuthullin shall be great or dead!

> *Fingal* (1761), Bk 1

2 In peace thou art the gale of spring. In war the mountain-storm.

> *Fingal* (1761), Bk 6

3 We rose on the wave with songs. We rushed, with joy, through the foam of the deep.

> *Fingal* (1761), Bk 6 (closing words of the epic)

4 The human passions lie, in some degree, concealed behind forms and artificial manners; and the powers of the soul, without an opportunity of exerting them, lose their vigour. The times of regular government and polished manners are, therefore, to be looked for by the feeble and weak in mind. An unsettled state, and those convulsions which attend it, is the proper field for an exalted character, and the exertion of great parts. Merit there rises always superior; no fortuitous event can raise the timid and mean into power.

> 'Dissertation concerning the Poems of Ossian', written as a preface to *Temora* (1763)

5 If tradition could be depended upon, it is only among a people from all time free from intermixture with foreigners. . . Such are the inhabitants of the mountains of Scotland. . . Their language is pure and original, and their manners are those of an ancient and unmixed race of men.

> On the power of isolation to preserve tradition. 'Dissertation concerning the Poems of Ossian', written as a preface to *Temora* (1763)

MacPherson, John (known as 'the Glendale Martyr') ?1845–1924
Crofter and leading agitator for land reform in the Highlands

1 . . . if the present land laws exist much longer the whole population will be paupers except the ministers, factors and landlords.

> Reported in the *North British Daily Mail* (14 May 1886). Quoted in Malcolm MacLean and Christopher Carrell (eds), *As an Fhearann* (*From the Land*, 1986)

MacPherson, Mary
see **Màiri Mhór nan Oran**

MacQueen, Robert see **Braxfield, Lord**

MacRae, Allan
Chairman of the Assynt Crofters Trust

1 It seems we have won our land. It certainly is a moment to savour, but my immediate thoughts are that some of our forbears should have been here to share it. It is an historic blow for people on the land throughout the Highlands and Islands.

> Speech in Stoer Primary School, following the sale of the North Lochinver Estate to the Assynt Crofters Trust (8 Dec 1992). Quoted in David Ross, 'The Assynt Crofters', *Scottish Affairs* No.3 (Spring 1993)

Macrae, (John) Duncan 1905–67
Actor and comedian

1 . . . The third craw was greetin' for his Maw, On a cold an' frosty mornin'.

O but the fourth craw, he wisna there at a'. . .

> 'The Three Craws', st.4–5
>> Traditional street song, popularised by Macrae

2 A wee cock sparra sat on a tree, Chirpin awa as blithe as could be.

> 'The Wee Cock Sparra', st.1
>> His version of this song, based on the original by Hugh Frater, an Edinburgh lawyer, was substantially 'Glaswegianised'

3 The man hit the boy though he wisnae his farra, And the boy stood and glowered, he was hurt to the marra.

> 'The Wee Cock Sparra', st.7

MacRae, John
see **Iain Mac Mhurchaidh**

McSporran, Alastair
Football writer and enthusiast

1 Slim Jim had everything required of a great Scottish footballer. Outrageously skilled, totally irresponsible, supremely arrogant and thick as mince.

> On Rangers player Jim Baxter, *The Absolute Game* fanzine (1990). Quoted in Kenny MacDonald, *Scottish Football Quotations* (1994)

2 The reason why we all go back, despite the rain, despite the urine, despite the macaroon bars,

despite the turgid football, despite the Pandas, despite the awful conditions, is that every so often something happens which makes it all worthwhile. . . We're Scottish! We like a bit of suffering with our pleasure! Whether Hampden is converted into a people's palace or left to rot as a gigantic folly, I somehow doubt if its unique ability to lift you out of the mundane into the realms of real cerebral ecstasy can be recaptured in any other context. . . You either got soul or you don't. Hampden had it.

> On Hampden Park, Glasgow. *The Absolute Game* fanzine (Oct 1992)

MacTaggart, John 1791–1830
Writer and Galloway folklorist

In the pingle or the pan,
Or the haurnpan o' man,
Boil the heart's bluid o' the tade,
Wi' the tallow o' the Gled. . .

> Opening lines of a witch's incantation or 'cantrip rhyme', collected by MacTaggart in *The Scottish Gallovidian Encyclopaedia* (1824)

Once, too, Curiosity dragged me to see the execution of a young man, when in Edinburgh, but she'll drag well if she drags me back again to see such a spectacle. I was not myself, Mactaggart, for a month afterwards, my mind was so disordered with the sight. . . I felt an inclination, both during night, when dream after dream whirled through my brain's airy halls, and in the day-time, to do some crime or other, that I might meet with a similar fate. Whether this is ever the way with any other person, I cannot tell, but so it operated on me, and which has caused me ever since to say, that *hanging*, instead of scaring from crime, has a strong tendency the other way. May God keep me far from seeing again any in the *dead-throws*.

> Entry on 'deads-thraws', in *The Scottish Gallovidian Encyclopaedia* (1824). Cf. Frances Wright 1

Weel aff are they aneath the mools,
They never fin' the caul ava,
But in their lanely narrow beds
Do snugly doze and rot awa.

The frost may bite, the hail may nip,
The rain may steep us to the skin,
But thae aneath the auld green truffs
The waes o' weather never fin'.

> Rhyme (st.3–4), quoted in entry on 'raw-weather', in *The Scottish Gallovidian Encyclopaedia* (1824)

SMEERIKIN – The sweetest of all kisses; the kiss one lover gives another, when they are quivering in one another's arms: few joys on earth exceed a *smeerikin*.

> Definition given in *The Scottish Gallovidian Encyclopaedia* (1824)

McTaggart, William 1835–1910
Painter

1 After all, it is not grand scenery that makes a fine landscape. You don't find the best artists working in the Alps. It's the heart that's the thing. You want to express something that appeals to our common humanity, not something extraordinary. . .

> Interview in *Black and White* (1905). Quoted in Lindsay Errington, *McTaggart* (1989)

2 No amount of finish would ever make a lie a truth.

> Quoted in William Hardie, *Scottish Painting: 1837 to the Present* (1990), ch.5, p.69

MacThòmais, Ruaraidh (Derick Thomson) 1921–
Poet

1 A' snìomh cainnte 's a' snìomh bhruadar,
ghoid siud mo shuaimhneas uam fad mo rè,
's an snìomh a rinn mi air t' òr-fhalt dualach
b'e siud am buaireadh bu mhò fon ghrèin.

† Weaving words and weaving dreams has stolen my peace from me all my days, but weaving your golden curls has brought me the greatest trouble under the sun.

> 'A' snìomh cainnte' ('Weaving words and weaving dreams'), *An Dealbh Briste* (1951), st.1

2 'S ma ruigeas mo dhùthaich-sa slànachd
cha seachainn i dànachd,
's cha chaill i a nàir'
airson gealtachd is crìonachd a dòigh,
ach cuireas i sròn ris a' gharbhlaich,
's ri crìdh na droch-aimsir,
ag èirigh air sgiathan neo-chearbach
a-mach ás a' cheò. . .
gun coisinn i fiughair
na grèine air mullach nan sgòth.

† And if my country attains wholeness
it will not shun boldness,
it will not lose its shame
for the cowardliness and barren wisdom of
its ways,
but will turn its nose to the heights,
and the heart of the storm,
rising on confident wings
out of the mist. . .
it will win the hope
of the sun above the clouds.

> 'Fàgail Leòdhais, 1949' ('Leaving Lewis, 1949'), *An Dealbh Briste* (1951), st.5

3 'Nam dhachaigh eadar dhà dhùthaich
chì thu air bùird càiricht
sligean iomallach na tràghad
is air a' bhalla, dealbh siùrsaich

is i 'na seasamh aig oisinn stràide.

† In my house, between two countries, you may
see, arrayed on tables, the far shells of the
sea-shore, and on the wall, the picture of a
harlot, standing at a street corner.

> ''Nam dhachaigh eadar dhà dhùthaich' ('In my
> house between two countries'), *An Dealbh Briste*
> (1951), st.1

4 'Nam sgrìobhadh eadar dhà chànain
chì thu ri deàlradh daoimein
cladhaicht á mèin an aoibhneis,
's a' ghrùid 's am morghan làmh riuth'
a' mùchadh, air uair, am boillsgeadh.

† In my writing, between two tongues, you can
see, gleaming, diamonds dug from the mine
of ecstasy, with the scum and the gravel by
them, choking at times their shining.

> ''Nam dhachaigh eadar dhà dhùthaich' ('In my
> house between two countries'), *An Dealbh Briste*
> (1951), st.2

5 Bidh eagal orm roimh do mhànran
's gum fàg a mhìlseachd ni leòinte
taobh-muigh do sheòmair san fhuar-ghaoth
tha reodhadh mo chainnte fuadain
's tha sgailceadh mo chridhe luainich.

† I shall be afraid of your wooing, lest its
sweetness leave me wounded, in the cold wind
outwith your chamber, freezing my fleeting
language, and splitting my heart unstable.

> ''Nam dhachaigh eadar dhà dhùthaich' ('In my
> house between two countries'), *An Dealbh Briste*
> (1951), st.4

6 . . . gluasad bithbhuan a' bhaile, am bàs 's
an ùrtan,
an ùrnaigh 's an t-suirghe, is mìle cridhe
ag at 's a' seacadh, is ann an seo
tha a' churracag a' ruith 's a' stad, 's a' ruith
's a' stad.

† . . . the everlasting movement of the village,
death and christening, praying and courting,
and a thousand hearts swelling and shrinking,
and here, the plover runs and stops, and runs
and stops.

> 'Pabail' ('Bayble'), *An Dealbh Briste* (1951), st.2

7 Cha do sguir na fir-chlis bho thàinig am
Faoilleach
a streap ri ceanglaichean dubha nan àrd-neul,
is bidh iad a' cluiche mar sin gun chaochladh
ged a chailleadh an t-eilean seo cuimhne air a
chànain. . .

† The Merry Dancers have not stopped, all
February,
climbing the black rafters of the clouds,
and will be playing like that, unchanging,
though this island should lose its
language. . .

> 'Fir-chlis' ('Merry Dancers'), *An Dealbh
> Briste* (1951)

8 . . . ach mo thruaighe an t-iomair sin thall
'na laighe,
ri dol don talamh 's gun neach ri buain ann.

† . . . but alas for the rigs over yonder lying,
returning to earth, with no one to scythe them.

> 'Ged bha ghaoth a-raoir a' sèideadh' ('Though
> the wind last night was blowing'), *An Dealbh
> Briste* (1951)

9 Nuair sheall mi 'na h-aodann preasach
chunnaic mi 'n raineach a' fàs mu thobar
a sùilean
's ga fhalach bho shireadh 's bho rùintean,
's ga dhùnadh 's ga dhùnadh.

† When I looked in her lined face
I saw the bracken growing round the well of
her eyes,
and hiding it from seeking and from desires,
and closing it, closing it.

> 'An Tobar' ('The Well'), *An Dealbh Briste*
> (1951), st.1

10 Air feasgar meallta a-measg nan adag,
is pàirt gun a bhuain, thàinig tu 'n rathad,
is chuir mi mo speal an sin am falach
air eagal gun dèanadh am faobhar do ghearradh.

† One deceptive evening, among the sheaves,
with some of the corn uncut, you came by,
and I put my scythe then in hiding, for fear
that the edge of the blade would cut you.

> 'Achadh-bhuana' ('Harvest field'), *An Dealbh
> Briste* (1951), st.1

11 A chionn 's gu bheil an dealbh briste
cuiridh mi bhuam e, chan eil buannachd
ann a bhith ga amharc, no slàinte,
a chionn 's gu bheil am balla sgàinte.

† Since the picture is broken I will put it from
me; there is no profit in looking at it, nor
healing, since the wall is cracked.

> 'A chionn 's gu bheil' ('Since the picture is
> broken'), *An Dealbh Briste* (1951), st.1

12 'S e cliù do bheatha a sheinninn,
eilein bhig riabhaich, O eilein
a thoinn do fhraoch mu mo theanga,
's a shaill le do shiaban m' anail,
is dh' iarrainn a seinn an Gàidhlig
ach am faic na thig is na thàinig
nach do mharbhadh uile gu lèir sinn
a dh' aindeoin Airm agus Nèibhi.

† It's your living praise I would sing,
brown little island, O island
that wound your heath round my tongue
and salted my breath with your brine,
and I want to sing it in Gaelic
so that people now and later
can see we were not killed entirely
in spite of the Army and Navy.

> 'Rannan air an sgrìobhadh as dèidh an ath
> chogaidh' ('Verses written after the next war'),
> *Eadar Samhradh is Foghar* (1967), st.4

An gàire mar chraiteachan salainn
ga fhroiseadh bho 'm beul,
an sàl 's am picil air an teanga,
's na miaran cruinne, goirid a dheanadh
  giullachd,
no a thogadh leanabh gu socair, cuimir,
seasgair, fallain,
gun mhearachd,
's na sùilean cho domhainn ri fèath.

Their laughter like a sprinkling of salt
showered from their lips,
brine and pickle on their tongues,
and the stubby short fingers that could
  handle fish,
or lift a child gently, neatly,
safely, wholesomely,
unerringly,
and the eyes that were as deep as a calm.

'Clann-nighean an sgadain' ('The herring girls'),
Eadar Samhradh is Foghar (1967), st.1

Cuil-lodair, is Briseadh na h-Eaglaise,
is briseadh nan tacannan −
lamhachas-làidir dà thrian de ar comas;
'se seòltachd tha dhìth oirnn.

Culloden, the Disruption,
and the breaking up of the tack-farms −
two thirds of our power is violence;
it is cunning we need.

'Cruaidh?' ('Steel?'), *Eadar Samhradh is Foghar*
(1967), st.1

. . . 's nuair a ruigeas tu Tir a' Gheallaidh,
mura bi thu air t'aire,
coinnichidh Sasannach riut is plìon air,
a dh'innse dhut gun tug Dia, bràthair athar,
  còir dha anns an fhearann.

. . . and when you reach the Promised Land,
unless you are on your toes,
a bland Englishman will meet you,
and say to you that God, his uncle, has given
  him a title to the land.

'Cruaidh?' ('Steel?'), *Eadar Samhradh is Foghar*
(1967), st.2

Is anns an sgoil eile cuideachd,
san robh saoir na h-inntinn a' locradh,
cha tug mi 'n aire do na cisteachan-laighe,
ged a bha iad 'nan suidhe mun cuairt orm;
cha do dh' aithnich mi 'm brèid Beurla,
an lìomh Gallda bha dol air an fhiodh,
cha do leugh mi na facail air a' phràis,
cha do thuig mi gu robh mo chinneadh
  a' dol bàs.

And in the other school also,
where the joiners of the mind were planing,
I never noticed the coffins,
though they were sitting all around me;
I did not recognise the English braid,
the Lowland varnish being applied to the wood,
I did not read the words on the brass,

I did not understand that my race was dying.

'Cisteachan-laighe' ('Coffins'), *Eadar Samhradh
is Foghar* (1967), st.3

17 'Se 'm peacadh as motha
a bhith càrnadh a' ghràis gu lèir 'na do
  chliabh fhèin.

† The greatest sin
is to pile all of the Grace in your own creel.

'A' cluich air football le fàidh' ('Playing football
with a prophet'), *An Rathad Cian* (1970)

18 O, nan tigeadh soisgeulaiche
a lorgadh ceann-teagaisg air na seann
  chreagan seo,
anns a riasg donn,
ann a flùraichean na machrach,
nar cainnt fhìn.

† O for an evangelist
who would find a text on these ancient rocks,
in the brown peat,
in the flowers of the machair,
in our own tongue.

'Dùsgadh' ('Re-awakening'), *An Rathad
Cian* (1970)

19 . . . iolach a' Ghaidheil
a' tighinn á cliabh na Galldachd;
nam biodh seasmhachd ás a lasair
sgrìobhte 'Saorsa' air nèamh Alba fhathast.

† . . . the Gael's exultant cry
coming from the chest of the Lowlands;
if only the flame lasted
it would write 'Freedom' on Scotland's sky yet.

On John Maclean. 'Armann' ('Warrior'), *Saorsa
agus an Iolaire* (1977)

20 Nuair a theid an Crann an àird
bidh Seoc an Aonaidh air a mhàs,
nuair a bheir tuath-ghaoth dha crathadh
bidh Seoc bochd ás aonais plathaidh,
bidh rudhadh ann an gruaidhean Seoc
nuair mhaoidheas an Crann air a shoc,
nuair chì sinn a' chrois air a' chrann
nì sinn ri ar dùthaich bann.

† When we run the Saltire up
the Union Jack will get a bump,
when the north wind makes it flutter,
Jack's old flaps will sound like butter,
and Jack's cheeks will blush right red
when the Saltire's brandished at his head,
when we see the cross on the flag-tree
we shall make a band with our land to be free.

'An Crann' ('The Plough'), *Saorsa agus an Iolaire*
(1977), Part 8

The puns in this poem are not readily
translatable. 'Crann' can mean 'plough,
cross, mast, lot, harp-key, Saltire' etc.

21 Dearg, dearg tha fuil mo bheatha,
sin an fhuil anns a bheil slàint,

nuair a laigheas làn a' bhotail
air mo sgòrnan anns a' mhadainn
tha e mar gun d'fhuair mi gràs,
dearg, dearg tha fuil a' bhotail
air mo chuisle, fuil mo ghràidh.

† Red, red is my life's blood,
that's the blood that's full of health,
when the brimming bottle lies
on my gullet in the morning
then I feel I've found grace,
red, red is the bottle's blood
on my veins, the blood I love.

'An Turas' ('The Journey'), *Saorsa agus an Iolaire* (1977), Part 3

22 . . . ceòl mìn aig deireadh an latha,
ceòl mòr anns a' chuimhne.

† . . . soft music at the end of the day,
big music in the memory.

'Adhlacadh Uistein MhicDhiarmaid 13.9.78' ('Hugh MacDiarmid's Burial 13.9.78'), *Creachadh na Clàrsaich* (1982)

23 'Se Glaschu an Eiphit a bh' agaibh
's chaidh cuid agaibh ann nur n-òige
nuair a thàinig a' chaoile air an tìr. . .

† Glasgow was your Egypt
and some of you migrated there in your youth
when the lean years came on your land. . .

'Airc a' Choimhcheangail' ('The Ark of the Covenant'), Part 16, *Creachadh na Clàrsaich* (1982)

24 Tha drùis cho eadar-nàiseanta ri Glaschu fhèin
's cho feumach
air cùil gun chuimhne,
air bàthadh
ann an cluaidh nàire.

† Lust is as international as Glasgow itself,
and a neglected corner
needs drowning
in a clyde of shame.

'Sprùilleach na drùis' ('Detritus of lust'), *Meall Garbh* (*The Rugged Mountain*, 1995)

McWilliam, Candia 1955–
Novelist

1 They had been avoiding their shared country. Talking about Scotland so far from it would be like starting on a bender; they might end up where they did not wish to.

Debatable Land (1994), ch.6

2 I was very jealous of buildings. [My father] was always trying to save them and I remember him putting me in front of bulldozers and saying 'If you're going to hurt the building you can run her over first.'

Quoted in the *Sunday Telegraph* (Jun 1994)

Magnusson, Magnus 1929–
Icelandic-born writer and broadcaster

1 I've started so I'll finish.

Catchphrase used as questionmaster on BBC Television's *Mastermind* (from 1972)

Màiri Mhór nan Oran ('Big Mary of the Songs', or Màiri Nic a' Phearsain, Mary MacPherson) 1821–98
Poet and songwriter closely associated with the agitation for land reform

1 Cuimhnichibh ur cruadal,
Is cumaibh suas ur stròil,
Gun teid an roth an cuairt duibh,
Le neart is cruas nan dòrn;
Gum bi ur crodh air bhuailtean,
'S gach tuathanach air dòigh,
'S na Sasunnaich air fuadach,
A Eilean uaine 'Cheò.

† Bear in mind your hardiness and keep your satin [banners] flying: the wheel will turn in your favour through the strength and hardness of fists; your cattle will be in folds [of pasture] and every farmer in good circumstances; and the English driven out of the green isle of mist [Skye].

'Eilean a' Cheò' ('The Isle of Mist')

2 Beannachd leibh, a chàirdean,
Anns gach cèarn tha fo na nèoil,
Gach mac is nighean màthar
A Eilean àrd a' Cheò.
Is cuimhnichidh sibh Màiri,
'Nuair bhios i cnàmh fo'n fhòid –
'S e na dh'fhuiling mi de thàmailt
A thug mo bhàrdachd beò.

† Farewell, friends, in every quarter of the earth below the clouds, every mother's son and daughter from the high Island of Mist [Skye]: you will remember Mairi when she is wasting beneath the sod: it was the humiliation of insult I endured that brought my poetry into life.

'Eilean a' Cheò' ('The Isle of Mist')

3 BEAN OIS: Bheir mi comhairle ort, a Mhàiri,
'N ainm an Aigh thoir suas do chèol
Mas bi sinn air ar nàrachad
Le gràisg nach tuig ar dòigh;
Tha'n sluagh air fàs cho iongantach
'S gur cruithneachd leotha bròn,
'S mur teid thu ann am faochaig dhaibh,
Chan fhaodadh tu bhith bèo.
MAIRI: Cha teid sinn ann am faochaig dhaibh,
Is faodaidh sinn bhith bèo
Ged nach cuir sinn aodainn oirnn,
No caochladh air ar nèoil;

Le osnaich chneadaich chiùranaich,
'S gun sùgh annt' ach an sgleò,
A dh'fhiach an creid an saoghal
Gu bheil caochladh air tigh'nn òirnn.
LADY OF OS: I'll give you advice, Mairi;
For goodness sake give up your music
Lest we be shamed by a rabble
Who do not understand our ways;
The people have become so strange
That sorrow to them is wheat,
And if you don't go into a whelk-shell for them
You cannot stay alive.
MAIRI: We will not go into a whelk-shell
  for them
And we can stay alive,
Although we shall not put on [long] faces
Or wear a look of gloom
With groans and plaintive sighing
That have no substance in them but vapour,
So the world may believe
A change has come upon us.

'Cogadh Sìobhalta eadar Bean Ois agus Màiri'
('A "Civilised War" between the Lady of Os
and Mairi')

4 'Sa cheàrn 's na dh'àithneadh dhuinn le Dia,
Chan fhaod sinn triall air sliabh no gaineimh,
A h-uile nì 'n robh smear no luach,
Gun spùinn iad uainn le lagh an fhearainn.

In the country given to us by God
we may not wander the moor or shore;
the best of everything, all of value,
they deprived us of by the law of the land.

'Brosnachadh nan Gaidheal' ('Incitement of the
Gaels'), st.4

Campaigning song for the crofters put forward
as candidates by the Highland Land Law
Reform Association in the general election of
1885. The 'law of the land' refers, literally,
to the laws of land ownership and rights

5 . . . Bhiodh òigridh ghreannmhor ri ceòl is
dannsa,
Ach dh'fhalbh an t-ám sin 's tha 'n gleann
fo bhròn;
Bha 'n tobht aig Anndra, 's e làn de fheanntaig,
Toirt 'na mo chuimhne nuair bha mi òg.

. . . there'd be young folk singing and dancing,
but that time's past and the glen's
in gloom;
Andrew's croft, overgrown with nettles,
reminding me of when I was young.

'Nuair Bha Mi Og' ('When I was Young'). Quoted
in Catherine Kerrigan (ed.), An Anthology of
Scottish Women Poets (1991), and translated by
Meg Bateman

Maitland, John
see **Lauderdale, Duke of**

Maitland (of Lethington), Sir Richard
1496–1586
Satirical poet, courtier and judge

1 Some wifis of the burrows-toun
Sa wonder vain are and wantoun,
In warld they wat not what to wear,
On claithis they wair mony a croun;
And all for newfangilness of gear.

'Satire on the Toun Ladies', st.1

Maitland, William c.1528–73
*Secretary of State to Mary of Guise and to
Mary, Queen of Scots*

1 God is a bogle of the nursery.

Attrib. But Sir John Skelton, in *Maitland of
Lethington and the Scotland of Mary Queen of Scots*
(1894), Vol.2, p.395, could find no evidence for
the attribution

Major (or **Mair**), John 1469–1550
Scholar and historian

1 It is the food of almost all the inhabitants of
Wales, of the northern English (as I learned
some seven years back) and of the Scottish
peasantry; and yet the main strength of the
Scottish and English armies is in men who have
been tillers of soil – a proof that oaten bread
is not a thing to be laughed at.

On bread made from oats, *Historia Majoris
Britanniae* (*A History of Greater Britain*, 1521;
translated by A Constable, 1892), Bk 1, ch.2.
Cf. Samuel Johnson 1

2 In courage, in prudence, in all virtues of this
nature, Englishmen do not think themselves
the lowest of mankind; and if, in a foreign land,
they happen upon a man of parts and spirit,
' 'tis pity,' they say, 'he's not an Englishman.'

Historia Majoris Britanniae (*A History of Greater
Britain*, 1521; translated by A Constable, 1892),
Bk 1, ch.5

3 A King has not the same unconditional
possession of his kingdom as you have of your
coat. . . It is the free people who first give
power to the King, and his power depends on
the whole people.

Historia Majoris Britanniae (1521). Quoted in
Agnes Mure Mackenzie, *Scottish Pageant*, Vol.1
(1946), p.71

Major, John 1943–
*English Conservative politician, British Prime
Minister (1990–)*

1 After the election, we will take stock.

On plans to improve the government of Scotland,

while remaining opposed to a Scottish parliament.
Interview on BBC Radio Scotland (22 Feb 1992)

2 The Act of Union was a remarkable political
development. The Union it enshrined is an
enduring achievement which is to the credit
of our people. As we all advance towards its
three hundredth anniversary, in 2007, we must
reaffirm our faith in the Union and work to
ensure that it flowers and flourishes in its fourth
century.

Introduction to the White Paper, *Scotland in the
Union* (Mar 1993)

Malloch (or Mallet), David 1700–65
Poet

1 For soon the winter of the year,
And age, life's winter, will appear. . .
Our taste of pleasure then is o'er;
The feather'd songsters love no more;
And when they droop, and we decay,
Adieu the birks of Invermay.

'The Birks of Invermay', st.2

On going to London in 1723 as tutor to
the sons of the Duke of Montrose, Malloch
changed his name to Mallet, anglicised his
speech, collaborated with James Thomson
in writing 'Rule, Britannia', and became,
according to Dr Johnson, 'the only Scot whom
Scotchmen did not commend'

2 'This is the dumb and dreary hour,
When injur'd ghosts complain. . . '

'William and Margaret', st.7

3 'The hungry worm my sister is,
This winding sheet I wear;
And cold and weary lasts our night
Till that last morn appear.'

'William and Margaret', st.13

Manning, J L
Sports journalist

1 Fans with typewriters.

On Scottish football reporters. Quoted in the
Daily Mail (1950s)

Marr, Andrew
*Political journalist and broadcaster, editor of
The Independent (1996–)*

1 Those who live by the hype shall die by
the hype.

On the heady predictions by pro–Home Rule
politicians and journalists of political change at
the 1992 General Election. *The Battle for Scotland*
(1992), ch.6. Cf. Ian Bell 2, Scottish National Party 2

2 Yet again the Scottish political world had
slithered from delusion to disillusion – it had
accomplished its familiar water-slide into cold
porridge.

On the 1992 General Election result. *The Battle
for Scotland* (1992), ch.6

3 A Scotland genuinely at ease with itself would
be an argumentative, grown-up Scotland with
a lively parliament as well as a strong economy
– a conscience and a tongue, as well as limbs
and a body. And when it does speak, its voice
will be sharp and fresh. And its views will
perhaps surprise us.

The Battle for Scotland (1992), concluding words

Marra, Michael
Singer and songwriter

1 Mincing wi' Chairlhi

Title of song (1981)

2 Mother Glasgow's succour is perpetual
Nestling the Billy and the Tim –
I dreamt I took a dander with St Mungo,
To try to catch a fish that couldnae swim.
For the tree and the bird and the fish and
the bell –
Let Glasgow Flourish.

'Mother Glasgow' (1988), sung by Pat Kane
during Glasgow's City of Culture year (1990).
Cf. Anonymous 55

3 Under the Ullapool moon
Jimmy and Moira were bathing their gloom
The palm trees were sulking
The gulls were in tears
She threw a tantrum
And he disappeared. . .

'Under the Ullapool Moon' (written for Ullapool's
bicentenary, 1988)

4 Up at Tannadice
Framed in woodwork cool as ice
Keeping out the wolves in his particular way
A smile and a wave, a miraculous save they say
Out runs Hamish and the ball's in
Invergowrie Bay

'Hamish', on *On Stolen Stationery* (1991)

On the Dundee United goalkeeper, Hamish
McAlpine

5 Up at Tannadice
Watching as their fortunes rise
Smiling when he hears 'Ah it's only a game,
Win, lose or draw you get home to your bed
just the same'
But Hamish stokes young men's dreams into
a burning flame.

'Hamish', on *On Stolen Stationery* (1991)

6 Hermless hermless
There's never nae bather fae me

I ging tae the libry, I tak oot a book
And then I go hame for my tea

'Hermless', on *On Stolen Stationery* (1991)

Martyn, John (originally Iain MacGeachy) 1948–

Singer, songwriter and guitarist

1 May you never lay your head down
Without a hand to hold,
May you never make your bed
Out in the cold.

'May You Never' (1973) (Warlock Music Ltd)

Mary of Guise (or of Lorraine) 1515–60

Wife of James V, mother of Mary, Queen of Scots, Regent from 1554

1 Whair is now Johne Knox his God? My God is now stronger than his, yea even in Fyff.

On learning of a French victory over Protestant rebels in a skirmish at Kinghorn in Fife (Jan 1560). Quoted in John Knox, *History of the Reformation in Scotland* (1586), Bk 3

Mary (Stewart), Queen of Scots 1542–87

Queen of Scotland, the daughter of James V and mother of James VI

1 MARY: . . . ye are not the Kirk that I will nourish. I will defend the Kirk of Rome for I think it is the true Kirk of God.
KNOX: Your will, Madam, is no reason; neither doth your thought make that Roman harlot to be the true and immaculate spouse of Jesus Christ.

At their first meeting (4 Sep 1561). Quoted in John Knox, *History of the Reformation in Scotland* (1586), Bk 4

2 What have ye to do with my mariage? Or what ar ye within this Commonwealth?

To John Knox (May/Jun 1563). Quoted in John Knox, *History of the Reformation in Scotland* (1586), Bk 4

To the second question, Knox made the reply, 'A subject borne within the same, Madam. And albeit I neather be Erle, Lord nor Barroun within it, yitt hes God maid me (how abject that ever I be in your eyes) a profitable member within the same. . . '

3 No more tears now; I will think on revenge.

Said after the murder of her secretary David Riccio, in her presence, by her husband Lord Darnley and the Protestant nobility (9 Mar 1566)

Quoted in Claude Nau, *Memorials of Mary Stewart* (ed. J Stevenson, 1883), p.4

4 Look to your consciences and remember that the theatre of the world is wider than the realm of England.

To the commissioners appointed to try her at Fotheringay (13 Oct 1586). Quoted in Antonia Fraser, *Mary Queen of Scots* (1969), ch.25

5 O Domine Deus speravi in Te.
O care mi Jesu nunc libera me.

† O Lord God, I have put my hope in thee.
O my dear Jesus, now liberate me.

Attrib.

Supposedly composed on the morning of her execution (8 Feb 1587)

6 Thou knowest, Melville, that all this world is but vanity and full of troubles and sorrows: carry this message from me to my friends, that I die a true woman to my religion, and like a true Scottish woman and a true French woman.

To Sir James Melville on the morning of her execution (8 Feb 1587). From an official account written for the English government by Robert Wingfield, quoted in Agnes Mure Mackenzie, *Scottish Pageant*, Vol.2 (1948), p.197

7 En ma fin est mon commencement.

† In my end is my beginning.

Embroidered motto. See Antonia Fraser, *Mary Queen of Scots* (1969), ch.21

Massie, Allan 1938–

Journalist and novelist

1 'Let Scotland be as independent as they wish, it will not alter the fact that there's little. . . to keep talent here. Of course a political framework would retain a few – but how many? Ireland is governed by grocers. . . Scotland will grow ever less Scottish and ever less stimulating; we live in a withered culture. Sounds of energy are the energy of the death-rattle. The Union may not have been the end of an auld sang, but it led us into the last verse.'

One Night in Winter (1984), Part 1, ch.8 (Ebenezer to Dallas). Cf. James Ogilvy 1

2 He was a fervent Scottish patriot, jealous of any encroachment on the liberties of his country; no man did more to feed national pride, and yet no man did more to reconcile Scots to the Union with England. About that he could not be other than ambivalent: his reason assented to it; his sentiment rejected it.

On Walter Scott. *101 Great Scots* (1987)

3 The question for Scottish Unionists now is whether to die in the last ditch. . .

They can't all go into exile, and few would wish to do so. They can't sensibly turn their backs on public life. Nor can they pretend that a parliament, once established in Edinburgh, will ever be abolished.

'Unionists Heading for the Last Ditch', *The Scotsman* (13 Jun 1994)

> On the declining Conservative and Unionist vote in Scotland, and the growing likelihood of a future Labour government establishing a Scottish parliament

4 [There are those] who would rather be in the last ditch, denying realities rather than submit to them. . . . I expect the last ditch to be a crowded place, littered with Unionist corpses, honourably dead of course, but very dead.

'Unionists Heading for the Last Ditch', *The Scotsman* (13 Jun 1994)

Matheson, Donald 1719–82

Poet

1 Tha mi 'faicinn iongantas
Air tighinn anns an àm;
Chan eil againn ach bhi 'g éisdeachd
Na chanas Esan ruinn.
Buinidh nitheanan follaiseach
Dhuinne 'us do'r cloinn,
Ach na nitheanan tha uaigneach
'S e 'dhiamhaireachds' tha ann.

Ach tha mi 'faicinn faileas
De nithean bh' ann bho chéin,
Dar bha pobull Israel
'S an Eiphit ann am péin;
Thug e le làmh làidir iad
A mach bho Pharaoh féin;
'S dh'fhosgail e an cuan doibh
Dar luathaich e 'n déidh.

† I see a wonder
happening at this time;
we have but to listen
to what He is telling us.
Obvious matters pertain
to us and to our children,
but what is mysterious
is His own secret.

I see a reflection
of what happened long ago,
when the Israelites were
in Egypt in distress.
He brought them with a strong hand
away from Pharaoh himself,
and divided the sea for them
when he pursued them.

'Tha mi 'faicinn iongantas' ('I see a wonder'). Quoted in Margaret MacDonell, *The Emigrant Experience: Songs of Highland Emigrants in North America* (1982), st.1–2

> The identification of the Gaels with the Children of Israel, explicit here, has a long history in Gaelic tradition

2 'S ged theidheadh iad do Char'lina
No do mhìr tha fo'n ghréin,
Cha b' urra dhoibh tachairt
Ach ann an talamh féin.
'S iad oighreachan nan geallaidhnean
'S bithidh an solumas da réir,
'S ged thigeadh iad gu cruaidh-chas
Theid fuasgladh orr' 'nam feum.

† If they should go to Carolina
or to any land under the sun,
they could meet
only on their own land.
They are heirs of the promises;
their reward will be as ordained;
and although they should be in distress
relief will come in their need.

'Tha mi 'faicinn iongantas' ('I see a wonder'). Quoted in Margaret MacDonell, *The Emigrant Experience: Songs of Highland Emigrants in North America* (1982), st.5

Matheson, George 1842–1906

Church of Scotland minister and hymnwriter

1 O Love that wilt not let me go,
I rest my weary soul in Thee. . .

Hymn, 'O Love that wilt not let me go', st.1

2 Make me a captive, Lord,
And then I shall be free;
Force me to render up my sword,
And I shall conqueror be.

Hymn, 'Make me a captive, Lord', st.1

Matheson, John fl.1840

Evangelical Presbyterian from North Uist

1 Creideam an crodh is an caoraich
Creideam an stìopanaibh mór
Creideam san duais tha mi faotainn
An t-airgead, an glìob, is an t-òr
Creideam anns an uachdaran thìmeil
An aghaidh an nì a deir Pòl.

† I believe in cattle and sheep
I believe in great stipends
I believe in the rewards I receive
Silver and glebe and gold
I believe in the temporal lord
In the face of what Paul declares.

'Oran mu'n Eaglais' ('Song on the Church', 1846)

> Matheson's satirical verses were directed against the established Church of Scotland minister's creed

Matheson, Kay 1928–

Teacher, one of the four students who recovered the Stone of Destiny from Westminster Abbey in 1950

1 Ian hadn't closed the boot properly. The Stone had landed in the middle of the road. I had to

lift it back in again. Luckily I had the muscle – from carrying the peats.

> On driving the Stone of Destiny through Knightsbridge on 25 December 1950. Quoted in Pat Gerber, 'Kay Matheson and the Stone of Destiny', in *Chapman* No.77 (1994). Cf. Ian Hamilton 3

We were supposed to be a united kingdom, but the further north you go away from London, from the centre of government, the dearer things become and the worse the roads are. If it's united, then everything should be equal.

> Quoted in Pat Gerber, 'Kay Matheson and the Stone of Destiny', in *Chapman* No.77 (1994)

Well, they will never know if it's the real Stone they got back or not, now. I most definitely *didn't* think it should be given back to England. I hoped then, and I'm *still* hoping, that we will get self-government.

> Quoted in Pat Gerber, 'Kay Matheson and the Stone of Destiny', in *Chapman* No.77 (1994)

Maxton, James 1885–1946

Labour MP, one of the group of 'Red Clydesiders'

. . . we will not go back to our people and tell them they are to starve in peace and quietness. We will not do so. . . I am as great a constitutionalist as any member on that Front Bench or this Front Bench, but there is a point where constitutionalists have to give way before human necessity. I tell the working-class people of the West of Scotland that this House has nothing to give them. . .

> Speech in the House of Commons (8 Dec 1922)

My criticism of the politician is not that he fails to keep order but that he does it too well. He regards the suppression of discontent as his job, when his real duty is to analyse discontent, to find out the causes of discontent, to express discontent, and to establish a world order that is more in keeping with the intelligence and the ethics of the men and women who live in the great age in which we are living.

> Quoted in *Radical Scotland* No.9 (Jun/Jul 1984)

In the interests of economy they condemned hundreds of children to death and I call it murder. I call the men who walked into the lobby in support of that policy murderers. They have blood on their hands – the blood of infants. It is a fearful thing for any man to have on his soul a cold, callous deliberate crime in order to save money. We are prepared to destroy children in the interests of dividends. We put children out in front of the fighting line.

> Speech in the House of Commons (27 Jun 1923)

denouncing the withdrawal of child benefits, including the supply of milk

> His accusations, which he refused to withdraw, caused outrage in Parliament. Maxton, to many 'the beloved rebel', was also described by Winston Churchill as 'the greatest gentleman of the House of Commons'

4 If my friend cannot ride two horses then he should not be in the bloody circus.

> Speaking (Jan 1931) against the Scottish Independent Labour Party's proposed disaffiliation from the Labour Party. Quoted in Gordon Brown, *Maxton* (1986), ch.30

5 Sit down, man. You're a bloody tragedy.

> Attrib. Said to Ramsay MacDonald, who was making his last speech to the House of Commons (1935)

6 You elected me to protest, and I will protest for you until I die.

> To his Bridgeton constituents (1945)

Maxwell, James Clerk 1831–79

Physicist

1 All the mathematical sciences are founded on relations between physical laws and laws of numbers, so that the aim of exact science is to reduce the problems of nature to the determination of quantities by operations with numbers.

> 'On Faraday's Lines of Force' (1856)

2 . . . the only laws of matter are those which our minds must fabricate, and the only laws of mind are fabricated for it by matter.

> 'Analogies in Nature' (1856)

3 Light consists in the transverse undulations of the same medium which is the cause of electric and magnetic phenomena.

> 'On Physical Lines of Force' (1861–2)
>
> > This was Maxwell's earliest statement of his electromagnetic theory of light

4 When at last this little instrument appeared, consisting, as it does, of parts every one of which is familiar to us, and capable of being put together by an amateur, the disappointment arising from its humble appearance was only partially relieved on finding that it was really able to talk.

> 'The Telephone' (1878)

5 Either be a machine and see nothing but 'phenomena' or else try to be a man, feeling your life interwoven, as it is, with many others, and strengthened by them whether in life or death.

> Letter to R B Litchfield (1879), following the death of his friend R H Pomeroy. Quoted in Ivan Tolstoy, *James Clerk Maxwell* (1981), ch.7

6 Gin a body meet a body
Flyin' through the air,
Gin a body hit a body,
Will it fly? and where?
Ilka impact has its measure,
Ne'er a ane hae I,
Yet a' the lads they measure me,
Or, at least, they try.

'Rigid Body Sings', in Maurice Lindsay (ed.),
Scottish Comic Verse (1981), st.1. Cf. Robert Burns 136

Maxwell wrote light verse throughout his life,
often parodying Burns

Maxwell, Jane see Gordon, Duchess of

Meadowbank, 1st Lord (Allan Maconochie) 1748–1816

Judge

1 Declaim, Sir! why don't you declaim? Speak
to me as if I were a popular assembly!

Wearying of the dry statement made by Thomas
Walker Baird, advocate. Quoted in Lord
Cockburn, *Memorials of his Time* (1856), ch.2

Meadowbank, 2nd Lord (Alexander Maconochie-Welwood) 1777–1861

Judge, son of the above

1 The clouds have been dispelled – the *darkness
visible* has been cleared away – and the Great
Unknown – the minstrel of our native land
– the mighty magician who has rolled back
the current of time, and conjured up before
our living senses the men and the manners
of days which have long since passed away,
stands revealed to the eyes and the hearts of
his affectionate and admiring countrymen.

On Walter Scott. Speech at a Theatrical Fund
charity dinner, Edinburgh (23 Feb 1827). Quoted
in J G Lockhart, *Memoirs of the Life of Sir Walter
Scott, Bart.* (1837–8), ch.73

On this occasion Scott first publicly acknowledged himself author of the Waverley Novels

Melville, Andrew 1545–1622

Presbyterian reformer

1 God's silly vassal.

Said of (and to) James VI (1596)

As reported in his nephew James Melville's
Diary: 'Mr Andrew boir him doun and utterit
the commissioun as from the michtie God,
calling the King bot Goddis sillie vassal, and
taking him by the sleive. . . '

2 And Sir, when ye war in your swadling cloutis,
Christ Jesus rang frielie in this land, in spite
of all his enemeis. . .

To James VI (1596). Quoted in James
Melville's *Diary*

Melville, Elizabeth (Lady Culross, the Younger) fl.1600

Poet

1 'Lord Jesus cum and saif thy awin Elect,
For Sathan seiks our simpill sauls to slay;
The wickit warld dois stranglie us infect,
Most monsterous sinnes increasses day be day:
Our luif grows cauld, our zeill is worne away,
Our faith is faillit, and we ar lyke to fall;
The Lyon roares to catch us as his pray,
Mak haist, O Lord! befoir wee perish all.'

'Ane Godlie Dreame, Compylit in Scotish Meter,
be M M Gentlewoman in Culros, at the Requeist
of her Friendes' (1603)

Melville, Frances Helen 1873–1962

*Educationalist and churchwoman, first woman
to graduate as Bachelor of Divinity in Scotland (1910)*

1 If ordination continues to be withheld and the
Church does not accept the services of men
and women on equal terms, there is a real
and grave danger of our finest, most energetic
and intellectual young women throwing their
energies into the work of organisations which
may have a Christian basis, but which are
neverthless outside the Church.

1931. Quoted in N M Cameron, D F Wright
et al., *Dictionary of Scottish Church History and
Theology* (1993)

Ordination of women was not finally allowed
by the Church of Scotland until 1968

Mendelssohn(-Bartholdy), (Jakob Ludwig) Felix 1809–47

German composer

1 NEXT AUGUST I AM GOING TO
SCOTLAND, with a rake for folksongs, an
ear for the lovely, fragrant countryside, and a
heart for the bare legs of the natives.

Letter to Karl Klingemann (26 Mar 1829). Quoted
in G Selden-Goth (ed.), *Felix Mendelssohn: Letters*
(1945; 1973 edition)

2 Long before you arrive at a place you hear
it talked of; the rest is heath with red or
brown heather, withered fir branches and white
stones between, or black moors where they
shoot grouse.

On travelling in the Highlands. Letter to his
family (15 Aug 1829). Quoted in G Selden-
Goth (ed.), *Felix Mendelssohn: Letters* (1945; 1973
edition)

Menuhin, Yehudi 1916–

American-born British violinist

Their music knows no detour – it goes straight
to our feet if dance we must, to our eyes
if cry we must and always directly to our
hearts evoking every shade of joy, sorrow or
contentment. . .

On the playing of Scottish fiddlers. Foreword to
James Hunter, *The Fiddle Music of Scotland* (1988)

Mercer, Wallace

Football manager

When we came to the end of the agenda and
I handed them the letter saying I was going,
there were tears in my eyes.

On leaving Heart of Midlothian Football Club.
Quoted in *The Scotsman* (1 Jun 1993)

Metrical Psalms

The Lord's my shepherd, I'll not want.
He makes me down to lie
In pastures green: he leadeth me
the quiet waters by.
My soul he doth restore again;
and me to walk doth make
Within the paths of righteousness,
ev'n for his own name's sake.

Yea, though I walk in death's dark vale,
yet will I fear none ill:
For thou art with me; and thy rod
and staff me comfort still.

Psalm 23 (1650), st.1–2

God is our refuge and our strength,
in straits a present aid;
Therefore, although the earth remove,
we will not be afraid. . .

Psalm 46 (1650), st.1

How lovely is thy dwelling-place
O Lord of hosts, to me!
The tabernacles of thy grace
how pleasant, Lord, they be!

Psalm 84 (1650), st.1

All people that on earth do dwell,
Sing to the Lord with cheerful voice.
Him serve with mirth, his praise forth tell,
Come ye before him and rejoice.
Know that the Lord is God indeed;
Without our aid he did us make:
We are his flock, he doth us feed,
And for his sheep he doth us take.

Psalm 100 (1650), st.1

I to the hills will lift mine eyes,
from whence doth come mine aid.

My safety cometh from the Lord,
Who heav'n and earth hath made.

Psalm 121 (1650), st.1

Mill, James 1773–1836

*Journalist, historian and philosopher, father
of John Stuart Mill*

1 One thing is pretty clear, that all those
individuals whose interests are indisputably
included in those of other individuals, may
be struck off without inconvenience. In this
light. . . women may be regarded, the interest
of almost all of whom is involved either in that
of their fathers or in that of their husbands.

On who should be eligible to vote. *Essay on
Government* (1824)

Millar, J(ohn) H(epburn) 1864–1929

Lawyer and literary historian

1 If to-day in Scotland hardly the humblest
rag is without its study of native life, and if
ne'er a Free Kirk probationer, too modest to
aspire to the smug heresies and complacent
latitudinarianism of its teachers, but manfully
resolves that he too will storm the world with
his 'Cameos from the Cowcaddens' or his
'Glimpses of the Goose-dubs', it is Mr Barrie's
doing. . . The Chronicles of the Kailyard are
ill at ease in the flower garden.

'The Literature of the Kailyard', *The New Review*
(Apr 1895)

Millar, in this article, was the first to describe
the sentimental parochial fiction of J M Barrie
and others, several of whom were Free Kirk
ministers, as 'Kailyard'. Cf. George Douglas
Brown 7

2 The circulating libraries became charged to
overflowing with a crowd of ministers, precen-
tors, and beadles, whose dry and 'pithy' wit had
plainly been recruited at the fountain-head of
Dean Ramsay; while the land was plangent with
the sobs of grown men, vainly endeavouring to
stifle their emotion by an elaborate affectation
of 'peching' and 'hoasting'.

On the Kailyard School. *A Literary History of
Scotland* (1903), ch.12. Cf. Dean Ramsay

Miller, Christian 1920–

Writer

1 . . . in the life of the castle, shooting came,
in theory, second only to religion. In fact,
of course, it took precedence over absolutely
everything.
As the summer wore on and the grain
ripened in the broad meadows, the thoughts

of all the male inhabitants of the castle turned inexorably to slaughter. Killing was not only their favourite pastime; it was also the activity for which they had had the most intensive training and for which their upbringing and tradition best suited them.

A Childhood in Scotland (1981)

Miller, Hugh 1802–56

Geologist, newspaper editor and writer

1 . . . though the interior of the county was thus *improved* into a desert, in which there are many thousands of sheep, but few human habitations, let it not be supposed by the reader that its population was in any degree lessened. . . The county has not been depopulated – its population has been merely arranged after a new fashion. The late Duchess found it spread equally over the interior and the sea-coast, and in very comfortable circumstances; – she left it compressed into a wretched selvage of poverty and suffering that fringes the county on its eastern and western shores. . .

'Sutherland as it was and is: or, How a country may be ruined' (1843), ch.1

2 . . . The Irish are buying guns and will be, by the bye, shooting magistrates and clergymen by the score: and Parliament will in consequence do a great deal for them. But the poor Highlander will shoot no-one. . . Government will yield nothing to justice but a great deal to fear.

1846. Quoted in Malcolm MacLean and Christopher Carrell (eds), *As an Fhearann (From the Land*, 1986)

3 If the Scottish people yield up to his Grace [the Duke of Atholl] their right of way through Glen Tilt, they will richly deserve to be shut out of their country altogether. . . If one proprietor shut up Glen Tilt, why may not a combination of proprietors shut up Perthshire? Or if one sporting tenant bar against us the Grampians, why, when the system of shooting-farms and game-parks has become completed, might not the sporting tenants united shut up against us the entire Highlands?

'Glen Tilt Tabooed', *The Witness* (1 Sep 1847)

The then Duke of Atholl had tried to bar the route between Blair Atholl and Braemar

4 . . . it was not until I had learned to detect among the ancient sandstone strata of this quarry exactly the same phenomena as those which I used to witness in my walks with Uncle Sandy in the ebb, that I was fairly excited to examine and inquire. It was the necessity which made me a quarrier that taught me to be a geologist.

On his first day as an apprentice stonemason. *My Schools and Schoolmasters* (1854), ch.8

5 For some little time she stood before me without speaking, and then abruptly asked – 'What makes *you* work as a mason?' I made some commonplace reply; but it failed to satisfy her. 'All your fellows are real masons,' she said; 'but you are merely in the disguise of a mason; and I have come to consult you about the deep matters of the soul.'

My Schools and Schoolmasters (1854), ch.9

The woman, Isabel Mackenzie, considered insane by her neighbours, met Miller in 1821 when he was serving his apprenticeship as a stonemason

6 For the cultivation of a shrewd common sense, a bank office is one of perhaps the best schools in the world. . . ingenuities, plausibilities, special pleadings, all that make the stump-orator great, must be brushed aside by the banker. The question with him comes always to be a sternly naked one: – Is, or is not, Mr— a person fit to be trusted with the bank's money?

My Schools and Schoolmasters (1854), ch.23

Miller was the Commercial Bank's agent in Cromarty from 1835 to 1839

7 Presbyterianism without the animating life is a poor shrunken thing: it never lies in state when it is dead; for it has no body of fine forms, or trapping of imposing ceremonies, to give it bulk or adornment: without the vitality of evangelism it is nothing. . .

The Cruise of the Betsey (1858), ch.6

8 I do not much like extermination carried out so thoroughly and on system; – it seems bad policy; and I have not succeeded in thinking any the better of it though assured by the economists that there are more than enough people in Scotland still.

On the clearances in Rum. *The Cruise of the Betsey* (1858), ch.8

9 A foundering land under a severe sky, beaten by tempests and lashed by tides, with glaciers half choking up its cheerless valleys, and with countless icebergs brushing its coasts and grating over its shallows. . .

On Scotland in the ice age. *Sketch-Book of Popular Geology* (1859), 'Lecture Second'

10 It is said that modern science is adverse to the exercise and development of the imaginative faculty. But is it really so? . . . Because science flourishes, must poesy decline? The complaint serves but to betray the weakness of the class who urge it. . . whenever a truly great poet arises, – one that will add a profound intellect to a powerful imagination, – he will find science not his enemy, but an obsequious caterer and a devoted friend. He will find sermons in stones, and more of the suggestive and the sublime in

a few broken scaurs of clay, a few fragmentary shells, and a few green reaches of the old coast line, than versifiers of the ordinary calibre in their once fresh gems and flowers, – in sublime ocean, the broad earth, or the blue firmament and all its stars.

Sketch-Book of Popular Geology (1859), 'Lecture Second'. Cf. Hugh MacDiarmid 37

. . . the abyss beneath, where all is fiery and yet dark, – a solitary hell, without suffering or sin. . .

On the molten state of the earth in its earliest stage. Sketch-Book of Popular Geology (1859), 'Lecture Sixth'

Miller, William 1810–72
Poet, known as the 'Laureate of the nursery' for his children's rhymes

Wee Willie Winkie rins through the toun,
Up stairs and doun stairs in his nicht-gown,
Tirling at the window, crying at the lock,
'Are the weans in their bed, for it's now ten
o' clock?'

'Willie Winkie' (1841), st.1

Milne, John C 1897–1962
Poet

I wadna be an orra loon
For a' the warld's gear!
I wadna be an orra loon,
I'd raither stick te lear!

'I wadna be an orra loon', *The Orra Loon* (1946), st.1

Folk wha say their say and speir their speir,
Gedder gey birns o' bairns and gey muckle gear,
And gang their ain gait wi' a lach or a spit
or a sweir.

On Buchan folk. 'Fut like folk?', *Poems* (1963)

O Lord look doon on Buchan
And a' its fairmer chiels!
For there's nae in a' Yer warld
Mair contermashious deils!

'O Lord look doon on Buchan', *Poems* (1963), st.1

Mitchell, James Leslie
see **Gibbon, Lewis Grassic**

Mitchell, Lilias d.1940
Suffragette

Never shall I forget the blazing warmth of that meeting. . . I was twenty-three at the time and was more than ready for an opening for work of this kind. In fact, after that meeting, the hockey, reading, music clubs, violin lessons, even dances, seemed sheer nonsense when the Vote had yet to be won.

On attending a meeting in Edinburgh addressed by Mrs Pankhurst (probably 12 Mar 1909). 'Suffrage Days', unpublished memoir, quoted in Leah Leneman, *A Guid Cause: The Women's Suffrage Movement in Scotland* (1991), ch.5

Mitchison, Naomi Margaret (*née* Haldane) 1897–
Novelist and poet

1 . . . I can imagine a communist society. . . It was after all, the peasant women rather than the peasant men. . . who so liked the idea of communal farms under the Plan [in Soviet Russia], who so cheerfully forsook the traditions that women are supposed to like so much. I am afraid women are rather dangerous people. I am afraid they are responsible for the cracks in the plaster of the home.

'Breaking Up the Home', *Twentieth Century*, Promethean Society, 3 (17 Jul 1932)

2 I call it war when people are being physically and mentally crippled, deprived of life either suddenly or gradually, and reduced to a war mentality of distrust and despair, by inadequate food, housing, and education and unnecessary industrial risks.

On class war, in 'Letters to the Editor', *Time and Tide* (29 Feb 1936)

3 . . . effective contraception. . . was itself part of women's emancipation.

You May Well Ask: A Memoir 1920–1940 (1979), Part 1, 'Patterns of Loving'

4 Being married is a value; it is bread and butter; but it may make one less able to provide the cake.

You May Well Ask: A Memoir 1920–1940 (1979), Part 1, 'Patterns of Loving'

5 I was told I could keep the word 'button' if I omitted the word 'trouser'!

You May Well Ask: A Memoir 1920–1940 (1979), Part 3, 'Why Write: A Note on the Literary Decencies'

On the reaction of Jonathan Cape to one of the passages in her novel, *We Have Been Warned* (1935). She ended a 10-year publishing relationship with Cape over disputes about this novel, which deals frankly with sex and contraception. It was eventually published by Constable, although they also cut passages from it

6 In Scottish culture nothing beats a good-going funeral. It takes the mind off other things. . .

You May Well Ask: A Memoir 1920–1940 (1979), Part 4, 'Storm Warning'

7 ... during the 18th and 19th centuries, kings were the enemies for many intelligent people, combining in some people's minds with priests. But now we know only too well that strangling the last king in the guts of the last priest isn't going to do the trick.

> Diary entry (27 Jul 1940), *Among You Taking Notes: The Wartime Diary of Naomi Mitchison 1939–45* (ed. Dorothy Sheridan, 1985)
>
> Paraphrasing French priest Jean Meslier (c.1644–1733), often quoted as having said 'Je voudrais... que le dernier des rois fût étranglé avec les boyaux du dernier prêtre' (I should like... the last of the kings to be strangled with the guts of the last priest'). Cf. Neal Ascherson 7, Tom Nairn 2

8 [Nationalism] does not want to conquer other nations. It wants to develop its own.... I am almost sure that nationalism is on the whole good for people, that it corresponds with something they want, and that it is not incompatible with internationalism or with peace.

> Diary entry (4 Aug 1940), *Among You Taking Notes: The Wartime Diary of Naomi Mitchison 1939–45* (ed. Dorothy Sheridan, 1985)

9 Nobody can be a power in their age unless they are part of its voice.

> Diary entry (2 Mar 1941), *Among You Taking Notes: The Wartime Diary of Naomi Mitchison 1939–45* (ed. Dorothy Sheridan, 1985)

10 ... my feminism is deeper in me than, say, nationalism or socialism: it is more irrational, harder to argue about, nearer the hurting core.

> Diary entry (22 Dec 1941), *Among You Taking Notes: The Wartime Diary of Naomi Mitchison 1939–45* (ed. Dorothy Sheridan, 1985)

11 It is always a bore being ahead of one's time...

> Diary entry (21 Jan 1942), *Among You Taking Notes: The Wartime Diary of Naomi Mitchison 1939–45* (ed. Dorothy Sheridan, 1985)

12 ... I find love, or sex, interesting, but as part of something else: of society, of one's life and work, above all of general tenderness and *agape*. By itself it's no better than sugar alone with no other ingredients. Naturally if you take it by itself in this way, you find it a bit sick-making.

> Diary entry (19 Mar 1943), *Among You Taking Notes: The Wartime Diary of Naomi Mitchison 1939–45* (ed. Dorothy Sheridan, 1985)

13 This hellish business of being a woman always with half an ear for babies or husbands or god knows what.

> Diary entry (13 May 1944), *Among You Taking Notes: The Wartime Diary of Naomi Mitchison 1939–45* (ed. Dorothy Sheridan, 1985)

14 ... All the time one keeps on thinking of this bomb, and what it may make the future look like. A perpetual menace over everything but may be as salutary as hell fire was in its time. I wonder.

> Diary entry (10 Aug 1945), *Among You Taking Notes: The Wartime Diary of Naomi Mitchison 1939–45* (ed. Dorothy Sheridan, 1985)
>
> On 6 August 1945, the first atom bomb was dropped on Hiroshima, Japan. A second one was dropped on Nagasaki on 8 August. The Japanese surrendered on 14 August (VJ Day)

15 I... try to write for my own race, to write intelligibly for the ordinary man and woman in Scotland, to shake them out of their bad dream of respectability.

> 'Writers in the USSR', *New Statesman and Nation* (6 Sep 1952)

16 No one can travel light with a house on their back, not even a snail.

> *Travel Light* (1952), Part 3, ch.3

17 Somewhere without colour, without beauty, without sunlight,
Amongst this cautious people,
some unhappy and some hungry,
There is a thing being born as it was
born once in Florence:
So that a man, fearful, may find his mind fixed on tomorrow.

> 'The Scottish Renaissance in Glasgow: 1935', *The Cleansing of the Knife and Other Poems* (1978)

18 Living in a village is walking
Among snare wire, being
The bulge-eyed rabbit, ware of
The light heart, dancing gossip-stoats, the blood-lipped,
Biding their time.

> 'Living in a Village', *The Cleansing of the Knife and Other Poems* (1978)

19 I know now that I speak
With a voice not of mine,
Knowledge beyond books:
I speak with the voice of Scotland...

> 'The Cleansing of the Knife', *The Cleansing of the Knife and Other Poems* (1978)

20 When we begin to think
Of the Highland clearances,
Of lairds and money and sheep,
We had best forget and drink
And the drink has need to be deep.

> 'The Cleansing of the Knife', *The Cleansing of the Knife and Other Poems* (1978)

21 ... he had the same quality of wonderful encouraging light-heartedness mixed with spasms of deep gloom which I had found in some of my fishermen friends; he had a deeply poetic way of looking at things, but with sharp knife-thrusts of understanding which could lead to action.

> On Neil Gunn, with whom she corresponded

regularly from the early 1940s. *Naomi Mitchison: Saltire Self-Portraits* (1986)

2 They were against village halls, the singing of songs other than religious or Gaelic, and promiscuous – that is to say boys and girls – dancing. I asked in a shocked voice if they preferred men dancing together; this was picked up with a few friendly twinkles by other Panel members but not by the deputation, buggery being uncommon in the Islands where, I think, sheep are preferred, or small cows.

Naomi Mitchison: Saltire Self-Portraits (1986)

> On the 'deputation' that came to remonstrate with the Highland Panel (an advisory body established in 1947 by the Labour government, and of which she was a member for more than 20 years). The deputation she remembers was made up of Free Presbyterian ministers

3 We went on to Mull, 'the colonels' mess' as some people called it. . .

Naomi Mitchison: Saltire Self-Portraits (1986)

4 The smelter ruins and the unemployment around Invergordon should teach us not to put our trust in the princes of industry. Trees and cows are more predictable.

Naomi Mitchison: Saltire Self-Portraits (1986)

5 In some ways my writing is old-fashioned, but I doubt if that matters much except in the literary fashion market where one has to wear the latest gear, however unbecoming. I know I can handle words, the way other people handle colours or computers or horses.

Naomi Mitchison: Saltire Self-Portraits (1986)

6 . . . until there is some form of public landownership in Scotland, and above all in the Highlands and Islands, there will still be a problem of rural unemployment and unhappiness.

Naomi Mitchison: Saltire Self-Portraits (1986)

7 Schools were supposed to teach words, not meanings. But sometimes they taught meanings by mistake, and that usually made for wrong answers in the exam. Once meanings get loose, kids pick them up. Those books ought to have been put right away where nobody could get at them.

'Somewhere Else', in *Chapman* No.50–1 (Summer 1987)

Mitchison, Rosalind (Mary) (*née Wrong*) 1919–

English-born historian

1 Go and stand on the castle rock of Stirling and look about you. That is the quickest way to comprehend the basic features that have dictated Scottish history. You will see the Highland line, one of the great geological faults to which Scotland owes its shape, a wall of hills rising sharply from the plain a few miles to the north. . . To pass in reasonable safety and comfort from southern to northern Scotland a man must cross the Forth within a mile or two of Stirling. Stirling is the brooch that holds together the two parts of the country.

A History of Scotland (1970), ch.1. Cf. Alexander Smith 10

Monboddo, Lord (James Burnett) 1714–99

Judge, philosopher and eccentric

1 There are many in Scotland who call themselves improvers, but who I think are rather *desolators* of the country. Their method is to take into their possession several farms, which no doubt they improve by cultivation. But after they have done so they set them off all to one tenant, instead of perhaps five or six who possessed them before.

Antient Metaphysics (1779–99), Vol.5, p.309

2 More matter, fewer words, Master C.

> Provoked in a large company dominated by the conversation of a silly lawyer. Quoted in John Ramsay of Ochtertyre, *Scotland and Scotsmen in the Eighteenth Century* (1888 edition), Vol.1, p.355, footnote

3 I have not, my lord. You write a good deal faster than I am able to read.

> On being asked by Lord Kames whether he had read his latest work, *The Elements of Criticism* (1762). Quoted in John Ramsay of Ochtertyre, *Scotland and Scotsmen in the Eighteenth Century* (1888 edition), Vol.1, p.356, footnote

4 Show me any of your French cooks who can make a dish like this.

> On a boiled egg. Quoted in John Kay, *Original Portraits* (1877 edition), Vol.1, p.21

5 I have forgot a great deal more than most other men know.

> Said in his latter years. Quoted in John Ramsay of Ochtertyre, *Scotland and Scotsmen in the Eighteenth Century* (1888 edition), Vol.1, p.357, footnote

Montgomerie, Alexander c.1545–1611

Poet

1 Adeu nou be treu nou
Sen that we must depairt.
Forget not, and set not
At licht my constant hairt.

> 'Adieu to his Mistress', st.1

2 O Lady for thy Constancie
   A faithfull servand sall I be,
   Thyn honour to defend
   And I sall surelie for thy saik
   As doth the turtle for her maik
   Love to my lyfis end.
      'Adieu to his Mistress', st.4

3 A bonny No, with smyling looks agane
   I wald ye leirnd, sen they so comely ar.
      'An Admonition to Young Lasses', or 'A Bonny
      No', st.1

4 For folou love, they say, and it will flie.
   Wald ye be lov'd, this lessone mon ye leir:
   Flie whylome love, and it will folou thee.
      'An Admonition to Young Lasses', or 'A Bonny
      No', st.3

5 Too late Experience dois teiche,
   The Schule-maister of fulis:
   Too late to fynde the nest I seik,
   When all the birdis are flowin:
   Too late the stable dore I steik,
   When all the steids are stowin. . .
      'The Cherry and the Slae', st.13

6 In throu the windoes of myn ees –
   A perillous and open pairt –
   Hes Cupid hurt my hevy hairt,
   Whilk daylie dwynes bot nevir dees,
   Throu poyson of his deidly dairt.
      'In throu the windoes of myn ees', st.1

7 What sall I say? This warld will away.
   Anis on a day I seimd a semely sight;
   Thou wants the wight that never said thee nay.
   Adeu for ay. This is a lang guidnicht.
      'A Lang Guidnicht', ll.37–40

8 So swete a kis yistrene fra thee I reft,
   In bowing down thy body on the bed,
   That evin my lyfe within thy lippis I left. . .
      'So Sweet a Kiss'

9 Lyk as the dum
   Solsequium,
   With cair ouercum,
   And sorow, when the sun goes out of sight,
   Hings doun his head,
   And droups as dead,
   And will not spread,
   But louks his leavis throu langour of
     the nicht. . .

   So fairis with me,
   Except I be
   Whair I may se
   My lamp of licht, my Lady and my Love.
      'The Solsequium', st.1–2
        solsequium: sunflower

10 The Lord most hie,
    I know, will be

An heyrde to me:
I can not long have stresse, nor stand in neede.
He makes my lare
In feelds so fare,
That without care
I do repose and at my pleasure feede.
   'The Twenty-third Psalm', st.1

Montgomery, Catriona
see NicGumaraid, Catriona

Montgomery, Mary
see NicGumaraid, Màiri

Montrose, James Graham, Marquis of
1612–50

*Soldier and poet, executed by the Covenanters
after his failure to secure Scotland for Charles II*

1 My dear and only Love, I pray
   This noble World of thee,
   Be govern'd by no other Sway
   But purest Monarchie.
      'My Dear and Only Love', or 'To His Mistress'
      (c.1642), st.1, as published in James Watson, *A
      Choice Collection of Comic and Serious Scots Poems
      Both Ancient and Modern* (1711)

        Although in the form of love verses, this
        poem is in fact a statement of Montrose's
        political beliefs, for which he would lay down
        his life. Variants on the above lines are also
        frequently printed: 'That little world of thee'
        in l.2; 'Than purest Monarchie' in l.4

2 He either fears his Fate too much,
   Or his Deserts are small,
   That puts it not unto the Touch,
   To win or lose it all.
      'My Dear and Only Love' or 'To His Mistress'
      (c.1642), st.2, as published in James Watson, *A
      Choice Collection of Comic and Serious Scots Poems
      Both Ancient and Modern* (1711)

        As above, variants for the last two lines are
        frequently printed: 'That dares not put it to
        the touch/To gain or lose it all'

3 . . . I'll tune Thy Elegies to Trumpet-sounds,
   And write Thy Epitaph in Blood and Wounds!
      'His Metrical Vow' or 'Lines on the Execution
      of King Charles I' (1649), as published in James
      Watson, *A Choice Collection of Comic and Serious
      Scots Poems Both Ancient and Modern* (1711)

        A common variant reading of these lines
        is: 'I'll sing thine obsequies with trumpet
        sounds/And write thine epitaphs with blood
        and wounds'

4 Let them bestow on ev'ry Airth a Limb;
   Open all my Veins, that I may swim

To Thee, my Saviour, in that Crimson Lake;
Then place my pur-boil'd Head upon a Stake;
Scatter my Ashes, throw them in the Air:
Lord (since Thou know'st where all these
    Atoms are)
I'm hopeful, once Thou'lt recollect my Dust,
And confident Thou'lt raise me with the Just.

'His Metrical Prayer' or 'Lines Composed on
the Eve of his Execution' (c.1650), as published
in James Watson, *A Choice Collection of Comic
and Serious Scots Poems Both Ancient and
Modern* (1711)

The legend is that Montrose scratched these
lines on the window of his cell the night before
his execution, using the point of a diamond.
There is no more evidence for this than for
the more improbable story that he wrote 'His
Metrical Vow' with the point of his sword

5 My head is still my own. Tonight, when it will
be yours, treat it as you please.

To Sir Archibald Johnston of Wariston, on the
morning of his execution (21 May 1650). Quoted
in John Buchan, *Montrose* (1928), ch.17. Cf. W E
Aytoun 2

Johnston, one of the strictest Covenanters,
had reproved Montrose for combing his long
hair with such care and seeming vanity in the
face of death. The sentence was that he should
be hanged, his body quartered, and his head
displayed on the Edinburgh tolbooth

6 What, am I still a terror to them? Let them
look to themselves; my ghost will haunt them.

On learning of the strong guard arranged for his
execution (21 May 1650) to prevent the possibility
of a rescue. Quoted in John Buchan, *Montrose*
(1928), ch.17

Moon, Lorna (pseudonym of Helen Nora Wilson Low) 1886–1930

*Novelist, short-story writer, and Hollywood
scriptwriter*

1 She'd stop her drinking, this would be the last.
She'd be looked up to and respected; she'd go
to kirk, she'd make red petticoats for naked
heathens, she'd stop her drinking. . . She'd
stop her drinking, break the bottle – break it
on the wall – but first she'd drink – No use
to waste good whisky – this would be the last
– the very last – the last.

'Wantin' a Hand', *Doorways in Drumorty* (1926)

Morgan, Edwin 1920–

Poet

1 Go from the grave. The shrill flutes
are silent, the march dispersed.
Deplore what is to be deplored,
and then find out the rest.

'King Billy', *The Second Life* (1968)

2 How shall the race be served?
It shall be served by anguish
as well as by children at play.
It shall be served by loneliness
as well as by family love.

'Glasgow Green', *The Second Life* (1968)

3 . . . the beds of married love
are islands in a sea of desire.

'Glasgow Green', *The Second Life* (1968)

4 Is it true that we come alive
not once, but many times?
We are drawn back to the image
of the seed in darkness, or the greying skin
of the snake that hides a shining one. . .

'The Second Life', *The Second Life (1968)*

5 There were never strawberries
like the ones we had
that sultry afternoon
sitting on the step
of the open french window
facing each other
your knees held in mine
the blue plates in our laps
the strawberries glistening
in the hot sunlight. . .

'Strawberries', *The Second Life* (1968)

6 In my smoochy corner
take me on a cloud
I'll wrap you round
and lay you down
in smoky tinfoil
rings and records
sheets of whisky
and the moon all right
old pal all right
the moon all night

'In Glasgow', *From Glasgow to Saturn* (1973)

7 A mean wind wanders through the back-
    court trash.
Hackles on puddles rise, old mattresses
puff briefly and subside.

'Glasgow Sonnets', *From Glasgow to Saturn*
(1973), No.1

8 The man lies late since he has lost his job,
smokes on one elbow, letting his coughs fall
thinly into an air too poor to rob.

'Glasgow Sonnets', *From Glasgow to Saturn*
(1973), No.1

9 A shilpit dog fucks grimly by the close.

'Glasgow Sonnets', *From Glasgow to Saturn*
(1973), No.2

10 'Let them eat cake' made no bones about it.
But we say let them eat the hope deferred
and that will sicken them. We have preferred
silent slipways to the riveters' wit.

'Glasgow Sonnets', *From Glasgow to Saturn*
(1973), No.5

11 . . . stalled lives never budge.
They linger in the single-ends that use
their spirit to the bone, and when they trudge
from closemouth to laundrette their steady shoes
carry a world that weighs us like a judge.

'Glasgow Sonnets', *From Glasgow to Saturn*
(1973), No.10

12 The planets move, and earth is one, I know.
Blue with endlessly moving seas,
white with clouds endlessly moving,
and the continents creep on plates
endlessly moving soundlessly.
How should we be exempt
or safe from change, we walk
on mercury from birth to death.

'The Planets', *The New Divan* (1977)

13 The planets lift their bones
and roar like megalosaurs.
Time has entered space.
Earth is again the centre
and the favoured place.

'The Worlds', *Star Gate: Science Fiction
Poems* (1979)

14 . . . Immensities
are mind, not ice, as the bright straths unfreeze.

'Post-Glacial', *Sonnets from Scotland* (1984)

15 Where are the eyes that should peer from
    those dens?
Marsh-lights, yes, mushroom-banks, leaf-mould,
    rank ferns,
and up above, a sense of wings, of flight,
of clattering, of calls through fog. Yet men,
going about invisible concerns,
are here, and our immoderate delight
waits to see them, and hear them speak, again.

'Silva Caledonia', *Sonnets from Scotland* (1984)

Morgan, Tommy 1898–1958
Comedian

1 Clairty, Clairty.

Catchphrase, derived from the phrase 'I declare
to Goodness.'

2 He may bomb and bomb and bomb us,
But we'll never turn a hair,
For there'll always be a Rothesay at the Ferr.

Anti-Hitler song performed during the Clyde blitz

Morison, Sir Alexander 1779–1866
Physician, pioneer of psychiatric medicine

1 Although diseases of the mind do not directly
affect the life of the sufferers, they too often
deprive them of everything that can render life
desirable, and more lasting distress and enduring

regret to friends and relatives are occasioned
by them than by any other diseased state,
or indeed by death itself, which under such
circumstances is often hailed to be a blessing.

*Lectures on the Nature, Causes and Treatment of
Insanity* (1848). Quoted in Sir David Kennedy
Henderson, *The Evolution of Psychiatry in Scotland*
(1964), p.36

Morison, Roderick see Clàrsair Dall, An

Morrison, Nancy Brysson ?1907–86
Novelist and biographer

1 '. . . Ye should bide as though to-day was mebbe
going to be your last, and then ye wouldna
be tethered to this earth wi' things that graw
bigger to ye than life itsel'.'

The Gowk Storm (1933), Bk 1, ch.3 (Nannie)

2 'There's worse things than being an auld maid,'
said Nannie. . . 'Marriage ne'er yet cured ill
temper and self-mindedness. Ma graundmither
used to say lang-back-seen, "Ne'er marry for
siller or ye'll carry a heart heavy as gold and
always mind that 'mithers' laddies' mak' the
puirest husbands."'

The Gowk Storm (1933), Bk 1, ch.3

3 'There are some wha have their doors and
windows opened wider than ithers. . . and then
some things are bound to come ben to them,
and there are ithers wha's clocks always gang
a wee thing fast. But whate'er happens to ye,
it's God's will and happens for the best.'

Nannie on second sight. *The Gowk Storm* (1933),
Bk 1, ch.8

4 When I saw the sweep of sky joining the sea
at the pale horizon, I thought of the light,
waning to wax, imprisoned in the globe of
the world. And as my thoughts ebbed and
flowed to the drow of the sea, I thought of
the earth after millions of years when life has
left it, like a shell worn with holes, filled only
with windy vibrations: the faint echo of the
sea, the whisper of spent rain, a weak sighing
of prayer.

The Gowk Storm (1933), Bk 3, ch.2 (Lisbet)

5 You could look at a woman, sit at the same
table with her, every day of your life, and not
see her. That was what he had done. He had
taken her as much for granted in his life as he
took a piece of furniture in a room he used
every day.

'No Letters, Please', in *Casual Columns: The
Glasgow Herald Miscellany* (1955)

Morrison, Wullie 1922–

Ayrshire grocer and Burns enthusiast

1 Ye canna recite Burns juist oot o yer heid. . .
If it disna come frae yer hert and up through
yer heid it's no worth sayin. . . because it must
touch the hert, because Burns touched the hert
aa the time.

> Speaking to Billy Kay, *At Hame Wi Burns*, BBC
> Radio Scotland (broadcast 25 Jan 1996)

>> He was referring specifically to Burns's lines
>> in the 'Epistle to J. Lapraik', 'My Muse, tho'
>> hamely in attire/May touch the heart.'

Morton, 4th Earl of (James Douglas) c.1616–81

Regent of Scotland from 1572

1 Here lieth a man who neither feared nor
flattered any flesh.

> On John Knox, at his burial (26 Nov 1572).
> Quoted in Introduction to Knox's *History of the
> Reformation in Scotland* (ed. W C Dickinson,
> 1949), Vol.1, p.lxviii. Cf. John Knox 12

>> Many variants on this epitaph exist, for
>> example in John Howie, *The Scots Worthies*
>> (1774): 'There lies one who in his life never
>> feared the face of man, who hath often been
>> threatened with dag and dagger, but hath
>> ended his days in peace and honour.'
>> Cf. William Skirving 1

Morton, H V 1892–1979

English travel writer

1 It is the most familiar bridge in the world. It is
seen on posters, framed in railway carriages and
in all kinds of books. To see the Forth Bridge
is rather like meeting a popular actress, but
with this difference: it exceeds expectations.

> *In Search of Scotland* (1929), ch.3, Part 3

2 Dundee has Calcutta in its pocket. There are
men now in Calcutta thinking only of retiring
on Dundee. To understand the wealth of this
city you must go and look at the houses at
Broughty Ferry, Carnoustie, and Newport. No
city in the world could have been kinder to its
rich ones.

> *In Search of Scotland* (1929), ch.4, Part 6

>> Dundee was the capital of the jute industry,
>> and thus had vital trade links with India

3 The superior person will perhaps sniff if I
suggest that no man since Sir Walter Scott has
warmed the world's heart to Scotland more
surely than Sir Harry Lauder. His genius is a
thing apart.

> On his meeting in Aberdeen (1928) with Harry
> Lauder. *In Search of Scotland* (1929), ch.6, Part 5

4 There is no sunlight in the poetry of exile.
There is only mist, wind, rain, the cry of
whaups, and the slow clouds above damp
moorland. That is the real Scotland; that is the
Scotland whose memory wrings the withers
of the far-from-home; and, in some way that
is mysterious, that is the Scotland that even a
stranger learns to love.

> *In Search of Scotland* (1929), ch.7, Part 4

5 . . . it is, like all the wild mountains of Scotland,
a lesson in humility. Man has never existed
for it; it is, at least in sunlight, not unfriendly
so much as utterly oblivious of humanity. . .
Here is a landscape without mercy. So far as
Glencoe is concerned the first germ of life has
never struggled from the warm slime. It is still
dreaming of geological convulsions.

> On Glencoe. *In Search of Scotland* (1929),
> ch.10, Part 2

6 The City of Reality.

> On Glasgow. *In Search of Scotland* (1929), ch.11,
> contents summary

7 Glasgow plays the part of Chicago to
Edinburgh's Boston. Glasgow is a city of
the glad hand and the smack on the back;
Edinburgh is a city of silence until birth or
brains open the social circle. In Glasgow a
man is innocent until he is found guilty; in
Edinburgh a man is guilty until he is found
innocent.

> *In Search of Scotland* (1929), ch.11, Part 2

8 Steel-workers at home are probably kind to their
children and to their wives. They probably love
dogs and grow vegetables. There is nothing
human about them at work! They are merely
the fingers of uncanny machinery.

> On the steelworks at Motherwell (Ravenscraig).
> *In Search of Scotland* (1929), ch.12, Part 1

>> 'All I know,' Morton concluded, 'is that at
>> Motherwell they seem to have a volcano under
>> complete control.'

9 'There is something in Burns for every moment
of a man's life, good days and bad. I shall find
his sympathy here. Burns would have known
what I feel now. . .'

> *In Search of Scotland* (1929), ch.12, Part 3

>> This remark was made to Morton by the
>> curator of the museum beside Burns's cottage
>> at Alloway. While pointing out some of the
>> exhibits, he was called away by someone,
>> and returned to his task without any of
>> the enthusiasm he had previously shown.
>> Finally he explained that he had just been
>> informed of the death of his wife during an
>> operation

Morton, Tom 1955–
Broadcaster and journalist

1 Dolphinsludge, Queen of the Highland
Fleshpots.
   On Inverness. *The Scotsman* (20 Jul 1994)

2 . . . Cumbernauld in a kilt – a description
somewhat unfair on poor old Cumbernauld.
   On Inverness. *The Scotsman* (20 Jul 1994)

Motherwell, William 1797–1835
Poet

1 I've wandered east, I've wandered west,
Through mony a weary way;
But never, never can forget
The luve o' life's young day!
   'Jeannie Morrison', st.1

Muir, Edwin 1887–1959
*Poet, critic and, with his wife Willa Muir,
translator of Franz Kafka*

1 Airdrie and Motherwell are the most improbable
places imaginable in which to be left with
nothing to do; for only rough work could
reconcile anyone to living in them.
   Scottish Journey (1935), Foreword

2 . . . the conventions on which a society
rests easily become sacred; and so a wholesale
invasion of Princes Street by the poor would be
felt not only as an offence against good taste,
but as a blasphemy.
   Scottish Journey (1935), ch.1, 'Edinburgh'

3 . . . Scottish people drink spasmodically and
intensely, for the sake of a momentary but
complete release, whereas the English like to
bathe and paddle about bucolically in a mild
puddle of beer.
   Scottish Journey (1935), ch.1, 'Edinburgh'

4 Nowhere that I have been is one so bathed
and steeped and rolled about in floating sexual
desire as in certain streets of Glasgow and
Edinburgh.
   Scottish Journey (1935), ch.1, 'Edinburgh'

5 . . . most of the. . . small towns I have
seen in Scotland are contentedly or morosely
lethargic, sunk in a fatalistic dullness broken
only by scandal-mongering and such alarums as
drinking produces; a dead silence punctuated
by malicious whispers and hiccups.
   Scottish Journey (1935), ch.2, 'The South'
      Muir excepted the Borders towns, with their
      'curiously wakeful and vivid air', from this
      criticism

6 If one wanted a rough-and-ready generalisation
to express the difference between a Glasgow
man and an Edinburgh man, one might say
that every Edinburgh man considers himself
a little better than his neighbour, and every
Glasgow man just as good as his neighbour.
   Scottish Journey (1935), ch.4, 'Glasgow', section 7

7 Scots has survived to our time as a language
for simple poetry and the simpler kind of
short story, such as *Thrawn Janet*; all its other
uses have lapsed, and it expresses therefore
only a fragment of the Scottish mind. One
can go further than this, however, and assert
that its very use is a proof that the Scottish
consciousness is divided. For, reduced to its
simplest terms, this linguistic division means
that Scotsmen feel in one language and think
in another; that their emotions turn to the
Scottish tongue, with all its associations of local
sentiment, and their minds to a standard English
which for them is almost bare of associations
other than those of the classroom.
   Scott and Scotland (1936), ch.1, 'Language'
      This is Muir's interpretation of Gregory
      Smith's idea of the 'Caledonian Antisyzygy';
      but whereas Smith described the relationship
      between Scottish feeling and intellect as a
      'combination of opposites', Muir sees an
      'irreconcilable' split. Cf. G Gregory Smith 1

8 The curse of Scottish literature is the lack of a
whole language, which finally means the lack
of a whole mind.
   Scott and Scotland (1936), ch.1, 'Language'

9 Dialect is to a homogeneous language what the
babbling of children is to the speech of grown
men and women; it is blessedly ignorant of
the wider spheres of thought and passion. . .
Scottish dialect poetry is a regression to
childhood, an escape from the responsibility
of the whole reason to the simplicity and
irresponsibility of the infant mind.
   Scott and Scotland (1936), ch.3, 'Comparative'

10 . . . The hills and towers
Stood otherwise than they should stand,
And without fear the lawless roads
Ran wrong throughout the land.
   'Hölderlin's Journey', *Journeys and Places*
   (1937), st.11

11 Courage beyond the point and obdurate pride
Made us a nation, robbed us of a nation.
   'Scotland 1941', *The Narrow Place* (1943)

12 Burns and Scott, sham bards of a sham
   nation. . .
   'Scotland 1941', *The Narrow Place* (1943)

13 All through that summer at ease we lay,
And daily from the turret wall

We watched the mowers in the hay
And the enemy half a mile away.
They seemed no threat to us at all.

'The Castle', *The Voyage* (1946), st.1

14 . . . my soul has birdwings to fly free.

'The Labyrinth', *The Labyrinth* (1949)

15 Oh these deceits are strong almost as life.
Last night I dreamt I was in the labyrinth,
And woke far on. I did not know the place.

'The Labyrinth', *The Labyrinth* (1949)

16 . . . We have seen
Good men made evil wrangling with the evil,
Straight minds grown crooked fighting crook-
ed minds.
Our peace betrayed us; we betrayed our peace.
Look at it well. This was the good town once.

'The Good Town', *The Labyrinth* (1949)

17 . . . the tormented wood
Will cure its hurt and grow into a tree
In a green springing corner of young Eden,
And Judas damned take his long journey
backward
From darkness into light and be a child
Beside his mother's knee, and the betrayal
Be quite undone and never more done.

'The Transfiguration', *The Labyrinth* (1949)

The 'tormented wood' is the cross of Christ

18 One foot in Eden still, I stand
And look across the other land.
The world's great day is growing late,
Yet strange these fields that we have planted
So long with crops of love and hate.

'One Foot in Eden', *One Foot in Eden* (1956)

19 The windless northern surge, the sea-gull's
scream,
And Calvin's kirk crowning the barren brae.

'The Incarnate One', *One Foot in Eden* (1956)

20 Barely a twelvemonth after
The seven days war that put the world
to sleep,
Late in the evening the strange horses came.

'The Horses', *One Foot in Eden* (1956)

21 . . . men of sorrow and acquainted with
Grieve . . .

On Scottish writers. Quoted in Karl Miller,
'Romantic Town', in Karl Miller (ed.), *Memoirs
of a Modern Scotland* (1970)

Referring to C M Grieve (Hugh MacDiarmid),
who became a bitter enemy of Muir after his
assertion in *Scott and Scotland* (1936), that
'Scotland can only create a national literature
by writing in English'

Muir, John 1838–1914

*Naturalist and founder of the National Parks
system in the USA*

1 Orchestral harmony of the storm, the wind in
fine tune, the whole sky one waterfall.
How gentle much of storms really is, though
apt to go unnoticed! Storms are never counted
among the resources of a country, yet how far
they go towards making brave people . . .
The tender hearts, the delights delicious
of storms!

*John of the Mountains: the Unpublished Journals
of John Muir* (1938, ed. L M Wolfe), 'Alaska
Fragments' (Jul 1890)

2 The clearest way into the Universe is through
a forest wilderness.

*John of the Mountains: the Unpublished Journals
of John Muir* (1938, ed. L M Wolfe), 'Alaska
Fragments' (Jul 1890)

3 The mountains are fountains of men as well as
of rivers, of glaciers, of fertile soil. The great
poets, philosophers, prophets, able men whose
thought and deeds have moved the world, have
come down from the mountains – mountain-
dwellers who have grown strong there with the
forest trees in Nature's workshops.

*John of the Mountains: the Unpublished Journals
of John Muir* (1938, ed. L M Wolfe), 'Alaska
Fragments' (Jul 1890)

4 In God's wilderness lies the hope of the world
– the great fresh unblighted, unredeemed
wilderness. The galling harness of civilisation
drops off, and the wounds heal ere we are aware.

*John of the Mountains: the Unpublished Journals
of John Muir* (1938, ed. L M Wolfe), 'Alaska
Fragments' (Jul 1890)

5 Most people are *on* the world, not in it – have no
conscious sympathy or relationship to anything
about them – undiffused, separate, and rigidly
alone like marbles of polished stone, touching
but separate.

*John of the Mountains: the Unpublished Journals
of John Muir* (1938, ed. L M Wolfe)

6 The tendency nowadays to wander in
wildernesses is delightful to see. Thousands of
tired, nerve-shaken, over-civilised people are
beginning to find out that going to the mountains is going home; that wildness is a necessity;
and that mountain parks and reservations are
useful not only as fountains of timber and
irrigating rivers, but as fountains of life.

Our National Parks (1901), ch.1, 'The Wild Parks
and Forest Reservations of the West'. Cf. Frank
Fraser Darling 4

7 The forests of America, however slighted by
man, must have been a great delight to God;
for they were the best he ever planted.

Our National Parks (1901), ch.10, 'The American

Forests' (first published in *Atlantic Monthly*,
Aug 1897)

8 Any fool can destroy trees. . . It took more
than three thousand years to make some of the
trees in these Western woods, trees that are
still standing in perfect strength and beauty,
waving and singing in the mighty forests of
the Sierra. Through all the wonderful, eventful
centuries since Christ's time – and long before
that – God has cared for these trees, saved
them from drought, disease, avalanches, and
a thousand straining, levelling tempests and
floods; but he cannot save them from fools –
only Uncle Sam can do that.

Our National Parks (1901), ch.10, 'The American
Forests' (first published in *Atlantic Monthly*,
Aug 1897)

9 On my lonely walks I have often thought how
fine it would be to have the company of Burns.
And indeed he was always with me, for I had
him by heart. On my first long walk from
Indiana to the Gulf of Mexico I carried a copy
of Burns's poems and sang them all the way.
The whole country and the people, beasts and
birds, seemed to like them. . .

Wherever a Scotsman goes, there goes Burns.
His grand whole, catholic soul squares with the
good of all; therefore we find him in everything
everywhere.

John of the Mountains: the Unpublished Journals
of John Muir (ed. L M Wolfe, 1938), 'Thoughts
Written on the Birthday of Robert Burns' (25
Jan 1906)

10 These temple destroyers, devotees of ravaging
commercialism, seem to have a perfect contempt
for Nature, and, instead of lifting their eyes
to the God of the mountains, lift them to the
Almighty Dollar.

Dam Hetch Hetchy! As well as dam
for water-tanks the people's cathedrals and
churches, for no holier temple has ever been
consecrated by the heart of man.

Opposing the plan to flood Hetch Hetchy Valley,
in the National Park, for San Francisco's water
supply. *The Yosemite* (1912), ch.15, 'Hetch
Hetchy Valley'

11 When we contemplate the whole globe as
one great dewdrop, striped and dotted with
continents and islands, flying through space with
other stars all singing and shining together as
one, the whole universe appears as an infinite
storm of beauty.

Travels in Alaska (1915), ch.1, 'The Puget Sound
and British Columbia'

12 Let a Christian hunter go to the Lord's woods
and kill his well-kept beasts, or wild Indians,
and it is well, but let an enterprising specimen of
these proper, predestined victims go to houses

and fields and kill the most worthless person of
the vertical godlike killers – oh! that is horribly
unorthodox, and on the part of the Indians
atrocious murder! Well, I have precious little
sympathy for the selfish propriety of civilised
man, and if a war of races should occur between
the wild beasts and Lord Man, I would be
tempted to sympathise with the bears.

A Thousand-Mile Walk to the Gulf (1916), ch.5,
'Through Florida Swamps and Forests'

Muir (of Huntershill), Thomas 1765–99
Lawyer and radical reformer

1 Gentlemen, from my infancy to this moment I
have devoted myself to the cause of the people.
It is a good cause – it shall ultimately prevail
– it shall finally triumph.

Speech at his trial for sedition (30 Aug 1793).
Cf. Lord Braxfield 2

Muir, Willa (*née* Anderson) 1890–1970
*Novelist, essayist and, with her husband Edwin
Muir, translator of Franz Kafka*

1 . . . the conventionalised ideal of the ignorant
good woman is the deepest disability laid upon
women in a men's State.

Women: An Inquiry (1925)

2 The more men deny the rights of women in
public, the more they are delivered over to
the obscure dissatisfaction of their women in
private. The conventional women whom men
evoke for their own protection have in the end
a more fatal, because a thwarted, influence on
human life than the fearless women. . . Women
are not merely inferior imitations of men: they
create men or destroy them.

Women: An Inquiry (1925)

3 Human life is so intricate in its relationships
that newcomers. . . cannot be dropped into a
town like glass balls into plain water. . .

Imagined Corners (1931), Part 1, ch.1

4 'All crises in women's lives seem to be
punctuated by cups of tea. . .'

Imagined Corners (1931), Part 2, ch.9 (Elizabeth).
Cf. Margaret Oliphant 18

5 Between poetic passion and intellectual passion
there lies a difficult and obscure space, in which
many people spend their whole lives. . .

Imagined Corners (1931), Part 3, ch.4

6 'You and I, Elizabeth, would make one damned
fine woman between us.'

Imagined Corners (1931), Part 3, ch.14 (Elise)

7 It is relatively easy to be proud and poor
when everybody of consequence is poor; it

is far from easy when money begins to spread itself.

> *Mrs Grundy in Scotland* (1936), ch.2, 'Mrs Grundy Comes to Scotland'

8 Sex is at all times to be concealed, but on Sundays it is anathema.

> *Mrs Grundy in Scotland* (1936), ch.3, 'Mrs MacGrundy'

9 The 'puir auld mithers' of Scotland, in their enduring patience, have reared a brood of aggressive, egotistical children who despise them even while they are dependent on them.

> *Mrs Grundy in Scotland* (1936), ch.6, 'Scots-women'

10 The Reformation was a kind of spiritual strychnine of which Scotland took an overdose.

> *Mrs Grundy in Scotland* (1936), ch.9, 'Interlude on Strychnine'

11 ... a Scotswoman who is too timid to utter a word in public may tongue-lash her family in private with great efficiency.

> 'Women in Scotland', *Left Review* (Oct 1936)

Mulgrew, Gerry (Gerard)

Actor, founder member of Communicado Theatre Company

1 Poverty (in the theatre) has become fashionable but it is dangerous to equate it with artistic worth, or worthiness. This breeds a patronising attitude and a belief that since these artists are going to do what they do whether they get paid or not, we won't bother paying them. 'Poor theatre', as it has come to be known, doesn't mean the actors have to eat dog food.

> 'The Poor Mouth?', in *Chapman* No.43–4 (Spring 1986)

2 Big fish need little fish to clean up their mess. The big theatre companies in Scotland need the small angry ones to show them where to go next.

> 'The Poor Mouth?', in *Chapman* No.43–4 (Spring 1986)

3 There's no tradition of theatre in Scotland, so why not make one?

> Quoted in Tom McGrath, 'Wealth or Wasteland', in K Cargill (ed.), *Scotland 2000* (1987)

Mull Herdsman, The
see **Aireach Muileach, An t-**

Mulrine, Stephen 1937–
Poet

1 Whit'll ye dae when the wee Malkies come, if they dreep doon affy the wash-hoose dyke,

an pit the hems oan the sterrheid light, an play wee heidies oan the clean close-wa, an bloo'er yir windae in wi the baw, missis, whit'll ye dae?

> 'The Coming of the Wee Malkies' (1967), st.1

2 ... when ye hear thum shauchlin doon yir loaby, chantin, 'Wee Malkies – the gemme's a bogey!' – Haw, missis, whit'll ye dae?

> 'The Coming of the Wee Malkies' (1967), st.3

Munro, Neil 1863–1930
Journalist and novelist

1 'If Dougie wass here he would tell you. She would not take in wan cup of watter unless it wass for synin' oot the dishes. She wass that dry she would not wet a postage stamp unless we slung it over the side in a pail. She wass sublime, chust sublime!'

> *The Vital Spark* (1906), ch.1, 'Para Handy, Master Mariner' (Para Handy on the *Vital Spark*)

2 'There's not mich that iss wholesomer than a good herrin',' said Para Handy. 'It's a fush that's chust sublime.'

> *The Vital Spark* (1906), ch.7, 'The Sea Cook'

3 'It's either a rise in pay,' he told himself, 'or he's heard aboot the night we had in Campbeltown. That's the worst of high jeenks; they're aye stottin' back and hittin' you on the nose; if it's no' a sore heid, you've lost a pound-note, and if it's nothing you lost, it's somebody clypin' on you.'

> *The Vital Spark* (1906), ch.11, 'Para Handy's Apprentice' (Para Handy on being summoned to the owner's office). Cf. Walter Scott 40

4 'It's a fine thing a drap watter,' said Para Handy, gasping.
'No' a worse thing you could drink,' said Hurricane Jack. 'It rots your boots; what'll it no' do on your inside? Watter's fine for sailin' on – there's nothing better – but it's no' drink for sailors.'

> *The Vital Spark* (1906), ch.22, 'Three Dry Days'

5 'It means the end of many things, I doubt, not all to be despised, – the last stand of Scotland, and she destroyed. And yet – and yet, this New Road will some day be the Old Road, too, with ghosts on it and memories.'

> *The New Road* (1914), ch.28, 'The Return' (Aeneas to Janet)
>
> On General Wade's military road-building in the 18th century

6 'The Congo's no' to be compared wi' the West o' Scotland when it comes to insects,' said

Para Handy. 'There's places here that's chust deplorable whenever the weather's the least bit warm. Look at Tighnabruaich! – they're that bad there, they'll bite their way through corrugated iron roofs to get at ye!. . . There iss a spachial kind of mudge in Dervaig, in the Isle of Mull, that hass aal the points o' a Poltalloch terrier, even to the black nose and cocked lugs, and sits up and barks at you.'

Hurricane Jack of the Vital Spark (1923), ch.14, ' "Mudges" '

7 'There iss nothing that the mudges likes to see among them better than an English towerist with a kilt: the very tops wass eaten off his stockin's.'

Hurricane Jack of the Vital Spark (1923), ch.14, ' "Mudges" '

8 Are you not weary in your distant places,
Far, far from Scotland of the mist and storm;
In drowsy airs, the sun-smite on your faces,
The days so long and warm?
When all around you lie the strange fields sleeping,
The dreary woods where no fond memories roam,
Do not your sad hearts over seas come leaping
To the highlands and the lowlands of
your Home?

'To Exiles', *The Poetry of Neil Munro* (1931), st.1

Munro, Rona 1959–
Playwright

1 NORA: Och you're killing yourself with those.
CASSIE: And what are *you* doing? Bit of interior decor? Tar-filled lungs: what the best dressed bodies are wearing.

On smoking. *Bold Girls* (1991), Scene 1

2 DEIRDRE: The whole town's a prison, smash chunks off the walls 'cause we're all in a prison.

On Belfast. *Bold Girls* (1991), Scene 2

3 LISA: You look like a wee china doll, a tiny pure and perfect bit of Victorian porcelain and you're wearing *black silk*. Their neanderthal brains will just explode.

Your Turn to Clean the Stair (1995), Act 1

4 LISA: . . . show me someone happy who hasn't been drawn by Disney.

Your Turn to Clean the Stair (1995), Act 2

Murray, Charles 1864–1941
Poet

1 Here on the Rand we freely grant
We're blest wi' sunny weather;

Fae cauld an' snaw we're weel awa',
But man, we miss the heather.

Hamewith (1900), epigraph

2 He cut a sappy sucker from the muckle rodden-tree,
He trimmed it, an' he wet it, an' he thumped it on his knee;
He never heard the teuchat when the harrow broke her eggs,
He missed the craggit heron nabbin' puddocks in the seggs,
He forgot to hound the collie at the cattle when they strayed,
But you should hae seen the whistle that the wee herd made!

'The Whistle', *Hamewith* (1900), st.1

3 The feet o' ilka man an' beast gat youkie when he played –
Hae ye ever heard o' whistle like the wee herd made?

'The Whistle', *Hamewith* (1900), st.5

4 Her teethless mou' was like a bell,
Her tongue the clangin' clapper.

'The Miller', *Hamewith* (1900)

5 *Bring them alang, the young, the strang,*
The weary an' the auld;
Feed as they will on haugh or hill,
This is the only fauld.

Dibble them doon, the laird, the loon,
King an' the cadgin' caird,
The lady fine beside the queyn,
A' in the same kirkyaird.

'A Green Yule', *Hamewith* (1900), st.9–10

6 Foreign fashions, lad, allure you,
Hamespun happit I would be;
Bring nae mair, for I assure you
Ferlies only scunner me.

Fancy tartans, clanless, gaudy,
Mention them nae mair, I say;
Best it suits your service, laddie,
An' my drinkin', hodden-grey.

'Horace in Scots', Car.1, 38, *Hamewith* (1900)

7 It wasna his wyte he was beddit sae late
An' him wi' sae muckle to dee,
He'd the rabbits to feed an' the fulpie to kame
An' the hens to hish into the ree. . .

'It Wasna His Wyte', *In the Country Places* (1920), st.1

8 Noo that cauldrife Winter's here
There's a pig in ilka bed,
Kindlin's scarce an' coals is dear;
Noo that cauldrife Winter's here
Doddy mittens we maun wear,
Butter skites an' winna spread;

Noo that cauldrife Winter's here
There's a pig in ilka bed.

'Winter', *In the Country Places* (1920)

9 Gin I was God, sittin' up there abeen,
Weariet nae doot noo a' my darg was deen,
Deaved wi' the harps an' hymns oonendin'
ringin,
Tired o' the flockin' angels hairse wi' singin',
To some clood-edge I'd dauner furth an', feth,
Look ower an' watch hoo things were
gyaun aneth.

'Gin I Was God', *In the Country Places* (1920)

0 Then mak' my bed in Aiberdeen
An' tak' me back; I'll no compleen
Tho' a' my life I lie my leen
In Aiberdeen awa'.

'Aiberdeen Awa'!', *In the Country Places*
(1920), st.1

1 Bauld Ben Muich Dhui towers, until
Ben Nevis looms the laird o' a';
But Bennachie! Faith, yon's the hill
Rugs at the hairt when ye're awa'!

'Bennachie', *In the Country Places* (1920), st.1

Murray, Chic (Charles Thomas McKinnon Murray) 1919–85
Comedian

1 A Scot is a man who keeps the Sabbath, and
everything else he can lay his hands on.

'There was a Scotsman. . . (Part Two)', in Miles
Kington (ed.), *Punch on Scotland* (1977)

2 There are only two rules for drinking
whisky. First, never take whisky without
water, and second, never take water without
whisky.

'There was a Scotsman. . . (Part Two)',
in Miles Kington (ed.), *Punch on Scotland* (1977)

Murray, George 1819–68
Poet

1 The gude auld Kirk o' Scotland,
She's nae in ruins yet!

'The Auld Kirk o' Scotland', st.1

Murray, Sir James 1837–1915
First editor of the Oxford English Dictionary

1 Knowledge is power.

Written on the flyleaf of his copy of Cassell's
Popular Educator. Quoted in Elizabeth Murray,
Caught in the Web of Words (1977), ch.1.
Cf. Samuel Smiles 6

2 Language is mobile and liable to change. . .
it is a free country, and a man may call a
vase a *vawse*, a *vahse*, a *vaze*, or a *vase*, as he
pleases. And why should he not? We do not
all think alike, walk alike, dress alike, write
alike, or dine alike; why should not we use our
liberty in speech also, so long as the purpose
of speech, to be intelligible, and its grace, are
not interfered with?

Letter (5 Jan 1895) to unnamed correspondent

3 The Dictionary is to me. . . the work that God
has found for me and for which I see that all my
sharpening of intellectual tools was done and
it becomes to me a high and sacred devotion.

Writing about his life's work on his 70th birthday
(7 Feb 1907)

Murray, Robert F 1863–94
Poet

1 Would you like to see a city given over,
Soul and body, to a tyrannising game?
If you would, there's no need to be a rover,
For St Andrews is the abject city's name.

'The City of Golf', *The Scarlet Gown* (1891)

N

Nairn, Tom 1932–

Sociologist and political commentator

1 In fact, there is no Stalinist like a Scottish Stalinist. . .

'The Three Dreams of Scottish Nationalism' in Karl Miller (ed.), *Memoirs of a Modern Scotland* (1970)

2 As far as I'm concerned, Scotland will be reborn when the last minister is strangled with the last copy of the *Sunday Post.*

'The Three Dreams of Scottish Nationalism' in Karl Miller (ed.), *Memoirs of a Modern Scotland* (1970). Cf. Neal Ascherson 7, Naomi Mitchison 7

Nairne, Lady Carolina (*née* Oliphant, pseudonym Mrs Bogan of Bogan) 1766–1845

Songwriter

1 Oh the auld house, the auld house,
What tho' the rooms were wee!
Oh! kind hearts were dwelling there,
And bairnies fu' o' glee;
The wild rose and the jessamine
Still hang upon the wa',
How mony cherish'd memories
Do they sweet flowers reca'!

'The Auld House', st.1

2 Wha'll buy my caller herrin'?
They're bonnie fish and halesome farin';
Wha'll buy my caller herrin',
New drawn frae the Forth?

'Caller Herrin' ', chorus

3 Wha'll buy my caller herrin'?
Oh, ye may ca' them vulgar farin';
Wives and mithers, maist despairin',
Ca' them lives o' men.

'Caller Herrin' ', st.3. Cf. Walter Scott 50

4 There's cauld kail in Aberdeen,
There's castocks in Stra'bogie,
And, morn and e'en, they're blythe and bein,
That haud them frae the cogie. . .

'Cauld Kail in Aberdeen', st.1. Cf. Alexander Gordon 1

5 Ye shouldna ca' the Laird daft, though daft like he may be;
Ye shouldna ca' the Laird daft, he's just as wise as me;

Ye shouldna ca' the Laird daft, his bannet has a *bee,* –
He's just a wee bit Fifish, like some Fife Lairds that be.

'The Fife Laird', st.1

6 Wi' a hundred pipers an' a', an' a',
Wi' a hundred pipers an' a', an' a';
We'll up an' gie them a blaw, a blaw,
Wi' a hundred pipers an' a', an' a'.

'The Hundred Pipers', chorus. Cf. Alexander Scott (1920–89) 1

7 The laird o' Cockpen, he's proud an' he's great,
His mind is ta'en up wi' things o' the State;
He wanted a wife his braw house to keep,
But favour wi' wooin' was fashious to seek.

Down by the dyke-side a lady did dwell,
At his table head he thought she'd look well,
McClish's ae daughter o' Claverse-ha' Lee,
A penniless lass wi' a lang pedigree.

'The Laird o' Cockpen', st.1–2

8 An' when she cam ben he bowed fu' low,
An' what was his errand he soon let her know;
Amazed was the laird when the lady said 'Na,'
And wi' a laigh curtsie she turned awa'.

Dumfounder'd was he, nae sigh did he gie,
He mounted his mare – he rade cannily;
And aften he thought, as he gaed thro' the glen,
She's daft to refuse the laird o' Cockpen.

'The Laird o' Cockpen', st.6–7. Cf. Robert Burns 117

9 I'm wearin' awa', John,
Like snaw-wreaths in thaw, John,
I'm wearin' awa'
To the land o' the leal.

There's nae sorrow there, John,
There's neither cauld nor care, John,
The day is aye fair
In the land o' the leal.

'The Land o' the Leal', st.1–2

10 Oh! Rowan Tree, Oh! Rowan Tree, thou'lt aye be dear to me,
Intwin'd thou art wi' mony ties o' hame and infancy.
Thy leaves were aye the first o' spring, thy flow'rs the simmer's pride;
There was nae sic a bonny tree, in a' the countrie side.
Oh! Rowan Tree.

'The Rowan Tree', st.1

1 There grows a bonnie brier bush in our
kail-yard,
And white are the blossoms o't in our
kail-yard...

> 'There Grows a Bonnie Brier Bush', st.1

>> Reworked from an old song collected by
Robert Burns. These opening lines were, with
slight alteration ('on't' for 'o't') used as an
epigraph by 'Ian Maclaren' (John Watson,
1850–1907) for his collection of stories *Beside
the Bonnie Brier Bush* (1894). Hence came the
opprobrious term 'Kailyard' to describe the
sentimental fiction of Maclaren, J M Barrie,
S R Crockett and others. Cf. J H Millar 1

2 Come thro' the heather, around him gather,
Ye're a' the welcomer early;
Aroud him cling wi' a' your kin;
For wha'll be king but Charlie?

> 'Wha'll be King but Charlie?', chorus

3 Bonnie Charlie's now awa,
Safely owre the friendly main;
Mony a heart will break in twa,
Should he ne'er come back again.

Will ye no come back again?
Will ye no come back again?
Better lo'ed ye canna be,
Will ye no come back again?

> 'Will Ye No Come Back Again?', st.1 and chorus

4 Sweet's the laverock's note and lang,
Lilting wildly up the glen;
But aye to me he sings ae sang, –
Will ye no come back again?

> 'Will Ye No Come Back Again?', st.5

Naughton, Charles and Gold, Jimmy
1887–1976 (Naughton), 1886–1967 (Gold)
Comedians

1 Turn it around the other way.

> Catchphrase

Neaves, Lord (Charles Neaves) 1800–76
Judge and man of letters

1 We zealots made up of stiff clay,
The sour-looking children of sorrow,
While not over jolly to-day,
Resolve to be wretched to-morrow.
We can't for a certainty tell
What mirth may molest us on Monday;
But, at least, to begin the week well,
Let us all be unhapy on Sunday.

> 'Let us all be Unhappy on Sunday', *Songs and
Verses: Social and Scientific* (1872), st.1

2 Abroad we forbid folks to roam,
For fear they get social or frisky;
But of course they can sit still at home,

And get dismally drunk upon whisky.

> 'Let us all be Unhappy on Sunday', *Songs and
Verses: Social and Scientific* (1872), st.5

3 Stuart Mill on Mind and Matter,
All our old Beliefs would shatter:
Stuart Mill exerts his skill
To make an end of Mind and Matter.

> 'Stuart Mill on Mind and Matter', *Songs and
Verses: Social and Scientific* (1872) st.1

4 David Hume could Mind and Matter
Ruthlessly assault and batter...

> 'Stuart Mill on Mind and Matter', *Songs and
Verses: Social and Scientific* (1872), st.3

5 Mutton old and claret good were Caledonia's
forte,
Before the Southron taxed her drink and
poisoned her with port.

> 'Beef and Potatoes', *Songs and Verses: Social and
Scientific* (4th edition, 1875), st.5. Cf. John Home 2

Neil, Rob(ert) 1963–
Interior designer and socialite

1 I suppose there's nothing wrong with living
life in the bus-lane.

> Attrib.

2 My face leaves at midnight. Be on it.

> Attrib. Responding to a suggestion that he was
'out of his face'

Neill, A(lexander) S(utherland)
1883–1973
Writer and educator

1 I shall henceforth try to make my bairns realise.
Yes, realise is the word... I want to make them
realise what life means... Most of the stuff I
teach them will be forgotten in a year or two,
but an attitude remains with one throughout
life. I want these boys and girls to acquire the
habit of looking honestly at life.

> *A Dominie's Log* (1915), ch.1

2 I find that I am on the side of the bairns. I am
against law and discipline; I am all for freedom
of action.

> *A Dominie's Log* (1915), ch.11

3 ... the first thing a child should learn is to
be a rebel.

> *A Dominie Dismissed* (1917), ch.5

4 'Casting Out Fear' ought to be the motto over
every school door.

> *The Problem Child* (1926), ch.12

5 There is never a problem child; there is only
a problem parent.

> *The Problem Parent* (1932), opening sentence

6 Oh parents, I know that you need sympathy
and understanding, but I am so weary of you!
You are the problems. I try to help some of
the children that you make problems, and they
become happy and efficient children, but you
have no school in which to learn. . . You are
all problem children, and the greatest need in
education today is the setting up of schools for
problem parents.

> *The Problem Parent* (1932), closing paragraph

7 The only thing certain is that we must keep
freedom for kids going until they shoot us at
the dusk of civilisation.

> Letter to Bill Currie (Jun 1940). Quoted
> in Jonathan Croall, *Neill of Summerhill: the
> Permanent Rebel* (1983), ch.13

8 The future of Summerhill itself may be of
little import. But the future of the Summerhill
idea is of the greatest importance to humanity.
New generations must be given the chance to
grow in freedom. The bestowal of freedom is
the bestowal of love. And only love can save
the world.

> *Summerhill: a Radical Approach to Child-Rearing*
> (1960), 'The Future of Summerhill'

> Summerhill was the experimental school
> established by Neill in Dorset in 1924

9 When I lost my leather tawse for ever I lost my
fear of my pupils and they lost their fear of me.

> Quoted in Jonathan Croall, *Neill of Summerhill:
> the Permanent Rebel* (1983), ch.4

Neill, William 1922–
Poet

1 They could not read, or would not read
except what they read in the sky, on the moor
  and the hills
and the noise of ploughshares ripping the
  winter turf
was a kind of music to them.

> 'Ayrshire Farm', *Four Points of a Saltire* (1970)

2 Broken on a wheel
a hare rests by the road verge,
shrouded by his guts,
his strong hind legs still striving
to beat that sly tortoise, death.

> 'Last Race', *Making Tracks* (1988)

3 Wyce bairns shuin lairn; sair airses an split heids
smoor oot the gust fir owre-heroic deeds.

> 'Prudence', *Making Tracks* (1988)

4 Now, poets write books that Scotland does
  not buy,
shrink, in their eyes, to the status of eccentric.
Poetry's drowned out by every parrot-cry

feeding the multitude the latest cantrip.
They value verses less than a clownish trick;
once a year only within a phantom nation
they shrink your head to fit a social occasion.

> 'Mr Burns for Supper', in P Fortune & B
> Hodgson (eds), *Mr Burns for Supper: Contem-
> porary Poetry from Ayrshire and Dumfries &
> Galloway* (1996), st.7

New Testament in Scots 1983
*Translation of the New Testament from the
original Greek, made between 1957 and 1967
by the classical scholar William Laughton
Lorimer (1885–1967)*

1 'Nae man can sair twa maisters: aither he will
ill-will the tane an luve the tither, or he will
grip til the tane and lichtlifie the tither. Ye
canna sair God and Gowd baith.'

> Matthew 6.24

2 'Black s' be your faa, Doctors o the Law an
Pharisees, hypocrites at ye ar! Ye ar like white-
wuishen graffs, at luiks bonnie an braw outside,
but inside is fu o deid men's banes an aa kin
o filth an fulyie.'

> Matthew 23.27

3 Jesus fell agreitin, an the Jews said, 'Man, wisna
he fain o him?'

> John 11.35–6

4 . . . knawledge maks big, luve biggs up.

> 1 Corinthians 8.1

5 Luve keeps nae nickstick o the wrangs it drees;
finnds nae pleisur i the ill wark o ithers; is
ey liftit up whan truith dings lies; kens ey tae
keep a caum souch; is ey sweired tae misdout;
ey howps the best; ey bides the warst.

> 1 Corinthians 13.4–7

6 Bairnies, latna our luve be frae the teeth outwith:
lat us luve ilk ither frae the hairt, an in deeds!

> 1 John 3.18

Nic a' Phearsain, Màiri
see **Màiri Mhór nan Oran**

Nic Fhearghais, Cairistìona
(Christina Ferguson) 18th century
*Widow of William Chisholm, who was killed
at Culloden*

1 Och a Thèarlaich òig Stiùbhairt, 's e do chùis
  rinn mo léireadh:
Thug thu bhuam gach nì bh'agam ann an
  cogadh nad adhbhar;
Cha chrodh is cha chàirdean tha gam chràdh
  ach mo chéile,

On la dh'fhàg thu mi 'm aonar gun sìon san
 t-saoghal ach léine –
Mo rùn geal òg.

Có nis thogas an claidheamh no nì chathair a
 lìonadh?
'S gann gur h-e tha air m'aire o nach maireann
 mo chiad ghràdh,
Ach ciamar gheibhinn o m'nàdur a bhith 'g
 àicheadh na 's miann leam
Is mo thogradh cho làidir thoirt gu àite mo
 righ math? –
Mo rùn geal òg.

Alas, young Charles Stewart, it is your cause
that has left me desolate: you took from me
everything that I had in a war in your cause;
it is not cattle or friends that have pained me
but my spouse, since the day that you left me
alone, with nothing in the world but my shift
– my fair young love.

  Who will now lift the sword or fill the chair?
It scarcely matters to me, since my first love
is dead, but how could I find it in my nature
to deny what I desire, when my wish is so
strong to take my good king to his rightful
place – my fair young love.

   'Mo rùn geal òg' ('My fair young love'), st.1–2

NicGumaraid, Catriona (Catriona Montgomery) 1947–

Poet

1 Ochòin, a Rìgh, 'n e sabaid fhalamh
a bhith sgrìobadh na fìrinn às an talamh?
Alas, but it's an empty fight
to scratch truth from the earth aright.

   'Gun Stiùir' ('Rudderless'), in C Whyte (ed.),
   An Aghaidh na Sìorraidheachd (*In the Face of
   Eternity*, 1991)

2 Nuair a bheir an fheannag
an t-sùil às a' chaora mu dheireadh,
bidh mi ri farchluais
air d' uinneagan,
rid osagan ag ochanaich,
's na guthan cruaidh Sasannach
a' dol an aghaidh na gaoith.
  When the hoodie-crow takes
the eye out of the last sheep
I will be eavesdropping at your windows
listening to your breezes sighing
and the harsh English voices clashing with
 the wind.

   'Ròdhag, 2000 AD' ('Roag, 2000 AD'), in C Whyte
   (ed.), *An Aghaidh na Sìorraidheachd* (*In the Face
   of Eternity*, 1991)

3 Mi 'm fiachan gu mo chluasan
is rùcail na mo chaolain
le acras; mo ghlùinean bleith a chèile an
 còmhnaidh;

gun tòin a chumas fhèileadh
air mo chnàmhan bochda, caola
nach cùm creapaillt mo stocainn an àirde.

Ur tòinean-se cho àlainn,
le saill iad cruinn is deàrrsach –
nach gabh sibh truas ri ceann-feadhna Chlann
 Dòmhnaill?

† I am in debt up to my ears
and my gut rumbling with hunger,
my knees knocking ceaselessly,
without a backside to hold my kilt up
on my poor thin bones;
no garter will hold up my stockings.

You have splendid buttocks
round and shining with fat;
will you not take pity on the last chief of Clan
Donald?

   'Gu Dòmhnallaich Aimeireagaidh' ('To the
   American Macdonalds'), in C Whyte (ed.),
   An Aghaidh na Sìorraidheachd (*In the Face of
   Eternity*, 1991)

NicGumaraid, Màiri (Mary Montgomery) 1955–

Poet

1 Feumaidh mi leabhar bhith deas air mo shùil
de bhriathran nan làithean a dh'fhalbh,
feumaidh mi leughadh fa chomhair an àm
tha cànan an cunnart dhol balbh.

† I must have a book for my eyes
of the words of the days gone by
I must read it when facing the time
a language threatens to go dumb.

   'An Taigh-tasgaidh 's an Leabhar' ('The Museum
   and the Book'), in C Whyte (ed.), *An Aghaidh
   na Sìorraidheachd* (*In the Face of Eternity*, 1991)

2 'S fheàrr leam nuair a tha iad borb
tha iad nas fhasa 'n sgrios nam smuain
faodaidh fois bhith aig mo chogais. . .

† I prefer it when they're rude
because they're easier to destroy in my
 thoughts
and my conscience can be at peace. . .

   'Na Sasannaich' ('The English'), in C Whyte
   (ed.), *An Aghaidh na Sìorraidheachd* (*In the Face
   of Eternity*, 1991)

3 an luach a th'ac' ga stòraigeadh
each one for himself
's e tha falbh lem dhùthaich
's e tha gam fàgail ann.

† the kind of value they lay store by
is each one for himself
that's what's going away with my country
and what leaves them in it.

   'Na Sasannaich' ('The English'), in C Whyte
   (ed.), *An Aghaidh na Sìorraidheachd* (*In the Face
   of Eternity*, 1991)

Nicholson, James 1822–97

Poet

1 Jenny wi' the lang poke,
  Haste ye owre the main,
  Lampin' wi' yer lang legs,
  Plashin' through the rain.
  Here's a waukrife laddie
  Winna steek his ee,
  Pit him in yer lang poke,
  An' dook him in the sea!

> 'Jenny wi the Lang Poke', st.1. Cf. Alexander
> Anderson 2

North, Christopher (pseudonym of John Wilson) 1785–1854

Critic and essayist, Professor of Moral Philosophy at the University of Edinburgh

1 The stars are shining cheerily, cheerily,
  Ho ro Mhairi dhu, turn ye to me;
  The sea-mew is moaning drearily, drearily,
  Ho ro Mhairi dhu, turn ye to me.

> 'Turn Ye To Me', st.1

2 Minds like ours, my dear James, must always be above national prejudice, and in all companies it gives me true pleasure to declare, that, as a people, the English are very little indeed inferior to the Scotch.

> 'Noctes Ambrosianae' No.28, *Blackwood's
> Magazine* (Oct 1826)

3 His Majesty's dominions, on which the sun never sets.

> 'Noctes Ambrosianae' No.42, *Blackwood's
> Magazine* (Apr 1829)

4 Laws were made to be broken.

> 'Noctes Ambrosianae' No.49, *Blackwood's
> Magazine* (May 1830)

5 It may be divided into three parts; in one you cannot hear, in another you cannot see, and in the third you can neither see nor hear. I remember once sitting alone in the third division – and never before or since have I had such a profound feeling of the power of solitude.

> On the Theatre Royal, Glasgow. 'Noctes
> Ambrosianae' No.64, *Blackwood's Magazine*
> (Nov 1832)

6 Such accidents will happen in the best-regulated families.

> 'Noctes Ambrosianae' No.67, *Blackwood's
> Magazine* (Aug 1834)

O

Oban Times 1861–
Newspaper

Those who have entered on the path of land laws reform in the Highlands cannot now look back. . . The sunken thousands in our cities cry daily for justice which the operation of one-sided laws has denied them. They must make common cause out of their common misery. The present cry for redress is the cry of humanity. It cannot be stifled. It will continue to be heard until all the fortresses of excessive privilege and class laws are laid in ruins.

> Editorial (27 Mar 1886). Quoted in Malcolm MacLean and Christopher Carrell (eds), *As an Fhearann (From the Land*, 1986)

Ogilvie, John 1579–1615
Jesuit priest, martyr and saint

If the King will be to me as his predecessors were to mine, I will obey and acknowledge him for my King, but if he do otherwise and play the runagate from God, as he and you all do, I will not acknowledge him more than this old hat.

> At his trial for high treason (Mar 1615)
>
> > Ogilvie refused to take an oath of allegiance to King James VI and I, which would effectively have meant him denying the spiritual supremacy of the Pope. He was hanged at Glasgow Cross. He was beatified in 1927, and canonised in 1976

Ogilvie, Will(iam) H(enry) 1869–1963
Poet

The hill road to Roberton's a steep road to climb,
But where your foot has crushed it you can smell the scented thyme,
And if your heart's a Border heart, look down to Harden Glen,
And hear the blue hills ringing with the restless hoofs again.

> 'The Hill Road to Roberton', st.6

Last night a wind from Lammermoor came roaring up the glen
With the tramp of trooping horses and the laugh of reckless men,
And struck a mailed hand on the gate and cried in rebel glee:

'Come forth, come forth, my Borderer, and ride the March with me!'

> 'The Raiders', st.1

Ogilvy (of Clova), Dorothea Maria 1823–95
Poet

1 Spinnin', spinnin', ever spinnin',
Never endin', aye beginnin';
Hard at wark wi' hand and fit,
Oh, the weary spinnin' o't!

> 'The Weary Spinnin' O't', *Poems of Dorothea Maria Ogilvy* (2nd edition, 1873), st.1

Ogilvy, James (1st Earl of Seafield) 1644–1730
Advocate and MP, a member of the Scottish commission which negotiated the Union of Parliaments

1 Now there's ane end of ane old song.

> Said in 1707, on signing, as Chancellor, the Treaty of Union between Scotland and England. Quoted in George Lockhart of Carnwath, *Memoirs* (1817 edition), Vol.1, p.223. Cf. Allan Massie 1
>
> > Lockhart refers to this as 'this despising and contemning remark'. Frequently given as 'ane auld sang'

Oliphant, Carolina
see **Nairne, Lady Carolina**

Oliphant, Caroline 1807–31
Poet, niece of Lady Nairne

1 Dreams bring the shadow back on Time's hard dial:
Shake the full hour-glass, and the golden sands
Run once again their sparkling course.

> 'Lines on Dreams', ll.6–8

Oliphant, Mrs Margaret (*née* Wilson) 1828–97
Novelist and critic

1 . . . remember those of you who have independent ambition those who have not: To

endure hardship and labour demands a kind of heroism – to endure to be useless is the hardest fate of woman.

The Melvilles (1852), ch.5

2 Woman's rights will never grow into a popular agitation, yet woman's wrongs are always picturesque and attractive. They are indeed so good to make novels and poems about. . . that we fear any real redress of grievance would do more harm to the literary world than it would do good to the feminine.

'The Laws Concerning Women' (book review), *Blackwood's Edinburgh Magazine* (Apr 1856)

3 The 'marriage of true minds' may be as rare as it is lofty and fortunate. The marriage of interests, hopes, and purposes is universal. The more independent the husband and wife are of each other, the less sure is the basis of society.

'The Laws Concerning Women' (book review), *Blackwood's Edinburgh Magazine* (Apr 1856)

4 Outside lies a world in which every event is an enigma, where nothing that comes offers any explanation of itself; where God does not show himself always kind, but by times awful, terrible – a God who smites and does not spare. It is easy to make a harmonious balance of doctrine; but where is the interpretation of life?

Salem Chapel (1863), ch.40

5 The beautiful new world of love and goodness into which the happy bride supposes herself to be entering comes to bear after a while so extraordinary a resemblance to the ordinary mediocre world which she has quitted that the young woman stands aghast and bewildered.

A Son of the Soil (1865), ch.46

6 I am almost sorry to say I don't feel myself much sillier than the majority of men I meet, though perhaps that may be because the men in Windsor are not lofty specimens.

Letter to John Blackwood (1876), National Library of Scotland manuscript 4349. Quoted in Elisabeth Jay, *Mrs Oliphant: A Fiction to Herself* (1995), p.235

7 . . . intellectualism like any other *ism* is monotonous. . . Scholarship is a sort of poison tree and kills everything.

Letter to John Blackwood (16 Mar 1879). Quoted in *Autobiography and Letters of Mrs Margaret Oliphant* (ed. Mrs Harry Coghill, 1899)

8 Happiness dies, love fails, but art is forever.

Within the Precincts (1879), ch.34

9 A man is none the worse for things that would ruin a girl for ever.

Within the Precincts (1879), ch.36

10 I think it is highly absurd that I should not have a vote, if I want one.

'The Grievances of Women', *Fraser's Magazine* (May 1880)

11 Real life has no ending save in death – it is a tangle of breakings off and addings on, of new beginnings overlapping the old, of ties arbitrarily cut and arbitrarily pieced together again, and nothing to make the picture, as painters say, 'compose'.

Review of several new novels, in *Blackwood's Edinburgh Magazine* (Sep 1880)

12 'Hester', he said, 'that is not what a man wants in a woman; not to go and explain it all to her with pen and ink, tables and figures, to make her understand as he would have to do with a man. What he wants, dear, is very different – just to lean upon you – to know that you sympathise, and think of me, and feel for me, and believe in me, and that you will share whatever comes.'

Hester said nothing, but her countenance grew very grave.

Hester (1883), ch.36 (Edward to Hester)

13 '. . . unfortunately, however high-minded we are, we can do nothing without it. It means of course show and luxury, and gaiety, and all the things you despise; but at the same time. . . it means ease of mind, so that a man can rise every day without anxiety, knowing that he has enough for every claim upon him.'

On money. *Hester* (1883), ch.36 (Roland to Hester)

14 Great scandals are not in the way of the ordinary and commonplace people among whom, all the same, the greatest tragedies may be enacted.

Review of Guy de Maupassant's novel, *Pierre et Jean*, in *Blackwood's Edinburgh Magazine* (Sep 1888)

15 Life is no definite thing with a beginning and an end, a growth and a climax; but a basket of fragments, passages that lead to nothing, curious incidents which look of importance at first, but which crumble and break in pieces, dropping into ruins.

Review of Henry James's *A London Life*, in *Blackwood's Edinburgh Magazine* (Jun 1889)

16 They were unlucky accidents, tares among the wheat, handmaids who might be useful about the house, but who had no future, no capabilities of advancing the family, creatures altogether of no account. . . Mr Douglas felt that every farthing spent upon the useless female portion of his household was so much taken from the boys, and the consequence was that the girls grew up without even the meagre education then considered necessary for women. . .

Kirsteen: The Story of a Scotch Family Seventy

Years Ago (1890), ch.5 (Mr Douglas of
Drumcarro's opinion of his daughters)

'I have got a trade, an occupation. Women with
that are better not to marry.'

Diana Trelawney, The History of a Great Mistake
(1892), ch.13

Tea singularly changed the face of affairs.
Gossip may be exchanged over the teacups, but
to come fully prepared for mortal combat, and
in the midst of it to be served by your antagonist
with a cup of tea, is terribly embarrassing. . .
It was more than female virtue was equal to,
to refuse that deceiving cup.

Old Mr Tredgold (1895), ch.8. Cf. Willa Muir 4

When people comment upon the number of
books I have written, and I say that I am so
far from being proud of that fact that I should
like at least half of them forgotten, they stare
– and yet it is quite true. . .

*Autobiography and Letters of Mrs Margaret
Oliphant* (ed. Mrs Harry Coghill, 1899), ch.1,
'1 Feb 1885'

Her prolific output included over 100 novels.
Her income from her writing had to support
not only her own children but eventually also
her brother and his family

How I have been handicapped in life! Should
I have done better if I had been kept, like her,
in a mental greenhouse and taken care of?

Comparing herself to George Eliot. *Autobiography
and Letters of Mrs Margaret Oliphant* (ed. Mrs
Harry Coghill, 1899), ch.1, '1 Feb 1885'

She felt that George Eliot lived in a 'carefully
regulated atmosphere into which nothing from
the outer world save the most delicate incense
with just the flavour that suited her, was
allowed to enter' (*Edinburgh Review*, Apr 1885)

I acknowledge frankly that there is nothing in
me – a fat, little, commonplace woman, rather
tongue-tied – to impress any one; and yet there
is a sort of whimsical injury in it which makes
me sorry for myself.

*Autobiography and Letters of Mrs Margaret
Oliphant* (ed. Mrs Harry Coghill, 1899), ch.1,
'1 Feb 1885'

I was reading of Charlotte Brontë the other
day, and could not help comparing myself
with the picture more or less as I read. I don't
suppose my powers are equal to hers – my work
to myself looks perfectly pale and colourless
besides hers – but yet I have had far more
experience and, I think, a fuller conception
of life. I have learned to take perhaps more a
man's view of mortal affairs – to feel that the
love between men and women, the marrying
and giving in marriage, occupy in fact so small
a portion of either existence or thought.

Autobiography and Letters of Mrs Margaret

Oliphant (ed. Mrs Harry Coghill, 1899), ch.2,
'Christmas Night, 1894'

23 I am no more interested in my own characters
than I am in Jeanie Deans, and do not remember
them half so well, nor do they come back to me
with the same steady interest and friendship.

*Autobiography and Letters of Mrs Margaret
Oliphant* (ed. Mrs Harry Coghill, 1899),
ch.4, '1894'

Jeanie Deans: the central character in Walter
Scott's novel *The Heart of Midlothian*

24 I made on the whole a large income – and spent
it, taking no great thought of the morrow. . .
It would have been better if I could have
added the grace of thrift, which is said to
be the inheritance of the Scot, to the faculty
of work.

*Autobiography and Letters of Mrs Margaret
Oliphant* (ed. Mrs Harry Coghill, 1899),
ch.4, '1894'

25 God help us all! what is the good done by
any such work as mine, or even better than
mine. . . An infinitude of pains and labour,
and all to disappear like the stubble and hay.
Yet who knows? The little faculty may grow
a bigger one in the more genial land to come,
where one will have no need to think of the
boiling of the daily pot.

*Autobiography and Letters of Mrs Margaret
Oliphant* (ed. Mrs Harry Coghill, 1899),
ch.4, '1894'

She was realistic enough to recognise that
many of her novels were, to some extent,
simply 'pot-boilers'

Outram, George 1805–56

Lawyer, publisher and editor of The Glasgow
Herald

1 She hurkles by her ingle-side,
An' toasts an' tans her wrunkled hide –
Lord kens how lang she yet may bide
To ca' for her annuity!

'The Annuity', *Lyrics, Legal and Miscellaneous*
(1874), st.4

2 It's pay me here – an' pay me there –
An' pay me, pay me, evermair. . .

'The Annuity', *Lyrics, Legal and Miscellaneous*
(1874), st.18

3 But noo his broo is bricht,
An' his een are orbs o' licht,
An' his nose is just a sicht
Wi' drinkin' drams.

'Drinkin' Drams', *Lyrics, Legal and Miscellaneous*
(1874), st.5

Owens, Agnes 1926–

Novelist and short-story writer

1 Sometimes I consider saving up for a different face, but that might be tempting fate. Who knows what face I would get. Besides, I have acquired a taste for the good things in life, like cigarettes and vodka. So I take my chances and confront the world professionally equipped in a fur jacket and high black boots, trailing my boa feathers behind me.

'A Change of Face', *Lean Tales* (1985)

P

Pagan, Isobel (known as 'Tibbie')
1741–1821
Songwriter, a contemporary of Robert Burns

1 I was born near four miles from Nith-head,
Where fourteen years I got my bread;
My learning it can soon be told,
Ten weeks when I was seven years old,
With a good old religious wife
Who lived a quiet and sober life. . .

'Account of the Author's Lifetime'

2 Ca' the yowes to the knowes,
Ca' them whare the heather grows,
Ca' them whare the burnie rowes,
My bonie dearie.

'Ca the Yowes', st.1. Cf. Robert Burns 128

> She is credited with the original composition
> of this song, or at least with the original
> reworking of an older song. Born deformed,
> she is remembered chiefly for her Ayrshire
> howff where she sold smuggled whisky, and
> for her fine singing voice

3 Ilka lassie has a laddie she lo'es aboon the rest,
Ilka lassie has a laddie, if she like to confess't,
That is dear unto her bosom whatever be
his trade,
But my love's aye the laddie that wears the
crook and plaid.

'The Crook and Plaid', st.1

4 Time, swift as it flies,
Gives strength to her truth,
And adds to her mind
What it steals from her youth.

My Jeanie and me,
My Jeanie and me,
And who lives so happy
As Jeanie and me?

'My Jeanie and Me'

5 You're *borin'* awa, I see?

Attrib. Said to a minister preaching vehemently
at an open-air meeting at Muirkirk. Quoted
in D C Cuthbertson, *Quaint Scots of Bygone
Days* (1939)

Paolozzi, Eduardo Luigi 1924–
Sculptor and printmaker

1 Modernism is the acceptance of the concrete
landscape and the destruction of the human
soul.

'Junk and the new Arts and Crafts Movement',
in *Eduardo Paolozzi: Collages Prints Sculptures*
(Talbot Rice Gallery, 1979)

2 I feel that man's position in general is his feeling
and his attitude towards the machine. You can
retreat from it or you can wrestle with it. . .
I think it hangs like a great shadow over all
our lives.

The Development of the Idea (1979). Quoted in
Eduardo Paolozzi: Nullius in Verba (Talbot Rice
Gallery, 1989)

3 . . . a wheel, a jet engine, a bit of a machine is
beautiful, if one chooses to see it that way. . .
For instance, something like the jet engine is
an exciting image if you're a sculptor. I think
it can quite fairly sit in the mind as much an
art image as an Assyrian wine jar.

In television interview with Jakob Bronowski.
Quoted in William Hardie, *Scottish Painting:
1837 to the Present* (1990), ch.11, p.192

Park, Mungo 1771–1806
Explorer

1 . . . the Foulah suddenly put his hand to
his mouth, exclaiming *Soubahan alluhi* (God
preserve us!), and to my great surprise I then
perceived a large red lion at a short distance
from the bush, with his head couched between
his fore-paws. I expected he would instantly
spring upon me. . . But it is probable the lion
was not hungry, for he quietly suffered us to
pass, though we were fairly within his reach.

*Travels in the Interior Districts of Africa, Performed
in the Years 1795, 1796 and 1797* (1799), journal
entry (28 Jul 1796)

2 I shall set sail for Africa with the fixed resolution
to discover the termination of the Niger or
perish in the attempt.

Letter to Lord Camden (17 Nov 1805)

> By the time this letter was received Park
> was dead, probably drowned in early 1806
> at Bussa Falls on the Niger, along with the
> few surviving members of his expedition.
> Cf. David Livingstone 3

Paton, Sir Joseph Noël 1821–1901
*Painter, appointed Queen's Limner for Scot-
land in 1865*

1 . . . why men professing to be artists can
devote their lives to recording dirt, vulgarity

and utter ugliness is beyond my powers of comprehension.

> On the exhibits of the 'Glasgow Boys' at the 1898 Royal Scottish Academy exhibition

Pattison, Ian 1950–

Television scriptwriter, creator of Rab C. Nesbitt

1 . . . in Glasgow there is no such word as 'happy'. The nearest we have is 'giro' or 'blootered'.

> Nesbitt talking, back-cover blurb, *Rab C. Nesbitt: The Scripts* (1990)

2 NESBITT: Work, eh. What a stupid way to earn a living. Christ, every bugger I know that's in work is up to the eyes in debt. So am I right enough, but at least my time's my ain to express myself.

> At the Job Centre. *Rab C. Nesbitt: The Scripts* (1990), 'Work', sc.5

3 MARY: This is the bit I hate. It's not so much a checkout queue this, it's more the Day of Judgement. And it disnae matter how jazzy a headscarf yi wear, it disnae take the poor look away from your groceries.

> Queueing at a supermarket checkout. *Rab C. Nesbitt: The Scripts* (1990), 'Rat', sc.10

4 NESBITT: In the West of Scotland we don't actually have sex. We just stand in wur underwear and throw chips at each other across the floor. My weans were actually conceived from a bit of bacteria on a mutton pie.

> *Rab C. Nesbitt: The Scripts* (1990), 'Holiday', sc.15

5 GASH: It's magic being abroad, in't it. For once in your life you feel normal. Instead of being Scottish.
FIRST GIRL: I know what you mean. But I'm determined not to enjoy it too much. Coz I'll just feel all the more miserable when I get back.

> *Rab C. Nesbitt: The Scripts* (1990), 'Holiday', sc.17

Pennant, Thomas 1726–98

Welsh naturalist, antiquarian and traveller

1 Midwives give new-born babes a small spoonful of earth and whisky, as the first food they taste.

> *A Tour in Scotland in 1769* (1771)

2 The common women are in general most remarkably plain, and soon acquire an old look, and by being much exposed to the weather without hats, such a grin, and contraction of the muscles, as heightens greatly their natural hardness of features: I never saw so much plainness among the lower ranks of females,

but the *ne plus ultra* of hard features is not found till you arrive among the fish-women of Aberdeen.

> In the north-east. *A Tour in Scotland in 1769* (1771)

3 The manners of the native Highlanders may justly be expressed in these words: indolent to a high degree, unless roused to war, or to any animating amusement. . . hospitable to the highest degree, and full of generosity: are much affected with the civility of strangers, and have in themselves a natural politeness and address, which often flows from the meanest when least expected.

> *A Tour in Scotland in 1769* (1771)

Petrie, Alexander Wyllie ('The Clincher') c.1853–1937

Glasgow eccentric and publisher of The Glasgow Clincher *(1897–1912), a newspaper in which he made scathing attacks on the City Council*

1 It takes a Brain to become insane, and I know it because I am not an Imbecile. I am simply a self-conscious Fool, which is the highest Art, higher than Music, or Painting.

> *The Glasgow Clincher* (Nov 1897)

> Petrie caused the Council so much grief that he was twice locked up as a lunatic. He then had himself diagnosed sane, and thereafter made a point of declaring that he was 'the only certified sane man in Glasgow'

2 Education is an admirable thing, but there is nothing worth knowing that can be taught. One has to learn it for one's self – even going right daft.

> *The Glasgow Clincher* (Jan 1898)

3 I exclaim, humour is the greatest gift the Creator can bestow upon the creature. Verily, verily, humour is a flash of eternity bursting through time.

> *The Glasgow Clincher* (Jun 1898)

4 Be kind to your granny, and gie her plenty of whisky.

> Quoted in 'Cliff Hanley's Notable Scots', *The Sunday Mail Story of Scotland* (1988), No.17

Pettie, John 1839–93

Painter

1 I felt about colour, then, like a boy looking at all the bright bottles in a sweetie shop window, that it was something to be bought when I had saved up a pennyworth of drawing.

> On his early ability as a draughtsman, but not as

a painter. Quoted in Martin Hardie, *John Pettie* (1908), ch.1

> Later, after proving himself as a painter, he said 'Colour may be in you, and it has to be *dragged* out; but it must be in you first!' (See Hardie, ch.1)

Phillips, Mary E b.1880
Suffragette, columnist for Forward

1 There are said to be three forms of baptism, through any of which one may pass in order to be dignified by the proud title. . . of Suffragette. One is to be thrown out of a Cabinet Minister's meeting; another to go to prison; the third to fight in a bye-election. I have now passed through all these ordeals in turn, and I can unhesitatingly say that the last is by far the hardest of all.

> *Forward* (2 May 1908). Quoted in Leah Leneman, *A Guid Cause: The Women's Suffrage Movement in Scotland* (1991), ch.4

Picken, Joanna 1798–1859
Poet

1 I say na 'tis *best* to be single,
But ae thing's to me unco clear:
Far better sit *lane* by the ingle
Than thole what some wives hae to bear.
It's braw to be dancin' and gaffin'
As lang as nae trouble befa' –
But hech! she is sune ower wi' daffin'
That's woo'd, an' married, an a'.

> 'An Auld Friend wi' a New Face', st.1. Quoted in Tom Leonard (ed.), *Radical Renfrew* (1990). Cf. Joanna Baillie 15, Alexander Ross 1

2 The married maun aft bear man's scornin',
An' humour his capers an' fykes;
But the single can rise in the mornin',
An' gang to her bed when she likes. . .

> 'An Auld Friend wi' a New Face', st.4. Quoted in Tom Leonard, *Radical Renfrew* (1990)

Pinkerton, Allan 1819–84
Glasgow-born American private detective

1 We never sleep

> Motto of the Chicago-based detective agency he founded (1852)

Pinkerton, John 1758–1826
Antiquary, historian and critic

1 . . . none can more sincerely wish a total extinction of the Scotish *colloquial* dialect than I do, for there are few *modern* Scoticisms which are not barbarisms. . . Yet, I believe, no man of either kingdom would wish an extinction of the Scotish dialect in poetry.

> Preface to *Ancient Scotish Poems, never before in print* (1786). Cf. Mrs Anne Grant (of Laggan) 3

> The scholar J Derrick McClure coined the phrase 'the Pinkerton syndrome' for modern-day teachers and academics who perpetuate this attitude to Scots. See *Chapman* No.41 (Summer 1985)

Playfair, John 1748–1819
Mathematician and geologist

1 We felt ourselves necessarily carried back to the time when the schistus on which we stood was set at the bottom of the sea, and when the sandstone before us was only beginning to be deposited, in the shape of sand and mud, from the waters of a superincumbent ocean. . . Revolutions still more remote appeared in the distance of this extraordinary perspective. The mind seemed to grow giddy by looking so far into the abyss of time. . . and we became sensible how much further reason may sometimes go than imagination can dare to follow.

> On viewing the geological unconformity at Siccar Point, Cockburnspath, with James Hutton and James Hall. 'Life of Dr Hutton', *Transactions of the Royal Society of Edinburgh* (1805), Vol.5, Part 3

2 Ardour and even enthusiasm, in the pursuit of science, great rapidity of thought, and much animation, distinguished Dr Hutton on all occasions. Great caution in his reasonings, and a coolness of head that even approached to indifference, were characteristic of Dr Black. . . Dr Black dreaded nothing so much as error and Dr Hutton dreaded nothing so much as ignorance: the one was always afraid of going beyond the truth and the other of not reaching it. . . Dr Black was correct, respecting at all times prejudices and fashions of the world; Dr Hutton was more careless, and was often found in direct collision with both.

> On the respective characters of Joseph Black and James Hutton. 'Life of Dr Hutton', *Transactions of the Royal Society of Edinburgh* (1805), Vol.5, Part 3

Polkemmet, Lord (William Baillie) c.1735–1816
Judge

1 Maister Jemmy, dinna dunt; ye may think ye're dunting it *intill me*, but ye're juist *dunting it oot o' me*, man.

> Interrupting James Ferguson, later Lord Kilkerran, who as an advocate was making a forceful point to the Bench by beating violently

on the table. Quoted in George Morton & D
MacLeod Malloch, *Law and Laughter* (1913)

2 Well, Maister Erskine, I heard you, and I thocht
ye were richt; syne I heard you, Dauvid, and
I thocht ye were richt; and noo I hae heard
Maister Clerk, and I think he's richtest amang
ye a'. That bauthers me, ye see! Sae I maun
e'en tak hame the process an' wimble-wamble
it i' ma wame a wee ower ma toddy, and syne
ye's hae ma interlocutor.

> Said after hearing various opinions of counsel
> from Henry Erskine, John Clerk and others.
> Quoted in George Morton & D MacLeod
> Malloch, *Law and Laughter* (1913)

3 Ou ay, it's a cauf; when we kill a beast we just
eat up ae side, and down the tither.

> Said to guests at his table who were surprised
> that their dinner consisted of 'veal broth, a
> roast fillet of veal, veal cutlets, a florentine
> (an excellent old Scottish dish composed of
> veal), a calf's head, calf's foot jelly.' Quoted in
> Dean Ramsay, *Reminiscences of Scottish Life and
> Character* (1857), ch.5

Pollok, Robert 1798–1827
Poet

1 With one hand he put
A penny in the urn of poverty,
And with the other took a shilling out.

> On a landlord. *The Course of Time* (1827), Bk 8

Proclaimers, The
(Charlie and Craig Reid) 1962–
Twin brothers, pop songwriters and performers

1 The question doesn't matter
The answer's always 'aye'
The best view of all
Is where the land meets the sky

> 'The Joyful Kilmarnock Blues', on *This is the
> Story* (1987)

2 Do we have to roam the world
To prove how much it hurts?

> 'Letter from America', on *This is the Story* (1987)

3 Bathgate no more
Linwood no more
Methil no more
Irvine no more

> 'Letter from America', on *This is the Story* (1987)

4 This is the story of our first teacher
Shetland made her jumpers
And the devil made her features. . .

> 'Over and Done With', on *This is the Story* (1987)

5 I'm just going to have to learn to hesitate
To make sure my words
On your Saxon ears don't grate
But I wouldn't know a single word to say

If I flattened all the vowels
And threw the 'R' away.

> 'Throw the "R" away', on *This is the Story* (1987)

6 I can't understand
Why we let someone else
Rule our land
Cap in hand.

> 'Cap in Hand', on *Sunshine on Leith* (1988)

7 What do you do when democracy fails you?
What do you do when minority means you?

> 'What Do You Do', on *Sunshine on Leith* (1988)
> (All lyrics courtesy of Reid–Reid/Warner
> Chappell Music Ltd)

Punch 1841–1992
English humorous periodical

1 PEEBLES BODY (to townsman who was supposed
to be in London on a visit): 'E-eh Mac! ye're
sune hame again!'
MAC: 'E-eh, it's just a ruinous place, that! Mun,
a had na' been the-erre abune twa hoours
when – *bang* – went saxpence!!!'

> Caption by Birket Foster to a cartoon by Charles
> Keene, titled 'Thrift' (5 Dec 1868)
>
> > Robert Ford, in his collection of Scots humour
> > *Thistledown* (1914), wrote that 'no *Punch*
> > artist. . . ever drew a Scotsman in "his manner
> > as he lived." The originals of the pictures
> > may have appeared in London Christmas
> > pantomimes, but certainly nowhere else. Then
> > the language which in their guileless innocence
> > they expect will pass muster as Scotch, is a
> > hash-up alike revolting to the ears of gods
> > and men.'

Purser, John 1942–
Composer, broadcaster and writer

1 It has had heaped upon its head more appalling
and ignorant performances than any song has
a right to bear. Its subject-matter is one of
bitter and ironic tragedy. . . This is usually
rendered by singers and arrangers with an
inane chirpiness more suited to selling washing-
up liquid.

> On 'The Bonnie Banks o' Loch Lomond', *Scotland's
> Music* (1992), ch.12. Cf. Traditional songs 13

2 It was always a wretched tune, rhythmically
unimaginative, as square as a box and accompanied by words insulting to half of the land
mass to which it is supposed to apply.

> On the anthem 'God Save The King', *Scotland's
> Music* (1992), ch.14. Cf. Anonymous 26

3 It is sung today, largely by people who
would not offer their nation so much as a
nose-bleed. . .

> On Burns's revolutionary song, 'Scots Wha Hae
> [wi' Wallace bled]', *Scotland's Music* (1992), ch.14

R

Radical Scotland 1983–91
Political magazine

The Doomsday Scenario

> Phrase coined (No.25, Feb/Mar 1987) to describe the political situation that would arise in the wake of a third Conservative election victory in the UK as a whole (in 1987) in which the Conservatives were nonetheless defeated in Scotland

>> The Scenario came true as predicted; and again in 1992

Rae, David see Eskgrove, Lord

Ramsay, Allan 1686–1758
Poet and bookseller

When we were weary'd at the gowff,
Then Maggy Johnston's was our howff;
Now a' our gamesters may sit dowff,
Wi' hearts like lead,
Death wi' his rung rax'd her a yowff,
And sae she died.

> 'Elegy on Maggy Johnston, who died Anno 1711' (1718), st.7

>> Maggy Johnston brewed a famous ale at her farm on the south side of Edinburgh beyond Bruntsfield Links, where the citizens played golf

Whene'er ye meet a man that's fow,
That ye're a maiden gar him trow,
Seem nice, but stick to him like glew;
And whan set down,
Drive at the jango till he spew,
Syne he'll sleep soun.

When he's asleep, then dive and catch
His ready cash, his rings or watch;
And gin he likes to light his match
At your spunk-box,
Ne'er stand to let the fumbling wretch
E'en take the pox.

> 'Lucky Spence's Last Advice' (1718), st.4–5

>> Lucky Spence was, according to Ramsay's note to this poem, 'a famous bawd who flourished about the beginning of the eighteenth century; she had her lodgings near Holyrood-house'. In a footnote, Ramsay wrote of the phrase *light his match*: 'I could give a large annotation on this sentence, but do not incline to explain every thing, lest I disoblige future criticks by leaving nothing for them to do'

3 She made many a benefit to herself by putting a trade in the hands of young lasses that had a little pertness, strong passions, abundance of laziness, and no fore-thought.

> Footnote to 'Lucky Spence's Last Advice' (1718)

4 Look up to Pentland's towring taps,
Buried beneath great wreaths of snaw. . .

> 'To the Phiz an Ode' (1720), st.1

>> 'The Phiz' was an Edinburgh club to which some of Ramsay's friends belonged

5 Then fling on coals, and ripe the ribs,
And beek the house baith butt and ben,
That mutchken stoup it hads but dribs,
Then let's get in the tappit hen.

Good claret best keeps out the cauld,
And drives away the winter soon,
It makes a man baith gash and bauld,
And heaves his saul beyond the moon.

> 'To the Phiz an Ode' (1720), st.3–4

6 When these good old Bards wrote, we had not yet made Use of imported Trimmings upon our Cloaths, nor of Foreign Embroidery in our Writings. Their Poetry is the Product of their own Country, not pilfered and spoiled in the Transportation from abroad: Their Images are native, and their Landskips domestick: copied from the Fields and Meadows we every Day behold.

> Preface to *The Ever Green* (1724), his two-volume anthology of early Scots poetry

>> The 'good old Bards' referred to include William Dunbar, Robert Henryson, and Gavin Douglas

7 JENNY: O! 'tis a pleasant thing to be a bride;
Syne whingeing getts about your ingle-side,
Yelping for this or that wi' fasheous din:
To mak them brats, then ye maun toil and spin.
Ae wean fa's sick, ane scads itsell wi' broe,
Ane breaks its shin, anither tynes his shoe;
The *Deil gaes o'er Jock Wabster*, hame grows hell,
And Pate misca's ye waur than tongue can tell!

> *The Gentle Shepherd* (1725), Act 1, sc.2

8 JENNY: A dish o' married love right soon grows cauld,
And dosens down to nane, as fouk grow auld.

> *The Gentle Shepherd* (1725), Act 1, sc.2

9 My Peggy is a young thing,
Just enter'd in her teens,

Fair as the day, and sweet as May,
Fair as the day, and always gay.
My Peggy is a young thing,
And I'm nae very auld,
Yet weel I like to meet her at
The wauking o' the fauld.

'My Peggy is a Young Thing' (1729), st.1

This became the opening song in the ballad
opera version of Ramsay's pastoral comedy
The Gentle Shepherd

10 The Scarlet Whore, indeed, they snarl at
but like right well a whore in scarlet. . .

'Epistle to Mr H S at London, November 1738'

On Edinburgh hypocrites (the Scarlet Whore
being the Church of Rome)

11 The lass o' Patie's mill,
So bonny, blythe, and gay,
In spite of all my skill,
Hath stole my heart away.

'The Lass o' Patie's Mill', *Poems of Allan Ramsay*
(1800), st.1

12 Gie me a lass with a lump of land,
And we for life shall gang thegither;
Tho' daft or wise I'll never demand,
Or black or fair it maks na whether.

'The Lass with the Lump of Land', *Poems of
Allan Ramsay* (1800), st.1

13 Fareweel to Lochaber, fareweel to my Jean,
Where heartsome wi' her I hae mony days been;
For Lochaber no more, Lochaber no more,
We'll maybe return to Lochaber no more.

'Lochaber No More', or 'The Soldier's Farewell
to His Love', *Poems of Allan Ramsay* (1800), st.1

14 At Polwart on the green
If you'll meet me the morn,
Where lassies do convene
To dance about the thorn.

'Polwart on the Green', *Poems of Allan Ramsay*
(1800), st.1

Ramsay, Allan 1713–84
Portrait painter and essayist, son of the above

1 The agreeable cannot be separated from the
exact; and a posture in painting must be a
just resemblance of what is graceful in nature,
before it can hope to be esteemed graceful.

On Ridicule (1753)

2 Lines and colours are of a more determined
nature, and strike the mind more immediately than words; which, before they can
produce any effect, must be form'd by the
mind itself, into pictures; and consequently
require a more tedious, and more difficult
process.

On Ridicule (1753)

3 We find that nonsense of every kind is received
with applause, when it happens to drop from
what is called *a great Name*; and that it is
sometimes, on the same account, transmitted
from age to age, like the toe-nail-pairings of
ST NICOLAS, with religious veneration and
astonishment.

On proverbs and quotations. *On the Naturalisation
of Foreigners* (1754)

4 In every elegant Art, there is a point beyond
which rules cannot carry us. Here the deficiency
must be supplied by Taste, which will always
advantageously distinguish those artists who
happen to be blest with it, and, perhaps nothing
tends more to debase any art, and to render
it inelegant, than an attempt to subject any
particular Grace in it to a particular Rule.

Unpublished essay, 'An enquiry into the
Principles of English Versification with some
analogous remarks upon the versification of the
Ancients'. Quoted in I G Brown, *Poet and Painter:
Allan Ramsay, Father and Son 1684–1784* (1984)

Ramsay, Dean Edward Bannerman
1793–1872
Episcopalian clergyman and essayist

1 [Lord Cockburn] was sitting on the hill-side
with the shepherd [on his estate of Bonaly],
and observing the sheep reposing in the coldest
situation, he observed to him, 'John, if I were
a sheep, I would lie on the other side of the
hill.' The shepherd answered, 'Ay, my lord,
but if ye had been a sheep ye would hae had
mair sense.'

Reminiscences of Scottish Life and Character
(1858), ch.2

2 At a prolonged drinking bout, one of the party
remarked, 'What gars the laird of Garskadden
look sae gash?' 'Ou,' says his neighbour, the laird
of Kilmardinny, 'deil meane him! Garskadden's
been wi' his Maker these twa hours; I saw
him step awa, but I didna like to disturb gude
company!'

Reminiscences of Scottish Life and Character
(1858), ch.3

3 A recorded reply of old Lady Perth to a French
gentleman is quaint and characteristic. They
had been discussing the respective merits of
the cookery of each country. The Frenchman
offended the old Scottish peeress by some
disparaging remarks on Scottish dishes, and
by highly preferring those of France. All
she would answer was, 'Weel, weel, some
fowk like parritch and some like paddocks
[puddocks].'

Reminiscences of Scottish Life and Character
(1858), ch.6

A very strong-minded lady. . . had been asking from a lady the character of a cook she was about to hire. The lady naturally entered upon her moral qualifications, and described her as a very decent woman; the response to which was, 'Oh, damn her decency; can she make good collops?'

Reminiscences of Scottish Life and Character (1858), ch.6. Cf. Robert Louis Stevenson 92

Then how quaint the answer of old Mrs Robison, widow of the eminent professor of natural philosophy, and who entertained an inveterate dislike to everything which she thought savoured of *cant*. She had invited a gentleman to dinner on a particular day, and he had accepted, with the reservation, 'If I am spared.' – 'Weel, weel,' said Mrs Robison; 'if ye're deed, I'll no expect ye.'

Reminiscences of Scottish Life and Character (1858), ch.6

'Ae, ae, but oh, I'm sair hadden doun wi' the bubbly jock.'

Reminiscences of Scottish Life and Character (1858), ch.7

The reported grievance of a man Ramsay described as a 'parochial idiot' or 'natural', whose life on a farm was comfortable and without care, but for his fear of the turkey-cock

Ramsay (of Ochtertyre), John 1736–1814
Agricultural improver and diarist

To think that lads flushed with money, and accustomed betimes to the manners of a profligate overgrown metropolis, will acquire either virtue or useful knowledge, is surely expecting a great deal too much. Most of them returned complete coxcombs, without any principle or learning, and with a smattering of the graces.

On the sending of sons to be educated in Paris. *Scotland and Scotsmen in the Eighteenth Century* (1888 edition), Vol.1, p.369, footnote

Ransford, Tessa 1938–
Poet, director of the Scottish Poetry Library, editor of Lines Review *(1988–)*

Under Plato or NATO
Must we live by bread alone?
We eat to live but live to give
The world its fill – of song.

'Ways and Means', *Fools and Angels* (1983)

Joy is my element.
I pass it through the test
of water, fire, air

and bring it back to earth.

'My Indian Self', *A Dancing Innocence* (1988), st.5

3 Ideas belong to humankind. They are the sphere in which we specifically belong as humans. They are as water is to fish or air to birds. They are not for censoring, cornering, privatising, possessing, selling, buying or marketing.

'The Case of the Intellectual Woman', in *Chapman* No.74–5 (Autumn/Winter 1993)

Redfern, June 1951–
Painter

1 I wish I could paint like people make music – paint an aria!

'Artist's comment', in Bill Hare, *Contemporary Painting in Scotland* (1992), p.184

Redpath, Anne 1895–1965
Painter

1 I do with a spot of red or yellow in a harmony of grey what my father did in his tweeds.

Quoted in Patrick Bourne, *Anne Redpath 1895–1965: Her Life and Work* (1989), ch.1

Her father was a textile weaver who became Head of Design in the Glebe Mills, Hawick

Reid, Alastair 1926–
Poet and essayist

1 . . . St Andrews, that placid centre of non-learning. . .

'Borderlines', in Karl Miller (ed.), *Memoirs of a Modern Scotland* (1970)

2 The Borders loom in my mind as a small archipelago of stony towns in a placid sea of grass, woods and furrows, small, bristling islands in a state of armed truce with one another, with their village satellites, their lumbering bus-ferries, their pugnacious localisms.

'Borderlines', in Karl Miller (ed.), *Memoirs of a Modern Scotland* (1970)

3 I can remember coming bursting in from just having glimpsed eternity in a grain of sand and being told, curtly: 'Your tea's cold.' It may be that tea is the reality and glimpses of eternity only a temporary foolishness. If I ever thought so, it might be possible to give up resisting and to belong.

On growing up in Selkirk. 'Borderlines', in Karl Miller (ed.), *Memoirs of a Modern Scotland* (1970)

4 It was a day peculiar to this piece of the planet, when larks rose on long thin strings of singing and the air shifted with the shimmer of actual angels.

'Scotland', *Weathering* (1978)

Reid, Charlie and Craig
see **Proclaimers, The**

Reid, Jimmy 1932–
Trade unionist and journalist

1 The world is witnessing the first of a new tactic on behalf of workers. We're not going to strike. We're not even having a sit-in strike. We're taking over the yards because we refuse to accept that faceless men, or any group of men in Whitehall, or anyone else, can take decisions that devastate our livelihoods with impunity. They're not on...

> Address to the Upper Clyde Shipbuilders workforce (30 Jul 1971). Quoted on BBC television news
>
>> The UCS work-in attracted worldwide publicity and eventually led to a sale of the John Brown shipyards rather than their closure

2 ... there will be no hooliganism. There will be no vandalism. There will be no bevvying, because the world is watching us, and it's our responsibility to conduct ourselves responsibly and with dignity and with maturity.

> Address to the UCS workforce (30 Jul 1971). Quoted on BBC television news

3 We don't only build ships, we build men. They have taken on the wrong people and we will fight.

> To the press (30 Jul 1971). Quoted in J McGill, *Crisis on the Clyde* (1973), ch.11

Reid, Marion (*née* Kirkland) fl.1843
Campaigner for women's rights

1 We shall be disposed to acknowledge that woman's influence has been sufficient to obtain her justice, when it has obtained for her... perfectly just and equal rights with the other sex. When this is the case, we shall expect to see each woman wakened up into a sense of her individual responsibilities and duties: finding herself no longer classed with children and idiots, we may reasonably expect to see her rousing herself up, and applying, with renewed energy, to all her duties ...

> *A Plea for Woman* (1843), ch.2. Cf. Catherine Carswell 18

2 No pure and noble-minded woman can long love affectionately, and submit passively to, a vicious and dissipated, – or even to a good and virtuous tyrant, – without having her own mind greatly deteriorated.

> *A Plea for Woman* (1843), ch.3

3 To leave the liberty of one-half of the human race at the mercy of the convenience of the other, amounts to an annihilation of the rights of that half.

> *A Plea for Woman* (1843), ch.5

4 ... are puddings and pies, roasting and boiling, dusting and washing, or even the rearing and educating her children, so entirely to engross her attention, that her heart and mind can never expand beyond her own little domestic circle? Nay, if her mind never does so expand, will she be able properly to regulate the concerns even of that little circle?

> *A Plea for Woman* (1843), ch.6

5 The grand plea for woman sharing with man all the advantages of education is, that every rational being is worthy of cultivation, for his or her own individual sake. The first object in the education of every mind ought to be its own development.

> *A Plea for Woman* (1843), ch.10. Cf. Frances Wright 11

6 ... the influence of woman – where any freedom of social intercourse is allowed between the sexes – is highly favourable to civilisation. She advances refinement and civilisation, and is, in turn, advanced by them.

> *A Plea for Woman* (1843), ch.11

7 ... if we take politics in the large and high sense in which it stands for patriotism and philanthropy, the assertion that an interest in it is out of place in the breast of the very gentlest of her sex, – in other words, that it is improper and unbecoming in a woman to take a deep interest in the affairs of her country and of humanity, – is made with more boldness and confidence, than regard to reason and truth.

> *A Plea for Woman* (1843), ch.11

Reid, Thomas 1710–96
Philosopher, leading figure of the 'Common Sense' school

1 I am persuaded, that the unjust *live by faith* as well as the *just*; that, if all belief could be laid aside, piety, patriotism, friendship, parental affection, and private virtue, would appear as ridiculous as knight-errantry; and that the pursuits of pleasure, of ambition, and of avarice, must be grounded upon belief, as well as those that are honourable or virtuous.

> *An Inquiry into the Human Mind on the Principles of Common Sense* (1764), 'Dedication'

2 It is genius, and not the want of it, that adulterates philosophy, and fills it with error and false theory.

> *An Inquiry into the Human Mind on the Principles of Common Sense* (1764), ch.1, section 2

... when I look within, and consider the Mind itself... if it is indeed what the *Treatise of Human Nature* makes it, I find I have been only in an enchanted castle, imposed upon by spectres and apparitions... If this is the philosophy of human nature, my soul enter thou not into her secrets. It is surely the forbidden tree of knowledge; I no sooner taste of it, than I perceive myself naked, and stript of all things, yea even of my very self.

An Inquiry into the Human Mind on the Principles of Common Sense (1764), ch.1, section 6

Suppose that... [a sensible man] meets with a modern philosopher, and wants to be informed, what smell in plants is. The philosopher tells him, that there is no smell in plants, nor in any thing but in the mind; that it is impossible there can be smell but in a mind; and that all this hath been demonstrated by modern philosophy. The plain man will, no doubt, be apt to think him merry: but if he finds that he is serious, his next conclusion will be, that he is mad...

An Inquiry into the Human Mind on the Principles of Common Sense (1764), ch.2, section 7

To what purpose is it for philosophy to decide against common sense... ? The belief of a material world is older, and of more authority, than any principles of philosophy. It declines the tribunal of reason, and laughs at all the artillery of the logician.

An Inquiry into the Human Mind on the Principles of Common Sense (1764), ch.5, section 7

Methinks, therefore, it were better to make a virtue of necessity; and, since we cannot get rid of the vulgar notion and belief of an external world, to reconcile our reason to it as well as we can; for, if Reason, should stomach and fret ever so much at this yoke, she cannot throw it off; if she will not be the servant of Common Sense she must be her slave.

An Inquiry into the Human Mind on the Principles of Common Sense (1764), ch.5, section 7.
Cf. David Hume 7

In fact, Reid misdirected his fire at Hume in supposing him to deny the existence of an outer world. 'We may well ask, *What causes induce us to believe in the existence of body?*' wrote Hume, 'but 'tis in vain to ask, *Whether there be body or not?* That is a point, which we must take for granted in all our reasonings.' (*A Treatise of Human Nature*, Bk 1, Part 4, section 2)

There is no greater impediment to the advancement of knowledge than the ambiguity of words.

Essays on the Intellectual Powers of Man (1785), Essay 1, ch.1, 'Explication of Words'

8 Prove to me the existence of other minds, and I will prove to you the existence of God.

To David Hume. *Works* (ed. William Hamilton, 2 Vols, 1846–63), p.461

His argument was that belief in God was as rational and legitimate as belief in one's neighbour

Reith, Lord (John Charles Walsham Reith, 1st Baron Reith of Stonehaven) 1889–1971

Pioneer of radio broadcasting, Director-General of the BBC (1927–38)

1 The BBC has secured and holds the goodwill and affection of the people. It has been trusted to do the right thing at all times. Its influence is widespread. It is a national institution and a national asset. If it be commandeered or unduly hampered or manipulated now, the immediate purpose of such action is not only unserved but prejudiced. This is not a time for dope, even if the people could be doped... As to suppression, from the panic of ignorance comes far greater danger than from the knowledge of facts.

On the BBC's role during the General Strike (1926). Quoted in Ian McIntyre, *The Expense of Glory* (1993), ch.7

2 ... life's for living... I had never been told it when young, and... I haven't fully learnt it yet; but at least I now realise how much I've missed, and how many mistakes I've made...

Prize-giving speech at Glasgow Academy. Quoted in *The Glasgow Herald* (23 Jun 1960)

3 ... the carrying into the greatest possible number of homes, everything that is best in every department of human knowledge, endeavour, and achievement.

On the role of the BBC. Quoted in David Hutchison, 'The Public Forum', *The Sunday Mail Story of Scotland* (1988), No.49

4 You can't think rationally on an empty stomach, and a whole lot of people can't do it on a full one either.

Attrib.

Renwick, James 1662–88

Covenanter and preacher

1 Ye that are the people of God, do not weary to maintain the testimony of the day in your stations and places; and whatever ye do, make sure of an interest in Christ; for there is a storm coming that shall try your foundation. Scotland must be rid of Scotland before the delivery come...

Speech on the scaffold in Edinburgh's Grassmarket (17 Feb 1688)

Renwick was the last Covenanter to be publicly executed for his faith

Riddell, Henry Scott 1798–1870
Shepherd, minister and poet

1 Then Scotland's right, and Scotland's might,
  And Scotland's hills for me;
  We'll drink a cup to Scotland yet,
  Wi' a' the honours three.

> 'Scotland Yet', st.4

Ritchie, Murray
Journalist

1 Newspapers carry their own, deliberate balance
  which in some eyes is bias. Politicians only
  complain when that bias does not suit them.

> *The Glasgow Herald* (19 Feb 1990)

Ritchie-Calder, Peter (Baron Ritchie-Calder of Balmashannar)
1906–82
Educationist and writer

1 Today, freedom is not enough. . . Flags are not
  enough; national anthems are not enough. . .
  On the morning after liberation, people wake
  up. They have had their 'do'. They have had
  their excitement; they have had their dancing
  and their fireworks. . . – and they have a
  hangover. They are free, but they are just as
  poor, just as sick, just as hungry and just as
  illiterate as before. Freedom, in that sense,
  has changed nothing. Freedom begins with
  breakfast. If people do not have the substance
  of freedom, freedom becomes a 'will-o'-the-
  wisp'; the freed slave dies of hunger in the
  ditch of freedom.

> On the need for 'freedom from want'. *On Human
> Rights*, inaugural H G Wells Memorial Lecture,
> London (7 Dec 1967). Cf. John Boyd Orr 1

2 Democracy is a word that rumbles meaninglessly
  in empty bellies.

> *On Human Rights*, inaugural H G Wells Memorial
> Lecture, London (7 Dec 1967)

Rob Donn (Robert Mackay) 1714–78
Sutherland poet

1 'N an luidhe so gu h-ìosal
  Far na thiodhlaic sinn an triùir,
  Bha fallain, làidir, inntinneach
  'N uair dh' intrig a' bhliadhn' ùr;
  Cha deachaidh seachad fhathast

Ach deich latha dhith o thùs; –
Ciod fhios nach tig an teachdair-s' oirnn
Ni 's braise na th' air ar dùil?

† Here they lie where we buried the three who
  were healthy and strong and in good spirits
  when the New Year came in. Only ten days
  of it have passed yet from its beginning – who
  knows but this messenger may come upon us
  more swiftly than we think?

> 'To the Rispond Misers', st.1

> Hew Morrison, in *Songs and Poems in the
> Gaelic Language by Rob Donn* (1899), wrote:
> 'These were two old bachelors who had lived
> together all their life, with an old maid for
> housekeeper. They were reported to be rich,
> but very miserly. . . Their death and that
> of their housekeeper took place in the same
> week. Only a few nights previous to the death
> of the oldest (who died first), a poor creature
> asking alms was turned from their door without
> receiving anything.'

2 Daoine nach d' rinn briseadh iad,
  Is e fiosrachail do chàch;
  'S cha mhò a rinn iad aon dad
  Ris an can an saoghal gràs;
  Ach ghineadh iad, is rugadh iad,
  Is thogadh iad, is dh'fhàs –
  Chaidh stràchd d'an t-saoghal thairis orr',
  'S mu dheireadh fhuair iad bàs.

† They were two who never caused dissension,
  so far as anyone knew; and neither did they
  do one single thing that the world calls grace;
  but they were conceived and born and reared
  and grew – a swathe of time passed over them
  and in the end they died.

> 'To the Rispond Misers', st.4

3 'S maith a tha i air do chùlaibh
  'S tha i ni 's ro ùrraichd air t' uchd,
  Bu chaomh leam i bhi leathann trom,
  Mur deanadh i call no lochd;
  Ach chan eil putan innt', no toll,
  Nach do chost bonn do dhuine bochd.

† It's good on you behind; it's even better on
  your front. I'd like it to be broad and heavy,
  if it didn't cause any loss or mischief. But
  there isn't a button or a buttonhole in it that
  didn't cost a coin for some poor person.

> 'The Factor's New Suit'

4 Falbh 'n an cuideachd 's 'n an còmhradh,
  Is gheibh thu mòran do 'n phac ud,
  Dheanadh ceannaich no seòldair,
  Dheanadh dròbhair no factoir,
  Dheanadh tuathanach crionnda,
  Dheanadh stiùbhard neo-chaithiseach,
  'S mach o 'n cheard air 'n do mhionnaich iad,
  Tha na h-uile ni gasd' ac.

† Go into their company and converse and you
  will find many of that crew who would make
  a merchant or sailor, a drover or factor; who'd

make a prudent farmer, a thrifty steward –
and, apart from the profession in which they've
taken their vows, they have everything perfect.

'To the Presbytery'

> The poem refers to the Moderate Presbyterian
> clergy, who were keen on and knowledgeable
> about land and stock, and were regarded by
> the Evangelicals as worldly men

Robert I see Bruce, Robert

Robert III c.1340–1406
King of Scotland from 1390

Let these men who strive in this world for the
pleasures of honour have shining monuments.
I on the other hand should prefer to be buried
at the bottom of a midden, so that my soul
may be saved in the day of the Lord. Bury
me therefore, in a midden, and write for my
epitaph: 'Here lies the worst of kings and the
most wretched of men in the whole kingdom.'

> Said in his last days to his Queen, who had
> asked him why he was not making arrangements
> for a splendid tomb. Quoted in Walter Bower,
> *Scotichronicon* (1440–9), Vol.8, Bk 15, ch.19
>
> > Robert III's reign was characterised by feud,
> > anarchy and a complete absence of royal
> > authority

Roberton, Sir Hugh Stevenson
1874–1952
*Founder (in 1906) and conductor of the
Glasgow Orpheus Choir, and life-long pacifist*

War and Art is an impossible combination,
impossible as love and hate. War is in an
insidious position. It sears and brutalises us
unconsciously. . .

> In *Lute* (1916). Quoted in W Knox (ed.), *Scottish
> Labour Leaders 1918–39* (1984)

We have a history, a tradition, all of our own. . .
and I am sure it comes out in our singing. . .
English choirs on the whole are probably more
competent than Scottish ones: they are also
more facile. . . their work wants roots. . .

> On Scottish choral singing. In H S and
> K Roberton, *Orpheus with his Lute* (1963).
> Quoted in W Knox (ed.), *Scottish Labour
> Leaders 1918–39* (1984)

Step we gaily, on we go,
Heel for heel and toe for toe,
Arm in arm and row on row,
All for Mairi's wedding.

Plenty herring, plenty meal,
Plenty peat to fill her creel,

Plenty bonnie bairns as weel,
There's the toast for Mairi.

> 'Lewis Bridal Song', popularly known as 'Mairi's
> Wedding', chorus and st.3

4 Hill you ho, boys; let her go boys,
Bring her head round, now all together.
Hill you ho, boys; let her go, boys,
Sailing home, home to Mingulay.

> 'Mingulay Boat Song', chorus

5 Come along, come along,
Let us foot it out together,
Come along, come along,
Be it fair or stormy weather,
With the hills of home before us
And the purple of the heather,
Let us sing in happy chorus,
Come along, come along.

> 'Uist Tramping Song', chorus
>
> > Translated from the Gaelic of Archibald
> > MacDonald of Uist

6 And it's westering home, and a song in the air,
Light in the eye, and it's goodbye to care.
Laughter o' love, and a welcoming there,
Isle of my heart, my own one.

7 Where are the folk like the folk o' the west?
Canty and couthy and kindly, the best.
There I would hie me and there I would rest
At hame wi' my ain folk in Islay.

> 'Westering Home', chorus and st.2
>
> > Chorus from the singing of Donald McIsaac

Roberts, David 1796–1864
Painter

1 Who are ye to attack me? Ye are just a damned
scribbling snob! Ye tried to paint yerself and
ye couldna!

> Attrib. Said to John Ruskin, who was highly
> critical of Roberts's technique and subject
> matter. Quoted in Paul Harris and Julian Halsby,
> *The Dictionary of Scottish Painters 1600–1960*
> (1990)

Robertson, Alexander
(13th Baron of Struan) 1668–1741
Jacobite and clan chief

1 At length the bondage I have broke
Which gave me so much pain;
I've slipt my heart out of the yoke,
Never to drudge again;
And, conscious of my long disgrace,
Have thrown my chain at Cupid's face.

If ever he attempt again
My freedom to enslave,

I'll court the Godhead of champagne
Which makes the coward brave;
And, when that deity has heal'd my soul,
I'll drown the little Bastard in my bowl.

> 'Liberty Preserved; or, Love Destroyed'. Quoted
> in Maurice Lindsay (ed.), *Scottish Comic
> Verse* (1981)

Robertson, George 1946–

*Labour politician, Shadow Secretary of State
for Scotland (1993–   )*

1 If this government was an individual, it would
be locked up in the interests of public safety.

> On the Conservative government of John Major.
> Speech at the Labour Party Conference, Brighton
> (1993). Quoted in *The Independent* (1 Oct 1993)

2 For the pensioner it will be her parliament.
For the handicapped child it will be her
parliament. For the business executive it will
be his parliament.

> Speech at the launch of the Scottish Constitu-
> tional Convention's document on Home Rule,
> *Scotland's Parliament, Scotland's Right* (30 Nov
> 1995). Quoted in *The Scotsman* (1 Dec 1995)

Robertson, Jeannie
see **Traditional songs**

Robertson, John c.1770–1810

Paisley weaver and poet

1 Sedition daurna now appear,
In reality or joke;
For ilka chiel maun mourn wi' me,
O' a hingin', toom meal pock. . .

> 'The Toom Meal Pock', st.1

Robertson, John 19th century

Journalist

1 For a century [the Highlanders'] privileges
have been lessening; they dare not now hunt
the deer, or shoot the grouse or the blackcock;
they have no longer the range of the hills for
their cattle and their sheep; they must not
catch a salmon in the stream: in earth, air and
water, the rights of the laird are greater, and
the rights of the people are smaller, than they
were in the days of their forefathers.

> Article in *The Glasgow National* (Aug 1844), on
> the clearance of the Rosses from Glencalvie, Ross-
> shire, the so-called 'Massacre of the Rosses'

2 Some Legislatures have made the right of
the people superior to the right of the chief;
British law-makers made the rights of the
chief everything, and those of their followers
nothing. . . Of this there cannot be a doubt,
however, the chiefs would not have had the
land at all, could the clansmen have foreseen
the present state of the Highlands – their
children in mournful groups going into exile
– the faggots of legal myrmidons in the thatch
of the feal cabin – the hearths of their homes
and their lives the green sheep-walks of the
stranger.

> Article in *The Glasgow National* (Aug 1844)

3 Most mournful will it be, should the clansmen
of the Highlands have been cleared away,
ejected, exiled, in deference to a political, a
moral, a social, and an economical mistake, – a
suggestion not of philosophy but of mammon,
– a system in which the demon of sordidness
assumed the shape of the angel of civilisation
and of light.

> Article in *The Glasgow National* (Aug 1844)

Robertson, William 1721–93

*Historian, minister and Moderator of the 1763
General Assembly of the Church of Scotland*

1 Formed with the qualities which we love,
not with the talents that we admire; she
was an agreeable woman, rather than an
illustrious queen.

> On Mary, Queen of Scots, *History of Scotland*
> (1759), Bk.8

2 Mary's friends have violently censured me for
my sentiments regarding her conduct; they do
not consider that but for the sake of historical
truth it would have been a principal object
with me to have made her innocent as she
was beautiful and accomplished; she was the
natural heroine of my book had not my historical
impartiality forbidden it.

> On Mary, Queen of Scots, whom he criticised
> in his *History of Scotland* (1759). Said to Henry
> Mackenzie, and quoted in Mackenzie's *Anecdotes
> and Egotisms* (ed. H W Thompson, 1927)

3 Thus, during the whole 17th century, the
English were gradually refining their language
and their taste; in Scotland the former was
much debased, and the latter almost entirely
lost. . . Even after science had once dawned
upon them, the Scots seemed to be shrinking
back into ignorance and obscurity; and active
and intelligent as they naturally are, they
continued, while other nations were eager in
the pursuit of fame and knowledge, in a state
of languor. This, however, must be imputed
to the unhappiness of their political situation,
not to any defect of genius; for no sooner was
the one removed in any degree, than the other
began to display itself.

> *History of Scotland* (1759), Bk 8

Rockville, Lord (Alexander Gordon)
1739–92

Judge

1 Gentlemen, I have just met with the most wonderful adventure that ever befell a human being. As I was walking along the Grassmarket, all of a sudden the street rose up and struck me in the face.

> Announced, on arriving the worse for drink, to his fellow-members of the 'Crochallan Fencibles', a convivial Edinburgh club 'which held its nocturnal revels in Daniel Douglas's tavern, Anchor Close.' Quoted in John Kay, *Original Portraits* (1877 edition), Vol.1, p.72

Rodger, Alexander 1784–1846

Poet

1 Sawney, now the king's come,
Sawney, now the king's come,
Kneel, and kiss his gracious bum,
Sawney now the king's come.

Tell him he is great and good,
And come o' Scottish royal blood –
To your hunkers – lick his fud –
Sawney, now the king's come.

> 'Sawney, Now the King's Come' (1822), chorus and st.2

>> Written as a parody of Walter Scott's 'Carle, Now the King's Come' for George IV's visit to Edinburgh. Cf. Walter Scott 80

2 Behave yoursel' before folk,
Behave yoursel' before folk,
Whate'er you do when out o' view,
Be cautious aye before folk!

> 'Behave Yoursel' Before Folk', *Poems and Songs, Humorous and Satirical* (1838), st.1

3 O! I'll awa hame to my mither, I will,
An' I'll awa hame to my mither, I will;
Gin I tarry wi' you I may meet wi' some ill,
Then I'll awa hame to my mither, I will.

> 'I'll Awa Hame to my Mither, I Will', *Poems and Songs, Humorous and Satirical* (1838), chorus

Rorie, David 1867–1946

Poet and doctor

1 Aiberdeen an twal' mile roon,
Fife an a' the lands aboot it,
Ta'en frae Scotland's runkled map
Little's left, an' wha will doot it?

Few at least 'at maitters ony,
Orra folk, it's easy seen,
Folk 'at dinna come frae bonny
Fife or canny Aiberdeen.

> 'A Per Se', *The Lum Hat Wantin' the Croon and other poems* (1935)

2 The burn was big wi' spate,
An' there cam' tum'lin' doon
Tapsalteerie the half o' a gate,
Wi' an auld fish-hake an' a great muckle skate,
An' a lum hat wantin' the croon.

> 'The Lum Hat Wantin' the Croon', *The Lum Hat Wantin' the Croon and other poems* (1935), st.1

>> Originally written in the 1890s, this poem was a favourite with Scots troops in the Boer War and First World War, and with expatriates throughout the world

3 He wore a sporran an' a dirk,
An' a beard like besom bristles,
He was an elder o' the kirk
And he hated kists o' whistles.
Hech mon! The pawky duke!
An' doon on kists o' whistles!
They're a' reid-heidit fowk up North
Wi' beards like besom bristles.

> 'The Pawky Duke', *The Lum Hat Wantin' the Croon and other poems* (1935), st.3. Cf. Sheena Blackhall 5

>> In a note to this poem, Rorie wrote, 'It is hoped that all Scottish characteristics known to the Southron are here: pawkiness and pride of race; love of the dram; redness of hair; eldership of, and objection to instrumental music in, the Kirk; hatred of the Sassenach; inability to see a joke, etc. etc. An undying portrait is thus put on record of the typical Scot of the day.'

4 But they brocht a joke, they did indeed,
Ae day for his eedification,
An' they needed to trephine his heid,
Sae he deed o' the operation.
Hech mon! The pawky duke!
Wae's me for the operation!
For weel I wot this typical Scot
Was a michty loss to the nation.

> 'The Pawky Duke', *The Lum Hat Wantin' the Croon and other poems* (1935), st.8. Cf. J M Barrie 13, Sydney Smith 4

Rose, Dilys 1954–

Short-story writer and poet

1 . . . So they linger,
the ugly unlovable glut of dull-eyed waifs
clutching the filthy hem of the world's skirt.

They sleep a lot: their dreams are crammed
with sides of beef, mountains of rice.

> 'Dream Feast', *Original Prints II: New Writing from Scottish Women* (1987). Reprinted in *Beauty is a Dangerous Thing* (1988)

2 . . . formal service, casual service, bar service, brisk service, service always with a smile. You name it, mister, I'll do it. I can sing, dance, rollerskate.

> 'I Can Sing, Dance, Rollerskate', *Our Lady of the Pickpockets* (1989)

3 Secrets. Those private chips of information which have to be – on occasion, under restricted circumstances – tested in the world, like newly discovered chemicals.

> 'The Original Version', *Our Lady of the Pickpockets* (1989)

4 History, whether we like it or not, presses itself upon us like an uninvited guest when we find great-aunt Lizzie's vase at the back of a cupboard.

> 'The Price of Tea', *Our Lady of the Pickpockets* (1989)

5 Sorry, I don't know, don't remember, am not in control of what I'm doing because I've had too much to drink – The national excuse for everything, from bad-mouthing to murder.

> 'Barely an Incident', *Red Tides* (1993)

Ross, Alexander 1699–1784
Schoolmaster and poet

1 Woo'd and married and a',
Married and woo'd and a';
The dandilly toast of the parish
Is woo'd and married and a'.

> 'Woo'd and Married and A'', st.1. Cf. Joanna Baillie 15 and Joanna Picken 1, both of whom reworked the song from a woman's viewpoint

Ross, Ricky 1957–
Rock singer and songwriter

1 Raintown

> Title of Deacon Blue song and album (1988)

2 Fergus Sings the Blues

> Title of Deacon Blue song, on *When the World Knows Your Name* (1989)

3 Real Gone Kid

> Title of Deacon Blue song, on *When the World Knows Your Name* (1989)

Rothes, 7th Earl and 1st Duke of (John Leslie) 1630–1681
Anti-covenanter and Privy Councillor

1 Vie in this cingdum ar will ffull, proud, and nesiesitus eivin to begarie. . .

> Quoted in Rosalind Mitchison, *A History of Scotland* (1970), ch.14

>> Rothes was commenting on opposition to the episcopalian church settlement of the Restoration, and the Act of 1663 which imposed fines on dissenters for non-attendance at the parish kirk. Rosalind Mitchison remarks that he was 'the worst speller of Scottish history and one of the heaviest drinkers'

Roxburgh, Andy 1943–
Scotland football team national coach (1986–94)

1 J B Priestley said football was both hurtling with conflict, and yet passionate and beautiful in its art. Now to me that's Scottish football. It was a remarkable statement, especially as the guy was English.

> *Only a Game?*, BBC documentary (1985)

2 Until a generation ago, kids would happily play football in the streets until it was too dark to see the ball. Now they can stage matches on the home computer and if they did go out for a kick-about in the street, there is a good chance they would be run over by a juggernaut.

> On a possible reason for the dwindling supply of first-class Scottish football players. Quoted in Roddy Forsyth, *The Only Game: The Scots and World Football* (1990), ch.5

3 Pressure to me is being homeless or unemployed. This isn't pressure, it's pleasure.

> On struggling to find available players for a match against Germany (1993). Quoted in Kenny MacDonald, *Scottish Football Quotations* (1994)

Runrig
Rock band

1 Dance Called America

> Title of song (1985). Cf. James Boswell 6

2 Cuibhlean stòlda mu dheas
Na fàsaichean a tuath
An taigh-mór falamh an Dun-Eideann
Gun chumhachd gun ghuth. . .

Ach 's math dhomh bhith seo an dràsd
A' cur fàilt air a' bhlàs
'San tìr a tha cho ùr dhomh an diugh
Is a bha i nuair bha mi 'nam phàisd

† I see the wheels of industry at a standstill
And the northern lands wasted
And the empty house in Edinburgh
Without authority or voice. . .

But it's good for me to be here now
As I welcome the warmth
In this land that's as exciting for me today
As it was the day I was born

> 'Alba' ('Scotland'), st.4, 6 (Chrysalis Music Ltd, 1987)

>> Composed by Calum Macdonald and Rory Macdonald

3 Once in a lifetime
You live and love
Once in a lifetime
You die
Once in a lifetime

The sun goes down
Protect and survive

> 'Protect and Survive', chorus (Chrysalis Music Ltd, 1987)
>> Composed by Calum Macdonald

4 Seididh gaoth is dearrsaidh grian
Tro mheas nan craobhan linn gu linn
Ach thig an là is thig an t-am
Airson an ubhal as airde
Air a' chraobh a bhuain

† The winds will blow
And the sun will shine
From generation to generation
Through the trees of the garden
But the day and the hour
Will surely come
To take the highest apple
From the knowledge tree

> 'An Ubhal as Airde' ('The Highest Apple'), chorus (Chrysalis Music Ltd, 1987)
>> Composed by Calum Macdonald

Rushforth, (Margaret) Winifred (*née* Bartholomew) 1885–1983

Psychiatrist, pioneer of psychotherapy

1 Equality is the high road of life. . .

> *Ten Decades of Happenings: The Autobiography of Winifred Rushforth* (1984), 'Second Decade'

2 . . . it would be quite impossible to analyse everyone, but for a start I would suggest the parents of young children and candidates for political office. Think how differently our country would be governed if all our MPs became aware of the motivation of their conduct.

> *Ten Decades of Happenings: The Autobiography of Winifred Rushforth* (1984), 'Sixth Decade'

3 They shall know we are old not by the frailty of the body but by the strength and creativity of the psyche.

> Quoted in Rosemary Goring (ed.), *Chambers Scottish Biographical Dictionary* (1992)

Russell, Jessie b.1850

Glasgow servant, dressmaker and poet

1 But a life for a life, and the murderer's hung, and we think not the law inhuman,
Then why not the lash for the man who kicks or strikes a defenceless woman?

> 'Woman's Rights *versus* Woman's Wrongs', *The Blinkin' o' the Fire and Other Poems* (1877)

In 1875 a parliamentary report recommended that men who beat or otherwise assaulted their wives should be lashed, but the proposal did not result in any legislation being passed.
Cf. Marion Bernstein 2

Rutherford, Samuel 1600–61

Covenanter, theologian and political theorist

1 Christ got a charter of Scotland from His Father; and who will bereave Him of His heritage, or put our Redeemer out of His mailing until His tack be run out?

> Letter to Marion M'Naught (20 Aug 1633)

2 My shallow and ebb thoughts are not the compass which Christ saileth by.

> Letter to J— R— (16 Jun 1637)

3 . . . there is not such a glassy, icy and slippery piece of way betwixt you and heaven, as Youth. . . The devil in his flowers (I mean the hot, fiery lusts and passions of youth) is much to be feared: better yoke with an old grey-haired, withered, dry devil.

> Letter to William Gordon of Earlston (16 Jun 1637)

4 All Christ's good bairns go to heaven with a broken brow, and with a crooked leg.

> Letter to William Gordon of Earlston (16 Jun 1637)

5 If my creditor, Christ, should take from me what He hath lent, I should not long keep the causeway. . . I think it manhood to play the coward, and jouk in the lee-side of Christ. . .

> Letter to William Gordon of Earlston (16 Jun 1637)

6 Lex Rex

† Law is King

> Title of book (1644)

7 I have got summons already before a Superior Judge and Judicatory, and I behove to answer to my first summons, and ere your day come, I will be where few kings and great folks come.

> Said when terminally ill (1661), on being summoned to appear before Parliament on a charge of treason. Quoted in N M Cameron, D F Wright et al., *Dictionary of Scottish Church History and Theology* (1993)

S

Sage, Donald 1789–1869

Minister at Achness in Strathnaver, witness to the Sutherland clearances

1 I preached and the people listened. . . At last all restraints were compelled to give way. The preacher ceased to speak, the people to listen. All lifted up their voices and wept, mingling their tears together. It was indeed the place of parting, and the hour. The greater number parted never again to behold each other in the land of the living.

> On his final sermon held in Langdale, Strathnaver, before the eviction of his congregation to make way for sheep (1819). From his journal, *Memorabilia Domestica* (1889), quoted in Ian Grimble, *The Trial of Patrick Sellar* (1962), ch.11

Salmond, Alex 1955–

Nationalist politician, MP and Scottish National Party leader (1990–   )

1 Nobody ever celebrated Devolution Day.
> Said during the run-up to the 1992 general election. Quoted in *The Independent* (2 Apr 1992)

2 It won't be 'In Heaven by '97'.
> On being asked what the SNP's campaign slogan would be in the next general Election (*The Scotsman*, 1995). Quoted by Peter MacMahon in *The Scotsman* (22 Jul 1996). Cf. Scottish National Party 2

Sanderson, William

Songwriter

1 What though in the ha's o' the great we may meet,
Wi' men o' high rank and braw orders,
Oor hearts sigh for hame
And nae music sae sweet
As the soft lowland tongue o' the Borders.
> 'Sweet Lowland Tongue o' The Borders', chorus

Scholey, Sir Robert 1921–

Chairman of British Steel (1986–92), nick-named 'Black Bob'

1 I love you all! I love you all!
> *Reporting Scotland* (BBC television, 29 Jul 1992)
> Scholey's 'last words' to the Scottish media on his retiral as chairman of British Steel.

Ravenscraig Steelworks in Motherwell had been closed in January 1992

Scotsman, The 1817–

Edinburgh-based national newspaper

1 Before proceeding to the ordinary business of our paper, we beg to observe that we have not chosen the name of SCOTSMAN to preserve an invidious distinction, but with the view of rescuing it from the odium of servility. With that stain removed, a Scotsman may well claim brotherhood with an Englishman, and there ought now to be no rivalry between them, but in the cause of regulated freedom.
> Opening words of the first edition (25 Jan 1817)

Scott, Alexander c.1515–83

Poet

1 Sum luvis, new cum to toun,
With jeigis to mak thame joly;
Sum luvis dance up and doun,
To meiss thair malancoly. . .
> 'Ballat Maid to the Derisioun and Scorne of Wantoun Wemen', st.8
> > This is the first occurrence of the word 'jig' (jeigis: jigs) being used to refer to a dance. See John Purser, *Scotland's Music* (1992), ch.9

2 Hence hairt, with her that must departe,
And hald thee with thy soverane,
For I had lever want ane harte
Nor haif the hairt that dois me pane;
Thairfor go, with thy lufe remane,
And lat me leif thus unmolest;
And see that thou come not agane,
But byde with her thou luvis best.
> 'Hence hairt, with her that must departe', st.1

3 Luve is ane fervent fire,
Kendillit without desire:
Short plesour, lang displesour,
Repentance is the hire;
Ane puir tressour without mesour:
Luve is ane fervent fire.

To luve and to be wise,
To rege with gude advice,
Now thus, now than, so goes the game,
Incertain is the dice:
There is no man, I say, that can
Both luve and to be wise.
> 'A Rondel of Luve', st.2–3

4 To luve unluvit is ane pane;
For scho that is my soverane,
Some wantoun man so hie has set hir
That I can get no lufe agene,
Bot breks my hairt, and nocht the bettir.
'To Luve Unluvit', st.1

The Bannatyne manuscript adds, at the end
of this poem, 'Quo Scott, Quhen His Wyfe
Left Him'

Scott, Alexander 1920–89
Poet

1 A hunder pipers canna blaw
Our trauchled times awa,
Drams canna droun them out, nor sang
Hap their scarecrow heids for lang.
'Calvinist Sang', *The Latest in Elegies* (1949),
st.1. Cf. Lady Nairne 6

2 I walkit air, I walkit late
By craigs o gloamin-coloured stane,
I heard the sea-maws skirl and keen
Like sclate-pens scraichan ower a sclate.
'Scrievin', *The Latest in Elegies* (1949), st.1

3 Waement the deid
I never did,
Owre gled I was ane o the lave
That somewey baid alive
To trauchle my thowless hert
Wi ithers' hurt.
'Coronach', *Mouth Music* (1954), st.1

4 The sea-gray toun, the stane-gray sea. . .
On Aberdeen. 'Heart of Stone', *Cantrips*
(1968), 1.12

5 The couthie country fat and fou o ferms. . .
On the countryside round Aberdeen. 'Heart of
Stone', *Cantrips* (1968), 1.65

6 *Scotch God*
Kent His
Faither.
'Scotched', *Double Agent* (1972)

7 *Scotch Religion*
Damn
Aa.
'Scotched', *Double Agent* (1972)

8 *Scotch Education*
I tellt ye
I tellt ye.
'Scotched', *Double Agent* (1972)

9 *Scotch Passion*
Forgot
Mysel.
'Scotched', *Double Agent* (1972)

Scott, Lady John
see **Spottiswoode, Alicia Anne**

Scott, Mike 1958–
Songwriter, lead singer with The Waterboys

1 I saw the rain dirty valley
you saw Brigadoon
I saw the crescent
you saw the Whole of the Moon
'The Whole of the Moon' (1985) (Dizzy Heights
Music Publ Ltd/Chrysalis Music Ltd)

Single recorded by The Waterboys, on *This
Is The Sea* (1985)

Scott, Tom 1918–95
Poet

1 A prime king like a rat wes stang til daeth.
And coorsely wes avenged:
His heir by his burst cannon tint his braeth
And had his throne, tae, singed.
His again, a priest gied his quietus
By a battle-field:
The fowrth saw Flodden utterly defeat us:
The fifth a bairn's birth killed.
'Fergus', *The Ship and Ither Poems* (1963)
On the fates of the first five King Jameses

2 The human race is a group o climbers roped
Thegither, aa for ane, and ane for aa,
Faced by the problem rock reality is. . .
At the Shrine o the Unkent Sodger (1968; revised
version in *Collected Shorter Poems*, 1993), section 6

3 The jauggy ruins o whit wes in its time
Europe's grandest cathedral, no even York
Milan, nor Rheims, nor Köln surpassan it –
There oor culture, oor Renaissance fell
And we, Sant-Aundraes, aa oor fowk fell wi't!
'Johnie Brand's Prologue', *Brand the Builder*
(1975)

4 Doun by the sea
Murns the white swaw owre the wrack
ayebydanlie.
'Brand the Builder', *Brand the Builder* (1975)

5 The warld ootside
Like a lug-held seashell, sings wi the rinnan tide.
'Brand the Builder', *Brand the Builder* (1975)

6 And this is aa the life he kens there is?
'Brand the Builder', *Brand the Builder* (1975)

7 Poets are not the unacknowledged legislators
of the world, but they ought to be the
acknowledged counsellors, the men of values
and vision, exposing the idiocies of their age, the
crimes against nature and mankind, promoting
a true religious vision of reality.
'Vive MacDiarmid', in *Chapman* No.22 (Winter
1978)

'Poets are the unacknowledged legislators of the world' was said by Shelley in *A Defence of Poetry*

Scott, Sir Walter 1771–1832

Novelist and poet

1 The way was long, the wind was cold,
The Minstrel was infirm and old;
His withered cheek, and tresses grey,
Seemed to have known a better day;
The harp, his sole remaining joy,
Was carried by an orphan boy.
The last of all the Bards was he,
Who sung of Border chivalry.

The Lay of the Last Minstrel (1805), Introduction

2 He poured, to lord and lady gay,
The unpremeditated lay...

The Lay of the Last Minstrel (1805), Introduction

3 If thou wouldst view fair Melrose aright,
Go visit it by the pale moonlight;
For the fair beams of lightsome day
Gild, but to flout, the ruins grey.

The Lay of the Last Minstrel (1805), Canto 2, I

4 And said I that my limbs were old,
And said I that my blood was cold,
And that my kindly fire was fled,
And my poor withered heart was dead,
And that I might not sing of Love?

The Lay of the Last Minstrel (1805), Canto 3, I

5 The Harper smiled, well pleased; for ne'er
Was flattery lost on poet's ear:
A simple race! they waste their toil
For the vain tribute of a smile.

The Lay of the Last Minstrel (1805), Canto 4, Conclusion

6 Call it not vain; – they do not err
Who say, that when the Poet dies,
Mute Nature mourns her worshipper,
And celebrates his obsequies...

The Lay of the Last Minstrel (1805), Canto 5, I

7 Breathes there the man, with soul so dead,
Who never to himself hath said,
This is my own, my native land!
Whose heart hath ne'er within him burned,
As home his footsteps he hath turned
From wandering on a foreign strand!
If such there be, go, mark him well;
For him no Minstrel raptures swell;
High though his titles, proud his name,
Boundless his wealth as wish can claim;
Despite those titles, power, and pelf,
The wretch, concentred all in self,
Living, shall forfeit fair renown,
And doubly dying, shall go down

To the vile dust, from whence he sprung,
Unwept, unhonoured, and unsung.

The Lay of the Last Minstrel (1805), Canto 6, I

8 O Caledonia! stern and wild,
Meet nurse for a poetic child!
Land of brown heath and shaggy wood,
Land of the mountain and the flood,
Land of my sires! what mortal hand
Can e'er untie the filial band,
That knits me to thy rugged strand!

The Lay of the Last Minstrel (1805), Canto 6, II.
Cf. Lord Byron 48

9 No, no – 'tis no laughing matter; little by little,
whatever your wishes may be, you will destroy
and undermine, until nothing of what makes
Scotland Scotland shall remain.

Said in 1806, rebuking Francis Jeffrey and other
liberals, whose schemes for legal reform he saw
as destructive of Scottish institutions. Quoted in
J G Lockhart, *Memoirs of the Life of Sir Walter
Scott, Bart.* (1837–8), ch.15

10 I do not at all like the task of reviewing &
have seldom myself undertaken it – in poetry
never – because I am sensible there is a greater
difference in tastes in that department than
in any other and that there is much excellent
poetry which I am not now-a-days able to read
without falling asleep... Now I think there is
something hard in blaming the poor cook for
the fault of one's own palate or deficiency of
appetite...

Letter to Anna Seward (23 Nov 1807)

11 November's sky is chill and drear,
November's leaf is red and sear...

Marmion (1808), Canto 1, Introduction

12 And come he slow, or come he fast,
It is but Death who comes at last.

Marmion (1808), Canto 2, xxx

13 O, young Lochinvar is come out of the west,
Through all the wide Border his steed was
the best;
And save his good broadsword he weapon
had none,
He rode all unarmed, and he rode all alone.
So faithful in love, and so dauntless in war,
There never was knight like the young
Lochinvar.

Marmion (1808), Canto 5, xii, 'Lochinvar' (Lady
Heron's Song)

14 'She is won! we are gone, over bank, bush,
and scaur;
They'll have fleet steeds that follow,' quoth
young Lochinvar.

Marmion (1808), Canto 5, xii, 'Lochinvar' (Lady
Heron's Song)

15 Heap on more wood! – the wind is chill;
But let it whistle as it will,

We'll keep our Christmas merry still.
Marmion (1808), Canto 6, Introduction

6 'And dar'st thou then
To beard the lion in his den,
The Douglas in his hall?'
Marmion (1808), Canto 6, XIV

7 Oh what a tangled web we weave,
When first we practise to deceive!
Marmion (1808), Canto 6, XVII

8 O Woman! in our hours of ease,
Uncertain, coy, and hard to please,
And variable as the shade
By the light quivering aspen made;
When pain and anguish wring the brow,
A ministering angel thou!
Marmion (1808), Canto 6, XXX

9 The stubborn spearmen still made good
Their dark impenetrable wood,
Each stepping where his comrade stood
The instant that he fell.
Marmion (1808), Canto 6, XXXIV

0 . . . the poor fellow has just talent enough to
spoil him for his own trade without having
enough to support him by literature.
On James Hogg, in a letter to Lady Dalkeith
(14 Aug 1810)
Scott enclosed a copy of Hogg's book, *The
Forest Minstrel, a Selection of Songs*, with
the letter

1 . . . life is too short for the indulgence of
animosity.
Letter to Lady Dalkeith (14 Aug 1810)

2 The stag at eve had drunk his fill,
Where danced the moon on Monan's rill,
And deep his midnight lair had made
In lone Glenartney's hazel shade. . .
The Lady of the Lake (1810), Canto 1, I

3 Hail to the Chief who in honour advances!
Honoured and bless'd be the evergreen Pine!
The Lady of the Lake (1810), Canto 2, XIX,
'Boat Song'

4 Time rolls his ceaseless course.
The Lady of the Lake (1810), Canto 3, I

5 He is gone on the mountain,
He is lost to the forest,
Like a summer-dried fountain,
When our need was the sorest.
The font, reappearing,
From the raindrops shall borrow;
But to us comes no cheering,
To Duncan no morrow!
The Lady of the Lake (1810), Canto 3, XVI,
'Coronach'

26 Like the dew on the mountain,
Like the foam on the river,
Like the bubble on the fountain,
Thou art gone, and for ever!
The Lady of the Lake (1810), Canto 3, XVI,
'Coronach'

27 Merry it is in the good greenwood,
When the mavis and merle are singing,
When the deer sweeps by, and the hounds
are in cry,
And the hunter's horn is ringing.
The Lady of the Lake (1810), Canto 4, XII,
'Alice Brand'

28 . . . I make it a rule to cheat nobody but
Booksellers, a race on whom I have no mercy.
Letter to Thomas Sheridan (19 Sep 1811)
At the time, 'bookseller' was virtually
synonymous with 'publisher'

29 'A weary lot is thine, fair maid,
A weary lot is thine!
To pull the thorn thy brow to braid,
And press the rue for wine!'
Rokeby (1813), Canto 3, XXVIII, 'Song'

30 So, now the danger dared at last,
Look back, and smile at perils past!
The Bridal of Triermain (1813), Introduction, II

31 False love, and hast thou play'd me thus
In summer among the flowers?
I will replay thee back again
In winter among the showers.
Waverely (1814), ch.9 (David Gellatley's song)

32 Hie away, hie away,
Over bank and over brae,
Where the copsewood is the greenest,
Where the fountains glisten sheenest,
Where the lady-fern grows strongest,
Where the morning dew lies longest,
Where the black-cock sweetest sips it,
Where the fairy latest trips it. . .
Waverley (1814), ch.12 (David Gellatley's song
to the deerhounds)

33 'He that steals a cow from a poor widow, or
a stirk from a cottar, is a thief; he that lifts a
drove from a Sassenach laird, is a gentleman-
drover. And, besides, to take a tree from the
forest, a salmon from the river, a deer from the
hill, or a cow from a Lowland strath, is what
no Highlander need ever think shame upon.'
Waverley (1814), ch.18 (Evan Dhu Maccombich
to Edward Waverley)

34 There's nought in the Highlands but syboes
and leeks,
And lang-leggit callants gaun wanting
the breeks;
Wanting the breeks, and without hose
and shoon,

But we'll a' win the breeks when King Jamie
comes hame!

> *Waverley* (1814), ch.28 (David Gellatley's song)

>> In a note, Scott claimed these lines as
>> ancient, and sung to the tune of 'There'll
>> Never be Peace till Jamie Comes Hame'.
>> Cf. Robert Burns 121

35 What a miserable thing it is that our royal
family cannot be quiet and decent at least if
not correct and moral in their deportment. Old
farmer George's manly simplicity modesty of
expence and domestic virtue saved this country
at its most perilous crisis for it is inconceivable
the number of persons whom these qualities
united in his behalf who would have felt but
coldly the abstract duty of supporting a crown
less worthily worn.

> Letter to John Morritt (28 Jul 1814)

>> George III ('Farmer George') was still alive
>> but insane: his son acted as Prince Regent
>> from 1810 to 1820, a period in which court
>> scandal was rife

36 I am heartily glad you continued to like
Waverley to the end – the hero is a sneaking
piece of imbecility and if he had married Flora
she would have set him up upon the chimney-
piece as Count Boralaski's wife used to do
with him.

> Letter to John Morritt (28 Jul 1814)

>> Joseph Borowlaski, a Polish dwarf, came
>> from France to the British Isles, where he
>> gave recitals at fairs and in concert halls,
>> and was much in demand as a curiosity in
>> wealthy social circles. He eventually retired
>> on the proceeds of his self-exploitation, and
>> is buried at Durham Cathedral. His memoirs
>> were among the first volumes produced by
>> Scott's friend and business associate James
>> Ballantyne

37 But ruffian stern, and soldier good,
The noble and the slave,
From various cause the same wild road,
On the same bloody morning, trode,
To that dark inn – the Grave!

> *The Lord of the Isles* (1815), Canto 6, XXVI

38 'Pro-di-gi-ous!'

> *Guy Mannering* (1815), ch.8. (Dominie Sampson's
> catchword)

39 'That sounds like nonsense, my dear.'
'Maybe so, my dear; but it may be very good
law for all that.'

> *Guy Mannering* (1815), ch.9 (Mrs and Mr Bertram
> in conversation)

40 . . . the frolicsome company had begun to
practise the ancient and now forgotten pastime
of *High Jinks*.

> *Guy Mannering* (1815), ch.36. Cf. Neil Munro 3

41 'A lawyer without history or literature is a
mechanic, a mere working mason; if he possesses
some knowledge of these, he may venture to
call himself an architect.'

> *Guy Mannering* (1815), ch.37 (Mr Pleydell to
> Colonel Mannering, referring to his own library)

42 'In civilised society, law is the chimney through
which all that smoke discharges itself that used
to circulate through the whole house, and put
every one's eyes out – no wonder, therefore,
that the vent itself should sometimes get a
little sooty.'

> *Guy Mannering* (1815), ch.39 (Mr Pleydell to
> Colonel Mannering)

43 *'Because the Hour's come, and the Man.'*

> *Guy Mannering* (1815), ch.54

>> The phrase is Meg Merrilies' signal for Dandie
>> Dinmont and Bertram to seize the villain Dirk
>> Hatteraick. In ch.53, Meg has forewarned
>> them that the signal will be *'The hour and the
>> man are baith come'*. Cf. Walter Scott 65

44 Then strip, lads, and to it, though sharp be
the weather,
And if, by mischance, you should happen to fall,
There are worse things in life than a tumble
on heather,
And life is itself but a game at football.

> 'Lines on the Lifting of the Banner of the House
> of Buccleuch, at a Great Football Match at
> Carterhaugh' (1815), st.5

45 To see foreign parts gives I think more the
feelings of youth to those of an advanced age
than anything they can engage [in].

> Letter to Matthew Weld Hartstonge
> (28 Nov 1816)

46 'Why weep ye by the tide, ladie?
Why weep ye by the tide?
I'll wed ye to my youngest son,
And ye sall be his bride:
And ye sall be his bride, ladie,
Sae comely to be seen' –
But aye she loot the tears down fa'
For Jock of Hazeldean.

> 'Jock of Hazeldean' (1816), st.1

>> In spite of the text, this song is invariably
>> known and sung as 'Jock o' Hazeldean'

47 'A chain of gold ye sall not lack,
Nor braid to bind your hair;
Nor mettled hound, nor managed hawk,
Nor palfrey fresh and fair. . . '

> 'Jock of Hazeldean' (1816), st.3

48 They sought her baith by bower and ha';
The ladie was not seen!
She's o'er the Border and awa'
Wi' Jock of Hazeldean.

> 'Jock of Hazeldean' (1816), st.4

9 'Prætorian here, prætorian there, I mind the bigging o't.'

> *The Antiquary* (1816), ch.4 (Edie Ochiltree to Jonathan Oldbuck, the Antiquary, disputing his theory that they stood on the site of a Roman camp)

0 'It's no fish ye're buying – it's men's lives.'

> *The Antiquary* (1816), ch.11 (Maggie Mucklebackit to Jonathan Oldbuck). Cf. Lady Nairne 3

1 'It's weel wi' you gentles, that can sit in the house wi' handkerchers at your een when ye lose a friend; but the like o' us maun to our wark again, if our hearts were beating as hard as my hammer.'

> *The Antiquary* (1816), ch.34 (Saunders Mucklebackit to Jonathan Oldbuck)

2 One crowded hour of glorious life
Is worth an age without a name.

> *Old Mortality* (1816), ch.34 (chapter motto)

3 'I'll no say but it may be possible that I might hae been there.'

> *Old Mortality* (1816), ch.36 (Cuddie Headrigg's cautious response to the question, 'Were you at the battle of Bothwell Brigg?')

4 . . . bookselling [is] the most ticklish and unsafe and hazardous of all professions scarcely with the exception of horse-jockeyship.

> Letter to Lord Montagu (8 Jun 1817)

>> At the time 'bookseller' was virtually synonymous with 'publisher'

5 To live the life of a mere author for bread is perhaps the most dreadful fate that can be encountered. Booksellers like other men drive the best of bargains they can: with those who have no independent means of support they make them very narrow indeed & sometimes contrive to evade fulfilling them. Besides they become masters of your time & your labour as well as dictators of the subjects on which they are to be employed and working under their direction a man who has got a reputation is in all probability forced upon some undertaking unfavourable to his talents by which he loses it.

> Letter to James Bailey (21 Jun 1817)

>> See entry above

6 'He that is without name, without friends, without coin, without country, is still at least a man; and he that has all these is no more.'

> *Rob Roy* (1817), ch.21 (Rob Roy to Francis Osbaldistone)

7 '. . . if your honour disna ken when ye hae a gude servant, I ken when I hae a gude master, and the deil be in my feet gin I leave ye. . . '

> *Rob Roy* (1817), ch.24 (Andrew Fairservice to Francis Osbaldistone)

58 Honour is a homicide and a bloodspiller, that gangs about making frays in the street; but Credit is a decent honest man, that sits at hame, and makes the pat play.'

> *Rob Roy* (1817), ch.26 (Bailie Nicol Jarvie to Francis Osbaldistone)

59 '. . . it's ill taking the breeks aff a Hielandman.'

> *Rob Roy* (1817), ch.27 (Andrew Fairservice to Bailie Nicol Jarvie)

>> In *The Fortunes of Nigel* (1822), ch.5, Scott has James VI and I say to Geordie Heriot, 'It's ill taking the breeks aff a wild Highlandman.'

60 'Whisht, sir! – whisht! it's ill-scraped tongues like yours that make mischief atween neighbourhoods and nations. There's naething sae gude on this side o' time but it might hae been better, and that may be said o' the Union. Nane were keener against it than the Glasgow folk, wi' their rabblings and their risings, and their mobs, as they ca' them nowadays. But it's an ill wind blaws naebody gude. Let ilka ane roose the ford as they find it – I say, Let Glasgow flourish! whilk is judiciously and elegantly putten round the town's arms by way of by-word. Now, since St Mungo catched herrings in the Clyde, what was ever like to gar us flourish like the sugar and tobacco trade? Will ony body tell me that, and grumble at the treaty that opened us a road west-awa' yonder?'

> *Rob Roy* (1817), ch.27 (Bailie Nicol Jarvie to Andrew Fairservice)

61 '. . . there's a gude time coming.'

> *Rob Roy* (1817), ch.32 (Rob Roy to the Duke of Montrose)

62 'Speak out, sir, and do not Maister or Campbell me – my foot is on my native heath, and my name is MacGregor!'

> *Rob Roy* (1817), ch.34 (Rob Roy to Francis Osbaldistone)

63 'It's a maxim of a wise man never to return by the same road he came, providing another's free to him.'

> *Rob Roy* (1817), ch.35 (Rob Roy to Bailie Nicol Jarvie)

64 '. . . ye ken weel eneugh that women and gear are at the bottom of a' the mischief in this warld. . . '

> *Rob Roy* (1817), ch.35 (Rob Roy to Francis Osbaldistone)

65 'The hour's come, but not the man.'

> *The Heart of Midlothian* (1818), ch.4 (chapter motto). Cf. Walter Scott 43

66 'I dinna ken muckle about the law,' answered Mrs Howden; 'but I ken, when we had a king, and a chancellor, and parliament-men o' our

ain, we could aye peeble them wi' stanes when they werena gude bairns – But naebody's nails can reach the length o' Lunnon.'

The Heart of Midlothian (1818), ch.4

67 'Better tyne life, since tint is gude fame.'

The Heart of Midlothian (1818), ch.7 (Effie Deans, refusing the chance to escape from the Tolbooth)

68 'Jock, when ye hae naething else to do, ye may aye be sticking in a tree; it will be growing, Jock, when ye're sleeping.'

The Heart of Midlothian (1818), ch.8 (the laird of Dumbiedikes to his son)

69 'Never mind my grace, lassie; just speak out a plain tale, and show you have a Scotch tongue in your head.'

The Heart of Midlothian (1818), ch.35 (the Duke of Argyle to Jeanie Deans)

70 Proud Maisie is in the wood,
Walking so early;
Sweet Robin sits on the bush,
Singing so rarely.

The Heart of Midlothian (1818), ch.40 (Madge Wildfire's song, st.1)

71 'Look not thou on beauty's charming, –
Sit thou still when kings are arming, –
Taste not when the wine-cup glistens, –
Speak not when the people listens, –
Stop thine ear against the singer, –
From the red gold keep thy finger, –
Vacant heart, and hand, and eye, –
Easy live and quiet die.'

The Bride of Lammermoor (1819), ch.3 (Lucy Ashton's song)

72 I was not long, however, in making the grand discovery, that in order to enjoy leisure, it is absolutely necessary it should be preceded by occupation.

The Monastery (1820), Introductory Epistle (Captain Clutterbuck)

73 March, march, Ettrick and Teviotdale,
Why the deil dinna ye march forward in order?
March, march, Eskdale and Liddesdale,
All the Blue Bonnets are bound for the Border.

The Monastery (1820), ch.25

74 In truth I have long given up poetry. I had my day with the public and being no great believer in poetical immortality I was very well pleased to rise a winner without continuing the game till I was beggared of any credit I had acquired with the public. Besides I felt the prudence of giving way before the more forcible and powerful genius of Byron.

Letter to Countess Pürgstall (1821)

75 But no one shall find me rowing against the stream. I care not who knows it – I write for the general amusement. . .

The Fortunes of Nigel (1822), Introductory Epistle (the 'Author of Waverley' to Captain Clutterbuck)

76 . . . I think there is a demon who seats himself on the feather of my pen when I begin to write, and leads it astray from the purpose. Characters expand under my hand; incidents are multiplied; the story lingers, while the materials increase; my regular mansion turns out a Gothic anomaly. . .

The Fortunes of Nigel (1822), Introductory Epistle (the 'Author of Waverley' to Captain Clutterbuck)

77 '. . . there canna be a waur prospective for a lawfu' king, wha wishes to reign in luve, and die in peace and honour, than to have naked swords flashing in his een. I am accounted as brave as maist folks; and yet I profess to ye I could never look on a bare blade without blinking and winking.'

The Fortunes of Nigel (1822), ch.5 (James VI and I to George Heriot)

78 'For a con-si-de-ra-tion.'

The Fortunes of Nigel (1822), ch.22 (Trapbois's catchphrase)

79 'And, my lords and lieges, let us all to our dinner, for the cock-a-leekie is cooling.'

The Fortunes of Nigel (1822), ch.37 (James VI and I, having just knighted Richie Moniplies; the final words of the novel)

80 Carle, now the King's come!
Carle, now the King's come!
Thou shalt dance, and I will sing,
Carle, now the King's come!

'Carle, Now the King's Come' (1822)

Adapted from an old song for George IV's visit to Edinburgh, which was largely stage-managed by Scott. Cf. Alexander Rodger 1

81 'A true Scot! Plenty of blood, plenty of pride, and right great scarcity of ducats, I warrant thee.'

Quentin Durward (1823), ch.2 ('Maitre Pierre' on Quentin Durward)

82 '. . . and what for no?'

St Ronan's Well (1823), ch.1 (Meg Dods's catchphrase)

83 'Fat, fair, and forty,' said Mr Winterblossom; 'that's all I know of her – a mercantile person.'

St Ronan's Well (1823), ch.7 (on Mrs Blower)

The phrase 'fat, fair and forty' was in common currency as a description of the attributes of a good wife. John O'Keeffe (1747–1833), the Irish playwright, used it in his play *The Irish Mimic* (1795)

84 '. . . it's ill speaking between a fou man and a fasting.'

Redgauntlet (1824), letter 11, ('Wandering Willie's Tale'). Cf. Robert Lindsay of Pitscottie 2

5 'The tae half of the warld thinks the tither daft.'

> *Redgauntlet* (1824), ch.7 (Peter Peebles to Justice Foxley). Cf. Tobias Smollett 10

6 'Then, gentlemen,' said Redgauntlet, clasping his hands together as the words burst from him, 'the cause is lost for ever!'

> *Redgauntlet* (1824), ch.23

7 Woman's faith, and woman's trust –
Write the characters in dust;
Stamp them on the running stream,
Print them on the moon's pale beam,
And each evanescent letter
Shall be clearer, firmer, better,
And more permanent, I ween,
Than the thing those letters mean.

> *The Betrothed* (1825), ch.20

8 They are certainly a very odd people and but for that ugly humour of murdering which is in full decline they would be the most amusing & easy to live with in the world.

> On the Irish. Letter to John Morritt (25 Aug 1825)

89 A third rogue writes to tell me, rather of the latest if the matter was of consequence, that he approves of the first three volumes of the *H. of Midlothian* but totally condemns the fourth. Doubtless he thinks his opinion worth the sevenpence Sterling which his letter costs. However an author should be reasonably well pleased when three fourths of his works are acceptable to the reader.

> *Journal* (10 Dec 1825)
>
> *The Heart of Midlothian* had been published seven years earlier

90 . . . from the earliest time I can remember, I preferred the pleasures of being alone to waiting for visitors, and have often taken a bannock and a bit of cheese to the wood or hill to avoid dining with company. As I grew from boyhood to manhood I saw that this would not do and that to gain a place in men's esteem I must mix and bustle with them. . . Still if the question was eternal company without the power of retiring within yourself or Solitary confinement for life I should say 'Turnkey, Lock the cell.'

> *Journal* (27 Dec 1825)

91 Came through cold roads to as cold news.

> *Journal* (16 Jan 1826)
>
> His publisher, Constable, had become bankrupt, and as their financial affairs were inextricably linked, this meant that Scott too was ruined

92 . . . I will involve no friend either rich or poor – My own right hand shall do it. . .

> On being offered financial support by friends to mitigate the effects of his bankruptcy. *Journal* (22 Jan 1826)
>
> Lord Cockburn, in *Memorials of His Time* (1856), ch.7, quotes Scott as saying, 'No! This right hand shall work it all off!'

93 The love of solitude increases with indulgence. I hope it will not diverge into misanthropy.

> *Journal* (14 Feb 1826)

94 If I can but get the sulky Scottish spirit set up the Devil won't turn them.

> *Journal* (25 Feb 1826)
>
> He was about to start writing the *Letters of Malachi Malagrowther* in opposition to government proposals to restrict the Scottish banks' issue of paper currency

95 That young lady had a talent for describing the involvements and feelings and characters of ordinary life, which is to me the most wonderful I ever met with. The Big Bow-wow strain I can do myself like any now going; but the exquisite touch, which renders ordinary commonplace things and characters interesting, from the truth of the description and the sentiment, is denied to me.

> On Jane Austen. *Journal* (14 Mar 1826)

96 Scotland, completely liberalised, as she is in a fair way of being, will be the most dangerous neighbour to England that she has had since 1639. There is yet time to make a stand, for there is yet a great deal of good and genuine feeling left in the country. But if you *unscotch* us you will find us damned mischievous Englishmen.

> Letter to J W Croker (19 Mar 1826). Cf. Lord Byron 48, Hugh MacDiarmid 52

97 J.G.L. [Lockhart] kindly points out some solecisms in my stile – as *amid* for *amidst*, *scarce* for *scarcely*. *Whose* he says is the proper genitive of *which* only at such times as *which* retains its quality of impersonification. Well! I will try to remember all this. But after all I write grammar as I speak, to make my meaning known, and a solecism in point of composition like a Scotch word in speaking is indifferent to me.

> *Journal* (22 Apr 1826)

98 Our passions are wild beasts. God grant us power to muzzle them.

> *Journal* (25 Jun 1826)
>
> He had learned that his old friend Richard Heber, book-collector and MP for Oxford University, had fled abroad after being 'detected in unnatural [ie homosexual] practices'

99 Many a clever boy is flogged into a dunce and many an original composition corrected into mediocrity.

> *Journal* (28 Jun 1826). Cf. Lord Kames 15

100 . . . a man of eighty and upwards may be allowed to talk long because in the nature of things he cannot have long to talk.

Journal (29 Jul 1826)

101 Long life to thy fame and peace to thy soul, Rob Burns. When I want to express a sentiment which I feel strongly, I find the phrase in Shakespeare or thee. The blockheads talk of my being like Shakespeare – not fit to tie his brogues.

Journal (11 Dec 1826)

102 We had better remain in union with England, even at the risk of becoming a subordinate species of Northumberland, as far as national consequence is concerned, than remedy ourselves by even hinting the possibility of a rupture. But there is no harm in wishing Scotland to have just so much ill-nature, according to her own proverb, as may keep her good-nature from being abused . . .

Letters of Malachi Malagrowther on the Proposed Change of Currency (1826), Letter 1

103 'Patience is a good nag, but she will bolt.'

Woodstock (1826), ch.2 (Sir Henry Lee)

See Shakespeare, Henry V, Act 2, sc.1: 'Though patience be a tired mare, yet she will plod'

104 At Court, and waited to see the poisoning woman. She is clearly guilty, but as one or two witnesses said the poor wench hinted an intention to poison herself, the jury gave that bastard verdict, Not proven. I hate that Caledonian medium quid. One who is not proven guilty is innocent in the eye of law.

Journal (20 Feb 1827)

The trial, at Edinburgh, was of a Mrs Mary Smith, who was accused of murdering a servant by poison. Lord Cockburn, whose client she was, later recalled that on her acquittal Scott remarked, 'Well, sirs! all I can say is, that if that woman was my wife, I should take good care to be my own cook.' See Cockburn, Circuit Journeys (12 Apr 1838)

105 . . . of what use is philosophy, and I have always pretended to a little [of it] of a practical character, if it cannot teach us to do or suffer?

Journal (2 Nov 1827)

106 I believe in God who can change evil into good and I am confident that what befalls us is always ultimately for the best.

Journal (3 Nov 1827)

107 . . . he who talks a great deal about fighting is seldom a brave soldier, and he who always speaks about wealth is seldom a rich man at bottom.

The Surgeon's Daughter (1827), ch.5

108 The state of society now leads so much to great accumulations of humanity that we cannot wonder if it ferment and reek like a compost dunghill. Nature intended that population should be diffused over the soil in proportion to its extent. We have accumulated in huge cities and smothering manufactures the numbers which should be spread over the face of a country and what wonder that they should be corrupted?

Journal (20 Feb 1828)

109 But who cares for the whipped cream of London society?

Journal (23 Apr 1828)

110 Nothing in life can be more ludicrous or contemptible than an old man aping the passions of his youth.

Journal (30 May 1828)

111 Among all the provinces in Scotland, if an intelligent stranger were asked to describe the most varied and the most beautiful, it is probable he would name the county of Perth.

The Fair Maid of Perth (1828), ch.1

112 'Another for Hector!'

The Fair Maid of Perth (1828), ch.34 (Torquil urging his sons forward, one after another, in defence of Hector or Eachin, chief of Clan Quhele, at the Battle of the North Inch)

113 'I fought for my own hand,' said the Smith indifferently, and the expression is still proverbial in Scotland.

The Fair Maid of Perth (1828), ch.34 (Harry Smith of the Wynd, who made up the numbers in the North Inch battle between the rival clans Quhele and Chattan)

114 . . . London licks the butter off our bread by opening a better market for ambition. Were it not for the difference of the religion and the laws poor Scotland could hardly keep a man that is worth having . . .

Journal (24 Mar 1829)

115 . . . the misfortune of writing fast is that one cannot at the same time write concisely.

Journal (28 Apr 1829)

116 To the Lords of Convention 'twas Claver'se who spoke,
'Ere the King's crown shall fall there are crowns to be broke;
So let each Cavalier who loves honour and me,
Come follow the bonnet of Bonny Dundee.'

The Doom of Devorgoil (1830), 'Bonny Dundee', st.1

117 Come fill up my cup, come fill up my can,
Come saddle your horses, and call up your men;

Come open your gates, and let me gae free,
For it's up with the bonnets of Bonny Dundee!

> *The Doom of Devorgoil* (1830), 'Bonny Dundee',
> final chorus

This gifted personage, besides having great talents, has conversation the least *exigeante* of any author, female at least, whom I have ever seen among the long list I have encountered with – simple, full of humour, and exceedingly ready at repartee; and all this without the least affectation of the blue-stocking.

> On Susan Ferrier. *Journal* (12 May 1831)

Surely chess-playing is a sad waste of brains.

> Quoted in J G Lockhart, *Memoirs of the Life
> of Sir Walter Scott, Bart.* (1837–8), ch.4.
> Cf. James VI and I 12

No repose for Sir Walter but in the grave. Friends, don't let me expose myself – get me to bed – that's the only place.

> Spoken in 1832, shortly before his death. Quoted
> in J G Lockhart, *Memoirs of the Life of Sir Walter
> Scott, Bart.* (1837–8), ch.83

My dear, be a good man – be virtuous – be religious – be a good man. Nothing else will give you any comfort when you come to lie here.

> Last words, spoken to Lockhart, as reported by
> him in his *Memoirs of the Life of Sir Walter Scott,
> Bart.* (1837–8), ch.83

Scott-Moncrieff, Ann (*née* Agnes Shearer) 1914–43

Journalist, poet and short-story writer, wife of George Scott-Moncrieff

1 Ye canna mak a pudden oot o' pig's meat,
Ye canna big a hoose wi' twa-three stays,
Ye canna plant a tattie when the grund's weet,
Ye canna ploo the hillside wi' yer taes!
And is it like, my love, to be
Thoo'll kin to mak a wife o' me?

> Poem dated *January 1933*. Quoted in *Chapman*
> No.38 (Spring 1984)

Scott-Moncrieff, George 1910–74

Writer and editor, husband of Ann Scott-Moncrieff

1 If Skye does produce great men nowadays it is only in the rather shameful ranks of the industrialists. For, although you may not spend your money in delight, West Highland Calvinism does not forbid you pleasure in amassing it: indeed, it encourages you, for it has a strong respect for Mammon, and making money may keep man from carnal mischief.

> 'Skye', in George Scott-Moncrieff (ed.), *Scottish
> Country* (1935)

Scottish National Party

Political party formed in 1934 by the merger of the National Party of Scotland with the Scottish Party

1 It's Scotland's Oil

> Slogan of campaign (launched Sep 1972)

2 Free by '93

> Campaign slogan for the 1992 general election.
> Cf. Andrew Marr 1, Alex Salmond 2

Scougal, Henry 1650–78

Theologian, Professor of Divinity, King's College, Aberdeen from 1674

1 The true religion is an Union of the soul with God. . .

> *The Life of God in the Soul of Man* (1677)

Scroggie, George 19th century

Miller and songwriter

1 Farewell tae Tarwathie, adieu Mormond Hill
Dear land of my fathers I bid you farewell
I'm bound for Greenland and ready to sail
In hope to find riches in hunting the whale.

> 'Farewell to Tarwathie' (1850s), st.1

2 The cold land of Greenland is barren and bare
No seed time or harvest is ever known there
The birds here sing sweetly on mountain
  and dale
But there's nae a birdie to sing to the whale.

> 'Farewell to Tarwathie' (1850s)

Seafield, 1st Earl of see Ogilvy, James

Sellar, Patrick 1780–1851

Lawyer, factor on the estate of the 1st Duke of Sutherland

1 It is of no great consequence that our new Sheriff be no 'Gael' nor 'Mac' – but a plain, honest, industrious *South* countryman.

> Attrib. (1816). On the appointment of a sheriff
> in Sutherland

2 I was at once a convert to the principle now almost universally acted on in the highlands of Scotland, viz. that the people should be employed in securing the natural riches of the sea-coast; that the mildew of the interior should be allowed to fall upon grass, and not upon corn; and that several hundred miles of Alpine plants, flourishing in these districts, in curious succession at all seasons,

and out of the reach of anything but sheep, be converted into wool and mutton for the English manufacturer.

> From his account of his work (1820). Quoted in Ian Grimble, *The Trial of Patrick Sellar* (1962), ch.2

3 In place of the few scores (perhaps from two to three scores) of highland families who have since emigrated, I am convinced there are five scores of south families imported; and that a trial will show no diminution of people in 1820.

> From his account of his work (1820). Quoted in Ian Grimble, *The Trial of Patrick Sellar* (1962), ch.2

Sempill, Francis ?1616–1682
Poet, son of Robert Sempill

1 Wha wadna be in love
Wi' bonnie Maggie Lauder?

> 'Maggie Lauder', st.1
>
> > He is attributed with the authorship of this song, but probably reworked it from older versions

2 'Weel hae you play'd your part,' quo' Meg,
'Your cheeks are like the crimson;
There's nane in Scotland plays sae weel,
Since we lost Habbie Simson.
I've liv'd in Fife, baith maid and wife,
These ten years and a quarter;
Gin you should come to Anster Fair,
Speir ye for Maggie Lauder.'

> 'Maggie Lauder', st.5. Cf. Robert Sempill 1, William Tennant 1

Sempill, Robert ?1595–?1665
Poet, father of Francis Sempill

1 Kilbarchan now may say alas!
For she hath lost her game and grace,
Both *Trixie* and *The Maiden Trace*;
But what remead?
For no man can supply his place:
Hab Simson's dead.

> 'The Life and Death of Habbie Simson, the Piper of Kilbarchan' (c.1640), st.1. Cf. Francis Sempill 2
>
> > The verse-form in this poem, given the name 'Standart Habby' by Allan Ramsay in 'Familiar Epistles Between Lieutenant William Hamilton and Allan Ramsay', became almost obligatory in Scots verse as practised by Ramsay, Robert Fergusson, Robert Burns and a host of others

Shairp, John Campbell 1819–85
Poet and critic

1 Will ye gang wi' me and fare
To the bush aboon Traquair?

> 'The Bush Aboon Traquair', st.1

Shakespeare, William 1564–1616
English playwright and poet

1 KING HENRY: We do not mean the coursing snatchers only,
But fear the main intendment of the Scot,
Who hath been still a giddy neighbour to us:
For you shall read, that my great-grandfather
Never went with his forces into France,
But that the Scot on his unfurnish'd kingdom
Came pouring, like the tide into a breach. . .

> *Henry V* (c.1599), Act 1, sc.1

2 WESTMORELAND: But there's a saying, very old and true,
'If that you will France win,
Then with Scotland first begin':
For once the eagle England being in prey,
To her unguarded nest the weasel Scot
Comes sneaking, and so sucks her princely eggs;
Playing the mouse in absence of the cat,
To teare and havoc more than she can eat.

> *Henry V* (c.1599), Act 1, sc.1

3 MACDUFF: Stands Scotland where it did?
ROSSE: Alas, poor country!
Almost afraid to know itself. It cannot
Be call'd our mother, but our grave; where nothing,
But who knows nothing, is once seen to smile;
Where sighs, and groans, and shrieks that rent the air,
Are made, not mark'd; where violent sorrow seems
A modern ecstasy. . .

> *Macbeth* (c.1606), Act 4, sc.3

Shand, Jimmy 1908–
Accordionist

1 I jist watch the feet o' the best dancers in the hall.

> On the Shand 'dunt', his immaculate sense of musical timing. Quoted in Robbie Shepherd, 'Dance', in P H Scott (ed.), *Scotland: A Concise Cultural History* (1993)

2 Elated? I have never been elated in my life. But I am quite pleased.

> On getting to No.15 in the music-video charts. Quoted in *The Independent* (4 Dec 1995)

Shankly, Bill (William) 1913–81
Football player and manager

1 John, you're immortal.

> Said to Jock Stein (25 May 1967) in the Celtic dressing-room after Celtic had become the first British team to win the European Cup by beating Inter Milan in Lisbon. Quoted by Hugh McIlvanney in *The Observer* (28 May 1967)

The trouble with referees is that they know the rules but they don't know the game.

> During a referees' campaign against foul play (1971)

Some people think football is a matter of life and death. I don't like that attitude. I can assure them it is much more serious than that.

> Quoted in *The Sunday Times* (4 Oct 1981)

I'm a people's man – only the people matter.

> Quoted in Hugh McIlvanney, 'A Man with more than Education', *The Observer* (4 Oct 1981). Reprinted in *McIlvanney on Football* (1994).

Me havin' no education, I had to use my brains.

> Quoted in Hugh McIlvanney, 'A Man with more than Education', *The Observer* (4 Oct 1981). Reprinted in *McIlvanney on Football* (1994).

He merges them all together. They're all helping each other. It's a form of socialism without the politics.

> On Jock Stein's team-training. Quoted in *Only a Game?*, BBC television documentary (1985)

At school we were brought up on tales of Bruce, Wallace and Burns. They were the greatest. Our village was the greatest. Our school was the greatest. And the English were vilified. We thought England was our enemy and the English were poison.
Later on, when I became an international footballer, I was like all Scots when confronted by England, the Auld Enemy. We tend to revert to being savages for ninety minutes on those occasions. We become Wallace and Bruce and Sir James Douglas – the Black Douglas – when we put on the blue jersey.

> Quoted in Roddy Forsyth, *The Only Game: The Scots and World Football* (1990), ch.3. Cf. Jim Sillars 3

Shanks, Norman 1942–

Church of Scotland minister, leader of the Iona Community

Yes, this is a political agenda, but it is God's agenda, because no area of human activity is beyond the scope of God's grace.

> On the Iona Community's support for the poor, and its stance against nuclear weapons. Speech at the General Assembly of the Church of Scotland (May 1996). Quoted in *The Scotsman* (25 May 1996). Cf. George MacLeod 6

Shaw, David d.1856

Forfar weaver

If it wasna for the weavers what wad they do?
They wadna hae claith made oot o'
  oor woo',

They wadna hae a coat neither black nor blue,
Gin it wasna for the wark o' the weavers.

> 'The Wark o' the Weavers', chorus. Quoted in Norman Buchan, *101 Scottish Songs* (1962). Cf. Billy Connolly 1

Shaw, George Bernard 1856–1950

Irish playwright

1 PROTEUS: God help England if she had no Scots to think for her!

> *The Apple Cart* (1929), Act 2

Shepherd, Nan (Anna) 1893–1981

Novelist and poet

1 Martha said it over and over to herself: *Scotland is bounded on the south by England, on the east by the rising sun, on the north by the Arory-bory-Alice, and on the west by Eternity.*

> *The Quarry Wood* (1928), ch.3

2 She perceived that the folk who had made history were not necessarily aware of the making, might indeed be quite ignorant of it: folk to whom a little valley and a broken hilltop spelt infinity and who from that width and reasonableness of life had somehow been uninvolved in the monstrous and sublime unreason of purposes beyond their own intention.

> *The Quarry Wood* (1928), ch.9. Cf. A L Kennedy 1

3 'Good Lord!' she exclaimed. 'Am I such a slave as that? Dependent on a man to complete me! I thought I couldn't be anything without him – I can be my own creator.'

> *The Quarry Wood* (1928), ch.17 (Martha)

4 'It's a grand thing to get leave to live.'

> *The Quarry Wood* (1928), ch.19 (Geordie)

5 There was no false sentiment about Miss Annie: nothing flimsy. She was hard-knit, like a home-made worsted stocking, substantial, honest and durable.

> *The Weatherhouse* (1930), 'The Prologue'

6 Life is an entertainment hard to beat when one's affections are not engaged.

> *The Weatherhouse* (1930), 'The Prologue'

7 O, licht amo' the hills,
  S'uld ye gang oot,
  To what na dark the warld'll fa'.

> 'O, licht amo' the hills', *In the Cairngorms* (1934)

8 The inaccessibility of this loch is part of its power. Silence belongs to it. If jeep finds it out, or if a funicular railway disfigures it, part of its meaning will be gone. The good of the greatest

number is not here relevant. It is necessary to be sometimes exclusive, not on behalf of rank or wealth, but of those human qualities that can apprehend loneliness.

> On Loch Avon, in the Cairngorms. *The Living Mountain* (written in the 1940s, published in 1977), ch.2. Cf. T C Smout 2

9 Walking barefoot has gone out of fashion since Jeanie Deans trudged to London, but no country child grows up without its benediction. Sensible people are reviving the habit.

> *The Living Mountain* (written in the 1940s, published in 1977), ch.11

10 . . . I now understand in some small measure why the Buddhist goes on pilgrimage to a mountain. The journey is in itself part of the technique by which the god is sought. It is a journey into Being; for as I penetrate more deeply into the mountain's life, I penetrate also into my own. . . I am not out of myself, but in myself. I am. To know Being, this is the final grace accorded from the mountain.

> *The Living Mountain* (written in the 1940s, published in 1977), closing lines

Shepherd, Robbie (Robert Horne)
1936–

Broadcaster and Scottish dance music expert

1 Aye, even folk with two left feet (self-styled) can get that special inner feeling which the music and the dance excites in us. Take away our music and dance, and part of our heritage is gone. What was it that is oft quoted on the Scot? – 'The best way to dish out punishment to an enemy who is Scottish is to nail his boot to the floor and make him listen to a Jimmy Shand record.'

> 'Dance', in P H Scott (ed.), *Scotland: A Concise Cultural History* (1993)

2 The combination of Scottish music and dance have always had a perfect marriage, and, indeed, we find in our culture today remnants of the past with enthusiasts retaining the oral tradition in Gaelic circles of *Port a Beul* – 'mouth music', also known in the north-east of Scotland as 'diddling'. 'Give us the lilt and we will give you the dance' is the motto.

> 'Dance', in P H Scott (ed.), *Scotland: A Concise Cultural History* (1993)

Shinwell, Manny (Emmanuel)
1884–1986

Labour politician, one of the group of 'Red Clydesiders'

1 There is a link between the Scots and the Jews. In fact I'm not sure myself that Scotland isn't the twelfth tribe of Israel. We always lost a tribe somehow or other. Why? It was on the rampage – off on its own – independent, constructive, destructive; it must have been the Scots tribe.

> Quoted in Tom Steel, 'South With Steel', *The Sunday Mail Story of Scotland* (1988), No.9

Shirrefs, Andrew 1762–1800
Poet

1 A cogie o' yill
And a pickle aitmeal,
And a dainty wee drappie o' whisky,
Was our forefathers' dose
For to sweel down their brose,
And keep them aye cheery and frisky.

> 'A Cogie o' Yill', st.1

2 What John Bull despises,
Our better sense prizes;
He denies eatin' blanter ava, man;
But by eatin' o' blanter,
His mare's grown, I'll warrant her,
The manliest brute o' the twa, man.

> 'A Cogie o' Yill', st.5
>
> > A riposte to Dr Johnson's definition of *oats* (blanter). Cf. Robert Fergusson 21, Samuel Johnson 1

Shorter Catechism, The 1643
The Presbyterian catechism as agreed by the Assembly of Divines at Westminster in 1643

1 QUESTION I: What is the chief end of man? ANSWER: Man's chief end is to glorify God, and to enjoy him for ever.

> Cf. Robert Louis Stevenson 70

Shortreed, Robert 1762–1829
Sheriff-Substitute of Roxburghshire and lifelong friend of Walter Scott

1 He was *makin' himsell* a' the time, but he didna ken maybe what he was about till years had passed: At first he thought o' little, I dare say, but the queerness and the fun.

> On Walter Scott's 'raids' into Liddesdale in the 1790s. Quoted in J G Lockhart, *Memoirs of the Life of Sir Walter Scott, Bart.* (1837–8), ch.7
>
> > On these 'raids' Scott gathered ballads and tales later used in the *Minstrelsy of the Scottish Border* and the Waverley novels. Shortreed knew Liddesdale well, acted as his guide, and introduced him to various local 'characters'

Sillars, Jim (James) 1937–

Labour, and later Nationalist, politician and MP, and political columnist

1 Don't Butcher Scotland's Future

> Title of pamphlet, co-written with Alex Eadie (1968)

>> At this time he was a Labour MP. While the pamphlet made the case for Scottish government reform, its most striking feature was the violence of its attack on the idea of an independent Scotland. This contributed to Sillars becoming known as 'the Hammer of the Nats'

2 The days of being patronised, lectured to, bullied and insulted are over. Opinion in England counts for nothing. It is what we believe about ourselves that is proving decisive. We'll soon be saying goodbye, Mr Pearce. We'll wave to you and yours as we pass you on the fast lane in Europe.

> *The Scotsman* (30 Jan 1992)

>> In the run-up to the 1992 general election, he was responding to English journalist Ed Pearce who had written in the *Guardian* (29 Jan 1992), 'Scotland costs us, nags us and grinds on. She may be surprised at how easily and comfortably we let her go'. In the event, Sillars lost his Govan seat in the election and Scotland remained part of the UK

3 The great problem is that Scotland has too many ninety-minute patriots whose nationalist outpourings are expressed only at major sporting events.

> Interview on Scottish Television after the 1992 general election. Quoted in *The Herald* (24 Apr 1992). Cf. Bill Shankly 7

Simple Minds

Pop group, fronted by Jim Kerr

1 Promised You a Miracle

> Title of song (1982)

2 Someone, Somewhere in Summertime

> Title of song (1982)

3 Don't You (Forget About Me)

> Title of song (1983)

Simpson, Sir James Young 1811–70

Obstetrician

1 This is far better and stronger than ether.

> Said on waking (4 Nov 1847), prostrate on the floor, after experimenting with the inhalation of chloroform. Quoted in E B Simpson, *Sir James Y Simpson* (1896), ch.4

>> Having first used ether as an anaesthetic in childbirth, Simpson discovered the more effective properties of chloroform, not without danger to his own health

2 I feel that the greater good I can accomplish for my profession and humanity, the greater will always be the temporary blame attempted to be heaped on me by the bigoted portion of the profession.

> Quoted in E B Simpson, *Sir James Y Simpson* (1896), ch.4

>> His work on relieving the pain of childbirth drew fierce criticism from doctors and clerics alike, who claimed it went against Holy Scripture ('In sorrow thou shalt bring forth children', Genesis 3:16). But, as Rosalind K Marshall points out, Simpson's patients were delighted by the introduction of chloroform: '[His] first patient was so overwhelmed that she christened her baby girl "Anaesthesia" '. (*Virgins and Viragos*, 1983, ch.13)

Simpson, James 1934–

Minister, Moderator of the General Assembly of the Church of Scotland (1994)

1 Just as you can't feed poison to cattle and not expect a bad effect, we also have to be wary about how we feed the minds of children. Feeding the mind is as important as feeding the body. Children often learn more from television than they do from their parents. I'm not against TV, but I am against it when it is totally uncontrolled. Children are often being raised by three parents and sometimes the most dominant one is the one sitting in the corner of the living room – the TV set.

> Drawing a parallel with 'the BSE scare'. Quoted in *The Inverness Courier* (12 Apr 1996)

Sinclair (of Ulbster), Sir John 1754–1835

Agriculturist and politician, organiser of the first Statistical Account of Scotland

1 ... the education of females, when it is considered only as a preparation for fashionable life, seldom leads to a happy result, for... the great objects of attention too often are merely to hold up the head, to point the toes, to learn a smattering of French and Italian, to play on some musical instrument, to draw and to receive instructions in the more useless and flimsy parts of needlework to the almost total neglect of mental attainments and of moral and religious principles.

> *Analysis of the Statistical Account of Scotland* (1826)

Skinner, John 1721–1807

Jacobite songwriter and Episcopalian minister

1 The ewie wi' the crookit horn,
Wha that kent her might hae sworn,
Sic a ewe was never born,
Here about, nor far awa'.

'The Ewie Wi' The Crookit Horn', st.1

2 Come gie's a sang, Montgomery cry'd,
And lay your disputes a' aside,
What signifies 't for folks to chide
For what's been done afore them.
Let Whig an' Tory a' agree,
Whig an' Tory, Whig an' Tory,
Whig an' Tory a' agree,
Tae drop their whigmigmorum.
Let Whig an' Tory a' agree
Tae spend this nicht wi' mirth an' glee,
An' cheerfu' sing alang wi' me
The Reel o' Tullochgorum.

'Tullochgorum', st.1

Robert Burns called this 'the best Scotch song
Scotland ever saw'

Skirving, Adam 1719–1803

Jacobite songwriter

1 Hey, Johnnie Cope, are ye waukin' yet?
Or are your drums a-beating yet?
If ye were waukin' I wad wait
Tae gang tae the coals i' the mornin'.

Cope sent a challenge frae Dunbar:
'Charlie, meet me an ye daur,
An' I'll learn ye the art o' war
If ye'll meet me i' the mornin'.'

When Charlie looked the letter upon
He drew his sword the scabbard from:
'Come, follow me, my merry men,
And we'll meet Johnnie Cope i' the morning.'

'Johnnie Cope', chorus and st.1–2

The song commemorates the Battle of
Prestonpans in 1745, which Skirving, an East
Lothian farmer, may have witnessed. He
was a canny man: challenged to a duel by
a Lieutenant Smith whose less than heroic
actions during the battle he had mocked in
another song, 'Trant Muir', he said: 'Tell
him to come here an I'll tak a look at him. If
I think I am fit to fecht him, I'll fecht him.
Gin no, I'll dae as he did – I'll rin awa.'

Skirving, William 18th century

Political radical

1 It is altogether unavailing for your lordship to
menace me; for I have long learned to fear not
the face of man.

To Lord Braxfield, before whom he was on trial

for sedition (1794). Quoted in John Kay, *Original
Portraits* (1877 edition), Vol.1, p.169. Cf. 4th
Earl of Morton 1

In a typical display of his disregard for fair
play when it came to 'radicals', Braxfield said
of Skirving to the jury, 'It would be very
difficult for me to conceive it possible that this
man, now at the bar, can be found not guilty.'
Quoted in Lord Cockburn, *An Examination
of the Trials for Sedition* (1888), Vol.1, p.286

Slessor, Mary Mitchell 1848–1915

*Missionary, who spent much of her life in
Calabar, Nigeria*

1 Creeds and ministers and books are all good
enough but look you to Jesus!

Letter to 'Maggie' (17 Apr 1887), in Dundee
Museum. Quoted in James Buchan, *The
Expendable Mary Slessor* (1980), ch.5

After her death, T D Maxwell, Justice of the
Supreme Court of Calabar, wrote of her: 'Her
outlook on this life – and on the next – was
never narrow. Her religion was above religion
– certainly above religious differences.' (See
Buchan, 'Epilogue')

2 To give an idea of the drink traffic here would
baffle my pen. There is nothing like it anywhere
I have ever been. I have seen about five shillings
worth of legal trade done here with Calabar and
I have seen barrels of rum and boxes of gin by
the score. *Everybody* drinks. I have lain down
at night knowing that not a sober man and
hardly a sober woman was within miles of me.

On the drink problems of the Okoyong people.
Quoted in James Buchan, *The Expendable Mary
Slessor* (1980), ch.8

3 God and one are always a majority.

Handwritten note in one of her Bibles, held in
Dundee Museum. Quoted in James Buchan, *The
Expendable Mary Slessor* (1980), ch.8.

The words 'Un homme avec Dieu est toujours
dans la majorité' ('A man with God is always in
the majority') are inscribed on the Reformation
Monument in Geneva, and are sometimes
attributed to John Knox

4 What a strange thing is sympathy. Undefinable,
untranslatable, and yet the most real thing
and the greatest power in human life. How
strangely our souls leap out to other souls
without our choosing or knowing the why. The
man or woman who possesses this subtle gift
of sympathy, possesses the most precious thing
on earth.

Quoted in James Buchan, *The Expendable Mary
Slessor* (1980), ch.11

5 It will be trying to get back to the home kind of
life and of language. . . I shall just want to find
a place to hide in: away from conventionalities
and all the paraphernalia of civilisation.

Anticipating a visit to Scotland in 1898. Quoted

in James Buchan, *The Expendable Mary Slessor* (1980), ch.12

> At the end of this trip to Scotland, she refused requests that she extend her leave, saying to the Foreign Missions Committee, 'If ye dinna send me back, I'll swim back'

Money is something I do not understand because I've never had to deal with it. What's money to God? The difficult thing is to make men and women. Money lies all about us in the world and He can turn it on to our path as easily as He sends a shower of rain.

> Reply to a friend who asked her what she would do for money. Quoted in James Buchan, *The Expendable Mary Slessor* (1980), ch.14

Without the Gospel. . . the very men you are educating with guns and motors and telegraph will one day turn you all out and keep Africa for the Africans.

> Letter to Charles Partridge (7 Jul 1909). Quoted in James Buchan, *The Expendable Mary Slessor* (1980), ch.16

I'm lame, feeble and foolish; the wrinkles are wonderful – no concertina is so wonderfully folded and convoluted. I'm a wee, wee, wifie, very little buikit but I grip on well none the less.

> Letter to friends, on completing 36 years as a missionary (Sep 1912). Quoted in James Buchan, *The Expendable Mary Slessor* (1980), ch.17

> The writer Mary Kingsley had written, after spending several days with her, '. . . the type of man Miss Slessor represents is rare. There are but few who have the power of resistance to the malarial climate, and of acquiring the language and an insight into the negro mind, so perhaps after all it is no great wonder that Miss Slessor stands alone as she certainly does.' (*Travels in West Africa*, 1897)

Don't grow up to be a nervous old maid. Gird yourself up for the battle outside somewhere, and keep your heart young. Give up your whole being to create music everywhere, in the light places, and in the dark places, and your life will make melody. . .

> Letter to a woman in Scotland (1914). Quoted in James Buchan, *The Expendable Mary Slessor* (1980), ch.18

Smellie, William 1740–95

Printer, antiquary and co-founder of the Encyclopaedia Britannica

'Here I stand at what is called the *Cross of Edinburgh*, and can, in a few minutes, take fifty men of genius and learning by the hand.'

> Quoting 'Mr Amyat, King's Chemist, a most sensible and agreeable English gentleman', *Literary and Characteristic Lives of Gregory, Kames, Hume, and Smith* (1800), pp.161-2

2 I wrote most of it, my lad, and snipped out from books enough material for the printer. With paste-pot and scissors I composed it.

> On editing the first edition of the *Encyclopaedia Britannica*. Quoted in Alan Taylor, ' "Aa" to "Zyglophyllum" ', *The Sunday Mail Story of Scotland* (1988), No.25

Smiles, Samuel 1812–1904

Moralist, social reformer and surgeon, who published works encouraging self-improvement

1 The spirit of self-help is the root of all genuine growth in the individual.
> *Self-help* (1859), ch.1

2 . . . the man who is always hovering on the verge of want is in a state not far removed from slavery. He is in no sense his own master, but is in constant danger of falling under the bondage of others, and accepting the terms which they dictate to him. He cannot help being, in a measure, servile, for he dares not look the world boldly in the face. . .
> *Self-help* (1859), ch.10

3 Self-respect is the noblest garment with which a man may clothe himself – the most elevating feeling with which the mind can be inspired.
> *Self-help* (1859), ch.11

4 We learn wisdom from failure much more than from success. We often discover what *will* do, by finding out what will not do; and probably he who never made a mistake never made a discovery.
> *Self-help* (1859), ch.11

5 Thrift began with civilisation. It began when men found it necessary to provide for to-morrow, as well as for to-day. It began long before money was invented.
> *Thrift* (1875), ch.1

6 We often hear that 'Knowledge is Power'; but we never hear that Ignorance is Power. And yet Ignorance has always had more power in the world than Knowledge. Ignorance dominates. . .
> Ignorance arms men against each other; provides gaols and penitentiaries; police and constabulary. All the physical force of the State is provided by Ignorance; is required by Ignorance; is very often wielded by Ignorance.
> *Thrift* (1875), ch.4. Cf. James Murray 1

7 A place for everything, and everything in its place.
> *Thrift* (1875), ch.5

8 'It will do!' is the common phrase of those who neglect little things. 'It will do!' has

blighted many a character, blasted many a
fortune, sunk many a ship, burnt down many
a house, and irretrievably ruined thousands
of hopeful projects of human good. It always
means stopping short of the right thing. It is
a makeshift. It is a failure and defeat.

Thrift (1875), ch.9

9 That terrible Nobody! How much he has to answer for. More mischief is done by Nobody than
by all the world besides. Nobody adulterates
our food. Nobody poisons us with bad drink.
Nobody supplies us with foul water. Nobody
spreads fever in blind alleys and unswept lanes.
Nobody leaves towns undrained. . .

Nobody has a theory too – a dreadful theory.
It is embodied in two words – *Laissez faire* –
Let alone.

Thrift (1875), ch.15

10 'Let the common people be taught,' was one of
John Knox's messages. His advice was followed,
and the results were great. . . The parish and
burgh schools of Scotland, and the education
given there, are but the lengthened shadow of
John Knox.

Autobiography (1905), ch.1

Smith, Adam 1723–90

Economist and philosopher

1 How selfish soever man may be supposed, there
are evidently some principles in his nature,
which interest him in the fortune of others,
and render their happiness necessary to him
though he derives nothing from it except the
pleasure of seeing it.

Theory of Moral Sentiments (1759), Part 1, Section
1, ch.1, 'Of Sympathy'

2 Though our brother is upon the rack, as long
as we ourselves are at our ease, our senses will
never inform us of what he suffers. They never
did, and never can, carry us beyond our own
person, and it is by the imagination only that
we can form any conception of what are his
sensations.

Theory of Moral Sentiments (1759), Part 1, Section
1, ch.1, 'Of Sympathy'

3 Were it possible that a human creature could
grow up to manhood in some solitary place,
without any communication with his own
species, he could no more think of his own
character, of the propriety or demerit of his
own sentiments and conduct, of the beauty or
deformity of his own mind, than of the beauty
or deformity of his own face.

The Theory of Moral Sentiments (1759), Part 3,
ch.1, 'Of the Principle of Self-approbation and
Self-disapprobation'. Cf. David Hume 5

4 The division of labour, from which so many
advantages are derived, is not originally the
effect of any human wisdom, which foresees and
intends that general opulence to which it gives
occasion. It is the necessary, though very slow
and gradual consequence of a certain propensity
in human nature which has in view no such
extensive utility; the propensity to truck, barter,
and exchange one thing for another.

*An Inquiry into the Nature and Causes of the
Wealth of Nations* (1776), Bk 1, ch.2

5 It is not from the benevolence of the butcher,
the brewer, or the baker, that we expect our
dinner, but from their regard to their own
interest. We address ourselves, not to their
humanity but to their self-love, and never talk
to them of our own necessities but of their
advantages.

*An Inquiry into the Nature and Causes of the
Wealth of Nations* (1776), Bk 1, ch.2

6 Labour. . . is the real measure of the
exchangeable value of all commodities.

The real price of everything, what everything
really costs to the man who wants to acquire
it, is the toil and trouble of acquiring it.

*An Inquiry into the Nature and Causes of the
Wealth of Nations* (1776), Bk 1, ch.5

7 Labour was the first price, the original purchase-
money that was paid for all things. It was not
by gold or by silver, but by labour, that all the
wealth of the world was originally purchased;
and its value, to those who possess it, and who
want to exchange it for some new productions,
is precisely equal to the quantity of labour which
it can enable them to purchase or command.

*An Inquiry into the Nature and Causes of the
Wealth of Nations* (1776), Bk 1, ch.5

8 The world neither ever saw, nor ever will
see, a perfectly fair lottery; or one in which
the whole gain compensated the whole loss;
because the undertaker could make nothing by
it. . . The soberest people scarce look upon it
as a folly to pay a small sum for the chance
of gaining ten or twenty thousand pounds. . .
In order to have a better chance for some of
the great prizes, some people purchase several
tickets, and others, small share in a still greater
number. There is not, however, a more certain
proposition in mathematics than that the more
tickets you adventure upon, the more likely
you are to be a loser. Adventure upon all the
tickets in the lottery, and you lose for certain;
and the greater number of your tickets the
nearer you approach to this certainty.

*An Inquiry into the Nature and Causes of the
Wealth of Nations* (1776), Bk 1, ch.10, Part 1

9 People of the same trade seldom meet
together, even for merriment and diversion,
but the conversation ends in a conspiracy

against the public, or in some contrivance to raise prices.

An Inquiry into the Nature and Causes of the Wealth of Nations (1776), Bk 1, ch.10, Part 2

It is the highest impertinence and presumption. . . in kings and ministers, to pretend to watch over the economy of private people, and to restrain their expense, either by sumptuary laws, or by prohibiting the importation of foreign luxuries. They are themselves always, and without any exception, the greatest spendthrifts in the society.

An Inquiry into the Nature and Causes of the Wealth of Nations (1776), Bk 2, ch.3

He [the investor of capital in the domestic market] generally, indeed, neither intends to promote the public interest, nor knows how much he is promoting it. . . he intends only his own gain, and he is in this, as in many other cases, led by an invisible hand to promote an end which was no part of his intention.

An Inquiry into the Nature and Causes of the Wealth of Nations (1776), Bk 4, ch.2

> This is the only mention of the famous 'invisible hand' in the entire work

To found a great empire for the sole purpose of raising up a people of customers may at first sight appear a project fit only for a nation of shopkeepers. It is, however, a project altogether unfit for a nation of shopkeepers; but extremely fit for a nation that is governed by shopkeepers.

An Inquiry into the Nature and Causes of the Wealth of Nations (1776), Bk 4, ch.7, Part 3

In the progress of the division of labour, the employment of the far greater part of those who live by labour, that is, of the great body of people, comes to be confined to a few very simple operations; frequently to one or two. . . The man whose whole life is spent in performing a few simple operations, of which the effects are, perhaps, always the same, or very nearly the same, has no occasion to exert his understanding, or to exercise his invention in finding out expedients for removing difficulties which never occur. He naturally loses, therefore, the habit of such exertion, and generally becomes as stupid and ignorant as it is possible for a human creature to become.

An Inquiry into the Nature and Causes of the Wealth of Nations (1776), Bk 5, ch.1

Science is the great antidote to the poison of enthusiasm and superstition.

An Inquiry into the Nature and Causes of the Wealth of Nations (1776), Bk 5, ch.1

Upon the whole, I have always considered him, both in his lifetime and since his death, as approaching as nearly to the idea of a perfectly wise and virtuous man, as perhaps the nature of human frailty will permit.

> On David Hume. Letter to William Strahan, who published it in 1777, together with Hume's 'My Own Life', under the title *The Life of David Hume Esq., Written by Himself*
>
> > Smith's comments, which followed a description of his friend's great equanimity in dying not believing in an afterlife, infuriated those who considered Hume's philosophy morally subversive

Smith, Alexander 1830–67

Poet

1 City! I am true son of thine;
Ne'er dwelt I where great mornings shine
Around the bleating pens;
Ne'er by the rivulets I strayed,
And ne'er upon my childhood weighed
The silence of the glens.
Instead of shores where ocean beats,
I hear the ebb and flow of streets.

'Glasgow', *City Poems* (1857), st.2

2 In thee, O City! I discern
Another beauty, sad and stern.

'Glasgow', *City Poems* (1857), st.6

3 And through thy heart, as through a dream,
Flows on that black disdainful stream;
All scornfully it flows,
Between the huddled gloom of masts,
Silent as pines unvexed by blasts –
'Tween lamps in streaming rows.
O wondrous sight! O stream of dread!
O long dark river of the dead!

'Glasgow', *City Poems* (1857), st.11

4 A sacredness of love and death
Dwells in thy noise and smoky breath.

'Glasgow', *City Poems* (1857), st.17

5 It is not of so much consequence what you say, as how you say it. Memorable sentences are memorable on account of some single irradiating word.

'On the Writing of Essays', *Dreamthorp* (1863)

6 A man gazing on the stars is proverbially at the mercy of the puddles on the road.

'Men of Letters', *Dreamthorp* (1863)

7 . . . death is the most ordinary thing in the world. . . But the difference between death and other forms of human experience lies in this, that we can gain no information about it. The dead man is wise, but he is silent.

'On Death and the Fear of Dying', *Dreamthorp* (1863)

8 If you wish to make a man look noble, your best course is to kill him. What superiority he may

have inherited from his race, what superiority
nature may have personally gifted him with,
comes out in death.

> 'On Death and the Fear of Dying',
> *Dreamthorp* (1863)

9 . . . a man's real possession is his memory.
In nothing else is he rich, in nothing else is
he poor.

> 'On Death and the Fear of Dying',
> *Dreamthorp* (1863)

10 Stirling, like a huge brooch, clasps Highlands
and Lowlands together.

> *A Summer in Skye* (1865), 'Stirling and the
> North'. Cf. Rosalind Mitchison 1

Smith, Alison 1962–
Short-story writer

1 I don't find labels at all helpful. Where do
you start and where do you stop? Scottish,
lesbian, right-handed, Catholic, Invernesian. . .
everything is relevant and none of them is more
relevant than the other, not really.

> Interviewed in Caroline Gonda, 'An Other
> Country?': Mapping Scottish/Lesbian/Writing',
> in Christopher Whyte (ed.), *Gendering the Nation:
> Studies in Modern Scottish Literature* (1995)

Smith, G(eorge) Gregory 1823–1910
Literary critic and scholar

1 . . . the literature [of Scotland] is remarkably
varied, and. . . becomes, under the stress
of foreign influence and native division and
reaction, almost a zigzag of contradictions. The
antithesis need not, however, disconcert us.
Perhaps in the very combination of opposites
– what either of the two Sir Thomases, of
Norwich and Cromarty, might have been willing
to call 'the Caledonian antisyzygy' – we have a
reflection of the contrasts which the Scot shows
at every turn, in his political and ecclesiastical
history, in his polemical restlessness, in his
adaptability. . . in his practical judgement.

> *Scottish Literature: Character and Influence* (1919),
> ch.1, 'Two Moods' Cf. Edwin Muir 7

2 . . . the Scot, in that medieval fashion which
takes all things as granted, is at his ease
in both 'rooms of life', and turns to fun,
and even profanity, with no misgivings. For
Scottish literature is more medieval in habit
than criticism has suspected, and owes some
part of its picturesque strength to this freedom
in passing from one mood to another. It takes
some people more time than they can spare
to see the absolute propriety of a gargoyle's
grinning at the elbow of a kneeling saint.

> *Scottish Literature: Character and Influence* (1919),
> ch.1, 'Two Moods'.

Smith, Iain Crichton
(Iain Mac a' Ghobhainn) 1928–
Poet, novelist and short-story writer

1 Some days were running legs and joy
and old men telling tomorrow would be
a fine day surely: for sky was red
at setting of sun between the hills.

> 'Some Days Were Running Legs', *The Long
> River* (1955), st.1

2 Gun fhios dhomh tha thu air aigeann m'inntinn
mar fhear-tadhail grunnd na mara
le chlogaid 's a dhà shùil mhóir
's chan aithne dhomh ceart d' fhiamh no
do dhòigh
an déidh còig bliadhna shiantan
tìme dòrtadh eadar mise 's tù. . .

† Without my knowing it you are at the bottom
of my mind
like one who visits the bottom of the sea
with his helmet and his two great eyes
and I do not rightly know your appearance or
your manner
after five years of showers
of time pouring between me and you. . .

> 'Tha thu air Aigeann m'Inntinn' ('You are at the
> Bottom of my Mind'), *Bùrn is Aran* (1960), st.1

3 . . . 'se 'n rùm-sa sgàthan a cuid smaointean,
armachd ás nach tig ceòl fàsmhor.

Oir 'se 'n ceòl a sheinneas e ri chéile
an òige fhéin nach till tuilleadh.
Tha a sùil a' sguabadh nan sràidean,
tha tìm 'na chrùban anns an uinneig.

† . . . this room is the mirror of her thoughts,
armoury from which no growing music
will come.

For the music that will harmonise it
is youth itself that will never return.
Her eye is sweeping the streets.
Time is crouching in the window.

> 'A' Chailleach' ('The Old Woman'), *Bùrn is Aran*
> (1960), st.4–5

4 Am màireach théid mi dhachaidh do m'eilean
a' fiachainn ri saoghal a chur an dìochuimhn'.

† Tomorrow I shall go home to my island
trying to put a world into forgetfulness.

> 'A' Dol Dhachaidh' ('Going Home'), *Bùrn is
> Aran* (1960), st.1

5 Ach bidh mi smaointinn. . .
air an teine mhór th'air cùl ar smuain,
Nagasàki 's Hiroshìma,
is cluinnidh mi ann an rùm leam fhìn
taibhs' no dhà a' sìor-ghluasad,

taibhs' gach mearachd, taibhs' gach cionta,
taibhs' gach uair a ghabh mi seachad
air fear leòint' air rathad clachach. . .

But I will be thinking. . .
of the great fire at the back of our thoughts,
Nagasaki and Hiroshima,
and I will hear in a room by myself
a ghost or two ceaselessly moving,

the ghost of each error, the ghost of each guilt,
the ghost of each time I walked past
a wounded man on a stony road. . .

'A' Dol Dhachaidh' ('Going Home'), *Bùrn is
Aran* (1960), st.3–4

And she, being old, fed from a mashed plate
as an old mare might droop across a fence
to the dull pastures of her ignorance.
Her husband held her upright while he prayed

to God who is all-forgiving to send down
some angel somewhere who might land perhaps
in his foreign wings among the gradual crops.
She munched, half dead, blindly searching
the spoon.

'Old Woman', *Thistles and Roses* (1961), st.1–2

Sunday of wrangling bells – and salt in the air –
I passed the tall black men and their women
walking
over the tight-locked streets which were
all on fire
with summer ascendant. The seas were talking
and talking. . .

'Sunday Morning Walk', *Thistles and Roses*
(1961), st.1

Deer on the high peaks, calling, calling,
you speak of love, love of the mind and body.
Your absolute heads populate the hills

like daring thoughts, half-in, half-out of
this world,
as a lake might open, and a god peer
into a room where failing darkness glows.

'Deer on the High Hills: A Meditation', *Deer on
the High Hills* (1962), section 9, st.1–2

More than this I do not love you,
Hume of the reasonable mind.
There was an otter crossed the sound,
a salmon in his cold teeth.

'Hume', *The Law and the Grace* (1965)

It's law they ask of me and not grace.
'Conform,' they say, 'your works are not
enough.
Be what we say you should be,' even if
graceful hypocrisy obscures my face.

'The Law and the Grace', *The Law and the Grace*
(1965), st.1

Tha am muir an nochd mar shanas-reice,
leabhar an déidh leabhair a' deàlradh.
Tha m' fhaileas a' ruith sìos do 'n chuan.
Tha mo chraiceann dearg is uaine.

Có sgrìobh mi? Có tha dèanamh bàrdachd

shanas-reice de mo chnàmhan?
Togaidh mi mo dhòrn gorm riutha:
'Gàidheal calma le a chànan.'

† Tonight the sea is like an advertisement,
book after book shining.
My shadow is running down to the sea.
My skin is red and green.

Who wrote me? Who is making a poetry
of advertisements from my bones?
I will raise my blue fist to them:
'A stout Highlander with his language.'

'An t-Oban' ('Oban'), *Bìobuill is Sanasan-Reice*
(1965), section 3

12 Ach 'se lomnochd ghrinn Leòdhais
a rinn obair mo chinn
mar bheart làn de cheòlraidh
mhìorbhail 's mhórachd ar linn.

† But it was the fine bareness of Lewis
that made the work of my head
like a loom full of the music
of the miracles and nobility of our time.

'Ochd Orain airson Céilidh Uir' ('Eight Songs
for a New Ceilidh'), No.2, *Bìobuill is Sanasan-
Reice* (1965)

13 All poetry's made by love and his life shows it.
An ordinary man unable to read or write,
this corrie in Argyllshire made him a poet.
Whatever it was that made that glen all light
worked in his heart till speech was necessary.

'Duncan Ban Macintyre', *Lines Review* No.28
(Mar 1969), st.3

On Duncan Ban Macintyre's poem 'Oran
Coire a' Cheathaich' ('The Song of the Misty
Corrie'). Cf. Donnchadh Bàn Mac an t-Saoir 8

14 Am fear a chailleas a chànain,
caillidh e a shaoghal.
An Gaidheal a chailleas a chànain,
caillidh e an saoghal.

† He who loses his language loses his world.
The Highlander who loses his language loses
the world.

'Am Faigh a' Ghàidhlig Bas?' ('Shall Gaelic
Die?'). In *Lines Review* No.29 (Jun 1969), section 5

15 You lived in Glasgow many years ago.
I do not find your breath in the air.
It was, I think, in the long-skirted thirties
when idle men stood at every corner
chewing their fag-ends of a failed culture.

'You Lived in Glasgow', *Love Poems and
Elegies* (1972)

The poem addresses the poet's mother

16 What love he must have lost to write so much.

'At the Scott Exhibition, Edinburgh Festival',
Love Poems and Elegies (1972)

On Walter Scott

17 The grass is waving now in stranger winds
and I feel sorrow more than I feel joy

as all must do who see the phantom boy
that they once were, scrambling among
the pools,
in his breeze-filled jersey, or among sea shells
entirely concentrate.

'Return to Lewis', *Lines Review* No.51 (Dec
1974), section 4

18 Làrna-mhàireach thachair Cairistìona riùm 's
i dol a thadhal air bean Mhurchaidh Mhóir.
Boireannach dona Crìosdaidh. Chan eil i call
nan òrdaighean uair sam bith, le a sròin bheag
bhiorach 's a bial beag a tha dol gun sgur, 's i
'n còmhnaidh 'na h-aodach dubh.

† The following day I met Christina going to
visit Big Murdoch's wife. A wicked Christian
woman. She never misses the Communions,
with her little, sharp nose and her little mouth
that's on the go without stop; always dressed
in her black clothes.

An t-Aonaran (1976), ch.2

19 'Uill,' ars ise, 'feumaidh mi dhol a thigh
Mhurchaidh Mhóir, air tòir copan siùcair.'
Sheall mi ás a déidh. Dh'fheumadh i siùcar
gu leòr, an dearbh thé. Bha ceòl na mara 'nam
chluasan. 'S fhèarr leam e na cèol dhaoine.

† 'Well,' she said, 'I'll have to go to Big
Murdoch's house to get a cupful of sugar.'
I looked at her as she left. She'd need plenty
of sugar, that one. The music of the sea was
in my ears. I like it better than the music of
mankind.

An t-Aonaran (1976), ch.2

20 A liuthad soitheach a dh'fhàg ar dùthaich
le sgiathan geala a' toirt Chanada orra.
Tha iad mar neapaigearan 'nar cuimhne
's an sàl mar dheòirean,
's anns na croinn aca seòladairean a' seinn
mar eòin air gheugan.

† The many ships that left our country
with white wings for Canada.
They are like handkerchiefs in our memories
and the brine like tears
and in their masts sailors singing
like birds on branches.

'Na h-Eilthirich' ('The Exiles'). In Donald
MacAulay (ed.), *Nua-Bhàrdachd Ghàidhlig*
(*Modern Scottish Gaelic Poems*, 1976)

21 ... I sometimes have a nightmare in which I
think that there are more teachers in Scotland
than there are pupils, and I yearn for the love
of ideas for their own sake: for the free play
of the mind.

'Between Sea and Moor', in Maurice Lindsay
(ed.), *As I Remember* (1979)

22 It is not a witticism to say 'Shall Gaelic die?'
What that means is 'Shall we die?' For on the
day that I go home to the island and speak

to my neighbour in English it is not only the
language that has died but in a sense the two
who no longer speak it. We would be elegies
on the face of the earth, empty and without
substance.

'Real People in a Real Place' (1982), *Towards the
Human* (1986)

23 The sea is blazing with a bitter flame.
'When are you leaving? When did you
come home?'
The island is the anvil where was made
the puritanical heart. The daisies foam
out of the summer grass. The rigid dead
sleep by the Braighe, tomb on separate tomb.

A Life (1986), 'Lewis 1928–45'

24 Canada to me was a very impressive country
but without resonance. It was like a house too
new to have random and ancient creakings.
Day after day the weather was hot and the sky
a stainless blue, but I longed for the corrupt
history of Scotland, for its rains and its historical
labyrinthine darkness.

'Bouquets and Brickbats', *The Sunday Mail Story
of Scotland* (1988), No.29

25 Even with all the complexities of the modern
world I find the idea of community important... Any community is very complex as a
family is. In a community everyone knows who
you are, what you are. You are labelled as a
worker or a dreamer or an idiot. Scotland's 'I
kent your faither' syndrome is often mocked.
I am not sure that there isn't a deep truth in
it, a deep democratic truth...
I think it is not the cult of the individual we
require and certainly not in Scotland. It is the
cult of community and anything which serves
it should be helped.

'Me and the Little White Rose' (1st *Cencrastus*
Hugh MacDiarmid Annual Memorial Lecture,
30 Nov 1989), published in *Cencrastus* No.36
(Spring 1990)

26 Now at a certain time, the potato and the
herring come together on the one plate...
Was it predestined that that particular herring
and that particular potato should meet – the
herring that was roving the sea in its grey
dress and the potato that was lying in the
earth in its brown dress? That is a very
deep question. And the herring cannot do
without the potato, nor for that matter can the
potato do without the herring. For they need
each other.

'Murdo and the Potato', *Thoughts of Murdo*
(1993). Cf. Traditional songs 70

27 When the Access card is lost, there shall be
sorrow in the glen...
The man who sings through the nose will signal
the downfall of the Mod...

The end of the world is near when the
MacBrayne's ship will be on time.

From 'Murdo's Prophecies', *Thoughts of
Murdo* (1993)

The oral tradition? I remember that we used to
sit around the fire in the ceilidh house reading
The Guns of Navarone aloud. It took three
weeks. Before that we had *Where Eagles Dare*...
I listen to Scottish Dance Music as I am
immune to it now, and it doesn't affect me.

'Seordag's Interview with the BBC, by Murdo',
Thoughts of Murdo (1993)

As I grow older I have learned to love light and
flowers and Aberdeen for me is the flower of
cities. It is easy to call it parochial. But what
one is looking for is a different word. 'Cities
that have been good to us we love. The rest we
are resigned to,' I once wrote about Aberdeen.
My love for it will not fade, for it was here that
my mind expanded, and I learnt about poetry
and ideas.

'A Maze and Grace', in *The Scotsman*, 'Weekend'
(15 Jun 1996)

Smith, Irvine
Sheriff

Do you not speak English? If you think aye in
Scots means yes, it doesn't.

Quoted in *The Scotsman* (29 Apr 1994)

Said to a woman appearing before him at
a means inquiry court in Stirling. She had
answered 'Aye' when asked by the depute
sheriff clerk to confirm that her name was
correctly given

Smith, James 1824–87
Children's poet

Wee Joukydaidles,
Toddlin' out an' in:
Oh but she's a cuttie,
Makin' sic a din!
Aye sae fou o' mischief,
An' minds na what I say:
My verra heart gangs loup, loup,
Fifty times a day!

'Wee Joukydaidles', st.1

Smith, John 1938–94
*Labour politician, MP and Labour Party leader
(1992–4)*

There is, as all aficionados will testify,
something special about Iona... Heaven, for
me, is walking on the springy machair at the

edge of a white Hebridean beach, watching the
summer sun sparkle on the ultramarine sea.

'Mr Smith Goes to Town', *The Sunday Mail
Story of Scotland* (1988), No.47

After his untimely death in May 1994, John
Smith was buried on the island of Iona

2 I am a doer and I want to do things, but there
exists the terrible possibility in politics that
you might never win.

Quoted in *You* magazine (22 Mar 1992), prior to
the 1992 General Election. Reprinted in Andy
McSmith, *John Smith: A Life 1938–1994* (1993,
updated 1994), Foreword

3 I don't think brains are terribly important in
politics or in anything else. You just need a
necessary minimum.

Quoted in *The Independent* (24 Mar 1992)

4 Today we are embarking on a great journey,
a journey to eliminate poverty, injustice
and homelessness; a journey to build lasting
sustainable prosperity; a journey to persuade
millions of the strength of our vision, the
relevance of our policies, the urgency of our
demand for change...

Speech on being elected leader of the Labour
Party (Jul 1992)

5 Unfinished business...

His phrase for establishing a Scottish parliament,
a policy to which he was consistently committed

Smith, Mrs M C (*née* Edgar)
1869–?1938
Poet

1 Whit wey does the engine say *Toot-toot?*
Is it feart to gang in the tunnel?
Whit wey is the furnace no pit oot
When the rain gangs doon the funnel?
What'll I hae for my tea the nicht?
A herrin', or maybe a haddie?
Has Gran'ma gotten electric licht?
Is the next stop Kirkcaddy?

'The Boy in the Train', st.1

2 For I ken mysel' by the queer-like smell
That the next stop's Kirkcaddy!

'The Boy in the Train', st.4

Kirkcaldy's linoleum industry has always
produced a strong and distinctive smell,
for which the 'Lang Toun' is still famous

Smith, Sydney 1771–1845
*English writer and co-founder of the
Edinburgh Review*

1 When shall I see Scotland again? Never shall
I forget the happy days I passed there amidst
odious smells, barbarous sounds, bad suppers,

excellent hearts, and the most enlightened and cultivated understandings.

Letter to Francis Jeffrey (27 Mar 1814)

2 I look upon Switzerland as a sort of inferior Scotland.

Letter to Lord Holland (1815), in N C Smith (ed.), *Letters of Sydney Smith* (1953)

3 The Scotch, whatever other talents they may have, can never condense; they always begin a few days before the flood, and come *gradually* down to the reign of George III, forgetful of nothing but the shortness of human life, and the volatility of human attention.

Letter to Lady Holland (1819)

4 It requires a surgical operation to get a joke well into a Scotch understanding. Their only idea of wit, which prevails occasionally in the north and . . . is so infinitely distressing to people of good taste, is laughing immoderately at stated intervals.

Quoted in Lady Holland, *Memoir of the Reverend Sydney Smith* (1855), Vol.1, ch.2. Cf. J M Barrie 13, David Rorie 4

Smith stayed in Edinburgh from 1798 to 1803, and his remark should be seen as good-natured banter rather than malicious prejudice

5 That garret of the earth – that knuckle-end of England – that land of Calvin, oat-cakes, and sulphur.

On Scotland. Quoted in Lady Holland, *Memoir of the Reverend Sydney Smith* (1855), Vol.1, ch.2

Smith, Sydney Goodsir 1915–75
New Zealand-born poet

1 We've come intil a gey queer time
Whan scrievin Scots is near a crime,
'There's no one speaks like that', they fleer,
– But wha the deil spoke like King Lear?

'Epistle to John Guthrie', *Skail Wind* (1941), st.1

2 Did Johnnie Keats whan he was drouth
Ask 'A beaker full o the warm South'?
Fegs no, he leaned across the bar
An called for 'A point of bitter, Ma!'

'Epistle to John Guthrie', *Skail Wind* (1941), st.5

3 My bonie Edinburrie,
Auld Skulduggerie!
Flat on her back sevin nichts o' the week,
Earnan her breid wi her hurdies' sweit.

Under the Eildon Tree (1948; 1954), Elegy 13, 'The Black Bull o' Norroway', Part 4

4 This rortie wretched city
Sair come doun frae its auld hiechts
– The hauf o't smug, complacent,

Lost til all pride of race or spirit,
The tither wild and rouch as ever
In its secret hairt . . .

On Edinburgh. *Kynd Kittock's Land* (1965), Part 1

5 Some dreams are sleepin in the bottom
o' a glass,
Some ride in the freezing winds of space,
Some snore in the dampest oxter o' a tree . . .

Kynd Kittock's Land (1965), Part 6

6 Wha'd hae daith when there's life?
Wha'd tak a corp in his teeth
When there's livin lips to pree?

'Three', *Fifteen Poems and a Play* (1969)

7 Wha seeks eternity in a rotten flouer?
Wha racks the mountains faa like stour
When nane there'll be to see it?

Wha'd dae this and wha'd dae yon
When end is nocht but naething?
You. Me. Anither.

'Three', *Fifteen Poems and a Play* (1969)

The poem has as its epigraph Lenin's words, 'Three men make a revolution'

Smith, Walter Chalmers 1824–1908
Clergyman and hymnwriter

1 Immortal, invisible, God only wise,
In light inaccessible hid from our eyes,
Most blessèd, most glorious, the Ancient
of Days,
Almighty, victorious, Thy great Name
we praise.

Hymn, 'Immortal, invisible, God only wise', st.1

2 One thing I of the Lord desire, –
For all my way hath miry been –
Be it by water or by fire,
O make me clean!

Hymn, 'One thing I of the Lord desire', st.1

Smith, Sir William Alexander 1854–1914
Founder of the Boys' Brigade (1883)

1 Sure and Stedfast.

Motto of the Boys' Brigade

Appearing with the emblem of an anchor, the motto, complete with Biblical spelling, is from Hebrews 6:19: 'Which hope we have as an anchor of the soul, both sure and stedfast . . .' Smith's aim was 'the advancement of God's Kingdom among Boys'

Smollett, Tobias (George) 1721–71
Novelist

1 Mourn, hapless Caledonia, mourn
Thy banish'd peace, thy laurels torn!

Thy sons, for valour long renown'd,
Lie slaughter'd on their native ground;
Thy hospitable roofs no more
Invite the stranger to the door;
In smoky ruins sunk they lie,
The monuments of cruelty...

On the aftermath of Culloden. 'The Tears of
Scotland' (1746), st.1

What foreign arms could never quell,
By civil rage and rancour fell.

'The Tears of Scotland' (1746), st.3

...some folks are wise, and some are otherwise.

The Adventures of Roderick Random (1748), ch.6

'We have been jeered, reproached, buffeted,
pissed upon, and at last stript of our money;
and I suppose by and by we shall be stript of
our skins.'

The Adventures of Roderick Random (1748), ch.15
(Hugh Strap)

'London is the devil's drawing-room.'

The Adventures of Roderick Random (1748), ch.18
(Hugh Strap)

'...he spoke little, and seemed to have
no reserve; for what he said was ingenuous,
sensible, and uncommon. In short,' said she,
'he was formed for the ruin of our sex.'

The Adventures of Roderick Random (1748), ch.22
(Miss Williams)

'As I have no estate to leave behind me, I am not
troubled with the importunate officiousness of
relations, or legacy hunters, and I consider the
world as made for me, not me for the world:
It is my maxim therefore to enjoy it while I
can, and let futurity shift for itself.'

The Adventures of Roderick Random (1748), ch.45
(Mr Medlar)

I am heartily tired of this Land [England]
of Indifference and Phlegm where the finer
Sensations of the Soul are not felt, and Felicity
is held to consist in stupifying Port and
overgrown Buttocks of Beef, where Genius is
lost, Learning undervalued, and Taste altogether
extinguished, and Ignorance prevails to such a
degree that one of our Chelsea Club asked me
if the weather was good when I crossed the
Sea from Scotland...

Letter to Alexander Carlyle (1 Mar 1754), in
L M Knapp (ed.), The Letters of Tobias Smollett
(1970), p.33

...that great Cham of Literature, Samuel
Johnson.

Letter to John Wilkes (16 Mar 1759). Quoted
in James Boswell, Life of Dr Johnson (1793
edition), Vol.1

In a footnote Boswell wrote: 'In my first

edition this word was printed Chum... and
I animadverted on Dr Smollett's ignorance;
for which let me propitiate the manes of that
ingenious and benevolent gentleman. CHUM
was certainly a mistaken reading for CHAM,
the title of the Sovereign of Tartary, which
is well applied to Johnson, the Monarch of
Literature...'

10 'I think for my part one half of the nation is
mad – and the other not very sound – I don't
see why I ha'n't as good a right to be mad as
another man...'

The Adventures of Sir Launcelot Greaves (1762),
ch.6 (Captain Crowe). Cf. Walter Scott 85

11 I desire you'll clap a pad-luck on the wind-
seller, and let none of the men have excess
to the strong bear – don't forget to have the
gate shit every evening before dark... and I
hope you'll have a watchful eye over the maids.
I know that hussy, Mary Jones, loves to be
rumping with the men.

The Expedition of Humphry Clinker (1771), Letter
from Tabitha Bramble, 2 Apr (instructions to
Mrs Gwyllim, her housekeeper)

12 'Heark ye, Clinker, you are a most notorious
offender – You stand convicted of sickness,
hunger, wretchedness, and want...'

The Expedition of Humphry Clinker (1771), Letter
from Jery Melford, 24 May (Matthew Bramble
to Humphry Clinker)

13 I am inclined to think, no mind was ever
wholly exempt from envy; which, perhaps, may
have been implanted, as an instinct essential
to our nature.

The Expedition of Humphry Clinker (1771), Letter
from Matthew Bramble, 2 Jun

14 'The Scots... have a slight tincture of letters,
with which they make a parade among people
who are more illiterate than themselves; but they
may be said to float on the surface of science,
and they have made very small advances in
the useful arts... Those who affected to extol
the Scots for superior merit, were no friends
to that nation.'

The Expedition of Humphry Clinker (1771), Letter
from Matthew Bramble, 15 Jul (Lieutenant
Lismahago)

15 Edinburgh is a hot-bed of genius.

The Expedition of Humphry Clinker (1771), Letter
from Matthew Bramble, 8 Aug

16 ...I am not yet Scotchman enough to relish
their singed sheep's-head and haggice...
The first put me in mind of the history
of Congo, in which I had read of negroes'
heads sold publickly in the markets; the last,
being a mess of minced lights, livers, suet,
oat-meal, onions, and pepper, inclosed in a

sheep's stomach, had a very sudden effect upon mine. . .

The Expedition of Humphry Clinker (1771), Letter from Jery Melford, 8 Aug

Smout, T(homas) C(hristopher) 1933–

English-born social and economic historian, Professor of Scottish History at St Andrews University (1980–91), Historiographer Royal for Scotland

1 The age of great industrial triumphs was an age of appalling social deprivation. . . I am astounded by the intolerance, in a country boasting of its high moral standards and basking in the spiritual leadership of a Thomas Chalmers, of unspeakable urban squalor, compounded by drink abuse, bad housing, low wages, long hours and sham education.

A Century of the Scottish People 1830–1950 (1986), Introduction

2 Only very good quality tourist development will ever succeed in bringing business or prosperity to the Highlands. Pushing the summer-time equivalent of Blackpool Tower up Scotland's second highest mountain at extreme public expense is not it.

Letter to *The Scotsman* (10 May 1996), opposing plans for a funicular railway on Cairn Gorm. Cf. Nan Shepherd 8

> He was writing in a personal capacity, but the letter was published only three days after Scottish Natural Heritage, of which he was Deputy Chairman, gave its conditional approval to the proposed development

Somerville, Mary (*née* Fairfax) 1780–1872

Mathematician and scientific writer

1 . . . one of the greatest improvements in education is that teachers are now fitted for their duties by being taught the art of teaching.

'Benevolence', *Physical Geography* (1848)

2 A few days after my arrival, although perfectly straight and well-made, I was enclosed in stiff stays with a steel busk in front, while, above my frock, bands drew my shoulders back till the shoulder-blades met. Then a steel rod, with a semi-circle which went under the chin, was clasped to the steel busk in my stays. In this constrained state I, and most of the younger girls, had to prepare our lessons.

> On her experience of Miss Primrose's school in Musselburgh which she attended from age 10 to 11, and where she was 'utterly wretched'. Quoted in Martha Somerville (ed.), *Personal Recollections from Early Life to Old Age of Mary Somerville* (1873), ch.1

3 In our play-hours we amused ourselves with playing at ball, marbles, and especially at 'Scotch and English', a game which represented a raid on the debatable land, or Border between Scotland and England, in which each party tried to rob the other of their playthings. The little ones were always compelled to be English, for the bigger girls thought it too degrading.

> On Miss Primrose's school in Musselburgh. Quoted in Martha Somerville (ed.), *Personal Recollections from Early Life to Old Age of Mary Somerville* (1873), ch.1

4 I was annoyed that my turn for reading was so much disapproved of, and thought it unjust that women should have been given a desire for knowledge if it were wrong to acquire it.

> Quoted in Martha Somerville (ed.), *Personal Recollections from Early Life to Old Age of Mary Somerville* (1873), ch.2

5 I had. . . gone through the first six books of Euclid. . . My father came home for a short time and, somehow or other, finding out what I was about, said to my mother, 'Peg, we must put a stop to this, or we shall have Mary in a strait jacket one of these days. . . '

> Quoted in Martha Somerville (ed.), *Personal Recollections from Early Life to Old Age of Mary Somerville* (1873), ch.3

6 After my marriage I did not dance, for in Scotland it was thought highly indecorous for a married woman to dance. Waltzing, when first introduced, was looked upon with horror, and even in England it was then thought improper.

> Quoted in Martha Somerville (ed.), *Personal Recollections from Early Life to Old Age of Mary Somerville* (1873), ch.9

7 A man can always command his time under the plea of business, a woman is not allowed any such excuse.

> Quoted in Martha Somerville (ed.), *Personal Recollections from Early Life to Old Age of Mary Somerville* (1873), ch.11

8 . . . all the disturbances arising from the reciprocal attraction of the planets and satellites are periodical, whatever the length of the periods may be, so that the stability of the solar system is insured for unlimited ages. The perturbations are only the oscillations of that immense pendulum of Eternity which beats centuries as ours beats seconds.

> Quoted in Martha Somerville (ed.), *Personal Recollections from Early Life to Old Age of Mary Somerville* (1873), ch.11

> Her interest in astronomy had led to her translation (1831, 'The Mechanism of the Heavens') of Pierre Simon Laplace's *Mécanique Céleste*. In 1822, the Irish novelist Maria Edgeworth had written to a friend: 'Mrs

Somerville is the lady who, Laplace says, is the only woman who understands his works. She draws beautifully, and while her head is among the stars her feet are firm upon the earth.'

Age has not abated my zeal for the emancipation of my sex from the unreasonable prejudice too prevalent in Great Britain against a literary and scientific education for women.

Quoted in Martha Somerville (ed.), *Personal Recollections From Early Life to Old Age of Mary Somerville* (1873), ch.17

. . . I firmly believe that the living principle is never extinguished. Since the atoms of matter are indestructible, as far as we know, it is difficult to believe that the spark which gives to their union life, memory, affection, intelligence, and fidelity, is evanescent.

Quoted in Martha Somerville (ed.), *Personal Recollections From Early Life to Old Age of Mary Somerville* (1873), ch.17

Sad to say, no savages are more gross than the lowest ranks in England, or treat their wives with more cruelty.

Quoted in Martha Somerville (ed.), *Personal Recollections From Early Life to Old Age of Mary Somerville* (1873), ch.17

Sorley, Charles Hamilton 1895–1915
Poet, killed in action at Loos (Oct 1915)

All the hills and vales along
Earth is bursting into song,
And the singers are the chaps
Who are going to die perhaps.

'All the hills and vales along', *Marlborough and other poems* (1916), st.1

Such, such is Death: no triumph: no defeat:
Only an empty pail, a slate rubbed clean,
A merciful putting away of what has been.

'Such, such is Death', *Marlborough and other poems* (1916)

When you see millions of the mouthless dead
Across your dreams in pale battalions go,
Say not soft things as other men have said,
That you'll remember. For you need not so.
Give them not praise. For deaf, how should they know
It is not curses heaped on each gashed head?
Nor tears. Their blind eyes see not your tears flow.
Nor honour. It is easy to be dead.

'When you see millions of the mouthless dead', *Marlborough and other poems* (1916)

Soutar, William 1898–1943
Poet, confined to his bed for the last thirteen years of his life with spondylitis

1 As I enter up my thought for each day on the day following there can be no entry for the day on which I die. Let me write it down now. 'To accept life is to give it beauty.'

Diary entry (14 May 1930). Quoted in *Chapman* No.53 (Summer 1988)

2 Somebody nippit me,
Somebody trippit me,
Somebody grippit me roun' and roun':
I ken it was Bawsy Broon:
I'm shair it was Bawsy Broon.

'Bawsy Broon' (1930), *Poems of William Soutar* (ed. W R Aitken, 1988), st.1

3 If the Doric is to come back alive, it will come on a cock-horse.

On the importance of writing in Scots for children. Letter to Hugh MacDiarmid (1931), quoted in Alexander Scott, *Still Life* (1958), p.116

4 Just now as I lifted my eyes to the hillside I saw the trees waving like a wall of fire. If only one could respond to life as the earth to the sun – but the heart is so often a trim little garden with neither the luxuriance nor the conflict of the jungle. It is so easy to retreat within the safe walls of mediocrity.

Diary entry (29 Jun 1932), *Diaries of a Dying Man* (ed. Alexander Scott, 1954)

His father, a joiner, redesigned the window of his room so that he had a view from his bed of the garden and hill beyond

5 Accept your fate; but, if life has set you on a bypath, do not deceive yourself into the belief that this is the best environment for you. Life is no loving father, but a force with which we must contend and to which we must adapt the self.

Diary entry (19 Aug 1932), *Diaries of a Dying Man* (ed. Alexander Scott, 1954)

6 Half doun the hill, whaur fa's the linn
Far frae the flaught o' fowk,
I saw upon a lanely whin
A lanely singin' gowk:
Cuckoo, cuckoo;
And at my back
The howie hill stüde up and spak:
Cuckoo, cuckoo.

'The Gowk' (1932), *Poems of William Soutar* (ed. W R Aitken, 1988), st.1

7 O luely, luely cam she in
And luely she lay doun;
I kent her be her caller lips
And her breists sae sma' an' roun'.

'The Tryst' (1932), *Poems of William Soutar* (ed. W R Aitken, 1988), st.1

8 Sae luely, luely cam she in
Sae luely was she gaen
And wi' her a' my simmer days
Like they had never been.

'The Tryst' (1932), *Poems of William Soutar* (ed.
W R Aitken, 1988), st.4

9 One rarely hears a radio talk or reads an article
on Scottish literature nowadays without meeting
the Calvinistic bogey. Why has our art been
so meagre for 100's of years – *ergo*, because of
Calvinism: and that's that. But surely we are
over-easily contented with this solution which
is but half-a-solution. . . One does not turn
round and blame a creeping creed in itself but
the men who submit to it. If for far too long
Scotland has accepted Calvinism – there can
be no doubt that at one time, and for a lengthy
period, Calvinism was acceptable.

Diary entry (24 Nov 1933), *Diaries of a Dying
Man* (ed. Alexander Scott, 1954). Cf. Fionn
MacColla 3

10 Snow makes us aware of silence, for in such a
multitudinous falling we expect sound.

Diary entry (27 Jan 1935), *Diaries of a Dying
Man* (ed. Alexander Scott, 1954)

11 Whaur yon broken brig hings owre;
Whaur yon water maks nae soun';
Babylon blaws by in stour:
Gang doun wi' a sang, gang doun.

'Song' (1935), *Poems of William Soutar* (ed.
W R Aitken, 1988), st.1

12 Out of the darkness of the womb
Into a bed, into a room:
Out of a garden into a town,
And to a country, and up and down
The earth; the touch of women and men
And back into a garden again:
Into a garden; into a room;
Into a bed and into a tomb;
And the darkness of the world's womb.

'Autobiography' (1937), *Poems of William Soutar*
(ed. W R Aitken, 1988)

13 No dead man is a stranger anywhere:
His speech is silence:
His body native to the earth and air:
His peace beyond pretence:
Look well upon a dead man's innocence;
The truth is there.

'Beyond Country' (1938), *Poems of William Soutar*
(ed. W R Aitken, 1988), st.1

14 Before the emblem of a dead man's face
All banners must bow;
All boundaries arrive at their meeting-place
In the blank of his brow. . .

'Beyond Country' (1938), *Poems of William Soutar*
(ed. W R Aitken, 1988), st.3

15 They only are the wise who claim
This for their foolishness:

To love the beast they cannot tame
Yet cheer the unending chase.

'The Unicorn' (1938), *Poems of William Soutar*
(ed. W R Aitken, 1988), st.3

16 Though the desire for women troubles the body
and the mind, I am yet glad that desire is still
so alive in me, for its death would be ominous
of creative moribundity. . . We gather the
world into the compass of our speculation; and
when our sensuous scope is small, we can keep
contact with the world only by quintessential
symbol. . . there are for me three dominant
images which are as doors into fuller life; and
these are woman, tree and the unicorn.

Diary entry (19 Apr 1939), *Diaries of a Dying
Man* (ed. Alexander Scott, 1954)

17 Wha wud be a tattie-bogle
Dringin oot his days:
Wha wud be a tattie-bogle
In castawa claes?

'Wha wud be a Tattie-Bogle' (1941), *Poems of
William Soutar* (ed. W R Aitken, 1988), st.1

18 John Knox in destination
Warsl'd wi' kirk and state;
And the souchin' o' his spirit
Blaws about Scotland yet.

'John Knox' (1942), *Poems of William Soutar* (ed.
W R Aitken, 1988), st.4

Spalding, Julian 1947–

*English director of Glasgow Museums
and Art Galleries (1989–   )*

1 There are no jobs for the girls. We must be
democratic and make jobs open for all.

Quoted in *The Glasgow Herald* (17 Apr 1990)

He reorganised his department and created a
new post of Keeper of Social History, which
was widely expected to go to Elspeth King,
who had been Keeper of the People's Palace
social history museum for sixteen years. His
remark was interpreted by many as part of a
campaign against King. In *The Sunday Times*
'Ecosse' (21 Apr 1996), Spalding gave his
version of the story: 'I said, "There's no jobs
for the boys." Then I made a joke I've come
to regret. . . "Or for the girls."'

2 The future is artists who want to communicate.
You can be popular and profound. You can be
radical and appeal to a lot of people.

Defending the artistic thinking behind his
selection of works for the Gallery of Modern
Art, Glasgow, opened in March 1996. Quoted
in *The Sunday Times* 'Ecosse' (21 Apr 1996)

3 Modern art is a conspiracy against people. It
operates in its own ridiculous little world. The
establishment sees itself as an arbiter of taste.

If the public don't like what they're given, they're told they don't understand it. . . If the work is unpopular with the public, the art establishment thinks it must be at the cutting edge. And if a work is popular, they won't promote it.

Profile in *The Big Issue* No.75 (26 Apr–9 May 1996). Cf. J D Fergusson 3

Spark, Muriel Sarah (*née* Camberg) 1918–

Novelist and short-story writer

Parents learn a lot from their children about coping with life. It is possible for parents to be corrupted or improved by their children.

The Comforters (1957), ch.6

'Being over seventy is like being engaged in a war. All our friends are going or gone and we survive amongst the dead and the dying as on a battlefield.'

Memento Mori (1959), ch.4 (Miss Taylor to Dame Lettie Colston)

There was altogether too much candour in married life; it was an indelicate modern idea, and frequently led to upsets in a household, if not divorce.

Memento Mori (1959), ch.12

'. . . all my pupils are the crème de la crème.'

The Prime of Miss Jean Brodie (1961), ch.1

'Give me a girl at an impressionable age, and she is mine for life.'

The Prime of Miss Jean Brodie (1961), ch.1

'One's prime is elusive. You little girls, when you grow up, must be on the alert to recognise your prime at whatever time of your life it may occur. You must then live it to the full.'

The Prime of Miss Jean Brodie (1961), ch.1

'Art and religion first; then philosophy; lastly science. That is the order of the great subjects of life, that's their order of importance.'

The Prime of Miss Jean Brodie (1961), ch.2

'To me education is a leading out of what is already there in the pupil's soul. To Miss Mackay it is a putting in of something that is not there, and that is not what I call education, I call it intrusion. . . '

The Prime of Miss Jean Brodie (1961), ch.2

'Whoever has opened the window has opened it too wide,' said Miss Brodie. 'Six inches is perfectly adequate. More is vulgar.'

The Prime of Miss Jean Brodie (1961), ch.3

The Girls of Slender Means

Title of novel (1963)

11 It was Edinburgh that bred within me the conditions of exiledom; and what have I been doing since then but moving from exile to exile? It has ceased to be a fate, it has become a calling.

'What Images Return', in Karl Miller (ed.), *Memoirs of a Modern Scotland* (1970)

12 All grades of society constructed sentences bridged by 'nevertheless'. It would need a scientific study to ascertain whether the word was truly employed more frequently in Edinburgh at the time than anywhere else. It is my own instinct to associate the word, as the core of a thought-pattern, with Edinburgh particularly. I can see the lips of tough elderly women in musquash coats taking tea at MacVittie's, enunciating this word of final justification, I can see the exact gesture of head and chin and gleam of the eye that accompanied it. . . I find that much of my literary composition is based on the nevertheless idea. I act upon it. It was on the nevertheless principle that I turned Catholic.

'What Images Return', in Karl Miller (ed.), *Memoirs of a Modern Scotland* (1970)

13 'There isn't any war and peace any more, no good and evil, no communism, no capitalism, no fascism. There's only one area of conflict left and that's between absurdity and intelligence.'

The Hothouse by the East River (1973), ch.4 (Pierre Hazlett to his father Paul)

14 '*Peter Pan* is a very obscene play.'

The Hothouse by the East River (1973), ch.4 (Pierre Hazlett to his father Paul)

15 'Sex,' she says, 'is a subject like any other subject. Every bit as interesting as agriculture.'

The Hothouse by the East River (1973), ch.5 (Elsa to Paul)

16 It is one of the secrets of Nature in its mood of mockery that fine weather lays a heavier weight on the mind and hearts of the depressed and the inwardly tormented than does a really bad day with dark rain snivelling continuously and sympathetically from a dirty sky.

Territorial Rights (1979), ch.3

17 A Far Cry from Kensington

Title of novel (1988)

Spence, (James) Lewis 1874–1955

Poet and anthropologist

1 As haars the windless waters find
The unguarded instant falls a prey
To sakeless shadows o' the mind,
And a' my life rins back to Tay.

'Great Tay of the Waves', *Plumes of Time* (1926), st.3

2 A hoose is but a puppet-box
  To keep life's images frae knocks,
  But mannikins scrieve oot their sauls
  Upon its craw-steps and its walls;
  Whaur hae they writ them mair sublime
  Than on yon gable-ends o' time?

    'The Prows o' Reikie', *Plumes of Time* (1926)

3 If a' the bluid shed at thy Tron,
  Embro', Embro';
  If a' the bluid shed at thy Tron
  Were sped into a river,
  It wad ca' the mills o' Bonnington,
  Embro', Embro',
  It wad ca' the mills o' Bonnington
  For ever and for ever.

    'Capernaum', *Plumes of Time* (1926), st.1

    Inspired by the Biblical verse, 'And thou,
    Capernaum, which art exalted unto heaven,
    shalt be brought down to hell. . .'
    (Matthew 11.23)

Spottiswoode, Alicia Anne (Lady John Scott) 1810–1900

Composer and songwriter

1 Maxwellton braes are bonnie,
  Where early fa's the dew,
  And it's there that Annie Laurie
  Gi'ed me her promise true;
  Gi'ed me her promise true,
  That ne'er forgot sall be,
  But for bonnie Annie Laurie,
  I'd lay doun my head and dee.

  Her brow is like the snawdrift,
  Her neck is like the swan. . .

    'Annie Laurie' (1835), st.1–2. Cf. William Douglas 1

    Edwin Muir, in *Scottish Journey* (1935), ch.2,
    disparaged this version of 'Annie Laurie' as
    'a symbol of modern Scotland. . . an almost
    unique anthology of hackneyed similes'. He
    also wrote that it was 'a sign that true folk
    sentiment in Scotland has for a long time
    been degenerating, so that a sham substitute
    is more pleasing to Scottish ears than the
    real thing', but it is unclear whether he knew
    William Douglas's original version

2 We'll meet nae mair at sunset, when the weary
  day is dune,
  Nor wander hame thegither, by the lee licht
  o' the mune!

    'Durisdeer', st.1

Stair, 1st Earl of (John Dalrymple) 1648–1707

Judge, Lord Advocate and Secretary of State

1 Just now, my lord Argyll tells me that Glencoe
  hath not taken the oaths, at which I rejoice. It's

a great work of charity to be exact in rooting
out that damnable sept, the worst in all the
Highlands.

    On learning that Alasdair MacIain, chief of the
    Glencoe MacDonalds, had been too late in taking
    an oath of loyalty to King William. Letter to Sir
    Thomas Livingston (11 Jan 1692)

Stair, 1st Viscount (James Dalrymple) 1619–95

Jurist

1 . . . we do always prefer the sense, to the
  subtilty, of law, and do seldom trip by niceties
  or formalities.

    Institutions of the Law of Scotland (1681),
    Dedication to the King

2 Law is the dictate of reason, determining
  every rational being to that which is congruous
  and convenient for the nature and condition
  thereof. . .

    Institutions of the Law of Scotland (1681), Bk 1, 1, 1

3 Liberty. . . is the most native and delightful
  right of man, without which he is capable of no
  other right. . . and the encroachments upon,
  and injuries against, the right of liberty, of all
  others are the most bitter and atrocious.

    Institutions of the Law of Scotland (1681), Bk 1, 2, 2

Stark (or Stirk), Helen (married name Ronaldson) d.1544

Only known woman martyr of the Scottish Reformation

1 They sit in that place quietly who are the cause
  of our death this day, but He who seeth this
  execution upon us all shall, by the grace of
  God, shortly see their nest shaken.

    Reported words on passing the Franciscan
    Greyfriars' house in Perth, on her way to be
    drowned in the Tay (25 Jan 1544). Quoted in
    D P Thomson, *Women of the Scottish Church*
    (1975), ch.1

    She was condemned to death, along with her
    husband, James, and four other men, in the
    heresy trials revived in 1543 by Cardinal David
    Beaton. Her words can be seen as prophetic of
    John Knox's sermon against idolatry made in
    St John's Kirk, Perth (11 May 1559), in which
    he said 'The true way to banish the rooks is
    to pull down their nests, and the rooks will
    fly off'. The friars' houses were one of the
    prime targets of the Protestant Reformers

Statistical Account of Scotland 1791–9

A social survey of every parish in Scotland composed of reports by the Church of Scotland's ministers, organised by Sir John Sinclair of Ulbster

1 Nay, even the scarlet mantle, which lately was

a badge of distinction among the daughters of farmers, is now despised; and, *O tempora! O mores!* the silk-worms of the East must be pillaged, to deck the heads and shoulders of our milk-maids.

William Logan, minister of Symington, Ayrshire, *Statistical Account of Scotland* (1793), Vol.5, p.404

As early as February 1791 George Dempster of Dunnichen wrote to Sinclair that the *Account* would be more read and referred to than any book since the Domesday Book: 'the older it gets, the more valuable it will prove'

2 Thou knowest that the silly snivelling body is not worthy even to keep a door to thy house. Cut him down as a cumberer of the ground; tear him up root and branch, and cast the wild rotten stump out of thy vineyard. Thresh him, O Lord, and dinna spare! O thresh him tightly, with the flail of thy wrath, and mak' a strae wisp o' him to stap the mouth of Hell!

James Finlayson, minister of Symington, Lanarkshire, *Statistical Account of Scotland* (1793), Vol.8, p.589–90, footnote

He was quoting an example of a Seceder preacher's opinion of the established Church's minister, from an open-air meeting conducted some years earlier

3 The use of tobacco may almost be said to be excessive, especially among the female sex; there is scarce a young woman, by the time she has been taught to spin, but has also learned to smoke.

James Adamson, minister of Abernyte, Perthshire, *Statistical Account of Scotland* (1793), Vol.9, p.149

4 Above 20 times more tea is used now than 20 years ago. Bewitched by the mollifying influence of an enfeebling potion, the very poorest classes begin to regard it as one of the necessaries of life, and for its sake resign the cheaper and more invigorating nourishment which the productions of their country afford.

Robert Stirling, minister of Crieff, *Statistical Account of Scotland* (1793), Vol.9, p.594, footnote

5 Their amusements are of the masculine kind. On holidays they frequently play at *golf*; and on Shrove Tuesday there is a standing match at *foot-ball*, between the married and unmarried women, in which the former are always victors.

Alexander Carlyle, minister of Inveresk, East Lothian, *Statistical Account of Scotland* (1795), Vol.16, p.20

Steel, Sir David Martin Scott 1938–

Politician, MP and last leader of the Liberal Party (1976–88)

1 I have the good fortune to be the first Liberal leader for over half a century who is able to say to you at the end of our annual assembly: go back to your constituencies and prepare for government.

Speech at the Liberal Party conference (18 Sep 1981). Cf. Jo Grimond 1

2 To listen to some people in politics, you'd think 'nice' was a four-letter word.

Party political broadcast (1987)

3 We can echo Tennyson and say, 'Come my friends, 'tis not too late to seek a newer world'. In another decade or two, it may be too late.

Speech at the Liberal Democrats conference, Torquay (1993), urging reform and increased support of the United Nations. Quoted in *The Independent* (23 Sep 1993)

Tennyson's words appear in 'Ulysses' (1842)

4 I hope you are under no illusion. I hope you recognise it is the settled will of the majority of people in Scotland that they want not just the symbol, but the substance of the return of democratic control over [their] internal affairs.

Said to Prime Minister John Major in the House of Commons, following his announcement that the Stone of Destiny would be returned to Scotland later in the year. Quoted in *The Scotsman* (4 Jul 1996)

Stein, Jock (John) 1922–85

Football player, and manager of Celtic (1965–78) and Scotland (1978–85)

1 We can be as hard and professional as anybody, but I mean it when I say we don't just want to win this cup. We want to win it playing good football, to make neutrals glad we've done it, glad to remember how we did it.

Speaking before the European Cup final in Lisbon (25 May 1967) when Celtic beat Inter Milan 2–1, becoming the first British club to win the Cup. Quoted by Hugh McIlvanney in *The Observer* (28 May 1967)

2 We do have the greatest fans in the world but I've never seen a fan score a goal.

On Scotland's World Cup campaign in Spain (1982)

3 There are Prime Ministers and Sports Ministers and other Ministers who are trying to tell us how to administer football. They know nothing at all about the game of football. They're trying to run football and most of them have never been to a football game.

Only a Game?, BBC television documentary (1985)

4 Down there for eight hours you're away from God's fresh air and sunshine and there's nothing that can compensate for that. There's nothing as dark as the darkness down a pit, the blackness

that closes in on you if your lamp goes out. You'd think you would see some kind of shapes but you can see nothing, nothing but the inside of your head. I think everybody should go down the pit at least once to learn what darkness is.

Quoted in Hugh McIlvanney's obituary of Stein, *The Observer* (15 Sep 1985)

He worked as a miner for 11 years, from the age of 16

5 Look at you, you're like the gable end of a pound note.

Said to comedian Billy Connolly, on his thinness. As quoted by Connolly on his *World Tour of Television 1* (broadcast on BBC2 television, 27 May 1996)

6 We all end up yesterday's men in this business. You're very quickly forgotten.

Quoted in Archie Macpherson, *The Great Derbies: Blue and Green* (1989)

Steinbeck, John 1902–68

American novelist

1 You talked of Scotland as a lost cause and that is not true. Scotland is an *unwon* cause.

Letter (28 Feb 1964) to Mrs John F Kennedy, in Elaine Steinbeck and Robert Wallsten (eds), *Steinbeck: A Life in Letters* (1975)

Stephen, Jessie fl.1913

Domestic servant and militant suffragette

1 I was able to drop acid into the postal pillar boxes without being suspected, because I walked down from where I was employed in my cap, muslin apron, and black frock. . . nobody would ever suspect me of dropping acid through the box.

Describing her leading role in a militant campaign by the Scottish Women's Social and Political Union (Feb 1913). The contents of pillar boxes throughout Glasgow were destroyed by bottles of acid posted in envelopes into the boxes. Quoted in Elspeth King, *The Scottish Women's Suffrage Movement* (1978), p.24

Steuart, Sir James 1712–80

Economist and Jacobite

1 Pipers, blue bonnets, and oat meal, are known in Swabia, Auvergne, Limousin, and Catalonia, as well as in Lochaber: numbers of idle, poor, useless hands, multitudes of children, whom I have found to be fed, nobody knows how, doing almost nothing at the age of fourteen, keeping of cattle and going to school, the only occupations possible for them. If you

ask why they are not employed, their parents will tell you because commerce is not in the country: they talk of commerce as if it was a man, who comes to reside in some countries in order to feed the inhabitants. The truth is it is not the fault of these poor people, but of those whose business it is to find out employment for them.

An Inquiry into the Principles of Political Oeconomy (1767), Bk 1, ch.16

2 Were all the strumpets in London received into a large and convenient building, whither the dissolute might repair for a while in secrecy and security, in a short time, no loose women would be found in the streets. And it cannot be doubted, but that by having them all together under certain regulations, which might render their lives more easy than they are at present, the progress of debauchery, and its hurtful consequences, might in great measure be prevented.

An Inquiry into the Principles of Political Oeconomy (1767), Bk 2, ch.27

3 If the money raised be more beneficially employed by the state, than it would have been by those who have contributed it, then I say the public has gained, in consequence of the burden laid upon individuals; consequently the statesman has done his duty, both in imposing the taxes, and in rightly expending them.

On taxation. *An Inquiry into the Principles of Political Oeconomy* (1767), Bk 5, ch.7

As a Jacobite who lived in exile for many years, he developed views against the trend of economic thought as typified by Adam Smith, but he anticipated many Keynesian ideas, including state intervention and the redistribution of wealth through taxation and public subsidy

Stevenson, Robert Louis 1850–94

Novelist, poet, essayist and travel writer

1 An opera is far more *real* than real life to me. . . I wish that life was an opera. I should like to *live* in one; but I don't know in what quarter of the globe I shall find a Society so constituted.

Letter to his mother, Margaret Stevenson (Aug 1872)

2 For will anyone dare to tell me that business is more entertaining than fooling among boats? He must have never seen a boat, or never seen an office, who says so. And for certain the one is a great deal better for the health.

An Inland Voyage (1878), 'The Royal Sport Nautique'. Cf. Kenneth Grahame 1

3 If a man knows he will sooner or later be robbed upon a journey, he will have a bottle

of the best in every inn, and look upon all his extravagances as so much gained upon the thieves.

An Inland Voyage (1878), 'The Oise in Flood'

4 The most patient people grow weary at last with being continually wetted with rain; except, of course, in the Scottish Highlands, where there are not enough fine intervals to point the difference.

An Inland Voyage (1878), 'Down the Oise: to Compiègne'

5 For my part, I travel not to go anywhere, but to go. I travel for travel's sake. The great affair is to move; to feel the needs and hitches of our life more nearly; to come down off this feather-bed of civilisation, and find the globe granite underfoot and strewn with cutting flints.

Travels with a Donkey (1879), 'Cheylard and Luc'

6 I own I like definite form in what my eyes are to rest upon; and if landscapes were sold, like the sheets of characters of my boyhood, one penny plain and twopence coloured, I should go the length of twopence every day of my life.

Travels with a Donkey (1879), 'Father Apollinaris'

7 . . . to live out of doors with the woman a man loves is of all lives the most complete and free.

Travels with a Donkey (1879), 'A Night Among the Pines'

8 To wash in one of God's rivers in the open air seems to me a sort of cheerful solemnity or semi-pagan act of worship. To dabble among dishes in a bedroom may perhaps make clean the body; but the imagination takes no share in such a cleansing.

Travels with a Donkey (1879), 'In the Valley of the Tarn'

9 . . . after an hospital, what uglier place is there in civilisation than a court of law? Hither come envy, malice, and all uncharitableness to wrestle it out in public tourney; crimes, broken fortunes, severed households, the knave and his victim, gravitate to this low building with the arcade. To how many has not St Giles's bell told the first hour after ruin? I think I see them pause to count the strokes, and wander on again into the moving High Street, stunned and sick at heart.

Edinburgh: Picturesque Notes (1879), 'The Parliament Close'

10 When I suffer in mind, stories are my refuge; I take them like opium; and I consider one who writes them as a sort of doctor of the mind. And frankly, Meiklejohn, it is not Shakespeare we take to, when we are in a hot corner; nor, certainly, George Eliot – no, not even Balzac. It is Charles Reade, or old Dumas, or the Arabian Nights, or the best of Walter Scott. . . We want incident, interest, action: to the devil with your philosophy.

Letter to John Meiklejohn (1 Feb 1880)

11 Some like drink
In a pint pot,
Some like to think;
Some not.

Some like Poe,
And others like Scott,
Some like Mrs Stowe;
Some not.

'Not I', *Not I and other poems* (1880), st.1, 3

12 The fact is, we are much more afraid of life than our ancestors, and cannot find it in our hearts either to marry or not to marry. Marriage is terrifying, but so is a cold and forlorn old age.

Virginibus Puerisque (1881), 'Virginibus Puerisque', section 1

13 In marriage, a man becomes slack and selfish, and undergoes a fatty degeneration of his moral being.

Virginibus Puerisque (1881), 'Virginibus Puerisque', section 1

14 I see women marry indiscriminately with staring burgesses and ferret-faced, white-eyed boys, and men dwell in contentment with noisy scullions, or taking into their lives acidulous vestals.

Virginibus Puerisque (1881), 'Virginibus Puerisque', section 1

15 And you have only to look these happy couples in the face, to see they have never been in love, or in hate, or in any other high passion all their days.

Virginibus Puerisque (1881), 'Virginibus Puerisque', section 1

16 . . . even if we take marriage at its lowest, even if we regard it as no more than a sort of friendship recognised by the police. . .

Virginibus Puerisque (1881), 'Virginibus Puerisque', section 1

17 You could read Kant by yourself, if you wanted; but you must share a joke with some one else. You can forgive people who do not follow you through a philosophical disquisition; but to find your wife laughing when you had tears in your eyes, or staring when you were in a fit of laughter, would go some way towards a dissolution of the marriage.

Virginibus Puerisque (1881), 'Virginibus Puerisque', section 1

18 Lastly (and this is, perhaps, the golden rule) no woman should marry a teetotaller, or a man who does not smoke.

Virginibus Puerisque (1881), 'Virginibus Puerisque', section 1

19 Marriage is a step so grave and decisive that it attracts light-headed, variable men by its very awfulness.

Virginibus Puerisque (1881), 'Virginibus Puerisque', section 1

20 . . . marriage is like life in this — that it is a field of battle, and not a bed of roses.

Virginibus Puerisque (1881), 'Virginibus Puerisque', section 1

21 Times are changed with him who marries; there are no more by-path meadows, where you may innocently linger, but the road lies long and straight and dusty to the grave. Idleness, which is often becoming and even wise in the bachelor, begins to wear a different aspect when you have a wife to support.

Virginibus Puerisque (1881), 'Virginibus Puerisque', section 2

22 To marry is to domesticate the Recording Angel. Once you are married, there is nothing left for you, not even suicide, but to be good.

Virginibus Puerisque (1881), 'Virginibus Puerisque', section 2

23 The cruellest lies are often told in silence. A man may have sat in a room for hours and not opened his teeth, and yet come out of that room a disloyal friend or a vile calumnator.

Virginibus Puerisque (1881), 'Truth of Intercourse'

24 Most of our pocket wisdom is conceived for the use of mediocre people, to discourage them from ambitious attempts, and generally console them in their mediocrity.

Virginibus Puerisque (1881), 'Crabbed Age and Youth'

25 Old and young, we are all on our last cruise.

Virginibus Puerisque (1881), 'Crabbed Age and Youth'

26 . . . it is better to be a fool than to be dead.

Virginibus Puerisque (1881), 'Crabbed Age and Youth'

27 For God's sake give me the young man who has brains enough to make a fool of himself!

Virginibus Puerisque (1881), 'Crabbed Age and Youth'

28 Books are good enough in their own way, but they are a mighty bloodless substitute for life.

Virginibus Puerisque (1881), 'An Apology for Idlers'

29 Extreme *busyness*, whether at school or college, kirk or market, is a symptom of a deficient vitality; and a faculty for idleness implies a catholic appetite and a strong sense of personal identity.

Virginibus Puerisque (1881), 'An Apology for Idlers'

30 There is no duty we so much underrate as the duty of being happy. By being happy we sow anonymous benefits upon the world, which remain unknown even to ourselves, or when they are disclosed, surprise nobody so much as the benefactor.

Virginibus Puerisque (1881), 'An Apology for Idlers'

31 We live the time that a match flickers; we pop the cork of a ginger-beer bottle, and the earthquake swallows us on the instant. Is it not odd, is it not incongruous, is it not, in the highest sense of human speech, incredible, that we should think so highly of the ginger-beer, and regard so little the devouring earthquake?

Virginibus Puerisque (1881), 'Aes Triplex'

32 Think of the heroism of Johnson, think of that superb indifference to mortal limitation that set him upon his dictionary, and carried him through triumphantly until the end! Who, if he were wisely considerate of things at large, would ever embark upon any work much more considerable than a halfpenny post-card? Who would project a serial novel, after Thackeray and Dickens had each fallen in mid-course? Who would find heart enough to begin to live, if he dallied with the consideration of death?

Virginibus Puerisque (1881), 'Aes Triplex'

33 It is better to lose health like a spendthrift than to waste it like a miser. It is better to live and be done with it than to die daily in the sick-room. By all means begin your folio; even if the doctor does not give you a year, even if he hesitates about a month, make one brave push and see what can be accomplished in a week.

Virginibus Puerisque (1881), 'Aes Triplex'

34 . . . to travel hopefully is a better thing than to arrive, and the true success is to labour.

Virginibus Puerisque (1881), 'El Dorado'

35 In the child's world of dim sensation, play is all in all. 'Making believe' is the gist of his whole life, and he cannot so much as take a walk except in character.

Virginibus Puerisque (1881), 'Child's Play'

36 . . . though we are mighty fine fellows nowadays, we cannot write like Hazlitt.

Virginibus Puerisque (1881), 'Walking Tours'

In the same essay, Stevenson describes Hazlitt's 'Going a Journey' as 'so good that there should be a tax levied on all who have not read it'

37 We are in such haste to be doing, to be writing, to be gathering gear, to make our voice audible a moment in the derisive silence of eternity, that we forget that one thing, of which these are but the parts — namely, to live.

Virginibus Puerisque (1881), 'Walking Tours'

38 Politics is perhaps the only profession for which no preparation is thought necessary...

Familiar Studies of Men and Books (1882), 'Yoshida-Torajiro'

39 'Fifteen men on a dead man's chest –
Yo-ho-ho, and a bottle of rum!
Drink and the devil had done for the rest –
Yo-ho-ho, and a bottle of rum!'

Treasure Island (1883), ch.1, 'The Old Sea-Dog at the "Admiral Benbow"'

40 'Pieces of eight!'

Treasure Island (1883), ch.10, 'The Voyage'

41 'You mightn't happen to have a piece of cheese about you, now? No? Well, many's the long night I've dreamed of cheese – toasted, mostly – and woke up again, and here I were.'

Treasure Island (1883), ch.15, 'The Man of the Island' (Ben Gunn to Jim Hawkins)

42 Scotland is indefinable; it has no unity except upon the map.

The Silverado Squatters (1883), 'The Scot Abroad'

43 And though I think I would rather die elsewhere, yet in my heart of hearts I long to be buried among good Scots clods. I will say it fairly, it grows on me with every year: there are no stars so lovely as Edinburgh street-lamps. When I forget thee, Auld Reekie, may my right hand forget its cunning!

The Silverado Squatters (1883), 'The Scot Abroad'

See Psalms 137.5: 'If I forget thee, O Jerusalem, let my right hand forget her cunning.' Cf. Catherine Carswell 1

44 The happiest lot on earth is to be born a Scotsman. You must pay for it in many ways, as for all other advantages on earth. You have to learn the Paraphrases and the Shorter Catechism; you generally take to drink; your youth, as far as I can find out, is a time of louder war against society, of more outcry and tears and turmoil, than if you had been born, for instance, in England. But somehow life is warmer and closer; the hearth burns more redly; the lights of home shine softer on the rainy street; the very names, endeared in verse and music, cling nearer round our hearts.

The Silverado Squatters (1883), 'The Scot Abroad'

45 Sight-seeing is the art of disappointment.

The Silverado Squatters (1883), 'The Petri-fied Forest'

46 There is but one art – to omit! O if I knew how to omit, I would ask no other knowledge. A man who knew how to omit would make an *Iliad* of a daily paper.

Letter to R A M Stevenson (Oct 1883)

47 In winter I get up at night
And dress by yellow candle-light.

In summer, quite the other way,
I have to go to bed by day.

I have to go to bed and see
The birds still hopping on the tree,
Or hear the grown-up people's feet
Still going past me in the street.

'Bed in Summer', *A Child's Garden of Verses* (1885), st.1–2

48 A child should always say what's true,
And speak when he is spoken to,
And behave mannerly at table:
At least as far as he is able.

'Whole Duty of Children', *A Child's Garden of Verses* (1885)

49 Whenever the moon and stars are set,
Whenever the wind is high,
All night long in the dark and wet,
A man goes riding by.

'Windy Nights', *A Child's Garden of Verses* (1885), st.1

50 When I am grown to man's estate
I shall be very proud and great,
And tell the other girls and boys
Not to meddle with my toys.

'Looking Forward', *A Child's Garden of Verses* (1885)

51 Whenever Auntie moves around,
Her dresses make a curious sound;
They trail behind her on the floor,
And trundle after through the door.

'Auntie's Skirts', *A Child's Garden of Verses* (1885)

52 I have a little shadow that goes in and out with me,
And what can be the use of him is more than I can see.

'My Shadow', *A Child's Garden of Verses* (1885), st.1

53 The world is so full of a number of things,
I'm sure we should all be as happy as kings.

'Happy Thought', *A Child's Garden of Verses* (1885)

54 Children, you are very little,
And your bones are very brittle;
If you would grow great and stately,
You must try to walk sedately.

'Good and Bad Children', *A Child's Garden of Verses* (1885), st.1

55 My tea is nearly ready and the sun has left the sky;
It's time to take the window to see Leerie going by;
For every night at tea-time and before you take your seat,
With lantern and with ladder he comes posting up the street.

'The Lamplighter', *A Child's Garden of Verses* (1885), st.1

56 Must we to bed indeed? Well then,
    Let us arise and go like men,
    And face with an undaunted tread
    The long black passage up to bed.

    'North-West Passage', 1, 'Good Night', *A Child's
    Garden of Verses* (1885), st.3

57 Then, when mamma goes by to bed,
    She shall come in with tip-toe tread,
    And see me lying warm and fast
    And in the Land of Nod at last.

    'North-West Passage', 3, 'In Port', *A Child's
    Garden of Verses* (1885), st.3

58 'David,' said he, 'I love you like a brother. And
    O, man,' he cried in a kind of ecstasy, 'am I
    no a bonny fighter?'

    Kidnapped (1886), ch.10 (Alan Breck to David
    Balfour)

59 'No, sir, I make it a rule of mine: the more it
    looks like Queer Street, the less I ask.'

    The Strange Case of Dr Jekyll and Mr Hyde
    (1886), 'Story of the Door' (Mr Enfield to Mr
    Utterson)

60 With every day, and from both sides of my
    intelligence, the moral and the intellectual, I
    thus drew steadily nearer to that truth, by
    whose partial discovery I have been doomed
    to such a dreadful shipwreck: that man is not
    truly one, but truly two.

    The Strange Case of Dr Jekyll and Mr Hyde (1886),
    'Henry Jekyll's Full Statement of the Case'

61 My devil had been long caged, he came out
    roaring.

    The Strange Case of Dr Jekyll and Mr Hyde (1886),
    'Henry Jekyll's Full Statement of the Case'

62 We have a butler! He doesn't buttle, but the
    point of the thing is the style. When Fanny
    gardens, he stands over her and looks genteel.
    He opens the door, and I am told waits at table.
    Well, what's the odds; I shall have it on my
    tomb – 'He ran a butler'.

    Letter to Sidney Colvin (Apr 1886)

63 The great thing is to know as much science
    as your mind will stand without turning into
    a man of science (a common professor), just
    as it is to know as much of the world as your
    heart will bear without turning into a man of
    the world. In all these things there is an easy
    rule, which I believe infallible. As long as any
    study continues to add, pursue it; as soon as
    it begins to subtract, have done with it. We
    want to round out our globe of experience
    and sympathy on all sides; not to contract into
    the cube.

    Letter to Garrett Droppers (5 Apr 1887)

64 The gauger walked with willing foot,
    And aye the gauger played the flute;

And what should Master Gauger play
But *Over the hills and far away*?

    'A Song of the Road' (dated 'Forest of Montargis,
    1878'), *Underwoods* (1887), Bk 1, st.1

65 Under the wide and starry sky,
    Dig the grave and let me lie.
    Glad did I live and gladly die,
    And I laid me down with a will.

    This be the verse you grave for me:
    Here he lies where he longed to be,
    Home is the sailor, home from sea,
    And the hunter home from the hill.

    'Requiem' (dated 'Hyères, May 1884'), *Under-
    woods* (1887), Bk 1

    The poem is engraved on Stevenson's tomb
    on Mount Vaea, Samoa, but with the third
    line of the second stanza reading 'Home is
    the sailor, home from *the* sea'. It is frequently
    quoted in this way

66 Out of the sun, out of the blast,
    Out of the world, alone I passed
    Across the moor and through the wood
    To where the monastery stood.

    'Our Lady of the Snows', *Underwoods* (1887), Bk 1

67 . . . To plant a star for seamen, where was then
    The surfy haunt of seals and cormorants. . .

    'Skerryvore', *Underwoods* (1887), Bk 1

    The lines refer to the building of the lighthouse
    on Skerryvore, off Tiree, by his uncle
    Alan Stevenson, Engineer to the Northern
    Lighthouse Board (1843–53)

68 A mile an' a bittock, a mile or twa,
    Abüne the burn, ayont the law,
    Davie an' Donal' an' Cherlie an' a',
    An' the müne was shinin' clearly!

    'A Mile an' a Bittock', *Underwoods* (1887),
    Bk 2, st.1

69 History is much decried; it is a tissue of
    errors, we are told, no doubt correctly; and
    rival historians expose each other's blunders
    with gratification. Yet the worst historian has
    a clearer view of the period he studies than the
    best of us can hope to form of that in which
    we live. The obscurest epoch is to-day. . .

    'The Day After To-morrow' (1887), *Ethical
    Studies* (first published in *Contemporary Review*)

70 About the very cradle of the Scot there goes a
    hum of metaphysical divinity; and the whole
    of two divergent systems is summed up, not
    merely speciously, in the two first questions
    of the rival catechisms, the English tritely
    inquiring, 'What is your name?' the Scottish
    striking at the very roots of life with 'What is
    the chief end of man?' and answering nobly, if
    obscurely, 'To glorify God and to enjoy Him
    for ever.'

    Memories and Portraits (1887), 'The Foreigner at

Home' (first published in *The Cornhill Magazine*, 1882). Cf. Shorter Catechism 1

71 The fact remains: in spite of the difference of blood and language, the Lowlander feels himself the sentimental countryman of the Highlander. When they meet abroad, they fall upon each other's necks in spirit; even at home there is a kind of clannish intimacy in their talk. But from his compatriot in the south the Lowlander stands consciously apart. He has had a different training; he obeys different laws; he makes his will in other terms, is otherwise divorced and married; his eyes are not at home in an English landscape or with English houses; his ear continues to remark the English speech; and even though his tongue acquire the Southern knack, he will still have a strong Scots accent of the mind.

Memories and Portraits (1887), 'The Foreigner at Home' (first published in *The Cornhill Magazine*, 1882)

72 The first step for all is to learn to the dregs our own ignoble fallibility.

Memories and Portraits (1887), 'Old Mortality', Part 2 (first published in *Longman's Magazine*, 1884)

73 I have thus played the sedulous ape to Hazlitt, to Lamb, to Wordsworth, to Sir Thomas Browne, to Defoe, to Hawthorne, to Montaigne, to Baudelaire and to Obermann.

Memories and Portraits (1887), 'A College Magazine'

74 Each has his own tree of ancestors, but at the top of all sits Probably Arboreal; in all our veins there run some minims of his old, wild, tree-top blood; our civilised nerves still tingle with his rude terrors and pleasures; and to that which would have moved our common ancestor, all must obediently thrill.

Memories and Portraits (1887), 'Pastoral' (first published in *Longman's Magazine*, 1887)

75 Marriage is one long conversation, chequered by disputes. The disputes are valueless; they but ingrain the difference; the heroic heart of woman prompting her at once to nail her colours to the mast. But in the intervals, almost unconsciously and with no desire to shine, the whole material of life is turned over and over, ideas are struck out and shared, the two persons more and more adapt their notions one to suit the other, and in process of time, without sound or trumpet, they conduct each other into new worlds of thought.

Memories and Portraits (1887), 'Talk and Talkers', Part 2 (first published in *The Cornhill Magazine*, 1882)

76 Faith means holding the same opinions as the person employing the word.

Memories and Portraits (1887), 'Selections from his Notebook'

77 Scientific men, who imagine that their science affords an answer to the problems of existence, are perhaps the most to be pitied of mankind; and *contemned*.

Memories and Portraits (1887), 'Selections from his Notebook'

78 Every one lives by selling something, whatever be his right to it.

'Beggars', *Scribner's Magazine* (1888)

79 If your morals make you dreary, depend upon it they are wrong.

'A Christmas Sermon', Part 2, *Ethical Studies* (first published in *Scribner's Magazine*, 1888)

80 The sight of a pleasure in which we cannot or else will not share moves us to a peculiar impatience. It may be because we are envious, or because we are sad, or because we dislike noise and romping – being so refined, or because – being so philosophic – we have an overweighing sense of life's gravity: at least, as we go on in years, we are all tempted to frown on our neighbour's pleasures.

'A Christmas Sermon', Part 2, *Ethical Studies* (first published in *Scribner's Magazine*, 1888)

81 No baggage – there was the secret of existence.

The Wrecker (1892), ch.4, 'Extremes of Fortune'

82 Life is not all Beer and Skittles. The inherent tragedy of things works itself out from white to black and blacker, and the poor things of a day look ruefully on. Does it shake my cast-iron faith? I cannot say it does. I believe in an ultimate decency of things: ay, and if I woke in hell, should still believe it!

Letter to Sidney Colvin (23 Aug 1893)

83 Give to me the life I love,
Let the lave go by me,
Give the jolly heaven above
And the byway nigh me.
Bed in the bush with the stars to see,
Bread I dip in the river –
There's the life for a man like me,
There's the life for ever.

'The Vagabond', *Songs of Travel* (1894), st.1

84 Wealth I ask not, hope nor love,
Nor a friend to know me.
All I ask, the heaven above,
And the road below me.

'The Vagabond', *Songs of Travel* (1894), st.4

85 I will make you brooches and toys for your delight
Of bird-song at morning and star-shine at night.
I will make a palace fit for you and me
Of green days in forests and blue days at sea.

'I will make you brooches. . . ', *Songs of Travel* (1894), st.1

86 In the highlands, in the country places,
   Where the old plain men have rosy faces,
   And the young fair maidens
   Quiet eyes. . .

   'In the highlands. . . ', *Songs of Travel* (1894), st.1

87 Blows the wind to-day, and the sun and rain
   are flying,
   Blows the wind on the moors to-day and now,
   Where about the graves of the martyrs the
   whaups are crying,
   My heart remembers how!

   'To S R Crockett (in reply to a dedication)',
   Songs of Travel (1894), st.1

88 Be it granted to me to behold you again
   in dying,
   Hills of home! and to hear again the call;
   Hear about the graves of the martyrs the
   peeweets crying,
   And hear no more at all.

   'To S R Crockett (in reply to a dedication)',
   Songs of Travel (1894), st.3

89 And all that I could think of, in the darkness
   and the cold,
   Was just that I was leaving home and my folks
   were growing old.

   'Christmas at Sea' (1894), st.11

90 If I had to begin again. . . I believe I should
   try to honour Sex more religiously. The worst
   of our education is that Christianity does not
   recognise and hallow Sex. It looks askance
   at it, over its shoulder, oppressed as it is
   by reminiscences of hermits and Asiatic self-
   tortures.

   Letter to R A M Stevenson (Sep 1894)

91 I saw rain falling and the rainbow drawn
   On Lammermuir. Hearkening I heard again
   In my precipitous city beaten bells
   Winnow the keen sea wind. And here afar,
   Intent on my own race and place, I wrote.

   Weir of Hermiston (1894, first published 1896),
   dedication 'To My Wife'

92 'What do I want with a Christian faim'ly? I
   want Christian broth! Get me a lass that can
   plain-boil a potato, if she was a whüre off the
   streets.'

   Weir of Hermiston (1894, first published 1896),
   ch.1, 'Life and Death of Mrs Weir' (Lord
   Hermiston to his wife Mrs Weir). Cf. Dean
   Ramsay 4

   The character of Lord Hermiston was based
   on the real 'Hanging Judge', Lord Braxfield

93 'You have taken this so calmly, sir, that I cannot
   but stand ashamed,' began Archie.
   'I'm nearer voamiting, though, than you
   would fancy,' said my lord.

   Weir of Hermiston (1894, first published 1896),

ch.3, 'In the Matter of the Hanging of Duncan
Jopp' (Archie and his father, Lord Hermiston)

94 'My poor, dear boy!' observed Glenalmond.
   'My poor, dear and, if you will allow me to say
   so, very foolish boy! You are only discovering
   where you are; to one of your temperament, or
   of mine, a painful discovery. The world was
   not made for us; it was made for ten hundred
   millions of men, all different from each other
   and from us; there's no royal road there, we
   just have to sclamber and tumble.'

   Weir of Hermiston (1894, first published 1896),
   ch.4, 'Opinions of the Bench' (Lord Glenalmond
   to Archie)

95 For that is the mark of the Scot of all classes:
   that he stands in an attitude towards the past
   unthinkable to Englishmen, and remembers and
   cherishes the memory of his forebears, good
   and bad; and there burns alive in him a sense
   of identity with the dead even to the twentieth
   generation.

   Weir of Hermiston (1894, first published 1896),
   ch.5, 'Winter on the Moors: A Border Family'

96 It seemed unprovoked, a wilful convulsion of
   brute nature. . .

   Weir of Hermiston (1894, first published 1896),
   ch.9, 'At the Weaver's Stone'

   These are the last words of the published
   version of the unfinished novel, dictated by
   Stevenson, ironically, hours before his death
   from a blood-clot on the brain

97 The problem of education is twofold: first to
   know, and then to utter. Every one who lives
   any semblance of an inner life thinks more nobly
   and profoundly than he speaks; and the best of
   teachers can impart only broken images of the
   truth they perceive. Speech which goes from
   one to another between two natures, and, what
   is worse, between two experiences, is doubly
   relative. The speaker buries his meaning; it is
   for the hearer to dig it up again; and all speech,
   written or spoken, is in a dead language until
   it finds a willing and prepared hearer.

   Lay Morals (first published in *Works*, ed.
   S Colvin, 1895–8), ch.1

98 So long as we love we serve; so long as we are
   loved by others, I would almost say that we
   are indispensable; and no man is useless while
   he has a friend.

   Lay Morals (first published in *Works*, ed.
   S Colvin, 1895–8), ch.4

99 Though we steer after a fashion, yet we must
   sail according to the winds and currents.

   'Reflections and Remarks on Human Life' (first
   published in *Works*, ed. S Colvin, 1895–8), Part 8

100 Last night we had a thunderstorm in style.
    Our God the Father fell down-stairs,

The stark blue lightning went its flight
the while,
The very rain you might have heard a mile –
The strenuous faithful buckled to their
prayers.

'New Poems' (published posthumously), LXXV

01 Love – what is love? A great and aching heart
Wrung hands; and silence; and a long despair
Life – what is life? Upon a moorland bare
To see love coming and see love depart.

'New Poems' (published posthumously), LXXXVI

02 The *bourgeoisie's* weapon is starvation. If as a
writer or artist you run counter to their narrow
notions they simply and silently withdraw your
means of subsistence. I sometimes wonder how
many people of talent are executed in this way
every year.

Quoted in Lloyd Osbourne, 'The Death of
Stevenson', preface to the Tusitala edition of *Weir
of Hermiston* (1924). Cf. Hugh MacDiarmid 42

03 The saddest object in civilisation, and to my
mind the greatest confession of its failure, is
the man who can work, who wants work, and
who is not allowed to work.

Quoted in Lloyd Osbourne, 'The Death of
Stevenson', preface to the Tusitala edition of
Weir of Hermiston (1924). Cf. Thomas Carlyle 34

04 What's that? Do I look strange?

Last words. Quoted in Lloyd Osbourne,
'Account of the Death and Burial of R L
Stevenson', in the Tusitala edition of his
Letters, Vol.5 (1924)

Stewart, Belle 1906–

*Traveller and traditional singer, one of the
Stewarts of Blairgowrie*

1 Noo there's some who earn a pound or twa,
some cannae earn their keep,
And some wad pick fae morn tae nicht, an'
some wad raither sleep.
But there's some wha has tae pick or stairve,
and some wha dinnae care,
And there's some wha bless, an' some wha
curse, the berryfields o' Blair.

'The Berryfields o' Blair', st.4. Quoted in Ailie
Munro, *The Folk Music Revival in Scotland*
(1984), ch.4

2 Travellers will aye exist to the end o' time, and
you'll never get them to change their ways,
and you'll never get rid o' Tinkers. They'll be
there till doomsday in the afternoon.

Quoted in Ewan MacColl & Peggy Seeger, *Till
Doomsday in the Afternoon* (1986)

Stewart, Prince Charles Edward
1720–88

*Claimant to the British throne; known, depend-
ing on political viewpoint, as 'Bonnie Prince
Charlie', the 'Young Chevalier' or the 'Young
Pretender'*

1 Let what will, happen, the stroke is struck and
I have taken a firm resolution to conquer or
to die and stand my ground as long as I have
a man remaining with me.

Letter to his father (1745)

His father, who had made an attempt on the
throne in 1715, tried to dissuade him from
landing in Scotland

2 I am come home.

Responding to Alexander MacDonald of
Boisdale's suggestion that he abandon his attempt
and go home (4 Aug 1745, Eriskay). Quoted in
Henry Patton (ed.), *The Lyon in Mourning* (1895),
Vol.1, p.205

3 Behold my war chest!

Showing the single guinea coin left of his funds
on entering Perth (4 Sep 1745). Quoted in
F McLynn, *Charles Edward Stuart: a Tragedy
in Many Acts* (1988), ch.11

4 You ruin, abandon and betray me if you do
not march on!

Said to his war council as they were about to
decide to retreat from Derby (5 Dec 1745).
Quoted in R C Jarvis, *Collected Papers on the
Jacobite Risings* (1972), Vol.2, p.100

5 When I came into Scotland I knew well enough
what I was to expect from my enemies, but I little foresaw what I meet with from my friends...
Everyone knew before he engaged in the cause,
what he was to expect in case it miscarried, and
should have stayed at home if he could not face
death in any shape... At least I am the only
person upon whose head a price has already been
set, and therefore I cannot indeed threaten at
every other word to throw down my arms and
make my peace with the government... my
authority may be taken from me by violence,
but I shall never resign it like an idiot.

Letter responding to Lord George Murray's
criticisms of his leadership (Jan 1746). Quoted
in W B Blaikie, *Itinerary of Prince Charles Stuart*
(1897), pp.74–5

6 Indeed, Miss, if we shall happen with any that
will go so narrowly to work in searching me
as what you mean, they will certainly discover
me at any rate.

To Flora MacDonald, who objected to his
carrying a pistol beneath his petticoat when
disguised as her servant Betty Burke (27 Jun 1746,
North Uist). Quoted in Compton Mackenzie,
Prince Charlie's Ladies (1934), p.88. Cf. 4th Duke
of Argyll 1

7 For all that has happened, I hope, Madam, we shall meet in St James's yet.

> His parting words to Flora MacDonald on Skye (30 Jun 1746). Quoted in Henry Patton (ed.), *The Lyon in Mourning* (1895), Vol.2, p.25

Stewart (of Garth), David 1772–1829
Soldier and author

1 The respectable gentlemen who, in so many cases, had formerly been entrusted with the management of Highland property, resigned, and their places were supplied by persons cast in a coarser mould, and generally strangers to the country who, detesting the people, and ignorant of their character, capability and language, quickly surmounted every obstacle, and hurried on the change, without reflecting on the distress of which it might be productive...

> On those responsible for implementing the Highland Clearances. *Sketches of the Character, Manners, and Present State of the Highlanders of Scotland...* (1822). Quoted in Alexander Mackenzie, *The History of the Highland Clearances* (1883). Cf. James Loch 1, Patrick Sellar 1

Stewart, Ena Lamont 1912–
Playwright

1 LILY: . . . It seems tae me, Maggie, that the mair ye cairry on wi ither men, the mair yer ain man thinks o ye. If ye sit at hame washin oot the nappies an blackleadin yer grate, all the attention ye'll get's a bashin on a Saturday.

> *Men Should Weep* (1947), Act 1, sc.1

2 LILY: . . . ony wumman'll tell ye that there's nae system ever inventit that disna go a tae Hell when ye've a hoose-fu o weans an a done aul granny tae look efter.

> *Men Should Weep* (1947), Act 1, sc.1

3 JOHN: . . . Weans! They roast the heart an liver oot ye!

> *Men Should Weep* (1947), Act 1, sc.2

Stirling Journal 1833–1970
Newspaper

1 . . . boys are beating their fathers. This is not how it should be. So long as we have football in winter and cricket in summer, golf should be forbidden to all males under 25 or 30. . . Let the young not be middle-aged too soon.

> Editorial on golf (17 Apr 1896). Quoted in Neil Tranter, 'Women and Sport in Nineteenth Century Scotland', in Grant Jarvie and Graham Walker (eds), *Scottish Sport in the Making of a Nation* (1994)

Stowe, Harriet Elizabeth Beecher (*née* Beecher) 1811–96
American novelist, author of Uncle Tom's Cabin *(1852)*

1 To my view it is an almost sublime instance of the benevolent employment of superior wealth and power in shortening the struggles of civilisation, and elevating in a few years a whole community to a point of education and material prosperity, which, unassisted, they might never have obtained.

> On the so-called 'Sutherland Improvements', in *Sunny Memories of Foreign Lands* (1854)

>> Rossal stonemason Donald MacLeod responded in his *Gloomy Memories* (1857), 'Yes, indeed, the shortest process of civilisation recorded in the history of nations. Oh, marvellous! From the year 1812 to 1820, the whole interior of the county of Sutherland . . . converted to a solitary wilderness, where the voice of man praising God is not be heard, nor the image of God upon man to be seen . . . This is the advancement of civilisation, is it not, madam?'

Strange, Lady 18th century
Staunch Jacobite supporter

1 *Pretender*, indeed, and be damned to ye!

> Said to a man who was disparaging Charles Edward Stewart in her presence. Quoted in Harry Graham, *A Group of Scottish Women* (1908, 2nd edition), ch.15

Stuart, Jamie
Writer

1 'Come oan then, ya bunch o nae-users! Pick oot a fechter for me an ah'll settle this stramash in wan square go!'

> *Auld Testament Tales* (1993). (Goliath challenges the Israelites)

Stuart, Muriel 1885–1967
Poet

1 . . . 'He who hears
Loud noise of Carnival about his ears,
How shall he heed the foot with silence shod,
Or listen for the small still voice of God?'

> 'Christ at Carnival', *Christ at Carnival and other poems* (1916)

2 'Behold Christ's milky mouth in the china cup,
Christ's hand that tips the blue-rimmed porridge bowl!'

> 'Christ at Carnival', *Christ at Carnival and other poems* (1916)

3 The world is changed between us, never more
Shall the dawn rise and seek another mate
Over the hill-tops; never can the shore
Spread out her ragged tresses to the roar
Of the sea passionate,
Moon-chained, and for a season love-forbid. . .

'The Dead Moment', *Christ at Carnival and other poems* (1916)

4 The muddy cough of the stream that strives
To free its throat from the clot of reed. . .

'Wild Geese Across the Moon', *Christ at Carnival and other poems* (1916), st.1

5 Here in their safe and simple house of death,
Sealed in their shells a million roses leap;
Here I can blow a garden with my breath,
And in my hand a forest lies asleep.

'The Seed Shop', *Poems* (1922), st.4

6 My faded mouth will never flower again,
Under the paint the wrinkles fret my eyes,
My hair is dull beneath its henna stain,
I have come to the last ramparts of disguise.

'Mrs Effingham's Swan Song', *Poems* (1922)

7 . . . Men who have longer, fuller lives to live,
Who are not stopped and broken in their prime,
With their faces still to summer. Men do
  not know
What Age says to a woman.

'Mrs Effingham's Swan Song', *Poems* (1922)

8 Not love, not love! Love was our first undoing,
We have lived too long on heart-beats.

'Andromeda Unfettered', *Poems* (1922)

Sully, Duc de (Maximilien de Béthune)
1559–1641
Minister in the government of Henri IV of France

1 The wisest fool in Christendom.

Attrib. On James VI and I

Sulter, Maud 1960–
Poet

1 As a blackwoman
every act is a personal act
every act is a political act

As a blackwoman
the personal is political
holds no empty rhetoric.

'As a Blackwoman', *As a Blackwoman* (1985)

2 Exile
self imposed
is not exile
my friend
it is fear.

'East', *Zabat: Poetics of a Family Tree* (1989)

3 . . . Civilisation can never
be written in the blood and bones of slavery.

'Historical Objects', *Zabat: Poetics of a Family Tree* (1989)

4 The whole dynamic of 'it's okay as long as it's from somewhere else' is endemic in British society. Black people are okay as long as they come from somewhere else.

Interview with Rebecca E Wilson, in Gillean Somerville-Arjat and Rebecca E Wilson (eds), *Sleeping with Monsters: Conversations with Scottish and Irish Women Poets* (1990)

5 . . . the fact that Black people have been in Scotland for over four hundred years has also to be taken on board. . . It's. . . disheartening. . . that in a country that claims to have such a radical, rebellious nature as Scotland, there is such a hesitation to take on board other people's voices.

Interview with Rebecca E Wilson, in Gillean Somerville-Arjat and Rebecca E Wilson (eds), *Sleeping with Monsters: Conversations with Scottish and Irish Women Poets* (1990)

6 The power of oratory, the power of memory, the power of keeping lines of communication open, is very much a role that women fulfil, and have every right to do so.

Interview with Rebecca E Wilson, in Gillean Somerville-Arjat and Rebecca E Wilson (eds), *Sleeping with Monsters: Conversations with Scottish and Irish Women Poets* (1990)

Responding to the idea that poetry is 'a male preoccupation'

Swan, Annie S 1859–1943
Novelist

1 It isn't Skye, but it really is a lovely place, only spoiled by the people. Far too many of them. Thank God, Skye will never be overrun. It's too difficult to get at, and there's nowhere for people to go when they get there, unless they sleep on the heather or up among the crags.

On Oban. *Macleod's Wife* (1924), ch.8

2 'All war is senseless and cruel, my dear,' Sheldon said grimly. 'It's got to be stopped at the source, which is in the hearts of men.'

Who are the Heathen? (1942), ch.28

Symon, Mary 1863–1938

Poet

1   Gie me a hill wi' the heather on't,
    An' a reid sun drappin' doon,
    Or the mists o' the mornin' risin' saft
    Wi' the reek owre a wee grey toon.

'The Soldiers' Cairn', *Deveron Days* (1933), st.1

2   Far awa' is the Flanders land
    Wi' fremmit France atween,
    But mony a howe o' them baith the day
    Has a hap o' the Gordon green;
    It's them we kent that's lyin' there,
    An' it's nae wi' stane or airn,
    But wi' brakin' herts, an' mem'ries sair,
    That we're biggin' the Soldiers' Cairn.

'The Soldiers' Cairn', *Deveron Days* (1933), st.2

T

Tait, Peter Guthrie 1831–1901
Scientist and mathematician, collaborator with Lord Kelvin

1 Perhaps to the student there is no part of elementary mathematics so repulsive as is spherical trigonometry.

> Article on 'Quaternions' in *Encyclopaedia Britannica* (11th edition, 1911)

Tannahill, Robert 1774–1810
Poet and songwriter

1 Let us go, lassie, go
To the braes o' Balquhither?
Where the blaeberries grow,
'Mang the bonnie Highland heather...

> 'The Braes o' Balquhither', st.1

>> This song (now usually known as 'The Braes o' Balquhidder') was adapted by Irish piper Francis McPeake, who set a slightly modified version of the lyrics to music: it is known as 'Wild Mountain Thyme' or 'Will Ye Go, Lassie Go?'

2 I will twine thee a bow'r
By the clear siller fountain,
An' I'll cover it o'er
Wi' the flowers o' the mountain...

Now the simmer is in prime,
Wi' the flowers richly blooming,
An' the wild mountain thyme
A' the moorlands perfuming.

> 'The Braes o' Balquhither', st.2, 4
> See entry above

3 For, O gin I saw but my bonny Scots callan,
The dark days o' winter were simmer to me!

> 'The Braes o' Gleniffer', st.3

4 Gloomy winter's now awa',
Saft the westlan' breezes blaw;
'Mang the birks o' Stanley shaw
The mavis sings fu' cheerie, O.

> 'Gloomy Winter's Now Awa'', st.1

5 The sun has gane down o'er the lofty Benlomond,
And left the red clouds to preside o'er the scene,
While lanely I stray, in the calm simmer gloamin',
To muse on sweet Jessie, the flower o' Dunblane.

How sweet is the brier wi' its saft faulding blossom,
And sweet is the birk, wi' its mantle o' green;
Yet sweeter, and fairer, and dear to this bosom,
Is lovely young Jessie, the flower o' Dunblane.

> 'Jessie, the Flower o' Dunblane', st.1–2

6 O! Are ye sleepin, Maggie?
O! Are ye sleepin, Maggie?
Let me in, for loud the linn
Is roarin o'er the warlock craigie!

> 'O! Are Ye Sleepin, Maggie?', st.1

Taylor, Rachel Annand 1876–1960
Poet

1 'Wherefore the mask of silken lace
Tied with a golden band?'
*Poverty walks with wanton grace
In my land.*

'Why do you softly, richly speak
Rhythm so sweetly-scanned?'
*Poverty hath the Gaelic and Greek
In my land.*

> 'The Princess of Scotland', st.3–4

>> Taylor came from Aberdeen: 'Greek' refers to the 'Doric', or Scots

Tennant, William 1784–1848
Poet and scholar, Professor of Oriental Languages at St Andrews University from 1835

1 My pulse beats fire – my pericranium glows,
Like baker's oven with poetic heat;
A thousand bright ideas, spurning prose,
Are in a twinkling hatch'd in Fancy's seat...

> *Anster Fair* (1812), Canto 1, st.7

>> This long comic poem set in Anstruther, Fife, was inspired by the poem 'Maggie Lauder'. Cf. Francis Sempill 2

2 His ev'ry finger, to its place assign'd,
Mov'd quiv'ring like the leaf of aspen tree,
Now shutting up the skittish squeaking wind,
Now op'ning to the music passage free;
His cheeks, with windy puffs therein confin'd,
Were swoln into a red rotundity,
As from his lungs into the bag was blown
Supply of needful air to feed the growling drone.

> On Rob the Ranter's bagpipe-playing. *Anster Fair* (1812), Canto 4, st.73

3 Pellmell in random couples they engage,
And boisterously wag their bodies' trunk,
Till from their heated skin the sweat out-squirts,
And soaks with clammy dew their goodly
   Holland shirts.

> On the dancers inspired by Rob the Ranter's
> bagpipe-playing. *Anster Fair* (1812), Canto 4, st.81

4 I sing the steir, strabush, and strife,
Whan, bickerin' frae the towns o' Fife,
Great bangs of bodies, thick and rife,
Gaed to Sanct Androis town,
And, wi' John Calvin i' their heads,
And hammers i' their hands and spades,
Enrag'd at idols, mass, and beads,
Dang the Cathedral down. . .

> *Papistry Storm'd, or the Dingin' Down o' the
> Cathedral* (1827), Sang First, ll.1–8
>
> > This mock-epic celebrates the destruction
> > of St Andrews Cathedral by the Protestant
> > mob in 1559

5 Than skippers, tailzeours, lairds, and hinds,
Fludes o' mad burghers a' kinkinds,
Dissim'lar men, but sim'lar minds,
In formidable sailyie,
Cam' whurrin' in like cats on rattens,
Swappin' their handspakes and their battens,
And ither mad artailyie. . .

> *Papistry Storm'd, or the Dingin' Down o' the
> Cathedral* (1827), Sang Sixth, ll.379–85

6 Great, gourlie, goustrous-lookin' clouds
Seem'd jundyin' i' the air wi' thuds,
And on the towns, and fields, and woods,
Out frae their fissures pour'd the floods
They'd borrow't frae the sea. . .

> *Papistry Storm'd, or the Dingin' Down o' the
> Cathedral* (1827), Sang Sixth, ll.682–5

Thatcher, Margaret Hilda, Baroness (*née* Roberts) 1925–

English Conservative politician, British Prime Minister (1979–90)

1 We English, who are marvellous people, are
really very generous to Scotland. We English
are the most underestimated people in the UK.

> Speech at a Young Conservatives Conference in
> Torquay. Quoted in *The Times* (12 Feb 1990)
>
> > She was commenting on the higher proportion
> > of central government funding spent on local
> > government in Scotland and Wales than in
> > England

2 Some part of this unpopularity must be
attributed to the national question on which
the Tories are seen as an English party and
on which I myself was apparently seen as a
quintessential English figure. About the second
point I could – and I can – do nothing. I am
what I am and I have no intention of wearing
tartan camouflage.

> *The Downing Street Years* (1993), ch.20,
> 'Thatcherism Rebuffed – The Case of Scotland'

Theroux, Paul Edward 1941–

American novelist and travel writer

1 I came to hate Aberdeen more than any other
place I saw. Yes, yes, the streets were clean;
but it was an awful city.
   Perhaps it had been made awful and was
not naturally that way. It had certainly been
affected by the influx of money and foreigners.
I guessed that in the face of such an onslaught
the Aberdonians had found protection and
solace by retreating into the most unbearable
Scottish stereotypes. It was only in Aberdeen
that I saw kilts and eightsome reels and the
sort of tartan tight-fistedness that made me
think of the average Aberdonian as a person
who would gladly pick a halfpenny out of a
dunghill with his teeth.

> On the effect of the oil industry on Aberdeen.
> *The Kingdom by the Sea* (1983), ch.20

2 It was a cold, stony-faced city. It did not even
look prosperous. That was some measure of
the city's mean spirit – its wealth remained
hidden. It looked over-cautious, unwelcoming
and smug, and a bit overweight like a rich uncle
in dull sensible clothes, smelling of mildew and
ledgers, who keeps his wealth in an iron chest
in the basement. The windows and doors of
Aberdeen were especially solid and unyielding;
it was a city of barred windows and burglar
alarms, of hasps and padlocks and Scottish
nightmares.

> On Aberdeen. *The Kingdom by the Sea*
> (1983), ch.20

3 Old Dundee had been destroyed and new
Dundee was an interesting monstrosity. It was
certainly an excellent example of a hard-edged
horror – the prison-like city of stony-faced
order – that I associated with the future.

> *The Kingdom by the Sea* (1983), ch.21

Thom, William 1798–1848

Poet

1 The mitherless bairn gangs till his lane bed,
Nane covers his cauld back, or haps his
   bare head;
His wee hackit heelies are hard as the airn,
An' litheless the lair o' the mitherless bairn!

> 'The Mitherless Bairn' (c.1841), st.2

Thomas the Rhymer
(Thomas of Ercildoune) c.1220–97
Seer

1 On the morrow, afore noon, shall blaw the greatest wind that ever wes heard afore in Scotland.

> Attrib. Prophecy made on the day of the death of Alexander III (19 Mar 1286)
>
> > On the morning of 20 March, the day being calm, Thomas was summoned to court in Edinburgh to explain his apparent mistake. Just before noon a messenger arrived from Fife bearing the news of the King's death in a fall from his horse during the night. 'Yon is the wind that shall blaw, to the great calamity and trouble of all Scotland', said the Rhymer. See John Bellenden, *History and Chronicles of Scotland* (1536), Bk 13, ch.21

2 The Burn o Breid
Sall rin fu reid.

> Attrib. Rhyme foretelling the Battle of Bannockburn

3 Tide, tide, whate'er betide,
There's aye be Haigs at Bemersyde.

> Attrib. Rhyme concerning the Haig family, who have held land at Bemersyde for 700 years

4 The teeth of the sheep shall lay the plough on the shelf.

> Attrib. Prophecy supposed to refer to the Highland Clearances

Thompson, Sir D'Arcy Wentworth
1860–1948
Zoologist, mathematician and classical scholar

1 Cell and tissue, shell and bone, leaf and flower, are so many portions of matter, and it is in obedience to the laws of physics that their particles have been moved, moulded and confirmed. They are no exceptions to the rule that God always geometrises. Their problems of form are in the first instance mathematical problems, their problems of growth are essentially physical problems, and the morphologist is, *ipso facto*, a student of physical science.

> *On Growth and Form* (1917)

2 Form is a diagram of forces.

> *On Growth and Form* (1917)

3 It behoves us always to remember that in physics it has taken great men to discover simple things. They are very great names indeed which we couple with the explanation of the path of a stone, the droop of a chain, the tints of a bubble, the shadows in a cup.

> *On Growth and Form* (1917)

Thomson, Derick
see **MacThòmais, Ruaraidh**

Thomson, Geddes 1939–
Poet

1 Susan, Sandra, Velma, Valerie,
Tennent's lager girlie gallery,
I've been drinking you for years
With thoughts that lie too deep for tears.

> 'Canonisation', *Four Scottish Poets* (1983), st.1

2 When I am taken
Do not blame the traitor
Or think that English gold
Has bought my body.

Do not, like the priests,
Elevate the idea
Above the people.

Question rather the idea.

> '1305', *Four Scottish Poets* (1983)
>
> > The poem refers to the betrayal and capture of William Wallace in 1305

Thomson, James 1700–48
Poet

1 When Britain first, at heaven's command,
Arose from out the azure main,
This was the charter of the land,
And guardian angels sung this strain:
'Rule, Britannia, rule the waves;
Britons never will be slaves.'

> *Alfred: a Masque* (1740), Act 2, sc.5
>
> > Composed in collaboration with David Malloch (or Mallet)

2 Delightful task! to rear the tender thought,
To teach the young idea how to shoot.

> *The Seasons* (1746), 'Spring'

3 An elegant sufficiency, content,
Retirement, rural quiet, friendship, books,
Ease and alternate labour, useful life,
Progressive virtue, and approving Heaven!

> *The Seasons* (1746), 'Spring'

4 Poor is the triumph o'er the timid hare!

> *The Seasons* (1746), 'Autumn'

5 Welcome, kindred glooms!
Congenial horrors, hail!

> *The Seasons* (1746), 'Winter'

6 There studious let me sit,
And hold high converse with the mighty dead.

> *The Seasons* (1746), 'Winter'

7 A little round, fat, oily man of God,

Was one I chiefly marked among the fry:
He had a roguish twinkle in his eye,
And alone all glittering with ungodly dew,
If a tight damsel chanced to trippen by:
Which when observed he shrunk into his mew,
And strait would recollect his piety of new.

The Castle of Indolence (1748), Canto 1, st.69

The model for this image was the Rev Patrick
Murdoch, a friend of Thomson and author
of various works of Newtonian philosophy

Thomson, James ('BV') 1834–82
Poet, journalist and critic

1 Give a man a horse he can ride,
Give a man a boat he can sail;
And his rank and wealth, his strength
 and health,
On sea nor shore shall fail.

Give a man a pipe he can smoke,
Give a man a book he can read;
And his home is bright with a calm delight,
Though the rooms be poor indeed.

'Sunday Up the River' (1869)

2 The City is of Night; perchance of Death,
But certainly of Night.

The City of Dreadful Night (1874), Part 1, st.1

3 The City is of Night, but not of Sleep;
There sweet Sleep is not for the weary brain;
The pitiless hours like years and ages creep,
A night seems termless hell.

The City of Dreadful Night (1874), Part 1, st.11

4 As I came through the desert thus it was,
As I came through the desert: All was black,
In heaven no single star, on earth no track;
A brooding hush without a stir or note;
The air so thick it clotted in my throat. . .

The City of Dreadful Night (1874), Part 4, st.2

5 Yet I strode on austere;
No hope could have no fear.

The City of Dreadful Night, (1874), Part 4, st.2

6 I find no hint throughout the Universe
Of good or ill, of blessing or of curse;
I find alone Necessity Supreme. . .

The City of Dreadful Night, (1874), Part 14, st.13

Thomson, John 1837–1921
Photographer, traveller and writer

1 The camera should be a power in this
age of instruction for the instruction
of the age.

1875. Quoted in Rosemary Goring (ed.), *Chambers
Scottish Biographical Dictionary* (1992)

Thomson, Roy (Baron Thomson of Fleet) 1894–1976
Canadian businessman and media tycoon

1 . . . it's just like having a licence to print your
own money!

On winning the licence (Aug 1957) to operate
Scottish Television. Quoted in R Braddon, *Roy
Thomson* (1965), ch.32

Thomson, Sir William see Kelvin, Lord

Torrington, Jeff 1935–
Novelist

1 Something really weird was happening in the
Gorbals – from the battered hulk of the Planet
Cinema in Scobie Street, a deepsea diver was
emerging.

Swing Hammer Swing! (1992), opening sentence

Traditional Gaelic tales

1 Is math a dhannsas tu. Ma dhannsas tu cho
math sin air oidhche na bainnseadh agad ri
nighean chamadhubh mhishealbhach Loch Ial,
cha bhi bheag aig duine sam bith ri thogail ort.

† You dance well. If you dance as well as that
on the night of your wedding to that devious
dark luckless daughter of Lochiel, no one will
have very much to criticise you for.

Said by the warrior MacIain to his younger
brother, whom he had just shot with an arrow,
causing him to stagger and stumble like one
dancing

There was a feud between the Camerons and
the MacIains, in spite of which the younger
brother had been courting Lochiel's daughter.
When MacIain heard of this, he put a stop
to it with the arrow. The brother died

2 An e creithleag a bhuail mi?

† Was that a cleg that bit me?

The dying words of MacIain

MacIain was killed on a hot summer's day
when he removed his helmet to wipe his brow.
Two bowmen were concealed in a nearby
birch grove. 'Nach math a laigheadh saighead
air bathais Mhic Iain (how nicely an arrow
would alight on MacIain's brow),' said one.
'Seadh (that is so),' said the other, 'ach chan
e do shùil chorrach no do làmh leibideach a
dhèanadh e (but it isn't your unsteady eye
nor your inept hand that could do it).' The
first man proved his skill by shooting MacIain
between the eyes. MacIain pulled the arrow
out, flung it away, made his remark, and
dropped dead

3 Se gaisgeach mór a bh' ann an Iain Odhar. Nuair
a bha e air leabaidh a' bhàis thainig nàbaidh a

choimhead air. Bha e crom os a chionn nuair a mhothaich e làmh an fhir eile a' tighinn chuige le sgithinn. Leum e bhuaithe. 'An ann as do chiall a tha thu?' ars esan. 'Chan ann,' thuirt Iain Odhar. 'Bhàth Abhainn Ruaidh fichead duine ri mo shaoghal fhìn agus mharbh mise fichead. Na robh mi air thusa fhaighinn, bha aon duine air fhichead agam is bha mi na b'fhearr na an abhainn.'

John the Sallow was a great warrior. When he was on his deathbed a neighbour came to see him. When he was bending over him he noticed his hand coming at him with a knife. He leapt away. 'Are you out of your mind?' he said. 'No,' said John the Sallow. 'During my lifetime the River Roy drowned twenty people and I killed twenty. If I had got you, I'd have twenty-one and I'd be better than the river.'

An oidhche rugadh Alasdair mac Colla bha na làirean a' tilgeil na searrach, bha na targaidean a' gliongarsaich ris a' bhalla, bha na claimhtean a' leum as na truaillean, is thuirt a' bhean-ghlùine: 'Is cinnteach gur h-e gaisgeach mór a bhios a seo.'

The night that Alasdair MacColla [Alexander Colkitto] was born, the mares were casting their foals, the shields clashed against the wall, and the swords leapt from their scabbards, and the midwife said: 'Truly this will be a great warrior.'

Traditional (17th century)

Alasdair MacColla (d.1647) was indeed a great soldier, and lieutenant to Montrose during his campaign of 1644–5

Traditional songs

1 Alasdair mhic Cholla ghasda,
As do làimh-sa dh'earbainn tapachd,
Mharbhadh Tighearn' Ach' nam Breac leat,
Thiolaigeadh e an oir an lochain...

† Splendid Alasdair, son of Colla,
From your arm I'd expect valour,
Auchinbreck's laird was killed by you,
And was buried at the lochside...

'Alasdair mhic Colla' ('Alasdair, son of Colla'). In J L Campbell & F Collinson (eds), *Hebridean Folksongs*, Vol.2 (1977)

Song in praise of Alasdair MacDonald, Montrose's lieutenant. Sir Duncan Campbell of Auchinbreck was killed at the Battle of Inverlochy (1645)

2 Ceannard an airm an tùs a' bhatail,
Sheinneadh pìob leat mhór air chnocan,
Dh'òladh fion leat dearg am portaibh.
Chuala mi 'n dé sgeul nach b'àit liom,
Glaschu bheag bhith 'na lasair,
'S Obar-eadhain an déidh a chreachadh.

† Army leader foremost in battle,
You'd play the great pipes on a hillock,
You would drink red wine in houses.
I heard today a tale amazing,
That little Glasgow is a-blazing,
And Aberdeen has been plundered.

'Alasdair mhic Colla' ('Alasdair, son of Colla'). In J L Campbell & F Collinson (eds), *Hebridean Folksongs*, Vol.2 (1977)

3 Noo I've aft times heard it said by my faither an' my mither,
That tae gang tae a waddin' is the makins o' anither.
If this be true, then I'll gang wi'-oot a biddin',
O kind Providence won't you send me tae a waddin'.

For it's Oh, dear me! Whit will I dae,
If I dee an auld maid in a garret.

'An Auld Maid in the Garret', st.1 and chorus. In Norman Buchan, *101 Scottish Songs* (1962)

4 Let howlet Whigs do what they can,
The Stuarts will be back again.
Wha cares for a' their creeshy duds,
And a' Kilmarnock sowen suds?
We'll wauk their hides and fyle their fuds,
And bring the Stuart back again.

'The Auld Stuarts Back Again' (c.1715), st.1. In James Hogg (ed.), *The Jacobite Relics of Scotland* (1st series, 1819)

5 Oh, there's meal and there's ale whaur the Gadie rins,
Wi' the yellow broom and the bonnie whins,
There's meal and there's ale whaur the Gadie rins,
At the back o' Bennachie.

'The Back o' Bennachie', chorus. In Norman Buchan and Peter Hall (eds), *The Scottish Folksinger* (1973)

John Ord's *Bothy Songs and Ballads* (1930) gives the older words, 'Oh! gin I were where Gaudie rins, where Gaudie rins,/Oh! gin I were where Gaudie rins, at the fit o' Bennachie'. The authorship is often ascribed to John Park (1804–65)

6 O, the ball, the ball,
The ball o Kirriemuir,
O, the buckin o the sweetie-wife
It wis an awfu tear.

The minister's dochter she wis there
And she was worst of a',
She cockit up her wooden leg
And pished against the wa'.

'The Ball of Kirriemuir' (19th-century version), chorus and verse

Perhaps the best known bawdy song in the world, it has countless verses and many versions

7 Four-and-twenty virgins
Came down from Inverness.
By the time the Ball was over
There were four-and-twenty less.

Sing balls to your partner,
Arse against the wall.
If ye canna get fucked on a Saturday night
Ye'll never get fucked at all!

'The Ball of Kirriemuir' (20th-century version),
st.1 and chorus

8 So, bonnie lassie, will ye gang,
And shear wi' me the hale day lang,
And love will cheer us as we gang
To join the band o' shearers.

'The Band o' Shearers', chorus. In John Ord,
Bothy Songs and Ballads (1930)

9 As I cam' in tae Turra Market,
Turra Market for tae fee,
It's I fell in wi' a wealthy fairmer,
The Barnyards o' Delgaty.

He promised me the ae best pair,
That was in a' the kintra roon,
Fan I gaed hame tae the Barnyards
There was naething there but skin and bone.

'The Barnyards o' Delgaty', st.1–2. In Norman
Buchan, *101 Scottish Songs* (1962)

Variations of these appear as stanzas 4–5 in
John Ord's *Bothy Songs and Ballads* (1930),
with stanza 4 as follows: 'As I cam' in by
Netherdale/At Turra Market for to fee/I fell
in wi' a farmer chiel/Frae the Barnyards o'
Delgaty'

10 There's some say that we wan,
And some say that they wan,
And some say that nane wan at a', man;
But ae thing I'm sure,
That at Sheriffmuir
A battle there was that I saw, man.
And we ran and they ran, and they ran
and we ran,
And we ran and they ran awa', man.

'The Battle of Sheriffmuir' (18th century)

The battle was fought on 13 November 1715
between Jacobite forces under the Earl of Mar
and a government force under the Duke of
Argyll. Although both sides claimed victory,
the battle's inconclusiveness effectively put
an end to this Jacobite rising

11 . . . The explosion was heard, all the women
and children
With pale anxious faces they haste to the mine.
When the truth was made known, the hills
rang with their mourning,
Three-hundred-and-ten young miners were
slain.

'The Blantyre Explosion', st.2. In Ewan MacColl,
Folk Songs and Ballads of Scotland (1965)

On 22 October 1877, in Scotland's worst

mining disaster, 207 miners were killed in an
explosion at Dixon's Colliery, High Blantyre,
Lanarkshire

12 'O lassie, lassie, do you remember
The ships that sailed by the Broomielaw,
And the sailor laddies they all admired
The bleacher lassie on Kelvinhaugh?'

'The Bleacher Lass o' Kelvinhaugh', st.3. In
Norman Buchan, *101 Scottish Songs* (1962)

13 O ye'll tak the high road, and I'll tak the
low road,
And I'll be in Scotland afore ye,
But me and my true love will never meet again
On the bonnie, bonnie banks o' Loch Lomond.

By yon bonnie banks and by yon bonnie braes,
Where the sun shines bright on Loch
Lomond. . .

'The Bonnie Banks o' Loch Lomond', chorus
and st.1. In Robert Ford (ed.), *Vagabond Songs
and Ballads of Scotland* (1904). Cf. John Purser 1

The speaker in the song is thought to be a
Jacobite soldier awaiting execution after the
retreat from Derby: it is his spirit that will
be travelling 'the low road'

14 'Twas there that we parted in yon shady glen,
On the steep, steep side o' Ben Lomond. . .

'The Bonnie Banks o' Loch Lomond' (19th
century), st.2. In Robert Ford (ed.), *Vagabond
Songs and Ballads of Scotland* (1904)

15 Noo there's mony a bonnie lass in the Howe
o' Auchterless,
There's mony a bonnie lass in the Garioch-o.
There's mony a bonnie Jean in the toon o'
Aiberdeen,
But the floo'er o' them a' is in Fyvie-o.

'The Bonnie Lass o' Fyvie', st.2. In Norman
Buchan, *101 Scottish Songs* (1962)

16 Green grow the birk upon bonnie Ythanside
An' law lies the lawlands o' Fyvie-o,
The captain's name was Ned an' he died
for a maid;
He died for the bonnie lass o' Fyvie-o.

'The Bonnie Lass o' Fyvie', st.13. In Norman
Buchan, *101 Scottish Songs* (1962)

17 So be cheerful, my lads,
Let your courage never fail,
While the bonnie ship the Diamond
Goes a-fishing for the whale.

'The Bonnie Ship the Diamond', chorus. In John
Ord, *Bothy Songs and Ballads* (1930)

The *Diamond* was one of 20 whaling ships
lost in the ice off the west coast of
Greenland in 1830

18 What's the spring breathing jess'mine and rose,
What's the summer, with all its gay train,
Or the plenty of autumn to those

Who've barter'd their freedom for gain?

Let the love of our king's sacred right,
To the love of our country succeed;
Let friendship and honour unite,
And flourish on both sides the Tweed.

> 'Both Sides the Tweed', st.1 and chorus. In James Hogg (ed.), *The Jacobite Relics of Scotland* (1st series, 1819)
>
>> Dick Gaughan updated these words on his album *Handful of Earth* (1981), 'to make it of more contemporary relevance'

Think him poorest who can be a slave,
Him richest who dares to be free.

> 'Both Sides the Tweed', st.3. In James Hogg (ed.), *The Jacobite Relics of Scotland* (1st series, 1819)

So, come all ye weavers, ye Calton weavers,
Come all ye weavers where e'er ye be;
Beware of Whisky, Nancy Whisky,
She'll ruin you as she ruined me.

> 'The Calton Weaver', st.10. In John Ord, *Bothy Songs and Ballads* (1930)

Cam ye ower frae France?
Cam ye doun by Lunnon?
Saw ye Geordie Whelps
And his bonnie woman?
Were ye at the place
Ca'd the Kittle Housie?
Saw ye Geordie's grace
Ridin' on a goosie?

> 'Cam Ye Ower Frae France?' (18th century), st.1
>
>> Jacobite song lampooning the Hanoverian George I as a frequenter of London brothels

The Campbells are comin', oho, oho!

> 'The Campbells are Comin'' (18th century)

Chaidil mi raoir air a' bhuailidh
Dh'fhairich mi crith 's cha chrith fuachd e
Dh'fhairich mi grìs 's cha ghrìs ruaidhe
Dh'fhairich mi fear làimhe fuaire
'S gliogadaich nan crios 'gam fuasgladh
'S a bhith cur nan arm an taobh shuas dhiom. . .

† Last night I slept at the cowfold
I felt a tremor, and not from shivering
I felt gooseflesh, but not from erysipelas
I perceived a man with a cold hand
And the noise of belts being loosened
And of weapons being put beside me. . .

> 'Chaidil mi raoir' ('Last night I slept'). In J L Campbell & F Collinson (eds), *Hebridean Folksongs*, Vol.2 (1977)

Thuirt e rium gu robh mi duathail
Thuirt mi ris nach robh mi suarach.

† He said to me that I was stubborn
I said to him that I was not disreputable.

> 'Chaidil mi raoir' ('Last night I slept'). In J L Campbell & F Collinson (eds), *Hebridean Folksongs*, Vol.2 (1977)

25 Ach mur h-è gur bean mo mhàthair
'S gur h-è mo mhuime rinn m'àrach
Dh'innsinn sgeul bheag air na mnài dhuibh
Tha iad sgeigeil, bleideil, bàrdail
'S an aigne mar ghaoth a' Mhàrta
Mar uan Chéitein anns a' mhèilich
Mar laogh féidh an déidh a mhàthar
Mar mhuir a' lìonadh 's a' tràghadh
Mar liaghan air leaca bàna
Mar easgann an lodan làthchadh.

† But were not my mother a woman
And the fostermother who reared me
I'd tell you a little tale of women
They are mocking, teasing, scolding
Their minds are like the March wind blowing
Like a lamb in May a-bleating
Like a fawn following its mother
Like the tide ebbing and flowing
Like the tangles on the white rocks
Like an eel in a muddy puddle.

> 'Chailin òig as stiùramaiche'. In J L Campbell & F Collinson (eds), *Hebridean Folksongs*, Vol.2 (1977)

26 Chan eil mi gun mhulad orm,
Ch-uile h-aon a' pòsadh,
'S tha mise gun phòsadh fhathast;
Seann-duine cha ghabh mi idir,
Bidh e fada 'g eirigh,
Fada dol 'na éideadh,
Fada cur a churraic air,
Cha déid e mach gun am bata,
Cha dig e steach gun an ad air. . .

† I am not unsorrowful, everyone is marrying, and yet I'm unmarried still; an old man I will not take, he'll be long in rising, long in putting on his clothes, long in putting on his cap, he won't go out without a stick, he won't come in without his hat on. . .

> 'Chan eil mi gun mhulad orm' ('I am not unsorrowful'). In J L Campbell & F Collinson (eds), *Hebridean Folksongs*, Vol.3 (1981)

27 B'annsa balach sgiobalta
A thogadh mi 's a leagadh mi,
'S a bheireadh mi a féithe.

† A tidy youth I would prefer, who'd lift me up and put me down, and from the bog would take me.

> 'Chan eil mi gun mhulad orm' ('I am not unsorrowful'). In J L Campbell & F Collinson (eds), *Hebridean Folksongs*, Vol.3 (1981)

28 Shiùbhlainn, shiùbhlainn, shiùbhlainn fhéin leat,
Shiùbhlainn Alba leat is Eirinn,
Shiùbhlainn machaire fada réidh leat,
Shiùbhlainn ro' choill' mhór nan geug leat
Ged bhiodh do bhean òg an eud rium –
Raghainn air sin 's a bhith réidh rium.

† I'd go, I'd go, I would go with you,
I'd go through Scotland and Ireland with you,
I'd walk the long smooth sandhills with you,
I'd go through the great leafy wood with you,

Though your young wife were jealous of me;
Her choice is that or to be at peace with me.

> 'Chuala mi 'n dé sgeul nach b' ait liom'
> ('Yesterday I heard a tale unjoyful'). In J L
> Campbell & F Collinson (eds), *Hebridean
> Folksongs*, Vol.2 (1977)

29 Chunna mise mo leannan
'S cha do dh'aithnich e an dé mi
Cha do dh'fhiosraich 's cha d'fharraid
'S cha do ghabh e mo sgeula
'Sann a ghabh e orm seachad
Air each glas nan ceum eudrom.

† I saw my lover and he did not recognise me
yesterday; he neither asked nor enquired nor
sought to find out how I was – he rode on
past me on a grey light-stepping horse.

> 'Chunna mise mo leannan' ('I saw my lover')
>
> Some versions of this song are associated with
> the Battle of Auldearn (1645)

30 Cock up your beaver and cock it fu' sprush,
We'll ower the Border and gie them a brush,
There's somebody there we'll teach better
behaviour,
Hey, brave Johnnie lad, cock up your beaver.

> 'Cock up your Beaver' (18th century), chorus

31 Coisich a rùin, lùb nan geal làmh
'S bheir soiridh bhuam dha na Hearadh
Go Seon Caimbeal donn, mo leannan.
Bu thric a laigh mi fo t'earradh.

† Come away, dear, white-handed gallant,
Bear my greetings to Harris
To John Campbell my handsome lover.
Often have I lain beneath your cloak.

> 'Coisich a rùin' ('Come away, dear'). In
> K C Craig (ed.), *Orain Luaidh* (1949)

32 Being pursuit by the dragoons,
Within my bed he was laid doon,
And weel I wot he was worth his room
He was a dainty Davie.

Leese me on your curly pow,
Bonnie Davie, dainty Davie,
Leese me on your curly pow
My ain dear dainty Davie!

> 'Dainty Davie' (17th century), st.1 and chorus
>
> This song refers to David Williamson, a
> Covenanting minister who hid from govern-
> ment troops in the bed of Lady Cherrytrees'
> daughter, and while there made her pregnant.
> He subsequently married her

33 Sooner than sell our country for a pension,
Down among the dead men,
Down among the dead men,
Down, down, down, down,
Down among the dead men let us lie.

> 'Down Among the Dead Men'. In James
> Hogg (ed.), *The Jacobite Relics of Scotland* (1st
> series, 1819)

34 My name's Duncan Campbell, from the shire
of Argyle,
I've travelled this country for many a mile,
I've travelled thro' England, and Ireland an' a',
And the name I go under's bold Erin-go-Bragh.

> 'Erin-go-Bragh', st.1. In Robert Ford (ed.),
> *Vagabond Songs and Ballads of Scotland* (1904)

35 Eudail a Rìgh! bu mhi bronag
'S mi dol 'na chlachan Di-Dòmhnaich
Chan ann le m' raghainn a dh'òigeir
Le fear odhar, bodhar, breòite. . .

† My dear God! I am so wretched
Going to church on Sunday
Not with the youth I would have chosen
But with a dun, deaf, broken-down fellow. . .

> 'Eudail a Rìgh! bu mhi brònag' ('My dear God! I
> am so wretched'). In J L Campbell & F Collinson
> (eds), *Hebridean Folksongs*, Vol.2 (1977)

36 'S tric mi shealltainn on chnoc as airde,
Dh'fheuch am faic mi fear a' bhàta:
An tig thu 'n diugh, na 'n tig thu màireach?
'S mar tig thu idir, gur truagh a tà mi.

Fhir a' bhàta, na hóro-éile. . .
Mo shoraidh slàn dut 's gach àit' an téid thu.

† From the highest hill I look out often
To try if I can see the Boatman:
Come you today, or come you tomorrow?
And sad am I if you come never.

O, the Boatman, *na hóro éile. . .*
My long farewell where you may go to.

> 'Fear a' Bhàta', st.1 and chorus. In K H Jackson,
> *A Celtic Miscellany* (1951)

37 So come fill up your glasses of brandy and wine
Whatever it costs I will pay;
So be easy an' free when you're drinkin' wi' me,
For I'm a man youse don't meet every day.

> 'For Ma Name is Jock Stewart', st.4. In Ailie
> Munro, *The Folk Music Revival in Scotland*
> (1984), ch.3
>
> As sung by Jeannie Robertson (1908–75)

38 Charlie, Charlie, rise and rin,
The fisher wives is makin' din,
It's best to sleep in a hale skin,
It'll be a bluidy mornin'.

> 'The Fraserburgh Meal Riot', st.1
>
> A riot took place in Fraserburgh on 6 March
> 1813. The export of grain ('meal') during a
> time of food scarcity was violently opposed,
> especially by the fisherwomen. The verse is
> derived from Adam Skirving's Jacobite song,
> 'Johnnie Cope'

39 The servant gaed where the dochter lay;
The sheets were cauld and she was away;
And fast to the guidwife she did say
'She's aff wi' the gaberlunzie man.'

> 'The Gaberlunzie Man', st.4. In Norman Buchan,
> *101 Scottish Songs* (1962)

Sometimes attributed to James V. First published in Allan Ramsay, *The Tea-Table Miscellany* (1724–37)

Oh, the Gallowa' hills are covered wi' broom,
Wi' heather bells, in bonnie bloom,
Wi' heather bells an' rivers a',
An' I'll gang oot owre the hills tae Gallowa'.

'The Gallowa' Hills', chorus. In Norman Buchan, *101 Scottish Songs* (1962)

As sung by Jeannie Robertson (1908–75), based on 'The Braes of Galloway' by wandering minstrel, William Nicholson (1783–1849)

Bheir mi óro bhanó,
Bheir mi óro bhan i,
Bheir mi óru o hó,
'Smith a brònach's tu'm dhìth.

Vair me oro van o
Vair me oro van ee,
Vair me oru o ho,
Sad am I without thee.

'Gradh Geal mo Chridh' ('Eriskay Love Lilt')

English adaptation by Marjory Kennedy-Fraser

As I cam in by Auchindoon,
A little wee bit frae the toon,
When tae the Hielands I was boun',
Tae view the Haughs o' Cromdale,
I met a man in tartan trews,
And speir'd at him what was the news.
Quo he, 'The Hieland army rues
That e'er we cam tae Cromdale.'

'The Haughs o' Cromdale', st.1. In Norman Buchan, *101 Scottish Songs* (1962)

The song conflates the events of two battles, one Montrose's victory at Auldearn (1645), the other a Jacobite defeat at Cromdale (1690)

I once loved a lad, and I loved him sae weel
I hated all others that spoke o' him ill,
But noo he's rewarded me weel for my love
For he's gaun tae be wad tae anither.

'I Once Loved a Lad', st.1

Or 'lass', whatever your persuasion

Far distant, far distant, lies Scotia, the brave!
No tombstone memorial to hallow his grave;
His bones now lie scattered on the rude soil of Spain,
For young Jamie Foyers in battle was slain.

'Jamie Foyers', st.1. In Robert Ford (ed.), *Vagabond Songs and Ballads of Scotland* (1904)

Apparently based on the story of Sergeant James Foyers, who was born in Stirlingshire and killed at the siege of Burgos in 1812. Ewan MacColl wrote another version of this song to mark the Spanish Civil War

My name is Jamie Raeburn, frae Glasgow toon I came;
My place and habitation I'm forced tae leave wi' shame;

From my place and habitation I now maun gang awa',
Far frae the bonnie hills and dales o' Caledonia.

'Jamie Raeburn' (c.1820), st.1. In Norman Buchan, *101 Scottish Songs* (1962). Cf. Norman Buchan 2

Jamie Raeburn was reputedly a Glasgow baker who was charged with petty theft, and subsequently transported to a convict settlement

46 And wi you, and wi you,
And wi you, Johnnie lad,
I'll dance the buckles aff my shoon
Wi you, my Johnnie lad.

'Johnnie Lad', chorus

47 And we'll gang nae mair a-roving
Sae late into the nicht;
And we'll gang nae mair a-roving, boys,
Let the mune sheen ne'er sae bricht.

'The Jolly Beggar', chorus

Traditional song, also known as 'We'll Gang Nae Mair A-Roving'. Associated with James V, who habitually travelled through his kingdom in disguise. Cf. Lord Byron 32

48 The lad that I hae chosen
I'll therewith be content;
The saut sea sall be frozen
Before that I repent.
Repent me will I never
Until the day I dee,
Though the Lawlands o' Holland
Hae twined my Love and me.

'The Lawlands o' Holland' (18th century), st.1

49 First fan I cam' tae the toon
They ca'd me proud and saucy,
But noo they've changed my name,
Ca' me the leaboy's lassie.

'The Leaboy's Lassie', st.2

Another version of this song is 'The Lichtbob's Lassie'

50 As I came in by Inverness,
The simmer sun was sinking down;
O there I saw the weel-faur'd lass,
And she was greeting through the town.
The gray-hair'd men were a' i' the streets,
And auld dames crying (sad to see!)
'The flower o' the lads o' Inverness
Lie bluidy on Culloden lee!'

'The Lovely Lass of Inverness', st.2. In James Hogg (ed.), *The Jacobite Relics of Scotland* (2nd series, 1821)

51 Make your way to Stornoway
On the road to Orinsay
Where my thoughts return each day
By lovely Stornoway

'Lovely Stornoway', st.1

Words by Robert Halfin and Calum Kennedy

52 Ah wis ludgin' wi Big Aggie,
Jist me an' ither ten,
An' we a' slept thegither
In a wee bit single-en';
We had nae beds at a'
We jist slept agin' the wa';
In oor ain wee hoose,
In oor ain wee hoose.

> 'Ludgin' Wi' Big Aggie', st.1. In Norman
> Buchan and Peter Hall (eds), *The Scottish Folk
> Singer* (1973)
>
> > Traditional Clydeside song which parodies
> > cosy, kailyard sentiments. Cf. Elizabeth Hamilton 7,
> > Traditional songs 73

53 But my blue een wi' sorrow are streamin'
For him who will never return, MacCrimmon.

No more, no more, no more MacCrimmon
In war nor in peace shall return MacCrimmon,
Till dawns the sad day of doom and burnin'
MacCrimmon is home no more returnin'.

> 'MacCrimmon's Lament', st.1 and chorus
>
> > The song is based on the events of 16 February
> > 1746, when at the so-called Rout of Moy, a
> > small Jacobite force clashed with government
> > troops led by the MacLeod of MacLeod, near
> > Inverness. His piper MacCrimmon, who was
> > the only person killed, had composed a lament
> > for his own death before leaving Skye. The
> > words are supposed to have been written by
> > his sister

54 Marbhaisg air a' mhulad, 's buan e
'S tric ugam e, 's ainneamh bhuam e
Dh'fhairlich orm a chur air fuadach
Chur a deas no chur a tuath bhuam
Chur a chuideachda nan uaislean
Chur a choimhideachd an guaillean.

† A curse on sorrow, it is lasting.
Oft 'tis with me, seldom absent,
I have failed to drive it from me,
To send it south or northwards from me,
To keep company with the gentry,
To overlook their shoulders.

> 'Marbhaisg air a' mhulad' ('A curse on sorrow').
> In J L Campbell & F Collinson (eds), *Hebridean
> Folksongs*, Vol.1 (1969)

55 Far frae my hame I wander, but still my
thoughts return
To my ain folk ower yonder, in the shieling
by the burn. . .

> 'My Ain Folk', st.1
>
> Words by Wilfrid Mills

56 And it's oh! but I'm longing for my ain folk,
Tho' they be but lowly, puir and plain folk;
I am far beyond the sea, but my heart
will ever be
At hame in dear auld Scotland, wi' my ain folk.

> 'My Ain Folk', chorus
>
> Words by Wilfrid Mills

57 The Northern Lights of Old Aberdeen mean
Home Sweet Home to me,
The Northern Lights of Aberdeen are what I
long to see;
I've been a wand'rer all of my life and many
a sight I've seen,
God speed the day when I'm on my way
To my home in Aberdeen.

> 'The Northern Lights of Old Aberdeen', chorus
>
> Words by Mel and Mary Webb

58 O sing to me the auld Scotch sangs
In the braid Scottish tongue,
The sangs my father lov'd to hear,
The sangs my mother sung,
When she sat beside my cradle
Or croon'd me on her knee
And I wadna sleep she sang so sweet
The auld Scotch sangs to me.

> 'O Sing to Me the Auld Scotch Sangs', st.1

59 O the shearin's no for you my bonnie lassie o,
O the shearin's no for you my bonnie lassie o,
O the shearin's no for you, for your belly's
round and fu'
And your back it winna boo, my bonnie lassie o.

> 'O the Shearin's no for You', st.1.
> Cf. Thomas Lyle 1
>
> > These words originally accompanied the tune
> > to which Lyle's 'Kelvingrove' was set during
> > the 19th century. Depicting a young woman
> > being too pregnant to bend to shear the corn,
> > they were considered improper for public
> > performance

60 The piper cam to our toun,
To our toun, to our toun,
The piper cam to our toun,
And he play'd bonnilie.
He play'd a spring, the laird to please,
A spring brent new, frae 'yont the seas,
And then he ga'e his bags a wheeze,
And played anither key.

And wasna he a roguey,
A roguey, a roguey,
And wasna he a roguey,
The piper o' Dundee?

> 'The Piper o' Dundee' (18th century), st.1 and
> chorus. Cf. Bairn rhymes 1

61 Cauld winter was howling o'er muir and o'er
mountain
And wild was the surge on the dark rolling
sea,
When I met, about daybreak, a bonnie
young lassie,
Wha asked me the road and the miles to
Dundee.

> 'The Road and the Miles to Dundee' (19th
> century), st.1. In John Ord, *Bothy Songs and
> Ballads* (1930)

338

So here's to the lassie – I ne'er can forget her –
And ilka young laddie that's listening to me,
And never be sweer to convoy a young lassie,
Though it's only to show her the road to
  Dundee.

'The Road and the Miles to Dundee' (19th
century), st.7. In John Ord, *Bothy Songs and
Ballads* (1930)

The shuttle rins, the shuttle rins,
The shuttle rins wi' speed;
Oh sweetly may the shuttle rin,
That wins the bairn's bread.

'The Shuttle Rins', chorus. In Henry Syme,
*Poems and Songs Chiefly for the Encouragement
of the Working Classes* (1849). Cf. John Ewen 1

Time is sic a precious thing,
Time brings a' things tae yer mind,
And time wi' its labours along wi' a' its joys
Oh time brings a' things tae an end.

'Sprig o' thyme', chorus. In Ailie Munro, *The
Folk Music Revival in Scotland* (1984), ch.4

Let kings and courtiers rise and fa;
This world has mony turns,
But brightly beams aboon them a'
The star o' Robbie Burns.

'The Star o' Robbie Burns', chorus. Cf. Norman
Buchan 1

Words by James Thomson. Usually sung as
'star o' Rabbie Burns'

Doon by yon green bushes by Calder's
  clear stream,
Where I an' my Annie sae aften hae been,
The hours they flew past us, richt happy
  were we;
It was little she thocht that a soldier I'd be.

'Sweet Calder Burn', or 'Bonnie Woodha'', st.1.
In John Ord, *Bothy Songs and Ballads* (1930)

Aft-times when I weary I think o' lang syne,
When I was a collier and wrought in the mine,
An' the tears they do trickle an' doon
  they do fa',
Like the dew on the gowans at bonnie Woodha'.

'Sweet Calder Burn', or 'Bonnie Woodha'', st.7.
In John Ord, *Bothy Songs and Ballads* (1930)

O' a' the trades that I do ken,
The beggin' is the best,
For when a beggar's weary,
He can aye sit doon an' rest.

Tae the beggin' I will go, will go,
Tae the beggin' I will go.

'Tae the Beggin'', st.1 and chorus. In Norman
Buchan, *101 Scottish Songs* (1962)

In winter when the rain rain'd cauld,
And frost and snaw on ilka hill,
And Boreas wi' his blasts sae bauld,
Was threat'ning a' our kye to kill;

Then Bell my wife, wha lo'es nae strife,
She said to me right hastily,
'Get up, gudeman, save Crummie's life,
And tak' your auld cloak about ye.'

'Tak' your Auld Cloak about Ye' (18th
century), st.1

70 Tatties and herrin', tatties and herrin',
Your natural food it is tatties and herrin'.

'Tatties an' Herrin''. In Norman Buchan and
Peter Hall (eds), *The Scottish Folksinger* (1973).
Cf. Iain Crichton Smith 26

71 Tha caolas eadar mi is Iain
Cha chaol a th'ann ach cuan domhain
Truagh nach tràghadh e fo latha
Nach biodh ann ach loch no abhainn
Fiach am faighinn a dhol tarsainn
Far a bheil mo leannan falaich.

† A sound there is between me and Ian
No sound it is, but a deep ocean
Would that it ebbed before the day
That it were only a loch or river
For me to try to get across
Over to my secret lover.

'Tha caolas eadar mi is Iain' ('A sound there is
between me and Iain'). In J L Campbell & F
Collinson (eds), *Hebridean Folksongs*, Vol.2 (1977)

72 Tha sneachd air na beannaibh Diùrach,
Cha doir uisge no ceò dhiù e:
A Rìgh! ma thà, gu dé sin dhuinne?
Cha truimid iad fhéin a ghiùlain!

† Snow lies on the mountains of Jura,
Rain nor mist will not remove it:
If it does, what does it matter?
The hills themselves feel it no burden!

'Tha sneachd air na beannaibh Diùrach' ('Snow
lies on the mountains of Jura'). In J L Campbell
& F Collinson (eds), *Hebridean Folksongs*,
Vol.2 (1977)

73 O this is no my ain house,
I ken by the biggin o't;
For bow-kail thrave at my door-cheek,
And thistles on the riggin o't.

'This is no my Ain House' (18th century).
Cf. Norman Buchan 1

74 When I hae a saxpence under my thoomb,
Then I get credit in ilka toun,
But aye when I'm puir they bid me gang by;
O! poverty parts gude companie.
Todlen hame, todlen hame,
Cou'dna my luv come todlen hame?

'Todlen Hame', (18th century), st.1.
Cf. Joanna Baillie 12

75 Oh, come a' ye tramps an' hawkers an'
  gaitherers o' bla',
That tramps the countrie roon' an roon', come
  listen ane and a'.
I'll tell tae you a rovin' tale and sights that I
  have seen,

Far up into the snowy North and South by Gretna Green.

'Tramps an' Hawkers', st.1. In Norman Buchan and Peter Hall (eds), *The Scottish Folksinger* (1973)

76 Twa recruitin' sairgeants cam' frae the Black Watch –
To markets and fairs some recruits for to catch;
An' a' that they listed was forty an' twa,
So list bonnie laddie, an' come awa'.

'Twa Recruitin' Sairgeants', st.1. In Norman Buchan, *101 Scottish Songs* (1962)

As sung by Jeannie Robertson (1908–75)

77 O waly, waly, up the bank,
And waly, waly, doun the brae,
And waly, waly, yon burn-side,
Where I and my Love wont to gae!
I lean'd my back unto an aik,
I thocht it was a trustie tree;
But first it bow'd, and syne it brak –
Sae my true love did lichtlie me.

'Waly, Waly' (18th century), st.1

78 O waly, waly, gin love be bonnie
A little time while it is new!
But when 'tis auld it waxeth cauld,
And fades awa' like morning dew.

'Waly, Waly' (18th century), st.2

79 But had I wist, before I kist,
That love had been sae ill to win,
I had lock'd my heart in a case o' gowd,
And pinn'd it wi' a siller pin.

'Waly, Waly' (18th century), st.4

80 Noo the cream o' the joke still remains tae be tellt,
Fur the bloke that was turnin' them aff on the belt
At the peak o' production was so sorely pressed
That the real yin got bunged in alang wi' the rest.

So if ever ye come on a stane wi' a ring
Jist sit yersel doon and appoint yersel King
Fur there's nane wud be able tae challenge yir claim
That ye'd croont yersel King on the Destiny Stane.

'The Wee Magic Stane', st.8–9. In Norman Buchan, *101 Scottish Songs* (1962)

Written by John McEvoy, the song celebrates the taking of the Stone of Destiny from Westminster Cathedral in 1950. Cf. Ian Hamilton 3, Kay Matheson 3

81 For we're no awa to bide awa,
We're no awa to leave ye,
We're no awa to bide awa,
We'll aye come back and see ye.

'We're no Awa' to Bide Awa'', chorus

Words adapted by Ian Macpherson

82 Wha wadna fecht for Charlie?
Wha wadna draw the sword?
Wha wadna up and rally
At the royal prince's word?

'Wha Wadna Fecht for Charlie?', st.1

83 O he's a ranting roving blade!
O he's a brisk and a bonnie lad!
Betide what may, my heart is glad
To see my lad wi' his white cockade.

'The White Cockade' (18th century), chorus

84 As I cam' in by Ythanside,
Where swiftly flows the rolling tide,
A fair young maid passed by my side,
She looked at me and smiled.

'Ythanside', st.1. In John Ord, *Bothy Songs and Ballads* (1930)

Traquair, Phoebe Anna 1852–1936

Irish embroiderer, enameller and illustrator, who lived in Edinburgh and was at the forefront of the Arts and Crafts movement

1 To the artist, be he the poet, painter or musician, the world is a great treasure house, stored with endless material for him to use; teach yourself to match the beauty of red-tipped buds, sunlight through green leaves, the yellow gorse on the hill, the song of wild birds, so on, step by step, the world opens out. This is life. This is to live, the perfection comes when one's own life is in harmony with this beauty . . .

Letter to her nephew Willie Moss (c.1893). Epigraph in Elizabeth Cumming, *Phoebe Anna Traquair* (1993)

She was married to Ramsay Traquair (1840–1912), the head of Natural History in the Royal Scottish Museum, Edinburgh

2 Perfect harmony, is not that what we all strive after? . . .

Letter to her nephew Willie Moss (11 Dec 1893), National Library of Scotland manuscript 8122 fol.40. Quoted in Elizabeth Cumming, *Phoebe Anna Traquair* (1993)

3 An artist's work in this world is to sing, music is his world, at times strong discords, passions which have not yet found their harmonies rush in, but it is all music, down deep at the foundation of all things the great Eternal Harmonies for every sound . . .

Letter to her nephew Willie Moss (15 Mar 1896), National Library of Scotland manuscript 8122 fol.67. Quoted in Elizabeth Cumming, *Phoebe Anna Traquair* (1993)

Trocchi, Alexander 1925–84

Novelist

1 Loose ends, things unrelated, shifts, nightmare journeys, cities arrived at and left, meetings,

desertions, betrayals, all manner of unions, adulteries, triumphs, defeats. . . these are the facts.

> *Cain's Book* (1960)

2 I often wondered how far out a man could go without being obliterated.

> *Cain's Book* (1960)

3 Invisible Insurrection of a Million Minds

> Title of essay published in *New Saltire Review* (Jun 1962)

4 We are concerned not with the *coup-d'état* of Trotsky and Lenin, but with the *coup-du-monde*, a transition of necessity more complex, more diffuse than the other, and so more gradual, less spectacular. . .

Political revolt is and must be ineffectual precisely because it must come to grips at the prevailing level of political process. Beyond the backwaters of civilisation it is an anachronism. Meanwhile, with the world at the edge of extinction, we cannot afford to wait for the mass. Nor to brawl with it.

> 'Invisible Insurrection of a Million Minds', *New Saltire Review* (Jun 1962)

5 A great deal of what is pompously called 'juvenile delinquency' is the inarticulate response of youth incapable of coming to terms with leisure. The violence associated with it is a direct consequence of the alienation of man from himself brought about by the Industrial Revolution. Man has forgotten how to play.

> 'Invisible Insurrection of a Million Minds', *New Saltire Review* (Jun 1962)

6 Of what is interesting in Scottish writing in the past twenty years or so, I have written it all!

> Speaking at the Edinburgh International Writers' Conference (21 Aug 1962)
>
> He clashed memorably at the conference with Hugh MacDiarmid, over their respective literary achievements. MacDiarmid called him 'cosmopolitan scum' while Trocchi called the discussion on Scottish writing 'turgid, petty, provincial, stale, cold-porridge, Bible-clasping nonsense.'

7 Set a bourgeois architect to design homes for the working class and without fail he will design homes for sardines!

> 'Wolfie', in Andrew Murray Scott (ed.), *Invisible Insurrection of a Million Minds: A Trocchi Reader* (1991)

Turberville, Ruby 1922–

Dancer, journalist and broadcaster

1 People talk about the glamour of show business. But they forget about the grotty digs which you often had to put up with, and living out of a suitcase, mending fishnet tights, and sewing ballet shoes and washing your costumes over the weekend. The glamour was on the stage when the lights came up; the rest of it was hard grind.

> Quoted in Vivien Devlin, *Kings, Queens and People's Palaces: An Oral History of the Scottish Variety Theatre, 1920–1970* (1991), ch.2

Turner, Sir James 1615–c.1686

Royalist soldier, known to his opponents as 'Bloody Bite-the-Sheep'

1 The house of death hath many doores, and thorough one or ane other of them we must all enter. . . If a man enjoy the inward peace of his mind, it is no matter whether a feaver, a pistoll, a dagger, a hatchet, or a halter, usher him to his grave.

> Said to his Covenanter captors (25 Nov 1666) when threatened with execution by them during the Pentland Rising. *Memoirs of His Own Life and Times* (1829 edition)

Twain, Mark (pseudonym of Samuel Langhorne Clemens) 1835–1910

American writer

1 It was Sir Walter [Scott] that made every gentleman in the South a Major or a Colonel, or a General or a Judge, before the war; and it was he, also, that made these gentlemen value these bogus decorations. For it was he that created rank and caste down there, and also reverence for rank and caste, and pride and pleasure in them. Enough is laid on slavery, without fathering upon it these creations and contributions of Sir Walter.

Sir Walter had so large a hand in making Southern character, as it existed before the war, that he is in great measure responsible for the war.

> *Life on the Mississippi* (1883), ch.46, 'Enchantments and Enchanters'

Tytler, James 1747–1805

Poet, editor of the Encyclopaedia Britannica *(2nd edition), and balloonist, known as 'Balloon' Tytler*

1 Lost are my wishes, lost is all my care,
And all my projects flutter in the air.

> 'To Mr Lunardi, on his successful aerial voyages from Edinburgh, Kelso, and Glasgow' (1786). Quoted in Sir James Fergusson, *Balloon Tytler* (1972), ch.5
>
> Published by the Italian balloonist Vincent

Lunardi in his *Account of Five Aerial Voyages in Scotland* (1786), this tribute to him also refers to Tytler's own earlier, mostly failed, ballooning attempts

2 . . . you must consider the House of Commons as your enemies. They affect to consider themselves as the *democratical* part of the constitution. They are not; they are a vile junto of aristocrats. The majority of them are landowners; and every landowner is a despot, in the most true and literal sense of the word.

'To the People and their Friends' (Nov 1792).

Quoted in Sir James Fergusson, *Balloon Tytler* (1972), Appendix

For publishing this broadside, Tytler was arrested and charged with seditious libel in December 1792. Released on bail, he fled the country to Ireland, and after two years there emigrated to America, where he lived for the rest of his life

3 The bonnie bruckit lassie,
She's blue beneath the een:
She was the fairest lassie
That dansit on the green.

'The Bonnie Bruckit Lassie' (1793), st.1.
Cf. Hugh MacDiarmid 2

U

Urquhart, Fred 1912–95
Novelist and short-story writer

'You just take a look at the *News of the World* any Sunday. It's the only newspaper you'll find any mention of this so-called heinous crime. Other papers never mention it. That's why people are ignorant of it, and suspicious, and narrow-minded. The lower classes don't understand it. Maybe, in fifty years they will. And a lot of the so-called, upper classes, don't understand it either. It's only intelligent people who understand it, and the mass of people are profoundly unintelligent. You've only got to look around you to see that.'

> On homosexuality. *Time Will Knit* (1938) (Cinnamon)

Proud Lady in a Cage

> Title of short story, first published in G Gordon (ed.), *Prevailing Spirits* (1976)

My Grandfather Willie was fond of a dram. It was a failing he bequeathed to me, along with a fondness for young men in uniform.

> 'My Many Splendoured Pavilion', in Maurice Lindsay (ed.), *As I Remember* (1979)

Urquhart, Sir Thomas 1611–60
Author, linguist, Royalist and eccentric

... the loxogonospherical triangles whether amblygonospherical or oxygonospherical are either monurgetick or disergetick.

> *The Trissotetras: or a most Exquisite Table for Resolving all Manner of Triangles. . .* (1645)

... the never-too-much-to-be-admired Crichtoun. . .

On James 'the Admirable' Crichton (1560–c.1583), adventurer and traveller, who was killed in a duel in Mantua. *The Jewel* (1652)

3 To speak of her *hirquitalliency* at the *elevation* of the *pole* of his *Microcosm*, or of his luxuriousness to erect a *gnomon* on her *horizontal* dial, will perhaps be held by some to be expressions full of obsceneness, and offensive to the purity of chaste ears. . .

> On 'the Admirable Crichton's' seduction of his Italian mistress. *The Jewel* (1652)

4 Words are the signs of things; it being to signify that they were instituted at first; nor can they be, as such, directed to any other end, whether they be articulate or inarticulate.

> *Logopandecteision, or an Introduction to the Universal Language* (1653), Book 1

> Urquhart claimed to have invented a language capable of expressing every fact, thought and emotion with the utmost clarity and precision

5 These two did oftentimes do the two-backed beast together, joyfully rubbing and frotting their bacon against one another, in so far, that at last she became great with child of a fair son. . .

> On the coupling of Gargantua's parents, in Urquhart's translation (1653) of Rabelais's *Gargantua and Pantagruel*, Book 1, ch.3

6 ... of all torcheculs, arsewisps, bumfodders, tail napkins, bung-hole cleansers, and wipe-breeches, there is none in the world comparable to the neck of a goose, that is well downed, if you hold her head betwixt your legs.

> Gargantua's personal hygiene, in Urquhart's translation (1653) of Rabelais's *Gargantua and Pantagruel*, Book 1, ch.13

V

Victoria, Queen 1819–1901

Queen of Great Britain (1837–1901)

1 Lord Aberdeen was quite touched when I
told him I was so attached to the dear, dear
Highlands and missed the fine hills so much.
There is a great peculiarity about the Highlands
and Highlanders; and they are such a chivalrous,
fine, active people.

> Journal entry (3 Oct 1844) *Our Life in the
> Highlands. . .* (1868, 1884)

2 . . . when we turned the corner to go into the
renowned Fingal's Cave, the effect was splendid,
like a great entrance into a vaulted hall. . . The
sea is immensely deep in the cave. The rocks,
under water, were all colours – pink, blue,
and green – which had a most beautiful and
varied effect. It was the first time the British
standard with a Queen of Great Britain, and
her husband and children, had ever entered
Fingal's Cave, and the men gave three cheers,
which sounded very impressive there.

> Journal entry (19 Aug 1847), *Our Life in the
> Highlands* (1868, 1884)

3 . . . the finest sight imaginable, about thirty
or forty hinds with four or five stags, one in
particular, a magnificent one, with fine horns.
Albert aimed, and shot twice, and he fell; the
others going back into the wood, one amongst

them being wounded. The noble animal never
rose, but struggled and groaned, so that Albert
went and gave him another shot, which killed
him at once. It was a most exciting sight.

> Journal entry (26 Sep 1853), *Our Life in the
> Highlands* (1868, 1884)

4 . . . I feel a sort of reverence in going over
these scenes in this most beautiful country,
which I am proud to call my own, where there
was such devoted loyalty to the family of my
ancestors – for Stuart blood is in my veins, and
I am now their representative, and the people
are as devoted and loyal to me as they were to
that unhappy race.

> On 'the scenes made historical by Prince Charles'
> wanderings'. Journal entry (1873), *Our Life in
> the Highlands* (1868, 1874)

5 I thought I never saw a lovelier or more
romantic spot, or one which told its history so
well. What a scene it must have been in 1745!
And here was *I*, the descendant of the Stuarts
and of the very king whom Prince Charles
sought to overthrow, sitting and walking about,
quite privately and peaceably.

> On Glenfinnan, where the Stewart standard was
> raised in 1745. Journal entry (1873), *Our Life in
> the Highlands* (1868, 1874)

W

Walker, Frances 1930–

Painter

You paint because you are lonely. You paint because you are unhappy. I believe that is often so, but it sounds negative – for although painting is a solitary and, by its nature, isolating occupation, you are also, of course, by painting at all, making a very positive assertion that you do not want to die – yet.

'Artist's comment', in Bill Hare, *Contemporary Painting in Scotland* (1992), p.200

Wallace, Angus

Orthopaedic surgeon

We sterilised it all with five-star brandy and when the operation was over, I drank the rest. I can tell you, I needed it.

On the emergency operation he carried out, using a coat-hanger, scissors and sticky tape, on a passenger with a collapsed lung, on a flight from Hong Kong to London (21 May 1995). Quoted in *The Independent* (28 May 1995)

Wallace, William c.1270–1305

Champion of Scottish independence, Guardian of Scotland from 1298

1 Tell your people that we have not come here to gain peace, but are prepared for battle, to avenge and deliver our country. Let them come up when they like, and they will find us ready to meet them even to their beards.

Attrib. To the English envoys, rejecting the Earl of Surrey's demands prior to the Battle of Stirling Bridge (11 Sep 1297). Quoted in J Fergusson, *William Wallace, Guardian of Scotland* (1938), pp.54–5

2 I have brought you to the ring; dance the best you can.

Attrib. To the Scottish army, before the Battle of Falkirk (22 Jul 1298). Quoted in James Mackay, *William Wallace, Brave Heart* (1995)

Variants, also quoted by Mackay, include 'Lo, I have brought you to the ring: revel the best that you know' (as chronicled by Matthew of Westminster); and 'I haif brocht you to the ring, hap gif ye cun' (Lord Hailes, *Annals of Scotland*)

3 Thy coward sloth is cause of all; thou didst lay claim to the throne, I never; all that I have done

I did for this reason only: that I am a soldier, and that I love my country. For I resolved to spare no strain to drive out of this kingdom every single Englishman; and had I not been met at every turn by the opposition of our nobles, 'tis beyond a doubt that I would have done it. . .

To Robert Bruce, after the defeat at Falkirk (22 Jul 1298), as quoted in John Major, *Historia Majoris Britanniae* (*A History of Greater Britain*, 1521; translated by A Constable, 1892), Bk 4, ch.14

4 Dico tibi verum, libertas optima rerum; numquam servili sub nexu vivito fili.

† I tell you truly, liberty is the best of things; never live under the halter of slavery.

Traditionally associated with Wallace, this maxim was taught to him as a youth, and, in different forms, often repeated by him. See, for example, *Liber Pluscardensis*, Bk 9, ch.2

Waters, Robert 1930–

General Secretary of the Congregational Church of Scotland (1971–   )

1 I married a prostitute. . . This analogy is the only one I can find to describe my position as a Scotsman [who lives in a land where] the imposition of foreign monetarist culture has driven out God in favour of Mammon.

Speech at the launch of the Scottish Constitutional Convention's document on Home Rule, *Scotland's Parliament, Scotland's Right* (30 Nov 1995). Quoted by Lesley Riddoch in *The Scotsman* (1 Dec 1995)

Waterston, Jane Elizabeth 1843–1932

Missionary and doctor, who worked in South Africa

1 . . . a woman's life can never be the broad, strong thing a man's may become but still, you might allow her to do what she can in the way of living. I like to live. I don't like to exist.

Letter to Dr James Stewart (1869), in Sheila M Brock, 'A Broad, Strong Life: Dr Jane Waterston', in Jenni Calder (ed.), *The Enterprising Scot: Scottish Adventure and Achievement* (1986)

2 Civilisation bores me and luxury does not suit me.

Quoted in Sheila Brock, 'Scotland's Single

Agents', *The Sunday Mail Story of Scotland*
(1988), No.39

3 . . . we don't get angels to take care of but girls
often knowing more evil at ten than women of
sixty in Scotland, and their language matches.

Quoted in Sheila Brock, 'Scotland's Single
Agents', *The Sunday Mail Story of Scotland*
(1988), No.39

Watson, Adam 1930–

Scientist and naturalist

1 Wilderness is important not just because
it's valuable from the standpoint of nature
conservation. It's important as a place to be
in and to enjoy. It's important to people just
to know it's there. It's important in a spiritual
sense. Wilderness, then, isn't just a geographical
area. It's a perception of the human mind.

Quoted in James Hunter, 'Against the Grain',
in K Cargill (ed.), *Scotland 2000* (1987)

Watson, John see Maclaren, Ian

Watson, Roderick 1943–

Scholar, critic and poet

1 National identity grows from the stories we
tell to ourselves about ourselves, and indeed
the nation itself can be seen as an 'imagined
community'. It is no surprise, then, that
literature should play a large part in that
imagining, and in fact the main 'state' left to a
'stateless nation' may well be its state of mind,
and in that territory it is certainly literature
which maps the land.

'Dialects of "Voice" and "Place": Literature in
Scots and English from 1700', in P H Scott (ed.),
Scotland: A Concise Cultural History (1993).
Cf. Joy Hendry 1

Watt, Christian 1833–1923

Domestic servant and fishwife

1 After Royalty came Deeside was ruined. The
rich came and built huge palaces to try to
outshine Easter Balmoral. . . In our fisher
dress a group of us stood by the roadside near
Crathie. The Queen came by, she looked so
sour you could have hung a jug on her mouth.

On Queen Victoria. *The Christian Watt Papers*
(ed. David Fraser, 1983), ch.2, 'Fishing Sales
and Highland Clearances (1843–1849)'

2 I cannot understand why any young woman
could ever marry an old man for money, I
think the idea is so repulsive, what with their
ruptures and prostate glands.

The Christian Watt Papers (ed. David

Fraser, 1983), ch.3, 'Philorth and First Love
(1849–1851)'. Cf. Elizabeth Grant 8

3 . . . it is stupid to marry young and have bairns
strung round your neck like tinkies pails and
be bogged down for the rest of your life. For
as hard as all the county folk work the crofter
is the hardest, it is one slave and traughle from
the marriage bed to the grave.

The Christian Watt Papers (ed. David Fraser,
1983), ch.4, 'Mormond Tam (1852)'

4 I always found, in male aristocrats, their Eton
and public school education set their minds like
treacle candy. Nothing but a good hammering
can break it.

The Christian Watt Papers (ed. David Fraser,
1983), ch.4, 'Mormond Tam (1852)'

5 . . . Scotland is now one vast playground for
the wealthy.

On the effect of the Highland Clearances. *The
Christian Watt Papers* (ed. David Fraser, 1983),
ch.5, 'A Voyage to America (1854–1857)'

6 . . . a handful of greedy blockhead peers should
never have had the power to vote to sell an
independent minded nation for English gold.

The Christian Watt Papers (ed. David Fraser,
1983), ch.5, 'A Voyage to America (1854–1857)'

On the Union of 1707, which was accomplished
by the bribery of some Scottish peers.
Cf. Robert Burns 120

7 . . . I find when working men climb the paling
into another class they do not knock down the
paling to let their friends through but build it
higher to keep them out.

The Christian Watt Papers (ed. David Fraser,
1983), ch.7, 'Return to Broadsea (1860–1869)'

8 . . . the Victorian age was one of complete
selfishness and immorality in high places.

The Christian Watt Papers (ed. David Fraser,
1983), ch.8, 'A Time of Sorrows (1871–1878)'

9 The nursing profession is to medicine what
a pair of glasses are to failing eyesight. It
is scandalous those quinies are paid with
sweeties for doing such a noble job, and in
some places they have to put up with awful
inferior food.

The Christian Watt Papers (ed. David Fraser,
1983), ch.9, 'The Breaking of a Mind (1878–1879)'

10 [Illegitimacy] is a word that should be erased
from the English language.

The Christian Watt Papers (ed. David Fraser,
1983), ch.10, 'Cornhill (1879–1892)'

11 It was not a victory but man's greatest defeat.

On World War I. *The Christian Watt Papers* (ed.
David Fraser, 1983), ch.11, 'Public Tragedies
and Private Reflections (1892–1918)'

Watt, James 1736–1819

Engineer and inventor

It was in the Green of Glasgow. . . I was thinking upon the engine at the time and had gone as far as the Herd's house when the idea came into my mind, that as steam was an elastic body it would rush into a vacuum, and if a communication was made between the cylinder and an exhausted vessel, it would rush into it, and might there be condensed without cooling the cylinder. . . I had not walked further than the Golf-house when the whole thing was arranged in my mind.

> Recalling the moment when, in May 1765, he had the idea of a separate condenser in a steam-driven engine. As told to Robert Hart, c.1813, and quoted in H W Dickinson, *James Watt, Craftsman and Engineer* (1935), ch.3

I think I shall not long to have anything to do with the House of Commons again – I never saw so many wrong-headed people on all sides gathered together. . . I believe *the Deevil* has possession of them.

> Letter to his wife (Mar 1767), on his failure to persuade Parliament to support his plans for a canal linking the firths of Clyde and Forth between Dumbarton and Bo'ness by way of Loch Lomond

Watt, John

Songwriter

Oh, she's just a Kelty Clippie,
She'll no' tak' nae advice;
It's 'Ach drap deid, awa' bile yer heid,
Ah'll punch yer ticket twice.'
Her faither's jist a waister,
Her mither's on the game,
She's jist a Kelty clippie
But I love her just the same.

> 'The Kelty Clippie', chorus. Quoted in Norman Buchan and Peter Hall (eds), *The Scottish Folksinger* (1973)

2 Oh I gang wi' a lass frae Pittenweem,
She's every fisher laddie's dream;
She guts the herrin' doon on the quay,
And saves her kisses just for me.

> 'My Pittenweem Jo', st.1. Quoted in Norman Buchan, *101 Scottish Songs* (1962)

Wedderburn, James, John and Robert see Gude and Godlie Ballatis, The

Weir, Lord (William Kenneth James Weir) 1933–

Businessman, chairman of the Weir Group (1966–)

1 . . . like Peru, without the sunshine.

> On what he imagined an independent Scotland would be like. Quoted in Maurice Smith, *Paper Lions: The Scottish Press and National Identity* (1994), ch.2

Wells, Allan 1952–

Sprinter and long-jumper

1 When I stood on the winner's podium my one regret was that the national anthem, and not 'Flower of Scotland', was ringing round the ground. There can be no better moment in a man's life, and the truth is I felt very Scottish. I would have liked this to be obvious on such a memorable occasion for me.

> On receiving his gold medal after winning the Olympic 100m sprint in Moscow (Jul 1980). As told to Alex Cameron, and quoted in Rodger Baillie (ed.), *One Hundred Years of Scottish Sport* (1994), 'Strike for Gold'

Wells, Nannie K(atharin) b.1875

Novelist, playwright, journalist and poet

1 There are mountains that are more to me
than men,
There are rivers that are more to me
than love. . .

> 'Scotland My Lover', *The Golden Eagle* (1962), st.1

2 When the Scots are bad, they are verra,
verra bad,
But when they are guid they are horrid.

> 'Epigrams for Scots', *The Golden Eagle* (1962)
>
> > Based on Longfellow's rhyme to his daughter which ends with 'When she was good she was very, very good/But when she was bad she was horrid.'

3 I have come back to the trees.
I am tired of the fight,
the fruitless effort, the mind's un-ease.
Trees live, and reign, in their own right.

> 'The Trees', *The Golden Eagle* (1962), st.1

4 In the dark there grows
a mighty cedar in my room.

> 'The Trees', *The Golden Eagle* (1962), st.5

5 God, give us the grace to hate
our unemancipated state,
and to wipe from Scotland's face
her intellectual disgrace.

The eye that peers forth cannily,
how can it reach the stars on high?
The ear that waits on market price
obeys the voice of cowardice.

'A Prayer', st.1–2. Quoted in Catherine Kerrigan
(ed.), *An Anthology of Scottish Women Poets* (1991)

Welsh, Irvine 1957–

Novelist

1 This internal sea. The problem is that this
beautiful ocean carries with it loads ay
poisonous flotsam and jetsam. . .
   Syringe, needle, spoon, candle, lighter, packet
ay powder. It's all okay, it's all beautiful; but
ah fear that this internal sea is gaunnae subside
soon, leaving this poisonous shite washed up,
stranded up in ma body.

Trainspotting (1993), 'Junk Dilemmas No.63'

2 Society invents a spurious convoluted logic tae
absorb and change people whae's behaviour is
outside its mainstream. . . Choose us. Choose
life. Choose mortgage payments; choose washing
machines; choose cars; choose sitting oan a
couch watching mind-numbing and spirit-
crushing game shows, stuffing fuckin junk food
intae yir mooth. Choose rotting away, pishing
and shiteing yersel in a home, a total fuckin
embarrassment tae the selfish, fucked-up brats
ye've produced. Choose life.

Trainspotting (1993), 'Blowing it: Searching for
the Inner Man'

3 In the Eighties, the drug of choice for people
changed from being alcohol and tobacco, sort
of legal drugs, to illegal drugs – that was a
major cultural sea-change in Britain. . .

In Your Face: Irvine Welsh (television profile,
first broadcast on BBC2, 27 Nov 1995)

4 All the political correctness thing, it is kind
of middle-class freemasonry, it's a kind of
attempt to sort of circumscribe or control
behaviour that a powerful section of society
find unacceptable. . .

In Your Face: Irvine Welsh (television profile,
first broadcast on BBC2, 27 Nov 1995)

5 . . . a symbol of all that's perfectly hideous
about Scotland.

On Hugh MacDiarmid. Quoted in *Scotland on
Sunday* (28 Jan 1996), 'Shooting Star'

6 A Scottish George Best of literature.

On Alexander Trocchi. Quoted in *Scotland on
Sunday* (28 Jan 1996), 'Shooting Star'

7 It's bad enough being an old punk
from Muirhouse, but an old hippy from
Silverknowes? No way! They'll be saying I'm
a Jambo next. Now that would be damaging.

On newspaper reports after his arrest at a football

match in Glasgow, which mistakenly gave his age
as 44. Letter to *The Big Issue* (No.71, 1–14 Mar
1996), which he closed 'Yours in sport and Hibs'

White, Kenneth 1936–

Poet

1 I have grown chrysanthemums in the
   dung of God
I have blacked my boots with the Bible
and walked all over the world

'At the Solstice' (1966), *The Bird Path: Collected
Longer Poems* (1989), section 3

2 for long the world was an inn
an ale-house back of heaven
where all were benighted and lost
but I say the world is a range of possibles
and the flight of wild poems

'At the Solstice' (1966), *The Bird Path: Collected
Longer Poems* (1989), section 3

3 to build a boat is good
to sail the faraway seas is good
but to write a poem on which
the minds of men could sail for centuries
that was his ambition now
with a long lifetime behind him

'Brandan's Last Voyage' (1986), *The Bird Path:
Collected Longer Poems* (1989), section 11

4 There's nothing much in the rue d'Ecosse
that dark little cul-de-sac –
just the full moon and a stray cat.

'Rue d'Ecosse' (Hill of Saint-Geneviève, Paris),
*Handbook for the Diamond Country: Collected
Shorter Poems 1960–90* (1990)

5 I'm a landowner myself after all –
I've got twelve acres of white silence
up at the back of my mind.

'My Properties', *Handbook for the Diamond
Country: Collected Shorter Poems 1960–90* (1990)

Whyte, Christopher 1952–

Poet, editor and lecturer in Scottish literature

1 Will those who come after us
gaze dumb at an outstretched map
tracing the far off lines of distant hills
unable to say the name of even one?
How long are we to continue being
supereducated illiterates of our own culture?

'The Importance of Gaelic', in *Chapman* No.35–6
(Jul 1983), st.2

2 Culture has to be rooted in the here and now
of our predicament. . . Just now Scotland
is a bundle of fragments, of contradictions
and antagonisms which, if allowed to find
expression, will add up to an identity much
richer and more tolerant than anything we

348

could invent: Highland and Lowland, Gaelic and English-speaking, a Scots-speaking working class and a highly Anglicised middle class, Catholic and Protestant, European and Asiatic, Irish and Scottish and English, and two cities so geographically close yet different in character as Glasgow and Edinburgh... A new Scottish identity won't exclude the experience of women, of gays, of children...

'Out of a Predicament', *Radical Scotland*, No.5 (Oct/Nov 1983)

3 Brisibh bannan bhur cuinge, gur saoradh fhèin bho ghrabadh bochdainn, cràbhachd, sloinntearachd!
Tha 'n saoghal ga liubhairt dhuibh às ùr an diugh.
Lìonaibh sràidean a' bhaile ler dannsaireachd!
Cumaibh fèill na daonndachd, is bithidh mi an glaicibh mo ghaoil a' gluasad nur measg.

† Snap the cords that bind you, free yourselves from shackles of religion, poverty and class!
Today the world is given to you again.
Fill the streets of the city with your dancing!
Keep the feast of humanity, and I will move among you in my lover's arms.

'Beul an Latha' ('Dawn'). In C Whyte (ed.), *An Aghaidh na Sìorraidheachd* (*In the Face of Eternity*, 1991), st.6

4 Tha maireannachd na carraige aig a' bheàirn a dh'fhàg thu.

† The gap you have left is as lasting as a rock face.

'Uinneag ann am Buccleuch Street' ('A Window in Buccleuch Street'), section 3. In A L Kennedy & J McGonigal (eds), *A Sort of Hot Scotland: New Writing Scotland 12* (1994)

5 Tha fhios ann.
Chan eil ceangal àraidh againn ris an fhear a chuireas peatroil anns a' chàr no, sa bhùth mhór, a chanas ruinn na dh'fheumas sinn a phàigheadh.
Ach, a-measg nan companach a roinneas sinn ar gaol 's ar gràin eatorra, is beag dhiubh nach do choinnich sinn a cheana.

† It's common knowledge.
Nothing special links us to the man who puts petrol in the car or tells us, in the supermarket, how much we have to pay.
But there are very few of those we share our love and loathing out among that we haven't met before.

'Uinneag ann am Buccleuch Street' ('A Window in Buccleuch Street'), section 6. In A L Kennedy & J McGonigal (eds), *A Sort of Hot Scotland: New Writing Scotland 12* (1994)

6 Those who hold power are perfectly willing to concede certain spaces to 'minorities' provided the reins of power remain firmly in their hands.

So they can demonstrate their moral superiority and feel good about themselves without taking any genuine risks.

'Not(e) from the Margin', in *Chapman* No.80 (1995)

Wilkie, Sir David 1785–1841
Painter

1 There is very genteel society in Inverary [*sic*]. The castle itself is a complete importation, and disappointed me much. I expected a Highland residence, in place of which it is Bond Street or Brighton, both within and without, and has nothing in it at all belonging to the Highlands, the situation and country adjoining excepted.

Letter to his brother, Thomas Wilkie (21 Aug 1817). Quoted in Allan Cunningham, *Life of Sir David Wilkie* (1843), Vol.1, ch.12

2 Here England is a theme of interest with all, and all try to speak a little English; but Scotland, above all, they look upon as the land of romance and of poetry. The Waverley Novels, as familiar to them as to us, have made our native country, in their eyes, the Arcadia of Europe...

Letter from Carlsbad to Miss Wilkie (1 Sep 1826). Quoted in Allan Cunningham, *Life of Sir David Wilkie* (1843), Vol.2, ch.8

3 On Christmas day we had a grand dinner given by young Severn... He wanted a Scotch dish for me... our cook said he could make three, and was, therefore, ordered to make the one he thought the best. Accordingly a most superb dinner was produced, and, for the Scotch dish, the veritable *Haggis!* – a true chieftain in Imperial Rome! He was soon operated upon to his demolition, and was left in a state that, to an Italian eye, must have looked very like as if we had dined off the bagpipe of a pifferara.

Letter from Rome to Miss Wilkie (1 Jan 1827). Quoted in Allan Cunningham, *Life of Sir David Wilkie* (1843), Vol.2, ch.8

4 ... as Scottish artists the younger students should be aware that no art that is not intellectual can be worthy of Scotland. Bleak as are her mountains, and homely as are her people, they have yet in their habits and occupations a characteristic acuteness and feeling.

Speech at a dinner held in his honour in Rome (Jan 1827). Quoted in Allan Cunningham, *Life of Sir David Wilkie*, Vol.2 (1843), ch.9

5 If my history shall ever be written, it will be found, though in a different way, quite as wonderful as that of Benvenuto Cellini.

Letter from Rome to Thomas Wilkie (25 Jan 1827). Quoted in Allan Cunningham, *Life of Sir David Wilkie* (1843), Vol.2, ch.9

Benvenuto Cellini (1500–71): Italian goldsmith

and sculptor, well-known for his autobiography (1558–62). He was imprisoned on several occasions for the assault or murder of his rivals

6 If true art were but an exact representation of nature, it could be practised with absolute certainty and assurance of success; but the duty of art is of a higher kind. . . Art is only art when it adds mind to form. . . .

'Remarks on painting', Introduction (1836). Quoted in Allan Cunningham, *Life of Sir David Wilkie* (1843), Vol.3, ch.5

7 The use of art to memory can never be doubted by any intelligent being. That which conveys ideas, forms, and appearances, clear and distinct, when language is lost or unintelligible – which speaks all tongues, living or dead, polite or barbarous, – proclaims its own usefulness.

'Remarks on painting', Introduction (1836). Quoted in Allan Cunningham, *Life of Sir David Wilkie* (1843), Vol.3, ch.5

Williams, Gordon 1934–
Novelist

1 From Scenes Like These
Title of novel (1968). Cf. Robert Burns 4

2 We knew our country was a smalltime dump where nothing ever happened and there was nothing to do.
And nobody had a name like Jelly Roll Morton.
'A Scots Burgh Boy's Dream of America', introductory poem to *Walk Don't Walk* (1972)

Williamson, Roy 1936–90
Folksinger and musician, who formed The Corries with Ronnie Browne

1 O flower of Scotland, when will we see your like again,
that fought and died for your wee bit hill and glen
and stood against him, proud Edward's army,
and sent him homeward tae think again.
'O Flower of Scotland' (1968), st.1 (Corries Music Ltd)

Willis, Dave (originally David Williams) 1895–1973
Comedian

1 Way way uppa kye.
Catchphrase

Willis, Denny 1922–
Comedian, son of Dave Willis

1 Scottish comics have a definite sense of humour. They have a sense of humour in other places but you can't make a name for yourself elsewhere

in Scotland, only in Glasgow. No matter how good you are in Edinburgh, or Aberdeen, if you don't make it in Glasgow, then you can't do it.
Quoted in Vivien Devlin, *Kings, Queens and People's Palaces: An Oral History of the Scottish Variety Theatre, 1920–1970* (1991), ch.10

Wilson, George 1818–59
First director of the Industrial Museum of Scotland, Professor of Technology at Edinburgh University (1854–9)

1 Half of the Industrial Arts are the result of our being born without clothes; the other half of our being born without tools.
Quoted in Marinell Ash, 'New Frontiers: George and Daniel Wilson', in Jenni Calder (ed.), *The Enterprising Scot: Scottish Adventure and Achievement* (1986)

Wilson, Jocky (John Thomas) 1951–
Darts player, twice world champion (in 1982 and 1989)

1 If darts come off TV for good then I'm off to Japan to take up sumo wrestling.
Quoted in *The Daily Telegraph* (31 Dec 1990)

Wilson, John 1720–89
Poet and schoolmaster

1 Thy arching groves, O Clyde, thy fertile plains,
Thy towns and villas, claim my filial strains.
'Clyde' (1764). Cf. Douglas Dunn 8

Wilson, John see North, Christopher

Wilson, Margaret c.1667–1685
Covenanting martyr

1 What do I see but Christ in one of his members wrestling there? Think you that we are the sufferers? No, it is Christ in us, for He sends none on a warfare at their own charges.
Her last words (11 May 1685). Quoted in D P Thomson, *Women of the Scottish Church* (1975), ch.8

She was the younger of two women known as the Wigtown Martyrs, drowned in the Solway Firth tied to stakes driven into the sands below high water. She and an elderly widow, Margaret Lachlane, were found guilty by a Commission of Justiciary of attending conventicles and refusing to take an oath renouncing the right of resistance to the government. Lachlane was tied further out

so that Wilson might be persuaded by her
struggles to take the oath, but her only response
was that given above. Her gravestone bears
the words, 'Within the sea ty'd to a stake/She
suffered for Christ Jesus sake'

Wilson, Richard

Actor

1 I am a socialist and even now I'm a rich,
fat bastard who can afford the odd bottle of
champagne, I believe in doing what I can for
my fellow man.

> Campaigning for the rectorship of Glasgow
> University (9 Feb 1996). Quoted in *The Scotsman*
> (10 Feb 1996)

Wilson, 'Scottie' (Louis) 1888–1972

Painter

1 Life! – It's all writ out for you – the moves
you make.

> Quoted in George Melly, *It's All Writ Out
> For You: the Life and Work of Scottie Wilson*
> (1986), p.14

2 God? Of course I believe in God! – who else
should I believe in? Macmillan? Khrushchev?

> Quoted in George Melly, *It's All Writ Out
> For You: the Life and Work of Scottie Wilson*
> (1986), p.56

Wilson, William 1817–50

Weaver and poet

1 If kings were just a harmless thing like thee,
A form on paper, not in real life,
Then would this suffering world be free
From many a bloody scene of strife.

> 'Lines on Looking at the Picture of a King', st.1

Winters, Larry 1943–77

*Convicted murderer, who died of a drug
overdose in the Barlinnie Special Unit*

1 I live in an ashtray
where smoke
curls faintly up
from glowing embers,
my life was stolen before
I was born. . .

> 'The Summing Up', *The Silent Scream* (1979)

Wishart, Ruth

Journalist and broadcaster

1 In our secret heart of hearts we acknowledge
that Argentina '78 stands for pain, humiliation
and bitter disappointment. But in public we

are prepared to discuss only whether or not
Gemmell's goal was the best of that tournament,
or the best of any.

It is optimism of the truly kamikaze variety,
and there is no known antidote.

> Review of Kevin McCarra, *Scottish Football*, in
> *Radical Scotland* No.12 (Dec/Jan 1985)

Witherspoon, John 1723–94

*Minister who emigrated to become President
of the College of New Jersey (now Princeton
University)*

1 I willingly embrace the opportunity of declaring
my opinion without hesitation that the cause
in which America is now in arms is the cause
of justice and liberty.

> Sermon at Princeton (17 May 1776)
>
> He helped to frame, and was the only Christian
> minister to sign, the American Declaration of
> Independence (4 Jul 1776). He had a major
> influence on the American education system

Wode, Thomas fl.1562–92

Priest and musicologist

1 To ane great man that has bot ane resonable
gripe of musike; thir fyve bukis wer worthy
thair wayght of gould.

> *Tenor Partbook*, pp.166–7
>
> Without his five partbooks much of our
> knowledge of Scotland's 16th century music
> would be lost

2 I cannot understand bot musike sall pereische
in this land alutterlye. . .

> Marginal note in *Tenor Partbook*, pp.166–7
>
> He wrote in despair at what he saw as the
> cultural vandalism of the Reformation

Wodehouse, P(elham) G(renville) 1881–1975

English novelist

1 It is never difficult to distinguish between a
Scotsman with a grievance and a ray of sunshine,
and Lord Emsworth, gazing upon the dour
man, was able to see at once into which category
Angus McAllister fell.

> *Blandings Castle and Elsewhere* (1935), 'The
> Custody of the Pumpkin'

Wodrow, Robert 1679–1734

Minister of Eastwood and church historian

1 'For lying, backbeiting, and slandering of my
nighbours, which the world thinks but little
off, I am, by the righteous judgment of God,
condemned eternally to the flames of Hell!'

> Quoting (in 1707) the last words of an Edinburgh

woman, who, according to witnesses, sat up in bed to say them several hours after her death (in 1693). *Analecta, or Materials for a History of Remarkable Providences* (1842–3), Vol.1, pp.117–18

2 King James the Sixth was an unclean pultron.

Analecta, or Materials for a History of Remarkable Providences (1842–3), Vol.2, p.326 (Aug 1717)

3 Mr Neil Gillies, in the Tron Kirk, Glasgow, when he heard 'twixt sermons, on a Sabbath day, that Mr Robert Langlands. . . was dead; after singing, when he began prayer, said to this purpose: 'Lord, what wilt thou do with us? It seems Thou art resolved to flit from among us, when Thou art packing up some of thy best plennishing!'

Analecta, or Materials for a History of Remarkable Providences (1842–3), Vol.2, p.336 (Aug 1719)

Wolfe, General James 1727–59
British general

1 . . . they are hardy, intrepid, accustomed to a rough country, and no great mischief if they fall.

On Highland soldiers in the British Army. Letter to a fellow officer in Canada (Jun 1751). Cf. Fionn MacColla 4

Wood, Wendy 1892–1981
English-born Scottish Patriot and nationalist

1 Take the blood-stained rag you fight for. . . You disgrace your tartan, you soil the name of Scotland, who fly and fight under the flag of her bondage.

Reported words to soldiers guarding Stirling Castle (1932) when, following that year's Bannockburn meeting of the National Party of Scotland, held in King's Park, Stirling, she and her supporters ripped down the Union Jack flying at the castle and replaced it with the Lion Rampant. Quoted in her book, *I Like Life* (1938), ch.12

2 . . . I am in the habit of sacrificing sheets by halves to Scotland's cause. When they are not confiscated, they become pillow-slips, and as the lettering always has to be waterproof, guests may find their faces, and perhaps their dreams, patterned with statements about the Stone of Destiny or the Key of the Castle.

On her banners. *I Like Life* (1938), ch.14

3 It will be a land of lively crofting communities, cheap food, good houses, roads, canals, bridges; a country where experts govern. Assuredly we must cut our coat to suit the cloth, and the cloth is the tartan.

Her vision of Scotland. *I Like Life* (1938), ch.14

4 There is no place where Sunday is more real than among the hills. . . If I went up silent,

I come down singing – and that is Sunday in the hills.

Yours Sincerely for Scotland (1970), ch.11

5 . . . political nationalism is not going to be enough to express the nation of Scotland and retain an identity which alone is the *raison d'être* of independence. . . If we permit this separation of Scottish minds from things Scottish, and launch into a form of government that echoes the English party outlook, we shall be only 'regional minded' even under our own government. . . Freedom will not be complete until we have a sense of national entity in every Scot.

Yours Sincerely for Scotland (1970), ch.17

6 . . . working for the independence of Scotland not only keeps the blood birling, but also means being interested in every facet of national life to the extent that you haven't time to see whether you are putting your shoes on the right foot.

Yours Sincerely for Scotland (1970), ch.17

7 Faith, hope, love and lettuce; faith in God, hope of independence, love of fellow men and women – and a green salad every day.

Her creed, as quoted in Cliff Hanley, 'Notable Scots', *The Sunday Mail Story of Scotland* (1988), No.51

Woolaston, Graeme
Writer

1 There are, it seems, to me, some very intriguing parallels between being Scottish and being lesbian or gay. Both are minority experiences sustained in the face of a massive hegemonic presence: heterosexuality, English domination of the Union. . .

To be gay, as to be Scottish, is to doubt yourself.

'Lesbians and Gays in the Scottish Republic', in Joanne Winning (ed.), *The Crazy Jig: Gay and Lesbian Writing from Scotland 2* (1992)

2 To counter the miasma of doubts and misgivings which can always threaten to descend like the famous mists of our land, we should repeat to ourselves as if it were a mantra: Scotland must be free, and lesbians and gays must be free within it.

'Lesbians and Gays in the Scottish Republic', in Joanne Winning (ed.), *The Crazy Jig: Gay and Lesbian Writing from Scotland 2* (1992)

Woolf, Virginia 1882–1941
English novelist

1 Skye is often raining, but also fine: hardly embodied; semi-transparent; like living in a jelly fish lit up with green light.

Postcard to Duncan Grant (27 Jun 1938)

2 We are now in Oban, which is, as far as I have seen it, the Ramsgate of the Highlands. . . On every lamp post is a notice, 'Please do not spit on the pavement'.

Letter to Vanessa Bell (28 Jun 1938)

Wordsworth, Dorothy 1771–1855

Journal writer, sister and companion of William Wordsworth

1 Scotland is the country above all others that I have seen, in which a man of imagination may carve out his own pleasures. There are so many *inhabited* solitudes. . .

Journal entry (20 Aug 1803), *Recollections of a Tour Made in Scotland* AD 1803 (1874)

The Wordsworths made this tour accompanied by the poet Samuel Taylor Coleridge

2 We had not climbed far before we were stopped by a sudden burst of prospect, so singular and beautiful that it was like a flash of images from another world. . . The sun shone, and the distant hills were visible, some through sunny mists, others in gloom with patches of sunshine; the lake was lost under the low and distant hills, and the islands lost in the lake, which was all in motion with travelling fields of light, or dark shadows under rainy clouds. There are many hills, but no commanding eminence at a distance to confine the prospect, so that the land seemed endless as the water.

On Loch Lomond. Journal entry (25 Aug 1803), *Recollections of a Tour Made in Scotland* AD 1803 (1874)

3 At the beginning of this our second walk we passed through the town, which is but a doleful example of Scotch filth. . . dirty people living in two-storied stone houses, with dirty sash windows, are a melancholy spectacle anywhere, giving the notion either of vice or the extreme of wretchedness.

On Inveraray, the model new town built in the 18th century. Journal entry (30 Aug 1803), *Recollections of a Tour Made in Scotland* AD 1803 (1874)

4 We thought it the grandest mountain we had seen, and on saying to the man who was with us that it was a fine mountain, 'Yes', he replied, 'it is an excellent mountain.'

On Ben Cruachan, near Dalmally. Journal entry (31 Aug 1803), *Recollections of a Tour Made in Scotland* AD 1803 (1874)

5 The sun had been set for some time, when, being within a quarter of a mile of the ferryman's hut, our path having led us close to the shore of the calm lake, we met two neatly dressed women, without hats, who had probably been taking their Sunday evening's walk. One of them said to us in a friendly, soft tone of voice,

'What! you are stepping westward?' I cannot decribe how affecting this simple expression was in that remote place, with the western sky in front, yet glowing with the departed sun.

In the Trossachs. Journal entry (11 Sep 1803), *Recollections of a Tour Made in Scotland* AD 1803 (1874)

6 The old town, with its irregular houses, stage above stage, seen as we saw it, in the obscurity of a rainy day, hardly resembles the work of men, it is more like a piling up of rocks, and I cannot attempt to describe what we saw so imperfectly, but must say that, high as my expectations had been raised, the city of Edinburgh far surpassed all expectation.

Journal entry (16 Sep 1803), *Recollections of a Tour Made in Scotland* AD 1803 (1874)

Wormald, Jenny (*née* Brown)

Historian

1 . . . the traditional 'thud and blunder' approach which has permeated Scottish historiography.

Book review in *English Historical Review*, No.92 (1977)

Wright, Frances (Fanny, married name d'Arusmont) 1795–1852

Dundee-born American reformer, abolitionist and campaigner for women's rights

1 Executions, where they are frequent, have been found to render the mind callous to the last mortal sufferings of the offender; and thus to leave it with no effect but what is decidedly vicious. To familiarise the human eye to blood is to render savage the human heart.

Letter 5 (Philadelphia, May 1819), *Views of Society and Manners in America* (1821). Cf. John MacTaggart 2

2 Knowledge, which is the bugbear of tyranny, is to liberty, the sustaining staff of life.

Letter 9 (Albany, Jul 1819), *Views of Society and Manners in America* (1821)

3 Before leaving Vermont, I would observe, that the Scotch emigrant would probably find it peculiarly suited to his habits and constitution . . . Our sons of the mist might here see their Grampians and Cheviots swelling out of a better soil, and smiling under a purer heaven.

Letter 17 (Burlington, Vermont, Oct 1819), *Views of Society and Manners in America* (1821)

4 . . . it is better to see a woman, as in Scotland, bent over the glebe, mingling the sweat of her brow with that of her churlish son, than to see her gradually sinking into the childish dependence of a Spanish *donna*.

Letter 23 (New York, Mar 1820), *Views of Society and Manners in America* (1821)

5 The sight of slavery is revolting everywhere, but to inhale the impure breath of its pestilence in the free winds of America is odious beyond all that the imagination can conceive.

Letter 28 (Washington, Apr 1820), *Views of Society and Manners in America* (1821)

6 ... that worst species of quackery, practised under the name of religion ...

Course of Popular Lectures (1830), Preface

7 It is not as of yore. Eve puts forth her hand to gather the fair fruit of knowledge. The wily serpent now hath better learned his lesson; and, to secure his reign in the garden, beguileth her *not* to eat.

Lecture 1, 'On the Nature of Knowledge', *Course of Popular Lectures* (1830)

8 Equality is the soul of liberty; there is, in fact, no liberty without it ...

Lecture 2, 'Of Free Inquiry, considered as a means for obtaining just Knowledge', *Course of Popular Lectures* (1830)

9 ... women, wherever placed, however high or low in the scale of cultivation, hold the destinies of humankind. Men will ever rise or fall to the level of the other sex; and from some causes in their conformation, we find them, however armed with power or enlightened with knowledge, still held in leading strings even by the least cultivated female.

Lecture 2, 'Of Free Inquiry, considered as a means for obtaining just Knowledge', *Course of Popular Lectures* (1830)

10 Did the knowledge of each individual embrace all the discoveries made by science, all the truths exacted by philosophy from the combined experience of ages, still would inquiry be in its infancy, improvement in its dawn. Perfection for man is in no time, no place. The law of his being, like that of the earth he inhabits, is *to move always, to stop never.*

Lecture 2, 'Of Free Inquiry, considered as a means for obtaining just Knowledge', *Course of Popular Lectures* (1830). Cf. Adam Ferguson 2

11 Oh! then, let us gird up our minds in courage, and compose them in peace. Let us cast aside fear and suspicion, suspend our jealousies and disputes, acknowledge the rights of others and assert our own. And oh! let us understand that the first and noblest of these rights is, the cultivation of our reason.

Lecture 2, 'Of Free Inquiry, considered as a means for obtaining just Knowledge', *Course of Popular Lectures* (1830). Cf. Marion Reid 5

12 I have wedded the cause of human improvement; staked it on my reputation, my fortune, and my life ...

Lecture 3, 'Of the more Important Divisions and

Essential Parts of Knowledge', *Course of Popular Lectures* (1830)

13 I am not going to question your opinions. I am not going to meddle with your belief. I am not going to dictate to you mine. All that I say is, examine, inquire. Look into the nature of things. Search out the grounds of your opinions, the *for* and the *against*. Know *why* you believe, understand *what* you believe, and possess a reason for the faith that is in you.

Lecture 3, 'Of the more Important Divisions and Essential Parts of Knowledge', *Course of Popular Lectures* (1830)

14 We have seen that from Maine to Missouri – from hence each way to our antipodes – the hired preachers of all sects, creeds, and religions, never do, and never can, teach anything but what is in conformity with the opinions of those who pay them.

Lecture 3, 'Of the more Important Divisions and Essential Parts of Knowledge', *Course of Popular Lectures* (1830)

15 ... so far from entrenching human conduct within the gentle barriers of peace and love, religion has ever been, and now is, the deepest source of contentions, wars, persecutions for conscience sake, angry words, angry feelings, backbitings, slanders, suspicions, false judgments, evil interpretations, unwise, unjust, injurious, inconsistent actions.

Lecture 5, 'Morals', *Course of Popular Lectures* (1830)

Wright, Canon Kenyon Edward 1932–

Methodist minister, General Secretary of the Scottish Council of Churches (1981–90), Chairman of the Scottish Constitutional Convention (1989–)

1 What if that other single voice we know so well [Prime Minister Margaret Thatcher] responds by saying, 'We say no, and we are the state'? Well, we say yes – and we are the people.

Speech at the inaugural meeting of the Scottish Constitutional Convention (30 Mar 1989), established to produce a plan for a Scottish parliament

2 If you take God out of politics, then you're taking God out of life.

Quoted in *The Scotsman* (21 Oct 1995)

3 Today may be Scotland's decisive day, our D-Day, but the victory is not yet won. There may be battles ahead but we sense that a decisive turning point has been reached, that the victory is no longer in doubt.

Speech at the launch of the Scottish Constitutional Convention's document on Home Rule, *Scotland's Parliament, Scotland's Right* (30 Nov 1995). Quoted in *The Scotsman* (1 Dec 1995)

Y

Young, Douglas 1913–73
Poet, scholar and nationalist

1 They libbit William Wallace,
he gart them bleed.
They dinna libb MacFoozle,
they dinna need.

> 'On a North British Devolutionary', *A Braird of Thristles* (1947)

2 The Minister said it wald dee,
the cypress-buss I plantit.
But the buss grew till a tree,
naething dauntit.

It's growan, stark and heich,
derk and straucht and sinister,
kirkyairdielike and dreich.
But whaur's the Minister?

> 'Last Lauch', *Auntran Blads* (1943)

KEYWORD INDEX

KEYWORD INDEX

This index is arranged alphabetically by keyword – with phrases containing that word listed beneath it, together with a shortened version of the author/speaker's name, followed by the relevant quotation number and page number.

Airlie: the bonnie house o' Airlie — BALLAD 8, 39
airth: Let them bestow on ev'ry Airth a Limb — MONTRO 4, 254
airts: Of a' the airts the wind can blaw — BURNS 70, 71
aits: aits in England are a feast — R FERG 21, 129
Aladdin: a kind of folk-tale . . . rather like Aladdin — C MACKEN 8, 225
Alasdair: Alasdair mhic Cholla ghasda — TRAD 1, 333
Splendid Alasdair, son of Colla — TRAD 1, 333
Albert: Albert aimed, and shot twice — VICTO 3, 344
alcoholic: Advocaat: the alcoholic's omelette — CONNOL 6, 100
I'd be an 18-stone alcoholic bricklayer — GORAM 1, 145
alder: I wish he were yew-wood and not alder — ALASD 1, 23
Aldivalloch: Roy's wife of Aldivalloch — E GRANT(1) 1, 148
ale: Gude ale hauds my heart aboon — CUNN 4, 104
ale-house: an ale-house back of heaven — WHITE 2, 348
Alexander: Quhen Alexander our kynge was dede — ANON 2, 26
alien: alien affectations are treated very harshly — BRIDIE 9, 58
alienation: world where alienation awaits us — LAING 1, 190
alive: Being alive is important — AL KENNE 5, 186
gaelic is alive — MACNEA 2, 236
Is it true that we come alive / not once — MORGAN 4, 255
most men hardly ever are alive — CUNN G. 16, 106
Allan: it is long since Allan was gallows-ripe — FIONN 2, 133
Ally: Ally, bally, ally bally bee — COLTAR 1, 98
We're on the road wi Ally's Army — A CAMER 1, 79
almond: The golden hands with the almond nails — LOCHI 1, 198
alone: alone on the face of the earth – drinking claret — HERMAN 5, 162
I can truly see only when alone — CARSW 15, 92
We are the most alone people in the world — CONNOL 13, 101
along: Come along, come along — ROBERTO 5, 283
altar: the altar of their incompetence — Ju DAVID 1, 108
toaffs that could afford tae kneel oan God's altar — T MCGRAT 1, 221
ambiguity: the ambiguity of words — T REID 7, 281
ambition: fearfulest malady, that of Ambition — CARLYL 30, 86
amble: A short story . . . is seldom an easy amble — E DAVIE 4, 109
Amen: Pisky, Pisky, say Amen — BAIRN 15, 37
amenity: an amenity, like soft toilet-paper — J MCGRAT 6, 221
America: Dance Called America — RUNRIG 1, 286
forests of America, however slighted by man — J MUIR 7, 259
There won't be any revolution in America — LINKLA 1, 197
American: bastard child of an American serviceman — FAIRB 2, 126
amicable: they would have to be a lot more amicable — DOCH 2, 111
amphibian: one should be an amphibian — LAWRE 1, 193
amusement: instrument for the purpose of rational
amusement — BREWST 1, 57
I write for the general amusement — SCOTT 75, 294
song alone, was the sole amusement — HOGG 16, 164
anaemia: a sort of smiling anaemia — MACLEN 1, 231
anaesthetic: Glasgow humour is disbelief under anaesthetic — W MCILV 12, 223
gleefully painful social anaesthetic — AL KENNE 7, 186
analyse: quite impossible to analyse everyone — RUSHF 2, 287
anam: sgrìobh thu air m' anam / do nàdur, a bhidse gun
chridhe — MACNEA 1, 236
anama: staid chaillte a h-anama thruaigh — MACGIL 8, 217
anarchist: this is an anarchist landscape — G GUNN 3, 153
anarchy: Sex Pistols' idea of anarchy — J FORS 1, 135
anathema: Those who live by the anathema — W MCILV 14, 224
anchors: An old ship without anchors, without oak — BARD 1, 43
ancient: an ancient and unmixed race of men — Ja MACPHE 5, 238
the Ancient of Days — WC SMITH 1, 310
Anderson: John Anderson, my jo — ANON 36, 29
John Anderson my jo — BURNS 86, 72
anecdotage: Beware, I'm in my anecdotage — MACCAI 42, 207
anewch: He hes anewch that is content — DUNBAR 18, 119
angel: A ministering angel thou — SCOTT 18, 291
domesticate the Recording Angel — STEVEN 22, 320
the angel of mechanical destruction — COCKBU 6, 97
to die in a night-shirt looking like an angel — BRIDIE 3, 58
angels: shimmer of actual angels — A REID 4, 279
we don't get angels to take care of — WATERST 3, 346
Anglicanised: completely Anglicanised by Whitehall — F BALF 4, 38
angst: enough angst here to keep me busy — LAING 6, 190
anguish: In anguish we uplift / A new unhallowed song — Jo DAVID(2) 4, 108
Angus: abune the Angus straths I saw the wild geese flee — JACOB 7, 174
animals: English are better animals than the Scots — BOSWEL 3, 54
'human stories', which by definition concerned animals — J CAMER 3, 80
animated: animated only when dance music or jazz is played — HOUSE 2, 165
animosity: the indulgence of animosity — SCOTT 21, 291
anither: You. Me. Anither — SG SMITH 7, 310

annibaptist: annibaptist is a thing I am not a member of — M FLEM 6, 134
Annie: Annie's got a bairnie / That hasna got a daddy — CRUICK 1, 103
for bonnie Annie Laurie — W DOUGL 1, 115
for bonnie Annie Laurie — SPOTT 1, 316
annoyed: annoyed that my turn for reading was so much
disapproved — SOMERV 4, 312
annuity: To ca' for her annuity — OUTRAM 1, 271
anomaly: being Black and Scottish is always treated as a
kind of anomaly — J KAY 2, 182
mansion turns out a Gothic anomaly — SCOTT 76, 294
anradh: Mar mheas air ghéig ri h-anradh garbh — BOTHCH 4, 55
Anster: Gin you should come to Anster Fair — F SEMP 2, 298
answer: The answer's always 'aye' — PROCL 1, 276
answers: When are you going to publish the answers? — MACCAI 41, 205
antagonist: make the person of an antagonist odious — HUME 6, 166
ant-hill: like an ant-hill beginning to move — BOTHCH 3, 55
anthology: anthology of hackneyed similes — SPOTT 1, 316
anti-life: if not unmanly, at least anti-life — HERDM 1, 161
antique: disgusting cult of antique fear — GIBBON 15, 143
Quho that Antique Stories reidis — D LINDS 6, 195
antiquity: that Gibraltar of antiquity — GALT 4, 139
antisyzygy: the Caledonian antisyzygy — G SMITH 1, 306
anus: Do not retain the urine, nor press forcibly your anus — ANON 19, 27
anvil: religion on the anvil of the will of the people — F BALF 3, 38
aodann: Tha aodann ga mo thathaich — MACGIL 18, 218
aoibhneis: daoimein / cladhaicht á mèin an aoibhneis — MACTHO 4, 240
aonach: Bha mi 'n dé 'san aonach — MACANT 4, 204
apathy: thunderous apathy of the devolution vote — J MCGRAT 4, 221
ape: played the sedulous ape to Hazlitt — STEVEN 73, 323
apill: He gaiff to hir ane apill rubye — DUNBAR 11, 119
Apollo: The youth that's favour'd by Apollo — R FERG 19, 129
TO APOLLO. / HIS MUSIC. HIS MISSILES — 1H FINL 17, 132
apology: No apology is thought necessary for murdering a
tree — COCKBU 17, 98
apostrophes: coyness larded with apostrophes and Doricisms — J CAMER 2, 80
appearance: disappointment arising from its humble
appearance — MAXWEL 4, 247
appeasement: Munich has not brought appeasement — ATHOLL 5, 33
appendage: the appendage to any soups or pearls — FERRI 12, 130
appetite: carnal appetite in man resembles his appetite for food — KAMES 6, 181
appetites: Men were simply victims of their own appetites — H KENNE 1, 186
applauded: heights of the applauded mediocre — J CAMER 8, 80
apple: O apple tree, may God be with thee — CARMIN 15, 89
To take the highest apple / From the knowledge tree — RUNRIG 4, 287
apples: apples began to be golden-skinned — Jo DAVID(2) 6, 108
Curse you apples on that tree — JACKS 1, 173
dangerous apples of the separate sciences — P GEDD 12, 142
appoint: Jist sit yersel doon and appoint yersel King — TRAD 80, 340
approval: a tiny approval smirks, ashamed of itself — MACCAI 23, 206
aqua vitae: wherewith to make aqua vitae — ANON 8, 27
arboreal: at the top of all sits Probably Arboreal — STEVEN 74, 323
arc: arc of the sky over us is as wide — GRIERS 3, 151
Arcadia: the Arcadia of Europe — WILKIE 2, 349
archipelago: archipelago of stony towns — A REID 2, 279
architects: Artists (I mean of course Architects) must be as
select — MACKINT 3, 228
architecture: architecture has the biggest programme — MACKINT 4, 228
architecture, to be real, must not be a mere envelope — MACKINT 5, 228
how are you to judge architecture — MACKINT 6, 228
less cosmopolitan and rather more national in our
Architecture — MACKINT 2, 228
argument: Argument from authority is, in general, the weakest — JEFFR 3, 177
Argyleshire: Argyleshire stots make the stupidest jurymen — COCKBU 4, 97
Argyll: Argyll has raised an hundred men — BALLAD 8, 39
aria: paint an aria — REDFE 1, 279
Ariosto: the Ariosto of the North — BYRON 18, 77
aristocracies: when aristocracies crack and proletariats
crumble — J BUCHAN 6, 64
aristocracy: Aristocracy of the Moneybag — CARLYL 24, 86
aristocrats: a vile junto of aristocrats — TYTLER 2, 342
arm: A guid cause maks a strong arm — ANON 46, 30
hir arm was sone brokiṅ in schonder — BELLEN 3, 48
armachd: armachd ás nach tig ceòl fàsmhor — IC SMITH 3, 306
armies: God damn all other armies — J MACLEA 2, 230
armoury: armoury from which no growing music will come — IC SMITH 3, 306
arms: arms stuck out sideyways when they ran — BYRNE 2, 75
ármuinn: Lochlannaigh is ármuinn iad — ARTÚR 1, 31
army: A silent conquering army, / The island dead — GM BROWN 11, 61

rag-tag army of ordinary people to destroy a bad law	I BELL 1, 47
arraheids: urnae arraheids / but a show o grannies' tongues	JAMIE 3, 176
arrive: Long before you arrive at a place	MENDEL 2, 248
travel hopefully is a better thing than to arrive	STEVEN 34, 320
arrogance: strength without arrogance	H MCILV 8, 222
arrogant: most arrogant man in the world	KAMES 2, 181
supremely arrogant and thick as mince	MCSPOR 1, 238
arrow: a steed that keeps pace ever with an arrow	FIONN 3, 133
arse: And never rises off his arse	CORRIE 8, 102
doesn't know its arse from its political elbow	GALLO 7, 138
he's a pain in the arse	CUMMI 1, 104
Lord pity the arse that's clagged	HUTTON 2, 169
they shall also see my arse	JAMES 23, 176
arselickers: a nation of arselickers	GRAY 9, 150
arses: they rattle i' their ranks, / At ither's arses	BURNS 16, 67
arsewisps: of all torcheculs, arsewisps, bumfodders	T URQU 6, 343
art: Art and religion first	SPARK 7, 315
Art is a common impulse	HANNAH 1, 157
Art is only art when it adds mind to form	WILKIE 6, 350
Art is the flower – Life is the green leaf	MACKINT 8, 229
art itself is natural to man	A FERG 1, 127
art more sacred than a million domesticities	CARSW 4, 91
art of seeing	P GEDD 11, 142
Art that stops short at art	IH FINL 7, 131
art which will be pregnant with Idea	MCCANC 1, 207
as much an art image as an Assyrian wine jar	PAOLO 3, 273
gardening is an Art	IH FINL 14, 132
great White Hope of European art	MCCANC 1, 207
instant tits and bottom line of art	DUFFY 5, 118
It is to art and religion that we must look	MACMUR 4, 235
love fails, but art is forever	OLIPH 8, 270
Modern art is a conspiracy against people	SPALD 3, 314
no art that is not intellectual can be worthy	WILKIE 4, 349
one great invisible quality in all art, soul	MACKINT 6, 228
Scotland should have an independent art	JD FERG 3, 127
the life-blood of all real art	HANNAH 1, 157
the only possible art for all	MACKINT 9, 229
There is but one art – to omit	STEVEN 46, 321
the Royal Academy – the dregs of the art world	BELLAN 3, 48
use of art to memory	WILKIE 7, 350
Violence is an art form practised in and for itself	T MCGRAT 2, 221
War and Art is an impossible combination	ROBERTO 1, 283
artful: who so artful as to put it by?	R BLAIR(2) 3, 51
articulate: Communism is hunger becoming articulate	BOYD OR 3, 56
artificial: my lord, do you require artificial heat	HAILES 2, 155
artist: An artist's work in this world is to sing	TRAQU 3, 340
give everyone the outlook of the artist	P GEDD 11, 142
obliterate the narrator, get rid of the artist	KELMAN 2, 183
this man ought to be an artist!	GUTHR 1, 154
To earn the name artist it seems clear that one must *create*	JD FERG 1, 127
artists: artists are all the better for hardship	MACDIA 42, 212
Artists (I mean of course Architects) must be as select	MACKINT 3, 228
The future is artists who want to communicate	SPALD 2, 314
arts: Industrial Arts are the result of our being born without clothes	G WILS 1, 350
Arts Council: Arts Councils are the insane asylums of bureaucracy	IH FINL 5, 131
hear the words 'Arts Council' I reach for my water-pistol	IH FINL 4, 131
ashtray: life is like an ashtray	CONNOL 3, 100
Asiatic: hermits and Asiatic self-tortures	STEVEN 90, 324
asking: Three things come without asking: fear, jealousy and love	ANON 22, 28
asklent: Look'd asklent and unco skeigh	BURNS 113, 73
asleep: in my hand a forest lies asleep	M STUA 5, 327
aspen: quiv'ring like the leaf of aspen tree	TENNAN 3, 329
aspirations: He saw the great horse of his aspirations	MACGIL 28, 219
assassin: call him a hired assassin	BROOKS 2, 59
assassination: mutual defence / Against assassination	BERNS 2, 48
assembly: Speak to me as if I were a popular assembly	MEAD(1) 1, 248
asses: They gang in stirks, and come out asses	BURNS 9, 67
windy polemics like asses they bray	BROOKS 3, 59
asset: Ignorance is not an asset	FINNIS 4, 132
Assyrian: as much an art image as an Assyrian wine jar	PAOLO 3, 273
astronaut: you're not an astronaut / Just a poet	V GRIEV 1, 151
asylum: an asylum of railway lunatics	COCKBU 5, 97
asylums: Arts Councils are the insane asylums of bureaucracy	IH FINL 5, 131
atheist: I was born an atheist	MACCAI 37, 207
Athole: He dearly lo'ed the Athole Brose	LYON 1, 201

atrocity: sink of atrocity, which no moral flushing	COCKBU 9, 97
Atropos: No more than I can he Atropos fly	Je ADAM 1, 23
attack: Attack me wha daur!	J BAILL 13, 36
attention: all the attention ye'll get's a bashin on a Saturday	E STEW 1, 326
Sit at attention?	MACCAI 40, 207
attitude: an attitude remains with one throughout life	A NEILL 1, 265
attitude towards the machine	PAOLO 2, 273
Scotland's an attitude of mind	M LINDS 2, 196
Auchindoon: As I cam in by Auchindoon	TRAD 42, 337
Auchterless: mony a bonnie lass in the Howe o' Auchterless	TRAD 15, 334
Auchtermuchty: In Auchtermuchty thair dwelt ane man	ANON 14, 27
audience: audience that goes to a play like they'd go to a pub	D CAMPB 1, 81
the cigar-smoking audience	D CAMPB 1, 81
audiences: Working-class audiences like laughs	J MCGRAT 5, 221
auld: cup o' kindness yet / For auld lang syne	BURNS 66, 70
Oh the auld house, the auld house	NAIRNE 1, 264
sheuk hands and parted wi' auld Reikie	BURNS 44, 69
Should auld acquaintance be forgot	BURNS 65, 70
the guid auld days	BROOKS 1, 59
when 'tis auld it waxeth cauld	TRAD 78, 340
worse things than being an auld maid	MORRIS 2, 256
Auld Reikie: Auld Reikie! wale o' ilka town	R FERG 9, 128
auntie: Whenever Auntie moves around	STEVEN 51, 321
aunty: Steps, like an aunty, forward	MACCAI 10, 205
austerity: austerity in the flat clean wind-swept lands	N GUNN 2, 153
author: author should be reasonably well pleased	SCOTT 89, 295
ever dream of marrying an Author	CARLYL 9, 83
live the life of a mere author	SCOTT 55, 293
authority: Argument from authority is, in general, the weakest	JEFFR 3, 177
hidden under a bushel of alien authority	CLYDE 1, 96
my authority may be taken from me by violence	C STEW 5, 325
the empty house in Edinburgh / Without authority or voice	RUNRIG 2, 286
autobiography: Autobiography is an attempted jail-break	HOOD 1, 165
autonomy: I want political autonomy but not cultural	M GRAY 2, 150
autumn: autumn wind's asteer	JACOB 4, 174
friends / Drop off, like leaves in autumn	R BLAIR(2) 4, 51
link the Autumn of our own Age	P GEDD 3, 141
avarice: a personified compound of avarice, indecency	COCKBU 7, 97
Avarice, the spur of industry	HUME 11, 166
best excuse that can be made for avarice	HUME 14, 166
her avarice was as large as her a—	J BOSWEL 1, 53
awa: We're no awa to bide awa	TRAD 81, 340
awake: men are awake with me, doing their work	N MACLEO 1, 233
awful: a more awful thing to be born than to die	GALT 10, 139
a reviving, as well as awful idea	COLQUH 2, 98
awful and dreary blank in creation	CARLYL 3, 83
awkward: Don't let the Awkward Squad fire over me	BURNS 140, 75
awoke: awoke one morning and found myself famous	BYRON 54, 78
aye: If you think aye in Scots means yes	I SMITH 1, 309
The answer's always 'aye'	PROCL 1, 276
Ayr: Auld Ayr, wham ne'er a town surpasses	BURNS 91, 72
Babbity-Bowster: Wha learnt ye tae dance, Babbity-Bowster	BAIRN 2, 36
babies: We must begin with the babies	M MCMIL 1, 234
baby: a little baby thing / That made a woman cry	Ge MACDON 7, 214
I was a midnight baby after all	J KAY 3, 182
Babylon: the Great Scarlet Whore of Babylon	CARLYL 1, 82
Bach: Bach is for me the bread and wine	CARSW 11, 92
bachelor: Idleness, which is often becoming and even wise in the bachelor	STEVEN 21, 320
backbeiting: lying, backbeiting, and slandering	WODROW 1, 351
backcourt: mean wind wanders through the backcourt	MORGAN 7, 255
backs: With our backs to the wall	HAIG 3, 155
backwart: the Thrie Estaits gangs all backwart	D LINDS 13, 195
bacon: rubbing and frotting their bacon	T URQU 5, 343
bad: I may have been repulsive, but I was not bad	BRIDIE 10, 58
When the Scots are bad	N WELLS 2, 347
Badenoch: Badenoch in simmer, wi nae clegs about	GARIOC 3, 140
bag: a narrow crooked bag, half-full of slavers	MACCOD 2, 208
We let out of the bag who we are	LOCHH 3, 199
baggage: No baggage	STEVEN 81, 323
bagpipe: a bag pipe to play a spryng	DUNBAR 25, 120
dined off the bagpipe of a pifferara	WILKIE 3, 349
bagpipes: the bubblyjock swallowed the bagpipes	MACDIA 10, 210
Baikie: O Baikie, my beloved, my washpot	BRIDIE 15, 59
baile: baile glas gun ghathadh gréine	MACGIL 3, 216
bailie: a cuff o' the neck like ony Glasgow bailie's	GALT 15, 139
She frightens the bailie	J BAILL 14, 36
bairn: a bairn brocht up in vanitie	M BOYD 1, 55

Earth, thou bonnie broukit bairn	MACDIA 2, 210
like a barfit bairn, stauns nicht	BLACKH 2, 49
litheless the lair o' the mitherless bairn	THOM 1, 330
Our past is an auld-farrant bairn we cairry	MCDONA 3, 214
bairned: bairned up a close in Coatbridge	DONAL 2, 112
bairnie: Annie's got a bairnie / That hasna got a daddy	CRUICK 1, 103
bairnies: The bairnies cuddle doon at nicht	ANDERS 1, 24
bairns: All Christ's good bairns	RUTHER 4, 287
I am on the side of the bairns	A NEILL 2, 265
Plenty bonnie bairns as weel	ROBERTO 3, 283
Wyce bairns shuin lairn	W NEILL 3, 266
bairny: Singing till her Bairny	ANON 27, 28
bake: She wadna bake, nor she wadna brew	BALLAD 13, 40
baker: Like baker's oven with poetic heat	TENNAN 1, 329
balach: B'annsa balach sgiobalta / A thogadh mi	TRAD 27, 335
balbh: an àm / tha cànan an cunnart dhol balbh	M NICGU 1, 267
balderdash: this flatulent balderdash	N DOUGL 4, 115
Balgounie: Balgounie's Brig's *black wall*	BYRON 47, 78
ball: The ball o Kirriemuir	TRAD 6, 333
ballads: if a man were permitted to make all the ballads	FLETCH 1, 134
ballattis: Off sangis, ballattis, and of playis	DUNBAR 14, 119
balloons: fule hizzies – blawn oot like balloons	Ja HAMIL 6, 156
ballot: Jesus never got a ballot vote	MCGAH 2, 205
balls: balls to your partner	TRAD 7, 334
Balmaquhapple: what's to become of poor Balmaquhapple	HOGG 11, 163
Balquhither: go / To the braes o' Balquhither	TANNAH 1, 329
banana: big banana feet	BAIRN 17, 37
If someone falls on a banana skin	B FORS 3, 135
banc: Fra banc to banc, fra wod to wod, I rin	M BOYD 1, 55
band: The Band Played Waltzing Matilda	BOGLE 1, 52
To join the band o' shearers	TRAD 8, 334
banes: deid men's banes an aa kin o filth an fulyie	NEW TES 2, 266
bang: *bang* – went saxpence	PUNCH 1, 276
bank: fit to be trusted with the bank's money	MILLER 6, 250
hie away, / Over bank and over brae	SCOTT 32, 291
banks: The pleasant banks of Clyde	LITHGO 1, 197
Ye banks and braes o' bonnie Doon	BURNS 107, 73
banners: All banners must bow	SOUTAR 14, 314
bannock: The buttered bannock of the moon	GM BROWN 4, 61
bantracht: bantracht an aigne aimhréidh	BARD 2, 43
baptism: said to be three forms of baptism	PHILL 1, 275
barbares: allutterlie barbares	JAMES 7, 175
barbaric: a barbaric continent	ASCHER 2, 32
barbarism: methods of barbarism	CAMPB-B. 1, 82
Scotland gradually extricates herself from the slough of barbarism	CROSL 5, 103
barbarisms: few *modern* Scoticisms which are not barbarisms	J PINKER 1, 275
barbarous: barbarous dialects of Yorkshire or Devon	JEFFR 2, 177
barbarous with gulls	GM BROWN 2, 60
those times which we call barbarous	H BLAIR 1, 50
barbed: barred us by barbed wire fences	T JOHNST 3, 179
like carrying a bundle of barbed wire	GILLI 2, 144
bardie: A certain Bardie's rantin, drinkin	BURNS 20, 68
bardies: Amang the writers and the bardies	R FERG 20, 129
bards: last of all the Bards was he	SCOTT 1, 290
sham bards of a sham nation	E MUIR 12, 258
When these good old Bards wrote	A RAMS(1) 6, 277
barefitted: barefitted in ragged claes	BROOKS 1, 59
barefoot: rather go barefoot than wear Daddy's shoes	JACKS 2, 173
Walking barefoot has gone out of fashion	SHEPH 9, 300
bareness: it was the fine bareness of Lewis / that made the work of my head	IC SMITH 12, 307
barley: ay we'll taste the barley bree	BURNS 79, 71
Corn rigs, an' barley rigs	BURNS 33, 68
Barleycorn: Inspiring bold John Barleycorn	BURNS 97, 72
John Barleycorn was a hero bold	BURNS 55, 70
barnacles: Hell like their Nation feeds on Barnacles	CLEVE 2, 96
barnyards: The Barnyards o' Delgaty	TRAD 9, 334
barred: barred us by barbed wire fences	T JOHNST 3, 179
barren: A barren soil where Nature's germs	BYRON 9, 76
she's as barren as Rannoch Moor	LINGA 1, 197
Barrie: sentimental slop of Barrie, and Crockett	GD BROWN 7, 60
bar-room: as soon tell a funny story in a churchyard as in a bar-room	LEACO 2, 193
bars: see the stars without seeing bars	BOYLE 2, 56
barter: propensity to truck, barter	SMITH 4, 304
bashin: all the attention ye'll get's a bashin on a Saturday	E STEW 1, 326

bastard: bastard child of an American servicemen	FAIRB 2, 126
I'll drown the little Bastard in my bowl	A ROBERTSO 1, 283
Memory. A bastard really	GALLO 3, 138
that bastard verdict, *Not proven*	SCOTT 104, 296
well I know within that bastard land	BYRON 9, 76
bata: Cha déid e mach gun am bata	TRAD 26, 335
batalis: The batalis and the man I wil discrive	G DOUGL 2, 114
Bathgate: Bathgate no more	PROCL 3, 276
bathroom: can't feel fierce and revolutionary in a bathroom	LINKLA 1, 197
battalions: in pale battalions	SORLEY 3, 313
battering: yesterday she was battering at a university door	T JOHNST 5, 180
battle: field of battle, and not a bed of roses	STEVEN 20, 320
battle-axe: I have broken my good battle-axe	R BRUCE 1, 62
bauchle: shilpet wee bauchle, the glaiket big dreep	MCNAUG 2, 236
bawbee: bawbee-worshipping bailie-bodies	P GEDD 6, 141
Greetin' for anither bawbee	COLTAR 1, 98
bawis: Thy bawis hingis throw thy breik	DUNBAR 5, 118
Bawsy: ken it was Bawsy Broon	SOUTAR 2, 313
bazaar: ready for the opening of the Kirk Bazaar	GORDON 2, 146
BBC: an unctuous BBC Broth	FINDL 2, 133
The BBC has secured and holds the goodwill	REITH 1, 281
be: What she had been, what I should be	BARRIE 1, 43
beak-stab: gannets rest a beak-stab apart	GILLI 3, 144
bean: Ní math bean gan bheith náireach	MACDHU 2, 209
bear: a polar bear eating an Eskimo	GIBBON 13, 143
beard: beard like besom bristles	RORIE 3, 285
beard the lion in his den	SCOTT 16, 291
beards: ready to meet them even to their beards	W WALLA 1, 345
Then came the beards, proliferating	E MACCOL 4, 209
bears: sympathise with the bears	J MUIR 12, 260
beast: do the two-backed beast	T URQU 5, 343
that vile Beast Pod	HUME 1, 166
To love the beast they cannot tame	SOUTAR 15, 314
beastie: Wee sleekit, cow'rin, tim'rous beastie	BURNS 17, 67
beasts: Our passions are wild beasts	SCOTT 98, 295
beast-taming: Beast-taming seems to me / Not quite a woman's mission	BERNS 2, 48
beating: If beating can reform a wife	BERNS 3, 48
beautiful: a jet engine, a bit of a machine is beautiful	PAOLO 3, 273
beautiful, in its monstrous way	J CAMER 4, 80
How beautiful is Dunfermline	CARNEG 3, 90
Ingigerth is the most beautiful	ANON 1, 26
innocent as she was beautiful	W ROBERTSO 2, 284
Moral conduct *is* beautiful	MACMUR 3, 235
the Beautiful is more useful than the Useful	P GEDD 15, 142
beauty: Another beauty, sad and stern	SMITH 2, 305
Beauty, whether moral or natural, is felt	HUME 20, 167
infinite storm of beauty	J MUIR 11, 260
Look not thou on beauty's charming	SCOTT 71, 294
scenic beauty of empty glens	N GUNN 5, 153
She walks in beauty, like the night	BYRON 28, 77
the deer of your gentle beloved beauty	MACGIL 14, 218
To accept life is to give it beauty	SOUTAR 1, 313
beaver: cock up your beaver	TRAD 30, 336
bed: 'A bed, a bed,' Clerk Saunders said	BALLAD 12, 39
Are the weans in their bed	MILLER 1, 251
Bed in the bush with the stars to see	STEVEN 83, 323
Best bloody place is bloody bed	ANON 52, 30
'Come to your bed,' says Johnie Faa	BALLAD 26, 40
field of battle, and not a bed of roses	STEVEN 20, 320
gang to her bed when she likes	PICKEN 2, 275
get me to bed – that's the only place	SCOTT 120, 297
He is lying in his bed – and he is seik and sair	GOWDIE 3, 146
I'd make my bed in the heather tonight	ANON 24, 28
I have to go to bed by day	STEVEN 47, 321
mak' my bed in Aiberdeen	MURRAY 10, 263
May you never make your bed / Out in the cold	MARTYN 1, 245
nicer to lie in bed	LAUDER 8, 192
Oh, mother, mother, mak my bed	BALLAD 2, 39
put them out of doors, or to bed	CARLYL 2, 82
Quhen gone to bed war Vesper and Lucyne	DUNBAR 6, 118
The long black passage up to bed	STEVEN 56, 322
The muse has felled me in this bed	WS GRAH 4, 147
There's a pig in ilka pane	MURRAY 8, 262
women know talent when they share a bed with it	CARSW 13, 92
beds: All beds have ghosts	AL KENNE 3, 185
beds of married love	MORGAN 3, 255
bedtime: A good gulp of whisky at bedtime	A FLEM 6, 133

you etched your nature / on my spirit, heartless bitch — MACNEA 1, 236
you ugly old English bitch — LOVAT 1, 200
bitches: Fare ye a' weel, ye bitches! — KAMES 16, 182
bitchify'd: I gat myself sae notouriously bitchify'd — BURNS 45, 69
bites: mute hound that bites the hardest — DOYLE 14, 116
bitter: A point of bitter, Ma — SG SMITH 2, 310
God is not in the bitter divisione — W DRUM 10, 117
If actors became bitter every time a theatre folded — E MACCOL 5, 209
bitterlie: she wept right bitterlie — BALLAD 15, 40
bittock: A mile an' a bittock — STEVEN 68, 322
bizarre: more bizarre a thing is the less mysterious — DOYLE 7, 116
black: being Black and Scottish is always treated as a kind of anomaly — J KAY 2, 182
black disdainful stream — SMITH 3, 305
Black people are okay as long as — SULTER 4, 327
Black people have been in Scotland — SULTER 5, 327
refuse to have anything to do with *black* — JD FERG 2, 127
black-cock: Where the black-cock sweetest sips it — SCOTT 32, 291
blackest: the blackest day of my life — LAW 1, 193
blackguard: the most blackguard place in Scotland — COCKBU 9, 97
blackguardism: Dundee, the palace of Scottish blackguardism — COCKBU 3, 97
Blackpool Tower: equivalent of Blackpool Tower up Scotland's second highest mountain — SMOUT 2, 312
blackwoman: As a blackwoman / the personal is political — SULTER 1, 327
blade: could never look on a bare blade without blinking — SCOTT 77, 294
keep a chib over the door an a blade in ma bedroom — T MCGRAT 3, 221
Blair: the berryfields o' Blair — B STEW 1, 325
blaming: something hard in blaming the poor cook — SCOTT 10, 290
blank: In the blank of his brow — SOUTAR 14, 314
blanket: up goeth the blew-blanket — JAMES 8, 175
blankets: with their despicable blankets over their heads — DOMHN R 1, 112
blanter: eatin' o' blanter — SHIRR 2, 300
blasphemy: let God call it blasphemy — MACGIL 20, 218
blast: Out of the sun, out of the blast — STEVEN 66, 322
To meet cauld poortith's nipping blast — MACNEI 1, 237
blàth: ar blàth chòmhnaradh fo fhéidh — P MACGRE 1, 221
blaw: A hunder pipers canna blaw — A SCOTT(2) 1, 289
blayguards: Where the money is, there will the blayguards — JACOB 1, 173
blaze: go out / in a last wild blaze — FELL 3, 127
bleacher: The bleacher lassie on Kelvinhaugh — TRAD 12, 334
bleeding: The old physicians were fond of bleeding people — LAMONT 1, 190
bless: Bless this house, wherever it is — W MCILV 6, 223
blessing: Sweet was its blessing, kind its caressing — A COCKBU 1, 96
the blessing of a cup of cold water — GALT 5, 139
the fatal blessing of prosperity — GM BROWN 8, 61
blessings: count one's blessings, even if it implies one's conceit — KENNAW 2, 185
Self-conceit is none of the smallest blessings — KAMES 2, 181
blind: quhair the blind the blind dois gyde — GUDE 7, 152
blinds: the brave will not pull down the blinds — M MCMIL 3, 234
blinking: could never look on a bare blade without blinking — SCOTT 77, 294
blizzards: like ploughmen / In blizzards of gulls — GM BROWN 3, 61
blockhead: handful of greedy blockhead peers — WATT 6, 346
blockheads: blockheads talk of my being like Shakespeare — SCOTT 101, 296
blokes: There's roughly three kinds o blokes — R MCMIL 1, 235
blonaig: mionach seilcheig a bha annta air a mheasgadh ri blonaig cait — LAMONT 2, 191
blood: blood enough upon your penal code — BYRON 11, 76
Blood is pumping through my whole body — BOYLE 1, 56
capitalism dripping with blood — J MACLEA 3, 230
Civilisation can never / be written in the blood — SULTER 3, 327
Clydeside, / Webbed in its foundries and loud blood — WS GRAH 3, 147
doesn't get enough blood to his brain — Jo BELL 3, 47
Flame and blood is always the cement — GM BROWN 14, 61
if you do but taste his blood — BURNS 55, 70
keeps the blood birling — WOOD 6, 352
Notice the blood. It is also red — KENNAW 8, 185
redder his cheeks than calf's blood — DEAN 3, 110
red, red is the bottle's blood — MACTHO 21, 241
stained with the best blood of the Highlands — BRAHAN 3, 56
Stuart blood is in my veins — VICTO 4, 344
the moon will be as if blood had been spilt on her — BOTHCH 4, 55
the blood fondly says, 'This is my land,' — N GUNN 9, 153
the lochs of the blood of the children of men — MACGIL 13, 217
the old accustomed tax of common blood — HAY 4, 158
To familiarise the human eye to blood — WRIGHT 1, 353
To say *ach!* correctly you need generations of Scots blood — R DOUGL 1, 115

write Thy Epitaph in Blood and Wounds — MONTRO 3, 254
Yet still the blood is strong — ANON 41, 29
bloodless: bloodless lay th' untrodden snow — T CAMPB 7, 81
mighty bloodless substitute for life — STEVEN 28, 320
blood-stained: Take the blood-stained rag you fight for — WOOD 1, 352
bloodthirsty: Bloodthirsty Dee — BAIRN 8, 37
bloody: In bloody Orkney — ANON 51, 30
bloom: my bloom will be slight and meagre — ISEAB 1, 172
blossom: the blossom to the bee — CUNN 7, 105
blow: an historic blow for people on the land — A MACRAE 1, 238
each blow / Be given with the kitchen poker — BERNS 3, 48
blud: This blud is myn, that hurtis most my thocht — BLIND 3, 52
yon Scot ettis his awn blud — BLIND 3, 52
blude: The blude of all my body to my hert — JAMES I 5, 174
blue: Blue with endlessly moving seas — MORGAN 12, 256
find a true blue secretary for Scotland — F BALF 4, 38
green days in forests and blue days at sea — STEVEN 85, 323
He who first met the Highlands' swelling blue — BYRON 52, 78
man who was growing blue carrots — J HAYN 2, 159
bluebell: Mary, ma Scotch Bluebell — LAUDER 3, 192
blues: Fergus Sings the Blues — R ROSS 2, 286
bluestocking: absurd as a bluestocking — A GRANT 1, 148
no objection to the blue-stocking — F JEFFR 1, 177
without the least affectation of the blue-stocking — SCOTT 118, 297
bluid: a' the bluid shed at thy Tron — SPENCE 3, 316
Why dois your brand sae drap wi bluid — BALLAD 19, 40
bluidy: lads o' Inverness / Lie bluidy on Culloden lee — TRAD 50, 337
blunder: 'thud and blunder' approach — WORMAL 1, 353
blyth: Be blyth and blisfull, burgh of Aberdeen — DUNBAR 27, 120
boar: Love of the Lion, loathing of the Boar — A MACDON 1, 233
the bald boar dull and worthless — FIONN 1, 132
boat: Black boat, perfect Greek — MACGIL 10, 217
my heart's a boat in tow — BOULT 2, 55
Speed, bonnie boat, like a bird on the wing — BOULT 1, 55
that big boat on the horizon, / the Cuillin — MACGIL 27, 219
ye'll get a fishie when the boat comes in — BAIRN 7, 37
boatie: O weel may the boatie row — EWEN 1, 124
boatman: Boatman, do not tarry — T CAMPB 8, 81
O, the Boatman, *na hóro éile* — TRAD 36, 336
boats: business is more entertaining than fooling among boats? — STEVEN 2, 318
messing about in boats — K GRAH 1, 147
bobby: cannot expect the ordinary 'bobby' — Jo BELL 3, 47
bodie: he's juist a bodie — GD BROWN 2, 60
body: Feeding the mind is as important as feeding the body — J SIMP(2) 1, 301
Gin a body hit a body, / Will it fly? and where? — MAXWEL 6, 248
Gin a body meet a body / Comin thro' the rye — BURNS 136, 75
They shall know we are old not by the frailty of the body — RUSHF 3, 287
'tis in vain to ask, *Whether there be body or not?* — T REID 6, 281
bog: This Bolshevik bog! Suits me doon to the grun'! — MACDIA 33, 211
bogey: the Calvinistic bogey — SOUTAR 9, 314
Wee Malkies – the gemme's a bogey! — MULRIN 2, 261
bogle: God is a bogle of the nursery — W MAIT 1, 243
bogs: bogs do not require a level surface — N DOUGL 5, 115
boil: Then does the boil fester on the thigh — CLARS 4, 95
boiling: puddings and pies, roasting and boiling — M REID 4, 280
the boiling of the daily pot — OLIPH 25, 271
boils: satan has not geven me boils — M FLEM 2, 134
boireannach: Boireannach dona Crìosdaidh — IC SMITH 18, 308
bold: bold man who first swallowed an oyster — JAMES 27, 176
Bolshevik: I must be a Bolshevik / Before the Revolution — MACDIA 55, 213
This Bolshevik bog! Suits me doon to the grun'! — MACDIA 33, 211
bomb: monstrous regiment of the damned bomb — G MACLEO 7, 233
Bond: one is not Bond — CONNER 1, 100
bondage: We can't do away with the bondage — S GLOV 1, 145
bone: flesh of my flesh / And bone of my bone — A GRAY 1, 150
My fingers are so wore to the bone — BURNS 83, 72
bones: bones of slavery — SULTER 3, 327
full of dead men's bones — R BLAIR(2) 5, 51
stripped from her bones / and spat to herring gulls — E BURNS 1, 66
bonkers: The reason they think I'm bonkers — FAIRB 4, 126
bonn: chan eil putan innt', no toll, / Nach do chost bonn — ROB DON 3, 282
bonnet: follow the bonnet of Bonny Dundee — SCOTT 116, 296
bonnets: Blue Bonnets are bound for the Border — SCOTT 73, 294
nane but Hielan bonnets here — C CAMPB 2, 81
Pipers, blue bonnets, and oat meal — STEUAR 1, 318
bonnie: bonnie brier bush in our kail-yard — NAIRNE 11, 265
Bonnie Charlie's now awa — NAIRNE 13, 265
Bonnie Kilmeny gaed up the glen — HOGG 5, 163

bonnie Maggie Lauder | F SEMP **1**, 298
Bonnie Saint Johnston stands upon Tay | BALLAD **44**, 42
bonnie ship the Diamond / Goes a-fishing for the whale | TRAD **17**, 334
By the bonnie mill-dams o' Binnorie | BALLAD **5**, 39
By yon bonnie banks | TRAD **13**, 334
Dance to your daddy, my bonnie laddie | BAIRN **7**, 37
Earth, thou bonnie broukit bairn | MACDIA **2**, 210
for bonnie Annie Laurie | W DOUGL **1**, 115
for bonnie Annie Laurie | SPOTT **1**, 316
heather creep, creepin' / Ower the bonnie dryin' green | ANGUS **2**, 25
in Scotland's bonnie bounds | A GRANT **2**, 148
Let us haste to Kelvin Grove, bonnie lassie | LYLE **1**, 201
Maxwellton braes are bonnie | SPOTT **1**, 316
Maxwelton banks are bonnie | W DOUGL **1**, 115
met, about daybreak, a bonnie young lassie | TRAD **61**, 338
O waly, waly, gin love be bonnie | TRAD **78**, 340
O wha will shoe my bonnie foot? | BALLAD **31**, 41
shearin's no for you my bonnie lassie | TRAD **59**, 338
So list bonnie laddie, an' come awa' | TRAD **76**, 340
Speed, bonnie boat, like a bird on the wing | BOULT **1**, 55
The bonnie bloomin' heather | LAUDER **3**, 192
the bonnie, bonnie broom | BALLAD **11**, 39
The bonnie bruckit lassie | TYTLER **3**, 342
the bonnie house o' Airlie | BALLAD **8**, 39
the bonnie lass o' Fyvie-o | TRAD **16**, 334
The bonnie muir hen | BAIRN **4**, 36
yellow broom and the bonnie whins | TRAD **5**, 333
bonnily: The work gangs bonnily on | DICKS **1**, 111
bonny: A bonny No, with smyling looks agane | MONTGO **3**, 254
am I no a bonny fighter? | STEVEN **58**, 322
Bonny Bobbie Shafto | BAIRN **3**, 36
fathered between a kailyard and a bonny brier bush | GIBBON **2**, 142
follow the bonnet of Bonny Dundee | SCOTT **116**, 296
was nae sic a bonny tree | NAIRNE **10**, 264
book: A Book's a Book, altho' there's nothing in't | BYRON **6**, 76
a language in which no book was ever written | LOCH **2**, 198
any fool can write a book | A MACLEA **1**, 230
book is a friend whose face | A LANG **4**, 191
every time I've been in Scotland I write a book | CARTL **1**, 93
only good purpose of a book | FERRI **2**, 130
books: Bad books perish, but good books survive | FRAZER **4**, 137
books are all good enough but look you to Jesus | SLESS **1**, 302
Books are good enough in their own way | STEVEN **28**, 320
cover a great deal of country in books | A LANG **6**, 191
Criticism in Scotland, of books | CRUICK **9**, 104
In Books lies the *soul* of the whole Past | CARLYL **4**, 82
magic preservation in the pages of Books | CARLYL **41**, 87
number of books I have written | OLIPH **19**, 271
Some books are lies frae end to end | BURNS **5**, 67
University of these days is a Collection of Books | CARLYL **42**, 87
booksellers: cheat nobody but Booksellers | SCOTT **28**, 291
bookselling: bookselling [is] the most ticklish | SCOTT **54**, 293
book-tongue: Scots can only survive as a book-tongue | A BUCHAN **3**, 63
boots: I have blacked my boots with the Bible | WHITE **1**, 348
rots your boots | MUNRO **4**, 261
borb: 'S fheàrr leam nuair a tha iad borb | M NICGU **2**, 267
bord: Gach bord cho mìn ri cluaimh nan eala | CARMIN **14**, 89
border: Blue Bonnets are bound for the Border | SCOTT **73**, 294
if your heart's a Border heart | W OGILVI **1**, 269
She's o'er the Border and awa' / Wi' Jock of Hazeldean | SCOTT **48**, 292
we haven't even crossed the border | J KAY **5**, 183
Borderer: come forth, my Borderer | W OGILVI **2**, 269
Borders: soft lowland tongue o' the Borders | SANDER **1**, 288
bore: always a bore being ahead of one's time | MITCHI **11**, 252
Life would indeed be a bore | N DOUGL **4**, 115
Boreas: Boreas wi' his blasts sae bauld | TRAD **69**, 339
bores: 21 millions of the greatest bores | LIVING **2**, 198
the greatest of bores | CARLYL **10**, 83
borin': You're *borin'* awa | PAGAN **5**, 273
born: a more awful thing to be born than to die | GALT **10**, 139
a thing being born as it was / born once in Florence | MITCHI **17**, 252
happiest lot on earth is to be born a Scotsman | STEVEN **44**, 321
I was born an atheist | MACCAI **37**, 207
borrowed: We are on borrowed time | CONN **2**, 99
boss: the power of some to be a boss | Jo DAVID(2) **1**, 108
bother: Nae bother at aw! | ANTHON **1**, 31
bottle: red, red is the bottle's blood | MACTHO **21**, 241
She'd stop her drinking, break the bottle | MOON **1**, 255

Twelve and a tanner a bottle | FYFFE **2**, 137
bottles: bright bottles in a sweetie shop window | PETTIE **1**, 274
the sad glugs in your bottles | DUNN **7**, 121
bottom: no bottom and a social conscience | S MACDON **2**, 215
boucheouris: Like boucheouris hakkand on thair stokkis | D LINDS **9**, 195
bought: We're bought and sold for English gold | BURNS **120**, 74
bound: A Working Boy though not bound | CARNEG **1**, 89
bounded: *Scotland is bounded on the south by England* | SHEPH **1**, 299
bounder: she is a bounder, a liar, a deceiver | DALYE **6**, 108
bourgeois: Two rosy bourgeois howling at each other | MACCAI **9**, 205
bourgeoisie: The *bourgeoisie's* weapon is starvation | STEVEN **102**, 325
boustius: a boustius berne | D LINDS **2**, 195
bowed: when she cam ben he bowed fu' low | NAIRNE **8**, 264
bowels: no complete misery in the world that does not emanate from the bowels | J CARLYL **5**, 83
bower: when I'm in my father's bower | BALLAD **10**, 39
bowl: Christ's hand that tips the blue-rimmed porridge bowl | M STUA **2**, 326
bow'r: I will twine thee a bow'r / By the clear siller fountain | TANNAH **2**, 329
bow-wow: The Big Bow-wow strain | SCOTT **95**, 295
boxes: drop acid into the postal pillar boxes | STEPH **1**, 318
boy: A Working Boy though not bound | CARNEG **1**, 89
boy who is flogged into grammar-rules | KAMES **15**, 182
clever boy is flogged into a dunce | SCOTT **99**, 295
God send a smilinge boy | JAMES **21**, 176
the phantom boy / that they once were | IC SMITH **17**, 307
this boy will be surrounded by sycophants and flatterers | HARDIE **1**, 157
boyhood: two great subjects between us in my boyhood | BARRIE **1**, 43
boys: boys will suffer *more* from the absence of the girls | J GRANT **3**, 149
ferret-faced, white-eyed boys | STEVEN **14**, 319
God's Kingdom among Boys | W A SMITH **1**, 310
Hill you ho, boys | ROBERTO **4**, 283
bra: I won't throw my bra away yet | Jo BEAT **2**, 46
bracken: I saw the bracken growing round the well of her eyes | MACTHO **9**, 240
brae: Calvin's kirk crowning the barren brae | E MUIR **19**, 259
hie away, / Over bank and over brae | SCOTT **32**, 291
braes: go / To the braes o' Balquhither | TANNAH **1**, 329
think nae mair on the braes of Yarrow | W HAMIL(2) **1**, 157
We twa hae run about the braes | BURNS **67**, 70
brain: better store of love than brain | AYTON **3**, 34
Come, lamefoot brain, and dance | O FRAS **1**, 136
doesn't get enough blood to his brain | Jo BELL **3**, 47
It takes a Brain to become insane | PETRIE **1**, 274
sweet Sleep is not for the weary brain | Ja THOMS(2) **3**, 332
brains: beat out his brains on account of their constipation | CARLYL **4**, 82
brains came to be their chief item of commerce | LEACO **3**, 193
brains enough to make a fool of himself | STEVEN **27**, 320
chess-playing is a sad waste of brains | SCOTT **119**, 297
don't think brains are terribly important | Jo SMITH **3**, 309
expenditure of chalk is often a saving of brains | KELVIN **9**, 184
havin' no education, I had to use my brains | SHANKL **5**, 299
last Druid whose brains should be knocked out | ASCHER **7**, 32
sans brains for anything at all | FERRI **13**, 130
Their neanderthal brains will just explode | MUNRO **3**, 262
brand: Why dois your brand sae drap wi bluid | BALLAD **19**, 40
brandy: Brandy makes me dull and dizzy | CUNN **4**, 104
fill up your glasses of brandy and wine | TRAD **37**, 336
some are fou o' brandy | BURNS **13**, 67
sterilised it all with five-star brandy | A WALLA **1**, 345
brave: Scotland the brave | HANLEY **1**, 157
the brave will not pull down the blinds | M MCMIL **3**, 234
Braveheart: *Braveheart* is pure Australian shite | CONNOL **12**, 100
breacain: Gheibhte breacain charnaid | MACANT **2**, 203
breacana: Cha bhi oirnn ach ad is casag / An àite nam breacana dearga | MACANT **5**, 204
bread: Bread I dip in the river | STEVEN **83**, 323
going from hunger away, / To a land that promised me bread | CORRIE **7**, 102
oaten bread is not a thing to be laughed at | MAJOR(1) **1**, 243
bread-knife: I dream of poems like the bread-knife | MACDIA **49**, 212
break: Better to break the law than break the poor | ANON **58**, 31
breakaway: mak oor land republican / In a Scottish breakaway | BLYTH **1**, 52
breakfast: Dinner is the English meal, breakfast the Scotch | COCKBU **1**, 97
Freedom begins with breakfast | RITCH-C **1**, 282
Greyhound for Breakfast | KELMAN **3**, 183
breakings: a tangle of breakings off and addings on | OLIPH **11**, 270
breast: Wasp waist and cone breast | LOCHH **4**, 199
breasts: Yet lie all night between my breasts | W HAMIL(2) **2**, 157
breath: I can blow a garden with my breath | M STUA **5**, 327

thy noise and smoky breath	SMITH 4, 305
where every breath may bring infection	COLQUH 4, 98
breathes: Breathes there the man, with soul so dead	SCOTT 7, 290
breathing: the trick is to keep breathing	GALLO 2, 138
breeches: belly-band of his regimen-tal breeches	ESKGR 5, 124
God's wounds, I will pull down my breeches	JAMES 23, 176
breeks: But the hose and but the breeks	CUNN 2, 104
callants gaun wanting the breeks	SCOTT 34, 291
ill taking the breeks aff a Hielandman	SCOTT 59, 293
breid: Earnan her breid wi her hurdies' sweit	SG SMITH 3, 310
Nonsense at this time o' day / That breid-and-butter problems	MACDIA 31, 211
The Burn o Breid / Sall rin fu reid	THOMAS 2, 331
breik: Thy bawis hingis throw thy breik	DUNBAR 5, 118
brevity: Study brevity	MACCAI 45, 207
brew: She wadna bake, nor she wadna brew	BALLAD 13, 40
brewer: benevolence of the butcher, the brewer	SMITH 5, 304
bribed: Half our nation was bribed	JOHNS 4, 178
brick-lanes: Unsightly brick-lanes smoke, and clanking engines gleam	T CAMPB 9, 82
bricklayer: I'd be an 18-stone alcoholic bricklayer	GORAM 1, 145
brickwall: the brickwall you are these days	LOCHH 7, 199
bride: busk ye, my bonny, bonny bride	W HAMIL(2) 1, 157
O wha's the bride that cairries the bunch	MACDIA 17, 210
The bride she is winsome and bonny	J BAILL 15, 36
bridegroom: Like a bridegroom from his room	AYTOUN 2, 34
bridge: Beautiful Railway Bridge of the Silv'ry Tay	MCGON 4, 220
brier: bonnie brier bush in our kail-yard	NAIRNE 11, 265
fathered between a kailyard and a bonny brier bush	GIBBON 2, 142
Brigadoon: I saw the rain dirty valley / you saw Brigadoon	M SCOTT 1, 289
bright: bright bottles in a sweetie shop window	PETTIE 1, 274
Where the pools are bright and deep	HOGG 14, 163
briseadh: Daoine nach d' rinn briseadh iad	ROB DON 2, 282
briseadh-cridhe: nist tha mi a' faicinn nad shùilean / briseadh-cridhe na cùise	BATE 2, 45
brissit: Brissit brawnis and brokin banis	ANON 9, 27
Britannia: Rule, Britannia, rule the waves	Ja THOMS(1) 1, 331
singing Rule Britannia in the heavenly choirs	CUNN G. 16, 106
brither: Tam lo'ed him like a vera brither	BURNS 93, 72
British: British institutions are in terminal decay	ASCHER 6, 32
easily combine with British patriotism	A BALF 2, 38
Briton: Though a mere Briton, I triumphed here	J BRUCE 1, 62
broad: woman's life can never be the broad, strong thing	WATERST 1, 345
brogue: to hear the Scotch brogue – oh, heavens!	FERRI 9, 130
brogues: not fit to tie his brogues	SCOTT 101, 296
broke: with research you may make a failure, then another failure, then others, but you never go broke	A FLEM 4, 133
broken: A broken heart is what I have	DUNN 11, 122
Laws were made to be broken	NORTH 4, 268
broken-heartedness: strangest disease I have seen in this country seems really to be broken-heartedness	LIVING 5, 198
brokin: hir arm was sone brokin in schonder	BELLEN 3, 48
bròn: cruithneachd leotha bròn	MAIRI 3, 242
brònach: 'Smitha brònach's tu'm dhìth	TRAD 41, 337
brònag: bu mhi brònag / 'S mi dol 'na chlachan Di-Dòmhnaich	TRAD 35, 336
brooch: Stirling is the brooch	MITCHI 1, 253
Stirling, like a huge brooch	SMITH 10, 306
brooches: I will make you brooches and toys	STEVEN 85, 323
brood: brood of aggressive, egotistical children	W MUIR 9, 261
broom: The broom of the Cowdenknowes	BALLAD 11, 39
the Gallowa' hills are covered wi' broom	TRAD 40, 337
When the pods went pop on the broom	Jo DAVID(2) 6, 108
yellow broom and the bonnie whins	TRAD 5, 333
Broomielaw: The ships that sailed by the Broomielaw	TRAD 12, 334
Broon: ken it was Bawsy Broon	SOUTAR 2, 313
brosgal: Cha b'e an creideamh ach am brosgal	AIREAC 1, 23
broth: an unctuous BBC Broth	FINDL 2, 131
I want Christian broth	STEVEN 92, 324
brother: By far my elder brother in the Muse	BURNS 52, 69
my elder brother in misfortune	BURNS 52, 69
Though our brother is upon the rack	SMITH 2, 304
brotherhood: a Scotsman may well claim brotherhood with an Englishman	SCOTS 1, 288
brothers: countless unborn sisters and brothers	DONAL 4, 113
Man to Man the warld o'er, / Shall brothers be	BURNS 134, 75
brow: go to heaven with a broken brow	RUTHER 4, 287
Her brow is like the snawdrift	SPOTT 1, 316

In the blank of his brow	SOUTAR 14, 314
pull the thorn thy brow to braid	SCOTT 29, 291
brows: Gathering her brows like gathering storm	BURNS 90, 72
Bruce: Bruce was a spectacular success	M FORS 1, 135
Scots, wham Bruce has aften led	BURNS 126, 74
bruckit: The bonnie bruckit lassie	TYTLER 3, 342
Bruichladdich: Glenfiddich, Bruichladdich and Glengrant	MACCAI 8, 205
brunstane: torment o the lowin brunstane pit	R MCLEL 3, 231
brute: Yet the brute did die	BIRNIE 1, 49
brybour: Iersch brybour baird, vyle beggar	DUNBAR 3, 118
bryght: with your bryght lanternis	JAMES I 2, 174
bubbly-jock: like a bubbly-jock wi a chuckie in its thrapple	R MCLEL 4, 231
Rax me a spaul o' that bubbly jock	D GORD 2, 145
sair hadden doun wi' the bubbly jock	D RAMS 6, 279
the bubblyjock swallowed the bagpipes	MACDIA 10, 210
Buchan: O Lord look doon on Buchan	MILNE 3, 251
buckles: I'll dance the buckles aff my shoon	TRAD 46, 337
Buddhist: I fyles chant Buddhist mantras / An read René Magritte	BLACKH 5, 50
why the Buddhist goes on pilgrimage to a mountain	SHEPH 10, 300
budge: stalled lives never budge	MORGAN 11, 256
buffeted: reproached, buffeted, pissed upon	SMOLL 4, 311
bug: him that leads the life of a bug	HAILES 1, 155
bugbear: Knowledge, which is the bugbear of tyranny	WRIGHT 2, 353
buggery: buggery being uncommon in the Islands	MITCHI 22, 253
buik: Scots disna bide in a buik	BLACKH 3, 50
building: Why have slums when half the building trade are unemployed?	MCGAH 2, 216
buildings: plenty of ruined buildings in the world but no ruined stones	MACDIA 36, 211
very jealous of buildings	MCWIL 2, 242
bukis: bukis wer worthy thair wayght of gould	WODE 1, 351
bullet: a vehement bullet will come from the gun of Love	MACGIL 26, 219
bulletin: six o'clock bulletin is a tiresome postponement of the football results	C MACKEN 5, 225
bum: Kneel, and kiss his gracious bum	RODGER 1, 285
leave her bum sticking out	CONNOL 2, 100
bumfodders: of all torcheculs, arsewisps, bumfodders	T URQU 6, 343
bumper: Life is a bumper filled by fate	BLACKL 1, 50
bundle: like carrying a bundle of barbed wire	GILLI 2, 144
bungaloids: When the bungaloids burgeon and gowfers gowf	BRIDIE 15, 59
burden: the burning of the noontide heat / And the burden of the day	CLEPH 1, 96
bureaucracy: Arts Councils are the insane asylums of bureaucracy	IH FINL 5, 131
burglar: a city of barred windows and burglar alarms	THERO 2, 330
burial-field: a spacious burial-field unwall'd	R BLAIR(2) 5, 51
buried: long to be buried among good Scots clods	STEVEN 43, 321
Burke: Burke and Hare, / They were a pair	BAIRN 5, 37
Burke's the butcher, Hare's the thief	BAIRN 6, 37
burlesque: a burlesque with evil undertones	CAIRNS 1, 79
burn: in the shieling by the burn	TRAD 55, 338
jist ae wee woman, / The kind they used tae burn	BROOKS 8, 59
she has lived too long; let her burn	D MACLEO 1, 231
The Burn o Breid / Sall rin fu reid	THOMAS 2, 331
The burn was big wi' spate	RORIE 2, 285
burnin': sad day of doom and burnin'	TRAD 53, 338
burning: the burning of the noontide heat / And the burden of the day	CLEPH 1, 96
Burns: Burns orgies detestable	CRUICK 8, 104
Burns, originally virtuous	H MACKEN 7, 226
Burns touched the hert aa the time	MORRIS 1, 257
canna recite Burns juist oot o yer heid	MORRIS 1, 257
more intellectual honesty at Murrayfield than at a Burns Supper	GARIOC 8, 140
Robert Burns knelt and kissed the mool	GARIOC 5, 140
something in Burns for every moment	H MORT 9, 257
The star o' Robbie Burns	TRAD 65, 339
Wherever a Scotsman goes, there goes Burns	J MUIR 9, 260
burnys: And burnys hurlys all thar bankis downe	G DOUGL 5, 114
bus-ferries: lumbering bus-ferries	A REID 2, 279
bush: the bush aboon Traquair	SHAIRP 1, 298
bushel: hidden under a bushel of alien authority	CLYDE 1, 96
business: always the factor who does the dirty business	BLACKI 1, 50
business is more entertaining than fooling among boats?	STEVEN 2, 318
For the business executive it will be his parliament	G ROBERTSO 2, 284
man can always command his time under the plea of business	SOMERV 7, 312

carraige: Tha maireannachd na carraige / aig a' bheàirn a
dh'fhàg thu — WHYTE 4, 349
carrots: it's the diced carrots — CONNOL 5, 100
  man who was growing blue carrots — J HAYN 2, 159
carrying: seemed to me to be 'carrying coals to Newcastle' — ARNOLD 3, 31
cars: cars were to be the great means of propulsion — F BALF 7, 39
Carterhaugh: To come or gae by Carterhaugh — BALLAD 41, 41
carving: Carving has ever been esteemed one of the minor arts — DODS 1, 112
cas: Chuir iad cas air reachd na firinn — CLARK 1, 95
casag: Cha bhi oirnn ach ad is casag / An àite nam breacana
dearga — MACANT 5, 204
cash-payment: Cash-payment is not the sole nexus of man — CARLYL 49, 87
castawa: Wha wud be a tattie-bogle / In castawa claes — SOUTAR 17, 314
castle: By yon castle wa' — BURNS 121, 74
  castle itself is a complete importation — WILKIE 1, 349
  enchanted castle, imposed upon by spectres — T REID 3, 281
  where the key shall not keep the castle — JAMES I 1, 174
castock: a kail-whittle in a castock — BURNS 45, 69
castocks: castocks in Stra'bogie — NAIRNE 4, 264
cat: I am he who will bell the cat — A DOUGL 1, 114
  just the full moon and a stray cat — WHITE 4, 348
  snail's entrails mixed with cat's fat — LAMONT 2, 191
  two inferior members, a maid and a cat — HUME 25, 167
cat-fish: cat-fish that vitalises the other torpid denizens — MACDIA 44, 212
cataract: cataract of drivel for which Conan Doyle — Jo BELL 1, 47
catastrophe: wickedest man-made catastrophe — J CAMER 7, 80
catch: catch it on Monday, you're cured on Tuesday — A FLEM 5, 133
  Catch the Wind — DONOV 1, 114
catechism: reared on porridge and the Shorter Catechism — MCNEI 1, 237
cathedral: Dang the Cathedral down — TENNAN 4, 330
  Jesus was not crucified in a cathedral — G MACLEO 6, 233
cathedrals: dam for water-tanks the people's cathedrals — J MUIR 10, 260
  monument of the pre-Reformation spirit is cathedrals — F MACCOL 1, 209
Catholic: agree to become Rangers' first Catholic — M JOHNST 1, 179
cats: whurrin' in like cats on rattens — TENNAN 5, 330
cattle: I believe in cattle and sheep — J MATHES 1, 246
  Men, even the good ones, are kittle cattle — A BUCHAN 1, 63
  The sky moves like cattle — JAMIE 5, 177
cauf: Ou ay, it's a cauf — POLKEM 3, 276
cauld: Cauld blaws the wind frae east to west — BURNS 57, 70
  Cauld blaws the wind frae north to south — Jo HAMIL(2) 1, 156
  cauld in the clay — J ELLIO 2, 123
  cauld kail in Aberdeen — NAIRNE 4, 264
  Cauld winter was howling — TRAD 61, 338
  Good claret best keeps out the cauld — A RAMS(1) 5, 277
  Oh wert thou in the cauld blast — BURNS 139, 75
  There's cauld kail in Aberdeen — A GORD 1, 145
  when 'tis auld it waxeth cauld — TRAD 78, 340
cauldrife: Noo that cauldrife Winter's here — MURRAY 8, 262
cause: A guid cause maks a strong arm — ANON 46, 30
  cause of the 'shrieking sisterhood' — BAILIE 1, 35
  Scotland is an unwon cause — STEINB 1, 318
  the cause of justice and liberty — WITHER 1, 351
  the cause is lost for ever — SCOTT 86, 295
  the cause of the people — T MUIR 1, 260
causes: No causes whatsoever . . . ever acted — LYELL 1, 201
caution: Great caution in his reasonings — PLAYF 2, 275
cautious: Be cautious in displaying your good sense — GREGOR 1, 151
  Be very cautious of your friendships — COLQUH 3, 98
cave: the renowned Fingal's Cave — VICTO 2, 344
caveful: swaying caveful of half- / seas over oil-men — LOCHH 9, 199
ceangal: Chan eil ceangal àraidh againn / ris an fhear a
chuireas peatroil — WHYTE 5, 349
ceann: A Cheit, tog an ceann — DOMHN D 1, 112
  'S a' phlangaid shuarach 's i suas mun ceann — DOMHN R 1, 112
ceann-teagaisg: O, nan tigeadh soisgeulaiche / a lorgadh
ceann teagaisg — MACTHO 18, 241
cedar: a mighty cedar in my room — N WELLS 4, 347
ceilidh: in the ceilidh house reading The Guns of Navarone — IC SMITH 28, 309
celestial: an unsleeping celestial sneak-thief — GIBBON 15, 143
cell: Turnkey, Lock the cell — SCOTT 90, 295
Cellini: as wonderful as that of Benvenuto Cellini — WILKIE 5, 349
Celtic: anti-Pinkerton, and delight in the Celtic — A GRANT 3, 148
  Celtic races, with their melancholy and unprogressiveness — ARNOLD 2, 31
  I am a Celtic man through and through — M JOHNST 2, 179
cement: a cement of political strength — DUNDAS 2, 120
centuries: handclapping centuries / Of his one minute on
earth — WS GRAH 2, 147

ceòl: armachd ás nach tig ceòl fàsmhor — IC SMITH 3, 306
  Bha ceòl na mara 'nam chluasan — IC SMITH 19, 308
  Ceól as mó rugas do roghainn — DEAN 2, 110
  ceòl mòr anns a' chuimhne — MACTHO 22, 242
cesspool: London, that great cesspool — DOYLE 1, 116
chagnadh: cha sguir thu gu bràth de chagnadh nan
Caimbeulach? — IAIN L 2, 170
chaidil: Chaidil mi raoir air a' bhuailidh — TRAD 23, 335
chain: A chain of gold ye sall not lack — SCOTT 47, 292
chair: Who will now lift the sword or fill the chair? — NIC FHE 1, 266
Chairlhi: Mincing wi' Chairlhi — MARRA 1, 244
Chairlie: haill Toun sterts to talk like Chairlie — R MCLEL 6, 231
chalk: draw a chalk circle round every individuality — CARLYL 12, 84
  expenditure of chalk is often a saving of brains — KELVIN 9, 186
cham: great Cham of Literature — SMOLL 9, 311
Chamberlain: Chamberlain was right at Munich — HOME 5, 165
chance: You are allowed one chance in Scotland — B FORS 1, 134
chandeliers: Throw all your stagey chandeliers — CRAWFO 2, 103
change: Change and decay in all around I see — LYTE 2, 202
  John, we'll soon change all this — KIRKWO 1, 187
  Language is mobile and liable to change — J MURRAY 2, 263
change-house: Out o' the change-house an' the pawn — Ja HAMIL 2, 156
channerin': The channerin' worm doth chide — BALLAD 47, 42
chapman: as ane chapman beris his pak, / I bure thy Grace — D LINDS 3, 195
  When chapman billies leave the street — BURNS 90, 72
chaps: the chaps / Who are going to die perhaps — SORLEY 1, 313
character: his character in stone and lime — GD BROWN 6, 60
  'It will do!' has blighted many a character — SMILES 8, 303
  pathological cracks in his character — BOLD 4, 53
characters: no more interested in my own characters than I
am in Jeanie Deans — OLIPH 23, 271
  The characters we think we 'create' — BARRIE 23, 45
charger: knight on a white charger is never going to come — GALLO 6, 138
charity: It's a great work of charity — STAIR(1) 1, 316
Charles: If Charles were to descend on us — MACANT 2, 203
Charlie: Bonnie Charlie's now awa — NAIRNE 13, 265
  Charlie, Charlie, rise and rin — TRAD 38, 336
  Charlie he's my darling — BURNS 135, 75
  Charlie he's my darling — HOGG 6, 163
  Charlie, meet me an ye daur — A SKIR 1, 302
  wae's me for Prince Charlie — GLEN 1, 145
  wha'll be king but Charlie? — NAIRNE 12, 265
  Wha wadna fecht for Charlie? — TRAD 82, 340
Char'lina: 'S ged theidheadh iad do Char'lina — D MATHES 2, 246
charm: What is charm, exactly, Maggie? — BARRIE 9, 44
charter: Christ got a charter of Scotland — RUTHER 1, 287
château: he should be château-bottled — FAIRB 7, 126
chathair: Có nis thogas an claidheamh no nì chathair
a lìonadh? — NIC FHE 1, 266
chatterers: we chatterers in the Central Belt — I BELL 2, 47
cheat: cheat nobody but Booksellers — SCOTT 28, 291
checkmate: That's checkmate to you, Matthew! — KAMES 9, 181
checkout: not so much a checkout queue this, it's more the
Day of Judgement — PATTIS 3, 274
cheeks: redder his cheeks than calf's blood — DEAN 3, 110
  Your cheeks are like the crimson — F SEMP 2, 298
cheese: many's the long night I've dreamed of cheese — STEVEN 41, 321
Cheit: A Cheit, tog an ceann — DOMHN D 1, 112
cheque: shair of his cheque at the month's end — GARIOC 2, 140
chess-playing: chess-playing is a sad waste of brains — SCOTT 119, 297
chest: Behold my war chest! — C STEW 3, 325
  Fifteen men on a dead man's chest — STEVEN 39, 321
chewing gum: Does Your Chewing Gum Lose Its Flavour — DONEG 1, 113
chianti: running Scotland over pasta and chianti — HESELT 2, 162
chib: keep a chib over the door an a blade in ma bedroom — T MCGRAT 3, 221
chief: Hail to the Chief who in honour — SCOTT 23, 291
  I see a chief, the last of his house — BRAHAN 4, 56
chieftain: A chieftain to the Highlands bound — T CAMPB 8, 81
  Great chieftain o' the puddin'-race — BURNS 34, 68
chiel': Ye're a verra clever chiel', man — BRAXF 9, 57
chield: A chield's amang you takin' notes — BURNS 125, 74
chiels: facts are chiels that winna ding — BURNS 25, 68
child: A child should always say what's true — STEVEN 48, 321
  child's world of dim sensation — STEVEN 35, 320
  Child, with many a childish wile — J BAILL 4, 35
  Educate every child as if he were your own — M MCMIL 9, 235
  first thing a child should learn is to be a rebel — A NEILL 3, 265
  It's a naked child against a hungry wolf — Jo DAVID(2) 3, 108

comedy: I see life as a comedy   **CAIRNS 1**, 79
   the great art of all comedy   **CARR 1**, 90
   traditions of Scottish comedy lie in homeliness   **CARR 2**, 90
comers: rich new Comers / Hae changed to frost their ance
   warm summers   **MACNEI 1**, 237
comfort: thy rod / and staff me comfort still   **METRIC 1**, 249
   We leeve in the sewers o' ither bastards' comfort   **W MCILV 3**, 223
còmhradh: Falbh 'n an cuideachd 's 'n an còmhradh   **ROB DON 4**, 282
comics: Graveyard of English comics   **LOGAN 3**, 200
   majority of Scots comics have come from Glasgow   **S BAXT 4**, 46
command: command him by obeying him   **CARLYL 4**, 85
commencement: En ma fin est mon commencement   **MARY(2) 7**, 245
commend: the only Scot whom Scotchmen did not
   commend   **MALLOC 1**, 244
commentators: I do not care three farthings for
   Commentators   **BURNS 76**, 71
commerce: brains came to be their chief item of commerce   **LEACO 3**, 193
   commerce and Christianity   **LIVING 4**, 198
   culture is opposed not to commerce   **J ANDERS 2**, 25
   they talk of commerce as if it was a man   **STEUAR 1**, 318
commercialism: devotees of ravaging commercialism   **J MUIR 10**, 260
   the vomit of a cataleptic commercialism   **GIBBON 1**, 142
commitment: kind of commitment Scots invest in football   **W MCILV 7**, 223
commodity: tragedy of the Highlands has become a saleable
   commodity   **J MCGRAT 2**, 220
common: common cause out of their common misery   **OBAN 1**, 269
   common women are in general most remarkably plain   **PENNA 2**, 274
   the common people, humanised by Christianity   **CHALM 3**, 93
commonplace: 'Common-place,' said Holmes   **DOYLE 2**, 116
   fat, little, commonplace woman   **OLIPH 21**, 271
Commons: consider the House of Commons as your enemies   **TYTLER 2**, 342
   The Commons, faithful to their system   **MACKINT 1**, 229
common sense: cultivation of a shrewd common sense   **MILLER 6**, 250
   don't believe in common sense, we believe in intelligence   **DUNN 9**, 121
   if she will not be the servant of Common Sense   **T REID 6**, 281
   philosophy to decide against common sense   **T REID 5**, 281
   the etherealisation of common sense   **KELVIN 19**, 185
common weal: govern according to the common weal   **JAMES 22**, 176
commonwealth: families fatal to the ruin of the
   Commonwealth   **W DRUM 11**, 117
common-weil: Quhat is the caus the Common-weil is
   crukit?   **D LINDS 13**, 195
communicate: The future is artists who want to communicate   **SPALD 2**, 314
communication: keeping lines of communication open   **SULTER 6**, 327
communism: back to communism and forward to
   communism   **J MACLEA 5**, 230
   Communism is hunger becoming articulate   **BOYD OR 3**, 56
communist: I can imagine a communist society   **MITCHI 1**, 251
communists: Communists don't infiltrate unions   **MCGAH 1**, 216
   I do not hate the Communists   **G MACLEO 4**, 232
communities: I even dream of ideal communities   **DUNN 2**, 121
community: A disgrace to the community   **MACDIA 47**, 212
   for the good of the community   **CARNEG 7**, 90
   I find the idea of community important   **IC SMITH 25**, 308
companion: a delicious companion to a man   **KAMES 14**, 182
company: didna like to disturb gude company   **D RAMS 2**, 278
   Go into their company and converse   **ROB DON 4**, 282
   poverty parts good company   **J BAILL 12**, 36
   when the liquor is done there is an end to the company   **J MACLAR 1**, 229
compass: compass which Christ saileth by   **RUTHER 2**, 287
compelled: The little ones were always compelled to be
   English   **SOMERV 3**, 312
competition: a competition for who was to be hindmost   **GD BROWN 4**, 60
complexion: spoil your eyes and complexion   **FERRI 3**, 130
composing: composing a Scotch song is a trifling business   **BURNS 49**, 69
comrades: I hae been blythe wi' Comrades dear   **BURNS 32**, 68
Conan Doyle: cataract of drivel for which Conan Doyle   **Jo BELL 1**, 47
conceit: count one's blessings, even if it implies one's conceit   **KENNAW 2**, 185
   curst conceit o' bein' richt   **MACDIA 15**, 210
   Guid gi'e us a guid conceit o' oursel's   **BRIDIE 8**, 58
concentration: shortest way to a concentration camp   **N GUNN 8**, 153
concrete: Modernism is the acceptance of the concrete   **PAOLO 1**, 273
condemned: The honourable mouth that condemned you   **HAY 5**, 158
condense: Scotch, whatever other talents they may have,
   can never condense   **S SMITH 3**, 310
conduct: Moral conduct *is* beautiful   **MACMUR 3**, 235
   the odour of a stinking Conduct   **HUME 1**, 166
cone: Wasp waist and cone breast   **LOCHH 4**, 199

confessions: hellish, unembellished / True Confessions   **LOCHH 12**, 199
conflict: Conflict is one of the givens of the universe   **1H FINL 10**, 132
congenial: Congenial horrors, hail!   **Ja THOMS(1) 5**, 331
Congo: Congo's no' to be compared   **MUNRO 6**, 261
congregation: Congregation to elect their Minister   **DISCIP(1) 1**, 111
   intruded or thrust in upon any congregation   **DISCIP(1) 2**, 111
Connery: Sean Connery would become king of Scotland   **HUSTON 1**, 169
conquer: I have taken a firm resolution to conquer or to die   **C STEW 1**, 325
conscience: between the poet's conscience and the rights
   of the public   **MACKINN 2**, 227
   Conscience, Madam, requyres knowlege   **KNOX 6**, 188
   nae plaster for a wounded conscience   **GALT 8**, 139
   no bottom and a social conscience   **S MACDON 2**, 215
conscientious: spectacle of the conscientious journalist   **J CAMER 6**, 80
conscious: civil suffering conscious me   **JACKS 1**, 173
   greatest of faults, I should say, is to be conscious of none   **CARLYL 39**, 86
conscripts: children are conscripts   **DONAL 1**, 113
consequence: trained up to be a person of consequence   **FERRI 22**, 131
consideration: For a con-si-de-ra-tion   **SCOTT 78**, 294
conspiracy: a conspiracy against the public   **SMITH 9**, 304
   Civilisation is a conspiracy   **J BUCHAN 3**, 63
   Modern art is a conspiracy against people   **SPALD 3**, 314
constancie: O Lady for thy Constancie   **MONTGO 2**, 254
constipation: beat out his brains on account of their
   constipation   **CARLYL 4**, 82
constituencies: back to your constituencies and prepare for
   government   **STEEL 1**, 317
constitutionalists: constitutionalists have to give way
   before human necessity   **MAXTON 1**, 247
constitutions: delicate minds and delicate constitutions   **A GRANT 10**, 148
consumebatur: Nec tamen consumebatur   **ANON 23**, 28
consumed: And yet it was not consumed   **ANON 23**, 28
contemned: most to be pitied of mankind; and *contemned*   **STEVEN 77**, 323
contemplating: divine grace has bestowed the gift of
   contemplating   **COLUMB 1**, 99
contempt: contempt of the idler for the hard worker   **CARSW 12**, 92
   Your contempt for the weak – I called it virility   **BARRIE 17**, 44
content: He hes anewch that is content   **DUNBAR 18**, 119
contentment: I do not think the road to contentment
   lies in despising   **Ge MACDON 4**, 214
contermashious: contermashious deils   **MILNE 3**, 251
continents: believe their greed holds up the continents   **GRAY 4**, 150
continually: continually wedded to his errors   **A FERG 1**, 127
contraception: contraception... was itself part of women's
   emancipation   **MITCHI 3**, 251
contradictions: Take away the contradictions / and what's
   left? Heaven   **MACCAI 39**, 207
contrivance: some contrivance to raise prices   **SMITH 9**, 304
controversies: state-papers, controversies and abstractions of
   men   **CARLYL 31**, 86
convention: To the Lords of Convention   **SCOTT 116**, 296
conventional: Folk-song has no use for the conventional   **HENDER 7**, 160
conversation: humour is less apparent in conversation   **CARLYL 3**, 82
   Marriage is one long conversation, chequered by disputes   **STEVEN 75**, 323
converse: Go into their company and converse   **ROB DON 4**, 282
   hold high converse with the mighty dead   **Ja THOMS(1) 6**, 331
   I am not afraid to converse with anybody   **D GORD 1**, 145
convicted: convicted of sickness   **SMOLL 12**, 311
conviction: fornicates gravely but without conviction   **CUNN G. 7**, 106
convulsion: wilful convulsion of brute nature   **STEVEN 96**, 324
coof: He's but a coof for a' that   **BURNS 133**, 75
cook: Cook, like the Surgeon, must first look on   **DODS 2**, 112
   something hard in blaming the poor cook   **SCOTT 10**, 290
   take good care to be my own cook   **SCOTT 104**, 296
cookery: easily satisfied with the cookery   **E GRANT(2) 7**, 149
cooks: Show me any of your French cooks   **MONBOD 4**, 253
cooper: There was a wee cooper who lived in Fife   **BALLAD 13**, 40
coorie: Coorie doon and dream   **MCGINN 1**, 219
coos: if I don't get ye, the coos'll get ye   **LORNE 2**, 200
Cope: we'll meet Johnnie Cope i' the morning   **A SKIR 1**, 302
copulate: The number of people who can copulate properly   **MACDIA 23**, 211
corbies: I heard twa corbies making a mane   **BALLAD 43**, 42
corn: Corn rigs, an' barley rigs   **BURNS 33**, 68
   Plain corn countries   **A COCKBU 2**, 97
corner: green springing corner of young Eden   **E MUIR 17**, 259
   In my smoochy corner / take me on a cloud   **MORGAN 6**, 255
corporation: government in every country should be just like a
   corporation   **BRAXF 2**, 57

corpses: a crowded place, littered with Unionist corpses	MASSIE 4, 246
corran: Cuiridh mi làmh air corran na gealaich	MACGIL 20, 218
corrected: corrected into mediocrity	SCOTT 99, 295
correspondent: best war correspondent is he who can tell	HAIG 1, 155
corrie: The Misty Corrie of hinds aye roving	MACANT 8, 204
Corrivrekin: Where Corrivrekin's surges roar	LEYDEN 1, 194
corrupt: corrupt history of Scotland	IC SMITH 24, 308
corruption: *petticoat-tails* is a corruption of the French	DODS 3, 112
that school of corruption	E GRANT(2) 2, 148
Coshieville: The west wind blows to Coshieville	S MACGRE 2, 222
cosmopolitan: cosmopolitan scum	TROCCHI 6, 341
less cosmopolitan and rather more national in our Architecture	MACKINT 2, 228
cottages: thatched cottages and honey still for tea	ASCHER 3, 32
cotton-spinning: All work, even cotton-spinning, is noble	CARLYL 48, 87
cotton wool: effect of having lived in a world of cotton wool	KAMES 3, 181
cough: muddy cough of the stream that strives	M STUA 4, 327
Coulter: Tae buy mair Coulter's candy	COLTAR 1, 98
counsellors: Two counsellors there were, short of stature, and not speaking	CLARS 3, 95
countenance: her countenance grew very grave	OLIPH 12, 270
When dismal grew his countenance	BALLAD 15, 40
countrie: hame, to my ain countrie	CUNN 5, 105
In my ain countrie	CUNN 6, 105
countries: wave to the waving citizens / of all those other countries	JAMIE 4, 176
country: a country where experts govern	WOOD 3, 352
Alas, poor country	SHAKES 3, 298
And if my country attains wholeness	MACTHO 2, 239
country consists of two things, stone and water	JOHNS 5, 178
cover a great deal of country in books	A LANG 6, 191
desolators of the country	MONBOD 1, 253
every country has need of Scotchmen	A BALF 7, 38
heard the feet of my country / Breaking into a run	CRAWFO 5, 102
how differently our country would be governed	RUSHF 2, 287
impressive country but without resonance	IC SMITH 24, 308
indifference is a mortal sign for the country	BOSWEL 7, 54
In the highlands, in the country places	STEVEN 86, 324
knew our country was a smalltime dump	G WILLIA 2, 350
Lord have mercy on my poor country	FLETCH 4, 134
not another country on earth where such a deed could have been done	JEFFR 9, 177
Poet of this Country – perhaps of mankind	CARSW 8, 91
proletarian has no country	CUNN G. 14, 106
self-expression is the life of any free country	JD FERG 5, 128
Semiconductor country	CRAWFO 3, 102
strangers to the country who, detesting	D STEW 1, 326
the language of a whole country	JEFFR 2, 177
There is no passport to this country	HERBER 1, 161
This is my country, / The land that begat me	A GRAY 1, 150
This was a peasant country before the Union	FAIRB 3, 126
What I have been to my country	KNOX 15, 189
when we take thought of our own small country	GRIERS 3, 151
countryside: the smiling and beautiful countryside	DOYLE 10, 116
county: the county was thus *improved* into a desert	MILLER 1, 250
countynance: ane rycht malancolious countynance	D LINDS 2, 195
coup: one way street to the coup of the mind	T BUCHAN 2, 65
coup-d'état: concerned not with the *coup-d'état* of Trotsky	TROCCHI 4, 341
courage: All goes if courage goes	BARRIE 20, 44
Courage beyond the point and obdurate pride	E MUIR 11, 258
Courage, brother! do not stumble	N MACLEO 2, 233
Courage is a common quality in men of little sense	LINKLA 8, 197
courage to write about himself as he is	C MACKEN 2, 225
courage wise, and wisedome should be stoute	JAMES VI 1, 171
League of Nations grows in moral courage	R MACDON 1, 215
let us gird up our minds in courage	WRIGHT 11, 354
'Twill make your courage rise	BURNS 55, 70
Whistling aloud to bear his courage up	R BLAIR(2) 1, 51
court: the court of the poisoned rose	ANGUS 1, 25
what uglier place is there in civilisation than a court of law?	STEVEN 9, 319
courteous: The women are courteous in the extreme	AYALA 1, 33
courtiers: Let kings and courtiers rise and fa	TRAD 65, 339
courts: Courts for cowards were erected	BURNS 26, 68
Pleasant are Thy courts above	LYTE 3, 202
couthie: couthie country fat and fou o ferms	A SCOTT(2) 5, 289
couthy: Canty and couthy and kindly	ROBERTO 7, 283
covet: covet the mydding and not the skyis	LESLIE 1, 194

inclined to believe what they covet	BYRON 23, 77
cow: He that steals a cow	SCOTT 33, 291
coward: Thy coward sloth is cause of all	W WALLA 3, 345
cowardice: cowardice in the heart / and belief in nothing	MACGIL 1, 216
Cowdenknowes: The broom of the Cowdenknowes	BALLAD 11, 39
cowfold: Last night I slept at the cowfold	TRAD 23, 335
cowhubye: Gramercye! my sweit cowhubye	DUNBAR 11, 119
cows: sheep are preferred, or small cows	MITCHI 22, 253
Trees and cows are more predictable	MITCHI 24, 253
coxcombs: coxcombs, without any principle	J RAMS 1, 279
coyness: coyness larded with apostrophes and Doricisms	J CAMER 2, 80
cradle: claim Scotland as the cradle of football	A MCGRE 1, 221
craga: fir nach cruaidhe na craga	GIOL Co 4, 144
craigie: roarin o'er the warlock craigie	TANNAH 6, 329
Craigo: Craigo Woods, wi' the splash	JACOB 4, 174
crank: Accept. Admit you're a bit of a crank	LOCHH 5, 199
crann: Bheirteadh gach seòl a bhiodh aice / Am bàrr nan crann dith	ALASD 3, 24
Nuair a theid an Crann an àird	MACTHO 20, 241
crap: Stop applauding things that are crap	M GRAY 3, 151
cratur: Davie's a fine gude-natured cratur	HUME 16, 167
craw: The third craw was greetin' for his Maw	D MACRAE 1, 238
crawl: crawl a little longer in this evil world	LOVAT 4, 201
crazy: he's fitba' crazy	J MACGRE 1, 221
cream: whipped cream of London society	SCOTT 109, 296
create: create men or destroy them	W MUIR 2, 260
The characters we think we 'create'	BARRIE 23, 45
To earn the name artist it seems clear that one must *create*	JD FERG 1, 127
creation: awful and dreary blank in creation	CARLYL 3, 83
cause of my creation was as high	Je ADAM 1, 23
mystery and miracle of the creation	KELVIN 13, 184
creative: there is no creative soul	CARSW 20, 92
creator: I can be my own creator	SHEPH 3, 299
creatures: just two creatures I would envy	BURNS 50, 69
Mankind are by nature benevolent creatures	BURNS 80, 71
credit: Credit is a decent honest man	SCOTT 58, 293
creditor: my creditor, Christ	RUTHER 5, 287
creed: first creed that comes to hand	JEFFR 8, 177
stark, sure creed that will cut like a knife	GIBBON 7, 143
creeds: hired preachers of all sects, creeds, and religions	WRIGHT 14, 354
most insular and isolationist of all creeds	ASCHER 1, 32
creel: pile all of the Grace in your own creel	MACTHO 17, 241
creideam: Creideam an crodh is an caoraich	J MATHES 1, 246
creideamh: Cha b'e an creideamh ach am brosgal	AIREAC 1, 23
creithleag: An e creithleag a bhuail mi?	TRAD GA 2, 332
crème: my pupils are the crème de la crème	SPARK 4, 315
Cresseid: fair Cresseid, the flour and A per se / Of Troy	HENRYS 11, 161
crew: a ship and a crew, a ship and a crew	HAY 2, 155
Crichtoun: the never-too-much-to-be-admired Crichtoun	T URQU 2, 343
Crieff: visit the ancient town of Crieff	MCGON 5, 220
crime: crime which is of all others the most mysterious	G MACKEN 5, 225
hanging, instead of scaring from crime	MACTAG 2, 239
the Napoleon of crime	DOYLE 13, 116
crimes: featureless crimes which are really puzzling	DOYLE 7, 116
witchcraft be the greatest of crimes	G MACKEN 5, 225
crimson: Your cheeks are like the crimson	F SEMP 2, 298
Crìosdaidh: Boireannach dona Crìosdaidh	IC SMITH 18, 308
crippled: call it war when people are being physically and mentally crippled	MITCHI 2, 251
crith: Dh'fhairich mi crith 's cha chrith fuachd e	TRAD 23, 335
critic: one good critic is precisely what we do not have	E BOYD 1, 55
criticism: Criticism in Scotland, of books	CRUICK 9, 104
Criticism is good for a movement	G MACLEO 3, 232
critics: critics all are ready made	BYRON 7, 76
crodh: Creideam an crodh is an caoraich	J MATHES 1, 246
croich: Croich is binn air aird gach cnocain	CLARK 1, 95
crois: Thàinig oirnn a dh'Albainn crois	AILEAN 1, 23
cromak: As step I wi' my cromak to the Isles	MACLEOI 3, 234
Cromdale: Tae view the Haughs o' Cromdale	TRAD 42, 337
crook: laddie that wears the crook and plaid	PAGAN 3, 273
crooked: Straight minds grown crooked	E MUIR 16, 259
crookit: ewie wi' the crookit horn	SKINN 1, 302
croppis: The birdis sang upon the tender croppis	DUNBAR 7, 119
crops: crops of love and hate	E MUIR 18, 259
foreign wings among the gradual crops	IC SMITH 6, 307
cross: Cross be raised again at the centre of the market-place	G MACLEO 6, 233
May God bless thy cross / Before thou go over the sea	CARMIN 1, 88

daonndachd: Cumaibh fèill na daonndachd — WHYTE 3, 349
dark: nothing as dark as the darkness down a pit — STEIN 4, 317
  We look into the dark and see the faces — KENNAW 3, 185
darkness: learn what darkness is — STEIN 4, 317
  Men die in darkness at thy side — BONAR 3, 53
  Out of the darkness of the womb — SOUTAR 12, 314
  The darkness deepens; Lord, with me abide — LYTE 1, 202
darling: Charlie he's my darling — HOGG 6, 163
daughter: George's daughter / would not allow my pocket
  to be empty — MACANT 3, 203
daughters: their daughters and their sons are a wood — MACGIL 25, 219
dauntless: so dauntless in war — SCOTT 13, 290
Davie: My ain dear dainty Davie — TRAD 32, 336
day: Scho draif the day unto the nicht — ANON 15, 27
  Scotland's decisive day, our D-Day — WRIGHT 3, 354
  the blackest day of my life — LAW 1, 193
  The bright day of my death — CARMIN 7, 88
  you can do without the day if you've a lamp — GIBBON 5, 143
dayis: In to thir dirk and drublie dayis — DUNBAR 14, 119
days: as we grow older, the days seem shorter — J BUCHAN 14, 64
  early days of a better nation — GRAY 6, 150
  Some days were running legs — IC SMITH 1, 306
  the Ancient of Days — WC SMITH 1, 310
dazzle: dazzle us with their fastidious pomp — BURNS 61, 70
D-Day: Scotland's decisive day, our D-Day — WRIGHT 3, 354
Dé: Guth an Dé mhóir — CARMIN 5, 88
de-Tibetanization: de-Tibetanization of the Highlands and
  Islands — MACDIA 45, 212
dead: A silent conquering army, / The island dead — GM BROWN 11, 61
  better to be a fool than to be dead — STEVEN 26, 320
  Dark Cuthullin shall be great or dead — Ja MACPHE 1, 238
  dead man is wise, but he is silent — SMITH 7, 305
  Dead matter cannot become living — KELVIN 6, 184
  Down among the dead men let us lie — TRAD 33, 336
  Fifteen men on a dead man's chest — STEVEN 39, 321
  her coat so dead — G GUNN 1, 152
  hold high converse with the mighty dead — Ja THOMS(1) 6, 331
  I'd have been dead by dinner time — EVARI 1, 124
  I happen at this moment to be dead — J BUCHAN 1, 63
  I saw a dead man win a fight — BALLAD 4, 39
  It is easy to be dead — SORLEY 3, 313
  long dark river of the dead — SMITH 3, 305
  Look well upon a dead man's innocence — SOUTAR 13, 314
  millions of the mouthless dead — SORLEY 3, 313
  No dead man is a stranger — SOUTAR 13, 314
  sense of identity with the dead — STEVEN 95, 324
  silent wheels that raised the dead — CORRIE 5, 102
  Sitting dead in 'Death Valley' — MACGIL 23, 218
  the advantage / of not being dead yet — MACCAI 13, 205
dead-born: It fell dead-born from the press — HUME 33, 168
dead-throws: seeing again any in the dead-throws — MACTAG 2, 239
dealbh: A chionn 's gu bheil an dealbh briste / cuiridh mi
  bhuam e — MACTHO 11, 240
Deans: no more interested in my own characters than I am
  in Jeanie Deans — OLIPH 23, 271
dear: Rowan Tree, thou'lt aye be dear to me — NAIRNE 10, 264
  the dear, dear Highlands — VICTO 1, 344
dearg: dearg, dearg tha fuil a' bhotail — MACTHO 21, 241
dearie: My ain kind dearie, O — BURNS 116, 73
deary: Mine ain kind deary O — R FERG 22, 129
death: contrive to doubt of Death — CARLYL 13, 84
  dallied with the consideration of death — STEVEN 32, 320
  Death is the sade Estranger — W DRUM 8, 117
  Death's shafts fly thick — R BLAIR(2) 3, 51
  Death to Privilege — CARNEG 13, 90
  football is a matter of life and death — SHANKL 3, 299
  house of death hath many doores — TURNER 1, 341
  in order to avoid the loneliness of death — KENNAW 6, 185
  It is but Death who comes at last — SCOTT 12, 290
  no fear of death — KESSON 8, 187
  Poverty! Thou half-sister of Death — BURNS 103, 73
  Scotland / rolling down and up on death's yoyo — HERBER 1, 161
  such is Death: no triumph: no defeat — SORLEY 2, 313
  that sly tortoise, death — W NEILL 2, 266
  The bright day of my death — CARMIN 7, 88
  The City is of Night; perchance of Death — Ja THOMS(2) 2, 332
  There's Death in the cup — BURNS 137, 75
  the road to dusty death — BARRIE 8, 44

till death comes to fetch me — KAMES 17, 182
  Who laid the stones, put death into his wars? — M LINDS 3, 196
  You have tasted of death now — Ge MACDON 5, 214
death-rattle: the energy of the death-rattle — MASSIE 1, 245
Death Valley: Sitting dead in 'Death Valley' — MACGIL 23, 218
deaved: Deaved wi' the harps an' hymns — MURRAY 9, 263
deaving: Knox deaving us a' with his clavers — ELPHIN 1, 123
debatable: lugged backwards / through the Debatable
  Lands of history — MACCAI 15, 206
deboshed: like a deboshed waister — JAMES 11, 175
debt: We can only pay our debt to the past — J BUCHAN 9, 64
decadence: pass, through Decadence, towards Renascence — P GEDD 3, 141
decay: British institutions are in terminal decay — ASCHER 6, 35
  Change and decay in all around I see — LYTE 2, 202
  Decay of language is always the symptom — GM BROWN 6, 61
  feeling's dull decay — BYRON 29, 77
deceits: these deceits are strong almost as life — E MUIR 15, 259
deceive: When first we practise to deceive — SCOTT 17, 291
deceiver: she is a bounder, a liar, a deceiver — DALYE 6, 108
December: mirk December's dowie face — R FERG 4, 128
decency: believe in an ultimate decency of things — STEVEN 82, 323
  damn her decency; can she make good collops? — D RAMS 4, 279
  Decency is in knowing about what's happened — DUNN 13, 122
decision: the brief decision of ignorance — HAILES 1, 155
deck: we fall, face forward, fighting, on the deck — Jo DAVID(2) 3, 108
declaim: Declaim, Sir! why don't you declaim? — MEAD(1) 1, 248
decorum: Let them cant about decorum / Who have
  characters to lose — BURNS 27, 68
dede: Thy dede sall be to Sotheroun full der sauld — BLIND 4, 52
Dee: Ae mile o' Don's worth twa o' Dee — BAIRN 9, 37
  Bloodthirsty Dee — BAIRN 8, 37
  broad abundant dying sprawl of the Dee — GS FRAS 1, 135
deed: if ye're deed, I'll no expect ye — D RAMS 5, 279
deeds: smoor oot the gust fir owre-heroic deeds — W NEILL 3, 266
deep: The deep, unutterable woe — AYTOUN 5, 34
deepest: deepest rivers make least din — ALEX 2, 31
deer: Deer on the high peaks — IC SMITH 8, 307
  let none disturb the deer — BLACKI 7, 50
  long unbroken moor, / sanctuary of deer — MACANT 7, 204
  My heart's in the Highlands a chasing the deer — BURNS 88, 72
  Our sheltered fields are under deer — P MACGRE 1, 221
  sooner be a wild deer — KEATS 1, 183
  the deer of your gentle beloved beauty — MACGIL 14, 218
  the deer that goes dizzily — MACGIL 26, 219
  Time, the deer, is in the wood of Hallaig — MACGIL 24, 219
Deeside: After Royalty came Deeside was ruined — WATT 1, 346
deevil: believe the Deevil has possession of them — Ja WATT 2, 347
defeat: not a victory but man's greatest defeat — WATT 11, 346
defeatism: paralysing ideology of defeatism — MACDIA 46, 212
defeats: triumphs, defeats . . . these are the facts — TROCCHI 1, 340
defence: that is no defence: that makes you worse — JOHNS 4, 178
deficiency: the deficiency must be supplied by Taste — A RAMS(2) 4, 278
degeneration: fatty degeneration of his moral being — STEVEN 13, 319
deid: A livin' man upon a deid man thinks — MACDIA 29, 211
  But the rowan's deid — JACOB 10, 174
  Damn few, and they're aa deid — ANON 53, 30
  Quhat is this lyfe bot ane straucht way to deid — DUNBAR 19, 119
  Sen for the deid remeid is none — DUNBAR 13, 119
  Waement the deid — A SCOTT(2) 3, 289
  ye canny spend a dollar when ye're deid — MACK 1, 224
deil: Deil gaes o'er Jock Wabster — A RAMS(1) 7, 277
  The Deil's Awa wi' th' Exciseman — BURNS 112, 73
  Wha the deil hae we got for a king — CUNN 2, 104
  wha the deil spoke like King Lear — S G SMITH 1, 310
deils: contermashious deils — MILNE 3, 251
deith: dolent deith, allace, did hym devore — D LINDS 4, 195
deity: soaring and grovelling, dirt and deity — BYRON 25, 77
delectation: Wild life does not exist for man's delectation — FRAS D. 5, 136
delicate: delicate minds and delicate constitutions — A GRANT 10, 148
delicious: a delicious companion to a man — KAMES 14, 182
delight: his home is bright with a calm delight — Ja THOMS(2) 1, 332
delighted: just delighted to be joining the club — M JOHNST 3, 179
delights: the delights delicious of storms — J MUIR 1, 259
delusion: from delusion to disillusion — MARR 2, 244
demands: help our children meet the demands which we
  impose — DONAL 2, 113
democracy: Democracy is a word that rumbles
  meaninglessly — RITCH-C 2, 282

liberty, patriotism, democracy and all their dreary clan — MACCAI 31, 207
never have Socialism without complete democracy — T JOHNST 1, 179
What do you do when democracy fails you? — PROCL 7, 276
democratic: a thoroughly democratic dish — MCNEI 2, 237
democratic intellectualism — W ELLIO 2, 123
folk tradition is a shared and democratic — S DOUGL 1, 115
The Democratic Intellect — G DAVIE 1, 109
demon: demon of sordidness — J ROBERTSO(2) 3, 284
demon who seats himself on the feather — SCOTT 76, 294
denationalised: health service which is being covertly denationalised — D BLACK 1, 49
denner: joost when they were sitten doon to their denner — ESKGR 3, 124
deoch: Dh' olainn deoch ge b'oil le m' chàirdibh — CHAIMB 1, 93
fuath liom deoch anbhfann 's í daor — MACDHU 3, 209
deoch-an-doris: Just a wee deoch-an-doris — LAUDER 5, 192
Deòrsa: Cha leigeadh nighean Deòrsa mo phòca falamh — MACANT 3, 203
'S e Deòrsa rinn an eucoir — MACANT 1, 203
dependence: the childish dependence of a Spanish *donna* — WRIGHT 4, 353
deplore: Deplore what is to be deplored — MORGAN 1, 255
deprivation: an age of appalling social deprivation — SMOUT 1, 312
Sleep deprivation is now widely recognised — KING 3, 187
der: In till hir tym scho was als der to me — BLIND 2, 52
derisive: derisive silence of eternity — STEVEN 37, 320
Dervaig: spachial kind of mudge in Dervaig — MUNRO 6, 261
desert: As I came through the desert — Ja THOMS(2) 4, 332
more often than not we are looking at a man-made desert — FRAS D. 3, 136
our young affections run to waste, / Or water but the desert — BYRON 19, 77
Scotland free or a desert — ANON 38, 29
the county was thus *improved* into a desert — MILLER 1, 250
they make a desert and call it peace — GALGAC 1, 138
deserts: he makes deserts as spectacularly as any horde of locusts — FRAS D. 1, 136
desire: floating sexual desire — E MUIR 4, 258
islands in a sea of desire — MORGAN 3, 255
One thing I of the Lord desire — WC SMITH 2, 310
desolating: The desolating and the unfamiliar — E DAVIE 6, 109
desolators: *desolators* of the country — MONBOD 1, 253
despair: bottom of every joke is a piece of despair — B FORS 1, 135
life is a puddle o' perfect despair — HOGG 17, 164
desperation: a metaphor for their desperation — H MCILV 5, 222
despise: luxury, and gaiety, and all the things you despise — OLIPH 13, 270
despot: every landowner is a despot — TYTLER 2, 342
destination: John Knox in destination — SOUTAR 18, 314
destiny: statements about the Stone of Destiny — WOOD 2, 352
ye'd croont yersel King on the Destiny Stane — TRAD 80, 340
destitute: He is, but does not know it, destitute — DUNN 6, 121
destroy: create men or destroy them — W MUIR 2, 260
I want to destroy your system — BOYLE 1, 56
rag-tag army of ordinary people to destroy a bad law — I BELL 1, 47
the way the English destroy a people — MACCAI 34, 207
destroyed: the land of the north is utterly destroyed — AILEAN 1, 23
destruction: prefer the destruction of the whole world to the scratching of my finger — HUME 8, 166
the angel of mechanical destruction — COCKBU 6, 97
desyre: feidis in his hairt a mad desyre — M BOYD 1, 55
detached: a detached and a solitary being — A FERG 4, 127
difficult to be more detached from life than I am — HUME 34, 168
detesting: strangers to the country who, detesting — D STEW 1, 205
detour: Their music knows no detour — MENUH 1, 249
development: development of submissiveness — J ANDERS 3, 25
devil: devil in his flowers — RUTHER 3, 287
Drink and the devil had done for the rest — STEVEN 39, 321
grey-haired, withered, dry devil — RUTHER 3, 287
London is the devil's drawing-room — SMOLL 5, 311
My devil had been long caged — STEVEN 61, 322
Shetland made her jumpers / And the devil made her features — PROCL 4, 276
sweatt morsall for the Devillis mouth — KNOX 11, 188
that is the devil himself — J BAILL 5, 35
The Devil, the World and the Flesh — BURNS 63, 70
The prime devil of the Gael is dead — FIONN 1, 132
to the devil with your philosophy — STEVEN 10, 319
Wi' usquabae, we'll face the devil — BURNS 97, 72
devilish: The most Devilish thing is 8 times 8 — M FLEM 1, 133
devill: I gif him to the Devill of hell — DUNBAR 2, 119
The Devill wold giv us the brawest lyk money — GOWDIE 2, 146
why do we not denie God and adore the Devill — JAMES 13, 175
devolution: difference between devolution and evolution — BAIN 1, 36

Nobody ever celebrated Devolution Day — SALMO 1, 288
thunderous apathy of the devolution vote — J MCGRAT 4, 221
devolved: continue to legislate on subjects which had been devolved — DALYE 1, 107
devore: dolent deith, allace, did hym devore — D LINDS 4, 195
devotees: devotees of ravaging commercialism — J MUIR 10, 260
dew: glittering with ungodly dew — Ja THOMS(1) 7, 331
Like the dew on the gowans at bonnie Woodha' — TRAD 67, 339
Like the dew on the mountain — SCOTT 26, 291
dewdrop: globe as one great dewdrop — J MUIR 11, 260
dextrous: dextrous Similitude of Acting — CARLYL 44, 87
dhannsadh: tha iad gu dìcheallach 'ga dhannsadh gus an là' an diugh — MACKINN 3, 227
dhannsas: Is math a dhannsas tu — TRAD GA 1, 332
dhaolag: A dhaolag, a dhaolag, / An cuimhne leat an la 'n dé — CARMIN 3, 88
Dhia: cha mhór a ghaoil ghil nach dug 's mo Dhia bhuam — ANON 20, 28
dhìt: 'm beul onorach a dhìt thu — HAY 5, 158
dhiùghaidh: Nach b'e sin an dà dhiùghaidh gun aon roghainn — C MACDON 1, 213
Dhòmhaill: Dhòmhaill mhóir bhochd! / Tha 'm pathadh ort! — CARMIN 9, 88
dhùthaich-sa: 'S ma ruigeas mo dhùthaich-sa slànachd — MACTHO 2, 239
Dia: canadh Dia gur h-e an toibheum — MACGIL 20, 218
Gum beannaicheadh Dia bùrn Loch Hàstain — MACCOD 1, 208
Gum beannaicheadh Dia do chrois / Mun téid thu thar lear — CARMIN 1, 88
gun tug Dia, bràthair athar, còir dha anns an fhearann — MACTHO 15, 241
diabhal: Theast aon diabhal na nGaoidheal — FIONN 1, 132
diagram: Form is a diagram of forces — THOMPS 2, 331
dialect: dialect poetry is a regression to childhood — E MUIR 9, 258
humour has so much to do with dialect — S BAXT 5, 46
one nation's language is another's corrupt dialect — B KAY 3, 182
she will inevitably shed her uncouth dialect — CROSL 5, 103
dialects: barbarous dialects of Yorkshire or Devon — JEFFR 2, 177
diamond: bonnie ship the Diamond / Goes a-fishing for the whale — TRAD 17, 334
diamonds: diamonds dug from the mine of ecstasy — MACTHO 4, 240
dibble: Dibble them doon, the laird, the loon — MURRAY 5, 262
dìcheallach: tha iad gu dìcheallach 'ga dhannsadh gus an là' an diugh — MACKINN 3, 227
dicks: Peaceful dicks — S MACDON 3, 215
die: a more awful thing to be born than to die — GALT 10, 139
Easy live and quiet die — SCOTT 71, 294
I die a Christian — CHARL I 3, 94
I have taken a firm resolution to conquer or to die — C STEW 1, 325
Learning to live and practising to die — MACCAI 7, 205
Men die in darkness at thy side — BONAR 3, 53
no man fit to live that is not fit to die — BALMER 1, 42
Sure 'tis a serious thing to die — R BLAIR(2) 2, 51
That any Scot would *choose* to die and be buried in England — A BUCHAN 4, 63
'tis not so difficult to die — BYRON 34, 78
To die will be an awfully big adventure — BARRIE 6, 44
to learn to die / Were no concern of ours — R BLAIR(2) 4, 51
whether to die in the last ditch — MASSIE 3, 245
difference: difference between us and the English — BARRIE 12, 44
difficult: 'tis not so difficult to die — BYRON 34, 78
digestion: if Mr Carlyle's digestion had been better — CARLYL 17, 84
dignity: all dignity is painful — CARLYL 48, 87
When I'm a queen, I shall hold it to be my dignity to go slow — COCKBU 8, 97
dilettanteism: dilettanteism and drains — MACKINT 4, 228
diligently: they dance it diligently to the present day — MACKINN 3, 227
dìlseachd: mheud 's a thaisbean sibh dur dìlseachd — ALASD 2, 23
diminution: a trial will show no diminution of people — SELLAR 3, 298
a diminution of Glasgow — W MCILV 11, 223
din: deepest rivers make least din — ALEX 2, 24
The fisher wives is makin' din — TRAD 38, 336
dined: dined off the bagpipe of a pifferara — WILKIE 3, 349
dinner: Dinner is the English meal, breakfast the Scotch — COCKBU 1, 97
I'd have been dead by dinner time — EVARI 1, 124
dinners: Dinners are commonly dull things — FERRI 1, 130
dìochuimhn': a' fiachainn ri saoghal a chur an dìochuimhn' — IC SMITH 4, 306
directors: The ideal board of directors — DOCH 1, 111
dirk: In to thir dirk and drublie dayis — DUNBAR 14, 119
dirt: recording dirt, vulgarity and utter ugliness — PATON 1, 273
soaring and grovelling, dirt and deity — BYRON 25, 77
dirty: always the factor who does the dirty business — BLACKI 6, 50
dirty old town — E MACCOL 1, 208
though I do not toil nor engage in dirty labour — MACANT 3, 203
disadvantage: disadvantage of perpetually living in a crowd — HAMIL 1, 155
disappointment: disappointment from humble appearance — MAXWEL 4, 247

Sight-seeing is the art of disappointment STEVEN **45**, 321
disapproved: annoyed that my turn for reading was so much
disapproved SOMERV **4**, 312
disaster: hidden trap-doors of disaster BURNS **81**, 71
disbelief: disbelief in great men CARLYL **38**, 86
Glasgow humour is disbelief under anaesthetic W MCILV **12**, 223
male disbelief in our capacity cannot be argued away INGLIS **4**, 171
discimus: Vivendo discimus P GEDD **1**, 141
Vivendo discimus P GEDD **1**, 141
disciple: can the disciple of Christ here seek for
enjoyment? COLQUH **4**, 98
discontent: real duty is to analyse discontent MAXTON **2**, 247
discover: discover the termination of the Niger or perish PARK **2**, 273
they will certainly discover me C STEW **6**, 325
discovery: never made a mistake never made a discovery SMILES **4**, 303
disease: football's a lovely incurable disease DOCH **3**, 111
strangest disease I have seen in this country seems really
to be broken-heartedness LIVING **5**, 198
the disease is larger than me BOYLE **4**, 56
the remedy's / inside the disease JACKS **7**, 173
diseases: diseases of the mind do not directly affect MORIS **1**, 256
disenchantments: disenchantments / Settle round me like a
cold fog DUNN **1**, 121
disgrace: A disgrace to the community MACDIA **47**, 212
disgrace for a woman never to lose her virginity CARSW **3**, 91
wages that are an international disgrace COOK **2**, 101
we were a disgrace in that first half LAMBIE **2**, 190
You disgrace your tartan WOOD **1**, 352
disgraced: nation will be disgraced whose women M MCMIL **4**, 234
disguise: merely in the disguise of a mason MILLER **5**, 250
the last ramparts of disguise M STUA **6**, 327
dish: a thoroughly democratic dish MCNEI **2**, 237
dishonour: Rycht grit dishonour upoun him self he takkis DUNBAR **8**, 119
disillusion: from delusion to disillusion MARR **2**, 244
disloyalty: A No vote need not imply any disloyalty HOME **3**, 164
futile grumbling and petty acts of disloyalty CROSL **9**, 103
dismal: Professors of the Dismal Science CARLYL **54**, 87
When dismal grew his countenance BALLAD **15**, 40
dismally: dismally drunk upon whisky NEAVES **2**, 265
Disney: someone happy who hasn't been drawn by Disney MUNRO **4**, 262
disputes: Marriage is one long conversation, chequered by
disputes STEVEN **75**, 323
disreputable: I said to him that I was not disreputable TRAD **24**, 335
dissension: They were two who never caused dissension ROB DON **2**, 282
dissim'lar: Dissim'lar men, but sim'lar minds TENNAN **5**, 330
dissipation: dissipation of mechanical energy KELVIN **1**, 183
the mist of his dissipation H MACKEN **7**, 226
distance: distance lends enchantment to the view T CAMPB **2**, 81
distant: Far distant, far distant, lies Scotia, the brave! TRAD **44**, 337
distinction: distinction of 'Scottish education' F MACCOL **2**, 209
disturb: didna like to disturb gude company D RAMS **2**, 278
ditch: whether to die in the last ditch MASSIE **3**, 245
Diùrach: Tha sneachd air na beannaibh Diùrach TRAD **72**, 339
divided: the world's ill divided BROOKS **5**, 59
divil: he is a greeting divil R BLAIR(1) **2**, 51
divines: three centuries and more of diabologiac Divines P GEDD **6**, 141
divinity: controversial divinity BURNS **59**, 70
hum of metaphysical divinity STEVEN **70**, 322
division: division of labour SMITH **4**, 304
divisione: God is not in the bitter divisione W DRUM **10**, 117
dizzily: the deer that goes dizzily MACGIL **26**, 219
dizziness: Love's like a dizziness HOGG **18**, 164
do: 'It will do!' has blighted many a character SMILES **8**, 303
This will never do JEFFR **4**, 177
dobrón: fuath liom dobrón i dtigh n-óil MACDHU **3**, 209
dochter: The minister's dochter she wis there TRAD **6**, 333
doctor: Any really good doctor Jo BELL **2**, 47
if the doctor does not give you a year STEVEN **33**, 320
worst of being a doctor is that one's mistakes matter INGLIS **9**, 172
doctors: doctors and kirkyards would go out of fashion HOGG **13**, 163
Doctors, like mini-cab drivers, are the other idiots KENNAW **9**, 185
documentary: Documentary can achieve an intimacy of
knowledge GRIERS **4**, 151
dodo: a dodo / Wha'd drappit doon deid BLACKH **3**, 50
doer: I am a doer and I want to do things Jo SMITH **2**, 309
dog: curious incident of the dog in the night DOYLE **11**, 116
I was a Dog much in Respect W HAMIL(1) **1**, 157
rather have a man dog M FLEM **4**, 134

shilpit dog fucks grimly MORGAN **9**, 255
wherever I went was my poor dog Tray T CAMPB **1**, 81
dog food: doesn't mean the actors have to eat dog food MULGR **1**, 261
dogs: she loved little dogs / And parrots ANGUS **1**, 25
the mild mad dogs of my poetry MACGIL **14**, 218
Twa dogs, that were na thrang at hame BURNS **39**, 69
doleful: a doleful example of Scotch filth WORDS **3**, 353
dollar: ye canny spend a dollar when ye're deid MACK **1**, 224
Dolphinsludge: Dolphinsludge, Queen of the Highland
Fleshpots T MORT **1**, 258
domesticate: domesticate the Recording Angel STEVEN **22**, 320
domesticities: art more sacred than a million domesticities CARSW **4**, 91
Domhnach: Ní math siubhal san Domhnach MACDHU **1**, 209
Dòmhnall: eadar Dòmhnall Gorm 's a léine ANON **21**, 28
dominie: *Dominie, Dominie, / There was nane like John
Maclean* MCGINN **4**, 219
dominions: dominions, on which the sun never sets NORTH **3**, 268
Don: Ae mile o' Don's worth twa o' Dee BAIRN **9**, 37
dona: Boireannach dona Críosdaidh IC SMITH **18**, 308
Donald: between Donald Gorm and his shirt ANON **21**, 28
It is no joy without Clan Donald GIOL Co **3**, 144
Poor big Donald! / You are thirsty! CARMIN **9**, 88
will you not take pity on the last chief of Clan Donald? C NICGU **3**, 267
donna: the childish dependence of a Spanish *donna* WRIGHT **4**, 353
doocoots: our spires and doocoots JAMIE **4**, 176
dool: To flee the Dool upo' the Stool ANON **27**, 28
doolie: Ane doolie sessoun to ane cairfull dyte HENRYS **10**, 161
doom: sad day of doom and burnin' TRAD **53**, 338
doomsday: Doomsday Scenario RADIC **1**, 277
till doomsday in the afternoon B STEW **2**, 325
door: door slammed in the deepest hollows of the sea J CAMER **4**, 80
Get up and bar the door BALLAD **20**, 40
I told them they could slip it under the door J JEFF **1**, 177
Lock the door, Lariston HOGG **3**, 163
doores: house of death hath many doores TURNER **1**, 341
doors: doors into fuller life SOUTAR **16**, 314
put them out of doors, or to bed CARLYL **2**, 82
some wha have their doors and windows opened wider MORRIS **3**, 256
doots: grave doots about the minister FORD **3**, 134
dope: This is not a time for dope REITH **1**, 281
Doric: I am a Doric stereotype BLACKH **5**, 50
If the Doric is to come back alive SOUTAR **3**, 313
Doricisms: coyness larded with apostrophes and Doricisms J CAMER **2**, 80
doubt: contrive to doubt of Death CARLYL **13**, 84
I think faith and doubt are co-active HOLLOW **1**, 164
model of order, even if set in a space filled with doubt IH FINL **3**, 131
To be gay, as to be Scottish, is to doubt WOOLAS **1**, 352
Douglas: The Black Douglas shall not get ye BAIRN **10**, 37
The Douglas in his hall SCOTT **16**, 291
Doune: Look owre the castle Doune BALLAD **7**, 39
dour: dour and practical and canny BARRIE **19**, 44
down-stairs: God the Father fell down-stairs STEVEN **100**, 324
doze: snugly doze and rot awa MACTAG **3**, 239
dozing: lownging and dozing, which I call thinking HUME **30**, 168
drag: she'll drag well if she drags me back MACTAG **2**, 239
drains: dilettanteism and drains MACKINT **4**, 228
There are such things as drains I MACLAR **2**, 229
dramatic: life is constantly dramatic KELMAN **5**, 183
drams: Drams canna droun them out A SCOTT(2) **1**, 289
nose is just a sicht / Wi' drinkin' drams OUTRAM **3**, 271
draper: land of the millionaire draper T BUCHAN **1**, 65
drawing-room: London is the devil's drawing-room SMOLL **5**, 311
dread: like troop trains without the dread H MCILV **10**, 223
dream: bad dream of respectability MITCHI **15**, 252
Dreamed a dream by the old canal E MACCOL **1**, 208
hunger that makes mortals strive, / And dream CORRIE **6**, 102
I even dream of ideal communities DUNN **2**, 121
I have dreamed a dreary dream BALLAD **4**, 39
Yestreen I dream'd a dolefu' dream BALLAD **18**, 40
dreamed: nothing dreamed of but the dress making E GRANT(2) **5**, 149
dreamers: dreamers of another existence . . . and spectators
of this BYRON **24**, 77
dreams: Hamish stokes young men's dreams MARRA **5**, 244
Some dreams are sleepin SG SMITH **5**, 310
support us in our dreams and in our nightmares AL KENNE **3**, 185
Sweet Dreams (Are Made of This) LENNOX **2**, 193
their dreams are crammed / with sides of beef ROSE **1**, 285
Weaving words and weaving dreams MACTHO **1**, 239

A Scotland genuinely at ease with itself	MARR 3, 244
easgann: Mar easgann an lodan làthchadh	TRAD 25, 335
east: You took the east from me and you took the west from me	ANON 20, 28
easy: be easy an' free when you're drinkin' wi' me	TRAD 37, 336
Easy live and quiet die	SCOTT 71, 294
easy to be proud and poor	W MUIR 7, 260
It is easy to be dead	SORLEY 3, 313
eat: eat up ae side, and down the tither	POLKEM 3, 276
let them eat the hope deferred	MORGAN 10, 255
like to taste my friends but not to eat them	N DOUGL 3, 115
Some hae meat and canna eat	ANON 29, 29
they would eat me in penny pies	D MACLEO 2, 232
We eat to live but live to give	RANSF 1, 279
eathar: an t-eathar mór ud air an fhàire, / An Cuilithionn	MACGIL 27, 219
ebb: ebb and flow of streets	SMITH 1, 305
eccentricities: keep alive a good measure of our eccentricities	CARST 2, 91
ecchoes: Onlie the Ecchoes, which hee made relent	W DRUM 5, 117
echo: Echo is dejected	CLARS 1, 95
economic: economic AIDS	FINNIS 5, 132
When I have to read economic documents	HOME 1, 164
economist: economist may be grossly ignorant of administration	CAIRNC 2, 79
Ecossais: Fier comme un Ecossais	ANON 3, 26
Ecosse: nothing much in the rue d'Ecosse	WHITE 4, 348
ecstasies: This journey over endless ecstasies	BOLD 5, 53
ecstasy: diamonds dug from the mine of ecstasy	MACTHO 4, 240
Eden: green springing corner of young Eden	E MUIR 17, 259
One foot in Eden still	E MUIR 18, 259
Edens: create Edens in the heart of mean streets	M MCMIL 6, 235
education: Education! pooh!	FERRI 6, 130
Edina: Edina! Scotia's darling seat	BURNS 21, 68
They kindly shower Edina's roses	R FERG 10, 128
Edinburgh: difference between a Glasgow man and an Edinburgh man	E MUIR 6, 258
Edinburgh far surpassed all expectation	WORDS 6, 353
Edinburgh is a hot-bed of genius	SMOLL 15, 311
favourite food of the Edinburgh reviewers	LUCAS 1, 201
in Edinburgh a man is guilty until he is found innocent	H MORT 7, 257
no one really alive in Edinburgh yet	MACDIA 54, 213
no stars so lovely as Edinburgh street-lamps	STEVEN 43, 321
thank God for the Edinburgh Festival	DEMARC 1, 111
the empty house in Edinburgh / Without authority or voice	RUNRIG 2, 286
What is Edinburgh for? To be a city	ASCHER 9, 32
Edinburrie: My bonie Edinburrie, / Auld Skulduggerie	SG SMITH 3, 310
educate: Educate every child as if he were your own	M MCMIL 9, 235
educated: educated at a far better place, Glasgow	FINNIS 1, 132
want to be educated go to bloody university	CONTI 1, 101
education: distinction of 'Scottish education'	F MACCOL 2, 209
education... is a battlefield between liberality and illiberality	J ANDERS 4, 25
education is less of a boon than an outrage	M MCMIL 2, 234
education is a leading out	SPARK 8, 315
Education is not merely by and for the sake of thought	P GEDD 4, 141
Education makes a people easy to lead	BROUGH 4, 60
havin' no education, I had to use my brains	SHANKL 5, 299
literary and scientific education for women	SOMERV 9, 313
My education down about my knees	MACCAI 7, 205
not what I call education, I call it intrusion	SPARK 8, 315
public school education set their minds like treacle	WATT 4, 346
educational: unChristian as the Scottish educational system	R MACKEN 1, 226
Edward: See approach proud Edward's power	BURNS 126, 74
eejit: ye'r an eejit, shanter	FITT 2, 133
eel: Like an eel in a muddy puddle	TRAD 25, 335
een: my blue een wi' sorrow are streamin'	TRAD 53, 338
Effen: stung by a big Effen bee	MCGINN 5, 220
eggs: believe themselves to be poached eggs	HERDM 2, 161
Egypt: Glasgow was your Egypt	MACTHO 23, 242
worse than the ten plagues of Egypt	BURNS 63, 70
eight: Pieces of eight	STEVEN 40, 321
Eildon: riding down by the Eildon Tree	BALLAD 42, 41
eilean: na Sasunnaich air fuadach, / A Eilean uaine 'Cheò	MAIRI 1, 242
Siud an t-eilean ás an t-sealladh	MACAMH 3, 203
eilein: O eilein / a thoinn do fhraoch mu mo theanga	MACTHO 12, 240
Eiphit: 'Se Glaschu an Eiphit a bh' agaibh	MACTHO 3, 240
elastic: as steam was an elastic body	Ja WATT 1, 347
elated: never been elated in my life	SHAND 2, 298
elbow: doesn't know its arse from its political elbow	GALLO 7, 138
elect: Congregation to elect their Minister	DISCIP(1) 1, 111
Lord Jesus cum and saif thy awin Elect	E MELV 1, 248
elegant: An elegant sufficiency	Ja THOMS(1) 3, 331
A scientific hypothesis is elegant	LYELL 2, 201
elegies: elegies on the face of the earth	IC SMITH 22, 308
tune Thy Elegies to Trumpet-sounds	MONTRO 3, 254
element: Joy is my element	RANSF 2, 279
elementary: 'Elementary,' said he	DOYLE 12, 116
Elginbrodde: Here lie I, Martin Elginbrodde	Ge MACDON 3, 214
élitist: He was an élitist; a platform man	BELLAN 2, 48
Elsinore: By thy wild and stormy steep, / Elsinore	T CAMPB 6, 81
elusive: One's prime is elusive	SPARK 6, 315
emancipation: contraception... was itself part of women's emancipation	MITCHI 3, 251
embarrassment: Love/Emotion = embarrassment	GALLO 1, 138
emblem: emblem is a passing stream, not a stagnating pool	A FERG 2, 127
Embro: in Embro to the ploy	GARIOC 1, 140
embroidery: Foreign Embroidery in our Writings	A RAMS(1) 6, 277
emigrant: Scotch emigrant would probably find it peculiarly suited	WRIGHT 3, 353
emotion: Guilt is of course not an emotion	AL KENNE 7, 186
Love/Emotion = embarrassment	GALLO 1, 138
emotional: such a mixture of the practical and the emotional	BARRIE 14, 44
empire: I look upon Scotland as part of the British Empire	J HILL 1, 162
that Empire of which Scotland is no small part	A BALF 6, 38
the House of Terror, the Glasgow Empire	DODD 1, 112
employ: Never employ one of these rioters	CARNEG 9, 90
employers: trouble with employers is that they like ballots as long as you lose them	KNAPP 1, 188
employment: benevolent employment of superior wealth	STOWE 1, 326
tho' fatigu'd wi' close employment	BURNS 42, 69
emptiness: The emptiness. The human lack	BOLD 2, 52
empty: He could start a party in an empty room	DEWAR 1, 111
enchanted: enchanted castle, imposed upon by spectres	T REID 3, 281
end: ane end of ane old song	J OGILVY 1, 269
In my end is my beginning	MARY(2) 7, 245
Man's chief end is to glorify God	SHORTE 1, 300
no vestige of a beginning, no prospect of an end	HUTTON 4, 169
time brings a' things tae an end	TRAD 64, 339
endeavour: Land of my high endeavour	HANLEY 1, 157
endure: to endure to be useless	M OLIPH 1, 269
enemies: consider the House of Commons as your enemies	TYTLER 2, 342
enemies are among us, born without imagination	CUNN G. 11, 106
enemies of Scottish nationalism are not the English	CUNN G. 11, 106
enemy: England was our enemy and the English were poison	SHANKL 7, 299
energy: dissipation of mechanical energy	KELVIN 1, 183
Energy is as real and indestructible as *Matter*	KELVIN 4, 184
the energy of the death-rattle	MASSIE 1, 245
enough: we just do weel eneugh	HAMIL 4, 155
enfeebling: mollifying influence of an enfeebling potion	STATIS 4, 317
engine: a jet engine, a bit of a machine is beautiful	PAOLO 3, 273
Whit wey does the engine say *Toot-toot?*	M SMITH 1, 309
engines: our resistless engines	CARLYL 8, 85
Unsightly brick-lanes smoke, and clanking engines gleam	T CAMPB 9, 82
England: England, their England	MACDONN 1, 215
England! thy beauties are tame and domestic	BYRON 2, 75
England was our enemy and the English were poison	SHANKL 7, 299
God help England if she had no Scots	G SHAW 1, 299
knuckle-end of England	S SMITH 5, 310
language is all I expect to learn in England	BRAXF 3, 57
My feet they travel England	JACOB 6, 174
Scotland is bounded on the south by England	SHEPH 1, 299
That any Scot would *choose* to die and be buried in England	A BUCHAN 4, 63
theatre of the world is wider than the realm of England	MARY(2) 4, 245
English: difference between us and the English	BARRIE 12, 44
enemies of Scottish nationalism are not the English	CUNN G. 11, 106
English are a justice-loving people	GALT 20, 140
English are better animals than the Scots	BOSWEL 3, 54
English are very little indeed inferior to the Scotch	NORTH 2, 268
English towerist with a kilt	MUNRO 7, 262
English words so sharp and clean	GIBBON 3, 142
especially if he went among the English	BARRIE 10, 44
foreign language, which the English dialect is to us	CARLYL 3, 82
Graveyard of English comics	LOGAN 3, 200
Rioting is at least as English	ASCHER 3, 32
Scots is like English in its underwear	W MCILV 4, 223
the English driven out of the green isle of mist	MAIRI 1, 242
The little ones were always compelled to be English	SOMERV 3, 312

ne'er / Was flattery lost on poet's ear	SCOTT 5, 290
flattrie: Thou feinyeit Flattrie, the Feind fart in thy face	D LINDS 14, 196
flatulent: this flatulent balderdash	N DOUGL 4, 115
flech: a' the warks gae round the *flech*	C GRAH 1, 146
fled: they're all fled with thee, / Robin Adair	KEPPEL 1, 186
fleet: Tall men are arraying the fleet	ARTÚR 1, 31
flesche: flatter no flesche upoun the face of the earth	KNOX 12, 189
The flesche is brukle, the Fend is sle	DUNBAR 12, 119
flesh: flesh of my flesh / And bone of my bone	A GRAY 1, 150
Mass shall encounter mass / Of shuddering human flesh	Jo DAVID(2) 5, 108
neither feared nor flattered any flesh	J MORT 1, 257
The Devil, the World and the Flesh	BURNS 63, 70
flesh-Garment: Language is the Flesh-Garment, the Body, of Thought	CARLYL 17, 85
flesh-hook: wield a flesh-hook rather than a sword	J BAILL 2, 35
fleshpots: Dolphinsludge, Queen of the Highland Fleshpots	T MORT 1, 258
flie: Flie whylome love, and it will folou thee	MONTGO 4, 254
fling: fling the hale fukn religious thing oot	MACMIL 3, 234
flit: seems Thou art resolved to flit	WODROW 3, 352
float: float on the surface of science	SMOLL 14, 311
Flodden: Flodden and Culloden are much better worth remembering	CROSL 10, 103
flogged: boy who is flogged into grammar-rules	KAMES 15, 182
flood: Land of the mountain and the flood	SCOTT 8, 290
floodtide: the incomprehensible ocean fills / With floodtide	MACGIL 21, 218
floor: 'Tis on the floor of the big house I was born	CARMIN 10, 89
Florence: a thing being born as it was / born once in Florence	MITCHI 17, 252
floschis: floschis, dubbis, myre and clay	G DOUGL 6, 115
flotsam: poisonous flotsam and jetsam	WELSH 1, 348
flouer: eternity in a rotten flouer	S G SMITH 7, 310
flour: Nocht is your fairnes bot ane faiding flour	HENRYS 12, 161
floure: The fairest or the freschest yonge floure	JAMES I 5, 174
flourish: And flourish on both sides the Tweed	TRAD 18, 334
flow: Flow gently, sweet Afton	BURNS 77, 71
flower: Aberdeen for me is the flower of cities	IC SMITH 29, 309
Art is the flower – Life is the green leaf	MACKINT 8, 229
between a man and his vision of a flower	N GUNN 8, 153
lad that pu'd yon flower	JACOB 3, 173
My faded mouth will never flower again	M STUA 6, 327
O flower of Scotland	R WILLIA 1, 350
sweet Jessie, the flower o' Dunblane	TANNAH 5, 329
flowers: devil in his flowers	RUTHER 3, 287
Did the pipes play 'The Flowers o' the Forest'?	BOGLE 3, 52
flowers wither wherever they are driven	F BALF 7, 39
The Flowers of the Forest	J ELLIO 1, 123
flown: all the birds are flown	CHARL I 1, 94
flow'r: Wee, modest, crimson-tipped flow'r	BURNS 38, 69
flowre: Flowre of the Seasons, Season of the Flowrs	W DRUM 4, 117
flute: And aye the gauger played the flute	STEVEN 64, 322
played the flute and had something to do with fish	I ANDERS 1, 25
flutter: all my projects flutter in the air	TYTLER 1, 341
fly: fly into the arms of a tiger	FERRI 5, 130
Have I three kingdoms and thou must needs fly	JAMES 26, 176
flying: managed to set up a flying faceache	ARNOLD 4, 31
foe: honourable thing to deal stoutly wi' the foe	GALT 19, 140
fog: disenchantments / Settle round me like a cold fog	DUNN 1, 121
folk: Behave yoursel' before folk	RODGER 2, 285
comic tartan-wearing country folk	A CAMPB 1, 80
folk tradition is a shared and democratic	S DOUGL 1, 115
Folk wha say their say and speir their speir	MILNE 2, 251
folk who had made history	SHEPH 2, 299
If folk think I'm mean	LAUDER 12, 193
In our cities the folk tradition	HENDER 4, 159
not possible to take politics out of folk music	GAUGH 1, 141
oh! but I'm longing for my ain folk	TRAD 56, 338
stories aboot folk gettin' their heids cut aff	J J BELL 2, 47
the folk like the folk o' the west	ROBERTO 7, 283
folk-tale: a kind of folk-tale...rather like Aladdin	C MACKEN 8, 225
folks: I was leaving home and my folks were growing old	STEVEN 89, 324
some folks are wise	SMOLL 3, 311
where few kings and great folks come	RUTHER 7, 287
folk-song: Folk-song has no use for the conventional	HENDER 7, 160
follie: over wise and Philosophicke a follie	JAMES 12, 175
folow: Folow fortoun, and all hir fers owtrage	BLIND 1, 51
fond: because I was so fond of him	BATE 1, 45
fondness: a fondness for young men in uniform	F URQU 3, 343
food: favourite food of the Edinburgh reviewers	LUCAS 1, 201
fool: a fool to ask grace at a graceless face	BALLAD 25, 40

Any fool can destroy trees	J MUIR 8, 260
any fool can write a book	A MACLEA 1, 230
better to be a fool than to be dead	STEVEN 26, 320
brains enough to make a fool of himself	STEVEN 27, 320
Do not marry a fool	GREGOR 2, 151
Scotchman stands confessed a sentimental fool	CUNN G. 7, 106
wisest fool in Christendom	SULLY 1, 327
fooling: business is more entertaining than fooling among boats?	STEVEN 2, 318
foolishe: foolishe, madde, and phrenetike shal governe	KNOX 2, 188
fools: Fools are my theme	BYRON 5, 76
If honest Nature made you fools	BURNS 8, 67
foot: heed the foot with silence shod	M STUA 1, 326
my foot is on my native heath	SCOTT 62, 293
One foot in Eden still	E MUIR 18, 259
They placed their foot on the rule of truth	CLARK 1, 95
football: claim Scotland as the cradle of football	A MCGRE 1, 221
foot-ball, between the married and unmarried women	STATIS 5, 317
football is a matter of life and death	SHANKL 3, 299
Football management these days is like a nuclear war	DOCH 5, 112
football's a lovely incurable disease	DOCH 3, 111
Jimmy Hill is to football what King Herod was	DOCH 4, 111
kids would happily play football in the streets	ROXBUR 3, 286
kind of commitment Scots invest in football	W MCILV 7, 223
know anything about football, you'll never talk alone	R FORS 1, 135
know nothing at all about the game of football	STEIN 3, 317
life is itself but a game at football	SCOTT 44, 292
Now to me that's Scottish football	ROXBUR 1, 286
six o'clock bulletin is a tiresome postponement of the football results	C MACKEN 5, 225
win it playing good football	STEIN 1, 317
footprints: nothing but / cigarette packets and footprints	MACCAI 20, 206
forbidden: golf should be forbidden to all males under 25	STIRL 1, 326
force: two apparently irreconcilables – force and goodwill	W ELLIO 5, 123
forces: Form is a diagram of forces	THOMPS 2, 331
foreign: Foreign Embroidery in our Writings	A RAMS(1) 6, 277
Foreign fashions, lad, allure you	MURRAY 6, 262
foreign language, which the English dialect is to us	CARLYL 3, 82
foreign wings among the gradual crops	IC SMITH 6, 307
going foreign and coming home again	I HAMIL 2, 156
Her children grow up with foreign accents	LOCHH 1, 198
To see foreign parts	SCOTT 45, 292
forest: Did the pipes play 'The Flowers o' the Forest'?	BOGLE 3, 52
in my hand a forest lies asleep	M STUA 5, 327
It's a peatbog, it's a daurk forest	LOCHH 17, 200
forests: forests of America, however slighted by man	J MUIR 7, 259
green days in forests and blue days at sea	STEVEN 85, 323
fore-thought: abundance of laziness, and no fore-thought	A RAMS(1) 3, 277
forever: I'm coming near to Forever and Ever	ANGUS 4, 26
forget: Don't You (Forget About Me)	SIMPLE 3, 301
let my right hand forget its cunning	CARSW 1, 91
forgetfulness: trying to put a world into forgetfulness	IC SMITH 4, 306
forgot: Forgot / Mysel	A SCOTT(2) 9, 289
forgot a great deal more than most other men know	MONBOD 5, 253
forjesket: forjesket and forniaw'd as a forfoughten cock	BURNS 44, 69
form: Art is only art when it adds mind to form	WILKIE 6, 350
Form is a diagram of forces	THOMPS 2, 331
forms: they'll all be at their posts, filling in forms	R MACKEN 2, 226
fornicates: fornicates gravely but without conviction	CUNN G. 7, 106
forrit: haud forrit MacDiarmid	V GRIEV 2, 152
Forth: gateway of Scotland is the Firth of Forth	W ELLIO 1, 123
the siller tides rin up the Firth o' Forth	JACOB 6, 174
Forth Bridge: see the Forth Bridge is rather like meeting a popular actress	H MORT 1, 257
fortoun: Folow fortoun, and all hir fers owtrage	BLIND 1, 51
fortresses: fortresses of excessive privilege	OBAN 1, 269
fortune: Guid fortune's blate	JACOB 9, 174
I've seen the smiling of Fortune beguiling	A COCKBU 1, 96
saddest sight that Fortune's inequality	CARLYL 34, 86
forty: Fat, fair, and forty	SCOTT 83, 294
forward: Bring forward the tartan!	C CAMPB 3, 81
fou: Am I fou yet?	MACDOU 1, 215
every Piper was fou	R BUCHANA 2, 65
getting fou and unco happy	BURNS 90, 72
I amna fou' sae muckle as tired	MACDIA 12, 210
ill speaking between a fou man and a fasting	SCOTT 84, 294
I was na fou, but just had plenty	BURNS 6, 67
na talk to be had betuix ane fou man and ane fastand	R LINDS 2, 196

On blythe Yule-Night when we were fou	BURNS 113, 73
some are fou o' brandy	BURNS 13, 67
some are fou o' love divine	BURNS 13, 67
They had been fou for weeks thegither	BURNS 93, 72
We are na fou, we're nae that fou	BURNS 79, 71
foul: Foul as their soil	BYRON 10, 76
foul rain that rains on poverty	GS FRAS 2, 135
foundation: a storm coming that shall try your foundation	RENWIC 1, 281
foundering: A foundering land under a severe sky	MILLER 9, 250
foundries: Clydeside, / Webbed in its foundries and loud blood	WS GRAH 3, 147
fountain: I will twine thee a bow'r / By the clear siller fountain	TANNAH 2, 329
fountains: fountains of life	J MUIR 6, 259
mountains are fountains of men	J MUIR 3, 259
fourth: a *Fourth Estate* more important far	CARLYL 43, 87
fowlys: al small fowlys syngis on the spray	G DOUGL 9, 115
fox: The Paip is the fox, Rome is the rox	GUDE 9, 152
Foyers: young Jamie Foyers in battle was slain	TRAD 44, 337
frailty: They shall know we are old not by the frailty of the body	RUSHF 3, 287
framed: came to the conclusion that Eve had been framed	H KENNE 1, 186
France: Cam ye ower frae France?	TRAD 21, 335
The sun rises bright in France	CUNN 6, 105
Francie: Francie and Josie were ethnic	FULTON 1, 137
fre: Till we have maid our cuntre fre	BARBOU 3, 42
fredom: In thee was wyt, fredom, and hardines	BLIND 4, 52
fredome: A! fredome is a noble thing!	BARBOU 2, 42
They lyve in fredome everich in his kynd	JAMES I 3, 174
free: be easy an' free when you're drinkin' wi' me	TRAD 37, 336
Free by '93	SCOTTI 2, 297
free play of the mind	IC SMITH 21, 308
I see a Free and Independent Kingdom delivering up	BELHAV 1, 46
lesbians and gays must be free	WOOLAS 2, 352
Momentous things may happen in a man's free time	A FLEM 1, 133
my soul has birdwings to fly free	E MUIR 14, 259
privatisation would set the people free	T BLAIR 1, 51
Scotland free or a desert	ANON 38, 29
The Free kirk, the wee kirk	ANON 44, 30
The glaid gangs free, my bonnie lad	MCDONA 1, 213
Free Church: Who cares about the Free Church	CHALM 6, 94
freedom: an alien / freedom I don't understand	MACAMH 1, 203
choice between freedom and security	MACMUR 6, 236
fight in the end between FREEDOM and GOD	GIBBON 9, 143
freedom alone that we fight and contend for	DECLAR 1, 110
Freedom an' whisky gang thegither	BURNS 24, 68
Freedom begins with breakfast	RITCH-C 1, 282
Freedom depends upon Reality	MACMUR 2, 235
Freedom or sand	FRATER 1, 136
Freedom will not be complete until	WOOD 5, 352
freed slave dies of hunger in the ditch of freedom	RITCH-C 1, 282
Here's freedom to him that wad read	BURNS 114, 73
I am all for freedom of action	A NEILL 2, 265
O come all ye at hame wi freedom	HENDER 6, 159
old freedom of the Scots	R BRUCE 2, 62
safety of our Homes and the Freedom of mankind	HAIG 3, 155
Ultimately, the *need* is for freedom	BOYLE 3, 56
freedoms: four freedoms or four sandwiches	BOYD OR 1, 55
freemasonry: middle-class freemasonry	WELSH 4, 348
free-thinker: better to be a free-thinker than a slavish thinker	BUCKLE 5, 66
free-thinkers: Do not be afraid of being free-thinkers	KELVIN 14, 184
freiris: I heir freiris say that reiding dois na gude	D LINDS 16, 196
French: French Revolution / Scorned circumlocution	1H FINL 8, 131
petticoat-tails or a corruption of the French	DODS 3, 112
Show me any of your French cooks	MONBOD 4, 253
frenzy: Fashion is an epidemical frenzy	A GRANT 8, 148
freynd: To God be humill, and to thy freynd be kynd	DUNBAR 15, 119
friend: book is a friend whose face	A LANG 4, 191
no man is useless while he has a friend	STEVEN 98, 324
Nothing endears so much a friend	HUME 13, 166
The people have lost a friend	DEWAR 2, 111
friends: friends / Drop off, like leaves in autumn	R BLAIR(2) 4, 51
Friends and lovers are the most important	J HAYN 1, 159
friends leave us they take away our shores	1H FINL 11, 132
like to taste my friends but not to eat them	N DOUGL 3, 115
little foresaw what I meet with from my friends	C STEW 5, 325
We have friends all over the world	CONNER 3, 100
friendship: all meaningful action for the sake of friendship	MACMUR 7, 236

Married female friendship – / An art form	GUTTE 1, 154
peace, friendship, and needlework	A GRANT 5, 148
precise moment when friendship is formed	BOSWEL 8, 54
sort of friendship recognised by the police	STEVEN 16, 319
friendships: Be very cautious of your friendships	COLQUH 3, 98
frigid: frigid as their snows	BYRON 10, 76
frivolous: a frivolous old age	CARSW 19, 92
frivolous work of polished idleness	MACKINT 5, 229
frogs: I love frogs that sit / like Buddha	MACCAI 12, 205
never saw more frogs / than once at the back of Ben Dorain	MACCAI 18, 206
frontier: one king and one bloody frontier have gone	JACKS 4, 173
frost: rich new Comers / Hae changed to frost their ance warm summers	MACNEI 1, 237
frosty: The frosty regioun ryngis of the yer	G DOUGL 5, 114
frotting: rubbing and frotting their bacon	T URQU 5, 343
frown: frown on our neighbour's pleasures	STEVEN 80, 323
fruit: like fruit on a branch in a raging storm	BOTHCH 4, 55
the fair fruit of knowledge	WRIGHT 7, 354
frying: the 'Frying Scotsman' All Night Chipperama	J MCGRAT 3, 220
fual: Na connuiph co fada ar fual	ANON 19, 27
fuck: 'fuck' can be used in about 17 different ways	KELMAN 8, 183
fucks: shilpit dog fucks grimly	MORGAN 9, 255
Fuehrer: the right and the joy / that he got from his Fuehrer	MACGIL 23, 218
fuil: bidh ghealach mar gun dòirt oirr' fuil	BOTHCH 4, 55
dearg, dearg tha fuil a' bhotail	MACTHO 21, 241
deirge a ghruadh ioná fuil laoigh	DEAN 3, 110
fule: Grit fule is he that puttis in dangeir	HENRYS 8, 161
fules: fules and tawpies	FERRI 15, 130
fulis: The Schule-maister of fulis	MONTGO 5, 254
fulyie: deid men's banes an aa kin o filth an fulyie	NEW TES 2, 266
fumes: brown air fumes at the shop windows	MACCAI 6, 205
funeral: nothing beats a good-going funeral	MITCHI 6, 251
funicular: if a funicular railway disfigures it	SHEPH 8, 299
funny: as soon tell a funny story in a churchyard as in a bar-room	LEACO 2, 193
Funny peculiar or funny ha-ha?	1 HAY 1, 159
not funny after the tenth time	S BAXT 3, 45
furnace: Whit wey is the furnace no pit oot	M SMITH 1, 309
furniture: every last stick of furniture	GM BROWN 13, 61
fury: Manhede but prudence is ane fury blind	BELLEN 1, 48
fush: a fush that's chust sublime	MUNRO 2, 261
futball: futball and golf be utterly cryit downe	JAMES II 1, 174
fute-ball: Thir are the bewteis of the fute-ball	ANON 9, 27
future: Don't Butcher Scotland's Future	SILLA 1, 301
future is bound up with the fortunes of science	FRAZER 2, 137
The future is artists who want to communicate	SPALD 2, 314
futurity: let futurity shift for itself	SMOLL 7, 311
Fyfe: scho waistit all the wodis in Fyfe	R LINDS 3, 196
Fyvie: the bonnie lass o' Fyvie-o	TRAD 16, 334
gaberlunzie: aff wi' the gaberlunzie man	TRAD 39, 336
gable: you're like the gable end of a pound note	STEIN 5, 318
gable-ends: yon gable-ends o' time	SPENCE 2, 316
Gadie: whaur the Gadie rins	TRAD 5, 333
Gael: no real Gael, in his heart, believes in the Mod	N GUNN 6, 153
our new Sheriff be no 'Gael' nor 'Mac'	SELLAR 1, 297
the Gael's exultant cry / coming from the chest of the Lowlands	MACTHO 19, 241
Gaelic: gaelic is alive	MACNEA 2, 236
Gaelic people would be extirpated root and branch	D MACLEO 3, 232
Poverty hath the Gaelic and Greek	TAYLOR 1, 329
Gaels: my beloved hardy Gaels	ALASD 2, 23
gae-ups: twa gae-ups for ae gae-down	ANON 36, 29
Gàidheal: Gàidheal calma le a chànan	IC SMITH 11, 307
Gàidhlig: tha gàidhlig beò	MACNEA 2, 236
gaiety: luxury, and gaiety, and all the things you despise	OLIPH 13, 270
gaily: Step we gaily, on we go	ROBERTO 3, 283
gaineimh: Chan fhaod sinn triall air sliabh no gaineimh	MAIRI 4, 225
gainmheach: Saorsa no gainmheach	FRATER 1, 136
gàire: An gàire mar chraiteachan salainn	MACTHO 13, 241
gaisgeach: Ach 's gaisgeach esan a bheir buaidh / Air eagal beatha	BOTHCH 1, 54
Is cinnteach gur h-e gaisgeach mór a bhios a seo	TRAD GA 4, 333
gal: thug e gal beag air mo shùilean	MACGIL 22, 218
gale: In peace thou art the gale of spring	Ja MACPHE 2, 218
Gall: Is dú éirghe i n-aghaidh Gall	DEAN 5, 110
Gallagh: ye can never tell wi a Gallagh	G GUNN 2, 152
gallant: Come away, dear, white-handed gallant	TRAD 31, 336
You have spoiled a better face than your own	BALLAD 7, 39

gallantry: What men call gallantry, and gods adultery — BYRON 35, 78
Galldachd: iolach a' Ghaidhein / a' tighinn á cliabh na Galldachd — MACTHO 19, 241
galley: this loathsome Galley of the World — W DRUM 9, 117
Gallowa: the Gallowa' hills are covered wi' broom — TRAD 40, 337
gallows: a gallows and sentence on the summit of every hillock — HENDER 6, 159
Dings the fell gallows o the burghers doon — HENDER 6, 159
gallows-ripe: it is long since Allan was gallows-ripe — FIONN 2, 133
galravitchings: sinful possets and galravitchings — GALT 1, 138
game: a tyrannising game — R MURRAY 1, 263
Golf has ceased to be a peculiarly national game — F BALF 6, 38
gaming: [the noise of] gaming was the sweetest music — DEAN 1, 109
gang: Gang doun wi' a sang — SOUTAR 11, 314
gang tae the coals i' the mornin' — A SKIR 1, 302
ganging: A ganging point compos'd a line — R FERG 12, 129
gangrel: but haiks its gangrel body, whaur / eternities cry doun — MCDONA 1, 213
Ye need a cheery hert / To play the gangrel pairt — ANNAND 5, 26
gannets: gannets rest a beak-stab apart — GILLI 3, 144
gaoir: gaoir na h-Eòrpa — MACGIL 2, 216
gaoith: guthan cruaidh Sasannach / a' dol an aghaidh na gaoith — C NICGU 2, 267
gaol: Thig trì nithean gun iarraidh: / An t-eagal, an t-iadach, 's an gaol — ANON 22, 28
gap: The gap you have left / is as lasting as a rock face — WHYTE 4, 349
garb: garb of old Gaul is no doubt very fetching — CROSL 8, 103
In the garb of old Gaul — H ERSK 1, 124
garden: Garden Centres must become the Jacobin Clubs — IH FINL 16, 132
I can blow a garden with my breath — M STUA 5, 327
may the perfume of her garden — E BURNS 1, 66
gardening: gardening is an Art — IH FINL 14, 132
gardens: where the people have miniature wharfs instead of gardens — LINKLA 5, 197
gargantuan: common-minded sort of gargantuan Governess — FINDL 2, 131
gargoyle: gargoyle's grinning at the elbow of a kneeling saint — G SMITH 2, 306
garment: Self-respect is the noblest garment — SMILES 3, 303
garret: If I dee an auld maid in a garret — TRAD 3, 333
this lord's station, who does not live in a garret — BROUGH 2, 60
gas: the Gas Chamber of the Scots — F MACCOL 4, 209
yer gas in a peep — MCNAUG 2, 236
gash: What gars the laird of Garskadden look sae gash? — D RAMS 2, 278
gate: don't forget to have the gate shit — SMOLL 11, 311
gateway: gateway of Scotland is the Firth of Forth — W ELLIO 1, 123
gathering: many a noble gathering in the cause of liberty — MCLAR 1, 229
gaucheries: any of your Scotch *gaucheries* — BRUNT 1, 63
gauger: And aye the gauger played the flute — STEVEN 64, 322
Gaul: garb of old Gaul is no doubt very fetching — CROSL 8, 103
In the garb of old Gaul — H ERSK 1, 124
gaunt: gaunt church, gaunt people — E BURNS 3, 66
gay: Lesbians and gay men are, for the most part, invisible — CANT 1, 82
To be gay, as to be Scottish, is to doubt — WOOLAS 1, 352
gays: lesbians and gays must be free — WOOLAS 2, 352
gaze: gaze dumb at an outstretched map — WHYTE 1, 348
gealaich: Cuiridh mi làmh air corran na gealaich — MACGIL 20, 218
gealtachd: gealtachd anns a' chrìdh, / gun chreideamh an aon ni — MACGIL 1, 216
gear: all for newfangilness of gear — R MAIT 1, 243
That I for grace an' gear may shine — BURNS 15, 67
women and gear are at the bottom of a' the mischief — SCOTT 64, 293
Geddie: like other men Mr Geddie grows old — J FRAS 1, 135
geese: abune the Angus straths I saw the wild geese flee — JACOB 7, 174
Skeins o geese write a word — JAMIE 5, 177
geis: wild geis claking eik by nyghtis tyde — G DOUGL 7, 115
gemme: Wee Malkies — the gemme's a bogey! — MULRIN 2, 261
generation: Glencalvie people the wicked generation — ANON 42, 30
generous: the Scot can be stupidly generous — S BAXT 1, 45
Geneva: The grim Geneva ministers — AYTOUN 3, 34
genius: Edinburgh is a hot-bed of genius — SMOLL 15, 311
fifty men of genius and learning — SMELLI 1, 303
genius, and not the want of it, that adulterates philosophy — T REID 2, 280
His genius is a thing apart — H MORT 3, 257
Poetic Genius of my Country — BURNS 51, 69
powerful genius of Byron — SCOTT 74, 294
talent instantly recognises genius — DOYLE 15, 116
genteel: avoided God with a shudder of genteel taste — GIBBON 14, 143
gentle: How gentle much of storms really is — J MUIR 1, 259
gentleman: fine gentleman whose father toils with a muck-fork — CROSL 1, 103
greatest gentleman of the House of Commons — MAXTON 3, 247

kill himself that he may be a country gentleman — CARLYL 30, 86
Show'd him the gentleman an' scholar — BURNS 40, 69
Swearing was thought the right, and the mark, of a gentleman — COCKBU 12, 97
gentlemen: for the gentlemen that don't like it, whisky — KENNAW 1, 185
gentles: It's weel wi' you gentles — SCOTT 51, 293
gentry: I winna be gentry! — JJ BELL 1, 47
What care some gentry if they're weel — E JOHNST 3, 179
genuine: only two classes, the genuine and the humbug — CUNN G. 15, 106
geographical: Wilderness, then, isn't just a geographical area — A WATSON 1, 346
geographie: Rags of Geographie — CLEVE 1, 96
geography: Geography is people — W MCILV 1, 223
geologist: necessity which made me a quarrier that taught me to be a geologist — MILLER 4, 250
geology: what happens to the world's geology / Is not irrelevant to us — MACDIA 38, 211
geometrises: God always geometrises — THOMPS 1, 331
Geordie: muckin' o' Geordie's byre — BALLAD 36, 41
Saw ye Geordie's grace / Ridin' on a goosie? — TRAD 21, 335
George: Christ had his John and I have my George — JAMES 19, 176
George's daughter / would not allow my pocket to be empty — MACANT 3, 203
'Tis George has done the unfair thing — MACANT 1, 203
German: The wee, wee German lairdie — CUNN 2, 104
Germanie: My luve's in Germanie, send him hame — MACNEI 4, 237
Germany: Germany wallowing in a viler mud than the Middle Ages — J BUCHAN 10, 64
get: if I don't get ye, the coos'll get ye — LORNE 2, 200
Keep what you get, and get what you can — KAMES 7, 181
Ghàidhealaibh: Ghàidhealaibh calma mo ghràidh — ALASD 2, 23
Ghaidheil: iolach a' Ghaidheil / a' tighinn á cliabh na Galldachd — MACTHO 19, 241
gháire: ní math súgradh gan gháire — MACDHU 2, 209
ghaist: I gang like a ghaist — A LINDS 2, 194
ghaoil: thig peileir dian á gunna Ghaoil — MACGIL 26, 219
ghealach: bidh ghealach mar gun dòirt oirr' fuil — BOTHCH 4, 55
Fàilte dhut, a ghealach ùr — CARMIN 6, 88
ghetto-makars: Ghetto-makars, tae the knackirs' — CRAWFO 1, 102
ghettos: I want to be in all the ghettos — GALFO 1, 138
ghnùis: ge nach fhaicte mo ghnùis, / chluinnte aca 'san Dùn mo ghuth — CLARS 2, 95
ghost: being a ghost is worse than seeing them — BARRIE 18, 44
the ghost of each error, the ghost of each guilt — IC SMITH 5, 306
ghosts: All beds have ghosts — AL KENNE 3, 185
Ghosts of a primeval race — CUNN G. 3, 105
Our ghosts outnumber us — DUNN 14, 120
When injur'd ghosts complain — MALLOC 2, 244
ghràidh: I mo chridhe, I mo ghràidh — COLUMB 5, 99
ghràis: càrnadh a' ghràis gu lèir 'na do chliabh fhèin — MACTHO 17, 241
Ghreugaich: A bhàta dhuibh, a Ghreugaich choimhlionta — MACGIL 10, 217
ghrian: chuir thu do bhois / eadar do shùilean 's a' ghrian — MACAMH 2, 203
Ghriogóir: Clann Ghriogóir an dream nach tréith — DUBH 1, 118
ghruadh: deirge a ghruadh ioná fuil laoigh — DEAN 3, 110
ghruaim: más ar ghruaim bhitheas an rath — DEAN 6, 110
ghuth: An taigh-mór falamh an Dun-Eideann / Gun chumhachd gun ghuth — RUNRIG 2, 286
ge nach fhaicte mo ghnùis, / chluinnte aca 'san Dùn mo ghuth — CLARS 2, 95
Mairg duine do chaill a ghuth — DONN Mo 1, 113
Gibraltar: that Gibraltar of antiquity — GALT 4, 139
giddy: a giddy neighbour — SHAKES 1, 298
gie: gie her plenty of whisky — PETRIE 4, 274
gil: Is gil thu na 'n eal air loch làthaich — CARMIN 2, 88
Gilnockie: Some time called Laird of Gilnockie — BALLAD 24, 40
Gilsanquhar: coupin' gless for gless / Wi' Cruivie and Gilsanquhar — MACDIA 12, 210
gin-mules: make gin-mules of their fathers — CROSL 2, 103
ginger beer: the said snail-tainted ginger beer — DONOGH 1, 113
think so highly of the ginger-beer — STEVEN 31, 320
gird: let us gird up our minds in courage — WRIGHT 11, 354
girl: Girl of the yellow, heavy-yellow, gold-yellow hair — MACGIL 2, 216
Girl under the dominion of the Kirk — KEATS 1, 183
Give me a girl at an impressionable age — SPARK 5, 315
man is none the worse for things that would ruin a girl — OLIPH 9, 270
girlie: Tennent's lager girlie gallery — G THOMS 1, 331
girls: boys will suffer *more* from the absence of the girls — J GRANT 3, 149
no jobs for the girls — SPALD 1, 314
The Girls of Slender Means — SPARK 10, 315

girns: greets a' winter, and girns a' simmer	C GRAH 2, 147
giro: Not Not While the Giro	KELMAN 1, 183
glaciers: Glaciers, grinding West, gouged out	MACCAI 19, 206
glad: glad that I was born on the other side the Tweed	CARLYL 7, 83
Glaic a' Bhàis: 'Na shuidhe marbh an 'Glaic a' Bhàis'	MACGIL 23, 218
glaid: The glaid gangs free, my bonnie lad	MCDONA 1, 213
glamour: talk about the glamour of show business	TURBER 1, 341
glas: baile glas gun ghathadh gréine	MACGIL 3, 216
is glas a cadal suain an nochd	MACGIL 8, 217
Glaschu: Glaschu bheag bhith 'na lasair	TRAD 2, 333
'Se Glaschu an Eiphit a bh' agaibh	MACTHO 23, 242
Tha drùis cho eadar-nàiseanta ri Glaschu fhèin	MACTHO 24, 242
Glasgow: Academy I found in the Glasgow streets	BONE 1, 53
a cuff o' the neck like ony Glasgow bailie's	GALT 15, 139
a diminution of Glasgow	W MCILV 11, 223
butchers of Glasgow have all got their pride	MCGINN 6, 220
difference between a Glasgow man and an Edinburgh man	E MUIR 6, 258
educated at a far better place, Glasgow	FINNIS 1, 132
Glasgow exists as a music-hall song	GRAY 3, 149
Glasgow humour is disbelief under anaesthetic	W MCILV 12, 223
Glasgow invention of square-toed shoes	HOUSE 3, 165
Glasgow is kind. Glasgow is cruel	W MCILV 11, 223
Glasgow's greatest export	W MCILV 13, 224
Glasgow's Miles Better	ANON 57, 30
Glasgow was your Egypt	MACTHO 23, 242
I belong to Glasgow	FYFFE 1, 137
if you don't make it in Glasgow, then you can't do it	De WILLIS 1, 350
In Glasgow a man is innocent until he is found guilty	H MORT 7, 257
In Glasgow half the fans hate you	T BURNS 1, 75
in Glasgow there is no such word as 'happy'	PATTIS 1, 274
little Glasgow is a-blazing	TRAD 2, 333
Lust is as international as Glasgow itself	MACTHO 24, 242
majority of Scots comics have come from Glasgow	S BAXT 4, 46
Mother Glasgow's succour is perpetual	MARRA 2, 244
Oh where is the Glasgow that I used tae know	MCNAUG 2, 236
only certified sane man in Glasgow	PETRIE 1, 274
real Glasgow faggots	H COCKBU 2, 97
sense of proportion is anathema to the Glasgow drinker	H MCILV 1, 222
You lived in Glasgow	IC SMITH 15, 307
glass: dropped into a town like glass balls	W MUIR 3, 260
glasses: fill up your glasses of brandy and wine	TRAD 37, 336
gleann: Gleann a' mhìltich as lìonmhor mang	MACANT 8, 204
glebe: better to see a woman, as in Scotland, bent over the glebe	WRIGHT 4, 353
glen: glen of arrow-grass that's full of fawns	MACANT 8, 204
Glen of Weeping	MACAUL 1, 204
Not a glen but it has its but and ben	N BUCHAN 1, 64
we parted in yon shady glen	TRAD 14, 334
Glenartney: lone Glenartney's hazel shade	SCOTT 22, 291
Glencalvie: Glencalvie people the wicked generation	ANON 42, 30
Glenco: McDonalds of Glenco	DUNCAN 1, 120
Glenfiddich: Glenfiddich, Bruichladdich and Glengrant	MACCAI 8, 205
Glengrant: Glenfiddich, Bruichladdich and Glengrant	MACCAI 8, 205
Glenkindie: Glenkindie was ance a harper gude	BALLAD 21, 40
Glenleevit: Gie me the real Glenleevit	HOGG 13, 163
glens: scenic beauty of empty glens	N GUNN 5, 153
Glesca: drivin intae Glesca in my soor-mulk cairt	T JOHNST 1, 181
gless: coupin' gless for gless / Wi' Cruivie and Gilsanquhar	MACDIA 12, 210
glib: between the imperative and the glib	J CAMER 8, 80
glitter: Glitter of mica at the windy corners	GS FRAS 1, 135
glittering: glittering with ungodly dew	Ja THOMS(1) 7, 331
gloamin': roamin' in the gloamin'	LAUDER 6, 192
globe: globe as one great dewdrop	J MUIR 11, 260
round out our globe of experience	STEVEN 63, 322
gloom: if grace goes with gloom	DEAN 6, 110
light-heartedness mixed with spasms of deep gloom	MITCHI 21, 252
The torch that lights time's thickest gloom	BONAR 3, 53
Ye are the owls, who from the gloom	J BAILL 8, 35
glooms: Welcome, kindred glooms!	Ja THOMS(1) 5, 331
gloomy: Gloomy winter's now awa'	TANNAH 4, 329
glorify: glorify God in the Grassmarket	LAUDER 2, 193
Man's chief end is to glorify God	SHORTE 1, 300
glory: glory dwelleth / In Immanuel's land	COUSIN 2, 102
not glory, it is not riches, neither is it honour	DECLAR 1, 110
The Child of glory	M MACDON 1, 214
glove: wha will glove my hand?	BALLAD 31, 41
gluasad: gluasad bithbhuan a' bhaile	MACTHO 6, 240
glugs: the sad glugs in your bottles	DUNN 7, 121
gnawing: It's not gnawing at you that I find hard	IAIN L 2, 170
will you never cease gnawing at the Campbells?	IAIN L 2, 170
gnomon: erect a gnomon on her horizontal dial	T URQU 3, 343
go: You will go no further, nor touch the man	COLUMB 2, 99
goal: I don't know why the ref ruled out that goal	A MACPHE 1, 237
I've never seen a fan score a goal	STEIN 2, 317
goals: Hampden Roar is the equivalent of two goals	HOUSE 4, 165
goats: goats in the Sahara and sheep in the Highlands	R MCLEL 7, 231
God: a God who smites and does not spare	OLIPH 4, 270
almost, white love, you took my God from me	ANON 20, 28
a political agenda, but it is God's agenda	SHANKS 1, 299
as for God, I will take Him in my own hands	J GRAH 1, 147
avoided God with a shudder of genteel taste	GIBBON 14, 143
Be war, I am ane Jelous God	GUDE 6, 152
bound by the laws of God and nature to help	GALT 19, 140
Fegs, God's no blate gin he stirs up	MACDIA 5, 210
fight in the end between FREEDOM and GOD	GIBBON 9, 143
forced by science to the belief in God	KELVIN 14, 184
Gin I was God	MURRAY 9, 263
glorify God in the Grassmarket	LAUDER 2, 193
God always geometrises	THOMPS 1, 331
God and one are always a majority	SLESS 3, 302
God and Sanct Petir	ANON 16, 27
God damn all other armies	J MACLEA 2, 230
God gives not Kings the stile of Gods in vaine	JAMES 3, 175
God, give us the grace to hate / our unemancipated state	N WELLS 5, 347
God grant that Marshal Wade	ANON 26, 28
God grant that thai, that cummyne ar	BARBOU 6, 43
God help England if she had no Scots	G SHAW 1, 299
God, his uncle, has given him a title to the land	MACTHO 15, 241
God is a bleak fact	GRAY 12, 150
God is a bogle of the nursery	W MAIT 1, 243
God is not in the bitter divisione	W DRUM 10, 117
God's Kingdom among Boys	WA SMITH 1, 310
God send a smilinge boy	JAMES 21, 176
God's silly vassal	A MELV 1, 248
God the Father fell down-stairs	STEVEN 100, 324
God through the wrong end of a telescope	MACDIA 34, 211
God to man doth speak in solitude	BLACKI 2, 50
Good morning, God	BARRIE 25, 45
grown chrysanthemums in the dung of God	WHITE 1, 348
he made you a little God	JAMES 4, 175
Immortal, invisible, God	WC SMITH 1, 310
Know that the Lord is God indeed	METRIC 4, 249
let God call it blasphemy	MACGIL 20, 218
'Let there be Licht,' said God	MACDIA 20, 211
listen for the small still voice of God	M STUA 1, 326
Man is but a thought of God	Ge MACDON 6, 214
Man's chief end is to glorify God	SHORTE 1, 300
May God bless the water of Loch Hasten	MACCOD 1, 208
May God bless thy cross / Before thou go over the sea	CARMIN 1, 88
ME, made after the image o' God	CORRIE 1, 101
monetarist culture has driven out God in favour of Mammon	WATERS 1, 345
not the much diminished perfect work of God	D HILL 1, 162
play the runagate from God	J OGILVI 1, 269
prayer, which is nothing else but a friendly talking with God	JAMES 5, 175
prove to you the existence of God	T REID 8, 281
religion is an Union of the soul with God	SCOUG 1, 297
round, fat, oily man of God	Ja THOMS(1) 7, 331
Success is hearing the voice of God	G MACLEO 2, 232
sucked in the being and attributes of God	HERMAN 3, 161
take God out of politics, then you're taking God out of life	WRIGHT 2, 354
thank God for the Edinburgh Festival	DEMARC 1, 111
Thank you for having me, God	M LINDS 4, 196
These stones go through Man, straight to God	MACDIA 37, 211
The voice of the great God	CARMIN 5, 88
toaffs that could afford tae kneel oan God's altar	T MCGRAT 1, 221
To God be humill, and to thy freynd be kynd	DUNBAR 15, 119
Trust in God and do the right	N MACLEO 2, 233
Whair is now Johne Knox his God?	MARY(1) 1, 245
What's money to God?	SLESS 6, 303
why do we not denie God and adore the Devill	JAMES 13, 175
will of God, takes precedence over the laws of the state	A MCLEL 2, 231
with God's help, I run faster	LIDDEL 2, 194
Ye canna sair God and Gowd baith	NEW TES 1, 266
godly: sinner fu' and the godly stairv't	JACOB 9, 174
gods: no gods and precious few heroes	HENDER 2, 159

There's too many Gods	MACMIL **3**, 234
Goethe: open thy Goethe	CARLYL **1**, 84
Goill: B'e a' cheud aon a sheinn am port so do na Goill	MACKINN **3**, 227
gold: A beggar's mantle fringed with gold	JAMES **24**, 176
A chain of gold ye sall not lack	SCOTT **47**, 292
He that hes gold and grit riches	DUNBAR **1**, 118
liquid gold carried by the *Cabinet Minister*	C MACKEN **7**, 225
not by gold or by silver, but by labour	SMITH **7**, 304
Pure gold is pure gold	CARSW **14**, 92
to find the source of the gold, he must be wise	JF CAMPB **1**, 81
we bought the hills with English gold	BLACKI **7**, 50
We're bought and sold for English gold	BURNS **120**, 74
golden: The golden hands with the almond nails	LOCHH **1**, 198
golf: [Golf] is an intensely Presbyterian activity	HANLEY **2**, 157
futball and golf be utterly cryit downe	JAMES II **1**, 174
Golf has ceased to be a peculiarly national game	F BALF **6**, 38
Golf is an indispensable adjunct to high civilisation	CARNEG **12**, 90
Golf is a thoroughly national game	A LANG **5**, 191
golf should be forbidden to all males under 25	STIRL **1**, 326
On holidays they frequently play at *golf*	STATIS **5**, 317
gone: Thou art gone, and for ever	SCOTT **26**, 291
good: A great good is coming to us all	Ge MACDON **11**, 214
be a good man – be virtuous	SCOTT **121**, 297
Even good men like to make the public stare	BYRON **44**, 78
Good night, an' joy be wi' you a'	HOGG **8**, 163
Let us acknowledge all good	Ge MACDON **4**, 214
nothing left for you, not even suicide, but to be good	STEVEN **22**, 320
so good that there should be a tax levied	STEVEN **36**, 320
The good of eye be thine, / The good of liking be thine	CARMIN **4**, 88
This was the good town once	E MUIR **16**, 259
We have seen / Good men made evil	E MUIR **16**, 259
goodbye: it's goodbye to care	ROBERTO **6**, 283
goodwill: The BBC has secured and holds the goodwill	REITH **1**, 281
two apparently irreconcilables – force and goodwill	W ELLIO **5**, 123
goose: Drops into Styx, and turns a Soland-Goose	CLEVE **2**, 96
goosie: Saw ye Geordie's grace / Ridin' on a goosie?	TRAD **21**, 335
Gorbals: Gorbals life goes on its way	MCARTH **2**, 204
Lermontov and Proust in the Gorbals	HAVER **1**, 158
Something really weird was happening in the Gorbals	TORRIN **1**, 332
Gordon: a hap o' the Gordon green	SYMON **2**, 328
gory: Hamlet, Hamlet! Aw the gory!	MCNAUG **5**, 236
gospel: the true gospel concerning wealth	CARNEG **8**, 90
Gothic: mansion turns out a Gothic anomaly	SCOTT **76**, 294
gould: bukis wer worthy thair wayght of gould	WODE **1**, 351
gourlie: gourlie, goustrous-lookin' clouds	TENNAN **6**, 330
govern: a country where experts govern	WOOD **3**, 352
easy to govern but impossible to enslave	BROUGH **4**, 60
govern according to the common weal	JAMES **22**, 176
Here I sit and govern Scotland with my pen	JAMES **17**, 176
governe: foolishe, madde, and phrenetike shal governe	KNOX **2**, 188
governed: how differently our country would be governed	RUSHF **2**, 287
governess: common-minded sort of gargantuan Governess	FINDL **2**, 131
government: back to your constituencies and prepare for government	STEEL **1**, 317
Good government can never be a substitute for government by the people	CAMPB-B. **3**, 82
government in every country should be just like a corporation	BRAXF **2**, 57
Government will yield nothing to justice	MILLER **2**, 250
If this government was an individual	G ROBERTSO **1**, 284
Like People like Government	CARLYL **50**, 87
only 'regional minded' even under our own government	WOOD **5**, 352
times of regular government and polished manners	Ja MACPHE **4**, 238
governs: He governs by law, she by persuasion	KAMES **13**, 182
Gow: Gow beat time, now time's beat Gow	GOW **3**, 146
Gow's delightful violin	E GRANT(2) **1**, 148
gowan: gowan glitters on the sward	J BAILL **10**, 35
gowans: Like the dew on the gowans at bonnie Woodha'	TRAD **67**, 339
pou'd the gowans fine	BURNS **67**, 70
gowd: I had lock'd my heart in a case o' gowd	TRAD **79**, 340
The man's the gowd for a' that	BURNS **131**, 75
Ye canna sair God and Gowd baith	NEW TES **1**, 266
gowfers: When the bungaloids burgeon and gowfers gowf	BRIDIE **15**, 59
gowff: When we were weary'd at the gowff	A RAMS(1) **1**, 277
gowk: A lanely singin' gowk	SOUTAR **6**, 313
Daft gowk, in macaroni dress	R FERG **17**, 129
I'm feared he turn out to be a conceited gowk	HOGG **9**, 163
gowks: if a' the gowks in the world were brought together	CHALM **7**, 94
gown: Toga and gown walk the pier	G BRUCE **4**, 62

grace: a fool to ask grace at a graceless face	BALLAD **25**, 40
as ane chapman beris his pak, / I bure thy Grace	D LINDS **3**, 195
God, give us the grace to hate / our unemancipated state	N WELLS **5**, 347
if grace goes with gloom	DEAN **6**, 110
It's law they ask of me and not grace	IC SMITH **10**, 307
ministers without grace and women without shame	BRAHAN **1**, 56
pile all of the Grace in your own creel	MACTHO **17**, 241
Poverty walks with wanton grace	TAYLOR **1**, 329
That I for grace an' gear may shine	BURNS **15**, 67
the grace of thrift	OLIPH **24**, 271
graces: smattering of the graces	J RAMS **1**, 279
grádh: Is mairg dá ngalar an grádh	ISEAB **1**, 172
grammar: I write grammar as I speak	SCOTT **97**, 295
grammar-rules: boy who is flogged into grammar-rules	KAMES **15**, 182
grammars: What sairs your grammars?	BURNS **8**, 67
gramophone: Lenin's gramophone	J MACLEA **7**, 230
Grampians: Our sons of the mist might here see their Grampians	WRIGHT **3**, 353
grandeur: What a selfish cold-hearted thing is grandeur	FERRI **11**, 130
grandmother: It was the day my grandmother exploded	BANKS **2**, 42
granitette: natural, washable, plastic granitette	J MCGRAT **3**, 220
grannie: aged and worthy grannie of the papistry	GALT **18**, 139
His grannie keepit a sweetie-shop in Strathbungo	GD BROWN **3**, 60
We'll no hae grannie lang noo!	HISLOP **1**, 162
grannies: urnae arraheids / but a show o grannies' tongues	JAMIE **3**, 176
granny: a hoose-fu o weans an a done aul granny	E STEW **2**, 325
Be kind to your granny	PETRIE **4**, 274
Not a granny but she is old and frail	N BUCHAN **1**, 64
granted: He had taken her as much for granted	MORRIS **5**, 256
grass: Let grass grow over works	CARNEG **9**, 90
love better the rustle of the grass	CUNN G. **3**, 105
The grass is waving now in stranger winds	IC SMITH **17**, 307
Grassmarket: As I was walking along the Grassmarket	ROCKV **1**, 285
glorify God in the Grassmarket	LAUDER **2**, 193
grate: Get up and clean the grate	WS GRAH **4**, 147
only the stranger / Hissing in the grate	WS GRAH **5**, 147
grave: her countenance grew very grave	OLIPH **12**, 270
Marriage is a step so grave	STEVEN **19**, 320
quiet as the grave – or Peebles	COCKBU **18**, 98
Romantic Scotland's in the grave	GS FRAS **3**, 135
that dark inn – the Grave	SCOTT **37**, 292
gravel: bag of gravel is a history	HUTTON **1**, 169
gravelie: gravelie, like a Minister	JAMES **11**, 175
graves: about the graves of the martyrs the whaups	STEVEN **87**, 324
the graves will suddenly pour out their dead	BOTHCH **3**, 55
graveyard: Graveyard of English comics	LOGAN **3**, 200
gravity: gravity of a Barcelonian bishop	J BOSWEL **1**, 53
true centre of gravity is in the mind	J BUCHAN **13**, 64
great: Dark Cuthullin shall be great or dead	Ja MACPHE **1**, 238
disbelief in great men	CARLYL **38**, 86
it has taken great men to discover simple things	THOMPS **3**, 331
greatest: Like Muhammad Ali – you're the greatest	V GRIEV **2**, 152
greatness: fervid exaltation and dreary greatness	CARLYL **1**, 84
Man's Unhappiness as I construe, comes of his Greatness	CARLYL **18**, 85
what is the hall-mark of greatness?	BRIDIE **1**, 58
greed: believe their greed holds up the continents	GRAY **4**, 150
Greek: Black boat, perfect Greek	MACGIL **10**, 217
Poverty hath the Gaelic and Greek	TAYLOR **1**, 329
they think to climb Parnassus / By dint o' Greek	BURNS **9**, 67
green: a hap o' the Gordon green	SYMON **2**, 328
At Polwart on the green	A RAMS(1) **14**, 278
green days in forests and blue days at sea	STEVEN **85**, 323
Green grow the rashes O	ANON **34**, 29
Green grow the rashes, O	R BURNS **2**, 66
green springing corner of young Eden	E MUIR **17**, 259
in the lee of a house with green shutters	GIBBON **2**, 142
people and earth / are aware of a green spirit	CAIMB **2**, 79
spare the green and take the ripe	R CAMER **1**, 80
greenhouse: kept, like her, in a mental greenhouse	OLIPH **20**, 271
Greenland: The cold land of Greenland is barren and bare	SCROGG **2**, 297
greenwood: Merry it is in the good greenwood	SCOTT **27**, 291
greet: Ah! gentle dames! it gars me greet	BURNS **92**, 72
How should I greet thee? – / With silence and tears	BYRON **30**, 77
greeting: he is a greeting divil	R BLAIR(1) **2**, 51
greets: greets a' winter, and girns a' simmer	C GRAH **2**, 147
Gregor: The race of Gregor is a folk not weak	DUBH **1**, 118
gréin: Meic Uí Mhoichéirghe, lá samhraidh / iarras gréin	GIOL Co **2**, 144
Gretna Green: snowy North and South by Gretna Green	TRAD **75**, 339

In hell they'll roast thee like a herrin	BURNS 100, 72
it's hell's mouth	BIRD 4, 49
reward of dansaris, and that will be drynk in hell	KNOX 10, 188
scaling heaven with ladders fetched out of hell	LEIGHT 1, 193
Sends ane to Heaven, an' ten to Hell	BURNS 14, 67
hellish: hellish, unembellished / True Confessions	LOCHH 12, 199
This hellish business of being a woman	MITCH1 13, 252
help: Help of the helpless, O abide with me	LYTE 1, 202
hen: A hen stares at nothing with one eye	MACCAI 2, 205
let's get in the tappit hen	A RAMS(1) 5, 277
The bonnie muir hen	BAIRN 4, 36
henna: we will henna our hair / like Colette	FELL 3, 127
hens: hens to hish into the ree	MURRAY 7, 262
herd: whistle that the wee herd made	MURRAY 1, 262
heredity: there is a birth independent of heredity	CARSW 20, 92
heretics: If laws and lawgivers did not make heretics	G MACKEN 3, 225
herisie: Herisie, herisie! Fire, fire incontinent!	D LINDS 11, 195
heritage: always banging on about 'our heritage'	L KENNED 2, 186
hermits: hermits and Asiatic self-tortures	STEVEN 90, 324
hermless: Hermless hermless / There's never nae bather fae	
me	MARRA 6, 244
hero: A hero is he who has subdued the fears of life	BOTHCH 1, 54
Herod: greatest respect for the character of *Herod*	BYRON 8, 76
heroes: Heroes have gone out; quacks have come in	CARLYL 44, 87
no gods and precious few heroes	HENDER 2, 159
heroic: a heroic poem of its sort	CARLYL 25, 86
heroism: labour demands a kind of heroism	M OLIPH 1, 269
Think of the heroism of Johnson	STEVEN 32, 320
herrin: In hell they'll roast thee like a herrin	BURNS 100, 72
'I see herrin'.' – I hear the glad cry	MACDIA 39, 211
ma heid's as caller as a herrin	GARIOC 7, 140
She guts the herrin' doon on the quay	Jo WATT 2, 347
Wha'll buy my caller herrin'	NAIRNE 2, 264
Your natural food it is tatties and herrin'	TRAD 70, 339
herring: For the dead herring / On the living water	G BRUCE 1, 62
Plenty herring, plenty meal	ROBERTO 3, 283
the herring cannot do without the potato	IC SMITH 26, 308
we hunted for the shoals of herring	E MACCOL 3, 208
herrings: Mungo catched herrings in the Clyde	SCOTT 60, 293
hert: Burns touched the hert aa the time	MORRIS 1, 257
Lourd on my hert as winter	MACDIA 24, 211
sair his hert wi döl and wae	BALLAD 27, 40
The blude of all my body to my hert	JAMES I 5, 174
Ye need a cheery hert / To play the gangrel pairt	ANNAND 5, 26
heterodoxy: Orthodoxy or *My-doxy* and Heterodoxy or	
Thy-doxy	CARLYL 21, 85
heterosexual: When did you first realise you were	
heterosexual?	I MCGRE 2, 221
heym-folk: I laek da heym-folk at bide by da sea	B ANDERS 2, 25
hiccups: silence punctuated by malicious whispers and hiccups	E MUIR 5, 258
hidden: hidden trap-doors of disaster	BURNS 81, 71
hide: just want to find a place to hide in	SLESS 5, 302
hideous: all that's perfectly hideous about Scotland	WELSH 5, 348
women in the House of Commons are mostly hideous	FAIRB 9, 126
hie: hie away, / Over bank and over brae	SCOTT 32, 291
Hielan: nane but Hielan bonnets here	C CAMPB 2, 81
Hieland: distant and imaginary hieland hame	N BUCHAN 1, 60
Hielandman: ill taking the breeks aff a Hielandman	SCOTT 59, 293
Hielands: As for the Hie-lands, I shortly comprehend them	JAMES 7, 175
Will ye gang to the Hielands, Lizie Lindsey?	BALLAD 32, 41
high: High Church is high only in the sense that game is	KELVIN 21, 185
worst of high jeenks	MUNRO 3, 261
Highland: A 'Highland welcome' all the wide world over	BYRON 45, 78
all the objective restraint of the Highland Light Infantry	H MCILV 2, 222
Dolphinsludge, Queen of the Highland Fleshpots	T MORT 1, 258
For Highland Harry back again	BURNS 85, 72
I'll ask no more / Than just a Highland welcome	BURNS 54, 69
just returned from a Highland expedition	A COCKBU 2, 97
Our Highland hearts are true and leal	HOGG 6, 163
where is your Highland laddie gone?	A GRANT 1, 148
Highlander: A stout Highlander with his language	IC SMITH 11, 307
Lowlander feels himself the sentimental countryman of the	
Highlander	STEVEN 71, 323
no Highlander need ever think shame	SCOTT 33, 291
Highlanders: The manners of the native Highlanders	PENNA 3, 274
Highlands: A chieftain to the Highlands bound	T CAMPB 8, 81
clasps Highlands and Lowlands together	SMITH 10, 306
de-Tibetanization of the Highlands and Islands	MACDIA 45, 212

extent of the Highlands gives a sense of vastness	ARNOLD 1, 31
goats in the Sahara and sheep in the Highlands	R MCLEL 7, 231
He who first met the Highlands' swelling blue	BYRON 52, 78
Highlands may be said to open for the season	FERRI 20, 131
Highlands, where there are not enough fine intervals	STEVEN 4, 319
In the highlands, in the country places	STEVEN 86, 324
My heart's in the Highlands a chasing the deer	BURNS 88, 72
nothing in it at all belonging to the Highlands	WILKIE 1, 349
nought in the Highlands but syboes and leeks	SCOTT 34, 291
shut up against us the entire Highlands	MILLER 3, 250
stained with the best blood of the Highlands	BRAHAN 3, 56
Sufferings have been inflicted in the Highlands	D MACLEO 4, 232
the dear, dear Highlands	VICTO 1, 344
the Ramsgate of the Highlands	WOOLAS 2, 353
tragedy of the Highlands has become a saleable commodity	J MCGRAT 2, 220
Ye Highlands and ye Lawlands	BALLAD 6, 39
hikers: There are also the 'hikers'	HOUSE 5, 165
Hill: burning hatred for Jimmy Hill is a poor substitute	J MCMIL 2, 234
hill: Bennachie! Faith, yon's the hill	MURRAY 11, 263
Gie me a hill wi' the heather on't	SYMON 1, 328
Hill you ho, boys	ROBERTO 4, 283
No hill is dull between the sunset and the sea	H BROWN 1, 61
She gaed up yon high, high hill	BALLAD 18, 40
The hill road to Roberton	W OGILVI 1, 269
the hunter home from the hill	STEVEN 65, 322
When o'er the hill the eastern star	BURNS 116, 73
hills: All the hills and vales along	SORLEY 1, 313
although people might come together, the hills would not	
stir	MACLEOI 2, 233
behold you again in dying, / Hills of home	STEVEN 88, 324
I to the hills will lift mine eyes	METRIC 5, 249
licht amo' the hills	SHEPH 7, 299
no hills high enough to intercept it	LINKLA 4, 197
Over the hills and far away	STEVEN 64, 322
Sunday in the hills	WOOD 4, 352
we bought the hills with English gold	BLACKI 7, 50
Who owns these ample hills?	BLACKI 1, 50
With the hills of home before us	ROBERTO 5, 283
Your absolute heads populate the hills	IC SMITH 8, 307
hillside: Ye canna ploo the hillside wi' yer taes	A SCOTT-M 1, 297
hindmost: a competition for who was to be hindmost	GD BROWN 4, 60
hippis: cum behind and kis hir hippis	DUNBAR 17, 119
Hiroshima: After Hiroshima / You ask a poet to sing	BOLD 1, 52
hirquitalliency: To speak of her *hirquitalliency*	T URQU 3, 343
hissing: only the stranger / Hissing in the grate	WS GRAH 5, 147
historians: the lawful prey of Historians & Poets	BURNS 104, 73
historic: an historic blow for people on the land	A MACRAE 1, 238
historical: this the historical nation	HUME 31, 168
history: bag of gravel is a history	HUTTON 1, 169
corrupt history of Scotland	IC SMITH 24, 308
folk who had made history	SHEPH 2, 299
Go into any place where history is stored	AL KENNE 1, 185
History a distillation of Rumour	CARLYL 20, 85
History can show few benign mergings	GM BROWN 14, 61
History is littered with dead opinion polls	I LANG 4, 192
History is the essence of innumerable Biographies	CARLYL 14, 85
History, whether we like it or not, presses itself	ROSE 4, 286
humour may reflect the history of Scotland	FULTON 2, 137
it wasn't history but memory / great mary macpherson	MACNEA 4, 236
lawyer without history or literature	SCOTT 41, 292
lugged backwards / through the Debatable Lands of	
history	MACCAI 15, 206
not learning from our history but merely living in it	T BLAIR 4, 51
sentimentality, militarism and bogus history	HOOD 2, 165
the world's history written in stone	MACKINT 1, 228
what passed for Scottish history	GALLO 4, 138
You yield to history nothing	G BRUCE 2, 62
Hitler: Herr Hitler has recently reminded us	ATHOLL 2, 33
hit-or-miss: I'm a spontaneous hit-or-miss writer	MACCAI 24, 206
hizzies: fule hizzies – blawn oot like balloons	Ja HAMIL 6, 156
hoasting: 'peching' and 'hoasting'	MILLAR 2, 249
hocus: Hocus was an old cunning attorney	ARBUTH 2, 31
Holland: Lawlands o' Holland / Hae twined my Love and me	TRAD 48, 337
hollows: door slammed in the deepest hollows of the sea	J CAMER 4, 80
Holmes: My name is Sherlock Holmes	DOYLE 9, 116
holocaust: A holocaust of children	BARRIE 8, 44
holy: Holy Willies of Scottish life	HENDER 7, 160
Sae pious and sae holy	BURNS 22, 68

ken when ye hae a gude servant	SCOTT 57, 293
Kennedy: Cuntbittin crawdoun Kennedy	DUNBAR 3, 118
kens: What a man *kens* he *cans*	CARLYL 23, 85
Kensington: A Far Cry from Kensington	SPARK 17, 315
kent: Kent His / Faither	A SCOTT(2) 6, 289
key: Are ye needin ony guisers / wha sing in a minor key?	MCDONA 2, 214
where the key shall not keep the castle	JAMES I 1, 174
Khrushchev: who else should I believe in? Macmillan?	
Khrushchev?	S WILS 2, 351
kick: allow me my last dying kick	CHURCH 2, 94
nothing but a kick could ever have hardened her heart	FERRI 5, 130
yir erse is the right shape fur a kick	LOCHH 16, 200
kid: Ah'll kid oan that Ah'm a daftie	MCNAUG 4, 236
Real Gone Kid	R ROSS 3, 286
kids: kids would happily play football in the streets	ROXBUR 2, 286
Once meanings get loose, kids pick them up	MITCHI 27, 253
Kilbarchan: Kilbarchan now may say alas	R SEMP 1, 298
kill: kill himself that he may be a country gentleman	CARLYL 30, 86
to make a man look noble, your best course is to kill him	SMITH 8, 305
Killiecrankie: On the braes o' Killiecrankie, O!	BURNS 87, 72
killing: Killing No Murder	HARDIE 4, 158
The killing, the dying, it was all done in vain	BOGLE 2, 52
Kilmeny: Bonnie Kilmeny gaed up the glen	HOGG 5, 163
kilt: Cumbernauld in a kilt	T MORT 2, 258
English towerist with a kilt	MUNRO 7, 262
since he deprived us of the kilt	MACANT 1, 203
That's the reason noo I wear the kilt	LAUDER 4, 192
wiggle, wiggle-waggle o' the kilt	LAUDER 9, 192
kind: Be kind to your granny	PETRIE 4, 274
kindness: cup o' kindness yet / For auld lang syne	BURNS 66, 70
kindnesses: in a series of kindnesses there is at last one	BOSWEL 8, 54
king: A good king, evil used	R BLAIR(1) 1, 51
A prime king like a rat wes stang	T SCOTT 1, 289
At morne, ane king with sceptour	D LINDS 5, 195
Carle, now the King's come	SCOTT 80, 294
difference betwixt a lawfull good King and a usurping Tyrant	JAMES 6, 175
get to be a man and kill a king	CARNEG 10, 90
It was a' for our rightfu' King	BURNS 138, 75
Jist sit yersel doon and appoint yersel King	TRAD 80, 340
Law is King	RUTHER 6, 287
No bishop, no king	JAMES 16, 176
one king and one bloody frontier have gone	JACKS 4, 173
sa lang as the king is young	R LINDS 1, 196
Sawney, now the king's come	RODGER 1, 285
Sean Connery would become king of Scotland	HUSTON 1, 169
strangling the last king in the guts of the last priest	MITCHI 7, 252
The King doesn't care for Ewen	E CAMER 1, 80
The King ower the Water	ANON 28, 29
The king sits in Dumfermline town	BALLAD 37, 41
to live an exiled king	AYTOUN 6, 34
wha'll be king but Charlie?	NAIRNE 12, 265
Wha the deil hae we got for a king	CUNN 2, 104
kingdom: God's Kingdom among Boys	W A SMITH 1, 310
I see a Free and Independent Kingdom delivering up	BELHAV 1, 46
possession of his kingdom as you have of your coat	MAJOR(1) 3, 243
Scot on his unfurnish'd kingdom	SHAKES 1, 298
We were supposed to be a united kingdom	K MATHES 2, 247
kingdoms: Have I three kingdoms and thou must needs fly	JAMES 26, 176
kings: constantly withstand their kings, and as constantly	
succumb to their clergy	BUCKLE 1, 65
God gives not Kings the stile of *Gods* in vaine	JAMES 3, 175
Here lies the worst of kings	ROBERT 1, 283
If kings were just a harmless thing	W WILS 1, 351
Kings may be blest but Tam was glorious	BURNS 95, 72
Let kings and courtiers rise and fa	TRAD 65, 339
old Scots kings and dancing fairies	JAMIE 4, 176
we should all be as happy as kings	STEVEN 53, 321
where few kings and great folks come	RUTHER 7, 287
kirk: At Chrystis Kirk on the grene	ANON 11, 27
Calvin's kirk crowning the barren brae	E MUIR 19, 259
every severall Kirk have one School-maister	DISCIP(1) 3, 111
Girl under the dominion of the Kirk	KEATS 1, 183
gude auld Kirk o' Scotland	G MURRAY 1, 263
heid and onlie monarche in this kirk	DISCIP(2) 1, 111
Marie Hamilton's to the kirk gane	BALLAD 34, 41
not the Kirk that I will nourish	MARY(2) 1, 245
ready for the opening of the Kirk Bazaar	GORDON 2, 146
The Free kirk, the wee kirk	ANON 44, 30

The kirk, in a gale of psalms	GM BROWN 4, 61
Kirkcaddy: the next stop's Kirkcaddy	M SMITH 2, 309
Kirkconnell: where Helen lies, / On fair Kirkconnell lea	BALLAD 22, 40
kirkyaird: A' in the same kirkyaird	MURRAY 5, 262
Canongate kirkyaird in the failing year	GARIOC 4, 140
kirkyards: doctors and kirkyards would go out of fashion	HOGG 13, 163
Kirriemuir: The ball o Kirriemuir	TRAD 6, 333
kis: Johne, cum kis me now	GUDE 4, 152
kis and withe her go in grippis	DUNBAR 17, 119
So swete a kis yistrene	MONTGO 8, 254
kiss: Ae fond kiss, and then we sever	BURNS 105, 73
dawmned villain! does he kiss and tell!	COCKBU 15, 98
Dusty was the kiss / That I got frae the Miller	BURNS 68, 70
every Duchess in London will be wanting to kiss me	R MACDON 3, 215
Kneel, and kiss his gracious bum	RODGER 1, 285
The price was a kiss o' the mou	MACNEI 3, 237
wasn't a woman who betrayed Jesus with a kiss	CARSW 5, 91
kist: wantoning to the sound o' the kist fu' o' whistles	GALT 13, 139
kittle: Men, even the good ones, are kittle cattle	A BUCHAN 1, 63
knackered: I want everything to be knackered	IMLACH 2, 171
knackirs: Ghetto-makars, tae the knackirs'	CRAWFO 1, 102
knaves: braceless, breechless knaves	CUNN G. 2, 105
knawledge: knawledge maks big, luve biggs up	NEW TES 4, 266
knew: he knew so much, he realised how little	KELVIN 12, 184
knife: Lamkin's tane a sharp knife	BALLAD 30, 41
sharp knife-thrusts of understanding	MITCHI 21, 252
stark, sure creed that will cut like a knife	GIBBON 7, 143
knight: knight on a white charger is never going to come	GALLO 6, 138
knitted: Knitted Claymore	JACKS 5, 173
Knockhaspie: I wad gie a' Knockhaspie's land	BURNS 85, 72
knot: The Double Knot in the Peeny	J HENDR 3, 160
know: first to know, and then to utter	STEVEN 97, 324
forgot a great deal more than most other men know	MONBOD 5, 253
Know that the Lord is God indeed	METRIC 4, 249
my business to know what other people don't know	DOYLE 9, 116
knowes: Ca' the yowes to the knowes	PAGAN 2, 273
knowing: Decency is in *knowing* about what's happened	DUNN 13, 122
nothing worth knowing that can be taught	PETRIE 2, 274
knowledge: Documentary can achieve an intimacy of	
knowledge	GRIERS 4, 151
everything that is best in every department of human	
knowledge	REITH 3, 281
knowledge calculated to improve the human mind	J GRANT 2, 149
knowledge is an infinite progression	FRAZER 3, 137
Knowledge is power	J MURRAY 1, 263
Knowledge, which is the bugbear of tyranny	WRIGHT 2, 353
the fair fruit of knowledge	WRIGHT 7, 354
To take the highest apple / From the knowledge tree	RUNRIG 4, 287
knowlege: Conscience, Madam, requyres knowlege	KNOX 6, 188
Knox: John Knox in destination	SOUTAR 18, 314
Knox deaving us a' with his clavers	ELPHIN 1, 123
Let Scott thank John Knox	CARLYL 29, 86
the lengthened shadow of John Knox	SMILES 10, 304
was not Knox a traitor?	G MACLEO 7, 233
Whair is now Johne Knox his God?	MARY(1) 1, 245
knuckle-end: knuckle-end of England	S SMITH 5, 310
kow: a saddil upon the back of ane unrewly kow	KNOX 4, 188
krö: Hae we, or hae we no, a krö	B ANDERS 1, 25
Kwik-Fit: in love with a Kwik-Fit fitter	FARMER 1, 126
kye: Way way uppa kye	Da WILLIS 1, 350
woo a bonny lassie when the kye comes hame	HOGG 7, 163
Kyle: There was a lad was born in Kyle	BURNS 56, 70
labels: I don't find labels at all helpful	A SMITH 1, 306
labour: An infinitude of pains and labour	OLIPH 25, 271
division of labour	SMITH 4, 304
Every thing in the world is purchased by labour	HUME 23, 167
Go, labour on: spend and be spent	BONAR 2, 53
Labour . . . is the real measure	SMITH 6, 304
labour demands a kind of heroism	M OLIPH 1, 269
not by gold or by silver, but by labour	SMITH 7, 304
only thing is they all vote Labour	CARTL 1, 93
though I do not toil nor engage in dirty labour	MACANT 3, 203
true success is to labour	STEVEN 34, 320
labourer: right of the labourer to his hundred dollars	CARNEG 6, 90
labyrinth: a clue to the labyrinth	FRAZER 2, 137
I dreamt I was in the labyrinth	E MUIR 15, 259
lack: The emptiness. The human lack	BOLD 2, 52
the lack of a whole mind	E MUIR 8, 258

listen: listen for the small still voice of God — **M STUA 1**, 326
literary: literary and scientific education for women — **SOMERV 9**, 313
literate: To be so randy . . . and so literate — **S BAXT 6**, 46
literature: curse of Scottish literature — **E MUIR 8**, 258
  great Cham of Literature — **SMOLL 9**, 311
  lawyer without history or literature — **SCOTT 41**, 292
  Literature lay all puking and sprawling — **CARLYL 28**, 86
  one of the qualities of great literature — **BRIDIE 13**, 58
  People most distinguish'd for Literature in Europe — **HUME 27**, 167
  real literature can exist only when it's produced / By madmen — **MACDIA 55**, 213
  Scottish George Best of literature — **WELSH 6**, 348
  something in the literature of the sea — **MACLEOI 1**, 233
litheless: litheless the lair o' the mitherless bairn — **THOM 1**, 330
litill: gif I haif litill, I haif als litill to fear — **HENDER 1**, 160
litreachas: rud-eigin an litreachas na mara — **MACLEOI 1**, 233
live: a grand thing to get leave to live — **SHEPH 4**, 299
  All that is left, is to live lovingly — **CONN 2**, 99
  By leaves we live — **P GEDD 9**, 142
  Easy live and quiet die — **SCOTT 71**, 294
  find heart enough to begin to live — **STEVEN 32**, 320
  if to live / Is to be all one's possibilities — **MACCAI 7**, 205
  I like to live. I don't like to exist — **WATERST 1**, 345
  Learning to live and practising to die — **MACCAI 7**, 205
  live out of doors with the woman a man loves — **STEVEN 7**, 319
  live the time that a match flickers — **STEVEN 31**, 320
  no man fit to live that is not fit to die — **BALMER 1**, 42
  Trees live, and reign, in their own right — **N WELLS 3**, 347
  We eat to live but live to give — **RANSF 1**, 279
liver: Weans! They roast the heart an liver oot ye! — **E STEW 3**, 326
lives: Ca' them lives o' men — **NAIRNE 3**, 264
  Every one lives by selling — **STEVEN 78**, 323
  no fish ye're buying – it's men's lives — **SCOTT 50**, 293
  stalled lives never budge — **MORGAN 11**, 256
  We have small lives, easily lost — **AL KENNE 2**, 185
  will not leave me, the lives of other people — **DUNN 4**, 121
livin': A livin' man upon a deid man thinks — **MACDIA 29**, 211
living: believe that the living principle is never extinguished — **SOMERV 10**, 313
  By living we learn — **P GEDD 1**, 141
  expert in the art of living — **BRIDIE 7**, 58
  he poured the full violence of living — **CARSW 6**, 91
  life's for living — **REITH 2**, 281
  living, its mysteriousness and its absurdity — **E DAVIE 6**, 109
  Look to the living, love them — **DUNN 15**, 122
  Work, eh. What a stupid way to earn a living — **PATTIS 2**, 274
Lizie Lindsey: Will ye gang to the Hielands, Lizie Lindsey? — **BALLAD 32**, 41
loathsome: this loathsome Galley of the World — **W DRUM 9**, 117
lobby: does he stay in the lobby / like a hatstand? — **MACCAI 40**, 207
location: Drink's the king in oor location — **Ja HAMIL 3**, 156
loch: Between my feet a loch shines in the brown — **MACCAI 4**, 205
Lochaber: by Tummel and Loch Rannoch and Lochaber — **MACLEOI 3**, 234
  Fareweel to Lochaber — **A RAMS(1) 13**, 278
  return to Lochaber no more — **A RAMS(1) 13**, 278
Loch na Garr: steep frowning glories of dark Loch na Garr — **BYRON 2**, 75
Loch Hàstain: Gum beannaicheadh Dia bùrn Loch Hàstain — **MACCOD 1**, 208
Loch Hasten: May God bless the water of Loch Hasten — **MACCOD 1**, 208
Lochiel: Lochiel! beware of the day — **T CAMPB 5**, 81
Loch Inch: What ship is this on Loch Inch — **BARD 1**, 43
Loch Inse: Créad í an long-sa ar Loch Inse — **BARD 1**, 43
Lochinvar: young Lochinvar is come out of the west — **SCOTT 13**, 290
Lochlannaigh: Lochlannaigh is ármuinn iad — **ARTÚR 1**, 31
Loch Lomond: the bonnie, bonnie banks o' Loch Lomond — **TRAD 13**, 334
lochan: lochan fala clann nan daoine — **MACGIL 13**, 217
lochs: the lochs of the blood of the children of men — **MACGIL 13**, 217
lock: Lock the door, Lariston — **HOGG 3**, 163
locks: Your locks are like the snaw — **BURNS 86**, 72
locusts: he makes deserts as spectacularly as any horde of locusts — **FRAS D. 1**, 136
lodan: Mar easgann an lodan làthchadh — **TRAD 25**, 335
lo'ed: Better lo'ed ye canna be — **NAIRNE 13**, 265
logic: More ships have been lost by bad logic — **KELVIN 16**, 184
loingse: Fir arda ag eagar na loingse — **ARTÚR 1**, 31
lomnochd: 'se lomnochd ghrinn Leòdhais / a rinn obair mo chinn — **IC SMITH 12**, 307
London: effect which the instrument excited in London — **BREWST 2**, 58
  London is the devil's drawing-room — **SMOLL 5**, 311
  London – it is a damned place — **BYRON 31**, 77
  London licks the butter off our bread — **SCOTT 114**, 296

London! Pompous Ignorance sits enthroned there — **BRIDIE 4**, 58
London, that great cesspool — **DOYLE 1**, 116
London, thou art of townes *A per se* — **ANON 13**, 27
London, thou art the flour of Cities all — **ANON 13**, 27
lowest and vilest alleys in London — **DOYLE 10**, 116
man in London is not quite so good a creature — **GALT 7**, 139
Were all the strumpets in London received — **STEUAR 2**, 318
whipped cream of London society — **SCOTT 109**, 296
loneliness: human qualities that can apprehend loneliness — **SHEPH 8**, 299
  in order to avoid the loneliness of death — **KENNAW 6**, 185
  served by loneliness / as well as by family love — **MORGAN 2**, 255
lonely: count the beatings of the lonely heart — **FERRI 19**, 131
  to be lonely is largely one's own fault — **A BUCHAN 2**, 63
  You paint because you are lonely — **WALKER 1**, 345
long: Fágmaid ar an sruth síonach / an long dhona dhroichdhíonach — **BARD 2**, 43
  long is sgioba, long is sgioba — **HAY 2**, 158
long-fo-thuinn: Togaidh long-fo-thuinn a turraid — **MACGIL 29**, 219
long-sa: Créad í an long-sa ar Loch Inse — **BARD 1**, 43
longing: oh! but I'm longing for my ain folk — **TRAD 56**, 338
long-skirted: the long-skirted thirties — **IC SMITH 15**, 307
long-term: Really valuable research is a long-term affair — **A FLEM 2**, 133
look: Look to the living, love them — **DUNN 15**, 122
loon: Dibble them doon, the laird, the loon — **MURRAY 5**, 262
  I wadna be an orra loon — **MILNE 1**, 251
loose: a loose and unformed state of society — **LOCH 1**, 198
  no loose women would be found in the streets — **STEUAR 2**, 318
lord: And sae the Lord be thankit — **ANON 29**, 29
  But Lord, remember me and mine — **BURNS 15**, 67
  The Lord most hie, / I know, will be — **MONTGO 10**, 254
  The Lord's my shepherd, I'll not want — **METRIC 1**, 249
  this lord's station, who does not live in a garret — **BROUGH 2**, 60
  Unworthy war he suld be a lord or a maister — **G HAY 2**, 159
  Ye see yon birkie ca'd a lord — **BURNS 133**, 75
lordly: lordly piece of Self-consequence — **BURNS 82**, 71
lords: House of Lords is composed largely of descendants of successful pirates — **T JOHNST 4**, 179
  Some speiks of lords, some speiks of lairds — **BALLAD 24**, 40
  To the Lords of Convention — **SCOTT 116**, 296
lose: puts it not unto the Touch, / To win or lose it all — **MONTRO 2**, 254
loser: a loser and he knows it — **BOLD 4**, 53
lost: the cause is lost for ever — **SCOTT 86**, 295
  We have small lives, easily lost — **AL KENNE 2**, 185
Lothian: West Lothian Question — **DALYE 1**, 107
lottery: Adventure upon all the tickets in the lottery — **SMITH 8**, 304
  a perfectly fair lottery — **SMITH 8**, 304
lottery-ticket: from a lottery-ticket up to a passport to Paradise — **BYRON 23**, 77
loun: Sam, the lying loun — **R FERG 21**, 129
loup: My verra heart gangs loup, loup — **Ja SMITH 1**, 309
lourd: Lourd on my hert as winter — **MACDIA 24**, 211
lov'd: Had we never lov'd sae kindly — **BURNS 106**, 73
love: Alas for him whose sickness is love — **ISEAB 1**, 172
  All poetry's made by love — **IC SMITH 13**, 307
  And I lo'e Love / Wi' a scunner in't — **MACDIA 8**, 210
  a vehement bullet will come from the gun of Love — **MACGIL 26**, 219
  beds of married love — **MORGAN 3**, 255
  better forms of love than brain — **AYTON 3**, 34
  crops of love and hate — **E MUIR 18**, 259
  dish o' married love right soon grows cauld — **A RAMS(1) 8**, 277
  Faith, hope, love and lettuce — **WOOD 7**, 352
  False love, and hast thou play'd me thus — **SCOTT 31**, 291
  Flie whylome love, and it will folou thee — **MONTGO 4**, 254
  Has owning anything to do with love? — **MACCAI 19**, 206
  if we were of the buchan, it would love us — **E BUCHAN 2**, 63
  I loved thee once; I'll love no more — **AYTON 2**, 33
  I love you all — **SCHOL 1**, 288
  Iona of my heart, Iona of my love — **COLUMB 5**, 99
  Laughter o' love, and a welcoming there — **ROBERTO 6**, 283
  law cannot make two people continue to love — **J MACKAY 1**, 224
  Look to the living, love them — **DUNN 15**, 122
  love for the pleasure of loving — **KAMES 3**, 181
  Love/Emotion = embarrassment — **GALLO 1**, 138
  love better the rustle of the grass — **CUNN G. 3**, 105
  love fails, but art is forever — **OLIPH 8**, 270
  love his fellows before he loves their liberty — **JEFFR 6**, 177
  Love is a Stranger — **LENNOX 1**, 193
  Love is a very papithatick thing — **M FLEM 7**, 134

Love is the Alpha and the Omega of human enjoyment	**BURNS 74,** 71	Luve keeps nae nickstick	**NEW TES 5,** 266
Love makes buildings home	**DUFFY 2,** 118	My luve's in Germanie, send him hame	**MACNEI 4,** 237
love of solitude increases	**SCOTT 93,** 295	O my luve's like a red, red rose	**BURNS 130,** 74
Love's like a dizziness	**HOGG 18,** 164	The luve o' life's young day	**MOTHER 1,** 258
Love was our first undoing	**M STUA 8,** 327	To luve and to be wise	**A SCOTT(1) 3,** 288
Love – what is love?	**STEVEN 101,** 325	To luve unluvit is ane pane	**A SCOTT(1) 4,** 289
Man's love is of his life a thing apart	**BYRON 38,** 78	luvis: byde with her thou luvis best	**A SCOTT(1) 2,** 288
Marriage from love, like vinegar from wine	**BYRON 42,** 78	luxury: Civilisation bores me and luxury does not suit me	**WATERST 2,** 345
Men can and often *do* love their wives	**CARSW 17,** 92	luxury, and gaiety, and all the things you despise	**OLIPH 13,** 270
More than this I do not love you	**IC SMITH 9,** 307	luxury to blame ourselves for the mess we are in	**GRAY 9,** 150
My dear and only Love, I pray	**MONTRO 1,** 254	lycht: In obscure lycht, quhair mune may nocht be kend	**G DOUGL 4,** 114
my fair young love	**NIC FHE 1,** 266	Welcum the lord of lycht and lamp of day	**G DOUGL 9,** 115
My love, say you'll come with me	**DUNN 12,** 122	lyfe: Quhat is this lyfe bot ane straucht way to deid	**DUNBAR 19,** 119
My love, she's but a lassie yet	**BURNS 89,** 72	lying: improved somewhat my technique in lying	**BRIDIE 11,** 58
never been in love, or in hate	**STEVEN 15,** 319	lying, backbeiting, and slandering	**WODROW 1,** 351
No pure and noble-minded woman can long love	**M REID 2,** 280	lyon: Lyon roares to catch us as his pray	**E MELV 1,** 248
O Love that wilt not let me go	**G MATHES 1,** 246	lyoun: O lamit lyoun, liggand heir sa law	**HENRYS 7,** 160
Once in a lifetime / You live and love	**RUNRIG 3,** 286	lyric: Better a'e gowden lyric / Than a social problem solved	**MACDIA 27,** 211
only love can save the world	**A NEILL 8,** 266	MA: And you an MA!	**BARRIE 2,** 43
O waly, waly, gin love be bonnie	**TRAD 78,** 340	Mac: our new Sheriff be no 'Gael' nor 'Mac'	**SELLAR 1,** 297
rivers that are more to me than love	**N WELLS 1,** 347	Mac-alla: Tha Mac-alla fo ghruaim	**CLARS 1,** 95
served by loneliness / as well as by family love	**MORGAN 2,** 255	macaroni: Daft gowk, in macaroni dress	**R FERG 17,** 129
So faithful in love	**SCOTT 13,** 290	MacBrayne: And they are all MacBrayne's	**ANON 49,** 30
So long as we love we serve	**STEVEN 98,** 324	end of the world is near when the MacBrayne's ship	**IC SMITH 27,** 308
some are fou o' love divine	**BURNS 13,** 67	McBride: For Willie McBride it all happened again	**BOGLE 2,** 52
Strange is the love you have for your children	**E MACCOL 6,** 209	MacCrimmon: no more MacCrimmon	**TRAD 53,** 338
that I might not sing of Love	**SCOTT 4,** 290	MacDiarmid: haud forrit MacDiarmid	**V GRIEV 2,** 152
the natural love of your native cuntre	**COMPL 1,** 99	MacFoozle: They dinna libb MacFoozle	**YOUNG 1,** 355
This love will I freely sing	**JH MACKAY 1,** 224	MacGill-Eain: Iain mór MacGill-Eain, / ceann is fèitheam ar	
Thou shamrock of love	**CARMIN 3,** 89	sgeula	**MACGIL 11,** 217
Three things come without asking: fear, jealousy and love	**ANON 22,** 28	machaire: Shiùbhlainn machaire fada réidh leat	**TRAD 28,** 335
Tobacco is like love	**HUME 2,** 168	machine: a jet engine, a bit of a machine is beautiful	**PAOLO 3,** 273
To love the beast they cannot tame	**SOUTAR 15,** 314	attitude towards the machine	**PAOLO 2,** 273
violence masquerading as love	**LAING 3,** 190	Either be a machine and see nothing but 'phenomena'	**MAXWEL 5,** 247
What love he must have lost	**IC SMITH 16,** 307	machine for converting the Heathen	**CARLYL 9,** 85
loved: I once loved a lad, and I loved him sae weel	**TRAD 43,** 337	machinery: merely the fingers of uncanny machinery	**H MORT 8,** 257
lovelier: never saw a lovelier or more romantic spot	**VICTO 5,** 344	the Age of Machinery	**CARLYL 7,** 85
lovely: a lovely place, only spoiled by the people	**SWAN 1,** 327	Maclean: *Dominie, Dominie, / There was nane like John*	
How lovely is thy dwelling-place	**METRIC 3,** 249	*Maclean*	**MCGINN 4,** 219
lover: I saw my lover and he did not recognise me yesterday	**TRAD 29,** 336	great John Maclean, / the top and hem of our story	**MACGIL 11,** 217
no real lady would make her lover talk about his wife	**BRIDIE 5,** 58	great John Maclean has come hame tae the Clyde	**HENDER 8,** 159
lovers: Friends and lovers are the most important	**J HAYN 1,** 159	To the wedding of Shon Maclean	**R BUCHANA 2,** 65
loves: live out of doors with the woman a man loves	**STEVEN 7,** 319	MacLeod: Why did he leave the Land of MacLeod	**MACGIL 27,** 219
loving: by loving, and not by being loved	**Ge MACDON 2,** 214	Macmillan: who else should I believe in? Macmillan?	
lovingly: All that is left, is to live lovingly	**CONN 2,** 99	Khrushchev?	**S WILS 2,** 351
lowland: soft lowland tongue o' the Borders	**SANDER 1,** 288	MacVittie: taking tea at MacVittie's	**SPARK 12,** 315
Lowlander: Lowlander feels himself the sentimental		mad: half of the nation is mad	**SMOLL 10,** 311
countryman of the Highlander	**STEVEN 71,** 323	If you're poor you're plain mad	**KESSON 3,** 187
Lowlands: clasps Highlands and Lowlands together	**SMITH 10,** 306	mad wi' drink and whoring	**BURNS 43,** 69
He was the first to play this melody for the Lowlands	**MACKIN 3,** 227	Some deemed him wondrous wise, and some believed him	
I find the humdrum lowlands interesting enough	**CAMPB-B. 2,** 82	mad	**Ja BEAT 1,** 46
the Gael's exultant cry / coming from the chest of the		The world outside us can't be mad	**MACMUR 1,** 235
Lowlands	**MACTHO 19,** 241	What doe you thinke? The man was mad	**AYTON 1,** 33
lownging: lownging and dozing, which I call thinking	**HUME 30,** 168	maddened: maddened by swarms of midges	**F BALF 5,** 39
loxogonospherical: loxogonospherical triangles	**T URQU 1,** 343	madman: pretty certain that I had to deal with a madman	**J BUCHAN 1,** 63
luach: an luach a th'ac' ga stòraigeadh / *each one for himself*	**M NICGU 3,** 267	madmen: real literature can exist only when it's produced /	
luaidh: A sheamarag mo luaidh	**CARMIN 13,** 89	By madmen	**MACDIA 55,** 213
lùb: Coisich a rùin, lùb nan geal làmh	**TRAD 31,** 336	madness: Madness need not be all breakdown	**LAING 4,** 190
lucidity: rocky road to lucidity	**MACCAI 41,** 207	Maggie: Are ye sleepin, Maggie?	**TANNAH 6,** 329
luck: there's nae luck about the house	**Je ADAM 2,** 23	bonnie Maggie Lauder	**F SEMP 1,** 298
luely: O luely, luely cam she in	**SOUTAR 7,** 313	magic: It's magic being abroad	**PATTIS 5,** 274
lufe: tak gude heid about / Quhome that ye lufe	**HENRYS 13,** 161	magic is not science	**MCNEI 5,** 237
luferay: My luferay salbe reid, blew, and grene	**D LINDS 10,** 195	Magic is not religion	**MCNEI 5,** 237
lug: Dost thou say mass at my lug	**J GEDD 1,** 141	Proper, sheer, naked, magic	**HIGGIN 1,** 162
lum hat: lum hat wantin' the croon	**RORIE 2,** 285	magician: magician who has rolled back the current of time	**MEAD(2) 1,** 248
lungs: daungerous to the Lungs	**JAMES 15,** 176	magnifico: *omne ignotum pro magnifico est*	**GALGAC 1,** 138
lungs for urban industrial populations	**FRAS D. 4,** 136	magnified: everything unknown is magnified	**GALGAC 1,** 138
Tar-filled lungs	**MUNRO 1,** 262	Magritte: I fyles chant Buddhist mantras / An read René	
wonderful lungs of leather	**R BUCHANA 3,** 65	Magritte	**BLACKH 5,** 50
Lunnon: naebody's nails can reach the length o' Lunnon	**SCOTT 66,** 293	magryme: So sair the magryme dois me menyie	**DUNBAR 24,** 120
lust: Lust is as international as Glasgow itself	**MACTHO 24,** 242	Mag Uidhir: Mag Uidhir as mion meanma	**GIOL Cr 1,** 144
lute: Sound hoarse sad Lute, true Witnesse of my Woe	**W DRUM 2,** 117	Maguire: Maguire of paltry spirit	**GIOL Cr 1,** 144
With lute in hand, syne, sweitlie	**D LINDS 1,** 194	Mahoun: ilka wife cries, 'Auld Mahoun'	**BURNS 111,** 73
luve: And trew luve rysis fro the splene	**DUNBAR 20,** 119	maid: A weary lot is thine, fair maid	**SCOTT 29,** 291
knawledge maks big, luve biggs up	**NEW TES 4,** 266	Don't grow up to be a nervous old maid	**SLESS 9,** 303
latna our luve be frae the teeth outwith	**NEW TES 6,** 266	If I dee an auld maid in a garret	**TRAD 3,** 333
Luve gi'es wi' a lauch an' a sang	**ANGUS 3,** 25	two inferior members, a maid and a cat	**HUME 25,** 167
Luve is ane fervent fire	**A SCOTT(1) 3,** 288	worse things than being an auld maid	**MORRIS 2,** 256

My Mary's asleep by the murmuring stream — BURNS **77**, 71
my sweet Highland Mary — BURNS **115**, 73
we shall have Mary in a strait jacket — SOMERV **5**, 312
Ye are na Mary Morison — BURNS **124**, 74
mason: Lamkin was a mason good — BALLAD **28**, 41
  merely in the disguise of a mason — MILLER **5**, 250
masquerade: 'Tis but / The truth in masquerade — BYRON **49**, 78
mass: Dost thou say mass at my lug — J GEDD **1**, 141
  Mass shall encounter mass / Of shuddering human flesh — Jo DAVID(2) **5**, 108
massacre: a 'bloody massacre' — CUNN G. **2**, 105
  the title-deeds are rapine, murder, massacre — T JOHNST **4**, 179
  We massacre every town tree — COCKBU **16**, 98
mast: And bends the gallant mast, my boys — CUNN **1**, 104
masts: masts, / Silent as pines — SMITH **3**, 305
match: live the time that a match flickers — STEVEN **31**, 320
matches: I have to have a box of matches — HOME **1**, 164
material: not finally judge one another by material standards — W MCILV **9**, 223
  our best and most valuable raw material — ATHOLL **1**, 33
mates: ye never sell yer mates — W MCILV **3**, 223
màthair: 'S tu màthair àigh nan reul — CARMIN **4**, 88
mathas: Mathas sùla dhuit, / Mathas ùidhe dhuit — CARMIN **4**, 88
mathematics: art of reading mathematics is judicious skipping — KELVIN **20**, 185
  Mathematics is the only true metaphysics — KELVIN **18**, 185
Matilda: The Band Played Waltzing Matilda — BOGLE **1**, 52
matter: David Hume could Mind and Matter — NEAVES **4**, 265
  Dead matter cannot become living — KELVIN **6**, 184
  Energy is as real and indestructible as *Matter* — KELVIN **4**, 184
  make an end of Mind and Matter — NEAVES **3**, 265
  More matter, fewer words — MONBOD **2**, 253
  only laws of mind are fabricated for it by matter — MAXWEL **4**, 247
mavis: The mavis sings fu' cheerie, O — TANNAH **4**, 329
  When the mavis and merle are singing — SCOTT **27**, 291
Maxwellton: Maxwellton braes are bonnie — SPOTT **1**, 316
Maxwelton: Maxwelton banks are bonnie — W DOUGL **1**, 115
May: Worschippe, ye that loveris bene, this May — JAMES I **4**, 174
may: O may she comes — BALLAD **9**, 39
  There ance was a may, and she loo'd na men — G BAILL **1**, 35
mayhem: There is mayhem in my smile — LOCHH **6**, 199
meal: Plenty herring, plenty meal — ROBERTO **3**, 283
mean: create Edens in the heart of mean streets — M MCMIL **6**, 235
  If folk think I'm mean — LAUDER **12**, 193
  Small and mean though this place is — COLUMB **3**, 99
  The legend that Scots are mean — S BAXT **1**, 45
meanings: Once meanings get loose, kids pick them up — MITCHI **27**, 253
meanma: Mag Uidhir as mion meanma — GIOL Cr **1**, 144
meanness: land of meanness, sophistry and mist — BYRON **9**, 76
means: The Girls of Slender Means — SPARK **10**, 315
mearachd: taibhs' gach mearachd, taibhs' gach cionta — IC SMITH **5**, 306
Mearns: Lit a fire in the Mearns — CRUICK **2**, 104
measail: a chionn 's gu robh mi measail air — BATE **1**, 45
measure: Labour... is the real measure — SMITH **6**, 304
  measure what you are speaking about — KELVIN **7**, 184
meat: Some hae meat and canna eat — ANON **29**, 29
mechanical: If I can make a mechanical model I can understand — KELVIN **8**, 184
  man's / insolent mechanical ignorance — JACKS **8**, 173
  Men are grown mechanical in head and in heart — CARLYL **10**, 85
  the angel of mechanical destruction — COCKBU **6**, 97
meddle: Don't meddle with other people's ideas — MACKINT **7**, 229
  Not to meddle with my toys — STEVEN **50**, 321
  Wha daur meddle wi me? — ANON **56**, 30
medicine: nursing profession is to medicine — WATT **9**, 346
mediocre: heights of the applauded mediocre — J CAMER **8**, 80
  pocket wisdom is conceived for the use of mediocre people — STEVEN **24**, 320
mediocrity: corrected into mediocrity — SCOTT **99**, 295
  Mediocrity knows nothing higher than itself — DOYLE **15**, 116
  terrified of the celebration of mediocrity — M GRAY **2**, 150
  the safe walls of mediocrity — SOUTAR **4**, 313
  used to blame the English for our mediocrity — GRAY **10**, 150
mediterraneanise: do well to *mediterraneanise* ourselves — N DOUGL **1**, 115
meet: I hope, Madam, we shall meet in St James's yet — C STEW **7**, 326
  We'll meet nae mair at sunset — SPOTT **2**, 316
megalomaniac: a megalomaniac in every parish — GD BROWN **5**, 60
megalosaurs: The planets lift their bones / and roar like megalosaurs — MORGAN **13**, 256
meic Uí Mhoichéirghe: Meic Uí Mhoichéirghe, lá samhraidh / iarras gréin — GIOL Co **2**, 144

meit: To tender meit my stomok is ay usit — HENRYS **3**, 160
melancholy: Celtic races, with their melancholy and unprogressiveness — ARNOLD **2**, 31
  that pass is the most dreary and melancholy — MACAUL **1**, 204
mellow: Mellow Yellow — DONOV **2**, 114
melody: He was the first to play this melody for the Lowlands — MACKINN **3**, 227
  that saft-tongu'd melody / Which now lies dead — R FERG **7**, 128
  your life will make melody — SLESS **9**, 303
Melrose: If thou wouldst view fair Melrose — SCOTT **3**, 290
member: a profitable member within the same — MARY(2) **2**, 245
memorable: sentences are memorable on account of some single irradiating word — SMITH **5**, 305
memories: like handkerchiefs in our memories — IC SMITH **20**, 308
  memories of suffering and cruelty — M MCMIL **7**, 235
memory: big music in the memory — MACTHO **22**, 242
  great wealth of memory — LINKLA **2**, 197
  human without a memory is a helpless victim — GAUGH **2**, 141
  it wasn't history but memory / great mary macpherson — MACNEA **4**, 236
  man's real possession is his memory — SMITH **9**, 306
  Memory. A bastard really — GALLO **3**, 138
  use of art to memory — WILKIE **7**, 350
men: a fondness for young men in uniform — F URQU **3**, 343
  Ca' them lives o' men — NAIRNE **3**, 264
  Civilisation is the womanisation of brave men — T JOHNST **7**, 180
  create men or destroy them — W MUIR **2**, 260
  Dissim'lar men, but sim'lar minds — TENNAN **5**, 330
  Hamish stokes young men's dreams — MARRA **5**, 244
  If old men will marry young women — E GRANT(2) **8**, 149
  Let us arise and go like men — STEVEN **56**, 322
  Men are grown mechanical in head and in heart — CARLYL **10**, 85
  Men are never so good or so bad — MACKINT **6**, 229
  Men can and often *do* love their wives — CARSW **17**, 92
  Men do not know / What Age says to a woman — M STUA **7**, 327
  Men, even the good ones, are kittle cattle — A BUCHAN **1**, 63
  men, / going about invisible concerns — MORGAN **15**, 256
  men, in all other ways admirable — CARSW **18**, 92
  men in Windsor are not lofty specimens — OLIPH **6**, 270
  Men Talk — LOCHH **13**, 199
  men than whom the rocks were not harder — GIOL Co **4**, 144
  Men / Think First, Speak Later — LOCHH **14**, 199
  Men were simply victims of their own appetites — H KENNE **1**, 186
  Men will ever rise or fall — WRIGHT **9**, 354
  mountains that are more to me than men — N WELLS **1**, 347
  Sheep shall eat men — BRAHAN **2**, 56
  Some men are born to feast — J BAILL **2**, 35
  The best-laid schemes o' mice an' men — BURNS **18**, 67
  We all end up yesterday's men — STEIN **6**, 318
  We don't only build ships, we build men — J REID **3**, 280
  women are not behind any more than Scottish men — LADY'S **1**, 190
mended: mended now in a day — JAMES **18**, 176
mental: kept, like her, in a mental greenhouse — OLIPH **20**, 271
merchant: a tenement or a merchant's ha' — LOCHH **17**, 200
mercury: we walk / on mercury from birth to death — MORGAN **2**, 256
mercy: a landscape without mercy — H MORT **5**, 257
  at the mercy of the puddles — SMITH **6**, 305
  Lord have mercy on my poor country — FLETCH **4**, 134
  Thai ask mercy but nocht at yow — BARBOU **5**, 43
  Yon folk knelis till ask mercy — BARBOU **5**, 43
merit: no merit in many of my favourite tunes — BURNS **127**, 74
merle: When the mavis and merle are singing — SCOTT **27**, 291
merrie: No one in his wildest fits of patriotism ever talked of Merrie Scotland — CUNN G. **5**, 105
merry: Merry it is in the good greenwood — SCOTT **27**, 291
  plain man will, no doubt, be apt to think him merry — T REID **4**, 281
mess: looked at the mess in the morning — BROOKS **6**, 59
  Mull, 'the colonels' mess' — MITCHI **23**, 253
messe: One Messe.... was more fearful — KNOX **5**, 188
messenger: who knows but this messenger may come upon us — ROB DON **1**, 282
messing: messing about in boats — K GRAH **1**, 147
metaphor: a metaphor for their desperation — H MCILV **5**, 222
  Presbyterian faith is an incomparable metaphor — ASCHER **4**, 32
metaphysic: with metaphysic hand / Lift the farm like a lid — MACCAI **3**, 205
metaphysical: hum of metaphysical divinity — STEVEN **70**, 322
  racial aptitude for metaphysical — MCCANC **1**, 207
metaphysics: Mathematics is the only true metaphysics — KELVIN **18**, 185
  visitors to Scotland without a taste for metaphysics — G DAVIE **5**, 109

Moderatism: You don't know what Moderatism is — MCCHEY 1, 208
modernism: Modernism is the acceptance of the concrete — PAOLO 1, 273
modesty: mingle impudence on the hustings with modesty on the back benches — C MACKEN 3, 225
Not good is a woman without modesty — MACDHU 2, 209
She just wore / Enough for modesty – no more — R BUCHANA 1, 65
throw off all modesty — ESKGR 1, 124
mollifying: mollifying influence of an enfeebling potion — STATIS 4, 317
moment: no better moment in a man's life — A WELLS 1, 347
monaidhean: Muile nam monaidhean farsaing — CAIMB 1, 79
monarche: heid and onlie monarche in this kirk — DISCIP(2) 1, 111
monarchie: no other Sway / But purest Monarchie — MONTRO 1, 254
monetarist: monetarist culture has driven out God in favour of Mammon — WATERS 1, 345
money: gave money away as silently as a waiter falling — CONNOL 7, 100
If the money raised be more beneficially employed — STEUAR 3, 318
licence to print your own money — R THOMS 1, 332
making money may keep man from carnal mischief — G SCOTT-M 1, 297
Money . . . is none of the wheels of trade — HUME 12, 166
more money as a professional invalid — IMLACH 3, 171
Of lairds and money and sheep — MITCHI 20, 252
What's money to God? — SLESS 6, 303
Where the money is, there will the blayguards — JACOB 1, 173
moneybag: Aristocracy of the Moneybag — CARLYL 24, 86
mongol: the mongol quine / collogues / wi hersel — MACKIE 3, 227
monkish: that monkish rabble — BUCKLE 4, 66
monologue: Prayer is not a monologue — BARCLA 1, 43
monstrosity: new Dundee was an interesting monstrosity — THERO 3, 330
monstrous: beautiful, in its monstrous way — J CAMER 4, 80
monstrous regiment of the damned bomb — G MACLEO 7, 233
Montagu: Adieu, adieu, Monsure Montagu — BLACK Ag 1, 49
Montgomery: Come gie's a sang, Montgomery cry'd — SKINN 2, 302
monument: monument of the pre-Reformation spirit is cathedrals — F MACCOL 1, 209
monuments: monuments of cruelty — SMOLL 1, 310
mool: Robert Burns knelt and kissed the mool — GARIOC 5, 140
mools: Weel aff are they aneath the mools — MACTAG 3, 239
moon: Beneath the moon's unclouded light — BURNS 31, 68
Hail to thee, thou new moon — CARMIN 6, 88
her face was like the moon — CARLYL 1, 82
I saw the new moon late yestreen — BALLAD 39, 41
I will put a handle on the sickle of the moon — MACGIL 20, 218
just the full moon and a stray cat — WHITE 4, 348
moon and the stars were the gifts you gave — E MACCOL 2, 208
now nobody wants the moon — GRAY 11, 150
the moon will be as if blood had been spilt on her — BOTHCH 4, 55
The buttered bannock of the moon — GM BROWN 4, 61
Under the Ullapool moon — MARRA 3, 244
you saw the Whole of the Moon — M SCOTT 1, 289
moon-chained: the sea passionate, / Moon-chained — M STUA 3, 327
moonfuck: got rich by selling a quick moonfuck — GRAY 11, 150
moonlight: visit it by the pale moonlight — SCOTT 5, 290
moor: long unbroken moor, / sanctuary of deer — MACANT 7, 204
we may not wander the moor or shore — MAIRI 4, 243
Yesterday I was on the moor — MACANT 4, 204
moorcock: The moorcock springs on whirring wings — BURNS 30, 68
moorland: this was just a moorland and I had only a spade — 1H FINL 13, 132
moors: Mull of the spacious moors — CAIMB 1, 79
moral: fatty degeneration of his moral being — STEVEN 13, 319
grandest moral attribute of a Scotsman — BARRIE 12, 44
Moral conduct *is* beautiful — MACMUR 3, 235
Self-realisation is the true moral ideal — MACMUR 5, 235
Such moral culture is no slight art — KAMES 10, 181
moralist: Scotchman must be a very sturdy moralist — JOHNS 8, 178
morality: Morality of every Religion was bad — HUME 35, 168
morals: If your morals make you dreary — STEVEN 79, 323
morne: At morne, ane king with sceptour — D LINDS 5, 195
mornin': nice to get up in the mornin' — LAUDER 8, 192
Up in the mornin' early — Jo HAMIL(2) 1, 156
morning: Listen. Put on morning — WS GRAH 2, 147
looked at the mess in the morning — BROOKS 6, 59
Up in the morning's no for me — BURNS 57, 70
Morrison's: no Morrison's Pill for curing the maladies of Society — CARLYL 46, 87
morsall: sweatt morsall for the Devillis mouth — KNOX 11, 188
mortal: indifference is a mortal sign for the country — BOSWEL 7, 54
take perhaps more a man's view of mortal affairs — OLIPH 22, 271
mortar: never sacrificing mortar to foliage — COCKBU 16, 98

mother: Doesn't get tense, my mother, just can't park the car — S MACDON 4, 215
I see our Ancient Mother Caledonia — BELHAV 2, 46
Mother Glasgow's succour is perpetual — MARRA 2, 244
My mother bids me bind my hair — HUNTER 1, 168
Oh, mother, mother, mak my bed — BALLAD 2, 39
Old Mother Riley at the pawnshop door — BAIRN 13, 37
Thou art the glorious mother of the stars — CARMIN 8, 88
mother-in-law: untutored savage contemplates his mother-in-law — FRAZER 1, 137
motherless: he left us like motherless lambs — MACANT 6, 204
Motherwell: Airdrie and Motherwell are the most improbable places — E MUIR 1, 258
motion: The poetry of motion — K GRAH 2, 147
motto: 'Casting Out Fear' ought to be the motto — A NEILL 4, 265
mou': Her teethless mou' was like a bell — MURRAY 4, 262
Mound: Sermon on the Mound — L KENNED 2, 186
mountain: He is gone on the mountain — SCOTT 25, 291
it is an excellent mountain — WORDS 4, 353
Land of the mountain and the flood — SCOTT 8, 290
Like the dew on the mountain — SCOTT 26, 291
more to a mountain than the cairn on top of it — MACCAI 35, 207
robes the mountain in its azure hue — T CAMPB 2, 81
the mountain, which I little thought / would suffer transformation — MACANT 4, 204
why the Buddhist goes on pilgrimage to a mountain — SHEPH 10, 300
wild mountain thyme — TANNAH 2, 329
You remember your first mountain — M GRAY 1, 150
mountains: Caledonia! belov'd are thy mountains — BYRON 1, 75
going to the mountains is going home — J MUIR 6, 259
Having been bred amongst mountains — HOGG 1, 163
High mountains are a feeling — BYRON 15, 76
mountains are fountains of men — J MUIR 3, 259
mountains faa like stour — SG SMITH 7, 310
mountains that are more to me than men — N WELLS 1, 347
silence of people looking at stars or mountains — E DAVIE 3, 109
mountain-storm: In war the mountain-storm — Ja MACPHE 2, 238
mourn: Mourn, hapless Caledonia — SMOLL 1, 310
mouth: My faded mouth will never flower again — M STUA 6, 327
so sour you could have hung a jug on her mouth — WATT 1, 346
stopped my mouth and dung out several of my teeth — GRANGE 1, 147
The honourable mouth that condemned you — HAY 5, 158
mouthis: The sugurit mouthis with myndis thairfra — DUNBAR 23, 120
mouthless: millions of the mouthless dead — SORLEY 3, 313
move: great affair is to move — STEVEN 5, 319
movement: Criticism is good for a movement — G MACLEO 3, 232
'Movement' is meant to express — J/R ADAM 1, 23
Mozart: Mozart takes me to the Milky Way — CARSW 11, 92
muck-fork: fine gentleman whose father toils with a muck-fork — CROSL 1, 103
muckin': muckin' o' Geordie's byre — BALLAD 36, 41
muckle: An' him wi' sae muckle to dee — MURRAY 7, 262
Common-Ridin' day in the Muckle Toon — MACDIA 16, 210
Muckle he made o' that; he was hanget — BRAXF 4, 57
mucky-mucks: whole gang of high mucky-mucks, famous fatheads — MACDIA 45, 212
mud: Germany wallowing in a viler mud than the Middle Ages — J BUCHAN 10, 64
muddy: muddy cough of the stream that strives — M STUA 4, 327
mudge: spachial kind of mudge in Dervaig — MUNRO 6, 261
Muhammad Ali: Like Muhammad Ali – you're the greatest — V GRIEV 2, 152
Muile: Muile nam monaidhean farsaing — CAIMB 1, 79
muir: muir is misneach, muir is misneach — HAY 2, 158
Tha am muir an nochd mar shanas-reice — IC SMITH 11, 307
muir: Owre the muir amang the heather — J GLOV 1, 145
Mull: Mull of the spacious moors — CAIMB 1, 79
Mull, 'the colonels' mess' — MITCHI 23, 253
multitude: Multitude of the skies — MACGIL 4, 216
Papacy in a multitude may be as dangerous — CHARL I 2, 94
multitudes: We have multitudes of perceptions — HUTCH 3, 169
munadh: Munadh fada rèidh, / Cuilidh 'm faighte fèidh — MACANT 7, 204
mune: An' the mūne was shinin' clearly — STEVEN 68, 322
by the lee licht o' the mune — SPOTT 2, 316
In obscure lycht, quhair mune may nocht be kend — G DOUGL 4, 114
Mungo: I dreamt I took a dander with St Mungo — MARRA 2, 244
Mungo catched herrings in the Clyde — SCOTT 60, 293
Munich: Chamberlain was right at Munich — HOME 5, 165
Munich has not brought appeasement — ATHOLL 5, 33
murder: I call it murder — MAXTON 3, 247

Killing No Murder	HARDIE 4, 158	Such a parcel of rogues in a nation	BURNS 119, 73
the title-deeds are rapine, murder, massacre	T JOHNST 4, 179	this the historical nation	HUME 31, 168
murdering: that ugly humour of murdering	SCOTT 88, 295	**national:** Golf has ceased to be a peculiarly national game	F BALF 6, 38
murders: violent tale of murders, feuds and tribal revenge	DALYE 4, 107	less cosmopolitan and rather more national in our	
Murrayfield: more intellectual honesty at Murrayfield than		Architecture	MACKINT 2, 228
at a Burns Supper	GARIOC 8, 140	National identity grows from the stories	R WATSON 1, 346
muse: By far my elder brother in the Muse	BURNS 52, 69	National Theatre of Scotland is Pantomime	CASSON 1, 93
My Muse, tho' hamely in attire	BURNS 10, 67	too much to drink – The national excuse	ROSE 5, 286
The muse has felled me in this bed	WS GRAH 4, 147	**nationalism:** enemies of Scottish nationalism are not the	
muses: this Parnassus and bosom of the Muses	G MACKEN 6, 226	English	CUNN G. 11, 106
mushroom: soon make a mushroom o' ye	CORRIE 2, 101	my feminism is deeper in me than, say, nationalism	MITCHI 10, 252
music: animated only when dance music or jazz is played	HOUSE 2, 165	nationalism is on the whole good for people	MITCHI 8, 252
armoury from which no growing music will come	IC SMITH 3, 306	the best kind of nationalism	A MCLEL 1, 231
big music in the memory	MACTHO 22, 242	**nationalist:** every Scotsman should be a Scottish Nationalist	J BUCHAN 7, 64
harmony is now no more, / And music dead	R FERG 6, 128	**nationality:** if your nationality is the strongest suit you can	
If fiddling is music, that is enough	CLARS 5, 96	play	CONNOL 12, 100
I was the wrong music / The wrong guest	O FRAS 2, 136	I stand for nationality	LAUDER 10, 192
listen to Scottish Dance Music as I am immune	IC SMITH 28, 309	**nations:** League of Nations grows in moral courage	R MACDON 1, 215
my taste in Music must be inelegant & vulgar	BURNS 127, 74	there is nocht twa nations undir the firmament	COMPL 3, 99
She was skilled in music and the dance	ANGUS 1, 25	**native:** my foot is on my native heath	SCOTT 62, 293
the howling rhapsodies of the music halls	FORD 1, 134	This is my own, my native land	SCOTT 7, 290
Their music knows no detour	MENUH 1, 249	**natives:** a heart for the bare legs of the natives	MENDEL 1, 248
The music of the sea was in my ears	IC SMITH 19, 308	betrayal of our trusteeship to hand over natives	ATHOLL 3, 33
The music on which my choice has most fallen	DEAN 2, 110	**NATO:** Under Plato or NATO	RANSF 1, 279
TO APOLLO. / HIS MUSIC. HIS MISSILES	IH FINL 17, 132	**natty:** Natty in tattersall	LOCHH 8, 199
two types of music: rock and roll	HARVEY 1, 158	**natural:** natural outcome of a civilised society	BARRIE 4, 44
musike: musike sall pereische in this land	WODE 2, 351	whatever is natural is right	BARRIE 4, 44
mute: mute hound that bites the hardest	DOYLE 14, 116	**nature:** A barren soil where Nature's germs	BYRON 9, 76
mutton: Mutton old and claret good	NEAVES 5, 265	aim of exact science is to reduce the problems of nature	MAXWEL 1, 247
mydding: covet the mydding and not the skyis	LESLIE 1, 194	bound by the laws of God and nature to help	GALT 19, 140
mynd: a proud mynd, a crafty witt, and ane indurat hearte	KNOX 7, 188	genuine, unsophisticated nature	CARLYL 10, 83
myrmidons: faggots of legal myrmidons	J ROBERTSO(2) 2, 284	Gie me ae spark o' Nature's fire	BURNS 10, 67
myrth: Now leiff thy myrth	BLIND 1, 51	his nature within me als cold as spring-well-water	BREAD 1, 57
mysteries: He read mysteries and distributed the Scriptures		If honest Nature made you fools	BURNS 8, 67
among the schools	DALLAN 1, 107	I love not Man the less, but Nature more	BYRON 20, 77
mysterious: crime which is of all others the most		Mute Nature mourns her worshipper	SCOTT 6, 290
mysterious	G MACKEN 5, 225	nature in her awful simplicity	A COCKBU 2, 97
more bizarre a thing is the less mysterious	DOYLE 7, 116	Nature's workshops	J MUIR 3, 259
When you call a thing mysterious	KELVIN 17, 184	Set the child observing Nature	P GEDD 10, 142
mysteriousness: living, its mysteriousness and its absurdity	E DAVIE 6, 109	We war with rude Nature	CARLYL 8, 85
mystery: mystery and miracle of the creation	KELVIN 13, 184	wilful convulsion of brute nature	STEVEN 96, 324
mystery of radium, no doubt we shall solve it	KELVIN 15, 184	*Navarone:* in the ceilidh house reading *The Guns of*	
myth: A land without myth	G BRUCE 3, 62	*Navarone*	IC SMITH 28, 309
prefer the romantic myth to the complicated truth	DALYE 3, 107	**navel-string:** the navel-string of life	LINKLA 3, 197
nae-users: bunch o nae-users	J STUA 1, 326	**neanderthal:** Their neanderthal brains will just explode	MUNRO 3, 262
nag: Patience is a good nag	SCOTT 103, 296	**neapaigearan:** mar neapaigearan 'nar cuimhne	IC SMITH 20, 308
nail: ca'ing a nail intil the timber hip o' the Virgin Mary	GALT 18, 139	**neart:** Neart a' bhradain as braise leumas	ANON 21, 28
nails: naebody's nails can reach the length o' Lunnon	SCOTT 66, 293	**necessary:** a necessary minimum	Jo SMITH 3, 309
The golden hands with the almond nails	LOCHH 1, 198	**necessity:** constitutionalists have to give way before human	
náireach: Ní math bean gan bheith náireach	MACDHU 2, 209	necessity	MAXTON 1, 247
naitural: pardon the rest o us for juist bidin naitural	R MCLEL 5, 231	damning necessity of studying Selfishness	BURNS 80, 71
naked: A fine woman seen naked once	KAMES 4, 181	necessity which made me a quarrier that taught me to be a	
Proper, sheer, naked, magic	HIGGIN 1, 162	geologist	MILLER 4, 250
name: He that is without name	SCOTT 56, 293	Necessity Supreme	Ja THOMS(2) 6, 332
In the name o' the wee man!	LORNE 1, 200	wildness is a necessity	J MUIR 6, 259
My name is Sherlock Holmes	DOYLE 9, 116	**neck:** I must hing by the Neck / Without Remeed	W HAMIL(1) 1, 157
nothing but an empty name	J BAILL 9, 35	like ticks on a ewe's neck	GILLI 1, 144
your name shall be immortal	BURNS 64, 70	my neck being now about to be embraced by a halter	BRODIE 1, 59
names: datchie sesames, and names for nameless things	MACDIA 11, 210	**needlework:** more useless and flimsy parts of needlework	SINCLA 1, 301
Nancy: Beware of Whisky, Nancy Whisky	TRAD 20, 335	Needlework, good old court needlework	A GRANT 7, 148
Napoleon: the Napoleon of crime	DOYLE 13, 116	peace, friendship, and needlework	A GRANT 5, 148
narrator: obliterate the narrator, get rid of the artist	KELMAN 2, 183	**ne'erdoweels:** Spendthrifts and ne'erdoweels	FERRI 15, 130
nation: a kindly and long-suffering nation	ASCHER 8, 32	**neglect:** perpetual source of oppression and neglect	MACKINT 2, 229
a michty loss to the nation	RORIE 5, 285	**neglected:** NEGLECTED SCOTLAND shews her awful	
a nation of arselickers	GRAY 9, 150	BROW	DEFOE 1, 110
capital of a nation regaining the use of its limbs	ASCHER 10, 32	**neighbour:** a giddy neighbour	SHAKES 1, 298
chip of a nation	CRAWFO 4, 102	frown on our neighbour's pleasures	STEVEN 80, 323
early days of a better nation	GRAY 6, 150	most dangerous neighbour to England	SCOTT 96, 295
half of the nation is mad	SMOLL 10, 311	strong neighbour never shows much consideration	GM BROWN 13, 61
Half our nation was bribed	JOHNS 4, 178	Thou shalt not take thy neighbour's job	CARNEG 4, 90
nation goes on making and singing its own songs	I HAMIL 1, 156	**nemo:** Nemo me impune lacessit'	ANON 56, 30
nation of shopkeepers	SMITH 12, 305	**nerra:** We walk a nerra line	W MCILV 3, 233
nation will be disgraced whose women	M MCMIL 4, 234	**nervous:** Don't grow up to be a nervous old maid	SLESS 9, 303
no other nation that goes into trouble laughing	INGLIS 3, 171	**nesiesitus:** nesiesitus eivin to begarie	ROTHES 1, 286
offer their nation so much as a nose-bleed	PURSER 3, 276	**nest:** A nest of singing birds	COLUMB 4, 99
Scotland's a Nation Epidemicall	CLEVE 1, 96	see their nest shaken	STARK 1, 316
sham bards of a sham nation	E MUIR 12, 258	**nevertheless:** the nevertheless principle	SPARK 12, 315
such a nation will rise again	ASCHER 5, 32	**new:** New Road will some day be the Old Road	MUNRO 5, 261

Newcastle: a Scot, a rat, and a Newcastle grindstone   CUNN 8, 105
   seemed to me to be 'carrying coals to Newcastle'   ARNOLD 3, 31
newfangilness: all for newfangilness of gear   R MAIT 1, 243
news: Never did a thunder-clap daunt the heart like this news   GALT 3, 139
   through cold roads to as cold news   SCOTT 91, 295
newspapers: only true things in the newspapers are the
   advertisements   LAMONT 1, 191
Newton: As Shakespeare or Sir Isaac Newton   R FERG 1, 128
   intellect of Newton is the lowest degree   BREWST 3, 58
New Yeir: Prepair aganis this gude New Yeir   GUDE 5, 152
New York: I love short trips to New York   J CAMER 1, 80
nexus: Cash-payment is not the sole nexus of man   CARLYL 49, 87
Niagara: Niagara of eloquent commonplace talk   CARLYL 53, 87
   Niagara of sights, sounds and sensations   E DAVIE 4, 109
   one wouldn't *live* under Niagara   CARLYL 53, 87
nice: nice, but dampish and Northern   LAWRE 1, 193
   nice to get up in the mornin'   LAUDER 8, 192
   you'd think 'nice' was a four-letter word   STEEL 2, 317
nicht: Intil the pitmirk nicht we northwart sail   ANNAND 4, 26
   It's a braw bricht moonlicht nicht   LAUDER 5, 192
   like a barfit bairn, stauns nicht   BLACKH 2, 49
   Scho draif the day unto the nicht   ANON 15, 27
nichtis: Midsummer evin, mirriest of nichtis   DUNBAR 28, 120
nickstick: Luve keeps nae nickstick   NEW TES 5, 266
Nicolas: like the toe-nail-pairings of ST NICOLAS   A RAMS(2) 3, 278
Niel: Ye've surely heard o' famous Niel   LYON 1, 201
nievie: Nievie, nievie, nick, nack   BAIRN 12, 45
Niger: discover the termination of the Niger or perish   PARK 2, 273
niggard: thistle well betrays the niggard earth   BYRON 9, 76
nigger: What is a 'nigger'?   CUNN G. 6, 106
nighean: A nighean a' chùil bhuidhe   MACGIL 2, 216
   Cha leigeadh nighean Deòrsa mo phòca falamh   MAC ANT 3, 203
nigheanan: tha 'n nigheanan 's am mic 'nan coille   MACGIL 25, 219
night: A night seems termless hell   Ja THOMS(2) 3, 332
   Come before me, gentle night   MACGIL 16, 218
   Good night, an' joy be wi' you a'   HOGG 8, 163
   night tinkles like ice in glasses   MACCAI 6, 205
   She walks in beauty, like the night   BYRON 28, 77
   The City is of Night; perchance of Death   Ja THOMS(2) 2, 332
   the night is beastly derk   BRIDIE 17, 59
   the night was made for loving   BYRON 33, 78
night-shirt: to die in a night-shirt looking like an angel   BRIDIE 3, 58
nightmares: support us in our dreams and in our
   nightmares   AL KENNE 3, 185
nightmarish: Nightmarish regions, swathed in boreal mists   N DOUGL 5, 115
Nile: resemblance of law to the river Nile   KAMES 1, 181
nine: Nine Inch will Please a Lady   ANON 33, 29
nineteen: nineteen with a wardrobe full of clothes   BYRNE 3, 75
ninety: revert to being savages for ninety minutes   SHANKL 7, 299
   too many ninety-minute patriots   SILLA 3, 301
niosgaid: siod an niosgaid a' fàs / air an iosgaid   CLARS 4, 95
nipping: nipping blast of care   E JOHNST 2, 179
nippit: Somebody nippit me   SOUTAR 2, 313
nithean: Thig trì nithean gun iarraidh: / An t-eagal, an
   t-iadach, 's an gaol   ANON 22, 28
no: A bonny No, with smyling looks agane   MONTGO 3, 254
   and what for no?   SCOTT 82, 294
   A No vote need not imply any disloyalty   HOME 3, 164
   land of the omnipotent No   BOLD 3, 53
nobility: our Old Nobility is not noble   T JOHNST 4, 179
noble: All work, even cotton-spinning, is noble   CARLYL 48, 87
   many a noble gathering in the cause of liberty   MCLAR 1, 229
   to make a man look noble, your best course is to kill him   SMITH 8, 305
noblest: noblest prospect which a Scotchman ever sees   JOHNS 2, 178
nobody: That terrible Nobody   SMILES 9, 304
nod: in the Land of Nod at last   STEVEN 57, 322
noise: thy noise and smoky breath   SMITH 4, 305
nomad: shaky as small nomad tents / Within Victorian
   permanence   W MCILV 6, 223
non-learning: that placid centre of non-learning   A REID 1, 279
nonsense: Bible-clasping nonsense   TROCCHI 6, 341
   Mair nonsense has been uttered in his name   MACDIA 14, 210
   Nonsense at this time o' day / That breid-and-butter
   problems   MACDIA 31, 211
   nonsense when the Vote had yet to be won   MITCH 1, 251
   Religious Nonsense is the most nonsensical   BURNS 109, 73
   sounds like nonsense, my dear   SCOTT 39, 292
   What a glorious thing it is to speak nonsense   BRAXF 10, 57

normal: For once in your life you feel normal   PATTIS 5, 274
Noroway: To Noroway o'er the faem   BALLAD 38, 41
north: I'm deein' for the north   JACOB 6, 174
   the Ariosto of the North   BYRON 18, 77
   The cold infernal North   J BUCHAN 15, 64
   the land of the north is utterly destroyed   AILEAN 1, 23
   ugliest witch in the north countrie   BALLAD 1, 39
northern: The Northern Lights of Old Aberdeen   TRAD 57, 338
Northumberland: subordinate species of Northumberland   SCOTT 102, 296
Norval: My name is Norval   HOME 1, 165
nose: nose is just a sicht / Wi' drinkin' drams   OUTRAM 3, 271
nose-bleed: offer their nation so much as a nose-bleed   PURSER 3, 276
nostrum: never-failing nostrum of all state physicians   BYRON 11, 76
notes: A child's amang you takin' notes   BURNS 125, 74
   first he played da notes o noy   BALLAD 27, 40
nothing: this really has nothing to do with me   AL KENNE 4, 186
nothingness: the sound of nothingness   AL KENNE 1, 185
noticing: noticing the little apparent trifles   Jo BELL 2, 47
notorious: a most notorious offender   SMOLL 12, 311
nourice: the nourice was a fause limmer   BALLAD 29, 41
novel: what is the ordinary novel but a string   N DOUGL 4, 115
novelist: novelist should never have an axe of his own to
   grind   GD BROWN 7, 60
November: November's sky is chill and drear   SCOTT 11, 290
nuclear: Football management these days is like a nuclear war   DOCH 5, 112
numbers: express it in numbers   KELVIN 7, 184
   greatest happiness for the greatest numbers   HUTCH 2, 169
nurse: Meet nurse for a poetic child   SCOTT 8, 290
nursery: God is a bogle of the nursery   W MAIT 1, 243
   The wind hangs nursery rhymes on branches   MACCAI 5, 205
nursing: nursing profession is to medicine   WATT 9, 346
oak: An old ship without anchors, without oak   BARD 1, 43
oat: Pipers, blue bonnets, and oat meal   STEUAR 1, 318
oat-cakes: land of Calvin, oat-cakes, and sulphur   S SMITH 5, 310
oaten: oaten bread is not a thing to be laughed at   MAJOR(1) 1, 243
oatmeal: oatmeal cakes and oatmeal porridge have made
   Scotchmen   BLACKI 4, 50
   Scotland was an independent oatmeal republic   N FAIRB 1, 126
oats: OATS – A grain, which in England   JOHNS 1, 178
obair: Ge nach dèan mi saothair no obair shalach   MAC ANT 3, 203
   's e obair th'ann a bhith dannsa   MACNEA 3, 236
Obar-eadhain: Obar-eadhain an déidh a chreachadh   TRAD 2, 333
obdurate: Courage beyond the point and obdurate pride   E MUIR 11, 258
obedient: Women, destined by nature to be obedient   KAMES 12, 181
obeying: command him by obeying him   CARLYL 4, 85
objectivity: objectivity was of less importance than the truth   J CAMER 5, 80
obliterated: how far out a man could go without being
   obliterated   TROCCHI 2, 341
obscene: *Peter Pan* is a very obscene play   SPARK 14, 315
obscure: calm, though obscure, regions of philosophy   HUME 28, 168
obscurest: obscurest epoch is to-day   STEVEN 69, 322
obscurity: shrinking back into ignorance and obscurity   W ROBERTSO 3, 284
observe: You see, but you do not observe   DOYLE 5, 116
obstreperous: when the men grew obstreperous   CARLYL 2, 82
occupation: I have got a trade, an occupation   OLIPH 17, 271
ocean: Roll on, thou deep and dark blue ocean   BYRON 21, 77
   the incomprehensible ocean fills / With floodtide   MACGIL 4, 218
   The ocean churning, mixing, stirring   ALASD 4, 24
odd: I think we're basically all odd   B FORS 4, 135
odious: happy days I passed there amidst odious smells   S SMITH 1, 309
   make the person of an antagonist odious   HUME 6, 166
odium: the odium of servility   SCOTS 1, 288
odour: the odour of a stinking Conduct   HUME 1, 166
o-draochain: A' sparradh o-draochain / An earball o-
   dròchain   MACCOD 2, 208
odroochan: ramming *odroochan* in the tail of *odrochan*   MACCOD 2, 208
Odyssey: The surge and thunder of the Odyssey   A LANG 3, 191
offender: a most notorious offender   SMOLL 12, 311
offer: Now there's an offer of worthless alternatives   C MACDON 1, 213
office: harsh realities of the office furniture   BARRIE 19, 44
officiousness: importunate officiousness of relations   SMOLL 7, 311
òg: nuair bha mi òg   MAIRI 5, 243
oidhche: Thig am chomhair, oidhche chiùin   MACGIL 16, 218
oil: It's Scotland's Oil   SCOTTI 1, 297
oil-men: swaying caveful of half- / seas over oil-men   LOCHH 9, 199
oily: round, fat, oily man of God   Ja THOMS(1) 7, 331
okay: Black people are okay as long as   SULTER 4, 327
old: ane end of ane old song   J OGILVY 1, 269

two thirds of our power is violence; / it is cunning we need — MACTHO 14, 241
pox: let the fumbling wretch / E'en take the pox — A RAMS(1) 2, 277
poysonabill: puft up pryde, thow is full poysonabill — HENRYS 5, 160
prætorian: prætorian there, I mind the bigging o't — SCOTT 49, 293
practical: dour and practical and canny — BARRIE 19, 44
only practical approach to sport is the romantic one — H MCILV 6, 222
such a mixture of the practical and the emotional — BARRIE 14, 44
praise: claque delude with false praise — CRUICK 9, 104
Praise, my soul, the King of heaven — LYTE 4, 202
They may praise your braid roads — GOW 2, 146
praises: let me bash out praises – pass the tambourine — JAMIE 2, 176
praise-song: who will make a praise-song for you? — IAIN L 1, 170
pray: Some days, although we cannot pray — DUFFY 6, 118
prayer: highest form of prayer is silence — BARCLA 1, 43
Prayer is not a monologue — BARCLA 1, 43
prayer, which is nothing else but a friendly talking with God — JAMES 5, 175
Scotsman's most earnest prayer — BRIDIE 8, 58
prayers: strenuous faithful buckled to their prayers — STEVEN 100, 324
preacher: abetted by the preacher and the Press — MCGINN 4, 219
preacher ceased to speak, the people to listen — SAGE 1, 288
preachers: hired preachers of all sects, creeds, and religions — WRIGHT 14, 354
preaching: preaching earnestness to a nation which had plenty — ARNOLD 3, 31
precious: precious stuff mixed with dross — CARSW 14, 92
precipitous: In my precipitous city beaten bells — STEVEN 91, 324
predestination: predestination in the stride of yon connecting rod — W ELLIO 3, 123
pregnant: never done being pregnant — MACMIL 2, 234
preist: God send everie preist ane wyfe — GUDE 3, 152
The office of a Preist and Byschop — Jo HAMIL(1) 1, 156
preistis: I will na preistis for me sing — DUNBAR 25, 120
prejudice: story of Wallace poured a Scottish prejudice — BURNS 47, 69
whisky would be less damagin than prejudice — MACMIL 1, 234
preparation: only profession for which no preparation — STEVEN 38, 321
Presby: Presby, Presby, never bend — BAIRN 15, 37
Presbyterian: [Golf] is an intensely Presbyterian activity — HANLEY 2, 157
not a business to which the presbyterian mind is natively and nationally attuned — GRIERS 1, 151
Presbyterian faith is an incomparable metaphor — ASCHER 4, 32
Presbyterianism: he shook off Presbyterianism as a viper — G BURNET 1, 66
Presbyterianism without the animating life — MILLER 7, 250
preservation: magic preservation in the pages of Books — CARLYL 41, 87
press: abetted by the preacher and the Press — MCGINN 4, 219
It fell *dead-born from the press* — HUME 33, 168
pressure: This isn't pressure, it's pleasure — ROXBUR 3, 286
pretender: *Pretender*, indeed, and be damned to ye — STRAN 1, 326
Pretender's son passed over from the Isle — ARGYLL 1, 31
prey: the lawful prey of Historians & Poets — BURNS 104, 73
price: price of insubordination and insurrection — I MACGRE 1, 221
The real price of everything — SMITH 6, 304
prices: some contrivance to raise prices — SMITH 9, 304
pride: Courage beyond the point and obdurate pride — E MUIR 11, 258
cumbrous pomp of Saxon pride — BYRON 3, 76
starved pride — J BAILL 6, 35
Tam o' the Lin was fu' o' pride — J BAILL 13, 36
The fient a pride, nae pride had he — BURNS 40, 69
There are two kinds of pride — CHALM 1, 93
waving of flags was an empty pride — LINKLA 3, 197
priest: Churches built to please the priest — BURNS 26, 68
not good a priest lacking an eye — MACDHU 1, 209
one-a-side – one will be a priest and the other a minister — DALGL 2, 107
strangling the last king in the guts of the last priest — MITCHI 7, 252
priests: I like Roman Catholic priests better — BRIDIE 7, 58
Three priests' hearts, rotten, black as muck — BURNS 98, 72
prime: One's prime is elusive — SPARK 6, 315
Prime Minister: all the qualifications for a great Liberal Prime Minister — CUNN G. 9, 106
primitive: Primitive man was an intense realist — MCNEI 4, 237
primrose: primrose / And wood-sorrel, / The children's food — CARMIN 12, 89
prince: I will share the fate of my Prince — D CAMER 1, 79
Steel is Prince or Pauper — CARNEG 11, 90
Princes Street: invasion of Princes Street by the poor — E MUIR 2, 258
Princes Street or Paddy's Merkit — LOCHH 17, 200
principle: coxcombs, without any principle — J RAMS 1, 279
Principle built on piety is a pedestal — A GRANT 4, 148
the nevertheless principle — SPARK 12, 315
we go out on the Establishment principle — CHALM 5, 93
print: A milk maid poem-books to print — LITTLE 1, 197

licence to print your own money — R THOMS 1, 332
printing: Gunpowder, Printing, and the Protestant religion — CARLYL 5, 85
prison: The whole town's a prison — MUNRO 2, 262
prisoners: bring me prisoners, and I'll find them law — BRAXF 8, 57
privatisation: privatisation would set the people free — T BLAIR 1, 51
privilege: Death to Privilege — CARNEG 13, 90
fortresses of excessive privilege — OBAN 1, 269
spellbound while privilege picks its pockets — T JOHNST 4, 179
prizes: prizes that were ours for the taking — LOCHH 2, 198
problem: Better a'e gowden lyric / Than a social problem solved — MACDIA 27, 211
It is quite a three-pipe problem — DOYLE 8, 116
schools for problem parents — A NEILL 6, 266
There is never a problem child — A NEILL 5, 265
process: tak hame the process an' wimble-wamble it — POLKEM 2, 276
procession: a torchlight procession of one — MACCAI 28, 206
prodigious: Pro-di-gi-ous! — SCOTT 38, 292
profane: The sacred and profane go hand-in-hand — BELLAN 1, 47
profanity: I leave my testimony against profanity — ALISON 1, 24
profession: only profession for which no preparation — STEVEN 38, 321
the bigoted portion of the profession — J SIMP(1) 2, 301
professional: more money as a professional invalid — IMLACH 3, 171
professors: Professors of the Dismal Science — CARLYL 54, 87
profits: makes the profits something extraordinary — MACDONN 2, 215
profound: profound feeling of the power of solitude — NORTH 5, 268
You can be popular and profound — SPALD 2, 314
progedi: Noles ultra progedi, nec hominem tangas — COLUMB 2, 101
progress: life grows poorer as progress multiplies — GM BROWN 9, 61
Progress is a cheynge for the better — R MCLEL 6, 231
Progress is not a triumphant riding on — M MCMIL 8, 235
projects: all my projects flutter in the air — TYTLER 1, 341
proletarian: proletarian has no country — CUNN G. 14, 106
proletariats: when aristocracies crack and proletariats crumble — J BUCHAN 6, 64
promises: Wi' promises we're bocht — BROOKS 8, 59
Wonder for taking, acres of promises — W MCILV 5, 223
pronunciation: pronunciation is like ourselves, fiery — G MACKEN 4, 225
propensity: propensity to truck, barter — SMITH 4, 304
property: proper use of property is to make property useful — D MACLEO 5, 232
the sacredness of property — CARNEG 6, 90
propriety: selfish propriety of civilised man — J MUIR 12, 260
props: Shake off all the props — MACKINT 7, 229
propulsion: cars were to be the great means of propulsion — F BALF 7, 39
prospect: noblest prospect which a Scotchman ever sees — JOHNS 2, 178
prosperity: the fatal blessing of prosperity — GM BROWN 8, 61
prostate: so repulsive, what with their ruptures and prostate glands — WATT 2, 346
prostitute: I married a prostitute — WATERS 1, 345
prostitutes: all women would in effect be common prostitutes — KAMES 6, 181
protect: Protect and survive — RUNRIG 3, 286
protest: Fyrst I protest, beaw schirris — G DOUGL 1, 114
I will protest for you until I die — MAXTON 6, 247
Protestant: Gunpowder, Printing, and the Protestant religion — CARLYL 5, 85
protuberance: no more than a considerable protuberance — BOSWEL 5, 54
proud: better, a thousand-fold, for a proud man to fall — Ge MACDON 1, 214
easy to be proud and poor — W MUIR 7, 260
Proud Lady in a Cage — F URQU 2, 343
the proud title. . . of Suffragette — PHILL 1, 275
Proust: Lermontov and Proust in the Gorbals — HAVER 1, 158
prove: prove to you the existence of God — T REID 8, 281
you might prove anything by figures — CARLYL 32, 86
proven: that bastard verdict, *Not proven* — SCOTT 104, 296
province: beyond a woman's province — CHART 1, 94
provinces: Among all the provinces in Scotland — SCOTT 111, 296
provincial: I simply refuse to be provincial — R MCLEL 5, 231
provoking: tediousness of these people is certainly provoking — LAMB 2, 190
prudence: Manhede but prudence is ane fury blind — BELLEN 1, 48
prudence is very suitable at seventy — FERRI 1, 129
pryde: I say pryde is bot honestie — D LINDS 17, 196
puft up pryde, thow is full poysonabill — HENRYS 5, 160
The Paip, that pagane full of pryde — GUDE 7, 152
psalm: Dominie stickit the psalm — J BAILL 11, 36
psalms: The kirk, in a gale of psalms — GM BROWN 4, 61
psyche: troubled psyche that broods over the Scottish classroom — R MACKEN 1, 226
psychic: Song writing is like psychic wrestling — LENNOX 5, 193
pub: never been in a Rose Street pub — CRUICK 10, 104
public: a conspiracy against the public — SMITH 9, 304

noblest of these rights is, the cultivation of our reason   WRIGHT 11, 354
Reason is, and ought only to be the slave of the passions   HUME 7, 166
reasonable: Hume of the reasonable mind   IC SMITH 9, 307
   Man, being reasonable, must get drunk   BYRON 41, 78
reasonings: Great caution in his reasonings   PLAYF 2, 275
rebel: first thing a child should learn is to be a rebel   A NEILL 3, 265
   the beloved rebel   MAXTON 3, 247
rebellion: endless room for rebellion against ourselves   Ge MACDON 8, 214
rebellious: Rebellious Scots to crush   ANON 26, 28
reckoning: writing and reckoning, reckoning and writing   MACKINN 4, 228
recollection: lose all recollection of the habits and customs   LOCH 3, 198
reconcile: no man did more to reconcile Scots to the Union   MASSIE 2, 245
recruitin': Twa recruitin' sairgeants   TRAD 76, 340
red: Notice the blood. It is also red   KENNAW 8, 185
   red, red is the bottle's blood   MACTHO 21, 241
   spot of red or yellow in a harmony of grey   REDPA 1, 279
   the Red Duchess   ATHOLL 4, 33
redeemer: put our Redeemer out of His mailing   RUTHER 1, 287
reek: reek like a compost dunghill   SCOTT 108, 296
reeky: reeky mass of stones and lime and dung   CARLYL 2, 84
reel: a canty Highland reel   R FERG 5, 128
   dance a reel and a salsa   J KAY 1, 182
   Reel o' Tullochgorum   SKINN 2, 302
reelin': dinna haud me reelin' here   GOW 1, 146
reels: There's threesome reels, there's foursome reels   BURNS 112, 73
ref: I don't know why the ref ruled out that goal   A MACPHE 1, 237
referees: trouble with referees   SHANKL 2, 299
refinement: She advances refinement and civilisation   M REID 6, 280
reform: avert revolution by reform   MACKINT 4, 229
   Reform. That's what Scotland needs   M MCMIL 7, 235
reformation: of the Reformation spirit, industrial slums   F MACCOL 1, 209
   only solid, though a far slower reformation   CARLYL 13, 85
   Reformation was a kind of spiritual strychnine   W MUIR 10, 261
   what the Reformation did was to snuff out   F MACCOL 3, 209
reformations: perpetually busied in reformations   A FERG 1, 127
refrigerator: passing one's existence in a refrigerator   GIBBON 11, 143
refuge: God is our refuge and our strength   METRIC 2, 249
   stories are my refuge; I take them like opium   STEVEN 10, 319
refugee: more miserable than a refugee   LINKLA 7, 197
regiment: monstrous regiment of the damned bomb   G MACLEO 7, 233
regional: only 'regional minded' even under our own
   government   WOOD 5, 352
regression: dialect poetry is a regression to childhood   E MUIR 9, 258
regular: times of regular government and polished
   manners   Ja MACPHE 4, 238
regulations: rising torrent of acts, regulations   COOPER 1, 101
reid: The Burn o Breid / Sall rin fu reid   THOMAS 2, 331
   Your roising reid to rotting   HENRYS 12, 161
reiding: I heir freiris say that reiding dois na gude   D LINDS 16, 196
reign: Trees live, and reign, in their own right   N WELLS 3, 347
reik: the reik of Maister Patrik Hammyltoun hes infected   LYNDS 1, 201
Reikie: sheuk hands and parted wi' auld Reikie   BURNS 44, 69
relations: importunate officiousness of relations   SMOLL 7, 311
religion: a man's religion is the chief fact   CARLYL 36, 86
   Art and religion first   SPARK 3, 315
   errors in religion are dangerous   HUME 3, 166
   I die a true woman to my religion   MARY(2) 6, 245
   It is to art and religion that we must look   MACMUR 4, 235
   It was not religion but fawning   AIREAC 1, 23
   Magic is not religion   MCNEI 5, 237
   mine is the Religion of the bosom   BURNS 59, 70
   Morality of every Religion was bad   HUME 35, 168
   One's religion is whatever he is most interested in, and yours
   is Success   BARRIE 16, 44
   quackery, practised under the name of religion   WRIGHT 6, 354
   religion has ever been, and now is, the deepest source of
   contentions   WRIGHT 15, 354
   religion is an Union of the soul with God   SCOUG 1, 297
   religion on the anvil of the will of the people   F BALF 3, 38
   rum and true religion   BYRON 39, 78
   shooting came, in theory, second only to religion   MILLER 1, 249
religions: hired preachers of all sects, creeds, and religions   WRIGHT 14, 354
religious: fling the hale fukn religious thing oot   MACMIL 3, 234
   I hope I will be religious agoin   M FLEM 5, 134
   Religious Nonsense is the most nonsensical   BURNS 109, 73
   This is not a Religious age   CARLYL 11, 85
remark: despising and contemning remark   J OGILVY 1, 269
remedy: the remedy's / inside the disease   JACKS 7, 173

remeed: I must hing by the Neck / Without Remeed   W HAMIL(1) 1, 157
remeid: Sen for the deid remeid is none   DUNBAR 13, 119
remember'd: Which will be remember'd for a very long time   MCGON 4, 220
renaissance: Renaissance is also to be found / In the witches   CONN 1, 99
   There oor culture, oor Renaissance fell   T SCOTT 3, 289
renascence: pass, through Decadence, towards Renascence   P GEDD 3, 141
repent: repent, and from olde errours turne   W DRUM 5, 117
repose: No repose for Sir Walter   SCOTT 120, 297
reproached: reproached, buffeted, pissed upon   SMOLL 4, 311
republic: out for a Scottish Workers' Republic   J MACLEA 6, 230
   Scotland was an independent oatmeal republic   N FAIRB 1, 126
repulsive: her public persona almost totally repulsive   L KENNED 1, 186
   I may have been repulsive, but I was not bad   BRIDIE 10, 58
   so repulsive as is spherical trigonometry   TAIT 1, 329
   so repulsive, what with their ruptures and prostate glands   WATT 2, 346
research: Really valuable research is a long-term affair   A FLEM 2, 133
   with research you may make a failure, then another failure,
   then others, but you never go broke   A FLEM 4, 133
resign: would have resigned if I had anything to resign from   MCKEL 1, 224
resist: nothing can resist us   CARLYL 8, 85
resonance: impressive country but without resonance   IC SMITH 24, 308
respect: greatest respect for the character of *Herod*   BYRON 8, 76
   I was a Dog much in Respect   W HAMIL(1) 1, 157
   my respect for women more than this which made me a
   feminist   CRAWFU 1, 102
respectability: bad dream of respectability   MITCHI 15, 252
responses: Personal responses were irrelevant   W MCILV 2, 223
responsibility: the responsibility of being Scotch   CUNN G. 7, 106
responsible: he is in great measure responsible for the war   TWAIN 1, 341
rest: A blink o' rest's a sweet enjoyment   BURNS 42, 69
   when a beggar's weary, / He can aye sit doon an' rest   TRAD 68, 339
restraint: all the objective restraint of the Highland Light
   Infantry   H MCILV 2, 222
   over the top with restraint   MACLEN 1, 231
resurrection: we fed her cloth to take her up to / resurrection   ALASD 3, 24
return: never to return by the same road   SCOTT 63, 293
   return to Lochaber no more   A RAMS(1) 13, 278
reul: 'S tu màthair àigh nan reul   CARMIN 8, 88
revenge: I will think on revenge   MARY(2) 3, 245
   Sweet is revenge – especially to women   BYRON 36, 78
   violent tale of murders, feuds and tribal revenge   DALYE 4, 107
reverence: Reverence is the Dada of the 1980s   IH FINL 9, 131
reviewers: favourite food of the Edinburgh reviewers   LUCAS 1, 201
reviewing: do not at all like the task of reviewing   SCOTT 10, 290
reviving: a reviving, as well as awful idea   COLQUH 2, 98
revolt: Political revolt is and must be ineffectual   TROCCHI 4, 341
revolting: hash-up alike revolting to the ears   PUNCH 1, 276
   slavery is revolting everywhere   WRIGHT 5, 354
revolution: avert revolution by reform   MACKINT 4, 229
   French Revolution / Scorned circumlocution   IH FINL 8, 131
   seething in the pot of revolution   GALT 6, 139
   Terror is the piety of the revolution   IH FINL 18, 132
   There won't be any revolution in America   LINKLA 1, 197
   we are in the rapids of revolution   J MACLEA 1, 230
revolutionary: can't feel fierce and revolutionary in a
   bathroom   LINKLA 1, 197
   utter a Scots word you are making a revolutionary statement   J HENDR 2, 160
revulsion: a hundred horsepower revulsion from writing
   about myself   MACCAI 29, 206
rewards: rewards of any kind are but vulgarities   CUNN G. 8, 106
rex: Lex Rex   RUTHER 6, 287
rhapsodies: the howling rhapsodies of the music halls   FORD 1, 134
rich: got rich by selling a quick moonfuck   GRAY 11, 150
   rich will get the benefits and the poor will make the
   sacrifices   G BROWN 1, 61
   seldom a rich man at bottom   SCOTT 107, 296
   The man who dies thus rich dies disgraced   CARNEG 8, 90
   vicious selfishness of the rich   BIRD 3, 49
riches: not glory, it is not riches, neither is it honour   DECLAR 1, 110
   where the riches are in few hands   HUME 24, 167
richt: for the richt ilk man suld ficht   BARBOU 4, 42
   maynteyme richt and ek laute   BARBOU 6, 43
   The first is, that we have the richt   BARBOU 4, 42
ridge: 'Tis on the heather ridge I was born   CARMIN 10, 89
riding: A man goes riding by   STEVEN 49, 321
   Progress is not a triumphant riding on   M MCMIL 8, 235
rifles: Did the rifles fire o'er ye   BOGLE 3, 52
rigg: Time booed his rigg an shöre his tap   B ANDERS 1, 25

like a Scot to be real Scottish	MACDONN **2**, 215
mark of the Scot of all classes	STEVEN **95**, 324
Scot, exiled from his house of thought	W ELLIO **3**, 123
Scot but an uninspired Irishman	ANON **54**, 30
Scot is a man who keeps the Sabbath	C MURRAY **1**, 263
Scot on his unfurnish'd kingdom	SHAKES **1**, 298
That any Scot would *choose* to die and be buried in England	A BUCHAN **4**, 63
the horrid little Scot locked up inside	KENNAW **4**, 185
the Inarticulate Scot	B KAY **2**, 182
the only Scot whom Scotchmen did not commend	MALLOC **1**, 244
the Scot can be stupidly generous	S BAXT **1**, 45
the weasel Scot	SHAKES **2**, 298
typical Scot has bad teeth	BOLD **4**, 53
yon Scot ettis his awn blud	BLIND **3**, 52
Scotch: a doleful example of Scotch filth	WORDS **3**, 353
best Scotch song Scotland ever saw	SKINN **2**, 302
composing a Scotch song is a trifling business	BURNS **49**, 69
concede that the Scotch really do love learning	CROSL **2**, 103
English are very little indeed inferior to the Scotch	NORTH **2**, 268
I, the Scotch accent!	BYRON **4**, 76
No Scotchman of his time was more entirely Scotch	CARLYL **29**, 86
O sing to me the auld Scotch sangs	TRAD **58**, 338
Scotch are a wrong-resenting race	GALT **20**, 140
Scotch emigrant would probably find it peculiarly suited	WRIGHT **3**, 353
Scotch folks' humour	FORD **2**, 134
Scotch, whatever other talents they may have, can never condense	S SMITH **3**, 310
Scotch word in speaking	SCOTT **97**, 295
so vulgar as to sing Scotch songs	FERRI **18**, 130
The laddie has clear tint his Scotch	BRAXF **3**, 57
the last purely Scotch age	COCKBU **10**, 97
the responsibility of being Scotch	CUNN G. **7**, 106
to hear the Scotch brogue – oh, heavens!	FERRI **9**, 130
scotched: I '*scotched*, not killed,' the Scotchman	BYRON **48**, 78
Scotchman: Much may be made of a Scotchman	JOHNS **3**, 178
noblest prospect which a Scotchman ever sees	JOHNS **2**, 178
No Scotchman of his time was more entirely Scotch	CARLYL **29**, 86
Scotchman must be a very sturdy moralist	JOHNS **8**, 178
Scotchman stands confessed a sentimental fool	CUNN G. **7**, 106
the Scotchman's peculiar vanity	CROSL **7**, 103
what it is that makes a Scotchman happy	JOHNS **6**, 178
Scotchmen: been trying all my life to like Scotchmen	LAMB **1**, 190
every country has need of Scotchmen	A BALF **7**, 38
oatmeal cakes and oatmeal porridge have made Scotchmen	BLACKI **4**, 50
Scotchwomen: must be vulgar – all Scotchwomen are so	FERRI **9**, 130
Scotia: Edina! Scotia's darling seat	BURNS **21**, 68
Far distant, far distant, lies Scotia, the brave!	TRAD **44**, 337
From scenes like these, old Scotia's	BURNS **4**, 67
May Scotia's simmers ay look gay and green	R FERG **14**, 129
On Scotia's plains, in days of yore	R FERG **6**, 128
simple stone directs pale Scotia's way	BURNS **53**, 69
Scoticisms: few *modern* Scoticisms which are not barbarisms	J PINKER **1**, 275
Scotland: a better and truer Scotland	J GRANT **1**, 149
all that's perfectly hideous about Scotland	WELSH **5**, 348
Among all the provinces in Scotland	SCOTT **111**, 296
And, Scotland, this is all he knows of you	BLACKI **1**, 50
A Scotland genuinely at ease with itself	MARR **3**, 244
A song for Scotland this	G BRUCE **1**, 62
Auld Scotland wants nae skinking ware	BURNS **35**, 68
benefits derived to Scotland from the Union	BOSWEL **4**, 54
Black people have been in Scotland	SULTER **5**, 327
Calvinism has done more damage to Scotland than drugs	LAING **5**, 190
Christ got a charter of Scotland	RUTHER **1**, 287
come from Scotland, but I cannot help it	BOSWEL **2**, 54
corrupt history of Scotland	IC SMITH **24**, 308
could find nothing that looked like Scotland	A CAMPB **1**, 80
curse of Scotland is these wee hard men	GRAY **10**, 150
Don't Butcher Scotland's Future	SILLA **1**, 301
enrichment not only of the national life of Scotland	CHURCH **1**, 94
every time I've been in Scotland I write a book	CARTL **1**, 93
far from Scotland of the mist and storm	MUNRO **8**, 262
film will come to serve Scotland	GRIERS **2**, 151
find a true blue secretary for Scotland	F BALF **4**, 38
gude auld Kirk o' Scotland	G MURRAY **1**, 263
He canna Scotland see wha yet / Canna see the Infinite	MACDIA **21**, 211
Here I sit and govern Scotland with my pen	JAMES **17**, 176
humour may reflect the history of Scotland	FULTON **2**, 137
I felt I was fighting for Scotland	LYNCH **1**, 201
I look upon Scotland as part of the British Empire	J HILL **1**, 162
in Scotland a woman speaks of her 'man'	HARDIE **3**, 157
in Scotland's bonnie bounds	A GRANT **2**, 148
in Scotland we have no such thing as '*crusts*'	CARLYL **6**, 83
In the West of Scotland we don't actually have sex	PATTIS **4**, 274
I speak with the voice of Scotland	MITCHI **19**, 252
It's Scotland's Oil	SCOTTI **1**, 297
make Scotland a clearinghouse of ideas	R MACKEN **4**, 226
modern Scotland does not bear thinking of	G DAVIE **3**, 109
more than enough people in Scotland still	MILLER **8**, 250
my Scotland, two corners of the North-East	KESSON **9**, 187
NEGLECTED SCOTLAND shews her awful BROW	DEFOE **1**, 110
None can Destroy Scotland, save Scotland's self	BELHAV **4**, 47
No one in his wildest fits of patriotism ever talked of Merrie Scotland	CUNN G. **5**, 105
nothing of what makes Scotland Scotland	SCOTT **9**, 290
no tradition of theatre in Scotland	MULGR **3**, 261
O flower of Scotland	R WILLIA **1**, 350
'puir auld mithers' of Scotland	W MUIR **9**, 261
Reform. That's what Scotland needs	M MCMIL **7**, 235
Romantic Scotland's in the grave	GS FRAS **3**, 135
running Scotland over pasta and chianti	HESELT **2**, 162
sacrificing sheets by halves to Scotland's cause	WOOD **2**, 352
Scotland as a state of mind	MCCABE **3**, 205
Scotland free or a desert	ANON **38**, 29
Scotland gradually extricates herself from the slough of barbarism	CROSL **5**, 103
Scotland has suffered in the past	MACDONN **3**, 215
Scotland is an absolutely critical part of the UK	HESELT **1**, 162
Scotland is an *unwon* cause	STEINB **1**, 318
Scotland is bounded on the south by England	SHEPH **1**, 299
Scotland is European	W ELLIO **1**, 123
Scotland is indefinable	STEVEN **42**, 321
Scotland is not a place, of course	HANLEY **4**, 157
Scotland is one of the most intense talking-shops	W MCILV **10**, 223
Scotland is playing tartan waitress	EWING **1**, 124
Scotland lived, she could never die	GIBBON **4**, 143
Scotland must be rid of Scotland	RENWIC **1**, 281
Scotland / rolling down and up on death's yoyo	HERBER **1**, 161
Scotland's a Nation Epidemicall	CLEVE **1**, 96
Scotland's an attitude of mind	M LINDS **2**, 196
Scotland's decisive day, our D-Day	WRIGHT **3**, 354
Scotland's first recorded rape victim	KING **2**, 187
Scotland's greatest days have been since the Union	I LANG **1**, 191
Scotland should have an independent art	JD FERG **3**, 127
Scotland small?	MACDIA **56**, 213
Scotland the brave	HANLEY **1**, 157
Scotland the wee	T BUCHAN **1**, 65
Scotland! thy weather's like a modish wife!	A HILL **1**, 162
Scotland was an independent oatmeal republic	N FAIRB **1**, 126
Sean Connery would become king of Scotland	HUSTON **1**, 169
see if Scotland will go for it – or cop out	CONNER **3**, 100
Seeing Scotland, Madam, is only seeing a worse England	JOHNS **10**, 178
Stands Scotland where it did?	SHAKES **3**, 298
Switzerland as a sort of inferior Scotland	S SMITH **2**, 310
Talking about Scotland so far from it would be like starting on a bender	MCWIL **1**, 242
that Empire of which Scotland is no small part	A BALF **6**, 38
Traverse isn't in Scotland	J HAYN **2**, 159
Treacherous Scotland to no int'rest true	DRYDEN **1**, 118
two seasons in Scotland: June and winter	CONNOL **10**, 100
until there is a State of Scotland	J HENDR **1**, 160
Was never in Scotland hard nor sene	ANON **11**, 27
We'll drink a cup to Scotland yet	RIDDEL **1**, 282
with Scotland first begin	SHAKES **2**, 298
working for the independence of Scotland	WOOD **6**, 352
You are allowed one chance in Scotland	B FORS **1**, 134
Scotlande: Succoure Scotlande and ramede	ANON **2**, 26
Scotlanders: They are little Scotlanders	N FAIRB **1**, 126
Scotorum: Perfervidum ingenium Scotorum	ANON **4**, 26
Scotorum libertas prisca	R BRUCE **2**, 62
Scots: English are better animals than the Scots	BOSWEL **3**, 54
God help England if she had no Scots	G SHAW **1**, 299
If you think aye in Scots means yes	I SMITH **1**, 309
old freedom of the Scots	R BRUCE **2**, 62
Rebellious Scots to crush	ANON **26**, 28
Scots. . . have a slight tincture of letters	SMOLL **14**, 311
Scots can only survive as a book-tongue	A BUCHAN **3**, 63

Scots disna bide in a buik	**BLACKH 3**, 50
Scots down south either turn into Rob Roy McStrathspeyandreel	**AL KENNE 6**, 186
Scots for pleading	**G MACKEN 4**, 225
Scots is like English in its underwear	**W MCILV 4**, 223
Scots, wha hae wi' Wallace bled	**BURNS 126**, 74
Scots words to tell to your heart	**GIBBON 3**, 142
strong Scots accent of the mind	**STEVEN 71**, 323
that clackin Scots tongue	**G GUNN 2**, 152
The ardent temper of the Scots	**ANON 4**, 26
the Gas Chamber of the Scots	**F MACCOL 4**, 209
The legend that Scots are mean	**S BAXT 1**, 45
the Scots and the Jews	**SHINW 1**, 300
The Scots deserve no pity	**FLETCH 2**, 134
utter a Scots word you are making a revolutionary statement	**J HENDR 2**, 160
When the Scots are bad	**N WELLS 2**, 347
Scotsman: a Scotsman may well claim brotherhood with an Englishman	**SCOTS 1**, 288
a Scotsman on the make	**BARRIE 11**, 44
every Scotsman should be a Scottish Nationalist	**J BUCHAN 7**, 64
grandest moral attribute of a Scotsman	**BARRIE 12**, 44
happiest lot on earth is to be born a Scotsman	**STEVEN 44**, 321
Scotsman of your ability let loose upon the world	**BARRIE 10**, 44
Scotsman's most earnest prayer	**BRIDIE 8**, 58
Scotsman who has succeeded in becoming an Englishman	**BRIDIE 9**, 58
Scotsman with a grievance and a ray of sunshine	**WODEH 1**, 351
the 'Frying Scotsman' All Night Chipperama	**J MCGRAT 3**, 220
When a Scotsman says he'll see us out	**INGLIS 7**, 171
Wherever a Scotsman goes, there goes Burns	**J MUIR 9**, 260
Scott: great sick heart of a Sir Walter Scott	**CARLYL 52**, 87
half so flat as Walter Scott	**T ERSK 1**, 124
Let Scott thank John Knox	**CARLYL 29**, 86
Scotticisms: for fear of Scotticisms	**Ja BEAT 3**, 46
Scottis: ane ythyr scottis man in his bellye	**COMPL 2**, 99
onpossibil that scottis men and inglis men can remane in concord	**COMPL 3**, 99
Scottis sall bruke that realme	**ANON 6**, 26
Scottish: A new Scottish identity won't exclude	**WHYTE 2**, 348
being Black and Scottish is always treated as a kind of anomaly	**J KAY 2**, 182
countless Scottish women who perished in the witch-hunts	**KING 1**, 187
get the sulky Scottish spirit set up	**SCOTT 94**, 295
I never said to myself 'Oh, I'm Scottish.'	**J BAXT 2**, 45
like a Scot to be real Scottish	**MACDONN 2**, 215
no Stalinist like a Scottish Stalinist	**NAIRN 1**, 264
Now to me that's Scottish football	**ROXBUR 1**, 286
Of what is interesting in Scottish writing	**TROCCHI 6**, 341
out for a Scottish Workers' Republic	**J MACLEA 6**, 230
Scottish people drink spasmodically	**E MUIR 3**, 258
the truth is I felt very Scottish	**A WELLS 1**, 347
To be gay, as to be Scottish, is to doubt	**WOOLAS 1**, 352
We're not Scottish, we're northern European	**B FORS 5**, 135
women are not behind any more than Scottish men	**LADY'S 1**, 190
scrap-heap: Man, precariously perched on this rotating scrap-heap	**J BUCHAN 15**, 64
scratch: to scratch truth from the earth aright	**C NICGU 1**, 267
Screapadal: Ann an Screapadal mo chinnidh	**MACGIL 25**, 219
In Screapadal of my people	**MACGIL 25**, 219
screptra: Legais rúna, ro-chuaid eter scolaib screptra	**DALLAN 1**, 107
scribbling: damned scribbling snob	**ROBERTS 1**, 283
scriptures: He read mysteries and distributed the Scriptures among the schools	**DALLAN 1**, 107
scrutinise: scrutinise the Sense of a Vocable	**H MACKEN 3**, 226
scum: cosmopolitan scum	**TROCCHI 6**, 341
the scum is mounting uppermost	**GALT 6**, 139
treated like the scum of the earth	**J MCGRAT 1**, 220
scunner: And I lo'e Love / Wi' a scunner in't	**MACDIA 8**, 210
scythe: I put my scythe then in hiding	**MACTHO 10**, 240
sea: door slammed in the deepest hollows of the sea	**J CAMER 4**, 80
green days in forests and blue days at sea	**STEVEN 85**, 323
Home is the sailor, home from sea	**STEVEN 65**, 322
if we gang to sea, master	**BALLAD 39**, 41
my thoughts ebbed and flowed to the drow of the sea	**MORRIS 4**, 256
No hill is dull between the sunset and the sea	**H BROWN 1**, 61
sea and spirit, sea and spirit	**HAY 2**, 158
something in the literature of the sea	**MACLEOI 1**, 233
stabillit wyndis and the cawmyt sea	**G DOUGL 8**, 115
The music of the sea was in my ears	**IC SMITH 19**, 308
The old grey mist upon the old grey sea	**BLACKI 3**, 50

The sea-gray toun, the stane-gray sea	**A SCOTT(2) 4**, 289
The sea is blazing with a bitter flame	**IC SMITH 23**, 308
the sea passionate, / Moon-chained	**M STUA 3**, 327
this internal sea	**WELSH 1**, 348
Tonight the sea is like an advertisement	**IC SMITH 11**, 307
What comes from the sea should go to the people	**C MACKEN 6**, 225
Within the sea ty'd to a stake	**M WILS 1**, 350
sea-change: a major cultural sea-change in Britain	**WELSH 3**, 348
Seaforth: the last deaf and dumb Seaforth	**BRAHAN 4**, 56
seagreen: seagreen Incorruptible	**CARLYL 22**, 85
sealg: An t-sealg 's an t-iasgach bha sinne dìon dhaibh	**DOMHN R 1**, 112
seamen: To plant a star for seamen	**STEVEN 67**, 322
seams: seams of rich humanity	**H MCILV 9**, 222
seangain: mar dhùn an t-seangain dol 'na ghluas'	**BOTHCH 3**, 55
seanlong: Seanlong gan iarnaí gan dair	**BARD 1**, 43
seas: Blue with endlessly moving seas	**MORGAN 12**, 256
sad hearts over seas come leaping	**MUNRO 8**, 262
Till a' the seas gang dry	**BURNS 130**, 74
seashell: The warld ootside / Like a lug-held seashell	**T SCOTT 5**, 289
season: Flowre of the Seasons, Season of the Flowrs	**W DRUM 4**, 117
seasons: two seasons in Scotland: June and winter	**CONNOL 10**, 100
sea-water: mak drinkable toddy out o' sea-water	**HOGG 13**, 163
seclusion: idea that all seclusion is a grievance	**COCKBU 5**, 97
secreit: In secreit place this hyndir nycht	**DUNBAR 9**, 119
secretary: find a true blue secretary for Scotland	**F BALF 4**, 38
secrets: Secrets. Those private chips of information	**ROSE 3**, 286
You all have dark secrets	**BARRIE 21**, 44
sects: hired preachers of all sects, creeds, and religions	**WRIGHT 14**, 354
security: choice between freedom and security	**MACMUR 6**, 236
sedately: You must try to walk sedately	**STEVEN 54**, 321
sedition: Sedition daurna now appear	**J ROBERTSO(1) 1**, 284
sedulous: played the sedulous ape to Hazlitt	**STEVEN 73**, 323
see: I can truly see only when alone	**CARSW 15**, 92
You see, but you do not observe	**DOYLE 5**, 116
seeds: Let the seeds of independence be sown	**E JOHNST 2**, 179
seeing: art of seeing	**P GEDD 11**, 142
Seeing by wireless	**BAIRD 1**, 36
seeker: seeker, finder, reaper	**HAY 3**, 158
seen: Hast Thou seen her, great Jew	**MACGIL 7**, 217
seggs: nabbin' puddocks in the seggs	**MURRAY 2**, 262
seik: He is lying in his bed – and he is seik and sair	**GOWDIE 3**, 146
seilcheig: mionach seilcheig a bha annta air a mheasgadh ri blonaig cait	**LAMONT 2**, 191
self: self is but the shadow of life	**Ge MACDON 10**, 214
Self under self, a pile of selves I stand	**MACCAI 3**, 205
where this passionate self will go, God knows	**CRUICK 7**, 104
self-conceit: Self-conceit is none of the smallest blessings	**KAMES 2**, 181
self-consequence: lordly piece of Self-consequence	**BURNS 82**, 71
self-destructiveness: a World Cup for self-destructiveness	**H MCILV 4**, 222
self-help: spirit of self-help	**SMILES 1**, 303
self-realisation: Self-realisation is the true moral ideal	**MACMUR 5**, 235
self-respect: Self-respect is the noblest garment	**SMILES 3**, 303
self-tortures: hermits and Asiatic self-tortures	**STEVEN 90**, 324
selfish: How selfish soever man may be	**SMITH 1**, 304
selfish propriety of civilised man	**J MUIR 12**, 260
their patriotism was but a selfish passion	**BUCKLE 2**, 65
What a selfish cold-hearted thing is grandeur	**FERRI 11**, 130
selfishness: damning necessity of studying Selfishness	**BURNS 80**, 71
vicious selfishness of the rich	**BIRD 3**, 49
Victorian age was one of complete selfishness	**WATT 8**, 346
sell: not a man of law that has my tongue to sell	**KNOX 14**, 189
ye never sell yer mates	**W MCILV 3**, 223
selling: Every one lives by selling	**STEVEN 78**, 323
selvage: a wretched selvage of poverty and suffering	**MILLER 1**, 250
semiconductor: Semiconductor country	**CRAWFO 3**, 102
Senegal: It was in sweet Senegal	**BURNS 118**, 73
sensation: child's world of dim sensation	**STEVEN 35**, 320
sensations: Niagara of sights, sounds and sensations	**E DAVIE 4**, 109
sense: an unfathomable sense of the incongruous	**BRIDIE 6**, 58
Be cautious in displaying your good sense	**GREGOR 1**, 151
If a person speaks sense and truth	**FERRI 10**, 130
if ye had been a sheep ye would hae had mair sense	**D RAMS 1**, 278
It's soon', no' sense, that faddoms the herts o' men	**MACDIA 11**, 210
no landscape can make sense of my me	**MCCABE 1**, 205
prefer the sense, to the subtilty, of law	**STAIR(2) 1**, 316
senseless: All war is senseless and cruel	**SWAN 2**, 327
senses: as long as I keep my senses	**CARLYL 15**, 84
science is bounded by the five senses	**MCNEI 3**, 237

slipways: silent slipways to the riveters' wit	MORGAN **10**, 255
slop: sentimental slop of Barrie, and Crockett	GD BROWN **7**, 60
sloth: Thy coward sloth is cause of all	W WALLA **3**, 345
slow: slow as torture he discloses bit by bit	J KAY **3**, 182
slowe: be slowe in peace-making	JAMES **9**, 175
sluistreadh: An fhairge 'g a maistreadh 's 'g a sluistreadh	ALASD **4**, 24
slumber: Cease Leaden Slumber dreaming	HUME **1**, 168
slums: of the Reformation spirit, industrial slums	F MACCOL **1**, 209
Why have slums when half the building trade are unemployed?	MCGAH **3**, 216
sly: stabbed him on the sly	GD BROWN **1**, 60
small: Scotland small?	MACDIA **56**, 213
Small and mean though this place is	COLUMB **3**, 99
We have small lives, easily lost	AL KENNE **2**, 185
when we take thought of our own small country	GRIERS **3**, 151
small-minded: To be miniaturised is not small-minded	CRAWFO **4**, 102
smalltime: knew our country was a smalltime dump	G WILLIA **2**, 350
smaointean: mo shaothrach / bhith cur smaointean an cainnt bhàsmhoir	MACGIL **17**, 218
smashin': Smashin', in't it?	LOGAN **2**, 200
smattering: smattering of the graces	J RAMS **1**, 279
smeerikin: few joys on earth exceed a *smeerikin*	MACTAG **4**, 239
smell: queer-like smell	M SMITH **2**, 309
there is no smell in plants	T REID **4**, 281
the stale smell of spent euphoria	H MCILV **3**, 222
smells: happy days I passed there amidst odious smells	S SMITH **1**, 309
smiddy-vice: ye partan-handit, grip-and-haud smiddy-vice Mammon	GALT **16**, 139
smile: Look back, and smile at perils past	SCOTT **30**, 291
There is mayhem in my smile	LOCHH **6**, 199
the vain tribute of a smile	SCOTT **5**, 290
which boy had the sweetest smile	BARRIE **21**, 44
smites: a God who smites and does not spare	OLIPH **4**, 270
smoke: Give a man a pipe he can smoke	Ja THOMS(2) **1**, 332
horrible Stigian smoke of the pit	JAMES **15**, 176
marry a teetotaller, or a man who does not smoke	STEVEN **18**, 319
taught to spin, but has also learned to smoke	STATIS **3**, 317
smokey: A smokey house and a scolding wife	FERRI **16**, 130
smoky: thy noise and smoky breath	SMITH **4**, 305
smoochy: In my smoochy corner / take me on a cloud	MORGAN **6**, 255
smoor: smoor oot the gust fir owre-heroic deeds	W NEILL **3**, 266
smuain: an teine mhór th'air cùl ar smuain	IC SMITH **5**, 306
snail: snail's entrails mixed with cat's fat	LAMONT **2**, 191
snail-tainted: the said snail-tainted ginger beer	DONOGH **1**, 113
snake: skin / of the snake that hides a shining one	MORGAN **4**, 255
snare: Living in a village is walking / Among snare wire	MITCHI **18**, 252
snaw: Scharpe soppys of sleit and of the snypand snaw	G DOUGL **6**, 115
Ye're shairly no expectin snaw?	ANNAND **1**, 26
Your locks are like the snaw	BURNS **86**, 72
snawdrift: Her brow is like the snawdrift	SPOTT **1**, 316
sneachd: Tha sneachd air na beannaibh Diùrach	TRAD **72**, 339
sneaking: a sneaking piece of imbecility	SCOTT **36**, 292
sneak-thief: an unsleeping celestial sneak-thief	GIBBON **15**, 143
snìomh': A' snìomh cainnte 's a' snìomh bhruadar	MACTHO **1**, 239
snivelling: dark rain snivelling continuously	SPARK **16**, 315
snob: damned scribbling snob	ROBERTS **1**, 283
snooker: have to play unbelievable snooker to beat me	S HENDR **1**, 160
snore: snore in the dampest oxter o' a tree	SG SMITH **5**, 310
snout: as wise a snout on	R FERG **1**, 128
snow: bloodless lay th' untrodden snow	T CAMPB **7**, 81
Snow lies on the mountains of Jura	TRAD **72**, 339
Snow makes us aware of silence	SOUTAR **10**, 314
snuff: what the Reformation did was to snuff out	F MACCOL **3**, 209
snugly: snugly doze and rot awa	MACTAG **3**, 239
sober: not a sober man and hardly a sober woman	SLESS **2**, 302
what will he not do when he's sober?	HERMAN **2**, 161
sobhrach: sobhrach / 'S feada-coille, / Biadh na cloinne	CARMIN **12**, 89
sobs: plangent with the sobs of grown men	MILLAR **2**, 249
social: an age of appalling social deprivation	SMOUT **1**, 312
socialism: forced into the serfdom of Socialism	CHURCH **3**, 95
never have Socialism without complete democracy	T JOHNST **1**, 179
Socialism is an ideology often more successfully caricatured	G BROWN **3**, 61
socialism without the politics	SHANKL **6**, 299
To think of the socialism that we would turn back!	F DRUM **1**, 117
socialist: married woman and a socialist in a hurry	F DRUM **1**, 117
society: a loose and unformed state of society	LOCH **1**, 198
beyond the bounds of civilised society	BOYLE **5**, 56
greatest spendthrifts in the society	SMITH **10**, 305
I can imagine a communist society	MITCHI **1**, 251
natural outcome of a civilised society	BARRIE **4**, 44
no Morrison's Pill for curing the maladies of Society	CARLYL **46**, 87
one of the contradictions of our society	CHRIS **1**, 94
There is society, where none intrudes	BYRON **20**, 77
soda: Sermons and soda water the day after	BYRON **40**, 78
sodger: She's run off with a Sodger	KESSON **4**, 187
soil: A barren soil where Nature's germs	BYRON **9**, 76
rural pleasures of my native Soil	BURNS **51**, 69
soisgeulaiche: O, nan tigeadh soisgeulaiche / a lorgadh ceann-teagaisg	MACTHO **18**, 241
solder: nor solder for a broken heart	GALT **8**, 139
soldier: little she thocht that a soldier I'd be	TRAD **66**, 339
seldom a brave soldier	SCOTT **107**, 296
soldiers: we're biggin' the Soldiers' Cairn	SYMON **2**, 328
solitary: a detached and a solitary being	A FERG **4**, 127
grow up to manhood in some solitary place	SMITH **3**, 304
solitude: God to man doth speak in solitude	BLACKI **2**, 50
He makes a solitude – and calls it – peace	BYRON **26**, 77
love of solitude increases	SCOTT **93**, 295
profound feeling of the power of solitude	NORTH **5**, 268
solitude should teach us how to die	BYRON **17**, 77
solitudes: so many *inhabited* solitudes	WORDS **1**, 353
solitudinem: *solitudinem faciunt pacem appellant*	GALGAC **1**, 138
solsequium: Lyk as the dum / Solsequium	MONTGO **9**, 254
somebody: somebody goin' away, / Somebody gettin' home	JJ BELL **3**, 47
someone: Someone, Somewhere in Summertime	SIMPLE **2**, 301
somewhere: Someone, Somewhere in Summertime	SIMPLE **2**, 301
song: ane end of ane old song	J OGILVY **1**, 269
A song for Scotland this	G BRUCE **1**, 62
best Scotch song Scotland ever saw	SKINN **2**, 302
composing a Scotch song is a trifling business	BURNS **49**, 69
In anguish we uplift / A new unhallowed song	Jo DAVID(2) **4**, 108
let Satire be my song	BYRON **5**, 76
man who will sing any song	I LANG **2**, 191
sign of a bad song is that it calls Scotland 'Caledonia'	N BUCHAN **2**, 65
So fierce and sweet the song	GM BROWN **5**, 61
song alone, was the sole amusement	HOGG **16**, 164
Song writing is like psychic wrestling	LENNOX **5**, 193
the song of other shores	ANON **40**, 29
the song sold so many copies	A CAMER **2**, 79
songs: nation goes on making and singing its own songs	I HAMIL **1**, 156
so vulgar as to sing Scotch songs	FERRI **18**, 130
We rose on the wave with songs	Ja MACPHE **3**, 238
sonnets: would have written sonnets all his life	BYRON **43**, 78
sons: borne good sons to broken men	CORRIE **4**, 102
Our sons of the mist might here see their Grampians	WRIGHT **3**, 353
their daughters and their sons are a wood	MACGIL **25**, 219
sonsie: Fair fa' your honest, sonsie face	BURNS **34**, 68
soon': It's *soon*', *no* sense, that faddoms the herts o' men	MACDIA **11**, 210
soor-mulk: drivin intae Glesca in my soor-mulk cairt	T JOHNST **1**, 180
Sophia: Philo lov'd Sophia	AYTON **1**, 33
sophistry: land of meanness, sophistry and mist	BYRON **9**, 76
nothing but sophistry and illusion	HUME **21**, 167
sordidness: demon of sordidness	J ROBERTSO(2) **3**, 284
sore: this open sore of the world	LIVING **7**, 198
sorrow: A curse on sorrow, it is lasting	TRAD **54**, 338
He wirkis sorrow to him sell	DUNBAR **1**, 118
might never bid farewell to sin and sorrow	COLQUH **1**, 98
no sorrow in thy song, / No winter in thy year	M BRUCE **1**, 62
rising on the other side of sorrow	MACGIL **13**, 217
sorrow to them is wheat	MAIRI **3**, 242
this wrechit warld of sorrow	DUNBAR **15**, 119
Whene'er I forgather wi' Sorrow and Care	BURNS **129**, 74
sorrows: pour her sorrows o'er the Poet's dust	BURNS **53**, 69
sotheroun: Thy dede sall be to Sotheroun full der sauld	BLIND **4**, 52
soul: a human being, even if he be very poor, is a soul	M MCMIL **5**, 235
Breathes there the man, with soul so dead	SCOTT **7**, 290
come nearest the soul of another	Ge MACDON **2**, 214
either got soul or you don't. Hampden had it	MCSPOR **2**, 238
Equality is the soul of liberty	WRIGHT **8**, 354
In Books lies the *soul* of the whole Past	CARLYL **40**, 86
my soul has birdwings to fly free	E MUIR **14**, 259
one great invisible quality in all art, soul	MACKINT **6**, 228
Praise, my soul, the King of heaven	LYTE **4**, 202
problems o' the Scottish soul / Are nocht to Harry Lauder	MACDIA **25**, 211
religion is an Union of the soul with God	SCOUG **1**, 297
the lost state of her miserable soul	MACGIL **8**, 217

summertime: Someone, Somewhere in Summertime   SIMPLE 2, 301
sumo: I'm off to Japan to take up sumo wrestling   JT WILS 1, 350
sun: An' a reid sun drappin' doon   SYMON 1, 328
   as if under a single ray of the sun   COLUMB 1, 99
   dominions, on which the sun never sets   NORTH 3, 268
   Get intae the sun an' the fresh air   R MCMIL 2, 235
   man voyages, into the blackest sun   GM BROWN 10, 61
   Out of the sun, out of the blast   STEVEN 66, 322
   sun has gane down o'er the lofty Benlomond   TANNAH 5, 329
   tea is nearly ready and the sun has left the sky   STEVEN 55, 321
   The bleer-ey'd sun   R FERG 4, 128
   the shilpit sun is thin   JACOB 10, 174
   The sun leans ladders against the apple trees   MACCAI 5, 205
   The sun rises bright in France   CUNN 6, 105
   They are Early-rising-sons, who on a summer's day demand
     more sun   GIOL Co 2, 144
   What do I owe to ought below the sun   Je ADAM 1, 23
   you put your hand / between your eyes and the sun   MACAMH 2, 203
Sunday: It is not good to travel on Sunday   MACDHU 1, 209
   Let us all be unhappy on Sunday   NEAVES 1, 265
   Sunday – day of rest to the poor   FERRI 23, 131
   Sunday in the hills   WOOD 4, 352
   Sunday of wrangling bells   IC SMITH 7, 307
Sunday Post: last minister is strangled with the last copy
   of the Sunday Post   NAIRN 2, 264
sunlight: no sunlight in the poetry of exile   H MORT 4, 257
sunrise: Those who wait till evening for sunrise   HAMIL 5, 155
   you get out of touch with the sunrise   J BUCHAN 14, 64
sunset: No hill is dull between the sunset and the sea   H BROWN 1, 61
   We'll meet nae mair at sunset   SPOTT 2, 316
sunshine: like Peru, without the sunshine   WEIR 1, 347
   Scotsman with a grievance and a ray of sunshine   WODEH 1, 351
   We meet in cloud and sunshine   BORTH 1, 53
supereducated: supereducated illiterates of our own
   culture   WHYTE 1, 348
supper: supper is na ready   ANON 37, 29
suppers: Gang down to your suppers, ye daft limmers   GOW 1, 146
supreme: Necessity Supreme   Ja THOMS(2) 6, 332
sure: Sure and Stedfast   W A SMITH 1, 310
surge: The surge and thunder of the Odyssey   A LANG 3, 191
surgeon: Cook, like the Surgeon, must first look on   DODS 2, 112
surgical: surgical operation to get a joke   S SMITH 4, 310
surrender: What, is this an entire surrender?   BELHAV 5, 47
survival: laugh for survival's sake   B FORS 3, 135
   survival of the fittest in every department   CARNEG 5, 90
survive: Bad books perish, but good books survive   FRAZER 4, 137
   Protect and survive   RUNRIG 3, 286
swaddies: Puir bluidy swaddies are weary   HENDER 1, 159
swadling: Sir, when ye war in your swadling cloutis   A MELV 2, 248
swall: swall men's thochts wi' impurities   LOCHH 15, 199
swan: She's breastlit like the swan   W DOUGL 2, 116
   Thou art whiter than the swan on miry lake   CARMIN 2, 88
swans: Each plank of her smooth as the swans' plumage   CARMIN 14, 89
swaw: Murns the white swaw owre the wrack ayebydanlie   T SCOTT 4, 289
sway: no other Sway / But purest Monarchie   MONTRO 1, 254
swearing: swearing and drunkenness   COCKBU 12, 97
   Swearing was thought the right, and the mark, of a
     gentleman   COCKBU 12, 97
sweat: from their heated skin the sweat out-squirts   TENNAN 3, 330
sweet: Go sad or sweet or riotous with beer   GM BROWN 1, 60
   I wadna sleep she sang so sweet   TRAD 58, 338
   So fierce and sweet the song   GM BROWN 5, 61
   Sweet Dreams (Are Made of This)   LENNOX 2, 193
   Sweet is revenge – especially to women   BYRON 36, 78
   Sweet's the laverock's note and lang   NAIRNE 14, 265
   Sweet was its blessing, kind its caressing   A COCKBU 1, 96
sweetie: bright bottles in a sweetie shop window   PETTIE 1, 274
sweetie-shop: His grannie keepit a sweetie-shop in
   Strathbungo   GD BROWN 3, 60
swerd: I have my swerd undishonorit   HENDER 1, 160
swete: So swete a kis yistrene   MONTGO 8, 254
swim: If ye dinna send me back, I'll swim back   SLESS 5, 302
   to catch a fish that couldnae swim   MARRA 2, 244
Switzerland: Switzerland as a sort of inferior Scotland   S SMITH 2, 310
sword: putt all to the sword under seventy   DUNCAN 1, 120
   Who will now lift the sword or fill the chair?   NIC FHE 1, 266
   wield a flesh-hook rather than a sword   J BAILL 2, 35
swords: the swords leapt from their scabbards   TRAD GA 4, 333

syboes: nought in the Highlands but syboes and leeks   SCOTT 34, 291
sycophants: this boy will be surrounded by sycophants and
   flatterers   HARDIE 1, 157
symbol: they want not just the symbol, but the substance   STEEL 4, 317
symbols: All our lives are symbols   BANKS 1, 42
sympathise: sympathise with the bears   J MUIR 12, 260
sympathy: Sympathy, Synthesis and Synergy   P GEDD 14, 142
   What a strange thing is sympathy   SLESS 4, 302
syn: He may weill to the syn assent   DUNBAR 29, 120
syndrome: the Pinkerton syndrome   J PINKER 1, 275
synthesis: Will a synthesis be made of Fate   MACGIL 6, 216
system: I want to destroy your system   BOYLE 1, 56
table: behave mannerly at table   STEVEN 48, 321
tables: Tables are like cobwebs   CARLYL 33, 86
taibhs: taibhs' gach mearachd, taibhs' gach cionta   IC SMITH 5, 306
taigh: Air làr an taigh mhóir a rugadh mi   CARMIN 10, 89
taigh-mór: An taigh-mór falamh an Dun-Eideann / Gun
   chumhachd gun ghuth   RUNRIG 2, 286
tail: walk first that I may see your tail   KAMES 8, 181
tail-tree: Ye had as good a tail-tree   ANON 36, 29
talamh: a bhith sgriobadh na fìrinn às an talamh   C NICGU 1, 267
tale: speak out a plain tale   SCOTT 69, 294
talent: just talent enough to spoil him   SCOTT 20, 291
   talent instantly recognises genius   DOYLE 15, 116
   women know talent when they share a bed with it   CARSW 13, 92
talents: I prefer the talents of action   BYRON 24, 77
talk: know anything about football, you'll never talk alone   R FORS 1, 135
   man of eighty and upwards may be allowed to talk   SCOTT 100, 296
   Men Talk   LOCHH 13, 199
   Talk that does not end in any kind of action   CARLYL 55, 87
talking: more travelling and much less talking   I BELL 2, 47
   prayer, which is nothing else but a friendly talking with God   JAMES 5, 175
talking-shops: Scotland is one of the most intense talking-
   shops   W MCILV 10, 223
Tam: Tam o' the Lin was fu' o' pride   J BAILL 13, 36
Tam Lin: young Tam Lin is there   BALLAD 41, 41
tambourine: let me bash out praises – pass the tambourine   JAMIE 2, 176
tambours: tambours / For fifteen hours a day   Ja HAMIL 4, 156
tame: To love the beast they cannot tame   SOUTAR 15, 314
tangas: Noles ultra progedi, nec hominem tangas   COLUMB 2, 99
tangle: a tangle of breakings off and addings on   OLIPH 11, 270
   the tangle o' the Isles   MACLEOI 3, 234
tangled: Oh what a tangled web we weave   SCOTT 17, 291
Tannadice: Up at Tannadice / Framed in woodwork cool as
   ice   MARRA 4, 244
tanner: Twelve and a tanner a bottle   FYFFE 2, 137
tapestry: I wish people would begin to work tapestry again   A GRANT 9, 148
tap-mast: He strack the tap-mast wi his hand   BALLAD 16, 40
tappit: let's get in the tappit hen   A RAMS(1) 5, 277
tares: accidents, tares among the wheat, handmaids   OLIPH 16, 270
tar-filled: Tar-filled lungs   MUNRO 1, 262
targaidean: bha na targaidean a' gliongarsaich ris a' bhalla   TRAD GA 4, 333
tartan: Bring forward the tartan!   C CAMPB 3, 81
   comic tartan-wearing country folk   A CAMPB 1, 80
   cut our coat to suit the cloth, and the cloth is the tartan   WOOD 3, 352
   I have no intention of wearing tartan camouflage   THATCH 2, 330
   I met a man in tartan trews   TRAD 42, 337
   lily-livered, tartan-Tory half-wits   MCLEA 1, 230
   Scotland is playing tartan waitress   EWING 1, 124
   tartan tax   M FORS 3, 135
   You disgrace your tartan   WOOD 1, 352
   young poets waving tartan rattles   JACKS 5, 173
tartans: Fancy tartans, clanless, gaudy   MURRAY 6, 262
   red-tinted tartans could be got   MACANT 2, 203
   we shall wear only hat and long coat / instead of the scarlet
     tartans   MÀCANT 5, 204
Tarwathie: Farewell tae Tarwathie   SCROGG 1, 297
tassie: fill it in a silver tassie   BURNS 72, 71
taste: like to taste my friends but not to eat them   N DOUGL 3, 115
   my taste in Music must be inelegant & vulgar   BURNS 127, 74
   the deficiency must be supplied by Taste   A RAMS(2) 4, 278
tattersall: Natty in tattersall   LOCHH 8, 199
tattie: Ye canna plant a tattie when the grund's weet   A SCOTT-M 1, 297
tattie-bogle: Wha wud be a tattie-bogle / In castawa claes   SOUTAR 17, 314
tatties: Your natural food it is tatties and herrin'   TRAD 70, 339
tattoo: Edinburgh Tattoo   HOOD 2, 165
taught: Let the common people be taught   SMILES 10, 304
   nothing worth knowing that can be taught   PETRIE 2, 274

ticket: never saw a railway ticket	F BALF 2, 38
tickets: Adventure upon all the tickets in the lottery	SMITH 8, 304
tickling: stop yer tickling, Jock	LAUDER 2, 192
ticks: like ticks on a ewe's neck	GILLI 1, 144
tide: Why weep ye by the tide, ladie?	SCOTT 46, 292
tides: beaten by tempests and lashed by tides	MILLER 9, 250
tiger: fly into the arms of a tiger	FERRI 5, 130
tiger-shooting: no one I would rather have with me to go tiger-shooting	J BUCHAN 4, 64
tighearna: Is treasa tuath na tighearna	ANON 45, 30
tight-locked: tight-locked streets which were all on fire	IC SMITH 7, 307
Till: Says Tweed to Till	BAIRN 18, 37
tìm: Tha tìm, am fiadh, an Coille Hallaig	MACGIL 24, 219
tha tìm 'na chrùban anns an uinneig	IC SMITH 3, 306
time: Dwellers all in time and space	LYTE 5, 202
Gow beat time, now time's beat Gow	GOW 3, 146
humour is a flash of eternity bursting through time	PETRIE 3, 274
Momentous things may happen in a man's free time	A FLEM 1, 133
Nae man can tether time or tide	BURNS 96, 72
never-resting thing called Time	CARLYL 37, 86
Perfection for man is in no time, no place	WRIGHT 10, 354
so far into the abyss of time	PLAYF 1, 275
speech is shallow as Time	CARLYL 26, 86
the twin categories of time and space	J BUCHAN 11, 64
there's a gude time coming	SCOTT 61, 293
The sands of time are sinking	COUSIN 1, 102
The time is sick and out of joint	CARLYL 12, 85
Time booed his rigg an shöre his tap	B ANDERS 1, 25
time brings a' things tae an end	TRAD 64, 339
Time is crouching in the window	IC SMITH 3, 306
time knocking / Somewhere through the wall	WS GRAH 5, 147
Time rolls his ceaseless course	SCOTT 24, 291
Time's hard dial	C OLIPH 1, 269
Time, swift as it flies	PAGAN 4, 273
Time, the deer, is in the wood of Hallaig	MACGIL 24, 219
Time, which measures every thing	HUTTON 3, 169
We are on borrowed time	CONN 2, 99
yon gable-ends o' time	SPENCE 2, 316
you, poor Time, are an ancient measure	ANGUS 4, 26
timebombs: when they come out they are timebombs	BOYLE 5, 56
times: Times are changed with him who marries	STEVEN 21, 320
timid: Poor is the triumph o'er the timid hare	Ja THOMS(1) 4, 331
timor: *Timor mortis conturbat me*	DUNBAR 12, 119
Timothys: Why do we always get Julians and Timothys?	ANON 59, 31
timperacht: na h-eigin go laidir do timperacht	ANON 19, 27
tired: all readers can get tired with their paper	IRVINE 1, 172
tired of speaking to stones	HUTTON 2, 169
tiredness: Better is tiredness of feet after a bright deed	DEAN 4, 110
tireless: A tireless, tough, and God-fearing people	N GUNN 11, 154
tissue: a tissue of errors	STEVEN 69, 322
title-deeds: the title-deeds are rapine, murder, massacre	T JOHNST 4, 179
titles: anyone had told me I would win so many titles	S HENDR 2, 160
tits: instant tits and bottom line of art	DUFFY 5, 118
toad: A jewel in your head? Toad, / you've put one in mine	MACCAI 37, 205
toadies: toadies and lickspittles of the English Ascendancy	MACDIA 45, 212
toast: yon the toast of a' the town	BURNS 124, 74
tobacco: Tobacco is like love	HUME 2, 168
tobacco may almost be said to be excessive	STATIS 3, 317
To live upon Tobacco and on hope	AYTON 4, 34
to sit tossing of *Tobacco pipes*	JAMES 14, 176
tochts: Let aa tochts be lichthooses	JAMIES 1, 177
to-day: obscurest epoch is to-day	STEVEN 69, 322
toddy: mak drinkable toddy out o' sea-water	HOGG 13, 163
todlen: Cou'dna my luv come todlen hame?	TRAD 74, 339
toe-nail-pairings: like the toe-nail-pairings of ST NICOLAS	A RAMS(2) 3, 278
toga: Toga and gown walk the pier	G BRUCE 4, 62
toibheum: canadh Dia gur h-e an toibheum	MACGIL 20, 218
toilet-paper: an amenity, like soft toilet-paper	J MCGRAT 6, 221
tolerable: honorable & just warre is more tolerable	JAMES 9, 175
tomb: circular idea / Call'd vulgarly a tomb	ANON 39, 29
have it on my tomb – 'He ran a butler'	STEVEN 62, 322
tongue: a Scotch tongue in your head	SCOTT 69, 294
Her tongue the clangin' clapper	MURRAY 4, 262
his tongue only should be left at liberty	CARLYL 1, 83
my tongue / shedding its skin	DUFFY 3, 118
not a man of law that has my tongue to sell	KNOX 14, 189
O island / that wound your heath round my tongue	MACTHO 12, 240

soft lowland tongue o' the Borders	SANDER 1, 288
that clackin Scots tongue	G GUNN 2, 152
tongue-lash: may tongue-lash her family in private	W MUIR 11, 261
tongues: ill-scraped tongues like yours	SCOTT 60, 293
urnae arraheids / but a show o grannies' tongues	JAMIE 3, 176
tools: sharpening of intellectual tools	J MURRAY 3, 263
tool-using: Man is a Tool-using Animal	CARLYL 15, 85
toon: Common-Ridin' day in the Muckle Toon	MACDIA 16, 210
toot-toot: Whit wey does the engine say *Toot-toot?*	M SMITH 1, 309
top: I began my career at the top	GARDEN 1, 140
torch: The torch that lights time's thickest gloom	BONAR 3, 53
torcheculs: of all torcheculs, arsewisps, bumfodders	T URQU 6, 343
torchlight: a torchlight procession of one	MACCAI 28, 206
Tories: For the Tories to become believers in intervention	G BROWN 4, 61
torment: torment o the lowin brunstane pit	R MCLEL 3, 231
tormented: the tormented wood	E MUIR 17, 259
torrent: rising torrent of acts, regulations	COOPER 1, 101
tortoise: that sly tortoise, death	W NEILL 2, 266
torture: slow as torture he discloses bit by bit	J KAY 3, 182
Tory: Let Whig an' Tory a' agree	SKINN 2, 302
lily-livered, tartan-Tory half-wits	MCLEA 1, 230
not going to grovel to any Tory butcher	AIRLIE 1, 23
Voting Tory is like being in trouble with the police	C KENNE 1, 186
touch: puts it not unto the Touch, / To win or lose it all	MONTRO 2, 254
You will go no further, nor touch the man	COLUMB 2, 99
toun: haill Toun sterts to talk like Chairlie	R MCLEL 6, 231
The piper cam to our toun	TRAD 60, 338
There cam a man tae oor toun	BAIRN 1, 36
The sea-gray toun, the stane-gray sea	A SCOTT(2) 4, 289
toungis: The plesand toungis with hartis unplane	DUNBAR 23, 120
tourist: whims of a passing tourist	N GUNN 4, 153
tourists: like tourists in a foreign country	G BROWN 4, 61
tow: Up the lang ladder, / And doun the pickle tow	ANON 31, 29
towels: we manna pretend to towels	HAMIL 2, 155
towerist: English towerist with a kilt	MUNRO 7, 262
town: a grey town without darting sun	MACGIL 3, 216
dirty old town	E MACCOL 1, 208
dropped into a town like glass balls	W MUIR 3, 260
the finest three-day town on earth	J CAMER 1, 80
The whole town's a prison	MUNRO 2, 262
This was the good town once	E MUIR 16, 259
What's this dull town to me?	KEPPEL 1, 186
town-planning: Town-planning is not mere place-planning	P GEDD 8, 142
towns: archipelago of stony towns	A REID 2, 279
toys: I will make you brooches and toys	STEVEN 85, 323
Not to meddle with my toys	STEVEN 50, 321
trade: I'd trade a lot for tenderness	GALLO 5, 138
I have got a trade, an occupation	OLIPH 17, 271
trades: O' a' the trades that I do ken	TRAD 68, 339
tradition: folk tradition is a shared and democratic	S DOUGL 1, 115
In our cities the folk tradition	HENDER 4, 159
no tradition of theatre in Scotland	MULGR 3, 261
tradition, though infinitely more than mere fashion	A BALF 8, 38
traditions: traditions of Scottish comedy lie in homeliness	CARR 2, 90
tragedy: tragedy of the Highlands has become a saleable commodity	J MCGRAT 2, 220
You're a bloody tragedy	MAXTON 5, 247
trained: trained up to be a person of consequence	FERRI 22, 131
trains: like troop trains without the dread	H MCILV 10, 223
traitor: Away, away, thou traitor strang	BALLAD 25, 40
was not Knox a traitor?	G MACLEO 7, 233
When I am taken / Do not blame the traitor	G THOMS 2, 331
traivel: The road I traivel has nae end	MCDONA 3, 214
tramp: maunna tramp on the Scots thistle, Laddie	ANON 48, 30
tramp of trooping horses	W OGILVI 2, 269
tramps: come a' ye tramps an' hawkers	TRAD 75, 339
transformation: the mountain, which I little thought / would suffer transformation	MACANT 4, 204
transportation: Transportation from Paradise is one thing	H KENNE 2, 186
transvite: I know what they call you, transvite	J KAY 4, 182
trap: this Trap of their own making	FLETCH 2, 134
Traquair: the bush aboon Traquair	SHAIRP 1, 298
traughle: slave and traughle from the marriage bed to the grave	WATT 3, 346
travel: It is not good to travel on Sunday	MACDHU 1, 209
No one can travel light with a house on their back	MITCHI 16, 252
travel for travel's sake	STEVEN 5, 319
travel hopefully is a better thing than to arrive	STEVEN 34, 320
travelling: more travelling and much less talking	I BELL 2, 47

And I sae weary fu' o' care	BURNS 107, 73
A weary lot is thine, fair maid	SCOTT 29, 291
Oh, the weary spinnin' o't	D OGILVY 1, 269
Puir bluidy swaddies are weary	HENDER 1, 159
when a beggar's weary, / He can aye sit doon an' rest	TRAD 68, 339
weary'd: When we were weary'd at the gowff	A RAMS(1) 1, 277
weasel: the weasel Scot	SHAKES 2, 298
weather: fine weather lays a heavier weight on the mind	SPARK 16, 315
Scotland! thy weather's like a modish wife!	A HILL 1, 162
weaver: For – Jenny dang the Weaver	A BOSWEL 1, 53
weavers: come all ye weavers, ye Calton weavers	TRAD 20, 335
wasna for the wark o' the weavers	D SHAW 1, 299
weaving: Weaving words and weaving dreams	MACTHO 1, 239
web: Oh what a tangled web we weave	SCOTT 17, 291
wedded: I have wedded the cause of human improvement	WRIGHT 12, 354
wedding: All for Mairi's wedding	ROBERTO 3, 283
At Willie's wedding on the green	A BOSWEL 1, 53
has softened into wedding presents	H MACKEN 5, 226
To the wedding of Shon Maclean	R BUCHANA 2, 65
wedding-Day: Why Should I be Sad on my Wedding-Day?	ANON 25, 28
wee: And there I spied a wee wee man	BALLAD 45, 42
In the name o' the wee man!	LORNE 1, 200
Scotland the wee	T BUCHAN 1, 65
The Free kirk, the wee kirk	ANON 44, 30
week: a Christian on a Pound a Week	HARDIE 4, 157
weep: Why weep ye by the tide, ladie?	SCOTT 46, 292
weeping: Glen of Weeping	MACAUL 1, 204
he took a little weeping to my eyes	MACGIL 22, 218
weidis: Duill weidis I think hypocrisie	D LINDS 10, 195
weird: Something really weird was happening in the Gorbals	TORRIN 1, 332
welcome: A 'Highland welcome' all the wide world over	BYRON 45, 78
I'll ask no more / Than just a Highland welcome	BURNS 54, 69
welcum: Welcum the lord of lycht and lamp of day	G DOUGL 9, 115
well: Ane springing well of sinceir veritie	D LINDS 11, 195
I saw the bracken growing round the well of her eyes	MACTHO 9, 240
wellies: If it wasnae for yer wellies	CONNOL 1, 100
wemen: Wemen ar wemen, and sa will end and de	DUNBAR 8, 119
west: In the West of Scotland we don't actually have sex	PATTIS 4, 274
the folk like the folk o' the west	ROBERTO 7, 283
The west wind blows to Coshieville	S MACGRE 2, 222
You took the east from me and you took the west from me	ANON 20, 28
West End Perk: phentoms are dencing in the West End Perk	BRIDIE 17, 59
westering: And it's westering home	ROBERTO 6, 283
Westminster: In Westminster's hall o' fame	BROOKS 7, 59
westward: What! you are stepping westward?	WORDS 5, 353
wet: A wet sheet and a flowing sea	CUNN 1, 104
wetted: continually wetted with rain	STEVEN 4, 319
wha: O wha's been here afore me, lass	MACDIA 18, 210
whale: bonnie ship the Diamond / Goes a-fishing for the whale	TRAD 17, 334
hurrah! for the mighty monster whale	MCGON 3, 220
nae a birdie to sing to the whale	SCROGG 2, 297
whammy: That is a double whammy	I LANG 3, 192
wharfs: where the people have miniature wharfs instead of gardens	LINKLA 5, 197
whaups: about the graves of the martyrs the whaups	STEVEN 87, 324
wheat: accidents, tares among the wheat, handmaids sorrow to them is wheat	OLIPH 16, 270
	MAIRI 3, 242
wheels: silent wheels that raised the dead	CORRIE 5, 102
where: Oh where is the Glasgow that I used tae know	MCNAUG 2, 236
Whig: Let Whig an' Tory a' agree	SKINN 2, 302
Whigs: Let howlet Whigs do what they can	TRAD 4, 333
whims: whims of a passing tourist	N GUNN 4, 153
whine: lay down with a whine in the dirt	GIBBON 8, 143
whingeing: whingeing getts about your ingle-side	A RAMS(1) 7, 277
whisht: O Wind, hae maircy, haud yer whisht	JACOB 7, 174
whiskers: hair, a veritable Birnam Wood of whiskers	E MACCOL 4, 209
whisky: A good gulp of whisky at bedtime	A FLEM 6, 133
a small spoonful of earth and whisky	PENNA 1, 274
Beware of Whisky, Nancy Whisky	TRAD 20, 335
dainty wee drappie o' whisky	SHIRR 1, 300
dismally drunk upon whisky	NEAVES 2, 265
fareweel to whisky, O	LYON 1, 201
for the gentlemen that don't like it, whisky	KENNAW 1, 185
Freedom an' whisky gang thegither	BURNS 24, 68
gie her plenty of whisky	PETRIE 4, 274
Limited water and unlimited whisky	BIRD 2, 49
never take water without whisky	C MURRAY 2, 263

no Scottish family without its whisky skeletons	BRUCE L. 2, 63
O Whisky! soul o' plays an' pranks	BURNS 16, 67
vice more attractive than whisky	W ELLIO 4, 123
whisky has made us what we are	BRUCE L. 1, 62
Whisky is concerned about the limitations of the mind	N GUNN 1, 153
whisky would be less damagin than prejudice	MACMIL 1, 234
whispers: silence punctuated by malicious whispers and hiccups	E MUIR 5, 258
whistle: whistle o'er the lave o't	BURNS 102, 73
whistle that the wee herd made	MURRAY 2, 262
whistles: wantoning to the sound o' the kist fu' o' whistles	GALT 13, 139
whistling: Whistling aloud to bear his courage up	R BLAIR(2) 1, 51
white: as a silent leaf the white bird passes	F MACLEO 2, 232
Whitehall: completely Anglicanised by Whitehall	F BALF 4, 38
whiter: Thou art whiter than the swan on miry lake	CARMIN 2, 88
wholeness: And if my country attains wholeness	MACTHO 2, 239
whore: like right well a whore in scarlet	A RAMS(1) 10, 278
met with a monstrous big whore	J BOSWEL 1, 53
the Great Scarlet Whore of Babylon	CARLYL 1, 82
whoredom: Whoredom her trade, and vice her end	R FERG 11, 129
whoring: mad wi' drink and whoring	BURNS 43, 69
whurrin': whurrin' in like cats on rattens	TENNAN 5, 330
wicked: A wicked Christian woman	IC SMITH 18, 308
wickedest: wickedest man-made catastrophe	J CAMER 7, 80
widdefow: Wan wisage widdefow	DUNBAR 5, 118
widows: The widows they hae gashes O	ANON 34, 29
wife: a dune wife / Greetin' in her plaid	ANGUS 2, 25
A smokey house and a scolding wife	FERRI 16, 130
a waefu' wife and bairnies three	BALLAD 23, 40
crouching vassal to the tyrant wife	BURNS 78, 71
If beating can reform a wife	BERNS 3, 48
I fed my children and I loved my wife	DUNN 8, 121
if Laura had been Petrarch's wife	BYRON 43, 78
ilka wife cries, 'Auld Mahoun'	BURNS 111, 73
Lissy, I am looking out for a wife	BRAXF 6, 57
nevir curse his puir auld wife	HOGG 4, 163
no real lady would make her lover talk about his wife	BRIDIE 5, 58
Roy's wife of Aldivalloch	E GRANT(1) 1, 148
Scotland! thy weather's like a modish wife!	A HILL 1, 162
Tam o' the Lin he married a wife	J BAILL 14, 36
The husband frae the wife despises	BURNS 92, 72
There lived a wife at Usher's Well	BALLAD 46, 42
Thoo'll kin to mak a wife o' me?	A SCOTT-M 1, 297
Though your young wife were jealous of me	TRAD 28, 335
your wife laughing when you had tears in your eyes	STEVEN 21, 319
wifie: I'm a wee, wee, wifie	SLESS 8, 303
wild: By thy wild and stormy steep, / Elsinore	T CAMPB 6, 81
wild mountain thyme	TANNAH 2, 329
wilderness: formerly an insurrection, there is now a wilderness	JOHNS 7, 178
In God's wilderness lies the hope of the world	J MUIR 4, 259
What better than a Wilderness, to liberate the mind	CONN 3, 100
Wilderness, then, isn't just a geographical area	A WATSON 1, 346
wild life: Wild life does not exist for man's delectation	FRAS D. 5, 136
wildness: wildness is a necessity	J MUIR 6, 259
wilful: wilful convulsion of brute nature	STEVEN 96, 324
will: she bent her voice to her will	J KAY 6, 183
Willie: At Willie's wedding on the green	A BOSWEL 1, 53
For Willie McBride it all happened again	BOGLE 2, 52
Kind, honest-hearted Willie	BURNS 44, 69
rattlin, roarin Willie, / Ye're welcome hame to me	BURNS 71, 71
Wee Willie Winkie rins through the toun	MILLER 1, 251
Willie Wastle dwalt on Tweed	BURNS 122, 74
Willies: Holy Willies of Scottish life	HENDER 7, 160
Wilson: the fourteenth Mr Wilson	HOME 2, 164
wimble-wamble: tak hame the process an' wimble-wamble it	POLKEM 2, 276
win: anyone had told me I would win so many titles	S HENDR 2, 160
possibility in politics that you might never win	Jo SMITH 2, 309
puts it not unto the Touch, / To win or lose it all	MONTRO 2, 254
we'll a' win to it yet	JACOB 5, 174
win it playing good football	STEIN 1, 317
Winchburgh: Waterways in Winchester, but not in Winchburgh	DALYE 1, 107
Winchester: Waterways in Winchester, but not in Winchburgh	DALYE 1, 107
wind: autumn wind's asteer	JACOB 4, 174
Blows the wind to-day	STEVEN 87, 324
Catch the Wind	DONOV 1, 114

Scottish Toast

May the best you've ever seen.
Be the worst you'll ever see
May the mouse ne'er leave your girnal
Wi' a teardrap in it's ee.
May your lum keep blithely reekin'
Till ye're auld enough to dee
May you aye be just as happy
As I wish you now to be